W9-BTQ-643

U.S.News
& WORLD REPORT
2017 EDITION

Best
COLLEGES

HOW TO ORDER: Additional copies of U.S.News & World Report's Best Colleges 2017
guidebook are available for purchase at usnews.com/collegeguide or by calling (800) 836-6397.
To order custom reprints, please call (877) 652-5295 or email usnews@wrightsmedia.com.
For permission to republish articles, data or other content from this book, email permissions@usnews.com.

Colorado College
BRETT ZIEGLER FOR USN&WR

CONTENTS

WHY I PICKED...

WHAT TO EXPECT IN YOUR PAYCHECK

seeK U·T

Earnings by major of real UT graduates

www.utsystem.edu/seekut

THE UNIVERSITY of TEXAS SYSTEM
FOURTEEN INSTITUTIONS. UNLIMITED POSSIBILITIES.

REAL GRADUATES
REAL EARNINGS
REALISTIC EXPECTATIONS

seeK U·T
search · earnings · employment · knowledge
www.utsystem.edu/seekut
#seekUT @seekUT

Chapter Three

The U.S. News Rankings

154

142
CHASE
WATKINS
AND
CATHERINE
CASSEDY

What Great Minds Can Do

Cynthia Sularz, Class of 2016

- Fulbright Scholar
- U.S. Representative: G-20 Girls Summit in Australia
- Researcher: Genocide Prevention Project
- Study Abroad: Russia, Germany and Poland

www.shu.edu

SETON HALL UNIVERSITY

1856

@usnews.com

GETTING IN

COLLEGE ADMISSIONS PLAYBOOK

Get tips from Varsity Tutors, an academic tutoring and test-prep provider. This blog offers advice on mastering the SAT and ACT as well as the college application process.
usnews.com/collegeplaybook

STUDENTS ON HOW THEY MADE IT IN

Seniors from high schools across the country talk about their admissions experiences and offer advice to students getting ready to apply to college.
usnews.com/studentprofiles

COLLEGE VISITS

TAKE A ROAD TRIP

We've gone on numerous trips to visit campuses in case you can't. Check out our compendium of nearly 30 different trips to 100-plus schools.
usnews.com/roadtrips

RANKINGS INSIGHT

MORSE CODE BLOG

Get the inside scoop on the rankings – and the commentary and controversy surrounding them – from U.S. News' Bob Morse, the mastermind behind our education rankings projects.
usnews.com/morsecode

IN-DEPTH DATA

COLLEGE COMPASS

Gain access to the U.S. News College Compass, which offers comprehensive searchable data and tools for high school students starting down the path to campus. To get a 25 percent discount, subscribe at
usnews.com/compassoffer

PAYING FOR COLLEGE

RESEARCHING AID

Visit our guide to all your possible sources of college funds. Learn about your savings options and which schools meet students' full need.
usnews.com/payforcollege

SCHOLARSHIP SEARCH INSIDER

There's free money out there to help you finance a college education. Expert bloggers, including Cappex.com, offer tips on how to search, apply for and win scholarships.
usnews.com/scholarshipinsider

THE STUDENT LOAN RANGER

Don't fall into the trap of taking on too much debt. Bloggers from American Student Assistance provide guidance if you must turn to loans to pay for college.
usnews.com/studentloanranger

DISTANCE LEARNING

ONLINE EDUCATION

Do you need to balance school with work or other obligations? Consult our rankings of the best online degree programs for leads on how to get your diploma without leaving home.
usnews.com/online

FOR SCHOOLS ONLY

ACADEMIC INSIGHTS

U.S. News Academic Insights is an analytics dashboard intended for use by institutions that comprises all of the undergraduate and graduate historical rankings data we've collected. The dashboard allows for peer group comparisons and includes easy-to-understand visualizations.
ai.usnews.com

Helping students take the next step toward college

Over 1.4 million in Scholarships
10 $25,000 National Winners
42 $10,000 State Winners
300 $2,500 Community Winners

Over **$25** million awarded to more than **6,000** students

ONLINE APPLICATION
Deadline to apply:
December 15, 2016

Follow us

Are you active in your community? Have you led or initiated a project that benefits others? Have you overcome personal challenges or difficulties to achieve your goals?

If the answer to any of these questions is **"Yes"** then you **may already be an AXA Achiever.**

Find out what it takes to win an **AXA Achievement℠ Scholarship.** If you're headed for college, you could be one of our 2017 AXA Achievers.

To learn more and apply, visit
www.axa.com/achievers

AXA Achievement℠ The Official Scholarship of the U.S. News America's Best Colleges Guidebook

The AXA Achievement℠ Scholarship, in association with U.S. News & World Report, is a program of AXA Achievement – a philanthropic program dedicated to providing resources that help make college possible through access and advice. AXA Achievement is funded by the AXA Foundation, the philanthropic arm of AXA in the US.

Paying for college is one of the biggest risks families face – AXA Achievement℠ can help.

TAB STICKERS

AXA Achievement℠ can help you take the next step toward college.

Use these stickers to tab your college choices inside this issue.

Next steps toward college

Taking the right small steps today can help eliminate the risk of not being able to afford a college education

Filling out the FAFSA helps you minimize borrowing. It's a misconception that filling out the Free Application for Federal Student Aid (FAFSA) is the fast track to student loan debt. You risk losing need-based grants and scholarships from the university. The reason? The universities you selected on the FAFSA to receive your information use it to evaluate your financial aid eligibility.

To avoid losing need-based aid you might qualify for:

1. Fill out the FAFSA as early as possible. Some need-based aid is limited in numbers and available on a first-come first-served basis for those who qualify. Universities have a limited amount of grant aid. Applying late could mean you miss out.

2. Select schools. Always select schools that are being considered on the form. Otherwise, the information won't arrive at the colleges that need it. Amend the FAFSA form online if school choices change.

3. Fill out the special circumstances forms when needed. Whether you're applying for next year or are already in college, you need to fill out a special circumstances form if your income changes due to a number of reasons, such as a medical situation, a layoff, or a salary reduction.

4. Practice filling out the FAFSA on the FAFSA4caster site from the Department of Education as early as middle school. It's designed to roughly estimate financial aid years in advance.

5. Follow up with schools to make sure information is received and to check on financial aid availability. Bonus: you may find out about a scholarship you previously didn't know about during the phone call.

Choosing universities with the lowest listed tuition prices can sometimes cost you more money. A private school with "sticker price" that is four times more than that of a state school may offer scholarships and grants that make it the cheaper alternative. Find out which schools offer the best financial aid packages before applying. Net price calculators available on most college websites are one way to estimate what you would pay based on individual circumstances.

To better understand the relative costs of higher education:

1. Narrow college choices down to ten using factors such as majors, campus size and internship placement. Talk with your high school counselor early to start the process of college selection and career exploration.

2. Request information from each school on what's important to you. For instance, call the career center to ask about graduate employment rates.

3. Visit the websites of your top ten college choices. Find the net price calculator on their website by entering "net price calculator" into the search box on the school's home page. Enter information such as family income and number of children in college.

4. Call financial aid offices at your top five choices to see if there are any changes in grant awards for the year you will be attending. Available funds change, so you want to make sure you factor in the most recent information into your family's application decisions.

5. Use the net price calculator as a baseline. You may also qualify for merit-based aid.

To learn more and apply, visit www.axa.com/achievers

From the Editor's Desk

BY BRIAN KELLY

This college search thing can be a little intimidating, especially if you're going through it for the first time. This is our 32nd go-round at U.S. News, so we feel like we've got some experience worth sharing.

Over the years, we've improved our information and sharpened our focus, with our primary objective being to help students and their parents make one of life's most important - and costliest - decisions. Prospective students and their parents need objective measures that allow them to evaluate and compare schools. The U.S. News rankings are one tool to help them make choices,

along with all the other insights and guidance contained in these pages. This sort of assistance is more relevant than ever, with some private colleges now costing around $250,000 for a bachelor's degree. At the same time, many public high schools have greatly reduced their college counseling resources, leaving students and parents to educate themselves about the search and admission process.

Of course, we have adjusted our ranking methodology over the years to reflect changes in the world of higher education, and we make it clear that we are not doing peer-reviewed social science research, although we do maintain very high survey and data standards. We have always been open and transparent. We have always said that the rankings are not perfect. The first were based solely on schools' academic reputation among leaders at peer institutions; we later developed a formula in which reputation accounts for 22.5 percent of a school's score and important quantitative measures such as graduation and retention rates, average class size and student-faculty ratios account for the rest. Over time, we have shifted weight from inputs (indicators of the quality of students and resources) to outputs (success in graduating students). We operate under this guiding principle: The methodology is altered only if a change will better help our readers and web audience compare schools as they're deciding where to apply and enroll.

A starting point. It has helped us a great deal to have these principles to focus on as we have faced the inevitable criticisms from academia about our rankings' growing influence. One main critique remains: that it is impossible to reduce the complexities of a college's offerings and attributes to a single number. It's important to keep in mind that our information is a starting point. The next steps in a college search should include detailed research on a smaller list of choices, campus visits and conversations with students, faculty and alumni wherever you can find them. Feedback from academia has helped improve the

rankings over time. We meet with our critics, listen to their points of view, debate them on the merits of what we do, and make appropriate changes.

U.S. News is keenly aware that the higher education community is also a major audience for our rankings. We understand how seriously academics, college presidents, trustees and governing boards take our data. They study, analyze and use them in various ways, including benchmarking against peers, alumni fundraising, and advertising to attract students.

What does all of this mean in today's global information marketplace? U.S. News has become a respected unbiased source that higher education administrators and policymakers and the college-bound public worldwide turn to for reliable guidance. In fact, the Best Colleges rankings have become a key part of the evolving higher education accountability movement. Universities are increasingly being held responsible for their policies, how their funds are spent, the level of student engagement, and how much graduates have learned. The U.S. News rankings have become the annual public benchmark to measure the academic performance of the country's colleges and universities.

We know our role has limits. The rankings should only be used as one factor in the college search – we've long said that there is no single "best college." There is only the best college for you or, more likely, a handful of good options, one of which will turn out to be a great fit. Besides the rankings, we can help college-bound high school students and their parents by providing a wealth of information on all aspects of the application process, from getting in to getting financial aid. Our website, usnews.com, features thousands of pages of rankings, research, sortable data, photos, videos and a personalized tool called College Compass.

We've been doing this for over three decades, so we know the process is not simple. But our experience tells us the hard work is worth it in the end. ●

Study the
School

1

LS

**A DRAWING CLASS AT XAVIER
UNIVERSITY OF LOUISIANA**

BRETT ZIEGLER FOR USN&WR

A Focus on FRESHMAN Success!

Keep an eye out as you create your college list for programs that help students bond and thrive

BY CHRISTOPHER J. GEARON

Stepping onto Georgia State University's Atlanta campus as a freshman, Tyler Mulvenna knew the odds of graduating were stacked against him. A first-generation student from Newnan, Georgia, Mulvenna initially had been wait-listed, and he missed out on the state's Hope Scholarship because his high school GPA wasn't high enough. That forced him to take out loans, work up to 30 hours a week as a sales rep at a local YMCA, and commute from home by bus to pay for his courses. Moreover, the university, with its large population of low-income and first-generation students, had been losing 17 percent of freshmen before sophomore year and graduating only a bit over half of its students within six years. Yet today, Mulvenna is a senior on track to get his diploma on time. Freshman year, he says, was "a success."

Georgia State, like a growing number of colleges and universities nationwide, has stepped up its game in helping first-years make the transition to indepen-dent living and college-level work. A main motivation: to change the fact that 20 percent of full-time freshman nationwide don't return and that only 39 percent of students graduate in four years. The cost of not getting a degree is huge. A new report by Georgetown University's Center on Education and the Workforce shows that of the 11.6 million jobs created in the post-recession economy, only 80,000 went to people with a high school diploma or less.

Students have many reasons to drop out

or transfer, of course, from family problems to lack of funds. But one big factor that colleges can address is the lack of a strong connection to classmates and professors, or to the school itself. A number of innovative programs that have been shown to

---

GSU STUDENTS BRIANNA VALENTINE AND TYLER MULVENNA ON CAMPUS

help students thrive are worth looking for as you research schools:

Many colleges and universities aiming to make themselves "stickier" are building in a first-year experience as an introduction to campus life. Some are expanding orientation to include summer bonding trips, leadership institutes and reading programs intended to get students talking once on campus. Or your experience might entail a discussion-based and writing-intensive freshman seminar with a small group of other newbies and a professor you get to know well. At Appalachian State University in North Carolina, for example, freshmen pick a seminar from dozens of choices, from Our Global Energy Future to Boxing and American Culture. Other schools with notable first-year programs can be seen in the box at right.

Georgia State's first-year program puts freshmen in a learning community, a small group of students who typically take two or more classes together. Mulvenna and two dozen of his peers inter-

First-Year Experience

Many schools ease freshmen into college through programs that bond them to peers and a professor. The following (arranged alphabetically) got the most votes for having good first-year programs in the U.S. News survey; others can be found at usnews.com.

Appalachian State University (NC)*
College of William and Mary (VA)*
Elon University (NC)
Franklin and Marshall College (PA)
Georgia State University*
Ohio State University-Columbus*
Skidmore College (NY)
Stanford University (CA)

University of Michigan-Ann Arbor*
U. of North Carolina-Chapel Hill*
Univ. of South Carolina*
University of Texas-Austin*
University of Virginia*
Univ. of Wisconsin-Madison*
Vanderbilt University (TN)
Wagner College (NY)

(*Public)

ested in business spent first semester taking four courses together plus a class focused on solving problems, tapping campus resources, and living in Atlanta. The professor of that class also served as an adviser and mentor. "It was tremendously helpful," says Mulvenna of the support his community provided.

The common purpose of efforts to foster community is to get new students connected. But each college offers its own twist on the concept. Since 1933, Yale University has been placing new arrivals into a "residential college" where they'll live for all four years. Sort of like Gryffindor in the "Harry Potter" novels, each of the 12 colleges has a unique architecture, courtyard, dining hall, library and activity spaces such as

offerings. At the University of Maryland–College Park, for example, topics include globalization, women in engineering, and honors college programs in cybersecurity and entrepreneurship.

Each freshman at Franklin & Marshall

College in Pennsylvania is assigned to one of five "college houses" based on his or her choice of a first-semester "Connections" seminar; the 42 possibilities range from Rivers & Regions to Living Sustainably and The Business of Food. The college houses, where students can live for all four years, are each guided by an administrator and a faculty member who helps with academic concerns. "It's less of a building you live in than a home and community," says Emily Hawk, a

investigating Greek and Roman conceptions of rhetoric and virtue and applying those lessons by coaching local middle school debate teams and running a citywide debate league.

"One thing the college is great at is building community through service," says Jennie Caswell, a senior at the College of the Ozarks in Missouri who is majoring in secondary English education. The education classes involve such service activities as working on the college's Night to Shine gala for people with special needs and helping provide food for local families.

Colleges with first-year experiences and learning communities have often made a point of improving their freshman advising by having a seminar professor or faculty resident also fill the adviser role. Increasingly, schools are also using big data to support so-called intrusive advising. Rather than depend on greenhorns to proactively seek their adviser's help, for example, Georgia State has culled years' worth of data to see at what points students veer off the path to a timely graduation. Now its system raises an electronic flag when a student hits a danger zone, such as overlooking a course requirement. A prompt is sent to the student's adviser, who then reaches out.

Some 45,000 flags were raised last year at GSU. Timothy Renick, the university's vice provost, credits the first-year experience and intrusive advising for a jump in GSU's six-year graduation rate from 32 percent in 2003 to 54 percent in 2015.

At Indiana State University, advisers meet at least monthly with freshmen and interim grades are issued so students have a handle on their progress. Those who are first in their families to attend college get a faculty or staff mentor, and students who need extra support are appointed coaches who help with problem-solving and organization. "I'm shy and procrastinate a lot," says Loretta Stewart, a junior health sciences major from Indianapolis. "The coaching helped me become a better time manager and advocate for myself." Freshman retention, which was running only 58 percent in 2011, has risen to nearly 65 percent. Now graduation rates are ticking up, too. ●

Learning Communities

To better engage in school, students typically take two or more courses as a group and may live together. These schools got the most mentions for their programs in U.S. News' survey; others are cited at usnews.com.

Belmont University (TN)
Elon University (NC)
Evergreen State College (WA)*
Franklin and Marshall College (PA)

Georgia State University*
Indiana U.-Purdue U.-Indianapolis*
Michigan State University*
Ohio State University-Columbus*
Purdue Univ.-West Lafayette (IN)*
Syracuse University (NY)
Univ. of Maryland-College Park*
University of Michigan-Ann Arbor*
Univ. of South Carolina*
University of Washington*
Univ. of Wisconsin-Madison*
Vanderbilt University (TN)
Wagner College (NY)
Yale University (CT)

(*Public)

a movie theater, recording studio and gym. Two professors live in each college, dining with students, arranging speakers and other events, and acting as academic advisers. Social life is the focus, rather than academics. This is "the heartbeat of the Yale undergrad experience," notes Stephen Davis, a professor of religious studies, head of one of the colleges, and chair of the school's Council of Heads of College.

A more modern take on a purposeful housing arrangement is the themed living-and-learning community, in which students with a shared interest take a seminar or two together and also live together on the same dorm floor or in the same campus house. Social events and field trips often enrich the academic

2016 graduate in history and dance. She landed in the Brooks College House upon enrolling in Demons and Dancers, a class held in the residence that had her studying horror films and musicals with 15 other freshmen housemates.

Research shows that about half of freshmen now engage in some form of service learning, a key practice colleges use to engage first-year students in their studies and the local community while helping them bond with their peers. These programs link volunteer work with a class or other academic endeavor so students can integrate what they're learning with the hands-on experience. At Tulane University in New Orleans, for example, Persuasive Writing: Aristotle in New Orleans has participants

CHRISTOPHER NEWPORT
UNIVERSITY

SCHOLARSHIP ⫸ LEADERSHIP ⫸ SERVICE ⫸ HONOR

LEARN TO LEAD

Christopher Newport is different from many other colleges and universities because we care about minds and hearts. Our purpose is to form good citizens and leaders. We want our students to lead lives of meaning, consequence and purpose. We call that lives of significance.

That's why we study the liberal arts and sciences and emphasize leadership at Christopher Newport. That's why we have a rigorous core curriculum of seven required courses, including American history and government, mathematics, natural science, foreign language, composition, literature, and economics. That's why our students perform thousands of hours of community service. That's why we built a chapel and celebrate our speaking tradition and honor code. Come see us — there's no better way to experience Christopher Newport than to visit our beautiful campus.

1 AVENUE OF THE ARTS, NEWPORT NEWS, VA 23606   •   (757) 594-7015   •   CNU.EDU

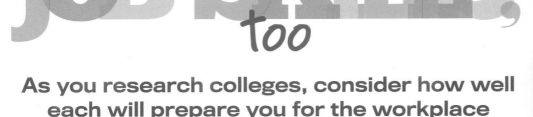

A DEGREE and JOB SKILLS, too

As you research colleges, consider how well each will prepare you for the workplace

BY CHRISTOPHER J. GEARON

B y the time Kristen Lundebjerg earns her degree in mechanical engineering, she'll also have a full year of work in the field to show prospective employers. This fall, she is serving as a test director in the Energy Test Systems Area at NASA's Johnson Space Center. That follows a four-month stint last winter and spring with NASA's external relations office, where she helped debrief International Space Station astronauts. And the summer after sophomore year, she interned as a "design-to-value" engineer at tool company Stanley Black & Decker. All in all, says Lundebjerg, a senior at Boston's Wentworth Institute of Technology, these opportunities gave her "really great hands-on experience."

Wentworth has long integrated career prep into its curriculum. Today, a growing number of colleges are following suit. The trend is not surprising, since higher education costs are a huge stressor on many families. The four-year tab now runs over $78,000 on average for in-state students at public universities and $175,000 at private colleges. With student debt at record levels, people are thinking hard about the value they're getting in return.

"Families and students are very focused on career readiness and career outcomes," observes Paul Timmins, career services director at the University of Minnesota's College of Liberal Arts and president-elect of the National Career Development Association, an organization of career counseling professionals. Meantime, governments are shining a brighter light on how well graduates are faring. A majority of states now peg some of their funding to measures like course completion and time to degree, according to the National Conference of State Legislatures. And the Obama administration's college "scorecard" (collegescorecard.ed.gov) provides information on cost, graduation rates and the salaries of graduates.

Most schools are not as far along the career-prep path as Wentworth, which requires undergrads to complete two semesters of cooperative education. "Co-op" programs typically alternate class time with work at a partnering employer so the experiences build on each other. Yet even traditional liberal arts colleges are giving greater emphasis to experience, expanding internship opportunities and service-learning coursework that melds academics with community service, for example. Many colleges are also punching up their career education programs. Some students are getting a healthy dose of career awareness as early as freshman year that includes how-tos on résumé writing, internship searches and networking. "If they are coming into career services for the first time as a senior, it's quite possibly too late" to do much good, says Timmins.

KRISTEN LUNDEBJERG, AT NASA'S JOHNSON SPACE CENTER

Internships

U.S. News asked college officials to nominate up to 10 schools with standout internship programs, practicums or co-op opportunities, in which one period of study typically alternates with one of work. The following (arranged alphabetically) got the most votes; additional schools are recognized at usnews.com.

Berea College (KY)
Butler University (IN)
Cornell University (NY)
Drexel University (PA)
Elon University (NC)
Georgia Institute of Technology*
Massachusetts Inst. of Technology
Messiah College (PA)
Northeastern University (MA)
Purdue Univ.-West Lafayette (IN)*
Rochester Inst. of Technology (NY)
University of Cincinnati*
Virginia Tech*
Worcester Polytechnic Inst. (MA)

(*Public)

practice internship application in the spring.

High-quality career prep is far from a given, however. Indeed, the National Association of Colleges and Employers reports that overall, budgets for career services were slashed during the lean years between 2007 and 2014. As families research colleges, they should "consider their return on investment," advises Susan Brennan, associate vice president of university career services at Bentley University in Massachusetts. "And that includes evaluating a school's commitment to career education and student outcomes."

Activities in the early years vary widely and may

lean more toward raising students' consciousness than required coursework. The University of Notre Dame in Indiana invites all incoming students to start filling a digital portfolio with their goals, plans and samples of their best work, for example. It's voluntary, but all 8,000 undergrads took advantage during the last academic year. Irere Romeo Kwihangana, a 2014 grad who is now an electrical engineer with General Electric's Aviation Systems division, recalls how the tool helped him reflect on and "engage with my adviser on skills I would need to develop." When he noticed sophomore year that good written and oral communication skills "came up in nearly every single job

At Minnesota, the liberal arts college has doubled the number of career counselors from five to 10 over the past year and assigned them to specific majors so they can get to know faculty and students in their areas. Counselors now have more time to help students explore their interests and strengths and find internships. The 2,500 freshmen in the college all must visit career services during their first semester, write a résumé, and take part in an informational interview or complete a

Dedicated to the noble pursuit of unmaking the world a better place.

There are two types of people. Those who accept the world for what it is, and those who refuse to see it for anything less than what it could become. Here at the University of California San Diego, we tend to attract the latter. The ever-curious ones. The defiant. These are the mischievous minds who will someday change our world simply because it demands change. We call them Breakers. Why? Because they are convinced that the only way to truly solve a problem is to first break it apart and examine every angle to discover what makes it tick. So when the pieces are reassembled, they will work better than before. Now, if tackling the world's ugliest issues with truckloads of creative problem solving  piques your interest, read on. We've got much to cover.

Like the most recent global financial crisis. And how our very own Writing professor Rae Armantrout wielded her poetry like a spiked club to crack Wall Street's greed wide open.

Dictatorial injustice? Well, Literature professor Luis Martín-Cabrera is fighting to protect Latin America's political, economic and cultural future by diving headfirst into people's memories of its oppressive past. And now that we have a stage to highlight what a few curious minds here on the clifftops have been up to, perhaps Professor Robert Brill can erect us a more elaborate one. After all, he already made Broadway do a double-take with sets that incorporate audiences directly into classic stage productions, like *Cabaret*. Of course, unconventional thinking like this is what each bright-eyed student should expect. That, and a grueling academic boot camp that thoroughly whips their impressionable minds into peak Breaker condition. So, before we send our army of motivated,  well-equipped grads off to conquer the world's biggest problems by applying solutions no one ever thought up before, first we'll cue the victory music. Perhaps a recording from Professor Roger Reynolds. He's famous for mashing together music and technology to create unique experiences that engage on multidimensional levels — smack dab in our collective "Breaker" comfort zone.

ucsd.edu/breakthingsbetter

posting," he joined a monologues group that soon had him speaking on stage.

Like the Minnesota college, some schools require at least a drop-by visit to the career center. Many offer résumé-writing workshops, career-focused seminars and opportunities to interview with alumni or role-play in different situations. At Bentley, first-year students take Career Development Introduction 101, an interactive class that helps them identify personal strengths and present themselves in a cover letter, LinkedIn profile and elevator pitch. That's the first step in Bentley's four-year "Hire Education" curriculum, a program of workshops, coaching and career exploration that leads to an internship and ideally, a job.

A five-week seminar during sophomore year prepped Lundebjerg for her co-op, offering material on networking in person and via social media, interviewing and landing a position. Employers separately came in to provide tips on appropriate workplace behavior as well as to conduct mock interviews. The tack taken by the University of Missouri-Kansas City is to focus on building the soft skills employers say they value. The school has revamped its core curriculum to emphasize critical thinking, communication and teamwork in first- and second-year coursework.

Service Learning

In the most recent U.S. News survey, these schools (arranged alphabetically) got the most votes for having fine service-learning programs, which use volunteer work as a teaching tool. Others can be found at usnews.com.

Belmont University (TN)
Berea College (KY)
Brown University (RI)
College of St. Benedict (MN)
College of the Ozarks (MO)
Duke University (NC)
Elon University (NC)
Indiana U.-Purdue U.-Indianapolis*
Michigan State University*
Northeastern University (MA)
Portland State University (OR)*
Stanford University (CA)
Tulane University (LA)
U. of Michigan-Ann Arbor*
U. of N. Carolina-Chapel Hill*
University of Notre Dame (IN)
University of Pennsylvania
Valparaiso University (IN)
Wagner College (NY)
Warren Wilson College (NC)

(*Public)

Liberal arts colleges, which pride themselves on imparting those soft skills, traditionally haven't concerned themselves so much with career prep. But many now are also going all in to help students connect their classroom learning to workplace experiences, notes Stacy Bingham, director of the career development office at Vassar College in New York. Many even provide funding so students can take unpaid internships. Vassar senior Matthew McCardwell,

FRESHMEN AT BENTLEY TAKE A CAREER DEVELOPMENT SEMINAR.

• • •

CONCRETE EVIDENCE OF HOW WE'RE ADDRESSING GLOBAL CLIMATE CHANGE.

As part of the UCLA Grand Challenges, Bruins are leading the way to make Los Angeles sustainable by 2050. Developing energy-generating water treatment plants. Inventing smarter electrical grids. And creating eco-friendly construction materials that have worldwide impact. Driving the effort behind carbon neutral "sustainable concrete," Associate Professor of Engineering Gaurav Sant is transforming a greenhouse gas into a reusable resource in the construction of roads, buildings and bridges. By turning something harmful into something valuable, he's laying the foundation for a greener future.

HOW WILL YOU SHAPE THE FUTURE?

UCLA.edu/optimists

UCLA

an art history major from Louisville, Kentucky, says the school's three-day Sophomore Career Connections conference gave him the chance "to speak with other creatives working in publishing, nonprofits and in computer software design. The biggest value for me was to see how many life paths, careers and fields are open to me."

The program spurred him to reach out to a college career counselor as well as to a friend's mother, an artist, who shared the behind-the-scenes aspects of working in an artist's studio. Those two contacts led him to identify and snag two internships this past summer in New York funded by Vassar. Most days he worked in development for a nonprofit arts organization; one day a week, he helped out in the curatorial department of the International Center for Photography.

As McCardwell's example shows, getting early exposure to career basics can inspire students to seek out hands-on experiences early, too. Julianne Falotico, a senior majoring in neuroscience at Colgate University in New York, began cultivating her workplace chops right away. The school's job-shadowing program, which gives students a taste of the professional lives of alumni, inspired the would-be doctor to shadow a clinical pharmacist during winter break of freshman year. "It showed me that when you're treating patients, it's much more multilayered than you think," she says.

Next, Falotico shadowed C-suite executives at a hospital near her home and landed an eight-week internship doing medical rounds.

WHERE THE MONEY IS

Members of the class of 2016 who majored in science, technology, engineering or mathematics were expected to nab the highest paychecks upon graduation: an average of $55,000 to $65,000, according to the National Association of Colleges and Employers.

Those who opted for business, natural resources, health care or communications were expected to land jobs around the $50,000 mark. At the top of the list? Engineering graduates, who will hit nearly $65,000. Computer science majors come in second, at $61,321, followed by math and science majors at $55,100.

STEM sweep. "A 'C' in STEM will make you more money than an 'A' in English," says Anthony Carnevale, director of Georgetown University's Center on Education and the Workforce. A 2015 center report showed that of the 25 highest-paid majors, only two, economics and business economics, are not in STEM fields.

Meanwhile, other research by the center shows just how important higher education is in the modern workplace. Of the 11.6 million jobs created since the recession, fully 11.5 million went to workers who had spent at least some time in college.

The industries that have added the largest number of jobs are consulting and business services, at 2.5 million. By occupation, management expanded the most, by 1.6 million positions, and the professional and technical health care fields came in a close second, adding 1.5 million jobs together. –C.J.G.

She capped those experiences this past summer doing research on the degeneration of intervertebral discs at Long Island's Feinstein Institute for Medical Research, thanks to $2,000 provided by Colgate. Now in its fourth year, Colgate's summer grant program has raised $2.6 million to make such experiences possible for students who otherwise might have to wait tables or work as camp counselors to make money. Besides Vassar and Colgate, others that do the same include Colorado College, Bard and Hamilton colleges in New York, Mount Holyoke College in Massachusetts, and the University of Richmond in Virginia.

Some schools have taken pains to build partnerships with employers, whose managers come to campus for educational programs and may

Two Years, No Tuition?

Some states are moving ahead with free community college

BY PETER RATHMELL

What's the latest on President Barack Obama's proposal to provide first-time college students two years of community college tuition-free? The idea, which he announced in early 2015, hasn't swayed Congress. But some states, beginning with Oregon and Tennessee, are starting to offer the benefit.

In Oregon, $10 million was appropriated this year to kick off the Oregon Promise program. "The benefits of higher education to the individual and the economy are significant," says Ben Cannon, executive director of the Oregon Higher Education Coordinating Commission. "We believe that this moderate investment economically will pay huge dividends for college availability and college success."

Bridging the gap. To receive Oregon Promise aid, students must have earned a high school diploma or a GED within the last six months and must file the Free Application for Federal Student Aid or the Oregon Student Aid Application. After the federal and state grants are applied (and students chip in a $50 copay),

even get involved in academic planning. The employers also hire interns or collaborate in co-op programs. Besides Wentworth, other institutions with robust co-op curricula include Northeastern University in Boston, Drexel University in Philadelphia, and the University of Cincinnati. In addition, Bentley, Colorado School of Mines, the University of Maryland-Baltimore County and the University of Minnesota have developed strong company partnerships. "We have an employer relations team that builds connections with employers who hire liberal arts graduates," says Timmins. Bentley's career services staffers double as "account managers" who learn the hiring needs of the companies they are assigned to. They then match students to those needs.

Clearly, the chance to get experience can make a big

difference to students' eventual path. Randi Williams, a 2016 UMBC graduate in computer engineering, is convinced that her three internships helped her get into the Massachusetts Institute of Technology's graduate program in media, arts and sciences, where she'll be working with the personal robots group. She spent one summer at Jawbone in San Francisco ("I loved learning about start-ups!"), another at NASA's Jet Propulsion Lab in Silicon Valley, and another at the MIT Media Lab.

"I loved CDI 101," says Alison Abrams, a 2016 Bentley math graduate, of the required career course freshman year. "I didn't know how beneficial it was until I delved into my internship." The course provided a foundation that over the next three years was followed by lots of assistance in job-search skills, attendance at networking events and career fairs, and a data analysis research fellowship at a Boston homeless shelter. That led to a paid internship the summer after her junior year at Liberty Mutual Insurance Co., where Abrams created a tool allowing the marketing analytics team to speed through six hours of work in 10 minutes. Before senior year, she was offered a $55,000 job upon graduation that would ramp up significantly in pay after a smooth entry period. "That," she says, "was a weight off my shoulders." •

the program covers the difference between that total and the average community college tuition. If grants already cover tuition, students receive a $1,000 stipend to help defray other expenses such as books, board or transportation.

The Tennessee Promise is a similar grant program for any student who files the FAFSA. One difference: Students in Tennessee have to meet periodically with career mentors and record eight volunteer hours per term.

More states may follow suit in the near future. Minnesota is piloting a program this school year for students from families making up to $90,000 annually, and seven other states – Oklahoma, Washington, New York, Massachusetts, Illinois, Hawaii and California – are considering legislation for similar plans. •

A SENSE OF Belonging

The appeal of attending a minority-serving institution

BY DARCY LEWIS

At first, Ileana Gonzalez of Houston hoped to go to Texas A&M University – until she visited campus. After attending a primarily white high school, one of her requirements was greater diversity, and the level she observed in College Station (the student body is about 60 percent white) didn't meet her target. So she took a trip to the University of Texas–San Antonio and found it "very welcoming" and with a mix (just over one-quarter white) that felt just right. Her time at UTSA, where she majored in business and entrepreneurship, culminated this year with a stint as president of the student body. "I was born in Mexico, and it was not easy to come to this country, attend college, and be the first in my family to graduate," she says. It was a gift to be able to "identify with those who have faced similar struggles."

Though Gonzalez didn't realize it at the time, she had chosen to attend a "Hispanic-serving institution," a Department of Education designation that means a school's population of full-time Hispanic undergrads has hit 25 percent. (The proportion at UTSA is twice that.) The 330 HSIs are one type of a broader category of school, minority-serving institutions, whose mission is not specifically to promote diversity but rather to provide greater educational op-portunities to students of a given group. Other types of MSIs include the country's 105 two- and four-year historically black colleges and universities plus another 50 "predominantly black institutions," 34 tribal colleges and universities, and 160 Asian-American and Native American Pacific Islander-serving institutions. All told, some 600 schools are now categorized as MSIs, says Marybeth Gasman, a professor of higher education and director of the Penn Center for Minority Serving Institutions at the University of Pennsylvania, which studies the schools. As of 2012, some 20 percent of all U.S. undergraduates attended one.

The HBCUs, which include such well-known schools as Howard University in Washington, D.C., and Morehouse and Spelman colleges in Atlanta, accounted for nearly all black college graduates in the country up through the 1960s, and today enroll 11 percent of black students. Tribal colleges are much newer: The first one, Diné College in Tsaile, Arizona, debuted in 1968. Most serve geographically isolated populations, though a few are near such metro areas as Albuquerque, New Mexico, and Seattle. Tribal college enrollment has consistently been about 85 percent native; a handful of schools require tribal membership to enroll.

The AANAPISIs, the newest category, must have at least 10 percent enrollment from the target population and a significant percentage of low-income students. The income requirement "excludes campuses with only affluent Asian-American students," says Gasman. Most University of California schools do not qualify, she notes, but 18 of 23 California State campuses do.

Besides providing a natural community for students who might feel isolated elsewhere, MSIs offer greater affordability, one reason out-of-group interest has been on the rise. White students now account for about 13 percent of enrollment at HBCUs, for ex-

ILEANA GONZALEZ (CENTER) PARTICIPATES IN FIESTA UTSA, PART OF SAN ANTONIO'S CELEBRATION OF ITS DIVERSE CULTURES.

ample. "People have figured out that MSIs are a really good value," says Gasman, who estimates that costs average at least $10,000 less per year at MSIs than at similar predominantly white schools. On the other hand, the schools typically have small endowments and can offer only limited financial aid beyond the federal Pell Grant and Stafford Loan programs. And you're less likely to be using cutting-edge technology or luxuriating in plush dorms and athletic facilities.

Recognizing that many minority students are the first in their families to go to college and that many arrive on campus unprepared for the academics, MSIs generally put great emphasis on easing the way. Cal State East Bay in Hayward, which is both an HSI and an AANAPISI, offers AANAPI students special academic counseling, peer tutoring, career training, and cultural events at every stage of their campus experience. Hispanic students have a similar support sys-

of color is intensely affirming for students of color, because it shows them what it is possible to achieve," notes William B. Harvey, founding president of the National Association of Diversity Officers in Higher Education and a professor in the department of leadership studies at North Carolina A&T State University, an HBCU. Sometimes these lessons come from off-campus experiences. Gonzalez attended the University of California's all-expenses-paid Summer Institute for Emerging Managers and Leaders, open only to HBCU and HSI students, which included networking opportunities and one-on-one meetings with the CEOs of several companies, members of minority groups themselves.

"Even the way buildings are named can send a message," says Anne-Marie Nuñez, until recently an associate professor of educational leadership and policy studies at UTSA. And whereas a predominantly white institution might boast just one or two cultural organiza-

"A SENSE OF *COMMUNITY* IS FOSTERED IN MANY WAYS, ACADEMIC AND SOCIAL."

tem, including a sophomore summer academy and learning community, and major-specific support networks.

And all students entering Paul Quinn College, an HBCU in Dallas, are required to attend a one-month, six-credit bridge program the summer before enrolling – regardless of their academic preparation – that includes personality assessments, etiquette training, mock interviews, and bonding activities. "The message is that your success is my success," says Gasman. "There is a spirit of cooperation and collectivism" often missing at more competitive institutions.

A sense of community is fostered in many ways, academic and social. At Haskell Indian Nations University in Lawrence, Kansas, courses include Fundamentals of Tribal Sovereignty, Environmental Protection in Indian Country, and Human Behavior in American Indian Communities. Music courses at Morehouse feature the great black artists in jazz and gospel, past and present, and criminal justice students at John Jay College in New York City (about 40 percent Latino) examine issues like Latino struggles for civil rights and their experiences with the U.S. legal system.

Moreover, students are regularly taught by people who share their background, a potentially powerful factor in their success. "Extensive research has shown that the presence of faculty

tions for a minority group, students at an MSI often have more nuanced choices, allowing them "to celebrate their unique aspects," says Robert T. Palmer, an HBCU expert and professor at Howard. Club options there range from the African Students Association and the Caribbean Students Association to a dance ensemble that celebrates Afro-jazz.

High-achievers considering an MSI may also be weighing generous offers from more elite schools looking to increase their diversity profile. David Hawkins, executive director for educational content and policy at the National Association for College Admission Counseling, notes that students who thrive at a very selective school can reap "enormous benefits later in life" but that underrepresented students can struggle with loneliness on such campuses. He advises focusing on finding the best fit. "There's no indication that students can't go just as far in their careers coming from a campus where they feel comfortable," Hawkins says.

Lauren Stanley, a member of the Cherokee Nation, considered several Cal State schools but found her fit at Haskell. A 2015 business grad, Stanley now works for Boston Financial Data Services in Lawrence. "I enjoyed no longer being the only Native American," she says. Having time with people of similar backgrounds "was special." ●

THIS IS A SMART CHOICE.

THIS IS AUBURN.

AUBURN
UNIVERSITY

Whether you've known about Auburn all your life or are just learning about this university, we invite you to discover the real Auburn.

This is a university whose alumni include the CEO of Apple, the founders of Habitat for Humanity and Wikipedia, an Oscar-winning actress, sports legends, and astronauts. Graduates are recruited by top companies around the globe.

This is a university where you will make friends for a lifetime with a 300,000-strong, worldwide network of alumni who will think of you as family.

This is a university that will surprise you, impress you, and propel you to success as it has for generations before you. **auburn.edu**

Taking *the* FAST Track

Should you save money by accelerating? BY CHRISS SWANEY

The only thing growing more quickly than the sticker price on a college education may be the debate around the value of a degree – particularly if a student takes on a big load of debt while majoring in something with no clear path to a decent job.

With an eye toward giving families a way to save time and money, colleges and universities nationwide are offering accelerated degree programs that scoot students through the ivy-covered halls of academia in three years, allow them to get both a bachelor's and master's degree in four or five years, and provide a streamlined path through law school or medical school. "Parents really perk up when they hear about the cost savings of an accelerated program," says Josh Boyd, associate professor and director of undergraduate studies at the Brian Lamb School of Communication at Purdue University in Indiana.

For Charlotte Tuggle, a mass communication major there from Winston, Georgia, the accelerated program will mean a savings of $20,000 in tuition by the time she graduates in 2017. And she still has been able to squeeze in broadcast internships, she notes.

Faith Finoli is "getting to finish my undergraduate and osteopathic medical degree in seven rather than eight years" by choosing a three-year bachelor's in biology at Seton Hill University in Pennsylvania coupled with a D.O. degree that takes an additional four years from partner school Lake Erie College of Osteopathic Medicine. She graduates in 2018.

What all these fast-track programs have in common is that they require a high level of focus and motivation and a stress-inducing course load, although students who choose to accelerate often take full advantage of Advanced Placement or International Baccalaureate credits. Is one of these programs for you?

Consider the three-year bachelor's

While some students have always opted to take extra courses on their own each semester and go to summer school to graduate early, a handful of institutions have set up formal three-year pathways in at least some disciplines that typically require students to carry 18 to 20 credits per semester. Purdue communication students without any AP credits take an extra course four out of six semesters and put in two summers. At Bates College in Maine, the accelerated option is open to anyone who is willing to take five courses instead of four per semester and a class in each one-month "short term" that closes out the spring. At Wesleyan in Connecticut, students can opt to graduate in three years by adding summer terms and taking advantage of one or two AP or IB courses.

By contrast, American University in Washington, D.C., has fashioned three rigorous three-year "Scholars" programs, complete with opportunities to study abroad, mentoring, and internships, for small cohorts of accomplished students interested in international service; public health; and politics, policy and law. The State University of New York at Potsdam lets students who arrive with a high school average of at least 95 and maintain a 3.25 GPA take accelerated tracks in majors ranging from biology and chemistry to economics and English literature.

CHARLOTTE TUGGLE IS IN HER FINAL YEAR OF PURDUE'S THREE-YEAR PROGRAM.

"I'll miss leaving my classmates a bit early, but the fast track has been worth it," says Cosima Compton, a 2016 business administration graduate of Hartwick College in Oneonta, New York, which offers a three-year plan in 22 majors. "My parents love saving $52,000 in tuition and fees." Students get priority in class selection as well as mentoring and special counseling. They also get a complete draft schedule of all courses they might take before they ever hit campus.

Most of these programs so far have drawn a very limited number of students. Only 15 of the 600 communication majors at Purdue are currently accelerating, and only 8 percent of students at Hartwick are participating in three-year options. Partly that's a function of the intense workload, and a desire to leave room in the day for athletics and other activities as well

A FEW SCHOOLS OFFER A *BACHELOR'S* PLUS **MBA**, DOABLE IN FOUR YEARS.

as down time with friends in the dorm. Experts also point out the advantages of having time to develop a network of peers and mentors in college and to explore the curriculum widely. Many students, they note, decide to switch majors at least once. Of course, plenty of people have to spend any extra time they have each week financing their education with a job.

On the other hand, for those who head to college clear about their career path – like Allyson Daniels, a 2016 graduate of Hartwick's nursing program from Pembroke, New Hampshire – the shortened time frame can be a big draw. "I wanted to beat the competition and get into the job market early," she says.

The bachelor's plus grad degree options

At many universities, high achievers in certain fields can apply to enter the fast track to a master's degree early enough in their undergraduate career to collect both diplomas in as little as four years. Among them: Brown University in Rhode Island, Emory University in Georgia, Northwestern University in Illinois, and Harvard and Brandeis universities in Massachusetts. More typically, fast trackers speed to that credential in five years instead of six. Students

at Duke University's Pratt School of Engineering can earn a bachelor's and a master of engineering in five years, for example – as long as they get a B in any graduate class taken as an undergrad and maintain a 3.0 overall in their grad courses. And a growing number of business schools allow an early start so the MBA can be earned in a fifth year.

The latest wrinkle: A few schools, including Quinnipiac University in Connecticut and La-Salle University in Philadelphia, have begun offering a combined bachelor's plus MBA that is possible to complete in four years. At Quinnipiac, students seeking the two degrees live with others in the program freshman year and follow a crammed course plan that packs in study abroad and internships. "I selected to do a week in Peru," says Erika Edlund of Albany, New York, who combined a bachelor's in health sciences and an MBA (taking five years) and landed a job at Qualdigm, a national health care consulting and research company. Tuition is frozen for four years, and those taking the shortest route save up to 25 percent compared to the traditional MBA route, the school estimates.

A host of programs similarly provide a streamlined path to other professions. Applicants to Drexel University in Philadelphia, for instance, can seek entry to programs leading to a law degree in six years or a medical degree in seven. And students already enrolled have the option of accelerated tracks to advanced degrees in physical therapy or physician assistant studies. Georgia State University offers an expedited law program to students who have completed 24 to 30 credits in AP courses before arriving. By contrast, students at the University of Denver's Sturm College of Law can earn a bachelor's and law degree in six years by double-counting graduate law classes as elective undergraduate credits.

Temple University in Pennsylvania offers a seven-year combo undergrad/doctor of pharmacy option. Besides Drexel, institutions that accept highly qualified high school seniors into accelerated programs that funnel directly into medical school (assuming the student stays highly qualified) include Boston University, Kent State in Ohio, the University of Southern Florida, the University of Missouri – Kansas City, George Washington University in the District of Columbia and Northwestern.

Such programs can clearly offer advantages to the right students. But college advisers caution that the choice should be made only after a clear-eyed assessment of the demands. ●

WHO SAYS

A **BLUE MAN** IS TOO COOL FOR SCHOOL?

The Blue Man Group founders (l. to r.) Phil Stanton, Chris Wink and Matt Goldman.

Clark University alumnus **Matt Goldman '83, M.B.A. '84,** motivates himself with three words:

MAKE IDEAS REAL.

In 1987 that simple mission statement drove him to co-found Blue Man Group, whose raucous and wry stagecraft turned the troupe's signature art into a cultural touchstone.

Matt and his partners have since turned their energies to Blue School, the Manhattan elementary and middle school he co-founded in 2007. The school reimagines education in a changing world by creating communities of learners "who use courageous and innovative thinking to build a harmonious and sustainable world."

The same spirit for inventive enterprise that drives Matt Goldman recently earned Clark a #16 ranking on Forbes magazine's list of the nation's most entrepreneurial research universities.

Matt exemplifies the Clark University motto, "Challenge Convention. Change Our World," which inspires all Clarkies to make ideas real. Here, we regard the status quo and say, "We can do better." **Can you?**

CLARK UNIVERSITY

FIAT LUX

MDCCCLXXXVII

CHALLENGE CONVENTION. CHANGE OUR WORLD.   clarku.edu

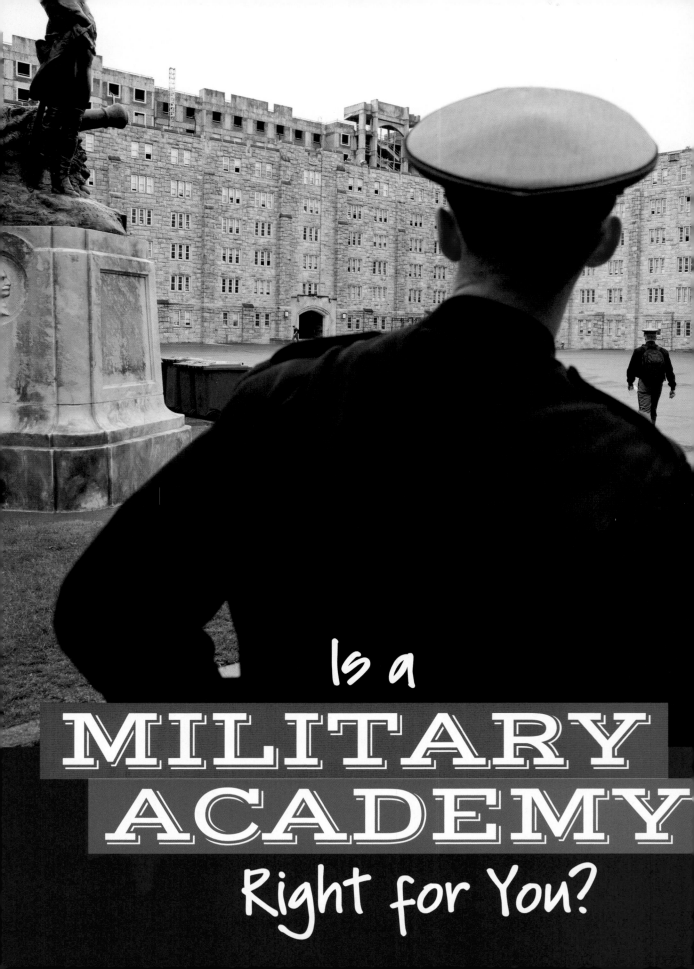

Is a

MILITARY
ACADEMY
Right for You?

WAITING FOR
LUNCH FORMATION
AT WEST POINT

You can get a great education tuition-free if you're willing to serve

BY MARGARET LOFTUS

During summers in college, Caroline Zotti spent time in Africa, Asia and the Mideast. Her travels weren't for fun – though she's the first to admit they were the "coolest part" of her academic career. Rather, they were part of her shipboard training as a midshipman at the U.S. Naval Academy. On these trips mids, as they're called, learn a range of skills from basic seamanship while sailing on one of the Navy's sloops to live-fire gunnery while aboard a guided-missile cruiser.

The USNA is one of the nation's five service academies, which are known for providing an education on par with elite colleges. Students are offered phenomenal opportunities for on-the-job experience like Zotti's. They undergo intensive leadership training and gain skills in areas as varied as submarine warfare, advanced cybersecurity, physical oceanography and aeronautical engineering that can serve as great stepping-stones to post-military careers. What's more, tuition and many other expenses are covered largely courtesy of Uncle Sam, and a job is typically waiting for you upon graduation. The catch? Be ready to trade your jeans and hoodies for uniforms and a multiyear service obligation following graduation.

In addition to the standard college application process, service academies require that applicants pass a fitness assessment, meet certain medical criteria – asthma and migraines are among the conditions that could rule you out – and (except for the Coast Guard) receive an appointment by their congressional representative or senator. Depending on what your skills and interests are, one of the service academies may well be able to match them.

U.S. Naval Academy
Annapolis, Maryland

With its Beaux Arts buildings, oak-lined streets, and the Chesapeake Bay as a backdrop, the Naval Academy and its location in historic Annapolis have wowed would-be midshipmen and their parents for generations. Says Zac Dannelly, who graduated last May, "None of the other service academies have a stronger connection to the city that they're a part of."

Still, despite the appealing locale, midshipmen spend most of their first year on campus adjusting to military life. It can be challenging even for those like recent USNA grad Zotti, who grew up in a Marine Corps family and whose mother is a professor at the academy. "The regimented schedule is a shock to the system," she says. From reveille at 6:30 a.m. to taps at midnight, weekdays are highly structured with two formations, six class periods, roughly two hours for sports or extracurriculars, and a mandatory study session in the evening. Free time depends on your year, ranging from the precious 12 hours of "town liberty" allotted to plebes (freshmen) on Saturdays to full weekends for first classmen (seniors).

While majors at the academy range from Arabic to quantitative economics, at least two-thirds of students are encouraged to major in one of the STEM fields – science, technology, engineering or mathematics – to meet the needs of the Navy. All students graduate with a Bachelor of Science degree.

Summer training throughout all four years is mandatory, starting with basic seamanship and military skills during "plebe summer" leading into freshman year. Each subsequent summer, mids are required to participate in "fleet cruises" to explore various career paths. First classmen, for instance, can choose from surface, submarine, aviation or other cruises, where they're expected to lead sailors and Marines as division officers in specialized training.

Mids must also take professional development courses each summer, which range from dive school to faculty-led cultural trips like one Zotti took to Ethiopia's South Omo Valley. First classmen submit their career preferences in August before their senior year and are assigned by November. All 4,400 midshipmen live under one roof – Bancroft Hall – that is the center of social life. "There's a forced unity in the sense

A LEADERSHIP CAMP SOLD CADET ALEX WERDEN (CENTER) ON WEST POINT.

that you can't leave," says Zotti, now a surface warfare officer stationed in San Diego. But it's not all homework and formations. Dannelly, who will be a cryptologic warfare officer after he wraps up a master's in technology policy at the University of Cambridge in England and a master's in management science and engineering at Stanford University, fondly recalls the annual Army-Navy game and going up to Baltimore's Camden Yards for Orioles games. "There's so much more you can do than studying calculus," he says.

U.S. Military Academy
West Point, New York

★ Alex Werden's first impression of West Point was right out of "Harry Potter." "It's like showing up at Hogwarts," he says. As a rising high school senior from Chapel Hill, North Carolina, he had gone to the storied Hudson Valley campus to participate in a summer leadership camp. Like the fictional school, West Point is an imposing "castle on a hill," he says, exemplifying its mission to groom the best and the brightest, albeit in leadership, not wizardry.

After the weeklong experience, the college became Werden's top choice, and today he is a junior majoring in international history. Not being from a military family, he took some time to adjust during the first summer of basic

training. But gone are the days when the seven-week program was designed to weed out students, says Lt. Col. Rance Lee, associate director of admissions. "Now we bring in 1,200 students, and we want every one of those kids to make it."

What sets West Point apart from other academies is how early cadets take on leadership roles, says Lee. "Within a year of graduating, you're more than likely going to be a platoon leader in charge of 30-some soldiers." Plus, the school offers a broader range of majors than most service academies, from philosophy to electrical engineering. Still, the core requirements make up most of the academic workload of the first two years, including three semesters each of math and science and two of information technology. Other requirements sprinkled throughout the curriculum: a semester apiece of military history, leadership, law and officership.

Cadets spend part of their summers on military skills-building, including cadet leader development training after their sophomore and junior years. Other summer opportunities are voluntary, from fellowships on Capitol Hill to language immersion programs. After graduation, cadets are commissioned as second lieutenants and must serve five years on active duty, in roles running the gamut from aviation to finance to military intelligence.

Lee says that the academy looks for well-rounded students, those who excel in the classroom and have shown themselves to be proven leaders and athletes. (The school boasts 28 intercollegiate sports – football and hockey are popular – as well as club sports.) But there's also room for kids who "have off-the-charts SATs but aren't the best athletes, or leaders who didn't score 800 on their SATs but did well enough academically" to meet the rigors of the workload, he says.

U.S. Air Force Academy
Colorado Springs, Colorado

★ As soon as he knew he'd be attending the Air Force Academy, Christopher Steele began rigorous workouts to ease acclimatization to life at 7,000 feet. Still, coming to the Rocky Mountains from near sea-level Aiken, South Carolina, he found the transition challenging. So too was the pounding on the door at 0400 to roust him for basic training. "It was shocking," he recalls, but well worth it for an opportunity to become an Air Force pilot.

At the USAFA, cadets can choose from 31 academic majors ranging from English to aeronautics engineering, but the core curriculum skews technical. Everyone has to take astronau-

DEGREES *for* DREAMERS DOERS *and* LEADERS

Whether you want to change the world or tell its stories, you'll find the right degree program for you at IU. Whatever your goal is, you'll get the support you need to succeed. And you'll leave prepared for whatever comes next.

Learn more at go.iu.edu/indiana

Ⅲ INDIANA UNIVERSITY
FULFILLING *the* **PROMISE**

tics, for example, as well as computer science. While your major obviously influences your career path, an aeronautical engineering degree is no guarantee that you'll be selected for flight training. Other factors include medical qualifications, class ranking and demand. The 19,000-acre base in the shadow of the Rockies seems like an ideal jumping-off point for ski breaks, but only about half of the weekends are free. Cadets spend the other half in military exercises such as wilderness training in the mountains. What the curriculum lacks in free time, it makes up for in togetherness. "In a normal college, you could go the whole way without talking to anyone. [Here] you're around people 24 hours a day," says Steele, now a senior. "You form a tight bond with others."

Summer opportunities are wide-ranging. A number are required, such as going through the Expeditionary Survival and Evasion Training program and stints at air force bases. Steele has spent his summers learning to fly a glider and a T-53 (a militarized version of a Cessna), shadowing officers at Malmstrom Air Force Base in Montana, and attending a language immersion program in France. After graduation in 2017, he plans to train as a pilot, which obligates him to 10 years of active duty (aviators must serve an extra five years on top of the standard commitment). But he hopes to spend his career in the Air Force. "I love it here," he says.

U.S. Merchant Marine Academy

Kings Point, New York

✯ The USMMA's mission is "to educate and graduate licensed merchant mariners and leaders of exemplary character who will serve America's marine transportation and defense needs in peace and war." For Midshipman First Class Brody Oakes, the chance to merge academics with shipboard experience is what sold him on the school – that, and the picturesque campus, which is set on a peninsula on the north shore of Long Island. "We have the best backyard of any college, if you ask me," Oakes notes.

All majors focus on the maritime industry, from marine transportation – a hybrid of nautical science and marine business management – to marine engineering and shipyard management. A big part of the experience is sea year: Midshipmen serve as deck or engine cadets aboard commercial, military or passenger vessels during two or more assignments that total over 300 days and are primarily spread across sophomore and junior years. Oakes sailed as a crewman on a Maersk K-class container ship, helping keep the engines running. Stops at ports in countries like Spain, Dubai, Pakistan and India only enhanced the experience, he says.

This past summer, sea year came under a cloud as the academy suspended it amid reports of sexual and other professional misconduct towards cadets, primarily by peers or other crewmen. The program has been reintroduced, although for now it will be conducted aboard military ships only.

The accrediting body responsible for the academy has also issued a warning, giving the USMMA two years to address academywide issues of sexual assault and harassment and governance. The school has instituted anti-harassment training and prevention, as well as a confidential reporting system so students can seek help without triggering an official investigation. Through a spokesperson, Rear Admiral James Helis, the USMMA superintendent, stressed to U.S. News that, "While there remains more work to do, we are committed to ensuring midshipmen training is conducted in an environment of safety, dignity, and respect."

While at the USMMA, students must also participate in two- to six-week internships that focus on their specialty. For instance, a marine engineering and shipyard management major may opt to intern at a shipping company or port facility. Grads leave the academy with a Bachelor of Science degree, a

Coast Guard license, and an officer's commission. They can satisfy their service obligation by working as licensed officers aboard U.S. flag vessels and spending eight years in a reserve unit of the nation's armed forces. Alternately, some 25 percent of graduates opt for five years of active duty in one of the armed forces or the National Oceanic and Atmospheric Administration Corps, which operates NOAA's ships and aircraft and aids in its research projects. Mids who decide to serve in the armed forces apply directly and, if offered a commission, will become an officer in that service. Oakes, who graduated in May, plans to work aboard an oil tanker.

U.S. Coast Guard Academy
New London, Connecticut

✯ Both of Aileen Fagan's parents attended the Coast Guard Academy. Nonetheless, Fagan's transition to military life during the eight-week indoctrination before freshman year known as Swab Summer came as a bit of a

WE GIVE YOU DIRECTION.
YOU LEAD THE WAY.

The University of Tampa's AACSB-accredited graduate business programs prepare students with the invaluable skills and career connections needed for success in today's rapidly evolving global economy. Students benefit from hands-on learning, one-on-one faculty mentoring and a degree from a private, top-ranked university. Within six months of graduation, 94 percent of alumni report achieving their goals, including a new job or a promotion.

THE UNIVERSITY OF TAMPA IS PROUD TO BE:

- Named by The Princeton Review as one of the 295 best business schools in the world
- Included on *Forbes'* annual ranking of America's Top Colleges
- Listed in *U.S. News & World Report* among the best graduate nursing and best part-time MBA programs
- Named the #7 best value business school in the U.S. by *Business Insider*
- Consistently named a military friendly university by *Military Advanced Education* and Victory Media

THE UNIVERSITY OF TAMPA

LEARN MORE AT UT.EDU/GRADINFO OR CALL (813) 258-7409

MBA | Professional MBA | Executive MBA | M.S. in Accounting | M.S. in Entrepreneurship
M.S. in Finance | M.S. in Marketing | Certificate in Nonprofit Management
M.Ed. in Educational Leadership | M.Ed. in Curriculum and Instruction
M.S. in Instructional Design and Technology | M.S. in Exercise and Nutrition Science
M.S. in Nursing | MFA in Creative Writing

shock. "One day you're a civilian and you just graduated from high school, and the next day you're doing pushups and getting yelled at," she says.

Like orientation at all service academies, that first summer is meant to instill core values in students and prepares them to enter the classroom and join the Corps of Cadets. But in some ways, the similarities to other military branches end there. The biggest difference is the Coast Guard's mission, which covers three broad categories: maritime safety, maritime security and maritime stewardship. "We see ourselves as guardians, not warriors," explains Susan Bibeau, associate director of admissions for marketing.

Women make up more than one-third of the most recent class, the highest among the academies (females make up 22 percent of West Point's Class of 2020, for example). And with a student population of about 900, the school vies annually with the USMMA for the distinction of smallest service academy and boasts a student-faculty ratio of 8-1.

Academics are rigorous, with a heavy dose of science and math. Save for a government and a management major, most options are STEM-related, ranging from civil engineering to marine and environmental science. Support is baked into the chain of command system, with the entire corps divided into companies, consisting of students from each year. Older students mentor and advocate for the younger ones in their companies, Fagan explains. "We're there for each other."

Summers bring opportunities for professional development and training programs, such as the required multiweek stint for sophomores sailing aboard the tall ship

RECENT GRAD AILEEN FAGAN AT THE COAST GUARD ACADEMY

Eagle that serves as a seamanship training platform. The experience also helps build leadership skills and challenges cadets' physical limits (climbing the rigging on a tall ship is no easy task). Depending on their year, cadets are required to participate in a mix of training, professional development and academic internships each summer. For instance, last summer, Fagan, a marine science major, did oceanic research in Iceland.

Graduates are obligated to five years of service. The majority are stationed on ships in the Coast Guard fleet, from polar ice breakers to national security cutters. Most grads focus either on commanding the movements of a ship and what goes on "topside" or on engineering, maintaining the physical plant of the ship. The actual missions of these new ensigns depend on the functions of the teams they're assigned to, which range from drug interdiction to search and rescue. A small percentage of graduates head either to flight school at Naval Air Station Pensacola in Florida for 18 months before moving on to a transition or "T" course, where they learn to fly a specific aircraft, or they are stationed at shore units of large U.S. ports, where they manage Coast Guard response and prevention operations. Pilots owe an extra nine years of service, not including flight training.

After graduation last May, Fagan was assigned to a Coast Guard cutter based in Port Angeles, Washington, monitoring offshore fisheries, enforcing quotas, and protecting endangered species. Reflecting on her academy experience, she observes how much more engaged in the world she has become. "It's made me a better person," she says ●

WHY I PICKED...

California Institute of Technology Pasadena

Suchita Nety, CLASS OF 2017

I was drawn to Caltech by the opportunity to study chemistry and to contribute to high-impact interdisciplinary research in a collaborative, close-knit environment. As a freshman, I joined a lab and have continued working year-round thanks to the support of Caltech's Summer Undergraduate Research Fellowships. My research thesis, which I started junior year, was on the development of noninvasive techniques to image biological function in humans. By serving as an editor for the institute's undergraduate research journal, I've been able to observe the work of my peers as they tackle exciting problems like detecting gravitational waves or optimizing tissue regeneration.

I've also benefited tremendously from opportunities to grow outside the realm of academics. Caltech's SanPietro Travel Prize allowed me to spend three weeks traveling through Greece to experience a foreign country – just because! As a dancer, I've found opportunities to explore diverse styles, including hip-hop and Indian classical dance, and even choreograph and stage my own pieces. My love of literature, combined with the encouragement of wonderful English professors, has led me to pursue an English minor along with my B.S. in chemistry. I am grateful to have found my place in such a nurturing community. ●

> **I AM GRATEFUL TO HAVE FOUND MY PLACE IN SUCH A NURTURING COMMUNITY.**

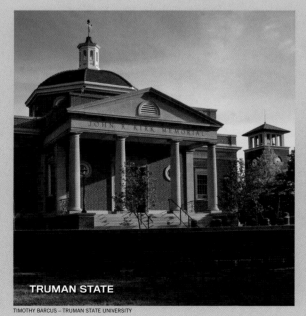

TRUMAN STATE

TIMOTHY BARCUS – TRUMAN STATE UNIVERSITY

Truman State University Kirksville, Missouri

Mackenzie Smith, CLASS OF 2017

I chose Missouri's Truman State because of its affordability, small classes and commitment to academic excellence. Initially, I did not know what to major in, so the school's liberal studies program turned out to be a great fit for me. It requires students to take a range of classes to broaden themselves. A public speaking course so engaged me that I decided to major in communications.

Truman faculty take a strong interest in their students, which is how I became a McNair Scholar. My professors encouraged me to apply to the McNair

TECH

Rutgers University
New Brunswick, New Jersey

Katherine Lau, CLASS OF 2016

I chose Rutgers because of its phenomenal school spirit (on game day the school is a sea of alumni and students wearing scarlet shirts), state-of-the-art facilities, and central location in the biopharma hub of America. On my first campus visit, I spent the most time during my tour in the gleaming Biomedical Engineering building where students can conduct research alongside professors in an ultramodern clean room.

Rutgers is a large school, but with 450-plus clubs and organizations, each student can easily find his or her own small community to settle in. As a biomedical engineering major, I found a home in the Engineering Governing Council and Phi Sigma Rho, the national engineering sorority. Because the university has great career services and supportive faculty and staff, I have been able to capitalize on great opportunities. As a sophomore, for example, I was able to start research in computational gene analysis. Then as a junior, I landed an internship at Chromocell Corporation, a biotechnology company. I was also awarded school research funding to develop a 3-D printed prosthetic hand for a 4-year-old girl in Las Vegas. The university's ties with top pharmaceutical corporations is a big plus, too, as I hope to join one of these companies after completing graduate school. ●

> EACH STUDENT CAN EASILY FIND HIS OR HER OWN SMALL COMMUNITY TO SETTLE IN.

program, which helps students who are the first in their family to attend college or who are from underrepresented groups to get access to research opportunities and faculty mentors who advise them on course planning and their research projects. The goal is to keep you on track for graduate school - something I had never dreamed of doing before reaching Truman. For my research, I'm examining how institutions approach intercultural communication. Fellow McNair Scholars have done projects in the hard sciences, the humanities and other fields. Truman students are extremely friendly, and it's easy to find classmates who share your passions. For me, the university has become a second home. ●

> THE SCHOOL'S LIBERAL STUDIES PROGRAM TURNED OUT TO BE A GREAT FIT FOR ME.

KATHERINE LAU, IN THE LAB AT RUTGERS

MARCHING BAND
PRACTICE, UNIVERSITY
OF CONNECTICUT

MATT SLABY – LUCEO FOR USN&WR

Take a
Road T

2

rip

2

TAKE A ROAD TRIP

Colorado

Enjoy Colorado's famously beautiful landscape as U.S. News begins it college tour at the University of Colorado–Boulder, then moves on to the University of Denver and the Colorado School of Mines in Golden before finishing up at Colorado College in the foothills of Pikes Peak. **BY CHRISTOPHER J. GEARON**

University of Colorado–Boulder

Colorado School of Mines

University of Denver

Colorado College

CU-Boulder

Tuscan vernacular architecture dominates the 318-acre main campus of Colorado's flagship university, expressed in sandstone and red tile roofs. The backdrop: the majestic Flatirons. The broader setting, usually sunny Boulder, often lands on lists of the most livable places, and skiing, snowboarding and other outdoor activities are big draws. "The first few weeks I got here I took up skydiving," says Aidan Rafferty, a senior from Greenwich, Connecticut, studying aerospace engineering.

Students choose from 150 fields of study, including programs considered among the nation's best in aerospace engineering, ceramics, geology, physical chemistry, quantum physics and environmental law. Eighteen astronauts have studied or worked here, and CU–Boulder faculty have been awarded five Nobel Prizes over the past few decades. It was the "really strong" physics education that kept Boulder native Oak Nelson, a 2016 grad, from accepting offers from Dartmouth or the Massachusetts Institute of Technology. The school

draws about 40 percent of its enrollment from outside Colorado, and the student population is approximately 30 percent minority and international.

Several programs make Colorado's largest university feel smaller and more welcoming to freshmen, part of an effort to raise the six-year graduation rate from 71 percent to 80 percent

UNDERGRADUATES
Full-time: 24,906

TOTAL COST*
In-State: $25,121
Out-of-State: $48,669

U.S. NEWS RANKING
National Universities: #92

*Tuition, fees and room & board for 2016-17

by 2020. Over half of students living on campus are enrolled in 14 themed residential academic programs, or RAPs, and six similar living-and-learning communities. The programs build communities around an interest such as global studies, fine arts, leadership and community service or sustainable design. For example, students in the humanities-focused Farrand RAP live in Farrand Hall and take a class each semester in which they examine texts, write and learn the research process as they connect with their peers and professor.

"Most of my friends I met in my RAP," says Daniel Peaslee, a 2016 graduate in film studies from Estes Park, Colorado, who joined the arts and film group.

Another way CU gets students engaged is by giving upperclassmen lots of opportunities to do research. "I got to command a spacecraft in my second year," says Maggie Williams, a 2016 aerospace engineering graduate from Highlands Ranch, Colo-rado; the command center for the Kepler spacecraft now surveying the Milky Way for potentially habitable planets is located at CU. "Half of our staff members are students," says Bill Possel, director of Mission Operations and Data Systems.

But that doesn't mean students don't cut loose. "If you're into the party scene," notes Ellysse Dick, a 2016 graduate in international affairs and German studies from Rapid City, South Dakota, "there are plenty of things to do." Nearby Pearl Street's restaurants and bars are popular destinations. Although cannabis is legal in Colorado, CU takes a zero-tolerance position in keeping with a smoke-free policy. Students enjoy cheering on their Buffaloes in an array of varsity sports in the Pac-12 Conference. The men's and women's ski teams are among the most competitive.

Sustainability is a major focus, with student-run recycling, the nation's first Division I zero-waste athletics program, and the new Sustainability, Energy and Environment Com-

BETWEEN CLASSES (TOP) AND AT WORK IN THE CU-BOULDER LIBRARY

plex, where a new major in environmental design will be headquartered.

Other points of pride are the school's entrepreneurial bent and an interdisciplinary approach to learning. At the BioFrontiers Institute, faculty from 10 departments from applied math to the geological sciences are partnering with industry to make their discoveries relevant. At the Idea Forge, engineering, business and humanities majors design, create and test products tackling societal needs and problems of companies. Some students find support through a summer startup accelerator that ends with "Shark Tank"-like pitches to potential investors. ●

University of Denver

Located five miles from downtown, the University of Denver, known as DU, is recognized for its international studies and business programs, particularly hospitality management; its access to skiing and other mountain pursuits; a vibrant study abroad program; and its national champion men's lacrosse team. "I needed to be close to the mountains, and I wanted to go to a good school as well," says Vermonter Connor Davis, a 2016 graduate in journalism,

UNDERGRADUATES
Full-time: 5,448

TOTAL COST*
$58,383

U.S. NEWS RANKING
National Universities: #86

*Tuition, fees and room & board for 2016-17

avid skier, and former editor of DU's newspaper.

"Study abroad was a big draw," says Jess Davidson, a 2016 graduate in political science who

studied in South Africa for a semester and worked on DU-sponsored research in Uganda one summer.

Founded in 1864, DU is the oldest and largest private university in the Rocky Mountain region. While the school's 76 percent admit rate seems high, officials say the caliber of student also is high, with the average GPA of entrants running 3.68. Less than a quarter of students hail from Colorado, with large numbers coming from the East and West Coasts, Illinois and Minnesota.

The student body is 68 percent white, although the new chancellor wants to increase diversity.

About one-third of undergrads major in business; many enter the university's formal dual bachelor's/graduate programs that allow them to start and complete their advanced degree sooner than is typical in such fields as business, engineering, public policy, education, social work and law. "I'm getting my master's in less than five years," says Davidson of Fort Collins, Colorado, who is continuing at DU for a master's in public policy analysis.

With at least two-thirds of undergrads choosing to study abroad, the Institute of International Education regularly puts DU at or near the top in the nation for overseas study. The question "isn't whether you are going to study abroad, but where you will go," notes Aaron Sanchez, a senior in marketing from Thornton, Colorado. DU has more than 150 programs in its global studies portfolio.

The emphasis is shifting toward collaborative and experiential learning, already big in the engineering program. Students do senior capstone projects that have involved, for example, helping a local biotech or

other firm solve problems or create new products. "A lot of students get jobs with these customers," says Bradley Davidson, a mechanical engineering assistant professor and director of DU's Human Dynamics Laboratory.

DU students are required to live on campus their first two years ("When you are in the freshmen dorms, you're waking up to the mountains," says Cameron Hickert, a 2016 graduate in physics and international studies from Colorado Springs), and freshmen have a choice of five theme-based living-and-learning communities that have them taking seminar classes together while living on the same floor. A quarter of students participate in the Greek system.

Cherished traditions include tailgating before lacrosse games, winter carnival, and camping out in line to get hockey tickets. "The Colorado College-DU game," says Jess Davidson, "is huge." ●

Colorado School of Mines

While the school has its roots in geology and mining, most students today come to the Golden public university for its engineering programs. Traditionally, Mines has been known for producing graduates who command handsome salaries six months after graduation (an average of $66,400 in 2015) and the culture of a suitcase school, deserted on weekends. That part has changed, says Brent Waller, director of residence life and housing. "Now it feels like a college."

Indeed, the campus leadership is bent on transformation, from increasing the number of women enrolled (about one-third of the class of 2019 is female, and the school now boasts the largest college chapter of the Society of Women Engineers) to undertaking a building boom. Mines also has beefed up its weekend and other social programming, along with efforts aimed at bonding students to the school. Among them: freshmen success seminars and learning communities organized around

UNDERGRADUATES
Full-time: 4,386

TOTAL COST*
In-State: $28,391
Out-of-State: $45,836

U.S. NEWS RANKING
National Universities: #82

*Tuition, fees and room & board
for 2015-16

such themes as the visual and performing arts, being a first-generation student, and tackling solutions to big engineering challenges.

"The academics are really top-notch, but the students have fun too," says Peter Consalvi, a senior from Hereford, Maryland, majoring in engineering physics. Fun ranges from Free Pour Fridays (which doesn't involve beer, but rather smelting things for fun at the campus foundry) and Greek life to intramural athletics and the mountain sports available minutes from campus. Still, says Gus Becker, a senior in engineering physics from Centennial, Colorado, the typical Mines student is a "nerd and proud."

Through sophomore year, Orediggers are fed a steady diet of core require-ments, typically entailing calculus I-III, differential equations, chemistry I-II, physics I-II, principles of economics, and two classes in which students work in teams to solve open-ended design problems. Professors are very helpful inside and outside of class and "want you to succeed," says Katie Schumacher, a recent environmental engineering grad from Murphy, Texas. Students in most majors must do at least one summer of fieldwork; petroleum engineering majors might work in the Rangely Oil Field and geology students in geomorphic regions of Colorado, for example. Senior year wraps up with a capstone project.

As students increasingly have sought "to understand the intersection of engineering and society," capstone projects have

THE MINES FOOTBALL SQUAD RUNNING PRACTICE DRILLS

----

often taken a more socially conscious focus, says Kevin Moore, dean of the College of Engineering and Computational Sciences. And Mines is rolling out a humanitarian engineering degree.

The changes notwithstanding, traditions are held dear. Freshmen bring rocks from their hometowns and hike as a class up nearby Mt. Zion, where they whitewash their rocks and place them into the huge "M" overlooking campus; students retrieve them upon graduation. Career Day brings hundreds of employers to campus twice a year, and the three-day spring blowout known as "E (for Engineering)

Days" features "the best fireworks show you'll ever see in your life," says Jennifer Jacobs, a 2016 graduate from Bremerton, Washington, majoring in computer science.

"The biggest complaint on campus is the food," says Cody Watters, a senior in computer science from Colorado Springs, who adds that it's getting better. Students are required to live on campus as freshmen, but tend to move into the surrounding area thereafter. There is housing and good food available in downtown Golden, described by one student as "a sleepy little town" 20 minutes from Denver. The Division II women's soccer team made it to the 2014 NCAA Final Four, and the football team was co-champ of its conference in 2014. ●

Colorado College

Colorado College, or CC, may be best known for its Block Plan, a curriculum that involves taking just one class at a time. Blocks run three-and-a-half weeks; students take eight blocks a year and need 32 to graduate. It was this arrangement plus the beautiful location at the foothills of 14,115-foot Pikes Peak and "the undergrad cadaver lab" that drew Ellen Gilbertson, a senior from Wellington, Colorado, majoring in biochemistry.

"We tend to get students who are passionate about things," says Regula Meyer Evitt, associate dean and associate professor of English. Those who do well, she says, "are students who love an intensive experience and who like to go deep." One day here "equals one week in a regular semester," says Alison Bemis, a history major and senior from Honolulu. Literature students, for example, devour "Beowulf" in two days. CC students are "known for being artsy and out there," adds Esther Chan, a 2016 graduate from California who, like dozens of other CC students, designed her own major – visual media and social change. Skiers and outdoor enthusiasts also are attracted to the campus.

The novel calendar also allows ample opportunity for field-based study. Bemis, for example, spent her first block of junior year in Paris, taking an art and cultural history class focused on the 19th century. Other field-based experiences entail studying the ecology of Patagonia in Chile and reading Homer's "The Odyssey" in the Greek Isles. "In every geology class, we spend up to a week in Wyoming or Texas or some other place," notes Cody Duckworth, a 2016 graduate in geology from Black Mountain, North Carolina.

The 90-acre campus features a hodgepodge of architecture ("It's a mix of 1960s cubism and turn-of-the-century Gothic," says

UNDERGRADUATES
Full-time: 2,096

TOTAL COST*
$62,560

U.S. NEWS RANKING
National Liberal Arts: #24

*Tuition, fees and room & board for 2016-17

studying sociology and pre-med.

Students allow that the intense schedule can be stressful, and some feel a bit isolated. "We're in a bubble in Colorado Springs," says Gilbertson. There are opportunities to broaden perspectives, however.

and delivering it to food pantries. Venture Grants from the school allow students to pursue individual research on campus or around the world. Lubchenco has twice been awarded $1,000 to travel to the Dominican Republic to interpret for doctors who didn't speak Spanish. Other grants have helped students investigate food security in India, study the psychology of climate change denial, and build a renewable energy market for African entrepreneurs.

Colorado College is a Division III school whose men's ice hockey and women's soccer teams

AN ECOLOGY CLASS AT CC

Laurie Laker, a 2012 grad who works as a writer at the school). But 16 buildings are on the state or national historical registries, and the location offers beautiful mountain views. The food, heavy on the healthy and organic, gets rave reviews. "It's so good!" says Cora Lubchenco, a senior from Glenwood Springs, Colorado,

CC's Innovation Institute helps students bring their tech or business or socially conscious ideas to fruition, for instance. The annual Big Idea competition has teams of students vying for $50,000 of seed funding to pull off projects such as saving and collecting edible food on and off campus that otherwise would have been tossed

play in Division I. (The women's soccer team played as Team USA at the World University Games in South Korea in 2015.) Three-quarters of students participate in intramurals, and plenty of other activities keep them busy, too, from working in the organic garden and doing community service to skiing and snowboarding. ●

Connecticut

Scenic fall foliage gives way to snowy New England winters in the Nutmeg State, which despite its small size is home to a diverse set of colleges. U.S. News paid a visit to UConn, in rural Storrs; Wesleyan, in suburban Middletown; and Yale and Connecticut College, in cities along the southern coast. **BY MICHAEL MORELLA**

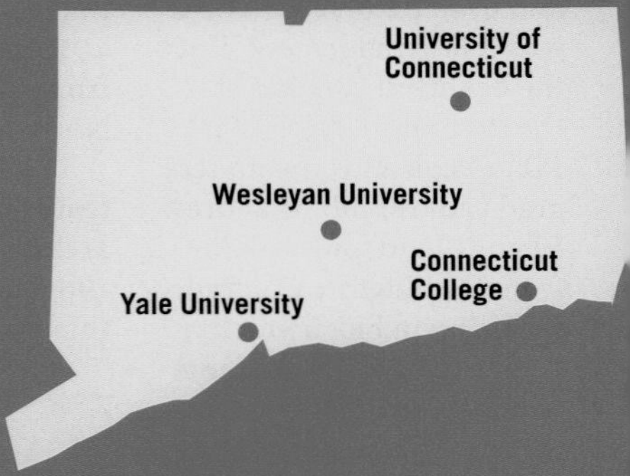

University of Connecticut

Wesleyan University

Connecticut College

Yale University

Yale University

Embedded in the heart of downtown New Haven, Yale University's campus features elegant Gothic architecture, plenty of well-kept green spaces, and amenities like several performance venues and the university art gallery, which includes more than 200,000 works. Founded more than 300 years ago, the country's third oldest college (after Harvard and William and Mary) is ranked No. 3 among national universities by U.S. News. It's also one of the most selective: Only about 6.7 percent of those who applied for the Class of 2019 were admitted.

While students are high-achieving and driven, "no one is rooting for anyone at Yale to fail," says senior Tobias Holden, a molecular, cellular, and developmental biology major from Greenville, South Carolina. "People actually are encouraged to work together."

That sense of community is fostered by Yale's residential college system. All first-year students are randomly assigned to one of 12 colleges, each with its own residence hall, dining facility, gym and library plus some distinct touches: Morse and Ezra Stiles colleges, for example, share

a music recording studio. Faculty members serve as so-called college heads and deans, living in the residences and hosting events at their homes such as teas featuring artists, ambassadors and other high-profile guests. Students often hang out at each facility's "buttery," a game room and common area that serves cheap late-night food. Two new residential colleges are under

construction and expected to open in the fall of 2017, adding space for about 800 undergraduates that Yale is adding to the student body by 2020.

About 84 percent of Yale's 5,500 undergrads live on the 343-acre central campus. All enroll at Yale College, which offers more than 80 majors. (The university has about 6,800 graduate students in 13 additional schools.) Undergrads must complete courses in the humanities and arts, sciences, social sciences, writing, quantitative reasoning, and a foreign language. About three-quarters of classes have fewer than 20 students, and with a 6-to-1 student-faculty ratio, "professors really are looking out for you," says senior Samantha Bensinger, a philos-

UNDERGRADUATES
Full-time: 5,509

TOTAL COST*
$64,650

U.S. NEWS RANKING
National Universities: #3

*Tuition, fees and room & board for 2016-17

OUTSIDE YALE'S
STERLING MEMORIAL LIBRARY

ophy major from Chicago. That said, "you have to make the first move" to get to know faculty members one-on-one or to pursue undergraduate research opportunities, says recent mechanical engineering grad Carlene Huard, from Danbury, New Hampshire. The school does offer plenty of

resources to help students navigate, from a network of faculty and peer advisers to Dwight Hall, Yale's center for public service and social justice, which helps students pursue community service opportunities.

Students say it's a myth that all Yalies are wealthy Northeasterners. In the

Class of 2019, for instance, about 11 percent of undergrads come from abroad, more than 40 percent identify as a minority, and about 1 in 7 are first-generation college students.

Entertainment options are plentiful, with hundreds of student-led organizations and more than 50 performance groups that put on plays, concerts, dances and other events. The Division I Bulldogs compete in the Ivy League in about three dozen sports. Yale is "large enough that you have those kinds of niche groups, but it's small enough that you really do know a lot

A MEDICAL DEVICE
ENGINEERING
CLASS AT YALE'S
BECTON CENTER

of people," says senior Joe English, a global affairs and ethnicity, race, and migration major from Galway, New York. And there are plenty of ways to escape the Yale "bubble." Students can hike, bike or picnic in East Rock Park, catch a concert at College Street Music Hall, or head to New York City, 80 miles away by car or train.

The annual Yale-Harvard football game is a must-attend event. Yalies also enjoy midnight snowball fights and traditions like the Yale Symphony Orchestra Halloween Show; costumed undergrads listen to the music group perform a soundtrack to a student-made silent film at midnight on Oct. 31. "We take our work seriously, but not ourselves seriously," Huard says. ●

A DANCE CLASS
AT WESLEYAN

Wesleyan University

Looking beyond the stately brownstone buildings and well-manicured lawns, students observe that a strong sense of activism and open-mindedness pervades Wesleyan's campus. This is a place that "pushes you to think critically about yourself and about the world," says 2016 grad Bulelani Jili, from South Africa, a College of Social Studies major. That spirit of critical inquiry has been a core university value since its founding in 1831, when its first president, Methodist educator Willbur Fisk, declared the goal of its teachings to focus on "the good of the individual educated and the good of the world." (Wesleyan no longer maintains a religious affiliation.)

Today most undergraduates live on the university's 316-acre campus, set on a hill overlooking Middletown, a city of about 48,000 along the Connecticut River. With about 2,800 undergraduates, the community is close-knit but not excessively so.

"I know everyone's face, but I don't know everything about everyone," says senior Courtney Laermer, a biology and government major from Princeton Junction, New Jersey. Students live in a mix of dorms, apartments and themed houses such

as the Women of Color House or Art House. Seniors typically move to the coveted wood-frame houses on the southern part of campus.

Just over 1 in 5 of those who apply are admitted. In 2014-15, Wesleyan stopped requiring most applicants to submit SAT and ACT scores, and nearly a third of those who joined the Class of 2019 didn't. More than 90 percent of students come from outside Connecticut, and about a third are students of color. "Different groups

AUTUMN LEAVES
COLOR WESLEYAN'S
316-ACRE CAMPUS.

mix and match very well," says Henry Martellier Jr., a sophomore from Brooklyn, New York, who is interested in mathematics and economics.

Students appreciate the 8-to-1 student-faculty ratio and the close relationships that can develop with professors, though doing so "still requires a certain amount of initiative," says junior Henry Prine, an American studies major from Burlington, Vermont.

The university offers 45 undergraduate majors, along with a handful of master's and Ph.D. programs. The open curriculum means that students only need to complete classes required by their major, though the school encourages them to fulfill certain general education courses in math and the sciences, arts and humanities, and social and behavioral sciences. Undergrads can enroll in student forums, small, for-credit courses taught by their peers, on topics like mass incarceration or food justice and sustainability.

Most agree academics are rigorous, but the environment isn't cutthroat. To relax, undergrads can catch a show from the student-run theater group Second Stage or see movies put on by the Wesleyan Film Series, which is affiliated with the university's film studies program. The outing club organizes camping, hiking and other trips throughout the region. In the winter, many students enjoy sledding down Foss Hill near the center of campus.

Some students say Wesleyan can at times feel a bit insular, while others wish it had more diversity. But typically "when there are problems, there's a lot of organizing and activism to change them," Prine says.

Indeed, students are passionate about politics and social issues. Undergrads can get involved in a range of local and global volunteer activities through the Jewett Center for Community Partnerships. And the Patricelli Center for Social Entrepreneurship offers grants for enterprising students and alumni who develop businesses and ideas that help others. Working with the Patricelli Center, sophomore computer science major Alvin Chitena recently founded Zim Code, which works to engage disadvantaged young people in computer programming in his native Zimbabwe. Here, he says, "if you have an idea, you always have someone you can talk to." ●

University of Connecticut

UNDERGRADUATES
Full-time: 18,131

TOTAL COST*
In-State: $26,502
Out-of-State: $48,294

U.S. NEWS RANKING
National Universities: #60

*Tuition, fees and room & board for 2016-17

The University of Connecticut got its start in 1881 as Storrs Agricultural School. Today, the state's flagship public university is part of a bustling college town where undergraduates can choose from more than 100 majors, get involved in cutting-edge research, and cheer on the Division I Huskies, particularly in men's and women's basketball.

Located in rural Storrs, about 30 miles east of Hartford, UConn spans nearly 4,100 acres and enrolls about 18,100 undergraduates. The university is "like a city within itself," where "there are things for everybody," says junior Antonio Salazar, a journalism and Latino studies major from Millburn, New Jersey. More than 600 academic, cultural, athletic, arts and other clubs keep students

-----

UCONN UNDERGRADS CAN PICK FROM MORE THAN 100 MAJORS.

engaged. "Some exist that I haven't even heard of" before, says 2016 molecular and cell biology grad Kayvon Ghoreshi, of Manchester, Connecticut.

The Student Union is one hub of activity, with an art gallery, movie theater, game room and several dining options. Inside are also the university's five cultural centers, which offer activities and support for female, minority and LGBTQ students. About 12 percent of undergrads join fraternities and sororities, which are active but don't dominate the social scene. "We're not a 'go Greek or go home' school," says Noor Afolabi, a 2016 grad in economics from Nigeria. Storrs Center, located just southeast of campus, has a range of shops and restaurants.

About half of students who apply to UConn are admitted, and close to a quarter of them come from outside Connecticut. Students must further apply for certain majors like engineering, business and nursing. With a 17-to-1 student-faculty ratio, undergrads can expect some large lecture classes, particularly in foundation courses, though those typically break out into small-group discussion sections.

Students can also choose from a range of first-year seminars and learning communities, where those with shared interests in public health or the arts, for instance, can live alongside their peers and take classes together. About 2,000 undergrads participate in the honors program, which offers its own

smaller seminars, advising and housing communities.

"It becomes much smaller once you make those key connections, but you definitely have to be proactive," says Michael Bond, a recent grad from Windsor, Connecticut, who double-majored in molecular and cell biology and chemical biology. Bond got involved with undergraduate cancer research as a freshman by seeking out advice from a peer and an instructor, contacting a professor who might be willing to take him on (being "a considerate pest," as Bond puts it), and later securing funding through the Office of Undergraduate Research.

The OUR offers a range of grants to support student-designed research or creative projects across all disciplines. Nathan Wojtyna, another 2016 grad from Willington, Connecticut, was impressed by "how diverse and how deep the resources are" at UConn. The resource economics and horticulture major did research on ways to improve harvesting of the chokeberry, an antioxidant-rich fruit.

Though some students wish there were more to do off campus, most find ways to keep busy no matter the season, from ice skating and hockey on Swan Lake and sledding down Horsebarn Hill in the winter to playing in the OOzeball (mud volleyball) tournament. Huskies also take pride in the campus Dairy Bar, which serves ice cream made from milk produced by UConn cows. ●

Connecticut College

Connecticut College in New London has a lot in common with a certain British capital, with its gray stone castlelike architecture and sweeping view of the Thames River. Founded in 1911 as Connecticut College for

Women, the private liberal arts school enrolls nearly 1,900 undergraduates, about 60 percent of whom are female. The 750-acre campus is an arboretum, with a wide range of trees, gardens, trails, an outdoor amphitheater for concerts and theater performances, and a pond that's often incorporated into science classes. Downtown New London, a historic whaling port of about 27,000, is two miles south of campus, and students venture there for food, entertainment, community service and beach time.

About 40 percent of those who apply to Conn College are admitted, and the school

UNDERGRADUATES
Full-time: 1,857

TOTAL COST*
$65,000

U.S. NEWS RANKING
National Liberal Arts: #50

*Tuition, fees and room & board for 2016-17

THE CONN COLLEGE SAILING TEAM ON THE THAMES RIVER

South Africa, say, or intern with the World Health Organization. A team of advisers will help students navigate.

Freshmen enroll in writing-intensive first-year seminars capped at 16 students, and the seminar professor typically serves as participants' pre-major adviser. As a freshman, Anna Marshall of Norridgewock, Maine, took a course called "Who Are You? Questions of Identity in Contemporary Literature and Culture," and she and her classmates got together with their professor for pizza and bowling even after the class was finished. Students can build strong connections with professors and peers so "it isn't just a face that you sit next to in class," says Marshall, a 2016 anthropology and environmental studies grad.

Indeed, the mostly small classes and 9-to-1 student-faculty ratio create a strong sense of community. Students speak highly of the nearly 100-year-old honor code, which preaches academic honesty and mutual respect and allows undergrads to self-schedule exams. Undergrads are also linked up with a career adviser from the start of their freshman year, and they have access to a range of resources and skill-development workshops (story, Page 20). Those who complete Conn's career development program are eligible for up to $3,000 to pursue a summer internship or research project. And 96 percent of alumni report they are employed or in graduate school one year after graduation.

Ninety-eight percent of students live on campus in one of 23 residence houses, which range from more traditional dorms and apartments to specialty housing based on foreign languages or sustainability. While some say campus can feel a bit like a fishbowl, "it's not small enough that you feel claustrophobic," says Luca Powell, a 2016 English grad from New Haven, Connecticut. "I feel like there are people I'm meeting every day."

More than 60 student-led clubs drive social life. The Division III Camels field 20 varsity sports teams. And each fall, students enjoy Camelympics, in which houses compete against each other in activities like basketball, shaving cream Wiffle ball, and Quidditch. ●

TAKING A STUDY BREAK BETWEEN CLASSES AT CONNECTICUT COLLEGE

does not require applicants to submit standardized test scores.

Beginning this fall, students will take classes according to the college's revamped Connections curriculum. Once the program is fully phased in, they will still complete majors – Conn offers 41 of them – but along the way, undergrads will pursue an interdisciplinary and interconnected track of courses and immersion experiences designed "to begin to get them to think integratively," says Jefferson Singer, dean of the college. Students will follow multifaceted pathways in subjects like sustainability and social justice, global capitalism, and peace and conflict. For example, an undergrad with an interest in worldwide epidemics like the Zika or Ebola viruses could follow the public health pathway, completing a biology degree while taking classes like health economics, health psychology, and social policy analysis in urban America. During or after her junior year, she could study abroad in

Louisiana& Mississippi

The Deep South offers plenty of distinctive college experiences, from Division I football to the music and nightlife of New Orleans. U.S. News traced a path east of the Mississippi River from Xavier University of Louisiana and Tulane in the Big Easy to Millsaps College and Ole Miss in the Magnolia State. **BY BRIANA BOYINGTON**

University of Mississippi

Millsaps College

Tulane University

Xavier Universi of Louis

Xavier University of Louisiana

Bright green roofs top many of the buildings at Xavier, marking the re-building that's been going on since Hurricane Katrina swept through New Orleans a decade ago. Founded in 1915 as a high school for Native Americans and African-Americans, XULA is today the country's only Catholic historically black college, known for its record of producing graduates in the sciences. The campus is surrounded by the city; popular New Orleans hotspots such as the French Quarter and Frenchman Street are an easy bus or Uber ride away. Even after seeing enrollment drop off after Katrina, Xavier (which now has about 2,250 students) still boasts the country's highest number of black graduates in both the biological and physical sciences and the highest number who go on to complete medical school.

One of Xavier's unique programs allows for students to graduate with a doctorate in pharmacy in six years. Students complete two years of the Pharm.D. program as an undergraduate before transferring to the school's College of Pharmacy. High school seniors can secure a spot in the program through the contingent admittance program; it's also possible to apply to the Pharm.D. program during sophomore year of college.

Starting freshman year, the academic advising of-fice makes sure students stay on track for success by laying out milestones for them to hit each year – when to meet with medical school recruiters and study for the MCAT, say, and when to apply to early acceptance programs. "The pre-med office is so structured and organized," says David Powell, a 2016 grad in chemistry from Bakersfield, California. He nabbed a spot at the University of Rochester's med-ical school during his ju-nior year through XULA's early assurance program, which allows underclass-men to apply to Rochester without taking the MCAT. "You're going to get in if you do everything that they tell you to do." Fellow 2016 grad Kandis Carter, who majored in chemis-try and is from Gonzales, Louisiana, credits the advising department's

UNDERGRADUATES
Full-time: 2,242

TOTAL COST*
$31,569

U.S. NEWS RANKING
Regional University
(South): #27

*Tuition, fees and room & board
for 2016-17

counsel on everything from when to start filling out applications to questions to expect in interviews with helping her get into seven dental schools.

While everyone is required to take six hours of theology, students say the campus is open and accepting to all; only about one-quarter identify as Catholic. African-Americans make up nearly 70 percent of the student body. More than half of students are from Louisiana, primarily the New Orleans area.

Still, students from elsewhere say the school does a good job of making them feel at home. "Being at an HBCU and being around a lot of warm hearts made it easier," recalls senior political science major Sierra Blanchard-Hodge of her transition to college in the South after arriving from Denver. "It kind of just felt like home," she says. "It's easier to make friends and almost family connections down here."

Xavier's 70 or so student groups range from the concert choir and the Black Magic Volleyball Team to the poetry and chess clubs. The school also has varsity tennis, basketball and track and field. And the location makes it easy for students to play hard as well as study. From jazz in the streets to Mardi Gras, there are endless ways to sample the food, art, culture and history that make New Orleans so hypnotizing.

And some students seize the opportunity "to make something that's not there," says Chandler Schexnayder, a fourth-year student in the pharmacy program from Patterson, Louisiana. He helped to create Project E.A.T. (for Evaluate, Attack and Triumph), whose mission is to increase the retention of black male students and mentor them to succeed academically, socially and financially. ●

JAZZ BAND PRACTICE AT XAVIER. JADA MACK (LEFT) STUDIES IN THE LIBRARY.

Tulane University

EXAMINING SOLAR CELLS IN THE LAB AT TULANE

T o fans of the movie "22 Jump Street" or Fox's "Scream Queens," Tulane's stately buildings and trees and well-manicured lawns might look familiar. Scenes from several popular shows and movies have been shot on the New Orleans campus. The surrounding Uptown area offers plenty to do; students can walk or catch a streetcar to the restaurants and bars on Maple, Oak, Magazine and Barrett streets. Across from the Tulane entrance, Audubon Park offers a jogging trail, golf and tennis; a bit farther on, along the Mississippi River, the Audubon Zoo is both an attraction and a source of research internships.

About 85 percent of Tulane's 6,500-plus undergraduates are from out-of-state, but students say the school does a great job of helping them make New Orleans home. First, freshman take a one-credit seminar that connects them with a small group of peers while preparing them for the academic rigors of college and exploring life in the city. Students can choose from more than 70 options, from songwriting to architecture. Will Dickson, a junior Latin major from Memphis who is in a special pre-med program giving him early acceptance into Tulane's medical school, notes that his "favorite thing" about the course was that "you get to make a friend on campus who isn't a student." You "really, really get to know your professor."

Second, Tulane requires two public service experiences to graduate, which often involve working with people in the city. One is a course that embeds service in the curriculum, and the second can be filled by any of more than 150 options from internships and service-focused study-abroad programs to faculty-sponsored research projects. Someone in a sociology of education class could tutor students at a school in New Orleans, for example. Those studying abroad in India might help Tibetan refugees learn English.

"You feel way more involved and like a piece of you is in New Orleans," says Richard Carthon, a 2016 graduate from Shreveport, Louisiana, who majored in legal studies in business and business management. To fulfill his second requirement, Carthon interned with a local nonprofit that feeds the

UNDERGRADUATES
Full-time: 6,624

TOTAL COST*
$64,854

U.S. NEWS RANKING
National Universities: #39

*Tuition, fees and room & board for 2016–17

homeless and provides cleaning services and transportation to middle-aged and elderly people with vision problems. He used his training to create a business plan for the organization and help secure funding.

Students can select their major from more than 70 offerings in any of Tulane's five undergraduate schools: architecture, business, liberal arts, public health and tropical medicine, or science and engineering. While many universities require separate admission to their business or architecture schools, say, that is not true here.

Traditions are a big part of the Tulane experience, especially the ones that bring the spirit of New Orleans onto campus. Each spring, 20,000 pounds of free crawfish, plus music, star at the student-run Crawfest festival. And after Mardi Gras, students add their colorful Mardi Gras beads to the huge oak tree behind the administration building for good luck. Tulane has over 200 student-run clubs and organizations, which include performance groups, Greek organizations, academic and service groups as well as a variety of sports clubs and intramural offerings. The 16 Division 1 varsity teams include baseball, basketball and tennis.

This is "a work hard-play hard school," says Lena Franklin, a 2016 grad from Boca Raton, Florida, who majored in music composition and business management. The "person you see at the bar is the same person that you see at the library." ●

Millsaps College

Grace McWatters didn't intend to apply to Millsaps College, but she forgot to cross the school off her list when she was filling out the Common Application. The Washington state native wanted to go to a small school that offered creative writing, economics and an opportunity to act, but she didn't have any desire to be in the South. Then she was offered a theater scholarship and experienced the school's Southern hospitality on a campus visit. "Everyone really cares about you," says McWatters, an economics major now in her final year.

The private liberal arts college sits in the heart of Jackson, the capital of Mississippi and its largest city. A large bell tower overlooks the easily walkable 100-acre campus. At its center, students gather and relax underneath the trees in the open space known as the Bowl. The school's enrollment is small, too: about 750 undergraduates, a little more than half of whom are out-of-state students. The average class size is 14, and the student-faculty ratio is 9-to-1.

Millsaps offers 34 degree programs, including an accelerated MBA that can be started senior year and completed 12 months after graduation. No matter what your major is, writing is a significant part of the curriculum. All students are required to complete a writing portfolio that includes six papers by the end of sophomore year and a reflection on their growth as writers and thinkers during their senior seminar. Among the study abroad options are programs in Yucatán, Mexico, where the college owns a nonprofit organization that operates a 4,000-acre tropical forest biocultural reserve. Students live there and take courses or conduct research in such disciplines as archaeology, ecology,

ENJOYING SOME OUTDOOR TIME AT MILLSAPS COLLEGE

geology and business. For students who prefer studying poetry and art in Paris, there's an option for that too.

Students say the small size and close-knit community make it easy for them to find their niche and nurture their interests. "You don't feel cloistered as long as you're doing what you should be doing, which is trying to be involved," says 2016 graduate Zachary Smith, an English literature and communications studies major from Madison, Mississippi. Millsaps boasts 75-plus organizations, from mock trial to acting groups, and more than 20 percent of students participate in intercollegiate sports on the 18 Division III sports teams.

But "you're not going to be just a football player," says Kendra Williams, a sophomore political science major from Houston. "You're going to be a football player who participates in Major Havoc [an improvisation group],

and is in a frat and goes to support LGBTQ. You're usually not just doing one thing."

Students like the fact that Jackson has a small-town feel but plenty of city amenities – museums, restaurants, shopping centers, live music and bars – within a 20-minute drive of campus. Freshmen who want to get involved in community service in the city can apply to participate in the Wellspring Living and Learning Community; they live with other first-years who are interested in service and volunteer at local schools and other organizations in the Midtown area.

Millsaps is "very deliberate" in making sure grads enter the workforce with the skills to be competitive, says Daniel Kees, a 2016 graduate in political science and economics from Vicksburg, Mississippi, who thinks his strong foundation in writing, critical thinking and teamwork will help him "stand out." Next up: He's been awarded a Fulbright grant to teach English in Mexico. ●

STUDENTS EXPLORE TOGETHER IN ORGANIC CHEMISTRY LAB.

University of Mississippi

A walk through the 990-acre campus of Ole Miss and its surroundings offers a peek into the history of the South and the civil rights movement. Several stately antebellum buildings served as hospitals during the

Civil War, and William Faulkner's home is a university museum nearby, south of the town square. At the heart of the first and largest university in Mississippi stand both a monument to Confederate soldiers and a statue of James Meredith, the first African-American student admitted to the segregated school in 1962 after he sued for the right to enroll. Bullet marks from the rioting that followed can still be seen on the Greek columns of the Lyceum, the university's first building.

Despite this history and the size of the school – the undergraduate population sits at just under 17,400 – students say that today the

environment feels open and welcoming. Black students now account for about 13 percent of the student body; a little over three-quarters are white. Over the last couple of years, students and the NAACP have called to have the Confederate monument and Mississippi state flag – which depicts a Confederate flag – removed; the state flag is gone, and a plaque adding historical context is being added to the monument.

"I have seen in my time here just such an inclusive style about the campus," says Cole Putman, a senior social work major from Brandon, Mississippi. He points to programs put on by the university's inclusion and cross-cultural engagement center on such topics as Native American and LGBT history and Black Lives Matter, for example.

Administrators keep an open-door policy so students can feel comfortable reaching out. Faculty, too, make themselves accessible. The result is the culture and feel of a smaller institution, students say. "They've told me since day one, 'We're here for you.' Ole Miss does a really good job at letting students know that they're not alone," Putman says. And it's only "about a 10-minute walk from anywhere across campus," says Ryley Blomberg, a junior majoring in

well as a final capstone year studying in the country that includes four months of an internship.

Athletics are a big part of the culture; the recently expanded football stadium seats 64,000. Tailgating on the Grove, a grassy area filled with trees, is a major attraction. Other than football, sports events are free for students.

Off campus, the city of Oxford, with a population of about 22,000, has lots to offer history buffs interested in Civil War-era sites and music lovers. The square downtown is a hub of boutiques, restaurants, bars and coffee shops. Nine bus lines run through the campus and throughout the city, and students ride for free. They can also rent a bike, helmet and lock for the semester for just $25. ●

math education from Belleville, Illinois.

Students can choose from over 100 degree options. One multidisciplinary opportunity can be found in the Haley Barbour Center for Manufacturing Excellence, which brings business, accountancy and engineering students together to learn the ins and outs of manufacturing. They get hands-on experience in a space that resembles a modern factory and learn the communication, management and marketing skills needed to run a successful manufacturing business. The center accepts 50 students each year.

Ole Miss is home to one of the country's 12 Chinese Language Flagship programs, part of the Department of Defense's effort to foster education in critical languages. Students who complete the five-year undergrad program become proficient in Mandarin while completing a major of their choice. They spend two summers in China as

The
U.S. NEWS
Rankin

Best National Universities 72
Best National Liberal Arts Colleges 80

BARNARD COLLEGE
GRADUATION CEREMONY

KRISANNE JOHNSON FOR USN&WR

gs

3

3

THE U.S. NEWS RANKINGS

How We Rank Colleges

College-bound students can make good use of our statistics

BY ROBERT J. MORSE AND ERIC M. BROOKS

The host of intangibles that make up the college experience cannot be measured by a series of data points. But for families concerned with finding the best academic value for their money, the U.S. News Best Colleges rankings, now in their 32nd year, provide an excellent starting point for the search. They help you compare at a glance the relative quality of institutions based on such widely accepted indicators of excellence as first-year retention rates, graduation rates and the strength of the faculty. As you check out the data for colleges already on your short list, you may discover unfamiliar schools with similar attributes and thus broaden your options.

Yes, many factors other than those spotlighted here will figure in your decision, including location and the feel of campus life; the range of academic offerings, activities and sports; and the cost plus the availability of financial aid. But if you combine the information in this book with campus visits, interviews and your own intuition, our rankings can be a powerful tool in your quest for the best fit.

How does the methodology work? The U.S. News ranking system rests on two pillars. The formula uses quantita-

UNIVERSITY OF COLORADO-BOULDER

tive and qualitative measures that education experts have proposed as reliable indicators of academic quality, and it is based on our researched view of what matters in education. First, schools are categorized by their mission, which is derived from the breakdown of types of higher education institutions originally developed by the Carnegie Foundation for the Advancement of Teaching. (An update of the Carnegie Classification of Institutions of Higher Education, now the responsibility of the Indiana University Center for Postsecondary Research, was released in February 2016.) The classification has been the basis of the Best Colleges ranking categories since our first ranking was published over three decades ago because it is used extensively by higher education researchers. The U.S. Department of Education and many higher education associations use the system to organize their data and to determine colleges' eligibility for grant money, for example.

The category names we use are our own: National Universities, National Liberal Arts Colleges, Regional Universities and Regional Colleges. But how schools are grouped relies on the Carnegie principles. As a result of the updated classifications, about 1 in 8 schools are ranked in a different category this year than in the past.

The national universities offer a full range of undergraduate majors plus master's and Ph.D. programs and emphasize faculty research (Page 72). The national liberal arts colleges focus almost exclusively on undergraduate education (Page 80). They award at least 50 percent of their degrees in the arts and sciences.

The regional universities (Page 88) offer a broad scope of undergraduate degrees and some master's degree programs but few, if any, doctoral programs. The regional colleges (Page 106) focus on undergraduate education but grant fewer than 50 percent of their degrees in liberal arts disciplines; this category also includes schools that have small bachelor's degree programs but primarily grant two-year associate degrees. The regional universities and regional colleges are further divided and ranked in four geographical groups: North, South, Midwest and West.

Next, we gather data from each college on up to 15 indicators of academic excellence. Each factor is assigned a weight that reflects our research about how much a measure matters. Finally, the colleges and universities in each category are ranked against their peers based on their composite weighted scores.

Some schools are not ranked and thus do not appear in the tables. The most common reason is that the school does not use ACT or SAT test scores in admissions decisions for first-time, first-year, degree-seeking applicants. (Schools with test-optional admission policies are included in the rankings because they do consider ACT or SAT scores when provided.) In fewer cases, colleges are not ranked because they received too few ratings in the peer assessment survey, had a total enrollment of fewer than 200 students, had a large proportion of nontraditional students, or had no first-year students (as is the situation at upper-division schools). As a result of these standards, many for-profit institutions are not ranked. We also did not rank the overall quality of a number of highly specialized schools in the arts, business and engineering.

Colleges report most of the data themselves, via the annual U.S. News statistical survey. This year, 93.5 percent of the 1,374 ranked colleges and universities returned their statistical information during our spring and summer 2016 data collection period.

For eligible colleges that declined to complete our survey, we made extensive use of the data they reported to the U.S. Department of Education's National Center for Education Statistics and other organizations. We obtained missing data on graduation rates from the National Collegiate Athletic Association and data on alumni giving from the Council for Aid to Education. The National Center for Education Statistics provided data on SAT and ACT scores, acceptance rates, retention and graduation rates, faculty, student-faculty ratios, and information on financial resources.

Data that schools did not report in this year's U.S. News survey are footnoted. Schools that did not submit their surveys altogether are identified as nonresponders. Estimates were used in the calculations when schools failed to report data not available from other sources, but these estimates are not displayed in this guidebook. Missing data are reported as N/A.

To ensure the highest possible quality of data used in the rankings, U.S. News conducted rigorous assessments by comparing schools' responses to those of their peers, to third party data, and to their own earlier statistics. Schools were also instructed to verify the accuracy of their final data.

The indicators we use to capture academic quality fall into a number of groupings: assessment by administrators

Weighing What's Important

The U.S. News rankings are based on several key measures of quality, listed below. Scores for each measure are weighted as shown to arrive at a final overall score. In the case of the national universities and national liberal arts colleges, the assessment figure represents input from both academic peers (15 percent) and high school guidance counselors (7.5 percent); for regional universities and colleges, it reflects peer opinion only.

The Scoring Breakdown

Graduation and retention rates	22.5%
Assessment of excellence	22.5%
Faculty resources	20%
Student selectivity	12.5%
Financial resources	10%
Graduation rate performance*	7.5%
Alumni giving	5%

*The difference between actual and predicted graduation rates.

at peer institutions (and, for national universities and liberal arts colleges, also by high school guidance counselors), how well schools retain and graduate students, the quality of and investment in their faculty, admissions selectivity, financial resources, and alumni giving. The indicators include input measures that reflect schools' student bodies, faculties and resources. They also include outcome measures that signal how well institutions are engaging and educating their students.

An explanation of the measures and their weightings in the ranking formula follows; more detail on the methodology can be found at usnews.com/collegemeth.

Retention (22.5 percent).

The higher the proportion of first-year students who return to campus for sophomore year and eventually graduate, the better a school most likely is at offering the classes and services that students need to succeed. This measure has two components: six-year graduation rate (80 percent of the retention score) and first-year retention rate (20 percent).

The graduation rate indicates the average proportion of a class earning a degree in six years or less. We consider freshman classes that started from fall 2006 through fall 2009. First-year student retention indicates the average proportion of freshmen who entered the school in the fall of 2011 through fall 2014 and returned the following fall.

Assessment by peers and counselors (22.5 percent).

The ranking formula integrates the opinions of those in a position to judge a school's undergraduate academic excellence. The academic peer assessment survey allows presidents, provosts and deans of admission to account for qualitative measures of peer institutions such as faculty dedication to teaching. The average academic peer scores are derived from using the two most recent sets of survey results, collected in spring 2015 and spring 2016. Using two years of data incorporates a larger number of respondents and reduces year-to-year volatility in the results.

For their views on the national universities and the national liberal arts colleges, we also surveyed 2,200 counselors at public high schools that appeared in a recent U.S. News ranking of Best High Schools.

Each person surveyed was asked to rate schools' academic programs on a 5-point scale from 1 (marginal) to 5 (distinguished). Those who did not know enough about a school to evaluate it fairly were instructed to mark "don't know." The score used in the rankings is the average of these scores; "don't knows" are not counted.

In the case of the national universities and national liberal arts colleges, the academic peer assessment accounts for 15 percentage points of the weighting, and 7.5 percentage points go to the counselors' ratings. Once again the three most recent years' results were combined to compute the average high school counselor score. For the full results of the high school counselors' ratings of the colleges, visit usnews.com/counselors. In terms of reputation, the regional universities and the regional colleges are judged by peers only.

To reduce the possible impact of strategic voting by re-

spondents, we eliminated the two highest and two lowest scores each school received before calculating the average score. Ipsos Public Affairs collected the most recent year's data in the spring of 2016; of the 4,635 academics who were sent questionnaires, 39.2 percent responded. The counselors' response rate for just this past spring was 9 percent.

Faculty resources (20 percent).

Research shows that the more satisfied students are about their contact with professors, the more they will learn and the more likely they are to graduate. We use five factors from the 2015-2016 academic year to assess a school's commitment to instruction.

Class size (40 percent of this measure) is a more nuanced factor than in the past. We have created an index that takes fuller advantage of the data schools report on class size. Schools receive the most credit in this index for their proportion of undergraduate classes with fewer than 20 students. Classes with 20-29 students score second highest; those with 30-39 students, third highest; and those with 40-49 students, fourth highest. Classes that have 50 or more students receive no credit. Faculty salary (35 percent) is the average faculty pay, plus benefits, during the 2014-2015 and 2015-2016 academic years, adjusted for regional differences in the cost of living using indexes from the consulting firm Runzheimer International.

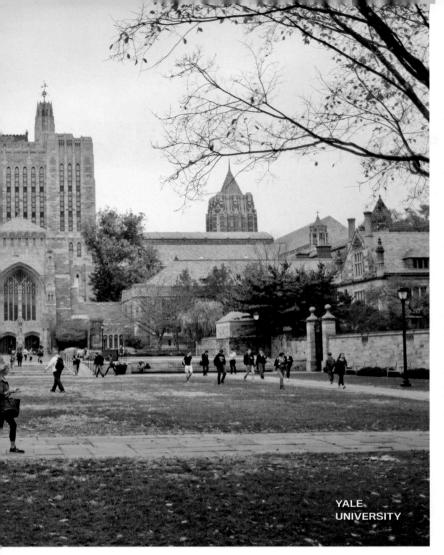
YALE
UNIVERSITY

in the summer of 2015) or schools that declined to tell us whether all students with scores were represented. We once again discounted the value of these schools' reported scores by 15 percent in the ranking model since the effect of leaving students out could be that lower scores are omitted. Also once again, if schools had under 75 percent of their 2015 entering class submitting both SAT and ACT scores then those scores were discounted by 15 percent.

Financial resources (10 percent). Generous per-student spending indicates that a college can offer a wide variety of programs and services. U.S. News measures financial resources by using the average spending per student on instruction, research, student services and related educational expenditures in the 2014 and 2015 fiscal years. Spending on sports, dorms and hospitals does not count.

Graduation rate performance (7.5 percent). This shows the effect of programs and policies on the graduation rate when controlling for spending per student, admissions selectivity, and the proportion of undergraduates receiving Pell grants. We compare a school's six-year graduation rate for the class that entered in 2009 relative to the graduation rate we predicted for that class based on a regression analysis. If the actual graduation rate is higher than the predicted rate, then the college is enhancing achievement.

Alumni giving rate (5 percent). This reflects the average percentage of living alumni with bachelor's degrees who gave to their school during 2013-2014 and 2014-2015 – an indirect measure of student satisfaction.

To arrive at a school's rank, we calculated the weighted sum of its standardized scores. The scores were rescaled so the top college or university in each category received a value of 100 and the other schools' weighted scores were calculated as a proportion of the top score. Final scores were rounded to the nearest whole number and ranked in descending order. Tied schools appear in alphabetical order.

Be sure to check out usnews.com regularly over the coming year, since we may add content to the Best Colleges pages as we obtain additional information. And as you mine the tables that follow for insights (a sense of which schools might be impressed enough by your SAT or ACT scores to offer some merit aid, for example, or where you will be apt to get the most attention from professors), keep in mind that the rankings provide a launching pad for more research, not an easy answer. ●

We also weigh the proportion of professors with the highest degree in their field (15 percent), the student-faculty ratio (5 percent), and the proportion of faculty who are full time (5 percent).

Student selectivity (12.5 percent). A school's academic atmosphere is determined in part by the abilities and ambitions of the students. We factor in the admissions test scores for all enrollees who took the critical reading and math portions of the SAT and the composite ACT score (65 percent of the selectivity score); the proportion of enrolled freshmen at national universities and national liberal arts colleges who graduated in the top 10 percent of their high school classes or in the top quarter at regional universities and regional colleges (25 percent); and the acceptance rate, or the ratio of students admitted to applicants (10 percent). The data are all for the fall 2015 entering class. While the ranking calculation takes account of both the SAT and ACT scores of all entering students, the table displays the score range for whichever test was taken by the most entering students. Footnotes clearly indicate the schools that did not report fall 2015 SAT and ACT test scores for all new students for whom they had scores (including athletes, international students, minority students, legacies, those admitted by special arrangement, and those who started

Best National Univer

						2015 graduation rate			
Rank School (State) (*Public)	Overall score	Peer assessment score (5.0=highest)	High school counselor assessment score	Graduation and retention rank	Average first-year student retention rate	Predicted	Actual	Over-performance (+) Under-performance (-)	F res
1. Princeton University (NJ)	100	4.8	4.9	1	98%	97%	97%	None	
2. Harvard University (MA)	98	4.9	5.0	1	97%	97%	98%	+1	
3. University of Chicago	97	4.6	4.8	11	99%	94%	92%	-2	
3. Yale University (CT)	97	4.8	5.0	1	99%	97%	97%	None	
5. Columbia University (NY)	95	4.6	4.9	4	99%	97%	96%	-1	
5. Stanford University (CA)	95	4.9	5.0	4	98%	95%	94%	-1	
7. Massachusetts Inst. of Technology	94	4.9	5.0	15	98%	97%	92%	-5	
8. Duke University (NC)	92	4.4	4.8	10	97%	95%	95%	None	
8. University of Pennsylvania	92	4.4	4.8	4	98%	97%	95%	-2	
10. Johns Hopkins University (MD)	91	4.6	4.9	15	97%	93%	94%	+1	
11. Dartmouth College (NH)	90	4.3	4.9	4	98%	95%	94%	-1	
12. California Institute of Technology	89	4.6	4.7	20	97%	98%	91%	-7	
12. Northwestern University (IL)	89	4.3	4.7	11	97%	96%	93%	-3	
14. Brown University (RI)	87	4.4	4.9	4	98%	95%	96%	+1	
15. Cornell University (NY)	85	4.5	4.8	15	97%	93%	93%	None	
15. Rice University (TX)	85	4.1	4.6	20	97%	93%	91%	-2	
15. University of Notre Dame (IN)	85	4.0	4.7	4	98%	95%	97%	+2	
15. Vanderbilt University (TN)	85	4.1	4.7	15	97%	94%	92%	-2	
19. Washington University in St. Louis	84	4.0	4.6	11	96%	97%	93%	-4	
20. Emory University (GA)	78	4.0	4.4	28	95%	93%	89%	-4	
20. Georgetown University (DC)	78	4.0	4.8	15	96%	95%	94%	-1	
20. University of California–Berkeley*	78	4.7	4.7	23	97%	93%	91%	-2	
23. Univ. of Southern California	77	4.0	4.4	23	97%	92%	92%	None	
24. Carnegie Mellon University (PA)	75	4.2	4.6	33	96%	91%	88%	-3	
24. Univ. of California–Los Angeles*	75	4.2	4.4	23	96%	90%	91%	+1	
24. University of Virginia*	75	4.2	4.5	11	97%	91%	93%	+2	
27. Tufts University (MA)	74	3.7	4.5	20	97%	93%	93%	None	
27. University of Michigan–Ann Arbor*	74	4.4	4.4	23	97%	91%	90%	-1	
27. Wake Forest University (NC)	74	3.5	4.3	36	94%	88%	88%	None	
30. U. of North Carolina–Chapel Hill*	71	4.0	4.5	28	97%	89%	90%	+1	
31. Boston College	70	3.6	4.4	23	95%	89%	92%	+3	
32. College of William and Mary (VA)*	68	3.7	4.3	28	96%	89%	90%	+1	
32. University of Rochester (NY)	68	3.4	3.9	38	96%	89%	88%	-1	
34. Brandeis University (MA)	67	3.5	4.2	32	93%	90%	87%	-3	
34. Georgia Institute of Technology*	67	4.1	4.5	47	96%	88%	85%	-3	1
36. New York University	66	3.8	4.5	47	92%	86%	84%	-2	
37. Case Western Reserve Univ. (OH)	65	3.6	4.3	60	93%	87%	81%	-6	
37. Univ. of California–Santa Barbara*	65	3.5	3.9	68	92%	86%	86%	None	
39. Boston University	64	3.5	4.3	44	93%	81%	85%	+4	
39. Northeastern University (MA)	64	3.2	4.3	47	96%	80%	84%	+4	
39. Rensselaer Polytechnic Inst. (NY)	64	3.5	4.4	47	94%	85%	81%	-4	
39. Tulane University (LA)	64	3.4	4.2	72	91%	84%	83%	-1	
39. University of California–Irvine*	64	3.6	4.1	38	93%	85%	88%	+3	
44. Lehigh University (PA)	63	3.2	4.1	33	95%	91%	88%	-3	
44. University of California–Davis*	63	3.8	4.2	47	93%	87%	88%	+1	1
44. Univ. of California–San Diego*	63	3.8	4.1	36	95%	89%	87%	-2	1
44. U. of Illinois–Urbana-Champaign*	63	3.9	3.9	44	94%	82%	85%	+3	
44. University of Miami (FL)	63	3.3	3.9	58	92%	84%	82%	-2	
44. Univ. of Wisconsin–Madison*	63	4.0	4.0	40	95%	81%	85%	+4	1
50. Pennsylvania State U.–Univ. Park*	62	3.7	4.0	40	93%	73%	86%	+13	1
50. Pepperdine University (CA)	62	3.3	4.4	55	93%	77%	84%	+7	
50. University of Florida*	62	3.6	3.8	33	96%	85%	87%	+2	
50. Villanova University (PA)†	62	3.2	4.2	31	95%	83%	90%	+7	1

Note: Key to footnotes, Page 79.

sities

...20 ('15)	% of classes of 50 or more ('15)	Student/faculty ratio ('15)	Selectivity rank	SAT/ACT 25th-75th percentile ('15)	Freshmen in top 10% of HS class ('15)	Acceptance rate ('15)	Financial resources rank	Alumni giving rank	Average alumni giving rate
%	11%	5/1	5	1390-1590	94%[5]	7%	10	1	63%
%	12%	7/1	5	1400-1600	95%[5]	6%	6	8	35%
%	6%	5/1	1	1440-1600	98%[5]	8%	5	3	41%
%	9%	6/1	3	1430-1600	97%[5]	7%	1	15	32%
%	9%	6/1	5	1400-1590	96%[5]	6%	13	13	33%
%	11%	4/1	5	1390-1580	96%[5]	5%	6	9	35%
%	13%	3/1	3	1430-1580	98%[5]	8%	3	6	37%
%	7%	6/1	13	1360-1550	91%[5]	12%	16	9	35%
%	10%	6/1	5	1380-1550	95%[5]	10%	11	9	35%
%	10%	8/1	10	1400-1550	92%[5]	13%	4	6	37%
%	8%	7/1	13	1330-1560	91%[5]	11%	15	2	45%
%	10%	3/1	1	1500-1600	99%[5]	9%	2	32	22%
%	6%	7/1	13	31-34	91%[5]	13%	9	19	27%
%	11%	7/1	10	1370-1560	91%[5]	9%	22	9	35%
%	17%	9/1	20	1330-1530	89%[5]	15%	17	18	29%
%	7%	6/1	13	1390-1560	89%[5]	16%	21	15	32%
%	9%	10/1	18	32-34	91%[5]	20%	28	3	41%
%	9%	8/1	10	32-35	91%[5]	12%	13	20	26%
%	11%	8/1	13	32-34	89%[5]	17%	6	28	24%
%	8%	8/1	23	1270-1490	83%[5]	24%	17	32	22%
%	7%	11/1	22	1320-1500	89%[5]	17%	32	17	30%
%	16%	17/1	20	1250-1500	98%	15%	36	88	12%
%	12%	9/1	32	1270-1500	88%[5]	18%	25	5	39%
%	12%	13/1	23	1360-1540	78%[5]	24%	32	54	16%
%	22%	17/1	23	1190-1470	97%	17%	20	152	8%
%	14%	15/1	29	1250-1460	89%[5]	30%	55	35	20%
%	8%	9/1	18	1370-1520	90%[4]	16%	28	41	20%
%	17%	15/1	29	29-33	73%[5]	26%	40	46	19%
%	1%	10/1	40	1200-1410[2]	77%[5]	29%	11	24	25%
%	14%	14/1	35	1200-1390	77%	30%	27	52	17%
%	7%	12/1	27	1260-1470	79%[4]	29%	66	22	25%
%	9%	12/1	32	1260-1460	81%[5]	34%	112	20	26%
%	12%	10/1	35	1240-1470[2]	68%[5]	34%	22	42	19%
%	11%	10/1	35	1250-1470	71%[5]	34%	48	30	23%
%	26%	19/1	27	1310-1500	81%[5]	32%	48	22	26%
%	8%	10/1	58	1250-1470	56%[5]	33%	32	136	9%
%	13%	11/1	32	30-33	71%[5]	36%	36	35	21%
%	19%	18/1	35	1130-1370	100%	33%	66	54	16%
%	14%	12/1	49	1200-1410	58%[5]	33%	48	115	10%
%	7%	14/1	31	31-34	70%[5]	28%	81	94	12%
%	12%	15/1	35	1280-1490	72%[5]	42%	53	88	12%
%	5%	8/1	42	29-32	55%[5]	31%	55	51	17%
%	21%	19/1	68	1040-1310	96%	39%	55	187	6%
%	12%	10/1	47	1230-1420	60%[5]	30%	55	35	21%
%	27%	19/1	49	1070-1340	100%	38%	36	162	7%
%	38%	19/1	23	1210-1450	100%	34%	22	202	6%
%	20%	18/1	58	26-31	53%[5]	66%	55	115	10%
%	7%	12/1	42	28-32	63%[4]	38%	26	62	15%
%	21%	17/1	54	27-31	54%[5]	49%	63	79	13%
%	15%	16/1	98	1090-1300	41%[5]	51%	55	68	14%
%	2%	13/1	74	1100-1320	48%[4]	38%	66	175	7%
%	16%	21/1	54	1170-1350	72%	48%	46	68	14%
%	4%	12/1	54	1200-1400	55%[5]	48%	103	24	25%

What Is a National University?

To assess more than 1,600 of the country's four-year colleges and universities, U.S. News first assigns each to a group of its peers, based on the categories of higher education institutions developed by the Carnegie Foundation for the Advancement of Teaching and recently revised. The National Universities category consists of 310 institutions (189 public, 114 private and seven for-profit) that offer a wide range of undergraduate majors as well as master's and doctoral degrees; some emphasize research. A list of the top 30 public national universities appears on Page 79.

Data on up to 15 indicators of academic quality are gathered from each institution and tabulated. Schools are ranked by total weighted score; those tied at the same rank are listed alphabetically. For a description of the methodology, see Page 68. For more on a college, turn to the directory at the back of the book.

Rank	School (State) (*Public)	Overall score	Peer assessment score (5.0=highest)	High school counselor assessment score	Average first-year student retention rate	2015 graduation rate Predicted	2015 graduation rate Actual	% of classes under 20 ('15)	% of classes of 50 or more ('15)	SAT/ACT 25th-75th percentile ('15)	Freshmen in top 10% of HS class ('15)	Acceptance rate ('15)	Average alumni giving rate
54.	Ohio State University–Columbus*	61	3.8	4.1	93%	76%	83%	30%	23%	27-31	62%	49%	14%
54.	University of Washington*	61	3.9	3.9	94%	84%	84%	38%	21%	1120-1370	92%[5]	53%	13%
56.	George Washington University (DC)	60	3.5	4.4	93%	85%	83%	53%	10%	1190-1390[2]	56%[5]	46%	9%
56.	Southern Methodist University (TX)	60	3.1	3.9	90%	77%	79%	58%	8%	28-32	44%[5]	49%	25%
56.	University of Georgia*	60	3.5	4.0	94%	79%	85%	42%	13%	1150-1330	53%	53%	11%
56.	University of Texas–Austin*	60	4.0	4.2	95%	83%	80%	35%	26%	1170-1390	72%	39%	12%
60.	Fordham University (NY)	59	3.2	4.2	90%	75%	81%	48%	2%	1170-1350	46%[5]	48%	15%
60.	Purdue Univ.–West Lafayette (IN)*	59	3.7	4.2	92%	70%	76%	40%	18%	1080-1330	43%[5]	59%	19%
60.	Syracuse University (NY)	59	3.3	4.0	92%	70%	81%	59%	9%	1090-1290	35%[5]	48%	16%
60.	University of Connecticut*	59	3.2	4.0	93%	75%	83%	53%	16%	1130-1340	50%[5]	53%	14%
60.	Univ. of Maryland–College Park*	59	3.6	4.1	95%	85%	86%	46%	17%	1210-1420	70%	45%	7%
60.	Worcester Polytechnic Inst. (MA)	59	3.0	3.8	96%	81%	85%	64%	11%	1210-1420[2]	65%	49%	13%
66.	Clemson University (SC)*	58	3.2	4.0	92%	76%	81%	53%	14%	27-31	56%	51%	23%
66.	Yeshiva University (NY)	58	2.8	3.3	90%	79%	92%	56%	1%	1130-1370	39%[4]	80%	15%
68.	Brigham Young Univ.–Provo (UT)	57	3.1	3.9	88%	78%	80%	56%	15%	27-31	54%	48%	13%
68.	University of Pittsburgh*	57	3.5	3.8	92%	78%	82%	40%	20%	1180-1350	50%	54%	10%
70.	Rutgers University–New Brunswick (NJ)*	56	3.4	4.0	92%	74%	80%	37%	21%	1110-1340	38%[5]	58%	8%
71.	Baylor University (TX)	55	3.2	4.0	88%	72%	70%	54%	9%	25-30	42%	44%	18%
71.	Stevens Institute of Technology (NJ)	55	2.8	3.8	94%	80%	82%	38%	9%	1240-1425[2]	66%[5]	44%	17%
71.	Univ. of Minnesota–Twin Cities*	55	3.7	3.8	92%	76%	77%	38%	20%	26-31	49%	45%	9%
74.	American University (DC)	54	3.1	4.0	89%	81%	81%	49%	1%	1150-1340[2]	36%[5]	35%	7%
74.	Clark University (MA)	54	2.8	3.6	89%	70%	83%	55%	6%	1120-1340[2]	44%[5]	55%	19%
74.	Texas A&M Univ.–College Station*	54	3.6	4.1	91%	76%	79%	21%	27%	1070-1310[3]	66%	66%	20%
74.	Univ. of Massachusetts–Amherst*	54	3.3	3.9	90%	67%	78%	50%	18%	1130-1310	32%[5]	58%	9%
74.	Virginia Tech*	54	3.5	4.0	93%	75%	83%	28%	21%	1100-1320	39%	73%	11%
79.	Miami University–Oxford (OH)*	53	3.2	3.9	90%	71%	80%	32%	10%	26-30	36%[5]	65%	21%
79.	Univ. of California–Santa Cruz*	53	3.1	3.8	90%	81%	81%	48%	24%	1070-1310	96%	51%	5%
79.	University of Delaware*	53	3.1	3.8	92%	73%	81%	32%	16%	1110-1310	33%[5]	63%	9%
82.	Colorado School of Mines*	52	3.3	4.3	92%	79%	77%	26%	21%	28-32	56%[5]	38%	14%
82.	Michigan State University*	52	3.5	3.9	92%	67%	77%	24%	24%	23-28	31%[5]	66%	8%
82.	Texas Christian University	52	2.9	3.7	90%	69%	76%	42%	6%	25-30	44%[5]	43%	19%
82.	University of Iowa*	52	3.5	3.6	86%	69%	72%	52%	13%	23-28	28%	81%	11%
86.	Binghamton University–SUNY*	51	2.9	3.7	91%	79%	81%	44%	14%	1230-1383	48%[4]	42%	7%
86.	Indiana University–Bloomington*	51	3.6	3.9	89%	70%	77%	35%	18%	1060-1290	34%[5]	78%	12%
86.	Marquette University (WI)	51	3.0	3.9	90%	72%	80%	40%	13%	24-30	34%[5]	74%	15%
86.	University of Denver	51	2.8	3.7	86%	75%	77%	53%	6%	23-30	45%[5]	73%	9%
86.	University of San Diego	51	2.9	3.8	89%	75%	79%	40%	0.4%	1110-1310	36%[5]	52%	13%
86.	University of Tulsa (OK)	51	2.7	3.7	89%	84%	69%	61%	3%	26-32	74%[5]	42%	20%
92.	Florida State University*	50	3.1	3.6	92%	70%	79%	33%	18%	25-29	38%	56%	18%
92.	North Carolina State U.–Raleigh*	50	3.1	3.6	93%	72%	76%	35%	17%	1160-1330	51%	50%	12%
92.	University of Colorado–Boulder*	50	3.5	3.7	85%	69%	71%	47%	16%	24-30	28%[5]	80%	7%
92.	University of Vermont*	50	3.0	3.6	86%	70%	77%	50%	15%	1100-1290	32%[5]	71%	10%
96.	Drexel University (PA)	49	3.0	3.9	85%	72%	68%	58%	9%	1095-1310	42%[5]	75%	7%
96.	Saint Louis University	49	2.9	3.8	89%	74%	74%	54%	9%	25-31	42%[5]	63%	12%
96.	Stony Brook–SUNY*	49	3.2	3.6	90%	71%	68%	43%	21%	1150-1380	46%[5]	41%	10%
99.	Auburn University (AL)*	48	3.3	3.8	90%	72%	73%	33%	15%	24-30	31%	78%	12%
99.	Loyola University Chicago	48	3.0	4.0	86%	71%	74%	45%	7%	24-29	33%[5]	71%	6%
99.	SUNY Col. of Envir. Sci. and Forestry*	48	2.7	3.5	85%	71%	75%	51%	11%	1120-1300	34%	52%	21%
99.	University at Buffalo–SUNY*	48	3.0	3.5	88%	67%	74%	36%	21%	1060-1260	30%[5]	60%	9%
103.	Illinois Institute of Technology	47	2.8	3.6	92%	77%	73%	54%	10%	25-30	56%[5]	53%	8%
103.	University of Alabama*	47	3.1	3.7	86%	69%	67%	39%	20%	22-31	37%	54%	34%
103.	University of Oregon*	47	3.3	3.7	87%	62%	72%	44%	22%	1000-1230	29%[5]	74%	9%
103.	University of Tennessee*	47	3.1	3.7	86%	72%	70%	28%	14%	24-30	54%[5]	76%	10%
107.	Rochester Inst. of Technology (NY)†	46	3.3	4.1	88%	71%	70%	47%	5%	1130-1350	36%	57%	6%
107.	University of New Hampshire*	46	2.8	3.6	86%	64%	79%	40%	17%	1010-1210	18%	79%	7%
107.	University of San Francisco	46	2.8	3.7	86%	63%	71%	48%	2%	1070-1260	25%[5]	65%	7%
107.	Univ. of South Carolina*	46	3.0	3.7	88%	69%	73%	34%	15%	1110-1290	30%	65%	15%
111.	Iowa State University*	45	3.3	3.6	87%	67%	71%	32%	24%	22-28	22%	87%	13%
111.	University of Dayton (OH)	45	2.6	3.4	90%	69%	79%	31%	5%	24-29	25%[5]	58%	14%
111.	Univ. of Missouri*	45	3.2	3.6	85%	69%	69%	40%	17%	24-29	28%	78%	15%
111.	Univ. of Nebraska–Lincoln*	45	3.2	3.6	84%	67%	67%	37%	17%	22-28	26%	76%	19%
111.	University of Oklahoma*	45	3.1	3.6	85%	71%	66%	43%	10%	24-29	37%	78%	18%
111.	University of the Pacific (CA)	45	2.5	3.7	85%	72%	70%	56%	5%	1010-1280	33%[5]	65%	9%
111.	University of Utah*	45	3.1	3.5	89%	63%	64%	41%	18%	21-28	25%[4]	81%	10%

Note: Key to footnotes, Page 79.

FUELING DIS-RUPTION.

WVU ENGINEER **DAN CARDER**
His team broke open the diesel vehicle
emissions scandal. Read more at
wvumag.wvu.edu/features/double-exposure

Here, we aren't afraid to
challenge assumptions.
Get our hands dirty. Tear
things apart. And ask the
tough questions — all in
the pursuit of progress.
In fact, at West Virginia
University, that's our job.
Because when staring down
convention, there are two
ways you can go.

MOUNTAINEERS GO FIRST.

West Virginia University

Rank	School (State) (*Public)	Overall score	Peer assessment score (5.0=highest)	High school counselor assessment score	Average first-year student retention rate	2015 graduation rate Predicted	2015 graduation rate Actual	% of classes under 20 ('15)	% of classes of 50 or more ('15)	SAT/ACT 25th-75th percentile ('15)	Freshmen in top 10% of HS class ('15)	Acceptance rate ('15)	Average alumni giving rate
118.	Michigan Technological University*	44	2.7	3.8	84%	69%	65%	45%	16%	24-29	28%	75%	11%
118.	Seton Hall University (NJ)	44	2.8	3.8	84%	57%	63%	49%	2%	1060-1230	30%[5]	76%	9%
118.	Temple University (PA)*	44	2.9	3.7	89%	60%	71%	38%	9%	1050-1250[2]	22%	56%	6%
118.	Univ. of California–Riverside*	44	3.0	3.6	90%	71%	73%	21%	34%	1020-1250	94%	56%	4%
118.	University of Kansas*	44	3.3	3.6	80%	67%	61%	48%	11%	22-28	26%	93%	14%
118.	University of St. Thomas (MN)	44	2.5	3.5	88%	65%	76%	40%	2%	24-29[3]	24%[5]	84%	16%
124.	Catholic University of America (DC)	43	2.8	3.6	84%	65%	69%	58%	4%	1020-1230[2]	N/A	79%	8%
124.	DePaul University (IL)	43	2.9	3.8	85%	64%	73%	35%	1%	22-28[2]	20%[5]	72%	7%
124.	Duquesne University (PA)	43	2.7	3.7	88%	63%	72%	40%	8%	1040-1210[2]	23%	76%	6%
124.	Howard University (DC)	43	2.9	3.8	84%	57%	60%	57%	5%	990-1220	24%[5]	49%	8%
124.	University of Arizona*	43	3.5	3.7	81%	64%	61%	40%	15%	960-1220[2]	28%[5]	76%	7%
129.	Arizona State University–Tempe*	42	3.3	3.5	84%	61%	66%	40%	18%	23-28[2]	29%	83%	10%
129.	Clarkson University (NY)	42	2.6	3.4	89%	68%	73%	42%	24%	1080-1290	36%	68%	14%
129.	Colorado State University*	42	2.9	3.6	86%	65%	67%	38%	19%	22-28	19%	81%	10%
129.	New School (NY)	42	2.8	3.8	83%	60%	66%	91%	1%	1000-1250[2]	15%[5]	67%	2%
133.	Hofstra University (NY)	41	2.8	3.7	79%	70%	60%	50%	4%	1090-1260[2]	27%[5]	61%	12%
133.	University of Kentucky*	41	3.0	3.7	82%	67%	61%	32%	16%	22-28	30%[5]	91%	15%
135.	Kansas State University*	40	3.0	3.5	82%	62%	62%	41%	13%	22-28[2]	22%	95%	23%
135.	Louisiana State Univ.–Baton Rouge*	40	2.8	3.5	84%	69%	67%	36%	22%	23-28	26%	77%	10%
135.	Mercer University (GA)†	40	2.3	3.9	83%	72%	61%	65%	4%	1110-1310	45%	67%	10%
135.	New Jersey Inst. of Technology*	40	2.6	3.5	85%	65%	61%	37%	6%	1110-1310	31%[5]	61%	8%
135.	Rutgers University–Newark (NJ)*	40	2.8	3.9	86%	60%	68%	28%	17%	930-1130	19%	65%	5%
135.	University of Arkansas*	40	2.9	3.3	82%	69%	62%	48%	17%	23-28	26%	60%	24%
135.	University of Cincinnati*	40	2.8	3.4	86%	64%	65%	41%	14%	23-28	21%	76%	13%
135.	University of Mississippi*	40	2.8	3.5	85%	58%	61%	43%	17%	21-28[2]	24%	79%	15%
143.	George Mason University (VA)*	39	3.0	3.9	87%	64%	69%	30%	14%	1040-1250[2]	21%[5]	80%	3%
143.	Oregon State University*	39	3.0	3.5	84%	59%	64%	28%	22%	970-1240	24%	78%	10%
143.	Washington State University*	39	3.0	3.5	80%	61%	64%	35%	20%	910-1150	34%[5]	80%	13%
146.	Adelphi University (NY)	38	2.2	3.3	83%	59%	67%	52%	2%	1010-1220[9]	23%[5]	72%	9%
146.	Ohio University*	38	3.0	3.6	79%	58%	67%	31%	18%	22-26	16%	74%	6%
146.	San Diego State University*	38	2.8	3.7	89%	51%	69%	28%	25%	1010-1230	33%[5]	34%	5%
146.	St. John Fisher College (NY)	38	2.2	3.2	85%	59%	70%	44%	1%	1000-1170	22%	62%	12%
146.	University at Albany–SUNY*	38	2.8	3.4	83%	62%	68%	30%	19%	1000-1170	16%[5]	56%	7%
146.	University of Texas–Dallas*	38	2.7	3.6	86%	72%	67%	26%	22%	1160-1370	33%	61%	3%
152.	Illinois State University*	37	2.4	3.4	82%	61%	73%	33%	11%	21-26	N/A	80%	7%
152.	Immaculata University (PA)	37	1.9	3.2	81%	41%	70%	86%	0.2%	860-1080	N/A	79%	10%
152.	Oklahoma State University*	37	2.7	3.6	80%	65%	62%	35%	16%	22-27	27%	75%	12%
152.	University of California–Merced*	37	2.7	3.5	84%[8]	52%	66%	30%	26%	900-1120	N/A	61%	11%
152.	University of Illinois–Chicago*	37	2.9	3.6	80%	63%	60%	35%	20%	21-26[3]	23%	77%	3%
152.	University of La Verne (CA)	37	1.9	3.4	86%	47%	64%	65%	1%	940-1120	18%[5]	47%	6%
152.	Univ. of Massachusetts–Lowell*	37	2.5	3.4	84%	57%	56%	59%	4%	1070-1270	20%	57%	11%
159.	Seattle Pacific University†	36	2.4	3.5	85%	64%	71%	48%	4%	1000-1230[3]	1%[5]	82%	6%
159.	University of Alabama–Birmingham*	36	2.7	3.3	81%	64%	55%	39%	18%	22-28	27%	87%	11%
159.	Univ. of Maryland–Baltimore County*	36	2.8	3.5	87%	67%	63%	39%	12%	1110-1310	27%	59%	4%
159.	University of Rhode Island*	36	2.7	3.5	82%	56%	63%	39%	9%	1010-1190[3]	19%	71%	6%
159.	University of South Florida*	36	2.7	3.3	89%	67%	68%	31%	16%	1070-1270	34%	45%	5%
164.	Biola University (CA)	35	1.9	3.6	86%	63%	72%	47%	5%	980-1240	30%[5]	73%	9%
164.	Maryville Univ. of St. Louis	35	1.8	3.2	88%	61%	71%	74%	1%	23-27[2]	25%	72%	7%
164.	Missouri Univ. of Science & Tech.*	35	2.6	3.5	84%[8]	76%	65%	27%	27%	25-31	44%	88%	15%
164.	St. John's University (NY)	35	2.7	3.7	79%	58%	58%	37%	6%	960-1180	21%[4]	65%	4%
164.	Virginia Commonwealth University*	35	2.8	3.6	86%	58%	62%	34%	16%	990-1200[2]	19%	72%	5%
169.	Union University (TN)†	34	1.8	3.0	89%	69%	69%	73%	0.2%	22-29	34%	69%	6%
169.	University of Hawaii–Manoa*	34	2.7	3.3	79%	62%	57%	50%	13%	980-1190	25%	81%	6%
171.	Edgewood College (WI)	33	1.8	3.2	81%	51%	60%	80%	0%	20-25	13%	77%	8%
171.	Florida Institute of Technology	33	2.3	3.3	79%	64%	57%	49%	4%	1080-1290	31%[5]	57%	4%
171.	University of Idaho*	33	2.7	3.3	78%	58%	57%	53%	9%	940-1170	17%	72%	10%
171.	University of Louisville (KY)*	33	2.8	3.4	79%	66%	53%	34%	9%	22-29[3]	11%[4]	72%	14%
171.	University of Wyoming*	33	2.6	3.4	75%	62%	55%	38%	10%	22-27	22%	96%	9%
176.	Ball State University (IN)*	32	2.5	3.3	80%	53%	61%	42%	6%	1010-1190[9]	19%	61%	11%
176.	Lipscomb University (TN)†	32	2.0	3.4	79%	63%	55%	57%	6%	23-29	29%[5]	61%	13%
176.	Mississippi State University*	32	2.5	3.3	80%	62%	60%[6]	40%	14%	20-27	26%	72%	16%[4]
176.	Montclair State University (NJ)*†	32	2.1	2.9	83%	47%	66%	39%	2%	870-1090[2]	10%[5]	70%	4%
176.	Texas Tech University*	32	2.8	3.4	82%	60%	60%	28%	21%	1030-1220	20%	63%	13%
176.	University of Central Florida*	32	2.6	3.2	88%	69%	71%	27%	25%	1080-1270	33%	49%	8%

Note: Key to footnotes, Page 79.

Rank	School (State) (*Public)	Overall score	Peer assessment score (5.0=highest)	High school counselor assessment score	Average first-year student retention rate	2015 graduation rate Predicted	2015 graduation rate Actual	% of classes under 20 ('15)	% of classes of 50 or more ('15)	SAT/ACT 25th-75th percentile ('15)	Freshmen in top 10% of HS class ('15)	Acceptance rate ('15)	Average alumni giving rate
176.	University of New Mexico*	32	2.7	3.5	79%	53%	47%	55%	10%	19-25	N/A	50%	4%
183.	Andrews University (MI)	31	1.7	3.4	79%	51%	54%	69%	3%	20-27	17%[5]	39%	6%
183.	Azusa Pacific University (CA)	31	2.0	3.4	85%	62%	68%	60%	2%	950-1180	25%[4]	81%	N/A
183.	University of Maine*	31	2.6	3.4	78%	57%	55%	41%	17%	960-1210	19%	91%	7%
183.	West Virginia University*	31	2.7	3.1	77%	58%	57%	50%	14%	21-27	20%[5]	86%	10%
183.	Widener University (PA)	31	2.2	3.1	75%	50%	57%	59%	1%	930-1120	12%[5]	68%	3%
188.	Kent State University (OH)*	30	2.5	3.3	80%	49%	56%	54%	9%	21-25	14%	85%	4%
188.	North Dakota State University*	30	2.5	3.5	79%	56%	54%	33%	20%	21-26	15%	94%	8%
188.	Pace University (NY)	30	2.3	3.5	77%	57%	52%	49%	2%	940-1160[2]	17%[5]	84%	5%
188.	Robert Morris University (PA)†	30	2.1	2.9	81%	49%	58%	51%	3%	940-1150	18%	78%	6%
188.	Suffolk University (MA)†	30	2.2	3.1	75%	50%	56%	42%	0.2%	910-1120[2]	11%[5]	82%	5%
188.	University of Hartford (CT)†	30	2.4	3.2	74%	57%	60%	70%	1%	940-1160	N/A	64%	4%
194.	Bowling Green State University (OH)*	29	2.5	3.4	74%	50%	56%	41%	9%	20-25	12%	76%	7%
194.	University of Houston*	29	2.6	3.3	85%	57%	51%	28%	24%	1050-1250	30%	60%	12%
194.	Western Michigan University*	29	2.4	3.2	76%	51%	54%	38%	10%	19-25	13%	82%	4%
197.	Indiana U.-Purdue U.-Indianapolis*	28	2.8	3.7	72%	51%	45%	37%	11%	890-1120	15%	70%	7%
197.	Lesley University (MA)†	28	2.0	3.1	78%[8]	54%	54%	75%	0%	960-1170	15%[5]	69%	N/A
197.	University of Alabama–Huntsville*	28	2.4	3.2	79%	67%	49%	45%	9%	24-30	31%[5]	81%	4%
197.	University of Colorado–Denver*	28	2.7	3.5	72%	58%	46%	36%	9%	20-25	31%[4]	67%	3%
197.	University of Nevada–Reno*	28	2.4	2.9	81%	60%	59%	33%	20%	970-1190	24%	86%	9%
202.	California State U.–Fullerton*†	27	2.5	3.2	89%	47%	62%	25%	9%	930-1130	23%	42%	2%[4]
202.	Central Michigan University*	27	2.2	3.2	77%	51%	59%	32%	8%	20-24	17%[5]	69%	5%
202.	Louisiana Tech University*	27	2.3	3.2	79%	56%	53%	49%	11%	21-27	24%	64%	12%
202.	South Dakota State University*	27	2.4	3.5	76%	56%	57%[8]	32%	15%	20-26	14%	92%	9%
202.	University of Alaska–Fairbanks*	27	2.4	3.2	76%	52%	42%	66%	4%	18-26	18%	73%	5%
202.	U. of North Carolina–Charlotte*	27	2.7	3.6	81%	53%	53%	25%	25%	1010-1180	22%	63%	4%
202.	University of North Dakota*	27	2.6	3.4	78%	72%	53%	40%	8%	21-26[3]	17%	82%	8%
202.	University of South Dakota*	27	2.5	3.4	76%	55%	52%	51%	6%	20-25[2]	21%	74%	7%[4]
210.	East Carolina University (NC)*	26	2.2	3.2	80%	53%	61%	30%	17%	980-1130	16%	69%	3%
210.	Montana State University*	26	2.5	3.2	76%	61%	52%	43%	14%	21-28	18%	83%	9%
210.	Old Dominion University (VA)*	26	2.6	3.5	81%	51%	53%	36%	10%	920-1140	8%	83%	5%
210.	Univ. of Missouri–Kansas City*	26	2.5	3.2	72%	64%	52%	55%	11%	21-28	32%	63%	6%
214.	Ashland University (OH)	25	1.8	3.2	74%	56%	57%	59%	0%	20-25	18%	74%	5%
214.	Dallas Baptist University†	25	1.8	2.8	71%	56%	58%	69%	2%	19-24	19%	42%	1%
214.	Northern Illinois University*	25	2.4	3.2	70%	53%	50%	46%	11%	19-25	13%	50%	4%
214.	Nova Southeastern University (FL)	25	1.8	2.8	74%	50%	44%	78%	0.4%	980-1225	31%	59%	2%
214.	Southern Illinois U.–Carbondale*	25	2.3	3.0	65%	51%	45%	53%	4%	19-25	10%	81%	5%
214.	University of Montana*	25	2.6	3.3	73%	56%	46%	51%	10%	20-27[3]	18%	92%	7%
220.	Benedictine University (IL)	24	2.0	3.3	71%	55%	53%	71%	0.2%	19-24[3]	12%[5]	79%	5%[4]
220.	California State Univ.–Fresno*†	24	2.4	3.2	83%	40%	58%	18%	11%	790-1010	15%	52%	3%
220.	Gardner-Webb University (NC)†	24	1.8	3.3	71%	50%	51%	69%	0%	850-1080	20%	79%	8%
220.	New Mexico State University*	24	2.4	3.4	74%	45%	42%	47%	11%	18-24	19%	65%	5%
220.	Shenandoah University (VA)†	24	1.8	3.0	77%	50%	54%	61%	2%	870-1123	15%	82%	6%
220.	Tennessee Technological Univ.*†	24	2.2	3.0	74%	57%	53%	41%	11%	21-27	33%	68%	8%
220.	Univ. of Massachusetts–Boston*	24	2.6	3.5	79%	56%	42%	42%	6%	950-1160	N/A	69%	5%
220.	Univ. of Massachusetts–Dartmouth*†	24	2.6	3.5	76%	55%	46%	37%	11%	920-1130	13%	76%	4%
220.	Univ. of Missouri–St. Louis*	24	2.4	3.2	77%	57%	41%	51%	6%	21-27	29%	76%	5%
220.	U. of North Carolina–Greensboro*	24	2.5	3.5	76%	52%	56%	25%	24%	940-1110	13%	59%	5%
220.	Univ. of Southern Mississippi*	24	2.2	3.0	73%	51%	50%	44%	9%	19-26	19%[4]	58%	8%
220.	Utah State University*	24	2.5	3.1	70%	61%	49%	42%	14%	20-27	21%	97%	6%

School (State) (*Public)	Peer assessment score (5.0=highest)	High school counselor assessment score	Average first-year student retention rate	2015 graduation rate Predicted	2015 graduation rate Actual	% of classes under 20 ('15)	% of classes of 50 or more ('15)	SAT/ACT 25th-75th percentile ('15)	Freshmen in top 10% of HS class ('15)	Acceptance rate ('15)	Average alumni giving rate
SECOND TIER (SCHOOLS RANKED 232 THROUGH 298 ARE LISTED HERE ALPHABETICALLY)											
American International College (MA)†	1.6	2.5	67%	40%	38%	51%	4%	790-980	N/A	64%	7%
Augusta University (GA)*†	2.0	3.3	72%[8]	63%	30%	N/A	N/A	930-1140[3]	N/A	74%	2%
Barry University (FL)	1.9	3.1	63%[8]	38%	33%	68%	1%	850-1020	N/A	55%	3%
Boise State University (ID)*†	2.5	3.4	74%	51%†	38%	35%	11%	920-1140[2]	15%	80%	7%
Cardinal Stritch University (WI)	1.7	3.1	69%[8]	52%	44%	78%	0.3%	20-24[2]	20%	77%	3%
Clark Atlanta University	2.1	3.3	63%	32%	38%	46%	6%	16-20	3%[5]	52%	N/A
Cleveland State University*	2.1	2.8	68%	45%	39%	35%	11%	19-25[3]	15%	91%	4%[4]
Eastern Michigan University*†	2.3	2.8	74%	46%	40%	41%	4%	19-25	13%	75%	2%

School (State) (*Public)	Peer assessment score (5.0=highest)	High school counselor assessment score	Average first-year student retention rate	2015 graduation rate Predicted	2015 graduation rate Actual	% of classes under 20 ('15)	% of classes of 50 or more ('15)	SAT/ACT 25th-75th percentile ('15)	Freshmen in top 10% of HS class ('15)	Accept-ance rate ('15)	Average alumni giving rate
SECOND TIER CONTINUED (SCHOOLS RANKED 232 THROUGH 298 ARE LISTED HERE ALPHABETICALLY)											
East Tennessee State University*	2.0	2.9	68%	52%	43%	46%	8%	20-26	20%	79%	3%
Florida A&M University*	2.1	3.4	82%	37%	39%	33%	13%	18-23	14%[5]	51%	5%
Florida Atlantic University*	2.2	3.1	76%	54%	49%	25%	16%	950-1140	11%	68%	3%
Florida International University*	2.3	3.2	84%	65%	58%	21%	22%	1030-1200	18%[5]	50%	5%
Georgia Southern University*	2.2	3.2	80%	56%	50%	25%	11%	1030-1180	17%[5]	60%	6%
Georgia State University*	2.6	3.5	82%	57%	54%	18%	18%	950-1160[3]	16%	58%	5%
Grand Canyon University[1] (AZ)†	1.7	2.9	61%[8]	19%	30%[6]	N/A	N/A	N/A[2]	N/A	58%[4]	N/A
Indiana State University*	2.4	3.3	63%	38%	41%	28%	11%	800-1020	8%	85%	5%
Indiana Univ. of Pennsylvania*	2.1	3.0	75%	45%	55%	34%	13%	860-1060[3]	8%	88%	6%
Jackson State University (MS)*	1.8	2.7	78%[8]	35%	40%	39%	10%	17-21	N/A	68%	4%[4]
Kennesaw State University (GA)*†	2.2	3.2	77%	55%	40%	32%	12%	1010-1180	35%	59%	4%
Lamar University (TX)*	1.9	2.8	57%	38%	32%	33%	11%	860-1070	16%	79%	2%
Liberty University (VA)†	1.7	2.8	77%	44%	49%	32%	4%	950-1190[3]	23%[5]	21%	2%
Lindenwood University (MO)†	1.7	3.0	70%	47%	49%	67%	0.1%	20-25[2]	10%	55%	9%
Middle Tennessee State Univ.*	2.1	3.0	71%	53%	44%	45%	7%	19-25	19%[4]	73%	4%
Morgan State University (MD)*	2.0	3.0	74%	37%	31%	41%	1%	840-970[2]	4%[4]	67%	11%
National Louis University (IL)	1.8	3.0	72%[8]	48%	37%[6]	N/A	N/A	N/A[2]	N/A	81%	N/A
North Carolina A&T State Univ.*	2.0	3.1	77%	36%	44%	30%	8%	830-990	9%	59%	8%
Northern Arizona University*	2.4	3.4	74%	53%	52%	30%	13%	920-1150[2]	22%	77%	4%
Oakland University (MI)*	2.1	3.2	76%	50%	44%	36%	14%	20-26	15%	80%	4%
Portland State University (OR)*	2.6	3.5	72%[8]	52%	41%	33%	16%	930-1160[2]	11%	86%	3%
Prairie View A&M University (TX)*†	1.8	2.6	67%	24%	34%	22%	6%	770-930	5%	86%	N/A
Regent University (VA)	1.8	3.3	78%	57%	48%	61%	0%	900-1150	14%	86%	4%
Sam Houston State University (TX)*	2.1	3.1	78%	47%	50%	29%	13%	880-1090	15%	73%	9%
San Francisco State University*†	2.6	3.4	82%	48%	51%	23%	17%	860-1090	N/A	68%	2%
Spalding University[1] (KY)	1.7	3.0	74%[8]	30%	41%[6]	N/A	N/A	860-1000[4]	N/A	46%[4]	N/A
Tennessee State University*	2.0	3.1	59%[8]	27%	38%	60%	1%	16-20[3]	N/A	53%[4]	N/A
Texas A&M University–Commerce*	2.1	3.5	70%	47%	42%	39%	4%	680-1080[3]	11%	47%	3%
Texas A&M Univ.–Corpus Christi*	2.1	3.6	58%	42%	37%	18%	20%	870-1070	10%	84%	2%
Texas A&M Univ.–Kingsville*	2.0	3.5	65%	34%	33%	38%	6%	17-22	16%	82%	10%
Texas Southern University*	1.9	3.1	54%	21%	19%	40%	15%	725-900[3]	5%	51%	2%
Texas State University*†	2.2	3.1	77%	54%	53%	29%	16%	930-1120	12%	71%	4%
Texas Woman's University*	2.1	3.3	69%	48%	41%	45%	10%	830-1050[2]	18%	75%	0.4%
Trevecca Nazarene University (TN)	1.5	3.1	76%	51%	51%	71%	4%	19-25[3]	N/A	73%	8%[4]
Trinity International Univ. (IL)	1.7	3.5	72%[8]	55%	45%	73%	0%	19-26	15%[5]	96%	N/A
University of Akron (OH)*	2.2	3.0	70%	46%	40%	43%	8%	19-26	16%	97%	13%
Univ. of Arkansas–Little Rock*	2.2	2.9	75%[8]	46%	27%	66%	4%	18-24	N/A	68%	3%
University of Louisiana–Lafayette*	2.1	3.2	75%	51%	46%	34%	9%	21-25	21%	55%	7%
University of Louisiana–Monroe*†	2.0	3.1	70%	44%	39%	34%	16%	20-25	22%	94%	4%
Univ. of Maryland–Eastern Shore*†	2.1	2.7	70%	28%	33%	55%	3%	750-930	N/A	49%	3%
University of Memphis*	2.4	3.1	77%	50%	45%	48%	10%	20-26	15%	92%	6%
University of Nebraska–Omaha*	2.5	3.3	75%	54%	46%	37%	10%	19-26	14%	76%	5%
University of Nevada–Las Vegas*	2.5	3.1	76%	53%	41%	26%	18%	890-1120	23%	88%	4%
University of New Orleans*	2.0	3.2	66%	52%	35%	37%	11%	20-24	14%	58%	2%
University of Northern Colorado*	2.2	3.3	68%	51%	48%	42%	11%	19-25[2]	13%	89%	4%
University of North Texas*	2.4	3.1	77%	58%	52%	24%	24%	990-1200[3]	21%	70%	5%
University of South Alabama*	2.0	2.8	70%	53%	35%	42%	10%	20-25[2]	N/A	78%	N/A
University of Texas–Arlington*	2.6	3.5	73%	55%	46%	32%	25%	950-1200	32%	64%	2%
University of Texas–El Paso*	2.3	3.2	70%[8]	37%	40%	31%	15%	820-1050	18%	100%	N/A
University of Texas–San Antonio*	2.4	3.4	65%	49%	31%	17%	32%	930-1150	19%	78%	5%[4]
University of the Cumberlands (KY)†	1.6	3.0	61%	46%	37%	67%	1%	19-25	17%	68%	11%
University of Toledo (OH)*	2.3	3.1	68%	47%	42%	36%	14%	20-26	16%	93%	3%
University of West Florida*	2.0	3.1	72%	55%	47%	36%	11%	20-26	14%	42%	4%
University of West Georgia*†	1.9	2.8	72%	41%	39%	34%	10%	860-1020	N/A	57%	4%
Univ. of Wisconsin–Milwaukee*	2.7	3.5	70%	50%	41%	44%	11%	20-25[2]	10%	73%	4%
Valdosta State University (GA)*†	1.9	3.0	69%	46%	36%	51%	4%	910-1080	N/A	50%	3%
Wayne State University (MI)*	2.5	3.3	76%	45%	35%	52%	8%	20-26	22%	80%	5%
Wichita State University (KS)*	2.4	3.3	72%	56%	43%	47%	11%	21-26[2]	20%	95%	7%
Wright State University (OH)*	2.2	3.2	63%	47%	40%	41%	15%	19-25	17%	96%	4%

UC-BERKELEY, THE NO. 1 PUBLIC

► The Top 30 Public National Universities

Rank School (State)	Rank School (State)	Rank School (State)	Rank School (State)
1. University of California–Berkeley	9. University of California–Irvine	16. University of Washington	25. Rutgers U.–New Brunswick (NJ)
2. Univ. of California–Los Angeles	10. University of California–Davis	18. University of Georgia	26. Univ. of Minnesota–Twin Cities
2. University of Virginia	10. Univ. of California–San Diego	18. University of Texas–Austin	27. Texas A&M Univ.–College Station
4. University of Michigan–Ann Arbor	10. U. of Illinois–Urbana-Champaign	20. Purdue Univ.–West Lafayette (IN)	27. Univ. of Massachusetts–Amherst
5. U. of North Carolina–Chapel Hill	10. Univ. of Wisconsin–Madison	20. University of Connecticut	27. Virginia Tech
6. College of William and Mary (VA)	14. Pennsylvania State U.–Univ. Park	20. Univ. of Maryland–College Park	30. Miami University–Oxford (OH)
7. Georgia Institute of Technology	14. University of Florida	23. Clemson University (SC)	30. Univ. of California–Santa Cruz
8. Univ. of California–Santa Barbara	16. Ohio State University–Columbus	24. University of Pittsburgh	30. University of Delaware

Footnotes:
1. School refused to fill out U.S. News statistical survey. Data that appear are from school in previous years or from another source such as the National Center for Education Statistics.
2. SAT and/or ACT not required by school for some or all applicants.
3. In reporting SAT/ACT scores, the school did not include all students for whom it had scores or refused to tell U.S. News whether all students with scores had been included.
4. Previous year's data was used in the ranking calculation.
5. Data based on fewer than 51 percent of enrolled freshmen.
6. Some or all data reported to the NCAA and/or the National Center for Education Statistics.
7. Data reported to the Council for Aid to Education.

8. This rate, normally based on four years of data, is given here for less than four years because school didn't report rate for the most recent year or years to U.S. News.
9. SAT and/or ACT may not be required by school for some or all applicants, and in reporting SAT/ACT scores, the school did not include all students for whom it had scores or refused to tell U.S. News whether all students with scores had been included.

† School's Carnegie classification has changed. It appeared in a different U.S. News ranking category last year.
N/A means not available.

Rank	School (State) (*Public)	Overall score	Peer assessment score (5.0=highest)	High school counselor assessment score	Graduation and retention rank	Average first-year student retention rate	2015 graduation rate			Fac reso ra
							Predicted	Actual	Over-performance (+) Under-performance (-)	
1.	**Williams College** (MA)	100	4.7	4.7	3	97%	96%	96%	None	
2.	**Amherst College** (MA)	95	4.7	4.5	1	98%	95%	95%	None	2
3.	**Wellesley College** (MA)	94	4.5	4.6	11	96%	93%	93%	None	1
4.	**Middlebury College** (VT)	93	4.4	4.4	4	96%	96%	94%	-2	2
4.	**Swarthmore College** (PA)	93	4.6	4.5	4	97%	96%	94%	-2	1
6.	**Bowdoin College** (ME)	92	4.4	4.6	4	97%	96%	93%	-3	3
7.	**Carleton College** (MN)	90	4.3	4.4	4	97%	94%	95%	+1	1
7.	**Pomona College** (CA)	90	4.4	4.4	1	98%	96%	94%	-2	3
9.	**Claremont McKenna College** (CA)	89	4.2	4.5	11	96%	96%	92%	-4	
9.	**Davidson College** (NC)	89	4.2	4.3	4	96%	94%	93%	-1	1
11.	**Washington and Lee University** (VA)	87	3.8	4.1	17	96%	96%	91%	-5	
12.	**Colby College** (ME)	86	4.0	4.3	17	93%	89%	94%	+5	1
12.	**Colgate University** (NY)	86	4.0	4.5	17	95%	91%	90%	-1	1
12.	**Hamilton College** (NY)	86	3.9	4.3	11	95%	95%	92%	-3	1
12.	**Haverford College** (PA)	86	4.1	4.4	4	97%	96%	90%	-6	5
12.	**Smith College** (MA)	86	4.3	4.6	37	93%	83%	87%	+4	2
12.	**United States Naval Academy** (MD)*	86	4.2	4.8	25	98%	87%	86%	-1	4
12.	**Vassar College** (NY)	86	4.2	4.6	11	95%	92%	91%	-1	3
19.	**Grinnell College** (IA)	85	4.3	4.2	28	94%	89%	86%	-3	1
19.	**United States Military Academy** (NY)*	85	4.1	4.8	46	95%	83%	83%	None	2
21.	**Harvey Mudd College** (CA)	84	4.4	4.6	11	98%	96%	92%	-4	10
21.	**Wesleyan University** (CT)	84	4.1	4.5	10	95%	92%	94%	+2	4
23.	**Scripps College** (CA)	82	3.8	4.3	28	93%	91%	92%	+1	1
24.	**Colorado College**	81	3.8	4.1	28	95%	89%	87%	-2	
24.	**Macalester College** (MN)	81	4.0	4.4	21	95%	89%	90%	+1	5
24.	**Oberlin College** (OH)	81	4.1	4.4	28	93%	90%	88%	-2	2
27.	**Barnard College** (NY)	80	4.0	4.4	17	96%	87%	91%	+4	7
27.	**Bates College** (ME)	80	4.0	4.3	21	94%	91%	88%	-3	6
27.	**Kenyon College** (OH)	80	3.9	4.3	25	95%	87%	87%	None	4
27.	**University of Richmond** (VA)	80	3.8	4.1	42	94%	86%	88%	+2	
31.	**Bryn Mawr College** (PA)	79	4.0	4.2	46	92%	86%	85%	-1	4
32.	**Bucknell University** (PA)	78	3.8	4.3	21	94%	87%	90%	+3	8
32.	**College of the Holy Cross** (MA)	78	3.6	4.1	11	95%	87%	92%	+5	5
32.	**Pitzer College** (CA)	78	3.6	4.2	37	92%	83%	90%	+7	2
32.	**United States Air Force Acad.** (CO)*	78	3.9	4.6	46	93%	89%	81%	-8	9
36.	**Lafayette College** (PA)	76	3.5	4.0	21	94%	87%	90%	+3	6
36.	**Mount Holyoke College** (MA)	76	3.9	4.2	53	91%	84%	85%	+1	
38.	**Skidmore College** (NY)	75	3.6	4.2	33	94%	79%	86%	+7	4
38.	**Trinity College** (CT)	75	3.6	4.1	43	89%	83%	86%	+3	4
38.	**Union College** (NY)	75	3.3	3.9	37	92%	84%	88%	+4	2
41.	**Dickinson College** (PA)	73	3.5	4.1	43	91%	81%	85%	+4	4
41.	**Soka University of America** (CA)	73	2.4	3.1	33	96%	80%	86%	+6	
41.	**Whitman College** (WA)	73	3.4	3.9	28	94%	87%	87%	None	3
44.	**Centre College** (KY)	72	3.5	4.1	43	90%	81%	86%	+5	9
44.	**Occidental College** (CA)	72	3.7	4.0	33	93%	83%	88%	+5	8
44.	**Rhodes College** (TN)	72	3.5	4.1	59	91%	72%	83%	+11	5
47.	**Franklin and Marshall College** (PA)	71	3.6	4.0	37	92%	90%	87%	-3	5
47.	**Sewanee–University of the South** (TN)	71	3.5	4.2	69	89%	81%	78%	-3	
49.	**Bard College** (NY)	70	3.4	4.1	87	87%	92%	78%	-14	1
50.	**Connecticut College**	69	3.5	4.1	46	90%	85%	83%	-2	7

Note: Key to footnotes, Page 86.

Arts Colleges

of ses r 20)	% of classes of 50 or more ('15)	Student/ faculty ratio ('15)	Selectivity rank	SAT/ACT 25th-75th percentile ('15)	Freshmen in top 10% of HS class ('15)	Acceptance rate ('15)	Financial resources rank	Alumni giving rank	Average alumni giving rate
%	3%	7/1	4	1330-1550	93%[5]	18%	5	2	56%
%	3%	8/1	5	1360-1560	86%[5]	14%	9	9	48%
%	0%	7/1	11	1290-1490	80%[5]	30%	7	4	52%
%	1%	8/1	9	1270-1500	79%[5]	17%	4	6	51%
%	3%	8/1	5	1340-1530	88%[5]	12%	10	18	40%
%	3%	9/1	7	1375-1535[2]	84%[5]	15%	11	2	56%
%	1%	9/1	14	29-33	71%[5]	21%	33	7	50%
%	1%	8/1	1	1360-1530	92%[5]	10%	7	46	31%
%	1%	8/1	21	1340-1530	73%[5]	11%	13	24	38%
%	0%	10/1	16	1260-1440	74%[5]	22%	24	4	52%
%	0%	8/1	8	30-33	85%[5]	24%	25	8	49%
%	1%	10/1	23	1270-1460[2]	63%[5]	23%	25	17	41%
%	2%	9/1	16	1250-1450	75%[5]	27%	29	16	41%
%	1%	9/1	11	1300-1470	77%[5]	25%	20	21	40%
%	3%	9/1	3	1320-1530	96%[5]	25%	13	14	42%
%	4%	9/1	33	1240-1460[2]	62%[5]	38%	13	34	34%
%	0.1%	8/1	31	1180-1380	58%	9%	3	117	19%
%	0.3%	8/1	14	1330-1490	72%	26%	18	52	30%
%	0%	7/1	9	30-33	81%[5]	25%	21	41	32%
%	0%	7/1	35	26-31	52%	10%	6	45	31%
%	9%	9/1	1	1400-1560	93%[5]	13%	13	52	30%
%	4%	8/1	19	1250-1470[2]	72%[5]	22%	47	25	38%
%	1%	10/1	16	1280-1448	72%[5]	28%	25	41	32%
%	0%	10/1	19	28-32[2]	68%[5]	17%	29	90	23%
%	0.4%	10/1	24	29-32	65%[5]	39%	50	30	35%
%	2%	9/1	26	1260-1450	61%[5]	29%	34	52	29%
%	10%	10/1	11	1260-1450	81%[5]	20%	53	70	25%
%	3%	10/1	21	1190-1416[2]	72%[5]	22%	45	14	42%
%	1%	10/1	26	1240-1420	61%[5]	24%	38	23	39%
%	0.1%	8/1	31	1220-1420	61%[5]	31%	29	74	24%
%	4%	8/1	33	1240-1460[2]	63%[5]	39%	19	27	37%
%	2%	9/1	26	1210-1390	65%[5]	25%	42	46	30%
%	1%	9/1	52	1220-1380[2]	61%[5]	37%	53	11	47%
%	0%	10/1	46	1250-1440[2]	60%[5]	13%	29	41	32%
%	0%	8/1	26	28-33	52%	17%	2	163	14%
%	1%	10/1	26	1200-1380	70%[5]	30%	34	41	32%
%	2%	10/1	35	1230-1465[2]	58%[5]	50%	38	38	32%
%	1%	8/1	50	1110-1343[2]	41%[5]	37%	47	90	23%
%	1%	9/1	43	1150-1340[2]	64%[5]	33%	25	52	29%
%	1%	10/1	24	1240-1400[2]	71%[5]	38%	50	36	33%
%	0%	9/1	46	1190-1380[2]	46%[4]	47%	59	59	27%
%	0%	8/1	68	1070-1390	33%[5]	46%	1	61	26%
%	0%	8/1	37	1200-1420	54%[5]	43%	53	38	33%
%	0%	10/1	43	26-31	54%	71%	76	12	46%
%	0.2%	10/1	38	1200-1380	55%[5]	45%	59	111	20%
%	0%	10/1	38	27-32	54%[5]	47%	99	29	36%
%	1%	9/1	62	1210-1400[2]	48%[5]	32%	38	61	26%
%	0.3%	10/1	58	26-30[2]	29%[5]	41%	59	34	34%
%	0.3%	10/1	70	1160-1370[2]	49%[5]	32%	13	30	35%
%	1%	9/1	64	1220-1400[2]	49%[5]	40%	45	70	25%

What Is a National Liberal Arts College?

The country's 239 liberal arts colleges emphasize undergraduate education and award at least half of their degrees in the arts and sciences, which include such disciplines as English, the biological and physical sciences, history, foreign languages, and the visual and performing arts but exclude professional disciplines such as business, education and nursing. There are 219 private and 20 public liberal arts colleges; none are for-profit. The top public colleges appear below.

The Top Public Colleges

Rank School (State)

1. **United States Naval Academy** (MD)
2. **United States Military Academy** (NY)
3. **United States Air Force Acad.** (CO)
4. **Virginia Military Institute**
5. **New College of Florida**
6. **St. Mary's College of Maryland**
7. **University of Minnesota–Morris**
8. **U. of North Carolina–Asheville**

Rank	School (State) (*Public)	Overall score	Peer assessment score (5.0=highest)	High school counselor assessment score	Average first-year student retention rate	2015 graduation rate Predicted	2015 graduation rate Actual	% of classes under 20 ('15)	% of classes of 50 or more ('15)	SAT/ACT 25th-75th percentile ('15)	Freshmen in top 10% of HS class ('15)	Acceptance rate ('15)	Average alumni giving rate
51.	Denison University (OH)	68	3.4	4.0	90%	84%	80%	69%	0%	26-31[2]	55%[5]	48%	22%
51.	Gettysburg College (PA)	68	3.4	4.0	90%	88%	83%	66%	0.3%	1210-1350	56%[5]	40%	24%
53.	DePauw University (IN)	67	3.4	3.8	92%	79%	82%	72%	0%	25-29	41%[5]	65%	24%
53.	Furman University (SC)	67	3.4	4.0	89%	85%	83%	57%	0.2%	1100-1320[2]	39%	65%	24%
53.	St. John's College (MD)	67	3.5	4.0	83%	84%	71%	99%	1%	1220-1450[2]	29%[5]	78%	23%
53.	St. Lawrence University (NY)	67	3.3	3.7	91%	77%	87%	62%	1%	1100-1310[2]	45%[5]	46%	25%
53.	St. Olaf College (MN)	67	3.6	4.0	93%	81%	87%	54%	3%	26-31	43%[5]	36%	21%
53.	Thomas Aquinas College (CA)	67	2.7	3.2	91%	71%	89%	100%	0%	1160-1380	44%[5]	63%	59%
59.	Sarah Lawrence College (NY)	66	3.4	4.2	85%	77%	79%	93%	0.3%	1170-1390[2]	37%[5]	53%	19%
60.	Berea College (KY)	65	3.4	3.7	83%	45%	63%	79%	1%	22-26	24%	37%	16%
60.	Lawrence University (WI)	65	3.2	3.9	89%	78%	76%	80%	2%	26-32[2]	42%[5]	68%	32%
62.	Beloit College (WI)	64	3.2	3.8	89%	75%	82%	69%	0%	24-30[2]	29%	69%	21%
62.	College of Wooster (OH)	64	3.3	3.8	89%	75%	82%	70%	1%	25-30	46%[5]	55%	23%
62.	Wheaton College (IL)	64	3.1	4.0	95%	84%	89%	57%	5%	27-32	54%[5]	71%	23%
65.	Hobart & William Smith Colleges (NY)	63	3.2	3.9	88%	78%	81%	65%	0%	1170-1340[2]	30%[5]	57%	28%
65.	Muhlenberg College (PA)	63	2.8	3.6	92%	79%	85%	78%	1%	1110-1320[2]	41%[5]	48%	19%
65.	Wabash College (IN)	63	3.3	3.8	86%	74%	73%	72%	2%	1040-1250	35%	61%	40%
68.	Earlham College (IN)	62	3.3	3.9	84%	73%	67%	79%	0.4%	1110-1390[2]	43%[5]	62%	25%
68.	Kalamazoo College (MI)	62	3.3	3.9	93%	79%	83%	61%	1%	26-30[2]	40%[5]	72%	26%
70.	Agnes Scott College (GA)	61	3.1	3.7	84%	69%	68%	70%	0%	1060-1330[2]	29%	62%	38%
70.	University of Puget Sound (WA)	61	3.2	3.6	87%	74%	78%	61%	1%	1100-1340[2]	37%[5]	79%	16%
72.	Hendrix College (AR)	60	3.3	3.9	85%	77%	68%	73%	0%	25-32	48%	82%	26%
72.	Illinois Wesleyan University	60	2.9	3.6	91%	78%	83%	65%	1%	25-30	34%[5]	62%	24%
72.	Spelman College (GA)	60	3.4	3.8	89%	60%	76%	58%	3%	920-1120	23%	48%	39%
72.	Virginia Military Institute*	60	3.1	3.9	87%	68%	74%	66%	0.1%	1040-1230[3]	17%	53%	30%
72.	Willamette University (OR)	60	3.2	3.8	86%	76%	79%	56%	0%	1100-1330	40%	78%	13%
77.	Allegheny College (PA)	59	3.1	3.6	85%	73%	75%	70%	1%	1013-1250[2]	35%	68%	23%
77.	Gustavus Adolphus College (MN)	59	3.2	3.7	90%	73%	83%	64%	0%	24-30[2]	30%	67%	20%
77.	Knox College (IL)	59	3.1	3.5	87%	75%	77%	71%	1%	23-29[2]	34%[5]	64%	31%
77.	St. John's University (MN)	59	3.2	3.8	87%	71%	77%	59%	0.4%	23-28	21%[5]	74%	25%
77.	Wheaton College (MA)	59	3.4	4.0	85%	82%	79%	68%	2%	1100-1330[2]	26%[5]	65%	22%
77.	Wofford College (SC)	59	3.1	3.7	89%	79%	82%	52%	0.2%	23-29	42%	72%	24%
83.	College of the Atlantic (ME)	58	2.5	3.4	81%	68%	70%	94%	0%	1130-1350[2]	26%[5]	76%	40%
83.	Hillsdale College (MI)	58	2.5	3.5	96%	82%	77%	73%	0.4%	27-31	50%[4]	50%	12%
83.	St. John's College (NM)	58	3.1	4.0	80%	70%	48%	100%	0%	1160-1420[2]	26%	81%	21%
83.	Transylvania University (KY)	58	2.8	3.5	86%	71%	73%	71%	0%	24-30[2]	39%	93%	35%
87.	College of St. Benedict (MN)	57	3.0	3.4	89%	71%	85%	59%	0.4%	22-27	31%	75%	19%
87.	Lewis & Clark College (OR)	57	3.3	3.8	86%	81%	72%	67%	1%	1190-1390[2]	48%[5]	63%	18%
87.	Reed College[1] (OR)	57	3.8	4.2	92%[8]	87%	78%[6]	N/A	N/A	1290-1480[4]	N/A	39%[4]	N/A
90.	Bennington College (VT)	56	2.9	3.7	83%	76%	68%	90%	0.4%	1140-1400[2]	N/A	63%	22%
90.	Cornell College (IA)	56	3.0	3.7	83%	70%	68%	81%	0%	23-29	22%	71%	23%
90.	Luther College (IA)	56	3.0	3.4	86%	71%	77%	60%	1%	23-29	31%	67%	25%
90.	Millsaps College (MS)	56	2.9	3.6	78%	72%	66%	84%	0%	23-28	34%	53%	23%
90.	New College of Florida*	56	3.0	4.0	81%	78%	71%	73%	2%	1170-1380	43%	61%	18%
95.	Ohio Wesleyan University	55	2.9	3.9	80%	73%	71%	72%	0.2%	22-28[2]	23%	75%	22%
95.	Southwestern University (TX)	55	2.9	3.5	85%	79%	75%	76%	1%	1040-1270	32%	44%	23%
95.	St. Mary's College (IN)	55	2.9	3.8	89%	73%	79%	53%	1%	22-28	28%[5]	80%	31%
95.	Ursinus College (PA)	55	2.9	3.4	89%	77%	78%	75%	1%	1040-1250[2]	25%[5]	83%	20%
99.	Augustana College (IL)	54	3.0	3.4	85%	73%	76%	64%	0%	23-28[2]	27%	49%	19%
99.	St. Mary's College of Maryland*	54	2.8	3.6	87%	77%	78%	72%	0%	1030-1260	N/A	79%	11%
99.	St. Michael's College (VT)	54	2.8	3.5	89%	70%	76%	59%	1%	1070-1260[2]	26%	76%	17%
99.	Washington and Jefferson Col. (PA)	54	2.9	3.5	N/A	70%	76%	66%	0%	1060-1250[2]	34%	43%	14%
99.	Washington College (MD)	54	2.8	3.5	83%	74%	75%	70%	1%	1070-1290	36%[5]	54%	17%
99.	Westmont College (CA)	54	2.7	3.3	86%	74%	77%	65%	2%	1050-1300	37%[5]	81%	20%
105.	Austin College (TX)	53	3.1	3.6	82%	73%	73%	67%	0.3%	22-28	36%	54%	7%[7]
105.	Hampden-Sydney College (VA)	53	2.8	3.5	80%	69%	63%	73%	0%	1000-1230	12%	55%	33%
105.	Hollins University (VA)	53	2.7	3.6	75%	62%	57%	89%	0%	990-1210	23%	61%	31%
108.	Drew University (NJ)	52	2.8	3.5	80%	71%	67%	72%	0.3%	990-1240[2]	27%[5]	70%	24%
108.	Hope College (MI)	52	3.0	3.5	89%	71%	76%	54%	2%	24-29	34%	72%	22%
108.	Juniata College (PA)	52	2.7	3.4	88%	74%	73%	72%	2%	1020-1250[2]	30%	77%	28%
108.	Lake Forest College (IL)	52	2.9	3.6	84%	70%	72%	62%	0%	23-28[2]	39%[5]	55%	24%
108.	Stonehill College (MA)	52	2.7	3.6	88%	78%	87%	49%	0.3%	1020-1220[2]	27%[5]	75%	15%
113.	Goucher College (MD)	51	3.0	3.8	82%	71%	69%	72%	1%	980-1220[2]	22%[5]	78%	19%
113.	Ripon College (WI)	51	2.6	3.2	85%	63%	69%	75%	1%	21-27	21%	66%	28%

Note: Key to footnotes, Page 86.

THE Winthrop Experience

43 degree programs

approximately **200** employers and community partners visited campus last year to recruit Winthrop students and alumni

30+ performing arts groups

2 ROTC partnership programs (Air Force and Army)

19 national Greek organizations

GREEK LIFE

35 recreational sports activities (intramurals)

18 NCAA Division I athletics teams

14 to 1 student/faculty ratio

160+ clubs and interest groups

ADMIT ONE

numerous events sponsored by Winthrop's award-winning DiGiorgio Student Union programming board

25 service learning courses

Asheville • Raleigh •
Charlotte •
Greenville • WINTHROP UNIVERSITY
Columbia •
Charleston •

Learn More

www.winthrop.edu/usnews
800/WINTHROP (946-8476)

IN THE HEART OF THE CAROLINAS

WINTHROP
UNIVERSITY

Rank	School (State) (*Public)	Overall score	Peer assessment score (5.0=highest)	High school counselor assessment score	Average first-year student retention rate	2015 graduation rate Predicted	2015 graduation rate Actual	% of classes under 20 ('15)	% of classes of 50 or more ('15)	SAT/ACT 25th-75th percentile ('15)	Freshmen in top 10% of HS class ('15)	Acceptance rate ('15)	Average alumni giving rate
115.	Concordia College–Moorhead (MN)	50	2.7	3.4	83%	67%	73%	61%	0%	22-28	31%	78%	18%
115.	Elizabethtown College (PA)†	50	2.5	3.2	82%	69%	78%	64%	1%	1000-1230	31%	71%	17%
115.	Principia College (IL)	50	2.2	2.9	84%	71%	80%	N/A	N/A	930-1198	21%[5]	75%	25%[4]
115.	St. Anselm College (NH)	50	2.6	3.2	88%	68%	73%	68%	3%	1070-1250[2]	31%[5]	73%	19%
119.	Coe College (IA)	49	2.9	3.4	79%	65%	67%	72%	1%	22-27	27%	61%	19%
119.	Presbyterian College (SC)	49	2.7	3.5	83%	70%	70%	66%	0%	970-1190[2]	27%	62%	15%
119.	Westminster College (PA)	49	2.5	3.3	83%	62%	71%	75%	1%	940-1070	24%	94%	17%[4]
122.	Albion College (MI)	48	2.7	3.4	80%	70%	65%	63%	0%	22-27	N/A	79%	20%
122.	Eckerd College (FL)	48	2.9	3.6	82%	63%	64%	52%	0%	1000-1210	N/A	73%	N/A
122.	Grove City College (PA)	48	2.4	3.3	90%	75%	85%	51%	4%	1076-1309	40%	81%	20%
122.	Hanover College (IN)	48	2.6	3.5	82%	69%	67%	73%	0.3%	22-27	20%	61%	14%
122.	Salem College (NC)	48	2.2	3.3	77%	52%	64%	88%	0%	21-29	37%	62%	24%
122.	Siena College (NY)	48	2.7	3.5	89%	66%	75%	40%	0%	980-1200[2]	21%[5]	56%	14%
128.	Illinois College	47	2.5	3.1	77%	64%	71%	75%	0%	18-25[2]	23%	61%	24%
128.	Linfield College (OR)	47	2.6	3.5	86%	64%	63%	72%	2%	950-1160	26%	84%	14%
128.	Marlboro College (VT)	47	2.2	3.3	73%	71%	61%	100%	0%	1090-1360[2]	17%[4]	94%	25%
128.	McDaniel College (MD)	47	2.7	3.4	81%	66%	70%	74%	0%	960-1180	26%	80%	16%
132.	Birmingham-Southern Col. (AL)	46	2.8	3.4	83%	73%	61%	65%	1%	21-25	21%	53%	18%
132.	Central College (IA)	46	2.6	3.2	81%	64%	67%	69%	0.3%	20-26	23%	64%	15%
132.	Randolph College (VA)	46	2.6	3.1	77%	69%	69%	85%	0.3%	910-1120	13%	81%	22%
132.	Randolph-Macon College (VA)	46	2.8	3.4	78%	65%	58%	63%	0%	1000-1180	21%	60%	36%
132.	St. Norbert College (WI)	46	2.7	3.3	83%	66%	73%	48%	0.3%	22-27	26%	78%	16%
132.	Susquehanna University (PA)	46	2.7	3.1	84%	66%	71%	57%	0%	1010-1220[2]	26%[5]	76%	12%
132.	Wartburg College (IA)	46	2.6	3.4	78%	65%	69%	60%	2%	21-27	26%	74%	21%
132.	Whittier College (CA)	46	3.0	3.2	84%	63%	66%	55%	1%	933-1170	25%[5]	63%	20%
140.	Roanoke College (VA)	45	2.9	3.3	80%	65%	66%	53%	0%	970-1200	15%	72%	22%
140.	Sweet Briar College (VA)	45	1.9	3.4	63%	70%	64%	98%	0%	935-1230	25%[5]	95%	25%
140.	University of Minnesota–Morris*	45	2.7	3.6	80%	62%	65%	66%	3%	22-28	24%	60%	12%
140.	Wesleyan College (GA)	45	2.6	3.6	78%	58%	59%	78%	1%	920-1140	N/A	42%	27%
144.	Bard College at Simon's Rock (MA)†	44	2.7	3.7	74%	78%	49%	97%	0%	1250-1400[2]	60%[5]	89%	N/A
144.	Houghton College (NY)	44	2.3	3.2	87%	65%	71%	69%	1%	990-1250	27%	94%	18%
146.	Alma College (MI)	43	2.5	3.2	81%	63%	59%	68%	1%	21-27	22%	68%	21%
146.	Centenary College of Louisiana	43	2.3	3.4	75%	69%	55%	86%	0%	21-28	27%	67%	13%
146.	Guilford College (NC)	43	2.9	3.5	71%	50%	59%	67%	0%	910-1170[2]	14%	63%	13%
149.	Doane University (NE)	42	2.1	3.1	74%	49%	61%	79%	0.2%	20-26	12%	77%	16%
149.	Hiram College (OH)	42	2.4	3.4	72%	57%	60%	80%	0%	20-27	17%	58%	12%
149.	Saint Vincent College (PA)	42	2.2	3.2	84%	62%	69%	49%	0%	950-1160	17%	70%	20%
149.	Simpson College (IA)	42	2.5	3.1	81%	62%	68%	70%	1%	21-27	24%	89%	15%
149.	Westminster College (MO)	42	2.5	3.3	81%	61%	66%	68%	0%	21-26	21%	64%	12%
154.	Carthage College (WI)	41	2.5	3.3	77%	60%	59%	57%	0.3%	22-28	33%[5]	70%	14%
154.	Lycoming College (PA)	41	2.5	3.2	80%	59%	64%	65%	2%	920-1140[2]	17%	71%	19%
154.	Meredith College (NC)†	41	2.3	3.9	76%	61%	62%	62%	0.2%	920-1130	20%	60%	21%
154.	William Jewell College (MO)	41	2.4	3.4	77%	71%	62%	73%	0.3%	23-28[2]	30%	49%	10%
154.	Wittenberg University (OH)	41	2.5	3.6	77%	69%	64%	53%	1%	22-28[2]	19%	77%	13%
159.	Alfred University (NY)†	40	2.6	3.4	73%	62%	60%	67%	3%	920-1150	15%	68%	12%
159.	Covenant College (GA)†	40	2.3	3.4	86%	62%	64%	56%	1%	24-29	32%[5]	94%	13%
159.	Hartwick College (NY)	40	2.7	3.4	74%	63%	56%	71%	0.2%	910-1110[2]	6%	81%	14%
159.	Monmouth College (IL)	40	2.5	3.1	76%	55%	58%	69%	0%	20-26	13%	59%	19%
159.	Moravian College (PA)	40	2.4	3.1	78%	65%	69%	61%	1%	930-1090	10%	75%	17%
159.	Morehouse College (GA)	40	3.2	3.7	82%	54%	51%	50%	1%	870-1100	11%	76%	13%
159.	Oglethorpe University[1] (GA)	40	2.6	3.5	77%[8]	60%	56%[8]	73%[4]	0%[4]	22-28[4]	29%[4]	78%[4]	12%[4]
159.	U. of North Carolina–Asheville*	40	2.9	3.6	79%	62%	60%	50%	1%	1050-1250	21%	79%	9%
159.	Warren Wilson College (NC)	40	2.5	3.4	67%	69%	53%	85%	0%	21-28[2]	17%[5]	84%	13%
168.	College of Idaho	39	2.5	3.1	85%	62%	68%	58%	1%	930-1190[2]	23%	90%	35%
168.	Franklin College (IN)†	39	2.4	3.5	77%	58%	60%	66%	0%	890-1080[3]	16%	70%	22%
168.	Georgetown College (KY)	39	2.4	3.5	73%	63%	57%	77%	0%	20-25	17%	68%	13%
171.	Fisk University (TN)	38	2.7	3.5	80%	54%	53%	72%	0.4%	17-23	15%[5]	81%	23%
171.	Gordon College (MA)	38	2.3	3.1	82%	70%	69%	60%	3%	950-1230[3]	26%[5]	93%	8%
171.	Ouachita Baptist University (AR)	38	2.2	3.1	76%	64%	65%	63%	1%	21-28	34%	60%	18%
174.	Elmira College (NY)†	37	2.4	3.2	76%	63%	55%	74%	1%	910-1130[2]	26%	76%	16%
174.	Emory and Henry College (VA)	37	2.6	3.4	72%	56%	54%	75%	0%	860-1090	10%[5]	76%	25%
174.	Northland College (WI)	37	2.3	3.0	71%	60%	58%	66%	0%	21-28	22%	57%	14%
174.	Wells College (NY)	37	2.5	3.5	73%	61%	46%	80%	1%	900-1090[9]	N/A	58%[4]	23%
174.	Young Harris College (GA)	37	2.1	3.7	67%	51%	60%	72%	0.2%	875-1080	8%	52%	11%

Note: Key to footnotes, Page 86.

WASHINGTON
AND LEE, NO. 11

School (State) (*Public)	Peer assessment score (5.0=highest)	High school counselor assessment score	Average first-year student retention rate	2015 graduation rate Predicted	2015 graduation rate Actual	% of classes under 20 ('15)	% of classes of 50 or more ('15)	SAT/ACT 25th-75th percentile ('15)	Freshmen in top 10% of HS class ('15)	Accept-ance rate ('15)	Average alumni giving rate
SECOND TIER (SCHOOLS RANKED 179 THROUGH 232 ARE LISTED HERE ALPHABETICALLY)											
Albright College (PA)	2.5	3.2	75%	58%	58%	61%	1%	960-1150[2]	16%	49%	9%
Alice Lloyd College (KY)†	2.1	3.0	63%	38%	30%	53%	3%	19-24	17%	N/A	43%
Allen University[1] (SC)	1.9	2.6	59%[8]	16%	24%[8]	N/A	N/A	N/A[2]	N/A	43%[4]	N/A
American Jewish University[1] (CA)	2.4	3.1	64%[8]	63%	66%[6]	N/A	N/A	970-1190[4]	N/A	58%[4]	N/A
Ave Maria University[1] (FL)	1.9	2.6	72%[8]	58%	55%[6]	N/A	N/A	980-1220[4]	N/A	52%[4]	N/A
Bethany College (WV)	2.3	3.1	62%	50%	41%	80%	2%	780-1010	5%	70%	16%
Bethany Lutheran College (MN)	2.0	2.9	72%	57%	49%	75%	1%	20-26	14%	85%	16%
Bethel College (KS)†	2.3	3.0	65%	65%	60%	71%	1%	18-24	22%	53%	20%
Bethune-Cookman University (FL)†	2.0	3.3	64%	29%	32%	44%	2%	15-18	3%	54%	5%
Bloomfield College (NJ)	2.0	2.5	68%	34%	31%	71%	0%	770-950	3%	60%	7%
Bridgewater College (VA)	2.3	3.2	76%	57%	53%	47%	0%	920-1125	15%	49%	15%
Bryn Athyn Col. of New Church (PA)	1.8	3.0	62%[8]	72%	77%	N/A	N/A	785-1105	N/A	42%	N/A
Burlington College[1] (VT)	2.1	3.3	46%[8]	51%	28%[6]	N/A	N/A	N/A[2]	N/A	78%[4]	N/A
Cheyney U. of Pennsylvania*†	1.7	2.8	54%[8]	30%	17%	N/A	N/A	N/A[2]	N/A	40%	N/A
Claflin University (SC)	2.2	3.1	73%	34%	42%	64%	1%	720-910	8%	41%	48%
Davis and Elkins College[1] (WV)†	2.2	3.4	60%[8]	45%	43%[6]	N/A	N/A	870-1080[4]	N/A	58%[4]	N/A
Dillard University (LA)	2.2	3.3	69%[8]	37%	38%	58%	1%	17-20	10%[5]	48%	13%
East-West University[1] (IL)	1.7	2.4	31%[8]	14%	10%[6]	N/A	N/A	N/A	N/A	N/A	N/A
Emmanuel College (MA)†	2.4	3.2	79%	60%	64%	40%	0%	1030-1210[2]	N/A	78%	11%
Erskine College (SC)	2.2	3.4	69%	65%	62%	78%	0%	880-1110	17%	64%	16%
Fort Lewis College (CO)*	2.5	3.1	62%	51%	40%	42%	3%	19-24[3]	11%	86%	2%
Heidelberg University (OH)†	2.4	3.4	65%	54%	39%	66%	0.3%	19-25	N/A	79%	19%
Holy Cross College (IN)	2.5	3.6	60%[8]	50%	25%	59%	0%	890-1170	16%[5]	91%	7%
Johnson C. Smith University (NC)	2.1	2.8	66%	36%	46%	74%	0%	700-880	5%	46%	17%
Judson College[1] (AL)	2.0	2.8	58%[8]	53%	40%[6]	N/A	N/A	N/A[2]	N/A	65%[4]	N/A
The King's College[1] (NY)	2.2	3.0	64%[8]	67%	57%[8]	41%[4]	0%[4]	23-27[4]	N/A	70%[4]	N/A
LaGrange College (GA)†	2.2	3.3	62%	57%	46%	70%	0.4%	20-24	18%	57%	16%
Louisiana State University–Alexandria*	2.1	3.2	57%	38%	26%	48%	5%	18-22	9%	68%	3%
Lyon College (AR)	2.3	3.1	70%	62%	38%	61%	0%	22-27	27%	59%	11%
Manhattanville College (NY)†	2.3	3.2	77%	63%	57%	63%	0.2%	960-1150[2]	7%[5]	74%	12%
Marymount Manhattan College (NY)	2.3	3.3	71%	61%	42%	63%	0%	930-1150	N/A	84%	11%
Maryville College (TN)	2.5	3.2	72%	57%	53%	55%	1%	20-26	20%[5]	67%	21%
Massachusetts Col. of Liberal Arts*	2.4	3.1	77%	55%	52%	64%	0%	890-1130	16%[5]	73%	10%
Pacific Union College (CA)	2.5	3.2	80%	55%	44%	64%	4%	850-1130	N/A	45%	7%
Paine College[1] (GA)†	2.0	3.0	58%[8]	24%	22%[6]	N/A	N/A	670-850[4]	N/A	22%[4]	N/A
Philander Smith College (AR)†	1.8	2.5	64%	34%	40%	75%	4%	14-19	5%	60%	10%
Pine Manor College (MA)	1.8	2.5	58%	42%	28%	81%	4%	680-860	N/A	71%	N/A
Purchase College–SUNY*	2.4	3.4	82%	60%	59%	62%	4%	960-1180	N/A	41%	5%
Schreiner University (TX)†	2.4	3.3	69%[8]	48%	40%	67%	0%	890-1090	11%	90%	4%
Shepherd University (WV)*†	2.2	3.8	66%	45%	48%	56%	2%	870-1093	N/A	90%	7%
Southern Virginia University[1]	1.9	3.4	70%[8]	34%	32%[6]	N/A	N/A	908-1163[4]	N/A	47%[4]	N/A
Spring Hill College (AL)†	2.3	3.3	76%	61%	53%	56%	0.3%	22-27	26%	41%	17%
Stillman College[1] (AL)	2.4	3.2	63%[8]	29%	19%[6]	N/A	N/A	753-990[4]	N/A	59%[4]	N/A
Thiel College (PA)†	2.1	3.3	67%	48%	41%	64%	1%	790-1010	9%	61%	14%
Tougaloo College (MS)	2.1	2.5	75%	47%	54%	70%	1%	15-20	19%	39%	19%
University of Maine–Machias*	2.1	2.9	68%	44%	29%	78%	0%	770-1010	N/A	87%	0.2%
University of Pikeville (KY)	1.8	3.1	54%	42%	36%	57%	3%	18-23	14%	100%	5%
Univ. of Science and Arts of Okla.*	2.4	3.1	73%	49%	42%	73%	4%	19-24	25%	66%	N/A
University of Virginia–Wise*	2.4	3.5	71%	47%	41%	69%	1%	850-1040	31%	77%	10%
Univ. of Wisconsin–Parkside*	2.0	3.1	71%	47%	33%	42%	7%	18-23[2]	12%	82%	1%
Virginia Union University†	2.2	3.1	53%	29%	32%	45%	1%	680-860	7%	49%	7%
Virginia Wesleyan College	2.4	3.2	66%	56%	47%	83%	0%	860-1090[2]	13%	93%	5%
West Virginia State University*	2.2	3.2	55%	38%	28%	52%	1%	17-22	N/A	94%	3%
William Peace University[1] (NC)	1.9	3.1	64%[8]	47%	41%[6]	N/A	N/A	790-990[4]	N/A	63%[4]	N/A

Footnotes:

1. School refused to fill out U.S. News statistical survey. Data that appear are from school in previous years or from another source such as the National Center for Education Statistics.
2. SAT and/or ACT not required by school for some or all applicants.
3. In reporting SAT/ACT scores, the school did not include all students for whom it had scores or refused to tell U.S. News whether all students with scores had been included.
4. Previous year's data was used in the ranking calculation.
5. Data based on fewer than 51 percent of enrolled freshmen.
6. Some or all data reported to the NCAA and/or the National Center for Education Statistics.
7. Data reported to the Council for Aid to Education.

8. This rate, normally based on four years of data, is given here for less than four years because school didn't report rate for the most recent year or years to U.S. News.
9. SAT and/or ACT may not be required by school for some or all applicants, and in reporting SAT/ACT scores, the school did not include all students for whom it had scores or refused to tell U.S. News whether all students with scores had been included.

† School's Carnegie classification has changed, and it appeared in a different U.S. News ranking category last year.
N/A means not available.

Best Regional Universities

What Is a Regional University?

Like the national universities, the institutions that appear here provide a full range of undergraduate majors and master's programs; the difference is that they offer few, if any, doctoral programs. The 653 universities in this category are not ranked nationally but rather against their peer group in one of four regions – North, South, Midwest and West – because in general they tend to draw students most heavily from surrounding states.

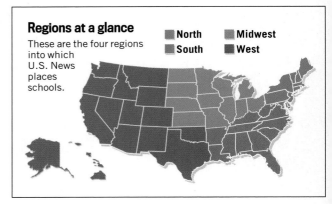

Regions at a glance
These are the four regions into which U.S. News places schools.
- North
- South
- Midwest
- West

NORTH ►

Rank School (State) (*Public)	Overall score	Peer assessment score (5.0=highest)	Average first-year student retention rate	2015 graduation rate Predicted	2015 graduation rate Actual	% of classes under 20 ('15)	% of classes of 50 or more ('15)	Student/ faculty ratio ('15)	SAT/ACT 25th-75th percentile ('15)	Freshmen in top 25% of HS class ('15)	Accept- ance rate ('15)	Average alumni giving rate
1. Providence College (RI)	100	3.7	91%	76%	85%	52%	3%	12/1	1050-1250[2]	69%[5]	57%	18%
2. Fairfield University (CT)	96	3.5	88%	79%	82%	43%	1%	12/1	1100-1270[2]	69%[5]	65%	14%
3. Bentley University (MA)	92	3.4	95%	83%	89%	26%	0%	12/1	1140-1330	72%[5]	42%	6%
3. College of New Jersey*	92	3.4	94%	85%	85%	43%	1%	13/1	1120-1310	79%[5]	49%	7%
3. Loyola University Maryland	92	3.6	88%	80%	81%	36%	1%	11/1	1110-1280[2]	62%[5]	61%	13%
6. Ithaca College (NY)	88	3.5	86%	73%	76%	60%	4%	11/1	1100-1270[2]	63%[5]	67%	9%
6. University of Scranton (PA)	88	3.2	89%	69%	80%	52%	0.1%	10/1	1030-1230	62%[5]	72%	11%
8. Emerson College (MA)	85	3.3	88%	80%	80%	67%	2%	13/1	1100-1310	67%[5]	49%	7%
9. Bryant University (RI)	83	3.0	89%	74%	80%	25%	0%	13/1	1090-1250[2]	58%[5]	72%	8%
9. Marist College (NY)	83	3.2	90%	74%	78%	46%	0%	16/1	1050-1250[2]	61%[5]	45%	13%
11. Quinnipiac University (CT)	81	3.3	87%	76%	76%	49%	3%	12/1	990-1180	69%	74%	7%
11. Simmons College (MA)	81	3.0	86%	69%	74%	71%	4%	10/1	1060-1240	72%[5]	58%	19%
11. St. Joseph's University (PA)	81	3.2	89%	71%	79%	31%	1%	13/1	1050-1230[2]	48%[5]	82%	11%
14. SUNY–Geneseo*	80	3.5	90%	84%	82%	29%	11%	20/1	1100-1290	74%[5]	73%	13%
15. Manhattan College (NY)	76	3.0	86%	65%	72%	46%	0.1%	13/1	990-1190[3]	51%[5]	67%	16%
16. Gallaudet University (DC)	72	3.1	70%	50%	46%	96%	0%	6/1	16-21	N/A	62%	N/A
16. Le Moyne College (NY)	72	2.9	87%	61%	68%	51%	2%	12/1	980-1170[2]	55%	62%	16%
18. Massachusetts Maritime Academy*†	70	3.2	89%	61%	72%	35%	2%	17/1	980-1160	N/A	74%	13%
18. SUNY Polytechnic Institute*	70	2.7	76%	53%	49%	62%	2%	17/1	960-1310	59%[5]	60%	5%
20. CUNY–Baruch College*	69	3.1	90%	61%	70%	19%	16%	17/1	1100-1320	78%	32%	4%
20. Rowan University (NJ)*	69	3.0	87%	65%	66%	40%	1%	18/1	1000-1230	N/A	56%	3%
20. SUNY–New Paltz*	69	3.0	89%	64%	73%	39%	2%	15/1	1025-1210	74%[5]	42%	3%
23. Assumption College (MA)	68	2.8	83%	63%	73%	46%	0.2%	12/1	1020-1210[2]	43%	76%	12%
23. Canisius College (NY)	68	2.8	83%	64%	70%	50%	1%	11/1	950-1180	50%	87%	11%
23. Lebanon Valley College (PA)†	68	2.5	85%	69%	74%	58%	1%	11/1	1000-1210[2]	69%	72%	14%
23. Rider University (NJ)	68	2.8	79%	61%	64%	52%	1%	12/1	910-1110	37%[5]	69%	10%
27. Mount St. Mary's University (MD)	67	2.8	78%	64%	69%	46%	0%	12/1	910-1130	31%[5]	67%	22%
27. Ramapo College of New Jersey*	67	2.8	88%	69%	74%	36%	0%	17/1	990-1195	25%[5]	53%	10%
27. Springfield College (MA)	67	2.7	85%	48%	72%	53%	2%	12/1	930-1140	33%	64%	10%
27. St. Bonaventure University (NY)	67	2.8	83%	56%	64%	57%	0%	11/1	930-1170	47%	66%	19%
27. St. Francis University (PA)	67	2.6	82%[8]	60%	71%	71%	1%	14/1	930-1160	58%	74%	17%
32. New York Inst. of Technology	66	2.9	73%	56%	46%	62%	1%	14/1	1060-1248	52%[5]	68%	14%
32. Rutgers University–Camden (NJ)*	66	3.1	82%	58%	57%	43%	10%	10/1	920-1120	44%	58%	3%
32. Salve Regina University (RI)	66	2.7	83%	67%	72%	49%	0.2%	13/1	1020-1170[2]	49%	73%	17%
35. La Salle University (PA)	65	3.0	80%	58%	63%	43%	1%	12/1	890-1100	36%	78%	11%
35. Roger Williams University (RI)	65	2.9	80%	65%	64%	53%	0%	14/1	1030-1200[2]	44%[4]	78%	5%
35. Wagner College (NY)	65	2.8	86%	73%	64%	62%	1%	15/1	1030-1230[2]	62%	69%	9%
38. CUNY–Queens College*	64	2.9	86%	57%	58%	33%	9%	14/1	1020-1200	66%[5]	40%	20%

Note: Key to footnotes Page 104.

SMALL CAMPUS & BIG CITY

Manhattan College
1853

When everything New York City holds lies just outside a
quintessential college campus, the opportunities are endless.

EXPERIENCE THE UNCOMMON
MANHATTAN.EDU

NORTH ▶

Rank School (State) (*Public)	Overall score	Peer assessment score (5.0=highest)	Average first-year student retention rate	2015 graduation rate Predicted	Actual	% of classes under 20 ('15)	% of classes of 50 or more ('15)	Student/ faculty ratio ('15)	SAT/ACT 25th-75th percentile ('15)	Freshmen in top 25% of HS class ('15)	Accept-ance rate ('15)	Average alumni giving rate
38. Hood College (MD)	64	2.8	77%	62%	63%	75%	0%	11/1	910-1170[2]	42%[5]	79%	17%
38. Monmouth University (NJ)	64	2.9	81%	63%	67%	39%	0%	14/1	950-1120	39%[5]	78%	5%
38. Nazareth College (NY)	64	2.5	82%	66%	73%	60%	0%	9/1	970-1170[2]	58%	76%	11%
42. Arcadia University (PA)	63	2.7	81%	62%	58%	72%	4%	10/1	996-1200	60%	59%	12%
42. CUNY–Hunter College*	63	3.2	85%	61%	54%	42%	6%	13/1	1070-1260	57%	39%	11%
44. Misericordia University (PA)	62	2.5	83%	57%	72%	44%	0%	12/1	970-1140[3]	56%	71%	18%
44. Molloy College (NY)	62	2.2	89%	59%	71%	65%	0.3%	10/1	970-1150	56%[5]	76%	11%
44. Niagara University (NY)	62	2.8	84%	55%	63%	52%	1%	13/1	930-1133	44%	48%	8%
44. Sacred Heart University (CT)	62	2.9	82%	64%	64%	39%	1%	15/1	961-1245[2]	35%[5]	59%	7%
44. Seton Hill University (PA)†	62	2.7	80%[8]	53%	61%	55%	0.4%	14/1	930-1170[2]	52%	76%	16%[4]
44. SUNY College–Oneonta*	62	2.8	86%	63%	72%	42%	5%	18/1	1000-1170[3]	54%[4]	49%	8%
44. SUNY–Oswego*	62	2.9	80%	59%	66%	56%	6%	17/1	1010-1190[3]	52%	51%	7%
51. Endicott College (MA)	61	2.6	83%	60%	71%	55%	0%	14/1	980-1170[2]	44%[5]	73%	14%
51. Gannon University (PA)	61	2.7	82%	56%	66%	53%	0%	13/1	923-1130	50%	76%	10%
51. Marywood University (PA)	61	2.4	82%	58%	70%	57%	0.2%	11/1	930-1120	48%[5]	71%	14%
51. Notre Dame of Maryland University	61	2.7	77%	59%	54%	93%	0%	12/1	960-1180	55%	52%	9%
51. Stockton University (NJ)*	61	2.7	86%	62%	73%	22%	2%	17/1	980-1180	54%	64%	3%
51. Towson University (MD)*	61	3.1	86%	60%	70%	30%	3%	17/1	1000-1170	45%[5]	73%	4%
57. King's College (PA)	60	2.5	75%	57%	66%	58%	0.2%	12/1	930-1130[2]	42%	72%	14%
57. Merrimack College (MA)†	60	2.8	82%	64%	71%	40%	1%	13/1	890-1100[2]	26%[5]	79%	10%
57. Wentworth Inst. of Technology (MA)†	60	3.0	83%	60%	66%	41%	2%	15/1	1010-1210	N/A	67%	5%
60. Philadelphia University	59	2.7	79%	63%	65%	68%	0.1%	13/1	980-1180	41%	64%	6%
61. College at Brockport–SUNY*	58	2.7	82%	56%	69%	33%	6%	16/1	930-1120	36%	53%	4%
61. DeSales University (PA)	58	2.4	82%	64%	70%	59%	2%	13/1	890-1180	47%[5]	78%	8%
61. Mercyhurst University (PA)	58	2.6	81%	56%	66%	60%	0%	13/1	910-1160[2]	25%[5]	82%	13%
61. SUNY College–Cortland*	58	2.7	81%	57%	73%	33%	6%	17/1	960-1110[2]	39%	51%	7%
61. SUNY–Fredonia*	58	2.7	78%	58%	65%	55%	5%	14/1	920-1160	38%	59%	5%
61. West Chester Univ. of Pennsylvania*	58	2.8	87%	55%	71%	23%	7%	19/1	980-1160	40%	59%	6%
67. College of Saint Rose (NY)	57	2.4	78%	56%	61%	57%	0.1%	14/1	950-1130[9]	40%	82%	17%
67. Fairleigh Dickinson Univ. (NJ)	57	3.0	76%	53%	53%	69%	1%	14/1	910-1130	41%[5]	65%	4%
67. Johnson & Wales University (RI)	57	2.9	78%	41%	55%	49%	0%	20/1	852-1070[2]	N/A	82%	N/A
67. Salisbury University (MD)*	57	2.8	82%	62%	67%	32%	3%	16/1	1080-1240[2]	54%[5]	61%	7%
67. Western New England Univ. (MA)	57	2.6	75%	63%	57%	53%	0%	12/1	960-1180	47%[5]	81%	6%
72. Chatham University (PA)	56	2.4	77%	60%	56%	78%	1%	10/1	955-1145[2]	53%	55%	13%
72. Keene State College (NH)*	56	2.7	76%	52%	63%	53%	1%	15/1	880-1100	23%[5]	79%	5%
72. SUNY–Plattsburgh*	56	2.6	82%	54%	65%	42%	4%	16/1	980-1200[3]	39%[5]	50%	7%
75. College of New Rochelle (NY)	55	2.3	73%	24%	47%	82%	0.4%	9/1	870-1030	47%	32%	17%
75. CUNY–Brooklyn College*	55	2.9	84%	55%	54%	27%	5%	16/1	970-1180	50%[5]	37%	6%
75. Iona College (NY)	55	2.7	81%	65%	66%	38%	0.2%	16/1	890-1100	25%[5]	91%	8%
75. Slippery Rock U. of Pennsylvania*	55	2.8	82%	52%	68%	16%	10%	21/1	910-1080	36%	68%	7%
75. Stevenson University (MD)	55	2.7	76%	56%	53%	68%	0%	14/1	900-1110	48%	60%	5%
80. Geneva College (PA)†	54	2.3	81%	53%	64%	65%	4%	13/1	900-1180	51%	73%	10%
80. Norwich University (VT)	54	2.7	75%	60%	56%	54%	2%	16/1	940-1160[2]	38%[5]	57%	7%
80. St. Joseph's College New York	54	2.3	85%	56%	68%	73%	0%	12/1	910-1110	N/A	68%	5%
80. SUNY Maritime College*†	54	3.0	83%	61%	56%	32%	3%	17/1	1030-1200	34%[5]	68%	4%
80. University of New England (ME)	54	2.7	76%	62%	65%	48%	5%	13/1	960-1170	N/A	85%	8%
85. CUNY–City College*	53	2.9	86%	49%	44%	37%	4%	12/1	970-1230[3]	N/A	40%	20%
85. Eastern Connecticut State Univ.*	53	2.6	76%	57%	56%	35%	0.3%	16/1	950-1140[9]	31%	64%	8%
85. The Sage Colleges (NY)	53	2.5	78%	50%	60%	58%	0%	13/1	850-1070[2]	48%	54%	11%
85. Waynesburg University (PA)	53	2.3	81%	52%	62%	72%	1%	12/1	905-1140	48%	86%	8%
85. Wheelock College (MA)	53	2.4	70%	56%	64%	57%	1%	10/1	810-1062	33%	95%	12%
85. Wilkes University (PA)	53	2.4	79%	59%	59%	54%	6%	15/1	930-1176	50%	82%	14%
91. Champlain College (VT)†	52	2.6	80%	59%	58%	68%[4]	0%[4]	13/1	1030-1260[3]	34%[5]	66%	4%
91. Eastern University (PA)	52	2.3	78%	58%	63%	86%	1%	10/1	920-1170	44%	52%	13%
91. University of St. Joseph (CT)	52	2.4	76%	55%	55%	71%	3%	11/1	820-1120[2]	47%	93%	14%
91. York College of Pennsylvania	52	2.4	76%	58%	57%	51%	0%	16/1	960-1150	30%	43%	8%
95. Millersville U. of Pennsylvania*	51	2.7	79%	57%	62%	27%	7%	20/1	900-1100	29%	73%	4%
95. Shippensburg U. of Pennsylvania*	51	2.8	71%	52%	57%	27%	6%	19/1	880-1080	28%	89%	12%
95. SUNY College–Potsdam*	51	2.6	76%	51%	55%	68%	2%	13/1	877-1150[2]	25%[5]	74%	8%
95. University of New Haven (CT)	51	2.5	78%	56%	54%	48%	3%	16/1	960-1160	40%	82%	9%
99. St. Peter's University (NJ)	50	2.5	79%	48%	54%	59%	0%	13/1	810-1010[2]	36%	67%	11%

Note: Key to footnotes Page 104.

Rank	School (State) (*Public)	Overall score	Peer assessment score (5.0=highest)	Average first-year student retention rate	2015 graduation rate Predicted	2015 graduation rate Actual	% of classes under 20 ('15)	% of classes of 50 or more ('15)	Student/ faculty ratio ('15)	SAT/ACT 25th-75th percentile ('15)	Freshmen in top 25% of HS class ('15)	Accept-ance rate ('15)	Average alumni giving rate
99.	St. Thomas Aquinas College (NY)	50	2.4	77%	46%	55%	59%	0.3%	15/1	830-1050	34%[5]	79%	16%
101.	College of Our Lady of the Elms (MA)†	49	2.0	82%	44%	67%	70%	0.3%	13/1	870-1070[3]	N/A	75%	15%
101.	Roberts Wesleyan College (NY)	49	2.4	81%	56%	62%	59%	4%	11/1	950-1180[3]	47%	66%	10%
101.	Southern New Hampshire University	49	2.7	74%	45%	60%	55%	0%	15/1	880-1090[9]	24%[5]	92%	3%
104.	Bloomsburg U. of Pennsylvania*	48	2.6	79%	51%	62%	24%	6%	21/1	880-1080	26%	88%	6%
104.	Caldwell University (NJ)	48	2.3	80%	52%	52%	65%	0%	13/1	830-1070	35%[5]	64%	14%
104.	Plymouth State University (NH)*	48	2.5	74%	46%	58%	49%	1%	17/1	880-1080[2]	21%	74%	6%
104.	William Paterson Univ. of N.J.*	48	2.5	76%	50%	49%	49%	0.4%	14/1	900-1080	N/A	74%	5%
108.	Albertus Magnus College (CT)	47	2.2	82%[8]	38%	59%	89%	0%	14/1	820-950	24%[4]	69%	N/A
108.	CUNY–John Jay Col. of Crim. Justice*	47	3.0	78%	36%	41%	32%	1%	16/1	860-1050	N/A	52%	2%[4]
110.	Central Connecticut State Univ.*	46	2.5	78%	54%	57%	41%	3%	15/1	920-1100	28%	59%	4%
110.	Mount St. Mary College (NY)	46	2.3	73%	50%	59%	51%	1%	14/1	880-1055	32%	90%	9%
110.	Point Park University (PA)	46	2.3	75%	51%	58%	74%	0.3%	13/1	880-1090	34%	71%	3%
110.	SUNY Buffalo State*	46	2.7	73%	49%	49%	48%	5%	16/1	800-990	28%[5]	62%	3%[4]
114.	Alvernia University (PA)	45	2.3	75%	47%	51%	71%	1%	12/1	900-1090	35%	74%	9%
114.	Delaware Valley University (PA)†	45	2.4	71%	57%	57%	60%	2%	14/1	870-1110[3]	35%	69%	8%
114.	LIU Post (NY)	45	2.2	72%	42%	49%	69%	1%	12/1	910-1110[3]	N/A	81%	2%
114.	Western Connecticut State Univ.*	45	2.4	75%	53%	49%	38%	1%	14/1	900-1090[2]	24%	57%	3%
118.	Bridgewater State University (MA)*	44	2.5	81%	52%	58%	42%	1%	19/1	890-1100	N/A	75%	7%
118.	Carlow University (PA)	44	2.2	74%	47%	50%	75%	0.3%	11/1	868-1063	38%	81%	9%
118.	Westfield State University (MA)*	44	2.4	79%	52%	63%	36%	2%	16/1	910-1090	25%	80%	2%
118.	Worcester State University (MA)*	44	2.5	79%	52%	51%	71%	0.2%	18/1	925-1110	N/A	69%	7%
122.	Bay Path University (MA)†	43	2.1	76%	40%	57%	83%	0%	12/1	850-1050[2]	42%	77%	6%
122.	College of St. Elizabeth (NJ)	43	2.1	70%	43%	49%	88%	0%	11/1	709-903	N/A	63%	11%
122.	Frostburg State University (MD)*	43	2.5	76%	46%	53%	47%	3%	17/1	860-1060	27%	63%	5%
122.	Georgian Court University (NJ)	43	2.1	73%	55%	53%	76%	0%	12/1	840-1050	28%	73%	11%
122.	Southern Connecticut State Univ.*	43	2.5	75%	50%	52%	44%	2%	14/1	820-1010	10%	65%	4%
122.	Utica College (NY)	43	2.5	70%	47%	42%	66%	0%	11/1	880-1100[2]	33%	83%	7%
128.	College of Mount St. Vincent (NY)	42	2.3	72%	45%	53%	47%	0%	14/1	810-990	19%[5]	86%	15%
128.	Delaware State University*	42	2.5	67%	42%	42%	49%	3%	15/1	810-970	30%	44%	9%
128.	Kutztown Univ. of Pennsylvania*	42	2.6	73%	48%	54%	26%	9%	19/1	860-1050	19%	81%	5%
131.	Cabrini University (PA)	41	2.2	75%	51%	54%	79%	0.4%	11/1	N/A[2]	17%[4]	72%	8%
131.	Centenary College (NJ)	41	2.1	76%	49%	59%	88%	0%	16/1	830-1020	31%[4]	87%	8%[4]
131.	East Stroudsburg Univ. of Pa.*	41	2.6	72%	50%	55%	35%	4%	22/1	840-1030[2]	23%	77%	4%
131.	Keuka College (NY)	41	2.2	73%	47%	53%	70%	0.3%	8/1	N/A[2]	26%[4]	77%	12%
131.	Lasell College (MA)†	41	2.3	74%	51%	52%	66%	0%	14/1	870-1060	N/A	78%	11%
131.	Mansfield Univ. of Pennsylvania*	41	2.3	74%	45%	50%	42%	7%	17/1	850-1070[2]	30%	86%	8%
137.	Cairn University (PA)	40	2.1	73%[8]	52%	57%	73%[4]	2%[4]	14/1[4]	850-1095[3]	27%[5]	99%	7%[4]
137.	Chestnut Hill College (PA)	40	2.2	73%	45%	49%	85%	0%	9/1	850-1080	28%	93%	13%
137.	Gwynedd Mercy University (PA)	40	2.3	78%	49%	57%	61%	4%	10/1	830-1010	25%	92%	5%
137.	Lock Haven U. of Pennsylvania*	40	2.4	70%	41%	50%	34%	11%	19/1	850-1050	29%	92%	5%
137.	Rhode Island College*	40	2.7	77%	47%	44%	48%	1%	14/1	800-1030[3]	35%	72%	5%
137.	Rosemont College (PA)	40	2.2	72%	46%	47%	76%	0%	10/1	780-1025	46%[5]	71%	13%
137.	St. Joseph's College[1] (ME)	40	2.4	75%[8]	52%	59%[6]	N/A	N/A	11/1[4]	870-1060[4]	N/A	79%[4]	N/A

School (State) (*Public)	Peer assessment score (5.0=highest)	Average first-year student retention rate	2015 graduation rate Predicted	2015 graduation rate Actual	% of classes under 20 ('15)	% of classes of 50 or more ('15)	Student/ faculty ratio ('15)	SAT/ACT 25th-75th percentile ('15)	Freshmen in top 25% of HS class ('15)	Accept-ance rate ('15)	Average alumni giving rate
SECOND TIER (SCHOOLS RANKED 144 THROUGH 187 ARE LISTED HERE ALPHABETICALLY)											
Anna Maria College (MA)	1.9	66%[8]	43%	45%[6]	77%[4]	0%[4]	11/1[4]	N/A[2]	N/A	80%	8%[4]
Bowie State University (MD)*†	2.3	72%	38%	34%[6]	45%	1%	16/1	810-960	N/A	53%	5%[4]
California U. of Pennsylvania*	2.2	77%	48%	52%	28%	11%	21/1	820-1020[3]	23%	83%	5%
Clarion U. of Pennsylvania*	2.2	74%	42%	50%	23%	6%	18/1	840-1030	27%	96%	7%
Coppin State University (MD)*	2.1	69%[8]	36%	19%	52%	2%	13/1	810-970	N/A	37%	11%[4]
CUNY–College of Staten Island*	2.6	82%	47%	43%	17%	9%	16/1	910-1100	N/A	100%	2%
CUNY–Lehman College*	2.7	83%	44%	38%	32%	5%	14/1	860-1000[3]	N/A	30%	1%
Curry College (MA)	2.2	70%	50%	47%	62%	0%	10/1	840-1030[2]	21%[5]	88%	6%
Daemen College (NY)	2.2	78%	52%	49%	61%	2%	13/1	920-1140	51%	50%	4%
Daniel Webster College[1] (NH)†	2.1	66%[8]	47%	51%[6]	N/A	N/A	14/1[4]	N/A	N/A	63%[4]	N/A
Dominican College (NY)	2.1	69%	43%	46%	60%	0%	16/1	780-960[3]	N/A	71%	N/A

NORTH ▶

SECOND TIER CONTINUED (SCHOOLS RANKED 144 THROUGH 187 ARE LISTED HERE ALPHABETICALLY)

School (State) (*Public)	Peer assessment score (5.0=highest)	Average first-year student retention rate	2015 graduation rate		% of classes under 20 ('15)	% of classes of 50 or more ('15)	Student/faculty ratio ('15)	SAT/ACT 25th-75th percentile ('15)	Freshmen in top 25% of HS class ('15)	Accept-ance rate ('15)	Average alumni giving rate
			Predicted	Actual							
Dowling College[1] (NY)	1.8	66%[8]	44%	42%[6]	81%[4]	0%[4]	13/1[4]	N/A[2]	N/A	78%[4]	N/A
D'Youville College (NY)	2.0	76%	54%	44%	63%	2%	10/1	900-1130	51%[4]	70%	13%
Eastern Nazarene College (MA)†	2.0	68%	49%	66%	79%[4]	4%[4]	13/1	840-1110	27%[4]	61%	N/A
Edinboro Univ. of Pennsylvania[1]*	2.4	70%[8]	40%	47%[8]	27%[4]	10%[4]	20/1[4]	16-22[4]	24%[4]	99%[4]	5%[4]
Felician College (NJ)	2.0	77%	42%	39%	72%	0.2%	13/1	790-970	30%	79%	2%
Fitchburg State University (MA)*	2.4	76%	52%	51%	42%	1%	14/1	890-1090	N/A	75%	4%
Framingham State University (MA)*	2.5	74%	54%	56%	41%	1%	15/1	870-1080	19%[5]	71%	5%
Franklin Pierce University (NH)	2.3	66%	50%	43%	65%	2%	12/1	830-1040	30%	80%	4%
Green Mountain College (VT)†	2.1	68%[8]	49%	38%	55%	0%	14/1[4]	N/A[2]	N/A	66%	10%
Harrisburg Univ. of Science and Tech. (PA)†	2.2	54%[8]	51%	6%	N/A	N/A	26/1	N/A[2]	N/A	N/A	N/A
Holy Family University (PA)	2.1	76%	48%	57%	55%	0%	12/1	820-1010	25%	74%	2%
Husson University (ME)	2.1	73%	40%	44%	53%	0%	15/1	860-1070	39%	78%	5%
Johnson State College (VT)*	2.2	N/A	42%	35%[6]	N/A	N/A	19/1	N/A[2]	N/A	N/A	N/A
Kean University (NJ)*	2.4	74%	45%	50%	35%	0%	17/1	840-1020	28%[5]	74%	3%
Lincoln University (PA)*	2.0	73%	33%	42%	63%	0.2%	18/1	740-930	19%[5]	91%	10%
Medaille College (NY)	1.9	N/A	41%	45%[6]	N/A	N/A	N/A	N/A	N/A	29%	N/A
Metropolitan College of New York	1.9	50%[8]	18%	36%	89%	0%	10/1	N/A[2]	N/A	53%	N/A
Neumann University (PA)	2.2	71%	50%	50%	64%	1%	14/1	820-990	N/A	91%	9%
New England College (NH)	2.3	60%	36%	35%	80%	0%	19/1	790-1020[2]	16%[5]	98%	6%
New Jersey City University*	2.2	71%	39%	29%	49%	0%	14/1	760-970	29%[5]	87%	3%[4]
Nyack College (NY)	2.1	67%	34%	46%	77%	1%	12/1	770-1030[2]	20%[5]	99%	6%
Post University (CT)†	2.1	42%	35%	30%	81%	0%	19/1	770-1000	N/A	81%	N/A
Rivier University[1] (NH)	2.1	76%[8]	50%	54%[6]	N/A	N/A	17/1[4]	880-1050[4]	N/A	63%[4]	N/A
Salem State University (MA)*	2.4	78%	49%	50%	47%	1%	15/1	880-1070	N/A	75%	5%
SUNY College–Old Westbury*†	2.4	80%	47%	40%	34%	1%	18/1	910-1080[3]	N/A	50%	N/A
Thomas College (ME)†	2.1	66%	34%	42%	57%	0%	19/1	22-24[4]	40%[4]	74%[4]	6%[4]
Touro College (NY)	1.8	69%	64%	59%	65%	8%	12/1	950-1240[2]	N/A	34%	2%
Trinity Washington University[1] (DC)	2.6	58%[8]	31%	36%[6]	N/A	N/A	9/1[4]	N/A[2]	N/A	91%[4]	N/A
University of Baltimore*	2.6	75%[8]	44%	32%	27%	0.3%	15/1	865-1080	N/A	60%	7%
University of Bridgeport (CT)	2.1	62%	41%	33%	69%	1%	17/1	830-1010	30%[5]	53%	2%
University of Southern Maine*	2.6	65%	51%	33%	50%	3%	16/1	860-1100	26%	88%	1%
Univ. of the District of Columbia*	1.9	54%[8]	48%	34%	69%	0.3%	8/1[4]	700-910[9]	22%[4]	35%	N/A
Washington Adventist University (MD)†	1.8	68%	51%	37%	85%	0%	7/1	700-930	N/A	37%	2%

SOUTH ▶

Rank	School (State) (*Public)	Overall score	Peer assessment score (5.0=highest)	Average first-year student retention rate	2015 graduation rate		% of classes under 20 ('15)	% of classes of 50 or more ('15)	Student/faculty ratio ('15)	SAT/ACT 25th-75th percentile ('15)	Freshmen in top 25% of HS class ('15)	Accept-ance rate ('15)	Average alumni giving rate
					Predicted	Actual							
1.	Elon University (NC)	100	4.0	90%	83%	83%	51%	0%	12/1	1110-1290	58%[5]	57%	21%
2.	Rollins College (FL)	97	3.8	85%	77%	71%	71%	0.4%	10/1	1105-1310[9]	66%[5]	60%	13%
3.	The Citadel (SC)*	90	3.9	85%	61%	67%	44%	2%	13/1	980-1180	34%	77%	26%
4.	Samford University (AL)	88	3.8	88%	77%	74%	62%	1%	12/1	23-29	52%[5]	93%	9%
5.	Stetson University (FL)	87	3.6	78%	66%	64%	54%	1%	13/1	1050-1260[2]	60%	63%	10%
6.	Belmont University (TN)	84	3.7	83%	74%	69%	40%	0.4%	13/1	23-28	58%[5]	80%	19%
7.	Berry College (GA)†	82	3.3	79%	72%	64%	59%	0%	12/1	24-29	62%	55%	16%
8.	James Madison University (VA)*	81	3.9	88%	70%	81%[8]	34%	12%	16/1	1040-1220[3]	41%	73%	7%[4]
9.	Appalachian State University (NC)*	78	3.6	87%	66%	71%	35%	8%	16/1	1060-1240	61%	66%	8%
10.	College of Charleston (SC)*	75	3.6	81%	72%	68%	37%	4%	15/1	1030-1210	54%	77%	7%
10.	Loyola University New Orleans	75	3.4	78%	75%	66%	54%	3%	12/1	22-28	20%[5]	90%	8%
12.	Bellarmine University (KY)	74	3.3	81%	67%	67%	54%	0.3%	12/1	22-27[3]	59%[5]	84%	16%
12.	Embry-Riddle Aeronautical U. (FL)	74	3.6	78%	61%	55%	26%	2%	15/1	1010-1240[2]	53%	69%	2%
14.	Asbury University (KY)†	73	3.1	81%	63%	62%	64%	1%	13/1	21-27	51%	57%	18%
14.	Christopher Newport Univ. (VA)*	73	3.1	86%	71%	70%	59%	3%	15/1	1070-1250[2]	53%	60%	16%
16.	Univ. of Mary Washington (VA)*	72	3.3	81%	68%	70%	53%	3%	14/1	1000-1210[2]	41%	83%	12%
16.	Univ. of North Carolina–Wilmington*	72	3.4	85%	68%	71%	30%	9%	17/1	23-27	63%	61%	5%
18.	Hampton University (VA)	70	2.9	77%	53%	65%	63%	3%	9/1	940-1090[2]	54%	69%	15%
18.	John Brown University (AR)†	70	3.0	83%	67%	61%	58%	1%	14/1	24-30[2]	59%	74%	15%
20.	Florida Southern College†	68	3.0	79%	58%	57%	60%	0%	13/1	1050-1230	59%[5]	45%	12%
21.	University of Tampa (FL)	67	3.2	74%	57%	56%	41%	2%	17/1	990-1170	45%[4]	51%	19%
22.	Milligan College (TN)†	66	2.7	81%	59%	62%	73%	1%	9/1	22-28	65%	65%	22%

Note: Key to footnotes Page 104.

WE'RE TOP RANKED
but you're
#1

Being No. 1 is about more than being the best. It's a distinction marked when a purposeful passion intersects with an unsettled desire for excellence that extends beyond yourself. It's not a rank blindly given. It's earned. Every day.

That's the kind of students we want at Rollins. Students who aren't content with the present state of the world. We want students who strive to be No. 1 in science, business, and art—not only for themselves but for the betterment of lives around them.

What's our passion? To graduate global citizens and responsible leaders who will do good in the world. Do you have what it takes to be No. 1? Join us, the No. 1 college in the South for 10 of the last 11 years, and find out.

Winter Park · Orlando, FL | rollins.edu/no1

ROLLINS

SOUTH ▶

Rank	School (State) (*Public)	Overall score	Peer assessment score (5.0=highest)	Average first-year student retention rate	2015 graduation rate		% of classes under 20 ('15)	% of classes of 50 or more ('15)	Student/ faculty ratio ('15)	SAT/ACT 25th-75th percentile ('15)	Freshmen in top 25% of HS class ('15)	Accept-ance rate ('15)	Average alumni giving rate
					Predicted	Actual							
22.	Queens University of Charlotte (NC)	66	2.9	72%	60%	53%	68%	0%	9/1	940-1150	44%	67%	23%
24.	Harding University (AR)	64	2.9	83%	61%	64%	55%	6%	17/1	22-28	51%	94%	10%
24.	Tuskegee University (AL)†	64	3.0	76%	49%	46%	57%	9%	14/1	18-23	60%	53%	18%
26.	Winthrop University (SC)*	63	3.3	75%	58%	55%	46%	3%	14/1	910-1130	51%	67%	7%
27.	Xavier University of Louisiana†	62	3.3	71%	43%	38%	41%	3%	14/1	20-26	57%	66%	17%
28.	Christian Brothers University (TN)	61	2.8	78%	57%	52%	67%	0.4%	12/1	21-27	60%	46%	16%
28.	Georgia College & State Univ.*	61	3.1	86%	61%	60%	36%	5%	17/1	23-27	N/A	76%	4%
30.	Campbell University (NC)	60	3.0	75%	58%	53%	59%	8%	16/1	900-1110	54%	74%	10%
31.	Converse College (SC)	59	2.7	71%[8]	61%	54%	86%	1%	12/1	20-25	48%	58%	12%
31.	Longwood University (VA)*	59	2.8	79%	59%	66%	53%	1%	16/1	890-1090	34%	79%	10%
31.	Mississippi College	59	3.0	73%	54%	54%	57%	2%	15/1	21-27[3]	60%	63%	6%
31.	Western Kentucky University*	59	3.0	72%	46%	50%	49%	6%	18/1	19-26	44%[5]	93%	10%
35.	Lynchburg College (VA)	58	2.7	74%	56%	56%	58%	0.3%	11/1	910-1120	N/A	69%	14%
35.	Murray State University (KY)*	58	3.1	72%	53%	48%	58%	3%	15/1	20-26	45%	91%	6%
37.	University of Montevallo (AL)*	56	3.0	77%	57%	45%	48%	1%	16/1	20-26	N/A	70%	13%
37.	Western Carolina University (NC)*	56	3.0	78%	55%	57%	28%	4%	16/1	20-24	38%	40%	6%
37.	Wheeling Jesuit University (WV)†	56	2.6	71%	62%	54%	69%	0%	11/1	20-25	39%	92%	13%
37.	Wingate University (NC)	56	2.8	73%	57%	54%	51%	0.3%	14/1	930-1130	49%	70%	10%
41.	Eastern Mennonite University (VA)†	55	2.4	77%	63%	61%	60%	2%	10/1	870-1130	N/A	62%	19%
41.	William Carey University (MS)	55	2.7	77%	40%	54%	71%	1%	15/1	20-27[3]	54%	57%	4%
43.	Columbia International Univ. (SC)	54	2.4	77%	57%	54%	72%	11%	14/1	930-1130	42%	34%	9%
43.	Freed-Hardeman University (TN)	54	2.5	74%	60%	58%	53%	2%	13/1	21-27	52%[5]	92%	11%
43.	Marymount University (VA)	54	2.8	75%	52%	50%	51%	0.2%	12/1	880-1110[2]	37%[5]	86%	4%
43.	Mississippi Univ. for Women*	54	3.0	74%	47%	49%	64%	2%	14/1	18-24	54%	96%	8%
47.	Columbia College (SC)	53	2.6	70%	46%	50%	75%	0%	12/1	840-1070	47%	89%	11%
47.	Marshall University (WV)*	53	3.3	72%	52%	45%	45%	4%	19/1	20-25	N/A	88%	6%
47.	Radford University (VA)*	53	3.0	76%	50%	59%	31%	10%	17/1	890-1050[2]	18%	83%	4%
47.	University of Tennessee–Martin*	53	2.8	73%	49%	46%	60%	4%	16/1	20-25	46%	70%	7%
47.	West Virginia Wesleyan College†	53	2.7	69%	56%	50%	58%	0.3%	13/1	20-25	53%	77%	18%
52.	Belhaven University (MS)	52	2.8	66%	41%	52%	84%	1%	14/1	20-24	43%	51%	4%
52.	Brenau University (GA)	52	2.7	64%	39%	48%	84%	0.2%	11/1	890-1090	N/A	66%	3%
52.	Mary Baldwin College (VA)	52	2.9	63%	48%	37%	70%	0.4%	11/1	860-1140	32%[5]	50%	16%[7]
52.	University of North Florida*	52	2.9	82%	56%	55%	30%	10%	18/1	22-27	42%	57%	6%
56.	Lee University (TN)	51	2.8	77%	52%	52%	54%	6%	17/1	21-27	47%	85%	8%
56.	Lenoir-Rhyne University (NC)†	51	2.7	66%	52%	48%	71%	0%	12/1	880-1100	39%[4]	84%	13%
58.	St. Thomas University (FL)	50	2.7	65%	39%	39%	70%	0%	12/1	870-1030	27%[5]	49%	2%
59.	Arkansas State University*	49	2.8	74%	38%	39%	49%	5%	17/1	21-26	49%	70%	10%
59.	Carson-Newman University (TN)†	49	2.9	66%	55%	45%	55%	0%	13/1	19-26	N/A	59%	7%
59.	Lincoln Memorial University (TN)	49	2.4	68%	52%	44%	82%[4]	1%[4]	13/1[4]	20-28	N/A	74%	6%
62.	Coastal Carolina University (SC)*	48	2.9	64%	50%	43%	35%	2%	18/1	910-1080	31%	60%	8%
62.	Jacksonville University (FL)	48	2.7	69%	56%	41%	74%	0.4%	11/1	890-1110[2]	N/A	54%	5%
62.	Palm Beach Atlantic University (FL)	48	2.7	73%	54%	44%	61%	2%	13/1	940-1180	N/A	93%	4%
62.	Saint Leo University (FL)	48	2.7	70%	39%	42%	43%	0%	15/1	910-1080[2]	32%	73%	5%
62.	Univ. of Tennessee–Chattanooga*	48	3.1	69%	54%	44%	38%	11%	20/1	21-26	47%[4]	79%	5%
67.	Anderson University (SC)†	47	2.9	75%	51%	49%	42%	7%	16/1	950-1183	62%	55%	7%
67.	Piedmont College (GA)	47	2.4	70%	44%	45%	75%	0%	11/1	870-1100	40%	57%	4%
69.	Midway University (KY)†	46	2.1	81%[8]	34%	53%	N/A	N/A	15/1	20-26	42%	58%	N/A
69.	Southern Adventist University (TN)†	46	2.4	76%	55%	48%	61%	7%	15/1	20-26	N/A	83%	11%
69.	Troy University (AL)*	46	2.8	70%[8]	36%	36%[6]	60%	5%	14/1	19-26	54%[4]	92%	7%[4]
72.	Bryan College (TN)†	45	2.4	67%	56%	56%	72%	2%	16/1	19-25	51%	46%	9%
72.	Morehead State University (KY)*	45	2.6	68%	47%	40%	55%	3%	18/1	20-25	44%	85%	8%
72.	North Carolina Central Univ.*	45	2.4	76%	32%	42%	39%	4%	16/1	800-940	22%	66%	13%
72.	University of Central Arkansas*	45	2.8	71%	55%	45%	45%	3%	17/1	20-26	44%	92%	6%
72.	University of Charleston (WV)†	45	2.9	66%	52%	47%	65%	1%	15/1	19-24	N/A	52%	6%
72.	University of North Georgia*	45	2.8	81%	54%	54%	30%	3%	21/1	1010-1190	42%[5]	64%	6%
72.	U. of South Florida–St. Petersburg*	45	2.8	67%	55%	38%	30%	9%	17/1	1010-1170	46%	47%	17%
79.	Austin Peay State University (TN)*	44	2.9	69%	41%	38%	52%	4%	18/1	19-24[2]	34%	88%	4%
79.	Eastern Kentucky University*	44	2.8	69%	49%	45%	57%	5%	16/1	19-25	35%	71%	5%
79.	Thomas More College (KY)	44	2.4	66%	56%	47%	71%	0.3%	16/1	20-24	31%	88%	13%
82.	Florida Gulf Coast University*	43	2.9	77%	51%	43%	16%	15%	22/1	970-1140	39%[5]	61%	7%
82.	Northern Kentucky University*	43	2.8	68%	50%	40%	38%	3%	19/1	20-26	32%	92%	5%

Note: Key to footnotes Page 104.

SOUTH ▶

Rank School (State) (*Public)	Overall score	Peer assessment score (5.0=highest)	Average first-year student retention rate	2015 graduation rate		% of classes under 20 ('15)	% of classes of 50 or more ('15)	Student/faculty ratio ('15)	SAT/ACT 25th-75th percentile ('15)	Freshmen in top 25% of HS class ('15)	Acceptance rate ('15)	Average alumni giving rate
				Predicted	Actual							
84. Francis Marion University (SC)*	42	2.6	67%	44%	42%	44%[4]	6%[4]	15/1	820-1030[3]	39%	59%	5%[4]
84. North Greenville University (SC)†	42	2.3	72%	53%	55%	72%	0.4%	14/1	22-30	37%	58%	5%
84. Pfeiffer University (NC)	42	2.3	68%	46%	43%	67%	0%	13/1	805-1060	28%	47%	11%
87. Methodist University (NC)†	41	2.6	62%[8]	48%	39%	64%	0.1%	12/1	18-23	33%	54%	10%
87. University of North Alabama*	41	2.8	72%	47%	38%	44%	4%	21/1	19-25	N/A	58%	5%
89. Alcorn State University (MS)*	40	2.3	72%	28%	34%	51%	4%	17/1	16-20	N/A	81%	9%
89. Elizabeth City State Univ. (NC)*†	40	1.9	75%[8]	29%	39%	69%	3%	15/1	760-940	8%	70%	N/A
91. Henderson State University (AR)*	39	2.7	59%	44%	34%	61%	1%	15/1	18-24	40%	64%	3%
91. King University (TN)	39	2.3	73%	51%	45%	75%	1%	14/1	19-25[3]	43%[5]	44%	8%
91. Lynn University (FL)†	39	2.6	70%	56%	44%	49%	0.2%	18/1	895-1090[2]	25%[5]	76%	5%
91. U. of North Carolina–Pembroke*	39	2.6	67%	36%	38%	47%	2%	16/1	830-990	34%	74%	4%
91. Winston-Salem State Univ.[1] (NC)*	39	2.5	79%[8]	36%	44%[6]	N/A	N/A	14/1[4]	800-930[4]	N/A	60%[4]	7%[7]
96. Southern Wesleyan University[1] (SC)	38	2.4	70%[8]	38%	49%[6]	N/A	N/A	18/1[4]	N/A[2]	N/A	63%[4]	N/A
97. Arkansas Tech University*	37	2.6	69%	43%	47%	41%	7%	19/1	18-25	34%	89%	4%
98. Campbellsville University (KY)	36	2.5	64%[8]	46%	37%	57%	0.2%	13/1	18-24	40%	76%	11%
98. Charleston Southern University (SC)	36	2.7	65%[8]	53%	39%	56%	4%	15/1	910-1110[3]	47%	60%	7%
98. Jacksonville State University (AL)*	36	2.8	71%	41%	31%	41%	6%	18/1	20-26[3]	45%	67%	9%
98. McNeese State University (LA)*	36	2.6	69%	45%	41%	44%	9%	20/1	20-24	41%	82%	7%
102. Alabama A&M University[1]*	35	2.3	65%[8]	34%	32%[8]	N/A	N/A	21/1[4]	15-19[4]	N/A	53%[4]	9%[4]
102. Fayetteville State University (NC)*	35	2.4	75%	29%	32%	38%	1%	17/1	790-930	20%	60%	2%
102. Nicholls State University (LA)*	35	2.5	68%[8]	46%	44%	40%	10%	19/1	20-24	42%	90%	5%
105. Columbus State University (GA)*	34	2.6	70%	42%	31%	46%	5%	18/1	850-1090	36%	56%	3%
105. Tusculum College (TN)	34	2.5	57%	38%	36%	80%	0.2%	17/1	18-23	N/A	69%	5%

School (State) (*Public)	Peer assessment score (5.0=highest)	Average first-year student retention rate	2015 graduation rate		% of classes under 20 ('15)	% of classes of 50 or more ('15)	Student/faculty ratio ('15)	SAT/ACT 25th-75th percentile ('15)	Freshmen in top 25% of HS class ('15)	Acceptance rate ('15)	Average alumni giving rate
			Predicted	Actual							
SECOND TIER (SCHOOLS RANKED 107 THROUGH 140 ARE LISTED HERE ALPHABETICALLY)											
Alabama State University*	2.3	60%	24%	32%	43%	0.3%	16/1	15-23	11%[5]	48%	3%
Albany State University (GA)*	2.3	71%	28%	31%	52%	2%	17/1	840-950[3]	37%	64%	5%
Amridge University (AL)†	2.1	N/A	37%	22%[6]	N/A	N/A	10/1	N/A[2]	N/A	N/A	N/A
Armstrong State University (GA)*	2.5	69%	44%	33%	41%	3%	18/1	910-1080	23%	74%	5%
Auburn University–Montgomery (AL)*	2.9	63%	47%	22%	43%	1%	16/1	19-23	40%	79%	3%
Bethel University (TN)	2.3	58%[8]	22%	31%	81%	1%	17/1	17-22[2]	N/A	84%	N/A
Clayton State University (GA)*†	2.4	70%	38%	32%	43%	3%	16/1	860-1020	N/A	39%	3%
Concord University (WV)*†	2.4	65%	42%	38%	62%	2%	16/1	19-24	46%	85%	4%
Cumberland University (TN)	2.4	66%	48%	45%	64%	3%	16/1	19-23	32%	49%	4%
Delta State University[1] (MS)*	2.5	66%[8]	44%	35%[8]	64%[4]	1%[4]	14/1[4]	N/A	N/A	92%[4]	N/A
Fairmont State University (WV)*	2.4	63%	34%	34%[6]	54%	5%	15/1	18-23	33%	66%	2%[4]
Faulkner University (AL)†	2.6	56%	28%	21%	74%	2%	15/1	18-24	19%[4]	57%	2%
Fort Valley State University (GA)*†	2.1	64%	31%	29%	63%	3%	14/1	16-20	13%	21%	13%
Georgia Southwestern State University*	2.4	68%	38%	33%	47%	2%	18/1	870-1040	40%	72%	2%
Grambling State University (LA)*	2.3	69%	28%	39%	44%	7%	20/1	16-20	19%	38%	N/A
Lindsey Wilson College (KY)	2.5	59%	29%	26%	57%	0%	16/1	19-24[2]	36%	72%	13%
Louisiana College†	2.2	60%	49%	32%	71%	0%	11/1	18-23	N/A	69%	N/A
Louisiana State U.–Shreveport*	2.5	66%	47%	37%	57%	8%	21/1	20-25[4]	N/A	81%	N/A
Mississippi Valley State Univ.*	2.3	66%[8]	25%	22%	61%	1%	16/1	16-19	N/A	76%	N/A
Montreat College (NC)	2.1	60%[8]	47%	38%[6]	81%	0%	12/1	850-1060	26%	54%	4%
Norfolk State University (VA)*	2.3	72%[8]	30%	33%	57%	1%	16/1	700-910	22%	79%	N/A
Northwestern State U. of La.[1]*	2.5	69%[8]	46%	37%[6]	N/A	N/A	20/1[4]	880-1100[4]	N/A	73%[4]	N/A
Savannah State University (GA)*†	2.4	66%[8]	25%	27%	25%	0.3%	21/1	770-920	N/A	83%	5%
South Carolina State University*†	2.0	60%	30%	36%	54%	1%	17/1	680-840	13%	95%	5%
Southeastern Louisiana University*	2.5	64%	46%	38%	35%	6%	21/1	20-24	31%	87%	5%
Southeastern University (FL)†	2.3	67%	46%	39%	52%	4%	20/1	840-1080[3]	N/A	46%	6%
Southern Arkansas University*	2.4	62%	40%	31%	43%	3%	17/1	18-24	38%	67%	6%
Southern Univ. and A&M College (LA)*	2.1	68%	37%	34%	N/A	N/A	16/1	17-21	7%	N/A	N/A
Southern University–New Orleans[1]*	2.2	54%[8]	24%	13%[6]	N/A	N/A	15/1[4]	660-1010[4]	N/A	21%[4]	N/A
South University[1] (GA)	1.9	45%[8]	51%	11%[6]	N/A	N/A	11/1[4]	N/A[2]	N/A	N/A	N/A
Thomas University (GA)†	2.0	55%	33%	28%	77%[4]	1%[4]	10/1	20-24[4]	N/A	32%	N/A
Union College[1] (KY)	2.5	62%[8]	35%	34%[6]	N/A	N/A	13/1[4]	18-23[4]	N/A	75%[4]	N/A
University of West Alabama*	2.5	60%	42%	28%	53%	2%	13/1	18-23	N/A	73%	4%
Virginia State University[1]*	2.4	63%[8]	34%	44%[6]	N/A	N/A	14/1[4]	760-920[4]	N/A	80%[4]	N/A

Note: Key to footnotes Page 104.

MIDWEST ▶

Rank School (State) (*Public)	Overall score	Peer assessment score (5.0=highest)	Average first-year student retention rate	2015 graduation rate		% of classes under 20 ('15)	% of classes of 50 or more ('15)	Student/ faculty ratio ('15)	SAT/ACT 25th-75th percentile ('15)	Freshmen in top 25% of HS class ('15)	Accept-ance rate ('15)	Average alumni giving rate
				Predicted	Actual							
1. Creighton University (NE)	100	4.2	91%	82%	79%	48%	6%	11/1	24-29	68%[5]	70%	14%
2. Butler University (IN)	98	4.1	90%	81%	76%	52%	3%	11/1	25-30	77%	70%	20%
3. Drake University (IA)	91	3.9	88%	76%	75%	52%	4%	13/1	24-30[2]	69%	67%	12%
4. Valparaiso University (IN)	88	3.8	85%	69%	67%	48%	4%	12/1	23-29	64%	82%	16%
4. Xavier University (OH)	88	3.8	83%	71%	74%	40%	0.4%	11/1	22-27[3]	53%[5]	72%	14%
6. Bradley University (IL)	87	3.6	87%	70%	74%	57%	3%	12/1	23-28	58%	66%	10%
7. John Carroll University (OH)	84	3.4	87%	62%	73%	49%	1%	14/1	22-28	41%[5]	82%	14%
8. Truman State University (MO)*	82	3.7	88%	79%	73%	49%	2%	16/1	25-30	79%	79%	8%
8. University of Evansville (IN)	82	3.4	84%	70%	69%	66%	1%	12/1	23-29[2]	66%	70%	13%
10. Elmhurst College (IL)	77	3.2	79%	64%	67%	59%	0.2%	14/1	21-26	54%[5]	55%	8%
11. Drury University (MO)	75	2.8	82%	61%	67%	70%	1%	10/1	20-31	59%	65%	13%
11. Millikin University (IL)†	75	3.6	77%	59%	60%	62%	1%	11/1	20-26	38%	60%	13%
11. Milwaukee School of Engineering	75	3.5	83%	77%	64%	42%	0%	16/1	25-30	N/A	65%	8%
11. Otterbein University (OH)	75	3.2	78%	61%	61%	68%	1%	10/1	21-26	60%	75%	14%
15. Baldwin Wallace University (OH)	74	3.1	81%	63%	67%	60%	1%	13/1	20-27[2]	45%	60%	9%
15. Nebraska Wesleyan University†	74	3.0	79%	66%	62%	75%	0%	12/1	22-27	50%	79%	18%
15. North Central College (IL)	74	3.1	79%	68%	67%	39%	0%	15/1	22-27	54%	57%	19%
15. Rockhurst University (MO)	74	3.1	87%	68%	72%	41%	2%	12/1	23-28	56%	74%	13%
15. St. Catherine University (MN)	74	3.1	82%	61%	64%	69%	1%	10/1	21-26	68%	67%	14%
20. Hamline University (MN)	73	3.3	81%	63%	63%	52%	3%	13/1	21-28	47%	72%	12%
20. University of Northern Iowa*	73	3.3	82%	60%	68%	36%	7%	17/1	20-25	48%	80%	9%
22. Bethel University (MN)	72	2.9	84%	66%	73%	54%	3%	12/1	22-27	57%	95%	8%
22. Franciscan Univ. of Steubenville (OH)	72	2.5	87%	67%	79%	52%	1%	14/1	23-28	55%[5]	79%	13%
24. Lewis University (IL)	71	2.8	83%	55%	66%	69%	0.3%	13/1	20-25	41%	62%	7%
24. University of Detroit Mercy	71	2.9	81%	66%	63%	53%	2%	10/1	22-27	45%	73%	10%
24. Webster University (MO)	71	2.8	79%	62%	62%	87%	0%	9/1	21-27	47%	56%	4%
27. Dominican University (IL)	69	2.8	81%	58%	59%	62%	0.2%	12/1	19-24	51%	63%	17%
27. Grand Valley State University (MI)*	69	3.1	83%	61%	67%[6]	24%	6%	17/1	21-26	46%	81%	5%
27. Indiana Wesleyan University	69	2.8	79%	57%	65%	66%	2%	14/1	21-27	58%	89%	7%
30. Augsburg College (MN)	68	3.0	79%	55%	56%	64%	0.4%	12/1	19-24	N/A	59%	10%
31. Kettering University (MI)	67	2.8	92%	79%	54%	58%	2%	14/1	24-29	65%	70%	3%
31. University of Indianapolis	67	3.1	74%	57%	56%	57%	1%	12/1	910-1120	55%	84%	11%
31. University of St. Francis (IL)	67	2.7	79%	60%	65%	71%	0%	11/1	21-25	43%	51%	6%
31. Univ. of Wisconsin–La Crosse*	67	3.1	86%	68%	69%	29%	11%	18/1	23-26	61%	80%	4%
35. College of St. Scholastica (MN)	66	2.8	84%	59%	70%	52%	3%	15/1	20-26	48%	61%	7%
35. St. Ambrose University (IA)	66	2.9	78%	55%	63%	71%	0.1%	10/1	20-25	40%	73%	6%
37. Univ. of Wisconsin–Eau Claire*	65	3.1	83%	64%	67%	23%	13%	21/1	22-26	49%	85%	8%
38. Anderson University (IN)	64	2.9	75%	56%	54%	68%	2%	11/1	940-1130	53%	60%	6%
38. Capital University (OH)	64	2.6	75%	63%	63%	56%	2%	12/1	22-28[3]	47%	72%	8%
40. Bethel College (IN)†	63	2.5	79%	51%	64%	66%	2%	12/1	19-26	47%	66%	10%
40. Concordia University (NE)	63	2.6	78%	58%	59%	51%	2%	14/1	20-27	43%	78%	21%
40. Eastern Illinois University*	63	2.6	77%	49%	58%	43%	3%	15/1	19-24	31%	50%	5%
40. Lawrence Technological Univ. (MI)	63	2.8	80%	58%	54%	76%	0.2%	12/1	22-29	50%	55%	4%
40. Marian University (IN)†	63	2.6	73%	47%	56%	68%	1%	13/1	20-26	43%	55%	13%
40. University of Michigan–Dearborn*	63	2.9	82%	61%	53%	30%	8%	15/1	21-27	59%	62%	9%
40. Univ. of Northwestern–St. Paul (MN)†	63	2.4	81%	59%	67%	56%[4]	3%[4]	18/1[4]	21-27	49%	87%	16%
47. Baker University (KS)	62	2.5	77%	56%	61%	67%	0.4%	13/1	20-25	43%	82%	15%
47. University of Minnesota–Duluth*	62	3.0	76%	60%	60%	34%	17%	17/1	22-26	44%	76%	6%
49. Mount Mercy University (IA)†	60	2.4	79%	60%	65%	57%	2%	11/1	19-23	37%	61%	12%
49. Olivet Nazarene University (IL)	60	2.7	76%	59%	61%	45%	9%	17/1	20-27	50%	77%	13%
49. St. Mary's Univ. of Minnesota†	60	2.6	78%	59%	61%	67%	0%	18/1	19-26	39%[5]	78%	10%
49. Univ. of Wisconsin–Stevens Point*	60	2.9	79%	56%	65%	29%	5%	21/1	20-25[9]	33%	74%	5%
49. Univ. of Wisconsin–Whitewater*	60	3.0	80%	50%	60%	38%	7%	22/1	20-26[3]	32%	81%	9%
49. Walsh University (OH)	60	2.4	76%	52%	60%	75%	0%	13/1	18-27	43%	80%	11%
49. Western Illinois University*	60	2.7	68%	49%	53%	51%	3%	14/1	18-23	31%	60%	4%
56. Aquinas College (MI)	59	2.5	79%	56%	58%	63%	1%	13/1	21-26	N/A	72%	14%
56. Carroll University (WI)	59	2.9	79%	61%	59%	49%	6%	16/1	21-26	50%	94%	10%
56. Concordia University Wisconsin	59	2.7	74%	48%	58%	51%	3%	12/1	20-26[3]	45%	69%	3%
56. Morningside College (IA)†	59	2.3	73%	54%	55%	64%	0%	13/1	20-26	43%	56%	23%
56. St. Xavier University (IL)	59	2.9	73%	53%	48%	41%	1%	13/1	19-23	53%	75%	7%
56. University of Findlay (OH)	59	2.7	79%[8]	62%	55%	53%	2%	16/1	20-25	45%	76%	9%

Note: Key to footnotes Page 104.

MIDWEST ▶

Rank	School (State) (*Public)	Overall score	Peer assessment score (5.0=highest)	Average first-year student retention rate	2015 graduation rate		% of classes under 20 ('15)	% of classes of 50 or more ('15)	Student/faculty ratio ('15)	SAT/ACT 25th-75th percentile ('15)	Freshmen in top 25% of HS class ('15)	Acceptance rate ('15)	Average alumni giving rate
					Predicted	Actual							
56.	Univ. of Nebraska–Kearney*	59	2.9	79%	52%	57%	48%	3%	14/1	20-25	41%	85%	7%
63.	Alverno College (WI)	58	3.0	72%	41%	42%	77%	0%	10/1	16-22	36%	77%	12%
63.	Muskingum University (OH)	58	2.6	70%	53%	52%	72%	0.2%	14/1	18-24[3]	33%	74%	16%
63.	Southern Illinois U.–Edwardsville*	58	2.9	72%	58%	49%	38%	12%	20/1	20-26	43%	88%	4%
63.	Spring Arbor University (MI)	58	2.6	77%	51%	52%	72%	1%	14/1	20-26	48%	69%	9%
63.	Univ. of Illinois–Springfield*	58	2.9	76%	59%	48%	51%	2%	14/1	20-26	46%	63%	5%
63.	Ursuline College (OH)	58	2.4	67%	48%	44%	91%	0%	7/1	19-24	45%	88%	15%
69.	Malone University (OH)	57	2.4	69%	55%	57%	63%	2%	12/1	19-25	42%	69%	9%
69.	University of Wisconsin–Stout*	57	2.9	74%	51%	57%	33%	1%	18/1	20-24	28%	84%	4%
71.	Missouri State Univ.[1]*	56	2.9	76%[8]	58%	54%[8]	27%[4]	13%[4]	20/1[4]	21-26[4]	54%[4]	85%[4]	7%[4]
71.	North Park University (IL)	56	2.7	77%	55%	52%	60%	2%	11/1	19-24	N/A	49%	9%[4]
71.	Winona State University (MN)*	56	2.9	78%	54%	59%	28%	8%	20/1	20-25	30%	62%	9%
74.	Ferris State University (MI)*	55	2.7	75%	49%	51%	42%	3%	16/1	19-24[3]	N/A	78%	3%
74.	Grace College and Seminary (IN)†	55	2.3	81%	56%	62%	57%	4%	20/1	910-1160[3]	53%	78%	14%
74.	Greenville College (IL)†	55	2.4	69%[8]	51%	57%	62%	4%	13/1	19-25	40%	72%	16%
74.	McKendree University (IL)	55	2.5	75%	56%	56%	77%	0%	14/1	19-24	34%	64%	7%
74.	Quincy University (IL)	55	2.5	70%	47%	52%	64%	0.3%	14/1	19-24	32%	63%	12%
79.	Cornerstone University (MI)	54	2.1	75%	52%	61%	56%	2%	15/1	20-25	37%	73%	34%
79.	Mount St. Joseph University (OH)	54	2.4	70%	52%	50%	58%	0%	12/1	19-24	34%	52%	9%
79.	Northern Michigan University*	54	2.8	73%	54%	49%	37%	8%	21/1	19-24[3]	N/A	70%	5%
79.	Stephens College (MO)†	54	2.4	68%	53%	50%	75%	0%	8/1	20-24[3]	45%	68%	12%
79.	University of Saint Francis (IN)	54	2.7	70%	50%	56%	63%	1%	11/1	860-1070	47%	95%	6%
79.	University of Sioux Falls (SD)†	54	2.6	67%†	54%	54%	65%	1%	14/1	20-25	35%	92%	3%
79.	Univ. of Wisconsin–Oshkosh*	54	2.8	76%	50%	51%	41%	9%	20/1	20-24	31%	68%	4%
86.	Madonna University (MI)	53	2.4	82%	52%	61%	69%	2%	11/1	20-24	43%	60%	2%

MIDWEST ▶

Rank	School (State) (*Public)	Overall score	Peer assessment score (5.0=highest)	Average first-year student retention rate	2015 graduation rate		% of classes under 20 ('15)	% of classes of 50 or more ('15)	Student/ faculty ratio ('15)	SAT/ACT 25th-75th percentile ('15)	Freshmen in top 25% of HS class ('15)	Accept-ance rate ('15)	Average alumni giving rate
					Predicted	Actual							
86.	Mount Mary University (WI)	53	2.4	71%	43%	43%	88%	0%	10/1	17-21	50%	53%	13%
86.	Mount Vernon Nazarene U. (OH)	53	2.3	78%	53%	58%	71%	3%	13/1	20-25	30%	78%	7%
86.	University of Central Missouri*	53	2.7	70%	49%	52%	46%	4%	20/1	19-24[2]	33%	79%	2%[7]
86.	Univ. of Wisconsin–Green Bay*	53	2.9	75%	52%	47%	32%	9%	21/1	21-25	N/A	85%	5%
91.	Fontbonne University (MO)	52	2.5	74%	52%	53%	83%	0%	11/1	20-25	N/A	97%	4%
91.	Univ. of Wisconsin–River Falls*	52	2.7	73%	50%	57%	43%	7%	22/1	20-25	33%	90%	7%
91.	William Woods University (MO)	52	2.4	76%	52%	46%	78%	0%	11/1	19-26	57%	93%	10%
94.	College of St. Mary[1] (NE)†	51	2.4	76%[8]	44%	42%[6]	74%[4]	0%[4]	10/1[4]	20-25[4]	52%[4]	N/A	18%[4]
94.	Judson University (IL)†	51	2.2	70%	56%	52%	74%	1%	10/1	21-26	41%	71%	4%
94.	Northwest Missouri State Univ.*	51	2.8	69%	48%	47%	44%	8%	21/1	20-25[3]	40%	75%	6%
94.	Pittsburg State University (KS)*	51	2.6	73%	49%	48%	45%	6%	18/1	19-24[3]	46%	82%	7%
94.	Robert Morris University (IL)	51	2.3	49%	24%	49%[8]	51%	1%	23/1	16-21[2]	17%	24%	1%
94.	University of Mary (ND)	51	2.4	76%[8]	49%	62%	70%	4%	13/1	20-26[3]	45%	82%	13%
94.	Univ. of Wisconsin–Platteville*	51	2.8	77%	50%	53%	20%	4%	20/1	21-26	35%	77%	N/A
94.	Washburn University (KS)*	51	2.8	67%	47%	36%	50%	2%	13/1	19-25	34%	99%	11%
94.	Wayne State College (NE)*	51	2.5	68%	43%	49%	47%	1%	19/1	18-25[2]	29%	100%	12%
103.	Concordia University–St. Paul (MN)	50	2.7	71%	43%	46%	75%	0%	16/1	18-24[3]	30%	55%	5%
103.	Minnesota State Univ.–Mankato*	50	2.7	73%	50%	48%	31%	9%	23/1	20-24	23%	67%	5%
103.	Mount Marty College (SD)†	50	2.2	69%	53%	47%	82%	0%	9/1	19-25	45%	73%	6%
103.	Northern State University (SD)*†	50	2.4	69%	50%	48%	60%	3%	18/1	19-25	24%	76%	11%
103.	Southeast Missouri State Univ.*	50	2.7	73%	53%	48%	42%	5%	21/1	20-25[3]	44%	84%	5%
108.	Dakota State University (SD)*	49	2.5	67%	51%	39%	54%	2%	18/1	20-25	22%	81%	9%
108.	Emporia State University (KS)*	49	2.7	72%	49%	42%	47%	7%	18/1	19-25[9]	36%	87%	9%
108.	Ohio Dominican University[1]	49	2.6	67%[8]	44%	41%[6]	57%[4]	0%[4]	15/1[4]	19-24[4]	42%[4]	47%[4]	7%[4]
108.	University of Dubuque (IA)	49	2.6	65%[8]	45%	41%	77%	0.3%	14/1	780-980[4]	25%	77%	10%
108.	University of Michigan–Flint*	49	2.7	75%	47%	38%	50%	1%	15/1	18-24	40%	74%	1%
113.	Graceland University (IA)	48	2.1	64%	50%	52%	66%	3%	15/1	18-24	18%	48%	18%
113.	Marian University (WI)	48	2.3	69%	44%	41%	78%	0.4%	12/1	17-23	28%	84%	6%
115.	Bemidji State University (MN)*	47	2.6	68%[8]	48%	46%[6]	41%	8%	19/1	19-24	23%	94%	5%
115.	Lake Erie College (OH)	47	2.0	68%	43%	50%	68%	0.4%	15/1	19-23[9]	N/A	56%	8%
115.	MidAmerica Nazarene University (KS)	47	2.3	74%[8]	55%	54%	75%	2%	13/1	22[3]	N/A	61%	N/A
115.	Minnesota State Univ.–Moorhead*	47	2.6	70%	47%	41%	40%	7%	18/1	20-25	35%	82%	5%
115.	Roosevelt University (IL)	47	2.4	62%	48%	37%	50%	1%	11/1	19-25	37%	72%	5%
115.	Southwestern College (KS)	47	2.1	64%	56%	44%	83%	0%	9/1	19-24	34%	91%	5%
115.	St. Cloud State University (MN)*	47	2.7	71%	49%	42%	42%	4%	19/1	19-25	20%	86%	3%
115.	Viterbo University[1] (WI)	47	2.6	76%[8]	52%	50%[6]	N/A	N/A	11/1[4]	910-1178[4]	N/A	69%[4]	N/A

School (State) (*Public)	Peer assessment score (5.0=highest)	Average first-year student retention rate	2015 graduation rate		% of classes under 20 ('15)	% of classes of 50 or more ('15)	Student/ faculty ratio ('15)	SAT/ACT 25th-75th percentile ('15)	Freshmen in top 25% of HS class ('15)	Accept-ance rate ('15)	Average alumni giving rate
			Predicted	Actual							
SECOND TIER (SCHOOLS RANKED 123 THROUGH 163 ARE LISTED HERE ALPHABETICALLY)											
Aurora University[1] (IL)	2.4	71%[8]	50%	56%[6]	N/A	N/A	16/1[4]	910-1100[4]	N/A	81%[4]	4%[7]
Avila University[1] (MO)	2.4	71%[8]	56%	47%[6]	N/A	N/A	12/1[4]	810-1030[4]	N/A	52%[4]	N/A
Black Hills State University (SD)*	2.5	60%[8]	41%	34%[6]	N/A	N/A	N/A	N/A[2]	N/A	N/A	N/A
Calumet College of St. Joseph (IN)	2.1	58%	38%	27%	75%	1%	10/1	785-1010[9]	14%	35%	3%
Chicago State University[1]*	1.8	52%[8]	28%	20%[8]	54%[4]	0%[4]	N/A	16-20[4]	N/A	30%[4]	N/A
Columbia College Chicago[1]	2.5	69%[8]	53%	42%[6]	N/A	N/A	13/1[4]	N/A[2]	N/A	89%[4]	N/A
Davenport University (MI)	2.1	71%	35%	37%	74%	0%	12/1	19-24[9]	N/A	89%	1%
DeVry University (IL)	1.5	N/A	40%	27%	17%	0%	15/1	N/A[2]	N/A	N/A	N/A
Evangel University (MO)†	2.2	72%[8]	53%	48%[6]	N/A	N/A	14/1	20-26	N/A	62%	N/A
Fort Hays State University (KS)*	2.5	68%[8]	46%	42%	43%	4%	16/1	N/A[2]	30%[4]	86%	N/A
Friends University (KS)	2.2	N/A	46%	33%[6]	N/A	N/A	N/A	19-24	37%	58%	9%
Governors State University[1] (IL)*	2.1	N/A	N/A	N/A	60%[4]	1%[4]	10/1[4]	770-995[4]	N/A	94%[4]	N/A
Herzing University[1] (WI)†	1.7	38%[8]	44%	35%[6]	N/A	N/A	15/1[4]	N/A[2]	N/A	100%[4]	N/A
Indiana University East*†	2.3	66%	34%	28%	64%	2%	15/1	860-1050	30%	62%	7%
Indiana University Northwest*	2.4	67%	34%	24%	37%	7%	15/1	805-1030	32%	79%	6%
Indiana U.-Purdue U.-Fort Wayne*	2.8	65%	40%	25%	51%	4%	17/1	870-1090	36%	92%	N/A
Indiana University–South Bend*	2.7	65%	37%	24%	49%	2%	13/1	840-1060	25%	76%	6%
Indiana University Southeast*	2.4	61%	40%	28%	50%	1%	14/1	830-1050	31%	85%	6%
Lakeland College[1] (WI)	2.1	70%[8]	50%	50%[6]	N/A	N/A	14/1[4]	858-925[4]	N/A	55%[4]	N/A

Note: Key to footnotes Page 104.

BUTLER UNIVERSITY,
NO. 2 IN THE MIDWEST

MIDWEST ▶

SECOND TIER CONTINUED (SCHOOLS RANKED 123 THROUGH 163 ARE LISTED HERE ALPHABETICALLY)

School (State) (*Public)	Peer assessment score (5.0=highest)	Average first-year student retention rate	2015 graduation rate Predicted	Actual	% of classes under 20 ('15)	% of classes of 50 or more ('15)	Student/faculty ratio ('15)	SAT/ACT 25th-75th percentile ('15)	Freshmen in top 25% of HS class ('15)	Acceptance rate ('15)	Average alumni giving rate
Lincoln University (MO)*	2.1	49%	41%	20%	47%	4%	17/1	15-19	23%	54%[4]	7%
Lourdes University (OH)	2.2	62%	35%	27%	66%	0%	10/1	18-24	24%	69%	N/A
Marygrove College[1] (MI)	2.2	55%[8]	16%	21%[6]	N/A	N/A	9/1[4]	14-19[4]	N/A	48%[4]	N/A
Metropolitan State University[1] (MN)*	2.2	66%[8]	46%	34%[6]	N/A	N/A	17/1[4]	N/A[2]	N/A	100%[4]	2%[7]
Minot State University (ND)*	2.4	69%	49%	42%	N/A	N/A	12/1	19-24	20%[5]	57%	4%
Missouri Baptist University[1]	2.1	61%[8]	44%	42%[6]	N/A	N/A	20/1[4]	820-1060[4]	N/A	60%[4]	N/A
Newman University (KS)	2.2	71%	55%	50%	69%	1%	14/1	20-27[9]	53%	56%	5%
Northeastern Illinois University*	2.4	61%	43%	22%	43%	1%	16/1	16-20	13%[5]	67%	2%
Notre Dame College of Ohio[1]†	2.4	61%[8]	43%	37%[6]	N/A	N/A	14/1[4]	780-980[4]	N/A	90%[4]	N/A
Park University (MO)	2.3	60%[8]	57%	29%	90%	0%	17/1	22[4]	35%	42%	1%
Rockford University (IL)	2.3	62%	50%	42%	82%	0.3%	10/1	19-24	N/A	54%	8%
Saginaw Valley State Univ. (MI)*	2.5	71%	45%	40%	33%	3%	18/1	19-25	43%	76%	3%
Siena Heights University (MI)	2.4	65%	47%	37%	79%	0%	11/1[4]	18-26[2]	32%	77%	5%
Silver Lake College[1] (WI)†	1.9	72%[8]	51%	39%[6]	95%[4]	0%[4]	7/1[4]	14-20[4]	25%[4]	83%[4]	5%[4]
Southwest Baptist University[1] (MO)	2.3	66%[8]	49%	42%[6]	N/A	N/A	15/1[4]	910-1220[4]	N/A	62%[4]	N/A
Southwest Minnesota State University*	2.3	68%	48%	39%	46%	4%	15/1	19-24	21%	64%	11%
Tiffin University (OH)	2.4	64%	35%	43%	56%	0.2%	11/1	18-23[9]	N/A	93%	7%
University of Southern Indiana*	2.5	70%	44%	41%	40%	3%	17/1	890-1100	33%	69%	4%
University of St. Mary (KS)	2.4	70%	52%	41%	68%	1%	8/1	19-23	34%	49%	N/A
Upper Iowa University	2.2	62%	38%	41%	82%	0.1%	17/1	17-22	19%	66%	3%
William Penn University[1] (IA)†	1.9	60%[8]	33%	32%[6]	N/A	N/A	17/1[4]	N/A[2]	N/A	60%[4]	N/A
Youngstown State University (OH)*	2.5	71%	38%	31%	39%	5%	17/1	18-24	30%	71%	4%

WEST ▶

Rank School (State) (*Public)	Overall score	Peer assessment score (5.0=highest)	Average first-year student retention rate	2015 graduation rate Predicted	Actual	% of classes under 20 ('15)	% of classes of 50 or more ('15)	Student/faculty ratio ('15)	SAT/ACT 25th-75th percentile ('15)	Freshmen in top 25% of HS class ('15)	Acceptance rate ('15)	Average alumni giving rate
1. Trinity University (TX)	100	4.1	89%	89%	83%	63%	2%	9/1	27-32	75%	48%	15%
2. Santa Clara University (CA)	95	3.9	95%	85%	84%	46%	1%	12/1	27-32	83%[5]	49%	21%
3. Loyola Marymount University (CA)	92	3.7	90%	77%	79%	51%	1%	11/1	1110-1300	76%[5]	51%	19%
4. Gonzaga University (WA)	86	3.9	94%	77%	83%	35%	2%	12/1	1090-1290	71%	73%	16%
5. Mills College (CA)	82	3.3	78%	70%	67%	73%	0.4%	10/1	1030-1290[2]	68%[5]	76%	24%
6. Chapman University (CA)	78	3.5	91%	76%	79%	45%	3%	14/1	1100-1290	79%[5]	48%	9%
7. University of Portland (OR)	76	3.7	90%	76%	78%	30%	1%	14/1	1090-1300	77%[5]	62%	12%
8. Seattle University	75	3.4	86%	73%	79%	57%	1%	12/1	1060-1280	68%[5]	73%	8%
9. Cal. Poly. State U.–San Luis Obispo*	72	3.9	93%	76%	79%	16%	13%	19/1	1130-1340[3]	84%[5]	31%	5%
9. St. Mary's College of California	72	3.4	89%	69%	71%	52%	0.2%	11/1	1010-1230	N/A	76%	14%
11. Whitworth University (WA)	71	3.5	86%	72%	75%	59%	1%	11/1	1060-1270[9]	N/A	62%	16%
12. University of Dallas	68	3.3	80%	73%	70%	66%	2%	10/1	1080-1340[3]	67%[5]	64%	16%
12. University of Redlands (CA)	68	3.1	88%	72%	72%	62%	1%	14/1	1020-1220	68%	68%	12%
14. St. Edward's University (TX)	67	3.4	83%	63%	63%	56%	1%	14/1	1040-1220	58%	77%	6%
15. Pacific Lutheran University (WA)	66	3.2	83%	68%	68%	53%	3%	12/1	980-1230	85%[5]	76%	11%
16. California Lutheran University	64	3.2	84%	67%	66%	61%	0.3%	15/1	1000-1200	72%[5]	62%	14%
17. Point Loma Nazarene University (CA)	62	3.0	86%	69%	75%	40%	3%	15/1	1020-1250	63%[5]	71%	9%
18. Abilene Christian University (TX)	61	3.3	77%	63%	61%	45%	8%	14/1	950-1180	58%	50%	10%
18. Western Washington University*	61	3.4	83%	63%	72%	37%	16%	18/1	1000-1220	54%	82%	5%
20. Westminster College (UT)	60	3.1	77%	68%	62%	72%	0%	9/1	22-27	53%	96%	13%
21. St. Mary's Univ. of San Antonio	59	3.0	73%	57%	60%	60%	1%	11/1	930-1130	53%	55%	10%
22. Pacific University (OR)	57	3.0	80%	68%	71%	60%	3%	11/1	990-1190	N/A	79%	10%
23. George Fox University (OR)	55	3.1	82%	62%	71%	67%	2%	14/1	960-1200	56%[5]	78%	3%
23. Mount Saint Mary's University (CA)	55	2.9	79%	43%	65%	63%	0%	13/1	830-1020	52%[5]	77%	11%
23. Oklahoma City University	55	3.0	82%	68%	60%	75%	2%	11/1	23-29	61%	70%	5%
23. Regis University (CO)	55	3.1	82%	63%	73%	64%	1%	14/1	21-27[3]	50%	66%	5%
27. LeTourneau University (TX)	54	2.9	77%	63%	54%	68%	2%	14/1	22-29[2]	53%[5]	45%	7%
27. N.M. Inst. of Mining and Tech.*	54	3.1	77%	79%	49%	56%	6%	12/1	23-29	68%	24%	N/A
29. University of St. Thomas (TX)	53	3.0	82%	65%	57%	65%	0%	9/1	980-1210	53%	79%	7%
30. Dominican University of California	52	2.7	83%	62%	66%	66%	0%	9/1	950-1140	55%[5]	79%	8%
31. Calif. State Poly. Univ.–Pomona*	50	3.5	90%	47%	63%	15%	13%	25/1	920-1180	N/A	39%	3%
32. Evergreen State College (WA)*	48	3.2	70%	50%	54%	36%	12%	22/1	940-1190	25%[5]	98%	5%

Note: Key to footnotes Page 104.

Rank School (State) (*Public)	Overall score	Peer assessment score (5.0=highest)	Average first-year student retention rate	2015 graduation rate		% of classes under 20 ('15)	% of classes of 50 or more ('15)	Student/ faculty ratio ('15)	SAT/ACT 25th-75th percentile ('15)	Freshmen in top 25% of HS class ('15)	Accept-ance rate ('15)	Average alumni giving rate
				Predicted	Actual							
33. Hardin-Simmons University (TX)	47	2.8	65%	55%	53%	69%	1%	12/1	19-25[3]	49%	60%	10%
33. San Jose State University (CA)*	47	3.2	86%	50%	57%	19%	16%	28/1	920-1180	N/A	55%	2%
35. California State U.–Long Beach*	46	3.1	89%	58%	67%	22%[4]	10%[4]	24/1	930-1170	N/A	34%	3%[4]
35. Master's Col. and Seminary (CA)†	46	2.6	82%	61%	69%	71%	5%	10/1	960-1210	52%[5]	95%	9%
37. California Baptist University	44	2.8	79%	52%	60%	55%	5%	17/1	830-1080	40%	65%	2%
37. California State Univ.–Chico*	44	2.8	86%	56%	64%	26%	14%	24/1	890-1110	76%[5]	65%	5%[7]
39. Univ. of Colo.–Colorado Springs*	43	3.2	68%	54%	44%	46%	7%	15/1	21-26	37%	92%	3%
40. St. Martin's University (WA)	42	2.7	79%	54%	49%	76%	0%	11/1	918-1150[3]	55%	93%	6%
41. Concordia University (CA)	41	2.6	76%	51%	61%	53%	1%	18/1	900-1130	49%	59%	5%
41. Oklahoma Christian U.	41	2.8	77%	59%	49%	54%	7%	13/1	21-28[3]	49%	59%	18%
41. Sonoma State University (CA)*	41	2.9	81%	47%	59%	29%	7%	25/1	880-1100	N/A	77%	1%
44. Central Washington University*	40	2.9	77%	49%	52%	46%	5%	20/1	870-1080[3]	N/A	81%	3%
44. Fresno Pacific University (CA)	40	2.5	81%	49%	55%	76%	1%	13/1	880-1077	64%	52%	N/A
44. Northwest Nazarene University (ID)	40	2.5	76%	57%	50%	67%	4%	15/1	920-1150	52%	55%	13%
44. Notre Dame de Namur University (CA)	40	2.7	76%	48%	42%	68%	0%	11/1	810-1025	39%[5]	87%	9%
44. Oral Roberts University (OK)	40	2.4	80%	55%	56%	62%	4%	14/1	19-24	38%	22%	8%
44. Univ. of the Incarnate Word (TX)	40	2.8	74%	49%	54%	54%	2%	13/1	860-1060	40%	92%	5%
50. La Sierra University (CA)	39	2.4	77%	51%	49%	72%	2%	14/1	840-1030	42%	45%	3%
50. Texas Wesleyan University	39	2.7	61%	42%	36%	63%	0%	16/1	928-1090	42%	46%	6%
52. Alaska Pacific University	38	2.5	66%[8]	62%	67%	N/A	N/A	8/1	830-1122[3]	N/A	69%	N/A
52. Chaminade Univ. of Honolulu	38	2.7	73%	40%	46%	57%	0.3%	10/1	865-1060	50%	82%	4%
52. Holy Names University (CA)	38	2.4	72%	42%	40%	75%	0%	10/1	770-950	39%	44%	8%
52. Humboldt State University (CA)*	38	2.8	75%	48%	46%	27%	14%	25/1	870-1110[2]	48%	75%	6%
52. Univ. of Mary Hardin-Baylor (TX)	38	2.8	68%	55%	43%	51%	3%	19/1	930-1130	50%	80%	6%
52. Walla Walla University (WA)	38	2.7	80%[8]	42%	50%	55%	7%	14/1	920-1160[3]	40%[5]	56%	9%[4]
58. California State U.–Monterey Bay*	37	2.8	82%	48%	53%	17%	7%	25/1	853-1100	51%	49%	2%
58. Woodbury University (CA)	37	2.3	80%	38%	46%	82%	0%	8/1	860-1060	N/A	58%	3%
60. Vanguard U. of Southern California†	36	2.5	76%	56%	56%	58%	4%	15/1	850-1090	44%	68%	6%
61. California State U.–Los Angeles*	35	2.9	83%	27%	45%	26%	8%	27/1	780-990[2]	N/A	68%	2%
61. Calif. State U.–San Bernardino*	35	2.7	88%	33%	52%	23%	20%	29/1	800-990[2]	N/A	65%	2%
61. California State U.–Stanislaus*	35	2.6	84%	42%	55%	19%	6%	20/1	800-1010[2]	N/A	71%	1%
61. Eastern Washington University[1]*	35	2.8	76%[8]	45%	45%[8]	37%[4]	11%[4]	22/1[4]	17-23[4]	N/A	74%[4]	3%[4]
61. Hawaii Pacific University	35	2.8	70%	57%	49%	57%	1%	13/1	876-1110	55%	68%	1%
61. University of Hawaii–Hilo*†	35	2.8	67%	48%	39%	49%	2%	12/1	830-1050	50%	71%	N/A
67. Western Oregon University*	34	2.7	70%	38%	45%	56%	3%	15/1	840-1070[2]	35%	88%	3%
68. California State U.–Northridge*	33	3.1	77%	38%	50%	11%	16%	27/1	800-1030	N/A	46%	5%[7]
68. Corban University (OR)†	33	2.2	76%	61%	57%	53%	2%	15/1	940-1160	60%	31%	5%
68. Northwest University (WA)†	33	2.5	79%	50%	50%	58%	5%	10/1	840-1075	N/A	64%	N/A
68. Southern Utah University*	33	2.5	65%	51%	39%	42%	7%	18/1	20-27	47%	72%	3%
68. Texas A&M International University*	33	2.7	79%	39%	41%	33%	15%	20/1	810-1010	50%	48%	3%
73. University of Alaska–Anchorage*	32	2.9	72%	48%	27%	56%	4%	12/1	880-1150[2]	34%	71%	4%
74. Oklahoma Wesleyan University†	31	2.7	55%	56%	45%	86%	2%	15/1	18-25	25%	95%	4%
74. University of Houston–Clear Lake*	31	2.7	71%[8]	N/A	N/A	27%	6%	15/1	940-1120	44%	66%	4%
76. Houston Baptist University	30	2.6	67%	53%	33%	58%	2%	16/1	960-1150	56%	33%	4%
76. Lubbock Christian University (TX)	30	2.5	70%	46%	42%	62%	3%	13/1	19-25[3]	43%	96%	5%
76. Our Lady of the Lake University (TX)†	30	2.7	63%	43%	38%	64%	0%	13/1	840-1020	26%	68%	14%
76. Southern Oregon University*	30	2.7	70%	43%	39%	41%	4%	23/1	910-1150	N/A	95%	2%
76. Stephen F. Austin State Univ. (TX)*	30	2.8	68%	44%	41%	29%	11%	19/1	890-1100	40%	62%	4%
76. Weber State University (UT)*	30	2.8	69%	40%	38%	47%	6%	20/1	18-24[2]	29%	100%	2%
82. California State U.–Channel Islands[1]*	29	2.6	77%[8]	54%	55%[6]	N/A	N/A	22/1[4]	N/A[2]	N/A	72%[4]	N/A
82. California State U.–Sacramento[1]*	29	3.0	82%[8]	43%	42%[6]	21%[4]	17%[4]	26/1[4]	830-1050[4]	N/A	73%[4]	3%[7]
82. Midwestern State University (TX)*	29	2.6	70%[8]	50%	44%	39%	13%	18/1	900-1090	39%	76%	5%
82. Prescott College (AZ)	29	2.4	71%[8]	38%	37%	100%	0%	10/1	900-1150	N/A	70%	N/A
82. Simpson University (CA)†	29	2.2	76%	43%	49%	78%	1%	9/1	893-1120	64%[4]	52%	5%
82. University of North Texas–Dallas*	29	2.8	69%[8]	N/A	N/A	40%	0.3%	15/1	830-987	24%[5]	58%	N/A
88. California State Univ.–San Marcos*	28	2.7	82%	46%	53%	15%	7%	25/1	850-1050	N/A	67%	1%[7]
88. University of Central Oklahoma*	28	2.8	65%	48%	39%	37%	2%	19/1	19-24	35%	70%	1%
88. University of Texas–Tyler*	28	2.7	63%	55%	41%	34%	11%	16/1[4]	970-1160	35%[5]	64%	1%
91. West Texas A&M University*	27	2.6	65%	48%	43%	30%	11%	21/1	18-23	39%	67%	3%
92. Western State Colorado University*†	26	2.5	68%	49%	42%	59%	1%	16/1	17-23	17%	98%	N/A
93. U. of Texas of the Permian Basin*	24	2.4	68%	51%	40%	28%	13%	24/1	880-1070	54%	84%	11%

BEST REGIONAL UNIVERSITIES

WEST ▶

School (State) (*Public)	Peer assessment score (5.0=highest)	Average first-year student retention rate	2015 graduation rate Predicted	2015 graduation rate Actual	% of classes under 20 ('15)	% of classes of 50 or more ('15)	Student/faculty ratio ('15)	SAT/ACT 25th-75th percentile ('15)	Freshmen in top 25% of HS class ('15)	Accept-ance rate ('15)	Average alumni giving rate
SECOND TIER (SCHOOLS RANKED 94 THROUGH 124 ARE LISTED HERE ALPHABETICALLY)											
Adams State University[1] (CO)*	2.4	57%[8]	25%	24%[6]	N/A	N/A	15/1[4]	888-1080[4]	N/A	65%[4]	N/A
Angelo State University (TX)*	2.4	60%	44%	37%	23%	10%	23/1	18-23	31%	77%	2%
California State Univ.–Bakersfield*	2.7	75%[8]	35%	41%	26%	12%	28/1	800-1010[9]	N/A	100%	1%[7]
California State U.–Dominguez Hills*	2.5	80%	31%	35%	23%	9%	23/1	750-940[2]	N/A	58%	2%
California State Univ.–East Bay*	2.6	78%	43%	45%	15%	19%	26/1	790-1000[9]	N/A	74%	N/A
Cameron University (OK)*	2.2	61%	30%	24%	47%	1%	18/1	17-22[2]	11%	100%	2%
Colorado Christian University[1]	2.5	71%[8]	54%	40%[6]	N/A	N/A	14/1[4]	N/A[2]	N/A	94%[4]	N/A
Colorado State University–Pueblo*	2.5	62%	37%	33%	26%	53%	20/1	18-23	32%	96%	2%
Concordia University Texas[1]	2.4	57%[8]	58%	35%[6]	N/A	N/A	11/1[4]	910-1120[4]	N/A	85%[4]	N/A
East Central University[1] (OK)*	2.3	65%[8]	37%	34%[6]	N/A	N/A	19/1[4]	810-1070[4]	N/A	97%[4]	N/A
Eastern New Mexico University[1]*	2.5	60%[8]	40%	29%[6]	N/A	N/A	19/1[4]	850-1080[4]	N/A	63%[4]	N/A
Eastern Oregon University*	2.4	61%	38%	26%	70%	3%	18/1	840-1050	37%	97%	1%
Hope International University (CA)†	2.0	74%	50%	42%	70%	0%	9/1	790-1030	36%	34%	7%
Metropolitan State Univ. of Denver*†	2.8	65%	50%	25%	38%	2%	18/1	17-23[3]	19%	65%	N/A
Montana State Univ.–Billings*	2.8	56%	44%	24%	53%	4%	17/1	18-24[2]	31%	100%	5%[4]
New Mexico Highlands University*	2.4	50%	29%	18%	70%	1%	14/1	15-20[2]	15%	100%	N/A
Northeastern State University (OK)*	2.5	63%	38%	26%	50%	4%	17/1	19-23[3]	47%	92%	2%
Northwest Christian University (OR)†	2.0	66%	51%	50%	67%	2%	12/1	910-1075	N/A	68%	5%
Northwestern Oklahoma State U.*	2.3	60%	36%	24%	58%	1%	17/1	18-22	27%	48%	4%
Sierra Nevada College (NV)	2.2	71%[8]	53%	40%	84%	0.4%	9/1	870-1100[3]	9%[5]	66%	N/A
Southeastern Oklahoma State U.*	2.4	60%	43%	29%	58%	3%	17/1	18-23	41%	72%	3%
Southern Nazarene University[1] (OK)	2.4	46%[8]	44%	45%[6]	N/A	N/A	N/A	N/A	N/A	37%[4]	N/A
Southwestern Assemblies of God University (TX)	2.2	69%[8]	34%	41%	N/A	N/A	14/1	18-23[3]	N/A	28%	1%
Southwestern Oklahoma State U.*	2.4	67%	44%	33%	49%	7%	18/1	19-24[2]	47%	81%	N/A
Sul Ross State University (TX)*	2.2	55%[8]	26%	19%	62%	3%	16/1	740-940	20%	80%	N/A
Tarleton State University (TX)*	2.5	68%	43%	44%	33%	9%	19/1	850-1050	37%	71%	2%[7]
Texas A&M University–Texarkana[1]*	2.5	48%[8]	N/A	N/A	N/A	N/A	15/1[4]	745-955[4]	N/A	48%[4]	N/A
University of Houston–Downtown*†	2.6	66%	36%	13%	27%	4%	20/1	810-990	29%	78%	2%
University of Houston–Victoria*	2.6	60%[8]	N/A	N/A	N/A	N/A	17/1	790-970[2]	N/A	53%	2%[7]
University of the Southwest[1] (NM)†	2.2	51%[8]	46%	18%[6]	N/A	N/A	17/1[4]	N/A	N/A	N/A	N/A
Wayland Baptist University (TX)	2.1	48%	59%	33%	85%	0.1%	10/1	16-23	26%	99%	1%

The Top Public Regional Universities ▶

NORTH

Rank School (State)

1. College of New Jersey
2. SUNY–Geneseo
3. Massachusetts Maritime Academy
3. SUNY Polytechnic Institute
5. CUNY–Baruch College
5. Rowan University (NJ)
5. SUNY–New Paltz
8. Ramapo College of New Jersey
9. Rutgers University–Camden (NJ)
10. CUNY–Queens College
11. CUNY–Hunter College
12. SUNY College–Oneonta
12. SUNY–Oswego
14. Stockton University (NJ)
14. Towson University (MD)

SOUTH

Rank School (State)

1. The Citadel (SC)
2. James Madison University (VA)
3. Appalachian State University (NC)
4. College of Charleston (SC)
5. Christopher Newport Univ. (VA)
6. U. of Mary Washington (VA)
6. U. of North Carolina–Wilmington
8. Winthrop University (SC)
9. Georgia College & State Univ.
10. Longwood University (VA)
10. Western Kentucky University
12. Murray State University (KY)
13. University of Montevallo (AL)
13. Western Carolina University (NC)
15. Mississippi Univ. for Women

MIDWEST

Rank School (State)

1. Truman State University (MO)
2. University of Northern Iowa
3. Grand Valley State University (MI)
4. Univ. of Wisconsin–La Crosse
5. Univ. of Wisconsin–Eau Claire
6. Eastern Illinois University
6. University of Michigan–Dearborn
8. University of Minnesota–Duluth
9. Univ. of Wisconsin–Stevens Point
9. Univ. of Wisconsin–Whitewater
9. Western Illinois University
12. Univ. of Nebraska–Kearney
13. Southern Illinois U.–Edwardsville
13. Univ. of Illinois–Springfield
15. University of Wisconsin–Stout

WEST

Rank School (State)

1. Cal. Poly. State U.–San Luis Obispo
2. Western Washington University
3. N.M. Inst. of Mining and Tech.
4. Calif. State Poly. Univ.–Pomona
5. Evergreen State College (WA)
6. San Jose State University (CA)
7. California State U.–Long Beach
8. California State Univ.–Chico
9. Univ. of Colo.–Colorado Springs
10. Sonoma State University (CA)
11. Central Washington University
12. Humboldt State University (CA)
13. California State U.–Monterey Bay
14. California State U.–Los Angeles
14. Calif. State U.–San Bernardino
14. California State U.–Stanislaus
14. Eastern Washington University[1]
14. University of Hawaii–Hilo

Footnotes:
1. School refused to fill out U.S. News statistical survey. Data that appear are from school in previous years or from another source such as the National Center for Education Statistics.
2. SAT and/or ACT not required by school for some or all applicants.
3. In reporting SAT/ACT scores, the school did not include all students for whom it had scores or refused to tell U.S. News whether all students with scores had been included.
4. Previous year's data was used in the ranking calculation.
5. Data based on fewer than 51 percent of enrolled freshmen.
6. Some or all data reported to the NCAA and/or the National Center for Education Statistics.
7. Data reported to the Council for Aid to Education.

8. This rate, normally based on four years of data, is given here for less than four years because school didn't report rate for the most recent year or years to U.S. News.
9. SAT and/or ACT may not be required by school for some or all applicants, and in reporting SAT/ACT scores, the school did not include all students for whom it had scores or refused to tell U.S. News whether all students with scores had been included.

† School's Carnegie classification has changed. It appeared in a different U.S. News ranking category last year.
N/A means not available.

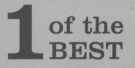

Best Regional Colleges

What Is a Regional College?

These schools focus almost entirely on the undergraduate experience and offer a broad range of programs in the liberal arts (which account for fewer than half of bachelor's degrees granted) and in fields such as business, nursing and education. They grant few graduate degrees. Because most of the 334 colleges in the category draw heavily from nearby states, they are ranked by region: North, South, Midwest, West.

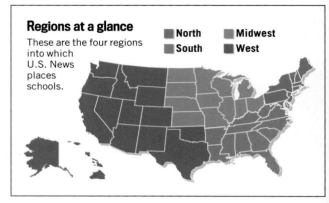

Regions at a glance
These are the four regions into which U.S. News places schools.
■ North ■ Midwest ■ South ■ West

NORTH ▶

Rank	School (State) (*Public)	Overall score	Peer assessment score (5.0=highest)	Average first-year student retention rate	2015 graduation rate		% of classes under 20 ('15)	% of classes of 50 or more ('15)	Student/faculty ratio ('15)	SAT/ACT 25th-75th percentile ('15)	Freshmen in top 25% of HS class ('15)	Acceptance rate ('15)	Average alumni giving rate
					Predicted	Actual							
1.	Cooper Union (NY)	100	4.0	94%[8]	85%	81%	70%	1%	9/1	1240-1510	90%[5]	13%	18%
2.	U.S. Coast Guard Acad. (CT)*	94	4.1	92%	85%	85%	78%	0%	8/1	1180-1350	79%	18%	N/A
3.	U.S. Merchant Marine Acad. (NY)*	82	3.8	92%[8]	76%	69%	N/A	N/A	13/1	1183-1351	68%	15%	N/A
4.	Messiah College (PA)	73	3.4	88%	68%	77%	46%	1%	12/1	1010-1250	63%	79%	12%
5.	Maine Maritime Academy*	69	3.5	81%	53%	58%	52%	0%	13/1	950-1150	44%	78%	18%
6.	Cedar Crest College (PA)	55	3.0	71%	57%	58%	75%	2%	10/1	830-1080	45%	68%	12%
7.	University of Maine–Farmington*	49	2.9	73%	48%	59%	63%	1%	14/1	870-1115[2]	40%	83%	4%
8.	Cazenovia College (NY)	46	2.7	71%	47%	58%	83%	0%	12/1	840-1060[2]	35%	81%	8%
9.	Castleton State College[1] (VT)*†	45	2.9	71%[8]	41%	46%[6]	70%[4]	2%[4]	10/1[4]	850-1070[4]	29%[4]	78%[4]	8%[4]
9.	St. Francis College (NY)	45	2.8	79%	39%	52%	51%	0.4%	17/1	810-1000	N/A	79%	11%
9.	Vaughn Col. of Aeron. and Tech. (NY)	45	2.6	74%	43%	56%	72%	0%	14/1	890-1121	N/A	74%	3%
12.	SUNY College of Technology–Alfred*	44	2.8	85%	41%	60%	46%	2%	18/1	840-1080[2]	N/A	57%	2%
13.	Pennsylvania College of Technology*	42	3.0	72%	47%	38%	62%	0.1%	14/1	840-1050[2]	22%	85%	1%
13.	Wilson College (PA)	42	2.5	68%	52%	39%	89%	0%	10/1	820-1050[2]	43%	46%	17%
15.	Unity College (ME)	40	2.6	73%	43%	54%	60%	1%	12/1	880-1150[2]	32%	91%	3%
16.	Vermont Technical College*	40	2.5	74%	46%	56%	70%	0.3%	12/1	830-1060[9]	14%[5]	68%	1%
17.	Farmingdale State College–SUNY*	39	2.9	80%	50%	49%	27%	1%	19/1	910-1080	25%[5]	44%	0.4%
17.	SUNY College of A&T–Cobleskill*	39	2.7	75%	41%	55%	42%	4%	19/1	760-1000[2]	17%	89%	5%
19.	Dean College (MA)	37	2.6	66%	34%	52%	46%	0%	15/1	720-940[2]	N/A	67%	7%
19.	SUNY College of Technology–Delhi*	37	2.7	70%	33%	52%	45%	3%	16/1	N/A[2]	18%[5]	54%	6%
21.	Morrisville State College (NY)*	36	2.4	70%	36%	32%	51%	3%	15/1	830-1010[9]	19%	58%	4%
22.	Concordia College (NY)	33	2.7	71%[8]	38%	41%	N/A	N/A	13/1	790-1000[2]	N/A	71%	7%
23.	La Roche College (PA)	32	2.3	72%[8]	38%	46%	62%	0%	12/1	830-1040	29%[5]	95%	4%
23.	SUNY College of Technology–Canton*	32	2.8	78%	29%	34%	52%	3%	17/1	800-1000[2]	16%	85%	3%
23.	University of Maine–Fort Kent*	32	2.5	64%	32%	39%	79%	2%	15/1	800-980[2]	7%	89%	6%
26.	Monroe College (NY)†	31	2.5	75%	48%	68%	50%	0.1%	18/1	715-870[9]	N/A	45%	3%
27.	Mount Ida College (MA)	30	2.5	62%	36%	40%	73%	0.2%	14/1	800-1010	N/A	63%	3%
27.	Univ. of Maine–Presque Isle*	30	2.5	62%	45%	45%	75%	0%	15/1	791-1060[2]	15%	77%	2%
29.	Keystone College (PA)	29	2.4	66%	32%	40%	73%[4]	0%[4]	11/1[4]	800-1010	17%[4]	98%	7%[7]
29.	Mount Aloysius College (PA)	29	2.8	66%[8]	36%	35%[6]	75%	0%	12/1	860-1020[3]	N/A	73%	N/A
31.	Fisher College (MA)	26	2.3	59%	26%	47%	74%	0%	18/1	700-920[2]	N/A	70%	2%
31.	Paul Smith's College[1] (NY)	26	2.7	69%[8]	41%	41%[6]	N/A	N/A	14/1[4]	N/A[2]	N/A	98%[4]	N/A
33.	University of Valley Forge[1] (PA)	25	2.2	74%[8]	40%	48%[6]	N/A	N/A	12/1[4]	790-1050[4]	N/A	93%[4]	N/A

School (State) (*Public)	Peer assessment score (5.0=highest)	Average first-year student retention rate	2015 graduation rate		% of classes under 20 ('15)	% of classes of 50 or more ('15)	Student/faculty ratio ('15)	SAT/ACT 25th-75th percentile ('15)	Freshmen in top 25% of HS class ('15)	Acceptance rate ('15)	Average alumni giving rate
			Predicted	Actual							
SECOND TIER (SCHOOLS RANKED 34 THROUGH 44 ARE LISTED HERE ALPHABETICALLY)											
Bay State College (MA)	2.2	N/A	32%	22%[6]	68%	0%	17/1[4]	N/A[2]	N/A	N/A	N/A
Becker College[1] (MA)	2.6	65%[8]	34%	28%[6]	N/A	N/A	16/1[4]	890-1120[4]	N/A	62%[4]	N/A

Note: Key to footnotes, Page 111.

NORTH ▶

School (State) (*Public)	Peer assessment score (5.0=highest)	Average first-year student retention rate	2015 graduation rate		% of classes under 20 ('15)	% of classes of 50 or more ('15)	Student/faculty ratio ('15)	SAT/ACT 25th-75th percentile ('15)	Freshmen in top 25% of HS class ('15)	Acceptance rate ('15)	Average alumni giving rate
			Predicted	Actual							
SECOND TIER CONTINUED (SCHOOLS RANKED 34 THROUGH 44 ARE LISTED HERE ALPHABETICALLY)											
College of St. Joseph (VT)†	2.4	55%[8]	31%	20%	97%	0%	N/A	783-923[9]	10%	70%	N/A
CUNY–Medgar Evers College*	2.4	N/A	24%	19%	3%	8%	17/1	690-860[2]	N/A	91%[4]	N/A
CUNY–New York City Col. of Tech.*	2.7	77%	28%	30%	28%	0.1%	17/1	740-950[2]	N/A	74%	1%
CUNY–York College*	2.6	75%[8]	30%	27%	28%	9%	19/1	770-950	N/A	63%	N/A
Five Towns College (NY)	2.3	63%	33%	30%	79%	0%	15/1	770-980	16%[5]	62%	N/A
Lyndon State College[1] (VT)*	2.5	63%[8]	34%	35%[6]	N/A	N/A	14/1[4]	820-1060[4]	N/A	99%[4]	N/A
Southern Vermont College[1]	2.5	62%[8]	33%	32%[6]	N/A	N/A	14/1[4]	770-940[4]	N/A	94%[4]	N/A
University of Maine–Augusta*	3.0	52%	37%	12%	76%	0.3%	16/1	780-1000[2]	14%[4]	97%	0.3%
Wesley College[1] (DE)	2.8	51%[8]	36%	26%[6]	N/A	N/A	14/1[4]	770-950[4]	N/A	57%[4]	N/A

SOUTH ▶

Rank	School (State) (*Public)	Overall score	Peer assessment score (5.0=highest)	Average first-year student retention rate	2015 graduation rate		% of classes under 20 ('15)	% of classes of 50 or more ('15)	Student/faculty ratio ('15)	SAT/ACT 25th-75th percentile ('15)	Freshmen in top 25% of HS class ('15)	Acceptance rate ('15)	Average alumni giving rate
					Predicted	Actual							
1.	High Point University (NC)	100	3.6	77%	55%	65%	61%	1%	13/1	1012-1196	54%[5]	72%	11%
2.	Flagler College (FL)	87	3.5	69%	54%	61%	54%	0%	16/1	960-1148	38%[4]	50%	16%
3.	University of the Ozarks (AR)	76	3.3	70%	54%	43%	68%	1%	13/1	20-25	39%	97%	14%
4.	Catawba College (NC)	67	2.9	71%	51%	47%	70%	0.3%	13/1	870-1110[9]	39%	32%	17%
5.	Univ. of South Carolina–Aiken*	63	3.1	68%	44%	43%	44%	3%	16/1	880-1080	43%	57%	5%
6.	Coker College (SC)	61	2.9	70%[8]	44%	52%	74%[4]	0%[4]	13/1	18-22	18%[4]	50%	N/A
7.	Blue Mountain College (MS)	60	2.6	72%	45%	55%	87%	1%	11/1	18-24	37%	38%	7%
8.	University of Mobile (AL)	57	3.0	76%	46%	48%	52%	0.3%	13/1	19-25	52%	61%	1%
9.	Bennett College (NC)†	56	2.5	56%	25%	44%	81%	0%	10/1	633-778	16%	95%	35%
10.	Belmont Abbey College (NC)	55	3.0	63%[8]	44%	43%	65%	0%	15/1	900-1130[9]	15%[4]	68%	8%
10.	Huntingdon College (AL)	55	2.7	64%	50%	41%	58%	0.3%	14/1	19-23	29%	58%	29%
10.	U. of South Carolina–Upstate*	55	3.0	69%	41%	40%	54%	1%	17/1	860-1040	35%	57%	1%
13.	Barton College (NC)	54	2.5	71%	43%	40%	67%	0.3%	11/1	850-1050	38%	42%	8%
13.	Kentucky Wesleyan College	54	2.8	63%	46%	35%	85%	0.3%	12/1	20-26[3]	39%[4]	N/A	15%
15.	Toccoa Falls College (GA)	53	2.6	70%	42%	46%	68%	1%	13/1	860-1090	43%	45%	3%
16.	Kentucky State University*†	52	2.9	51%	29%	22%	77%	0.3%	11/1	17-22	26%	38%	4%
16.	Newberry College (SC)	52	2.7	70%	44%	39%	64%	0%	12/1	850-1070	32%	56%	15%
16.	Tennessee Wesleyan College	52	2.6	N/A	47%	44%[6]	69%	4%	12/1	19-25	64%[4]	65%	8%
19.	Lander University (SC)*	51	2.7	65%	38%	46%	43%	4%	14/1	860-1060	40%	62%	10%
20.	Averett University (VA)	49	2.6	61%	38%	36%	80%	0%	11/1	800-1003	27%[5]	61%	4%
20.	Mars Hill University (NC)	49	2.9	57%	40%	34%	68%	0.2%	12/1	810-990[3]	19%	61%	11%
22.	Brevard College (NC)†	47	2.9	57%	43%	38%	68%	0%	11/1	840-1060[2]	18%	41%	6%
23.	Florida Memorial University†	45	2.6	69%[8]	24%	39%	N/A	N/A	15/1	16-20[2]	N/A	23%	N/A
23.	Keiser University (FL)	45	1.9	83%	24%	57%[6]	N/A	N/A	N/A	N/A[2]	N/A	N/A	N/A
23.	Lees-McRae College (NC)	45	2.7	61%	43%	36%	75%	0%	15/1	18-24[2]	27%	67%	10%
23.	Shorter University[1] (GA)†	45	2.9	66%[8]	47%	46%[6]	N/A	N/A	12/1[4]	840-1065[4]	N/A	69%[4]	N/A
23.	Williams Baptist College (AR)	45	2.7	59%[8]	43%	41%	65%	1%	14/1	19-24	34%	64%	4%
28.	West Liberty University (WV)*	44	2.5	69%	36%	48%	68%	0.3%	13/1	18-24	43%	72%	4%
29.	Emmanuel College (GA)	43	2.5	61%	33%	38%	68%	0%	13/1	790-1070	N/A	35%	5%
29.	Reinhardt University (GA)	43	2.7	62%	41%	35%	78%	1%	12/1	18-22	30%	91%	4%
31.	Welch College (TN)	42	2.3	69%	45%	44%	89%	2%	9/1	17-25	52%	69%	12%
32.	Brescia University (KY)	41	2.5	60%	43%	29%	92%	0%	13/1	19-24	N/A	48%	13%
32.	Everglades University (FL)	41	2.3	54%	22%	32%	97%	0%	10/1	N/A[2]	N/A	97%	N/A
32.	Ferrum College (VA)	41	2.9	51%	33%	31%	61%	0%	17/1	770-1000[2]	16%[5]	73%	6%
32.	Kentucky Christian University[1]	41	2.6	61%[8]	47%	38%[8]	72%[4]	0%[4]	12/1[4]	18-23[4]	33%[4]	48%[4]	5%[4]
32.	University of Mount Olive (NC)	41	2.5	63%	32%	39%	70%	0%	14/1	795-1020[9]	N/A	51%	3%
37.	Alderson Broaddus University (WV)	40	2.5	59%	47%	36%	62%	4%	17/1	19-23	31%	54%	13%
37.	Bluefield College (VA)	40	2.5	53%	40%	39%	75%	0%	16/1	802-1036	25%	93%	7%
37.	Univ. of South Carolina–Beaufort*	40	2.9	54%	39%	23%	48%	3%	20/1	830-1020	27%	63%	2%
40.	Central Baptist College (AR)	37	2.4	59%	39%	49%	80%	1%	10/1	18-23	30%	47%	8%
41.	Limestone College (SC)	36	2.2	57%	32%	37%	62%	0%	13/1	810-1010[3]	19%	52%	6%
42.	College of Coastal Georgia*	35	2.7	64%[8]	24%	35%	41%	1%	19/1	833-1040	N/A	95%	2%
42.	Univ. of Arkansas–Pine Bluff*	35	2.5	61%	22%	26%	54%	3%	15/1	16-20	36%	46%	7%
42.	Warner University (FL)†	35	2.5	61%	35%	36%	53%	0%	12/1	17-20	21%	42%	2%
45.	Ohio Valley University (WV)	34	2.3	54%	46%	27%	88%	0%	10/1	17-22	10%	47%	10%
45.	Point University (GA)	34	2.3	53%[8]	31%	48%	72%	2%	18/1	17-21	N/A	49%	N/A
47.	North Carolina Wesleyan College	33	2.6	54%	36%	23%	75%	0%	15/1	760-970[9]	30%	55%	3%
47.	Oakwood University (AL)	33	2.6	76%[8]	40%	42%	N/A	N/A	N/A	N/A	N/A	47%	N/A

SOUTH ▶

Rank	School (State) (*Public)	Overall score	Peer assessment score (5.0=highest)	Average first-year student retention rate	2015 graduation rate Predicted	2015 graduation rate Actual	% of classes under 20 ('15)	% of classes of 50 or more ('15)	Student/faculty ratio ('15)	SAT/ACT 25th-75th percentile ('15)	Freshmen in top 25% of HS class ('15)	Accept-ance rate ('15)	Average alumni giving rate
49.	St. Augustine's University (NC)	31	2.2	47%	21%	34%	72%[4]	0%[4]	12/1	14-18	N/A	58%	5%
50.	Glenville State College (WV)*	30	2.4	64%	32%	30%	68%	1%	16/1	17-22	26%	72%	4%
51.	Greensboro College[1] (NC)	29	2.7	56%[8]	46%	35%[6]	N/A	N/A	12/1[4]	780-980[4]	N/A	73%[4]	N/A
52.	Bluefield State College (WV)*	28	2.3	58%	31%	23%	77%	0.3%	14/1	17-22	56%[5]	77%	4%
52.	Chipola College[1] (FL)*	28	2.4	N/A	39%	42%[6]	N/A	N/A	18/1[4]	N/A	N/A	N/A	N/A
52.	Georgia Gwinnett College*	28	2.8	65%	35%	21%	28%	0%	18/1	800-1040[2]	9%	84%	3%
52.	Rust College (MS)†	28	2.4	60%[8]	20%	32%	N/A	N/A	18/1	14-18	N/A	16%	N/A
56.	Lane College (TN)†	27	2.3	51%	15%	24%	42%	1%	21/1	14-17	30%	55%	33%
56.	Our Lady of Holy Cross College[1] (LA)†	27	2.7	72%[8]	38%	27%[6]	N/A	N/A	16/1[4]	N/A[2]	N/A	56%[4]	N/A
56.	University of Arkansas–Fort Smith[1]*	27	2.7	64%[8]	41%	26%[6]	48%[4]	4%[4]	18/1[4]	19-25[4]	N/A	56%[4]	N/A

School (State) (*Public)	Peer assessment score (5.0=highest)	Average first-year student retention rate	2015 graduation rate Predicted	2015 graduation rate Actual	% of classes under 20 ('15)	% of classes of 50 or more ('15)	Student/faculty ratio ('15)	SAT/ACT 25th-75th percentile ('15)	Freshmen in top 25% of HS class ('15)	Accept-ance rate ('15)	Average alumni giving rate
SECOND TIER (SCHOOLS RANKED 59 THROUGH 75 ARE LISTED HERE ALPHABETICALLY)											
Abraham Baldwin Agricultural College[1] (GA)*	2.5	59%[8]	30%	16%[8]	26%[4]	3%[4]	N/A	17-22[4]	39%[4]	79%[4]	N/A
Benedict College[1] (SC)	2.2	58%[8]	24%	29%[6]	N/A	N/A	N/A	17[4]	N/A	73%[4]	N/A
Brewton-Parker College[1] (GA)	2.1	55%[8]	33%	19%[6]	N/A	N/A	14/1[4]	N/A[2]	N/A	N/A	N/A
Chowan University (NC)	2.6	48%	24%	24%	27%	0.2%	16/1	700-860	11%	62%	10%
Crowley's Ridge College[1] (AR)	2.1	50%[8]	32%	24%[6]	N/A	N/A	10/1[4]	N/A[2]	N/A	N/A	N/A
East Georgia State College*	2.3	N/A	12%	6%[6]	N/A	N/A	N/A	N/A[2]	N/A	59%	N/A
Edward Waters College[1] (FL)	2.0	51%[8]	21%	21%[6]	N/A	N/A	15/1[4]	720-930[4]	N/A	53%[4]	N/A
Florida College	2.4	N/A	53%	12%[6]	68%	6%	13/1	19-24[3]	N/A	81%	41%
Gordon State College (GA)*	2.5	N/A	17%	13%[6]	N/A	N/A	21/1	750-960	N/A	43%	N/A
Indian River State College (FL)*	2.6	N/A	37%	39%[6]	31%	2%	22/1[4]	N/A[2]	N/A	100%	N/A
LeMoyne-Owen College (TN)	2.4	43%[8]	23%	13%	76%	0%	N/A	13-17	N/A	100%	N/A
Livingstone College (NC)	2.1	53%	21%	24%	49%	1%	17/1	640-810[3]	7%	71%	10%
Middle Georgia State University[1]*	2.4	67%[8]	34%	19%[6]	N/A	N/A	21/1[4]	N/A[2]	N/A	100%[4]	N/A
Shaw University[1] (NC)	2.0	43%[8]	16%	27%[6]	N/A	N/A	15/1[4]	N/A[2]	N/A	59%[4]	N/A
Truett McConnell College (GA)	2.4	63%	32%	32%	65%	8%	19/1	838-1020	33%	91%	2%
Voorhees College[1] (SC)	2.2	46%[8]	24%	32%[6]	N/A	N/A	10/1[4]	N/A[2]	N/A	50%[4]	N/A
Webber International University[1] (FL)	2.4	50%[8]	37%	31%[6]	70%[4]	0%[4]	15/1[4]	860-1040[4]	N/A	57%[4]	N/A

MIDWEST ▶

Rank	School (State) (*Public)	Overall score	Peer assessment score (5.0=highest)	Average first-year student retention rate	2015 graduation rate Predicted	2015 graduation rate Actual	% of classes under 20 ('15)	% of classes of 50 or more ('15)	Student/faculty ratio ('15)	SAT/ACT 25th-75th percentile ('15)	Freshmen in top 25% of HS class ('15)	Accept-ance rate ('15)	Average alumni giving rate
1.	Calvin College (MI)†	100	4.0	87%	71%	74%	36%	1%	13/1	23-30	56%	74%	22%
1.	Taylor University (IN)	100	3.9	88%	70%	77%	59%	5%	13/1	24-30	65%[5]	85%	21%
3.	Augustana University (SD)	91	3.6	82%	65%	75%	50%	3%	11/1	23-28	59%	65%	16%
4.	College of the Ozarks (MO)	88	3.6	83%	52%	73%	58%	2%	14/1	21-25[3]	61%	12%	20%
5.	Goshen College (IN)†	87	3.4	79%	65%	66%	72%	1%	9/1	890-1178	46%	66%	22%
6.	Northwestern College (IA)	84	3.4	79%	63%	67%	68%	0.3%	11/1	22-28	57%	72%	20%
6.	Ohio Northern University	84	3.4	86%	70%	66%	60%	1%	11/1	23-28[3]	60%	69%	13%
8.	Dordt College (IA)	83	3.4	81%	63%	68%	61%	5%	13/1	23-29[3]	47%	71%	23%
8.	Marietta College (OH)	83	3.2	73%	62%	66%	80%	0.2%	10/1	21-27[3]	56%	72%	18%
10.	University of Mount Union (OH)	79	3.3	77%	51%	61%	52%	0.4%	13/1	21-26	50%	75%	19%
11.	Loras College (IA)	78	3.2	80%	59%	70%	45%	0%	12/1	21-26	46%	95%	21%
12.	Cedarville University (OH)	77	3.2	86%	68%	72%	63%	5%	13/1	23-28	61%	74%	11%
13.	Huntington University (IN)	76	3.1	80%	55%	68%	73%	1%	12/1	878-1140	49%	84%	16%
14.	Benedictine College (KS)	74	3.3	77%	54%	68%	52%	1%	13/1	21-28	49%[5]	99%	24%
15.	Adrian College (MI)	73	3.2	64%	53%	54%	71%	1%	13/1	19-24	60%	61%	14%
16.	Hastings College (NE)	72	3.1	71%	55%	58%	68%	0.3%	14/1	20-26	45%	71%	20%
17.	Clarke University (IA)	70	2.8	77%	53%	56%	69%	0.4%	11/1	20-25	42%	72%	15%
18.	Saint Mary-of-the-Woods College (IN)	69	3.0	80%	48%	53%	97%	0%	8/1	830-1030	31%	59%	22%
19.	Trinity Christian College (IL)	67	3.1	80%	55%	62%	54%	1%	11/1	21-27	31%[5]	88%	13%
20.	Wisconsin Lutheran College†	66	2.7	77%	63%	62%	70%	0.3%	11/1	21-27	37%	92%	17%
21.	Manchester University (IN)	62	3.1	69%	50%	54%	56%	1%	14/1	870-1100[2]	44%	74%	18%
22.	Cottey College (MO)	60	3.0	75%[8]	47%	7%	91%	0%	9/1	20-26	41%	74%	N/A
22.	Trine University (IN)	60	3.1	72%	55%	56%	48%	0.2%	13/1	21-27	54%	78%	8%
24.	Buena Vista University (IA)	59	3.0	74%	54%	51%	69%	1%	10/1	19-24	41%	68%	7%

Note: Key to footnotes, Page 111.

MIDWEST ▶

Rank	School (State) (*Public)	Overall score	Peer assessment score (5.0=highest)	Average first-year student retention rate	2015 graduation rate		% of classes under 20 ('15)	% of classes of 50 or more ('15)	Student/ faculty ratio ('15)	SAT/ACT 25th-75th percentile ('15)	Freshmen in top 25% of HS class ('15)	Accept- ance rate ('15)	Average alumni giving rate
					Predicted	Actual							
24.	University of Jamestown (ND)	59	3.1	68%	48%	45%	60%	3%	13/1	18-28	41%	65%	16%
26.	Central Methodist University (MO)	58	2.8	65%	45%	52%	66%	2%	13/1	20-25	42%	58%	8%
26.	Eureka College (IL)	58	2.6	68%[8]	49%	51%	75%	1%	12/1	18-29	35%	65%	17%
28.	St. Joseph's College (IN)	57	2.8	70%	49%	54%	78%	0.4%	12/1	19-24[3]	25%	71%	18%
29.	Bluffton University (OH)	56	2.8	69%	49%	45%	63%	0%	12/1	18-23	25%	54%	13%
30.	Briar Cliff University (IA)	53	2.8	62%	48%	48%	64%	2%	14/1	19-23	38%	53%	13%
30.	Culver-Stockton College (MO)	53	2.9	70%	51%	52%	60%	0%	15/1	18-23	27%	56%	17%
32.	Union College (NE)	52	2.4	72%	53%	50%	72%	3%	10/1	19-26	25%[5]	56%	22%
33.	Dakota Wesleyan University (SD)	51	2.9	69%[8]	42%	40%	61%	1%	11/1	18-24	34%	74%	16%
33.	Oakland City University (IN)†	51	2.1	74%	38%	48%	91%	0%	12/1	840-1010[2]	18%	55%	14%
33.	Valley City State University (ND)*	51	2.6	65%	42%	41%	78%	1%	11/1	18-23	25%[4]	86%	11%
36.	Blackburn College (IL)	49	2.5	68%	49%	42%	71%	0%	13/1	19-24	36%	55%	18%
36.	Univ. of Wisconsin–Superior*†	49	2.9	69%	49%	40%	60%	2%	14/1	19-23	21%	72%	5%
38.	Defiance College (OH)	48	2.6	57%	47%	41%	75%	0%	10/1	19-24	19%	66%	8%

COLLEGE OF THE OZARKS

MIDWEST ▶

Rank School (State) (*Public)	Overall score	Peer assessment score (5.0=highest)	Average first-year student retention rate	2015 graduation rate		% of classes under 20 ('15)	% of classes of 50 or more ('15)	Student/faculty ratio ('15)	SAT/ACT 25th-75th percentile ('15)	Freshmen in top 25% of HS class ('15)	Acceptance rate ('15)	Average alumni giving rate
				Predicted	Actual							
38. McPherson College[1] (KS)	48	2.5	57%[8]	48%	50%[6]	69%[4]	1%[4]	13/1[4]	18-25[4]	25%[4]	88%[4]	8%[4]
40. University of Minnesota–Crookston*	47	2.5	68%	45%	45%	62%	1%	16/1	19-25	37%	78%	5%
41. Grand View University (IA)	46	2.6	72%	43%	47%	70%	0.4%	13/1	18-23	33%	98%	4%
41. Tabor College (KS)	46	2.6	60%	45%	41%	70%	1%	12/1	19-25	36%	55%	8%
43. Dickinson State University (ND)*	43	2.3	56%[8]	42%	35%[6]	81%	0%	10/1	18-22[2]	N/A	62%	N/A
44. North Central University (MN)	41	2.4	68%	41%	43%	N/A	N/A	14/1	18-27	41%[5]	53%	N/A
45. Kansas Wesleyan University	40	2.4	59%	49%	41%	69%	1%	9/1	20-24	29%	62%	14%
45. Wilmington College[1] (OH)	40	2.7	75%[8]	44%	44%[6]	N/A	N/A	16/1[4]	18-23[4]	N/A	95%[4]	10%[7]
47. Ottawa University (KS)	39	2.5	61%	57%	47%	67%	1%	18/1	18-23[2]	28%	41%	12%
48. Crown College (MN)	38	2.4	53%[8]	49%	58%	48%	4%	18/1	19-25	N/A	51%	3%
48. Maranatha Baptist University (WI)	38	2.0	68%	46%	58%	71%	3%	13/1	20-26	26%	69%	N/A
48. Midland University (NE)	38	2.4	59%[8]	46%	43%	N/A	N/A	16/1	18-23	N/A	61%	7%
48. Olivet College (MI)	38	2.6	64%	33%	45%	64%	1%	16/1[4]	17-22[3]	N/A	57%	N/A
52. MacMurray College (IL)	37	2.3	70%	35%	33%	61%	0%	13/1	17-22	20%	63%	14%
53. Dunwoody College of Tech. (MN)	36	1.9	67%[8]	39%	42%[6]	89%	0%	10/1	N/A[2]	41%	N/A	4%
53. Lake Superior State University (MI)*	36	2.6	68%[8]	44%	35%	56%	6%	13/1	19-24[2]	35%	92%	3%
53. Mayville State University (ND)*	36	2.4	53%	38%	25%	77%	1%	13/1	17-22	N/A	54%	9%[4]
56. Bismarck State College (ND)*	35	2.3	N/A	41%	42%[6]	71%[4]	0.2%[4]	14/1	17-23[2]	11%	100%	3%
56. Sterling College (KS)	35	2.3	67%	44%	40%	70%[4]	0.4%[4]	14/1[4]	19-24[3]	20%	41%	N/A
58. Hannibal-LaGrange University (MO)	33	2.3	59%[8]	49%	49%[6]	81%	0.3%	14/1	N/A	N/A	61%	5%
58. Rochester College[1] (MI)	33	2.3	60%[8]	42%	38%[6]	85%[4]	0.3%[4]	11/1[4]	18-23[4]	N/A	41%[4]	N/A
60. Iowa Wesleyan University	32	2.1	49%	38%	18%	97%	0%	N/A	19-23	35%	50%	N/A
60. Kuyper College[1] (MI)	32	2.0	63%[8]	51%	53%[6]	N/A	N/A	11/1[4]	19-25[4]	N/A	71%[4]	N/A

School (State) (*Public)		Peer assessment score (5.0=highest)	Average first-year student retention rate	2015 graduation rate		% of classes under 20 ('15)	% of classes of 50 or more ('15)	Student/faculty ratio ('15)	SAT/ACT 25th-75th percentile ('15)	Freshmen in top 25% of HS class ('15)	Accept-ance rate ('15)	Average alumni giving rate
				Predicted	Actual							
SECOND TIER (SCHOOLS RANKED 62 THROUGH 80 ARE LISTED HERE ALPHABETICALLY)												
Bethany College (KS)		2.3	59%[8]	48%	41%	78%	0%	12/1	18-23	22%	99%	12%
Central Christian College (KS)		1.8	56%	34%	37%	55%	1%	9/1	17-24[2]	23%[5]	42%	14%
Central State University (OH)*		1.8	50%	26%	19%	59%	1%	13/1	14-18	20%	40%	14%
Finlandia University[1] (MI)		2.1	59%[8]	38%	43%[6]	N/A	N/A	9/1[4]	16-22[4]	N/A	45%[4]	N/A
Grace Bible College (MI)		1.6	61%[8]	34%	50%	86%	1%	13/1	19-23	30%	45%	12%
Grace University[1] (NE)		2.1	71%[8]	50%	47%[6]	N/A	N/A	14/1[4]	830-980[4]	N/A	45%[4]	N/A
Harris-Stowe State University (MO)*		1.7	46%	21%	7%	88%	0%	13/1	14-18	20%	51%	2%
Indiana University–Kokomo*		2.5	63%	37%	29%	49%	2%	16/1	840-1040	29%	71%	7%
Kendall College (IL)		2.2	62%	37%	20%	71%	0.3%	8/1	16-24[9]	N/A	74%	N/A
Lincoln College[1] (IL)		2.1	49%[8]	25%	8%[6]	N/A	N/A	18/1[4]	22-27[4]	N/A	56%[4]	N/A
Missouri Southern State University*		2.3	63%	36%	30%	49%	0%	18/1	19-25	39%	94%	6%
Missouri Valley College		1.9	44%[8]	33%	29%	N/A	N/A	14/1	N/A	37%	46%	N/A
Missouri Western State University[1]*		2.5	61%[8]	36%	33%[8]	52%[4]	6%[4]	17/1[4]	17-23[4]	26%[4]	99%[4]	6%[4]
Ohio Christian University		2.3	64%[8]	23%	33%[6]	N/A	N/A	10/1	17-22[4]	N/A	65%[4]	N/A
Purdue Univ.–North Central[1] (IN)*		2.9	60%[8]	32%	20%[8]	58%[4]	2%[4]	15/1[4]	18-23[4]	26%[4]	74%[4]	N/A
Shawnee State University (OH)*†		2.0	56%	35%	24%	54%	2%	16/1	N/A[2]	35%	75%	1%
Waldorf College[1] (IA)		2.0	50%[8]	36%	39%[6]	N/A	N/A	26/1[4]	820-1030[4]	N/A	69%[4]	N/A
Wilberforce University[1] (OH)		2.1	54%[8]	29%	43%[6]	N/A	N/A	8/1[4]	13-17[4]	N/A	38%[4]	N/A
York College (NE)		2.2	67%[8]	43%	35%	81%	0%	15/1	16-20	22%	46%	5%[4]

WEST ▶

Rank School (State) (*Public)	Overall score	Peer assessment score (5.0=highest)	Average first-year student retention rate	2015 graduation rate		% of classes under 20 ('15)	% of classes of 50 or more ('15)	Student/faculty ratio ('15)	SAT/ACT 25th-75th percentile ('15)	Freshmen in top 25% of HS class ('15)	Accept-ance rate ('15)	Average alumni giving rate
				Predicted	Actual							
1. Carroll College (MT)	100	3.5	82%	60%	63%	65%	1%	13/1	22-27	60%	64%	15%
2. Texas Lutheran University	87	3.5	70%	52%	47%	60%	0%	14/1	915-1115	49%	51%	14%
3. Oregon Inst. of Technology*	85	3.8	73%	52%	46%	56%	3%	15/1	920-1170	49%	57%	4%
4. Montana Tech of the Univ. of Mont.*	84	3.6	70%	54%	36%	62%	10%	15/1	23-27	56%	88%	14%
5. Oklahoma Baptist University	83	3.4	76%	57%	52%	68%	3%	13/1	20-25	49%	75%	7%
6. Warner Pacific College (OR)	76	3.0	67%	36%	55%	74%	1%	11/1	800-1070	7%	94%	4%
7. Howard Payne University (TX)	70	3.1	60%	45%	46%	73%	0.3%	10/1	850-1060	33%	86%	8%
8. University of Montana–Western*	66	2.9	71%	37%	41%	71%	0%	15/1	17-22[3]	21%	74%	3%
9. Rocky Mountain College (MT)	64	2.6	69%	47%	44%	74%	1%	11/1	20-25	38%	70%	7%
10. Brigham Young University–Idaho[1]	63	3.5	69%[8]	50%	52%[6]	N/A	N/A	25/1[4]	910-1130[4]	N/A	100%[4]	N/A

WEST ▶

Rank	School (State) (*Public)	Overall score	Peer assessment score (5.0=highest)	Average first-year student retention rate	2015 graduation rate Predicted	2015 graduation rate Actual	% of classes under 20 ('15)	% of classes of 50 or more ('15)	Student/faculty ratio ('15)	SAT/ACT 25th-75th percentile ('15)	Freshmen in top 25% of HS class ('15)	Acceptance rate ('15)	Average alumni giving rate
10.	California Maritime Academy[1]*	63	3.2	82%[8]	56%	57%[6]	N/A	N/A	14/1[4]	N/A	N/A	67%[4]	6%[7]
10.	East Texas Baptist University	63	3.0	56%	46%	46%	64%	0%	14/1	18-23	42%	55%	4%
13.	McMurry University (TX)	61	2.9	59%	43%	35%	73%	0.3%	11/1	790-980	28%	53%	9%
14.	Brigham Young University–Hawaii[1]	55	3.1	61%[8]	57%	49%[6]	N/A	N/A	15/1[4]	970-1170[4]	N/A	35%[4]	N/A
15.	San Diego Christian College†	52	3.2	67%[8]	39%	30%	79%	1%	17/1	813-1038[2]	31%[5]	52%	N/A
16.	Trinity Lutheran College[1] (WA)	49	2.7	58%[8]	48%	56%[6]	N/A	N/A	14/1[4]	N/A[2]	N/A	75%[4]	N/A
17.	St. Gregory's University (OK)	48	2.7	55%[8]	41%	45%	86%	0%	11/1	18-23	N/A	61%	N/A
18.	Marymount California University	46	3.4	58%[8]	48%	36%	59%	0%	18/1	800-1030[2]	N/A	60%	0.3%
19.	University of Great Falls (MT)	45	2.7	67%[8]	35%	29%[6]	67%	0%	14/1	17-22	N/A	84%	N/A
20.	Oklahoma St. U. Inst. of Tech.–Okmulgee*	39	2.9	56%	38%	34%	82%	0%	15/1	16-20[3]	16%	42%	1%
21.	Southwestern Adventist Univ.[1] (TX)	38	2.5	67%[8]	41%	36%[6]	N/A	N/A	12/1[4]	810-1020[4]	N/A	50%[4]	9%[7]
22.	Southwestern Christian University[1] (OK)	37	2.7	49%[8]	35%	35%[6]	N/A	N/A	11/1[4]	860-1180[4]	N/A	81%[4]	N/A
23.	Colorado Mesa University*†	36	2.7	66%	35%	37%	46%	8%	22/1	17-23	25%	83%	2%
23.	Huston-Tillotson University (TX)†	36	2.4	56%[8]	23%	22%	75%	0%	15/1	680-900	N/A	47%	N/A
23.	Lewis-Clark State College (ID)*	36	3.1	57%	36%	21%	64%	1%	14/1	820-1030[2]	23%	99%	N/A

School (State) (*Public)	Peer assessment score (5.0=highest)	Average first-year student retention rate	2015 graduation rate Predicted	2015 graduation rate Actual	% of classes under 20 ('15)	% of classes of 50 or more ('15)	Student/faculty ratio ('15)	SAT/ACT 25th-75th percentile ('15)	Freshmen in top 25% of HS class ('15)	Acceptance rate ('15)	Average alumni giving rate
SECOND TIER (SCHOOLS RANKED 26 THROUGH 31 ARE LISTED HERE ALPHABETICALLY)											
Bacone College[1] (OK)	2.3	N/A	25%	8%[6]	N/A	N/A	15/1[4]	725-925[4]	N/A	N/A	N/A
Jarvis Christian College (TX)	2.0	55%	19%	18%	49%	4%	22/1	16-22	14%	14%	3%
Montana State Univ.–Northern[1]*	2.9	59%[8]	38%	24%[6]	N/A	N/A	14/1[4]	860-1050[4]	N/A	100%[4]	N/A
Oklahoma Panhandle State Univ.[1]*	1.9	N/A	34%	34%[6]	N/A	N/A	N/A	17-21[4]	N/A	60%[4]	N/A
Rogers State University (OK)*	2.8	63%	38%	22%	51%	1%	19/1	16-18	33%	82%	N/A
Wiley College[1] (TX)	1.7	50%[8]	15%	19%[6]	N/A	N/A	18/1[4]	N/A[2]	N/A	N/A	N/A

The Top Public Regional Colleges ▶

NORTH
Rank School (State)

1. U.S. Coast Guard Acad. (CT)
2. U.S. Merchant Marine Acad. (NY)
3. Maine Maritime Academy
4. University of Maine–Farmington
5. Castleton State College[1] (VT)

SOUTH
Rank School (State)

1. U. of South Carolina–Aiken
2. U. of South Carolina–Upstate
3. Kentucky State University
4. Lander University (SC)
5. West Liberty University (WV)

MIDWEST
Rank School (State)

1. Valley City State University (ND)
2. Univ. of Wisconsin–Superior
3. University of Minnesota–Crookston
4. Dickinson State University (ND)
5. Lake Superior State University (MI)
5. Mayville State University (ND)

WEST
Rank School (State)

1. Oregon Inst. of Technology
2. Montana Tech of the Univ. of Mont.
3. University of Montana–Western
4. California Maritime Academy[1]
5. Oklahoma State University Institute of Technology–Okmulgee

Footnotes:
1. School refused to fill out U.S. News statistical survey. Data that appear are from school in previous years or from another source such as the National Center for Education Statistics.
2. SAT and/or ACT not required for some or all applicants.
3. In reporting SAT/ACT scores, the school did not include all students for whom it had scores or refused to tell U.S. News whether all students with scores had been included.
4. Previous year's data was used in the ranking calculation.
5. Data based on fewer than 51 percent of enrolled freshmen.
6. Some or all data reported to the NCAA and/or the National Center for Education Statistics.
7. Data reported to the Council for Aid to Education.

8. This rate, normally based on four years of data, is given here for less than four years because school didn't report rate for the most recent year or years to U.S. News.
9. SAT and/or ACT may not be required by school for some or all applicants, and in reporting SAT/ACT scores, the school did not include all students for whom it had scores, or refused to tell U.S. News whether all students with scores had been included.

† School's Carnegie classification has changed. It appeared in a different U.S. News ranking category last year.
N/A means not available.

Best
Historically Black Colleges

Increasingly, the nation's top historically black colleges and universities are an appealing option for applicants of all races; many HBCUs, in fact, now actively recruit Hispanic, international and white students in addition to African-American high school graduates. Which schools offer the best undergraduate education? U.S. News each year surveys administrators at the HBCUs, asking the president, provost and admissions dean at each to rate the academic quality of all other HBCUs with which they are familiar.

In addition to the two most recent years of survey results, reflected in the peer assessment score, the rankings below are based on nearly all the same ranking indicators (although weighted slightly differently) as those used in ranking the regional universities. These include graduation and retention rates, high school class standing, admission test scores, and the strength of the faculty, among others.

To be part of the universe, a school must be designated by the Department of Education as an HBCU, be a baccalaureate-granting institution that enrolls primarily first-year, first-time students, and have been part of this year's Best Colleges survey and ranking process. If an HBCU is unranked in the 2017 Best Colleges rankings, it is also unranked here; reasons that schools are not ranked vary, but include a school's policy not to use test scores in admissions decisions.

There are 80 HBCUs; 72 were ranked. HBCUs in the top three-quarters are numerically ranked, and those in the bottom quarter are listed alphabetically. For more detail, visit usnews.com/hbcu.

Key Measures

Graduation and retention rates	27.5%
Peer assessment	25%
Faculty resources	20%
Student selectivity	12.5%
Financial resources	10%
Alumni giving	5%

Rank	School (State) (*Public)	Overall score	Peer assessment score (5.0=highest)	Average first-year student retention rate	Average graduation rate	% of classes under 20 ('15)	% of classes of 50 or more ('15)	Student/ faculty ratio ('15)	% of faculty who are full time ('15)	SAT/ACT 25th-75th percentile ('15)	Freshmen in top 25% of HS class ('15)	Acceptance rate ('15)	Average alumni giving rate
1.	Spelman College (GA)	100	4.7	89%	73%	58%	3%	10/1	88%	920-1120	62%	48%	39%
2.	Howard University (DC)	89	4.6	84%	62%[6]	57%	5%	10/1	93%	990-1220	52%[5]	49%	8%
3.	Hampton University (VA)	83	4.6	77%	63%[6]	63%	3%	9/1	94%	940-1090[2]	54%	69%	15%
4.	Morehouse College (GA)	68	4.6	82%	54%	50%	1%	12/1	90%	870-1100	30%	76%	13%
4.	Tuskegee University (AL)	68	4.1	76%	45%[6]	57%	9%	14/1	98%	18-23	60%	53%	18%
6.	Xavier University of Louisiana	64	4.3	71%	44%	41%	3%	14/1	96%	20-26	57%	66%	17%
7.	Florida A&M University*	60	4.1	82%	40%[6]	33%	13%	15/1	90%	18-23	40%[5]	51%	5%
8.	Fisk University (TN)	57	3.6	80%	50%[6]	72%	0.4%	12/1	88%	17-23	46%[5]	81%	23%
9.	Claflin University (SC)	56	3.7	73%	45%	64%	1%	13/1	88%	720-910	26%	41%	48%
10.	North Carolina A&T State Univ.*	55	4.1	77%	44%	30%	8%	19/1	86%	830-990	33%	59%	8%
11.	Tougaloo College (MS)	54	3.5	75%	52%[6]	70%	1%	13/1	87%	15-20	25%	39%	19%
12.	Dillard University (LA)	50	3.6	69%[8]	38%[6]	58%	1%	14/1	76%	17-20	35%[5]	48%	13%
13.	North Carolina Central Univ.*	49	3.7	76%	43%	39%	4%	16/1	88%	800-940	22%	66%	13%
14.	Delaware State University*	47	3.4	67%	39%	49%	3%	15/1	84%	810-970	30%	44%	9%
15.	Johnson C. Smith University (NC)	46	3.3	66%	44%	74%	0%	12/1	80%	700-880	15%	46%	17%
16.	Jackson State University (MS)*	45	3.7	78%[8]	44%[6]	39%	10%	18/1	84%	17-21	N/A	68%	4%[4]
17.	Bennett College (NC)	44	3.2	56%	43%	81%	0%	10/1	91%	633-778	16%	95%	35%
18.	Clark Atlanta University	42	3.7	63%	39%[6]	46%	6%	17/1	81%	16-20	20%[5]	52%	N/A
19.	Elizabeth City State Univ. (NC)*	41	2.9	75%[8]	41%[6]	69%	3%	15/1	98%	760-940	8%	70%	N/A
20.	Lincoln University (PA)*	40	2.9	73%	40%[6]	63%	0.2%	18/1	71%	740-930	19%[5]	91%	10%
20.	Morgan State University (MD)*	40	3.6	74%	32%	41%	1%	14/1	84%	840-970[2]	9%[4]	67%	11%
22.	Tennessee State University*	39	3.5	59%[8]	36%[6]	60%	1%	16/1	90%	16-20[3]	N/A	53%[4]	N/A
22.	Univ. of Maryland–Eastern Shore*	39	3.3	70%	35%[6]	55%	3%	15/1	85%	750-930	N/A	49%	3%
24.	Alcorn State University (MS)*	37	3.1	72%	35%[6]	51%	4%	17/1	89%	16-20	N/A	81%	9%
24.	Bethune-Cookman University (FL)	37	3.4	64%	44%[6]	44%	2%	16/1	86%	15-18	16%	54%	5%
26.	Alabama A&M University[1]*	35	3.4	65%[8]	32%[8]	N/A	N/A	21/1[4]	98%[4]	15-19[4]	N/A	53%[4]	9%[4]
26.	Bowie State University (MD)*	35	3.3	72%	34%[6]	45%	1%	16/1	77%	810-960	N/A	53%	5%[4]
26.	Fayetteville State University (NC)*	35	3.2	75%	33%	38%	1%	17/1	90%	790-930	20%	60%	2%
29.	Kentucky State University*	34	3.0	51%	19%	77%	0.3%	11/1	98%	17-22	26%	38%	4%

Note: Key to footnotes, Page 104.

Rank	School (State) (*Public)	Overall score	Peer assessment score (5.0=highest)	Average first-year student retention rate	Average graduation rate	% of classes under 20 ('15)	% of classes of 50 or more ('15)	Student/faculty ratio ('15)	% of faculty who are full time ('15)	SAT/ACT 25th-75th percentile ('15)	Freshmen in top 25% of HS class ('15)	Acceptance rate ('15)	Average alumni giving rate
30.	Prairie View A&M University (TX)*	33	3.4	67%	36%[6]	22%	6%	18/1	93%	770-930	14%	86%	N/A
31.	Fort Valley State University (GA)*	32	3.0	64%	30%[6]	63%	3%	14/1	93%	16-20	13%	21%	13%
32.	Albany State University (GA)*	31	3.0	71%	38%[6]	52%	2%	17/1	92%	840-950[3]	37%	64%	5%
32.	Norfolk State University (VA)*	31	3.2	72%[8]	36%[6]	57%	1%	16/1	89%	700-910	22%	79%	N/A
32.	Winston-Salem State Univ.[1] (NC)*	31	3.2	79%[8]	44%[6]	N/A	N/A	14/1[4]	88%[4]	800-930[4]	N/A	60%[4]	7%[7]
35.	Alabama State University*	29	3.2	60%	27%[6]	43%	0.3%	16/1	83%	15-23	11%[5]	48%	3%
35.	Univ. of Arkansas–Pine Bluff*	29	3.1	61%	27%	54%	3%	15/1	93%	16-20	36%	46%	7%
37.	Florida Memorial University	26	2.7	69%[8]	39%[6]	61%	0%	15/1	90%	16-20[2]	N/A	23%	N/A
37.	Virginia State University[1]*	26	3.2	63%[8]	44%[6]	N/A	N/A	14/1[4]	85%[4]	760-920[4]	N/A	80%[4]	N/A
39.	Philander Smith College (AR)	25	2.7	64%	39%[6]	75%	4%	15/1	84%	14-19	28%	60%	10%
40.	Grambling State University (LA)*	23	3.0	69%	33%[6]	44%	7%	20/1	98%	16-20	19%	38%	N/A
40.	Huston-Tillotson University (TX)	23	3.0	56%[8]	26%[6]	75%	0%	15/1	77%	680-900	N/A	47%	N/A
40.	Southern U. and A&M College (LA)*	23	3.2	68%	32%[6]	N/A	N/A	16/1	89%	17-21	7%	N/A	N/A
43.	Bluefield State College (WV)*	22	2.6	58%	26%[6]	77%	0.3%	14/1	82%	17-22	56%[5]	77%	4%
44.	Mississippi Valley State Univ.*	21	2.7	66%[8]	25%[6]	61%	1%	16/1	92%	16-19	N/A	76%	N/A
44.	South Carolina State University*	21	2.3	60%	38%[6]	54%	1%	17/1	86%	680-840	13%	95%	5%
44.	Texas Southern University*	21	3.3	54%	16%	40%	15%	18/1	84%	725-900[3]	19%	51%	2%
47.	Savannah State University (GA)*	20	3.2	66%[8]	29%[6]	25%	0.3%	21/1	95%	770-920	N/A	83%	5%
47.	St. Augustine's University (NC)	20	2.7	47%	26%[6]	72%[4]	0%[4]	12/1	87%	14-18	N/A	58%	5%
49.	Oakwood University (AL)	19	2.9	76%[8]	40%[6]	N/A	N/A	N/A	N/A	N/A	N/A	47%	N/A
49.	Virginia Union University	19	3.1	53%	31%	45%	1%	15/1	78%	680-860	15%	49%	7%
51.	Central State University (OH)*	18	2.8	50%	23%	59%	1%	13/1	73%	14-18	20%	40%	14%
51.	Lincoln University (MO)*	18	2.9	49%	23%	47%	4%	17/1	86%	15-19	23%	54%[4]	7%
51.	West Virginia State University*	18	2.7	55%	23%[6]	52%	1%	16/1	79%	17-22	N/A	94%	3%
54.	Coppin State University (MD)*	16	2.9	69%[8]	17%[6]	52%	2%	13/1	75%	810-970	N/A	37%	11%[4]

School (State) (*Public)	Peer assessment score (5.0=highest)	Average first-year student retention rate	Average graduation rate	% of classes under 20 ('15)	% of classes of 50 or more ('15)	Student/faculty ratio ('15)	% of faculty who are full time ('15)	SAT/ACT 25th-75th percentile ('15)	Freshmen in top 25% of HS class ('15)	Acceptance rate ('15)	Average alumni giving rate
SECOND TIER (SCHOOLS RANKED 55 THROUGH 72 ARE LISTED HERE ALPHABETICALLY)											
Allen University[1] (SC)	2.4	59%[8]	24%[8]	N/A	N/A	14/1[4]	100%[4]	N/A[2]	N/A	43%[4]	N/A
Benedict College[1] (SC)	2.9	58%[8]	29%[6]	N/A	N/A	N/A	N/A	17[4]	N/A	73%[4]	N/A
Cheyney U. of Pennsylvania*	2.5	54%[8]	22%[6]	N/A	N/A	N/A	N/A	N/A[2]	N/A	40%	N/A
Edward Waters College[1] (FL)	2.3	51%[8]	21%[6]	N/A	N/A	15/1[4]	83%[4]	720-930[4]	N/A	53%[4]	N/A
Harris-Stowe State University (MO)*	2.6	46%	8%	88%	0%	13/1	49%	14-18	20%	51%	2%
Jarvis Christian College (TX)	2.5	55%	14%	49%	4%	22/1	72%	16-22	14%	14%	3%
Lane College (TN)	2.6	51%	30%[6]	42%	1%	21/1	97%	14-17	30%	55%	33%
LeMoyne-Owen College (TN)	2.4	43%[8]	15%[6]	76%	0%	N/A	N/A	13-17	N/A	100%	N/A
Livingstone College (NC)	2.5	53%	30%[6]	49%	1%	17/1	98%	640-810[3]	7%	71%	10%
Paine College[1] (GA)	2.6	58%[8]	22%[6]	N/A	N/A	12/1[4]	91%[4]	670-850[4]	N/A	22%[4]	N/A
Rust College (MS)	2.8	60%[8]	26%[6]	N/A	N/A	18/1	99%	14-18	N/A	16%	N/A
Shaw University[1] (NC)	2.7	43%[8]	27%[6]	N/A	N/A	15/1[4]	84%[4]	N/A[2]	N/A	59%[4]	N/A
Southern University–New Orleans[1]*	2.9	54%[8]	13%[6]	N/A	N/A	15/1[4]	85%[4]	660-1010[4]	N/A	21%[4]	N/A
Stillman College[1] (AL)	2.7	63%[8]	19%[6]	N/A	N/A	17/1[4]	100%[4]	753-990[4]	N/A	59%[4]	N/A
Univ. of the District of Columbia*	2.7	54%[8]	20%[6]	69%	0.3%	8/1[4]	71%[4]	700-910[9]	22%[4]	35%	N/A
Voorhees College[1] (SC)	2.5	46%[8]	32%[6]	N/A	N/A	10/1[4]	100%[4]	N/A[2]	N/A	50%[4]	N/A
Wilberforce University[1] (OH)	2.4	54%[8]	43%[6]	N/A	N/A	8/1[4]	58%[4]	13-17[4]	N/A	38%[4]	N/A
Wiley College[1] (TX)	2.7	50%[8]	19%[6]	N/A	N/A	18/1[4]	85%[4]	N/A[2]	N/A	N/A	N/A

Sources: Statistical data from the schools. Peer assessment data collected by Ipsos Public Affairs.

Best Business Programs

E ach year, U.S. News ranks undergraduate business programs accredited by the Association to Advance Collegiate Schools of Business; the results are based solely on surveys of B-school deans and senior faculty. Participants were asked to rate the quality of business programs with which they're familiar on a scale of 1 (marginal) to 5 (distinguished);

38 percent of those canvassed responded to the most recent survey conducted in the spring of 2016. Two years of data were used to calculate the peer assessment score. Deans and faculty members also were asked to nominate the 10 best programs in a number of specialty areas; the five schools receiving the most mentions in the 2016 survey appear on page 116.

Top Programs ▶

Rank	School (State) (*Public)	Peer assessment score (5.0=highest)
1.	University of Pennsylvania (Wharton)	4.8
2.	Massachusetts Inst. of Technology (Sloan)	4.6
2.	University of California–Berkeley (Haas)*	4.6
4.	University of Michigan–Ann Arbor (Ross)*	4.5
5.	New York University (Stern)	4.4
6.	Carnegie Mellon University (Tepper) (PA)	4.2
6.	University of Texas–Austin (McCombs)*	4.2
6.	University of Virginia (McIntire)*	4.2
9.	Cornell University (Dyson) (NY)	4.1
9.	Indiana University–Bloomington (Kelley)*	4.1
9.	U. of N. Carolina–Chapel Hill (Kenan-Flagler)*	4.1
9.	University of Notre Dame (Mendoza) (IN)	4.1
9.	Univ. of Southern California (Marshall)	4.1
14.	Washington University in St. Louis (Olin)	4.0
15.	Emory University (Goizueta) (GA)	3.9
15.	Georgetown University (McDonough) (DC)	3.9
15.	U. of Illinois–Urbana-Champaign*	3.9
15.	Univ. of Minnesota–Twin Cities (Carlson)*	3.9
19.	Ohio State University–Columbus (Fisher)*	3.8
19.	University of Arizona (Eller)*	3.8
19.	Univ. of Maryland–College Park*	3.8
19.	Univ. of Wisconsin–Madison*	3.8
23.	Michigan State University (Broad)*	3.7
23.	Pennsylvania State U.–Univ. Park (Smeal)*	3.7
23.	Purdue Univ.–West Lafayette (Krannert) (IN)*	3.7
23.	University of Washington (Foster)*	3.7
27.	Arizona State University–Tempe (Carey)*	3.6
27.	Boston College (Carroll)	3.6
27.	Texas A&M Univ.–College Station (Mays)*	3.6
27.	University of Florida (Warrington)*	3.6
27.	University of Georgia (Terry)*	3.6
32.	Babson College (MA)	3.5
32.	Brigham Young Univ.–Provo (Marriott) (UT)	3.5
32.	Georgia Institute of Technology (Scheller)*	3.5
32.	University of California–Irvine (Merage)*	3.5
32.	University of Colorado–Boulder (Leeds)*	3.5
32.	University of Iowa (Tippie)*	3.5
38.	Boston University	3.4
38.	Case Western Reserve U. (Weatherhead) (OH)	3.4
38.	George Washington University (DC)	3.4
38.	University of Pittsburgh*	3.4
38.	Wake Forest University (NC)	3.4
43.	College of William and Mary (Mason) (VA)*	3.3
43.	Syracuse University (Whitman) (NY)	3.3
43.	University of Arkansas (Walton)*	3.3
43.	Univ. of California–San Diego (Rady)*	3.3
43.	Virginia Tech (Pamplin)*	3.3
48.	Bentley University (MA)	3.2
48.	Miami University–Oxford (Farmer) (OH)*	3.2
48.	Pepperdine University (CA)	3.2
48.	Southern Methodist University (Cox) (TX)	3.2
48.	Temple University (Fox) (PA)*	3.2
48.	Tulane University (Freeman) (LA)	3.2
48.	United States Air Force Acad. (CO)*	3.2
48.	University of Connecticut*	3.2
48.	Univ. of Massachusetts–Amherst (Isenberg)*	3.2
48.	Univ. of Nebraska–Lincoln*	3.2
48.	University of Oklahoma (Price)*	3.2
48.	University of Oregon (Lundquist)*	3.2
48.	Univ. of South Carolina (Moore)*	3.2
48.	University of Tennessee (Haslam)*	3.2
48.	University of Utah (Eccles)*	3.2
63.	Auburn University (Harbert) (AL)*	3.1
63.	Baylor University (Hankamer) (TX)	3.1
63.	Clemson University (SC)*	3.1
63.	Florida State University*	3.1
63.	Georgia State University (Robinson)*	3.1
63.	Northeastern U. (D'Amore-McKim) (MA)	3.1
63.	Rensselaer Polytechnic Inst. (Lally) (NY)	3.1
63.	Santa Clara University (Leavey) (CA)	3.1
63.	Texas Christian University (Neeley)	3.1
63.	University of Alabama (Culverhouse)*	3.1
63.	University of Kansas*	3.1
63.	University of Miami (FL)	3.1
63.	Univ. of Missouri (Trulaske)*	3.1
63.	Villanova University (PA)	3.1
77.	American University (Kogod) (DC)	3.0
77.	CUNY–Baruch College (Zicklin)*	3.0
77.	DePaul University (Driehaus) (IL)	3.0
77.	Fordham University (Gabelli) (NY)	3.0
77.	George Mason University (VA)*	3.0
77.	Iowa State University*	3.0
77.	Loyola University Chicago (Quinlan)	3.0
77.	Marquette University (WI)	3.0
77.	Oklahoma State University (Spears)*	3.0
77.	Rochester Inst. of Technology (Saunders) (NY)	3.0
77.	Rutgers University–New Brunswick (NJ)*	3.0
77.	San Diego State University*	3.0
77.	University at Buffalo–SUNY*	3.0
77.	Univ. of California–Riverside*	3.0
77.	University of Illinois–Chicago*	3.0
77.	University of Kentucky (Gatton)*	3.0
77.	University of Richmond (Robins) (VA)	3.0
94.	Brandeis University (MA)	2.9
94.	Colorado State University*	2.9
94.	Creighton University (NE)	2.9
94.	Drexel University (LeBow) (PA)	2.9
94.	Lehigh University (PA)	2.9
94.	Louisiana State Univ.–Baton Rouge (Ourso)*	2.9
94.	Loyola Marymount University (CA)	2.9
94.	North Carolina State U.–Raleigh (Poole)*	2.9
94.	Rutgers University–Newark (NJ)*	2.9
94.	Saint Louis University (Cook)	2.9
94.	St. Joseph's University (Haub) (PA)	2.9
94.	Texas Tech University (Rawls)*	2.9
94.	University of Colorado–Denver*	2.9
94.	University of Delaware (Lerner)*	2.9
94.	University of Denver (Daniels)	2.9
94.	University of Houston (Bauer)*	2.9
94.	University of Louisville (KY)*	2.9
94.	University of San Diego	2.9
94.	University of Texas–Dallas (Jindal)*	2.9
94.	Washington State University (Carson)*	2.9
114.	Gonzaga University (WA)	2.8
114.	James Madison University (VA)*	2.8
114.	Kansas State University*	2.8
114.	Loyola University Maryland (Sellinger)	2.8
114.	Oregon State University*	2.8
114.	Seattle University (Albers)	2.8
114.	Seton Hall University (Stillman) (NJ)	2.8
114.	U.S. Coast Guard Acad. (CT)*	2.8
114.	University at Albany–SUNY*	2.8
114.	University of Alabama–Birmingham (Collat)*	2.8
114.	University of Cincinnati (Lindner)*	2.8
114.	University of Hawaii–Manoa (Shidler)*	2.8
114.	University of Mississippi*	2.8
114.	University of New Mexico (Anderson)*	2.8
114.	U. of North Carolina–Charlotte (Belk)*	2.8
114.	University of San Francisco	2.8
114.	Univ. of Wisconsin–Milwaukee (Lubar)*	2.8
114.	Virginia Commonwealth University*	2.8
114.	Washington and Lee University (Williams) (VA)	2.8
133.	Ball State University (Miller) (IN)*	2.7
133.	Binghamton University–SUNY*	2.7
133.	Bucknell University (PA)	2.7
133.	Butler University (IN)	2.7
133.	Cal. Poly. State U.–San Luis Obispo (Orfalea)*	2.7
133.	Elon University (Love) (NC)	2.7
133.	Hofstra University (Zarb) (NY)	2.7
133.	Howard University (DC)	2.7
133.	Ohio University*	2.7

Top Programs ▶

Rank School (State) (*Public)	Peer assessment score (5.0=highest)
133. **Rollins College** (FL)	2.7
133. **Rutgers University–Camden** (NJ)*	2.7
133. **San Jose State University** (Lucas) (CA)*	2.7
133. **Univ. of Colo.–Colorado Springs***	2.7
133. **University of Memphis** (Fogelman)*	2.7
133. **Univ. of Missouri–St. Louis***	2.7
133. **University of Texas–Arlington***	2.7
133. **Xavier University** (Williams) (OH)	2.7
150. **Boise State University** (ID)*	2.6
150. **Bradley University** (Foster) (IL)	2.6
150. **California State U.–Fullerton** (Mihaylo)*	2.6
150. **California State U.–Los Angeles***	2.6
150. **Chapman University** (Argyros) (CA)	2.6
150. **Clark University** (MA)	2.6
150. **Duquesne University** (Palumbo) (PA)	2.6
150. **Fairfield University** (Dolan) (CT)	2.6
150. **Georgia College & State Univ.** (Bunting)*	2.6
150. **Kennesaw State University** (Coles) (GA)*	2.6
150. **Mississippi State University***	2.6
150. **Northern Illinois University***	2.6
150. **Pace University** (Lubin) (NY)	2.6
150. **Quinnipiac University** (CT)	2.6
150. **St. John's University** (Tobin) (NY)	2.6
150. **University of Alabama–Huntsville***	2.6
150. **Univ. of Arkansas–Little Rock***	2.6
150. **University of Baltimore** (Merrick)*	2.6

Rank School (State) (*Public)	Peer assessment score (5.0=highest)
150. **University of Central Florida***	2.6
150. **University of Idaho***	2.6
150. **U. of Massachusetts–Boston***	2.6
150. **U. of Massachusetts–Dartmouth** (Charlton)*	2.6
150. **University of Minnesota–Duluth** (Labovitz)*	2.6
150. **University of Montana***	2.6
150. **University of Nebraska–Omaha***	2.6
150. **U. of North Carolina–Greensboro** (Bryan)*	2.6
150. **University of Portland** (Pamplin) (OR)	2.6
150. **University of Rhode Island***	2.6
150. **University of St. Thomas** (Opus) (MN)	2.6
150. **University of Tulsa** (Collins) (OK)	2.6
150. **University of Vermont***	2.6
150. **West Virginia University***	2.6
150. **Worcester Polytechnic Inst.** (MA)	2.6
184. **Bowling Green State University** (OH)*	2.5
184. **Bryant University** (RI)	2.5
184. **Calif. State Poly. Univ.–Pomona***	2.5
184. **California State U.–Long Beach***	2.5
184. **The Citadel** (SC)*	2.5
184. **Florida International University***	2.5
184. **John Carroll University** (Boler) (OH)	2.5
184. **Kent State University** (OH)*	2.5
184. **Loyola University New Orleans**	2.5
184. **Northern Arizona University** (Franke)*	2.5
184. **Old Dominion University** (Strome) (VA)*	2.5

Rank School (State) (*Public)	Peer assessment score (5.0=highest)
184. **Portland State University** (OR)*	2.5
184. **Providence College** (RI)	2.5
184. **San Francisco State University***	2.5
184. **Southern Illinois U.–Carbondale***	2.5
184. **Stevens Institute of Technology** (NJ)	2.5
184. **Trinity University** (TX)	2.5
184. **University of Dallas** (Gupta)	2.5
184. **University of Dayton** (OH)	2.5
184. **Univ. of Illinois–Springfield***	2.5
184. **University of Maine***	2.5
184. **Univ. of Massachusetts–Lowell** (Manning)*	2.5
184. **University of Michigan–Dearborn***	2.5
184. **Univ. of Missouri–Kansas City** (Bloch)*	2.5
184. **University of Nevada–Las Vegas** (Lee)*	2.5
184. **University of New Hampshire** (Paul)*	2.5
184. **U. of North Carolina–Wilmington** (Cameron)*	2.5
184. **University of Scranton** (Kania) (PA)	2.5
184. **University of South Florida** (Muma)*	2.5
184. **Univ. of Tennessee–Chattanooga***	2.5
184. **University of Texas–San Antonio***	2.5
184. **University of Wyoming***	2.5
184. **Utah State University** (Huntsman)*	2.5
184. **Valparaiso University** (IN)	2.5
184. **Western Michigan University** (Haworth)*	2.5

Note: Peer assessment survey conducted by Ipsos Public Affairs. To be ranked in a specialty, an undergraduate business school may have either a program or course offerings in that subject area. Extended undergraduate business rankings can be found at usnews.com/bestcolleges.

Best in the Specialties ▶

(*Public)

ACCOUNTING
1. **University of Texas–Austin** (McCombs)*
2. **U. of Illinois–Urbana-Champaign***
3. **Brigham Young Univ.–Provo** (Marriott) (UT)
4. **University of Pennsylvania** (Wharton)
5. **Univ. of Southern California** (Marshall)

ENTREPRENEURSHIP
1. **Babson College** (MA)
2. **Massachusetts Inst. of Technology** (Sloan)
3. **University of Pennsylvania** (Wharton)
4. **University of California–Berkeley** (Haas)*
4. **Univ. of Southern California** (Marshall)

FINANCE
1. **University of Pennsylvania** (Wharton)
2. **New York University** (Stern)
3. **Massachusetts Inst. of Technology** (Sloan)
4. **University of Michigan–Ann Arbor** (Ross)*
5. **University of Texas–Austin** (McCombs)*

INSURANCE/RISK MANAGEMENT
1. **St. Joseph's University** (Haub) (PA)
1. **University of Pennsylvania** (Wharton)
3. **University of Georgia** (Terry)*
4. **Georgia State University** (Robinson)*
5. **Univ. of Wisconsin–Madison***

INTERNATIONAL BUSINESS
1. **Univ. of South Carolina** (Moore)*
2. **New York University** (Stern)
3. **University of California–Berkeley** (Haas)*
4. **Univ. of Southern California** (Marshall)
5. **Florida International University***

MANAGEMENT
1. **University of Michigan–Ann Arbor** (Ross)*
2. **University of California–Berkeley** (Haas)*
3. **University of Pennsylvania** (Wharton)
4. **U. of North Carolina–Chapel Hill** (Kenan-Flagler)*
5. **University of Texas–Austin** (McCombs)*

MANAGEMENT INFORMATION SYSTEMS
1. **Massachusetts Inst. of Technology** (Sloan)
2. **Carnegie Mellon University** (Tepper) (PA)
3. **University of Arizona** (Eller)*
3. **Univ. of Minnesota–Twin Cities** (Carlson)*
5. **University of Texas–Austin** (McCombs)*

MARKETING
1. **University of Michigan–Ann Arbor** (Ross)*
2. **University of Pennsylvania** (Wharton)
3. **New York University** (Stern)
3. **University of California–Berkeley** (Haas)*
5. **University of Texas–Austin** (McCombs)*

PRODUCTION/OPERATIONS MANAGEMENT
1. **Massachusetts Inst. of Technology** (Sloan)
2. **Carnegie Mellon University** (Tepper) (PA)
3. **University of Pennsylvania** (Wharton)
4. **Purdue Univ.–West Lafayette** (Krannert) (IN)*
5. **University of Michigan–Ann Arbor** (Ross)*

QUANTITATIVE ANALYSIS/METHODS
1. **Massachusetts Inst. of Technology** (Sloan)
2. **Carnegie Mellon University** (Tepper) (PA)
3. **University of Pennsylvania** (Wharton)
4. **Purdue Univ.–West Lafayette** (Krannert) (IN)*
5. **University of California–Berkeley** (Haas)*

REAL ESTATE
1. **University of Pennsylvania** (Wharton)
2. **Univ. of Wisconsin–Madison***
3. **University of California–Berkeley** (Haas)*
4. **University of Georgia** (Terry)*
5. **Univ. of Southern California** (Marshall)

SUPPLY CHAIN MANAGEMENT/LOGISTICS
1. **Michigan State University** (Broad)*
2. **Massachusetts Inst. of Technology** (Sloan)
3. **University of Tennessee** (Haslam)*
4. **Ohio State University–Columbus** (Fisher)*
5. **Arizona State University–Tempe** (Carey)*
5. **Pennsylvania State U.–Univ. Park** (Smeal)*

Best Engineering Programs

O n these pages, U.S. News ranks undergraduate engineering programs accredited by ABET. The rankings are based solely on surveys of engineering deans and senior faculty at accredited programs. Participants were asked to rate programs with which they're familiar on a scale from 1 (marginal) to 5 (distinguished); the two most recent years' survey results were used to calculate the peer assessment score. Students who prefer a program that focuses on its undergrads can use the list below of top institutions whose terminal engineering degree is a bachelor's or master's; universities that grant doctorates in engineering, whose programs are ranked separately, may boast a wider range of offerings at the undergraduate level. For the spring 2016 surveys, 28 percent of those canvassed returned ratings of the group below; 48 percent did so for the doctorate group. Respondents were also asked to name 10 top programs in specialty areas; those mentioned most often in the 2016 survey alone appear here.

Top Programs ▶ AT ENGINEERING SCHOOLS WHOSE HIGHEST DEGREE IS A BACHELOR'S OR MASTER'S

Rank	School (State) (*Public)	Peer assessment score (5.0=highest)	Rank	School (State) (*Public)	Peer assessment score (5.0=highest)	Rank	School (State) (*Public)	Peer assessment score (5.0=highest)
1.	Rose-Hulman Inst. of Tech. (IN)	4.5	22.	San Jose State University (CA)*	3.2	42.	James Madison University (VA)*	2.8
2.	Harvey Mudd College (CA)	4.4	25.	Bradley University (IL)	3.1	42.	Loyola University Maryland	2.8
3.	Franklin W. Olin College of Engineering (MA)	4.2	25.	SUNY Polytechnic Institute*	3.1	42.	Mercer University (GA)	2.8
4.	United States Military Academy (NY)*	4.1	25.	Trinity University (TX)	3.1	42.	Montana Tech of the Univ. of Mont.*	2.8
5.	Cal. Poly. State U.–San Luis Obispo*	4.0	25.	Union College (NY)	3.1	42.	Northern Arizona University*	2.8
5.	United States Naval Academy (MD)*	4.0	25.	U.S. Merchant Marine Acad. (NY)*	3.1	42.	Penn State Univ.–Erie, Behrend Col.*	2.8
7.	Bucknell University (PA)	3.9	25.	Virginia Military Institute*	3.1	42.	University of Alaska–Anchorage*	2.8
7.	United States Air Force Acad. (CO)*	3.9	31.	LeTourneau University (TX)	3.0	42.	Wentworth Inst. of Technology (MA)	2.8
9.	Cooper Union (NY)	3.7	31.	Miami University–Oxford (OH)*	3.0	55.	California State U.–Fullerton*	2.7
10.	Milwaukee School of Engineering	3.6	31.	Ohio Northern University	3.0	55.	California State U.–Sacramento*	2.7
11.	Calif. State Poly. Univ.–Pomona*	3.5	31.	Seattle University	3.0	55.	Grand Valley State University (MI)*	2.7
12.	U. S. Coast Guard Acad. (CT)*	3.4	35.	Brigham Young University–Idaho	2.9	55.	Grove City College (PA)	2.7
13.	The Citadel (SC)*	3.3	35.	California State U.–Los Angeles*	2.9	55.	Hofstra University (NY)	2.7
13.	Embry-Riddle Aeronautical U.–Prescott (AZ)	3.3	35.	Oregon Inst. of Technology*	2.9	55.	Humboldt State University (CA)*	2.7
13.	Kettering University (MI)	3.3	35.	University of Minnesota–Duluth*	2.9	55.	Indiana U.-Purdue U.–Fort Wayne*	2.7
13.	Lafayette College (PA)	3.3	35.	University of Portland (OR)	2.9	55.	Manhattan College (NY)	2.7
13.	Loyola Marymount University (CA)	3.3	35.	University of St. Thomas (MN)	2.9	55.	Messiah College (PA)	2.7
13.	Smith College (MA)	3.3	35.	Univ. of Wisconsin–Platteville*	2.9	55.	Texas Christian University	2.7
13.	Swarthmore College (PA)	3.3	42.	California Maritime Academy*	2.8	55.	Trinity College (CT)	2.7
13.	University of San Diego	3.3	42.	California State U.–Northridge*	2.8	55.	University of New Haven (CT)	2.7
13.	Valparaiso University (IN)	3.3	42.	Calvin College (MI)	2.8	55.	University of the Pacific (CA)	2.7
22.	Gonzaga University (WA)	3.2	42.	Cedarville University (OH)	2.8	55.	West Virginia U. Inst. of Tech.*	2.7
22.	Rowan University (NJ)*	3.2	42.	Dordt College (IA)	2.8			

Best in the Specialties ▶

(*Public)

AEROSPACE/AERONAUTICAL/ASTRONAUTICAL
1. United States Air Force Acad. (CO)*

CHEMICAL
1. Rose-Hulman Inst. of Tech. (IN)

CIVIL
1. Rose-Hulman Inst. of Tech. (IN)
2. Bucknell University (PA)
3. Cal. Poly. State U.–San Luis Obispo*
4. United States Military Academy (NY)*

COMPUTER ENGINEERING
1. Rose-Hulman Inst. of Tech. (IN)

ELECTRICAL/ELECTRONIC/COMMUNICATIONS
1. Rose-Hulman Inst. of Tech. (IN)
2. Franklin W. Olin College of Engineering (MA)
3. Bucknell University (PA)
4. Cal. Poly. State U.–San Luis Obispo*
4. Harvey Mudd College (CA)
4. United States Air Force Acad. (CO)*

ENVIRONMENTAL/ENVIRONMENTAL HEALTH
1. Cal. Poly. State U.–San Luis Obispo*

MECHANICAL
1. Rose-Hulman Inst. of Tech. (IN)
2. Franklin W. Olin College of Engineering (MA)
3. Bucknell University (PA)
3. Harvey Mudd College (CA)
5. Cal. Poly. State U.–San Luis Obispo*

Note: Peer assessment survey conducted by Ipsos Public Affairs. To be ranked in a specialty, a school may have either a program or course offerings in that subject area; ABET accreditation of that program is not needed. Extended rankings can be found at usnews.com/bestcolleges.

Top Programs ▶ AT ENGINEERING SCHOOLS WHOSE HIGHEST DEGREE IS A DOCTORATE

Rank	School (State) (*Public)	Peer assessment score (5.0=highest)
1.	Massachusetts Inst. of Technology	4.9
2.	Stanford University (CA)	4.8
3.	University of California–Berkeley*	4.7
4.	California Institute of Technology	4.6
4.	Georgia Institute of Technology*	4.6
6.	U. of Illinois–Urbana-Champaign*	4.4
6.	University of Michigan–Ann Arbor*	4.4
8.	Carnegie Mellon University (PA)	4.3
9.	Cornell University (NY)	4.2
9.	Purdue Univ.–West Lafayette (IN)*	4.2
11.	Princeton University (NJ)	4.1
11.	University of Texas–Austin*	4.1
13.	Northwestern University (IL)	4.0
14.	Johns Hopkins University (MD)	3.9
14.	Univ. of Wisconsin–Madison*	3.9
16.	Texas A&M Univ.–College Station*	3.8
16.	Virginia Tech*	3.8
18.	Columbia University (NY)	3.7
18.	Duke University (NC)	3.7
18.	Pennsylvania State U.–Univ. Park*	3.7
18.	Rice University (TX)	3.7
18.	Univ. of California–Los Angeles*	3.7
18.	University of Washington*	3.7
24.	Univ. of California–San Diego*	3.6
24.	Univ. of Maryland–College Park*	3.6

Rank	School (State) (*Public)	Peer assessment score (5.0=highest)
24.	Univ. of Minnesota–Twin Cities*	3.6
24.	University of Pennsylvania	3.6
28.	Harvard University (MA)	3.5
28.	Ohio State University–Columbus*	3.5
28.	University of California–Davis*	3.5
28.	Univ. of Southern California	3.5
32.	North Carolina State U.–Raleigh*	3.4
32.	Rensselaer Polytechnic Inst. (NY)	3.4
32.	Univ. of California–Santa Barbara*	3.4
32.	University of Colorado–Boulder*	3.4
32.	University of Virginia*	3.4
37.	Arizona State University–Tempe*	3.3
37.	Case Western Reserve Univ. (OH)	3.3
37.	Iowa State University*	3.3
37.	University of Florida*	3.3
37.	University of Notre Dame (IN)	3.3
37.	Vanderbilt University (TN)	3.3
37.	Yale University (CT)	3.3
44.	Brown University (RI)	3.2
44.	Colorado School of Mines*	3.2
44.	Dartmouth College (NH)	3.2
44.	Lehigh University (PA)	3.2
44.	University of California–Irvine*	3.2
44.	Washington University in St. Louis	3.2
50.	Michigan State University*	3.1

Rank	School (State) (*Public)	Peer assessment score (5.0=highest)
50.	University of Arizona*	3.1
50.	University of Pittsburgh*	3.1
53.	Boston University	3.0
53.	Clemson University (SC)*	3.0
53.	Drexel University (PA)	3.0
53.	Northeastern University (MA)	3.0
53.	Rutgers University–New Brunswick (NJ)*	3.0
58.	Auburn University (AL)*	2.9
58.	Rochester Inst. of Technology (NY)	2.9
58.	Tufts University (MA)	2.9
58.	University of Delaware*	2.9
58.	University of Utah*	2.9
63.	Illinois Institute of Technology	2.8
63.	Michigan Technological University*	2.8
63.	Missouri Univ. of Science & Tech.*	2.8
63.	New York University	2.8
63.	Stony Brook–SUNY*	2.8
63.	University at Buffalo–SUNY*	2.8
63.	University of Connecticut*	2.8
63.	University of Illinois–Chicago*	2.8
63.	University of Iowa*	2.8
63.	Univ. of Massachusetts–Amherst*	2.8
63.	University of Tennessee*	2.8
63.	Worcester Polytechnic Inst. (MA)	2.8

Best in the Specialties ▶

(*Public)

AEROSPACE/AERONAUTICAL/ASTRONAUTICAL
1. Massachusetts Inst. of Technology
2. Georgia Institute of Technology*
3. University of Michigan–Ann Arbor*
4. Purdue Univ.–West Lafayette (IN)*
5. Stanford University (CA)

BIOLOGICAL/AGRICULTURAL
1. Iowa State University*
1. Purdue Univ.–West Lafayette (IN)*
3. U. of Illinois–Urbana-Champaign*
4. Texas A&M Univ.–College Station*
5. University of Florida*

BIOMEDICAL/BIOMEDICAL ENGINEERING
1. Georgia Institute of Technology*
2. Johns Hopkins University (MD)
3. Duke University (NC)
4. Massachusetts Inst. of Technology
5. Stanford University (CA)

CHEMICAL
1. Massachusetts Inst. of Technology
2. University of California–Berkeley*
3. University of Texas–Austin*
4. Georgia Institute of Technology*
4. Univ. of Minnesota–Twin Cities*

CIVIL
1. U. of Illinois–Urbana-Champaign*
2. Georgia Institute of Technology*
2. University of California–Berkeley*
4. University of Texas–Austin*
5. Massachusetts Inst. of Technology

COMPUTER ENGINEERING
1. Massachusetts Inst. of Technology
2. Stanford University (CA)
3. University of California–Berkeley*
4. U. of Illinois–Urbana-Champaign*
5. Carnegie Mellon University (PA)

ELECTRICAL/ELECTRONIC/COMMUNICATIONS
1. Massachusetts Inst. of Technology
1. Stanford University (CA)
3. University of California–Berkeley*
4. Georgia Institute of Technology*
5. U. of Illinois–Urbana-Champaign*

ENVIRONMENTAL/ENVIRONMENTAL HEALTH
1. Stanford University (CA)
2. University of Michigan–Ann Arbor*
3. University of California–Berkeley*
4. Georgia Institute of Technology*
5. U. of Illinois–Urbana-Champaign*

INDUSTRIAL/MANUFACTURING
1. Georgia Institute of Technology*
2. University of Michigan–Ann Arbor*
3. Purdue Univ.–West Lafayette (IN)*
4. University of California–Berkeley*
5. Virginia Tech*

MATERIALS
1. Massachusetts Inst. of Technology
2. U. of Illinois–Urbana-Champaign*
3. University of California–Berkeley*
4. Northwestern University (IL)
4. University of Michigan–Ann Arbor*

MECHANICAL
1. Massachusetts Inst. of Technology
2. Georgia Institute of Technology*
2. Stanford University (CA)
4. University of California–Berkeley*
5. University of Michigan–Ann Arbor*

PETROLEUM
1. University of Texas–Austin*
2. Texas A&M Univ.–College Station*
3. Colorado School of Mines*
4. University of Tulsa (OK)

Best
Online Degree Programs

When we surveyed colleges in 2015 about their online options, 300 schools reported having bachelor's programs that can be completed without showing up in person for class (though attendance may be required for testing, orientations or support services). These offerings, typically degree-completion programs aimed at working adults and community college grads, were evaluated on their success at engaging students, the credentials of their faculty, and the services and technologies made available remotely. The table below features some of the most significant ranking factors, such as the prevalence of faculty holding a Ph.D. or other terminal degree, class size, the percentages of new entrants who stayed enrolled and later graduated, and the debt load of recent graduates. The top half of programs are listed here. Ranks are determined by the institutions' rounded overall program score, displayed below. To see the rest of the ranked online bachelor's programs and to read the full methodology, visit usnews.com/online. You'll also find detail-rich profile pages for each of the schools and (in case you want to plan ahead) rankings of online MBA programs and graduate programs in engineering, nursing, education and more.

(*Public, **For profit)

Rank	School	Overall program score	Average peer assessment score (5.0=highest)	'15 total program enrollment	'15 - '16 tuition[1]	'15 full-time faculty with Ph.D.	'15 average class size	'15 retention rate	'15 graduation rate[2]	% graduates with debt ('15)	Average debt of graduates ('15)
1.	Embry-Riddle Aeronautical U.–Worldwide (FL)	100	3.6	14,259	$355	47%	21	77%	24%	18%	$3,826
1.	Pennsylvania State University–World Campus*	100	4.2	5,005	$535	54%	27	74%	40%	75%	$39,017
3.	Western Kentucky University*	97	3.1	2,519	$474	71%	15	83%	N/A	54%	$18,118
4.	University of Illinois–Chicago*	96	3.4	182	$519	43%	17	95%	90%	57%	$14,889
5.	University of Georgia*	95	3.4	35	$562	100%	35	65%	N/A	89%	$21,009
6.	Temple University* (PA)	94	3.6	193	$752	86%	25	81%	N/A	73%	$17,585
7.	Daytona State College* (FL)	93	3.2	1,778	$560	75%	29	80%	62%	49%	$23,063
7.	Ohio State University–Columbus*	93	3.5	260	$387	27%	N/A	68%	N/A	29%	$11,879
7.	Oregon State University*	93	3.5	3,989	$200	63%	29	71%	47%	69%	$26,706
7.	University of Wisconsin–Whitewater*	93	3.6	162	$389	70%	38	92%	73%	76%	N/A
11.	Arizona State University*	92	3.8	15,188	$490	68%	45	88%	N/A	68%	$25,228
11.	CUNY School of Professional Studies* (NY)	92	3.3	1,431	$275	88%	17	64%	33%	60%	$6,225
11.	Colorado State University–Global Campus*	92	3.3	9,164	$350	100%	13	69%	42%	61%	$24,110
11.	Pace University (NY)	92	3.1	376	$555	86%	14	76%	55%	65%	$28,111
11.	University of Florida*	92	3.5	1,570	$500	75%	49	92%	67%	58%	$17,697
11.	West Texas A&M University*	92	N/A	1,010	$284	70%	31	84%	66%	42%	$7,600
17.	Charleston Southern University (SC)	90	3.2	331	$490	60%	12	78%	N/A	95%	$30,862
17.	Regent University (VA)	90	3.2	2,569	$395	85%	18	69%	35%	74%	$30,156
17.	University of Nebraska–Omaha*	90	3.4	179	$409	N/A	25	64%	N/A	82%	$23,982
20.	Creighton University (NE)	89	3.4	98	$422	58%	11	87%	N/A	50%	$36,293
20.	University of Central Florida*	89	3.7	9,082	$642	68%	68	85%	77%	58%	$20,746
20.	University of Denver (CO)	89	3.3	138	$566	100%	9	75%	45%	58%	N/A
20.	Utah State University*	89	3.6	2,330	$299	47%	63	63%	49%	59%	$16,500
24.	Fort Hays State University* (KS)	88	3.0	7,179	$194	60%	24	89%	72%	23%	$24,203
24.	Savannah College of Art and Design (GA)	88	3.3	657	$766	39%	18	75%	48%	78%	$50,627
24.	University of La Verne (CA)	88	2.9	321	$592	88%	20	85%	58%	76%	$27,935
27.	City University of Seattle (WA)	87	2.7	2,557	$398	27%	10	59%	44%	26%	$9,790
27.	George Washington University (DC)	87	3.6	221	$560	82%	16	71%	58%	32%	$25,176
27.	SUNY College of Technology–Delhi* (NY)	87	3.3	937	$270	34%	16	73%	52%	34%	$16,822
30.	American InterContinental University** (IL)	86	N/A	16,788	$302	88%	22	83%	65%	82%	$29,853
30.	University of Illinois–Springfield*	86	3.5	1,029	$362	81%	22	77%	50%	60%	$22,879
30.	University of Maine–Augusta*	86	3.1	3,457	$271	66%	25	77%	24%	74%	$27,539
30.	University of Oklahoma*	86	3.4	1,311	$589	100%	17	82%	43%	N/A	N/A
34.	Ball State University* (IN)	85	3.5	583	$483	63%	31	66%	40%	63%	$32,200
34.	California Baptist University	85	3.4	2,228	$529	75%	18	72%	N/A	88%	$33,972
34.	Florida State University*	85	3.6	583	$776	N/A	32	87%	78%	N/A	N/A
34.	Palm Beach Atlantic University (FL)	85	3.0	64	$450	74%	10	78%	51%	79%	$32,539
34.	Washington State University*	85	3.5	2,242	$569	75%	40	61%	53%	60%	$22,799
39.	Indiana University– Online*	84	3.2	2,001	$303	63%	25	81%	N/A	78%	$22,515
39.	University of Massachusetts–Lowell*	84	3.4	2,049	$370	88%	26	85%	34%	58%	$28,579
39.	University of Wisconsin–Milwaukee*	84	3.4	2,705	$337	82%	25	76%	39%	67%	$21,551
39.	University of the Incarnate Word (TX)	84	2.5	1,667	$505	100%	19	72%	68%	N/A	N/A

(*Public, **For profit)

Rank	School	Overall program score	Average peer assessment score (5.0=highest)	'15 total program enrollment	'15 - '16 tuition[1]	'15 full-time faculty with Ph.D.	'15 average class size	'15 retention rate	'15 graduation rate[2]	% graduates with debt ('15)	Average debt of graduates ('15)
43.	Central Michigan University*	83	3.3	1,717	$415	77%	19	66%	36%	38%	$7,974
43.	Northeastern State University* (OK)	83	N/A	247	$430	71%	11	63%	65%	N/A	N/A
43.	St. Leo University (FL)	83	2.8	6,052	$470	82%	16	78%	21%	68%	$34,966
43.	University of Missouri–St. Louis*	83	3.2	103	$452	20%	20	87%	100%	53%	$6,176
47.	Brandman University (CA)	82	2.5	1,219	$500	88%	25	72%	57%	85%	$23,243
48.	Marist College (NY)	81	3.2	231	$625	72%	20	75%	73%	83%	$30,223
49.	Ferris State University* (MI)	80	2.8	885	$392	50%	19	75%	52%	53%	$17,510
49.	Georgia College & State University*	80	3.2	42	$289	86%	25	96%	N/A	54%	$10,717
49.	Graceland University (IA)	80	N/A	69	$395	29%	12	91%	80%	54%	$26,546
49.	New England Institute of Technology (RI)	80	N/A	79	$250	53%	13	85%	N/A	N/A	N/A
49.	North Carolina State University–Raleigh*	80	3.6	94	$940	72%	22	77%	44%	50%	$9,184
49.	Old Dominion University* (VA)	80	3.1	5,505	$345	61%	38	85%	57%	N/A	N/A
49.	SUNY College of Technology–Canton* (NY)	80	3.2	950	$680	60%	23	81%	71%	61%	$28,123
49.	University of Arkansas*	80	3.1	425	$266	73%	35	84%	73%	60%	$18,230
49.	University of Wisconsin–Platteville*	80	3.6	426	$370	3%	18	58%	N/A	N/A	N/A
58.	American Public University System** (WV)	79	2.7	61,283	$270	51%	16	51%	36%	32%	$25,821
58.	Lamar University* (TX)	79	2.6	1,089	$208	67%	N/A	75%	N/A	29%	$24,711
58.	Robert Morris University (PA)	79	2.7	126	$710	86%	12	78%	N/A	74%	$35,204
58.	Southeast Missouri State University*	79	3.3	787	$379	74%	25	73%	23%	N/A	N/A
58.	Westfield State University* (MA)	79	N/A	158	$280	86%	20	84%	77%	57%	$15,700
63.	Colorado Technical University**	78	2.9	27,678	$325	93%	23	89%	48%	81%	$28,320
63.	Eastern Kentucky University*	78	2.8	1,961	$400	77%	16	71%	25%	89%	$28,148
63.	Eastern Oregon University*	78	N/A	1,350	$210	90%	21	78%	42%	80%	$18,655
63.	Golden Gate University (CA)	78	N/A	354	$610	100%	14	N/A	N/A	N/A	N/A
63.	Linfield College (OR)	78	2.8	640	$465	67%	16	88%	62%	72%	$19,321
63.	University of Massachusetts–Amherst*	78	3.7	1,435	$385	63%	26	70%	65%	71%	$24,021
63.	University of Minnesota–Crookston*	78	3.4	1,184	$391	41%	25	73%	42%	74%	$22,016
70.	New England Col. of Business and Finance** (MA)	77	N/A	1,152	$340	50%	20	91%	48%	63%	$44,250
70.	University of Massachusetts–Dartmouth*	77	3.6	247	$313	67%	15	65%	N/A	N/A	N/A
72.	Bellevue University (NE)	76	2.3	6,760	$395	34%	14	75%	45%	79%	N/A
72.	Drexel University (PA)	76	3.4	1,588	$547	65%	22	81%	31%	65%	$11,371
72.	Norwich University (VT)	76	3.4	765	$375	75%	6	71%	N/A	32%	$9,170
72.	Sam Houston State University* (TX)	76	3.1	1,088	$215	76%	40	75%	N/A	68%	$26,139
72.	Siena Heights University (MI)	76	N/A	542	$480	70%	16	26%	84%	47%	$22,386
72.	University of West Georgia*	76	3.5	N/A	$264	75%	41	N/A	N/A	N/A	N/A
72.	Western Carolina University* (NC)	76	N/A	1,123	$480	79%	20	76%	N/A	44%	N/A
79.	Concordia University–St. Paul (MN)	75	2.5	979	$420	33%	11	75%	43%	79%	$18,863
79.	Granite State College* (NH)	75	N/A	2,060	$325	29%	16	75%	54%	70%	$21,210
79.	Herzing University (WI)	75	1.8	1,178	$540	27%	18	82%	28%	80%	$25,883
79.	Lawrence Technological University (MI)	75	N/A	93	$986	100%	13	65%	N/A	N/A	N/A
79.	Loyola University Chicago (IL)	75	3.3	364	$722	77%	18	82%	N/A	59%	$25,187
79.	Peirce College (PA)	75	N/A	1,146	$566	76%	13	66%	48%	82%	N/A
79.	Wayne State University* (MI)	75	3.2	48	$409	100%	19	91%	N/A	100%	$25,224
86.	Colorado State University*	74	3.3	469	$419	72%	21	N/A	69%	N/A	N/A
86.	St. John's University (NY)	74	3.2	27	$1,262	87%	19	70%	15%	67%	$11,839
86.	University at Buffalo–SUNY* (NY)	74	3.4	77	$898	100%	25	93%	N/A	N/A	N/A
86.	University of Alabama–Birmingham*	74	3.0	491	$667	83%	N/A	N/A	N/A	100%	$20,217
86.	University of Nebraska–Lincoln*	74	3.5	33	$535	95%	40	83%	N/A	18%	$21,125
86.	University of North Texas*	74	N/A	889	N/A	95%	N/A	71%	N/A	64%	$22,050
92.	Berkeley College** (NY)	73	2.5	1,509	$525	66%	22	65%	32%	90%	$36,013
92.	California State University–Dominguez Hills*	73	2.8	641	N/A	93%	N/A	N/A	40%	38%	$16,697
92.	Concordia University Chicago (IL)	73	N/A	133	$505	40%	8	78%	N/A	82%	$24,461
92.	Florida Institute of Technology	73	3.2	2,876	$510	72%	19	67%	14%	86%	$43,430
92.	Regis University (CO)	73	2.7	3,537	$470	55%	11	80%	41%	69%	$34,100
92.	Southwestern Oklahoma State University*	73	N/A	442	N/A	N/A	19	2%	90%	N/A	N/A
92.	University of Texas of the Permian Basin*	73	3.0	689	$203	78%	40	50%	N/A	81%	N/A
92.	Western Illinois University*	73	3.1	715	$293	75%	35	84%	58%	N/A	N/A
100.	Florida International University*	72	3.1	3,015	$279	87%	16	N/A	N/A	N/A	N/A
100.	Liberty University (VA)	72	2.7	41,999	$435	43%	24	71%	41%	73%	$30,024
100.	Stevenson University (MD)	72	N/A	610	$495	67%	14	83%	57%	32%	$21,347
100.	Texas Tech University*	72	3.4	N/A	$220	44%	30	N/A	N/A	N/A	N/A
100.	Troy University* (AL)	72	N/A	5,430	$338	59%	25	57%	1%	N/A	N/A

Note: Key to footnotes, Page 123.

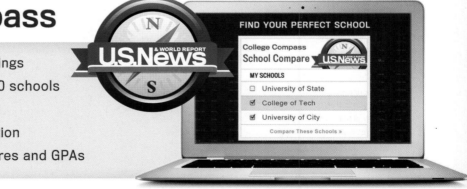

(*Public, **For profit)

Rank	School	Overall program score	Average peer assessment score (5.0=highest)	'15 total program enrollment	'15 - '16 tuition[1]	'15 full-time faculty with Ph.D.	'15 average class size	'15 retention rate	'15 graduation rate[2]	% graduates with debt ('15)	Average debt of graduates ('15)
100.	University of St. Francis (IL)	72	N/A	438	$599	67%	14	83%	54%	56%	$27,457
106.	Columbia College (MO)	71	2.8	13,542	$275	72%	19	75%	41%	60%	$28,136
106.	Franklin University (OH)	71	N/A	5,500	$484	88%	14	75%	27%	70%	$22,954
106.	Indiana University-Purdue U.–Fort Wayne*	71	3.6	419	$361	70%	N/A	85%	N/A	89%	$25,635
106.	St. Louis University (MO)	71	N/A	742	$620	88%	14	5%	9%	72%	$34,846
106.	University of Wisconsin–Green Bay*	71	3.3	1,557	$578	86%	29	N/A	N/A	56%	$22,028
111.	Bowling Green State University* (OH)	70	3.1	298	$390	79%	24	83%	N/A	66%	$27,811
111.	California University of Pennsylvania*	70	N/A	1,643	$300	100%	40	N/A	N/A	N/A	N/A
111.	University of Wisconsin–Stout*	70	3.3	871	$334	59%	25	N/A	N/A	89%	$21,342
114.	Dakota Wesleyan University (SD)	69	N/A	123	$325	63%	15	90%	N/A	48%	$7,298
114.	Dallas Baptist University (TX)	69	3.0	1,096	$813	91%	16	N/A	N/A	78%	N/A
114.	Georgia Southern University*	69	2.6	752	$204	69%	40	70%	N/A	72%	$24,288
114.	National University (CA)	69	1.8	N/A	$354	76%	18	62%	42%	N/A	N/A
114.	New England College (NH)	69	N/A	1,335	$405	46%	19	73%	N/A	62%	$11,914
114.	United States Sports Academy (AL)	69	2.4	267	$370	100%	7	61%	54%	76%	$26,833
120.	Clarion University of Pennsylvania*	68	N/A	548	$318	95%	25	N/A	N/A	79%	$20,501
120.	DeVry University** (IL)	68	2.0	22,202	$609	46%	26	79%	16%	78%	$41,346
120.	Malone University (OH)	68	N/A	118	$495	43%	19	88%	86%	86%	$21,136
120.	Marian University (IN)	68	N/A	220	$795	10%	51	66%	N/A	N/A	N/A
120.	Monroe College** (NY)	68	N/A	570	$552	10%	19	52%	56%	78%	$27,032

OREGON STATE
UNIVERSITY

Rank	School	Overall program score	Average peer assessment score (5.0=highest)	'15 total program enrollment	'15 - '16 tuition[1]	'15 full-time faculty with Ph.D.	'15 average class size	'15 retention rate	'15 graduation rate[2]	% graduates with debt ('15)	Average debt of graduates ('15)
120.	Sacred Heart University (CT)	68	N/A	409	$545	60%	13	N/A	N/A	N/A	$28,013
120.	University of Maine–Fort Kent*	68	N/A	368	$220	70%	23	82%	56%	N/A	N/A
120.	University of Toledo* (OH)	68	2.9	1,407	$385	69%	N/A	67%	N/A	72%	$26,423
128.	Chatham University (PA)	67	N/A	131	$805	100%	11	59%	72%	71%	$13,704
128.	John Brown University (AR)	67	2.1	193	$420	67%	13	79%	N/A	83%	$21,165
128.	Lynn University (FL)	67	2.5	662	$295	68%	16	76%	52%	36%	$29,299
128.	Missouri State University*	67	2.8	377	$285	62%	20	79%	N/A	N/A	N/A
128.	Slippery Rock University of Pennsylvania*	67	N/A	272	$300	100%	23	69%	79%	58%	$19,488
128.	University of South Carolina–Aiken*	67	3.1	141	$799	78%	15	86%	N/A	69%	$13,520
128.	Upper Iowa University	67	2.7	2,454	$423	38%	15	N/A	N/A	N/A	N/A
135.	Fitchburg State University* (MA)	66	N/A	161	$123	46%	14	90%	N/A	60%	N/A
135.	University of Missouri–Kansas City*	66	3.1	236	$711	N/A	22	N/A	N/A	N/A	N/A
137.	California State University–East Bay*	65	2.9	467	$297	100%	34	N/A	N/A	N/A	N/A
137.	Kaplan University** (IA)	65	1.8	22,169	$371	51%	24	84%	14%	85%	$25,974
137.	McKendree University (IL)	65	N/A	330	$360	88%	15	92%	N/A	56%	$16,062
137.	Oral Roberts University (OK)	65	2.9	393	$349	N/A	10	59%	35%	79%	$41,129
137.	University of North Florida*	65	2.9	82	$285	88%	40	N/A	N/A	N/A	N/A
137.	Wheeling Jesuit University (WV)	65	N/A	64	$390	74%	14	N/A	N/A	80%	$27,043
143.	Cornerstone University (MI)	64	N/A	N/A	$385	N/A	9	N/A	N/A	N/A	N/A
143.	Duquesne University (PA)	64	3.3	223	$815	100%	17	N/A	N/A	60%	N/A
143.	Kennesaw State University* (GA)	64	N/A	106	$277	67%	N/A	N/A	N/A	N/A	N/A
143.	Maranatha Baptist University (WI)	64	N/A	87	$376	47%	10	72%	N/A	52%	$7,029
143.	Neumann University (PA)	64	N/A	177	$589	N/A	13	79%	74%	N/A	N/A
143.	Northwestern State University of Louisiana*	64	N/A	N/A	$325	50%	23	76%	N/A	69%	$30,406
143.	Valley City State University* (ND)	64	N/A	N/A	$172	54%	11	N/A	N/A	N/A	N/A

▶ Best Online Bachelor's Programs For Veterans

Which programs offer military veterans and active-duty service members the best distance education? To ensure academic quality, all schools included in this ranking had to first qualify for a spot by being in the top three-quarters of the Best Online Degree Programs ranking, above. They had to be housed in a regionally accredited institution and were judged on a multitude of factors, including program reputation, faculty credentials, student graduation rate and graduate debt load. Secondly, because veterans and active-duty members often wish to take full advantage of federal benefits designed to make their coursework less expensive, programs also had to be certified for the GI Bill and participate in the Yellow Ribbon Program or charge in-state tuition that can be fully covered by the GI Bill to veterans from out of state. Qualifying programs were ranked in descending order based on their spot in the overall ranking.

Rank School (State)

1. Embry-Riddle Aeronautical University (FL)
1. Pennsylvania State University–World Campus*
3. Western Kentucky University*
4. University of Georgia*
5. Temple University* (PA)
6. Daytona State College* (FL)
6. Ohio State University–Columbus*
6. Oregon State University*
6. University of Wisconsin–Whitewater*
10. Arizona State University*
10. Colorado State University–Global Campus*
10. CUNY School of Professional Studies* (NY)

10. Pace University (NY)
10. University of Florida*
15. Charleston Southern University (SC)
15. Regent University (VA)
15. University of Nebraska–Omaha*
18. Creighton University (NE)
18. University of Central Florida*
18. University of Denver (CO)
18. Utah State University*
22. Fort Hays State University* (KS)
22. Savannah College of Art and Design (GA)
22. University of La Verne (CA)
25. City University of Seattle (WA)
25. George Washington University (DC)
25. SUNY College of Technology–Delhi* (NY)

28. American InterContinental University** (IL)
28. University of Maine–Augusta*
28. University of Oklahoma*
31. Ball State University* (IN)
31. California Baptist University
31. Florida State University*
31. Palm Beach Atlantic University (FL)
31. Washington State University*
36. Indiana University – Online*
36. University of Massachusetts–Lowell*
36. University of the Incarnate Word (TX)
36. University of Wisconsin–Milwaukee*
40. Central Michigan University*

40. Northeastern State University* (OK)
40. Saint Leo University (FL)
40. University of Missouri–St. Louis*
44. Brandman University (CA)
45. Marist College (NY)
46. Ferris State University* (MI)
46. Georgia College & State University*
46. New England Institute of Technology (RI)
46. North Carolina State University–Raleigh*
46. Old Dominion University* (VA)
46. SUNY College of Technology–Canton* (NY)
46. University of Arkansas*
46. University of Wisconsin–Platteville*

N/A=Data were not provided by the school. 1. Tuition is reported on a per-credit-hour basis. Out-of-state tuition is listed for public institutions. 2. Displayed here for standardization are six-year graduation rates.

Getting In

4

**A DANCE CLASS AT
COLORADO COLLEGE**

BRETT ZIEGLER FOR USN&WR

JACOB SIEGEL STUDIES
AT THE UNIVERSITY
OF WISCONSIN-MADISON.

GETTING IN

8 Ways to STAND OUT From the Crowd

Admissions deans and college counselors offer advice on getting in

BY COURTNEY RUBIN

NEWS YOU CAN USE — As a college admissions officer for nearly 30 years, Diane Anci has grown used to fielding questions from high school students anxious to improve their chances of being accepted. One that bothers her the most: "Would it be better if I took AP calculus and dropped band, even though I've been doing band my whole life?" Anci, vice president for enrollment management at Kenyon College in Ohio, says it makes her "so sad" to think applicants are "manipulating their whole life" to fit what they think she wants.

It's a common mistake. And every admissions officer invited by U.S. News to offer tips on standing out from the crowd insists that the key is not to reverse-engineer your life to fit some imagined ideal but to instead do the best possible job of presenting your true self. "I feel most persuaded by authenticity," Anci says. In other words, pursue extracurricular activities you're passionate about, write the way you sound (though not the way you sound in a text message!), and show sincere interest in your college choices.

Students who have watched older friends with perfect SAT scores and GPAs and plenty of passion get shut out of their top picks may find this hard to believe,

DARTMOUTH STUDENT TRACY GENG, AT DANCE PRACTICE

and it's true that the Ivy League and many other competitive schools have to turn away thousands of standout applicants each year, no matter how authentic.

But there's a movement afoot to change what's valued in admissions. A recent Harvard Graduate School of Education report written with the input of many admissions officers – "Turning the Tide: Inspiring Concern for Others and the Common Good Through College Admissions" – calls for shifting ideas of achievement to decrease emphasis on standardized tests and give more weight to depth of engagement in extracurriculars and service to family and community. The report has been endorsed by more than 50 schools, including all the Ivies. The education school project that produced the report will work widely with admissions folks and guidance counselors over the next two years to implement the recommendations.

Meantime, for more on how to make the best impression, read on.

Take the most challenging classes you can do well in

YOUR TRANSCRIPT MATTERS A LOT, and not only because it shows your grades. Colleges want to see that you've challenged yourself and taken advantage of your opportunities.

They can tell. Say there are two students with identical GPAs, test scores, recommendations, and high-quality essays. Student A took three Advanced Placement courses; Student B, two. Student A looks more impressive, right? Not so fast. She went to a large high school that offered 32 AP classes; Student B was from a small farming school that only offered two. "Context is everything," says Douglas Christiansen, Vanderbilt University's vice provost for university enrollment affairs and dean of admissions and financial aid.

And yes, colleges will have that context. They deal with the same high schools year after year, and they receive school profiles to remind them what AP and International Baccalaureate classes are offered. That doesn't mean that you need to take every one; rather, you should be taking the most rigorous courses that make sense given your talents and history. Keep in mind that a B in an AP history class may be more impressive than an A in a lower-level class; a C in a tough class is not.

Wondering about the merits of AP versus IB? Tracy Geng, 19, a sophomore at Dartmouth College from Eden Prairie, Minnesota, took both kinds of classes and thought the discussion-based IB format prepared her especially well for college. Her high school classmate Maddie Hoffmann, 19, a sophomore at Yale, credits the relative ease of writing her college application essay to her experience with the IB program, which requires essays even in math class, and a 4,000-word "extended essay." Hoffmann wrote hers about chemistry. "I got really comfortable writing," she says.

Show commitment in your extracurricular activities

IT'S ALREADY TRUE THAT MOST COLLEGES aren't interested in a lengthy list of activities proving only that you're a joiner. They want to see a significant, long-term investment of time in one or two that ideally includes leadership experience by junior or senior year. Indeed, the Harvard report calls upon colleges to "state plainly" in their applications that it's depth of experience and engagement, not the length of the "brag sheet," that matters. The report also suggests that colleges put more weight on endeavors that less privileged students often have to prioritize, such as working to contribute to household expenses or caring for younger siblings or an ill relative. Erica Johnson, director of admissions at Lewis & Clark College in Portland, Oregon, suggests including this sort of significant activity as an extracurricular if you don't want to write about it in your essay, so admissions officers know about it.

Should you do community service? Again, not if you are only going through the motions. Many colleges do value a service ethic and evidence of community engagement – and that may become more true where "Turning the Tide" recommendations are implemented. But the bottom line is still to be who you are. "Who am I to say that writing for the literary magazine is better than running track; or serving your high school community by being in student government is better or worse than community service [or] is better or worse than working at Subway?" Anci says. "What we're in the business of making judgments about is the student's ability to reflect on what that's meant to them."

Get to know your guidance counselor

JACOB SIEGEL, A 19-YEAR-OLD SOPHOMORE at the University of Wisconsin–Madison, watched as his older brother applied to college and decided he could do one thing better: Build a relationship with his high school counselor. If counselors know "even a little bit about you as a person – if when someone says your name they can picture your face and know you're a good guy who's on the sailing team, they're going to write a better recommendation than if they're just taking the information off a survey you filled out," Siegel figured. (The same principle holds true with the teachers you'll approach for a letter.) Starting junior year, Siegel made an appointment every few months to go in and ask about what he could be doing better. For example: "If I'm interested in engineering, should I be studying less history and more on engineering design?" Now he thinks that "building this relationship was one of the best things I did in my application process."

Heads up, Parents!
YOU'RE NOT IN CHARGE

Every admissions officer has a story about the overbearing parent who takes 100 percent control of the application process. Parents' appropriate role is to offer guidance, support and empathy during a complicated, emotionally taxing, and in some cases disappointing process. Here are our six best tips, which we tested recently during our son's college search (he's just started at Princeton):

1. **Work with your child to set a timetable.** This is a good place to take the lead, especially if your son or daughter is prone to procrastination or doesn't want to think about college yet. At the beginning of junior year, sit down together and plan a schedule. Things to calendar: making the initial list, visiting the colleges, taking the SAT or ACT, and writing the applications.

2. **Offer guidance in developing a preliminary list.** With thousands of choices, many students have no idea where to start. Help your child frame his preferences: big vs. small, near home or far away, city or rural. Once he has settled on a couple of choices, encourage him to locate colleges with similar characteristics using resources such as the comparison tools at usnews.com, the "choose a college" function at collegeresults.org, and college websites. Discuss pruning any schools you can't afford to avoid disappointment later.

3. **Help your child to find her "differentiator."** The holistic review used by many colleges rewards not only good grades and test scores but also accomplishments and activities that set a student apart. Brainstorm to locate your child's focal interest (preferably one showing her initiative and sustained commitment), then help her find ways to develop it. If she is interested in game design, you might point her to a summer internship with a game design company, a college course in graphic design or artificial intelligence, and a game design competition.

4. **Don't commandeer the college trips.** Encourage your child to take the initiative in setting up the information session, campus tour, lunch with a student, and, most important, visit to a class. Participate in the group activities, but let your child handle the class and interactions with students on her own. Be a sounding board.

5. **Be a calming influence.** The college search is a multiyear process, with moments of high stress and self-doubt. Kids are not used to this. Be empathetic and encourage your child to take things one step at a time.

6. **Let your child "own" the decision.** Remember, it's his life, not yours.

Lynn F. Jacobs and Jeremy S. Hyman are co-authors of "The Secrets of Picking a College (and Getting In!): Over 600 Tips, Techniques, and Strategies Revealed." You can download a free chapter at tsopac.com.

Choose schools wisely

IT MAY NOT SEEM LIKE IT, but the goal of the application process is to end up at a school that's the best fit for you. If you conduct your search that way – applying to five to eight schools you truly can see yourself attending – chances are you'll come across as a good candidate. As the Yale office of admissions tells prospective applicants on its website: "The more carefully and thoughtfully you've considered each possible college, the stronger your applications to those colleges will be." Lisa Sohmer, a college counselor for 20 years at the Garden School in Queens, New York, suggests coming up with a list of five attributes you want in a school, like an Italian minor, a rugby club, a change of seasons. And weigh questions like these from Anci: Do

Two Essays That Worked

What makes a college admissions essay successful? Below are two recent submissions that helped students get into Maryland's **Johns Hopkins University** with commentary from **Ellen Kim,** director of undergraduate admissions, about what these applicants did right. Remember, Kim advises, that "what works in these essays works because of who the student is" and how it fits into the rest of the application. In other words, you'll want to apply these principles to a topic that reveals something intriguing about you.

> "This title is interesting," Kim says. "But it's up to students to decide whether they want to title an essay." If nothing brilliant comes to mind, then you can skip.

More Than Thick Eyebrows
By Caroline

> The author takes a straightforward approach to starting, Kim says. "But you can tell you are going to get to know her."

Rarely have I studied a topic that flows from my ears to my brain to my tongue as easily as the Italian language. The Italian blood that runs through me is more than the genetics that gave me my dark hair and thick eyebrows. It is the work of the generation that traveled from Istria in the north and Sicilia in the south, meeting through friends in Chicago, and encouraging their children to study hard and make a living for their future families. In time, that influence would be passed on to me; finding my grandfather's meticulously-written electricity notes circa 1935 – filled with drawings and words I did not yet understand – inspired me to take Italian at my own high school.

> Many personal statements include short scenes, Kim notes. But the strongest essays are the ones that put those anecdotes toward a larger purpose, as the author does here. "She is helping us understand where she is in her journey with Italian," Kim says. "It's not just being descriptive for the sake of being descriptive."

The moment I realized that my Italian heritage was wholly a part of me was a rather insignificant one, yet to me is one of the most remarkable realizations of my life. The summer after my second year of Italian study, I was driving in my car, listening to a young trio of Italian teenagers, Il Volo, meaning "The Flight." As one of the tenors sang a solo, *Ti voglio tanto bene,* I realized that I could understand every word he was singing. Though it was a simple declaration of love and devotion in a beautiful tune, what mattered was that I was not just listening to three cute teenagers sing a song. I was fully engaged with the words and could finally sing along.

> The author chose to write about something very accessible and approachable, Kim notes. "Everyone can relate to family heritage," she says. "It would have been very easy to talk about the members of the family, but she does a good job of making it say something about herself," which is the goal.

After that moment, I sought out all the Italian I could get my hands on: watching *Cinema Paradiso* and *La Dolce Vita,* absorbing phrases of the language I felt I could now call my own. Even better, I felt confident enough in my skill that I could use it with my closest living Italian relative, my father's mother, *la mia nonna.* More than speaking the language, I discovered my family's past. In conversing with her and my father, I discovered that I will be only the third person in my paternal grandparents' family to attend college, that my grandmother had only a sixth-grade education, that my grandfather, despite never holding a degree in mathematics or physics, worked for three decades on CTA train cars as an electrician. The marriage of my grandparents in 195_ represented a synthesis of the culture of northern and southern Italy and America.

> In this paragraph, Kim says, "We learn not just about her intellectual appetite for something, but also about what she does when she is passionate."

Having now studied three full years of this language, I only want to consume more of it. I want to read Dante's *Divina Commedia* in its original vernacular, to watch my favorite Italian films without the subtitles, to sing every Italian refrain with fluid understanding of what the melody means, and to finally – finally! – visit my grandparents' childhood homes: the town of Trapani in Sicilia and the Istrian peninsula on the Adriatic coast. To me, the Italian language holds an essential connection to my past, but also a constant goal for the future. It is likely that I will never fully master the vernacular and colloquialisms, yet learning this language will stimulate me intellectually and culturally for life. I believe I can claim Italian as mine now, but there is still so much more to learn. Italian is a gift that I will hold dear forever, and I am glad that I received it so early in life.

> "This is a good way to close the essay, by describing why this matters to who she is as a person," Kim says.

you like the idea of being the smartest student in your class, or do you like being surrounded by really smart kids? Are you drawn to a highly collaborative environment or energized by a sense of competition?

One clue that you may not have chosen well: You find you're struggling to give a thoughtful answer to the school's question about why you want to attend.

5

Reveal yourself in your essay – and start it early

YOU MAY HAVE TO THROW OUT several ideas or half-written essays before you hit on the right spin on the right topic. Geng

String Theory
By Joanna

If string theory is really true, then the entire world is made up of strings, and I cannot tie a single one. This past summer, I applied for my very first job at a small, busy bakery and café in my neighborhood. I knew that if I were hired there, I would learn how to use a cash register, prepare sandwiches, and take cake orders. I imagined that my biggest struggle would be catering to demanding New Yorkers, but I never thought that it would be the benign act of tying a box that would become both my biggest obstacle and greatest teacher.

On my first day of work in late August, one of the bakery's employees hastily explained the procedure. It seemed simple: wrap the string around your hand, then wrap it three times around the box both ways, and knot it. I recited the anthem in my head, "three times, turn it, three times, knot" until it became my mantra. After observing multiple employees, it was clear that anyone tying the box could complete it in a matter of seconds. For weeks, I labored endlessly, only to watch the strong and small pieces of my pride unravel each time I tried.

As I rushed to discreetly shove half-tied cake boxes into plastic bags, I could not help but wonder what was wrong with me. I have learned Mozart arias, memorized the functional groups in organic chemistry, and calculated the anti-derivatives of functions that I will probably never use in real life – all with a modest amount of energy. For some reason though, after a month's effort, tying string around a cake box still left me in a quandary.

As the weeks progressed, my skills slowly began to improve. Of course there were days when I just wanted to throw all of the string in the trash and use Scotch tape; this sense of defeat was neither welcome nor wanted, but remarks like "Oh, you must be new" from snarky customers catapulted my determination to greater heights.

It should be more difficult to develop an internal pulse and sense of legato in a piece of music than it is to find the necessary rhythm required to tie a box, but this seemingly trivial task has clearly proven this. The lack of cooperation between my coordination and my understanding left me frazzled, but the satisfaction I felt when I successfully tied my first box was almost as great as any I had felt before.

Scientists developing string theory say that string can exist in a straight line, but it can also bend, oscillate, or break apart. I am thankful that the string I work with is not quite as temperamental, but I still cringe when someone asks for a chocolate mandel bread. Supposedly, the string suggested in string theory is responsible for unifying general relativity with quantum physics. The only thing I am responsible for when I use string is delivering someone's pie to them without the box falling apart. Tying a cake box may not be quantum physics, but it is just as crucial to holding together what matters.

I'm beginning to realize that I should not be ashamed if it takes me longer to learn. I persist, and I continue to tie boxes every weekend at work. Even though I occasionally backslide into feelings of exasperation, I always rewrap the string around my hand and start over because I have learned the most gratifying victories come from tenacity. If the universe really is comprised of strings, I am confident that I will be able to tie them together, even if I do have to keep my fingers crossed that knots hold up.

> Students should try to grab the reader's attention at the first sentence. "Her opening paragraph is interesting," says Kim. "You read it, and you aren't sure what the essay is going to be about. It makes you curious about what she is going to tell you."

> "A lot of times students feel like they need to write an essay about a life accomplishment or a life-changing event or something really extraordinary," Kim says. "But it's also possible to write a very effective personal statement about an ordinary thing. It's not the topic that has to be unique. It's what you say that has to be unique."

> The author does a good job of providing a window into her thought process, Kim notes. "You also see how she responds to a challenge in a very approachable way."

> In this instance, dropping in some academic references works with the theme of the essay, but students shouldn't think they have to follow suit, Kim cautions. It only works if it reinforces your central point.

> This essay, like all strong essays, was well-written, clear and error-free, Kim notes. The writing felt natural - not as though the author was reaching for a thesaurus. "This should sound like you," she says.

> Personal statements are called "personal" for a reason, Kim observes. They should tell the admissions committee something about the student. This essay does a good job of wrapping up the piece on a personal note.

started her essay for the Common Application in July before senior year. Her first draft was about her love of writing poetry "and it was really cheesy," she says. With time to rethink, she dug deeper. A creative writing workshop she had put on for young Chinese dancers offered an opportunity to weave in both her love of poetry and her Chinese heritage while also highlighting her initiative. Geng, who danced for 13 years, had come up with the idea for the workshop on her own.

Hoffmann decided what she wanted to write about – her desire to work in a science lab – and found a creative way to fit it to a Common App prompt asking for a story central to her identity. She made an analogy between her uncertainty about how to proceed and an episode of the TV show "Sherlock" in which the title character was inebriated and still trying to investigate. "It was about how I didn't really know what I was doing, but I knew I wanted to do it. I got the point across that I'm good at trying stuff," she says. "It was very me."

When you have a draft, read it out loud to avoid using language that's either clunky or too flowery. Your essay should sound like you, not you with a thesaurus on your lap (and definitely not like Mom). Next, get feedback from your English teacher or your school's writing center, experts advise. Finally, proofread. And don't rely on spell check.

Use social media to your advantage

AS A RULE, COLLEGE ADMISSIONS OFFICERS say they don't have a spare minute to look at social media. But sometimes they make the time. According to a survey conducted last year by Kaplan Test Prep, 40 percent of those asked had visited some applicants' social media accounts to learn about them, usually when they wanted to verify a noteworthy award or learn more about an interest. More than a third said they found details that boosted their opinion of the applicant. So be prepared and highlight your service or leadership roles and achievements. Photos should be tasteful and posts and comments should use proper grammar and spelling.

Before you post or tweet, consider: Is this the first thing I'd want a stranger to know about me? "I have seen kids tweet 'Ugh, on such a boring tour at school X,'" says Sohmer. She has also seen instances when overcompetitive parents or kids write to a school and say, "Before you think so-and-so is so great, you better take a look at her Facebook page."

Show sincere interest

A NATIONAL ASSOCIATION FOR COLLEGE ADMISSION Counseling survey found that, between 2003 and 2013, the percentage of colleges rating so-called demonstrated interest – emails, visits, attendance at college fairs – as "considerably impor-

Application Update
PLUG IN TO A NEW PORTAL

This year, the college application process is getting a bit of a makeover, thanks to a new online platform developed by a group of more than 90 selective universities across the country. The platform was created to "transform" the application experience by equipping students with a set of free tools that guide them through the college search process and allow them to create a portfolio of their work, customize their applications, and get feedback from teachers and friends, says Audrey Smith, vice president for enrollment at Smith College in Massachusetts. Smith is part of the group, which calls itself the Coalition for Access, Affordability, and Success. Also on board: all eight Ivy League universities and about three dozen public universities, including Clemson, Ohio State and the University of Florida.

The platform is also intended to improve college access for low-income students. To belong to the coalition, a private school must provide enough financial aid to meet the full demonstrated need of every U.S. student admitted, and a public must offer affordable tuition and need-based aid to in-state residents. Schools also must graduate at least 70 percent of undergraduates within six years. So far, approximately 90 out of the 140 or so colleges and universities that meet these qualifications have joined.

tant" jumped from 7 percent to 20 percent. A good plan is to first introduce yourself by email to the admissions representative for your geographic region, expressing your interest in the school, offering a bit about your background, and asking a question whose answer is not easily found on the college website. Introduce yourself with your high school, avoid text-speak, and sign with your first and last name. "I get a lot of emails written like texts and 'hey, quick question,'" says Lewis and Clark's Johnson. "It's a lost opportunity for the student. A properly written email is such an easy way to make a connection, and so many students don't do it," she says. But be judicious and "don't stalk the admissions officer," warns Christiansen.

Ideally, you can show up – taking the tour, sitting in on a class, staying a night in the dorms. But colleges understand that you may not be able to. If you do, it's best not to wear another college's sweatshirt. Who does that? It happens enough that some deans have a stock response:

Organizers of the coalition see their application portal as an alternative to, not a required replacement for, the Common Application, which is used by nearly 1 million applicants to 600-plus schools annually. A virtual "locker" will house students' papers, projects, awards, videos, artwork and other materials in one place, similar to Google Drive or Dropbox. Once a student has stored work in the locker, parents and teachers can be invited to take a look, share feedback, and suggest whether the material might enhance an application. The hope is that this collaborative tool will give students who attend high schools without strong counseling programs a way to get helpful guidance, says Barbara Gill, associate vice president for enrollment

management at the University of Maryland–College Park.

Students can start adding to their locker as early as ninth grade, a feature coalition leaders anticipate will inspire more top students from high-need schools to start planning for college sooner. (Some critics, though, have raised concerns that ninth grade is too early to start worrying about college.) "We want to signal to these students that there are a lot of schools where they are welcome" and might get generous aid, says James Nondorf, coalition president and vice president for enrollment and student advancement at the University of Chicago. The online platform will offer tools and application tips to students who might not have access to college-prep courses, Smith says.

Once a student is ready to apply, the coalition platform will allow him to seamlessly import background details and required documents into an application, while also permitting him to elect which items get shared from the locker on a school-by-school basis. Someone applying to a competitive music program, for instance, might opt to submit a recording of a performance to one school but not to another. The coalition will have a set of essay prompts that any school can use as part of its application requirements ("What is the hardest part of being a teenager now?" for example), but students will have to fulfill any extra requirements of a school and pay application fees for each; waivers may be available. Teachers and counselors will upload recommendation letters to the portal, and applicants can choose which letters to send to which schools. (You won't be able to read the recs, however.)

To learn more or to create an account and get started, visit coalitionforcollegeaccess.org. The coalition application opened in July, and more than 50 schools plan to start accepting it this fall. –*Lindsay Cates*

They point to the bookstore and cheerfully say, "I'm going to need you to go over there and get a new shirt."

A note about safety schools: Don't treat yours any less respectfully than the ones you would love to attend. "Sometimes we see very strong students who've put all their emphasis on very, very competitive schools" and haven't bothered to connect with the others, says Robert McCullough, director of undergraduate admission at Case Western Reserve in Cleveland. "And we pass up those students."

Be thoughtful about sharing your problems

THE DISCIPLINE ISSUE IS STRAIGHTFORWARD: The Common App asks about any behavior issues, and you'll need to sign and say the application is truthful. "If you leave the disciplinary part blank, you've got a problem if one of your recommenders mentions something and then says but now you're a model student," Christiansen says. Better to convey how you have grown from the experience.

On the other hand, experts say, only bring up any mental health issues if the knowledge will help admissions understand your experience or transcript, such as why a requirement was waived, or a sudden change in course level. Ideally, you should put out just those facts that will communicate what you've learned from the experience and how it's prepared you for college. One common mistake, admissions staffers say, is presenting a learning disability simply as an excuse for a mixed performance. Instead, explain: "Here's what this condition has taught me. Here's how I've been able to move forward." That shows grit and self-awareness – two qualities every college wants. ●

Race as a Factor in Admissions

In most states, colleges can weigh it along with other attributes as they seek diversity

BY PETER RATHMELL

What does the recent Supreme Court ruling on affirmative action in admissions mean to you? The court affirmed that race can be a factor in admissions – along with leadership and community service experiences, sports talent, and all the other personal attributes schools commonly weigh to diversify their student bodies.

In the case before the court, Abigail Fisher had sued the University of Texas–Austin several years ago claiming that she'd been denied admission unfairly in 2008 as a white applicant. The court upheld colleges' right to look at a range of attributes, including race when necessary to achieve diversity, rather than just sticking to academic performance and test scores. About one-third of colleges rely on such holistic reviews, says David Hawkins, executive director for educational content and policy at the National Association for College Admission Counseling. Beyond racial diversity, admissions counselors using holistic review look for signs that the student will be a good fit at the school and contribute to a well-rounded entering class. It "allows us to support our university mission to have a student body that engages people from across a variety of different life experiences, a variety of different points of view, a variety of different ways of interpreting the world," says Barbara Knuth, senior vice provost at Cornell University in New York.

A holistic review is unlikely to get anyone in whose academic record leaves doubt that he or she can handle college-level work, says Hawkins. And the ruling doesn't affect state laws. At schools in Michigan, California, Arizona, Oklahoma, Nebraska, Florida, New Hampshire and Washington, race cannot be considered.

A+ Schools for B Students

So you're a scholar with lots to offer and the GPA of a B student, and your heart is set on going to a great college. No problem. U.S. News has screened the universe of colleges and universities to identify those where nonsuperstars have a decent shot at being accepted and thriving – where spirit and hard work could make all the difference to the admissions office. To make this list, which is presented alphabetically, schools had to admit a meaningful proportion of applicants whose test scores and class standing put them in non-A territory (methodology, Page 139). Since many truly seek a broad and engaged student body, be sure to display your individuality and seriousness of purpose as you apply.

National Universities ▶

School (State) (*Public)	SAT/ACT 25th-75th percentile ('15)	Average high school GPA ('15)	Freshmen in top 25% of class ('15)
Adelphi University (NY)	1010-1220[9]	3.5	54%[5]
American University (DC)	1150-1340[2]	3.7	71%[5]
Andrews University (MI)	20-27	3.5	40%[5]
Arizona State University–Tempe*	23-28[2]	3.5	60%
Auburn University (AL)*	24-30	3.8	62%
Ball State University (IN)*	1010-1190[9]	3.5	50%
Baylor University (TX)	25-30	N/A	75%
Biola University (CA)	980-1240	3.5	59%[5]
Central Michigan University*	20-24	3.4	40%[5]
Clarkson University (NY)	1080-1290	3.7	72%
Clark University (MA)	1120-1340[2]	3.7	77%[5]
Colorado State University*	22-28	3.6	48%
DePaul University (IL)	22-28[2]	3.6	54%[5]
Drexel University (PA)	1095-1310	3.6	69%[5]
Duquesne University (PA)	1040-1210[2]	3.7	54%
East Carolina University (NC)*	980-1130	3.8	44%
Edgewood College (WI)	20-25	3.4	45%
Florida Institute of Technology	1080-1290	3.6	59%[5]
Florida State University*	25-29	3.9	75%
Fordham University (NY)	1170-1350	3.6	79%[5]
George Mason University (VA)*	1040-1250[2]	3.7	56%[5]
Hofstra University (NY)	1090-1260[2]	3.6	63%[5]
Howard University (DC)	990-1220	3.3	52%[5]
Indiana University–Bloomington*	1060-1290	3.6	68%[5]
Iowa State University*	22-28	3.5	54%
Kansas State University*	22-28[2]	3.5	47%
Lipscomb University (TN)	23-29	3.6	57%[5]
Louisiana State U.–Baton Rouge*	23-28	3.4	52%
Louisiana Tech University*	21-27	3.5	49%
Loyola University Chicago	24-29	3.7	70%[5]
Marquette University (WI)	24-30	N/A	68%[5]
Maryville University of St. Louis	23-27[2]	3.7	59%
Mercer University (GA)	1110-1310	3.8	73%
Miami University–Oxford (OH)*	26-30	3.8	68%[5]
Michigan State University*	23-28	3.7	67%[5]
Michigan Technological University*	24-29	3.7	62%
Mississippi State University*	20-27	3.3	52%
Montana State University*	21-28	3.3	42%
New Jersey Institute of Technology*	1110-1310	3.5	59%[5]
New School (NY)	1000-1250[2]	3.3	41%[5]
North Dakota State University*	21-26	3.4	41%
Ohio University*	22-26	3.5	43%
Oklahoma State University*	22-27	3.5	56%
Pepperdine University (CA)	1100-1320	3.6	80%[4]
Purdue University–West Lafayette (IN)*	1080-1330	3.7	79%[5]
Rochester Institute of Technology (NY)	1130-1350	N/A	70%
Rutgers U.–New Brunswick (NJ)*	1110-1340	N/A	76%[5]
San Diego State University*	1010-1230	3.7	73%[5]
Seton Hall University (NJ)	1060-1230	3.5	60%[5]
St. John Fisher College (NY)	1000-1170	3.5	57%
SUNY Col. of Environ. Sci. and Forestry*	1120-1300	3.6	72%
Syracuse University (NY)	1090-1290	3.6	70%[5]
Temple University (PA)*	1050-1250[2]	3.5	54%
Texas Christian University	25-30	N/A	76%[5]
Texas Tech University*	1030-1220	N/A	55%
Union University (TN)	22-29	3.7	59%
University at Albany–SUNY*	1000-1170	3.2	46%[5]
University at Buffalo–SUNY*	1060-1260	3.6	64%[5]
University of Alabama–Birmingham*	22-28	3.7	52%
University of Alabama–Huntsville*	24-30	3.7	58%[5]
University of Arkansas*	23-28	3.6	54%
University of Central Florida*	1080-1270	3.9	74%
University of Cincinnati*	23-28	3.5	47%
University of Colorado–Boulder*	24-30	3.6	57%[5]
University of Dayton (OH)	24-29	3.6	58%[5]
University of Delaware*	1110-1310	3.7	68%[5]
University of Denver	23-30	3.7	80%[5]
University of Hawaii–Manoa*	980-1190	3.5	56%
University of Houston*	1050-1250	N/A	64%
University of Illinois–Chicago*	21-26[3]	3.2	63%
University of Iowa*	23-28	3.7	60%
University of Kansas*	22-28	3.5	57%
University of Kentucky*	22-28	3.7	58%[5]
U. of Maryland–Baltimore County*	1110-1310	3.7	56%
University of Massachusetts–Amherst*	1130-1310	3.8	73%[5]
University of Massachusetts–Lowell*	1070-1270	3.5	49%
University of Mississippi*	21-28[2]	3.5	49%
University of Missouri*	24-29	N/A	58%
University of Missouri–St. Louis*	21-27	3.5	61%
University of Nebraska–Lincoln*	22-28	3.7	52%
University of New Hampshire*	1010-1210	3.4	45%
University of North Carolina–Charlotte*	1010-1180	3.3	57%
University of North Dakota*	21-26[3]	3.4	41%
University of Oklahoma*	24-29	3.6	68%
University of Oregon*	1000-1230	3.6	64%[5]
University of Rhode Island*	1010-1190[3]	3.5	50%
University of San Diego	1110-1310	3.8	71%[5]
University of San Francisco	1070-1260	3.6	67%[5]
University of South Carolina*	1110-1290	4.0	65%
University of South Dakota*	20-25[2]	3.3	42%
University of South Florida*	1070-1270	3.9	59%
University of St. Thomas (MN)	24-29[3]	3.6	56%[5]

National Universities (continued)

School (State) (*Public)	SAT/ACT 25th-75th percentile ('15)	Average high school GPA ('15)	Freshmen in top 25% of class ('15)
University of the Pacific (CA)	1010-1280	3.5	66%[5]
University of Utah*	21-28	3.6	53%[4]
University of Vermont*	1100-1290	3.5	74%[5]
University of Wyoming*	22-27	3.5	50%
Virginia Commonwealth University*	990-1200[2]	3.6	49%
Virginia Tech*	1100-1320	N/A	80%
West Virginia University*	21-27	3.5	46%[5]

National Liberal Arts Colleges ▶

School (State) (*Public)	SAT/ACT 25th-75th percentile ('15)	Average high school GPA ('15)	Freshmen in top 25% of class ('15)
Agnes Scott College (GA)	1060-1330[2]	3.7	62%
Allegheny College (PA)	1013-1250[2]	3.7	65%
Alma College (MI)	21-27	3.5	50%
Augustana College (IL)	23-28[2]	3.3	62%
Austin College (TX)	22-28	3.5	71%
Beloit College (WI)	24-30[2]	3.4	64%
Berea College (KY)	22-26	3.4	67%
Birmingham-Southern College (AL)	21-25	3.4	51%
Carthage College (WI)	22-28	3.3	58%[5]
Centenary College of Louisiana	21-28	3.4	54%
Central College (IA)	20-26	3.6	54%
Coe College (IA)	22-27	3.6	55%
College of St. Benedict (MN)	22-27	3.6	61%
College of the Atlantic (ME)	1130-1350[2]	3.6	47%[5]
College of Wooster (OH)	25-30	3.7	70%[5]
Concordia College–Moorhead (MN)	22-28	3.6	59%
Cornell College (IA)	23-29	3.4	45%
Covenant College (GA)	24-29	3.8	63%[5]
DePauw University (IN)	25-29	3.8	76%[5]
Drew University (NJ)	990-1240[2]	3.6	65%[5]
Elizabethtown College (PA)	1000-1230	N/A	63%
Furman University (SC)	1100-1320[2]	N/A	71%
Goucher College (MD)	980-1220[2]	3.2	47%[5]
Grove City College (PA)	1076-1309	3.7	68%
Gustavus Adolphus College (MN)	24-30[2]	3.6	65%
Hanover College (IN)	22-27	3.6	54%
Hobart and William Smith Colleges (NY)	1170-1340[2]	3.4	65%[5]
Hope College (MI)	24-29	3.7	65%
Houghton College (NY)	990-1250	3.5	61%
Illinois Wesleyan University	25-30	3.7	69%[5]
Juniata College (PA)	1020-1250[2]	3.7	58%
Kalamazoo College (MI)	26-30[2]	3.8	79%[5]
Knox College (IL)	23-29[2]	N/A	67%[5]
Lake Forest College (IL)	23-28[2]	3.7	64%[5]
Luther College (IA)	23-29	3.7	62%
Millsaps College (MS)	23-28	3.6	64%
Muhlenberg College (PA)	1110-1320[2]	3.3	71%[5]
Ohio Wesleyan University	22-28[2]	3.4	52%
Ouachita Baptist University (AR)	21-28	3.6	59%
Randolph-Macon College (VA)	1000-1180	3.7	56%
Ripon College (WI)	21-27	3.4	51%
Salem College (NC)	21-29	N/A	73%
Sewanee–University of the South (TN)	26-30[2]	3.7	64%[5]
Siena College (NY)	980-1200[2]	3.5	50%[5]
Simpson College (IA)	21-27	N/A	52%

School (State) (*Public)	SAT/ACT 25th-75th percentile ('15)	Average high school GPA ('15)	Freshmen in top 25% of class ('15)
Skidmore College (NY)	1110-1343[2]	N/A	72%[5]
Southwestern University (TX)	1040-1270	N/A	68%
St. Anselm College (NH)	1070-1250[2]	3.3	62%[5]
St. John's University (MN)	23-28	3.5	48%[5]
St. Lawrence University (NY)	1100-1310[2]	3.6	77%[5]
St. Mary's College (IN)	22-28	3.7	62%[5]
St. Michael's College (VT)	1070-1260[2]	3.5	56%
St. Norbert College (WI)	22-27	3.5	54%
Stonehill College (MA)	1020-1220[2]	3.3	59%[5]
Susquehanna University (PA)	1010-1220[2]	3.5	57%[5]
Transylvania University (KY)	24-30[2]	3.7	76%
University of Minnesota–Morris*	22-28	3.6	55%
University of North Carolina–Asheville*	1050-1250	3.4	52%
University of Puget Sound (WA)	1100-1340[2]	3.5	68%[5]
Ursinus College (PA)	1040-1250[2]	3.2	53%[5]
Virginia Military Institute*	1040-1230[3]	3.6	46%
Wabash College (IN)	1040-1250	3.7	71%
Wartburg College (IA)	21-27	3.5	58%
Washington College (MD)	1070-1290	3.7	60%[5]
Westminster College (MO)	21-26	3.3	40%
Westmont College (CA)	1050-1300	3.5	64%[5]
Wheaton College (MA)	1100-1330[2]	3.3	60%[5]
Willamette University (OR)	1100-1330	3.8	73%
William Jewell College (MO)	23-28[2]	3.8	59%
Wittenberg University (OH)	22-28[2]	3.4	46%
Wofford College (SC)	23-29	3.5	72%

Regional Universities ▶

School (State) (*Public)	SAT/ACT 25th-75th percentile ('15)	Average high school GPA ('15)	Freshmen in top 25% of class ('15)
NORTH			
Arcadia University (PA)	996-1200	3.6	60%
Assumption College (MA)	1020-1210[2]	3.4	43%
Bentley University (MA)	1140-1330	N/A	72%[5]
Bryant University (RI)	1090-1250[2]	3.4	58%[5]
College of New Jersey*	1120-1310	N/A	79%[5]
CUNY–Baruch College*	1100-1320	3.3	78%
CUNY–Hunter College*	1070-1260	3.4	57%
CUNY–Queens College*	1020-1200	3.5	66%[5]
Emerson College (MA)	1100-1310	3.6	67%[5]
Endicott College (MA)	980-1170[2]	3.3	44%[5]
Fairfield University (CT)	1100-1270[2]	3.4	69%[5]
Ithaca College (NY)	1100-1270[2]	N/A	63%[5]
Lebanon Valley College (PA)	1000-1210[2]	N/A	69%
Le Moyne College (NY)	980-1170[2]	3.5	55%
Loyola University Maryland	1110-1280[2]	3.4	62%[5]
Manhattan College (NY)	990-1190[3]	3.4	51%[5]
Marist College (NY)	1050-1250[2]	3.3	61%[5]
Philadelphia University	980-1180	3.5	41%
Providence College (RI)	1050-1250[2]	3.4	69%[5]
Quinnipiac University (CT)	990-1180	3.4	69%
Salisbury University (MD)*	1080-1240[2]	3.7	54%[5]
Salve Regina University (RI)	1020-1170[2]	3.3	49%
Simmons College (MA)	1060-1240	3.4	72%[5]
St. Joseph's University (PA)	1050-1230[2]	3.5	48%[5]
Stockton University (NJ)*	980-1180	N/A	54%

U.S. News & WORLD REPORT

Extra Help:
College Admissions

Parents: Your child may need help juggling high school classes and extracurriculars while researching and applying to colleges. Keep your teen on track with expert college admissions advice from U.S. News delivered to your email inbox twice a month.

To sign up, visit **http://www.usnews.com/extra-help**

Regional Universities (continued)

School (State) (*Public)	SAT/ACT 25th-75th percentile ('15)	Average high school GPA ('15)	Freshmen in top 25% of class ('15)
SUNY–Geneseo*	1100-1290	3.7	74%[5]
SUNY–New Paltz*	1025-1210	3.6	74%[5]
SUNY–Oswego*	1010-1190[3]	3.5	52%
Towson University (MD)*	1000-1170	3.6	45%[5]
University of Scranton (PA)	1030-1230	3.4	62%[5]
Wagner College (NY)	1030-1230[2]	3.5	62%
West Chester U. of Pennsylvania*	980-1160	3.5	40%
SOUTH			
Appalachian State University (NC)*	1060-1240	3.5	61%
Asbury University (KY)	21-27	3.6	51%
Bellarmine University (KY)	22-27[3]	3.5	59%[5]
Belmont University (TN)	23-28	3.5	58%[5]
Berry College (GA)	24-29	3.8	62%

School (State) (*Public)	SAT/ACT 25th-75th percentile ('15)	Average high school GPA ('15)	Freshmen in top 25% of class ('15)
Christian Brothers University (TN)	21-27	3.6	60%
Christopher Newport University (VA)*	1070-1250[2]	3.8	53%
College of Charleston (SC)*	1030-1210	3.9	54%
Elon University (NC)	1110-1290	4	58%[5]
Embry-Riddle Aeronautical U. (FL)	1010-1240[2]	3.6	53%
Florida Southern College	1050-1230	3.7	59%[5]
Harding University (AR)	22-28	3.5	51%
James Madison University (VA)*	1040-1220[3]	N/A	41%
John Brown University (AR)	24-30[2]	3.6	59%
Lee University (TN)	21-27	3.6	47%
Midway University (KY)	20-25	N/A	42%
Milligan College (TN)	22-28	3.8	65%
Rollins College (FL)	1105-1310[9]	3.3	66%[5]

MICHIGAN STATE UNIVERSITY

School (State) (*Public)	SAT/ACT 25th-75th percentile ('15)	Average high school GPA ('15)	Freshmen in top 25% of class ('15)
Samford University (AL)	23-29	3.6	52%[5]
Stetson University (FL)	1050-1260[2]	3.8	60%
University of Mary Washington (VA)*	1000-1210[2]	3.6	41%
U. of North Carolina–Wilmington*	23-27	4.0	63%
University of North Florida*	22-27	3.8	42%
University of North Georgia*	1010-1190	3.6	42%[5]
William Carey University (MS)	20-27[3]	3.6	54%
MIDWEST			
Baker University (KS)	20-25	3.4	43%
Baldwin Wallace University (OH)	20-27[2]	3.5	45%
Bethel University (MN)	22-27	3.5	57%
Bradley University (IL)	23-28	3.7	58%
Butler University (IN)	25-30	3.8	77%
Capital University (OH)	22-28[3]	3.5	47%
Carroll University (WI)	21-26	N/A	50%
College of St. Scholastica (MN)	20-26	3.5	48%
Concordia University (NE)	20-27	3.5	43%
Creighton University (NE)	24-29	3.8	68%[5]
Drake University (IA)	24-30[2]	3.7	69%
Elmhurst College (IL)	21-26	3.4	54%[5]
Franciscan U. of Steubenville (OH)	23-28	3.7	55%[5]
Grand Valley State University (MI)*	21-26	3.5	46%
Hamline University (MN)	21-28	3.4	47%
Indiana Wesleyan University	21-27	3.6	58%
John Carroll University (OH)	22-28	3.5	41%[5]
Kettering University (MI)	24-29	3.7	65%
Lawrence Technological U. (MI)	22-29	3.4	50%
Lewis University (IL)	20-25	3.3	41%
Madonna University (MI)	20-24	3.3	43%
Nebraska Wesleyan University	22-27	3.6	50%
North Central College (IL)	22-27	3.5	54%
Olivet Nazarene University (IL)	20-27	3.5	50%
Otterbein University (OH)	21-26	3.1	60%
Rockhurst University (MO)	23-28	3.6	56%
Spring Arbor University (MI)	20-26	3.5	48%
St. Ambrose University (IA)	20-25	3.3	40%
St. Catherine University (MN)	21-26	3.6	68%
Truman State University (MO)*	25-30	3.8	79%
University of Detroit Mercy	22-27	3.5	45%
University of Evansville (IN)	23-29[2]	3.7	66%
University of Findlay (OH)	20-25	3.5	45%
University of Illinois–Springfield*	20-26	3.4	46%
University of Mary (ND)	20-26[3]	3.5	45%
University of Michigan–Dearborn*	21-27	4.0	59%
University of Minnesota–Duluth*	22-26	3.5	44%
University of Nebraska–Kearney*	20-25	3.5	41%
University of Northern Iowa*	20-25	3.5	48%
U. of Northwestern–St. Paul (MN)	21-27	3.5	49%
University of St. Francis (IL)	21-25	3.4	43%
University of Wisconsin–Eau Claire*	22-26	N/A	49%
University of Wisconsin–La Crosse*	23-26	N/A	61%
Valparaiso University (IN)	23-29	3.7	64%
Webster University (MO)	21-27	3.5	47%
Xavier University (OH)	22-27[3]	3.6	53%[5]
WEST			
California Lutheran University	1000-1200	3.7	72%[5]
Chapman University (CA)	1100-1290	3.7	79%[5]

School (State) (*Public)	SAT/ACT 25th-75th percentile ('15)	Average high school GPA ('15)	Freshmen in top 25% of class ('15)
Gonzaga University (WA)	1090-1290	3.7	71%
LeTourneau University (TX)	22-29[2]	3.6	53%[5]
Loyola Marymount University (CA)	1110-1300	3.8	76%[5]
Mills College (CA)	1030-1290[2]	3.7	68%[5]
New Mexico Inst. of Mining and Technology*	23-29	3.7	68%
Oklahoma Christian University	21-28[3]	3.5	49%
Oklahoma City University	23-29	3.6	61%
Point Loma Nazarene University (CA)	1020-1250	3.8	63%[5]
Regis University (CO)	21-27[3]	3.5	50%
Seattle University	1060-1280	3.6	68%[5]
St. Edward's University (TX)	1040-1220	N/A	58%
University of Dallas	1080-1340[3]	3.8	67%[5]
University of Portland (OR)	1090-1300	3.7	77%[5]
University of Redlands (CA)	1020-1220	3.6	68%
University of St. Thomas (TX)	980-1210	3.5	53%
Western Washington University*	1000-1220	3.5	54%
Westminster College (UT)	22-27	3.6	53%

Regional Colleges ▶

School (State) (*Public)	SAT/ACT 25th-75th percentile ('15)	Average high school GPA ('15)	Freshmen in top 25% of class ('15)
NORTH			
Messiah College (PA)	1010-1250	3.7	63%
U.S. Coast Guard Academy (CT)*	1180-1350	3.8	79%
SOUTH			
High Point University (NC)	1012-1196	3.2	54%[5]
MIDWEST			
Augustana University (SD)	23-28	3.7	59%
Benedictine College (KS)	21-28	3.5	49%[5]
Calvin College (MI)	23-30	3.7	56%
Cedarville University (OH)	23-28	3.6	61%
Clarke University (IA)	20-25	3.4	42%
College of the Ozarks (MO)	21-25[3]	3.6	61%
Cottey College (MO)	20-26	3.6	41%
Dordt College (IA)	23-29[3]	3.6	47%
Loras College (IA)	21-26	3.6	46%
Northwestern College (IA)	22-28	3.7	57%
Ohio Northern University	23-28[3]	3.6	60%
Taylor University (IN)	24-30	3.7	65%[5]
University of Mount Union (OH)	21-26	3.4	50%
WEST			
Carroll College (MT)	22-27	3.6	60%
Oklahoma Baptist University	20-25	3.6	49%

Methodology: To be eligible, national universities, liberal arts colleges, regional universities and regional colleges all had to be ranked among the top three-quarters of their peer groups in the 2017 Best Colleges rankings. They had to admit a meaningful proportion of non-A students, as indicated by fall 2015 admissions data on SAT Critical Reading and Math or Composite ACT scores and high school class standing. The cutoffs were: The 75th percentile for the SAT had to be less than or equal to 1,350; the 25th percentile, greater than or equal to 980. The ACT composite range: less than or equal to 30 and greater than or equal to 20. The proportion of freshmen from the top 10 percent of their high school class had to be less than or equal to 50 percent (for national universities and liberal arts colleges only); for all schools, the proportion of freshmen from the top 25 percent of their high school class had to be less than or equal to 80 percent, and greater than or equal to 40 percent. Average freshman retention rates for all schools had to be greater than or equal to 75 percent. Average high school GPA itself was not used in the calculations identifying the A-plus schools. N/A means not available.

What if you get a

SPRING START?

A second-semester offer may well be worth taking

BY BETH BROPHY

Four years ago, when Madisen Keavy of Visalia, California, heard from her dream school – the University of Southern California – she was "devastated." She'd been admitted, but wouldn't have a spot until spring. After careful thought, Keavy passed up her other offers and said "yes" to USC, swayed by her interest in its journalism program. All fall, she lived at home, took a full load of community college classes that would transfer, drove three hours some weekends to attend USC home football games, and joined a

MADISEN KEAVY ANCHORS USC'S STUDENT-RUN NEWS SHOW.

Facebook group of other spring admits. She had to do some adjusting. "When my friends drove away in August, I felt I was at a standstill. My parents and brother became my new best friends. But my semester at home was a maturing process," says Keavy, 22, who graduated this year.

More families may find themselves facing a decision like Keavy's. While there is no definitive list of schools offering spring admission, "it's a growing phenomenon," says Jonathan Burdick, vice provost and dean of financial aid at the University of Rochester in New York, which has long had a spring program. Middlebury College in Vermont, a pioneer, has been offering spring admission for 40 years and this year enrolled 102 "Febs." Cornell University took its first bunch of 125 second-semester entrants this past January.

Other colleges with these programs include Brandeis University in Massachusetts, the University of California–Berkeley, the University of Maryland–College Park, Hamilton College in New York and Elon University in North Carolina.

Some colleges ask applicants to check a preference; others, like USC, simply relegate applicants to the spring pool without asking. "We want February admissions to be voluntary, and about 94 percent of it is," says Greg Buckles, dean of admissions at Middlebury, where students can indicate a choice of September only, February only, open to either but prefer September, or no preference. At York College of Pennsylvania, it's always up to the student.

While spring admissions may look like an extra shot at entry, admissions experts don't advise counting on it as a reach-school strategy. Many schools offering these programs are selective or highly selective, and they generally have way more qualified applicants than they can take; the standards for spring, deans at such schools say, are not different. "There really isn't a distinction. It just allows us to admit more students," says Jennifer Frey, senior assistant director of the program at USC, which uses spring admissions in place of a waiting list. "It's not easier to get in here for the spring," says Burdick.

Why do colleges do it? For them, it's always a win. The school can collect additional tuitions and fill the empty dorm rooms of students who study abroad second semester, transfer or drop out.

For students, a spring offer may be more of a mixed bag. Becca Brown, a junior at Middlebury whose preference was the February option, saw it as an opportunity, a chance to get a gap year type of experience. An international and global studies major with a focus on South Asia, she went to Nepal by herself for two months to work at a women's collective teaching English. "It solidified my interest in conflict resolution and gender issues," she says.

But plenty of questions arise for students

and parents. "Will coming late impede my adjustment? What if the other freshmen are already bonded and I don't make friends? Am I going to get decent housing? Will it affect the classes I can get into?" These are the possibilities that worry people, says Cyndy McDonald, a college and financial aid consultant in Visalia who helped Keavy. In fact, many schools strive to make the spring admits feel connected. They keep in touch with them before they arrive on campus, through Facebook groups, and by dispensing free sports tickets. They guide them through what courses to take during the fall to get credit when they arrive. They offer orientation programs before classes start and house them with or near other spring admits. Frey says her position was created in 2015 "to cater to this population" of about 500 students a year. "I'm a resource for support and feedback," she says.

Latecomers may also worry that their peers will look down on them. "I felt a stigma, but it was in my own head. No one else was ever negative," says Keavy. "I plunged into campus life, and within two weeks I was hosting my own morning talk show." She roomed with three older students, "who welcomed me, showed me around, and ate with me. Every semester is a clean slate." At Middlebury, Febs are an ingrained part of the culture and get a special winter commencement ceremony in which they ski down a slope in their caps and gowns.

One potential catch with these programs: While spring admits are

certainly eligible for financial aid, "we specify that aid might be constrained" and that it may be harder to land a work-study job midyear, says Burdick. McDonald advises looking closely at your package and asking about the future. "If your package is for half a year," she says, "ask what it will be for a full year" so you can try and avoid finding yourself in a difficult situation later.

It is always up to the spring admit to choose how to spend the fall term. "We don't have a preference. They can go to a community college, or work, or travel, or go on one of our partner study abroad programs in Paris, London, Rome or Switzerland," says Frey. It's a good idea to check with the college beforehand about what courses will transfer for credit and can be applied to graduation requirements. Buckles notes that credits earned during the fall from other colleges typically do not transfer to Middlebury.

At the University of Maryland, spring students have the option of taking classes in the fall through the office of extended studies, and they can even live on campus if they want to. They can take up to 17 credits that will end up on their Maryland transcript. The idea is to keep spring admits from "taking fall admission elsewhere," says Terrie Hruzd, director of programs in the office of extended studies.

A late start doesn't have to result in a delayed graduation. With so many options available to get course credits ahead of time, including Advanced Placement and International Baccalaureate credits, many spring admits graduate in seven semesters instead of eight, which can be a significant cost savings. These days, says Andrew Flagel, senior vice president of students and enrollment at Brandeis, "when you start college is less significant than where you finish." The path, he says, "is permeable and changing rapidly, serves diverse interests, and provides many opportunities with different entry points." Spring is one of them.

"If you love a school or a major, don't say no over a four-month wait," advises Keavy, with the benefit of hindsight. "You're not being demoted. There's no scarlet letter on your chest. You have accomplished getting in." ●

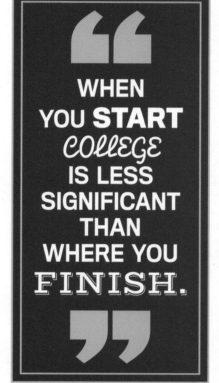

WHEN YOU **START** *College* IS LESS SIGNIFICANT THAN WHERE YOU FINISH.

WE DID IT!

How eight high school seniors got accepted

BY CHRISTOPHER J. GEARON

Choosing a college is one of life's big decisions, and the process of getting in is an exciting (but often stressful) rite of passage. To find out what that passage is really like, U.S. News visited T.R. Robinson High School in Tampa, Florida, in late April to ask a group of seniors what went into their calculus for deciding on a college. RHS is a neighborhood school whose International Baccalaureate diploma program attracts about one-third of the student body. Nearly a third are connected to the military, with family members stationed at nearby MacDill Air Force Base.

The school population is diverse: 47 percent of students are white; Hispanics comprise more than 21 percent; and African-American students account for 15 percent. Nearly half qualify for free or reduced-price lunch. Eighty-five percent of students go on to college. Here's how eight seniors found the right fit (and what it took for them make the cut):

Chase Watkins

With an eye toward studying mechanical engineering, Watkins was methodical in applying to college. He started with a list of 10 schools and checked them out by talking to college reps who visited T.R. Robinson and by consulting the U.S. News rankings. He whittled the choices to five Southeastern schools – the University of Florida, the University of Central Florida, the University of Alabama, Duke University and Georgia Institute of Technology. He decided the last two were too far from home and applied to the first three, all of which he visited at least twice and deemed "beautiful campuses." He got into all and then calculated "cost, the strength of the engineering program, and proximity to home" to settle on the "just perfect" University of Florida. He expects scholarships to cover about one-third of the cost. For example, Florida's Bright Futures scholarship provides up to $101 per credit hour for students with GPAs above 3.0 who go to Florida schools. The rest will be covered by his family and $4,500 in loans.
GPA: 3.85 unweighted
SAT/ACT scores: 660 math, 680 critical reading, 630 writing
Extracurrics: Student government, Latin Club and Feed America Club, which raises awareness about food insecurity.
Essay: Discussed his desire to pursue a career with NASA or Lockheed Martin and his record of achievement despite his father's death when he was starting high school.
Good move: He reached out to schools after submitting his applications to verify receipt and to inquire about honors programs. "They learn your

> STAY ON TOP OF THE PROCESS TO CUT DOWN ON STRESS.

name, and it was helpful to make sure I wasn't missing anything."
Regret: Not playing sports. A dislocated knee sophomore year prevented him from playing football.
Helpful: Getting off to a strong start as a high school freshman by attending two summer academic programs before ninth grade.
Advice: "Stay on top of the process" to cut down on the stress of dealing with so many details and deadlines.

Claire Chen

The top graduate of Robinson High School's IB program is headed to Johns Hopkins University to study political science, international studies or cognitive sciences – a major that got her attention on a visit to the Baltimore school. Eventually Chen would like to go to law school. She liked Hopkins' collaborative approach to learning and lack of a required core curriculum. She loved the city campus, too. In the end, her decision came down to JHU and Georgetown University, but she also got into the University of Florida and the University of South Florida; was wait-listed by Brown, Cornell and Duke universities; and was rejected by Columbia, Harvard, Stanford and the University of Pennsylvania. "I think my test scores helped" open the door at Hopkins, she says. Had she made more of her three-year leadership role as editor-in-chief of the school paper, she thinks she might have scored another outright acceptance. Still, she was pleased to commit to Hopkins the day after her visit. Chen's parents plan to cover the costs the first year, and she's considering loans along with their help in future years.
GPA: 3.91 unweighted
SAT/ACT scores: 750 math, 800 critical reading, 800 writing
Extracurrics: Besides the paper, Model UN and violinist in the orchestra (as well as the Tampa Metropolitan Youth Orchestra). She's also a pianist.
Essay: Learning from failure. Chen described messing up playing piano during one of three Tampa Bay Symphony concerts and her rebound for the last performance.
Oops: When she asked teachers for recommendations in the fall, some declined as they'd committed to other students.
Helpful step: Chen created an Excel spreadsheet of key deadlines, passwords, IDs and checklists for each school.
Visits: "Pictures and virtual tours are great, but I really got a sense of what it was like to be a student through walking around and visiting the dorms, din-

Chase
Watkins

ing halls and classrooms."

Resources: U.S. News and Forbes college guidance, books on writing admissions essays, and College Confidential.

Advice: "Start early." Chen didn't have a final list until October and was writing essays into December. Also, slow down occasionally during the crunch times and enjoy your life's "little moments."

Magnus Hanevik

The son of a Norwegian military officer on assignment to MacDill Air Force Base, Hanevik moved to Tampa at the start of junior year. Until last fall, college was not in the cards; he planned to return to Norway to complete the IB program and pursue a military career. "In Norway, a lot of people find work without going to college," he says.

But his girlfriend suggested he stay on, and a Norwegian friend recommended the University of South Florida. He applied, took the SAT in January, and got in. "I was very nonchalant about the process," he says. "I think it was the demographics – being Norwegian got me in." He now plans to study business or management. "The Norwegian military is looking for people with outside management" experience, he says. The degree also offers a backup in case the military doesn't work out. He knows getting a spot is highly competitive.

GPA: 3.4 unweighted

SAT/ACT scores: 610 math, 580 critical reading, 520 writing/24

Extracurrics: "I work out; I play games."

Essay: He didn't have to write one.

No regrets: "I could have done more, but I'm proud of what I've accomplished," he says. That includes fitting in at a

> START EARLY, AND SLOW DOWN ONCE IN A WHILE TO ENJOY LIFE.

Claire Chen

new school and taking AP and honors courses.

Best guidance: His girlfriend advised him to at least get an associate degree in the U.S. That provided him the motivation to go for a bachelor's.

Sweet: Most of the cost will be covered by Norway, which provides a yearly loan to residents that is partly converted to a scholarship upon graduation. It'll start sophomore year, since by Norway's standards he has a 13th year of high school to go.

Advice: Participate in community service, plays, sports and activities, as U.S. schools look at other things besides GPA.

Marlon Ausby Jr.

Ausby stuck with Florida and got into all five schools he applied to: UF, Florida State University, Florida Atlantic University, the University of Central Florida and the University of South Florida. He chose USF, considering it to have "the best premed program in the state." Ausby, who wants to be an orthopedic surgeon, says he did two things that helped his application shine despite suboptimal SAT and ACT scores. First, he earned an associate degree at Hillsborough Community College as well as a high school diploma by participating in a dual-enrollment program starting his sophomore summer. And he highlighted his commitment to service in his essay, which included helping out at a local clinic and at two

elementary schools. He also expected to get certified as a medical technician over the summer. Working will help pay for college, and

> GET INVOLVED IN COMMUNITY SERVICE, PLAYS SPORTS AND ACTIVITIES.

one-third of the $21,000 annual cost is covered by a scholarship.

GPA: 3.73

SAT/ACT scores: 600 math, 500 critical reading, 610 writing/25

Extracurrics: Founded the school's African-American Heritage Club, member of Feed America and Future Doctors of America clubs; shadowed a pharmacist to get a sense of a career in health.

Essay: The decisions and accomplishments of his parents to get to where they are today, with his father in the military and his mother a teacher, and continuing the family legacy of service.

Early start: Began working on his applications at the end of junior year and sent off his last app in early November.

Boost: The community college degree. "My test scores were low, but dual enrollment showed I can do the work."

Regret: Getting a liberal arts and sciences associate degree rather than one that would have allowed him to work as a surgical technician. The liberal arts credits transferred, but he thinks the work experience would have been helpful when he applies to medical school.

Advice: Do what his dad

key reasons she's staying in state include the less costly tuition and the fact that all the credits she has earned by being dually enrolled junior and senior year at Hillsborough Community College transfer. "I have enough credits for an associate degree," she says. Paight could finish a pre-med degree early with all those credits (she plans to be an anesthesiologist), but she wants to stick around to double major in psychology and biomed. And why not? She is getting 100 percent of the costs of her undergrad degree – at USF – covered by school and state scholarships. While the University of Florida did offer her some money, she says, it took several months to get information about scholarships, which left her "disheartened." USF reached out to her almost weekly.

GPA: 3.92

SAT/ACT scores: 750 math, 690 critical reading, 630 writing

Extracurrics: Volleyball, school service club, Feed America Club

Essay: USF doesn't require an essay. For a National Merit Scholarship essay, she discussed her growth through high school, a tumultuous time that involved three moves and a respiratory ailment.

Helpful: Quizlet, an online place where everyone can share knowledge in any

Magnus Hanevik

Marlon Ausby Jr.

advised: Be disciplined. That means "getting up when you don't feel like it and doing your work when you don't feel like it."

Ginger Paight

Virginia "Ginger" Paight

The top graduate among non-IB students applied to and got into just two schools: UF and USF. The

subject, "was great" as a resource that "helped me achieve my GPA."

Kind of helpful: "My dad tricked me into taking the SAT as a freshman." He signed her up and dropped her off, thinking the experience would help her later.

Best part: Not having to apply to a lot of schools; she knew in early fall that she was a National Merit Semifinalist and would get a full ride.

Do-over: Would have emphasized dual enrollment rather than take 13 AP classes. The college credit would have been more likely to be honored as a basis for placement in advanced math and science, she thinks.

Advice: Make connections with key teachers and staff well before senior year. While applying, you'll have to do "a lot of running around" to them asking for recommendations and transcripts.

Ana Rescala

An intended computer science major, Rescala bagged acceptances from five of the seven schools she applied to, including the Massachusetts Institute of Technology, Georgia Tech, the University of California–Los Angeles, the University of Southern California and her safety, UF. She was wait-listed by Stanford University and rejected by the University of California–Berkeley. She considered but passed on

> **STICK WITH A CLUB ALL FOUR YEARS SO YOU CAN LEAD IT SENIOR YEAR.**

MIT; "It felt too narrow," she says. "I wanted something bigger and more diverse." She chose USC after she "fell in love" with its California location and was offered a free ride. While she likes math and science, she also is passionate about art. "I'm very well-rounded," she says, and that's what she highlighted in her applications. But the thing she believes helped most was including a description of her service project, which involved getting girls and minority elementary school kids excited about STEM subjects.

GPA: 4.0

SAT/ACT scores: 740 math, 740 critical reading, 720 writing/35

Extracurrics: President of the Political Debate Club, co-president of Girls Who Code club, community service, taekwondo, flag football.

Essay: "How taekwondo has

developed me into who I am today."

Notable: While she liked Georgia Tech, she wanted a school with more courses in the arts and humanities.

Helpful: Colleges' websites, U.S. News, and being in touch with students at schools of interest.

Enjoyable: "Getting to know myself better" was the

> **START EARLY ENOUGH TO GIVE YOURSELF TIME TO REFLECT.**

best part of the process. "The essays are very valuable to me. This is who I am at 18."

Not to worry: "The college process is not as scary as people tell you it is," she says. "The process is very self-explanatory."

Advice: All four years of high school matter. Start freshman year on a good note and work hard; don't settle for B's or C's. And stick with a club for all four years so you can lead it by your senior year.

Abram Scharf

Wanting to be a writer, Scharf is headed to Brown University in Rhode Island to major in English. Since his particular interest is music criticism, he was looking for an open curriculum (one without a broad set of distribution requirements) or a "good music scene" or better yet, both. Brown is a two-fer; Providence is known for its strong and vibrant music life. While he got into the one Ivy he applied to, he

Ana Rescala and Abram Scharf

was denied by Amherst College and wait-listed by Vanderbilt and the University of Chicago; he also was accepted into the University of Florida's honors program. He considered other schools, but ruled them out after visits. "Williams College was a bit too touchy-feely for me, and that's saying a lot for a sensitive guy," he says. Nor did he warm to Princeton. One of the biggest challenges for the wannabe writer was trying to tell admissions about himself in so few words. "It was like being given one page in The New Yorker," he says.

GPA: 3.94

SAT/ACT scores: 730 math, 800 critical reading, 680 writing

Extracurrics: Varsity soccer, school spirit club, reviewed concerts for a Tampa magazine, and volunteered at a music festival.

Essay: "I found an obscure thing about each school and wrote how it applied to me." For Brown, he used the concept of the university's nudity week, a series of events exploring identity and the human body, to discuss who he really is when stripped down to his core.

Biggest help: A mother who volunteered at the school's writing center helped him focus his thoughts. "I probably would not have gotten into Brown without her help."

Visits: While they can help you rule a school in or out, he found that doing a five-college road trip was overwhelming. "It kind of becomes a farce of itself," he says, adding that "parents ask the most inane questions."

Advice: "Start early to give yourself time to reflect," he says, noting that he opened a College Board account on Aug. 1, the day the new Common Application was released.

GET FEEDBACK ON YOUR ESSAYS. YOU'LL ONLY IMPROVE THEM.

Catherine Cassedy

Though denied entry to her top choice, Georgetown University, Cassedy is stoked she has landed at Duke, where she'll either study computer science or economics. She applied to 11 colleges, knowing that "I wanted to get out of Florida for sure," though the University of Florida and Florida State University were among her picks. She got nods from both as well as the University of Virginia, Boston College and Tufts University. Princeton, Yale and Washington and Lee denied her, as did Trinity College in Dublin. (Cassedy's mother is from Ireland, and Cassedy has spent many summers there.) She portrayed herself as a leader in her applications, highlighting her officer status in several clubs and her participation in an anti-domestic abuse organization, Break the Silence. "I do feel colleges look for certain personalities, and

they pay attention to that."

GPA: 3.83

SAT/ACT scores: 730 math, 700 critical reading, 770 writing/31

Extracurrics: Captain of the lacrosse team, president

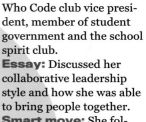

of National Honor Society and the sailing club, Girls Who Code club vice president, member of student government and the school spirit club.

Essay: Discussed her collaborative leadership style and how she was able to bring people together.

Smart move: She followed up with admissions in late January by sending an email with links to news coverage of a domestic violence awareness event she'd organized at school.

Commitment: Her passion for technology was "definitely reflected" in her application. Besides specifying an interest in computer science, she showcased her video editing for the spirit club and service as tech director of the Student Government Association and VP of Girls Who Code. "It's important that you draw parallels in your activities. Finding and highlighting that common theme throughout the application helps."

Lesson learned: Missed the early action deadline for Boston College and UVA by two and 10 minutes respectively, as "I waited until the last five minutes to submit." Trouble entering and processing her credit card info caused a delay, though she followed up with the schools to explain and squeaked in.

Insight: "I'm a procrastinator," she says. "Keeping your parents in the loop can help you stay on top of it all."

Advice: The Common App essay really needs to "shine a light on who you are." Get feedback on your essays – you'll only improve them by doing so. ●

Catherine Cassedy

To-Do List

FOR YOUR COLLEGE SEARCH BY NED JOHNSON

❯ Freshman Year

Get set for a great high school career. It's important to remember that what lies ahead is more than just a four-year audition for college. Still, it will help later to think now about what admissions staffers will look for three (short) years from now.

● **Plan your schedule carefully from the beginning.** Seek advice and teacher feedback when you map out your classes. Grades are important in ninth grade. But rigor is key, too, so don't just go for easy A's. Ask for help if you run into trouble, but if you earn a bad grade, accept it as constructive criticism, really read (or listen) to your teacher's comments, and figure out how to do better.

● **Read voraciously.** Books, newspapers, magazines, blogs – choose what engages you and remember to look up unfamiliar words.

● **Get involved.** In addition to academics, develop talents and interests outside the classroom. You'll find school is more fun and your preferred activity may just be the detail that catches a college's eye.

❯ Sophomore Year

Now that you're no longer a rookie, you'll want to focus on evolving as a learner. Besides studying the material, take note of what your teachers value, and consider how you can learn more efficiently – and better.

● **Refine your route.** Look ahead to the 11th and 12th grade courses you might be interested in taking and plan to work in any prerequisites.

● **Challenge yourself (wisely).** Remember to ask for help, if you need it. Create a balanced schedule. You want to strive for the best possible grades, but over-taxing yourself is bound to be counterproductive.

● **Consider a testing strategy.** Will you take the PSAT this year? You'll get a better sense of where you stand if you know what is on the exam before you take it. Also, consider whether an SAT subject test makes sense in the spring. If you're enrolled in an AP or hon-ors course now, the timing may be good. The College Board makes practice versions. Take at least one.

● **Put together a résumé.** Start jotting down your hobbies, jobs and extracurricular activities. For now, it's a way to keep track of what you have accomplished with thoughts of where you will go.

● **Make the most of your summer(s).** Work, volunteer, play sports, travel or take a class. Find an activity that builds on a favorite subject or extracurricular interest.

❯ Junior Year

Essays and testing and APs, oh my! Your grades, test scores and activities junior year constitute a big chunk of what colleges consider for admission. Do your best in class and truly prepare for the tests you take. Step forward as a leader and explore pursuits that interest you, not just because they'll look good on an application, but because they'll help you grow as a person.

● **Evaluate your approach.** As Albert Einstein al-legedly put it, insanity is "doing the same thing over and over again and expecting different results." So if you feel stuck in your studies and in need of a break-through, ask teachers, parents or friends for help in finding a new approach.

SAT prep
3:30

- **Speak up in class.** You will need to ask two junior-year teachers to write recommendations. They can't know you without hearing your thoughts, so make sure to contribute in class.

- **Sleep.** The average 16-year-old brain needs over nine hours of sleep to function at 100 percent, and that's exactly where you want to be.

- **Plan your testing calendar.** Test scores matter (along with grades), so talk with your parents and guidance counselor about which ones to take and when, and how to prepare for them. First up, the PSAT. If your 10th-grade scores put you in reach of a National Merit Scholarship, it might be wise to spend concentrated time prepping. Then take the SAT or ACT in winter or early spring. Don't worry if you don't get your ideal score; you can try again. The SAT subject tests are also an option for May or June in areas where you shine or in subjects you covered junior year.

- **Get involved.** It's great to show you've worked hard, are dedicated to an activity, play well with others – and can lead them. Start an arts discussion group that goes to museum openings, say, or be voted team captain.

- **Begin building your college list.** Once you have gotten your test scores, talk to a counselor and start putting together a list of target schools, reaches and safeties. Make use of new technology and apps to aid your research. Explore college websites and resources like ed.gov/finaid and usnews.com/bestcolleges. (While you're online, be sure to clean up your Facebook act. It might get a look from the college admissions folks.)

- **Make some campus visits.** Spring break and summer vacation are ideal times to check out a few campuses. Attend college fairs and talk with the people behind the tables. They can give you a feel for their school and some good future contacts.

- **Write.** Procrastination doesn't make for a good college essay. Aim to have first drafts done by Labor Day. Share them with an English teacher or counselor.

❯ Senior Year

You made it. Let's party! Well, not quite yet. This will also be a year of hard work and continued preparation. Colleges do consider senior-year transcripts. They can and will rescind offers to students who slack off, so stay focused.

- **Finish testing and check the boxes.** You're in the final stretch. If necessary, retake the SAT, ACT or subject tests. The early fall test dates will give you time to apply early. Also, make sure you're completing all graduation requirements as well as course requirements for your target colleges. Also, be very clear on the admissions testing policy of each school. Are they test-optional or do they require the SAT or ACT (and should you take the writing or subject tests)?

- **Ask for recommendations.** Early in the school year, ask two teachers if they are willing to write a letter of recommendation for you. Choose teachers with whom you have a good relationship and who will effectively communicate your academic and personal qualities. You will want people who can offer different perspectives on your performance. Be sure to update and polish your résumé, too; it will come in handy when you're filling out applications and preparing for admissions interviews.

- **Apply.** Fill out each application carefully and ask someone to look over your essays critically. Check that your colleges have received records and recs from your high school, and have your SAT or ACT scores sent from the testing organization. A month from the date you submit your application, call the college and confirm that your file is complete.

- **Follow the money.** Check with each college for specific financial aid application requirements. Dates and forms may vary.

- **Make a choice.** Try to visit the colleges where you've been accepted again. Talk with alumni, attend an accepted-student reception. Then confidently make your college choice official by sending in your deposit. Done!

Work w/ dad on FAFSA

Begin writing essay

Study!

Ned Johnson is founder of and tutor-geek at PrepMatters (prepmatters.com) where, along with colleagues, he torments teens with test prep, educational counseling and general attempts to help them thrive. He also is co-author of "Conquering the SAT: How Parents Can Help Teens Overcome the Pressure and Succeed."

WHY I PICKED...

Creighton University
Omaha, Nebraska

Ashley Weed, CLASS OF 2017

Creighton sent me a handwritten note to tell me I'd been accepted. This kind of warmth and personal attention – and the school's tradition of scholastic excellence, service and leadership – made it an easy decision to accept.

Once at Creighton, I entered the College of Arts and Sciences' four-year Honors Program. Freshman year we lived together on the same floor and shared the same core classes. I value this close-knit community of scholars and the flexibility we have in choosing classes to fulfill our requirements across all academic disciplines from the natural sciences to fine arts.

The university encourages students to pursue diverse interests, and mine range from psychology to art history. I've been able to build close relationships with my professors in the Classical and Near Eastern Studies and psychology departments, and they've helped me take advantage of different opportunities. Through the Center for Undergraduate Research and Scholarship, I studied ancient Roman artifacts including a first-century bust at Omaha's Joslyn Art Museum. As a sorority member, I led campus initiatives promoting academic achievement and wellness. These experiences have enabled me to get the kind of well-rounded liberal arts education Creighton emphasizes and which is so enriching. ●

> CREIGHTON SENT ME A HANDWRITTEN NOTE TO TELL ME I'D BEEN ACCEPTED.

RICE UNIVERSITY

BRANDON THIBODEAUX FOR USN&WR

Rice University
Houston

Griffin Thomas, CLASS OF 2017

I chose Rice because it melds an intimate liberal arts education with the research opportunities of much larger institutions. As a political science major, I've been able take small classes and develop relationships with professors who actively spend time with students outside of class, whether sharing a meal or inviting them to events off campus. At Rice, most students, regardless of their major, can do research. I spent last summer researching the operations of nonprofits in Salta, Argentina. I have met some of the world's

CREIGHTON
UNIVERSITY

preeminent political thinkers who've given speeches on campus and attended small lunches with renowned government officials that were sponsored by Rice's Baker Institute for Public Policy.

Nestled in the fourth largest city in the U.S., we never have a shortage of concerts, plays, cultural shows, parks and restaurants to explore. But the community is what I love most about Rice. The students here are endlessly collaborative. Many become volunteer advisers for their peers, providing academic, health and career guidance, among other things. And each night, if you wander into the residential commons, you'll find students tutoring each other for an exam, proofreading a paper, or discussing assignments. It's comforting. ●

> AT RICE, MOST STUDENTS, REGARDLESS OF THEIR MAJOR, CAN DO RESEARCH.

Colby College
Waterville, Maine

Lucas Lam, CLASS OF 2017

Growing up in Southern California, the coldest place I had ever visited before Colby was my refrigerator. But the school offered to pay my way for a campus visit, and I quickly felt at home despite the temperature shock.

There's no typical Colby student. Undergrads tend to have wide interests and reflect the diversity the college values. Our radio station, for example, is run by a biology and history double major. I am a Science, Technology and Society and physics double major headed to a career in government affairs and public policy. Professors are extremely accessible and involved. If you have a passion, they really want to help you achieve it. A professor once even offered me his frequent flier miles so I could go to a human rights conference. Colby also has a monthlong "Jan Plan" program each year in January. We can take a course, travel abroad, or intern off campus. Through Jan Plan, I have interned with a nonprofit working with disadvantaged students in LA County and pro bono lawyers helping clients with housing issues in San Francisco. It was a big leap leaving my comfort zone to come to Colby, but it was the best decision I ever made. ●

> THERE IS NO TYPICAL COLBY STUDENT. UNDERGRADS TEND TO HAVE WIDE INTERESTS.

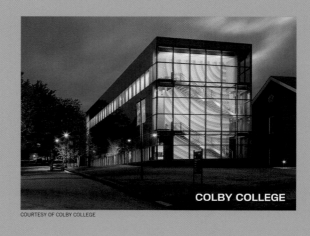

COLBY COLLEGE

Finding the Money

5

ON CAMPUS AT THE
UNIVERSITY OF MISSISSIPPI

BRETT ZIEGLER FOR USN&WR

9 Things You Need to Know to Get a

GREAT DEAL

You can improve your odds of getting the financial aid you need by understanding how the process works

BY ARLENE WEINTRAUB

NEWS YOU CAN USE

Want to nab your share of the $150 billion Uncle Sam will be handing out in financial aid as you head off to college? And a portion of the money your school of choice has set aside for its own awards? There are a multitude of details to consider when you're angling for aid, from the newly changed application deadlines to the complicated calculations schools make to arrive at their offers. Here are our top tips for navigating your way to success.

1

You must fill out the aid forms (and do it early)

THE FREE APPLICATION FOR FEDERAL STUDENT AID is a must-do for anyone hoping for help from the government. It asks parents to provide information about their own assets and those of their applicant and shoots back the "expected family contribution" that colleges use to assemble aid packages. It's essential to fill out this form as early as possible during senior year, because many schools award money on a first-come-first-served basis. And as of this year, the FAFSA calendar has moved up by three months, meaning those who will be college freshmen in the fall of 2017 can tackle the form as early as Oct. 1 of this year.

There are other changes to the FAFSA process that are important to understand, too. First, you no longer have to plug in figures from your most recent tax return. Previously, families who filed the FAFSA early in the new year had to estimate the numbers and then correct them after their return was finished. Now, you can instead use what's called prior-prior year tax information. So if you're applying in the fall of 2016 for the 2017-18 school year, you will use your 2015 tax information.

Be aware that some savings and investments that previously would not have counted against you in calculating

One Student's Strategy:
LIVE AT HOME AND WORK

AT WORK AT THE
COFFEE SHOP

Sarah Swainson
Chattanooga State Community College

Just before Sarah Swainson graduated from high school in Chattanooga, Tennessee, in 2014, she landed a job as a server at a coffee shop, Milk & Honey. She liked the job so much she decided to take a gap year between high school and college to work there full-time, eventually getting promoted to barista and then to manager. The $18,000 she saved from her salary and tips while living at home gave her a huge financial cushion when she enrolled at Chattanooga State Community College in 2015.

Swainson was able to win a HOPE Scholarship, too – an award funded by Tennessee's lottery and given out to students with a minimum of 21 on the ACT or 980 on the SAT and a GPA of at least 3.0. The scholarship covers her $2,000 per semester in tuition and will renew annually as long as she maintains the minimum 3.0 GPA. Swainson is still working 20 hours a week at the restaurant and living at home, earning up to $500 a week, which helps her cover the cost of books, gas and cellphone as well as chip in for the family's groceries.

Prepping to transfer. Swainson plans to transfer to the University of Tennessee at Chattanooga in the fall of 2017, a school that will cost her twice as much in tuition. But by continuing to live at home and work, while maintaining good spending habits (like resisting the urge to eat out several times a week with her friends), she has eased her concerns about being able to afford the tuition increase.

"I take about 20 to 30 percent of my paycheck and set it aside for spending money, and the rest is for savings," says Swainson. "I haven't had to touch the savings yet," she says, so her kitty now amounts to $22,000.

What's the best way to juggle a part-time job and a full-time education? Swainson, who is planning a career in recreation management, says she takes time at the beginning of each week to draw up a plan of how she'll need to allot her time: which hours she'll be working, when she'll be in class, and what pockets of each day will be left over for getting her studying done. –A.W.

your expected contribution may be included in the future. The amount of these so-called protected assets that families can hold without being penalized varies according to the age and marital status of the parents, but overall it's on a downward trend. For example, for a student whose eldest parent is 48, the limit plummeted from $30,300 in 2015-16 to $18,700 in 2016-17, according to Edvisors, an online college information site.

That said, there are some simple ways to plan your finances that should work to your advantage. Edvisors recommends that you balance any capital gains you report on your return with capital losses, avoid exercising stock options in the tax year that will be reflected on your FAFSA, and be strategic about taking distributions from 529 savings plans. Distributions from 529 plans that are owned by aunts, uncles or grandparents have to be reported as untaxed income, which can affect financial aid. Distributions from 529 plans owned by parents or students, on the other hand, won't count against you.

Heads up that you may need to fill out a second form as well as the FAFSA: the College Board's CSS/Financial Aid Profile. The CSS is a much more in-depth form required by about 300 colleges and scholarship programs to help these institutions determine which families should get their own nonfederal money. It's often due even earlier than the FAFSA, so be aware of each school's deadline.

The FAFSA doesn't require families to report the value of their home or retirement accounts; the Profile does. It gets at the value of a business and "splits out income, so you can see, for example, whether there is income or losses from a business," says Sara Beth Holman, director of financial aid at Lawrence University in Wisconsin. The CSS also takes into account factors like the cost of living in big cities vs. rural areas and allows for a larger proportion of income to be protected than the FAFSA does.

An elite private college might well cost less than a public university

"DON'T BE AFRAID OF ELITE UNIVERSITIES because of their high tuition prices. They also have a lot of aid and grants to give out," advises Laurie Martin, director of undergraduate and graduate consulting at Stratus Prep, a New York-based admissions consultancy. In fact, while public universities are struggling with tight budgets, tuition "discounting" by private colleges in the form of grants and scholarships reached an all-time high in the 2014-15 school year, according to a report from the National Association of College and University Business Officers. The average discount rate was 48 percent for freshmen, up from 46.4 percent the previous year. For all undergraduates, the discount rate rose from 39.8 percent to 41.6 percent. Furthermore, the proportion of freshmen at elite colleges who were receiving grant aid rose very slightly, to 89 percent.

Martin also notes that "universities are trying to address student debt more than ever before." Toward that end, a few schools have opted to become "no loan" universities, meaning their pockets are deep enough to meet your full need without any loans. Northwestern University joined the ranks of no-loan schools earlier this year, announcing that it would be eliminating loans for incoming undergrads thanks to more than $147 million in gifts and endowment earnings. "It's a huge step. Incoming students there won't even have to get Stafford loans," says Kevin Fudge, manager of consumer advocacy and government relations at American Student Assistance, a Boston-based nonprofit that educates students on the financial aspects of obtaining a college degree. Other schools with no-loan or minimal-loan policies include the University of Chicago, Davidson College in North Carolina, Vanderbilt University in Tennessee, and all of the Ivy League schools.

Sports Scholarships
CAN YOU GET PAID TO PLAY?

Here's what you need to know to catch a coach's eye

Rachel Scott knew back in middle school that she wanted to play softball for a top team in college and get a scholarship to do so. So as an eighth-grader, she drew up a list of universities whose teams she admired and started emailing the coaches. "I'd say, 'My name is Rachel Scott. I've attached my résumé, and I'm playing at this tournament near you,'" Scott says. "I did that through 10th grade."

Whether or not anyone ever showed up to watch her, Scott definitely got noticed. After her junior year playing for Plano East Senior High School in Texas, her coach started hearing from colleges she had targeted. She settled on the University of Texas–Austin, where she earned a partial sports scholarship to play for the Longhorns, a Division I team. Scott, who earned her bachelor's in business in 2015 and stayed on to get a master's in advertising, supplemented the award with a handful of other financial awards, including academic scholarships from the university and from her hometown church.

The competition for athletic scholarships can be as fierce as any encountered on the playing field, so winning a grant requires starting early. The probability of high school athletes competing on an NCAA Division I or II team ranges from 1 percent to 5 percent for men and 1 percent to 9 percent for women depending on the sport, according to the NCAA. (The probability of making a Division III team is higher, but those teams

Your family "need" may not be what you think

COLLEGES DETERMINE HOW MUCH aid students need based on the gap between the cost of attending the school and the expected family contribution. Many families are shocked

RACHEL
SCOTT, RIGHT

on't offer athletic scholarships.) The 250-plus colleges and universities that participate in the National Association of Intercollegiate Athletics also offer some $500 million in scholarships. The NAIA has added a variety of scholarship-eligible sports to the usual roster in recent years, including competitive cheer and lacrosse.

Game plan. So what's the best strategy? While NCAA coaches are not allowed to start recruiting high school students until the summer after junior year, they are certainly paying attention earlier. Coaches attend high school tournaments,

check out player stats online, and start making lists of potential future recruits. So it's important to get on the radar. Make sure any email you send is tailored to the school and coach, advises Julianne Soviero, who played Division I softball and is now a sports consultant and author of "Empowered Recruiting: A Student-Athlete's College Selection Guide." You could say "something like 'Congratulations on your recent win against UCLA. I was particularly excited to see Hofstra beat such a highly ranked school and advance in the playoffs.'" After that, she says, you should list your recent athletic ac-

to realize that they're expected to contribute $15,000 or $20,000 a year, and that the amount is not part of their need. It's also quite possible that each school a student applies to will decide what to do about his or her need completely differently than the others do. Some schools will come up with a package that meets a family's full need as determined by the FAFSA form. Others will not offer enough to cover all the costs that exceed the EFC, forcing the family to figure out how to manage even more than their expected contribution.

It's important to understand how packaging works

IT GOES WITHOUT SAYING that the more free money you can get in the form of grants and scholarships, the better. So you want to pay close attention to the components of

> **I have big dreams and big aspirations. That's why my scholarship was such a blessing.**
>
> – Quinton, Class of 2016

Quinton was putting in 20-hour days, balancing schoolwork with early morning cheerleading and aerial practice, and an after-school job. All of that hard work helped him win a scholarship from Sallie Mae®!

How will you turn your college dreams into reality?

Scholarships Our Scholarship Search is a great place to start. Access more than 5 million college scholarships, worth up to $24 billion. Not only is it free, but we're awarding $1,000 to one student each month, just for registering.*

SallieMae.com/ScholarshipMoney

Smart Option Student Loan® If you have to borrow money to pay for college, it's important to find a loan that fits your needs. This loan features competitive interest rates, three repayment options, and coverage of up to 100% of the school-certified cost of attendance.

SallieMae.com/SOSL

Sallie Mae Parent Loan℠ Your parents can give you the gift of education by financing your college expenses in their own name. This loan features competitive interest rates, two repayment options, and coverage of up to 100% of the school-certified cost of attendance.

SallieMae.com/ParentOptions

Find your way at SallieMae.com/USN

complishments and academic achievements.

Don't be afraid to brag about your grades and SAT scores. "We want to make sure our prospective student athletes are able to do well in college and that they have the foundation to succeed and to graduate," says David Schnase, vice president of academic and membership affairs for the NCAA. Towards that end, the NCAA has tightened its eligibility rules, mandating as of 2016 that all Division I recruits, for example, maintain a GPA of 2.3 throughout high school (vs. the old standard of 2.0) and that they complete 10 of 16 required core courses in English, math and science, for example, before the start of senior year. The rules vary by division. All student athletes are required to maintain certain academic standards in college for their scholarships to renew.

Most athletes don't get a full ride; the average award ranges from $12,359 to $17,529 per student per year for NCAA players and $12,537 in the NAIA, according to ScholarshipStats.com. But coaches often work with the financial aid office to add to the package. Even if you're not offered enough at the outset, the coach might entertain an appeal. "If a coach offers $10,000 every year, and Mom and Dad really need $15,000, it's OK to ask," says Tiffany Christian, assistant athletic director of compliance at the College of William and Mary, a Division I school. That's especially true if you have a better offer from another school. But be honest, advises Christian, who herself played soccer at Washington State and Boston universities. "It's a small business. Coaches will call each other" to check on reported offers, she says.

Is it smart to post an online résumé and video of yourself in action at one of the many sites that offer this service? It's not a bad idea, says NAIA spokesman Lynn Meredith. But he recommends including more than just the highlights. "If you're a football player, coaches want to see how quickly you get to the huddle," he says. "Put a whole game out there." The idea is to allow anyone you'd like to impress to see you giving it your all. –A. W.

funding sources for particular students. So if a college really wants that oboe-playing, straight-A student to fill an opening for an oboist in the school orchestra, her $20,000 package might include $3,000 in federal grants, $7,000 in scholarships, and $10,000 in loans while a kid who has the same GPA but plays volleyball instead is offered $2,000 in federal grants, $6,000 in scholarships, and $12,000 in loans.

Besides making the most of your talents as you search for scholarships, it's a good idea to apply to at least a handful of schools where your academic credentials will stand out. Those schools are good bets to make attractive aid offers. "I tell students to consider schools they might have otherwise overlooked," Fudge says.

5

Your external scholarships might count against you

REGARDLESS OF HOW RICH the financial aid package offered by your dream school is, experts advise supplementing your award by applying for private scholarships from companies, churches and the many other groups that offer them – provided your target schools endorse that strategy. The opportunities are vast: The online search tool Scholarships.com lists 3.7 million scholarships and grants totaling over $19 billion. Most people can and should apply for these opportunities every year of their college education, counselors say.

But you do need to ensure there won't be any ramifications, advises Kevin Ladd, Scholarships.com's chief operating officer. Federal law requires that universities lower financial aid packages when the sum of money from all sources is $300 or more above a family's calculated need. Be sure to specifically ask to review all outside scholarship policies. "You have to always make sure that the school you're going to isn't going to take whatever you win and rescind their financial aid offer," Ladd says. "They all have a policy in place, and they will tell you what it is."

Pell Grants aren't affected, he notes, and many colleges will work with you to first apply the outside scholarship funding to any unmet need. Then they often apply it to reducing your loan burden before resorting to lowering their initial offer.

your aid offers and not just focus on the bottom-line amounts. The typical financial aid package consists of scholarships from the school, if any, plus money from government sources such as the Pell Grant for low-income students, the Stafford loan and other loans that don't have to be repaid until after college, and the offer of a work-study job on campus. Parents might also be offered the opportunity to borrow up to the full cost of college via a PLUS loan.

But colleges can choose how they mix and match the

You can look for ways to save on costs beyond tuition

ROOM, BOARD, BOOKS and incidental expenses make up a substantial portion of college costs. Room and board expenses for four-year public colleges during the 2015-16 school year rose 3.6 percent on average to $10,138, according to the College Board. Those costs at private four-year colleges were up 3.2 percent to $11,516.

You can often shave your bill by carefully considering the various options available at your chosen university, notes Chris Collins, who recently retired as associate director of the office of financial aid and scholarships at San Diego State University. One example: You might forgo a meal plan that covers a fixed number of meals per week and opt for a flexible alternative such as a "declining balance" account. Such plans allow you to deposit a certain amount of money into an account that is tapped with a debit card

ON CAMPUS AT DUKE

One Student's Strategy:
FIND SCHOLARSHIPS

Jonathan Salazar

Duke and Yale

When Jonathan Salazar of Albuquerque, New Mexico, started looking for college scholarships, he was only in ninth grade – and, boy, did the early planning pay off. All told, he was offered $1.8 million by schools that accepted him, and ended up with $70,000 to use at $67,654-a-year Duke University. Salazar, an excellent student who wanted to study out of state but couldn't afford to without plenty of aid, says he knew "I would have to apply for a lot of scholarships."

In addition to getting academic and need-based awards from Duke to cover tuition and housing and $1,500 from the New Mexico National Honor Society, Salazar was named a Gates Millennium Scholar. Funded by Microsoft co-founder Bill Gates, the Millennium Scholars program supports 1,000 minority students a year. The rigorous application process – Salazar had to write eight 1,000-word essays over six

months – paid off with $10,000 for his freshman year alone. The Gates scholarship will renew every year, as his Duke award would have had he not decided to transfer to Yale this fall for sophomore year. (The Gates awards also renew through grad school in certain disciplines.)

The other grants and awards he brought to Duke included $5,000 from the Hearst Foundation, whose Senate Youth Program sent him on a weeklong trip to Washington, D.C.,

during high school. Salazar also received about $5,700 in needs-based grant funding from the federal government. The Gates scholarship follows him to Yale, and the university is offsetting the balance with grants and a scholarship.

Besides starting early, Salazar went out of his way to form bonds with his teachers. "They're going to be your recommenders," he says. It was those relationships that guided him to the Gates program. –A.W.

at eateries around campus. Many schools offer them with no fees or minimum balance requirements.

"We've found that a lot of students don't opt for two sit-down meals a day at their residence halls," Collins says. Paying for those meals will just be a waste of money.

Work-study opportunities can pay off in more ways than one

ABOUT 3,400 UNIVERSITIES receive federal funding to provide part-time work-study jobs, which eligible students are offered as part of their aid package. And some schools provide "co-op" opportunities, cooperative education jobs at partnering companies that allow students to earn money, gain credits towards their degrees, and get experience in their chosen field at the same time.

These work opportunities provide not just a funding boost but also valuable real-world experience that can kick-start a career. Work-study jobs may be available on or off campus and are often related to your area of study. Students earn at least the federal minimum wage and possibly more if the job requires special skills. The amount you can earn is limited by your aid award, though: Financial aid officers will determine how many hours you can work each week based on how much work-study funding per semester you're allotted. You should indicate on your FAFSA that you're interested in the opportunity.

Students who attend a school with co-ops, which typically involve periods of work interspersed with periods of class time so that the lessons learned build on each other, needn't worry about it affecting their financial aid going forward. "Because you're on a prear-ranged agreement between a company and the school, the earnings you get paid can be excluded from your earnings on the FAFSA," says Linda Fontaine, assistant director of financial aid at Michigan Technological University. About 18 percent of students there do a co-op.

Alex Ball, a Michigan Tech student set to graduate in 2018, opted for a full-year co-op in 2015 at American Axle & Manufacturing, a Detroit-based maker of auto supplies. It pushed his graduation back a year, but in addition to earning some credits and $60,000, "it gave me hands-on experience," says Ball, who is majoring in materials science and engineering and minoring in manufacturing. "In one class we learned about how inducing an electric current in a metal coil will create a magnetic field," he recalls. "When I got to this co-op, it showed me that what I was studying applied to the real world."

If you must borrow, it's best to choose federal loans first

IN GENERAL, FEDERAL LOANS OFFER the most attractive features. They don't have to be repaid until after graduation, they have fixed rates, and most are eligible for repayment plans that base monthly payments on income. And in some cases, the government will eventually forgive the loan, canceling the repayment requirement for people who have worked in public service careers for 10 years, for example. In recent years, private lenders have started to offer fixed-rate student loans and flexible repayment options, too, though the most favorable terms might require a parent to co-sign.

Students with demonstrated need can get subsidized federal Stafford loans, meaning the government pays the interest while you're in college. Students without demonstrated need can take out federal Stafford loans that aren't subsidized, meaning the interest will accumulate. The cur-

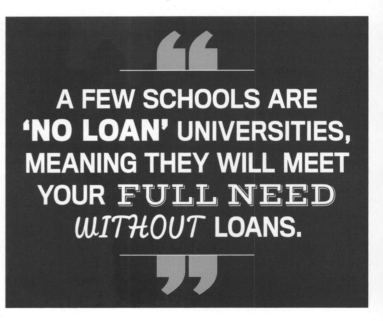

> A FEW SCHOOLS ARE 'NO LOAN' UNIVERSITIES, MEANING THEY WILL MEET YOUR FULL NEED WITHOUT LOANS.

rent cap for Stafford loans for freshmen who rely on their parents financially is $5,500, of which $3,500 can be subsidized. Freshmen who are not dependents can borrow up to $9,500. The caps increase in subsequent years.

You can appeal your package (respectfully)

WHEN A FINANCIAL AID OFFER doesn't measure up to what other universities are dangling, you may well be able to

successfully appeal for more money. Many colleges and universities are willing to compete for students they want and are open to hearing about a better offer from another institution. And if your circumstances have changed since you filled out the FAFSA, perhaps because of a job loss or onerous medical expense, financial aid officers certainly want to hear from you. Be specific about your reasons for wanting more. And it's best to be polite. You're unlikely to get happy cooperation from a demanding phone call.

You improve your odds by acting fast, says Lynne Martin, executive director of Students Rising Above, a San Francisco nonprofit that helps low-income first-generation students get into and through college. "Within 24 hours of receiving the offer, pick up the phone or write that financial aid officer and tell your story," Martin advises. "Get in there early. You want to be one of the first people for whom they're reconsidering" an award so you can receive as much of what's left as possible. ●

One Family's Strategy:
BE A LANDLORD

Paige Adams

Kennesaw State University

Paige Adams, who graduates from Kennesaw State University near Atlanta in 2017, has had 80 percent of her $7,000-a-year tuition paid for by the HOPE Scholarship she won from the state of Georgia for those with GPAs of at least 3.0, with another award covering the rest. Her other expenses? Before the start of freshman year, she looked for a way to live near the university without incurring thousands of dollars in housing fees.

Adams' mother and stepfather have a home just seven miles from campus, but they wanted to support her quest for independence. So the family came up with an innovative solution: Adams found a townhouse near campus that had gone into foreclosure, they snapped it up for $36,000 in cash, and Adams took charge of finding a roommate to help cover utilities, property taxes and maintenance. The $500 per month her roommate pays in rent goes most of the way, with her parents helping out some, too. And

ON HER TOWNHOUSE PORCH

Adams says that being a homeowner has offered her other benefits.

Handling the upkeep. "I learned a lot about the foreclosure process, and I had to manage renovations," says Adams, who plans to attend veterinary school after graduation. "I've learned to pay bills and do home maintenance." So far, she has removed wallpaper from the kitchen, stained the kitchen cabinets, landscaped the backyard, and changed out some doorknobs.

Adams also thinks her housing is more comfortable than a dorm or off-campus apartment would have been. "Some of my friends live five in a house," she says.

Her stepfather, Bruce Ailion, happens to be a real estate broker in Atlanta, but he says parents need no special training to use property ownership as a strategy for saving money on college. And it can pay off even after a child's graduation, depending on the location and purchase price. "If you own a property that's close to a major university, it will always be in demand from renters," Ailion says. And it could be a good investment. He estimates that the value of his family's townhome, a 1,200-square-foot two-bedroom unit, has skyrocketed to $85,000 in just four years. –A.W.

Scholarships for SCIENTISTS

Financial awards to reel students into STEM fields are multiplying, and an online search will turn up hundreds of sources. Below is a sampling of what students with the right qualifications can compete for; some are open to all STEM students, while others target members of underrepresented groups. Requirements vary. College-bound seniors can apply for many; a number are only for students already in college.

For all STEM students

■ **Buick Achievers Scholarship Program.** Fifty incoming or current college students get up to $25,000, renewable for up to four years (buickachievers.com).

■ **Great Lakes National Scholarship Program.** The student loan servicer offers up to 825 STEM scholarships of $2,500 (community.mygreatlakes.org).

■ **SMART Scholarship for Service Program.** This Department of Defense program provides full tuition and a stipend to students in STEM willing to work for the DOD upon graduation (smart.asee.org).

■ **Scholarship America Dream Award.** This renewable STEM award goes to students entering at least their second year of college (scholarshipamerica.org).

■ **American Society of Civil Engineers Scholarships.** Awards of $2,500 to $5,000 go to ASCE student members (asce.org).

■ **American Society of Mechanical Engineers awards.** ASME offers scholarships for current undergraduate students studying mechanical engineering or mechanical engineering technology (asme.org).

3 Reasons to Take the SAT®

1 It's accepted at all colleges.
2 It lets you show what you know.
3 You can practice for free online at Khan Academy®.

Register now:
sat.org/ready

■ **American Institute of Aeronautics and Astronautics awards.** For undergrads in aerospace-related or engineering programs (aiaa-awards.org).

■ **Siemens Competition in Math, Science & Technology.** Winners and finalists get from $1,000 to $100,000 (siemenscompetition.discoveryeducation.com).

■ **Regeneron Science Talent Search.** Hundreds of semifinalists win $2,000 each. Finalists compete for awards up to $250,000. (student.societyforscience.org).

■ **Thermo Fisher Scientific Antibody Scholarship Program.** Provides scholarships from $5,000 to $10,000 for undergraduate and graduate students to expand opportunities for future scientists (thermofisher.com).

For women

■ **Google Anita Borg Memorial Scholarship.** In honor of the founder of the Institute for Women and Technology, Google awards $10,000 to students of computer science or computer engineering (google.com/anitaborg).

■ **Palantir Women in Technology Scholarship.** The global software technology company offers 10 grants ranging from $1,500 to $10,000 to women studying computer science or STEM fields (palantir.com/college/scholarship).

■ **Society of Women Engineers awards.** Offers scholarships from $1,000 to $15,000 for women pursuing undergraduate and graduate degrees in engineering, engineering technology and computer science (swe.org).

■ **VIP Women in Technology Scholarship program.** Offers multiple scholarships of up to $2,500 each for women who are attending or are planning to attend a two- or four-year college (trustvip.com).

■ **Association for Women Geoscientists Awards and Scholarships.** AWG offers scholarships (and in some cases mentoring) to undergraduate women pursuing degrees and careers in the geosciences (awg.org).

■ **Women in Aviation International awards.** WAI provides dozens of scholarships and training opportunities for women working towards a degree either in aeronautical engineering or a related field (wai.org).

For underrepresented minorities

■ **Gates Millennium Scholars Program.** Tuition and expenses for undergraduate minority students with need in any field (gmsp.org).

■ **Xerox Technical Minority Scholarship Program.** Ranges between $1,000 and $10,000 for minority students in a technical or engineering field (xerox.com/jobs/minority-scholarships).

■ **National Action Council for Minorities in Engineering STEM Minority Scholarships.** For African-American, Latino or American Indian undergraduate students pursuing degrees in engineering (nacme.org/scholarships).

■ **National Society of Black Engineers awards.** NSBE and corporate partners such as Northrop Grumman and Chevron award engineering scholarships (nsbe.org).

■ **United Negro College Fund/Merck Science Initiative awards.** Scholarships for African-American students to further their science education (umsi.uncf.org).

■ **Society of Hispanic Professional Engineers awards.** The society offers a range of STEM-related scholarships for students (shpe.org).

■ **Hispanic Scholarship Fund.** Awards for Hispanic students in various majors, with an emphasis on STEM (hsf.net).

■ **HENAAC Scholars Program.** This organization offers scholarships ranging from $500 to $10,000 for college students who are of Hispanic descent (greatmindsinstem.org).

■ **The Google Lime Scholarship.** Google offers $10,000 scholarships for computer science or computer engineering students with disabilities (google.com/edu/students).

■ **The Generation Google Scholarship.** Students in underrepresented groups pursuing computer science or computer engineering or a closely related field are eligible for a $10,000 scholarship (google.com/edu/students).

■ **The National Institutes of Health Undergraduate Scholarship Program.** Up to $20,000, renewable for four years, for disadvantaged students pursuing biomedical, behavioral and social science health-related research (training.nih.gov/programs).

■ **Microsoft Scholarship Program.** Scholarships and internships for promising students in the STEM disciplines. Priority is given to minority students, women and people with disabilities (careers.microsoft.com/students).

■ **Ronald McDonald House Charities U.S. Scholarships.** Scholarship opportunities for African-American, Latino and Asian-American students in any field (rmhc.org). ●

MAKE BREAKFAST HAPPEN SO KIDS CAN BE HUNGRY FOR MORE

I was one of our nation's hungry kids growing up. Today, 1 in 5 children in America struggle with hunger. But when they get breakfast, their days are bigger and brighter. Learning, attention, memory and mood improve. Together, we have the power to get breakfast to kids in your neighborhood — let's make it happen. Go to hungeris.org and lend your time or your voice.

Viola
Viola Davis, Hunger Is Ambassador

HUNGER IS®

Great Schools, Great Prices

Which colleges and universities offer students the best value? The calculation used here takes into account a school's academic quality, based on its U.S. News Best Colleges ranking, and the 2015-16 net cost of attendance for a student who received the average level of need-based financial aid. The higher the quality of the program and the lower the cost, the better the deal. Only schools in or near the top half of their U.S. News ranking categories are included because U.S. News considers the most significant values to be among colleges that perform well academically.

National Universities ▶

Rank	School (State) (*Public)	% receiving grants based on need ('15)	Average cost after receiving grants based on need ('15)	Average discount from total cost ('15)
1.	Harvard University (MA)	55%	$15,867	75%
2.	Princeton University (NJ)	59%	$16,890	72%
3.	Yale University (CT)	49%	$18,485	72%
4.	Stanford University (CA)	47%	$19,677	70%
5.	Massachusetts Inst. of Technology	57%	$21,572	66%
6.	Columbia University (NY)	48%	$21,594	69%
7.	Dartmouth College (NH)	49%	$22,872	66%
8.	Duke University (NC)	40%	$21,628	67%
9.	California Institute of Technology	52%	$24,488	61%
10.	Brown University (RI)	44%	$22,815	65%
11.	University of Pennsylvania	47%	$25,202	62%
12.	U. of North Carolina–Chapel Hill*	41%	$18,207	63%
13.	University of Chicago	43%	$26,475	62%
14.	Rice University (TX)	37%	$22,478	62%
15.	Brigham Young Univ.–Provo (UT)	39%	$12,650	29%
16.	Cornell University (NY)	45%	$27,117	59%
17.	Emory University (GA)	39%	$23,618	63%
18.	Northwestern University (IL)	43%	$27,852	59%
19.	Clarkson University (NY)	82%	$32,957	47%
20.	Johns Hopkins University (MD)	44%	$29,459	55%
21.	Texas A&M Univ.–College Station*	63%	$23,794	45%
22.	St. John Fisher College (NY)	80%	$26,895	40%
23.	University of Rochester (NY)	51%	$27,879	57%
24.	Mercer University (GA)	70%	$25,115	50%
25.	University of Notre Dame (IN)	42%	$28,968	55%
26.	Univ. of California–Santa Cruz*	48%	$22,372	63%
27.	Clark University (MA)	58%	$25,262	51%
28.	Wake Forest University (NC)	31%	$23,738	63%
29.	Pepperdine University (CA)	53%	$29,271	56%
30.	Brandeis University (MA)	47%	$28,628	57%
31.	Washington University in St. Louis	41%	$31,111	55%
32.	Rensselaer Polytechnic Inst. (NY)	61%	$35,229	47%
33.	Rochester Inst. of Technology (NY)	70%	$31,067	39%
34.	Georgetown University (DC)	34%	$27,195	60%
35.	Tufts University (MA)	35%	$26,192	60%
36.	Illinois Institute of Technology	57%	$29,007	52%
37.	Duquesne University (PA)	65%	$28,689	41%
38.	Lehigh University (PA)	39%	$25,697	58%
39.	University of the Pacific (CA)	67%	$37,080	39%
40.	SUNY Col. of Envir. Sci. and Forestry*	67%	$27,275	21%
41.	Boston College	36%	$28,691	56%
42.	Worcester Polytechnic Inst. (MA)	62%	$38,264	37%
43.	Case Western Reserve Univ. (OH)	50%	$33,613	46%
44.	Syracuse University (NY)	50%	$32,807	46%
45.	Carnegie Mellon University (PA)	41%	$34,223	48%
46.	University of Virginia*	27%	$26,801	54%
47.	Loyola University Chicago	64%	$36,496	35%
48.	University of California–Irvine*	20%	$22,294	61%
49.	Yeshiva University (NY)	48%	$32,592	44%
50.	Marquette University (WI)	56%	$32,817	36%

National Liberal Arts Colleges ▶

Rank	School (State) (*Public)	% receiving grants based on need ('15)	Average cost after receiving grants based on need ('15)	Average discount from total cost ('15)
1.	Wellesley College (MA)	63%	$17,378	73%
2.	Amherst College (MA)	57%	$18,088	73%
3.	Virginia Military Institute*	52%	$12,216	76%
4.	Williams College (MA)	48%	$20,233	69%
5.	Pomona College (CA)	55%	$19,696	70%
6.	Swarthmore College (PA)	52%	$20,104	69%
7.	Vassar College (NY)	60%	$20,961	68%
8.	Soka University of America (CA)	92%	$21,801	53%
9.	Washington and Lee University (VA)	41%	$18,913	69%
10.	Grinnell College (IA)	68%	$22,886	63%
11.	Middlebury College (VT)	44%	$21,878	66%
12.	Haverford College (PA)	50%	$21,473	68%
13.	Bowdoin College (ME)	45%	$21,858	66%
14.	Principia College (IL)	70%	$15,011	64%
15.	Davidson College (NC)	51%	$22,754	64%
16.	College of the Atlantic (ME)	84%	$20,556	61%
17.	Earlham College (IN)	82%	$22,443	60%
18.	Colgate University (NY)	37%	$21,479	67%
19.	Colby College (ME)	37%	$21,444	66%
20.	Hamilton College (NY)	48%	$23,200	64%
21.	Macalester College (MN)	68%	$26,466	58%
22.	Smith College (MA)	59%	$26,409	59%
23.	Agnes Scott College (GA)	78%	$23,050	54%
24.	Thomas Aquinas College (CA)	67%	$20,747	42%
25.	Carleton College (MN)	56%	$27,913	57%
26.	University of Richmond (VA)	39%	$22,325	64%
27.	Hollins University (VA)	82%	$22,226	56%
28.	Wesleyan University (CT)	43%	$24,349	63%
29.	Ripon College (WI)	84%	$22,041	53%
30.	Knox College (IL)	77%	$23,816	55%
31.	St. Olaf College (MN)	68%	$24,898	55%
32.	Claremont McKenna College (CA)	38%	$25,544	61%
33.	Trinity College (CT)	43%	$23,451	65%
34.	Colorado College	34%	$23,062	64%
35.	Mount Holyoke College (MA)	65%	$27,545	53%
36.	Bryn Mawr College (PA)	50%	$25,803	60%
37.	Franklin and Marshall College (PA)	51%	$24,081	63%
38.	Bates College (ME)	43%	$24,657	62%
39.	Lake Forest College (IL)	76%	$23,387	58%
40.	Barnard College (NY)	41%	$24,600	62%

Methodology: The rankings were based on the following three variables: **1.** Ratio of quality to price: a school's overall score in the latest Best Colleges rankings divided by the net cost to a student receiving the average need-based scholarship or grant. The higher the ratio of rank to the discounted cost (tuition, fees, room and board, and other expenses less average scholarship or grant), the better the value. **2.** Percentage of all undergrads receiving need-based scholarships or grants during the 2015-16 year. **3.** Average discount: percentage of a school's total costs for 2015-16 covered by the average need-based scholarship or grant to undergrads. For public institutions, 2015-16 out-of-state tuition and percentage of out-of-state students receiving need-based scholarships or grants were used. Only those schools ranked in or near the top half of their U.S. News ranking categories were considered. Ranks were determined by standardizing scores achieved by every school in each of the three variables and weighting those scores. Ratio of quality to price accounted for 60 percent of the overall score; percentage of undergrads receiving need-based grants, for 25 percent; and average discount, for 15 percent. The school with the most total weighted points became No. 1 in its category.

Regional Universities ►

Rank School (State) (*Public)	% receiving grants based on need ('15)	Average cost after receiving grants based on need ('15)	Average discount from total cost ('15)
NORTH			
1. **Gallaudet University** (DC)	76%	$15,141	58%
2. **Lebanon Valley College** (PA)	85%	$28,299	47%
3. **Geneva College** (PA)	82%	$20,752	44%
4. **Le Moyne College** (NY)	82%	$26,986	43%
5. **Simmons College** (MA)	78%	$30,191	45%
6. **St. Bonaventure University** (NY)	72%	$23,967	46%
7. **Waynesburg University** (PA)	81%	$20,418	39%
8. **Canisius College** (NY)	76%	$27,027	46%
9. **Niagara University** (NY)	76%	$24,469	45%
10. **Gannon University** (PA)	76%	$24,675	44%
11. **Seton Hill University** (PA)	87%	$28,326	40%
12. **Springfield College** (MA)	80%	$28,307	42%
13. **Hood College** (MD)	78%	$28,440	44%
14. **Norwich University** (VT)	74%	$25,973	51%
15. **Arcadia University** (PA)	75%	$29,636	46%
SOUTH			
1. **The Citadel** (SC)*	43%	$14,947	61%
2. **William Carey University** (MS)	92%	$15,130	38%
3. **Berry College** (GA)	70%	$24,466	47%
4. **Milligan College** (TN)	79%	$21,342	47%
5. **West Virginia Wesleyan College**	78%	$19,329	55%
6. **Stetson University** (FL)	72%	$30,782	47%
7. **Converse College** (SC)	82%	$21,027	35%
8. **Coastal Carolina University** (SC)*	20%	$13,119	65%
9. **Harding University** (AR)	57%	$18,753	34%
10. **Wingate University** (NC)	76%	$21,663	47%
11. **Christian Brothers University** (TN)	69%	$21,753	47%
12. **Loyola University New Orleans**	70%	$27,974	49%
13. **Carson-Newman University** (TN)	81%	$20,729	46%
14. **Freed-Hardeman University** (TN)	76%	$20,481	40%
15. **Mary Baldwin College** (VA)	89%	$24,141	43%
MIDWEST			
1. **Valparaiso University** (IN)	74%	$22,368	55%
2. **Dominican University** (IL)	80%	$22,790	46%
3. **Aquinas College** (MI)	80%	$20,582	48%
4. **Elmhurst College** (IL)	75%	$24,718	48%
5. **Muskingum University** (OH)	84%	$21,236	45%
6. **Hamline University** (MN)	82%	$26,512	46%
7. **Olivet Nazarene University** (IL)	81%	$22,767	48%
8. **Milwaukee School of Engineering**	76%	$25,678	47%
9. **St. Xavier University** (IL)	88%	$24,622	45%
10. **Capital University** (OH)	78%	$23,794	48%
11. **Ursuline College** (OH)	83%	$22,437	45%
12. **Malone University** (OH)	84%	$22,596	45%
13. **University of Evansville** (IN)	68%	$25,283	47%
14. **Concordia University** (NE)	74%	$20,776	45%
15. **Marian University** (IN)	81%	$24,025	46%
WEST			
1. **Mills College** (CA)	69%	$27,956	54%
2. **Trinity University** (TX)	41%	$24,874	53%
3. **St. Mary's Univ. of San Antonio**	70%	$22,108	45%
4. **LeTourneau University** (TX)	83%	$25,097	40%
5. **Whitworth University** (WA)	68%	$28,137	46%
6. **Pacific Lutheran University** (WA)	74%	$28,610	45%
7. **St. Martin's University** (WA)	84%	$25,558	46%
8. **University of Dallas**	61%	$26,587	49%

Rank School (State) (*Public)	% receiving grants based on need ('15)	Average cost after receiving grants based on need ('15)	Average discount from total cost ('15)
9. **La Sierra University** (CA)	79%	$22,274	48%
10. **Univ. of the Incarnate Word** (TX)	73%	$21,836	49%
11. **Holy Names University** (CA)	87%	$28,462	46%
12. **Abilene Christian University** (TX)	66%	$25,871	42%
13. **Gonzaga University** (WA)	55%	$31,839	40%
14. **Westminster College** (UT)	59%	$25,078	44%
15. **Master's Col. and Seminary** (CA)	77%	$27,560	40%

Regional Colleges ►

Rank School (State) (*Public)	% receiving grants based on need ('15)	Average cost after receiving grants based on need ('15)	Average discount from total cost ('15)
NORTH			
1. **Cooper Union** (NY)	41%	$24,482	61%
2. **Cedar Crest College** (PA)	92%	$24,283	50%
3. **Messiah College** (PA)	70%	$28,061	38%
4. **Wilson College** (PA)	90%	$20,584	46%
5. **University of Maine–Farmington***	69%	$21,336	31%
6. **Unity College** (ME)	84%	$24,249	36%
7. **Cazenovia College** (NY)	91%	$32,730	30%
8. **St. Francis College** (NY)	70%	$28,150	31%
9. **Dean College** (MA)	73%	$31,001	42%
10. **Vaughn Col. of Aeron. and Tech.** (NY)	75%	$31,924	23%
SOUTH			
1. **University of the Ozarks** (AR)	75%	$15,867	57%
2. **Blue Mountain College** (MS)	73%	$12,459	38%
3. **Newberry College** (SC)	87%	$21,145	47%
4. **Toccoa Falls College** (GA)	86%	$19,738	42%
5. **Kentucky Wesleyan College**	83%	$19,276	45%
6. **Alderson Broaddus University** (WV)	84%	$17,947	49%
7. **Barton College** (NC)	91%	$25,339	41%
8. **Emmanuel College** (GA)	79%	$18,313	39%
9. **Tennessee Wesleyan College**	65%	$18,732	45%
10. **Huntingdon College** (AL)	74%	$22,890	38%
MIDWEST			
1. **College of the Ozarks** (MO)	93%	$13,989	52%
2. **Augustana University** (SD)	59%	$19,057	52%
3. **Goshen College** (IN)	71%	$22,263	49%
4. **Blackburn College** (IL)	89%	$14,997	48%
5. **Taylor University** (IN)	61%	$25,450	39%
6. **Manchester University** (IN)	85%	$20,559	51%
7. **Hastings College** (NE)	73%	$21,018	47%
8. **Clarke University** (IA)	87%	$23,248	46%
9. **University of Mount Union** (OH)	79%	$23,858	42%
10. **Dordt College** (IA)	68%	$23,891	42%
WEST			
1. **Texas Lutheran University**	81%	$18,843	54%
2. **Carroll College** (MT)	65%	$27,044	39%
3. **Howard Payne University** (TX)	69%	$21,182	43%
4. **Rocky Mountain College** (MT)	75%	$20,844	45%
5. **McMurry University** (TX)	84%	$22,661	41%
6. **Oklahoma Baptist University**	67%	$28,074	23%
7. **Warner Pacific College** (OR)	60%	$26,838	19%
8. **University of Montana–Western***	54%	$22,693	17%
9. **Montana Tech of the Univ. of Mont.***	24%	$27,529	18%
10. **East Texas Baptist University**	65%	$30,167	17%

The Payback Picture

With tuition rising and financial aid budgets shrinking, many undergrads have to borrow their way to a degree. U.S. News has compiled a list of the schools whose class of 2015 graduated with the heaviest and lightest debt loads. The data include loans taken out by students from their colleges, from private financial institutions, and from federal, state and local governments. Loans directly to parents are not included. The first data column indicates what percentage of the class graduated owing money and, by extrapolation, what percentage graduated debt-free. "Average amount of debt" refers to the cumulative amount borrowed by students who incurred debt; it's not an average for all students.

MOST DEBT

National Universities ▶

School (State) (*Public)	% of grads with debt	Average amount of debt
Stevens Institute of Technology (NJ)	75%	$48,244
Texas Southern University*	80%	$42,863
Suffolk University (MA)	75%	$42,584
Catholic University of America (DC)	58%	$42,458
Clark Atlanta University	96%	$40,815
Baylor University (TX)	56%	$40,721
University of St. Thomas (MN)	65%	$40,403
Boston University	53%	$40,365
University of Mississippi*	51%	$40,332
Prairie View A&M University (TX)*	88%	$40,269
Robert Morris University (PA)	77%	$39,402
Barry University (FL)	68%	$39,248
Duquesne University (PA)	73%	$38,437
Rochester Inst. of Technology (NY)	77%	$38,198
University of Pittsburgh*	63%	$38,045

Regional Universities ▶

School (State) (*Public)	% of grads with debt	Average amount of debt
NORTH		
Molloy College (NY)	76%	$49,408
Post University (CT)	80%	$48,077
Quinnipiac University (CT)	67%	$47,873
Sacred Heart University (CT)	72%	$47,715
Metropolitan College of New York	98%	$46,637
SOUTH		
Grambling State University (LA)*	99%	$51,887
Coastal Carolina University (SC)*	79%	$40,373
Francis Marion University (SC)*	78%	$40,244
Wheeling Jesuit University (WV)	75%	$35,355
Amridge University (AL)	100%	$35,238
MIDWEST		
College of St. Scholastica (MN)	76%	$46,383
University of Findlay (OH)	78%	$45,336
Alverno College (WI)	84%	$43,185
Lawrence Technological Univ. (MI)	69%	$42,025
St. Ambrose University (IA)	74%	$39,919
WEST		
Univ. of the Incarnate Word (TX)	76%	$43,998
Woodbury University (CA)	87%	$40,626
LeTourneau University (TX)	67%	$39,167
Hardin-Simmons University (TX)	71%	$38,354
St. Mary's Univ. of San Antonio	78%	$37,107

National Liberal Arts Colleges ▶

School (State) (*Public)	% of grads with debt	Average amount of debt
Wesleyan College (GA)	43%	$48,460
Dillard University (LA)	100%	$47,297
Bloomfield College (NJ)	95%	$46,574
Carthage College (WI)	79%	$42,697
Pacific Union College (CA)	75%	$41,706
Wartburg College (IA)	78%	$40,872
St. John's University (MN)	68%	$40,067
Wells College (NY)	85%	$39,910
College of St. Benedict (MN)	73%	$39,110
Gordon College (MA)	88%	$38,750
St. Anselm College (NH)	83%	$38,583
Ursinus College (PA)	74%	$38,282
Virginia Wesleyan College	86%	$38,107
Roanoke College (VA)	77%	$37,704
Emmanuel College (MA)	84%	$37,698

Regional Colleges ▶

School (State) (*Public)	% of grads with debt	Average amount of debt
NORTH		
Maine Maritime Academy*	82%	$49,272
Mount Ida College (MA)	92%	$47,636
Cedar Crest College (PA)	88%	$38,223
College of St. Joseph (VT)	100%	$36,719
Cazenovia College (NY)	86%	$36,060
SOUTH		
Chowan University (NC)	84%	$42,346
Livingstone College (NC)	95%	$40,857
High Point University (NC)	57%	$36,892
University of the Ozarks (AR)	61%	$36,411
Brevard College (NC)	77%	$34,348
MIDWEST		
Tabor College (KS)	84%	$47,172
MacMurray College (IL)	97%	$40,497
Marietta College (OH)	78%	$40,196
Clarke University (IA)	84%	$39,907
Benedictine College (KS)	88%	$39,272
WEST		
Texas Lutheran University	77%	$35,906
East Texas Baptist University	84%	$35,716
McMurry University (TX)	100%	$35,701
Jarvis Christian College (TX)	100%	$35,116
Howard Payne University (TX)	73%	$34,875

Note: Student debt data as of July 25, 2016

LEAST DEBT

National Universities ▶

School (State) (*Public)	% of grads with debt	Average amount of debt
Princeton University (NJ)	16%	$8,577
University of Texas–Arlington*	84%	$14,743
Yale University (CT)	17%	$15,521
Brigham Young Univ.–Provo (UT)	27%	$15,720
Harvard University (MA)	24%	$16,723
North Carolina State U.–Raleigh*	55%	$17,461
University of California–Berkeley*	38%	$17,869
California State Univ.–Fresno*	50%	$18,385
Florida International University*	48%	$18,918
University of Miami (FL)	40%	$19,000
University of Utah*	39%	$19,056
Duke University (NC)	35%	$19,104
Dartmouth College (NH)	43%	$19,135
Utah State University*	47%	$19,172
University of California–Davis*	56%	$19,588
University of New Orleans*	55%	$19,861
San Diego State University*	48%	$20,100
U. of North Carolina–Chapel Hill*	41%	$20,127
Florida Atlantic University*	53%	$20,458
University of California–Irvine*	59%	$20,628
California Institute of Technology	39%	$20,677
Boston College	49%	$20,849
Univ. of California–Santa Barbara*	56%	$20,978
Univ. of Maryland–Eastern Shore*	73%	$21,000
University of Florida*	43%	$21,028

National Liberal Arts Colleges ▶

School (State) (*Public)	% of grads with debt	Average amount of debt
Berea College (KY)	68%	$7,928
Alice Lloyd College (KY)	42%	$10,591
Erskine College (SC)	71%	$10,770
Wellesley College (MA)	49%	$12,455
Pomona College (CA)	39%	$13,381
University of Virginia–Wise*	65%	$14,424
New College of Florida*	48%	$14,929
Amherst College (MA)	25%	$15,756
Grinnell College (IA)	59%	$15,982
Williams College (MA)	43%	$16,593
Thomas Aquinas College (CA)	80%	$16,901
Hamilton College (NY)	39%	$17,654
Middlebury College (VT)	41%	$17,797
Vassar College (NY)	47%	$17,847
Swarthmore College (PA)	33%	$18,262
Louisiana State University–Alexandria*	61%	$18,326
Scripps College (CA)	44%	$18,692
Soka University of America (CA)	70%	$18,954
Haverford College (PA)	28%	$19,534
Bates College (ME)	39%	$19,917
Davidson College (NC)	27%	$19,929
Barnard College (NY)	44%	$20,008
Carleton College (MN)	41%	$20,063
Smith College (MA)	63%	$20,514
Warren Wilson College (NC)	71%	$20,768

Regional Universities ▶

School (State) (*Public)	% of grads with debt	Average amount of debt
NORTH		
CUNY–Baruch College*	16%	$13,600
CUNY–Brooklyn College*	18%	$14,313
CUNY–Lehman College*	69%	$15,000
CUNY–Queens College*	15%	$15,000
CUNY–City College*	22%	$16,942
SOUTH		
Univ. of Mary Washington (VA)*	50%	$17,500
Campbellsville University (KY)	72%	$18,641
William Carey University (MS)	67%	$19,000
University of North Florida*	49%	$19,396
U. of South Florida–St. Petersburg*	56%	$19,705
MIDWEST		
Northeastern Illinois University*	48%	$15,713
Univ. of Wisconsin–Platteville*	80%	$19,856
Southwest Minnesota State University*	93%	$20,234
Univ. of Nebraska–Kearney*	56%	$20,412
Southern Illinois U.–Edwardsville*	58%	$20,817
WEST		
California State Univ.–Bakersfield*	89%	$11,679
New Mexico Highlands University*	55%	$15,831
California State U.–Long Beach*	42%	$16,077
California State U.–Los Angeles*	51%	$16,402
U. of Texas of the Permian Basin*	50%	$16,776

Regional Colleges ▶

School (State) (*Public)	% of grads with debt	Average amount of debt
NORTH		
U.S. Merchant Marine Acad. (NY)*	35%	$5,500
Cooper Union (NY)	24%	$20,395
St. Francis College (NY)	64%	$23,702
University of Maine–Fort Kent*	81%	$24,012
Vermont Technical College*	78%	$24,496
SOUTH		
Blue Mountain College (MS)	70%	$17,928
Georgia Gwinnett College*	73%	$18,612
U. of South Carolina–Upstate*	74%	$19,896
Ohio Valley University (WV)	78%	$20,472
Bluefield State College (WV)*	59%	$20,499
MIDWEST		
College of the Ozarks (MO)	7%	$5,339
Maranatha Baptist University (WI)	63%	$20,461
Missouri Southern State University*	50%	$20,638
Indiana University–Kokomo*	78%	$24,440
Harris-Stowe State University (MO)*	95%	$24,968
WEST		
Oklahoma State U. Institute of Technology–Okmulgee*	48%	$13,775
Rogers State University (OK)*	51%	$16,164
University of Montana–Western*	67%	$20,669
Oklahoma Baptist University	63%	$25,262
Montana Tech of the Univ. of Mont.*	55%	$26,198

WHY I PICKED...

Gonzaga University
Spokane, Washington

Aaron Danowski, CLASS OF 2017

Gonzaga appealed to me because it offers tons of opportunities for students to discover how their talents can best serve communities around the world. I entered college as a business major and was admitted to the Gonzaga Honors Program. My first semester I helped a local Burmese refugee family improve their English as they adjusted to life in Spokane. Later, I spent spring break with Montana's Blackfeet Nation, immersing myself in the culture and listening to stories of the people. I spent part of one summer in Chennai, India, observing a social enterprise fighting caste discrimination of local "untouchables." Finally, I spent last fall in Cameroon studying international development and sociology.

> **I SPENT LAST FALL IN CAMEROON STUDYING INTERNATIONAL DEVELOPMENT.**

These experiences helped me realize I want to use social entrepreneurship to address the root causes of poverty, disease and environmental degradation. The university has encouraged my passion by sending me to conferences for social entrepreneurship in Washington, D.C., and Minneapolis, where I got to practice networking and deepen my knowledge of the field. The business school even let me create my own concentration in social enterprise development! Thanks to Gonzaga, I feel well-prepared to pursue a career I am passionate about. ●

STETSON UNIVERSITY

COURTESY OF STETSON UNIVERSITY

Stetson University
DeLand, Florida

Alexandra Shimalla, CLASS OF 2016

After visiting a few large universities, I realized I preferred a smaller school where I wouldn't be just a face in a crowd. In the end, I settled on Stetson. Located less than 45 minutes from world-class beaches and cities like Orlando, the university gave me a small school experience with access to larger metro areas. Since our class size is just 12-to-1, professors are extremely accessible. Stetson students have wide interests, and faculty and administrators seem to bend over backwards

GONZAGA
UNIVERSITY

to help us pursue our passions. Classmates have received grants from Stetson, for example, to do summer research with their biology professors, and my friends at our outstanding school of music perform with nationally known musicians.

In my case, after taking a terrific intro to journalism class, I realized how much I wanted to pursue writing and editing. The university offered me many opportunities to do so. I wrote a column about healthy living for the college newspaper and work as a peer tutor at the writing center. The head of the communications department helped me get an internship with a lifestyle magazine in Savannah, Georgia, to get on-the-job experience while earning credit. Stetson has been a perfect fit for me. ●

> **FACULTY AND ADMINISTRATORS SEEM TO BEND OVER BACKWARDS TO HELP US.**

Vassar College
Poughkeepsie, New York
Clairiola Manessa Etienne, CLASS OF 2018

I moved to the U.S. to attend high school three months after an earthquake devastated my hometown in Haiti. Looking at college websites, I was impressed to see that Vassar had a story about how its Haiti Project was aiding a village educationally, medically and environmentally. This enticed me to learn more. I discovered the college has a rich and diverse student body. Classes are small, encouraging open discussion and strong faculty-student relationships. I knew it was the place for me.

Since I hoped to go to medical school, freshman year I went back to Haiti on a spring break trip to get hands-on experience assisting a doctor and a nurse in a rural clinic built by the Haiti Project. No matter what your interests, Vassar has so much to offer. As a double major in biology and French, I've been able to study Caribbean writing, concentrating particularly on Haitian literature. Now as the school's director of the Haiti health initiative, I lead a student committee looking into solar power and laboratory equipment for the clinic, while serving as the liaison between U.S. doctors and the local staff. Vassar has helped me pave the path that will allow me to realize my ambitions to become a doctor. ●

> **I LEAD A STUDENT COMMITTEE LOOKING INTO SOLAR POWER AND LAB EQUIPMENT FOR THE CLINIC.**

VASSAR COLLEGE

TAMAR M. THIBODEAU – VASSAR COLLEGE

FIND
THE BEST
ONLINE
PROGRAM
FOR YOU

Search more than 1,000
online education
programs to find one
that best fits your needs

Start your search today: **usnews.com/education/online-education**

2017 EDITION

DIRECTORY OF COLLEGES AND UNIVERSITIES

INSIDE

The latest facts and figures on over
1,600 American colleges and universities,
including schools' U.S. News rankings

New data on tuition, admissions, the
makeup of the undergraduate student body,
popular majors and financial aid

Statistical profiles of freshman classes, including
entrance exam scores and high school class standing

Using the Directory

How to interpret the statistics in the following entries on more than 1,600 American colleges and universities – and how to get the most out of them

The snapshots of colleges and universities presented here, alphabetized by state, contain a wealth of helpful information on everything from the most popular majors offered to the stats on the freshman class that arrived in the fall of 2015. The statistics were collected in the spring and summer of 2016 and are as of Aug. 17, 2016; they are explained in detail below. A school whose name has been footnoted did not return the U.S. News statistical questionnaire, so limited data appear. If a college did not reply to a particular question, you'll see N/A, for "not available." By tapping our online directory at usnews.com/collegesearch, you can experiment with a customized search of our database that allows you to pick schools based on major, location and other criteria. To find a school of interest in the rankings tables, consult the index at the back of the book.

1. TELEPHONE NUMBER
This number reaches the admissions office.

2. U.S. NEWS RANKING
The abbreviation indicates which category of institution the school falls into: National Universities (Nat. U.), National Liberal Arts Colleges (Nat. Lib. Arts), Regional Universities (Reg. U.), or Regional Colleges (Reg. Coll.). The regional universities and regional colleges are further divided by region: North (N), South (S), Midwest (MidW), and West (W). "Business" refers to business specialty schools, and "Engineering" refers to engineering specialty schools. "Arts" refers to schools devoted to the fine and performing arts.

Next, you'll find the school's 2017 rank within its category. Colleges and universities falling in the top three-fourths of their categories are ranked numerically. Those ranked in the bottom 25 percent of their respective category are placed in the second tier, listed alphabetically. But remember: You cannot compare school ranks in different categories; U.S. News ranks schools only against their peers. Specialty schools that focus on business, engineering and the arts aren't ranked and are listed as unranked. Also unranked are schools with fewer than 200 students, a high percentage of older or part-time students, that don't use SAT or ACT test scores for admission decisions or that have received a very small number of peer assessment votes in a survey conducted in spring 2016.

3. WEBSITE
Visit the school's website to research programs, take a virtual tour, or submit an application. You can also find a link to each site at usnews.com.

4. ADMISSIONS EMAIL
You can use this email address to request information or to submit an application.

5. TYPE/AFFILIATION
Is the school public, private or for-profit? Affiliated with a religious denomination?

6. FRESHMAN ADMISSIONS
How competitive is the admissions process at this institution? Schools are designated "most selective," "more selective," "selective," "less selective" or "least selective." The more selective a school, the harder it will probably be to get in. All of the admissions statistics reported are for the class that entered in the fall of 2015. The 25/75 percentiles for the SAT Math and Critical Reading or ACT Composite show the range in which half the students scored: 25 percent of students scored at or below the lower end, and 75 percent scored at or below the upper end. If a school reported the averages and not the 25/75 percentiles, the average score is listed. The test score that is published represents the test that the greatest percentage of the entering students took.

7. EARLY DECISION/ EARLY ACTION DEADLINES
Applicants who plan to take the early decision route to fall 2017 enrollment will have to meet the deadline listed for the school. If the school offers an early action option, the application deadline and notification date are also shown.

8. APPLICATION DEADLINE
The date shown is the regular admission deadline for the academic year starting in the fall of 2017. "Rolling" means the school makes admissions decisions as applications come in until the class is filled.

9. UNDERGRADUATE STUDENT BODY
This section gives you the breakdown of full-time vs. part-time students, male and female enrollment, the ethnic makeup of the student body, in-state and out-of-state populations, the percentage of students living on campus, and the percentage in fraternities and sororities. All figures are for the 2015-16 academic year.

10. MOST POPULAR MAJORS
The five most popular majors appear, along with the percentage majoring in each among 2015 graduates with a bachelor's degree.

11. EXPENSES
The first figure represents tuition (including required fees); next is total room and board. Figures are for the 2016-17 academic year; if data are not available, we use figures for the 2015-16 academic year. For public schools, we list both in-state and out-of-state tuition.

12. FINANCIAL AID
The percentage of undergrads determined to have financial need and the amount of the average aid package (grants, loans and jobs) in 2015-16. We also provide the phone number of the financial aid office.

ALABAMA

Alabama Agricultural and Mechanical University[1]
Normal AL
(256) 372-5245
U.S. News ranking: Reg. U. (S), No. 102
Website: www.aamu.edu
Admissions email: admissions@aamu.edu
Public; founded 1875
Application deadline (fall): 7/15
Undergraduate student body: N/A full time, N/A part time
Expenses: 2015-2016: $9,096 in state, $16,596 out of state; room/board: $5,440
Financial aid: (256) 372-5400

Alabama State University
Montgomery AL
(334) 229-4291
U.S. News ranking: Reg. U. (S), second tier
Website: www.alasu.edu
Admissions email: mpettway@alasu.edu
Public; founded 1887
Freshman admissions: less selective; 2015-2016: 8,356 applied, 4,004 accepted. Either SAT or ACT required. ACT 25/75 percentile: 15-23. High school rank: 4% in top tenth, 11% in top quarter, 45% in top half
Early decision deadline: N/A, notification date: N/A
Early action deadline: N/A, notification date: N/A
Application deadline (fall): 7/30
Undergraduate student body: 4,377 full time, 387 part time; 38% male, 62% female; 0% American Indian, 0% Asian, 93% black, 1% Hispanic, 1% multiracial, 0% Pacific Islander, 2% white, 2% international; 69% from in state; 33% live on campus; 2% of students in fraternities, 3% in sororities
Most popular majors: 40% Secondary Education and Teaching; 20% Criminal Justice/Safety Studies; 20% Rehabilitation and Therapeutic Professions, Other; 10% Biology/Biological Sciences, General; 10% Computer Science
Expenses: 2016-2017: $8,720 in state, $15,656 out of state; room/board: $5,422
Financial aid: (334) 229-4323; 97% of undergrads determined to have financial need; average aid package $18,943

Amridge University
Montgomery AL
(800) 351-4040
U.S. News ranking: Reg. U. (S), second tier
Website: www.amridgeuniversity.edu/
Admissions email: admissions@amridgeuniversity.edu
Private; founded 1967
Affiliation: Church of Christ
Freshman admissions: less selective; 2015-2016: N/A applied, N/A accepted. Neither SAT nor ACT required. ACT 25/75 percentile: N/A. High school rank: N/A

Early decision deadline: N/A, notification date: N/A
Early action deadline: N/A, notification date: N/A
Application deadline (fall): rolling
Undergraduate student body: 167 full time, 141 part time; 43% male, 57% female; N/A American Indian, N/A Asian, 34% black, 2% Hispanic, N/A multiracial, 0% Pacific Islander, 21% white, N/A international
Most popular majors: 20% Human Development and Family Studies, General; 13% Bible/Biblical Studies; 9% Human Resources Management/Personnel Administration, General; 8% Business Administration and Management, General; 8% Business/Corporate Communications
Expenses: 2016-2017: $12,630; room/board: N/A
Financial aid: (800) 351-4040; 92% of undergrads determined to have financial need; average aid package $8,120

Athens State University
Athens AL
(256) 233-8217
U.S. News ranking: Reg. Coll. (S), unranked
Website: www.athens.edu/
Admissions email: N/A
Public; founded 1822
Freshman admissions: N/A; 2015-2016: N/A applied, N/A accepted. Neither SAT nor ACT required. ACT 25/75 percentile: N/A. High school rank: N/A
Early decision deadline: N/A, notification date: N/A
Early action deadline: N/A, notification date: N/A
Application deadline (fall): N/A
Undergraduate student body: 1,226 full time, 1,815 part time; 35% male, 65% female; 2% American Indian, 1% Asian, 12% black, 2% Hispanic, 2% multiracial, 0% Pacific Islander, 78% white, 1% international
Most popular majors: 17% Elementary Education and Teaching; 14% Business Administration and Management, General; 10% Accounting; 6% Liberal Arts and Sciences/Liberal Studies; 5% Business, Management, Marketing, and Related Support Services, Other
Expenses: 2015-2016: $6,270 in state, $11,790 out of state; room/board: N/A
Financial aid: (256) 233-8122; 71% of undergrads determined to have financial need; average aid package $9,666

Auburn University
Auburn AL
(334) 844-6425
U.S. News ranking: Nat. U., No. 99
Website: www.auburn.edu
Admissions email: admissions@auburn.edu
Public; founded 1856
Freshman admissions: more selective; 2015-2016: 19,414 applied, 15,077 accepted. Either SAT or ACT required. ACT 25/75 percentile: 24-30. High school

rank: 31% in top tenth, 62% in top quarter, 89% in top half
Early decision deadline: N/A, notification date: N/A
Early action deadline: 2/1, notification date: 10/15
Application deadline (fall): 6/1
Undergraduate student body: 19,738 full time, 2,048 part time; 51% male, 49% female; 1% American Indian, 2% Asian, 7% black, 3% Hispanic, 1% multiracial, 0% Pacific Islander, 84% white, 1% international; 66% from in state; 21% live on campus; 20% of students in fraternities, 39% in sororities
Most popular majors: 20% Business, Management, Marketing, and Related Support Services; 17% Engineering; 9% Biological and Biomedical Sciences; 9% Education; 6% Health Professions and Related Programs
Expenses: 2016-2017: $10,696 in state, $28,840 out of state; room/board: $12,898
Financial aid: (334) 844-4634; 36% of undergrads determined to have financial need; average aid package $10,530

Auburn University–Montgomery
Montgomery AL
(334) 244-3611
U.S. News ranking: Reg. U. (S), second tier
Website: www.aum.edu
Admissions email: vsamuel@aum.edu
Public; founded 1967
Freshman admissions: selective; 2015-2016: 2,494 applied, 1,963 accepted. Either SAT or ACT required. ACT 25/75 percentile: 19-23. High school rank: 16% in top tenth, 40% in top quarter, 76% in top half
Early decision deadline: N/A, notification date: N/A
Early action deadline: N/A, notification date: N/A
Application deadline (fall): 8/15
Undergraduate student body: 3,083 full time, 1,174 part time; 36% male, 64% female; 1% American Indian, 2% Asian, 35% black, 1% Hispanic, 3% multiracial, 0% Pacific Islander, 54% white, 3% international; 95% from in state; 20% live on campus; 2% of students in fraternities, 5% in sororities
Most popular majors: 25% Health Professions and Related Programs; 25% Business, Management, Marketing, and Related Support Services; 9% Education; 6% Biological and Biomedical Sciences
Expenses: 2016-2017: $9,640 in state, $20,710 out of state; room/board: $5,650
Financial aid: (334) 244-3571; 67% of undergrads determined to have financial need; average aid package $6,970

Birmingham-Southern College
Birmingham AL
(205) 226-4696
U.S. News ranking: Nat. Lib. Arts, No. 132
Website: www.bsc.edu
Admissions email: admission@bsc.edu
Private; founded 1856
Affiliation: United Methodist
Freshman admissions: more selective; 2015-2016: 3,683 applied, 1,957 accepted. Either SAT or ACT required. ACT 25/75 percentile: 21-25. High school rank: 21% in top tenth, 51% in top quarter, 85% in top half
Early decision deadline: N/A, notification date: N/A
Early action deadline: 11/15, notification date: 12/15
Application deadline (fall): 5/1
Undergraduate student body: 1,337 full time, 9 part time; 50% male, 50% female; 1% American Indian, 5% Asian, 11% black, 2% Hispanic, 1% multiracial, N/A Pacific Islander, 79% white, N/A international; 55% from in state; 87% live on campus; 38% of students in fraternities, 52% in sororities
Most popular majors: 22% Business Administration and Management, General; 12% Biology/Biological Sciences, General; 11% Psychology, General; 5% Teacher Education, Multiple Levels; 4% History, General
Expenses: 2016-2017: $34,448; room/board: $11,620
Financial aid: (205) 226-4688; 58% of undergrads determined to have financial need; average aid package $31,540

Concordia College[1]
Selma AL
(334) 874-5700
U.S. News ranking: Reg. Coll. (S), unranked
Website: www.ccal.edu/
Admissions email: admission@ccal.edu
Private; founded 1922
Affiliation: Lutheran
Application deadline (fall): N/A
Undergraduate student body: N/A full time, N/A part time
Expenses: 2015-2016: $10,320; room/board: $5,600
Financial aid: (334) 874-5700

Faulkner University
Montgomery AL
(334) 386-7200
U.S. News ranking: Reg. U. (S), second tier
Website: www.faulkner.edu
Admissions email: admissions@faulkner.edu
Private; founded 1942
Affiliation: Church of Christ
Freshman admissions: selective; 2015-2016: 1,712 applied, 981 accepted. Either SAT or ACT required. ACT 25/75 percentile: 18-24. High school rank: N/A
Early decision deadline: N/A, notification date: N/A
Early action deadline: N/A, notification date: N/A
Application deadline (fall): 8/1

Undergraduate student body: 1,771 full time, 793 part time; 39% male, 61% female; 1% American Indian, 0% Asian, 51% black, 2% Hispanic, 2% multiracial, 0% Pacific Islander, 40% white, 2% international; 86% from in state; 50% live on campus; 9% of students in fraternities, 10% in sororities
Most popular majors: 40% Business Administration and Management, General; 19% Human Resources Management/Personnel Administration, General; 16% Criminal Justice/Safety Studies; 3% Elementary Education and Teaching; 3% Sport and Fitness Administration/Management
Expenses: 2016-2017: $20,130; room/board: $7,230
Financial aid: (334) 386-7195; 63% of undergrads determined to have financial need; average aid package $6,215

Huntingdon College
Montgomery AL
(334) 833-4497
U.S. News ranking: Reg. Coll. (S), No. 10
Website: www.huntingdon.edu
Admissions email: admiss@huntingdon.edu
Private; founded 1854
Affiliation: Methodist
Freshman admissions: selective; 2015-2016: 1,839 applied, 1,061 accepted. Either SAT or ACT required. ACT 25/75 percentile: 19-23. High school rank: 9% in top tenth, 29% in top quarter, 69% in top half
Early decision deadline: N/A, notification date: N/A
Early action deadline: N/A, notification date: N/A
Application deadline (fall): rolling
Undergraduate student body: 896 full time, 270 part time; 50% male, 50% female; 1% American Indian, 1% Asian, 22% black, 3% Hispanic, 3% multiracial, 0% Pacific Islander, 63% white, 0% international; 80% from in state; 62% live on campus; 25% of students in fraternities, 43% in sororities
Most popular majors: 47% Business, Management, Marketing, and Related Support Services; 10% Education; 8% Biological and Biomedical Sciences; 8% Parks, Recreation, Leisure, and Fitness Studies; 5% Psychology
Expenses: 2016-2017: $25,450; room/board: $9,100
Financial aid: (334) 833-4519; 75% of undergrads determined to have financial need; average aid package $17,471

Jacksonville State University
Jacksonville AL
(256) 782-5268
U.S. News ranking: Reg. U. (S), No. 98
Website: www.jsu.edu
Admissions email: info@jsu.edu
Public; founded 1883
Freshman admissions: selective; 2015-2016: 3,085 applied, 2,056 accepted. Either SAT or ACT required. ACT 25/75

percentile: 20-26. High school rank: 20% in top tenth, 45% in top quarter, 75% in top half
Early decision deadline: N/A, notification date: N/A
Early action deadline: N/A, notification date: N/A
Application deadline (fall): rolling
Undergraduate student body: 5,461 full time, 1,922 part time; 43% male, 57% female; 1% American Indian, 1% Asian, 22% black, 1% Hispanic, N/A multiracial, 0% Pacific Islander, 70% white, 2% international; 83% from in state; 26% live on campus; 12% of students in fraternities, 17% in sororities
Most popular majors: 24% Registered Nursing/Registered Nurse; 6% Criminal Justice/Safety Studies; 6% Liberal Arts and Sciences/Liberal Studies; 5% Business Administration and Management, General; 5% Elementary Education and Teaching
Expenses: 2016-2017: $9,300 in state, $18,300 out of state; room/board: $7,128
Financial aid: (256) 782-5006; 88% of undergrads determined to have financial need; average aid package $9,339

Judson College[1]
Marion AL
(800) 447-9472
U.S. News ranking: Nat. Lib. Arts, second tier
Website: www.judson.edu/
Admissions email: admissions@judson.edu
Private
Application deadline (fall): N/A
Undergraduate student body: N/A full time, N/A part time
Expenses: 2015-2016: $16,868; room/board: $9,686
Financial aid: (334) 683-5170

Miles College[1]
Birmingham AL
(800) 445-0708
U.S. News ranking: Reg. Coll. (S), unranked
Website: www.miles.edu
Admissions email: admissions@mail.miles.edu
Private
Application deadline (fall): N/A
Undergraduate student body: N/A full time, N/A part time
Expenses: 2015-2016: $11,604; room/board: $7,042
Financial aid: (205) 929-1665

Oakwood University
Huntsville AL
(256) 726-7356
U.S. News ranking: Reg. Coll. (S), No. 47
Website: www.oakwood.edu
Admissions email: admissions@oakwood.edu
Private; founded 1896
Affiliation: Seventh-day Adventist
Freshman admissions: less selective; 2015-2016: 1,992 applied, 946 accepted. Either SAT or ACT required. ACT 25/75 percentile: N/A. High school rank: N/A
Early decision deadline: N/A, notification date: N/A

Early action deadline: N/A, notification date: N/A
Application deadline (fall): N/A
Undergraduate student body: 1,598 full time, 105 part time; 42% male, 58% female; 1% American Indian, 0% Asian, 84% black, 3% Hispanic, 0% multiracial, 0% Pacific Islander, 0% white, 7% international
Most popular majors: Information not available
Expenses: 2015-2016: $16,720; room/board: $9,700
Financial aid: (256) 726-7210

Samford University
Birmingham AL
(800) 888-7218
U.S. News ranking: Reg. U. (S), No. 4
Website: www.samford.edu
Admissions email: admission@samford.edu
Private; founded 1841
Affiliation: Baptist
Freshman admissions: more selective; 2015-2016: 3,196 applied, 2,982 accepted. Either SAT or ACT required. ACT 25/75 percentile: 23-29. High school rank: 27% in top tenth, 52% in top quarter, 84% in top half
Early decision deadline: N/A, notification date: N/A
Early action deadline: N/A, notification date: N/A
Application deadline (fall): 6/30
Undergraduate student body: 3,040 full time, 128 part time; 35% male, 65% female; 0% American Indian, 1% Asian, 7% black, 5% Hispanic, 2% multiracial, 81% white, 3% international; 33% from in state; 72% live on campus; 35% of students in fraternities, 53% in sororities
Most popular majors: 30% Health Professions and Related Programs; 16% Business, Management, Marketing, and Related Support Services; 7% Parks, Recreation, Leisure, and Fitness Studies; 6% Family and Consumer Sciences/Human Sciences
Expenses: 2016-2017: $29,402; room/board: $9,830
Financial aid: (205) 726-2905; 41% of undergrads determined to have financial need; average aid package $18,746

Spring Hill College
Mobile AL
(251) 380-3030
U.S. News ranking: Nat. Lib. Arts, second tier
Website: www.shc.edu
Admissions email: admit@shc.edu
Private; founded 1830
Affiliation: Catholic
Freshman admissions: more selective; 2015-2016: 7,393 applied, 3,055 accepted. Either SAT or ACT required. ACT 25/75 percentile: 22-27. High school rank: 26% in top tenth, 56% in top quarter, 82% in top half
Early decision deadline: N/A, notification date: N/A
Early action deadline: N/A, notification date: N/A
Application deadline (fall): 7/15
Undergraduate student body: 1,341 full time, 29 part time; 39% male, 61% female; 1% American

Indian, 1% Asian, 13% black, 4% Hispanic, 5% multiracial, 0% Pacific Islander, 68% white, 3% international; 39% from in state; 77% live on campus; 27% of students in fraternities, 36% in sororities
Most popular majors: 12% Psychology; 8% Biological and Biomedical Sciences; 8% Education; 7% Social Sciences
Expenses: 2016-2017: $35,798; room/board: $12,690
Financial aid: (251) 380-3460; 68% of undergrads determined to have financial need; average aid package $29,169

Stillman College[1]
Tuscaloosa AL
(205) 366-8837
U.S. News ranking: Nat. Lib. Arts, second tier
Website: www.stillman.edu
Admissions email: admissions@stillman.edu
Private; founded 1876
Affiliation: Presbyterian Church (USA)
Application deadline (fall): rolling
Undergraduate student body: N/A full time, N/A part time
Expenses: 2015-2016: $10,418; room/board: $7,056
Financial aid: (205) 366-8817

Talladega College[1]
Talladega AL
(256) 761-6235
U.S. News ranking: Reg. Coll. (S), unranked
Website: www.talladega.edu
Admissions email: admissions@talladega.edu
Private
Application deadline (fall): N/A
Undergraduate student body: N/A full time, N/A part time
Expenses: 2015-2016: $12,510; room/board: $6,504
Financial aid: (256) 761-6341

Troy University
Troy AL
(334) 670-3179
U.S. News ranking: Reg. U. (S), No. 69
Website: www.troy.edu/
Admissions email: admit@troy.edu
Public; founded 1887
Freshman admissions: selective; 2015-2016: 5,661 applied, 5,197 accepted. Either SAT or ACT required. ACT 25/75 percentile: 19-26. High school rank: N/A
Early decision deadline: N/A, notification date: N/A
Early action deadline: N/A, notification date: N/A
Application deadline (fall): rolling
Undergraduate student body: 8,951 full time, 5,113 part time; 41% male, 59% female; 1% American Indian, 1% Asian, 31% black, 4% Hispanic, 3% multiracial, 0% Pacific Islander, 54% white, 4% international; 67% from in state; 32% live on campus; 13% of students in fraternities, 15% in sororities
Most popular majors: 30% Business, Management, Marketing, and Related Support Services; 18% Homeland Security, Law Enforcement, Firefighting and Related

Protective Services; 14% Psychology; 8% Social Sciences; 6% Education
Expenses: 2015-2016: $9,646 in state, $18,256 out of state; room/board: $6,525
Financial aid: (334) 670-3186; 62% of undergrads determined to have financial need; average aid package $4,563

Tuskegee University
Tuskegee AL
(334) 727-8500
U.S. News ranking: Reg. U. (S), No. 24
Website: www.tuskegee.edu
Admissions email: admiweb@tusk.edu
Private; founded 1881
Freshman admissions: selective; 2015-2016: 7,529 applied, 3,987 accepted. Either SAT or ACT required. ACT 25/75 percentile: 18-23. High school rank: 20% in top tenth, 60% in top quarter, 100% in top half
Early decision deadline: N/A, notification date: N/A
Early action deadline: N/A, notification date: N/A
Application deadline (fall): rolling
Undergraduate student body: 2,430 full time, 55 part time; 38% male, 62% female; 0% American Indian, 0% Asian, 78% black, 0% Hispanic, 0% multiracial, 0% Pacific Islander, 0% white, 0% international
Most popular majors: 21% Engineering; 12% Psychology; 8% Biological and Biomedical Sciences; 8% Health Professions and Related Programs
Expenses: 2016-2017: $21,470; room/board: $9,104
Financial aid: (334) 727-8201; 78% of undergrads determined to have financial need; average aid package $19,250

University of Alabama
Tuscaloosa AL
(205) 348-5666
U.S. News ranking: Nat. U., No. 103
Website: www.ua.edu
Admissions email: admissions@ua.edu
Public; founded 1831
Freshman admissions: more selective; 2015-2016: 36,203 applied, 19,400 accepted. Either SAT or ACT required. ACT 25/75 percentile: 22-31. High school rank: 37% in top tenth, 57% in top quarter, 82% in top half
Early decision deadline: N/A, notification date: N/A
Early action deadline: N/A, notification date: N/A
Application deadline (fall): rolling
Undergraduate student body: 28,689 full time, 3,269 part time; 45% male, 55% female; 0% American Indian, 1% Asian, 11% black, 4% Hispanic, 3% multiracial, 0% Pacific Islander, 78% white, 2% international; 46% from in state; 26% live on campus; 26% of students in fraternities, 39% in sororities
Most popular majors: 30% Business, Management, Marketing, and Related Support Services; 10% Health Professions and Related Programs;

7% Engineering; 7% Family and Consumer Sciences/Human Sciences
Expenses: 2016-2017: $10,470 in state, $26,950 out of state; room/board: $9,550
Financial aid: (205) 348-2976; 43% of undergrads determined to have financial need; average aid package $13,271

University of Alabama–Birmingham
Birmingham AL
(205) 934-8221
U.S. News ranking: Nat. U., No. 159
Website: www.uab.edu
Admissions email: chooseuab@uab.edu
Public; founded 1969
Freshman admissions: more selective; 2015-2016: 5,335 applied, 4,641 accepted. Either SAT or ACT required. ACT 25/75 percentile: 22-28. High school rank: 27% in top tenth, 52% in top quarter, 82% in top half
Early decision deadline: N/A, notification date: N/A
Early action deadline: N/A, notification date: N/A
Application deadline (fall): rolling
Undergraduate student body: 8,297 full time, 3,214 part time; 41% male, 59% female; 0% American Indian, 6% Asian, 25% black, 3% Hispanic, 4% multiracial, 0% Pacific Islander, 59% white, 2% international; N/A from in state; 22% live on campus; N/A of students in fraternities, N/A in sororities
Most popular majors: 21% Health Professions and Related Programs; 18% Business, Management, Marketing, and Related Support Services; 10% Education; 9% Psychology; 7% Biological and Biomedical Sciences
Expenses: 2015-2016: $7,766 in state, $17,654 out of state; room/board: $10,809
Financial aid: (205) 934-8223; 60% of undergrads determined to have financial need; average aid package $10,063

University of Alabama–Huntsville
Huntsville AL
(256) 824-6070
U.S. News ranking: Nat. U., No. 197
Website: www.uah.edu
Admissions email: uahadmissions@uah.edu
Public; founded 1950
Freshman admissions: more selective; 2015-2016: 3,308 applied, 2,686 accepted. Either SAT or ACT required. ACT 25/75 percentile: 24-30. High school rank: 31% in top tenth, 58% in top quarter, 84% in top half
Early decision deadline: N/A, notification date: N/A
Early action deadline: N/A, notification date: N/A
Application deadline (fall): 8/17
Undergraduate student body: 4,774 full time, 1,239 part time; 57% male, 43% female; 1% American Indian, 4% Asian, 12% black, 4% Hispanic, 2% multiracial, N/A Pacific Islander, 70% white,

3% international; 87% from in state; 24% live on campus; N/A of students in fraternities, N/A in sororities
Most popular majors: 29% Engineering; 21% Business, Management, Marketing, and Related Support Services; 18% Health Professions and Related Programs; 7% Biological and Biomedical Sciences; 3% Computer and Information Sciences and Support Services
Expenses: 2016-2017: $9,128 in state, $20,622 out of state; room/board: $9,205
Financial aid: (256) 824-6241; 53% of undergrads determined to have financial need; average aid package $10,401

University of Mobile
Mobile AL
(251) 442-2273
U.S. News ranking: Reg. Coll. (S), No. 8
Website: www.umobile.edu
Admissions email: umadminfo@umobile.edu
Private; founded 1961
Affiliation: Southern Baptist
Freshman admissions: selective; 2015-2016: 1,180 applied, 714 accepted. Either SAT or ACT required. ACT 25/75 percentile: 19-25. High school rank: 23% in top tenth, 52% in top quarter, 79% in top half
Early decision deadline: N/A, notification date: N/A
Early action deadline: N/A, notification date: N/A
Application deadline (fall): rolling
Undergraduate student body: 1,283 full time, 159 part time; 37% male, 63% female; 2% American Indian, 1% Asian, 23% black, 2% Hispanic, 3% multiracial, 0% Pacific Islander, 62% white, 5% international; 75% from in state; 50% live on campus; N/A of students in fraternities, N/A in sororities
Most popular majors: 22% Education; 21% Health Professions and Related Programs; 16% Business, Management, Marketing, and Related Support Services; 6% Philosophy and Religious Studies
Expenses: 2015-2016: $20,470; room/board: $9,670
Financial aid: (251) 442-2385; 72% of undergrads determined to have financial need; average aid package $17,354

University of Montevallo
Montevallo AL
(205) 665-6030
U.S. News ranking: Reg. U. (S), No. 37
Website: www.montevallo.edu
Admissions email: admissions@montevallo.edu
Public; founded 1896
Freshman admissions: selective; 2015-2016: 2,024 applied, 1,417 accepted. Either SAT or ACT required. ACT 25/75 percentile: 20-26. High school rank: N/A
Early decision deadline: N/A, notification date: N/A
Early action deadline: N/A, notification date: N/A

Application deadline (fall): 8/15
Undergraduate student body: 2,302 full time, 264 part time; 33% male, 67% female; 1% American Indian, 1% Asian, 15% black, 4% Hispanic, 2% multiracial, 0% Pacific Islander, 72% white, 1% international; 93% from in state; N/A live on campus; N/A of students in fraternities, N/A in sororities
Most popular majors: Information not available
Expenses: 2016-2017: $12,040 in state, $24,310 out of state; room/board: $7,462
Financial aid: (205) 665-6050; 65% of undergrads determined to have financial need; average aid package $10,962

University of North Alabama
Florence AL
(256) 765-4608
U.S. News ranking: Reg. U. (S), No. 87
Website: www.una.edu
Admissions email: admissions@una.edu
Public; founded 1830
Freshman admissions: selective; 2015-2016: 3,319 applied, 1,925 accepted. Either SAT or ACT required. ACT 25/75 percentile: 19-25. High school rank: N/A
Early decision deadline: N/A, notification date: N/A
Early action deadline: N/A, notification date: N/A
Application deadline (fall): rolling
Undergraduate student body: 4,983 full time, 1,109 part time; 42% male, 58% female; 1% American Indian, 0% Asian, 14% black, 3% Hispanic, 3% multiracial, 0% Pacific Islander, 71% white, 4% international; 84% from in state; 26% live on campus; 10% of students in fraternities, 15% in sororities
Most popular majors: 23% Business, Management, Marketing, and Related Support Services; 15% Health Professions and Related Programs; 10% Education; 6% Social Sciences; 6% Visual and Performing Arts
Expenses: 2015-2016: $7,774 in state, $13,870 out of state; room/board: $6,516
Financial aid: (256) 765-4278; 71% of undergrads determined to have financial need; average aid package $7,996

University of South Alabama
Mobile AL
(251) 460-6141
U.S. News ranking: Nat. U., second tier
Website: www.southalabama.edu/departments/admissions/index.html
Admissions email: recruitment@southalabama.edu
Public; founded 1963
Freshman admissions: selective; 2015-2016: 6,650 applied, 5,203 accepted. Neither SAT nor ACT required. ACT 25/75 percentile: 20-25. High school rank: N/A
Early decision deadline: N/A, notification date: N/A

Early action deadline: N/A, notification date: N/A
Application deadline (fall): 7/15
Undergraduate student body: 9,380 full time, 2,144 part time; 44% male, 56% female; 1% American Indian, 3% Asian, 24% black, 3% Hispanic, 3% multiracial, 0% Pacific Islander, 59% white, 5% international; 82% from in state; 29% live on campus; N/A of students in fraternities, N/A in sororities
Most popular majors: 17% Registered Nursing/Registered Nurse; 5% Health/Medical Preparatory Programs, Other; 4% Elementary Education and Teaching; 4% Physical Education Teaching and Coaching
Expenses: 2016-2017: $9,446 in state, $18,468 out of state; room/board: $8,591
Financial aid: (251) 460-6231; 63% of undergrads determined to have financial need; average aid package $9,647

University of West Alabama
Livingston AL
(205) 652-3578
U.S. News ranking: Reg. U. (S), second tier
Website: www.uwa.edu
Admissions email: admissions@uwa.edu
Public; founded 1835
Freshman admissions: selective; 2015-2016: 1,195 applied, 878 accepted. Either SAT or ACT required. ACT 25/75 percentile: 18-23. High school rank: N/A
Early decision deadline: N/A, notification date: N/A
Early action deadline: N/A, notification date: N/A
Application deadline (fall): rolling
Undergraduate student body: 1,704 full time, 211 part time; 45% male, 55% female; 0% American Indian, 0% Asian, 40% black, 2% Hispanic, 2% multiracial, 0% Pacific Islander, 45% white, 6% international; 81% from in state; 46% live on campus; 9% of students in fraternities, 10% in sororities
Most popular majors: 26% Physical Education Teaching and Coaching; 18% Biology/Biological Sciences, General; 13% Teacher Education, Multiple Levels; 11% Kinesiology and Exercise Science
Expenses: 2016-2017: $7,144 in state, $14,288 out of state; room/board: $6,460
Financial aid: (205) 652-3576; 76% of undergrads determined to have financial need; average aid package $10,979

ALASKA

Alaska Pacific University
Anchorage AK
(800) 252-7528
U.S. News ranking: Reg. U. (W), No. 52
Website: www.alaskapacific.edu
Admissions email: admissions@alaskapacific.edu
Private; founded 1957
Affiliation: United Methodist

Freshman admissions: less selective; 2015-2016: 400 applied, 275 accepted. Either SAT or ACT required. SAT 25/75 percentile: 830-1122. High school rank: N/A
Early decision deadline: N/A, notification date: N/A
Early action deadline: N/A, notification date: N/A
Application deadline (fall): rolling
Undergraduate student body: 198 full time, 84 part time; 34% male, 66% female; 11% American Indian, 0% Asian, 4% black, 3% Hispanic, 9% multiracial, 0% Pacific Islander, 63% white, 0% international
Most popular majors: 23% Business Administration and Management, General; 17% Parks, Recreation and Leisure Studies; 12% Liberal Arts and Sciences/Liberal Studies; 6% Marine Biology and Biological Oceanography
Expenses: 2016-2017: $20,380; room/board: $7,260
Financial aid: (907) 564-8341

University of Alaska–Anchorage
Anchorage AK
(907) 786-1480
U.S. News ranking: Reg. U. (W), No. 73
Website: www.uaa.alaska.edu
Admissions email: enroll@uaa.alaska.edu
Public; founded 1954
Freshman admissions: selective; 2015-2016: 3,775 applied, 2,665 accepted. Neither SAT nor ACT required. SAT 25/75 percentile: 880-1150. High school rank: 14% in top tenth, 34% in top quarter, 63% in top half
Early decision deadline: N/A, notification date: N/A
Early action deadline: N/A, notification date: N/A
Application deadline (fall): 6/15
Undergraduate student body: 7,358 full time, 8,732 part time; 42% male, 58% female; 6% American Indian, 8% Asian, 4% black, 7% Hispanic, 11% multiracial, 1% Pacific Islander, 57% white, 2% international; 90% from in state; N/A live on campus; N/A of students in fraternities, N/A in sororities
Most popular majors: 19% Business, Management, Marketing, and Related Support Services; 16% Health Professions and Related Programs; 7% Engineering; 7% Social Sciences; 6% Psychology
Expenses: 2016-2017: $6,834 in state, $21,504 out of state; room/board: $10,600
Financial aid: (907) 786-1586; 53% of undergrads determined to have financial need; average aid package $8,847

University of Alaska–Fairbanks
Fairbanks AK
(800) 478-1823
U.S. News ranking: Nat. U., No. 202
Website: www.uaf.edu
Admissions email: admissions@uaf.edu

Public; founded 1917
Freshman admissions: selective; 2015-2016: 1,554 applied, 1,136 accepted. Either SAT or ACT required. ACT 25/75 percentile: 18-26. High school rank: 18% in top tenth, 38% in top quarter, 69% in top half
Early decision deadline: N/A, notification date: N/A
Early action deadline: N/A, notification date: N/A
Application deadline (fall): 6/15
Undergraduate student body: 3,398 full time, 4,212 part time; 42% male, 58% female; 14% American Indian, 1% Asian, 2% black, 6% Hispanic, 4% multiracial, 0% Pacific Islander, 42% white, 1% international; 86% from in state; 30% live on campus; N/A of students in fraternities, N/A in sororities
Most popular majors: 17% Engineering; 10% Business, Management, Marketing, and Related Support Services; 9% Biological and Biomedical Sciences; 7% Social Sciences; 6% Psychology
Expenses: 2016-2017: $7,799 in state, $22,469 out of state; room/board: $8,380
Financial aid: (907) 474-7256; 53% of undergrads determined to have financial need; average aid package $7,950

University of Alaska–Southeast[1]
Juneau AK
(907) 465-6350
U.S. News ranking: Reg. U. (W), unranked
Website: www.uas.alaska.edu
Admissions email: admissions@uas.alaska.edu
Public
Application deadline (fall): N/A
Undergraduate student body: N/A full time, N/A part time
Expenses: 2015-2016: $6,132 in state, $17,306 out of state; room/board: $8,194
Financial aid: (907) 796-6255

ARIZONA

American Indian College[1]
Phoenix AZ
(800) 933-3828
U.S. News ranking: Reg. Coll. (W), unranked
Website: www.aicag.edu
Admissions email: aicadm@aicag.edu
Private
Application deadline (fall): N/A
Undergraduate student body: N/A full time, N/A part time
Expenses: 2015-2016: $11,700; room/board: $6,202
Financial aid: (800) 933-3828

Arizona Christian University
Phoenix AZ
(602) 386-4100
U.S. News ranking: Reg. Coll. (W), unranked
Website: arizonachristian.edu/
Admissions email: admissions@arizonachristian.edu
Private; founded 1960

Affiliation: Nondenominational
Freshman admissions: N/A;
2015-2016: 486 applied, 249
accepted. Either SAT or ACT
required. ACT 25/75 percentile:
19-24. High school rank: N/A
Early decision deadline: N/A,
notification date: N/A
Early action deadline: 11/1,
notification date: 11/5
Application deadline (fall): 8/15
Undergraduate student body: 628
full time, 151 part time; 58%
male, 42% female; 1% American
Indian, 1% Asian, 12% black,
17% Hispanic, 6% multiracial,
1% Pacific Islander, 56% white,
3% international; 74% from in
state; 28% live on campus; N/A
of students in fraternities, N/A in
sororities
Most popular majors: 23%
Psychology; 21% Business,
Management, Marketing, and
Related Support Services;
19% Theology and Religious
Vocations; 16% Education
Expenses: 2016-2017: $23,896;
room/board: $10,080
Financial aid: N/A; 82% of
undergrads determined to have
financial need; average aid
package $17,070

Arizona State University–Tempe
Tempe AZ
(480) 965-7788
U.S. News ranking: Nat. U.,
No. 129
Website: www.asu.edu
Admissions email:
admissions@asu.edu
Public; founded 1885
Freshman admissions: more
selective; 2015-2016: 25,380
applied, 21,042 accepted.
Neither SAT nor ACT required.
ACT 25/75 percentile: 23-28.
High school rank: 29% in top
tenth, 60% in top quarter, 89%
in top half
Early decision deadline: N/A,
notification date: N/A
Early action deadline: N/A,
notification date: N/A
Undergraduate student body:
38,212 full time, 3,616 part
time; 57% male, 43% female;
1% American Indian, 7% Asian,
4% black, 19% Hispanic, 4%
multiracial, 0% Pacific Islander,
52% white, 12% international;
75% from in state; 22% live
on campus; 8% of students in
fraternities, 16% in sororities
Most popular majors: 23%
Business, Management,
Marketing, and Related Support
Services; 10% Social Sciences;
9% Biological and Biomedical
Sciences; 9% Engineering; 8%
Visual and Performing Arts
Expenses: 2015-2016: $10,158
in state, $25,458 out of state;
room/board: $11,061
Financial aid: (480) 965-3355;
55% of undergrads determined
to have financial need; average
aid package $14,754

Frank Lloyd Wright School of Architecture
Scottsdale AZ
(608) 588-4770
U.S. News ranking: Arts, unranked
Website: www.taliesin.edu/
Admissions email: N/A
Private; founded 1932
Freshman admissions: N/A;
2015-2016: N/A applied, N/A
accepted. Neither SAT nor ACT
required. SAT 25/75 percentile:
N/A. High school rank: N/A
Early decision deadline: N/A,
notification date: N/A
Early action deadline: N/A,
notification date: N/A
Application deadline (fall): 4/1
Undergraduate student body: N/A
full time, N/A part time; N/A
male, N/A female; N/A American
Indian, N/A Asian, N/A black, N/A
Hispanic, N/A multiracial, N/A
Pacific Islander, N/A white, N/A
international
Most popular majors: Information
not available
Expenses: 2016-2017: $40,500;
room/board: N/A
Financial aid: N/A

Grand Canyon University[1]
Phoenix AZ
(800) 800-9776
U.S. News ranking: Nat. U.,
second tier
Website: apply.gcu.edu
Admissions email:
golopes@gcu.edu
For-profit; founded 1949
Application deadline (fall): rolling
Undergraduate student body: N/A
full time, N/A part time
Expenses: 2015-2016: $17,050;
room/board: $8,550
Financial aid: (602) 639-6600

Northcentral University
Prescott Valley AZ
(888) 327-2877
U.S. News ranking: Nat. U.,
unranked
Website: www.ncu.edu
Admissions email:
admissions@ncu.edu
For-profit; founded 1996
Freshman admissions: N/A;
2015-2016: N/A applied, N/A
accepted. Neither SAT nor ACT
required. ACT 25/75 percentile:
N/A. High school rank: N/A
Early decision deadline: N/A,
notification date: N/A
Early action deadline: N/A,
notification date: N/A
Application deadline (fall): rolling
Undergraduate student body: 32
full time, 136 part time; 28%
male, 72% female; N/A American
Indian, N/A Asian, N/A black, N/A
Hispanic, N/A multiracial, N/A
Pacific Islander, N/A white, N/A
international
Most popular majors: Information
not available
Expenses: 2015-2016: $10,368;
room/board: N/A
Financial aid: (928) 541-7777

Northern Arizona University
Flagstaff AZ
(928) 523-5511
U.S. News ranking: Nat. U.,
second tier
Website: www.nau.edu
Admissions email: undergraduate.
admissions@nau.edu
Public; founded 1899
Freshman admissions: selective;
2015-2016: 28,937 applied,
22,299 accepted. Neither SAT
nor ACT required. SAT 25/75
percentile: 920-1150. High
school rank: 22% in top tenth,
53% in top quarter, 85% in
top half
Early decision deadline: N/A,
notification date: N/A
Early action deadline: N/A,
notification date: N/A
Application deadline (fall): rolling
Undergraduate student body:
20,357 full time, 4,763 part
time; 41% male, 59% female;
3% American Indian, 2% Asian,
3% black, 22% Hispanic, 5%
multiracial, 0% Pacific Islander,
59% white, 4% international;
71% from in state; 29% live
on campus; N/A of students in
fraternities, N/A in sororities
Most popular majors: 19%
Business, Management,
Marketing, and Related Support
Services; 12% Health Professions
and Related Programs; 11%
Liberal Arts and Sciences,
General Studies and Humanities;
10% Education; 8% Social
Sciences
Expenses: 2016-2017: $10,764
in state, $24,144 out of state;
room/board: N/A
Financial aid: (928) 523-4951

Prescott College
Prescott AZ
(877) 350-2100
U.S. News ranking: Reg. U. (W),
No. 82
Website: www.prescott.edu/
Admissions email: admissions@
prescott.edu
Private; founded 1966
Freshman admissions: selective;
2015-2016: 328 applied, 231
accepted. Either SAT or ACT
required. SAT 25/75 percentile:
900-1150. High school rank: N/A
Early decision deadline: 12/1,
notification date: 12/15
Early action deadline: N/A,
notification date: N/A
Application deadline (fall): 8/15
Undergraduate student body: 304
full time, 154 part time; 39%
male, 61% female; 4% American
Indian, 2% Asian, 3% black,
6% Hispanic, 5% multiracial,
0% Pacific Islander, 66% white,
1% international; 32% from in
state; 16% live on campus; N/A
of students in fraternities, N/A in
sororities
Most popular majors: 30%
Psychology; 13% Parks,
Recreation, Leisure, and Fitness
Studies; 11% Education; 7%
Liberal Arts and Sciences,
General Studies and Humanities
Expenses: 2016-2017: $28,943;
room/board: $8,374

Financial aid: (928) 350-1111;
70% of undergrads determined
to have financial need; average
aid package $19,856

Southwest University of Visual Arts[1]
Tucson AZ
(800) 825-8753
U.S. News ranking: Arts, unranked
Website: suva.edu/
Admissions email: N/A
For-profit
Application deadline (fall): N/A
Undergraduate student body: N/A
full time, N/A part time
Expenses: 2015-2016: $23,069;
room/board: N/A
Financial aid: N/A

University of Arizona
Tucson AZ
(520) 621-3237
U.S. News ranking: Nat. U.,
No. 124
Website: www.arizona.edu
Admissions email: admissions@
arizona.edu
Public; founded 1885
Freshman admissions: selective;
2015-2016: 35,408 applied,
27,061 accepted. Neither SAT
nor ACT required. SAT 25/75
percentile: 960-1220. High
school rank: 28% in top tenth,
54% in top quarter, 84% in
top half
Early decision deadline: N/A,
notification date: N/A
Early action deadline: N/A,
notification date: N/A
Application deadline (fall): 5/1
Undergraduate student body:
29,804 full time, 3,928 part
time; 49% male, 51% female;
1% American Indian, 6% Asian,
4% black, 25% Hispanic, 4%
multiracial, 0% Pacific Islander,
52% white, 6% international;
69% from in state; 20% live
on campus; N/A of students in
fraternities, N/A in sororities
Most popular majors: 16%
Business, Management,
Marketing, and Related Support
Services; 10% Biological and
Biomedical Sciences; 9% Social
Sciences; 7% Psychology; 7%
Health Professions and Related
Programs
Expenses: 2015-2016: $10,872
in state, $30,025 out of state;
room/board: N/A
Financial aid: (520) 621-5200;
54% of undergrads determined
to have financial need; average
aid package $12,340

University of Phoenix[1]
Phoenix AZ
(866) 766-0766
U.S. News ranking: Nat. U.,
unranked
Website: www.phoenix.edu
Admissions email: N/A
For-profit
Application deadline (fall): N/A
Undergraduate student body: N/A
full time, N/A part time
Expenses: 2015-2016: $10,554;
room/board: N/A
Financial aid: N/A

ARKANSAS

Arkansas Baptist College[1]
Little Rock AR
(501) 244-5104
U.S. News ranking: Reg. Coll. (S),
unranked
Website:
www.arkansasbaptist.edu
Admissions email: jocelyn.
spriggs@arkansasbaptist.edu
Private
Application deadline (fall): N/A
Undergraduate student body: N/A
full time, N/A part time
Expenses: 2015-2016: $8,760;
room/board: $8,826
Financial aid: (501) 374-0804

Arkansas State University
State University AR
(870) 972-3024
U.S. News ranking: Reg. U. (S),
No. 59
Website: www.astate.edu
Admissions email: admissions@
astate.edu
Public; founded 1909
Freshman admissions: more
selective; 2015-2016: 5,346
applied, 3,755 accepted. Either
SAT or ACT required. ACT 25/75
percentile: 21-26. High school
rank: 27% in top tenth, 49% in
top quarter, 74% in top half
Early decision deadline: N/A,
notification date: N/A
Early action deadline: N/A,
notification date: N/A
Application deadline (fall): 8/22
Undergraduate student body: 7,295
full time, 2,297 part time; 43%
male, 57% female; 0% American
Indian, 1% Asian, 14% black,
2% Hispanic, 2% multiracial,
0% Pacific Islander, 74% white,
6% international; 89% from in
state; 30% live on campus; 5%
of students in fraternities, 5% in
sororities
Most popular majors: 11% Liberal
Arts and Sciences, General
Studies and Humanities; 8%
Health Professions and Related
Programs; 7% Education; 4%
Psychology
Expenses: 2015-2016: $10,100
in state, $14,050 out of state;
room/board: $8,140
Financial aid: (870) 972-2310;
86% of undergrads determined
to have financial need; average
aid package $10,500

Arkansas Tech University
Russellville AR
(479) 968-0343
U.S. News ranking: Reg. U. (S),
No. 97
Website: www.atu.edu
Admissions email:
tech.enroll@atu.edu
Public; founded 1909
Freshman admissions: selective;
2015-2016: 4,619 applied,
4,116 accepted. Either SAT
or ACT required. ACT 25/75
percentile: 18-25. High school
rank: 13% in top tenth, 34% in
top quarter, 65% in top half
Early decision deadline: N/A,
notification date: N/A

Early action deadline: N/A, notification date: N/A
Application deadline (fall): rolling
Undergraduate student body: 7,065 full time, 4,126 part time; 45% male, 55% female; 1% American Indian, 1% Asian, 10% black, 6% Hispanic, 3% multiracial, 0% Pacific Islander, 76% white, 4% international; 96% from in state; 32% live on campus; 6% of students in fraternities, 7% in sororities
Most popular majors: 21% Multi-/Interdisciplinary Studies, Other; 10% Registered Nursing/Registered Nurse; 5% Business Administration and Management, General; 5% Psychology, General
Expenses: 2015-2016: $6,192 in state, $11,352 out of state; room/board: $7,098
Financial aid: (479) 968-0399; 68% of undergrads determined to have financial need; average aid package $9,235

Central Baptist College
Conway AR
(501) 329-6873
U.S. News ranking: Reg. Coll. (S), No. 40
Website: www.cbc.edu
Admissions email: admissions@cbc.edu
Private; founded 1952
Affiliation: Baptist Missionary Association of America
Freshman admissions: selective; 2015-2016: 358 applied, 170 accepted. Either SAT or ACT required. ACT 25/75 percentile: 18-23. High school rank: 18% in top tenth, 30% in top quarter, 61% in top half
Early decision deadline: N/A, notification date: N/A
Early action deadline: N/A, notification date: N/A
Application deadline (fall): rolling
Undergraduate student body: 635 full time, 246 part time; 53% male, 47% female; 2% American Indian, 0% Asian, 22% black, 3% Hispanic, 1% multiracial, 0% Pacific Islander, 69% white, 3% international
Most popular majors: 25% Bible/Biblical Studies; 19% Organizational Behavior Studies; 14% Psychology, General; 9% Psychology, Other; 7% General Studies
Expenses: 2016-2017: $15,000; room/board: $7,500
Financial aid: (501) 329-6872; 77% of undergrads determined to have financial need; average aid package $11,418

Crowley's Ridge College[1]
Paragould AR
(870) 236-6901
U.S. News ranking: Reg. Coll. (S), second tier
Website: www.crc.edu/
Admissions email: N/A
Private
Application deadline (fall): N/A
Undergraduate student body: N/A full time, N/A part time
Expenses: 2015-2016: $11,900; room/board: $6,100
Financial aid: N/A

Harding University
Searcy AR
(800) 477-4407
U.S. News ranking: Reg. U. (S), No. 24
Website: www.harding.edu
Admissions email: admissions@harding.edu
Private; founded 1924
Affiliation: Church of Christ
Freshman admissions: more selective; 2015-2016: 1,592 applied, 1,491 accepted. Either SAT or ACT required. ACT 25/75 percentile: 22-28. High school rank: 26% in top tenth, 51% in top quarter, 78% in top half
Early decision deadline: N/A, notification date: N/A
Early action deadline: 11/15, notification date: N/A
Application deadline (fall): rolling
Undergraduate student body: 4,105 full time, 345 part time; 45% male, 55% female; 1% American Indian, 1% Asian, 4% black, 3% Hispanic, 2% multiracial, 0% Pacific Islander, 83% white, 6% international; 31% from in state; 74% live on campus; 0% of students in fraternities, 0% of students in sororities
Most popular majors: 16% Business, Management, Marketing, and Related Support Services; 14% Health Professions and Related Programs; 13% Education; 8% Liberal Arts and Sciences, General Studies and Humanities; 7% Parks, Recreation, Leisure, and Fitness Studies
Expenses: 2016-2017: $18,635; room/board: $6,760
Financial aid: (501) 279-5278; 62% of undergrads determined to have financial need; average aid package $17,294

Henderson State University
Arkadelphia AR
(870) 230-5028
U.S. News ranking: Reg. U. (S), No. 91
Website: www.hsu.edu/admissions
Admissions email: admissions@hsu.edu
Public; founded 1890
Freshman admissions: selective; 2015-2016: 3,786 applied, 2,413 accepted. Either SAT or ACT required. ACT 25/75 percentile: 18-24. High school rank: 16% in top tenth, 40% in top quarter, 69% in top half
Early decision deadline: N/A, notification date: N/A
Early action deadline: N/A, notification date: N/A
Application deadline (fall): rolling
Undergraduate student body: 2,747 full time, 352 part time; 43% male, 57% female; 0% American Indian, 1% Asian, 24% black, 4% Hispanic, 4% multiracial, 0% Pacific Islander, 66% white, 1% international; 86% from in state; 50% live on campus; N/A of students in fraternities, N/A in sororities
Most popular majors: 17% Business, Management, Marketing, and Related Support Services; 14% Education; 13% Liberal Arts and Sciences,

General Studies and Humanities; 9% Psychology; 8% Visual and Performing Arts
Expenses: 2016-2017: $8,116 in state, $14,956 out of state; room/board: N/A
Financial aid: (870) 230-5148; 84% of undergrads determined to have financial need; average aid package $10,424

Hendrix College
Conway AR
(800) 277-9017
U.S. News ranking: Nat. Lib. Arts, No. 72
Website: www.hendrix.edu
Admissions email: adm@hendrix.edu
Private; founded 1876
Affiliation: United Methodist
Freshman admissions: more selective; 2015-2016: 1,714 applied, 1,412 accepted. Either SAT or ACT required. ACT 25/75 percentile: 25-32. High school rank: 48% in top tenth, 77% in top quarter, 96% in top half
Early decision deadline: N/A, notification date: N/A
Early action deadline: 11/15, notification date: 12/15
Application deadline (fall): 6/1
Undergraduate student body: 1,318 full time, 9 part time; 47% male, 53% female; 1% American Indian, 5% Asian, 5% black, 5% Hispanic, 3% multiracial, 0% Pacific Islander, 78% white, 3% international; 48% from in state; 92% live on campus; 0% of students in fraternities, N/A in sororities
Most popular majors: 19% Social Sciences; 18% Biological and Biomedical Sciences; 10% Psychology; 9% English Language and Literature/Letters; 7% Foreign Languages, Literatures, and Linguistics
Expenses: 2016-2017: $42,440; room/board: $11,580
Financial aid: (501) 450-1368; 64% of undergrads determined to have financial need; average aid package $32,743

John Brown University
Siloam Springs AR
(877) 528-4636
U.S. News ranking: Reg. U. (S), No. 18
Website: www.jbu.edu
Admissions email: jbuinfo@jbu.edu
Private; founded 1919
Affiliation: Interdenominational
Freshman admissions: more selective; 2015-2016: 1,166 applied, 860 accepted. Neither SAT nor ACT required. ACT 25/75 percentile: 24-30. High school rank: 33% in top tenth, 59% in top quarter, 81% in top half
Early decision deadline: N/A, notification date: N/A
Early action deadline: N/A, notification date: N/A
Application deadline (fall): rolling
Undergraduate student body: 1,529 full time, 597 part time; 43% male, 57% female; 2% American Indian, 2% Asian, 2% black, 6% Hispanic, 3% multiracial, 0% Pacific Islander, 74% white, 6% international; 41% from in

state; 75% live on campus; N/A of students in fraternities, N/A in sororities
Most popular majors: 42% Business, Management, Marketing, and Related Support Services; 10% Visual and Performing Arts; 8% Education; 5% Engineering; 5% Family and Consumer Sciences/Human Sciences
Expenses: 2016-2017: $25,324; room/board: $8,840
Financial aid: (479) 524-7115; 53% of undergrads determined to have financial need; average aid package $16,691

Lyon College
Batesville AR
(800) 423-2542
U.S. News ranking: Nat. Lib. Arts, second tier
Website: www.lyon.edu
Admissions email: admissions@lyon.edu
Private; founded 1872
Affiliation: Presbyterian
Freshman admissions: more selective; 2015-2016: 1,607 applied, 950 accepted. Either SAT or ACT required. ACT 25/75 percentile: 22-27. High school rank: 27% in top tenth, 57% in top quarter, 87% in top half
Early decision deadline: N/A, notification date: N/A
Early action deadline: N/A, notification date: N/A
Application deadline (fall): rolling
Undergraduate student body: 698 full time, 17 part time; 52% male, 48% female; 2% American Indian, 2% Asian, 6% black, 7% Hispanic, 0% multiracial, 0% Pacific Islander, 75% white, 2% international; 71% from in state; 74% live on campus; 18% of students in fraternities, 25% in sororities
Most popular majors: 22% Biology/Biological Sciences, General; 16% Business Administration and Management, General; 15% Psychology, General; 10% Social Sciences, General; 8% Visual and Performing Arts, General
Expenses: 2016-2017: $26,290; room/board: $8,440
Financial aid: (870) 698-4257; 74% of undergrads determined to have financial need; average aid package $21,345

Ouachita Baptist University
Arkadelphia AR
(870) 245-5110
U.S. News ranking: Nat. Lib. Arts, No. 171
Website: www.obu.edu
Admissions email: admissions@obu.edu
Private; founded 1886
Affiliation: Arkansas Baptist State Convention
Freshman admissions: more selective; 2015-2016: 1,993 applied, 1,200 accepted. Either SAT or ACT required. ACT 25/75 percentile: 21-28. High school rank: 34% in top tenth, 59% in top quarter, 85% in top half
Early decision deadline: N/A, notification date: N/A

Early action deadline: N/A, notification date: N/A
Application deadline (fall): rolling
Undergraduate student body: 1,455 full time, 83 part time; 49% male, 51% female; 1% American Indian, 1% Asian, 7% black, 4% Hispanic, 0% multiracial, 0% Pacific Islander, 85% white, 2% international; 65% from in state; 94% live on campus; 20% of students in fraternities, 30% in sororities
Most popular majors: 14% Biological and Biomedical Sciences; 13% Business, Management, Marketing, and Related Support Services; 12% Theology and Religious Vocations; 11% Visual and Performing Arts; 8% Education
Expenses: 2016-2017: $24,940; room/board: $7,380
Financial aid: (870) 245-5570; 61% of undergrads determined to have financial need; average aid package $22,041

Philander Smith College
Little Rock AR
(501) 370-5221
U.S. News ranking: Nat. Lib. Arts, second tier
Website: www.philander.edu
Admissions email: admissions@philander.edu
Private; founded 1877
Affiliation: United Methodist
Freshman admissions: less selective; 2015-2016: 4,291 applied, 2,562 accepted. Either SAT or ACT required. ACT 25/75 percentile: 14-19. High school rank: 5% in top tenth, 28% in top quarter, 50% in top half
Early decision deadline: N/A, notification date: N/A
Early action deadline: N/A, notification date: N/A
Application deadline (fall): 7/1
Undergraduate student body: 549 full time, 35 part time; 37% male, 63% female; 0% American Indian, 1% Asian, 90% black, 1% Hispanic, 2% multiracial, 0% Pacific Islander, 0% white, 5% international; 52% from in state; 60% live on campus; 2% of students in fraternities, 3% in sororities
Most popular majors: 40% Business/Commerce, General; 11% Health and Physical Education/Fitness, General; 9% Psychology, General; 8% Social Work; 7% Biology/Biological Sciences, General
Expenses: 2016-2017: $12,414; room/board: $9,064
Financial aid: (501) 370-5350; 89% of undergrads determined to have financial need; average aid package $13,375

Southern Arkansas University
Magnolia AR
(870) 235-4040
U.S. News ranking: Reg. U. (S), second tier
Website: www.saumag.edu
Admissions email: muleriders@saumag.edu
Public; founded 1909

Freshman admissions: selective; 2015-2016: 2,845 applied, 1,895 accepted. Either SAT or ACT required. ACT 25/75 percentile: 18-24. High school rank: 14% in top tenth, 38% in top quarter, 72% in top half
Early decision deadline: N/A, notification date: N/A
Early action deadline: N/A, notification date: N/A
Application deadline (fall): 8/27
Undergraduate student body: 2,691 full time, 432 part time; 44% male, 56% female; 1% American Indian, 1% Asian, 28% black, 3% Hispanic, 0% multiracial, 0% Pacific Islander, 63% white, 3% international; 76% from in state; 55% live on campus; 2% of students in fraternities, 2% in sororities
Most popular majors: 19% Business, Management, Marketing, and Related Support Services; 14% Education; 8% Biological and Biomedical Sciences; 8% Health Professions and Related Programs; 7% Psychology
Expenses: 2015-2016: $7,961 in state, $11,531 out of state; room/board: $6,422
Financial aid: (870) 235-4023

University of Arkansas
Fayetteville AR
(800) 377-8632
U.S. News ranking: Nat. U., No. 135
Website: www.uark.edu
Admissions email: uofa@uark.edu
Public; founded 1871
Freshman admissions: more selective; 2015-2016: 20,542 applied, 12,337 accepted. Either SAT or ACT required. ACT 25/75 percentile: 23-28. High school rank: 26% in top tenth, 54% in top quarter, 85% in top half
Early decision deadline: N/A, notification date: N/A
Early action deadline: 11/1, notification date: 12/15
Application deadline (fall): 8/1
Undergraduate student body: 19,607 full time, 2,552 part time; 48% male, 52% female; 1% American Indian, 2% Asian, 5% black, 8% Hispanic, 3% multiracial, 0% Pacific Islander, 77% white, 3% international; 60% from in state; 26% live on campus; 22% of students in fraternities, 37% in sororities
Most popular majors: 22% Business, Management, Marketing, and Related Support Services; 9% Engineering; 8% Health Professions and Related Programs; 7% Social Sciences
Expenses: 2015-2016: $8,522 in state, $23,320 out of state; room/board: $9,880
Financial aid: (479) 575-3806; 43% of undergrads determined to have financial need; average aid package $9,311

University of Arkansas–Fort Smith[1]
Fort Smith AR
(479) 788-7120
U.S. News ranking: Reg. Coll. (S), No. 56
Website: www.uafortsmith.edu/Home/Index
Admissions email: N/A
Public; founded 1928
Application deadline (fall): rolling
Undergraduate student body: N/A full time, N/A part time
Expenses: 2015-2016: $5,062 in state, $11,302 out of state; room/board: $8,077
Financial aid: (479) 788-7090

University of Arkansas–Little Rock
Little Rock AR
(501) 569-3127
U.S. News ranking: Nat. U., second tier
Website: www.ualr.edu/
Admissions email: admissions@ualr.edu
Public; founded 1927
Freshman admissions: selective; 2015-2016: 1,316 applied, 894 accepted. Either SAT or ACT required. ACT 25/75 percentile: 18-24. High school rank: N/A
Early decision deadline: N/A, notification date: N/A
Early action deadline: N/A, notification date: N/A
Application deadline (fall): 8/1
Undergraduate student body: 4,860 full time, 4,715 part time; 40% male, 60% female; 0% American Indian, 2% Asian, 27% black, 7% Hispanic, 9% multiracial, N/A Pacific Islander, 52% white, 2% international; 97% from in state; N/A live on campus; 4% of students in fraternities, 3% in sororities
Most popular majors: 17% Business, Management, Marketing, and Related Support Services; 15% Health Professions and Related Programs; 6% Homeland Security, Law Enforcement, Firefighting and Related Protective Services; 6% Psychology; 5% Biological and Biomedical Sciences
Expenses: 2015-2016: $8,165 in state, $19,235 out of state; room/board: $8,780
Financial aid: (501) 569-3035; 76% of undergrads determined to have financial need; average aid package $12,451

University of Arkansas–Monticello[1]
Monticello AR
(870) 460-1026
U.S. News ranking: Reg. Coll. (S), unranked
Website: www.uamont.edu
Admissions email: admissions@uamont.edu
Public
Application deadline (fall): N/A
Undergraduate student body: N/A full time, N/A part time
Expenses: 2015-2016: $6,446 in state, $12,296 out of state; room/board: $6,146
Financial aid: (870) 460-1050

University of Arkansas–Pine Bluff
Pine Bluff AR
(870) 575-8492
U.S. News ranking: Reg. Coll. (S), No. 42
Website: www.uapb.edu/
Admissions email: jonesm@uapb.edu
Public; founded 1873
Freshman admissions: less selective; 2015-2016: 4,452 applied, 2,055 accepted. Either SAT or ACT required. ACT 25/75 percentile: 16-20. High school rank: 18% in top tenth, 36% in top quarter, 66% in top half
Early decision deadline: N/A, notification date: N/A
Early action deadline: N/A, notification date: N/A
Application deadline (fall): rolling
Undergraduate student body: 2,312 full time, 233 part time; 44% male, 56% female; 0% American Indian, 0% Asian, 92% black, 1% Hispanic, 0% multiracial, 0% Pacific Islander, 4% white, 1% international; 62% from in state; 48% live on campus; N/A of students in fraternities, N/A in sororities
Most popular majors: 13% Criminal Justice/Safety Studies; 10% Biology/Biological Sciences, General; 10% Business Administration and Management, General; 8% General Studies; 7% Physical Education Teaching and Coaching
Expenses: 2016-2017: $6,676 in state, $12,706 out of state; room/board: N/A
Financial aid: (870) 575-8302; 86% of undergrads determined to have financial need; average aid package $12,036

University of Central Arkansas
Conway AR
(501) 450-3128
U.S. News ranking: Reg. U. (S), No. 72
Website: www.uca.edu
Admissions email: admissions@uca.edu
Public; founded 1907
Freshman admissions: selective; 2015-2016: 5,063 applied, 4,667 accepted. Either SAT or ACT required. ACT 25/75 percentile: 20-26. High school rank: 17% in top tenth, 44% in top quarter, 76% in top half
Early decision deadline: N/A, notification date: N/A
Early action deadline: N/A, notification date: N/A
Application deadline (fall): rolling
Undergraduate student body: 8,281 full time, 1,606 part time; 41% male, 59% female; 1% American Indian, 2% Asian, 18% black, 5% Hispanic, 4% multiracial, 0% Pacific Islander, 66% white, 4% international; 86% from in state; 36% live on campus; 20% of students in fraternities, 21% in sororities
Most popular majors: 21% Health Professions and Related Programs; 17% Business, Management, Marketing, and Related Support Services; 12% Education; 7% Visual and Performing Arts; 6% Psychology

Expenses: 2015-2016: $7,889 in state, $13,806 out of state; room/board: $5,778
Financial aid: (501) 450-3140

University of the Ozarks
Clarksville AR
(479) 979-1227
U.S. News ranking: Reg. Coll. (S), No. 3
Website: www.ozarks.edu
Admissions email: admiss@ozarks.edu
Private; founded 1834
Affiliation: Presbyterian
Freshman admissions: selective; 2015-2016: 744 applied, 720 accepted. Either SAT or ACT required. ACT 25/75 percentile: 20-25. High school rank: 15% in top tenth, 39% in top quarter, 74% in top half
Early decision deadline: N/A, notification date: N/A
Early action deadline: N/A, notification date: N/A
Application deadline (fall): rolling
Undergraduate student body: 633 full time, 18 part time; 48% male, 52% female; 1% American Indian, 0% Asian, 6% black, 10% Hispanic, 4% multiracial, 0% Pacific Islander, 66% white, 12% international; 67% from in state; 80% live on campus; N/A of students in fraternities, N/A in sororities
Most popular majors: 16% Business Administration and Management, General; 10% Physical Education Teaching and Coaching; 9% Biology/Biological Sciences, General; 8% Elementary Education and Teaching; 8% Marketing/Marketing Management, General
Expenses: 2016-2017: $23,750; room/board: $7,100
Financial aid: (479) 979-1221; 75% of undergrads determined to have financial need; average aid package $23,518

Williams Baptist College
Walnut Ridge AR
(800) 722-4434
U.S. News ranking: Reg. Coll. (S), No. 23
Website: www.wbcoll.edu
Admissions email: admissions@wbcoll.edu
Private; founded 1941
Affiliation: Southern Baptist Convention
Freshman admissions: selective; 2015-2016: 579 applied, 369 accepted. Either SAT or ACT required. ACT 25/75 percentile: 19-24. High school rank: 8% in top tenth, 34% in top quarter, 67% in top half
Early decision deadline: N/A, notification date: N/A
Early action deadline: N/A, notification date: N/A
Application deadline (fall): rolling
Undergraduate student body: 483 full time, 58 part time; 50% male, 50% female; 1% American Indian, 0% Asian, 9% black, 4% Hispanic, 0% multiracial, 0% Pacific Islander, 83% white, 3% international

Most popular majors: 22% Liberal Arts and Sciences/Liberal Studies; 13% Psychology, General; 7% Physical Education Teaching and Coaching; 6% Biology/Biological Sciences, General; 6% Elementary Education and Teaching
Expenses: 2016-2017: $17,320; room/board: $7,400
Financial aid: (870) 759-4112; 67% of undergrads determined to have financial need; average aid package $15,095

CALIFORNIA

Academy of Art University
San Francisco CA
(800) 544-2787
U.S. News ranking: Arts, unranked
Website: www.academyart.edu/
Admissions email: admissions@academyart.edu
For-profit; founded 1929
Freshman admissions: N/A; 2015-2016: 2,732 applied, 2,732 accepted. Neither SAT nor ACT required. SAT 25/75 percentile: N/A. High school rank: N/A
Early decision deadline: N/A, notification date: N/A
Early action deadline: N/A, notification date: N/A
Application deadline (fall): rolling
Undergraduate student body: 5,339 full time, 3,778 part time; 42% male, 58% female; 0% American Indian, 8% Asian, 7% black, 12% Hispanic, 3% multiracial, 1% Pacific Islander, 23% white, 28% international; 60% from in state; 15% live on campus; N/A of students in fraternities, N/A in sororities
Most popular majors: 15% Fashion/Apparel Design; 13% Animation, Interactive Technology, Video Graphics and Special Effects; 10% Cinematography and Film/Video Production; 7% Photography
Expenses: 2016-2017: $300; room/board: $15,250
Financial aid: (415) 274-2223; 42% of undergrads determined to have financial need; average aid package $11,252

Alliant International University
San Diego CA
(858) 635-4772
U.S. News ranking: Nat. U., unranked
Website: www.alliant.edu
Admissions email: admissions@alliant.edu
Private; founded 1969
Freshman admissions: N/A; 2015-2016: N/A applied, N/A accepted. Neither SAT nor ACT required. ACT 25/75 percentile: N/A. High school rank: N/A
Early decision deadline: N/A, notification date: N/A
Early action deadline: N/A, notification date: N/A
Application deadline (fall): rolling
Undergraduate student body: 180 full time, 1,047 part time; 44% male, 56% female; 1% American Indian, 4% Asian, 6% black,

25% Hispanic, 3% multiracial, N/A Pacific Islander, 32% white, 16% international
Most popular majors: 65% Business/Commerce, General; 14% Psychology, General; 9% Criminal Justice/Law Enforcement Administration
Expenses: 2015-2016: $16,800; room/board: $8,090
Financial aid: (858) 635-4700

American Jewish University[1]
Bel-Air CA
(310) 440-1247
U.S. News ranking: Nat. Lib. Arts, second tier
Website: www.aju.edu
Admissions email: admissions@aju.edu
Private; founded 1947
Affiliation: Jewish
Application deadline (fall): rolling
Undergraduate student body: N/A full time, N/A part time
Expenses: 2016-2017: $30,182; room/board: $16,112
Financial aid: (310) 476-9777; 68% of undergrads determined to have financial need; average aid package $28,416

Argosy University[1]
Orange CA
(800) 377-0617
U.S. News ranking: Nat. U., unranked
Website: www.argosy.edu/
Admissions email: N/A
For-profit
Application deadline (fall): N/A
Undergraduate student body: N/A full time, N/A part time
Expenses: 2015-2016: $13,560; room/board: N/A
Financial aid: (714) 620-3687

Art Center College of Design
Pasadena CA
(626) 396-2373
U.S. News ranking: Arts, unranked
Website: www.artcenter.edu
Admissions email: admissions@artcenter.edu
Private; founded 1930
Freshman admissions: N/A; 2015-2016: N/A applied, N/A accepted. Neither SAT nor ACT required. SAT 25/75 percentile: N/A. High school rank: N/A
Early decision deadline: N/A, notification date: N/A
Early action deadline: N/A, notification date: N/A
Application deadline (fall): rolling
Undergraduate student body: 1,613 full time, 302 part time; 50% male, 50% female; 0% American Indian, 36% Asian, 1% black, 12% Hispanic, 4% multiracial, 0% Pacific Islander, 18% white, 27% international
Most popular majors: 74% Visual and Performing Arts; 17% Engineering Technologies and Engineering-Related Fields; 4% Communications Technologies/Technicians and Support Services
Expenses: 2015-2016: $39,230; room/board: N/A
Financial aid: (626) 396-2215

Ashford University[1]
San Diego CA
(563) 242-4153
U.S. News ranking: Reg. U. (W), unranked
Website: www.ashford.edu
Admissions email: admissions@ashford.edu
For-profit
Application deadline (fall): N/A
Undergraduate student body: N/A full time, N/A part time
Expenses: 2015-2016: $10,720; room/board: $6,520
Financial aid: (563) 242-4023

Azusa Pacific University
Azusa CA
(800) 825-5278
U.S. News ranking: Nat. U., No. 183
Website: www.apu.edu
Admissions email: admissions@apu.edu
Private; founded 1899
Affiliation: Christian interdenominational
Freshman admissions: selective; 2015-2016: 6,084 applied, 4,922 accepted. Either SAT or ACT required. SAT 25/75 percentile: 950-1180. High school rank: N/A
Early decision deadline: N/A, notification date: N/A
Early action deadline: 11/15, notification date: 1/15
Application deadline (fall): 6/1
Undergraduate student body: 5,356 full time, 527 part time; 35% male, 65% female; 0% American Indian, 9% Asian, 5% black, 29% Hispanic, 8% multiracial, 1% Pacific Islander, 44% white, 2% international; 82% from in state; 62% live on campus; 0% of students in fraternities, 0% in sororities
Most popular majors: 23% Health Professions and Related Programs; 21% Business, Management, Marketing, and Related Support Services; 10% Psychology; 8% Liberal Arts and Sciences, General Studies and Humanities; 8% Visual and Performing Arts
Expenses: 2016-2017: $36,120; room/board: $9,492
Financial aid: (626) 815-6000

Biola University
La Mirada CA
(562) 903-4752
U.S. News ranking: Nat. U., No. 164
Website: www.biola.edu
Admissions email: admissions@biola.edu
Private; founded 1908
Affiliation: Christian, Interdenominational
Freshman admissions: selective; 2015-2016: 3,701 applied, 2,706 accepted. Either SAT or ACT required. SAT 25/75 percentile: 980-1240. High school rank: 30% in top tenth, 59% in top quarter, 88% in top half
Early decision deadline: N/A, notification date: N/A
Early action deadline: 11/15, notification date: 1/15
Application deadline (fall): rolling

Undergraduate student body: 4,073 full time, 152 part time; 37% male, 63% female; 0% American Indian, 18% Asian, 2% black, 19% Hispanic, 6% multiracial, 0% Pacific Islander, 49% white, 3% international; 78% from in state; 63% live on campus; 0% of students in fraternities, 0% in sororities
Most popular majors: 13% Business, Management, Marketing, and Related Support Services; 12% Visual and Performing Arts; 10% Theology and Religious Vocations; 10% Psychology
Expenses: 2016-2017: $36,696; room/board: $9,704
Financial aid: (562) 903-4742; 69% of undergrads determined to have financial need; average aid package $18,943

Brandman University[1]
Irvine CA
(877) 516-4501
U.S. News ranking: Reg. U. (W), unranked
Website: www.brandman.edu
Admissions email: apply@brandman.edu
Private; founded 1958
Application deadline (fall): rolling
Undergraduate student body: N/A full time, N/A part time
Expenses: 2015-2016: $12,480; room/board: N/A
Financial aid: (415) 575-6122

California Baptist University
Riverside CA
(877) 228-8866
U.S. News ranking: Reg. U. (W), No. 37
Website: www.calbaptist.edu
Admissions email: admissions@calbaptist.edu
Private; founded 1950
Affiliation: California Southern Baptist Convention
Freshman admissions: less selective; 2015-2016: 4,180 applied, 2,734 accepted. Either SAT or ACT required. SAT 25/75 percentile: 830-1040. High school rank: 12% in top tenth, 40% in top quarter, 75% in top half
Early decision deadline: N/A, notification date: N/A
Early action deadline: 12/15, notification date: 1/31
Application deadline (fall): rolling
Undergraduate student body: 5,674 full time, 956 part time; 37% male, 63% female; 1% American Indian, 5% Asian, 7% black, 34% Hispanic, 6% multiracial, 1% Pacific Islander, 39% white, 2% international; 94% from in state; 39% live on campus; N/A of students in fraternities, N/A in sororities
Most popular majors: 13% Business/Commerce, General; 10% Registered Nursing/Registered Nurse; 9% Psychology, General; 7% Liberal Arts and Sciences/Liberal Studies; 7% Kinesiology and Exercise Science
Expenses: 2016-2017: $31,372; room/board: $8,210

California College of the Arts
San Francisco CA
(800) 447-1278
U.S. News ranking: Arts, unranked
Website: www.cca.edu
Admissions email: enroll@cca.edu
Private; founded 1907
Freshman admissions: N/A; 2015-2016: 1,713 applied, 1,364 accepted. Neither SAT nor ACT required. SAT 25/75 percentile: N/A. High school rank: N/A
Early decision deadline: N/A, notification date: N/A
Early action deadline: N/A, notification date: N/A
Application deadline (fall): rolling
Undergraduate student body: 1,446 full time, 87 part time; 38% male, 62% female; 0% American Indian, 16% Asian, 4% black, 13% Hispanic, 0% multiracial, 1% Pacific Islander, 27% white, 31% international; 68% from in state; 29% live on campus; 1% of students in fraternities, N/A in sororities
Most popular majors: 12% Graphic Design; 12% Industrial and Product Design; 6% Animation, Interactive Technology, Video Graphics and Special Effects
Expenses: 2016-2017: $45,466; room/board: $12,220
Financial aid: (415) 703-9573; 54% of undergrads determined to have financial need; average aid package $29,781

California Institute of Integral Studies
San Francisco CA
(415) 575-6100
U.S. News ranking: Nat. U., unranked
Website: www.ciis.edu
Admissions email: N/A
Private; founded 1968
Freshman admissions: N/A; 2015-2016: N/A applied, N/A accepted. Neither SAT nor ACT required. ACT 25/75 percentile: N/A. High school rank: N/A
Early decision deadline: N/A, notification date: N/A
Early action deadline: N/A, notification date: N/A
Application deadline (fall): N/A
Undergraduate student body: 87 full time, 15 part time; 19% male, 81% female; N/A American Indian, N/A Asian, N/A black, N/A Hispanic, N/A multiracial, N/A Pacific Islander, N/A white, N/A international
Most popular majors: Information not available
Expenses: 2015-2016: $26,910; room/board: N/A
Financial aid: N/A

California Institute of Technology
Pasadena CA
(626) 395-6341
U.S. News ranking: Nat. U., No. 12
Website: www.caltech.edu
Admissions email: ugadmissions@caltech.edu

Financial aid: (951) 343-4236; 88% of undergrads determined to have financial need; average aid package $17,790

Private; founded 1891
Freshman admissions: most selective; 2015-2016: 6,506 applied, 573 accepted. Either SAT or ACT required. SAT 25/75 percentile: 1500-1600. High school rank: 99% in top tenth, 100% in top quarter, 100% in top half
Early decision deadline: N/A, notification date: N/A
Early action deadline: 11/1, notification date: 12/15
Application deadline (fall): 1/3
Undergraduate student body: 1,001 full time, 0 part time; 61% male, 39% female; 0% American Indian, 45% Asian, 1% black, 12% Hispanic, 5% multiracial, 0% Pacific Islander, 27% white, 8% international; 37% from in state; 86% live on campus; 0% of students in fraternities, 0% in sororities
Most popular majors: 35% Engineering; 23% Physical Sciences; 21% Computer and Information Sciences and Support Services; 12% Mathematics and Statistics; 8% Biological and Biomedical Sciences
Expenses: 2016-2017: $47,577; room/board: $14,100
Financial aid: (626) 395-6280; 52% of undergrads determined to have financial need; average aid package $42,932

California Institute of the Arts
Valencia CA
(661) 255-1050
U.S. News ranking: Arts, unranked
Website: www.calarts.edu
Admissions email: admiss@calarts.edu
Private; founded 1961
Freshman admissions: N/A; 2015-2016: 2,145 applied, 536 accepted. Neither SAT nor ACT required. SAT 25/75 percentile: N/A. High school rank: N/A
Early decision deadline: N/A, notification date: N/A
Early action deadline: N/A, notification date: N/A
Application deadline (fall): N/A
Undergraduate student body: 943 full time, 6 part time; 40% male, 60% female; 0% American Indian, 14% Asian, 6% black, 14% Hispanic, 5% multiracial, 1% Pacific Islander, 38% white, 14% international
Most popular majors: Information not available
Expenses: 2015-2016: $43,986; room/board: $12,000
Financial aid: (661) 253-7869

California Lutheran University
Thousand Oaks CA
(877) 258-3678
U.S. News ranking: Reg. U. (W), No. 16
Website: www.callutheran.edu
Admissions email: admissions@callutheran.edu
Private; founded 1959
Affiliation: Lutheran
Freshman admissions: selective; 2015-2016: 6,569 applied, 4,044 accepted. Either SAT or ACT required. SAT 25/75 percentile: 1000-1200. High

school rank: 30% in top tenth, 72% in top quarter, 93% in top half
Early decision deadline: N/A, notification date: N/A
Early action deadline: 11/1, notification date: 1/15
Application deadline (fall): N/A
Undergraduate student body: 2,675 full time, 135 part time; 43% male, 57% female; 1% American Indian, 6% Asian, 4% black, 27% Hispanic, 5% multiracial, 1% Pacific Islander, 49% white, 3% international; 87% from in state; 52% live on campus; 0% of students in fraternities, 0% in sororities
Most popular majors: 15% Business, Management, Marketing, and Related Support Services; 12% Psychology; 7% Homeland Security, Law Enforcement, Firefighting and Related Protective Services; 6% Parks, Recreation, Leisure, and Fitness Studies
Expenses: 2016-2017: $39,760; room/board: $13,060
Financial aid: (805) 493-3115; 69% of undergrads determined to have financial need; average aid package $29,980

California Maritime Academy[1]
Vallejo CA
(707) 654-1330
U.S. News ranking: Reg. Coll. (W), No. 10
Website: www.csum.edu
Admissions email: admission@csum.edu
Public; founded 1929
Application deadline (fall): rolling
Undergraduate student body: N/A full time, N/A part time
Expenses: 2015-2016: $6,558 in state, $17,718 out of state; room/board: $11,756
Financial aid: (707) 654-1275

California Polytechnic State University–San Luis Obispo
San Luis Obispo CA
(805) 756-2311
U.S. News ranking: Reg. U. (W), No. 9
Website: www.calpoly.edu
Admissions email: admissions@calpoly.edu
Public; founded 1901
Freshman admissions: more selective; 2015-2016: 46,820 applied, 14,651 accepted. Either SAT or ACT required. SAT 25/75 percentile: 1130-1340. High school rank: 49% in top tenth, 84% in top quarter, 98% in top half
Early decision deadline: 10/31, notification date: 12/15
Early action deadline: N/A, notification date: N/A
Application deadline (fall): 11/30
Undergraduate student body: 19,318 full time, 731 part time; 53% male, 47% female; 0% American Indian, 12% Asian, 1% black, 16% Hispanic, 7% multiracial, 0% Pacific Islander, 58% white, 2% international; 86% from in state; 36% live on campus; N/A of students in fraternities, N/A in sororities

Most popular majors: 24% Engineering; 15% Business, Management, Marketing, and Related Support Services; 6% Biological and Biomedical Sciences; 6% Social Sciences
Expenses: 2016-2017: $9,075 in state, $20,235 out of state; room/board: $12,507
Financial aid: (805) 756-2927; 42% of undergrads determined to have financial need; average aid package $9,864

California State Polytechnic University–Pomona
Pomona CA
(909) 869-5299
U.S. News ranking: Reg. U. (W), No. 31
Website: www.cpp.edu
Admissions email: admissions@cpp.edu
Public; founded 1938
Freshman admissions: selective; 2015-2016: 33,857 applied, 13,307 accepted. Either SAT or ACT required. SAT 25/75 percentile: 920-1180. High school rank: N/A
Early decision deadline: N/A, notification date: N/A
Early action deadline: N/A, notification date: N/A
Application deadline (fall): 11/30
Undergraduate student body: 19,619 full time, 2,538 part time; 56% male, 44% female; 0% American Indian, 24% Asian, 3% black, 40% Hispanic, 4% multiracial, 0% Pacific Islander, 19% white, 5% international; 98% from in state; 10% live on campus; 2% of students in fraternities, 1% in sororities
Most popular majors: 24% Business Administration and Management, General; 6% Hospitality Administration/Management, General; 4% Biology/Biological Sciences, General; 4% Civil Engineering, General; 4% Mechanical Engineering
Expenses: 2016-2017: $6,976 in state, $18,136 out of state; room/board: $15,238
Financial aid: (909) 869-3700; 69% of undergrads determined to have financial need; average aid package $10,658

California State University–Bakersfield
Bakersfield CA
(661) 654-3036
U.S. News ranking: Reg. U. (W), second tier
Website: www.csub.edu
Admissions email: admissions@csub.edu
Public
Freshman admissions: least selective; 2015-2016: 5,796 applied, 5,796 accepted. Neither SAT nor ACT required. SAT 25/75 percentile: 800-1010. High school rank: N/A
Early decision deadline: N/A, notification date: N/A
Early action deadline: N/A, notification date: 2/1
Application deadline (fall): 11/30

Undergraduate student body: 6,655 full time, 1,370 part time; 39% male, 61% female; 1% American Indian, 7% Asian, 7% black, 55% Hispanic, 3% multiracial, 0% Pacific Islander, 20% white, 4% international; 99% from in state; N/A live on campus; N/A of students in fraternities, N/A in sororities
Most popular majors: 29% Liberal Arts and Sciences, General Studies and Humanities; 9% Psychology; 8% Social Sciences; 8% Education; 7% Mathematics and Statistics
Expenses: 2016-2017: $6,841 in state, $18,001 out of state; room/board: $13,968
Financial aid: (661) 654-3016; 83% of undergrads determined to have financial need; average aid package $4,312

California State University–Channel Islands[1]
Camarillo CA
(805) 437-8500
U.S. News ranking: Reg. U. (W), No. 82
Website: www.csuci.edu
Admissions email: N/A
Public
Application deadline (fall): N/A
Undergraduate student body: N/A full time, N/A part time
Expenses: 2015-2016: $6,547 in state, $17,707 out of state; room/board: $14,858
Financial aid: (805) 437-8530

California State University–Chico
Chico CA
(800) 542-4426
U.S. News ranking: Reg. U. (W), No. 37
Website: www.csuchico.edu
Admissions email: info@csuchico.edu
Public; founded 1887
Freshman admissions: selective; 2015-2016: 22,321 applied, 14,441 accepted. Either SAT or ACT required. SAT 25/75 percentile: 890-1110. High school rank: 35% in top tenth, 76% in top quarter, 100% in top half
Early decision deadline: N/A, notification date: N/A
Early action deadline: N/A, notification date: N/A
Application deadline (fall): 11/30
Undergraduate student body: 14,552 full time, 1,575 part time; 48% male, 52% female; 1% American Indian, 6% Asian, 2% black, 29% Hispanic, 5% multiracial, 0% Pacific Islander, 45% white, 4% international; 99% from in state; 1% live on campus; 1% of students in fraternities, 1% in sororities
Most popular majors: 16% Business, Management, Marketing, and Related Support Services; 10% Social Sciences; 10% Health Professions and Related Programs; 8% Parks, Recreation, Leisure, and Fitness Studies; 7% Psychology
Expenses: 2016-2017: $8,580 in state, $19,736 out of state; room/board: $12,234

Financial aid: (530) 898-6451; 64% of undergrads determined to have financial need; average aid package $16,090

California State University–Dominguez Hills
Carson CA
(310) 243-3300
U.S. News ranking: Reg. U. (W), second tier
Website: www.csudh.edu
Admissions email: info@csudh.edu
Public; founded 1960
Freshman admissions: less selective; 2015-2016: 4,615 applied, 2,672 accepted. Neither SAT nor ACT required. SAT 25/75 percentile: 750-940. High school rank: N/A
Early decision deadline: N/A, notification date: N/A
Early action deadline: N/A, notification date: N/A
Application deadline (fall): rolling
Undergraduate student body: 9,172 full time, 3,390 part time; 37% male, 63% female; 0% American Indian, 9% Asian, 13% black, 59% Hispanic, 3% multiracial, 0% Pacific Islander, 8% white, 3% international
Most popular majors: 19% Business, Management, and Related Support Services; 14% Health Professions and Related Programs; 11% Psychology; 10% Social Sciences; 7% Liberal Arts and Sciences, General Studies and Humanities
Expenses: 2015-2016: $12,487 in state, $23,647 out of state; room/board: $12,790
Financial aid: (310) 243-3691

California State University–East Bay
Hayward CA
(510) 885-2784
U.S. News ranking: Reg. U. (W), second tier
Website: www.csueastbay.edu
Admissions email: admissions@csueastbay.edu
Public; founded 1957
Freshman admissions: less selective; 2015-2016: 14,776 applied, 10,938 accepted. Neither SAT nor ACT required. SAT 25/75 percentile: 790-1000. High school rank: N/A
Early decision deadline: N/A, notification date: N/A
Early action deadline: N/A, notification date: N/A
Application deadline (fall): 11/30
Undergraduate student body: 11,110 full time, 1,898 part time; 39% male, 61% female; 0% American Indian, 24% Asian, 11% black, 31% Hispanic, 6% multiracial, 1% Pacific Islander, 17% white, 6% international; 99% from in state; N/A live on campus; N/A of students in fraternities, N/A in sororities
Most popular majors: 21% Business Administration and Management, General; 18% Health Professions and Related Programs; 9% Social Sciences, General; 7% Psychology, General; 7% Public Administration and Social Service Professions, Other

Expenses: 2016-2017: $6,564 in state, $17,724 out of state; room/board: $14,184
Financial aid: (510) 885-2784; 67% of undergrads determined to have financial need; average aid package $10,882

California State University–Fresno
Fresno CA
(559) 278-2191
U.S. News ranking: Nat. U., No. 220
Website: www.csufresno.edu
Admissions email: tinab@csufresno.edu
Public; founded 1911
Freshman admissions: selective; 2015-2016: 19,935 applied, 10,404 accepted. Either SAT or ACT required. SAT 25/75 percentile: 790-1010. High school rank: 15% in top tenth, 80% in top quarter, 100% in top half
Early decision deadline: N/A, notification date: N/A
Early action deadline: N/A, notification date: N/A
Application deadline (fall): 11/30
Undergraduate student body: 17,806 full time, 3,676 part time; 43% male, 57% female; 0% American Indian, 15% Asian, 3% black, 48% Hispanic, 3% multiracial, 0% Pacific Islander, 21% white, 5% international; 99% from in state; 5% live on campus; 6% of students in fraternities, 6% in sororities
Most popular majors: 14% Business, Management, Marketing, and Related Support Services; 13% Health Professions and Related Programs; 8% Liberal Arts and Sciences, General Studies and Humanities; 7% Homeland Security, Law Enforcement, Firefighting and Related Protective Services; 7% Psychology
Expenses: 2016-2017: $6,313 in state, $17,209 out of state; room/board: $9,386
Financial aid: (559) 278-2182; 76% of undergrads determined to have financial need; average aid package $11,972

California State University–Fullerton
Fullerton CA
(657) 278-7788
U.S. News ranking: Nat. U., No. 202
Website: www.fullerton.edu
Admissions email: admissions@fullerton.edu
Public; founded 1957
Freshman admissions: selective; 2015-2016: 41,841 applied, 17,515 accepted. SAT required. SAT 25/75 percentile: 930-1130. High school rank: 23% in top tenth, 67% in top quarter, 96% in top half
Early decision deadline: N/A, notification date: N/A
Early action deadline: N/A, notification date: N/A
Application deadline (fall): 11/30
Undergraduate student body: 27,105 full time, 6,039 part time; 45% male, 55% female; 0% American Indian, 22% Asian, 2% black, 40% Hispanic, 4%

multiracial, 0% Pacific Islander, 22% white, 6% international; N/A from in state; 2% live on campus; 3% of students in fraternities, 5% in sororities
Most popular majors: 24% Business, Management, Marketing, and Related Support Services; 10% Health Professions and Related Programs; 7% Psychology; 6% Social Sciences
Expenses: 2016-2017: $6,436 in state, $17,596 out of state; room/board: $15,642
Financial aid: (714) 278-3128; 67% of undergrads determined to have financial need; average aid package $7,772

California State University– Long Beach
Long Beach CA
(562) 985-5471
U.S. News ranking: Reg. U. (W), No. 35
Website: www.csulb.edu
Admissions email: N/A
Public; founded 1949
Freshman admissions: selective; 2015-2016: 56,975 applied, 19,650 accepted. Either SAT or ACT required. SAT 25/75 percentile: 930-1170. High school rank: N/A
Early decision deadline: N/A, notification date: N/A
Early action deadline: N/A, notification date: N/A
Application deadline (fall): 11/30
Undergraduate student body: 26,727 full time, 5,352 part time; 44% male, 56% female; 0% American Indian, 23% Asian, 4% black, 39% Hispanic, 5% multiracial, 0% Pacific Islander, 19% white, 7% international; 99% from in state; 8% live on campus; N/A of students in fraternities, N/A in sororities
Most popular majors: 14% Business, Management, Marketing, and Related Support Services; 11% Health Professions and Related Programs; 10% Social Sciences; 8% Family and Consumer Sciences/Human Sciences
Expenses: 2016-2017: $6,452 in state, $16,124 out of state; room/board: $12,382
Financial aid: (562) 985-8403; 76% of undergrads determined to have financial need; average aid package $13,488

California State University– Los Angeles
Los Angeles CA
(323) 343-3901
U.S. News ranking: Reg. U. (W), No. 61
Website: www.calstatela.edu
Admissions email: admission@calstatela.edu
Public; founded 1947
Freshman admissions: less selective; 2015-2016: 31,855 applied, 21,704 accepted. Neither SAT nor ACT required. SAT 25/75 percentile: 780-990. High school rank: N/A

Early decision deadline: N/A, notification date: N/A
Early action deadline: N/A, notification date: N/A
Application deadline (fall): 11/30
Undergraduate student body: 20,378 full time, 3,061 part time; 42% male, 58% female; 0% American Indian, 15% Asian, 4% black, 63% Hispanic, 2% multiracial, 0% Pacific Islander, 7% white, 6% international; 99% from in state; 4% live on campus; 2% of students in fraternities, 1% in sororities
Most popular majors: 20% Business, Management, Marketing, and Related Support Services; 13% Social Sciences; 12% Health Professions and Related Programs; 6% Psychology
Expenses: 2016-2017: $6,345 in state, $17,505 out of state; room/board: $12,860
Financial aid: (323) 343-1784; 87% of undergrads determined to have financial need; average aid package $11,454

California State University– Monterey Bay
Seaside CA
(831) 582-3738
U.S. News ranking: Reg. U. (W), No. 58
Website: www.csumb.edu
Admissions email: admissions@csumb.edu
Public; founded 1994
Freshman admissions: selective; 2015-2016: 15,561 applied, 7,576 accepted. Either SAT or ACT required. SAT 25/75 percentile: 853-1100. High school rank: 15% in top tenth, 51% in top quarter, 88% in top half
Early decision deadline: N/A, notification date: N/A
Early action deadline: N/A, notification date: N/A
Application deadline (fall): 11/30
Undergraduate student body: 6,171 full time, 486 part time; 38% male, 62% female; 1% American Indian, 6% Asian, 7% black, 36% Hispanic, 7% multiracial, 1% Pacific Islander, 34% white, 4% international; 98% from in state; 46% live on campus; 3% of students in fraternities, 4% in sororities
Most popular majors: 17% Liberal Arts and Sciences, General Studies and Humanities; 16% Business, Management, Marketing, and Related Support Services; 12% Psychology; 11% Parks, Recreation, Leisure, and Fitness Studies; 6% Public Administration and Social Service Professions
Expenses: 2015-2016: $6,119 in state, $17,279 out of state; room/board: $10,542
Financial aid: (831) 582-5100; 68% of undergrads determined to have financial need; average aid package $11,069

California State University–Northridge
Northridge CA
(818) 677-3700
U.S. News ranking: Reg. U. (W), No. 68
Website: www.csun.edu
Admissions email: admissions.records@csun.edu
Public; founded 1958
Freshman admissions: less selective; 2015-2016: 34,444 applied, 15,706 accepted. Either SAT or ACT required. SAT 25/75 percentile: 800-1030. High school rank: N/A
Early decision deadline: N/A, notification date: N/A
Early action deadline: N/A, notification date: N/A
Application deadline (fall): 11/30
Undergraduate student body: 30,115 full time, 6,802 part time; 46% male, 54% female; 0% American Indian, 11% Asian, 5% black, 44% Hispanic, 3% multiracial, 0% Pacific Islander, 23% white, 9% international; 97% from in state; N/A live on campus; N/A of students in fraternities, N/A in sororities
Most popular majors: 17% Business, Management, Marketing, and Related Support Services; 13% Social Sciences; 10% Psychology; 8% Health Professions and Related Programs
Expenses: 2016-2017: $6,569 in state, $17,729 out of state; room/board: $9,962
Financial aid: (818) 677-4085

California State University– Sacramento[1]
Sacramento CA
(916) 278-3901
U.S. News ranking: Reg. U. (W), No. 82
Website: www.csus.edu
Admissions email: outreach@csus.edu
Public; founded 1947
Application deadline (fall): 11/30
Undergraduate student body: N/A full time, N/A part time
Expenses: 2015-2016: $6,648 in state, $17,808 out of state; room/board: N/A
Financial aid: (916) 278-6554

California State University– San Bernardino
San Bernardino CA
(909) 537-5188
U.S. News ranking: Reg. U. (W), No. 61
Website: www.csusb.edu
Admissions email: moreinfo@csusb.edu
Public; founded 1962
Freshman admissions: less selective; 2015-2016: 13,804 applied, 8,916 accepted. Neither SAT nor ACT required. SAT 25/75 percentile: 800-990. High school rank: N/A
Early decision deadline: N/A, notification date: N/A
Early action deadline: N/A, notification date: 5/1
Application deadline (fall): rolling

Undergraduate student body: 15,859 full time, 1,862 part time; 40% male, 60% female; 0% American Indian, 6% Asian, 6% black, 60% Hispanic, 3% multiracial, 0% Pacific Islander, 14% white, 7% international; 99% from in state; 8% live on campus; 4% of students in fraternities, 4% in sororities
Most popular majors: 23% Business, Management, Marketing, and Related Support Services; 14% Psychology; 10% Social Sciences; 9% Health Professions and Related Programs; 7% Homeland Security, Law Enforcement, Firefighting and Related Protective Services
Expenses: 2016-2017: $6,597 in state, $17,757 out of state; room/board: $12,966
Financial aid: (909) 537-7800; 83% of undergrads determined to have financial need; average aid package $8,439

California State University– San Marcos
San Marcos CA
(760) 750-4848
U.S. News ranking: Reg. U. (W), No. 88
Website: www.csusm.edu
Admissions email: apply@csusm.edu
Public; founded 1989
Freshman admissions: less selective; 2015-2016: 11,560 applied, 7,746 accepted. Either SAT or ACT required. SAT 25/75 percentile: 850-1050. High school rank: N/A
Early decision deadline: N/A, notification date: N/A
Early action deadline: N/A, notification date: N/A
Application deadline (fall): 11/30
Undergraduate student body: 9,578 full time, 2,599 part time; 39% male, 61% female; 0% American Indian, 10% Asian, 3% black, 42% Hispanic, 6% multiracial, 0% Pacific Islander, 30% white, 2% international; 100% from in state; 80% live on campus; N/A of students in fraternities, N/A in sororities
Most popular majors: 42% Parks, Recreation, Leisure, and Fitness Studies; 19% Social Sciences; 17% Business, Management, Marketing, and Related Support Services; 10% Family and Consumer Sciences/Human Sciences; 9% Health Professions and Related Programs
Expenses: 2016-2017: $7,378 in state, $16,306 out of state; room/board: $13,240
Financial aid: (760) 750-4850

California State University–Stanislaus
Turlock CA
(209) 667-3152
U.S. News ranking: Reg. U. (W), No. 61
Website: www.csustan.edu
Admissions email: Outreach_Help_Desk@csustan.edu
Public; founded 1957

Freshman admissions: less selective; 2015-2016: 7,080 applied, 5,001 accepted. Neither SAT nor ACT required. SAT 25/75 percentile: 800-1010. High school rank: N/A
Early decision deadline: N/A, notification date: N/A
Early action deadline: N/A, notification date: N/A
Application deadline (fall): 11/30
Undergraduate student body: 6,781 full time, 1,318 part time; 36% male, 64% female; 0% American Indian, 11% Asian, 2% black, 49% Hispanic, 4% multiracial, 1% Pacific Islander, 24% white, 3% international; 100% from in state; 8% live on campus; 7% of students in fraternities, 7% in sororities
Most popular majors: 20% Business Administration and Management, General; 14% Psychology, General; 9% Criminal Justice/Safety Studies; 8% Liberal Arts and Sciences/Liberal Studies; 7% Registered Nursing/Registered Nurse
Expenses: 2016-2017: $6,728 in state, $17,888 out of state; room/board: $8,567
Financial aid: (209) 667-3336; 77% of undergrads determined to have financial need; average aid package $12,192

Chapman University
Orange CA
(888) 282-7759
U.S. News ranking: Reg. U. (W), No. 6
Website: www.chapman.edu
Admissions email: admit@chapman.edu
Private; founded 1861
Affiliation: Christian Church (Disciples of Christ)
Freshman admissions: more selective; 2015-2016: 13,670 applied, 6,504 accepted. Either SAT or ACT required. SAT 25/75 percentile: 1100-1290. High school rank: 39% in top tenth, 79% in top quarter, 97% in top half
Early decision deadline: N/A, notification date: N/A
Early action deadline: 11/1, notification date: 1/10
Application deadline (fall): 1/15
Undergraduate student body: 6,080 full time, 283 part time; 40% male, 60% female; 1% American Indian, 0% Asian, 0% black, 14% Hispanic, 6% multiracial, 58% Pacific Islander, 10% white, 4% international; 74% from in state; 34% live on campus; 22% of students in fraternities, 40% in sororities
Most popular majors: 17% Business Administration and Management, General; 11% Cinematography and Film/Video Production; 8% Psychology, General
Expenses: 2016-2017: $49,060; room/board: $14,368
Financial aid: (714) 997-6741; 56% of undergrads determined to have financial need; average aid package $31,033

Claremont McKenna College

Claremont CA
(909) 621-8088
U.S. News ranking: Nat. Lib. Arts, No. 9
Website: www.claremontmckenna.edu
Admissions email: admission@cmc.edu
Private; founded 1946
Freshman admissions: most selective; 2015-2016: 7,156 applied, 784 accepted. Either SAT or ACT required. SAT 25/75 percentile: 1340-1530. High school rank: 73% in top tenth, 98% in top quarter, 100% in top half
Early decision deadline: 11/1, notification date: 12/15
Early action deadline: N/A, notification date: N/A
Application deadline (fall): 1/1
Undergraduate student body: 1,326 full time, 2 part time; 51% male, 49% female; 0% American Indian, 10% Asian, 4% black, 14% Hispanic, 7% multiracial, 0% Pacific Islander, 42% white, 17% international; 45% from in state; 97% live on campus; 0% of students in fraternities, 0% in sororities
Most popular majors: 27% Economics, General; 15% Political Science and Government, General; 13% Psychology, General; 8% Accounting; 8% International Relations and Affairs
Expenses: 2016-2017: $50,945; room/board: $15,740
Financial aid: (909) 621-8356; 40% of undergrads determined to have financial need; average aid package $43,315

Cogswell Polytechnical College[1]

Sunnyvale CA
(408) 541-0100
U.S. News ranking: Reg. Coll. (W), unranked
Website: www.cogswell.edu
Admissions email: info@cogswell.edu
Private; founded 1887
Application deadline (fall): rolling
Undergraduate student body: N/A full time, N/A part time
Expenses: 2015-2016: $16,640; room/board: $11,780
Financial aid: (408) 541-0100

Concordia University

Irvine CA
(949) 214-3010
U.S. News ranking: Reg. U. (W), No. 41
Website: www.cui.edu
Admissions email: admission@cui.edu
Private; founded 1972
Affiliation: Lutheran Church–Missouri Synod
Freshman admissions: selective; 2015-2016: 3,135 applied, 1,855 accepted. Either SAT or ACT required. SAT 25/75 percentile: 900-1130. High school rank: 23% in top tenth, 49% in top quarter, 78% in top half

Early decision deadline: N/A, notification date: N/A
Early action deadline: 12/1, notification date: 12/15
Application deadline (fall): rolling
Undergraduate student body: 1,721 full time, 218 part time; 38% male, 62% female; 0% American Indian, 6% Asian, 4% black, 21% Hispanic, 5% multiracial, 0% Pacific Islander, 46% white, 5% international; 86% from in state; 46% live on campus; N/A of students in fraternities, N/A in sororities
Most popular majors: 19% Business Administration and Management, General; 19% Registered Nursing/Registered Nurse; 9% Health and Physical Education/Fitness, General; 9% Liberal Arts and Sciences/Liberal Studies
Expenses: 2016-2017: $32,780; room/board: $10,240
Financial aid: (949) 854-8002; 71% of undergrads determined to have financial need; average aid package $19,781

Dominican University of California

San Rafael CA
(415) 485-3204
U.S. News ranking: Reg. U. (W), No. 30
Website: www.dominican.edu
Admissions email: enroll@dominican.edu
Private; founded 1890
Freshman admissions: selective; 2015-2016: 2,178 applied, 1,717 accepted. Either SAT or ACT required. SAT 25/75 percentile: 950-1140. High school rank: 24% in top tenth, 55% in top quarter, 87% in top half
Early decision deadline: N/A, notification date: N/A
Early action deadline: N/A, notification date: N/A
Application deadline (fall): rolling
Undergraduate student body: 1,180 full time, 203 part time; 28% male, 72% female; 1% American Indian, 22% Asian, 5% black, 20% Hispanic, 6% multiracial, 1% Pacific Islander, 36% white, 2% international; 91% from in state; 34% live on campus; N/A of students in fraternities, N/A in sororities
Most popular majors: 36% Health Professions and Related Programs; 18% Business, Management, Marketing, and Related Support Services; 12% Biological and Biomedical Sciences; 8% Psychology; 8% Social Sciences
Expenses: 2016-2017: $43,400; room/board: $13,650
Financial aid: (415) 257-1321; 77% of undergrads determined to have financial need; average aid package $15,295

Fashion Institute of Design & Merchandising

Los Angeles CA
(800) 624-1200
U.S. News ranking: Arts, unranked
Website: fidm.edu/
Admissions email: admissions@fidm.edu

Private; founded 1969
Freshman admissions: N/A; 2015-2016: 1,964 applied, 990 accepted. Neither SAT nor ACT required. SAT 25/75 percentile: N/A. High school rank: N/A
Early decision deadline: N/A, notification date: N/A
Early action deadline: 6/30, notification date: 8/1
Application deadline (fall): rolling
Undergraduate student body: 3,058 full time, 362 part time; 11% male, 89% female; 1% American Indian, 12% Asian, 5% black, 23% Hispanic, 3% multiracial, 1% Pacific Islander, 34% white, 15% international; 71% from in state; 0% live on campus; 0% of students in fraternities, 0% in sororities
Most popular majors: 99% Business, Management, Marketing, and Related Support Services, Other; 1% Industrial and Product Design
Expenses: 2015-2016: $29,930; room/board: N/A
Financial aid: N/A

Fresno Pacific University

Fresno CA
(559) 453-2039
U.S. News ranking: Reg. U. (W), No. 44
Website: www.fresno.edu
Admissions email: ugadmis@fresno.edu
Private; founded 1944
Affiliation: Mennonite Brethren
Freshman admissions: selective; 2015-2016: 709 applied, 366 accepted. Either SAT or ACT required. SAT 25/75 percentile: 880-1077. High school rank: 30% in top tenth, 64% in top quarter, 94% in top half
Early decision deadline: N/A, notification date: N/A
Early action deadline: N/A, notification date: N/A
Application deadline (fall): 7/31
Undergraduate student body: 2,010 full time, 519 part time; 30% male, 70% female; 1% American Indian, 4% Asian, 5% black, 43% Hispanic, 2% multiracial, 1% Pacific Islander, 35% white, 2% international; 98% from in state; 22% live on campus; 0% of students in fraternities, 0% in sororities
Most popular majors: 20% Business, Management, Marketing, and Related Support Services; 18% Liberal Arts and Sciences, General Studies and Humanities; 11% Family and Consumer Sciences/Human Sciences; 10% Psychology; 8% Health Professions and Related Programs
Expenses: 2016-2017: $29,170; room/board: $8,060
Financial aid: (559) 453-2027; 85% of undergrads determined to have financial need; average aid package $16,366

Golden Gate University[1]

San Francisco CA
(415) 442-7800
U.S. News ranking: Reg. U. (W), unranked
Website: www.ggu.edu
Admissions email: info@ggu.edu
Private; founded 1901
Application deadline (fall): rolling
Undergraduate student body: N/A full time, N/A part time
Expenses: 2015-2016: $14,640; room/board: N/A
Financial aid: (415) 442-7270

Harvey Mudd College

Claremont CA
(909) 621-8011
U.S. News ranking: Nat. Lib. Arts, No. 21
Website: www.hmc.edu
Admissions email: admission@hmc.edu
Private; founded 1955
Freshman admissions: most selective; 2015-2016: 4,119 applied, 534 accepted. Either SAT or ACT required. SAT 25/75 percentile: 1400-1560. High school rank: 93% in top tenth, 98% in top quarter, 100% in top half
Early decision deadline: 11/15, notification date: 12/15
Early action deadline: N/A, notification date: N/A
Application deadline (fall): 1/5
Undergraduate student body: 815 full time, 0 part time; 53% male, 47% female; 0% American Indian, 20% Asian, 2% black, 13% Hispanic, 8% multiracial, 0% Pacific Islander, 38% white, 13% international; 46% from in state; 99% live on campus; 0% of students in fraternities, 0% in sororities
Most popular majors: 30% Computer and Information Sciences and Support Services; 29% Engineering; 15% Multi/Interdisciplinary Studies; 12% Physical Sciences; 6% Mathematics and Statistics
Expenses: 2016-2017: $52,916; room/board: $17,051
Financial aid: (909) 621-8055; 50% of undergrads determined to have financial need; average aid package $43,723

Holy Names University

Oakland CA
(510) 436-1351
U.S. News ranking: Reg. U. (W), No. 52
Website: www.hnu.edu
Admissions email: admissions@hnu.edu
Private; founded 1868
Affiliation: Roman Catholic
Freshman admissions: less selective; 2015-2016: 854 applied, 375 accepted. Either SAT or ACT required. SAT 25/75 percentile: 770-950. High school rank: 16% in top tenth, 39% in top quarter, 77% in top half
Early decision deadline: N/A, notification date: N/A
Early action deadline: N/A, notification date: N/A
Application deadline (fall): rolling

Undergraduate student body: 546 full time, 110 part time; 35% male, 65% female; 0% American Indian, 13% Asian, 18% black, 37% Hispanic, 2% multiracial, 3% Pacific Islander, 21% white, 4% international; 93% from in state; 51% live on campus; N/A of students in fraternities, N/A in sororities
Most popular majors: 31% Health Professions and Related Programs; 15% Business, Management, Marketing, and Related Support Services; 12% Psychology; 11% Social Sciences; 9% Parks, Recreation, Leisure, and Fitness Studies
Expenses: 2016-2017: $37,074; room/board: $12,434
Financial aid: (510) 436-1327; 90% of undergrads determined to have financial need; average aid package $28,233

Hope International University

Fullerton CA
(714) 879-3901
U.S. News ranking: Reg. U. (W), second tier
Website: www.hiu.edu
Admissions email: admissions@hiu.edu
Private; founded 1928
Affiliation: Christian Churches/Churches of Christ
Freshman admissions: less selective; 2015-2016: 1,051 applied, 360 accepted. Either SAT or ACT required. SAT 25/75 percentile: 790-1030. High school rank: 12% in top tenth, 36% in top quarter, 69% in top half
Early decision deadline: N/A, notification date: N/A
Early action deadline: N/A, notification date: N/A
Application deadline (fall): rolling
Undergraduate student body: 634 full time, 241 part time; 46% male, 54% female; 1% American Indian, 3% Asian, 7% black, 21% Hispanic, 11% multiracial, 1% Pacific Islander, 42% white, 0% international; 90% from in state; 42% live on campus; N/A of students in fraternities, N/A in sororities
Most popular majors: 25% Theological and Ministerial Studies, Other; 21% Business Administration and Management, General; 13% Human Development and Family Studies, General; 13% Psychology, General; 10% Liberal Arts and Sciences/Liberal Studies
Expenses: 2016-2017: $30,550; room/board: $9,550
Financial aid: (714) 879-3901; 68% of undergrads determined to have financial need; average aid package $13,414

Humboldt State University

Arcata CA
(707) 826-4402
U.S. News ranking: Reg. U. (W), No. 52
Website: www.humboldt.edu
Admissions email: hsuinfo@humboldt.edu
Public; founded 1913

Freshman admissions: selective; 2015-2016: 13,017 applied, 9,765 accepted. Neither SAT nor ACT required. SAT 25/75 percentile: 870-1110. High school rank: 14% in top tenth, 48% in top quarter, 80% in top half
Early decision deadline: N/A, notification date: N/A
Early action deadline: N/A, notification date: N/A
Application deadline (fall): 11/30
Undergraduate student body: 7,710 full time, 532 part time; 44% male, 56% female; 1% American Indian, 3% Asian, 4% black, 33% Hispanic, 7% multiracial, 0% Pacific Islander, 44% white, 2% international; 94% from in state; 9% live on campus; 1% of students in fraternities, 1% in sororities
Most popular majors: 10% Biological and Biomedical Sciences; 10% Social Sciences; 9% Visual and Performing Arts; 8% Business, Management, Marketing, and Related Support Services
Expenses: 2016-2017: $7,210 in state, $18,370 out of state; room/board: $12,992
Financial aid: (707) 826-4321; 78% of undergrads determined to have financial need; average aid package $13,500

Humphreys College[1]
Stockton CA
(209) 478-0800
U.S. News ranking: Reg. Coll. (W), unranked
Website: www.humphreys.edu
Admissions email: ugadmission@humphreys.edu
Private
Application deadline (fall): N/A
Undergraduate student body: N/A full time, N/A part time
Expenses: 2015-2016: $13,212; room/board: N/A
Financial aid: (209) 478-0800

John F. Kennedy University[1]
Pleasant Hill CA
(925) 969-3330
U.S. News ranking: Reg. U. (W), unranked
Website: www.jfku.edu
Admissions email: proginfo@jfku.edu
Private; founded 1964
Application deadline (fall): rolling
Undergraduate student body: N/A full time, N/A part time
Expenses: 2015-2016: $23,292; room/board: N/A
Financial aid: (925) 969-3385

John Paul the Great Catholic University
Escondido CA
(858) 653-6740
U.S. News ranking: Reg. Coll. (W), unranked
Website: www.jpcatholic.com/
Admissions email: N/A
Private; founded 2006
Affiliation: Roman Catholic
Freshman admissions: N/A; 2015-2016: 122 applied, 116 accepted. Either SAT or ACT required. ACT 25/75 percentile: N/A. High school rank: N/A

Early decision deadline: N/A, notification date: N/A
Early action deadline: N/A, notification date: N/A
Application deadline (fall): rolling
Undergraduate student body: 193 full time, 13 part time; 57% male, 43% female; 0% American Indian, 4% Asian, 2% black, 23% Hispanic, 3% multiracial, 1% Pacific Islander, 54% white, N/A international; 50% from in state; 77% live on campus; N/A of students in fraternities, N/A in sororities
Most popular majors: 81% Visual and Performing Arts; 19% Business, Management, Marketing, and Related Support Services
Expenses: 2015-2016: $24,900; room/board: $10,980
Financial aid: N/A

Laguna College of Art and Design
Laguna Beach CA
(949) 376-6000
U.S. News ranking: Arts, unranked
Website: www.lcad.edu/
Admissions email: admissions@lcad.edu
Private; founded 1968
Freshman admissions: N/A; 2015-2016: 573 applied, 236 accepted. Neither SAT nor ACT required. SAT 25/75 percentile: N/A. High school rank: N/A
Early decision deadline: N/A, notification date: N/A
Early action deadline: 2/1, notification date: N/A
Application deadline (fall): 8/1
Undergraduate student body: 511 full time, 65 part time; 39% male, 61% female; 1% American Indian, 16% Asian, 2% black, 19% Hispanic, 2% multiracial, 1% Pacific Islander, 50% white, 4% international
Most popular majors: Animation, Interactive Technology, Video Graphics and Special Effects; Fine/Studio Arts, General; Game and Interactive Media Design; Graphic Design
Expenses: 2016-2017: $28,950; room/board: N/A
Financial aid: (949) 376-6000

La Sierra University
Riverside CA
(951) 785-2176
U.S. News ranking: Reg. U. (W), No. 50
Website: www.lasierra.edu
Admissions email: admissions@lasierra.edu
Private; founded 1922
Affiliation: Seventh-day Adventist
Freshman admissions: less selective; 2015-2016: 4,328 applied, 1,931 accepted. Either SAT or ACT required. SAT 25/75 percentile: 840-1030. High school rank: 13% in top tenth, 42% in top quarter, 81% in top half
Early decision deadline: N/A, notification date: N/A
Early action deadline: N/A, notification date: N/A
Application deadline (fall): 7/1
Undergraduate student body: 1,866 full time, 237 part time; 42% male, 58% female; 0% American Indian, 15% Asian, 6% black,

48% Hispanic, 4% multiracial, 2% Pacific Islander, 13% white, 11% international; 93% from in state; 30% live on campus; 0% of students in fraternities, 0% in sororities
Most popular majors: 12% Biomedical Sciences, General; 8% Criminal Justice/Safety Studies; 8% Kinesiology and Exercise Science; 8% Psychology, General; 6% Business Administration and Management, General
Expenses: 2016-2017: $31,590; room/board: $8,100
Financial aid: (909) 785-2175; 79% of undergrads determined to have financial need; average aid package $22,824

Loyola Marymount University
Los Angeles CA
(310) 338-2750
U.S. News ranking: Reg. U. (W), No. 3
Website: www.lmu.edu
Admissions email: admissions@lmu.edu
Private; founded 1911
Affiliation: Roman Catholic
Freshman admissions: more selective; 2015-2016: 13,288 applied, 6,748 accepted. Either SAT or ACT required. SAT 25/75 percentile: 1110-1300. High school rank: 44% in top tenth, 76% in top quarter, 93% in top half
Early decision deadline: N/A, notification date: N/A
Early action deadline: 11/1, notification date: 12/20
Application deadline (fall): 1/15
Undergraduate student body: 6,030 full time, 229 part time; 44% male, 56% female; 0% American Indian, 11% Asian, 6% black, 21% Hispanic, 8% multiracial, 0% Pacific Islander, 45% white, 9% international; 76% from in state; 51% live on campus; 22% of students in fraternities, 37% in sororities
Most popular majors: 23% Business/Commerce, General; 14% Social Sciences, General; 14% Visual and Performing Arts, General; 7% Psychology, General
Expenses: 2016-2017: $44,238; room/board: $14,485
Financial aid: (310) 338-2753; 55% of undergrads determined to have financial need; average aid package $29,305

Marymount California University
Rancho Palos Verdes CA
(310) 303-7311
U.S. News ranking: Reg. Coll. (W), No. 18
Website: www.marymountcalifornia.edu/
Admissions email: N/A
Private; founded 1933
Affiliation: Roman Catholic
Freshman admissions: less selective; 2015-2016: 1,483 applied, 886 accepted. Neither SAT nor ACT required. SAT 25/75 percentile: 800-1030. High school rank: N/A
Early decision deadline: N/A, notification date: N/A

Early action deadline: N/A, notification date: N/A
Application deadline (fall): rolling
Undergraduate student body: 1,012 full time, 47 part time; 46% male, 54% female; 0% American Indian, 5% Asian, 9% black, 37% Hispanic, 3% multiracial, 1% Pacific Islander, 17% white, 19% international; 92% from in state; 37% live on campus; N/A of students in fraternities, N/A in sororities
Most popular majors: 40% Business Administration and Management, General; 27% Liberal Arts and Sciences/Liberal Studies; 25% Psychology, General; 8% Digital Arts
Expenses: 2016-2017: $35,309; room/board: $14,262
Financial aid: N/A

Master's College and Seminary
Santa Clarita CA
(800) 568-6248
U.S. News ranking: Reg. U. (W), No. 35
Website: www.masters.edu
Admissions email: admissions@masters.edu
Private; founded 1927
Affiliation: Evangelical
Freshman admissions: selective; 2015-2016: 490 applied, 464 accepted. Either SAT or ACT required. SAT 25/75 percentile: 960-1210. High school rank: 29% in top tenth, 52% in top quarter, 81% in top half
Early decision deadline: N/A, notification date: N/A
Early action deadline: 11/15, notification date: 12/22
Application deadline (fall): rolling
Undergraduate student body: 990 full time, 264 part time; 54% male, 46% female; 0% American Indian, 6% Asian, 4% black, 10% Hispanic, 7% multiracial, 1% Pacific Islander, 64% white, 6% international; 65% from in state; 82% live on campus; 0% of students in fraternities, 0% in sororities
Most popular majors: 24% Theology and Religious Vocations; 22% Business, Management, Marketing, and Related Support Services; 14% Liberal Arts and Sciences, General Studies and Humanities; 7% Biological and Biomedical Sciences
Expenses: 2016-2017: $31,970; room/board: $10,600
Financial aid: (661) 259-3540; 79% of undergrads determined to have financial need; average aid package $22,383

Menlo College
Atherton CA
(800) 556-3656
U.S. News ranking: Business, unranked
Website: www.menlo.edu
Admissions email: admissions@menlo.edu
Private; founded 1927
Freshman admissions: N/A; 2015-2016: 2,445 applied, 931 accepted. Either SAT or ACT required. SAT 25/75 percentile: N/A. High school rank: N/A
Early decision deadline: N/A, notification date: N/A

Early action deadline: 11/15, notification date: 1/15
Application deadline (fall): 4/1
Undergraduate student body: 741 full time, 24 part time; 55% male, 45% female; 1% American Indian, 10% Asian, 6% black, 22% Hispanic, 7% multiracial, 2% Pacific Islander, 28% white, 14% international; 81% from in state; 60% live on campus; N/A of students in fraternities, N/A in sororities
Most popular majors: 31% Marketing/Marketing Management, General; 22% Accounting
Expenses: 2016-2017: $39,950; room/board: $13,150
Financial aid: (650) 543-3880; 67% of undergrads determined to have financial need; average aid package $22,614

Mills College
Oakland CA
(510) 430-2135
U.S. News ranking: Reg. U. (W), No. 5
Website: www.mills.edu
Admissions email: admission@mills.edu
Private; founded 1852
Freshman admissions: selective; 2015-2016: 839 applied, 639 accepted. Neither SAT nor ACT required. SAT 25/75 percentile: 1030-1290. High school rank: 28% in top tenth, 68% in top quarter, 96% in top half
Early decision deadline: N/A, notification date: N/A
Early action deadline: 11/15, notification date: 12/15
Application deadline (fall): 3/1
Undergraduate student body: 815 full time, 44 part time; 0% male, 100% female; 1% American Indian, 9% Asian, 7% black, 23% Hispanic, 10% multiracial, 0% Pacific Islander, 48% white, 1% international; 81% from in state; 57% live on campus; 0% of students in fraternities, 0% in sororities
Most popular majors: 21% Social Sciences; 15% English Language and Literature/Letters; 11% Visual and Performing Arts; 10% Psychology; 8% Biological and Biomedical Sciences
Expenses: 2016-2017: $45,635; room/board: $13,528
Financial aid: (510) 430-2000; 76% of undergrads determined to have financial need; average aid package $39,586

Mount Saint Mary's University
Los Angeles CA
(310) 954-4250
U.S. News ranking: Reg. U. (W), No. 23
Website: www.msmu.edu
Admissions email: admissions@msmu.edu
Private; founded 1925
Affiliation: Roman Catholic
Freshman admissions: less selective; 2015-2016: 2,407 applied, 1,842 accepted. Either SAT or ACT required. SAT 25/75 percentile: 830-1020. High school rank: 19% in top tenth, 52% in top quarter, 87% in top half

Early decision deadline: N/A,
notification date: N/A
Early action deadline: 12/1,
notification date: 1/30
Application deadline (fall): 8/1
Undergraduate student body: 2,143
full time, 645 part time; 7%
male, 93% female; 0% American
Indian, 16% Asian, 7% black,
60% Hispanic, 2% multiracial,
0% Pacific Islander, 11% white,
1% international; 98% from in
state; 22% live on campus; N/A
of students in fraternities, 1% in
sororities
Most popular majors: 39%
Health Professions and Related
Programs; 12% Psychology; 12%
Social Sciences; 11% Business,
Management, Marketing, and
Related Support Services; 5%
Public Administration and Social
Service Professions
Expenses: 2016-2017: $37,722;
room/board: $11,451
Financial aid: (310) 954-4191;
92% of undergrads determined
to have financial need; average
aid package $25,973

National University
La Jolla CA
(800) 628-8648
U.S. News ranking: Reg. U. (W),
unranked
Website: www.nu.edu
Admissions email: advisor@nu.edu
Private; founded 1971
Freshman admissions: N/A;
2015-2016: N/A applied, N/A
accepted. Neither SAT nor ACT
required. ACT 25/75 percentile:
N/A. High school rank: N/A
Early decision deadline: N/A,
notification date: N/A
Early action deadline: N/A,
notification date: N/A
Application deadline (fall): rolling
Undergraduate student body: 3,241
full time, 5,609 part time; 43%
male, 57% female; 1% American
Indian, 10% Asian, 11% black,
26% Hispanic, 5% multiracial,
2% Pacific Islander, 38% white,
1% international; 90% from in
state; 0% live on campus; 0%
of students in fraternities, 0% in
sororities
Most popular majors: 14%
Registered Nursing/Registered
Nurse; 11% Business
Administration and Management,
General; 10% Psychology,
General; 6% Criminal Justice/Law
Enforcement Administration
Expenses: 2015-2016: $12,744;
room/board: N/A
Financial aid: (858) 642-8500

NewSchool of Architecture and Design[1]
San Diego CA
(619) 684-7081
U.S. News ranking: Arts, unranked
Website: newschoolarch.edu/
Admissions email: N/A
For-profit
Application deadline (fall): N/A
Undergraduate student body: N/A
full time, N/A part time
Expenses: 2015-2016: $35,284;
room/board: $18,276
Financial aid: N/A

Notre Dame de Namur University
Belmont CA
(650) 508-3600
U.S. News ranking: Reg. U. (W),
No. 44
Website: www.ndnu.edu
Admissions email:
admissions@ndnu.edu
Private; founded 1851
Affiliation: Catholic
Freshman admissions: less
selective; 2015-2016: 1,710
applied, 1,482 accepted. Either
SAT or ACT required. SAT 25/75
percentile: 810-1025. High
school rank: 16% in top tenth,
39% in top quarter, 73% in
top half
Early decision deadline: N/A,
notification date: N/A
Early action deadline: 12/1,
notification date: 12/15
Application deadline (fall): rolling
Undergraduate student body: 788
full time, 309 part time; 33%
male, 67% female; 1% American
Indian, 12% Asian, 7% black,
39% Hispanic, 4% multiracial,
3% Pacific Islander, 25% white,
4% international
Most popular majors: 18%
Business, Management,
Marketing, and Related Support
Services; 18% Psychology;
14% Public Administration
and Social Service Professions;
7% Liberal Arts and Sciences,
General Studies and Humanities;
6% Biological and Biomedical
Sciences
Expenses: 2015-2016: $32,608;
room/board: $12,872
Financial aid: (650) 508-3600;
83% of undergrads determined
to have financial need; average
aid package $25,820

Occidental College
Los Angeles CA
(800) 825-5262
U.S. News ranking: Nat. Lib. Arts,
No. 44
Website: www.oxy.edu
Admissions email:
admission@oxy.edu
Private; founded 1887
Freshman admissions: more
selective; 2015-2016: 5,911
applied, 2,652 accepted. Either
SAT or ACT required. SAT 25/75
percentile: 1200-1380. High
school rank: 55% in top tenth,
90% in top quarter, 99% in
top half
Early decision deadline: 11/15,
notification date: 12/15
Early action deadline: N/A,
notification date: N/A
Application deadline (fall): 1/15
Undergraduate student body: 2,090
full time, 22 part time; 43%
male, 57% female; 0% American
Indian, 13% Asian, 5% black,
15% Hispanic, 9% multiracial,
0% Pacific Islander, 49% white,
5% international; 48% from in
state; 82% live on campus; 13%
of students in fraternities, 19%
in sororities
Most popular majors: 12%
Economics, General; 9% Political
Science and Government,
General; 7% Biology/Biological
Sciences, General; 7%
International Relations and
Affairs; 7% Psychology, General

Expenses: 2016-2017: $51,070;
room/board: $14,460
Financial aid: (323) 259-2548;
56% of undergrads determined
to have financial need; average
aid package $44,879

Otis College of Art and Design[1]
Los Angeles CA
(310) 665-6820
U.S. News ranking: Arts, unranked
Website: www.otis.edu
Admissions email:
admissions@otis.edu
Private; founded 1918
Application deadline (fall): rolling
Undergraduate student body: N/A
full time, N/A part time
Expenses: 2015-2016: $41,854;
room/board: $11,800
Financial aid: (310) 665-6880

Pacific Union College
Angwin CA
(707) 965-6336
U.S. News ranking: Nat. Lib. Arts,
second tier
Website: www.puc.edu
Admissions email: enroll@puc.edu
Private; founded 1882
Affiliation: Seventh-day Adventist
Freshman admissions: selective;
2015-2016: 2,041 applied, 923
accepted. Either SAT or ACT
required. SAT 25/75 percentile:
850-1130. High school rank: N/A
Early decision deadline: N/A,
notification date: N/A
Early action deadline: N/A,
notification date: N/A
Application deadline (fall): N/A
Undergraduate student body: 1,358
full time, 192 part time; 41%
male, 59% female; 0% American
Indian, 20% Asian, 9% black,
28% Hispanic, 7% multiracial,
2% Pacific Islander, 26% white,
3% international; 85% from in
state; 71% live on campus; N/A
of students in fraternities, N/A in
sororities
Most popular majors: 20%
Registered Nursing/Registered
Nurse; 14% Business/Commerce,
General; 7% Biology/Biological
Sciences, General; 5% Health
and Physical Education/Fitness,
General; 5% Biochemistry
Expenses: 2016-2017: $29,079;
room/board: $7,920
Financial aid: (707) 965-7200;
80% of undergrads determined
to have financial need; average
aid package $22,136

Pepperdine University
Malibu CA
(310) 506-4392
U.S. News ranking: Nat. U.,
No. 50
Website: www.pepperdine.edu
Admissions email: admission-
seaver@pepperdine.edu
Private; founded 1937
Affiliation: Church of Christ
Freshman admissions: more
selective; 2015-2016: 9,923
applied, 3,781 accepted. Either
SAT or ACT required. SAT 25/75
percentile: 1100-1320. High
school rank: 48% in top tenth,
80% in top quarter, 97% in
top half
Early decision deadline: N/A,
notification date: N/A

Early action deadline: N/A,
notification date: N/A
Application deadline (fall): 1/5
Undergraduate student body: 3,228
full time, 305 part time; 41%
male, 59% female; 0% American
Indian, 12% Asian, 6% black,
16% Hispanic, 5% multiracial,
0% Pacific Islander, 47% white,
10% international; 58% from in
state; 57% live on campus; 6%
of students in fraternities, 9% in
sororities
Most popular majors: 29%
Business, Management,
Marketing, and Related Support
Services; 12% Social Sciences;
8% Psychology; 7% Multi/
Interdisciplinary Studies
Expenses: 2016-2017: $50,022;
room/board: $14,330
Financial aid: (310) 506-4301;
54% of undergrads determined
to have financial need; average
aid package $40,575

Pitzer College
Claremont CA
(909) 621-8129
U.S. News ranking: Nat. Lib. Arts,
No. 32
Website: www.pitzer.edu
Admissions email:
admission@pitzer.edu
Private; founded 1963
Freshman admissions: most
selective; 2015-2016: 4,149
applied, 559 accepted. Neither
SAT nor ACT required. SAT
25/75 percentile: 1250-1440.
High school rank: 60% in top
tenth, 98% in top quarter, 100%
in top half
Early decision deadline: 11/15,
notification date: 12/18
Early action deadline: N/A,
notification date: N/A
Application deadline (fall): 1/1
Undergraduate student body: 1,036
full time, 31 part time; 43%
male, 57% female; 0% American
Indian, 9% Asian, 5% black,
15% Hispanic, 9% multiracial,
0% Pacific Islander, 48% white,
7% international; 49% from in
state; 76% live on campus; 0%
of students in fraternities, 0% in
sororities
Most popular majors: 10%
Psychology, General; 7% Political
Science and Government,
General; 5% English Language
and Literature, General
Expenses: 2015-2016: $48,660;
room/board: $15,210
Financial aid: (909) 621-8208

Point Loma Nazarene University
San Diego CA
(619) 849-2273
U.S. News ranking: Reg. U. (W),
No. 17
Website: www.pointloma.edu
Admissions email: admissions@
pointloma.edu
Private; founded 1902
Affiliation: Church of the Nazarene
Freshman admissions: selective;
2015-2016: 2,809 applied,
2,004 accepted. Either SAT
or ACT required. SAT 25/75
percentile: 1020-1250. High
school rank: 33% in top tenth,
63% in top quarter, 92% in
top half

Early decision deadline: N/A,
notification date: N/A
Early action deadline: 11/15,
notification date: 12/21
Application deadline (fall): 2/15
Undergraduate student body: 2,587
full time, 180 part time; 36%
male, 64% female; 1% American
Indian, 5% Asian, 2% black,
23% Hispanic, 8% multiracial,
1% Pacific Islander, 59% white,
1% international; 83% from in
state; 61% live on campus; N/A
of students in fraternities, N/A in
sororities
Most popular majors: 21%
Health Professions and Related
Programs; 19% Business,
Management, Marketing, and
Related Support Services; 9%
Psychology; 8% Biological and
Biomedical Sciences; 6% Visual
and Performing Arts
Expenses: 2016-2017: $33,500;
room/board: $9,950
Financial aid: (619) 849-2538;
68% of undergrads determined
to have financial need; average
aid package $21,542

Pomona College
Claremont CA
(909) 621-8134
U.S. News ranking: Nat. Lib. Arts,
No. 7
Website: www.pomona.edu
Admissions email: admissions@
pomona.edu
Private; founded 1887
Freshman admissions: most
selective; 2015-2016: 8,099
applied, 833 accepted. Either
SAT or ACT required. SAT 25/75
percentile: 1360-1530. High
school rank: 92% in top tenth,
100% in top quarter, 100% in
top half
Early decision deadline: 11/1,
notification date: 12/15
Early action deadline: N/A,
notification date: N/A
Application deadline (fall): 1/1
Undergraduate student body: 1,651
full time, 12 part time; 50%
male, 50% female; 0% American
Indian, 14% Asian, 7% black,
15% Hispanic, 8% multiracial,
0% Pacific Islander, 40% white,
10% international; 29% from in
state; 98% live on campus; 5%
of students in fraternities, 0% in
sororities
Most popular majors: 10%
Mathematics, General; 10%
Economics, General; 7% Biology/
Biological Sciences, General;
6% Neuroscience; 5% Political
Science and Government,
General
Expenses: 2016-2017: $49,352;
room/board: $15,605
Financial aid: (909) 621-8205;
55% of undergrads determined
to have financial need; average
aid package $47,888

Providence Christian College
Pasadena CA
(866) 323-0233
U.S. News ranking: Nat. Lib. Arts,
unranked
Website: www.providencecc.net/
Admissions email: N/A
Private; founded 2003

Freshman admissions: N/A; 2015-2016: 558 applied, 242 accepted. Neither SAT nor ACT required. ACT 25/75 percentile: N/A. High school rank: N/A
Early decision deadline: N/A, notification date: N/A
Early action deadline: N/A, notification date: N/A
Application deadline (fall): rolling
Undergraduate student body: 145 full time, 2 part time; 51% male, 49% female; 1% American Indian, 2% Asian, 7% black, 27% Hispanic, 1% multiracial, 1% Pacific Islander, 55% white, 6% international; 64% from in state; 85% live on campus; 0% of students in fraternities, 0% in sororities
Most popular majors: 100% Liberal Arts and Sciences/Liberal Studies
Expenses: 2016-2017: $28,164; room/board: $8,408
Financial aid: N/A; 83% of undergrads determined to have financial need; average aid package $24,000

San Diego Christian College
El Cajon CA
(619) 588-7747
U.S. News ranking: Reg. Coll. (W), No. 15
Website: www.sdcc.edu/
Admissions email: admissions@sdcc.edu
Private; founded 1970
Freshman admissions: less selective; 2015-2016: 433 applied, 224 accepted. Neither SAT nor ACT required. SAT 25/75 percentile: 813-1038. High school rank: 6% in top tenth, 31% in top quarter, 59% in top half
Early decision deadline: N/A, notification date: N/A
Early action deadline: N/A, notification date: N/A
Application deadline (fall): rolling
Undergraduate student body: 733 full time, 176 part time; 46% male, 54% female; 1% American Indian, 3% Asian, 12% black, 21% Hispanic, 6% multiracial, 1% Pacific Islander, 47% white, 1% international; 80% from in state; 23% live on campus; 0% of students in fraternities, 0% in sororities
Most popular majors: 20% Bible/Biblical Studies; 18% Business Administration and Management, General; 12% Human Development and Family Studies, General; 10% Kinesiology and Exercise Science; 9% Psychology, General
Expenses: 2015-2016: $28,470; room/board: $10,500
Financial aid: (619) 590-1786

San Diego State University
San Diego CA
(619) 594-6336
U.S. News ranking: Nat. U., No. 146
Website: www.sdsu.edu
Admissions email: admissions@sdsu.edu
Public; founded 1897
Freshman admissions: more selective; 2015-2016: 58,970

applied, 20,238 accepted. Either SAT or ACT required. SAT 25/75 percentile: 1010-1230. High school rank: 33% in top tenth, 73% in top quarter, 96% in top half
Early decision deadline: N/A, notification date: N/A
Early action deadline: N/A, notification date: N/A
Application deadline (fall): 11/30
Undergraduate student body: 26,005 full time, 3,229 part time; 46% male, 54% female; 0% American Indian, 14% Asian, 4% black, 31% Hispanic, 6% multiracial, 0% Pacific Islander, 34% white, 6% international; 92% from in state; 15% live on campus; 8% of students in fraternities, 10% in sororities
Most popular majors: 20% Business, Management, Marketing, and Related Support Services; 12% Social Sciences; 8% Health Professions and Related Programs; 8% Psychology; 7% Engineering
Expenses: 2016-2017: $7,084 in state, $18,244 out of state; room/board: $14,812
Financial aid: (619) 594-6323; 58% of undergrads determined to have financial need; average aid package $11,000

San Francisco Art Institute
San Francisco CA
(800) 345-7324
U.S. News ranking: Arts, unranked
Website: www.sfai.edu
Admissions email: admissions@sfai.edu
Private; founded 1871
Freshman admissions: N/A; 2015-2016: 563 applied, 368 accepted. Neither SAT nor ACT required. SAT 25/75 percentile: N/A. High school rank: N/A
Early decision deadline: N/A, notification date: N/A
Early action deadline: N/A, notification date: N/A
Application deadline (fall): rolling
Undergraduate student body: 385 full time, 27 part time; 41% male, 59% female; 1% American Indian, 4% Asian, 4% black, 17% Hispanic, 8% multiracial, 0% Pacific Islander, 47% white, 17% international; 60% from in state; 33% live on campus; N/A of students in fraternities, N/A in sororities
Most popular majors: 39% Painting; 33% Photography; 12% Sculpture; 9% Visual and Performing Arts, Other
Expenses: 2016-2017: $43,090; room/board: $11,600
Financial aid: (415) 749-4520; 60% of undergrads determined to have financial need; average aid package $28,702

San Francisco Conservatory of Music
San Francisco CA
(800) 899-7326
U.S. News ranking: Arts, unranked
Website: www.sfcm.edu
Admissions email: admit@sfcm.edu
Private; founded 1917
Freshman admissions: N/A; 2015-2016: 362 applied, 169

accepted. Neither SAT nor ACT required. SAT 25/75 percentile: N/A. High school rank: N/A
Early decision deadline: N/A, notification date: N/A
Early action deadline: N/A, notification date: N/A
Application deadline (fall): 12/1
Undergraduate student body: 156 full time, 2 part time; 56% male, 44% female; 1% American Indian, 11% Asian, 3% black, 6% Hispanic, 11% multiracial, 1% Pacific Islander, 32% white, 25% international; 59% from in state; 46% live on campus; 0% of students in fraternities, 0% in sororities
Most popular majors: 59% Stringed Instruments; 14% Woodwind Instruments; 10% Keyboard Instruments; 10% Voice and Opera; 7% Brass Instruments
Expenses: 2016-2017: $43,410; room/board: $15,700
Financial aid: (415) 759-3414; 85% of undergrads determined to have financial need; average aid package $33,600

San Francisco State University
San Francisco CA
(415) 338-6486
U.S. News ranking: Nat. U., second tier
Website: www.sfsu.edu
Admissions email: ugadmit@sfsu.edu
Public; founded 1899
Freshman admissions: selective; 2015-2016: 35,122 applied, 23,841 accepted. Either SAT or ACT required. SAT 25/75 percentile: 860-1090. High school rank: N/A
Early decision deadline: N/A, notification date: N/A
Early action deadline: N/A, notification date: N/A
Application deadline (fall): 11/30
Undergraduate student body: 22,206 full time, 4,700 part time; 44% male, 56% female; 0% American Indian, 28% Asian, 5% black, 29% Hispanic, 6% multiracial, 0% Pacific Islander, 21% white, 6% international; 99% from in state; 11% live on campus; N/A of students in fraternities, N/A in sororities
Most popular majors: 24% Business, Management, Marketing, and Related Support Services; 10% Social Sciences; 9% Health Professions and Related Programs; 7% Visual and Performing Arts
Expenses: 2016-2017: $6,484 in state, $17,644 out of state; room/board: N/A
Financial aid: (415) 338-7000; 71% of undergrads determined to have financial need; average aid package $14,863

San Jose State University
San Jose CA
(408) 283-7500
U.S. News ranking: Reg. U. (W), No. 33
Website: www.sjsu.edu
Admissions email: admissions@sjsu.edu
Public; founded 1857

Freshman admissions: selective; 2015-2016: 30,583 applied, 16,890 accepted. Either SAT or ACT required. SAT 25/75 percentile: 920-1180. High school rank: N/A
Early decision deadline: N/A, notification date: N/A
Early action deadline: N/A, notification date: N/A
Application deadline (fall): 11/30
Undergraduate student body: 21,638 full time, 5,184 part time; 52% male, 48% female; 0% American Indian, 36% Asian, 3% black, 26% Hispanic, 5% multiracial, 0% Pacific Islander, 19% white, 6% international; 99% from in state; 13% live on campus; N/A of students in fraternities, N/A in sororities
Most popular majors: 23% Business, Management, Marketing, and Related Support Services; 10% Engineering; 9% Health Professions and Related Programs; 8% Visual and Performing Arts; 6% Social Sciences
Expenses: 2016-2017: $9,284 in state, $13,066 out of state; room/board: $14,867
Financial aid: (408) 283-7500; 65% of undergrads determined to have financial need; average aid package $17,918

Santa Clara University
Santa Clara CA
(408) 554-4700
U.S. News ranking: Reg. U. (W), No. 2
Website: www.scu.edu
Admissions email: Admission@scu.edu
Private; founded 1851
Affiliation: Catholic
Freshman admissions: more selective; 2015-2016: 14,899 applied, 7,270 accepted. Either SAT or ACT required. ACT 25/75 percentile: 27-32. High school rank: 50% in top tenth, 83% in top quarter, 98% in top half
Early decision deadline: 11/1, notification date: 12/23
Early action deadline: 11/1, notification date: 12/23
Application deadline (fall): 1/7
Undergraduate student body: 5,303 full time, 82 part time; 51% male, 49% female; 0% American Indian, 16% Asian, 3% black, 17% Hispanic, 7% multiracial, 0% Pacific Islander, 49% white, 3% international; 73% from in state; 52% live on campus; 0% of students in fraternities, 0% in sororities
Most popular majors: 26% Business, Management, Marketing, and Related Support Services; 16% Social Sciences; 12% Engineering; 7% Psychology
Expenses: 2016-2017: $47,112; room/board: $13,965
Financial aid: (408) 554-4505; 47% of undergrads determined to have financial need; average aid package $32,052

Scripps College
Claremont CA
(909) 621-8149
U.S. News ranking: Nat. Lib. Arts, No. 23
Website: www.scrippscollege.edu/
Admissions email: admission@scrippscollege.edu
Private; founded 1926
Freshman admissions: most selective; 2015-2016: 2,613 applied, 729 accepted. Either SAT or ACT required. SAT 25/75 percentile: 1280-1448. High school rank: 72% in top tenth, 95% in top quarter, 98% in top half
Early decision deadline: 11/15, notification date: 12/15
Early action deadline: N/A, notification date: N/A
Application deadline (fall): 1/1
Undergraduate student body: 969 full time, 4 part time; 0% male, 100% female; N/A American Indian, 16% Asian, 4% black, 11% Hispanic, 8% multiracial, 0% Pacific Islander, 48% white, 4% international; 47% from in state; 100% live on campus; N/A of students in fraternities, N/A in sororities
Most popular majors: 14% Social Sciences; 11% Biological and Biomedical Sciences; 10% Psychology; 9% Multi/Interdisciplinary Studies
Expenses: 2016-2017: $50,983; room/board: $15,681
Financial aid: (909) 621-8275; 38% of undergrads determined to have financial need; average aid package $43,217

Simpson University
Redding CA
(530) 226-4606
U.S. News ranking: Reg. U. (W), No. 82
Website: www.simpsonu.edu
Admissions email: admissions@simpsonu.edu
Private; founded 1921
Affiliation: Christian and Missionary Alliance
Freshman admissions: selective; 2015-2016: 620 applied, 321 accepted. Either SAT or ACT required. SAT 25/75 percentile: 893-1120. High school rank: 27% in top tenth, 64% in top quarter, 91% in top half
Early decision deadline: N/A, notification date: N/A
Early action deadline: 8/31, notification date: 12/1
Application deadline (fall): rolling
Undergraduate student body: 927 full time, 36 part time; 36% male, 64% female; 4% American Indian, 4% Asian, 4% black, 12% Hispanic, 3% multiracial, 0% Pacific Islander, 60% white, 2% international; 90% from in state; 39% live on campus; N/A of students in fraternities, N/A in sororities
Most popular majors: 27% Business, Management, Marketing, and Related Support Services; 23% Psychology; 17% Health Professions and Related Programs; 9% Liberal Arts and Sciences, General Studies and Humanities; 8% Theology and Religious Vocations

Expenses: 2016-2017: $25,950; room/board: $7,950
Financial aid: (530) 226-4111; 89% of undergrads determined to have financial need; average aid package $19,119

Soka University of America

Aliso Viejo CA
(888) 600-Soka
U.S. News ranking: Nat. Lib. Arts, No. 41
Website: www.soka.edu
Admissions email: admission@soka.edu
Private; founded 1987
Freshman admissions: more selective; 2015-2016: 451 applied, 208 accepted. Either SAT or ACT required. SAT 25/75 percentile: 1070-1390. High school rank: 33% in top tenth, 88% in top quarter, 100% in top half
Early decision deadline: N/A, notification date: N/A
Early action deadline: 11/1, notification date: 12/1
Application deadline (fall): 1/15
Undergraduate student body: 432 full time, 1 part time; 38% male, 62% female; 0% American Indian, 17% Asian, 4% black, 10% Hispanic, 4% multiracial, 0% Pacific Islander, 20% white, 39% international; 55% from in state; 99% live on campus; 0% of students in fraternities, 0% in sororities
Most popular majors: 100% Liberal Arts and Sciences/Liberal Studies
Expenses: 2016-2017: $31,076; room/board: $11,812
Financial aid: N/A; 92% of undergrads determined to have financial need; average aid package $36,380

Sonoma State University

Rohnert Park CA
(707) 664-2778
U.S. News ranking: Reg. U. (W), No. 41
Website: www.sonoma.edu
Admissions email: student.outreach@sonoma.edu
Public; founded 1960
Freshman admissions: selective; 2015-2016: 15,265 applied, 11,686 accepted. Either SAT or ACT required. SAT 25/75 percentile: 880-1100. High school rank: N/A
Early decision deadline: N/A, notification date: N/A
Early action deadline: N/A, notification date: N/A
Application deadline (fall): 11/30
Undergraduate student body: 7,382 full time, 1,233 part time; 38% male, 62% female; 1% American Indian, 5% Asian, 2% black, 29% Hispanic, 7% multiracial, 0% Pacific Islander, 48% white, 2% international; N/A from in state; 22% live on campus; N/A of students in fraternities, N/A in sororities
Most popular majors: 19% Business Administration and Management, General; 10% Psychology, General; 8%

Sociology; 7% Liberal Arts and Sciences/Liberal Studies; 5% Criminology
Expenses: 2016-2017: $7,330 in state, $18,490 out of state; room/board: $12,814
Financial aid: (707) 664-2287; 58% of undergrads determined to have financial need; average aid package $10,085

Southern California Institute of Architecture[1]

Los Angeles CA
(800) 774-7242
U.S. News ranking: Arts, unranked
Website: www.sciarc.edu
Admissions email: admissions@sciarc.edu
Private
Application deadline (fall): 1/15
Undergraduate student body: N/A full time, N/A part time
Expenses: 2015-2016: $43,334; room/board: N/A
Financial aid: (213) 613-2200

Stanford University

Stanford CA
(650) 723-2091
U.S. News ranking: Nat. U., No. 5
Website: www.stanford.edu
Admissions email: admission@stanford.edu
Private; founded 1885
Freshman admissions: most selective; 2015-2016: 42,497 applied, 2,140 accepted. Either SAT or ACT required. SAT 25/75 percentile: 1390-1580. High school rank: 96% in top tenth, 99% in top quarter, 100% in top half
Early decision deadline: N/A, notification date: N/A
Early action deadline: 11/1, notification date: 12/15
Application deadline (fall): 1/3
Undergraduate student body: 6,999 full time, 0 part time; 52% male, 48% female; 1% American Indian, 20% Asian, 6% black, 15% Hispanic, 10% multiracial, 0% Pacific Islander, 37% white, 9% international; 39% from in state; 93% live on campus; 20% of students in fraternities, 20% in sororities
Most popular majors: 19% Engineering; 19% Multi/Interdisciplinary Studies; 14% Social Sciences; 13% Computer and Information Sciences and Support Services; 6% Biological and Biomedical Sciences
Expenses: 2016-2017: $47,940; room/board: $14,601
Financial aid: (650) 723-3058; 49% of undergrads determined to have financial need; average aid package $49,000

St. Mary's College of California

Moraga CA
(925) 631-4224
U.S. News ranking: Reg. U. (W), No. 9
Website: www.stmarys-ca.edu
Admissions email: smcadmit@stmarys-ca.edu
Private; founded 1863
Affiliation: Roman Catholic

Freshman admissions: selective; 2015-2016: 4,852 applied, 3,681 accepted. Either SAT or ACT required. SAT 25/75 percentile: 1010-1230. High school rank: N/A
Early decision deadline: N/A, notification date: N/A
Early action deadline: 11/15, notification date: 12/15
Application deadline (fall): 2/1
Undergraduate student body: 2,680 full time, 260 part time; 40% male, 60% female; 0% American Indian, 10% Asian, 4% black, 25% Hispanic, 7% multiracial, 1% Pacific Islander, 46% white, 2% international; 89% from in state; 56% live on campus; 0% of students in fraternities, 0% in sororities
Most popular majors: 32% Business, Management, Marketing, and Related Support Services; 10% Social Sciences; 9% Liberal Arts and Sciences, General Studies and Humanities; 6% Biological and Biomedical Sciences
Expenses: 2016-2017: $44,360; room/board: $14,880
Financial aid: (925) 631-4370; 70% of undergrads determined to have financial need; average aid package $27,902

Thomas Aquinas College

Santa Paula CA
(800) 634-9797
U.S. News ranking: Nat. Lib. Arts, No. 53
Website: www.thomasaquinas.edu
Admissions email: admissions@thomasaquinas.edu
Private; founded 1971
Affiliation: Catholic
Freshman admissions: more selective; 2015-2016: 189 applied, 119 accepted. Either SAT or ACT required. SAT 25/75 percentile: 1160-1380. High school rank: 44% in top tenth, 50% in top quarter, 75% in top half
Early decision deadline: N/A, notification date: N/A
Early action deadline: N/A, notification date: N/A
Application deadline (fall): rolling
Undergraduate student body: 377 full time, 0 part time; 50% male, 50% female; 0% American Indian, 1% Asian, 0% black, 15% Hispanic, 7% multiracial, 0% Pacific Islander, 72% white, 3% international; 42% from in state; 99% live on campus; 0% of students in fraternities, 0% in sororities
Most popular majors: 100% Liberal Arts and Sciences, General Studies and Humanities
Expenses: 2016-2017: $24,500; room/board: $7,950
Financial aid: (805) 525-4417; 75% of undergrads determined to have financial need; average aid package $21,350

Trident University International[1]

Cypress CA
(800) 579-3170
U.S. News ranking: Nat. U., unranked
Website: www.trident.edu
Admissions email: N/A
For-profit
Application deadline (fall): rolling
Undergraduate student body: N/A full time, N/A part time
Expenses: 2015-2016: $9,000; room/board: N/A
Financial aid: (877) 835-9818

United States University[1]

Chula Vista CA
(888) 422-3381
U.S. News ranking: Reg. Coll. (W), unranked
Website: www.usuniversity.edu/
Admissions email: N/A
For-profit
Application deadline (fall): N/A
Undergraduate student body: N/A full time, N/A part time
Expenses: N/A
Financial aid: N/A

University of California–Berkeley

Berkeley CA
(510) 642-3175
U.S. News ranking: Nat. U., No. 20
Website: students.berkeley.edu/admissions/
Admissions email: N/A
Public; founded 1868
Freshman admissions: most selective; 2015-2016: 78,924 applied, 12,048 accepted. Either SAT or ACT required. SAT 25/75 percentile: 1250-1500. High school rank: 98% in top tenth, 100% in top quarter, 100% in top half
Early decision deadline: N/A, notification date: N/A
Early action deadline: N/A, notification date: N/A
Application deadline (fall): 11/30
Undergraduate student body: 26,622 full time, 874 part time; 48% male, 52% female; 0% American Indian, 35% Asian, 2% black, 14% Hispanic, 5% multiracial, 0% Pacific Islander, 27% white, 14% international; 85% from in state; 26% live on campus; 10% of students in fraternities, 10% in sororities
Most popular majors: 20% Social Sciences; 13% Biological and Biomedical Sciences; 13% Engineering; 5% English Language and Literature/Letters
Expenses: 2015-2016: $13,431 in state, $38,139 out of state; room/board: $15,422
Financial aid: (510) 642-6442; 49% of undergrads determined to have financial need; average aid package $22,288

University of California–Davis

Davis CA
(530) 752-2971
U.S. News ranking: Nat. U., No. 44
Website: www.ucdavis.edu
Admissions email: undergraduateadmissions@ucdavis.edu
Public; founded 1905
Freshman admissions: more selective; 2015-2016: 64,510 applied, 24,614 accepted. Either SAT or ACT required. SAT 25/75 percentile: 1070-1340. High school rank: 100% in top tenth, 100% in top quarter, 100% in top half
Early decision deadline: N/A, notification date: N/A
Early action deadline: N/A, notification date: N/A
Application deadline (fall): 11/30
Undergraduate student body: 27,966 full time, 418 part time; 41% male, 59% female; 0% American Indian, 32% Asian, 2% black, 19% Hispanic, 5% multiracial, 0% Pacific Islander, 28% white, 11% international; 96% from in state; 25% live on campus; N/A of students in fraternities, N/A in sororities
Most popular majors: 9% Research and Experimental Psychology, Other; 7% Economics, General; 5% Biology/Biological Sciences, General; 5% Business/Managerial Economics; 4% Neurobiology and Anatomy
Expenses: 2016-2017: $14,046 in state, $40,728 out of state; room/board: $14,838
Financial aid: (530) 752-2396; 62% of undergrads determined to have financial need; average aid package $20,360

University of California–Irvine

Irvine CA
(949) 824-6703
U.S. News ranking: Nat. U., No. 39
Website: www.uci.edu
Admissions email: admissions@uci.edu
Public; founded 1965
Freshman admissions: more selective; 2015-2016: 71,768 applied, 27,764 accepted. Either SAT or ACT required. SAT 25/75 percentile: 1040-1310. High school rank: 96% in top tenth, 100% in top quarter, 100% in top half
Early decision deadline: N/A, notification date: N/A
Early action deadline: N/A, notification date: N/A
Application deadline (fall): 11/30
Undergraduate student body: 24,851 full time, 405 part time; 46% male, 54% female; 0% American Indian, 37% Asian, 2% black, 25% Hispanic, 4% multiracial, 0% Pacific Islander, 12% white, 16% international; 97% from in state; 41% live on campus; 9% of students in fraternities, 9% in sororities
Most popular majors: 10% Biology/Biological Sciences, General; 8% Public Health, Other; 8% Social Psychology; 6% Business/

Managerial Economics;
5% Political Science and
Government, General
Expenses: 2015-2016: $14,750
in state, $39,458 out of state;
room/board: $12,947
Financial aid: (949) 824-5337;
67% of undergrads determined
to have financial need; average
aid package $22,203

University of California–Los Angeles

Los Angeles CA
(310) 825-3101
U.S. News ranking: Nat. U.,
No. 24
Website: www.ucla.edu/
Admissions email:
ugadm@saonet.ucla.edu
Public; founded 1919
Freshman admissions: most
selective; 2015-2016: 92,728
applied, 16,016 accepted. Either
SAT or ACT required. SAT 25/75
percentile: 1190-1470. High
school rank: 97% in top tenth,
100% in top quarter, 100% in
top half
Early decision deadline: N/A,
notification date: N/A
Early action deadline: N/A,
notification date: N/A
Application deadline (fall): 11/30
Undergraduate student body:
29,004 full time, 581 part time;
44% male, 56% female; 0%
American Indian, 29% Asian,
3% black, 21% Hispanic, 5%
multiracial, 0% Pacific Islander,
27% white, 13% international;
89% from in state; 45% live
on campus; 15% of students in
fraternities, 15% in sororities
Most popular majors: 8% Social
Sciences; 7% Psychology; 7%
Social Sciences; 5% Biological
and Biomedical Sciences; 5%
Social Sciences
Expenses: 2016-2017: $12,836
in state, $39,518 out of state;
room/board: $15,069
Financial aid: (310) 206-0400;
55% of undergrads determined
to have financial need; average
aid package $22,490

University of California–Merced

Merced CA
(209) 228-7178
U.S. News ranking: Nat. U.,
No. 152
Website: www.ucmerced.edu/
Admissions email: N/A
Public; founded 2005
Freshman admissions: selective;
2015-2016: 18,862 applied,
11,444 accepted. Either SAT
or ACT required. SAT 25/75
percentile: 900-1120. High
school rank: N/A
Early decision deadline: N/A,
notification date: N/A
Early action deadline: N/A,
notification date: N/A
Application deadline (fall): 11/30
Undergraduate student body: 6,164
full time, 73 part time; 48%
male, 52% female; 0% American
Indian, 23% Asian, 5% black,
48% Hispanic, 4% multiracial,
1% Pacific Islander, 13% white,
5% international; 100% from in

state; 34% live on campus; 8%
of students in fraternities, 10%
in sororities
Most popular majors: 20%
Biological and Biomedical
Sciences; 20% Psychology;
16% Social Sciences; 15%
Engineering; 12% Business,
Management, Marketing, and
Related Support Services
Expenses: 2016-2017: $13,262
in state, $39,944 out of state;
room/board: $15,341
Financial aid: N/A; 87% of
undergrads determined to have
financial need; average aid
package $23,468

University of California–Riverside

Riverside CA
(951) 827-3411
U.S. News ranking: Nat. U.,
No. 118
Website: www.ucr.edu
Admissions email: admit@ucr.edu
Public; founded 1954
Freshman admissions: more
selective; 2015-2016: 38,505
applied, 21,608 accepted. Either
SAT or ACT required. SAT 25/75
percentile: 1020-1250. High
school rank: 94% in top tenth,
100% in top quarter, 100% in
top half
Early decision deadline: N/A,
notification date: N/A
Early action deadline: N/A,
notification date: N/A
Application deadline (fall): 11/30
Undergraduate student body:
18,279 full time, 329 part time;
48% male, 52% female; 0%
American Indian, 36% Asian,
4% black, 38% Hispanic, 5%
multiracial, 0% Pacific Islander,
13% white, 3% international;
99% from in state; 35% live
on campus; 6% of students in
fraternities, 10% in sororities
Most popular majors: 22% Social
Sciences; 16% Business,
Management, Marketing, and
Related Support Services; 13%
Biological and Biomedical
Sciences; 9% Psychology; 8%
Engineering
Expenses: 2016-2017: $13,581
in state, $40,263 out of state;
room/board: $14,550
Financial aid: (951) 827-3878;
79% of undergrads determined
to have financial need; average
aid package $21,638

University of California–San Diego

La Jolla CA
(858) 534-4831
U.S. News ranking: Nat. U.,
No. 44
Website: www.ucsd.edu/
Admissions email:
admissionsinfo@ucsd.edu
Public; founded 1960
Freshman admissions: most
selective; 2015-2016: 78,056
applied, 26,509 accepted. Either
SAT or ACT required. SAT 25/75
percentile: 1210-1450. High
school rank: 100% in top tenth,
100% in top quarter, 100% in
top half
Early decision deadline: N/A,
notification date: N/A
Early action deadline: N/A,
notification date: N/A

Application deadline (fall): 11/30
Undergraduate student body:
26,195 full time, 395 part time;
52% male, 48% female; 0%
American Indian, 34% Asian,
2% black, 15% Hispanic, 0%
multiracial, 0% Pacific Islander,
19% white, 23% international;
95% from in state; 43% live
on campus; 10% of students in
fraternities, 10% in sororities
Most popular majors: 18% Biology,
General; 14% Economics; 8%
Psychology; 7% Computer
Science; 5% Political Science
and Government, Other
Expenses: 2016-2017: $14,705
in state, $41,387 out of state;
room/board: $12,477
Financial aid: (858) 534-4480;
58% of undergrads determined
to have financial need; average
aid package $22,456

University of California–Santa Barbara

Santa Barbara CA
(805) 893-2485
U.S. News ranking: Nat. U.,
No. 37
Website: www.ucsb.edu
Admissions email: admissions@
sa.ucsb.edu
Public; founded 1909
Freshman admissions: more
selective; 2015-2016: 70,444
applied, 23,020 accepted. Either
SAT or ACT required. SAT 25/75
percentile: 1130-1370. High
school rank: 100% in top tenth,
100% in top quarter, 100% in
top half
Early decision deadline: N/A,
notification date: N/A
Early action deadline: N/A,
notification date: N/A
Application deadline (fall): 11/30
Undergraduate student body:
20,243 full time, 364 part time;
47% male, 53% female; 0%
American Indian, 19% Asian,
2% black, 26% Hispanic, 8%
multiracial, 0% Pacific Islander,
35% white, 7% international;
95% from in state; 35% live
on campus; 8% of students in
fraternities, 13% in sororities
Most popular majors: 25% Social
Sciences; 9% Biological and
Biomedical Sciences; 9%
Psychology; 6% Visual and
Performing Arts
Expenses: 2016-2017: $14,022
in state, $40,704 out of state;
room/board: $15,186
Financial aid: (805) 893-2432;
61% of undergrads determined
to have financial need; average
aid package $22,132

University of California–Santa Cruz

Santa Cruz CA
(831) 459-4008
U.S. News ranking: Nat. U.,
No. 79
Website: www.ucsc.edu
Admissions email:
admissions@ucsc.edu
Public; founded 1965
Freshman admissions: more
selective; 2015-2016: 45,544
applied, 23,403 accepted. Either
SAT or ACT required. SAT 25/75
percentile: 1070-1310. High

school rank: 96% in top tenth,
100% in top quarter, 100% in
top half
Early decision deadline: N/A,
notification date: N/A
Early action deadline: N/A,
notification date: N/A
Application deadline (fall): 11/30
Undergraduate student body:
15,823 full time, 408 part time;
47% male, 53% female; 0%
American Indian, 21% Asian,
2% black, 31% Hispanic, 7%
multiracial, 0% Pacific Islander,
33% white, 4% international;
97% from in state; 53% live
on campus; 5% of students in
fraternities, 7% in sororities
Most popular majors: 12%
Psychology, General; 6%
Business/Managerial Economics;
6% Cell/Cellular and Molecular
Biology; 6% Sociology
Expenses: 2016-2017: $13,559
in state, $40,241 out of state;
room/board: $15,385
Financial aid: (831) 459-2963;
68% of undergrads determined
to have financial need; average
aid package $24,180

University of La Verne

La Verne CA
(800) 876-4858
U.S. News ranking: Nat. U.,
No. 152
Website: www.laverne.edu
Admissions email:
admission@laverne.edu
Private; founded 1891
Freshman admissions: selective;
2015-2016: 8,179 applied,
3,859 accepted. Either SAT
or ACT required. SAT 25/75
percentile: 940-1120. High
school rank: 18% in top tenth,
54% in top quarter, 86% in
top half
Early decision deadline: N/A,
notification date: N/A
Early action deadline: N/A,
notification date: N/A
Application deadline (fall): rolling
Undergraduate student body: 2,775
full time, 89 part time; 41%
male, 59% female; 0% American
Indian, 6% Asian, 5% black,
51% Hispanic, 5% multiracial,
1% Pacific Islander, 25% white,
5% international; 96% from in
state; 31% live on campus; 8%
of students in fraternities, 12%
in sororities
Most popular majors: 21%
Business, Management,
Marketing, and Related Support
Services; 16% Social Sciences;
14% Psychology; 8% Education
Expenses: 2016-2017: $39,900;
room/board: $12,890
Financial aid: (800) 649-0160;
83% of undergrads determined
to have financial need; average
aid package $30,825

University of Redlands

Redlands CA
(800) 455-5064
U.S. News ranking: Reg. U. (W),
No. 12
Website: www.redlands.edu
Admissions email:
admissions@redlands.edu
Private; founded 1907

Freshman admissions: selective;
2015-2016: 4,790 applied,
3,234 accepted. Either SAT
or ACT required. SAT 25/75
percentile: 1020-1220. High
school rank: 38% in top tenth,
68% in top quarter, 90% in
top half
Early decision deadline: N/A,
notification date: N/A
Early action deadline: 11/15,
notification date: 1/15
Application deadline (fall): 1/15
Undergraduate student body: 2,709
full time, 784 part time; 44%
male, 56% female; 1% American
Indian, 6% Asian, 5% black,
27% Hispanic, 5% multiracial,
1% Pacific Islander, 48% white,
1% international
Most popular majors: 18%
Business/Commerce, General;
16% Business Administration
and Management, General; 7%
Liberal Arts and Sciences/Liberal
Studies; 7% Psychology, General;
6% Audiology/Audiologist and
Speech-Language Pathology/
Pathologist
Expenses: 2015-2016: $44,900;
room/board: $13,090
Financial aid: (909) 335-4047

University of San Diego

San Diego CA
(619) 260-4506
U.S. News ranking: Nat. U.,
No. 86
Website: www.SanDiego.edu
Admissions email: admissions@
SanDiego.edu
Private; founded 1949
Affiliation: Roman Catholic
Freshman admissions: more
selective; 2015-2016: 13,675
applied, 7,067 accepted. Either
SAT or ACT required. SAT 25/75
percentile: 1110-1310. High
school rank: 36% in top tenth,
71% in top quarter, 91% in
top half
Early decision deadline: N/A,
notification date: N/A
Early action deadline: N/A,
notification date: N/A
Application deadline (fall): 12/15
Undergraduate student body: 5,441
full time, 206 part time; 46%
male, 54% female; 0% American
Indian, 7% Asian, 3% black,
19% Hispanic, 6% multiracial,
0% Pacific Islander, 53% white,
7% international; 64% from in
state; 45% live on campus; 24%
of students in fraternities, 40%
in sororities
Most popular majors: 43%
Business, Management,
Marketing, and Related Support
Services; 11% Social Sciences;
11% Biological and Biomedical
Sciences; 5% Psychology
Expenses: 2016-2017: $46,140;
room/board: $12,302
Financial aid: (619) 260-4514;
53% of undergrads determined
to have financial need; average
aid package $32,397

University of San Francisco

San Francisco CA
(415) 422-6563
U.S. News ranking: Nat. U., No. 107
Website: www.usfca.edu
Admissions email: admission@usfca.edu
Private; founded 1855
Affiliation: Jesuit Catholic
Freshman admissions: more selective; 2015-2016: 15,360 applied, 9,946 accepted. Either SAT or ACT required. SAT 25/75 percentile: 1070-1260. High school rank: 25% in top tenth, 67% in top quarter, 94% in top half
Early decision deadline: 11/15, notification date: 1/1
Early action deadline: 11/15, notification date: 1/1
Application deadline (fall): rolling
Undergraduate student body: 6,448 full time, 334 part time; 38% male, 62% female; 0% American Indian, 21% Asian, 3% black, 20% Hispanic, 7% multiracial, 1% Pacific Islander, 27% white, 19% international; 80% from in state; 32% live on campus; 3% of students in fraternities, 4% in sororities
Most popular majors: 11% Registered Nursing/Registered Nurse; 8% Finance, General; 7% Psychology, General; 6% Business Administration and Management, General; 5% Biology/Biological Sciences, General
Expenses: 2016-2017: $44,494; room/board: $13,990
Financial aid: (415) 422-2620; 54% of undergrads determined to have financial need; average aid package $28,715

University of Southern California

Los Angeles CA
(213) 740-1111
U.S. News ranking: Nat. U., No. 23
Website: www.usc.edu/
Admissions email: admitusc@usc.edu
Private; founded 1880
Freshman admissions: more selective; 2015-2016: 51,924 applied, 9,181 accepted. Either SAT or ACT required. SAT 25/75 percentile: 1270-1500. High school rank: 88% in top tenth, 97% in top quarter, 100% in top half
Early decision deadline: N/A, notification date: N/A
Early action deadline: N/A, notification date: N/A
Application deadline (fall): 1/15
Undergraduate student body: 18,208 full time, 602 part time; 49% male, 51% female; 0% American Indian, 22% Asian, 4% black, 14% Hispanic, 5% multiracial, 0% Pacific Islander, 40% white, 13% international; 68% from in state; 30% live on campus; 26% of students in fraternities, 27% in sororities
Most popular majors: 24% Business, Management, Marketing, and Related Support Services; 14% Social Sciences; 12% Visual and Performing Arts; 9% Engineering

---

Expenses: 2016-2017: $52,217; room/board: $14,348
Financial aid: (213) 740-1111; 37% of undergrads determined to have financial need; average aid package $44,791

University of the Pacific

Stockton CA
(209) 946-2285
U.S. News ranking: Nat. U., No. 111
Website: www.pacific.edu
Admissions email: admissions@pacific.edu
Private; founded 1851
Freshman admissions: more selective; 2015-2016: 14,449 applied, 9,328 accepted. Either SAT or ACT required. SAT 25/75 percentile: 1010-1280. High school rank: 33% in top tenth, 66% in top quarter, 90% in top half
Early decision deadline: N/A, notification date: N/A
Early action deadline: 11/15, notification date: 1/15
Application deadline (fall): 1/15
Undergraduate student body: 3,636 full time, 99 part time; 48% male, 52% female; 0% American Indian, 35% Asian, 3% black, 18% Hispanic, 6% multiracial, 1% Pacific Islander, 27% white, 7% international; 93% from in state; 46% live on campus; 6% of students in fraternities, 6% in sororities
Most popular majors: 19% Business Administration and Management, General; 13% Biology/Biological Sciences, General; 10% Engineering, General; 7% Health and Physical Education/Fitness, General; 6% Curriculum and Instruction
Expenses: 2016-2017: $44,588; room/board: $12,858
Financial aid: (209) 946-2421; 69% of undergrads determined to have financial need; average aid package $30,775

University of the West[1]

Rosemead CA
(855) 469-3378
U.S. News ranking: Reg. Coll. (W), unranked
Website: www.uwest.edu
Admissions email: N/A
Private; founded 1991
Application deadline (fall): N/A
Undergraduate student body: N/A full time, N/A part time
Expenses: 2015-2016: $10,656; room/board: $6,920
Financial aid: (626) 571-8811

Vanguard University of Southern California

Costa Mesa CA
(800) 722-6279
U.S. News ranking: Reg. U. (W), No. 60
Website: www.vanguard.edu
Admissions email: admissions@vanguard.edu
Private; founded 1920
Affiliation: Assemblies of God
Freshman admissions: selective; 2015-2016: 1,487 applied, 1,015 accepted. Either SAT or ACT required. SAT 25/75

---

percentile: 850-1090. High school rank: 15% in top tenth, 44% in top quarter, 73% in top half
Early decision deadline: N/A, notification date: N/A
Early action deadline: 12/1, notification date: 1/15
Application deadline (fall): 8/1
Undergraduate student body: 1,482 full time, 399 part time; 36% male, 64% female; 0% American Indian, 4% Asian, 5% black, 35% Hispanic, 5% multiracial, 1% Pacific Islander, 47% white, 1% international; 88% from in state; 49% live on campus; N/A of students in fraternities, N/A in sororities
Most popular majors: 19% Psychology, General; 17% Business Administration and Management, General; 11% Nursing Administration; 8% Religion/Religious Studies, Other; 7% Sociology
Expenses: 2015-2016: $30,050; room/board: $9,010
Financial aid: (714) 556-3610

Westmont College

Santa Barbara CA
(800) 777-9011
U.S. News ranking: Nat. Lib. Arts, No. 99
Website: www.westmont.edu
Admissions email: admissions@westmont.edu
Private; founded 1937
Affiliation: Christian nondenominational
Freshman admissions: more selective; 2015-2016: 2,077 applied, 1,687 accepted. Either SAT or ACT required. SAT 25/75 percentile: 1050-1300. High school rank: 37% in top tenth, 64% in top quarter, 91% in top half
Early decision deadline: N/A, notification date: N/A
Early action deadline: 11/15, notification date: 1/5
Application deadline (fall): rolling
Undergraduate student body: 1,294 full time, 10 part time; 39% male, 61% female; 0% American Indian, 7% Asian, 1% black, 15% Hispanic, 7% multiracial, 0% Pacific Islander, 63% white, 1% international; 75% from in state; 84% live on campus; 0% of students in fraternities, 0% in sororities
Most popular majors: 16% Kinesiology and Exercise Science; 14% Business/Managerial Economics; 9% Psychology, General; 8% English Language and Literature, General
Expenses: 2016-2017: $42,900; room/board: $13,510
Financial aid: (805) 565-6063; 67% of undergrads determined to have financial need; average aid package $30,600

Whittier College

Whittier CA
(562) 907-4238
U.S. News ranking: Nat. Lib. Arts, No. 132
Website: www.whittier.edu
Admissions email: admission@whittier.edu
Private; founded 1887
Freshman admissions: selective; 2015-2016: 5,192 applied,

3,251 accepted. Either SAT or ACT required. SAT 25/75 percentile: 933-1170. High school rank: 25% in top tenth, 39% in top quarter, 93% in top half
Early decision deadline: N/A, notification date: N/A
Early action deadline: 11/15, notification date: 12/30
Application deadline (fall): rolling
Undergraduate student body: 1,623 full time, 27 part time; 44% male, 56% female; 0% American Indian, 10% Asian, 5% black, 44% Hispanic, 4% multiracial, 0% Pacific Islander, 31% white, 3% international; 84% from in state; 50% live on campus; 2% of students in fraternities, 3% in sororities
Most popular majors: 18% Business, Management, Marketing, and Related Support Services; 18% Social Sciences; 9% Parks, Recreation, Leisure, and Fitness Studies; 8% Psychology; 7% Foreign Languages, Literatures, and Linguistics
Expenses: 2016-2017: $44,574; room/board: $12,902
Financial aid: (562) 907-4285; 75% of undergrads determined to have financial need; average aid package $34,585

William Jessup University

Rocklin CA
(916) 577-2222
U.S. News ranking: Reg. Coll. (W), unranked
Website: www.jessup.edu
Admissions email: admissions@jessup.edu
Private; founded 1939
Affiliation: Nondenominational/Interdenominational
Freshman admissions: N/A; 2015-2016: 522 applied, 397 accepted. Either SAT or ACT required. ACT 25/75 percentile: 19-25. High school rank: 16% in top tenth, 41% in top quarter, 73% in top half
Early decision deadline: N/A, notification date: N/A
Early action deadline: N/A, notification date: N/A
Application deadline (fall): 8/13
Undergraduate student body: 906 full time, 191 part time; 42% male, 58% female; 1% American Indian, 4% Asian, 5% black, 19% Hispanic, 2% multiracial, 1% Pacific Islander, 66% white, 0% international; 94% from in state; 50% live on campus; N/A of students in fraternities, N/A in sororities
Most popular majors: 33% Psychology; 24% Business, Management, Marketing, and Related Support Services; 16% Theology and Religious Vocations; 10% Education; 7% English Language and Literature/Letters
Expenses: 2016-2017: $28,700; room/board: $10,650
Financial aid: N/A; 82% of undergrads determined to have financial need; average aid package $20,899

Woodbury University

Burbank CA
(818) 767-0888
U.S. News ranking: Reg. U. (W), No. 58
Website: www.woodbury.edu
Admissions email: info@woodbury.edu
Private; founded 1884
Freshman admissions: less selective; 2015-2016: 1,342 applied, 773 accepted. Either SAT or ACT required. SAT 25/75 percentile: 860-1060. High school rank: N/A
Early decision deadline: N/A, notification date: N/A
Early action deadline: N/A, notification date: N/A
Application deadline (fall): rolling
Undergraduate student body: 1,088 full time, 187 part time; 51% male, 49% female; 0% American Indian, 10% Asian, 4% black, 27% Hispanic, N/A multiracial, N/A Pacific Islander, 33% white, 25% international; 95% from in state; 30% live on campus; 7% of students in fraternities, 8% in sororities
Most popular majors: 14% Business Administration and Management, General; 7% Accounting; 6% Organizational Leadership; 5% Apparel and Accessories Marketing Operations
Expenses: 2016-2017: $37,906; room/board: N/A
Financial aid: (818) 767-0888; 85% of undergrads determined to have financial need; average aid package $23,103

COLORADO

Adams State University[1]

Alamosa CO
(800) 824-6494
U.S. News ranking: Reg. U. (W), second tier
Website: www.adams.edu
Admissions email: ascadmit@adams.edu
Public
Application deadline (fall): N/A
Undergraduate student body: N/A full time, N/A part time
Expenses: 2015-2016: $8,574 in state, $19,086 out of state; room/board: $8,696
Financial aid: (719) 587-7306

Art Institute of Colorado[1]

Denver CO
(800) 275-2420
U.S. News ranking: Arts, unranked
Website: www.artinstitutes.edu/denver/
Admissions email: N/A
For-profit
Application deadline (fall): N/A
Undergraduate student body: N/A full time, N/A part time
Expenses: 2015-2016: $17,628; room/board: $10,278
Financial aid: (800) 275-2420

Colorado Christian University[1]
Lakewood CO
(303) 963-3200
U.S. News ranking: Reg. U. (W), second tier
Website: www.ccu.edu
Admissions email: admission@ccu.edu
Private
Application deadline (fall): N/A
Undergraduate student body: N/A full time, N/A part time
Expenses: 2015-2016: $27,986; room/board: $10,580
Financial aid: (303) 963-3230

Colorado College
Colorado Springs CO
(719) 389-6344
U.S. News ranking: Nat. Lib. Arts, No. 24
Website: www.ColoradoCollege.edu
Admissions email: admission@ColoradoCollege.edu
Private; founded 1874
Freshman admissions: most selective; 2015-2016: 8,062 applied, 1,381 accepted. Neither SAT nor ACT required. ACT 25/75 percentile: 28-32. High school rank: 68% in top tenth, 91% in top quarter, 100% in top half
Early decision deadline: 11/15, notification date: 12/15
Early action deadline: 11/15, notification date: 12/18
Application deadline (fall): 1/15
Undergraduate student body: 2,096 full time, 22 part time; 46% male, 54% female; 0% American Indian, 5% Asian, 3% black, 9% Hispanic, 9% multiracial, 0% Pacific Islander, 64% white, 7% international; 18% from in state; 75% live on campus; 11% of students in fraternities, 11% in sororities
Most popular majors: 9% Economics, General; 7% Sociology; 6% Political Science and Government, General
Expenses: 2016-2017: $50,892; room/board: $11,668
Financial aid: (719) 389-6651; 35% of undergrads determined to have financial need; average aid package $45,707

Colorado Mesa University
Grand Junction CO
(800) 982-6372
U.S. News ranking: Reg. Coll. (W), No. 23
Website: www.coloradomesa.edu/
Admissions email: admissions@coloradomesa.edu
Public; founded 1925
Freshman admissions: selective; 2015-2016: 6,667 applied, 5,538 accepted. Either SAT or ACT required. ACT 25/75 percentile: 17-23. High school rank: 9% in top tenth, 25% in top quarter, 55% in top half
Early decision deadline: N/A, notification date: N/A
Early action deadline: N/A, notification date: N/A
Application deadline (fall): rolling
Undergraduate student body: 7,204 full time, 2,095 part time; 46% male, 54% female; 1% American Indian, 2% Asian, 3% black, 17% Hispanic, 4% multiracial, 1% Pacific Islander, 70% white, 1% international; 86% from in state; 25% live on campus; N/A of students in fraternities, N/A in sororities
Most popular majors: 17% Business/Commerce, General; 9% Registered Nursing/Registered Nurse; 8% Criminal Justice/Safety Studies; 7% Kinesiology and Exercise Science; 6% Biology/Biological Sciences, General
Expenses: 2015-2016: $8,008 in state, $19,363 out of state; room/board: $10,526
Financial aid: (970) 248-1396; 67% of undergrads determined to have financial need; average aid package $8,772

Colorado Mountain College[1]
Glenwood Springs CO
(800) 621-8559
U.S. News ranking: Reg. Coll. (W), unranked
Website: coloradomtn.edu/
Admissions email: N/A
Public
Application deadline (fall): N/A
Undergraduate student body: N/A full time, N/A part time
Expenses: 2015-2016: $2,756 in state, $9,140 out of state; room/board: $9,648
Financial aid: N/A

Colorado School of Mines
Golden CO
(303) 273-3220
U.S. News ranking: Nat. U., No. 82
Website: www.mines.edu
Admissions email: admit@mines.edu
Public; founded 1874
Freshman admissions: most selective; 2015-2016: 11,752 applied, 4,427 accepted. Either SAT or ACT required. ACT 25/75 percentile: 28-32. High school rank: 56% in top tenth, 90% in top quarter, 99% in top half
Early decision deadline: N/A, notification date: N/A
Early action deadline: N/A, notification date: N/A
Application deadline (fall): 5/1
Undergraduate student body: 4,386 full time, 222 part time; 72% male, 28% female; 0% American Indian, 5% Asian, 1% black, 7% Hispanic, 5% multiracial, 0% Pacific Islander, 75% white, 6% international; 65% from in state; 36% live on campus; 12% of students in fraternities, 21% in sororities
Most popular majors: 87% Engineering; 5% Computer and Information Sciences and Support Services; 5% Mathematics and Statistics; 2% Physical Sciences; 1% Social Sciences
Expenses: 2015-2016: $17,383 in state, $34,828 out of state; room/board: $11,008
Financial aid: (303) 273-3220; 50% of undergrads determined to have financial need; average aid package $12,359

Colorado State University
Fort Collins CO
(970) 491-6909
U.S. News ranking: Nat. U., No. 129
Website: www.colostate.edu
Admissions email: admissions@colostate.edu
Public; founded 1870
Freshman admissions: more selective; 2015-2016: 18,556 applied, 14,997 accepted. Either SAT or ACT required. ACT 25/75 percentile: 22-28. High school rank: 19% in top tenth, 48% in top quarter, 83% in top half
Early decision deadline: N/A, notification date: N/A
Early action deadline: 12/1, notification date: 2/1
Application deadline (fall): 2/1
Undergraduate student body: 21,764 full time, 2,669 part time; 49% male, 51% female; 1% American Indian, 2% Asian, 2% black, 11% Hispanic, 2% multiracial, 0% Pacific Islander, 73% white, 4% international; 79% from in state; 27% live on campus; 9% of students in fraternities, 12% in sororities
Most popular majors: 15% Business, Management, Marketing, and Related Support Services; 9% Biological and Biomedical Sciences; 9% Social Sciences; 8% Family and Consumer Sciences/Human Sciences; 7% Engineering
Expenses: 2016-2017: $11,080 in state, $28,374 out of state; room/board: $11,862
Financial aid: (970) 491-6321; 50% of undergrads determined to have financial need; average aid package $10,906

Colorado State University–Pueblo
Pueblo CO
(719) 549-2461
U.S. News ranking: Reg. U. (W), second tier
Website: www.csupueblo.edu
Admissions email: info@colostate-pueblo.edu
Public; founded 1933
Freshman admissions: selective; 2015-2016: 6,178 applied, 5,924 accepted. Either SAT or ACT required. ACT 25/75 percentile: 18-23. High school rank: 10% in top tenth, 32% in top quarter, 69% in top half
Early decision deadline: N/A, notification date: N/A
Early action deadline: N/A, notification date: N/A
Application deadline (fall): 8/1
Undergraduate student body: 3,398 full time, 1,608 part time; 47% male, 53% female; 1% American Indian, 1% Asian, 7% black, 33% Hispanic, 5% multiracial, 0% Pacific Islander, 48% white, 3% international
Most popular majors: 13% Sociology; 12% Business/Commerce, General; 9% Registered Nursing/Registered Nurse; 7% Kinesiology and Exercise Science
Expenses: 2016-2017: $11,216 in state, $25,798 out of state; room/board: $8,342
Financial aid: (719) 549-2753; 75% of undergrads determined to have financial need; average aid package $9,865

Colorado Technical University[1]
Colorado Springs CO
(888) 897-6555
U.S. News ranking: Reg. U. (W), unranked
Website: www.coloradotech.edu
Admissions email: info@ctuonline.edu
For-profit
Application deadline (fall): N/A
Undergraduate student body: N/A full time, N/A part time
Expenses: 2015-2016: $11,297; room/board: $9,603
Financial aid: (719) 598-2900

Fort Lewis College
Durango CO
(970) 247-7184
U.S. News ranking: Nat. Lib. Arts, second tier
Website: www.fortlewis.edu
Admissions email: admission@fortlewis.edu
Public; founded 1911
Freshman admissions: selective; 2015-2016: 3,105 applied, 2,669 accepted. Either SAT or ACT required. ACT 25/75 percentile: 19-24. High school rank: 11% in top tenth, 33% in top quarter, 70% in top half
Early decision deadline: N/A, notification date: N/A
Early action deadline: 1/15, notification date: 3/15
Application deadline (fall): 8/1
Undergraduate student body: 3,393 full time, 286 part time; 49% male, 51% female; 25% American Indian, 1% Asian, 1% black, 11% Hispanic, 7% multiracial, 0% Pacific Islander, 52% white, 1% international; 50% from in state; 40% live on campus; N/A of students in fraternities, N/A in sororities
Most popular majors: 17% Business, Management, Marketing, and Related Support Services; 13% Social Sciences; 10% Parks, Recreation, Leisure, and Fitness Studies; 8% Biological and Biomedical Sciences; 8% Physical Sciences
Expenses: 2016-2017: $7,601 in state, $17,817 out of state; room/board: $10,904
Financial aid: (970) 247-7142; 61% of undergrads determined to have financial need; average aid package $15,987

Metropolitan State University of Denver
Denver CO
(303) 556-3058
U.S. News ranking: Reg. U. (W), second tier
Website: www.mscd.edu
Admissions email: askmetro@mscd.edu
Public; founded 1963
Freshman admissions: less selective; 2015-2016: 5,995 applied, 3,913 accepted. Either SAT or ACT required. ACT 25/75 percentile: 17-23. High school rank: 6% in top tenth, 19% in top quarter, 50% in top half
Early decision deadline: N/A, notification date: N/A
Early action deadline: N/A, notification date: N/A
Application deadline (fall): 7/1
Undergraduate student body: 12,313 full time, 7,873 part time; 47% male, 53% female; 1% American Indian, 4% Asian, 6% black, 22% Hispanic, 4% multiracial, 0% Pacific Islander, 58% white, 0% international; 97% from in state; N/A live on campus; N/A of students in fraternities, N/A in sororities
Most popular majors: 19% Business, Management, Marketing, and Related Support Services; 9% Psychology; 8% Multi/Interdisciplinary Studies; 7% Public Administration and Social Service Professions; 6% Health Professions and Related Programs
Expenses: 2016-2017: $6,930 in state, $20,096 out of state; room/board: N/A
Financial aid: (303) 556-4741; 67% of undergrads determined to have financial need; average aid package $8,602

Naropa University
Boulder CO
(303) 546-3572
U.S. News ranking: Reg. U. (W), unranked
Website: www.naropa.edu
Admissions email: admissions@naropa.edu
Private; founded 1974
Freshman admissions: N/A; 2015-2016: 181 applied, 144 accepted. Neither SAT nor ACT required. ACT 25/75 percentile: N/A. High school rank: N/A
Early decision deadline: N/A, notification date: N/A
Early action deadline: N/A, notification date: N/A
Application deadline (fall): rolling
Undergraduate student body: 368 full time, 29 part time; 36% male, 64% female; 1% American Indian, 1% Asian, 2% black, 10% Hispanic, 10% multiracial, 0% Pacific Islander, 63% white, 2% international; 41% from in state; 19% live on campus; N/A of students in fraternities, N/A in sororities
Most popular majors: 40% Psychology, General; 13% Health and Physical Education/Fitness, Other; 11% Visual and Performing Arts, General; 9% Multi-/Interdisciplinary Studies, Other; 7% English Language and Literature, General
Expenses: 2016-2017: $31,170; room/board: $11,656
Financial aid: (303) 546-3565; 68% of undergrads determined to have financial need; average aid package $37,077

Regis University
Denver CO
(303) 458-4900
U.S. News ranking: Reg. U. (W), No. 23
Website: www.regis.edu
Admissions email: regisadm@regis.edu
Private; founded 1877
Affiliation: Roman Catholic (Jesuit)

Freshman admissions: selective; 2015-2016: 5,493 applied, 3,609 accepted. Either SAT or ACT required. ACT 25/75 percentile: 21-27. High school rank: 21% in top tenth, 50% in top quarter, 79% in top half
Early decision deadline: N/A, notification date: N/A
Early action deadline: N/A, notification date: N/A
Application deadline (fall): 8/1
Undergraduate student body: 2,419 full time, 2,080 part time; 39% male, 61% female; 1% American Indian, 5% Asian, 5% black, 19% Hispanic, 4% multiracial, 0% Pacific Islander, 59% white, 1% international; 63% from in state; N/A live on campus; N/A of students in fraternities, N/A in sororities
Most popular majors: 33% Health Professions and Related Programs; 27% Business, Management, Marketing, and Related Support Services; 6% Computer and Information Sciences and Support Services; 5% Social Sciences; 5% Biological and Biomedical Sciences
Expenses: 2016-2017: $33,710; room/board: $10,040
Financial aid: (303) 458-4066; 68% of undergrads determined to have financial need; average aid package $27,131

Rocky Mountain College of Art and Design[1]
Lakewood CO
(303) 225-8576
U.S. News ranking: Arts, unranked
Website: www.rmcad.edu/
Admissions email: admissions@rmcad.edu
For-profit; founded 1963
Application deadline (fall): rolling
Undergraduate student body: N/A full time, N/A part time
Expenses: 2015-2016: $16,370; room/board: $8,357
Financial aid: (303) 753-6046

United States Air Force Academy
USAF Academy CO
(800) 443-9266
U.S. News ranking: Nat. Lib. Arts, No. 32
Website: academyadmissions.com
Admissions email: rr_webmail@usafa.edu
Public; founded 1954
Freshman admissions: most selective; 2015-2016: 9,122 applied, 1,559 accepted. Either SAT or ACT required. ACT 25/75 percentile: 28-33. High school rank: 52% in top tenth, 81% in top quarter, 97% in top half
Early decision deadline: N/A, notification date: N/A
Early action deadline: N/A, notification date: N/A
Application deadline (fall): 12/31
Undergraduate student body: 4,111 full time, 0 part time; 77% male, 23% female; 0% American Indian, 5% Asian, 6% black, 10% Hispanic, 7% multiracial, 1% Pacific Islander, 63% white, 1% international; 12% from in

state; 100% live on campus; 0% of students in fraternities, 0% in sororities
Most popular majors: 32% Engineering; 21% Business, Management, Marketing, and Related Support Services; 16% Social Sciences; 9% Multi/Interdisciplinary Studies; 7% Biological and Biomedical Sciences
Expenses: N/A
Financial aid: (719) 333-3160; 0% of undergrads determined to have financial need; average aid package $0

University of Colorado–Boulder
Boulder CO
(303) 492-6301
U.S. News ranking: Nat. U., No. 92
Website: www.colorado.edu
Admissions email: apply@colorado.edu
Public; founded 1876
Freshman admissions: more selective; 2015-2016: 31,291 applied, 24,933 accepted. Either SAT or ACT required. ACT 25/75 percentile: 24-30. High school rank: 28% in top tenth, 57% in top quarter, 89% in top half
Early decision deadline: N/A, notification date: N/A
Early action deadline: 11/15, notification date: 2/1
Application deadline (fall): 1/15
Undergraduate student body: 24,906 full time, 2,104 part time; 55% male, 45% female; 0% American Indian, 5% Asian, 2% black, 11% Hispanic, 5% multiracial, 0% Pacific Islander, 71% white, 6% international; 60% from in state; 29% live on campus; 10% of students in fraternities, 19% in sororities
Most popular majors: 14% Biological and Biomedical Sciences; 14% Social Sciences; 12% Business, Management, and Related Support Services; 11% Engineering
Expenses: 2016-2017: $11,531 in state, $35,079 out of state; room/board: $13,590
Financial aid: (303) 492-5091; 36% of undergrads determined to have financial need; average aid package $16,146

University of Colorado–Colorado Springs
Colorado Springs CO
(719) 255-3383
U.S. News ranking: Reg. U. (W), No. 39
Website: www.uccs.edu
Admissions email: admrecor@uccs.edu
Public; founded 1965
Freshman admissions: selective; 2015-2016: 8,292 applied, 7,634 accepted. Either SAT or ACT required. ACT 25/75 percentile: 21-26. High school rank: 11% in top tenth, 37% in top quarter, 71% in top half
Early decision deadline: N/A, notification date: N/A
Early action deadline: N/A, notification date: N/A
Application deadline (fall): rolling

Undergraduate student body: 7,472 full time, 2,344 part time; 49% male, 51% female; 0% American Indian, 3% Asian, 4% black, 16% Hispanic, 7% multiracial, 0% Pacific Islander, 66% white, 1% international; 88% from in state; 14% live on campus; 1% of students in fraternities, 3% in sororities
Most popular majors: 17% Business Administration, Management and Operations; 15% Health Professions and Related Programs; 13% Social Sciences; 8% Psychology
Expenses: 2015-2016: $7,692 in state, $17,988 out of state; room/board: $9,900
Financial aid: (719) 262-3460; 61% of undergrads determined to have financial need; average aid package $8,469

University of Colorado–Denver
Denver CO
(303) 556-2704
U.S. News ranking: Nat. U., No. 197
Website: www.ucdenver.edu
Admissions email: admissions@ucdenver.edu
Public; founded 1912
Freshman admissions: selective; 2015-2016: 8,615 applied, 5,808 accepted. Either SAT or ACT required. ACT 25/75 percentile: 20-25. High school rank: 31% in top tenth, 55% in top quarter, 81% in top half
Early decision deadline: N/A, notification date: N/A
Early action deadline: N/A, notification date: N/A
Application deadline (fall): rolling
Undergraduate student body: 8,077 full time, 5,959 part time; 45% male, 55% female; 0% American Indian, 10% Asian, 5% black, 19% Hispanic, 5% multiracial, 0% Pacific Islander, 51% white, 8% international; 92% from in state; N/A live on campus; N/A of students in fraternities, N/A in sororities
Most popular majors: 16% Business Administration and Management, General; 11% Registered Nursing/Registered Nurse; 9% Biology/Biological Sciences, General; 7% Economics, General; 6% Psychology, General
Expenses: 2016-2017: $10,404 in state, $29,334 out of state; room/board: N/A
Financial aid: (303) 556-2886; 61% of undergrads determined to have financial need; average aid package $9,542

University of Denver
Denver CO
(303) 871-2036
U.S. News ranking: Nat. U., No. 86
Website: www.du.edu
Admissions email: admission@du.edu
Private; founded 1864
Freshman admissions: more selective; 2015-2016: 15,036 applied, 10,938 accepted. Either SAT or ACT required. ACT 25/75

percentile: 23-30. High school rank: 45% in top tenth, 80% in top quarter, 97% in top half
Early decision deadline: N/A, notification date: N/A
Early action deadline: 11/1, notification date: 1/15
Application deadline (fall): 1/17
Undergraduate student body: 5,448 full time, 310 part time; 46% male, 54% female; 0% American Indian, 4% Asian, 2% black, 10% Hispanic, 4% multiracial, 0% Pacific Islander, 68% white, 9% international; 41% from in state; 44% live on campus; 27% of students in fraternities, 29% in sororities
Most popular majors: 32% Business, Management, Marketing, and Related Support Services; 18% Social Sciences; 8% Psychology; 7% Biological and Biomedical Sciences
Expenses: 2016-2017: $46,362; room/board: $12,021
Financial aid: (303) 871-4020; 42% of undergrads determined to have financial need; average aid package $35,265

University of Northern Colorado
Greeley CO
(970) 351-2881
U.S. News ranking: Nat. U., second tier
Website: www.unco.edu
Admissions email: admissions.help@unco.edu
Public; founded 1890
Freshman admissions: selective; 2015-2016: 7,143 applied, 6,382 accepted. Neither SAT nor ACT required. ACT 25/75 percentile: 19-25. High school rank: 13% in top tenth, 35% in top quarter, 74% in top half
Early decision deadline: N/A, notification date: N/A
Early action deadline: N/A, notification date: N/A
Application deadline (fall): 8/1
Undergraduate student body: 8,180 full time, 1,214 part time; 37% male, 63% female; 0% American Indian, 2% Asian, 4% black, 18% Hispanic, 4% multiracial, 0% Pacific Islander, 55% white, 1% international; 86% from in state; 36% live on campus; 5% of students in fraternities, 6% in sororities
Most popular majors: 12% Multi/Interdisciplinary Studies; 10% Business, Management, and Related Support Services; 8% Health Professions and Related Programs; 8% Parks, Recreation, Leisure, and Fitness Studies; 6% Psychology
Expenses: 2016-2017: $8,416 in state, $20,002 out of state; room/board: $10,360
Financial aid: (970) 351-2502; 70% of undergrads determined to have financial need; average aid package $10,912

Western State Colorado University
Gunnison CO
(800) 876-5309
U.S. News ranking: Reg. U. (W), No. 92
Website: www.western.edu
Admissions email: discover@western.edu
Public; founded 1901
Freshman admissions: selective; 2015-2016: 1,631 applied, 1,592 accepted. Either SAT or ACT required. ACT 25/75 percentile: 17-23. High school rank: 4% in top tenth, 17% in top quarter, 42% in top half
Early decision deadline: N/A, notification date: N/A
Early action deadline: N/A, notification date: N/A
Application deadline (fall): rolling
Undergraduate student body: 1,883 full time, 536 part time; 57% male, 43% female; 1% American Indian, 1% Asian, 3% black, 10% Hispanic, 4% multiracial, 0% Pacific Islander, 75% white, 0% international; 72% from in state; 45% live on campus; N/A of students in fraternities, N/A in sororities
Most popular majors: 21% Business, Management, Marketing, and Related Support Services; 12% Parks, Recreation, Leisure, and Fitness Studies; 12% Social Sciences; 9% Biological and Biomedical Sciences; 9% Psychology
Expenses: 2016-2017: $9,193 in state, $20,497 out of state; room/board: $9,446
Financial aid: (970) 943-3085; 55% of undergrads determined to have financial need; average aid package $9,660

CONNECTICUT

Albertus Magnus College
New Haven CT
(800) 578-9160
U.S. News ranking: Reg. U. (N), No. 108
Website: www.albertus.edu
Admissions email: admissions@albertus.edu
Private; founded 1925
Affiliation: Roman Catholic
Freshman admissions: less selective; 2015-2016: 588 applied, 408 accepted. Either SAT or ACT required. SAT 25/75 percentile: 820-950. High school rank: N/A
Early decision deadline: N/A, notification date: N/A
Early action deadline: N/A, notification date: N/A
Application deadline (fall): rolling
Undergraduate student body: 1,023 full time, 174 part time; 34% male, 66% female; 0% American Indian, 0% Asian, 32% black, 17% Hispanic, 1% multiracial, 0% Pacific Islander, 40% white, 2% international; 96% from in state; 16% live on campus; 0% of students in fraternities, 0% in sororities
Most popular majors: 52% Business, Management, Marketing, and Related Support Services; 9% Social Sciences; 8% Homeland Security, Law

Enforcement, Firefighting and Related Protective Services; 8% Psychology; 3% Public Administration and Social Service Professions
Expenses: 2016-2017: $30,526; room/board: $14,016
Financial aid: (203) 773-8508; 96% of undergrads determined to have financial need; average aid package $16,655

Central Connecticut State University
New Britain CT
(860) 832-2278
U.S. News ranking: Reg. U. (N), No. 110
Website: www.ccsu.edu
Admissions email: admissions@ccsu.edu
Public; founded 1849
Freshman admissions: selective; 2015-2016: 8,686 applied, 5,096 accepted. Either SAT or ACT required. SAT 25/75 percentile: 920-1100. High school rank: 10% in top tenth, 28% in top quarter, 68% in top half
Early decision deadline: N/A, notification date: N/A
Early action deadline: N/A, notification date: N/A
Application deadline (fall): 5/1
Undergraduate student body: 7,763 full time, 2,170 part time; 53% male, 47% female; 0% American Indian, 4% Asian, 12% black, 13% Hispanic, 3% multiracial, 0% Pacific Islander, 65% white, 1% international; 97% from in state; 24% live on campus; 0% of students in fraternities, 0% in sororities
Most popular majors: 26% Business, Management, Marketing, and Related Support Services; 12% Social Sciences; 8% Education; 8% Psychology
Expenses: 2016-2017: $9,741 in state, $21,407 out of state; room/board: $11,462
Financial aid: (860) 832-2200; 77% of undergrads determined to have financial need; average aid package $9,871

Charter Oak State College
New Britain CT
(860) 832-3855
U.S. News ranking: Nat. Lib. Arts, unranked
Website: www.charteroak.edu
Admissions email: info@charteroak.edu
Public; founded 1973
Freshman admissions: N/A; 2015-2016: N/A applied, N/A accepted. Neither SAT nor ACT required. ACT 25/75 percentile: N/A. High school rank: N/A
Early decision deadline: N/A, notification date: N/A
Early action deadline: N/A, notification date: N/A
Application deadline (fall): rolling
Undergraduate student body: 329 full time, 1,406 part time; 32% male, 68% female; 0% American Indian, 1% Asian, 17% black, 14% Hispanic, 2% multiracial, 0% Pacific Islander, 59% white, 1% international; 80% from in

state; N/A live on campus; N/A of students in fraternities, N/A in sororities
Most popular majors: 93% Liberal Arts and Sciences/Liberal Studies; 7% Health/Health Care Administration/Management
Expenses: 2016-2017: $9,393 in state, $12,093 out of state; room/board: N/A
Financial aid: N/A

Connecticut College
New London CT
(860) 439-2200
U.S. News ranking: Nat. Lib. Arts, No. 50
Website: www.conncoll.edu
Admissions email: admission@conncoll.edu
Private; founded 1911
Freshman admissions: more selective; 2015-2016: 5,182 applied, 2,071 accepted. Neither SAT nor ACT required. SAT 25/75 percentile: 1220-1400. High school rank: 49% in top tenth, 79% in top quarter, 99% in top half
Early decision deadline: 11/15, notification date: 12/15
Early action deadline: N/A, notification date: N/A
Application deadline (fall): 1/1
Undergraduate student body: 1,857 full time, 61 part time; 38% male, 62% female; 0% American Indian, 4% Asian, 4% black, 9% Hispanic, 3% multiracial, 0% Pacific Islander, 71% white, 6% international; 18% from in state; 99% live on campus; 0% of students in fraternities, 0% in sororities
Most popular majors: 17% Economics, General; 11% Psychology, General; 7% Biology/Biological Sciences, General; 7% Political Science and Government, General; 6% International Relations and Affairs
Expenses: 2016-2017: $50,940; room/board: $14,060
Financial aid: (860) 439-2058; 55% of undergrads determined to have financial need; average aid package $39,225

Eastern Connecticut State University
Willimantic CT
(860) 465-5286
U.S. News ranking: Reg. U. (N), No. 85
Website: www.easternct.edu
Admissions email: admissions@easternct.edu
Public; founded 1889
Freshman admissions: selective; 2015-2016: 5,370 applied, 3,413 accepted. Neither SAT nor ACT required. SAT 25/75 percentile: 950-1140. High school rank: 11% in top tenth, 31% in top quarter, 73% in top half
Early decision deadline: N/A, notification date: N/A
Early action deadline: N/A, notification date: N/A
Application deadline (fall): rolling
Undergraduate student body: 4,267 full time, 830 part time; 46% male, 54% female; 0% American Indian, 3% Asian, 7% black, 10% Hispanic, 3% multiracial,

0% Pacific Islander, 67% white, 1% international; 95% from in state; 53% live on campus; N/A of students in fraternities, N/A in sororities
Most popular majors: 15% Business, Management, Marketing, and Related Support Services; 11% Liberal Arts and Sciences, General Studies and Humanities; 10% Psychology; 9% Social Sciences
Expenses: 2016-2017: $10,500 in state, $22,166 out of state; room/board: $12,559
Financial aid: (860) 465-5205; 66% of undergrads determined to have financial need; average aid package $8,737

Fairfield University
Fairfield CT
(203) 254-4100
U.S. News ranking: Reg. U. (N), No. 2
Website: www.fairfield.edu
Admissions email: admis@fairfield.edu
Private; founded 1942
Affiliation: Roman Catholic (Jesuit)
Freshman admissions: more selective; 2015-2016: 10,767 applied, 6,995 accepted. Neither SAT nor ACT required. SAT 25/75 percentile: 1100-1270. High school rank: 31% in top tenth, 69% in top quarter, 97% in top half
Early decision deadline: 11/15, notification date: 12/15
Early action deadline: 11/1, notification date: 12/20
Application deadline (fall): 1/15
Undergraduate student body: 3,704 full time, 266 part time; 40% male, 60% female; 0% American Indian, 2% Asian, 2% black, 7% Hispanic, 1% multiracial, 0% Pacific Islander, 76% white, 2% international; 28% from in state; 75% live on campus; N/A of students in fraternities, N/A in sororities
Most popular majors: 33% Business, Management, and Related Support Services; 13% Health Professions and Related Programs; 12% Social Sciences; 7% English Language and Literature/Letters
Expenses: 2016-2017: $46,000; room/board: $13,860
Financial aid: (203) 254-4125; 46% of undergrads determined to have financial need; average aid package $35,269

Lincoln College of New England–Southington[1]
Southington CT
(800) 328-6077
U.S. News ranking: Reg. Coll. (N), unranked
Website: www.lincolncollegene.edu/
Admissions email: N/A
For-profit
Application deadline (fall): N/A
Undergraduate student body: N/A full time, N/A part time
Expenses: 2015-2016: $19,950; room/board: $9,300
Financial aid: N/A

Mitchell College[1]
New London CT
(800) 443-2811
U.S. News ranking: Reg. Coll. (N), unranked
Website: www.mitchell.edu
Admissions email: admissions@mitchell.edu
Private
Application deadline (fall): N/A
Undergraduate student body: N/A full time, N/A part time
Expenses: 2015-2016: $31,000; room/board: $12,500
Financial aid: (860) 701-5061

Post University
Waterbury CT
(203) 596-4520
U.S. News ranking: Reg. U. (N), second tier
Website: www.post.edu
Admissions email: admissions@post.edu
For-profit; founded 1890
Freshman admissions: less selective; 2015-2016: 2,401 applied, 1,948 accepted. Either SAT or ACT required. SAT 25/75 percentile: 770-1000. High school rank: N/A
Early decision deadline: N/A, notification date: N/A
Early action deadline: N/A, notification date: N/A
Application deadline (fall): rolling
Undergraduate student body: 2,724 full time, 4,088 part time; 40% male, 60% female; 0% American Indian, 1% Asian, 21% black, 7% Hispanic, 4% multiracial, 0% Pacific Islander, 40% white, 0% international; 53% from in state; 20% live on campus; N/A of students in fraternities, N/A in sororities
Most popular majors: 38% Business Administration and Management, General; 12% Criminal Justice/Safety Studies; 8% Accounting; 8% Management Information Systems, General; 5% Psychology, General
Expenses: 2016-2017: $29,550; room/board: $10,600
Financial aid: (203) 596-4526; 83% of undergrads determined to have financial need; average aid package $12,748

Quinnipiac University
Hamden CT
(800) 462-1944
U.S. News ranking: Reg. U. (N), No. 11
Website: www.quinnipiac.edu
Admissions email: admissions@quinnipiac.edu
Private; founded 1929
Freshman admissions: selective; 2015-2016: 22,745 applied, 16,765 accepted. Either SAT or ACT required. SAT 25/75 percentile: 990-1180. High school rank: 37% in top tenth, 69% in top quarter, 94% in top half
Early decision deadline: 11/1, notification date: 12/1
Early action deadline: N/A, notification date: N/A
Application deadline (fall): 2/1
Undergraduate student body: 6,703 full time, 279 part time; 39% male, 61% female; 0% American Indian, 3% Asian, 5% black, 9% Hispanic, 2% multiracial, 0%

Pacific Islander, 77% white, 2% international; 30% from in state; 77% live on campus; 24% of students in fraternities, 25% in sororities
Most popular majors: 35% Health Professions and Related Programs; 22% Business, Management, Marketing, and Related Support Services; 6% Psychology; 4% Social Sciences
Expenses: 2016-2017: $43,940; room/board: $15,170
Financial aid: (203) 582-8750; 61% of undergrads determined to have financial need; average aid package $26,272

Sacred Heart University
Fairfield CT
(203) 371-7880
U.S. News ranking: Reg. U. (N), No. 44
Website: www.sacredheart.edu
Admissions email: enroll@sacredheart.edu
Private; founded 1963
Affiliation: Roman Catholic
Freshman admissions: selective; 2015-2016: 9,254 applied, 5,457 accepted. Neither SAT nor ACT required. SAT 25/75 percentile: 961-1245. High school rank: 10% in top tenth, 35% in top quarter, 77% in top half
Early decision deadline: 12/1, notification date: 12/15
Early action deadline: 12/15, notification date: 1/31
Application deadline (fall): rolling
Undergraduate student body: 4,435 full time, 770 part time; 36% male, 64% female; 0% American Indian, 2% Asian, 4% black, 8% Hispanic, 2% multiracial, 0% Pacific Islander, 71% white, 1% international; 39% from in state; 50% live on campus; 16% of students in fraternities, 31% in sororities
Most popular majors: 25% Health Professions and Related Programs; 23% Business, Management, Marketing, and Related Support Services; 11% Psychology; 5% Social Sciences
Expenses: 2016-2017: $38,300; room/board: $14,450
Financial aid: (203) 371-7980; 67% of undergrads determined to have financial need; average aid package $20,045

Southern Connecticut State University
New Haven CT
(203) 392-5656
U.S. News ranking: Reg. U. (N), No. 122
Website: www.southernct.edu/
Admissions email: information@southernct.edu
Public; founded 1893
Freshman admissions: less selective; 2015-2016: 8,113 applied, 5,241 accepted. Either SAT or ACT required. SAT 25/75 percentile: 820-1010. High school rank: 1% in top tenth, 10% in top quarter, 44% in top half
Early decision deadline: N/A, notification date: N/A
Early action deadline: N/A, notification date: N/A

Application deadline (fall): rolling
Undergraduate student body: 6,869 full time, 1,237 part time; 39% male, 61% female; 0% American Indian, 3% Asian, 17% black, 13% Hispanic, 2% multiracial, 0% Pacific Islander, 55% white, 1% international; 96% from in state; 32% live on campus; 1% of students in fraternities, 1% in sororities
Most popular majors: 14% Business Administration and Management, General; 14% Liberal Arts and Sciences/Liberal Studies; 9% Psychology, General; 6% Public Health, General; 6% Registered Nursing/Registered Nurse
Expenses: 2016-2017: $10,054 in state, $21,720 out of state; room/board: $11,870
Financial aid: (203) 392-5222; 75% of undergrads determined to have financial need; average aid package $13,906

Trinity College
Hartford CT
(860) 297-2180
U.S. News ranking: Nat. Lib. Arts, No. 38
Website: www.trincoll.edu
Admissions email: admissions.office@trincoll.edu
Private; founded 1823
Freshman admissions: more selective; 2015-2016: 7,570 applied, 2,530 accepted. Neither SAT nor ACT required. SAT 25/75 percentile: 1150-1340. High school rank: 64% in top tenth, 84% in top quarter, 98% in top half
Early decision deadline: 11/15, notification date: 12/15
Early action deadline: N/A, notification date: N/A
Application deadline (fall): 1/1
Undergraduate student body: 2,165 full time, 124 part time; 52% male, 48% female; 0% American Indian, 4% Asian, 6% black, 7% Hispanic, 3% multiracial, 0% Pacific Islander, 65% white, 10% international; 17% from in state; 91% live on campus; 21% of students in fraternities, 12% in sororities
Most popular majors: Economics, General; English Language and Literature, General; History, General; Political Science and Government, General; Psychology, General
Expenses: 2016-2017: $52,760; room/board: $13,680
Financial aid: (860) 297-2046; 45% of undergrads determined to have financial need; average aid package $45,859

United States Coast Guard Academy
New London CT
(800) 883-8724
U.S. News ranking: Reg. Coll. (N), No. 2
Website: www.uscga.edu
Admissions email: admissions@uscga.edu
Public; founded 1932
Freshman admissions: more selective; 2015-2016: 2,214 applied, 388 accepted. Either SAT or ACT required. SAT 25/75 percentile: 1180-1350. High

school rank: 45% in top tenth, 79% in top quarter, 96% in top half
Early decision deadline: N/A, notification date: N/A
Early action deadline: 11/15, notification date: 2/1
Application deadline (fall): 2/1
Undergraduate student body: 898 full time, 0 part time; 65% male, 35% female; 0% American Indian, 7% Asian, 4% black, 10% Hispanic, 8% multiracial, 0% Pacific Islander, 67% white, 2% international; 5% from in state; 100% live on campus; 0% of students in fraternities, 0% in sororities
Most popular majors: 38% Engineering; 20% Social Sciences; 19% Business, Management, Marketing, and Related Support Services; 17% Biological and Biomedical Sciences; 6% Mathematics and Statistics
Expenses: 2016-2017: $978 in state, $978 out of state; room/board: N/A
Financial aid: N/A

University of Bridgeport
Bridgeport CT
(203) 576-4552
U.S. News ranking: Reg. U. (N), second tier
Website: www.bridgeport.edu
Admissions email: admit@bridgeport.edu
Private; founded 1927
Freshman admissions: less selective; 2015-2016: 6,599 applied, 3,466 accepted. Either SAT or ACT required. SAT 25/75 percentile: 830-1010. High school rank: 10% in top tenth, 30% in top quarter, 58% in top half
Early decision deadline: N/A, notification date: N/A
Early action deadline: N/A, notification date: N/A
Application deadline (fall): rolling
Undergraduate student body: 2,112 full time, 785 part time; 36% male, 64% female; 1% American Indian, 3% Asian, 36% black, 18% Hispanic, 2% multiracial, 0% Pacific Islander, 24% white, 16% international; 61% from in state; 42% live on campus; 2% of students in fraternities, 2% in sororities
Most popular majors: 17% Business/Commerce, General; 15% Psychology, General; 14% General Studies; 10% Dental Hygiene/Hygienist; 9% Public Administration and Social Service Professions
Expenses: 2016-2017: $31,630; room/board: $13,200
Financial aid: (203) 576-4568; 81% of undergrads determined to have financial need; average aid package $26,304

University of Connecticut
Storrs CT
(860) 486-3137
U.S. News ranking: Nat. U., No. 60
Website: www.uconn.edu
Admissions email: beahusky@uconn.edu

Public; founded 1881
Freshman admissions: more selective; 2015-2016: 34,978 applied, 18,598 accepted. Either SAT or ACT required. SAT 25/75 percentile: 1130-1340. High school rank: 50% in top tenth, 85% in top quarter, 97% in top half
Early decision deadline: N/A, notification date: N/A
Early action deadline: N/A, notification date: N/A
Application deadline (fall): 1/15
Undergraduate student body: 18,131 full time, 695 part time; 50% male, 50% female; 0% American Indian, 10% Asian, 5% black, 9% Hispanic, 3% multiracial, 0% Pacific Islander, 61% white, 5% international; 77% from in state; 70% live on campus; 10% of students in fraternities, 15% in sororities
Most popular majors: 13% Business, Management, Marketing, and Related Support Services; 11% Health Professions and Related Programs; 11% Social Sciences; 9% Biological and Biomedical Sciences; 9% Engineering
Expenses: 2016-2017: $14,066 in state, $35,858 out of state; room/board: $12,436
Financial aid: (860) 486-2819; 55% of undergrads determined to have financial need; average aid package $14,074

University of Hartford
West Hartford CT
(860) 768-4296
U.S. News ranking: Nat. U., No. 188
Website: www.hartford.edu
Admissions email: admission@hartford.edu
Private; founded 1877
Freshman admissions: selective; 2015-2016: 15,093 applied, 9,585 accepted. Either SAT or ACT required. SAT 25/75 percentile: 940-1160. High school rank: N/A
Early decision deadline: N/A, notification date: N/A
Early action deadline: 11/15, notification date: 12/1
Application deadline (fall): rolling
Undergraduate student body: 4,533 full time, 713 part time; 49% male, 51% female; 0% American Indian, 3% Asian, 16% black, 12% Hispanic, 3% multiracial, 0% Pacific Islander, 56% white, 6% international; 49% from in state; 62% live on campus; 11% of students in fraternities, 10% in sororities
Most popular majors: 22% Visual and Performing Arts; 15% Health Professions and Related Programs; 13% Business, Management, Marketing, and Related Support Services; 11% Engineering; 7% Engineering Technologies and Engineering-Related Fields
Expenses: 2016-2017: $37,790; room/board: $11,986
Financial aid: (860) 768-4296

University of New Haven
West Haven CT
(203) 932-7319
U.S. News ranking: Reg. U. (N), No. 95
Website: www.newhaven.edu
Admissions email: adminfo@newhaven.edu
Private; founded 1920
Freshman admissions: selective; 2015-2016: 10,748 applied, 8,826 accepted. Either SAT or ACT required. SAT 25/75 percentile: 960-1160. High school rank: 16% in top tenth, 40% in top quarter, 78% in top half
Early decision deadline: 12/1, notification date: 12/15
Early action deadline: 12/15, notification date: 1/15
Application deadline (fall): rolling
Undergraduate student body: 4,611 full time, 391 part time; 50% male, 50% female; 0% American Indian, 3% Asian, 9% black, 11% Hispanic, 2% multiracial, 0% Pacific Islander, 59% white, 8% international; 43% from in state; 53% live on campus; N/A of students in fraternities, N/A in sororities
Most popular majors: 40% Homeland Security, Law Enforcement, Firefighting and Related Protective Services; 11% Business, Management, and Related Support Services; 9% Visual and Performing Arts; 8% Engineering; 7% Psychology
Expenses: 2016-2017: $37,060; room/board: $15,130
Financial aid: (203) 932-7315; 75% of undergrads determined to have financial need; average aid package $22,365

University of St. Joseph
West Hartford CT
(860) 231-5216
U.S. News ranking: Reg. U. (N), No. 91
Website: www.usj.edu
Admissions email: admissions@usj.edu
Private; founded 1932
Affiliation: Roman Catholic
Freshman admissions: less selective; 2015-2016: 751 applied, 697 accepted. Neither SAT nor ACT required. SAT 25/75 percentile: 820-1120. High school rank: 16% in top tenth, 47% in top quarter, 80% in top half
Early decision deadline: N/A, notification date: N/A
Early action deadline: N/A, notification date: N/A
Application deadline (fall): rolling
Undergraduate student body: 767 full time, 193 part time; 3% male, 97% female; 0% American Indian, 4% Asian, 16% black, 17% Hispanic, 2% multiracial, 0% Pacific Islander, 54% white, 0% international; 95% from in state; 29% live on campus; N/A of students in fraternities, N/A in sororities
Most popular majors: 33% Health Professions and Related Programs; 16% Public Administration and Social Service Professions; 11% Family and

Consumer Sciences/Human Sciences; 9% Biological and Biomedical Sciences; 9% Psychology
Expenses: 2016-2017: $36,930; room/board: $11,095
Financial aid: (860) 231-5223; 88% of undergrads determined to have financial need; average aid package $25,201

Wesleyan University
Middletown CT
(860) 685-3000
U.S. News ranking: Nat. Lib. Arts, No. 21
Website: www.wesleyan.edu
Admissions email: admissions@wesleyan.edu
Private; founded 1831
Freshman admissions: most selective; 2015-2016: 9,822 applied, 2,180 accepted. Neither SAT nor ACT required. SAT 25/75 percentile: 1250-1470. High school rank: 72% in top tenth, 91% in top quarter, 100% in top half
Early decision deadline: 11/15, notification date: 12/15
Early action deadline: N/A, notification date: N/A
Application deadline (fall): 1/1
Undergraduate student body: 2,820 full time, 77 part time; 47% male, 53% female; 0% American Indian, 8% Asian, 7% black, 11% Hispanic, 6% multiracial, 0% Pacific Islander, 53% white, 9% international; 8% from in state; 99% live on campus; 10% of students in fraternities, 3% in sororities
Most popular majors: 12% Psychology, General; 9% Economics, General; 9% Political Science and Government, General; 7% Biology/Biological Sciences, General; 7% Physiological Psychology/Psychobiology
Expenses: 2016-2017: $50,612; room/board: $13,950
Financial aid: (860) 685-2800; 45% of undergrads determined to have financial need; average aid package $46,529

Western Connecticut State University
Danbury CT
(203) 837-9000
U.S. News ranking: Reg. U. (N), No. 114
Website: www.wcsu.edu
Admissions email: admissions@wcsu.edu
Public; founded 1903
Freshman admissions: selective; 2015-2016: 5,235 applied, 2,999 accepted. Neither SAT nor ACT required. SAT 25/75 percentile: 900-1090. High school rank: 7% in top tenth, 24% in top quarter, 64% in top half
Early decision deadline: N/A, notification date: N/A
Early action deadline: N/A, notification date: N/A
Application deadline (fall): rolling
Undergraduate student body: 4,250 full time, 1,048 part time; 47% male, 53% female; 0% American Indian, 4% Asian, 12% black, 18% Hispanic, 1% multiracial, 0% Pacific Islander, 61% white,

0% international; 94% from in state; 33% live on campus; 4% of students in fraternities, 5% in sororities
Most popular majors: 25% Business, Management, Marketing, and Related Support Services; 11% Health Professions and Related Programs; 11% Homeland Security, Law Enforcement, Firefighting and Related Protective Services; 10% Psychology
Expenses: 2016-2017: $10,017 in state, $21,683 out of state; room/board: $12,089
Financial aid: (203) 837-8580; 69% of undergrads determined to have financial need; average aid package $8,176

Yale University
New Haven CT
(203) 432-9300
U.S. News ranking: Nat. U., No. 3
Website: www.yale.edu/
Admissions email: student.questions@yale.edu
Private; founded 1701
Freshman admissions: most selective; 2015-2016: 30,236 applied, 2,031 accepted. Either SAT or ACT required. SAT 25/75 percentile: 1430-1600. High school rank: 97% in top tenth, 99% in top quarter, 100% in top half
Early decision deadline: N/A, notification date: N/A
Early action deadline: 11/1, notification date: 12/15
Application deadline (fall): 1/1
Undergraduate student body: 5,509 full time, 23 part time; 51% male, 49% female; 1% American Indian, 17% Asian, 7% black, 11% Hispanic, 6% multiracial, 0% Pacific Islander, 47% white, 11% international; 7% from in state; 84% live on campus; N/A of students in fraternities, N/A in sororities
Most popular majors: 15% Economics, General; 10% Political Science and Government, General; 7% History, General; 6% Cell/Cellular and Molecular Biology; 5% Psychology, General
Expenses: 2016-2017: $49,480; room/board: $15,170
Financial aid: (203) 432-2700; 50% of undergrads determined to have financial need; average aid package $50,380

DELAWARE

Delaware State University
Dover DE
(302) 857-6353
U.S. News ranking: Reg. U. (N), No. 128
Website: www.desu.edu
Admissions email: admissions@desu.edu
Public; founded 1891
Freshman admissions: less selective; 2015-2016: 8,141 applied, 3,617 accepted. Either SAT or ACT required. SAT 25/75 percentile: 810-970. High school rank: 9% in top tenth, 30% in top quarter, 67% in top half
Early decision deadline: N/A, notification date: N/A

Early action deadline: N/A, notification date: N/A
Application deadline (fall): rolling
Undergraduate student body: 3,596 full time, 347 part time; 37% male, 63% female; 0% American Indian, 1% Asian, 70% black, 5% Hispanic, 4% multiracial, 0% Pacific Islander, 10% white, 4% international; 53% from in state; 59% live on campus; 3% of students in fraternities, 3% in sororities
Most popular majors: 13% Business, Management, Marketing, and Related Support Services; 12% Parks, Recreation, Leisure, and Fitness Studies; 11% Social Sciences; 7% Psychology
Expenses: 2016-2017: $7,732 in state, $16,597 out of state; room/board: $10,820
Financial aid: (302) 857-6250; 82% of undergrads determined to have financial need; average aid package $10,617

Goldey-Beacom College[1]
Wilmington DE
(302) 225-6248
U.S. News ranking: Business, unranked
Website: gbc.edu
Admissions email: admissions@gbc.edu
Private; founded 1886
Application deadline (fall): rolling
Undergraduate student body: N/A full time, N/A part time
Expenses: 2015-2016: $22,950; room/board: $7,453
Financial aid: (302) 225-6265

University of Delaware
Newark DE
(302) 831-8123
U.S. News ranking: Nat. U., No. 79
Website: www.udel.edu/
Admissions email: admissions@udel.edu
Public; founded 1743
Freshman admissions: more selective; 2015-2016: 24,881 applied, 15,567 accepted. Either SAT or ACT required. SAT 25/75 percentile: 1110-1310. High school rank: 33% in top tenth, 68% in top quarter, 94% in top half
Early decision deadline: N/A, notification date: N/A
Early action deadline: N/A, notification date: N/A
Application deadline (fall): 1/15
Undergraduate student body: 16,812 full time, 1,510 part time; 42% male, 58% female; 0% American Indian, 5% Asian, 5% black, 7% Hispanic, 3% multiracial, 0% Pacific Islander, 75% white, 4% international; 39% from in state; 43% live on campus; 19% of students in fraternities, 23% in sororities
Most popular majors: 20% Business, Management, Marketing, and Related Support Services; 11% Social Sciences; 10% Health Professions and Related Programs; 10% Engineering; 7% Education

Expenses: 2016-2017: $12,520 in state, $31,420 out of state; room/board: $11,830
Financial aid: (302) 831-8761; 49% of undergrads determined to have financial need; average aid package $12,504

Wesley College[1]
Dover DE
(302) 736-2400
U.S. News ranking: Reg. Coll. (N), second tier
Website: www.wesley.edu
Admissions email: admissions@wesley.edu
Private; founded 1873
Affiliation: United Methodist
Application deadline (fall): 4/30
Undergraduate student body: N/A full time, N/A part time
Expenses: 2015-2016: $25,020; room/board: $10,970
Financial aid: (302) 736-2321

Wilmington University
New Castle DE
(302) 328-9407
U.S. News ranking: Nat. U., unranked
Website: www.wilmu.edu
Admissions email: undergradadmissions@wilmu.edu
Private; founded 1967
Freshman admissions: N/A; 2015-2016: 1,866 applied, 1,866 accepted. Neither SAT nor ACT required. ACT 25/75 percentile: N/A. High school rank: N/A
Early decision deadline: N/A, notification date: N/A
Early action deadline: N/A, notification date: N/A
Application deadline (fall): rolling
Undergraduate student body: 3,831 full time, 5,451 part time; 37% male, 63% female; 1% American Indian, 2% Asian, 26% black, 4% Hispanic, 0% multiracial, 0% Pacific Islander, 54% white, 2% international
Most popular majors: Information not available
Expenses: 2016-2017: $10,670; room/board: N/A
Financial aid: (302) 328-9437

DISTRICT OF COLUMBIA

American University
Washington DC
(202) 885-6000
U.S. News ranking: Nat. U., No. 74
Website: www.american.edu
Admissions email: admissions@american.edu
Private; founded 1893
Affiliation: United Methodist
Freshman admissions: more selective; 2015-2016: 16,735 applied, 5,860 accepted. Neither SAT nor ACT required. SAT 25/75 percentile: 1150-1340. High school rank: 36% in top tenth, 71% in top quarter, 94% in top half
Early decision deadline: 11/10, notification date: 12/31
Early action deadline: N/A, notification date: N/A
Application deadline (fall): 1/10
Undergraduate student body: 7,540 full time, 369 part time; 38% male, 62% female; 0% American Indian, 7% Asian, 7% black,

12% Hispanic, 5% multiracial, 0% Pacific Islander, 58% white, 7% international; 19% from in state; N/A live on campus; 6% of students in fraternities, 9% in sororities
Most popular majors: 25% International Relations and Affairs; 12% Business Administration and Management, General; 8% Political Science and Government, General; 4% Economics, General
Expenses: 2016-2017: $44,853; room/board: $14,526
Financial aid: (202) 885-6100; 54% of undergrads determined to have financial need; average aid package $30,493

The Catholic University of America
Washington DC
(800) 673-2772
U.S. News ranking: Nat. U., No. 124
Website: www.cua.edu
Admissions email: cua-admissions@cua.edu
Private; founded 1887
Affiliation: Roman Catholic
Freshman admissions: selective; 2015-2016: 5,991 applied, 4,707 accepted. Neither SAT nor ACT required. SAT 25/75 percentile: 1020-1230. High school rank: N/A
Early decision deadline: 11/15, notification date: 12/20
Early action deadline: 11/1, notification date: 12/20
Application deadline (fall): 1/15
Undergraduate student body: 3,331 full time, 149 part time; 47% male, 53% female; 0% American Indian, 3% Asian, 5% black, 13% Hispanic, 5% multiracial, 0% Pacific Islander, 64% white, 5% international; 3% from in state; 57% live on campus; 1% of students in fraternities, 1% in sororities
Most popular majors: 11% Political Science and Government, General; 10% Registered Nursing/Registered Nurse; 9% Psychology, General
Expenses: 2016-2017: $42,536; room/board: $13,820
Financial aid: (202) 319-5307; 56% of undergrads determined to have financial need; average aid package $26,989

Gallaudet University
Washington DC
(202) 651-5750
U.S. News ranking: Reg. U. (N), No. 16
Website: www.gallaudet.edu
Admissions email: admissions.office@gallaudet.edu
Private; founded 1864
Freshman admissions: less selective; 2015-2016: 407 applied, 252 accepted. Either SAT or ACT required. ACT 25/75 percentile: 16-21. High school rank: N/A
Early decision deadline: N/A, notification date: N/A
Early action deadline: N/A, notification date: N/A
Application deadline (fall): rolling
Undergraduate student body: 959 full time, 52 part time; 47% male, 53% female; 1% American

Indian, 3% Asian, 13% black, 12% Hispanic, 11% multiracial, 0% Pacific Islander, 49% white, 8% international; 2% from in state; 80% live on campus; 11% of students in fraternities, 6% in sororities
Most popular majors: 10% Parks, Recreation, Leisure, and Fitness Studies; 10% Business, Management, Marketing, and Related Support Services; 9% Foreign Languages, Literatures, and Linguistics; 9% Public Administration and Social Service Professions
Expenses: 2016-2017: $16,078; room/board: $13,062
Financial aid: (202) 651-5290; 79% of undergrads determined to have financial need; average aid package $22,689

Georgetown University
Washington DC
(202) 687-3600
U.S. News ranking: Nat. U., No. 20
Website: www.georgetown.edu
Admissions email: guadmiss@georgetown.edu
Private; founded 1789
Affiliation: Roman Catholic (Jesuit)
Freshman admissions: most selective; 2015-2016: 19,478 applied, 3,358 accepted. Either SAT or ACT required. SAT 25/75 percentile: 1320-1500. High school rank: 89% in top tenth, 98% in top quarter, 100% in top half
Early decision deadline: N/A, notification date: N/A
Early action deadline: 11/1, notification date: 12/15
Application deadline (fall): 1/10
Undergraduate student body: 7,175 full time, 387 part time; 45% male, 55% female; 0% American Indian, 10% Asian, 6% black, 8% Hispanic, 5% multiracial, 0% Pacific Islander, 58% white, 12% international; 2% from in state; 65% live on campus; N/A of students in fraternities, N/A in sororities
Most popular majors: 35% Social Sciences; 25% Business, Management, Marketing, and Related Support Services; 5% Health Professions and Related Programs; 5% Multi/Interdisciplinary Studies; 5% Foreign Languages, Literatures, and Linguistics
Expenses: 2016-2017: $50,547; room/board: $15,568
Financial aid: (202) 687-4547; 38% of undergrads determined to have financial need; average aid package $42,314

George Washington University
Washington DC
(202) 994-6040
U.S. News ranking: Nat. U., No. 56
Website: www.gwu.edu
Admissions email: gwadm@gwu.edu
Private; founded 1821
Freshman admissions: more selective; 2015-2016: 19,837 applied, 9,216 accepted. Neither

SAT nor ACT required. SAT 25/75 percentile: 1190-1390. High school rank: 56% in top tenth, 86% in top quarter, 98% in top half **Early decision deadline:** 11/1, notification date: 12/15 **Early action deadline:** N/A, notification date: N/A **Application deadline (fall):** 1/1 **Undergraduate student body:** 10,163 full time, 994 part time; 44% male, 56% female; 0% American Indian, 10% Asian, 6% black, 8% Hispanic, 4% multiracial, 0% Pacific Islander, 56% white, 10% international; 3% from in state; 62% live on campus; 23% of students in fraternities, 27% in sororities **Most popular majors:** 34% Social Sciences; 18% Business, Management, Marketing, and Related Support Services; 9% Health Professions and Related Programs; 6% Psychology **Expenses:** 2016-2017: $51,950; room/board: $12,500 **Financial aid:** (202) 994-6620; 46% of undergrads determined to have financial need; average aid package $43,674

Howard University
Washington DC
(202) 806-2755
U.S. News ranking: Nat. U., No. 124
Website: www.howard.edu
Admissions email: admission@howard.edu
Private; founded 1867
Freshman admissions: selective; 2015-2016: 15,163 applied, 7,436 accepted. Either SAT or ACT required. SAT 25/75 percentile: 990-1220. High school rank: 24% in top tenth, 52% in top quarter, 83% in top half
Early decision deadline: N/A, notification date: N/A
Early action deadline: 11/1, notification date: 12/20
Application deadline (fall): 2/15
Undergraduate student body: 6,412 full time, 471 part time; 33% male, 67% female; 1% American Indian, 1% Asian, 91% black, 0% Hispanic, N/A multiracial, 0% Pacific Islander, 2% white, 5% international; 4% from in state; 59% live on campus; 3% of students in fraternities, 5% in sororities
Most popular majors: 14% Business, Management, Marketing, and Related Support Services; 11% Physical Sciences; 11% Social Sciences; 9% Biological and Biomedical Sciences
Expenses: 2016-2017: $24,908; room/board: $13,280
Financial aid: (202) 806-2762; 84% of undergrads determined to have financial need; average aid package $16,451

Strayer University[1]
Washington DC
(202) 408-2400
U.S. News ranking: Reg. U. (N), unranked
Website: www.strayer.edu
Admissions email: mzm@strayer.edu
For-profit; founded 1892

Application deadline (fall): N/A
Undergraduate student body: N/A full time, N/A part time
Expenses: 2015-2016: $12,975; room/board: N/A
Financial aid: (888) 311-0355

Trinity Washington University[1]
Washington DC
(202) 884-9400
U.S. News ranking: Reg. U. (N), second tier
Website: www.trinitydc.edu
Admissions email: admissions@trinitydc.edu
Private
Application deadline (fall): N/A
Undergraduate student body: N/A full time, N/A part time
Expenses: 2015-2016: $22,780; room/board: $10,080
Financial aid: (202) 884-9530

University of the District of Columbia
Washington DC
(202) 274-5010
U.S. News ranking: Reg. U. (N), second tier
Website: www.udc.edu/
Admissions email: N/A
Public; founded 1976
Freshman admissions: least selective; 2015-2016: 3,552 applied, 1,251 accepted. Neither SAT nor ACT required. SAT 25/75 percentile: 700-910. High school rank: N/A
Early decision deadline: N/A, notification date: N/A
Early action deadline: N/A, notification date: N/A
Application deadline (fall): rolling
Undergraduate student body: 1,937 full time, 2,548 part time; 40% male, 60% female; 0% American Indian, 1% Asian, 62% black, 10% Hispanic, 2% multiracial, 0% Pacific Islander, 4% white, 8% international
Most popular majors: 11% Business Administration, Management and Operations, Other; 8% Nursing Education; 7% Human Development and Family Studies, General; 6% Biology/Biological Sciences, General; 5% Accounting
Expenses: 2016-2017: $5,612 in state, $11,756 out of state; room/board: $16,425
Financial aid: (202) 274-5060; 65% of undergrads determined to have financial need; average aid package $8,639

University of the Potomac[1]
Washington DC
(202) 686-0876
U.S. News ranking: Business, unranked
Website: www.potomac.edu
Admissions email: admissions@potomac.edu
For-profit; founded 1989
Application deadline (fall): rolling
Undergraduate student body: N/A full time, N/A part time
Expenses: 2015-2016: $13,884; room/board: N/A
Financial aid: (888) 635-1121

FLORIDA

Ave Maria University[1]
Ave Maria FL
(877) 283-8648
U.S. News ranking: Nat. Lib. Arts, second tier
Website: www.avemaria.edu
Admissions email: N/A
Private; founded 2003
Affiliation: Catholic
Application deadline (fall): rolling
Undergraduate student body: N/A full time, N/A part time
Expenses: 2015-2016: $18,479; room/board: $10,137
Financial aid: N/A

Barry University
Miami Shores FL
(305) 899-3100
U.S. News ranking: Nat. U., second tier
Website: www.barry.edu
Admissions email: admissions@mail.barry.edu
Private; founded 1940
Affiliation: Roman Catholic
Freshman admissions: less selective; 2015-2016: 3,755 applied, 2,071 accepted. Either SAT or ACT required. SAT 25/75 percentile: 850-1020. High school rank: N/A
Early decision deadline: N/A, notification date: N/A
Early action deadline: N/A, notification date: N/A
Application deadline (fall): rolling
Undergraduate student body: 3,178 full time, 598 part time; 39% male, 61% female; 0% American Indian, 1% Asian, 33% black, 31% Hispanic, 2% multiracial, 0% Pacific Islander, 21% white, 8% international
Most popular majors: Information not available
Expenses: 2016-2017: $28,800; room/board: $10,600
Financial aid: (800) 899-3673; 78% of undergrads determined to have financial need; average aid package $20,319

Beacon College[1]
Leesburg FL
(706) 323-5364
U.S. News ranking: Reg. Coll. (S), unranked
Website: www.beaconcollege.edu/
Admissions email: admissions@beaconcollege.edu
Private
Application deadline (fall): N/A
Undergraduate student body: N/A full time, N/A part time
Expenses: 2015-2016: $34,680; room/board: $10,250
Financial aid: (352) 787-7660

Bethune-Cookman University
Daytona Beach FL
(800) 448-0228
U.S. News ranking: Nat. Lib. Arts, second tier
Website: www.bethune.cookman.edu
Admissions email: admissions@cookman.edu
Private; founded 1904
Affiliation: Methodist

Freshman admissions: less selective; 2015-2016: 8,766 applied, 4,693 accepted. Either SAT or ACT required. SAT 25/75 percentile: 15-18. High school rank: 3% in top tenth, 16% in top quarter, 60% in top half
Early decision deadline: N/A, notification date: N/A
Early action deadline: N/A, notification date: N/A
Application deadline (fall): rolling
Undergraduate student body: 3,497 full time, 182 part time; 41% male, 59% female; 0% American Indian, 0% Asian, 80% black, 3% Hispanic, 2% multiracial, 0% Pacific Islander, 2% white, 2% international; 74% from in state; 54% live on campus; 6% of students in fraternities, 13% in sororities
Most popular majors: 16% Corrections and Criminal Justice, Other; 13% Liberal Arts and Sciences/Liberal Studies; 9% Business Administration and Management, General; 9% Psychology, General
Expenses: 2015-2016: $14,410; room/board: $8,560
Financial aid: (386) 481-2620; 97% of undergrads determined to have financial need; average aid package $13,697

Broward College[1]
Fort Lauderdale FL
(954) 201-7350
U.S. News ranking: Reg. Coll. (S), unranked
Website: www.broward.edu/Pages/home.aspx
Admissions email: N/A
Public
Application deadline (fall): N/A
Undergraduate student body: N/A full time, N/A part time
Expenses: 2015-2016: $2,753 in state, $8,875 out of state; room/board: N/A
Financial aid: N/A

Chipola College[1]
Marianna FL
(850) 718-2211
U.S. News ranking: Reg. Coll. (S), No. 52
Website: www.chipola.edu
Admissions email: N/A
Public
Application deadline (fall): N/A
Undergraduate student body: N/A full time, N/A part time
Expenses: 2015-2016: $3,120 in state, $8,950 out of state; room/board: $4,560
Financial aid: (800) 433-3243

College of Central Florida
Ocala FL
(352) 853-2322
U.S. News ranking: Reg. Coll. (S), unranked
Website: www.cf.edu
Admissions email: admissions@cf.edu
Public; founded 1957
Affiliation: None
Freshman admissions: N/A; 2015-2016: 4,416 applied, 2,430 accepted. Neither SAT nor ACT required. ACT 25/75 percentile: N/A. High school rank: N/A

Early decision deadline: N/A, notification date: N/A
Early action deadline: N/A, notification date: N/A
Application deadline (fall): 8/12
Undergraduate student body: 3,036 full time, 4,895 part time; 37% male, 63% female; 2% American Indian, 3% Asian, 13% black, 14% Hispanic, 4% multiracial, 1% Pacific Islander, 59% white, 1% international; 84% from in state; N/A live on campus; N/A of students in fraternities, N/A in sororities
Most popular majors: Information not available
Expenses: 2015-2016: $2,570 in state, $10,126 out of state; room/board: N/A
Financial aid: N/A; 40% of undergrads determined to have financial need; average aid package $1,699

Daytona State College[1]
Daytona Beach FL
(386) 506-3059
U.S. News ranking: Reg. Coll. (S), unranked
Website: www.daytonastate.edu
Admissions email: N/A
Public; founded 1957
Application deadline (fall): rolling
Undergraduate student body: N/A full time, N/A part time
Expenses: 2015-2016: $3,282 in state, $12,352 out of state; room/board: N/A
Financial aid: (386) 506-3015

Eastern Florida State College
Cocoa FL
(321) 433-7300
U.S. News ranking: Reg. Coll. (S), unranked
Website: www.easternflorida.edu/
Admissions email: N/A
Public; founded 1960
Freshman admissions: N/A; 2015-2016: N/A applied, N/A accepted. Neither SAT nor ACT required. ACT 25/75 percentile: N/A. High school rank: N/A
Early decision deadline: N/A, notification date: N/A
Early action deadline: N/A, notification date: N/A
Application deadline (fall): rolling
Undergraduate student body: 5,560 full time, 10,033 part time; 41% male, 59% female; 1% American Indian, 3% Asian, 11% black, 12% Hispanic, 3% multiracial, 0% Pacific Islander, 68% white, 1% international
Most popular majors: 56% Liberal Arts and Sciences/Liberal Studies; 3% Business Administration, Management and Operations, Other; 3% Registered Nursing/Registered Nurse
Expenses: 2015-2016: $2,496 in state, $9,739 out of state; room/board: N/A
Financial aid: N/A

Eckerd College
St. Petersburg FL
(727) 864-8331
U.S. News ranking: Nat. Lib. Arts,
No. 122
Website: www.eckerd.edu
Admissions email:
admissions@eckerd.edu
Private; founded 1958
Affiliation: Presbyterian
Freshman admissions: selective;
2015-2016: 4,135 applied,
3,016 accepted. Either SAT
or ACT required. SAT 25/75
percentile: 1000-1210. High
school rank: N/A
Early decision deadline: N/A,
notification date: N/A
Early action deadline: 11/15,
notification date: 12/15
Application deadline (fall): rolling
Undergraduate student body: 1,748
full time, 41 part time; 38%
male, 62% female; 0% American
Indian, 2% Asian, 3% black,
9% Hispanic, 3% multiracial,
0% Pacific Islander, 77% white,
5% international; 23% from in
state; 87% live on campus; 0%
of students in fraternities, 0% in
sororities
Most popular majors: 12% Marine
Sciences; 9% Biology, General;
8% Psychology, General; 5%
International Business
Expenses: 2016-2017: $41,538;
room/board: $11,336
Financial aid: (727) 864-8334;
57% of undergrads determined
to have financial need; average
aid package $31,820

Edward Waters College[1]
Jacksonville FL
(904) 470-8200
U.S. News ranking: Reg. Coll. (S),
second tier
Website: www.ewc.edu
Admissions email:
admissions@ewc.edu
Private
Application deadline (fall): N/A
Undergraduate student body: N/A
full time, N/A part time
Expenses: 2015-2016: $12,525;
room/board: $7,282
Financial aid: (904) 470-8192

Embry-Riddle Aeronautical University
Daytona Beach FL
(800) 862-2416
U.S. News ranking: Reg. U. (S),
No. 12
Website: www.embryriddle.edu
Admissions email:
dbadmit@erau.edu
Private; founded 1926
Freshman admissions: selective;
2015-2016: 4,588 applied,
3,160 accepted. Neither SAT
nor ACT required. SAT 25/75
percentile: 1010-1240. High
school rank: 22% in top tenth,
53% in top quarter, 83% in
top half
Early decision deadline: N/A,
notification date: N/A
Early action deadline: N/A,
notification date: N/A
Application deadline (fall): rolling
Undergraduate student body: 4,876
full time, 402 part time; 81%
male, 19% female; 0% American
Indian, 4% Asian, 6% black,
4% Hispanic, 8% multiracial,
0% Pacific Islander, 54% white,
14% international; 37% from in
state; 37% live on campus; 9%
of students in fraternities, 16%
in sororities
Most popular majors: 24%
Aerospace, Aeronautical and
Astronautical/Space Engineering;
18% Airline/Commercial/
Professional Pilot and Flight
Crew; 14% Aeronautics/
Aviation/Aerospace Science and
Technology, General; 8% Air
Traffic Controller; 6% Homeland
Security
Expenses: 2016-2017: $33,886;
room/board: $10,826
Financial aid: (800) 943-6279;
62% of undergrads determined
to have financial need; average
aid package $18,528

Everglades University
Boca Raton FL
(888) 772-6077
U.S. News ranking: Reg. Coll. (S),
No. 32
Website:
www.evergladesuniversity.edu
Admissions email: N/A
Private; founded 2002
Freshman admissions: least
selective; 2015-2016: 122
applied, 118 accepted. Neither
SAT nor ACT required. ACT
25/75 percentile: N/A. High
school rank: N/A
Early decision deadline: N/A,
notification date: N/A
Early action deadline: N/A,
notification date: N/A
Application deadline (fall): rolling
Undergraduate student body: 1,296
full time, 8 part time; 48% male,
52% female; 1% American
Indian, 2% Asian, 18% black,
15% Hispanic, 4% multiracial,
0% Pacific Islander, 57% white,
0% international; 58% from in
state; N/A live on campus; N/A
of students in fraternities, N/A in
sororities
Most popular majors: 50%
Alternative and Complementary
Medicine and Medical Systems,
Other; 22% Aeronautics/
Aviation/Aerospace Science
and Technology, General; 13%
Construction Management; 7%
Business Administration and
Management, General
Expenses: 2016-2017: $15,848;
room/board: N/A
Financial aid: (888) 772-6077;
75% of undergrads determined
to have financial need; average
aid package $9,635

Flagler College
St. Augustine FL
(800) 304-4208
U.S. News ranking: Reg. Coll.
(S), No. 2
Website: www.flagler.edu
Admissions email:
admiss@flagler.edu
Private; founded 1968
Freshman admissions: selective;
2015-2016: 5,260 applied,
2,655 accepted. Either SAT
or ACT required. SAT 25/75
percentile: 960-1148. High
school rank: N/A
Early decision deadline: 11/1,
notification date: 12/15

Early action deadline:
N/A,
notification date: N/A
Application deadline (fall): 3/1
Undergraduate student body: 2,602
full time, 100 part time; 39%
male, 61% female; 0% American
Indian, 1% Asian, 4% black,
5% Hispanic, 3% multiracial,
0% Pacific Islander, 77% white,
3% international; 64% from in
state; 36% live on campus; N/A
of students in fraternities, N/A in
sororities
Most popular majors: 18%
Business, Management,
Marketing, and Related Support
Services; 13% Visual and
Performing Arts; 12% Social
Sciences; 11% Psychology
Expenses: 2016-2017: $17,500;
room/board: $10,120
Financial aid: (904) 819-6225;
61% of undergrads determined
to have financial need; average
aid package $12,166

Florida A&M University
Tallahassee FL
(850) 599-3796
U.S. News ranking: Nat. U.,
second tier
Website: www.famu.edu
Admissions email:
ugradmissions@famu.edu
Public; founded 1887
Freshman admissions: selective;
2015-2016: 5,832 applied,
2,998 accepted. Either SAT
or ACT required. ACT 25/75
percentile: 18-23. High school
rank: 14% in top tenth, 40% in
top quarter, 80% in top half
Early decision deadline: N/A,
notification date: N/A
Early action deadline: N/A,
notification date: N/A
Application deadline (fall): 5/15
Undergraduate student body: 6,967
full time, 1,161 part time; 37%
male, 63% female; 0% American
Indian, 1% Asian, 91% black,
2% Hispanic, 2% multiracial,
0% Pacific Islander, 3% white,
1% international; 85% from in
state; 73% live on campus; 4%
of students in fraternities, 4% in
sororities
Most popular majors: 25%
Health Professions and Related
Programs; 14% Business,
Management, Marketing, and
Related Support Services;
12% Homeland Security, Law
Enforcement, Firefighting and
Related Protective Services; 7%
Social Sciences; 5% Psychology
Expenses: 2015-2016: $5,784
in state, $17,726 out of state;
room/board: $10,120
Financial aid: (850) 412-7927;
84% of undergrads determined
to have financial need; average
aid package $13,157

Florida Atlantic University
Boca Raton FL
(561) 297-3040
U.S. News ranking: Nat. U.,
second tier
Website: www.fau.edu
Admissions email:
Admissions@fau.edu
Public; founded 1961

Florida College
Temple Terrace FL
(800) 326-7655
U.S. News ranking: Reg. Coll. (S),
second tier
Website: www.floridacollege.edu/
Admissions email: N/A
Private; founded 1946
Freshman admissions: selective;
2015-2016: 297 applied, 241
accepted. Either SAT or ACT
required. ACT 25/75 percentile:
19-24. High school rank: N/A
Early decision deadline: N/A,
notification date: N/A
Early action deadline: N/A,
notification date: N/A
Application deadline (fall): 8/1
Undergraduate student body: 537
full time, 13 part time; 46%
male, 54% female; 2% American
Indian, 0% Asian, 6% black, 6%
Hispanic, 5% multiracial, 0%
Pacific Islander, 77% white, 3%
international
Most popular majors: Information
not available
Expenses: 2016-2017: $16,550;
room/board: $8,230
Financial aid: N/A; 70% of
undergrads determined to have
financial need; average aid
package $10,640

Florida Gateway College[1]
Lake City FL
(138) 675-2182
U.S. News ranking: Reg. Coll. (S),
unranked
Website: www.fgc.edu/
Admissions email: N/A
Public
Application deadline (fall): N/A
Undergraduate student body: N/A
full time, N/A part time

Freshman admissions: selective;
2015-2016: 15,847 applied,
10,725 accepted. Either SAT
or ACT required. SAT 25/75
percentile: 950-1140. High
school rank: 11% in top tenth,
35% in top quarter, 77% in
top half
Early decision deadline: N/A,
notification date: N/A
Early action deadline: N/A,
notification date: N/A
Application deadline (fall): 5/1
Undergraduate student body:
16,116 full time, 9,355 part
time; 44% male, 56% female;
0% American Indian, 4% Asian,
20% black, 26% Hispanic, 4%
multiracial, 0% Pacific Islander,
43% white, 2% international;
95% from in state; 17% live
on campus; N/A of students in
fraternities, N/A in sororities
Most popular majors: 23%
Business, Management,
Marketing, and Related Support
Services; 9% Social Sciences;
8% Health Professions and
Related Programs; 7% Biological
and Biomedical Sciences;
7% Homeland Security, Law
Enforcement, Firefighting and
Related Protective Services
Expenses: 2016-2017: $5,432
in state, $19,432 out of state;
room/board: $12,006
Financial aid: (561) 297-3530;
63% of undergrads determined
to have financial need; average
aid package $13,229

Florida Gulf Coast University
Fort Myers FL
(239) 590-7878
U.S. News ranking: Reg. U. (S),
No. 82
Website: www.fgcu.edu
Admissions email:
admissions@fgcu.edu
Public; founded 1991
Freshman admissions: selective;
2015-2016: 13,608 applied,
8,244 accepted. Either SAT
or ACT required. SAT 25/75
percentile: 970-1140. High
school rank: 14% in top tenth,
39% in top quarter, 77% in
top half
Early decision deadline: N/A,
notification date: N/A
Early action deadline: N/A,
notification date: N/A
Application deadline (fall): 5/1
Undergraduate student body:
10,796 full time, 2,921 part
time; 45% male, 55% female;
0% American Indian, 2% Asian,
7% black, 19% Hispanic, 3%
multiracial, 0% Pacific Islander,
66% white, 2% international;
91% from in state; 36% live
on campus; N/A of students in
fraternities, N/A in sororities
Most popular majors: 8%
Business, Management,
Marketing, and Related Support
Services; 7% Psychology;
6% Business, Management,
Marketing, and Related Support
Services; 6% Homeland Security,
Law Enforcement, Firefighting
and Related Protective Services
Expenses: 2015-2016: $6,118
in state, $25,162 out of state;
room/board: $9,424
Financial aid: (239) 590-7920

Florida Institute of Technology
Melbourne FL
(800) 888-4348
U.S. News ranking: Nat. U.,
No. 171
Website: www.fit.edu
Admissions email:
admission@fit.edu
Private; founded 1958
Freshman admissions: more
selective; 2015-2016: 9,303
applied, 5,336 accepted. Either
SAT or ACT required. SAT 25/75
percentile: 1080-1290. High
school rank: 31% in top tenth,
59% in top quarter, 89% in
top half
Early decision deadline: N/A,
notification date: N/A
Early action deadline: N/A,
notification date: N/A
Application deadline (fall): rolling
Undergraduate student body: 3,253
full time, 333 part time; 71%
male, 29% female; 0% American
Indian, 2% Asian, 6% black,
7% Hispanic, 2% multiracial,
0% Pacific Islander, 42% white,
33% international; 51% from in
state; 42% live on campus; 3%
of students in fraternities, 5% in
sororities

Most popular majors: 13% Mechanical Engineering; 9% Electrical and Electronics Engineering; 8% Aerospace, Aeronautical and Astronautical/ Space Engineering; 8% Aviation/Airway Management and Operations; 6% Chemical Engineering
Expenses: 2016-2017: $40,446; room/board: $13,610
Financial aid: (321) 674-8070; 50% of undergrads determined to have financial need; average aid package $35,826

Florida International University
Miami FL
(305) 348-2363
U.S. News ranking: Nat. U., second tier
Website: www.fiu.edu
Admissions email: admiss@fiu.edu
Public; founded 1972
Freshman admissions: selective; 2015-2016: 15,834 applied, 7,874 accepted. Either SAT or ACT required. SAT 25/75 percentile: 1030-1200. High school rank: 18% in top tenth, 46% in top quarter, 84% in top half
Early decision deadline: N/A, notification date: N/A
Early action deadline: N/A, notification date: N/A
Undergraduate student body: 25,655 full time, 15,383 part time; 44% male, 56% female; 0% American Indian, 3% Asian, 12% black, 67% Hispanic, 2% multiracial, 0% Pacific Islander, 9% white, 6% international; 97% from in state; 8% live on campus; N/A of students in fraternities, N/A in sororities
Most popular majors: 29% Business, Management, Marketing, and Related Support Services; 12% Psychology; 9% Social Sciences; 7% Health Professions and Related Programs; 6% Biological and Biomedical Sciences
Expenses: 2015-2016: $6,556 in state, $18,954 out of state; room/board: $10,702
Financial aid: (305) 348-2431; 72% of undergrads determined to have financial need; average aid package $8,141

Florida Memorial University
Miami FL
(305) 626-3750
U.S. News ranking: Reg. Coll. (S), No. 23
Website: www.fmuniv.edu/
Admissions email: admit@fmuniv.edu
Private; founded 1879
Affiliation: Baptist
Freshman admissions: less selective; 2015-2016: 5,314 applied, 1,223 accepted. Neither SAT nor ACT required. ACT 25/75 percentile: 16-20. High school rank: N/A
Early decision deadline: 4/1, notification date: 4/1
Early action deadline: N/A, notification date: N/A
Application deadline (fall): rolling

Undergraduate student body: 1,332 full time, 67 part time; 38% male, 62% female; 0% American Indian, 0% Asian, 72% black, 4% Hispanic, 1% multiracial, 0% Pacific Islander, 0% white, 14% international
Most popular majors: 17% Elementary Education and Teaching; 11% Criminal Justice/ Law Enforcement Administration; 9% Psychology, General; 6% Accounting; 6% Finance, General
Expenses: 2015-2016: $15,280; room/board: $6,422
Financial aid: (305) 626-3745

Florida National University– Main Campus[1]
Hialeah FL
(786) 364-9514
U.S. News ranking: Reg. Coll. (S), unranked
Website: www.fnu.edu/
Admissions email: N/A
For-profit
Application deadline (fall): N/A
Undergraduate student body: N/A full time, N/A part time
Expenses: 2016-2017: $13,250; room/board: N/A
Financial aid: N/A

Florida Southern College
Lakeland FL
(863) 680-4131
U.S. News ranking: Reg. U. (S), No. 20
Website: www.flsouthern.edu
Admissions email: fscadm@flsouthern.edu
Private; founded 1883
Affiliation: United Methodist
Freshman admissions: more selective; 2015-2016: 6,190 applied, 2,806 accepted. Either SAT or ACT required. SAT 25/75 percentile: 1050-1230. High school rank: 24% in top tenth, 59% in top quarter, 91% in top half
Early decision deadline: 12/1, notification date: 12/15
Early action deadline: N/A, notification date: N/A
Application deadline (fall): rolling
Undergraduate student body: 2,260 full time, 59 part time; 37% male, 63% female; 1% American Indian, 2% Asian, 5% black, 11% Hispanic, 2% multiracial, 0% Pacific Islander, 74% white, 5% international; 63% from in state; 86% live on campus; 34% of students in fraternities, 35% in sororities
Most popular majors: 25% Business, Management, Marketing, and Related Support Services; 13% Health Professions and Related Programs; 12% Social Sciences; 9% Biological and Biomedical Sciences; 9% Education
Expenses: 2016-2017: $33,100; room/board: $10,680
Financial aid: (863) 680-4140; 68% of undergrads determined to have financial need; average aid package $25,242

Florida SouthWestern State College
Fort Myers FL
(800) 749-2322
U.S. News ranking: Reg. Coll. (S), unranked
Website: www.fsw.edu/
Admissions email: N/A
Public; founded 1962
Freshman admissions: N/A; 2015-2016: 5,525 applied, 4,500 accepted. Neither SAT nor ACT required. SAT 25/75 percentile: 840-1010. High school rank: N/A
Early decision deadline: N/A, notification date: N/A
Early action deadline: N/A, notification date: N/A
Application deadline (fall): 8/17
Undergraduate student body: 5,389 full time, 10,353 part time; 39% male, 61% female; 0% American Indian, 2% Asian, 11% black, 27% Hispanic, 2% multiracial, 0% Pacific Islander, 50% white, 2% international; 98% from in state; 2% live on campus; N/A of students in fraternities, N/A in sororities
Most popular majors: 36% Business, Management, Marketing, and Related Support Services; 29% Health Professions and Related Programs; 27% Education
Expenses: 2015-2016: $3,401 in state, $10,715 out of state; room/board: N/A
Financial aid: (239) 489-9127; 62% of undergrads determined to have financial need; average aid package $6,172

Florida State College–Jacksonville[1]
Jacksonville FL
(877) 633-5950
U.S. News ranking: Reg. Coll. (S), unranked
Website: www.fscj.edu
Admissions email: N/A
Public
Application deadline (fall): N/A
Undergraduate student body: N/A full time, N/A part time
Expenses: 2015-2016: $2,830 in state, $9,944 out of state; room/ board: N/A
Financial aid: (904) 359-5433

Florida State University
Tallahassee FL
(850) 644-6200
U.S. News ranking: Nat. U., No. 92
Website: www.fsu.edu
Admissions email: admissions@ admin.fsu.edu
Public; founded 1851
Freshman admissions: more selective; 2015-2016: 29,828 applied, 16,674 accepted. Either SAT or ACT required. ACT 25/75 percentile: 25-29. High school rank: 38% in top tenth, 75% in top quarter, 97% in top half
Early decision deadline: N/A, notification date: N/A
Early action deadline: N/A, notification date: N/A
Application deadline (fall): 1/15
Undergraduate student body: 29,185 full time, 3,521 part time; 45% male, 55% female; 0% American Indian, 2% Asian,

8% black, 19% Hispanic, 3% multiracial, 0% Pacific Islander, 64% white, 1% international; 90% from in state; 19% live on campus; 19% of students in fraternities, 25% in sororities
Most popular majors: 6% Criminal Justice/Safety Studies; 6% Psychology, General; 5% English Language and Literature, General; 4% Biology/Biological Sciences, General; 4% Finance, General
Expenses: 2016-2017: $9,507 in state, $24,673 out of state; room/board: $10,304
Financial aid: (850) 644-1993; 53% of undergrads determined to have financial need; average aid package $11,329

Gulf Coast State College[1]
Panama City FL
(850) 769-1551
U.S. News ranking: Reg. Coll. (S), unranked
Website: www.gulfcoast.edu/
Admissions email: N/A
Public
Application deadline (fall): N/A
Undergraduate student body: N/A full time, N/A part time
Expenses: 2015-2016: $2,765 in state, $10,072 out of state; room/board: N/A
Financial aid: N/A

Hodges University
Naples FL
(239) 513-1122
U.S. News ranking: Reg. U. (S), unranked
Website: www.hodges.edu
Admissions email: admit@hodges.edu
Private; founded 1990
Freshman admissions: N/A; 2015-2016: N/A applied, N/A accepted. Neither SAT nor ACT required. ACT 25/75 percentile: N/A. High school rank: N/A
Early decision deadline: N/A, notification date: N/A
Early action deadline: N/A, notification date: N/A
Application deadline (fall): rolling
Undergraduate student body: 991 full time, 496 part time; 38% male, 62% female; 0% American Indian, 2% Asian, 13% black, 35% Hispanic, 1% multiracial, 0% Pacific Islander, 46% white, 0% international
Most popular majors: 31% Health Professions and Related Programs; 27% Business, Management, Marketing, and Related Support Services; 16% Computer and Information Sciences and Support Services; 12% Homeland Security, Law Enforcement, Firefighting and Related Protective Services; 9% Legal Professions and Studies
Expenses: 2016-2017: $16,400; room/board: N/A
Financial aid: (239) 513-1122; 95% of undergrads determined to have financial need; average aid package $10,095

Indian River State College
Fort Pierce FL
(772) 462-7460
U.S. News ranking: Reg. Coll. (S), second tier
Website: www.irsc.edu
Admissions email: N/A
Public
Freshman admissions: least selective; 2015-2016: 1,755 applied, 1,755 accepted. Neither SAT nor ACT required. ACT 25/75 percentile: N/A. High school rank: N/A
Early decision deadline: N/A, notification date: N/A
Early action deadline: N/A, notification date: N/A
Application deadline (fall): rolling
Undergraduate student body: 5,876 full time, 12,328 part time; 40% male, 60% female; 0% American Indian, 2% Asian, 17% black, 20% Hispanic, 2% multiracial, 0% Pacific Islander, 55% white, 1% international
Most popular majors: Information not available
Expenses: 2016-2017: $2,640 in state, $9,890 out of state; room/ board: $5,700
Financial aid: (772) 462-7450; 65% of undergrads determined to have financial need; average aid package $4,892

Jacksonville University
Jacksonville FL
(800) 225-2027
U.S. News ranking: Reg. U. (S), No. 62
Website: www.jacksonville.edu
Admissions email: admissions@ju.edu
Private; founded 1934
Freshman admissions: selective; 2015-2016: 3,803 applied, 2,035 accepted. Neither SAT nor ACT required. SAT 25/75 percentile: 890-1110. High school rank: N/A
Early decision deadline: N/A, notification date: N/A
Early action deadline: N/A, notification date: N/A
Application deadline (fall): rolling
Undergraduate student body: 2,065 full time, 967 part time; 37% male, 63% female; 0% American Indian, 2% Asian, 15% black, 8% Hispanic, 2% multiracial, 0% Pacific Islander, 48% white, 4% international; 64% from in state; 33% live on campus; 4% of students in fraternities, 4% in sororities
Most popular majors: 57% Health Professions and Related Programs; 9% Business, Management, Marketing, and Related Support Services; 5% Biological and Biomedical Sciences; 5% Visual and Performing Arts; 4% Parks, Recreation, Leisure, and Fitness Studies
Expenses: 2016-2017: $33,930; room/board: $13,550
Financial aid: (904) 256-7060; 86% of undergrads determined to have financial need; average aid package $22,400

Keiser University

Ft. Lauderdale FL
(954) 776-4456
U.S. News ranking: Reg. Coll. (S),
No. 23
Website: www.keiseruniversity.edu
Admissions email: N/A
Private; founded 1977
Freshman admissions: least
selective; 2015-2016: N/A
applied, N/A accepted. Neither
SAT nor ACT required. ACT
25/75 percentile: N/A. High
school rank: N/A
Early decision deadline: N/A,
notification date: N/A
Early action deadline: N/A,
notification date: N/A
Application deadline (fall): rolling
Undergraduate student body: 9,040
full time, 6,070 part time; 32%
male, 68% female; 1% American
Indian, 4% Asian, 20% black,
25% Hispanic, 5% multiracial,
0% Pacific Islander, 41% white,
1% international
Most popular majors: 26%
Business Administration and
Management, General; 16%
Criminal Justice/Safety Studies;
16% Multi/Interdisciplinary
Studies; 11% Legal Professions
and Studies; 9% Health Services
Administration
Expenses: 2015-2016: $17,664;
room/board: $8,352
Financial aid: (954) 351-4456;
93% of undergrads determined
to have financial need; average
aid package $4,295

Lake-Sumter State College[1]

Leesburg FL
(352) 787-3747
U.S. News ranking: Reg. Coll. (S),
unranked
Website: www.lssc.edu/Pages/
default.aspx
Admissions email: N/A
Public
Application deadline (fall): N/A
Undergraduate student body: N/A
full time, N/A part time
Expenses: 2015-2016: $3,172
in state, $13,276 out of state;
room/board: N/A
Financial aid: N/A

Lynn University

Boca Raton FL
(800) 888-5966
U.S. News ranking: Reg. U. (S),
No. 91
Website: www.lynn.edu
Admissions email:
admission@lynn.edu
Private; founded 1962
Freshman admissions: less
selective; 2015-2016: 3,770
applied, 2,864 accepted. Neither
SAT nor ACT required. SAT
25/75 percentile: 895-1090.
High school rank: 10% in top
tenth, 25% in top quarter, 57%
in top half
Early decision deadline: N/A,
notification date: N/A
Early action deadline: 11/15,
notification date: 12/15
Application deadline (fall): rolling
Undergraduate student body: 1,867
full time, 136 part time; 52%
male, 48% female; 1% American
Indian, 2% Asian, 8% black,
15% Hispanic, 1% multiracial,
0% Pacific Islander, 44% white,

23% international; 47% from in
state; 45% live on campus; 4%
of students in fraternities, 5% in
sororities
Most popular majors: 43%
Business, Management,
Marketing, and Related Support
Services; 9% Homeland Security,
Law Enforcement, Firefighting
and Related Protective Services;
9% Psychology; 7% Visual and
Performing Arts
Expenses: 2016-2017: $36,350;
room/board: $11,640
Financial aid: (561) 237-7186;
45% of undergrads determined
to have financial need; average
aid package $20,850

Miami Dade College[1]

Miami FL
(305) 237-8888
U.S. News ranking: Reg. Coll. (S),
unranked
Website: www.mdc.edu/
Admissions email:
mdcinfo@mdc.edu
Public
Application deadline (fall): N/A
Undergraduate student body: N/A
full time, N/A part time
Expenses: 2015-2016: $2,834 in
state, $9,661 out of state; room/
board: N/A
Financial aid: (305) 237-6040

Miami International University of Art & Design[1]

Miami FL
(305) 428-5700
U.S. News ranking: Arts, unranked
Website: www.aimiu.aii.edu/
Admissions email: N/A
For-profit
Application deadline (fall): N/A
Undergraduate student body: N/A
full time, N/A part time
Expenses: 2015-2016: $17,700;
room/board: $7,800
Financial aid: N/A

New College of Florida

Sarasota FL
(941) 487-5000
U.S. News ranking: Nat. Lib. Arts,
No. 90
Website: www.ncf.edu
Admissions email:
admissions@ncf.edu
Public; founded 1960
Freshman admissions: more
selective; 2015-2016: 1,655
applied, 1,009 accepted. Either
SAT or ACT required. SAT 25/75
percentile: 1170-1380. High
school rank: 43% in top tenth,
79% in top quarter, 97% in
top half
Early decision deadline: N/A,
notification date: N/A
Early action deadline: 11/1,
notification date: 4/1
Application deadline (fall): 4/15
Undergraduate student body: 861
full time, 0 part time; 39% male,
61% female; 0% American
Indian, 3% Asian, 3% black,
16% Hispanic, 4% multiracial,
0% Pacific Islander, 69% white,
2% international; 87% from in
state; 76% live on campus; 0%
of students in fraternities, 0% in
sororities

Most popular majors: 100%
Liberal Arts and Sciences,
General Studies and Humanities,
Other
Expenses: 2016-2017: $6,916
in state, $29,944 out of state;
room/board: $9,060
Financial aid: (941) 359-4255;
52% of undergrads determined
to have financial need; average
aid package $13,506

Northwest Florida State College[1]

Niceville FL
(850) 729-6922
U.S. News ranking: Reg. Coll. (S),
unranked
Website: www.owcc.cc.fl.us/
Admissions email: N/A
Public
Application deadline (fall): N/A
Undergraduate student body: N/A
full time, N/A part time
Expenses: 2015-2016: $3,123
in state, $11,940 out of state;
room/board: N/A
Financial aid: (850) 729-5370

Nova Southeastern University

Ft. Lauderdale FL
(954) 262-8000
U.S. News ranking: Nat. U.,
No. 214
Website: www.nova.edu
Admissions email:
admissions@nova.edu
Private; founded 1964
Freshman admissions: selective;
2015-2016: 4,333 applied,
2,567 accepted. Either SAT
or ACT required. SAT 25/75
percentile: 980-1225. High
school rank: 31% in top tenth,
60% in top quarter, 88% in
top half
Early decision deadline: N/A,
notification date: N/A
Early action deadline: N/A,
notification date: N/A
Application deadline (fall): 7/21
Undergraduate student body: 3,194
full time, 1,447 part time; 30%
male, 70% female; 0% American
Indian, 9% Asian, 18% black,
32% Hispanic, 2% multiracial,
0% Pacific Islander, 31% white,
5% international; 83% from in
state; 23% live on campus; 8%
of students in fraternities, 7% in
sororities
Most popular majors: 33%
Health Professions and Related
Programs; 16% Biological
and Biomedical Sciences;
15% Business, Management,
Marketing, and Related Support
Services; 4% Psychology; 3%
Education
Expenses: 2016-2017: $27,660;
room/board: $11,540
Financial aid: (954) 262-3380;
74% of undergrads determined
to have financial need; average
aid package $26,189

Palm Beach Atlantic University

West Palm Beach FL
(888) 468-6722
U.S. News ranking: Reg. U. (S),
No. 62
Website: www.pba.edu
Admissions email: admit@pba.edu
Private; founded 1968

Affiliation: Christian
Interdenominational
Freshman admissions: selective;
2015-2016: 1,504 applied,
1,397 accepted. Either SAT
or ACT required. SAT 25/75
percentile: 940-1180. High
school rank: N/A
Early decision deadline: N/A,
notification date: N/A
Early action deadline: 3/31,
notification date: 4/15
Application deadline (fall): rolling
Undergraduate student body: 2,418
full time, 621 part time; 37%
male, 63% female; 0% American
Indian, 2% Asian, 12% black,
17% Hispanic, 3% multiracial,
0% Pacific Islander, 62% white,
4% international; 68% from in
state; 48% live on campus; 0%
of students in fraternities, 0% in
sororities
Most popular majors: 25%
Business, Management,
Marketing, and Related Support
Services; 15% Psychology; 11%
Theology and Religious Vocations;
10% Visual and Performing
Arts; 9% Health Professions and
Related Programs
Expenses: 2016-2017: $28,520;
room/board: $9,447
Financial aid: (561) 803-2000;
72% of undergrads determined
to have financial need; average
aid package $18,826

Palm Beach State College[1]

Lake Worth FL
(561) 207-5300
U.S. News ranking: Reg. Coll. (S),
unranked
Website:
www.palmbeachstate.edu/
Admissions email: N/A
Public
Application deadline (fall): N/A
Undergraduate student body: N/A
full time, N/A part time
Expenses: 2015-2016: $2,444 in
state, $8,732 out of state; room/
board: N/A
Financial aid: N/A

Pensacola State College[1]

Pensacola FL
(850) 484-2544
U.S. News ranking: Reg. Coll. (S),
unranked
Website: www.pensacolastate.edu/
Admissions email: N/A
Public
Application deadline (fall): N/A
Undergraduate student body: N/A
full time, N/A part time
Expenses: 2015-2016: $2,704
in state, $10,875 out of state;
room/board: N/A
Financial aid: N/A

Polk State College

Winter Haven FL
(863) 297-1000
U.S. News ranking: Reg. Coll. (S),
unranked
Website: www.polk.edu/
Admissions email: N/A
Public
Freshman admissions: N/A;
2015-2016: N/A applied, N/A
accepted. Neither SAT nor ACT
required. ACT 25/75 percentile:
N/A. High school rank: N/A

Early decision deadline: N/A,
notification date: N/A
Early action deadline: N/A,
notification date: N/A
Application deadline (fall): N/A
Undergraduate student body: 3,224
full time, 8,159 part time; 37%
male, 63% female; 0% American
Indian, 2% Asian, 17% black,
20% Hispanic, 2% multiracial,
0% Pacific Islander, 53% white,
1% international
Most popular majors: 87%
Business Administration,
Management and Operations,
Other; 13% Registered Nursing/
Registered Nurse
Expenses: 2015-2016: $3,366
in state, $12,271 out of state;
room/board: N/A
Financial aid: N/A

Ringling College of Art and Design

Sarasota FL
(800) 255-7695
U.S. News ranking: Arts, unranked
Website: www.ringling.edu
Admissions email:
admissions@ringling.edu
Private; founded 1931
Freshman admissions: N/A; 2015-
2016: 1,492 applied, 1,142
accepted. Neither SAT nor ACT
required. SAT 25/75 percentile:
N/A. High school rank: N/A
Early decision deadline: N/A,
notification date: N/A
Early action deadline: 10/1,
notification date: 12/15
Application deadline (fall): rolling
Undergraduate student body: 1,181
full time, 81 part time; 37%
male, 63% female; 1% American
Indian, 9% Asian, 3% black,
16% Hispanic, 2% multiracial,
0% Pacific Islander, 49% white,
15% international; 43% from in
state; 69% live on campus; 0%
of students in fraternities, 0% in
sororities
Most popular majors: 23%
Animation, Interactive
Technology, Video Graphics
and Special Effects; 8%
Graphic Design; 6% Fine/Studio
Arts, General; 6% Game and
Interactive Media Design
Expenses: 2016-2017: $42,990;
room/board: $14,390
Financial aid: (941) 351-5100;
64% of undergrads determined
to have financial need; average
aid package $23,141

Rollins College

Winter Park FL
(407) 646-2161
U.S. News ranking: Reg. U. (S),
No. 2
Website: www.rollins.edu
Admissions email:
admission@rollins.edu
Private; founded 1885
Freshman admissions: selective;
2015-2016: 4,922 applied,
2,972 accepted. Neither SAT
nor ACT required. SAT 25/75
percentile: 1105-1310. High
school rank: 34% in top tenth,
66% in top quarter, 88% in
top half
Early decision deadline: 11/15,
notification date: 12/15
Early action deadline: N/A,
notification date: N/A
Application deadline (fall): 2/15

Undergraduate student body: 1,948 full time, 0 part time; 41% male, 59% female; 0% American Indian, 3% Asian, 3% black, 14% Hispanic, 3% multiracial, N/A Pacific Islander, 66% white, 9% international; 53% from in state; 60% live on campus; 38% of students in fraternities, 42% in sororities
Most popular majors: 23% Social Sciences; 14% Business, Management, Marketing, and Related Support Services; 10% Psychology; 10% Visual and Performing Arts
Expenses: 2016-2017: $46,520; room/board: $14,450
Financial aid: (407) 646-2395; 50% of undergrads determined to have financial need; average aid package $34,934

Saint Johns River State College[1]
Palatka FL
(386) 312-4030
U.S. News ranking: Reg. Coll. (S), unranked
Website: sjrstate.edu/
Admissions email: N/A
Public
Application deadline (fall): N/A
Undergraduate student body: N/A full time, N/A part time
Expenses: 2015-2016: $2,830 in state, $9,166 out of state; room/board: N/A
Financial aid: N/A

Saint Leo University
Saint Leo FL
(800) 334-5532
U.S. News ranking: Reg. U. (S), No. 62
Website: www.saintleo.edu
Admissions email: admission@saintleo.edu
Private; founded 1889
Affiliation: Roman Catholic
Freshman admissions: selective; 2015-2016: 3,865 applied, 2,803 accepted. Neither SAT nor ACT required. SAT 25/75 percentile: 910-1090. High school rank: 10% in top tenth, 32% in top quarter, 69% in top half
Early decision deadline: N/A, notification date: N/A
Early action deadline: N/A, notification date: N/A
Application deadline (fall): rolling
Undergraduate student body: 2,275 full time, 95 part time; 46% male, 54% female; 0% American Indian, 2% Asian, 13% black, 19% Hispanic, 3% multiracial, N/A Pacific Islander, 45% white, 12% international; 71% from in state; 64% live on campus; 19% of students in fraternities, 10% in sororities
Most popular majors: 22% Business, Management, Marketing, and Related Support Services; 15% Homeland Security, Law Enforcement, Firefighting and Related Protective Services; 10% Computer and Information Sciences and Support Services; 8% Parks, Recreation, Leisure, and Fitness Studies; 8% Psychology
Expenses: 2016-2017: $21,130; room/board: $10,210

Financial aid: (352) 588-8270; 70% of undergrads determined to have financial need; average aid package $19,270

Santa Fe College[1]
Gainesville FL
(352) 395-7322
U.S. News ranking: Reg. Coll. (S), unranked
Website: www.sfcollege.edu/
Admissions email: N/A
Public
Application deadline (fall): N/A
Undergraduate student body: N/A full time, N/A part time
Expenses: 2015-2016: $2,541 in state, $9,189 out of state; room/board: N/A
Financial aid: N/A

Seminole State College of Florida[1]
Sanford FL
(407) 708-2050
U.S. News ranking: Reg. Coll. (S), unranked
Website: www.seminolestate.edu/
Admissions email: N/A
Public; founded 1965
Application deadline (fall): rolling
Undergraduate student body: N/A full time, N/A part time
Expenses: 2015-2016: $3,131 in state, $11,456 out of state; room/board: N/A
Financial aid: N/A

Southeastern University
Lakeland FL
(800) 500-8760
U.S. News ranking: Reg. U. (S), second tier
Website: www.seu.edu
Admissions email: admission@seu.edu
Private; founded 1935
Affiliation: Assemblies of God
Freshman admissions: less selective; 2015-2016: 3,823 applied, 1,777 accepted. Either SAT or ACT required. SAT 25/75 percentile: 840-1080. High school rank: N/A
Early decision deadline: N/A, notification date: N/A
Early action deadline: N/A, notification date: N/A
Application deadline (fall): 5/1
Undergraduate student body: 3,185 full time, 811 part time; 44% male, 56% female; 0% American Indian, 1% Asian, 14% black, 17% Hispanic, 0% multiracial, 1% Pacific Islander, 62% white, 2% international; 72% from in state; 43% live on campus; 0% of students in fraternities, 0% in sororities
Most popular majors: 24% Business, Management, Marketing, and Related Support Services; 22% Theology and Religious Vocations; 10% Education; 7% Visual and Performing Arts
Expenses: 2016-2017: $24,160; room/board: $9,562
Financial aid: (863) 667-5026; 84% of undergrads determined to have financial need; average aid package $15,707

South Florida State College
Avon Park FL
(863) 784-7416
U.S. News ranking: Reg. Coll. (S), unranked
Website: www.southflorida.edu/
Admissions email: N/A
Public; founded 1966
Freshman admissions: N/A; 2015-2016: N/A applied, N/A accepted. Neither SAT nor ACT required. ACT 25/75 percentile: N/A. High school rank: N/A
Early decision deadline: N/A, notification date: N/A
Early action deadline: N/A, notification date: N/A
Application deadline (fall): rolling
Undergraduate student body: 928 full time, 1,794 part time; 39% male, 61% female; 0% American Indian, 2% Asian, 11% black, 31% Hispanic, 2% multiracial, 0% Pacific Islander, 50% white, 2% international
Most popular majors: Information not available
Expenses: 2015-2016: $3,165 in state, $11,859 out of state; room/board: N/A
Financial aid: N/A

State College of Florida–Manatee-Sarasota[1]
Bradenton FL
(941) 752-5050
U.S. News ranking: Reg. Coll. (S), unranked
Website: www.scf.edu/
Admissions email: N/A
Public
Application deadline (fall): N/A
Undergraduate student body: N/A full time, N/A part time
Expenses: 2015-2016: $3,074 in state, $11,606 out of state; room/board: N/A
Financial aid: N/A

Stetson University
DeLand FL
(800) 688-0101
U.S. News ranking: Reg. U. (S), No. 5
Website: www.stetson.edu
Admissions email: admissions@stetson.edu
Private; founded 1883
Freshman admissions: more selective; 2015-2016: 11,216 applied, 7,119 accepted. Neither SAT nor ACT required. SAT 25/75 percentile: 1050-1260. High school rank: 28% in top tenth, 60% in top quarter, 88% in top half
Early decision deadline: N/A, notification date: N/A
Early action deadline: N/A, notification date: N/A
Application deadline (fall): N/A
Undergraduate student body: 3,037 full time, 47 part time; 43% male, 57% female; 1% American Indian, 2% Asian, 8% black, 15% Hispanic, 3% multiracial, 0% Pacific Islander, 65% white, 5% international; 68% from in state; 65% live on campus; 31% of students in fraternities, 32% in sororities
Most popular majors: 24% Business, Management, Marketing, and Related Support

Services; 11% Psychology; 11% Visual and Performing Arts; 11% Social Sciences; 9% Biological and Biomedical Sciences
Expenses: 2016-2017: $43,240; room/board: $12,326
Financial aid: (386) 822-7120; 73% of undergrads determined to have financial need; average aid package $33,881

St. Petersburg College[1]
St. Petersburg FL
(727) 341-4772
U.S. News ranking: Reg. Coll. (S), unranked
Website: www.spcollege.edu/
Admissions email: information@spcollege.edu
Public
Application deadline (fall): N/A
Undergraduate student body: N/A full time, N/A part time
Expenses: 2015-2016: $3,352 in state, $11,607 out of state; room/board: N/A
Financial aid: (727) 791-2442

St. Thomas University
Miami Gardens FL
(305) 628-6546
U.S. News ranking: Reg. U. (S), No. 58
Website: www.stu.edu
Admissions email: signup@stu.edu
Private; founded 1961
Affiliation: Roman Catholic
Freshman admissions: less selective; 2015-2016: 1,570 applied, 768 accepted. Either SAT or ACT required. SAT 25/75 percentile: 870-1030. High school rank: 13% in top tenth, 27% in top quarter, 54% in top half
Early decision deadline: N/A, notification date: N/A
Early action deadline: N/A, notification date: N/A
Application deadline (fall): rolling
Undergraduate student body: 849 full time, 2,333 part time; 41% male, 59% female; 0% American Indian, 0% Asian, 21% black, 46% Hispanic, 1% multiracial, 0% Pacific Islander, 10% white, 18% international; 90% from in state; 39% live on campus; 0% of students in fraternities, 0% in sororities
Most popular majors: 43% Business, Management, Marketing, and Related Support Services; 18% Homeland Security, Law Enforcement, Firefighting and Related Protective Services; 10% Biological and Biomedical Sciences; 6% Psychology; 4% Education
Expenses: 2015-2016: $28,710; room/board: $7,820
Financial aid: (305) 474-6960

University of Central Florida
Orlando FL
(407) 823-3000
U.S. News ranking: Nat. U., No. 176
Website: www.ucf.edu
Admissions email: admission@ucf.edu
Public; founded 1963

Freshman admissions: more selective; 2015-2016: 35,572 applied, 17,279 accepted. Either SAT or ACT required. SAT 25/75 percentile: 1080-1270. High school rank: 33% in top tenth, 74% in top quarter, 98% in top half
Early decision deadline: N/A, notification date: N/A
Early action deadline: N/A, notification date: N/A
Application deadline (fall): 5/1
Undergraduate student body: 37,596 full time, 16,917 part time; 45% male, 55% female; 0% American Indian, 6% Asian, 11% black, 24% Hispanic, 4% multiracial, 0% Pacific Islander, 53% white, 1% international; 95% from in state; 17% live on campus; 7% of students in fraternities, 7% in sororities
Most popular majors: 21% Business, Management, Marketing, and Related Support Services; 16% Health Professions and Related Programs; 9% Psychology; 7% Education; 7% Engineering
Expenses: 2015-2016: $6,368 in state, $22,467 out of state; room/board: $9,764
Financial aid: (407) 823-2827; 65% of undergrads determined to have financial need; average aid package $8,567

University of Florida
Gainesville FL
(352) 392-1365
U.S. News ranking: Nat. U., No. 50
Website: www.ufl.edu
Admissions email: N/A
Public; founded 1853
Freshman admissions: more selective; 2015-2016: 29,837 applied, 14,237 accepted. Either SAT or ACT required. SAT 25/75 percentile: 1170-1350. High school rank: 72% in top tenth, 96% in top quarter, 100% in top half
Early decision deadline: N/A, notification date: N/A
Early action deadline: N/A, notification date: N/A
Application deadline (fall): 11/1
Undergraduate student body: 30,907 full time, 4,136 part time; 45% male, 55% female; 0% American Indian, 8% Asian, 6% black, 21% Hispanic, 3% multiracial, 1% Pacific Islander, 57% white, 1% international; 95% from in state; 24% live on campus; 20% of students in fraternities, 24% in sororities
Most popular majors: 13% Engineering; 12% Business, Management, Marketing, and Related Support Services; 12% Social Sciences; 10% Biological and Biomedical Sciences
Expenses: 2016-2017: $6,389 in state, $28,666 out of state; room/board: $9,910
Financial aid: (352) 392-1271; 49% of undergrads determined to have financial need; average aid package $12,678

University of Miami
Coral Gables FL
(305) 284-4323
U.S. News ranking: Nat. U., No. 44
Website: www.miami.edu
Admissions email: admission@miami.edu
Private; founded 1925
Freshman admissions: most selective; 2015-2016: 33,415 applied, 12,624 accepted. Either SAT or ACT required. ACT 25/75 percentile: 28-32. High school rank: 63% in top tenth, 90% in top quarter, 97% in top half
Early decision deadline: 11/1, notification date: 12/20
Early action deadline: 11/1, notification date: 1/20
Application deadline (fall): 1/1
Undergraduate student body: 10,482 full time, 641 part time; 49% male, 51% female; 0% American Indian, 6% Asian, 8% black, 22% Hispanic, 3% multiracial, 0% Pacific Islander, 42% white, 14% international; 43% from in state; 37% live on campus; 16% of students in fraternities, 19% in sororities
Most popular majors: 19% Business, Management, Marketing, and Related Support Services; 15% Biological and Biomedical Sciences; 10% Engineering; 10% Social Sciences
Expenses: 2016-2017: $47,004; room/board: $13,310
Financial aid: (305) 284-5212; 19% of undergrads determined to have financial need; average aid package $40,319

University of North Florida
Jacksonville FL
(904) 620-2624
U.S. News ranking: Reg. U. (S), No. 52
Website: www.unf.edu
Admissions email: admissions@unf.edu
Public; founded 1965
Freshman admissions: more selective; 2015-2016: 10,901 applied, 6,171 accepted. Either SAT or ACT required. ACT 25/75 percentile: 22-27. High school rank: 19% in top tenth, 42% in top quarter, 78% in top half
Early decision deadline: N/A, notification date: N/A
Early action deadline: N/A, notification date: N/A
Application deadline (fall): rolling
Undergraduate student body: 9,562 full time, 4,255 part time; 45% male, 55% female; 0% American Indian, 4% Asian, 9% black, 10% Hispanic, 5% multiracial, 0% Pacific Islander, 69% white, 1% international; 97% from in state; 21% live on campus; N/A of students in fraternities, N/A in sororities
Most popular majors: 18% Business, Management, Marketing, and Related Support Services; 17% Health Professions and Related Programs; 11% Psychology; 7% Social Sciences
Expenses: 2016-2017: $6,394 in state, $20,112 out of state; room/board: $9,602

University of South Florida
Tampa FL
(813) 974-3350
U.S. News ranking: Nat. U., No. 159
Website: www.usf.edu
Admissions email: admission@admin.usf.edu
Public; founded 1956
Freshman admissions: more selective; 2015-2016: 30,386 applied, 13,563 accepted. Either SAT or ACT required. SAT 25/75 percentile: 1070-1270. High school rank: 34% in top tenth, 59% in top quarter, 69% in top half
Early decision deadline: N/A, notification date: N/A
Early action deadline: N/A, notification date: N/A
Application deadline (fall): 3/1
Undergraduate student body: 24,088 full time, 7,023 part time; 45% male, 55% female; 0% American Indian, 6% Asian, 11% black, 21% Hispanic, 4% multiracial, 0% Pacific Islander, 51% white, 5% international; 95% from in state; 21% live on campus; 6% of students in fraternities, 10% in sororities
Most popular majors: 7% Psychology, General; 7% Registered Nursing/Registered Nurse; 6% Biomedical Sciences, General; 5% Criminology; 4% Public Health, General
Expenses: 2016-2017: $6,410 in state, $17,325 out of state; room/board: $9,400
Financial aid: (813) 974-4700; 68% of undergrads determined to have financial need; average aid package $11,510

University of South Florida–St. Petersburg
St. Petersburg FL
(727) 873-4142
U.S. News ranking: Reg. U. (S), No. 72
Website: www.usfsp.edu
Admissions email: admissions@usfsp.edu
Public; founded 1965
Freshman admissions: selective; 2015-2016: 5,122 applied, 2,400 accepted. Either SAT or ACT required. SAT 25/75 percentile: 1010-1170. High school rank: 14% in top tenth, 46% in top quarter, 85% in top half
Early decision deadline: N/A, notification date: N/A
Early action deadline: 11/15, notification date: 12/1
Application deadline (fall): 4/15
Undergraduate student body: 2,657 full time, 1,466 part time; 39% male, 61% female; 0% American Indian, 4% Asian, 8% black, 16% Hispanic, 4% multiracial, 0% Pacific Islander, 65% white, 1% international; 97% from in state; 16% live on campus; 0% of students in fraternities, 0% in sororities

Most popular majors: 35% Business, Management, Marketing, and Related Support Services; 18% Social Sciences; 13% Psychology; 10% Education; 6% English Language and Literature/Letters
Expenses: 2016-2017: $5,830 in state, $16,746 out of state; room/board: $9,250
Financial aid: (727) 873-4128; 73% of undergrads determined to have financial need; average aid package $8,365

University of Tampa
Tampa FL
(888) 646-2738
U.S. News ranking: Reg. U. (S), No. 21
Website: www.ut.edu
Admissions email: admissions@ut.edu
Private; founded 1931
Freshman admissions: selective; 2015-2016: 18,712 applied, 9,499 accepted. Either SAT or ACT required. SAT 25/75 percentile: 990-1170. High school rank: 18% in top tenth, 45% in top quarter, 81% in top half
Early decision deadline: N/A, notification date: N/A
Early action deadline: 11/15, notification date: 12/15
Application deadline (fall): rolling
Undergraduate student body: 6,820 full time, 259 part time; 42% male, 58% female; 0% American Indian, 2% Asian, 5% black, 12% Hispanic, 3% multiracial, 0% Pacific Islander, 59% white, 11% international; 35% from in state; 58% live on campus; 8% of students in fraternities, 13% in sororities
Most popular majors: 29% Business, Management, and Related Support Services; 11% Social Sciences; 9% Health Professions and Related Programs; 8% Parks, Recreation, Leisure, and Fitness Studies
Expenses: 2016-2017: $27,740; room/board: $10,196
Financial aid: (813) 253-6219; 58% of undergrads determined to have financial need; average aid package $16,642

University of West Florida
Pensacola FL
(850) 474-2230
U.S. News ranking: Nat. U., second tier
Website: uwf.edu
Admissions email: admissions@uwf.edu
Public; founded 1963
Freshman admissions: more selective; 2015-2016: 7,104 applied, 2,951 accepted. Either SAT or ACT required. ACT 25/75 percentile: 20-26. High school rank: 14% in top tenth, 38% in top quarter, 74% in top half
Early decision deadline: N/A, notification date: N/A
Early action deadline: N/A, notification date: N/A
Application deadline (fall): 6/30
Undergraduate student body: 7,164 full time, 3,036 part time; 43% male, 57% female; 0% American

Indian, 3% Asian, 13% black, 9% Hispanic, 5% multiracial, 0% Pacific Islander, 65% white, 2% international; 91% from in state; 18% live on campus; N/A of students in fraternities, N/A in sororities
Most popular majors: 19% Health Professions and Related Programs; 13% Business Administration and Management, General; 8% Social Sciences, General; 6% Psychology, General
Expenses: 2016-2017: $8,960 in state, $21,841 out of state; room/board: $9,912
Financial aid: (850) 474-3127; 67% of undergrads determined to have financial need; average aid package $8,411

Valencia College[1]
Orlando FL
(407) 582-1507
U.S. News ranking: Reg. Coll. (S), unranked
Website: valenciacollege.edu/
Admissions email: N/A
Public
Application deadline (fall): N/A
Undergraduate student body: N/A full time, N/A part time
Expenses: 2015-2016: $2,474 in state, $9,383 out of state; room/board: N/A
Financial aid: N/A

Warner University
Lake Wales FL
(800) 309-9563
U.S. News ranking: Reg. Coll. (S), No. 42
Website: www.warner.edu
Admissions email: admissions@warner.edu
Private
Affiliation: Church of God, Anderson IN
Freshman admissions: less selective; 2015-2016: 708 applied, 296 accepted. Either SAT or ACT required. ACT 25/75 percentile: 17-20. High school rank: 8% in top tenth, 21% in top quarter, 52% in top half
Early decision deadline: N/A, notification date: N/A
Early action deadline: N/A, notification date: N/A
Application deadline (fall): rolling
Undergraduate student body: 904 full time, 151 part time; 54% male, 46% female; 0% American Indian, 1% Asian, 39% black, 12% Hispanic, 2% multiracial, 0% Pacific Islander, 41% white, 3% international; 94% from in state; 36% live on campus; N/A of students in fraternities, N/A in sororities
Most popular majors: 13% Business Administration, Management and Operations, Other; 12% Elementary Education and Teaching; 8% Theology/Theological Studies; 7% Business Administration and Management, General; 5% Sport and Fitness Administration/Management
Expenses: 2015-2016: $19,754; room/board: $7,924
Financial aid: (863) 638-7202

Webber International University[1]
Babson Park FL
(800) 741-1844
U.S. News ranking: Reg. Coll. (S), second tier
Website: www.webber.edu
Admissions email: admissions@webber.edu
Private; founded 1927
Application deadline (fall): 8/1
Undergraduate student body: N/A full time, N/A part time
Expenses: 2016-2017: $25,358; room/board: $8,942
Financial aid: (863) 638-2930; 68% of undergrads determined to have financial need; average aid package $20,535

GEORGIA

Abraham Baldwin Agricultural College[1]
Tifton GA
(800) 733-3653
U.S. News ranking: Reg. Coll. (S), second tier
Website: www.abac.edu/
Admissions email: N/A
Public; founded 1908
Application deadline (fall): 8/1
Undergraduate student body: N/A full time, N/A part time
Expenses: 2015-2016: $3,453 in state, $10,060 out of state; room/board: $7,200
Financial aid: (229) 391-4910

Agnes Scott College
Decatur GA
(800) 868-8602
U.S. News ranking: Nat. Lib. Arts, No. 70
Website: www.agnesscott.edu
Admissions email: admission@agnesscott.edu
Private; founded 1889
Affiliation: Presbyterian Church (USA)
Freshman admissions: more selective; 2015-2016: 1,461 applied, 902 accepted. Neither SAT nor ACT required. SAT 25/75 percentile: 1060-1330. High school rank: 29% in top tenth, 62% in top quarter, 93% in top half
Early decision deadline: 11/1, notification date: 12/1
Early action deadline: 11/15, notification date: 12/15
Application deadline (fall): 3/15
Undergraduate student body: 876 full time, 26 part time; 1% male, 99% female; 0% American Indian, 6% Asian, 34% black, 10% Hispanic, 8% multiracial, 0% Pacific Islander, 33% white, 8% international; 55% from in state; 87% live on campus; N/A of students in fraternities, N/A in sororities
Most popular majors: 19% Social Sciences; 14% Biological and Biomedical Sciences; 11% Psychology; 9% English Language and Literature/Letters; 9% Health Professions and Related Programs
Expenses: 2016-2017: $38,472; room/board: $11,520
Financial aid: (404) 471-6395; 78% of undergrads determined to have financial need; average aid package $33,793

Albany State University
Albany GA
(229) 430-4646
U.S. News ranking: Reg. U. (S), second tier
Website: www.asurams.edu/
Admissions email: admissions@asurams.edu
Public; founded 1903
Freshman admissions: less selective; 2015-2016: 2,196 applied, 1,399 accepted. Either SAT or ACT required. SAT 25/75 percentile: 840-950. High school rank: 10% in top tenth, 37% in top quarter, 66% in top half
Early decision deadline: N/A, notification date: N/A
Early action deadline: N/A, notification date: N/A
Application deadline (fall): 7/1
Undergraduate student body: 2,554 full time, 437 part time; 34% male, 66% female; 0% American Indian, 0% Asian, 90% black, 2% Hispanic, 1% multiracial, 0% Pacific Islander, 5% white, 0% international; 98% from in state; 47% live on campus; 7% of students in fraternities, 10% in sororities
Most popular majors: 11% Criminal Justice/Safety Studies; 10% Business Administration and Management, General; 7% Education, Other; 6% Social Work
Expenses: 2016-2017: $6,460 in state, $19,280 out of state; room/board: $7,788
Financial aid: (229) 430-4650; 87% of undergrads determined to have financial need

Armstrong State University
Savannah GA
(912) 344-2503
U.S. News ranking: Reg. U. (S), second tier
Website: www.armstrong.edu
Admissions email: adm-info@mail.armstrong.edu
Public; founded 1935
Freshman admissions: selective; 2015-2016: 2,328 applied, 1,721 accepted. Either SAT or ACT required. SAT 25/75 percentile: 910-1080. High school rank: N/A
Early decision deadline: N/A, notification date: N/A
Early action deadline: N/A, notification date: N/A
Application deadline (fall): 7/1
Undergraduate student body: 4,650 full time, 1,681 part time; 34% male, 66% female; 0% American Indian, 3% Asian, 25% black, 7% Hispanic, 5% multiracial, 0% Pacific Islander, 57% white, 2% international; 89% from in state; 20% live on campus; 5% of students in fraternities, 4% in sororities
Most popular majors: 44% Health Professions and Related Programs; 11% Education; 8% Biological and Biomedical Sciences; 6% Liberal Arts and Sciences, General Studies and Humanities; 5% Social Sciences
Expenses: 2016-2017: $6,332 in state, $19,152 out of state; room/board: $10,498

Financial aid: (912) 921-5990; 69% of undergrads determined to have financial need; average aid package $12,900

Art Institute of Atlanta[1]
Atlanta GA
(770) 394-8300
U.S. News ranking: Arts, unranked
Website: www.artinstitutes.edu/atlanta/
Admissions email: aiaadm@aii.edu
For-profit
Application deadline (fall): N/A
Undergraduate student body: N/A full time, N/A part time
Expenses: 2015-2016: $17,592; room/board: $11,268
Financial aid: (770) 394-8300

Atlanta Metropolitan State College[1]
Atlanta GA
(404) 756-4004
U.S. News ranking: Reg. Coll. (S), unranked
Website: www.atlm.edu/
Admissions email: N/A
Public
Application deadline (fall): N/A
Undergraduate student body: N/A full time, N/A part time
Expenses: 2015-2016: $3,250 in state, $9,588 out of state; room/board: N/A
Financial aid: N/A

Augusta University
Augusta GA
(706) 721-2725
U.S. News ranking: Nat. U., second tier
Website: www.georgiahealth.edu/
Admissions email: admissions@georgiahealth.edu
Public; founded 1828
Freshman admissions: selective; 2015-2016: 2,096 applied, 1,553 accepted. Either SAT or ACT required. SAT 25/75 percentile: 930-1140. High school rank: N/A
Early decision deadline: N/A, notification date: N/A
Early action deadline: N/A, notification date: N/A
Application deadline (fall): N/A
Undergraduate student body: 3,987 full time, 989 part time; 36% male, 64% female; 0% American Indian, 2% Asian, 25% black, 6% Hispanic, 4% multiracial, 0% Pacific Islander, 55% white, 1% international
Most popular majors: 17% Registered Nursing/Registered Nurse; 7% Kinesiology and Exercise Science; 7% Psychology, General
Expenses: 2016-2017: $8,422 in state, $23,130 out of state; room/board: $13,128
Financial aid: (706) 721-4901; 59% of undergrads determined to have financial need; average aid package $2,210

Bauder College[1]
Atlanta GA
(800) 241-3797
U.S. News ranking: Reg. Coll. (S), unranked
Website: www.bauder.edu
Admissions email: N/A
For-profit

Application deadline (fall): N/A
Undergraduate student body: N/A full time, N/A part time
Expenses: 2015-2016: $13,356; room/board: N/A
Financial aid: N/A

Berry College
Mount Berry GA
(706) 236-2215
U.S. News ranking: Reg. U. (S), No. 7
Website: www.berry.edu
Admissions email: admissions@berry.edu
Private; founded 1902
Freshman admissions: more selective; 2015-2016: 4,347 applied, 2,407 accepted. Either SAT or ACT required. ACT 25/75 percentile: 24-29. High school rank: 31% in top tenth, 62% in top quarter, 91% in top half
Early decision deadline: N/A, notification date: N/A
Early action deadline: N/A, notification date: N/A
Application deadline (fall): 7/22
Undergraduate student body: 2,078 full time, 45 part time; 38% male, 62% female; 0% American Indian, 1% Asian, 5% black, 7% Hispanic, 3% multiracial, 0% Pacific Islander, 81% white, 1% international; 69% from in state; 87% live on campus; 0% of students in fraternities, 0% in sororities
Most popular majors: 23% Business, Management, Marketing, and Related Support Services; 11% Biological and Biomedical Sciences; 8% Education; 7% Psychology
Expenses: 2016-2017: $33,556; room/board: $11,730
Financial aid: (706) 236-1714; 70% of undergrads determined to have financial need; average aid package $26,539

Brenau University
Gainesville GA
(770) 534-6100
U.S. News ranking: Reg. U. (S), No. 52
Website: www.brenau.edu
Admissions email: admissions@brenau.edu
Private; founded 1878
Freshman admissions: selective; 2015-2016: 2,324 applied, 1,525 accepted. Either SAT or ACT required. SAT 25/75 percentile: 890-1090. High school rank: N/A
Early decision deadline: N/A, notification date: N/A
Early action deadline: N/A, notification date: N/A
Application deadline (fall): rolling
Undergraduate student body: 986 full time, 586 part time; 10% male, 90% female; 0% American Indian, 2% Asian, 32% black, 8% Hispanic, 3% multiracial, 0% Pacific Islander, 51% white, 2% international; 94% from in state; 24% live on campus; N/A of students in fraternities, 12% in sororities
Most popular majors: 33% Health Professions and Related Programs; 31% Business, Management, Marketing, and Related Support Services; 11% Visual and Performing Arts; 4% Biological and Biomedical

Sciences; 3% Liberal Arts and Sciences, General Studies and Humanities
Expenses: 2016-2017: $27,152; room/board: $12,418
Financial aid: (770) 534-6176; 82% of undergrads determined to have financial need; average aid package $22,429

Brewton-Parker College[1]
Mount Vernon GA
(912) 583-3265
U.S. News ranking: Reg. Coll. (S), second tier
Website: www.bpc.edu
Admissions email: admissions@bpc.edu
Private; founded 1904
Affiliation: Baptist
Application deadline (fall): rolling
Undergraduate student body: N/A full time, N/A part time
Expenses: 2015-2016: $16,180; room/board: $7,665
Financial aid: (912) 583-3215

Clark Atlanta University
Atlanta GA
(800) 688-3228
U.S. News ranking: Nat. U., second tier
Website: www.cau.edu
Admissions email: cauadmissions@cau.edu
Private; founded 1988
Affiliation: Methodist
Freshman admissions: less selective; 2015-2016: 8,616 applied, 4,509 accepted. Either SAT or ACT required. ACT 25/75 percentile: 16-20. High school rank: 3% in top tenth, 20% in top quarter, 53% in top half
Early decision deadline: N/A, notification date: N/A
Early action deadline: N/A, notification date: N/A
Application deadline (fall): 6/1
Undergraduate student body: 2,629 full time, 112 part time; 26% male, 74% female; 0% American Indian, 0% Asian, 84% black, 0% Hispanic, N/A multiracial, N/A Pacific Islander, 0% white, 2% international; 37% from in state; 64% live on campus; 2% of students in fraternities, 3% in sororities
Most popular majors: 17% Business, Management, Marketing, and Related Support Services; 14% Psychology; 12% Homeland Security, Law Enforcement, Firefighting and Related Protective Services; 11% Biological and Biomedical Sciences
Expenses: 2016-2017: $22,396; room/board: $10,800
Financial aid: (404) 880-8111; 91% of undergrads determined to have financial need; average aid package $7,062

Clayton State University
Morrow GA
(678) 466-4115
U.S. News ranking: Reg. U. (S), second tier
Website: www.clayton.edu
Admissions email: ccsu-info@mail.clayton.edu

Public; founded 1969
Freshman admissions: less selective; 2015-2016: 2,816 applied, 1,100 accepted. Either SAT or ACT required. SAT 25/75 percentile: 860-1020. High school rank: N/A
Early decision deadline: N/A, notification date: N/A
Early action deadline: N/A, notification date: N/A
Application deadline (fall): 7/1
Undergraduate student body: 3,626 full time, 2,961 part time; 32% male, 68% female; 0% American Indian, 5% Asian, 66% black, 3% Hispanic, 3% multiracial, 0% Pacific Islander, 17% white, 1% international; 97% from in state; 14% live on campus; N/A of students in fraternities, N/A in sororities
Most popular majors: 11% Community Psychology; 11% Hospital and Health Care Facilities Administration/Management; 11% Liberal Arts and Sciences/Liberal Studies; 9% Registered Nursing/Registered Nurse; 5% Office Management and Supervision
Expenses: 2016-2017: $6,312 in state, $19,132 out of state; room/board: $10,156
Financial aid: (678) 466-4185; 87% of undergrads determined to have financial need; average aid package $9,137

College of Coastal Georgia
Brunswick GA
(912) 279-5730
U.S. News ranking: Reg. Coll. (S), No. 42
Website: www.ccga.edu
Admissions email: admiss@ccga.edu
Public; founded 1961
Freshman admissions: less selective; 2015-2016: 1,297 applied, 1,232 accepted. Either SAT or ACT required. SAT 25/75 percentile: 833-1040. High school rank: N/A
Early decision deadline: N/A, notification date: N/A
Early action deadline: N/A, notification date: N/A
Application deadline (fall): rolling
Undergraduate student body: 1,966 full time, 1,165 part time; 34% male, 66% female; 0% American Indian, 2% Asian, 18% black, 5% Hispanic, 4% multiracial, 0% Pacific Islander, 67% white, 1% international; 93% from in state; 14% live on campus; N/A of students in fraternities, N/A in sororities
Most popular majors: 21% Business/Commerce, General; 18% Registered Nursing/Registered Nurse; 14% Psychology, General; 10% Junior High/Intermediate/Middle School Education and Teaching; 8% Public Administration and Social Service Professions, Other
Expenses: 2016-2017: $4,434 in state, $12,692 out of state; room/board: $8,858
Financial aid: N/A; 69% of undergrads determined to have financial need; average aid package $8,463

Columbus State University

Columbus GA
(706) 507-8800
U.S. News ranking: Reg. U. (S), No. 105
Website: www.columbusstate.edu
Admissions email: admissions@columbusstate.edu
Public; founded 1958
Freshman admissions: selective; 2015-2016: 3,157 applied, 1,758 accepted. Either SAT or ACT required. SAT 25/75 percentile: 850-1090. High school rank: 15% in top tenth, 36% in top quarter, 67% in top half
Early decision deadline: N/A, notification date: N/A
Early action deadline: N/A, notification date: N/A
Application deadline (fall): 6/30
Undergraduate student body: 4,937 full time, 2,000 part time; 40% male, 60% female; 0% American Indian, 2% Asian, 37% black, 6% Hispanic, 2% multiracial, 0% Pacific Islander, 51% white, 1% international; 83% from in state; 20% live on campus; 5% of students in fraternities, 5% in sororities
Most popular majors: 25% Health Professions and Related Programs; 15% Business, Management, Marketing, and Related Support Services; 9% Education; 8% Homeland Security, Law Enforcement, Firefighting and Related Protective Services; 7% English Language and Literature/Letters
Expenses: 2016-2017: $7,076 in state, $20,294 out of state; room/board: $10,198
Financial aid: (706) 568-2036; 72% of undergrads determined to have financial need; average aid package $9,235

Covenant College

Lookout Mountain GA
(706) 820-2398
U.S. News ranking: Nat. Lib. Arts, No. 159
Website: www.covenant.edu
Admissions email: admissions@covenant.edu
Private; founded 1955
Affiliation: Presbyterian Church in America
Freshman admissions: more selective; 2015-2016: 615 applied, 578 accepted. Either SAT or ACT required. ACT 25/75 percentile: 24-29. High school rank: 32% in top tenth, 63% in top quarter, 87% in top half
Early decision deadline: N/A, notification date: N/A
Early action deadline: N/A, notification date: N/A
Application deadline (fall): rolling
Undergraduate student body: 999 full time, 45 part time; 42% male, 58% female; 0% American Indian, 2% Asian, 2% black, 3% Hispanic, 3% multiracial, 0% Pacific Islander, 87% white, 3% international; 24% from in state; 81% live on campus; 0% of students in fraternities, 0% in sororities
Most popular majors: 11% Education; 10% Business, Management, Marketing, and Related Support Services; 9%

Biological and Biomedical Sciences; 8% Psychology; 7% English Language and Literature/Letters
Expenses: 2016-2017: $32,230; room/board: $9,630
Financial aid: (706) 419-1126; 60% of undergrads determined to have financial need; average aid package $25,096

Dalton State College[1]

Dalton GA
(706) 272-4436
U.S. News ranking: Reg. Coll. (S), unranked
Website: www.daltonstate.edu/
Admissions email: N/A
Public
Application deadline (fall): N/A
Undergraduate student body: N/A full time, N/A part time
Expenses: 2015-2016: $4,052 in state, $12,302 out of state; room/board: $7,093
Financial aid: (706) 272-4545

Darton State College[1]

Albany GA
(866) 775-1214
U.S. News ranking: Reg. Coll. (S), unranked
Website: www.darton.edu/
Admissions email: N/A
Public
Application deadline (fall): N/A
Undergraduate student body: N/A full time, N/A part time
Expenses: 2015-2016: $3,395 in state, $9,470 out of state; room/board: $10,438
Financial aid: N/A

East Georgia State College

Swainsboro GA
(478) 289-2169
U.S. News ranking: Reg. Coll. (S), second tier
Website: www.ega.edu/
Admissions email: N/A
Public
Freshman admissions: less selective; 2015-2016: 3,394 applied, 1,997 accepted. Neither SAT nor ACT required. ACT 25/75 percentile: N/A. High school rank: N/A
Early decision deadline: N/A, notification date: N/A
Early action deadline: N/A, notification date: N/A
Application deadline (fall): 8/15
Undergraduate student body: 2,313 full time, 682 part time; 41% male, 59% female; 0% American Indian, 1% Asian, 44% black, 2% Hispanic, 5% multiracial, 0% Pacific Islander, 45% white, 2% international
Most popular majors: Information not available
Expenses: 2015-2016: $3,067 in state, $9,142 out of state; room/board: $7,082
Financial aid: N/A

Emmanuel College

Franklin Springs GA
(800) 860-8800
U.S. News ranking: Reg. Coll. (S), No. 29
Website: www.ec.edu
Admissions email: admissions@ec.edu

Private; founded 1919
Affiliation: International Pentecostal Holiness
Freshman admissions: less selective; 2015-2016: 1,560 applied, 539 accepted. Either SAT or ACT required. SAT 25/75 percentile: 790-1070. High school rank: N/A
Early decision deadline: N/A, notification date: N/A
Early action deadline: N/A, notification date: N/A
Application deadline (fall): 8/1
Undergraduate student body: 758 full time, 126 part time; 54% male, 46% female; 0% American Indian, 0% Asian, 17% black, 5% Hispanic, 2% multiracial, 1% Pacific Islander, 69% white, 6% international; 75% from in state; 60% live on campus; N/A of students in fraternities, N/A in sororities
Most popular majors: 22% Parks, Recreation, Leisure, and Fitness Studies; 18% Business, Management, Marketing, and Related Support Services; 13% Education; 12% Psychology; 10% Theology and Religious Vocations
Expenses: 2016-2017: $19,330; room/board: $7,200
Financial aid: (706) 245-2843; 79% of undergrads determined to have financial need; average aid package $14,759

Emory University

Atlanta GA
(404) 727-6036
U.S. News ranking: Nat. U., No. 20
Website: www.emory.edu
Admissions email: admission@emory.edu
Private; founded 1836
Affiliation: Methodist
Freshman admissions: most selective; 2015-2016: 20,492 applied, 4,851 accepted. Either SAT or ACT required. SAT 25/75 percentile: 1270-1490. High school rank: 83% in top tenth, 96% in top quarter, 99% in top half
Early decision deadline: 11/1, notification date: 12/15
Early action deadline: N/A, notification date: N/A
Application deadline (fall): 1/1
Undergraduate student body: 6,751 full time, 116 part time; 42% male, 58% female; 0% American Indian, 19% Asian, 9% black, 8% Hispanic, 3% multiracial, 0% Pacific Islander, 41% white, 17% international; 22% from in state; 64% live on campus; 26% of students in fraternities, 31% in sororities
Most popular majors: 15% Business Administration and Management, General; 11% Biology/Biological Sciences, General; 9% Economics, General; 7% Registered Nursing/Registered Nurse; 6% Neuroscience
Expenses: 2016-2017: $47,954; room/board: $13,486
Financial aid: (404) 727-6039; 43% of undergrads determined to have financial need; average aid package $43,224

Fort Valley State University

Fort Valley GA
(478) 825-6307
U.S. News ranking: Reg. U. (S), second tier
Website: www.fvsu.edu
Admissions email: admissap@mail.fvsu.edu
Public; founded 1895
Freshman admissions: less selective; 2015-2016: 4,925 applied, 1,010 accepted. Either SAT or ACT required. SAT 25/75 percentile: 16-20. High school rank: 3% in top tenth, 13% in top quarter, 42% in top half
Early decision deadline: N/A, notification date: N/A
Early action deadline: N/A, notification date: N/A
Application deadline (fall): 7/19
Undergraduate student body: 1,985 full time, 281 part time; 42% male, 58% female; 0% American Indian, 0% Asian, 93% black, 1% Hispanic, 0% multiracial, 0% Pacific Islander, 3% white, 0% international; 96% from in state; 45% live on campus; 35% of students in fraternities, 40% in sororities
Most popular majors: 13% Homeland Security, Law Enforcement, Firefighting and Related Protective Services; 11% Psychology; 10% Education; 9% Biological and Biomedical Sciences; 8% Health Professions and Related Programs
Expenses: 2015-2016: $5,594 in state, $15,850 out of state; room/board: $7,950
Financial aid: (478) 825-6351; 100% of undergrads determined to have financial need; average aid package $7,367

Georgia College & State University

Milledgeville GA
(478) 445-1283
U.S. News ranking: Reg. U. (S), No. 28
Website: www.gcsu.edu
Admissions email: info@gcsu.edu
Public; founded 1889
Freshman admissions: selective; 2015-2016: 3,968 applied, 3,002 accepted. Either SAT or ACT required. ACT 25/75 percentile: 23-27. High school rank: N/A
Early decision deadline: N/A, notification date: N/A
Early action deadline: 11/1, notification date: N/A
Application deadline (fall): 4/1
Undergraduate student body: 5,586 full time, 450 part time; 40% male, 60% female; 0% American Indian, 1% Asian, 5% black, 5% Hispanic, 3% multiracial, 0% Pacific Islander, 85% white, 1% international; 99% from in state; 36% live on campus; 6% of students in fraternities, 14% in sororities
Most popular majors: 10% Business Administration and Management, General; 8% Health Teacher Education; 8% Registered Nursing/Registered Nurse; 7% Marketing/Marketing Management, General
Expenses: 2016-2017: $9,202 in state, $27,550 out of state; room/board: $11,946

Financial aid: (478) 445-5149; 54% of undergrads determined to have financial need; average aid package $9,744

Georgia Gwinnett College

Lawrenceville GA
(877) 704-4422
U.S. News ranking: Reg. Coll. (S), No. 52
Website: www.ggc.edu
Admissions email: N/A
Public; founded 2005
Freshman admissions: less selective; 2015-2016: 3,612 applied, 3,041 accepted. Neither SAT nor ACT required. SAT 25/75 percentile: 800-1040. High school rank: 3% in top tenth, 9% in top quarter, 38% in top half
Early decision deadline: N/A, notification date: N/A
Early action deadline: N/A, notification date: N/A
Application deadline (fall): 5/2
Undergraduate student body: 7,794 full time, 3,674 part time; 44% male, 56% female; 0% American Indian, 9% Asian, 33% black, 16% Hispanic, 4% multiracial, 0% Pacific Islander, 34% white, 2% international; 98% from in state; 7% live on campus; 0% of students in fraternities, 0% in sororities
Most popular majors: 34% Business/Commerce, General; 12% Biology/Biological Sciences, General; 10% Psychology, General; 7% Information Technology
Expenses: 2016-2017: $5,558 in state, $16,062 out of state; room/board: $12,680
Financial aid: N/A; 78% of undergrads determined to have financial need; average aid package $7,438

Georgia Institute of Technology

Atlanta GA
(404) 894-4154
U.S. News ranking: Nat. U., No. 34
Website: admission.gatech.edu/information/
Admissions email: admission@gatech.edu
Public; founded 1885
Freshman admissions: most selective; 2015-2016: 27,277 applied, 8,775 accepted. Either SAT or ACT required. SAT 25/75 percentile: 1310-1500. High school rank: 81% in top tenth, 96% in top quarter, 99% in top half
Early decision deadline: N/A, notification date: N/A
Early action deadline: 10/15, notification date: 1/10
Application deadline (fall): 1/10
Undergraduate student body: 13,668 full time, 1,474 part time; 65% male, 35% female; 0% American Indian, 19% Asian, 7% black, 7% Hispanic, 4% multiracial, 0% Pacific Islander, 51% white, 11% international; 66% from in state; 53% live on campus; 25% of students in fraternities, 30% in sororities

Most popular majors: 61% Engineering; 13% Business, Management, Marketing, and Related Support Services; 9% Computer and Information Sciences and Support Services; 4% Biological and Biomedical Sciences; 2% Multi/Interdisciplinary Studies
Expenses: 2016-2017: $12,212 in state, $32,404 out of state; room/board: $13,640
Financial aid: (404) 894-4582; 41% of undergrads determined to have financial need; average aid package $14,758

Georgia Southern University

Statesboro GA
(912) 478-5391
U.S. News ranking: Nat. U., second tier
Website: www.georgiasouthern.edu/
Admissions email: admissions@georgiasouthern.edu
Public; founded 1906
Freshman admissions: selective; 2015-2016: 10,098 applied, 6,082 accepted. Either SAT or ACT required. SAT 25/75 percentile: 1030-1180. High school rank: 17% in top tenth, 49% in top quarter, 76% in top half
Early decision deadline: N/A, notification date: N/A
Early action deadline: N/A, notification date: N/A
Application deadline (fall): 5/1
Undergraduate student body: 15,872 full time, 2,091 part time; 50% male, 50% female; 0% American Indian, 2% Asian, 26% black, 5% Hispanic, 2% multiracial, 0% Pacific Islander, 62% white, 1% international; 96% from in state; 27% live on campus; 13% of students in fraternities, 17% in sororities
Most popular majors: 18% Business, Management, Marketing, and Related Support Services; 8% Liberal Arts and Sciences, General Studies and Humanities; 8% Parks, Recreation, Leisure, and Fitness Studies; 7% Education; 6% Health Professions and Related Programs
Expenses: 2016-2017: $6,796 in state, $18,692 out of state; room/board: $9,650
Financial aid: (912) 681-5413; 67% of undergrads determined to have financial need; average aid package $9,930

Georgia Southwestern State University

Americus GA
(229) 928-1273
U.S. News ranking: Reg. U. (S), second tier
Website: www.gsw.edu
Admissions email: admissions@gsw.edu
Public; founded 1906
Freshman admissions: selective; 2015-2016: 1,167 applied, 836 accepted. Either SAT or ACT required. SAT 25/75 percentile: 870-1040. High school rank: 18% in top tenth, 40% in top quarter, 72% in top half

Early decision deadline: N/A, notification date: N/A
Early action deadline: N/A, notification date: N/A
Application deadline (fall): 7/21
Undergraduate student body: 1,641 full time, 794 part time; 37% male, 63% female; 0% American Indian, 1% Asian, 29% black, 3% Hispanic, 2% multiracial, 0% Pacific Islander, 62% white, 2% international; 97% from in state; 32% live on campus; 11% of students in fraternities, 11% in sororities
Most popular majors: 18% Business Administration and Management, General; 15% Registered Nursing/Registered Nurse; 13% Accounting; 12% Adult and Continuing Education and Teaching; 6% Psychology, General
Expenses: 2016-2017: $6,234 in state, $19,054 out of state; room/board: $7,672
Financial aid: (229) 928-1378; 75% of undergrads determined to have financial need; average aid package $9,191

Georgia State University

Atlanta GA
(404) 413-2500
U.S. News ranking: Nat. U., second tier
Website: www.gsu.edu
Admissions email: admissions@gsu.edu
Public; founded 1913
Freshman admissions: selective; 2015-2016: 13,568 applied, 7,831 accepted. Either SAT or ACT required. SAT 25/75 percentile: 950-1160. High school rank: 16% in top tenth, 45% in top quarter, 83% in top half
Early decision deadline: N/A, notification date: N/A
Early action deadline: 11/16, notification date: 1/30
Application deadline (fall): 3/1
Undergraduate student body: 18,964 full time, 6,196 part time; 41% male, 59% female; 0% American Indian, 12% Asian, 42% black, 10% Hispanic, 5% multiracial, 0% Pacific Islander, 26% white, 2% international; 96% from in state; 18% live on campus; N/A of students in fraternities, N/A in sororities
Most popular majors: 26% Business, Management, Marketing, and Related Support Services; 11% Social Sciences; 8% Psychology; 7% Biological and Biomedical Sciences; 7% Visual and Performing Arts
Expenses: 2016-2017: $10,686 in state, $28,896 out of state; room/board: $14,084
Financial aid: (404) 651-2227; 80% of undergrads determined to have financial need; average aid package $11,163

Gordon State College

Barnesville GA
(678) 359-5021
U.S. News ranking: Reg. Coll. (S), second tier
Website: www.gordonstate.edu/
Admissions email: N/A
Public; founded 1852

Freshman admissions: less selective; 2015-2016: 2,480 applied, 1,068 accepted. Either SAT or ACT required. SAT 25/75 percentile: 750-960. High school rank: N/A
Early decision deadline: N/A, notification date: N/A
Early action deadline: N/A, notification date: N/A
Application deadline (fall): rolling
Undergraduate student body: 2,681 full time, 1,403 part time; 32% male, 68% female; 0% American Indian, 1% Asian, 42% black, 3% Hispanic, 3% multiracial, 0% Pacific Islander, 50% white, 0% international; 99% from in state; 24% live on campus; 0% of students in fraternities, 0% in sororities
Most popular majors: 27% Registered Nursing/Registered Nurse; 25% Elementary Education and Teaching; 15% Biology/Biological Sciences, General; 9% Health Information/Medical Records Administration/Administrator; 9% History, General
Expenses: 2016-2017: $2,632 in state, $6,761 out of state; room/board: $8,101
Financial aid: N/A

Kennesaw State University

Kennesaw GA
(770) 423-6300
U.S. News ranking: Nat. U., second tier
Website: www.kennesaw.edu
Admissions email: ksuadmit@kennesaw.edu
Public; founded 1963
Freshman admissions: selective; 2015-2016: 14,215 applied, 8,323 accepted. Either SAT or ACT required. SAT 25/75 percentile: 1010-1180. High school rank: 35% in top tenth, 45% in top quarter, 93% in top half
Early decision deadline: N/A, notification date: N/A
Early action deadline: N/A, notification date: N/A
Application deadline (fall): 5/6
Undergraduate student body: 22,974 full time, 7,506 part time; 51% male, 49% female; 0% American Indian, 4% Asian, 20% black, 9% Hispanic, 4% multiracial, 0% Pacific Islander, 58% white, 2% international; 93% from in state; 18% live on campus; 2% of students in fraternities, 4% in sororities
Most popular majors: 21% Business, Management, Marketing, and Related Support Services; 9% Education; 8% Computer and Information Sciences and Support Services; 7% Social Sciences
Expenses: 2016-2017: $8,276 in state, $21,732 out of state; room/board: $11,467
Financial aid: (770) 423-6074; 71% of undergrads determined to have financial need; average aid package $8,940

LaGrange College

LaGrange GA
(706) 880-8005
U.S. News ranking: Nat. Lib. Arts, second tier
Website: www.lagrange.edu
Admissions email: admission@lagrange.edu
Private; founded 1831
Affiliation: United Methodist
Freshman admissions: selective; 2015-2016: 1,530 applied, 876 accepted. Either SAT or ACT required. ACT 25/75 percentile: 20-24. High school rank: 18% in top tenth, 41% in top quarter, 75% in top half
Early decision deadline: N/A, notification date: N/A
Early action deadline: N/A, notification date: N/A
Application deadline (fall): rolling
Undergraduate student body: 856 full time, 56 part time; 50% male, 50% female; 0% American Indian, 1% Asian, 25% black, 2% Hispanic, 3% multiracial, N/A Pacific Islander, 68% white, 0% international; 82% from in state; 65% live on campus; 16% of students in fraternities, 35% in sororities
Most popular majors: 27% Registered Nursing/Registered Nurse; 10% Kinesiology and Exercise Science; 7% Business Administration and Management, General; 7% Psychology, General; 6% Elementary Education and Teaching
Expenses: 2016-2017: $28,460; room/board: $11,440
Financial aid: (706) 880-8229; 87% of undergrads determined to have financial need; average aid package $24,242

Mercer University

Macon GA
(478) 301-2650
U.S. News ranking: Nat. U., No. 135
Website: www.mercer.edu
Admissions email: admissions@mercer.edu
Private; founded 1833
Freshman admissions: more selective; 2015-2016: 4,559 applied, 3,049 accepted. Either SAT or ACT required. SAT 25/75 percentile: 1110-1310. High school rank: 45% in top tenth, 73% in top quarter, 95% in top half
Early decision deadline: N/A, notification date: N/A
Early action deadline: 11/1, notification date: 11/15
Application deadline (fall): 4/1
Undergraduate student body: 3,881 full time, 786 part time; 39% male, 61% female; 0% American Indian, 6% Asian, 31% black, 5% Hispanic, 3% multiracial, 0% Pacific Islander, 48% white, 3% international; 81% from in state; 69% live on campus; 23% of students in fraternities, 26% in sororities
Most popular majors: 20% Business, Management, Marketing, and Related Support Services; 16% Biological and Biomedical Sciences; 13% Engineering; 7% Social Sciences; 6% Psychology

Expenses: 2016-2017: $35,130; room/board: $11,916
Financial aid: (478) 301-2670; 71% of undergrads determined to have financial need; average aid package $34,307

Middle Georgia State University[1]

Macon GA
(800) 272-7619
U.S. News ranking: Reg. Coll. (S), second tier
Website: www.mga.edu/
Admissions email: N/A
Public
Application deadline (fall): 7/16
Undergraduate student body: N/A full time, N/A part time
Expenses: 2015-2016: $3,890 in state, $10,919 out of state; room/board: $7,870
Financial aid: (800) 272-7619

Morehouse College

Atlanta GA
(404) 215-2632
U.S. News ranking: Nat. Lib. Arts, No. 159
Website: www.morehouse.edu
Admissions email: admissions@morehouse.edu
Private; founded 1867
Freshman admissions: selective; 2015-2016: 2,288 applied, 1,738 accepted. Either SAT or ACT required. SAT 25/75 percentile: 870-1100. High school rank: 11% in top tenth, 30% in top quarter, 66% in top half
Early decision deadline: 11/1, notification date: 12/15
Early action deadline: 11/1, notification date: 12/15
Application deadline (fall): 2/15
Undergraduate student body: 2,069 full time, 98 part time; 100% male, 0% female; 0% American Indian, 0% Asian, 95% black, 1% Hispanic, 0% multiracial, 0% Pacific Islander, 0% white, 2% international; 32% from in state; 68% live on campus; 3% of students in fraternities, N/A in sororities
Most popular majors: 24% Business, Management, Marketing, and Related Support Services; 20% Social Sciences; 9% Biological and Biomedical Sciences; 7% Visual and Performing Arts
Expenses: 2016-2017: $26,742; room/board: $13,322
Financial aid: (404) 681-2800; 80% of undergrads determined to have financial need; average aid package $20,054

Oglethorpe University[1]

Atlanta GA
(404) 364-8307
U.S. News ranking: Nat. Lib. Arts, No. 159
Website: www.oglethorpe.edu
Admissions email: admission@oglethorpe.edu
Private; founded 1835
Application deadline (fall): rolling
Undergraduate student body: N/A full time, N/A part time
Expenses: 2015-2016: $33,800; room/board: $12,180
Financial aid: (404) 364-8356

Paine College[1]
Augusta GA
(706) 821-8320
U.S. News ranking: Nat. Lib. Arts, second tier
Website: www.paine.edu
Admissions email: admissions@paine.edu
Private; founded 1882
Affiliation: Christian Methodist Episcopal and United Methodist Churches
Application deadline (fall): 7/15
Undergraduate student body: N/A full time, N/A part time
Expenses: 2015-2016: $14,224; room/board: $6,662
Financial aid: (706) 821-8262

Piedmont College
Demorest GA
(800) 277-7020
U.S. News ranking: Reg. U. (S), No. 67
Website: www.piedmont.edu
Admissions email: ugrad@piedmont.edu
Private; founded 1897
Affiliation: Nat. Assoc. of Congreg. Christ. Churches & United Church of Christ
Freshman admissions: selective; 2015-2016: 1,135 applied, 647 accepted. Either SAT or ACT required. SAT 25/75 percentile: 870-1100. High school rank: 14% in top tenth, 40% in top quarter, 76% in top half
Early decision deadline: N/A, notification date: N/A
Early action deadline: N/A, notification date: N/A
Application deadline (fall): 7/1
Undergraduate student body: 1,133 full time, 151 part time; 34% male, 66% female; 0% American Indian, 1% Asian, 9% black, 5% Hispanic, 2% multiracial, 0% Pacific Islander, 71% white, 1% international; 91% from in state; 74% live on campus; N/A of students in fraternities, N/A in sororities
Most popular majors: 27% Education, General; 20% Health Professions and Related Programs; 17% Business, Management, Marketing, and Related Support Services; 14% Social Sciences; 10% Visual and Performing Arts
Expenses: 2016-2017: $23,112; room/board: $9,400
Financial aid: (706) 776-0114; 82% of undergrads determined to have financial need; average aid package $18,831

Point University
West Point GA
(706) 385-1202
U.S. News ranking: Reg. Coll. (S), No. 45
Website: www.point.edu
Admissions email: admissions@point.edu
Private; founded 1937
Affiliation: Christian Churches/Churches of Christ
Freshman admissions: less selective; 2015-2016: 862 applied, 423 accepted. Either SAT or ACT required. ACT 25/75 percentile: 17-21. High school rank: N/A
Early decision deadline: N/A, notification date: N/A

Early action deadline: N/A, notification date: N/A
Application deadline (fall): 8/5
Undergraduate student body: 1,191 full time, 391 part time; 50% male, 50% female; 0% American Indian, 0% Asian, 36% black, 6% Hispanic, 4% multiracial, 0% Pacific Islander, 44% white, 1% international; 71% from in state; 30% live on campus; N/A of students in fraternities, N/A in sororities
Most popular majors: Information not available
Expenses: 2016-2017: $19,200; room/board: $7,700
Financial aid: (800) 766-1222

Reinhardt University
Waleska GA
(770) 720-5526
U.S. News ranking: Reg. Coll. (S), No. 29
Website: www.reinhardt.edu/
Admissions email: admissions@reinhardt.edu
Private
Affiliation: United Methodist
Freshman admissions: selective; 2015-2016: 1,158 applied, 1,051 accepted. Either SAT or ACT required. ACT 25/75 percentile: 18-22. High school rank: 8% in top tenth, 30% in top quarter, 64% in top half
Early decision deadline: N/A, notification date: N/A
Early action deadline: N/A, notification date: N/A
Application deadline (fall): 8/15
Undergraduate student body: 1,137 full time, 125 part time; 53% male, 47% female; 1% American Indian, 1% Asian, 19% black, 6% Hispanic, 0% multiracial, 0% Pacific Islander, 68% white, 0% international
Most popular majors: Information not available
Expenses: 2016-2017: $21,644; room/board: $7,948
Financial aid: (770) 720-5667; 70% of undergrads determined to have financial need; average aid package $13,454

Savannah College of Art and Design
Savannah GA
(912) 525-5100
U.S. News ranking: Arts, unranked
Website: www.scad.edu
Admissions email: admission@scad.edu
Private; founded 1978
Freshman admissions: N/A; 2015-2016: 10,303 applied, 7,117 accepted. Either SAT or ACT required. SAT 25/75 percentile: N/A. High school rank: 22% in top tenth, 53% in top quarter, 77% in top half
Early decision deadline: N/A, notification date: N/A
Early action deadline: N/A, notification date: N/A
Application deadline (fall): rolling
Undergraduate student body: 8,372 full time, 1,813 part time; 34% male, 66% female; 1% American Indian, 8% Asian, 11% black, 8% Hispanic, 0% multiracial, 0% Pacific Islander, 52% white, 16% international; 22% from in

state; 42% live on campus; N/A of students in fraternities, N/A in sororities
Most popular majors: 10% Graphic Design; 9% Animation, Interactive Technology, Video Graphics and Special Effects; 6% Photography; 5% Fashion/Apparel Design
Expenses: 2016-2017: $35,690; room/board: $14,804
Financial aid: (912) 525-6104; 51% of undergrads determined to have financial need; average aid package $17,402

Savannah State University
Savannah GA
(912) 356-2181
U.S. News ranking: Reg. U. (S), second tier
Website: www.savannahstate.edu
Admissions email: admissions@savannahstate.edu
Public; founded 1890
Freshman admissions: least selective; 2015-2016: 2,950 applied, 2,438 accepted. Either SAT or ACT required. SAT 25/75 percentile: 770-920. High school rank: N/A
Early decision deadline: N/A, notification date: N/A
Early action deadline: N/A, notification date: N/A
Application deadline (fall): 7/15
Undergraduate student body: 4,062 full time, 583 part time; 42% male, 58% female; 0% American Indian, 0% Asian, 82% black, 8% Hispanic, 3% multiracial, 0% Pacific Islander, 4% white, 1% international; N/A from in state; 61% live on campus; N/A of students in fraternities, N/A in sororities
Most popular majors: 18% Business Administration and Management, General; 14% Biology/Biological Sciences, General; 13% Corrections and Criminal Justice, Other; 9% Political Science and Government, General
Expenses: 2016-2017: $6,616 in state, $19,436 out of state; room/board: $7,390
Financial aid: (912) 356-2253; 96% of undergrads determined to have financial need

Shorter University[1]
Rome GA
(800) 868-6980
U.S. News ranking: Reg. Coll. (S), No. 23
Website: www.shorter.edu
Admissions email: admissions@shorter.edu
Private
Application deadline (fall): N/A
Undergraduate student body: N/A full time, N/A part time
Expenses: 2015-2016: $20,846; room/board: $9,400
Financial aid: (706) 233-7227

South Georgia State College[1]
Douglas GA
(912) 260-4206
U.S. News ranking: Reg. Coll. (S), unranked
Website: www.sgsc.edu/
Admissions email: N/A

Public
Application deadline (fall): N/A
Undergraduate student body: N/A full time, N/A part time
Expenses: 2015-2016: $3,211 in state, $9,286 out of state; room/board: $8,250
Financial aid: N/A

South University[1]
Savannah GA
(912) 201-8000
U.S. News ranking: Reg. U. (S), second tier
Website: www.southuniversity.edu
Admissions email: cshall@southuniversity.edu
Private
Application deadline (fall): N/A
Undergraduate student body: N/A full time, N/A part time
Expenses: 2015-2016: $16,761; room/board: N/A
Financial aid: (912) 201-8000

Spelman College
Atlanta GA
(800) 982-2411
U.S. News ranking: Nat. Lib. Arts, No. 72
Website: www.spelman.edu
Admissions email: admiss@spelman.edu
Private; founded 1881
Freshman admissions: selective; 2015-2016: 5,051 applied, 2,441 accepted. Either SAT or ACT required. SAT 25/75 percentile: 920-1120. High school rank: 23% in top tenth, 62% in top quarter, 84% in top half
Early decision deadline: 11/1, notification date: 12/15
Early action deadline: 11/15, notification date: 12/31
Application deadline (fall): 2/1
Undergraduate student body: 2,090 full time, 54 part time; 0% male, 100% female; 0% American Indian, 0% Asian, 96% black, 0% Hispanic, 2% multiracial, N/A Pacific Islander, 0% white, 1% international; 27% from in state; 70% live on campus; 0% of students in fraternities, 1% in sororities
Most popular majors: 30% Social Sciences; 22% Psychology; 12% Biological and Biomedical Sciences; 9% English Language and Literature/Letters; 4% Mathematics and Statistics
Expenses: 2016-2017: $27,314; room/board: $12,795
Financial aid: (404) 270-5212; 83% of undergrads determined to have financial need; average aid package $14,175

Thomas University
Thomasville GA
(229) 227-6934
U.S. News ranking: Reg. U. (S), second tier
Website: www.thomasu.edu
Admissions email: rgagliano@thomasu.edu
Private; founded 1950
Freshman admissions: selective; 2015-2016: 361 applied, 117 accepted. Neither SAT nor ACT required. ACT 25/75 percentile: 20-24. High school rank: N/A
Early decision deadline: N/A, notification date: N/A

Early action deadline: N/A, notification date: N/A
Application deadline (fall): rolling
Undergraduate student body: 495 full time, 309 part time; 46% male, 54% female; 0% American Indian, 1% Asian, 24% black, 4% Hispanic, 0% multiracial, 0% Pacific Islander, 47% white, 5% international
Most popular majors: 30% Criminal Justice/Law Enforcement Administration; 23% Registered Nursing, Nursing Administration, Nursing Research and Clinical Nursing, Other; 16% Criminal Justice/Law Enforcement Administration; 14% Clinical/Medical Laboratory Science and Allied Professions, Other; 6% Business Administration and Management, General
Expenses: 2016-2017: $16,940; room/board: $9,820
Financial aid: (229) 227-6925; 89% of undergrads determined to have financial need; average aid package $10,500

Toccoa Falls College
Toccoa Falls GA
(888) 785-5624
U.S. News ranking: Reg. Coll. (S), No. 15
Website: www.tfc.edu
Admissions email: admissions@tfc.edu
Private; founded 1907
Affiliation: Christian and Missionary Alliance
Freshman admissions: selective; 2015-2016: 759 applied, 345 accepted. Either SAT or ACT required. SAT 25/75 percentile: 860-1090. High school rank: 25% in top tenth, 43% in top quarter, 65% in top half
Early decision deadline: N/A, notification date: N/A
Early action deadline: N/A, notification date: N/A
Application deadline (fall): rolling
Undergraduate student body: 732 full time, 205 part time; 46% male, 54% female; 0% American Indian, 9% Asian, 8% black, 4% Hispanic, 2% multiracial, 0% Pacific Islander, 76% white, 2% international; 62% from in state; 62% live on campus; 0% of students in fraternities, 0% in sororities
Most popular majors: 18% Missions/Missionary Studies and Missiology; 16% Counseling Psychology; 6% Business Administration and Management, General; 6% Elementary Education and Teaching; 6% Religious Education
Expenses: 2016-2017: $21,414; room/board: $7,628
Financial aid: (706) 886-6831; 87% of undergrads determined to have financial need; average aid package $18,438

Truett McConnell College
Cleveland GA
(706) 865-2134
U.S. News ranking: Reg. Coll. (S), second tier
Website: www.truett.edu
Admissions email: admissions@truett.edu

Private; founded 1946
Affiliation: Southern Baptist
Freshman admissions: less selective; 2015-2016: 485 applied, 442 accepted. Either SAT or ACT required. SAT 25/75 percentile: 838-1020. High school rank: 13% in top tenth, 33% in top quarter, 61% in top half
Early decision deadline: N/A, notification date: N/A
Early action deadline: N/A, notification date: N/A
Application deadline (fall): 8/1
Undergraduate student body: 733 full time, 1,264 part time; 45% male, 55% female; N/A American Indian, 1% Asian, 8% black, 4% Hispanic, N/A multiracial, N/A Pacific Islander, 84% white, 2% international; 92% from in state; 76% live on campus; N/A of students in fraternities, N/A in sororities
Most popular majors: 23% Theology and Religious Vocations; 22% Business, Management, Marketing, and Related Support Services; 18% Psychology; 11% Education; 9% Health Professions and Related Programs
Expenses: 2016-2017: $18,510; room/board: $7,220
Financial aid: (800) 226-8621; 87% of undergrads determined to have financial need; average aid package $14,760

University of Georgia
Athens GA
(706) 542-8776
U.S. News ranking: Nat. U., No. 56
Website: www.admissions.uga.edu
Admissions email: adm-info@uga.edu
Public; founded 1785
Freshman admissions: more selective; 2015-2016: 21,945 applied, 11,604 accepted. Either SAT or ACT required. SAT 25/75 percentile: 1150-1330. High school rank: 53% in top tenth, 93% in top quarter, 99% in top half
Early decision deadline: N/A, notification date: N/A
Early action deadline: 10/15, notification date: 12/1
Application deadline (fall): 1/15
Undergraduate student body: 25,906 full time, 1,641 part time; 43% male, 57% female; 0% American Indian, 10% Asian, 7% black, 5% Hispanic, 4% multiracial, 0% Pacific Islander, 71% white, 2% international; 92% from in state; 33% live on campus; 22% of students in fraternities, 31% in sororities
Most popular majors: 6% Psychology, General; 6% Finance, General; 6% Biology/Biological Sciences, General; 4% Marketing/Marketing Management, General; 3% Accounting
Expenses: 2016-2017: $11,634 in state, $29,844 out of state; room/board: $9,616
Financial aid: (706) 542-6147; 44% of undergrads determined to have financial need; average aid package $11,620

University of North Georgia
Dahlonega GA
(706) 864-1800
U.S. News ranking: Reg. U. (S), No. 72
Website: ung.edu/
Admissions email: bacheloradmissions@ung.edu
Public; founded 1873
Freshman admissions: selective; 2015-2016: 5,623 applied, 3,622 accepted. Either SAT or ACT required. SAT 25/75 percentile: 1010-1190. High school rank: 20% in top tenth, 42% in top quarter, 95% in top half
Early decision deadline: N/A, notification date: N/A
Early action deadline: 11/15, notification date: 12/15
Application deadline (fall): 2/15
Undergraduate student body: 11,756 full time, 4,973 part time; 45% male, 55% female; 0% American Indian, 3% Asian, 4% black, 11% Hispanic, 3% multiracial, 0% Pacific Islander, 77% white, 2% international; 97% from in state; 13% live on campus; 4% of students in fraternities, 6% in sororities
Most popular majors: 25% Education; 23% Business, Management, Marketing, and Related Support Services; 7% Biological and Biomedical Sciences; 7% Social Sciences; 6% Psychology
Expenses: 2016-2017: $7,178 in state, $20,720 out of state; room/board: $9,494
Financial aid: (706) 864-1412; 61% of undergrads determined to have financial need; average aid package $13,652

University of West Georgia
Carrollton GA
(678) 839-5600
U.S. News ranking: Nat. U., second tier
Website: www.westga.edu
Admissions email: admiss@westga.edu
Public; founded 1906
Freshman admissions: selective; 2015-2016: 7,679 applied, 4,381 accepted. Either SAT or ACT required. SAT 25/75 percentile: 860-1020. High school rank: N/A
Early decision deadline: N/A, notification date: N/A
Early action deadline: N/A, notification date: N/A
Application deadline (fall): 6/1
Undergraduate student body: 8,816 full time, 1,937 part time; 37% male, 63% female; 0% American Indian, 1% Asian, 37% black, 5% Hispanic, 3% multiracial, 0% Pacific Islander, 50% white, 1% international; 97% from in state; 29% live on campus; 3% of students in fraternities, 3% in sororities
Most popular majors: 22% Business, Management, Marketing, and Related Support Services; 15% Social Sciences; 14% Health Professions and Related Programs; 13% Education; 9% Psychology

Expenses: 2015-2016: $7,188 in state, $20,406 out of state; room/board: $8,998
Financial aid: (678) 839-6421; 76% of undergrads determined to have financial need; average aid package $8,927

Valdosta State University
Valdosta GA
(229) 333-5791
U.S. News ranking: Nat. U., second tier
Website: www.valdosta.edu
Admissions email: admissions@valdosta.edu
Public; founded 1906
Freshman admissions: selective; 2015-2016: 5,564 applied, 2,806 accepted. Either SAT or ACT required. SAT 25/75 percentile: 910-1080. High school rank: N/A
Early decision deadline: N/A, notification date: N/A
Early action deadline: N/A, notification date: N/A
Application deadline (fall): 6/15
Undergraduate student body: 7,256 full time, 1,540 part time; 41% male, 59% female; 0% American Indian, 1% Asian, 36% black, 5% Hispanic, 3% multiracial, 0% Pacific Islander, 50% white, 3% international; 93% from in state; 27% live on campus; 3% of students in fraternities, 4% in sororities
Most popular majors: 21% Business, Management, Marketing, and Related Support Services; 11% Education; 11% Health Professions and Related Programs; 9% Psychology
Expenses: 2016-2017: $7,342 in state, $20,560 out of state; room/board: $8,262
Financial aid: (229) 333-5935; 73% of undergrads determined to have financial need; average aid package $15,994

Wesleyan College
Macon GA
(800) 447-6610
U.S. News ranking: Nat. Lib. Arts, No. 140
Website: www.wesleyancollege.edu
Admissions email: admissions@wesleyancollege.edu
Private; founded 1836
Affiliation: United Methodist
Freshman admissions: selective; 2015-2016: 848 applied, 353 accepted. Either SAT or ACT required. SAT 25/75 percentile: 920-1140. High school rank: N/A
Early decision deadline: 11/15, notification date: 12/15
Early action deadline: 2/15, notification date: 3/15
Application deadline (fall): rolling
Undergraduate student body: 515 full time, 145 part time; 0% male, 100% female; 0% American Indian, 2% Asian, 27% black, 4% Hispanic, 3% multiracial, 0% Pacific Islander, 39% white, 24% international; 93% from in state; 85% live on campus; 0% of students in fraternities, 0% in sororities
Most popular majors: 22% Business Administration and Management, General; 19%

Registered Nursing/Registered Nurse; 9% Psychology, General; 8% Biology/Biological Sciences, General; 8% Social Sciences, General
Expenses: 2016-2017: $21,750; room/board: $9,290
Financial aid: (888) 665-5723; 69% of undergrads determined to have financial need; average aid package $19,728

Young Harris College
Young Harris GA
(706) 379-3111
U.S. News ranking: Nat. Lib. Arts, No. 174
Website: www.yhc.edu
Admissions email: N/A
Private; founded 1886
Affiliation: United Methodist
Freshman admissions: selective; 2015-2016: 2,232 applied, 1,165 accepted. Either SAT or ACT required. SAT 25/75 percentile: 875-1080. High school rank: 8% in top tenth, 23% in top quarter, 70% in top half
Early decision deadline: N/A, notification date: N/A
Early action deadline: N/A, notification date: N/A
Application deadline (fall): rolling
Undergraduate student body: 1,153 full time, 51 part time; 43% male, 57% female; 0% American Indian, 1% Asian, 7% black, 3% Hispanic, 2% multiracial, 0% Pacific Islander, 76% white, 8% international
Most popular majors: 20% Biology/Biological Sciences, General; 19% Business Administration and Management, General; 11% Psychology, General; 8% History, General
Expenses: 2015-2016: $28,012; room/board: $9,698
Financial aid: N/A

HAWAII

Brigham Young University–Hawaii[1]
Laie Oahu HI
(808) 293-3738
U.S. News ranking: Reg. Coll. (W), No. 14
Website: www.byuh.edu
Admissions email: admissions@byuh.edu
Private
Application deadline (fall): N/A
Undergraduate student body: N/A full time, N/A part time
Expenses: 2015-2016: $5,100; room/board: $5,802
Financial aid: (808) 293-3530

Chaminade University of Honolulu
Honolulu HI
(808) 735-4735
U.S. News ranking: Reg. U. (W), No. 52
Website: www.chaminade.edu
Admissions email: admissions@chaminade.edu
Private; founded 1955
Affiliation: Roman Catholic
Freshman admissions: selective; 2015-2016: 895 applied, 734 accepted. Either SAT or ACT required. SAT 25/75 percentile:

865-1060. High school rank: 17% in top tenth, 50% in top quarter, 82% in top half
Early decision deadline: N/A, notification date: N/A
Early action deadline: N/A, notification date: N/A
Application deadline (fall): rolling
Undergraduate student body: 1,200 full time, 26 part time; 29% male, 71% female; 1% American Indian, 38% Asian, 3% black, 4% Hispanic, 15% multiracial, 20% Pacific Islander, 13% white, 2% international; 68% from in state; 25% live on campus; N/A of students in fraternities, N/A in sororities
Most popular majors: 25% Criminal Justice/Safety Studies; 21% Registered Nursing/Registered Nurse; 11% Business Administration and Management, General; 9% Biology/Biological Sciences, General; 9% Psychology, General
Expenses: 2016-2017: $23,310; room/board: $12,690
Financial aid: (808) 735-4780; 71% of undergrads determined to have financial need; average aid package $18,794

Hawaii Pacific University
Honolulu HI
(808) 544-0238
U.S. News ranking: Reg. U. (W), No. 61
Website: www.hpu.edu
Admissions email: admissions@hpu.edu
Private; founded 1965
Freshman admissions: selective; 2015-2016: 4,631 applied, 3,153 accepted. Either SAT or ACT required. SAT 25/75 percentile: 876-1110. High school rank: 23% in top tenth, 55% in top quarter, 83% in top half
Early decision deadline: N/A, notification date: N/A
Early action deadline: 11/15, notification date: 12/31
Application deadline (fall): rolling
Undergraduate student body: 2,826 full time, 1,167 part time; 42% male, 58% female; 0% American Indian, 17% Asian, 5% black, 15% Hispanic, 16% multiracial, 2% Pacific Islander, 27% white, 11% international; 61% from in state; 11% live on campus; N/A of students in fraternities, N/A in sororities
Most popular majors: 26% Health Professions and Related Programs; 25% Business, Management, Marketing, and Related Support Services; 6% Psychology; 6% Biological and Biomedical Sciences
Expenses: 2016-2017: $23,440; room/board: $13,898
Financial aid: (808) 544-0253; 52% of undergrads determined to have financial need; average aid package $14,494

University of Hawaii–Hilo

Hilo HI
(800) 897-4456
U.S. News ranking: Reg. U. (W), No. 61
Website: www.uhh.hawaii.edu
Admissions email: uhhadm@hawaii.edu
Public; founded 1947
Freshman admissions: selective; 2015-2016: 1,534 applied, 1,091 accepted. Either SAT or ACT required. SAT 25/75 percentile: 830-1050. High school rank: 23% in top tenth, 50% in top quarter, 84% in top half
Early decision deadline: N/A, notification date: N/A
Early action deadline: N/A, notification date: N/A
Application deadline (fall): 7/1
Undergraduate student body: 2,548 full time, 712 part time; 39% male, 61% female; 1% American Indian, 17% Asian, 1% black, 13% Hispanic, 31% multiracial, 11% Pacific Islander, 22% white, 4% international; 72% from in state; N/A live on campus; N/A of students in fraternities, N/A in sororities
Most popular majors: 19% Health Professions and Related Programs; 11% Social Sciences; 10% Psychology; 9% Biological and Biomedical Sciences; 7% Business, Management, Marketing, and Related Support Services
Expenses: 2016-2017: $7,650 in state, $20,610 out of state; room/board: $10,418
Financial aid: (808) 974-7323

University of Hawaii–Manoa

Honolulu HI
(808) 956-8975
U.S. News ranking: Nat. U., No. 169
Website: www.manoa.hawaii.edu/
Admissions email: ar-info@hawaii.edu
Public; founded 1907
Freshman admissions: selective; 2015-2016: 7,658 applied, 6,234 accepted. Either SAT or ACT required. SAT 25/75 percentile: 980-1190. High school rank: 25% in top tenth, 56% in top quarter, 90% in top half
Early decision deadline: N/A, notification date: N/A
Early action deadline: N/A, notification date: N/A
Application deadline (fall): 3/1
Undergraduate student body: 11,413 full time, 2,276 part time; 45% male, 55% female; 0% American Indian, 41% Asian, 2% black, 2% Hispanic, 15% multiracial, 17% Pacific Islander, 20% white, 3% international; 74% from in state; 25% live on campus; 1% of students in fraternities, 1% in sororities
Most popular majors: 19% Business, Management, Marketing, and Related Support Services; 9% Social Sciences; 7% Biological and Biomedical Sciences; 7% Engineering; 7% Health Professions and Related Programs

Expenses: 2016-2017: $11,732 in state, $33,764 out of state; room/board: $13,030
Financial aid: (808) 956-7251; 57% of undergrads determined to have financial need; average aid package $14,759

University of Hawaii–Maui College[1]

Kahului HI
(800) 479-6692
U.S. News ranking: Reg. Coll. (W), unranked
Website: maui.hawaii.edu/
Admissions email: N/A
Public
Application deadline (fall): N/A
Undergraduate student body: N/A full time, N/A part time
Expenses: 2015-2016: $3,006 in state, $7,998 out of state; room/board: N/A
Financial aid: (808) 984-3277

University of Hawaii–West Oahu[1]

Kapolei HI
(808) 689-2900
U.S. News ranking: Reg. Coll. (W), unranked
Website: www.uhwo.hawaii.edu
Admissions email: uhwo.admissions@hawaii.edu
Public; founded 1976
Application deadline (fall): 8/1
Undergraduate student body: N/A full time, N/A part time
Expenses: 2015-2016: $7,380 in state, $19,620 out of state; room/board: N/A
Financial aid: (808) 689-2900

IDAHO

Boise State University

Boise ID
(208) 426-1156
U.S. News ranking: Nat. U., second tier
Website: www.BoiseState.edu
Admissions email: bsuinfo@boisestate.edu
Public; founded 1932
Freshman admissions: selective; 2015-2016: 8,155 applied, 6,490 accepted. Neither SAT nor ACT required. SAT 25/75 percentile: 920-1140. High school rank: 15% in top tenth, 40% in top quarter, 75% in top half
Early decision deadline: N/A, notification date: N/A
Early action deadline: N/A, notification date: N/A
Application deadline (fall): rolling
Undergraduate student body: 12,034 full time, 7,088 part time; 46% male, 54% female; 1% American Indian, 2% Asian, 2% black, 11% Hispanic, 4% multiracial, 0% Pacific Islander, 74% white, 5% international; 76% from in state; 14% live on campus; 1% of students in fraternities, 2% in sororities
Most popular majors: 21% Health Professions and Related Programs; 19% Business, Management, Marketing, and Related Support Services; 5% Engineering; 5% Psychology

Expenses: 2016-2017: $7,080 in state, $21,530 out of state; room/board: $7,780
Financial aid: (208) 426-1540; 60% of undergrads determined to have financial need; average aid package $9,457

Brigham Young University–Idaho[1]

Rexburg ID
(208) 496-1036
U.S. News ranking: Reg. Coll. (W), No. 10
Website: www.byui.edu
Admissions email: admissions@byui.edu
Private
Application deadline (fall): N/A
Undergraduate student body: N/A full time, N/A part time
Expenses: 2015-2016: $3,830; room/board: $4,850
Financial aid: (208) 496-1600

College of Idaho

Caldwell ID
(800) 224-3246
U.S. News ranking: Nat. Lib. Arts, No. 168
Website: www.collegeofidaho.edu
Admissions email: admissions@collegeofidaho.edu
Private; founded 1891
Freshman admissions: selective; 2015-2016: 955 applied, 863 accepted. Neither SAT nor ACT required. SAT 25/75 percentile: 930-1190. High school rank: 23% in top tenth, 27% in top quarter, 74% in top half
Early decision deadline: N/A, notification date: N/A
Early action deadline: 11/16, notification date: 12/21
Application deadline (fall): 2/16
Undergraduate student body: 1,007 full time, 32 part time; 49% male, 51% female; 1% American Indian, 2% Asian, 2% black, 14% Hispanic, 3% multiracial, 1% Pacific Islander, 66% white, 7% international; 75% from in state; 59% live on campus; 17% of students in fraternities, 18% in sororities
Most popular majors: 15% Business, Management, Marketing, and Related Support Services; 13% Psychology; 13% Social Sciences; 8% Health Professions and Related Programs; 8% Mathematics and Statistics
Expenses: 2016-2017: $27,425; room/board: $8,990
Financial aid: (208) 459-5307; 70% of undergrads determined to have financial need; average aid package $24,124

Idaho State University[1]

Pocatello ID
(208) 282-2475
U.S. News ranking: Nat. U., unranked
Website: www.isu.edu
Admissions email: info@isu.edu
Public
Application deadline (fall): N/A
Undergraduate student body: N/A full time, N/A part time

Expenses: 2015-2016: $6,784 in state, $20,182 out of state; room/board: $6,338
Financial aid: (208) 282-2756

Lewis-Clark State College

Lewiston ID
(208) 792-2210
U.S. News ranking: Reg. Coll. (W), No. 23
Website: www.lcsc.edu
Admissions email: admissions@lcsc.edu
Public; founded 1893
Freshman admissions: less selective; 2015-2016: 1,117 applied, 1,104 accepted. Neither SAT nor ACT required. SAT 25/75 percentile: 820-1030. High school rank: 6% in top tenth, 23% in top quarter, 46% in top half
Early decision deadline: N/A, notification date: N/A
Early action deadline: N/A, notification date: N/A
Application deadline (fall): 8/8
Undergraduate student body: 2,274 full time, 1,259 part time; 38% male, 62% female; 4% American Indian, 1% Asian, 1% black, 6% Hispanic, 2% multiracial, 0% Pacific Islander, 81% white, 3% international; 78% from in state; 14% live on campus; N/A of students in fraternities, N/A in sororities
Most popular majors: 24% Health Professions and Related Programs; 23% Business, Management, Marketing, and Related Support Services; 10% Public Administration and Social Service Professions; 9% Education; 6% Liberal Arts and Sciences, General Studies and Humanities
Expenses: 2016-2017: $6,156 in state, $17,656 out of state; room/board: $7,392
Financial aid: (208) 792-2224; 74% of undergrads determined to have financial need; average aid package $8,242

Northwest Nazarene University

Nampa ID
(208) 467-8000
U.S. News ranking: Reg. U. (W), No. 44
Website: www.nnu.edu
Admissions email: Admissions@nnu.edu
Private; founded 1913
Affiliation: Church of the Nazarene
Freshman admissions: selective; 2015-2016: 1,589 applied, 870 accepted. Either SAT or ACT required. SAT 25/75 percentile: 920-1150. High school rank: 26% in top tenth, 52% in top quarter, 80% in top half
Early decision deadline: N/A, notification date: N/A
Early action deadline: 12/15, notification date: 1/15
Application deadline (fall): 8/15
Undergraduate student body: 1,170 full time, 347 part time; 43% male, 57% female; 1% American Indian, 2% Asian, 2% black, 7% Hispanic, 4% multiracial, 0% Pacific Islander, 76% white, 3% international; 56% from in state; 70% live on campus; N/A

of students in fraternities, N/A in sororities
Most popular majors: 18% Business, Management, Marketing, and Related Support Services; 15% Health Professions and Related Programs; 8% Education; 8% Philosophy and Religious Studies; 6% Biological and Biomedical Sciences
Expenses: 2016-2017: $28,550; room/board: $6,800
Financial aid: (208) 467-8347; 80% of undergrads determined to have financial need; average aid package $18,806

University of Idaho

Moscow ID
(888) 884-3246
U.S. News ranking: Nat. U., No. 171
Website: www.uidaho.edu/admissions
Admissions email: admissions@uidaho.edu
Public; founded 1889
Freshman admissions: selective; 2015-2016: 6,212 applied, 4,476 accepted. Either SAT or ACT required. SAT 25/75 percentile: 940-1170. High school rank: 17% in top tenth, 42% in top quarter, 74% in top half
Early decision deadline: N/A, notification date: N/A
Early action deadline: N/A, notification date: N/A
Application deadline (fall): 8/1
Undergraduate student body: 7,400 full time, 1,716 part time; 52% male, 48% female; 1% American Indian, 1% Asian, 1% black, 10% Hispanic, 4% multiracial, 0% Pacific Islander, 76% white, 5% international; 78% from in state; 42% live on campus; 12% of students in fraternities, 10% in sororities
Most popular majors: 8% Psychology, General; 4% General Studies; 4% Marketing/Marketing Management, General; 4% Mechanical Engineering; 3% Sociology
Expenses: 2016-2017: $7,232 in state, $22,040 out of state; room/board: $8,354
Financial aid: (208) 885-6312; 64% of undergrads determined to have financial need; average aid package $13,598

ILLINOIS

American Academy of Art[1]

Chicago IL
(312) 461-0600
U.S. News ranking: Arts, unranked
Website: www.aaart.edu
Admissions email: N/A
For-profit
Application deadline (fall): N/A
Undergraduate student body: N/A full time, N/A part time
Expenses: 2015-2016: $31,220; room/board: N/A
Financial aid: N/A

American InterContinental University[1]
Hoffman Estates IL
(855) 377-1888
U.S. News ranking: Reg. U. (Mid. W), unranked
Website: www.aiuniv.edu
Admissions email: N/A
For-profit
Application deadline (fall): N/A
Undergraduate student body: N/A full time, N/A part time
Expenses: 2015-2016: $11,004; room/board: N/A
Financial aid: N/A

Augustana College
Rock Island IL
(800) 798-8100
U.S. News ranking: Nat. Lib. Arts, No. 99
Website: www.augustana.edu
Admissions email: admissions@augustana.edu
Private; founded 1860
Affiliation: Evangelical Lutheran Church in America
Freshman admissions: more selective; 2015-2016: 6,712 applied, 3,312 accepted. Neither SAT nor ACT required. ACT 25/75 percentile: 23-28. High school rank: 27% in top tenth, 62% in top quarter, 90% in top half
Early decision deadline: 11/1, notification date: 11/15
Early action deadline: 11/1, notification date: 12/1
Application deadline (fall): rolling
Undergraduate student body: 2,460 full time, 18 part time; 42% male, 58% female; 0% American Indian, 2% Asian, 4% black, 10% Hispanic, 4% multiracial, 0% Pacific Islander, 76% white, 4% international; 84% from in state; 70% live on campus; 25% of students in fraternities, 37% in sororities
Most popular majors: 23% Biology/Biological Sciences, General; 17% Business Administration and Management, General; 10% Psychology, General; 6% Communication Sciences and Disorders, General
Expenses: 2016-2017: $39,621; room/board: $10,037
Financial aid: (309) 794-7207; 77% of undergrads determined to have financial need; average aid package $29,389

Aurora University[1]
Aurora IL
(800) 742-5281
U.S. News ranking: Reg. U. (Mid. W), second tier
Website: www.aurora.edu
Admissions email: admission@aurora.edu
Private
Application deadline (fall): N/A
Undergraduate student body: N/A full time, N/A part time
Expenses: 2015-2016: $22,080; room/board: $9,052
Financial aid: (630) 844-5533

Benedictine University
Lisle IL
(630) 829-6000
U.S. News ranking: Nat. U., No. 220
Website: www.ben.edu
Admissions email: admissions@ben.edu
Private; founded 1887
Affiliation: Roman Catholic
Freshman admissions: selective; 2015-2016: 1,980 applied, 1,560 accepted. Either SAT or ACT required. ACT 25/75 percentile: 19-24. High school rank: 12% in top tenth, 30% in top quarter, 68% in top half
Early decision deadline: N/A, notification date: N/A
Early action deadline: N/A, notification date: N/A
Application deadline (fall): rolling
Undergraduate student body: 2,756 full time, 591 part time; 44% male, 56% female; 0% American Indian, 16% Asian, 9% black, 12% Hispanic, 0% multiracial, 0% Pacific Islander, 45% white, 1% international; 91% from in state; 23% live on campus; 0% of students in fraternities, 0% in sororities
Most popular majors: 25% Business, Management, Marketing, and Related Support Services; 25% Health Professions and Related Programs; 10% Psychology; 8% Social Sciences; 7% Biological and Biomedical Sciences
Expenses: 2016-2017: $32,170; room/board: $9,200
Financial aid: (630) 829-6108; 77% of undergrads determined to have financial need; average aid package $20,614

Blackburn College
Carlinville IL
(800) 233-3550
U.S. News ranking: Reg. Coll. (Mid. W), No. 36
Website: www.blackburn.edu
Admissions email: admit@mail.blackburn.edu
Private; founded 1837
Affiliation: Presbyterian
Freshman admissions: selective; 2015-2016: 1,078 applied, 598 accepted. Either SAT or ACT required. ACT 25/75 percentile: 19-24. High school rank: 14% in top tenth, 36% in top quarter, 67% in top half
Early decision deadline: N/A, notification date: N/A
Early action deadline: N/A, notification date: N/A
Application deadline (fall): rolling
Undergraduate student body: 561 full time, 24 part time; 46% male, 54% female; 0% American Indian, 1% Asian, 13% black, 2% Hispanic, 3% multiracial, 0% Pacific Islander, 80% white, N/A international; 90% from in state; 68% live on campus; N/A of students in fraternities, N/A in sororities
Most popular majors: 26% Business Administration, Management and Operations, Other; 14% Biology/Biological Sciences, General; 9% Criminal Justice/Safety Studies; 8% Sport and Fitness Administration/Management; 7% Accounting

Expenses: 2016-2017: $21,162; room/board: $7,364
Financial aid: (800) 233-3550; 90% of undergrads determined to have financial need; average aid package $18,678

Bradley University
Peoria IL
(800) 447-6460
U.S. News ranking: Reg. U. (Mid. W), No. 6
Website: www.bradley.edu
Admissions email: admissions@bradley.edu
Private; founded 1897
Freshman admissions: more selective; 2015-2016: 9,186 applied, 6,033 accepted. Either SAT or ACT required. ACT 25/75 percentile: 23-28. High school rank: 22% in top tenth, 58% in top quarter, 89% in top half
Early decision deadline: N/A, notification date: N/A
Early action deadline: N/A, notification date: N/A
Application deadline (fall): rolling
Undergraduate student body: 4,222 full time, 217 part time; 49% male, 51% female; 0% American Indian, 3% Asian, 5% black, 6% Hispanic, 1% multiracial, 0% Pacific Islander, 64% white, 1% international; 84% from in state; 51% live on campus; 34% of students in fraternities, 36% in sororities
Most popular majors: 17% Business, Management, Marketing, and Related Support Services; 15% Engineering; 13% Health Professions and Related Programs; 8% Education
Expenses: 2016-2017: $32,120; room/board: $10,010
Financial aid: (309) 677-3089; 72% of undergrads determined to have financial need; average aid package $20,463

Chicago State University[1]
Chicago IL
(773) 995-2513
U.S. News ranking: Reg. U. (Mid. W), second tier
Website: www.csu.edu
Admissions email: ug-admissions@csu.edu
Public; founded 1867
Application deadline (fall): rolling
Undergraduate student body: N/A full time, N/A part time
Expenses: 2015-2016: $9,994 in state; $16,954 out of state; room/board: $8,723
Financial aid: (773) 995-2304

Columbia College Chicago[1]
Chicago IL
(312) 344-7130
U.S. News ranking: Reg. U. (Mid. W), second tier
Website: www.colum.edu
Admissions email: admissions@colum.edu
Private
Application deadline (fall): N/A
Undergraduate student body: N/A full time, N/A part time
Expenses: 2015-2016: $24,344; room/board: $13,050
Financial aid: (312) 344-7054

DePaul University
Chicago IL
(312) 362-8300
U.S. News ranking: Nat. U., No. 124
Website: www.depaul.edu
Admissions email: admission@depaul.edu
Private; founded 1898
Affiliation: Roman Catholic
Freshman admissions: more selective; 2015-2016: 19,628 applied, 14,129 accepted. Neither SAT nor ACT required. ACT 25/75 percentile: 22-28. High school rank: 20% in top tenth, 54% in top quarter, 87% in top half
Early decision deadline: N/A, notification date: N/A
Early action deadline: 11/15, notification date: 1/15
Application deadline (fall): 2/1
Undergraduate student body: 13,664 full time, 2,297 part time; 47% male, 53% female; 0% American Indian, 8% Asian, 8% black, 18% Hispanic, 4% multiracial, 0% Pacific Islander, 55% white, 3% international; 77% from in state; 17% live on campus; 3% of students in fraternities, 6% in sororities
Most popular majors: 29% Business, Management, Marketing, and Related Support Services; 10% Liberal Arts and Sciences, General Studies and Humanities; 7% Social Sciences; 6% Computer and Information Sciences and Support Services
Expenses: 2016-2017: $37,626; room/board: $13,387
Financial aid: (312) 362-8091; 69% of undergrads determined to have financial need; average aid package $22,453

DeVry University
Downers Grove IL
(866) 338-7940
U.S. News ranking: Reg. U. (Mid. W), second tier
Website: www.devry.edu
Admissions email: N/A
For-profit; founded 1931
Freshman admissions: less selective; 2015-2016: N/A applied, N/A accepted. Neither SAT nor ACT required. ACT 25/75 percentile: N/A. High school rank: N/A
Early decision deadline: N/A, notification date: N/A
Early action deadline: N/A, notification date: N/A
Application deadline (fall): rolling
Undergraduate student body: 13,429 full time, 20,142 part time; 51% male, 49% female; 1% American Indian, 5% Asian, 22% black, 18% Hispanic, 1% multiracial, 1% Pacific Islander, 41% white, 1% international
Most popular majors: 42% Business Administration, Management and Operations, Other; 21% Business Administration and Management, General; 11% Computer Systems Analysis/Analyst; 8% Computer Systems Networking and Telecommunications; 4% Web Page, Digital/Multimedia and Information Resources Design
Expenses: 2015-2016: $19,568; room/board: $10,720
Financial aid: N/A

Dominican University
River Forest IL
(708) 524-6800
U.S. News ranking: Reg. U. (Mid. W), No. 27
Website: public.dom.edu/
Admissions email: domadmis@dom.edu
Private; founded 1901
Affiliation: Roman Catholic
Freshman admissions: selective; 2015-2016: 4,161 applied, 2,611 accepted. Either SAT or ACT required. ACT 25/75 percentile: 19-24. High school rank: 23% in top tenth, 51% in top quarter, 83% in top half
Early decision deadline: N/A, notification date: N/A
Early action deadline: N/A, notification date: N/A
Application deadline (fall): 7/1
Undergraduate student body: 2,076 full time, 196 part time; 34% male, 66% female; 0% American Indian, 3% Asian, 7% black, 48% Hispanic, 1% multiracial, 0% Pacific Islander, 38% white, 3% international; 93% from in state; 26% live on campus; 0% of students in fraternities, 0% in sororities
Most popular majors: 23% Business, Management, Marketing, and Related Support Services; 15% Health Professions and Related Programs; 10% Psychology; 8% Social Sciences; 4% Visual and Performing Arts
Expenses: 2016-2017: $31,570; room/board: $9,652
Financial aid: (708) 524-6809; 83% of undergrads determined to have financial need; average aid package $23,287

Eastern Illinois University
Charleston IL
(877) 581-2348
U.S. News ranking: Reg. U. (Mid. W), No. 40
Website: www.eiu.edu
Admissions email: admissions@eiu.edu
Public; founded 1895
Freshman admissions: selective; 2015-2016: 9,103 applied, 4,571 accepted. Either SAT or ACT required. ACT 25/75 percentile: 19-24. High school rank: 9% in top tenth, 31% in top quarter, 69% in top half
Early decision deadline: N/A, notification date: N/A
Early action deadline: N/A, notification date: N/A
Application deadline (fall): 8/15
Undergraduate student body: 6,255 full time, 947 part time; 40% male, 60% female; 0% American Indian, 1% Asian, 19% black, 6% Hispanic, 2% multiracial, 0% Pacific Islander, 68% white, 1% international; 96% from in state; 39% live on campus; 19% of students in fraternities, 18% in sororities
Most popular majors: 11% Business, Management, Marketing, and Related Support Services; 11% Education; 11% Parks, Recreation, Leisure, and Fitness Studies; 10% Liberal Arts and Sciences, General Studies and Humanities

Expenses: 2016-2017: $11,580 in state, $13,740 out of state; room/board: $9,546
Financial aid: (217) 581-3713; 68% of undergrads determined to have financial need; average aid package $11,574

East-West University[1]

Chicago IL
(312) 939-0111
U.S. News ranking: Nat. Lib. Arts, second tier
Website: www.eastwest.edu
Admissions email: seeyou@eastwest.edu
Private; founded 1980
Application deadline (fall): rolling
Undergraduate student body: N/A full time, N/A part time
Expenses: 2015-2016: $20,145; room/board: $13,491
Financial aid: (312) 939-0111

Elmhurst College

Elmhurst IL
(630) 617-3400
U.S. News ranking: Reg. U. (Mid. W), No. 10
Website: www.elmhurst.edu
Admissions email: admit@elmhurst.edu
Private; founded 1871
Affiliation: United Church of Christ
Freshman admissions: more selective; 2015-2016: 3,620 applied, 1,983 accepted. Either SAT or ACT required. ACT 25/75 percentile: 21-26. High school rank: 23% in top tenth, 54% in top quarter, 86% in top half
Early decision deadline: N/A, notification date: N/A
Early action deadline: N/A, notification date: N/A
Application deadline (fall): rolling
Undergraduate student body: 2,677 full time, 163 part time; 40% male, 60% female; 0% American Indian, 6% Asian, 5% black, 17% Hispanic, 3% multiracial, 0% Pacific Islander, 67% white, 0% international; 91% from in state; 32% live on campus; 10% of students in fraternities, 16% in sororities
Most popular majors: 21% Business, Management, Marketing, and Related Support Services; 14% Health Professions and Related Programs; 11% Psychology; 8% Education; 7% English Language and Literature/Letters
Expenses: 2016-2017: $35,500; room/board: $10,078
Financial aid: (630) 617-3075; 75% of undergrads determined to have financial need; average aid package $26,552

Eureka College

Eureka IL
(309) 467-6350
U.S. News ranking: Reg. Coll. (Mid. W), No. 26
Website: www.eureka.edu
Admissions email: admissions@eureka.edu
Private; founded 1855
Affiliation: Christian Church (Disciples of Christ)
Freshman admissions: selective; 2015-2016: 1,164 applied, 759 accepted. Either SAT or ACT required. ACT 25/75 percentile:

18-29. High school rank: 19% in top tenth, 35% in top quarter, 67% in top half
Early decision deadline: N/A, notification date: N/A
Early action deadline: N/A, notification date: N/A
Application deadline (fall): 8/1
Undergraduate student body: 657 full time, 38 part time; 45% male, 55% female; 0% American Indian, 1% Asian, 5% black, 3% Hispanic, 4% multiracial, 0% Pacific Islander, 84% white, 1% international; 95% from in state; 66% live on campus; 25% of students in fraternities, 25% in sororities
Most popular majors: 23% Business, Management, Marketing, and Related Support Services; 14% Education; 8% Homeland Security, Law Enforcement, Firefighting and Related Protective Services; 8% Visual and Performing Arts; 7% Psychology
Expenses: 2016-2017: $21,120; room/board: $9,100
Financial aid: (309) 467-6311; 75% of undergrads determined to have financial need; average aid package $16,411

Governors State University[1]

University Park IL
(708) 534-4490
U.S. News ranking: Reg. U. (Mid. W), second tier
Website: www.govst.edu/
Admissions email: GSUNOW@govst.edu
Public; founded 1969
Application deadline (fall): 4/1
Undergraduate student body: N/A full time, N/A part time
Expenses: 2015-2016: $10,246 in state, $18,406 out of state; room/board: $10,638
Financial aid: (708) 534-4480

Greenville College

Greenville IL
(618) 664-7100
U.S. News ranking: Reg. U. (Mid. W), No. 74
Website: www.greenville.edu
Admissions email: admissions@greenville.edu
Private; founded 1892
Affiliation: Free Methodist
Freshman admissions: selective; 2015-2016: 568 applied, 410 accepted. Either SAT or ACT required. ACT 25/75 percentile: 19-25. High school rank: 15% in top tenth, 40% in top quarter, 76% in top half
Early decision deadline: N/A, notification date: N/A
Early action deadline: N/A, notification date: N/A
Application deadline (fall): rolling
Undergraduate student body: 1,030 full time, 47 part time; 50% male, 50% female; 1% American Indian, 1% Asian, 10% black, 6% Hispanic, 0% multiracial, 0% Pacific Islander, 62% white, 2% international; 68% from in state; 90% live on campus; 0% of students in fraternities, 0% in sororities
Most popular majors: 24% Business, Management, Marketing, and Related Support

Services; 15% Education; 11% Biological and Biomedical Sciences; 7% Visual and Performing Arts; 5% Public Administration and Social Service Professions
Expenses: 2015-2016: $25,088; room/board: $8,288
Financial aid: (618) 664-7110

Illinois College

Jacksonville IL
(217) 245-3030
U.S. News ranking: Nat. Lib. Arts, No. 128
Website: www.ic.edu
Admissions email: admissions@ic.edu
Private; founded 1829
Affiliation: Presbyterian Church (USA) and United Church of Christ
Freshman admissions: selective; 2015-2016: 2,431 applied, 1,471 accepted. Neither SAT nor ACT required. ACT 25/75 percentile: 18-25. High school rank: 23% in top tenth, 51% in top quarter, 89% in top half
Early decision deadline: N/A, notification date: N/A
Early action deadline: 12/1, notification date: 12/23
Application deadline (fall): rolling
Undergraduate student body: 948 full time, 4 part time; 48% male, 52% female; 0% American Indian, 1% Asian, 12% black, 10% Hispanic, 4% multiracial, 0% Pacific Islander, 68% white, 4% international; 84% from in state; 84% live on campus; N/A of students in fraternities, N/A in sororities
Most popular majors: 21% Biological and Biomedical Sciences; 15% Multi/Interdisciplinary Studies; 13% Psychology; 10% Business, Management, Marketing, and Related Support Services; 9% Social Sciences
Expenses: 2016-2017: $31,660; room/board: $9,190
Financial aid: (217) 245-3035; 84% of undergrads determined to have financial need; average aid package $26,869

Illinois Institute of Art–Chicago[1]

Chicago IL
(800) 351-3450
U.S. News ranking: Arts, unranked
Website: www.artinstitutes.edu/chicago/
Admissions email: N/A
For-profit
Application deadline (fall): N/A
Undergraduate student body: N/A full time, N/A part time
Expenses: 2015-2016: $17,592; room/board: $12,897
Financial aid: N/A

Illinois Institute of Technology

Chicago IL
(800) 448-2329
U.S. News ranking: Nat. U., No. 103
Website: iit.edu/undergrad_admission
Admissions email: admission@iit.edu
Private; founded 1890

Freshman admissions: more selective; 2015-2016: 4,403 applied, 2,321 accepted. Either SAT or ACT required. ACT 25/75 percentile: 25-30. High school rank: 56% in top tenth, 84% in top quarter, 98% in top half
Early decision deadline: N/A, notification date: N/A
Early action deadline: N/A, notification date: N/A
Application deadline (fall): 8/1
Undergraduate student body: 2,790 full time, 201 part time; 70% male, 30% female; 0% American Indian, 13% Asian, 6% black, 16% Hispanic, 2% multiracial, 0% Pacific Islander, 33% white, 26% international; 79% from in state; 64% live on campus; 11% of students in fraternities, 15% in sororities
Most popular majors: 47% Engineering; 13% Computer and Information Sciences and Support Services; 5% Business, Management, Marketing, and Related Support Services; 4% Engineering Technologies and Engineering-Related Fields
Expenses: 2016-2017: $45,214; room/board: $11,612
Financial aid: (312) 567-7219; 58% of undergrads determined to have financial need; average aid package $36,732

Illinois State University

Normal IL
(309) 438-2181
U.S. News ranking: Nat. U., No. 152
Website: www.ilstu.edu
Admissions email: admissions@ilstu.edu
Public; founded 1857
Freshman admissions: selective; 2015-2016: 13,323 applied, 10,642 accepted. Either SAT or ACT required. ACT 25/75 percentile: 21-26. High school rank:
Early decision deadline: N/A, notification date: N/A
Early action deadline: N/A, notification date: N/A
Application deadline (fall): 4/1
Undergraduate student body: 17,151 full time, 1,275 part time; 45% male, 55% female; 0% American Indian, 2% Asian, 8% black, 9% Hispanic, 3% multiracial, 0% Pacific Islander, 77% white, 0% international; 98% from in state; 32% live on campus; 8% of students in fraternities, 17% in sororities
Most popular majors: 19% Business, Management, Marketing, and Related Support Services; 15% Education; 9% Health Professions and Related Programs; 6% Social Sciences
Expenses: 2015-2016: $13,296 in state, $20,886 out of state; room/board: $9,816
Financial aid: (309) 438-2231; 65% of undergrads determined to have financial need; average aid package $10,444

Illinois Wesleyan University

Bloomington IL
(800) 332-2498
U.S. News ranking: Nat. Lib. Arts, No. 72
Website: www.iwu.edu
Admissions email: iwuadmit@iwu.edu
Private; founded 1850
Affiliation: Methodist
Freshman admissions: more selective; 2015-2016: 3,744 applied, 2,318 accepted. Either SAT or ACT required. ACT 25/75 percentile: 25-30. High school rank: 34% in top tenth, 69% in top quarter, 97% in top half
Early decision deadline: N/A, notification date: N/A
Early action deadline: 11/15, notification date: 1/15
Application deadline (fall): rolling
Undergraduate student body: 1,828 full time, 14 part time; 44% male, 56% female; 0% American Indian, 4% Asian, 4% black, 7% Hispanic, 3% multiracial, 0% Pacific Islander, 71% white, 9% international; 87% from in state; 70% live on campus; 28% of students in fraternities, 32% in sororities
Most popular majors: 14% Business/Commerce, General; 11% Psychology, General; 8% Biological and Biomedical Sciences; 7% Accounting; 7% Registered Nursing/Registered Nurse
Expenses: 2016-2017: $44,142; room/board: $10,178
Financial aid: (309) 556-3096; 65% of undergrads determined to have financial need; average aid package $30,720

Judson University

Elgin IL
(800) 879-5376
U.S. News ranking: Reg. U. (Mid. W), No. 94
Website: www.judsonu.edu
Admissions email: admissions@judsonu.edu
Private; founded 1963
Affiliation: American Baptist
Freshman admissions: selective; 2015-2016: 653 applied, 461 accepted. Either SAT or ACT required. ACT 25/75 percentile: 21-26. High school rank: 15% in top tenth, 41% in top quarter, 75% in top half
Early decision deadline: N/A, notification date: N/A
Early action deadline: N/A, notification date: N/A
Application deadline (fall): rolling
Undergraduate student body: 739 full time, 371 part time; 41% male, 59% female; 0% American Indian, 2% Asian, 8% black, 16% Hispanic, 1% multiracial, 0% Pacific Islander, 58% white, 3% international; 76% from in state; 60% live on campus; 0% of students in fraternities, 0% in sororities
Most popular majors: 32% Business, Management, Marketing, and Related Support Services; 10% Public Administration and Social Service Professions; 8% Theology and Religious Vocations
Expenses: 2016-2017: $28,730; room/board: $9,650

Financial aid: (847) 628-2532; 64% of undergrads determined to have financial need; average aid package $18,502

Kendall College
Chicago IL
(877) 588-8860
U.S. News ranking: Reg. Coll. (Mid. W), second tier
Website: www.kendall.edu
Admissions email: admissions@kendall.edu
For-profit; founded 1934
Freshman admissions: less selective; 2015-2016: 176 applied, 131 accepted. Neither SAT nor ACT required. ACT 25/75 percentile: 16-24. High school rank: N/A
Early decision deadline: N/A, notification date: N/A
Early action deadline: N/A, notification date: N/A
Application deadline (fall): rolling
Undergraduate student body: 772 full time, 503 part time; 26% male, 74% female; 0% American Indian, 3% Asian, 17% black, 15% Hispanic, 2% multiracial, 0% Pacific Islander, 44% white, 16% international; 82% from in state; 11% live on campus; N/A of students in fraternities, N/A in sororities
Most popular majors: 40% Business, Management, Marketing, and Related Support Services; 30% Education; 30% Personal and Culinary Services
Expenses: 2015-2016: $19,459; room/board: $10,350
Financial aid: (312) 752-2028

Knox College
Galesburg IL
(800) 678-5669
U.S. News ranking: Nat. Lib. Arts, No. 77
Website: www.knox.edu
Admissions email: admission@knox.edu
Private; founded 1837
Freshman admissions: more selective; 2015-2016: 3,445 applied, 2,198 accepted. Neither SAT nor ACT required. ACT 25/75 percentile: 23-29. High school rank: 34% in top tenth, 67% in top quarter, 97% in top half
Early decision deadline: N/A, notification date: N/A
Early action deadline: 12/1, notification date: 1/15
Application deadline (fall): 1/15
Undergraduate student body: 1,368 full time, 29 part time; 41% male, 59% female; 0% American Indian, 6% Asian, 8% black, 14% Hispanic, 3% multiracial, 0% Pacific Islander, 52% white, 12% international; 55% from in state; 87% live on campus; 32% of students in fraternities, 18% in sororities
Most popular majors: 12% Economics, General; 9% Creative Writing; 9% Education, General; 7% Computer Science; 7% Psychology, General
Expenses: 2016-2017: $43,285; room/board: $9,330
Financial aid: (309) 341-7130; 79% of undergrads determined to have financial need; average aid package $34,769

Lake Forest College
Lake Forest IL
(847) 735-5000
U.S. News ranking: Nat. Lib. Arts, No. 108
Website: www.lakeforest.edu
Admissions email: admissions@lakeforest.edu
Private; founded 1857
Freshman admissions: more selective; 2015-2016: 3,373 applied, 1,855 accepted. Neither SAT nor ACT required. ACT 25/75 percentile: 23-28. High school rank: 39% in top tenth, 64% in top quarter, 91% in top half
Early decision deadline: 11/15, notification date: 12/15
Early action deadline: 11/15, notification date: 12/15
Application deadline (fall): 2/15
Undergraduate student body: 1,553 full time, 19 part time; 44% male, 56% female; 0% American Indian, 5% Asian, 7% black, 17% Hispanic, 3% multiracial, 0% Pacific Islander, 58% white, 8% international; 64% from in state; 74% live on campus; 19% of students in fraternities, 21% in sororities
Most popular majors: 20% Social Sciences; 10% Biological and Biomedical Sciences; 10% Business, Management, Marketing, and Related Support Services; 7% Psychology
Expenses: 2016-2017: $44,116; room/board: $9,810
Financial aid: (847) 735-5104; 77% of undergrads determined to have financial need; average aid package $36,745

Lewis University
Romeoville IL
(800) 897-9000
U.S. News ranking: Reg. U. (Mid. W), No. 24
Website: www.lewisu.edu
Admissions email: admissions@lewisu.edu
Private; founded 1932
Affiliation: Roman Catholic
Freshman admissions: selective; 2015-2016: 5,728 applied, 3,542 accepted. Either SAT or ACT required. ACT 25/75 percentile: 20-25. High school rank: 16% in top tenth, 41% in top quarter, 79% in top half
Early decision deadline: N/A, notification date: N/A
Early action deadline: N/A, notification date: N/A
Application deadline (fall): rolling
Undergraduate student body: 3,809 full time, 843 part time; 44% male, 56% female; 0% American Indian, 4% Asian, 6% black, 19% Hispanic, 3% multiracial, 0% Pacific Islander, 64% white, 1% international; 91% from in state; 26% live on campus; 4% of students in fraternities, 4% in sororities
Most popular majors: 16% Registered Nursing/Registered Nurse; 12% Criminal Justice/Safety Studies; 9% Business Administration and Management, General; 7% Aviation/Airway Management and Operations; 6% Psychology, General
Expenses: 2016-2017: $30,050; room/board: $10,320

Financial aid: (815) 836-5263; 76% of undergrads determined to have financial need; average aid package $21,292

Lincoln College[1]
Lincoln IL
(800) 569-0556
U.S. News ranking: Reg. Coll. (Mid. W), second tier
Website: www.lincolncollege.edu
Admissions email: admission@lincolncollege.edu
Private; founded 1865
Application deadline (fall): rolling
Undergraduate student body: N/A full time, N/A part time
Expenses: 2015-2016: $17,700; room/board: $7,100
Financial aid: (309) 452-0500

Loyola University Chicago
Chicago IL
(312) 915-6500
U.S. News ranking: Nat. U., No. 99
Website: www.luc.edu
Admissions email: admission@luc.edu
Private; founded 1870
Affiliation: Roman Catholic
Freshman admissions: more selective; 2015-2016: 21,555 applied, 15,360 accepted. Either SAT or ACT required. ACT 25/75 percentile: 24-29. High school rank: 33% in top tenth, 70% in top quarter, 92% in top half
Early decision deadline: N/A, notification date: N/A
Early action deadline: N/A, notification date: N/A
Application deadline (fall): rolling
Undergraduate student body: 9,774 full time, 1,305 part time; 35% male, 65% female; 0% American Indian, 12% Asian, 4% black, 14% Hispanic, 5% multiracial, 0% Pacific Islander, 58% white, 5% international; 65% from in state; 41% live on campus; 8% of students in fraternities, 14% in sororities
Most popular majors: 20% Business, Management, Marketing, and Related Support Services; 15% Biological and Biomedical Sciences; 12% Health Professions and Related Programs; 11% Psychology; 10% Social Sciences
Expenses: 2016-2017: $41,384; room/board: $13,770
Financial aid: (773) 508-3155; 67% of undergrads determined to have financial need; average aid package $31,932

MacMurray College
Jacksonville IL
(217) 479-7056
U.S. News ranking: Reg. Coll. (Mid. W), No. 52
Website: www.mac.edu
Admissions email: admissions@mac.edu
Private; founded 1846
Affiliation: United Methodist
Freshman admissions: selective; 2015-2016: 959 applied, 600 accepted. Either SAT or ACT required. ACT 25/75 percentile: 17-22. High school rank: 6% in top tenth, 20% in top quarter, 45% in top half

Early decision deadline: N/A, notification date: N/A
Early action deadline: N/A, notification date: N/A
Application deadline (fall): 8/30
Undergraduate student body: 544 full time, 26 part time; 49% male, 51% female; 0% American Indian, 6% Asian, 13% black, 6% Hispanic, 3% multiracial, 0% Pacific Islander, 74% white, 0% international
Most popular majors: 26% Registered Nursing/Registered Nurse; 14% Business Administration and Management, General; 13% Criminal Justice/Law Enforcement Administration; 11% Social Work; 7% Sport and Fitness Administration/Management
Expenses: 2016-2017: $25,110; room/board: $8,510
Financial aid: (217) 479-7041; 88% of undergrads determined to have financial need; average aid package $20,659

McKendree University
Lebanon IL
(618) 537-6831
U.S. News ranking: Reg. U. (Mid. W), No. 74
Website: www.mckendree.edu
Admissions email: inquiry@mckendree.edu
Private; founded 1828
Affiliation: Methodist
Freshman admissions: selective; 2015-2016: 1,904 applied, 1,209 accepted. Either SAT or ACT required. ACT 25/75 percentile: 19-24. High school rank: 12% in top tenth, 34% in top quarter, 71% in top half
Early decision deadline: N/A, notification date: N/A
Early action deadline: N/A, notification date: N/A
Application deadline (fall): rolling
Undergraduate student body: 1,820 full time, 522 part time; 46% male, 54% female; 1% American Indian, 1% Asian, 14% black, 5% Hispanic, 2% multiracial, 0% Pacific Islander, 68% white, 2% international; 79% from in state; 76% live on campus; 4% of students in fraternities, 16% in sororities
Most popular majors: 18% Registered Nursing/Registered Nurse; 16% Business Administration and Management, General; 7% Psychology, General; 6% Management Science; 5% Human Resources Management/Personnel Administration, General
Expenses: 2016-2017: $28,740; room/board: $9,200
Financial aid: (618) 537-6828; 81% of undergrads determined to have financial need; average aid package $20,294

Midstate College[1]
Peoria IL
(309) 692-4092
U.S. News ranking: Reg. Coll. (Mid. W), unranked
Website: www.midstate.edu/
Admissions email: jauer@midstate.edu
For-profit
Application deadline (fall): rolling
Undergraduate student body: N/A full time, N/A part time

Expenses: 2015-2016: $16,230; room/board: N/A
Financial aid: (309) 692-4092

Millikin University
Decatur IL
(217) 424-6210
U.S. News ranking: Reg. U. (Mid. W), No. 11
Website: www.millikin.edu
Admissions email: admis@millikin.edu
Private; founded 1901
Affiliation: Presbyterian
Freshman admissions: selective; 2015-2016: 3,540 applied, 2,124 accepted. Either SAT or ACT required. ACT 25/75 percentile: 20-26. High school rank: 17% in top tenth, 38% in top quarter, 73% in top half
Early decision deadline: N/A, notification date: N/A
Early action deadline: N/A, notification date: N/A
Application deadline (fall): rolling
Undergraduate student body: 1,984 full time, 79 part time; 42% male, 58% female; 0% American Indian, 1% Asian, 14% black, 6% Hispanic, 4% multiracial, 0% Pacific Islander, 73% white, 2% international; 86% from in state; 61% live on campus; 23% of students in fraternities, 27% in sororities
Most popular majors: 22% Business, Management, Marketing, and Related Support Services; 21% Visual and Performing Arts; 13% Health Professions and Related Programs; 11% Education
Expenses: 2016-2017: $31,824; room/board: $10,335
Financial aid: (217) 424-6343; 81% of undergrads determined to have financial need; average aid package $23,282

Monmouth College
Monmouth IL
(800) 747-2687
U.S. News ranking: Nat. Lib. Arts, No. 159
Website: www.monmouthcollege.edu/admissions
Admissions email: admissions@monmouthcollege.edu
Private; founded 1853
Affiliation: Presbyterian USA
Freshman admissions: selective; 2015-2016: 2,657 applied, 1,578 accepted. Either SAT or ACT required. ACT 25/75 percentile: 20-26. High school rank: 13% in top tenth, 36% in top quarter, 70% in top half
Early decision deadline: N/A, notification date: N/A
Early action deadline: N/A, notification date: N/A
Application deadline (fall): rolling
Undergraduate student body: 1,178 full time, 19 part time; 47% male, 53% female; 1% American Indian, 2% Asian, 10% black, 12% Hispanic, 2% multiracial, N/A Pacific Islander, 63% white, 6% international; 91% from in state; 92% live on campus; 18% of students in fraternities, 34% in sororities
Most popular majors: 20% Business, Management, Marketing, and Related Support Services; 10% Social Sciences; 8% Education; 8% Psychology

Expenses: 2016-2017: $35,300; room/board: $8,300
Financial aid: (309) 457-2129; 85% of undergrads determined to have financial need; average aid package $31,050

National Louis University
Chicago IL
(888) 658-8632
U.S. News ranking: Nat. U., second tier
Website: www.nl.edu
Admissions email: nluinfo@nl.edu
Private
Freshman admissions: selective; 2015-2016: 243 applied, 198 accepted. Neither SAT nor ACT required. ACT 25/75 percentile: N/A. High school rank: N/A
Early decision deadline: N/A, notification date: N/A
Early action deadline: N/A, notification date: N/A
Application deadline (fall): N/A
Undergraduate student body: 615 full time, 691 part time; 21% male, 79% female; 0% American Indian, 3% Asian, 35% black, 31% Hispanic, 2% multiracial, 0% Pacific Islander, 25% white, 1% international
Most popular majors: Information not available
Expenses: 2015-2016: $10,617; room/board: N/A
Financial aid: (847) 465-5350

North Central College
Naperville IL
(630) 637-5800
U.S. News ranking: Reg. U. (Mid. W), No. 15
Website: www.noctrl.edu
Admissions email: ncadm@noctrl.edu
Private; founded 1861
Affiliation: United Methodist
Freshman admissions: more selective; 2015-2016: 7,307 applied, 4,177 accepted. Either SAT or ACT required. ACT 25/75 percentile: 22-27. High school rank: 22% in top tenth, 54% in top quarter, 86% in top half
Early decision deadline: N/A, notification date: N/A
Early action deadline: N/A, notification date: N/A
Application deadline (fall): rolling
Undergraduate student body: 2,590 full time, 143 part time; 47% male, 53% female; 0% American Indian, 2% Asian, 4% black, 11% Hispanic, 3% multiracial, 0% Pacific Islander, 71% white, 2% international; 93% from in state; 56% live on campus; 0% of students in fraternities, 0% in sororities
Most popular majors: 13% Psychology, General; 6% Kinesiology and Exercise Science; 6% Marketing/Marketing Management, General; 5% Business Administration, Management and Operations, Other; 4% Sociology
Expenses: 2016-2017: $36,654; room/board: $10,356
Financial aid: (630) 637-5600; 77% of undergrads determined to have financial need; average aid package $23,604

Northeastern Illinois University
Chicago IL
(773) 442-4000
U.S. News ranking: Reg. U. (Mid. W), second tier
Website: www.neiu.edu
Admissions email: admrec@neiu.edu
Public; founded 1867
Freshman admissions: less selective; 2015-2016: 4,499 applied, 3,016 accepted. ACT required. ACT 25/75 percentile: 16-20. High school rank: 3% in top tenth, 13% in top quarter, 44% in top half
Early decision deadline: N/A, notification date: N/A
Early action deadline: N/A, notification date: N/A
Application deadline (fall): 7/1
Undergraduate student body: 4,502 full time, 3,593 part time; 44% male, 56% female; 0% American Indian, 9% Asian, 10% black, 37% Hispanic, 2% multiracial, 0% Pacific Islander, 33% white, 4% international; 99% from in state; 0% live on campus; 1% of students in fraternities, 1% in sororities
Most popular majors: 17% Business, Management, Marketing, and Related Support Services; 9% Public Administration and Social Service Professions; 8% Education; 8% Psychology; 7% Mathematics and Statistics
Expenses: 2016-2017: $10,659 in state, $17,959 out of state; room/board: N/A
Financial aid: (773) 442-5000; 72% of undergrads determined to have financial need; average aid package $8,342

Northern Illinois University
DeKalb IL
(815) 753-0446
U.S. News ranking: Nat. U., No. 214
Website: www.niu.edu/
Admissions email: admission@niu.edu
Public; founded 1895
Freshman admissions: selective; 2015-2016: 17,081 applied, 8,601 accepted. Either SAT or ACT required. ACT 25/75 percentile: 19-25. High school rank: 13% in top tenth, 36% in top quarter, 74% in top half
Early decision deadline: N/A, notification date: N/A
Early action deadline: N/A, notification date: N/A
Application deadline (fall): 8/1
Undergraduate student body: 13,224 full time, 1,803 part time; 51% male, 49% female; 0% American Indian, 5% Asian, 16% black, 15% Hispanic, 3% multiracial, 0% Pacific Islander, 57% white, 2% international; 97% from in state; 28% live on campus; 4% of students in fraternities, 4% in sororities
Most popular majors: 6% Registered Nursing/Registered Nurse; 6% Psychology, General; 5% Health/Medical Preparatory Programs, Other; 5% Accounting
Expenses: 2016-2017: $14,334 in state, $23,799 out of state; room/board: $10,776

Financial aid: (815) 753-1300; 73% of undergrads determined to have financial need; average aid package $12,773

North Park University
Chicago IL
(773) 244-5500
U.S. News ranking: Reg. U. (Mid. W), No. 71
Website: www.northpark.edu
Admissions email: admissions@northpark.edu
Private; founded 1891
Affiliation: Evangelical Covenant Church
Freshman admissions: selective; 2015-2016: 3,901 applied, 1,929 accepted. Either SAT or ACT required. ACT 25/75 percentile: 19-24. High school rank: N/A
Early decision deadline: N/A, notification date: N/A
Early action deadline: N/A, notification date: N/A
Application deadline (fall): 7/1
Undergraduate student body: 1,867 full time, 284 part time; 37% male, 63% female; 0% American Indian, 6% Asian, 8% black, 22% Hispanic, 4% multiracial, 1% Pacific Islander, 49% white, 5% international; 78% from in state; 38% live on campus; 0% of students in fraternities, 0% in sororities
Most popular majors: 21% Business Administration and Management, General; 19% Registered Nursing/Registered Nurse; 6% Biology/Biological Sciences, General; 6% Health and Physical Education/Fitness, General; 6% Non-Profit/Public/Organizational Management
Expenses: 2015-2016: $25,860; room/board: $8,980
Financial aid: (773) 244-5526

Northwestern University
Evanston IL
(847) 491-7271
U.S. News ranking: Nat. U., No. 12
Website: www.northwestern.edu
Admissions email: ug-admission@northwestern.edu
Private; founded 1851
Freshman admissions: most selective; 2015-2016: 32,122 applied, 4,248 accepted. Either SAT or ACT required. ACT 25/75 percentile: 31-34. High school rank: 91% in top tenth, 100% in top quarter, 100% in top half
Early decision deadline: 11/1, notification date: 12/15
Early action deadline: N/A, notification date: N/A
Application deadline (fall): 1/1
Undergraduate student body: 8,158 full time, 156 part time; 50% male, 50% female; 0% American Indian, 18% Asian, 6% black, 11% Hispanic, 5% multiracial, 0% Pacific Islander, 50% white, 9% international; 33% from in state; 40% live on campus; 29% of students in fraternities, 32% in sororities
Most popular majors: 14% Economics, General; 6% Psychology, General; 5% Political Science and Government,

General; 5% Biology/Biological Sciences, General
Expenses: 2016-2017: $50,855; room/board: $15,489
Financial aid: (847) 491-7400; 44% of undergrads determined to have financial need; average aid package $43,094

Olivet Nazarene University
Bourbonnais IL
(815) 939-5011
U.S. News ranking: Reg. U. (Mid. W), No. 49
Website: www.olivet.edu
Admissions email: admissions@olivet.edu
Private; founded 1907
Affiliation: Church of the Nazarene
Freshman admissions: selective; 2015-2016: 4,133 applied, 3,165 accepted. Either SAT or ACT required. ACT 25/75 percentile: 20-27. High school rank: 20% in top tenth, 50% in top quarter, 78% in top half
Early decision deadline: N/A, notification date: N/A
Early action deadline: N/A, notification date: N/A
Application deadline (fall): 8/1
Undergraduate student body: 3,043 full time, 360 part time; 39% male, 61% female; 0% American Indian, 2% Asian, 8% black, 7% Hispanic, 2% multiracial, 0% Pacific Islander, 79% white, 1% international; 65% from in state; 69% live on campus; 0% of students in fraternities, 0% in sororities
Most popular majors: 36% Registered Nursing/Registered Nurse; 7% Business Administration and Management, General; 6% Elementary Education and Teaching; 3% Teacher Education and Professional Development, Specific Subject Areas
Expenses: 2016-2017: $33,940; room/board: $7,900
Financial aid: (815) 939-5249; 81% of undergrads determined to have financial need; average aid package $25,369

Principia College
Elsah IL
(618) 374-5181
U.S. News ranking: Nat. Lib. Arts, No. 115
Website: www.principiacollege.edu
Admissions email: collegeadmissions@principia.edu
Private; founded 1910
Affiliation: Christian Science
Freshman admissions: selective; 2015-2016: 159 applied, 120 accepted. Either SAT or ACT required. SAT 25/75 percentile: 930-1198. High school rank: 21% in top tenth, 32% in top quarter, 84% in top half
Early decision deadline: N/A, notification date: N/A
Early action deadline: N/A, notification date: N/A
Application deadline (fall): 7/25
Undergraduate student body: 450 full time, 14 part time; 49% male, 51% female; 0% American Indian, 1% Asian, 2% black, 4% Hispanic, 2% multiracial, 0% Pacific Islander, 73% white,

16% international; 4% from in state; 98% live on campus; 0% of students in fraternities, 0% in sororities
Most popular majors: 19% Business Administration and Management, General; 9% Education, General; 7% Biology, General; 5% Computer Science
Expenses: 2016-2017: $27,980; room/board: $11,030
Financial aid: (618) 374-5186; 70% of undergrads determined to have financial need; average aid package $30,022

Quincy University
Quincy IL
(217) 228-5210
U.S. News ranking: Reg. U. (Mid. W), No. 74
Website: www.quincy.edu
Admissions email: admissions@quincy.edu
Private; founded 1860
Affiliation: Catholic
Freshman admissions: selective; 2015-2016: 1,553 applied, 984 accepted. Either SAT or ACT required. ACT 25/75 percentile: 19-24. High school rank: 8% in top tenth, 32% in top quarter, 75% in top half
Early decision deadline: N/A, notification date: N/A
Early action deadline: N/A, notification date: N/A
Application deadline (fall): rolling
Undergraduate student body: 1,024 full time, 116 part time; 45% male, 55% female; 0% American Indian, 1% Asian, 12% black, 5% Hispanic, 2% multiracial, 0% Pacific Islander, 70% white, 0% international; 68% from in state; 54% live on campus; N/A of students in fraternities, N/A in sororities
Most popular majors: 20% Business, Management, Marketing, and Related Support Services; 13% Health Professions and Related Programs; 8% Biological and Biomedical Sciences; 8% Education; 8% Psychology
Expenses: 2016-2017: $27,128; room/board: $10,000
Financial aid: (217) 228-5260; 83% of undergrads determined to have financial need; average aid package $24,970

Robert Morris University
Chicago IL
(312) 935-4400
U.S. News ranking: Reg. U. (Mid. W), No. 94
Website: www.robertmorris.edu/
Admissions email: enroll@robertmorris.edu
Private; founded 1913
Freshman admissions: selective; 2015-2016: 2,967 applied, 726 accepted. Neither SAT nor ACT required. ACT 25/75 percentile: 16-21. High school rank: 4% in top tenth, 17% in top quarter, 45% in top half
Early decision deadline: N/A, notification date: N/A
Early action deadline: N/A, notification date: N/A
Application deadline (fall): rolling
Undergraduate student body: 2,553 full time, 133 part time; 50%

male, 50% female; 0% American Indian, 3% Asian, 27% black, 29% Hispanic, 2% multiracial, 0% Pacific Islander, 36% white, 1% international; 91% from in state; 9% live on campus; N/A of students in fraternities, N/A in sororities
Most popular majors: 64% Business, Management, Marketing, and Related Support Services; 23% Multi/Interdisciplinary Studies; 7% Computer and Information Sciences and Support Services; 6% Visual and Performing Arts; Health Professions and Related Programs
Expenses: 2016-2017: $26,250; room/board: $13,875
Financial aid: (312) 935-4408; 91% of undergrads determined to have financial need; average aid package $16,377

Rockford University
Rockford IL
(815) 226-4050
U.S. News ranking: Reg. U. (Mid. W), second tier
Website: www.rockford.edu
Admissions email: Admissions@Rockford.edu
Private; founded 1847
Freshman admissions: selective; 2015-2016: 2,250 applied, 1,211 accepted. Either SAT or ACT required. ACT 25/75 percentile: 19-24. High school rank: N/A
Early decision deadline: N/A, notification date: N/A
Early action deadline: N/A, notification date: N/A
Application deadline (fall): 8/15
Undergraduate student body: 925 full time, 136 part time; 41% male, 59% female; 0% American Indian, 2% Asian, 9% black, 14% Hispanic, 3% multiracial, 0% Pacific Islander, 67% white, 1% international; 87% from in state; 36% live on campus; 0% of students in fraternities, 0% in sororities
Most popular majors: 23% Health Professions and Related Programs; 22% Business, Management, Marketing, and Related Support Services; 16% Education; 8% Social Sciences; 6% Biological and Biomedical Sciences
Expenses: 2016-2017: $29,180; room/board: $8,180
Financial aid: (815) 226-3396; 90% of undergrads determined to have financial need; average aid package $19,367

Roosevelt University
Chicago IL
(877) 277-5978
U.S. News ranking: Reg. U. (Mid. W), No. 115
Website: www.roosevelt.edu
Admissions email: admission@roosevelt.edu
Private; founded 1945
Freshman admissions: selective; 2015-2016: 3,303 applied, 2,387 accepted. Either SAT or ACT required. ACT 25/75 percentile: 19-25. High school rank: 13% in top tenth, 37% in top quarter, 68% in top half
Early decision deadline: N/A, notification date: N/A

Early action deadline: N/A, notification date: N/A
Application deadline (fall): rolling
Undergraduate student body: 2,569 full time, 670 part time; 36% male, 64% female; 0% American Indian, 5% Asian, 18% black, 23% Hispanic, 2% multiracial, 0% Pacific Islander, 46% white, 4% international; 85% from in state; 21% live on campus; 0% of students in fraternities, 2% in sororities
Most popular majors: 37% Business, Management, Marketing, and Related Support Services; 13% Psychology; 7% Biological and Biomedical Sciences; 7% Visual and Performing Arts; 6% Social Sciences
Expenses: 2016-2017: $28,119; room/board: $12,927
Financial aid: (312) 341-3565; 82% of undergrads determined to have financial need; average aid package $22,000

School of the Art Institute of Chicago
Chicago IL
(312) 629-6100
U.S. News ranking: Arts, unranked
Website: www.saic.edu
Admissions email: admiss@saic.edu
Private; founded 1866
Freshman admissions: N/A; 2015-2016: 4,210 applied, 2,799 accepted. Either SAT or ACT required. SAT 25/75 percentile: N/A. High school rank: N/A
Early decision deadline: N/A, notification date: N/A
Early action deadline: 12/1, notification date: 12/25
Application deadline (fall): 5/1
Undergraduate student body: 2,623 full time, 220 part time; 28% male, 72% female; 0% American Indian, 12% Asian, 3% black, 9% Hispanic, 2% multiracial, 0% Pacific Islander, 37% white, 32% international
Most popular majors: Information not available
Expenses: 2016-2017: $45,750; room/board: $13,100
Financial aid: (312) 629-6600

Shimer College[1]
Chicago IL
(312) 235-3500
U.S. News ranking: Nat. Lib. Arts, unranked
Website: www.shimer.edu
Admissions email: admission@shimer.edu
Private
Application deadline (fall): N/A
Undergraduate student body: N/A full time, N/A part time
Expenses: 2015-2016: $34,004; room/board: $11,000
Financial aid: (847) 249-7180

Southern Illinois University–Carbondale
Carbondale IL
(618) 536-4405
U.S. News ranking: Nat. U., No. 214
Website: www.siu.edu

Admissions email: admissions@siu.edu
Public; founded 1869
Freshman admissions: selective; 2015-2016: 10,645 applied, 8,602 accepted. Either SAT or ACT required. ACT 25/75 percentile: 19-25. High school rank: 10% in top tenth, 32% in top quarter, 61% in top half
Early decision deadline: N/A, notification date: N/A
Early action deadline: N/A, notification date: N/A
Application deadline (fall): 5/1
Undergraduate student body: 11,371 full time, 1,660 part time; 54% male, 46% female; 0% American Indian, 2% Asian, 19% black, 8% Hispanic, 3% multiracial, 0% Pacific Islander, 64% white, 4% international; 84% from in state; 30% live on campus; 5% of students in fraternities, 4% in sororities
Most popular majors: 14% Education; 8% Health Professions and Related Programs; 8% Business, Management, and Related Support Services; 7% Engineering Technologies and Engineering-Related Fields; 6% Social Sciences
Expenses: 2016-2017: $13,481 in state, $27,130 out of state; room/board: $10,186
Financial aid: (618) 453-4334; 71% of undergrads determined to have financial need; average aid package $14,646

Southern Illinois University–Edwardsville
Edwardsville IL
(618) 650-3705
U.S. News ranking: Reg. U. (Mid. W), No. 63
Website: www.siue.edu
Admissions email: admissions@siue.edu
Public; founded 1957
Freshman admissions: selective; 2015-2016: 7,786 applied, 6,869 accepted. Either SAT or ACT required. ACT 25/75 percentile: 20-26. High school rank: 17% in top tenth, 43% in top quarter, 73% in top half
Early decision deadline: N/A, notification date: N/A
Early action deadline: N/A, notification date: N/A
Application deadline (fall): 5/2
Undergraduate student body: 9,953 full time, 1,828 part time; 47% male, 53% female; 0% American Indian, 2% Asian, 15% black, 4% Hispanic, 3% multiracial, 0% Pacific Islander, 73% white, 1% international; 90% from in state; 27% live on campus; N/A of students in fraternities, N/A in sororities
Most popular majors: 13% Registered Nursing/Registered Nurse; 12% Business/Commerce, General; 6% Biology/Biological Sciences, General; 6% Psychology, General; 4% Criminal Justice/Safety Studies
Expenses: 2016-2017: $11,008 in state, $23,986 out of state; room/board: $9,180

Financial aid: (618) 650-3839; 65% of undergrads determined to have financial need; average aid package $11,151

St. Augustine College[1]
Chicago IL
(773) 878-3656
U.S. News ranking: Reg. Coll. (Mid. W), unranked
Website: www.staugustinecollege.edu/index.asp
Admissions email: info@staugustine.edu
Private
Application deadline (fall): N/A
Undergraduate student body: N/A full time, N/A part time
Expenses: 2015-2016: $9,840; room/board: N/A
Financial aid: (773) 878-3813

St. Xavier University
Chicago IL
(773) 298-3050
U.S. News ranking: Reg. U. (Mid. W), No. 56
Website: www.sxu.edu
Admissions email: admission@sxu.edu
Private; founded 1846
Affiliation: Roman Catholic
Freshman admissions: selective; 2015-2016: 7,883 applied, 5,886 accepted. Either SAT or ACT required. ACT 25/75 percentile: 19-23. High school rank: 22% in top tenth, 53% in top quarter, 87% in top half
Early decision deadline: N/A, notification date: N/A
Early action deadline: N/A, notification date: N/A
Application deadline (fall): rolling
Undergraduate student body: 2,615 full time, 383 part time; 33% male, 67% female; 0% American Indian, 3% Asian, 14% black, 32% Hispanic, 2% multiracial, 0% Pacific Islander, 45% white, 0% international; 94% from in state; 18% live on campus; 0% of students in fraternities, 0% in sororities
Most popular majors: 22% Business, Management, Marketing, and Related Support Services; 18% Health Professions and Related Programs; 11% Psychology; 10% Education; 7% Biological and Biomedical Sciences
Expenses: 2016-2017: $32,250; room/board: $11,060
Financial aid: (773) 298-3070; 89% of undergrads determined to have financial need; average aid package $24,699

Trinity Christian College
Palos Heights IL
(800) 748-0085
U.S. News ranking: Reg. Coll. (Mid. W), No. 19
Website: www.trnty.edu
Admissions email: admissions@trnty.edu
Private; founded 1959
Affiliation: Reformed
Freshman admissions: selective; 2015-2016: 861 applied, 755 accepted. Either SAT or ACT required. ACT 25/75 percentile:

21-27. High school rank: 11% in top tenth, 31% in top quarter, 66% in top half
Early decision deadline: N/A, notification date: N/A
Early action deadline: N/A, notification date: N/A
Application deadline (fall): rolling
Undergraduate student body: 1,032 full time, 205 part time; 32% male, 68% female; 0% American Indian, 1% Asian, 10% black, 13% Hispanic, 2% multiracial, 0% Pacific Islander, 65% white, 5% international; 71% from in state; 50% live on campus; N/A of students in fraternities, N/A in sororities
Most popular majors: 23% Education; 20% Business, Management, Marketing, and Related Support Services; 12% Health Professions and Related Programs; 10% Psychology; 5% Parks, Recreation, Leisure, and Fitness Studies
Expenses: 2016-2017: $27,450; room/board: $9,580
Financial aid: (708) 239-4706; 74% of undergrads determined to have financial need; average aid package $21,702

Trinity International University
Deerfield IL
(800) 822-3225
U.S. News ranking: Nat. U., second tier
Website: www.tiu.edu
Admissions email: tcadmissions@tiu.edu
Private; founded 1897
Affiliation: Evangelical Free Church of America
Freshman admissions: selective; 2015-2016: 380 applied, 364 accepted. Either SAT or ACT required. ACT 25/75 percentile: 19-26. High school rank: 15% in top tenth, 31% in top quarter, 54% in top half
Early decision deadline: N/A, notification date: N/A
Early action deadline: N/A, notification date: N/A
Application deadline (fall): rolling
Undergraduate student body: 758 full time, 308 part time; 49% male, 51% female; N/A American Indian, 2% Asian, 17% black, 12% Hispanic, 3% multiracial, 0% Pacific Islander, 52% white, 2% international
Most popular majors: 15% Religious Education; 13% Psychology, General; 12% Business/Commerce, General; 7% Elementary Education and Teaching
Expenses: 2016-2017: $30,130; room/board: $9,010
Financial aid: (847) 317-8060; 82% of undergrads determined to have financial need; average aid package $24,024

University of Chicago
Chicago IL
(773) 702-8650
U.S. News ranking: Nat. U., No. 3
Website: www.uchicago.edu
Admissions email: collegeadmissions@uchicago.edu
Private; founded 1890

Freshman admissions: most
selective; 2015-2016: 30,069
applied, 2,521 accepted. Either
SAT or ACT required. SAT 25/75
percentile: 1440-1600. High
school rank: 98% in top tenth,
99% in top quarter, 100% in
top half
Early decision deadline: N/A,
notification date: N/A
Early action deadline: 11/1,
notification date: 12/17
Application deadline (fall): 1/1
Undergraduate student body: 5,795
full time, 49 part time; 53%
male, 47% female; 0% American
Indian, 17% Asian, 5% black,
9% Hispanic, 3% multiracial,
0% Pacific Islander, 44% white,
11% international; 15% from in
state; 52% live on campus; 8%
of students in fraternities, 12%
in sororities
Most popular majors: 20%
Economics; 9% Biological
and Biomedical Sciences; 7%
Mathematics and Statistics; 5%
Public Policy Analysis
Expenses: 2016-2017: $52,491;
room/board: $15,093
Financial aid: (773) 702-8666;
44% of undergrads determined
to have financial need; average
aid package $46,961

University of
Illinois–Chicago
Chicago IL
(312) 996-4350
U.S. News ranking: Nat. U.,
No. 152
Website: www.uic.edu
Admissions email:
uicadmit@uic.edu
Public; founded 1965
Freshman admissions: selective;
2015-2016: 15,664 applied,
12,007 accepted. Either SAT
or ACT required. ACT 25/75
percentile: 21-26. High school
rank: 23% in top tenth, 63% in
top quarter, 95% in top half
Early decision deadline: N/A,
notification date: N/A
Early action deadline: N/A,
notification date: N/A
Application deadline (fall): 1/15
Undergraduate student body:
16,176 full time, 1,399 part
time; 50% male, 50% female;
0% American Indian, 22% Asian,
8% black, 28% Hispanic, 3%
multiracial, 0% Pacific Islander,
34% white, 2% international;
97% from in state; 16% live
on campus; 1% of students in
fraternities, 1% in sororities
Most popular majors: 15%
Business, Management,
Marketing, and Related Support
Services; 13% Biological and
Biomedical Sciences; 13%
Psychology; 12% Engineering;
8% Health Professions and
Related Programs
Expenses: 2016-2017: $13,670
in state, $26,526 out of state;
room/board: $10,882
Financial aid: (312) 996-3126;
77% of undergrads determined
to have financial need; average
aid package $14,536

University of
Illinois–Springfield
Springfield IL
(217) 206-4847
U.S. News ranking: Reg. U.
(Mid. W), No. 63
Website: www.uis.edu
Admissions email:
admissions@uis.edu
Public; founded 1969
Freshman admissions: selective;
2015-2016: 1,524 applied, 962
accepted. Either SAT or ACT
required. ACT 25/75 percentile:
20-26. High school rank: 19%
in top tenth, 46% in top quarter,
75% in top half
Early decision deadline: N/A,
notification date: N/A
Early action deadline: N/A,
notification date: N/A
Application deadline (fall): rolling
Undergraduate student body: 1,899
full time, 1,038 part time; 49%
male, 51% female; 0% American
Indian, 4% Asian, 16% black,
7% Hispanic, 3% multiracial,
0% Pacific Islander, 63% white,
5% international; 87% from in
state; 31% live on campus; N/A
of students in fraternities, N/A in
sororities
Most popular majors: 17%
Business Administration
and Management, General;
14% Computer Science; 8%
Psychology, General; 7%
Accounting
Expenses: 2016-2017: $11,413
in state, $20,938 out of state;
room/board: $9,700
Financial aid: (217) 206-6724;
67% of undergrads determined
to have financial need; average
aid package $13,407

University of Illinois–
Urbana-Champaign
Champaign IL
(217) 333-0302
U.S. News ranking: Nat. U.,
No. 44
Website: www.illinois.edu
Admissions email:
ugradadmissions@illinois.edu
Public; founded 1867
Freshman admissions: more
selective; 2015-2016: 34,277
applied, 22,471 accepted. Either
SAT or ACT required. ACT 25/75
percentile: 26-31. High school
rank: 53% in top tenth, 86% in
top quarter, 99% in top half
Early decision deadline: N/A,
notification date: N/A
Early action deadline: N/A,
notification date: N/A
Application deadline (fall): 12/1
Undergraduate student body:
31,989 full time, 1,379 part
time; 56% male, 44% female;
0% American Indian, 17% Asian,
6% black, 10% Hispanic, 3%
multiracial, 0% Pacific Islander,
48% white, 16% international;
86% from in state; 50% live
on campus; 21% of students in
fraternities, 27% in sororities
Most popular majors: 20%
Engineering; 12% Business,
Management, Marketing, and
Related Support Services; 8%
Social Sciences; 7% Biological
and Biomedical Sciences
Expenses: 2016-2017: $15,698
in state, $31,320 out of state;
room/board: $11,308

Financial aid: (217) 333-0100;
45% of undergrads determined
to have financial need; average
aid package $16,332

University
of St. Francis
Joliet IL
(800) 735-7500
U.S. News ranking: Reg. U.
(Mid. W), No. 31
Website: www.stfrancis.edu
Admissions email: admissions@
stfrancis.edu
Private; founded 1920
Affiliation: Roman Catholic
Freshman admissions: selective;
2015-2016: 1,423 applied, 719
accepted. Either SAT or ACT
required. ACT 25/75 percentile:
21-25. High school rank: 16%
in top tenth, 43% in top quarter,
77% in top half
Early decision deadline: N/A,
notification date: N/A
Early action deadline: N/A,
notification date: N/A
Application deadline (fall): 8/1
Undergraduate student body: 1,273
full time, 76 part time; 37%
male, 63% female; 0% American
Indian, 2% Asian, 7% black,
18% Hispanic, 3% multiracial,
0% Pacific Islander, 66% white,
2% international; 95% from in
state; 26% live on campus; N/A
of students in fraternities, 2% in
sororities
Most popular majors: 30%
Health Professions and Related
Programs; 11% Education;
8% Biological and Biomedical
Sciences; 8% Business,
Management, Marketing, and
Related Support Services; 6%
Public Administration and Social
Service Professions
Expenses: 2016-2017: $30,840;
room/board: $9,084
Financial aid: (815) 740-3403;
88% of undergrads determined
to have financial need; average
aid package $25,249

VanderCook
College of Music
Chicago IL
(800) 448-2655
U.S. News ranking: Arts, unranked
Website: www.vandercook.edu
Admissions email: admissions@
vandercook.edu
Private; founded 1909
Freshman admissions: N/A; 2015-
2016: 47 applied, 45 accepted.
Neither SAT nor ACT required.
SAT 25/75 percentile: N/A. High
school rank: 21% in top tenth,
29% in top quarter, 79% in
top half
Early decision deadline: N/A,
notification date: N/A
Early action deadline: N/A,
notification date: N/A
Application deadline (fall): rolling
Undergraduate student body: 96
full time, 58 part time; 58%
male, 42% female; 0% American
Indian, 2% Asian, 8% black,
21% Hispanic, 4% multiracial,
0% Pacific Islander, 62% white,
2% international
Most popular majors: Information
not available
Expenses: 2015-2016: $26,300;
room/board: $11,516
Financial aid: (312) 225-6288

Western Illinois
University
Macomb IL
(309) 298-3157
U.S. News ranking: Reg. U.
(Mid. W), No. 49
Website: www.wiu.edu
Admissions email:
admissions@wiu.edu
Public; founded 1899
Freshman admissions: selective;
2015-2016: 10,877 applied,
6,534 accepted. Either SAT
or ACT required. ACT 25/75
percentile: 18-23. High school
rank: 10% in top tenth, 31% in
top quarter, 67% in top half
Early decision deadline: N/A,
notification date: N/A
Early action deadline: N/A,
notification date: N/A
Application deadline (fall): 5/15
Undergraduate student body: 8,106
full time, 1,035 part time; 50%
male, 50% female; 0% American
Indian, 1% Asian, 19% black,
11% Hispanic, 2% multiracial,
0% Pacific Islander, 62% white,
2% international; 89% from in
state; 44% live on campus; 6%
of students in fraternities, 6% in
sororities
Most popular majors: 18%
Criminal Justice/Law
Enforcement Administration;
14% Business Administration
and Management, General;
12% Liberal Arts and Sciences,
General Studies and Humanities,
Other; 7% Parks, Recreation and
Leisure Facilities Management,
General
Expenses: 2016-2017: $11,245
in state, $11,245 out of state;
room/board: $9,770
Financial aid: (309) 298-2446;
75% of undergrads determined
to have financial need; average
aid package $11,291

Wheaton College
Wheaton IL
(630) 752-5005
U.S. News ranking: Nat. Lib. Arts,
No. 62
Website: www.wheaton.edu
Admissions email:
admissions@wheaton.edu
Private; founded 1860
Affiliation: Christian
nondenominational
Freshman admissions: more
selective; 2015-2016: 1,971
applied, 1,390 accepted. Either
SAT or ACT required. ACT 25/75
percentile: 27-32. High school
rank: 54% in top tenth, 81% in
top quarter, 96% in top half
Early decision deadline: N/A,
notification date: N/A
Early action deadline: 11/1,
notification date: 12/31
Application deadline (fall): 1/10
Undergraduate student body: 2,410
full time, 53 part time; 47%
male, 53% female; 0% American
Indian, 9% Asian, 3% black,
6% Hispanic, 5% multiracial,
0% Pacific Islander, 76% white,
3% international; 26% from in
state; 87% live on campus; N/A
of students in fraternities, N/A in
sororities
Most popular majors: 12% Social
Sciences; 10% Business,
Management, Marketing, and
Related Support Services; 10%
Visual and Performing Arts;

8% Theology and Religious
Vocations; 8% English Language
and Literature/Letters
Expenses: 2016-2017: $34,050;
room/board: $9,560
Financial aid: (630) 752-5021;
54% of undergrads determined
to have financial need; average
aid package $25,676

INDIANA

Anderson University
Anderson IN
(765) 641-4080
U.S. News ranking: Reg. U.
(Mid. W), No. 38
Website: www.anderson.edu
Admissions email:
info@anderson.edu
Private; founded 1917
Affiliation: Church of God
Freshman admissions: selective;
2015-2016: 2,620 applied,
1,562 accepted. Either SAT
or ACT required. SAT 25/75
percentile: 940-1130. High
school rank: 24% in top tenth,
53% in top quarter, 86% in
top half
Early decision deadline: N/A,
notification date: N/A
Early action deadline: N/A,
notification date: N/A
Application deadline (fall): rolling
Undergraduate student body: 1,610
full time, 297 part time; 39%
male, 61% female; 0% American
Indian, 1% Asian, 6% black,
2% Hispanic, 3% multiracial,
0% Pacific Islander, 80% white,
3% international; 75% from in
state; 77% live on campus; N/A
of students in fraternities, N/A in
sororities
Most popular majors: 17%
Business, Management,
Marketing, and Related Support
Services; 17% Health Professions
and Related Programs; 11%
Education; 9% Visual and
Performing Arts; 7% Psychology
Expenses: 2016-2017: $28,650;
room/board: $9,550
Financial aid: (765) 641-4180;
81% of undergrads determined
to have financial need; average
aid package $16,770

Ball State University
Muncie IN
(765) 285-8300
U.S. News ranking: Nat. U.,
No. 176
Website: www.bsu.edu
Admissions email: askus@bsu.edu
Public; founded 1918
Freshman admissions: selective;
2015-2016: 22,147 applied,
13,399 accepted. Neither SAT
nor ACT required. SAT 25/75
percentile: 1010-1190. High
school rank: 19% in top tenth,
50% in top quarter, 90% in
top half
Early decision deadline: N/A,
notification date: N/A
Early action deadline: N/A,
notification date: N/A
Application deadline (fall): 8/10
Undergraduate student body:
14,716 full time, 1,886 part
time; 41% male, 59% female;
0% American Indian, 1% Asian,
7% black, 4% Hispanic, 3%
multiracial, 0% Pacific Islander,
80% white, 2% international;

87% from in state; 41% live on campus; 13% of students in fraternities, 16% in sororities **Most popular majors:** 16% Business, Management, Marketing, and Related Support Services; 12% Education; 8% Health Professions and Related Programs; 8% Liberal Arts and Sciences, General Studies and Humanities **Expenses:** 2016-2017: $9,654 in state, $25,428 out of state; room/board: $9,936 **Financial aid:** (765) 285-5600; 66% of undergrads determined to have financial need; average aid package $12,206

Bethel College
Mishawaka IN
(800) 422-4101
U.S. News ranking: Reg. U. (Mid. W), No. 40
Website: www.bethelcollege.edu
Admissions email: admissions@bethelcollege.edu
Private; founded 1947
Affiliation: Missionary Church
Freshman admissions: selective; 2015-2016: 1,938 applied, 1,288 accepted. Either SAT or ACT required. ACT 25/75 percentile: 19-26. High school rank: 20% in top tenth, 47% in top quarter, 74% in top half
Early decision deadline: N/A, notification date: N/A
Early action deadline: N/A, notification date: N/A
Application deadline (fall): rolling
Undergraduate student body: 1,168 full time, 321 part time; 35% male, 65% female; 0% American Indian, 1% Asian, 11% black, 6% Hispanic, 3% multiracial, 0% Pacific Islander, 76% white, 1% international; 70% from in state; 51% live on campus; N/A of students in fraternities, N/A in sororities
Most popular majors: 26% Business, Management, Marketing, and Related Support Services; 14% Health Professions and Related Programs; 9% Education; 9% Liberal Arts and Sciences, General Studies and Humanities; 8% Theology and Religious Vocations
Expenses: 2016-2017: $27,390; room/board: $8,470
Financial aid: (574) 257-3316

Butler University
Indianapolis IN
(888) 940-8100
U.S. News ranking: Reg. U. (Mid. W), No. 2
Website: www.butler.edu
Admissions email: admission@butler.edu
Private; founded 1855
Freshman admissions: more selective; 2015-2016: 9,943 applied, 7,003 accepted. Either SAT or ACT required. ACT 25/75 percentile: 25-30. High school rank: 49% in top tenth, 77% in top quarter, 96% in top half
Early decision deadline: N/A, notification date: N/A
Early action deadline: 11/1, notification date: 12/20
Application deadline (fall): 2/1
Undergraduate student body: 3,978 full time, 50 part time; 40% male, 60% female; 0% American

Indian, 3% Asian, 4% black, 4% Hispanic, 2% multiracial, 0% Pacific Islander, 82% white, 0% international; 48% from in state; 66% live on campus; 26% of students in fraternities, 40% in sororities
Most popular majors: 27% Business, Management, Marketing, and Related Support Services; 11% Education; 11% Health Professions and Related Programs; 11% Visual and Performing Arts
Expenses: 2016-2017: $38,405; room/board: $12,947
Financial aid: (317) 940-8200; 61% of undergrads determined to have financial need; average aid package $24,532

Calumet College of St. Joseph
Whiting IN
(219) 473-4295
U.S. News ranking: Reg. U. (Mid. W), second tier
Website: www.ccsj.edu
Admissions email: admissions@ccsj.edu
Private; founded 1951
Affiliation: Roman Catholic
Freshman admissions: less selective; 2015-2016: 461 applied, 163 accepted. Neither SAT nor ACT required. SAT 25/75 percentile: 785-1010. High school rank: 6% in top tenth, 14% in top quarter, 40% in top half
Early decision deadline: N/A, notification date: N/A
Early action deadline: N/A, notification date: N/A
Application deadline (fall): rolling
Undergraduate student body: 532 full time, 349 part time; 55% male, 45% female; 0% American Indian, 1% Asian, 28% black, 29% Hispanic, 1% multiracial, 0% Pacific Islander, 40% white, 0% international; 54% from in state; 0% live on campus; N/A of students in fraternities, N/A in sororities
Most popular majors: 43% Criminal Justice/Safety Studies; 16% Business Administration, Management and Operations, Other; 10% Business Administration and Management, General; 6% Biology/Biological Sciences, General; 5% Legal Assistant/Paralegal
Expenses: 2016-2017: $17,570; room/board: N/A
Financial aid: (219) 473-4213; 81% of undergrads determined to have financial need; average aid package $13,404

DePauw University
Greencastle IN
(765) 658-4006
U.S. News ranking: Nat. Lib. Arts, No. 53
Website: www.depauw.edu
Admissions email: admission@depauw.edu
Private; founded 1837
Freshman admissions: more selective; 2015-2016: 5,182 applied, 3,356 accepted. Either SAT or ACT required. ACT 25/75 percentile: 25-29. High school rank: 41% in top tenth, 76% in top quarter, 96% in top half

Early decision deadline: 11/1, notification date: 12/1
Early action deadline: 12/1, notification date: 1/15
Application deadline (fall): 2/1
Undergraduate student body: 2,229 full time, 36 part time; 46% male, 54% female; 0% American Indian, 4% Asian, 5% black, 4% Hispanic, 7% multiracial, 0% Pacific Islander, 71% white, 8% international; 37% from in state; 97% live on campus; 79% of students in fraternities, 67% in sororities
Most popular majors: 20% Social Sciences; 11% Biological and Biomedical Sciences; 9% English Language and Literature/Letters; 8% Computer and Information Sciences and Support Services
Expenses: 2016-2017: $46,448; room/board: $12,160
Financial aid: (765) 658-4030; 56% of undergrads determined to have financial need; average aid package $37,235

Earlham College
Richmond IN
(765) 983-1600
U.S. News ranking: Nat. Lib. Arts, No. 68
Website: www.earlham.edu/admissions
Admissions email: admission@earlham.edu
Private; founded 1847
Affiliation: Quaker
Freshman admissions: more selective; 2015-2016: 2,549 applied, 1,571 accepted. Neither SAT nor ACT required. SAT 25/75 percentile: 1110-1390. High school rank: 43% in top tenth, 71% in top quarter, 92% in top half
Early decision deadline: 11/1, notification date: 12/1
Early action deadline: 1/15, notification date: 2/15
Application deadline (fall): 2/15
Undergraduate student body: 980 full time, 8 part time; 43% male, 57% female; 1% American Indian, 5% Asian, 12% black, 6% Hispanic, 0% multiracial, 0% Pacific Islander, 51% white, 21% international; 22% from in state; 96% live on campus; 0% of students in fraternities, 0% in sororities
Most popular majors: 21% Biology, General; 19% Multi/Interdisciplinary Studies, Other; 10% Social Sciences, General; 9% Psychology, General; 7% Visual and Performing Arts, General
Expenses: 2016-2017: $45,300; room/board: $9,570
Financial aid: (765) 983-1217; 82% of undergrads determined to have financial need; average aid package $40,987

Franklin College
Franklin IN
(317) 738-8062
U.S. News ranking: Nat. Lib. Arts, No. 168
Website: www.franklincollege.edu
Admissions email: admissions@franklincollege.edu
Private; founded 1834
Affiliation: American Baptist

Freshman admissions: selective; 2015-2016: 2,023 applied, 1,412 accepted. Either SAT or ACT required. SAT 25/75 percentile: 16% in top tenth, 43% in top quarter, 85% in top half
Early decision deadline: N/A, notification date: N/A
Early action deadline: N/A, notification date: N/A
Application deadline (fall): rolling
Undergraduate student body: 1,015 full time, 72 part time; 47% male, 53% female; 0% American Indian, 1% Asian, 4% black, 2% Hispanic, 4% multiracial, 0% Pacific Islander, 84% white, 2% international; 93% from in state; 79% live on campus; 34% of students in fraternities, 48% in sororities
Most popular majors: 10% Business/Commerce, General; 10% Social Sciences; 10% Biology/Biological Sciences, General; 9% Education
Expenses: 2016-2017: $30,025; room/board: $9,355
Financial aid: (317) 738-8075; 84% of undergrads determined to have financial need; average aid package $22,312

Goshen College
Goshen IN
(574) 535-7535
U.S. News ranking: Reg. Coll. (Mid. W), No. 5
Website: www.goshen.edu
Admissions email: admissions@goshen.edu
Private; founded 1894
Affiliation: Mennonite Church USA
Freshman admissions: selective; 2015-2016: 797 applied, 525 accepted. Either SAT or ACT required. SAT 25/75 percentile: 890-1178. High school rank: 22% in top tenth, 46% in top quarter, 83% in top half
Early decision deadline: N/A, notification date: N/A
Early action deadline: N/A, notification date: N/A
Application deadline (fall): 8/15
Undergraduate student body: 713 full time, 60 part time; 42% male, 58% female; 0% American Indian, 2% Asian, 4% black, 17% Hispanic, 2% multiracial, N/A Pacific Islander, 65% white, 9% international; 44% from in state; 64% live on campus; N/A of students in fraternities, N/A in sororities
Most popular majors: 21% Health Professions and Related Programs; 11% Business, Management, Marketing, and Related Support Services; 11% Visual and Performing Arts; 8% Biological and Biomedical Sciences; 8% Multi/Interdisciplinary Studies
Expenses: 2016-2017: $32,200; room/board: $10,300
Financial aid: (574) 535-7583; 73% of undergrads determined to have financial need; average aid package $25,492

Grace College and Seminary
Winona Lake IN
(574) 372-5100
U.S. News ranking: Reg. U. (Mid. W), No. 74
Website: www.grace.edu
Admissions email: enroll@grace.edu
Private; founded 1948
Affiliation: Fellowship of Grace Brethren Churches
Freshman admissions: selective; 2015-2016: 3,850 applied, 2,999 accepted. Either SAT or ACT required. SAT 25/75 percentile: 910-1160. High school rank: 22% in top tenth, 53% in top quarter, 81% in top half
Early decision deadline: N/A, notification date: N/A
Early action deadline: 12/1, notification date: 12/20
Application deadline (fall): 3/1
Undergraduate student body: 1,484 full time, 438 part time; 43% male, 57% female; 0% American Indian, 1% Asian, 6% black, 4% Hispanic, 2% multiracial, N/A Pacific Islander, 79% white, 0% international; 74% from in state; 50% live on campus; 0% of students in fraternities, 0% in sororities
Most popular majors: Information not available
Expenses: 2016-2017: $23,120; room/board: $8,404
Financial aid: (574) 372-5100; 75% of undergrads determined to have financial need; average aid package $14,231

Hanover College
Hanover IN
(812) 866-7021
U.S. News ranking: Nat. Lib. Arts, No. 122
Website: www.hanover.edu
Admissions email: admission@hanover.edu
Private; founded 1827
Affiliation: Presbyterian
Freshman admissions: more selective; 2015-2016: 3,355 applied, 2,056 accepted. Either SAT or ACT required. ACT 25/75 percentile: 22-27. High school rank: 20% in top tenth, 54% in top quarter, 92% in top half
Early decision deadline: N/A, notification date: N/A
Early action deadline: 12/1, notification date: 12/20
Application deadline (fall): rolling
Undergraduate student body: 1,127 full time, 6 part time; 41% male, 59% female; 1% American Indian, 2% Asian, 4% black, 2% Hispanic, 1% multiracial, 0% Pacific Islander, 82% white, 4% international; 68% from in state; 92% live on campus; 39% of students in fraternities, 32% in sororities
Most popular majors: 9% Biology/Biological Sciences, General; 9% Economics, General; 8% Kinesiology and Exercise Science; 7% Psychology, General
Expenses: 2016-2017: $35,514; room/board: $10,850
Financial aid: (800) 213-2178; 76% of undergrads determined to have financial need; average aid package $29,162

Holy Cross College
Notre Dame IN
(574) 239-8400
U.S. News ranking: Nat. Lib. Arts, second tier
Website: www.hcc-nd.edu/home
Admissions email: admissions@hcc-nd.edu
Private; founded 1966
Affiliation: Roman Catholic
Freshman admissions: selective; 2015-2016: 689 applied, 630 accepted. Either SAT or ACT required. SAT 25/75 percentile: 890-1170. High school rank: 16% in top tenth, 33% in top quarter, 64% in top half
Early decision deadline: N/A, notification date: N/A
Early action deadline: N/A, notification date: N/A
Application deadline (fall): rolling
Undergraduate student body: 509 full time, 69 part time; 58% male, 42% female; 1% American Indian, 2% Asian, 11% black, 10% Hispanic, 3% multiracial, 0% Pacific Islander, 65% white, 4% international; 51% from in state; 49% live on campus; 0% of students in fraternities, 0% in sororities
Most popular majors: 45% Business/Commerce, General; 7% Psychology, General; 7% English Language and Literature, General; 5% Elementary Education and Teaching
Expenses: 2015-2016: $27,950; room/board: $9,975
Financial aid: (574) 239-8408

Huntington University
Huntington IN
(800) 642-6493
U.S. News ranking: Reg. Coll. (Mid. W), No. 13
Website: www.huntington.edu
Admissions email: admissions@huntington.edu
Private; founded 1897
Affiliation: United Brethren in Christ
Freshman admissions: selective; 2015-2016: 942 applied, 790 accepted. Either SAT or ACT required. SAT 25/75 percentile: 878-1140. High school rank: 17% in top tenth, 49% in top quarter, 80% in top half
Early decision deadline: N/A, notification date: N/A
Early action deadline: N/A, notification date: N/A
Application deadline (fall): 8/1
Undergraduate student body: 890 full time, 122 part time; 43% male, 57% female; 0% American Indian, 1% Asian, 2% black, 4% Hispanic, 3% multiracial, 0% Pacific Islander, 85% white, 4% international; 67% from in state; 84% live on campus; 0% of students in fraternities, 0% in sororities
Most popular majors: 11% Business/Commerce, General; 8% Cinematography and Film/Video Production; 7% Psychology, General; 7% Special Education and Teaching, General; 7% Youth Ministry
Expenses: 2016-2017: $25,400; room/board: $8,456
Financial aid: (260) 359-4015; 87% of undergrads determined to have financial need; average aid package $19,050

Indiana Institute of Technology
Fort Wayne IN
(800) 937-2448
U.S. News ranking: Business, unranked
Website: www.indianatech.edu
Admissions email: admissions@indianatech.edu
Private; founded 1930
Freshman admissions: N/A; 2015-2016: 3,016 applied, 2,099 accepted. Either SAT or ACT required. SAT 25/75 percentile: N/A. High school rank: 8% in top tenth, 29% in top quarter, 62% in top half
Early decision deadline: N/A, notification date: N/A
Early action deadline: N/A, notification date: N/A
Application deadline (fall): rolling
Undergraduate student body: 4,141 full time, 2,730 part time; 39% male, 61% female; 0% American Indian, 0% Asian, 36% black, 3% Hispanic, 2% multiracial, 0% Pacific Islander, 35% white, 2% international
Most popular majors: 40% Business Administration and Management, General; 11% Business/Commerce, General; 8% Accounting; 6% General Studies; 6% Organizational Leadership
Expenses: 2016-2017: $26,370; room/board: $12,100
Financial aid: (260) 422-5561; 88% of undergrads determined to have financial need; average aid package $19,062

Indiana State University
Terre Haute IN
(812) 237-2121
U.S. News ranking: Nat. U., second tier
Website: web.indstate.edu/
Admissions email: admissions@indstate.edu
Public; founded 1865
Freshman admissions: less selective; 2015-2016: 11,819 applied, 10,104 accepted. Either SAT or ACT required. SAT 25/75 percentile: 800-1020. High school rank: 8% in top tenth, 24% in top quarter, 62% in top half
Early decision deadline: N/A, notification date: N/A
Early action deadline: N/A, notification date: N/A
Application deadline (fall): 8/15
Undergraduate student body: 9,659 full time, 1,598 part time; 47% male, 53% female; 0% American Indian, 1% Asian, 19% black, 4% Hispanic, 4% multiracial, 0% Pacific Islander, 66% white, 6% international; 85% from in state; 40% live on campus; 16% of students in fraternities, 15% in sororities
Most popular majors: 20% Business, Management, Marketing, and Related Support Services; 16% Health Professions and Related Programs; 11% Social Sciences; 9% Education; 9% Engineering Technologies and Engineering-Related Fields
Expenses: 2016-2017: $8,746 in state, $19,076 out of state; room/board: $9,785

Indiana University East
Richmond IN
(765) 973-8208
U.S. News ranking: Reg. U. (Mid. W), second tier
Website: www.iue.edu
Admissions email: eaadmit@indiana.edu
Public; founded 1971
Freshman admissions: less selective; 2015-2016: 1,311 applied, 816 accepted. Either SAT or ACT required. SAT 25/75 percentile: 860-1050. High school rank: 9% in top tenth, 30% in top quarter, 74% in top half
Early decision deadline: N/A, notification date: N/A
Early action deadline: N/A, notification date: N/A
Application deadline (fall): rolling
Undergraduate student body: 1,964 full time, 2,598 part time; 37% male, 63% female; 0% American Indian, 1% Asian, 4% black, 3% Hispanic, 3% multiracial, 0% Pacific Islander, 87% white, 1% international; 76% from in state; N/A live on campus; N/A of students in fraternities, N/A in sororities

Indiana University–Bloomington
Bloomington IN
(812) 855-0661
U.S. News ranking: Nat. U., No. 86
Website: www.iub.edu
Admissions email: iuadmin@indiana.edu
Public; founded 1820
Freshman admissions: more selective; 2015-2016: 34,483 applied, 26,892 accepted. Either SAT or ACT required. SAT 25/75 percentile: 1060-1290. High school rank: 34% in top tenth, 68% in top quarter, 95% in top half
Early decision deadline: N/A, notification date: N/A
Early action deadline: N/A, notification date: N/A
Application deadline (fall): rolling
Undergraduate student body: 31,728 full time, 6,636 part time; 49% male, 51% female; 0% American Indian, 4% Asian, 4% black, 5% Hispanic, 4% multiracial, 0% Pacific Islander, 71% white, 11% international; 67% from in state; 35% live on campus; 21% of students in fraternities, 19% in sororities
Most popular majors: 18% Business, Management, Marketing, and Related Support Services; 9% Social Sciences; 8% Biological and Biomedical Sciences; 8% Parks, Recreation, Leisure, and Fitness Studies
Expenses: 2016-2017: $10,388 in state, $34,246 out of state; room/board: $10,040
Financial aid: (812) 855-0321; 42% of undergrads determined to have financial need; average aid package $12,835

Financial aid: (812) 237-2215; 74% of undergrads determined to have financial need; average aid package $10,739

Most popular majors: 27% Business, Management, Marketing, and Related Support Services; 22% Health Professions and Related Programs; 11% Liberal Arts and Sciences, General Studies and Humanities; 7% Education; 6% Psychology
Expenses: 2016-2017: $7,073 in state, $18,683 out of state; room/board: N/A
Financial aid: (765) 973-8206; 80% of undergrads determined to have financial need; average aid package $8,866

Indiana University–Kokomo
Kokomo IN
(765) 455-9217
U.S. News ranking: Reg. Coll. (Mid. W), second tier
Website: www.iuk.edu
Admissions email: luadmiss@iuk.edu
Public; founded 1945
Freshman admissions: less selective; 2015-2016: 1,534 applied, 1,094 accepted. Either SAT or ACT required. SAT 25/75 percentile: 840-1040. High school rank: 6% in top tenth, 29% in top quarter, 66% in top half
Early decision deadline: N/A, notification date: N/A
Early action deadline: N/A, notification date: N/A
Application deadline (fall): rolling
Undergraduate student body: 2,160 full time, 1,784 part time; 34% male, 66% female; 1% American Indian, 1% Asian, 4% black, 5% Hispanic, 2% multiracial, 0% Pacific Islander, 84% white, 1% international; 99% from in state; N/A live on campus; N/A of students in fraternities, N/A in sororities
Most popular majors: 49% Health Professions and Related Programs; 9% Liberal Arts and Sciences, General Studies and Humanities; 9% Business, Management, Marketing, and Related Support Services; 6% Psychology; 5% Education
Expenses: 2016-2017: $7,073 in state, $18,683 out of state; room/board: N/A
Financial aid: (765) 455-9216; 73% of undergrads determined to have financial need; average aid package $8,551

Indiana University Northwest
Gary IN
(219) 980-6991
U.S. News ranking: Reg. U. (Mid. W), second tier
Website: www.iun.edu
Admissions email: admit@iun.edu
Public; founded 1948
Freshman admissions: less selective; 2015-2016: 1,573 applied, 1,247 accepted. Either SAT or ACT required. SAT 25/75 percentile: 805-1030. High school rank: 11% in top tenth, 32% in top quarter, 64% in top half
Early decision deadline: N/A, notification date: N/A
Early action deadline: N/A, notification date: N/A

Application deadline (fall): rolling
Undergraduate student body: 2,957 full time, 2,529 part time; 34% male, 66% female; 0% American Indian, 2% Asian, 18% black, 20% Hispanic, 3% multiracial, 0% Pacific Islander, 55% white, 0% international; 98% from in state; 0% live on campus; N/A of students in fraternities, N/A in sororities
Most popular majors: 31% Health Professions and Related Programs; 13% Liberal Arts and Sciences, General Studies and Humanities; 11% Business, Management, Marketing, and Related Support Services; 9% Psychology; 8% Homeland Security, Law Enforcement, Firefighting and Related Protective Services
Expenses: 2016-2017: $7,073 in state, $18,683 out of state; room/board: N/A
Financial aid: (877) 280-4593; 69% of undergrads determined to have financial need; average aid package $8,110

Indiana University-Purdue University–Fort Wayne
Fort Wayne IN
(260) 481-6812
U.S. News ranking: Reg. U. (Mid. W), second tier
Website: www.ipfw.edu
Admissions email: ask@ipfw.edu
Public; founded 1964
Freshman admissions: less selective; 2015-2016: 3,506 applied, 3,231 accepted. Either SAT or ACT required. SAT 25/75 percentile: 870-1090. High school rank: 13% in top tenth, 36% in top quarter, 72% in top half
Early decision deadline: N/A, notification date: N/A
Early action deadline: N/A, notification date: N/A
Application deadline (fall): 8/1
Undergraduate student body: 6,656 full time, 5,504 part time; 45% male, 55% female; 0% American Indian, 3% Asian, 5% black, 5% Hispanic, 3% multiracial, 0% Pacific Islander, 82% white, 2% international; 97% from in state; 6% live on campus; 1% of students in fraternities, N/A in sororities
Most popular majors: 18% Business Administration and Management, General; 13% General Studies; 13% Health Professions and Related Programs; 7% Education; 7% Public Administration and Social Service Professions
Expenses: 2015-2016: $8,199 in state, $19,565 out of state; room/board: $9,270
Financial aid: (260) 481-6820

Indiana University-Purdue University–Indianapolis
Indianapolis IN
(317) 274-4591
U.S. News ranking: Nat. U., No. 197
Website: www.iupui.edu
Admissions email: apply@iupui.edu

Public; founded 1969
Freshman admissions: selective; 2015-2016: 13,529 applied, 9,425 accepted. Either SAT or ACT required. SAT 25/75 percentile: 890-1120. High school rank: 15% in top tenth, 43% in top quarter, 86% in top half
Early decision deadline: N/A, notification date: N/A
Early action deadline: N/A, notification date: N/A
Application deadline (fall): 5/1
Undergraduate student body: 17,051 full time, 4,934 part time; 44% male, 56% female; 0% American Indian, 7% Asian, 10% black, 6% Hispanic, 4% multiracial, 0% Pacific Islander, 72% white, 4% international; 97% from in state; 9% live on campus; N/A of students in fraternities, N/A in sororities
Most popular majors: 18% Health Professions and Related Programs; 16% Business, Management, Marketing, and Related Support Services; 10% Liberal Arts and Sciences, General Studies and Humanities; 6% Engineering; 5% Psychology
Expenses: 2016-2017: $9,205 in state, $29,791 out of state; room/board: $8,370
Financial aid: (317) 274-4162; 68% of undergrads determined to have financial need; average aid package $10,373

Indiana University–South Bend
South Bend IN
(574) 520-4839
U.S. News ranking: Reg. U. (Mid. W), second tier
Website: www.iusb.edu
Admissions email: admissions@iusb.edu
Public; founded 1922
Freshman admissions: less selective; 2015-2016: 2,299 applied, 1,752 accepted. Either SAT or ACT required. SAT 25/75 percentile: 840-1060. High school rank: 7% in top tenth, 25% in top quarter, 64% in top half
Early decision deadline: N/A, notification date: N/A
Early action deadline: N/A, notification date: N/A
Application deadline (fall): rolling
Undergraduate student body: 3,851 full time, 3,165 part time; 39% male, 61% female; 0% American Indian, 1% Asian, 8% black, 9% Hispanic, 3% multiracial, 0% Pacific Islander, 74% white, 3% international; 96% from in state; 7% live on campus; N/A of students in fraternities, N/A in sororities
Most popular majors: 19% Business, Management, Marketing, and Related Support Services; 17% Health Professions and Related Programs; 13% Liberal Arts and Sciences, General Studies and Humanities; 10% Education
Expenses: 2016-2017: $7,073 in state, $18,683 out of state; room/board: N/A
Financial aid: (574) 237-4357; 75% of undergrads determined to have financial need; average aid package $8,533

Indiana University Southeast
New Albany IN
(812) 941-2212
U.S. News ranking: Reg. U. (Mid. W), second tier
Website: www.ius.edu
Admissions email: admissions@ius.edu
Public; founded 1941
Freshman admissions: less selective; 2015-2016: 1,930 applied, 1,632 accepted. Either SAT or ACT required. SAT 25/75 percentile: 830-1050. High school rank: 9% in top tenth, 31% in top quarter, 70% in top half
Early decision deadline: N/A, notification date: N/A
Early action deadline: N/A, notification date: N/A
Undergraduate student body: 3,452 full time, 2,302 part time; 41% male, 59% female; 0% American Indian, 1% Asian, 6% black, 4% Hispanic, 3% multiracial, 0% Pacific Islander, 85% white, 0% international; 70% from in state; 7% live on campus; 1% of students in fraternities, 1% in sororities
Most popular majors: 18% Business, Management, Marketing, and Related Support Services; 12% Health Professions and Related Programs; 12% Liberal Arts and Sciences, General Studies and Humanities; 11% Education; 10% Psychology
Expenses: 2016-2017: $7,073 in state, $18,683 out of state; room/board: N/A
Financial aid: (812) 941-2246; 69% of undergrads determined to have financial need; average aid package $7,996

Indiana Wesleyan University
Marion IN
(866) 468-6498
U.S. News ranking: Reg. U. (Mid. W), No. 27
Website: www.indwes.edu
Admissions email: admissions@indwes.edu
Private; founded 1920
Affiliation: Wesleyan Church
Freshman admissions: selective; 2015-2016: 2,569 applied, 2,274 accepted. Either SAT or ACT required. ACT 25/75 percentile: 21-27. High school rank: 28% in top tenth, 58% in top quarter, 83% in top half
Early decision deadline: N/A, notification date: N/A
Early action deadline: N/A, notification date: N/A
Application deadline (fall): rolling
Undergraduate student body: 2,688 full time, 245 part time; 34% male, 66% female; 0% American Indian, 1% Asian, 3% black, 4% Hispanic, 3% multiracial, 0% Pacific Islander, 88% white, 1% international; 57% from in state; 82% live on campus; 0% of students in fraternities, 0% in sororities
Most popular majors: 22% Registered Nursing/Registered Nurse; 6% Elementary Education and Teaching; 5% Business Administration and Management,

General; 4% Psychology, General; 4% Theology and Religious Vocations, Other
Expenses: 2016-2017: $25,346; room/board $8,148
Financial aid: (765) 677-2116; 77% of undergrads determined to have financial need; average aid package $28,160

Manchester University
North Manchester IN
(800) 852-3648
U.S. News ranking: Reg. Coll. (Mid. W), No. 21
Website: www.manchester.edu
Admissions email: admitinfo@manchester.edu
Private; founded 1889
Affiliation: Church of the Brethren
Freshman admissions: selective; 2015-2016: 2,822 applied, 2,079 accepted. Neither SAT nor ACT required. SAT 25/75 percentile: 870-1100. High school rank: 15% in top tenth, 44% in top quarter, 82% in top half
Early decision deadline: N/A, notification date: N/A
Early action deadline: N/A, notification date: N/A
Application deadline (fall): rolling
Undergraduate student body: 1,235 full time, 11 part time; 48% male, 52% female; 0% American Indian, 1% Asian, 6% black, 6% Hispanic, 3% multiracial, N/A Pacific Islander, 80% white, 3% international; 88% from in state; 75% live on campus; N/A of students in fraternities, N/A in sororities
Most popular majors: 23% Business, Management, Marketing, and Related Support Services; 13% Parks, Recreation, Leisure, and Fitness Studies; 11% Health Professions and Related Programs; 9% Education; 7% Psychology
Expenses: 2016-2017: $30,802; room/board: $9,620
Financial aid: (260) 982-5066; 85% of undergrads determined to have financial need; average aid package $27,294

Marian University
Indianapolis IN
(317) 955-6300
U.S. News ranking: Reg. U. (Mid. W), No. 40
Website: www.marian.edu
Admissions email: admissions@marian.edu
Private; founded 1851
Affiliation: Roman Catholic
Freshman admissions: selective; 2015-2016: 2,072 applied, 1,148 accepted. Either SAT or ACT required. ACT 25/75 percentile: 20-26. High school rank: 18% in top tenth, 43% in top quarter, 82% in top half
Early decision deadline: N/A, notification date: N/A
Early action deadline: N/A, notification date: N/A
Application deadline (fall): 8/1
Undergraduate student body: 1,686 full time, 410 part time; 38% male, 62% female; 0% American Indian, 2% Asian, 12% black, 5% Hispanic, 2% multiracial, 0% Pacific Islander, 72% white,

1% international; 82% from in state; 38% live on campus; 0% of students in fraternities, 0% in sororities
Most popular majors: 49% Registered Nursing/Registered Nurse; 14% Business Administration and Management, General; 7% Education; 5% Kinesiology and Exercise Science; 4% Biology/Biological Sciences, General
Expenses: 2016-2017: $31,500; room/board: $9,720
Financial aid: (317) 955-6040; 81% of undergrads determined to have financial need; average aid package $24,285

Martin University[1]
Indianapolis IN
(317) 543-3243
U.S. News ranking: Nat. Lib. Arts, unranked
Website: www.martin.edu
Admissions email: bshaheed@martin.edu
Private
Application deadline (fall): N/A
Undergraduate student body: N/A full time, N/A part time
Expenses: 2015-2016: $12,536; room/board: N/A
Financial aid: (317) 543-3258

Oakland City University
Oakland City IN
(800) 737-5125
U.S. News ranking: Reg. Coll. (Mid. W), No. 33
Website: www.oak.edu
Admissions email: admission@oak.edu
Private; founded 1885
Affiliation: General Association of General Baptist
Freshman admissions: less selective; 2015-2016: 832 applied, 460 accepted. Neither SAT nor ACT required. SAT 25/75 percentile: 840-1010. High school rank: 4% in top tenth, 18% in top quarter, 58% in top half
Early decision deadline: N/A, notification date: N/A
Early action deadline: N/A, notification date: N/A
Application deadline (fall): rolling
Undergraduate student body: 620 full time, 621 part time; 44% male, 56% female; 0% American Indian, 0% Asian, 9% black, 2% Hispanic, 1% multiracial, 0% Pacific Islander, 70% white, 4% international; 76% from in state; 37% live on campus; N/A of students in fraternities, N/A in sororities
Most popular majors: 43% Business, Management, Marketing, and Related Support Services; 20% Homeland Security, Law Enforcement, Firefighting and Related Protective Services; 14% Education; 6% Biological and Biomedical Sciences; 5% Psychology
Expenses: 2015-2016: $22,800; room/board: $9,030
Financial aid: (812) 749-1224

Purdue University–North Central[1]
Westville IN
(219) 785-5505
U.S. News ranking: Reg. Coll. (Mid. W), second tier
Website: www.pnc.edu/admissions
Admissions email: admissions@pnc.edu
Public; founded 1946
Application deadline (fall): rolling
Undergraduate student body: N/A full time, N/A part time
Expenses: 2015-2016: $7,358 in state, $17,516 out of state; room/board: $8,128
Financial aid: (219) 785-5653

Purdue University–West Lafayette
West Lafayette IN
(765) 494-1776
U.S. News ranking: Nat. U., No. 60
Website: www.purdue.edu
Admissions email: admissions@purdue.edu
Public; founded 1869
Freshman admissions: more selective; 2015-2016: 45,023 applied, 26,524 accepted. Either SAT or ACT required. SAT 25/75 percentile: 1080-1330. High school rank: 43% in top tenth, 79% in top quarter, 97% in top half
Early decision deadline: N/A, notification date: N/A
Early action deadline: 11/1, notification date: 12/12
Application deadline (fall): rolling
Undergraduate student body: 28,131 full time, 1,366 part time; 57% male, 43% female; 0% American Indian, 6% Asian, 3% black, 4% Hispanic, 2% multiracial, 0% Pacific Islander, 64% white, 18% international; 66% from in state; 38% live on campus; 19% of students in fraternities, 21% in sororities
Most popular majors: 23% Engineering; 17% Business, Management, Marketing, and Related Support Services; 12% Liberal Arts and Sciences, General Studies and Humanities; 5% Engineering Technologies and Engineering-Related Fields
Expenses: 2016-2017: $10,002 in state, $28,804 out of state; room/board: $10,030
Financial aid: (765) 494-5090; 43% of undergrads determined to have financial need; average aid package $13,566

Rose-Hulman Institute of Technology
Terre Haute IN
(812) 877-8213
U.S. News ranking: Engineering, unranked
Website: www.rose-hulman.edu
Admissions email: admissions@rose-hulman.edu
Private; founded 1874
Freshman admissions: N/A; 2015-2016: 4,331 applied, 2,503 accepted. Either SAT or ACT required. SAT 25/75 percentile: N/A. High school rank: 69% in top tenth, 90% in top quarter, 99% in top half

Early decision deadline: N/A, notification date: N/A
Early action deadline: 11/1, notification date: 12/15
Application deadline (fall): 2/1
Undergraduate student body: 2,241 full time, 29 part time; 77% male, 23% female; 0% American Indian, 4% Asian, 2% black, 3% Hispanic, 4% multiracial, 0% Pacific Islander, 74% white, 12% international; 36% from in state; 57% live on campus; 35% of students in fraternities, 36% in sororities
Most popular majors: 28% Mechanical Engineering; 17% Chemical Engineering; 11% Electrical and Electronics Engineering; 8% Computer Science; 8% Computer Software Engineering
Expenses: 2016-2017: $44,010; room/board: $13,293
Financial aid: (812) 877-8259; 62% of undergrads determined to have financial need; average aid package $28,789

Saint Mary-of-the-Woods College

St. Mary-of-the-Woods IN
(800) 926-7692
U.S. News ranking: Reg. Coll. (Mid. W), No. 18
Website: www.smwc.edu
Admissions email: smwcadms@smwc.edu
Private; founded 1840
Affiliation: Roman Catholic
Freshman admissions: less selective; 2015-2016: 283 applied, 168 accepted. Either SAT or ACT required. SAT 25/75 percentile: 830-1030. High school rank: 2% in top tenth, 31% in top quarter, 71% in top half
Early decision deadline: N/A, notification date: N/A
Early action deadline: N/A, notification date: N/A
Application deadline (fall): rolling
Undergraduate student body: 400 full time, 273 part time; 5% male, 95% female; 1% American Indian, 1% Asian, 5% black, 2% Hispanic, 1% multiracial, 0% Pacific Islander, 75% white, 1% international; 14% from in state; N/A live on campus; 0% of students in fraternities, 0% in sororities
Most popular majors: 26% Education; 15% Business, Management, Marketing, and Related Support Services; 14% Psychology; 9% Public Administration and Social Service Professions
Expenses: 2016-2017: $28,932; room/board: $10,700
Financial aid: (812) 535-5109; 95% of undergrads determined to have financial need; average aid package $25,121

St. Joseph's College

Rensselaer IN
(219) 866-6170
U.S. News ranking: Reg. Coll. (Mid. W), No. 28
Website: www.saintjoe.edu
Admissions email: admissions@saintjoe.edu
Private; founded 1889
Affiliation: Roman Catholic

Freshman admissions: selective; 2015-2016: 1,596 applied, 1,136 accepted. Either SAT or ACT required. ACT 25/75 percentile: 19-24. High school rank: 13% in top tenth, 25% in top quarter, 63% in top half
Early decision deadline: N/A, notification date: N/A
Early action deadline: N/A, notification date: N/A
Application deadline (fall): rolling
Undergraduate student body: 944 full time, 68 part time; 44% male, 56% female; 0% American Indian, 0% Asian, 10% black, 5% Hispanic, 3% multiracial, 0% Pacific Islander, 80% white, 2% international; 75% from in state; 67% live on campus; 0% of students in fraternities, 0% in sororities
Most popular majors: 27% Registered Nursing/Registered Nurse; 16% Business/Commerce, General; 13% Health and Physical Education/Fitness, General; 11% Biology/Biological Sciences, General; 6% Psychology, General
Expenses: 2016-2017: $30,080; room/board: $9,480
Financial aid: (219) 866-6163; 73% of undergrads determined to have financial need; average aid package $29,247

St. Mary's College

Notre Dame IN
(574) 284-4587
U.S. News ranking: Nat. Lib. Arts, No. 95
Website: www.saintmarys.edu
Admissions email: admission@saintmarys.edu
Private; founded 1844
Affiliation: Roman Catholic
Freshman admissions: more selective; 2015-2016: 1,722 applied, 1,384 accepted. Either SAT or ACT required. ACT 25/75 percentile: 22-28. High school rank: 28% in top tenth, 62% in top quarter, 90% in top half
Early decision deadline: 11/15, notification date: 12/15
Early action deadline: N/A, notification date: N/A
Application deadline (fall): rolling
Undergraduate student body: 1,558 full time, 61 part time; 1% male, 99% female; 0% American Indian, 2% Asian, 2% black, 11% Hispanic, 3% multiracial, 0% Pacific Islander, 78% white, 1% international; 27% from in state; 86% live on campus; 0% of students in fraternities, 0% in sororities
Most popular majors: 16% Registered Nursing/Registered Nurse; 9% Business Administration and Management, General; 7% Elementary Education and Teaching; 7% Psychology, General
Expenses: 2016-2017: $38,880; room/board: $11,720
Financial aid: (574) 284-4557; 66% of undergrads determined to have financial need; average aid package $31,880

Taylor University

Upland IN
(765) 998-5134
U.S. News ranking: Reg. Coll. (Mid. W), No. 1
Website: www.taylor.edu
Admissions email: admissions_u@taylor.edu
Private; founded 1846
Affiliation: Christian interdenominational
Freshman admissions: more selective; 2015-2016: 1,716 applied, 1,460 accepted. Either SAT or ACT required. ACT 25/75 percentile: 24-30. High school rank: 36% in top tenth, 65% in top quarter, 88% in top half
Early decision deadline: N/A, notification date: N/A
Early action deadline: N/A, notification date: N/A
Application deadline (fall): rolling
Undergraduate student body: 1,854 full time, 273 part time; 44% male, 56% female; 1% American Indian, 3% Asian, 3% black, 3% Hispanic, 0% multiracial, 0% Pacific Islander, 86% white, 5% international; 39% from in state; 88% live on campus; N/A of students in fraternities, N/A in sororities
Most popular majors: 18% Business, Management, Marketing, and Related Support Services; 14% Education; 8% Parks, Recreation, Leisure, and Fitness Studies; 8% Visual and Performing Arts
Expenses: 2016-2017: $31,472; room/board: $8,845
Financial aid: (765) 998-5358; 62% of undergrads determined to have financial need; average aid package $20,783

Trine University

Angola IN
(260) 665-4100
U.S. News ranking: Reg. Coll. (Mid. W), No. 22
Website: www.trine.edu
Admissions email: admit@trine.edu
Private; founded 1884
Freshman admissions: more selective; 2015-2016: 3,217 applied, 2,498 accepted. Either SAT or ACT required. ACT 25/75 percentile: 21-27. High school rank: 21% in top tenth, 54% in top quarter, 85% in top half
Early decision deadline: N/A, notification date: N/A
Early action deadline: N/A, notification date: N/A
Application deadline (fall): 8/1
Undergraduate student body: 1,719 full time, 1,436 part time; 58% male, 42% female; 0% American Indian, 1% Asian, 3% black, 4% Hispanic, 2% multiracial, 0% Pacific Islander, 78% white, 9% international; 61% from in state; 69% live on campus; 26% of students in fraternities, 19% in sororities
Most popular majors: 33% Engineering, General; 14% CAD/CADD Drafting and/or Design Technology/Technician; 9% Criminal Justice/Law Enforcement Administration; 9% Kinesiology and Exercise Science; 7% Education, General
Expenses: 2016-2017: $30,960; room/board: $10,350

Financial aid: (260) 665-4175; 88% of undergrads determined to have financial need; average aid package $25,700

University of Evansville

Evansville IN
(812) 488-2468
U.S. News ranking: Reg. U. (Mid. W), No. 8
Website: www.evansville.edu
Admissions email: admission@evansville.edu
Private; founded 1854
Affiliation: United Methodist
Freshman admissions: more selective; 2015-2016: 4,167 applied, 2,906 accepted. Neither SAT nor ACT required. ACT 25/75 percentile: 23-29. High school rank: 33% in top tenth, 66% in top quarter, 93% in top half
Early decision deadline: N/A, notification date: N/A
Early action deadline: 12/1, notification date: 12/15
Application deadline (fall): rolling
Undergraduate student body: 2,140 full time, 191 part time; 46% male, 54% female; 0% American Indian, 1% Asian, 3% black, 3% Hispanic, 2% multiracial, 0% Pacific Islander, 73% white, 13% international; 59% from in state; 63% live on campus; 30% of students in fraternities, 29% in sororities
Most popular majors: 14% Health Professions and Related Programs; 13% Business, Management, Marketing, and Related Support Services; 10% Parks, Recreation, Leisure, and Fitness Studies; 8% Social Sciences; 8% Visual and Performing Arts
Expenses: 2016-2017: $33,966; room/board: $11,690
Financial aid: (812) 488-2364; 69% of undergrads determined to have financial need; average aid package $27,256

University of Indianapolis

Indianapolis IN
(317) 788-3216
U.S. News ranking: Reg. U. (Mid. W), No. 31
Website: www.uindy.edu
Admissions email: admissions@uindy.edu
Private; founded 1902
Affiliation: United Methodist
Freshman admissions: selective; 2015-2016: 5,729 applied, 4,799 accepted. Either SAT or ACT required. SAT 25/75 percentile: 910-1120. High school rank: 21% in top tenth, 55% in top quarter, 87% in top half
Early decision deadline: N/A, notification date: N/A
Early action deadline: N/A, notification date: N/A
Application deadline (fall): rolling
Undergraduate student body: 3,469 full time, 731 part time; 36% male, 64% female; 0% American Indian, 1% Asian, 9% black, 4% Hispanic, 3% multiracial, 0% Pacific Islander, 70% white, 9% international

Most popular majors: 21% Registered Nursing/Registered Nurse; 12% Psychology, General; 11% Business Administration and Management, General; 6% Liberal Arts and Sciences/Liberal Studies; 5% Kinesiology and Exercise Science
Expenses: 2016-2017: $27,420; room/board: $10,362
Financial aid: (317) 788-3217; 71% of undergrads determined to have financial need; average aid package $19,276

University of Notre Dame

Notre Dame IN
(574) 631-7505
U.S. News ranking: Nat. U., No. 15
Website: www.nd.edu
Admissions email: admissions@nd.edu
Private; founded 1842
Affiliation: Roman Catholic
Freshman admissions: most selective; 2015-2016: 18,157 applied, 3,595 accepted. Either SAT or ACT required. ACT 25/75 percentile: 32-34. High school rank: 91% in top tenth, 98% in top quarter, 100% in top half
Early decision deadline: N/A, notification date: N/A
Early action deadline: 11/1, notification date: 12/21
Application deadline (fall): 1/1
Undergraduate student body: 8,450 full time, 12 part time; 52% male, 48% female; 0% American Indian, 6% Asian, 4% black, 11% Hispanic, 4% multiracial, 0% Pacific Islander, 69% white, 6% international; 7% from in state; 79% live on campus; 0% of students in fraternities, 0% in sororities
Most popular majors: 11% Finance, General; 7% Accounting; 6% Economics, General; 5% Political Science and Government, General; 5% Psychology, General
Expenses: 2016-2017: $49,685; room/board: $14,358
Financial aid: (574) 631-6436; 45% of undergrads determined to have financial need; average aid package $44,507

University of Saint Francis

Fort Wayne IN
(260) 399-8000
U.S. News ranking: Reg. U. (Mid. W), No. 79
Website: www.sf.edu
Admissions email: admis@sf.edu
Private; founded 1890
Affiliation: Roman Catholic
Freshman admissions: less selective; 2015-2016: 991 applied, 944 accepted. Either SAT or ACT required. SAT 25/75 percentile: 860-1070. High school rank: 17% in top tenth, 47% in top quarter, 78% in top half
Early decision deadline: N/A, notification date: N/A
Early action deadline: N/A, notification date: N/A
Application deadline (fall): rolling
Undergraduate student body: 1,502 full time, 302 part time; 29% male, 71% female; 0% American

Indian, 1% Asian, 7% black, 6% Hispanic, 2% multiracial, 0% Pacific Islander, 81% white, 1% international; 91% from in state; 22% live on campus; N/A of students in fraternities, N/A in sororities
Most popular majors: 34% Registered Nursing/Registered Nurse; 13% Health and Wellness, General; 11% Business Administration and Management, General; 5% Biology/Biological Sciences, General; 4% Social Work
Expenses: 2016-2017: $28,310; room/board: $9,090
Financial aid: (260) 434-3283; 87% of undergrads determined to have financial need; average aid package $18,373

University of Southern Indiana
Evansville IN
(812) 464-1765
U.S. News ranking: Reg. U. (Mid. W), second tier
Website: www.usi.edu
Admissions email: enroll@usi.edu
Public; founded 1965
Freshman admissions: selective; 2015-2016: 6,216 applied, 4,310 accepted. Either SAT or ACT required. SAT 25/75 percentile: 890-1100. High school rank: 12% in top tenth, 33% in top quarter, 71% in top half
Early decision deadline: N/A, notification date: N/A
Early action deadline: N/A, notification date: N/A
Application deadline (fall): 7/1
Undergraduate student body: 6,869 full time, 1,261 part time; 39% male, 61% female; 0% American Indian, 1% Asian, 4% black, 3% Hispanic, 2% multiracial, 0% Pacific Islander, 87% white, 2% international; 89% from in state; 31% live on campus; 10% of students in fraternities, 11% in sororities
Most popular majors: 25% Health Professions and Related Programs; 17% Business, Management, Marketing, and Related Support Services; 6% Education; 6% Parks, Recreation, Leisure, and Fitness Studies
Expenses: 2016-2017: $7,178 in state, $16,959 out of state; room/board: $8,176
Financial aid: (812) 464-1767; 62% of undergrads determined to have financial need; average aid package $9,331

Valparaiso University
Valparaiso IN
(888) 468-2576
U.S. News ranking: Reg. U. (Mid. W), No. 4
Website: www.valpo.edu
Admissions email: undergrad.admission@valpo.edu
Private; founded 1859
Affiliation: Lutheran
Freshman admissions: more selective; 2015-2016: 6,657 applied, 5,452 accepted. Either SAT or ACT required. ACT 25/75 percentile: 23-29. High school rank: 35% in top tenth, 64% in top quarter, 91% in top half

Early decision deadline: N/A, notification date: N/A
Early action deadline: N/A, notification date: N/A
Application deadline (fall): rolling
Undergraduate student body: 3,098 full time, 81 part time; 48% male, 52% female; 0% American Indian, 2% Asian, 6% black, 8% Hispanic, 3% multiracial, 0% Pacific Islander, 72% white, 7% international; 42% from in state; 66% live on campus; 20% of students in fraternities, 18% in sororities
Most popular majors: 18% Registered Nursing/Registered Nurse; 5% Biology/Biological Sciences, General; 4% Electrical and Electronics Engineering; 4% Finance, General; 4% Psychology, General
Expenses: 2016-2017: $37,450; room/board: $10,920
Financial aid: (219) 464-5015; 74% of undergrads determined to have financial need; average aid package $29,069

Vincennes University
Vincennes IN
(800) 742-9198
U.S. News ranking: Reg. Coll. (Mid. W), unranked
Website: www.vinu.edu
Admissions email: N/A
Public; founded 1801
Freshman admissions: N/A; 2015-2016: 6,261 applied, 5,108 accepted. Neither SAT nor ACT required. ACT 25/75 percentile: N/A. High school rank: N/A
Early decision deadline: N/A, notification date: N/A
Early action deadline: N/A, notification date: N/A
Application deadline (fall): rolling
Undergraduate student body: 5,773 full time, 12,938 part time; 54% male, 46% female; 0% American Indian, 1% Asian, 12% black, 3% Hispanic, 3% multiracial, 0% Pacific Islander, 73% white, 1% international; 81% from in state; 25% live on campus; N/A of students in fraternities, N/A in sororities
Most popular majors: Information not available
Expenses: 2015-2016: $5,375 in state, $12,709 out of state; room/board: $8,732
Financial aid: (812) 888-4361

Wabash College
Crawfordsville IN
(800) 345-5385
U.S. News ranking: Nat. Lib. Arts, No. 65
Website: www.wabash.edu
Admissions email: admissions@wabash.edu
Private; founded 1832
Freshman admissions: more selective; 2015-2016: 1,247 applied, 766 accepted. Either SAT or ACT required. SAT 25/75 percentile: 1040-1250. High school rank: 35% in top tenth, 71% in top quarter, 95% in top half
Early decision deadline: 10/15, notification date: 11/16
Early action deadline: 11/1, notification date: 12/7
Application deadline (fall): rolling

Undergraduate student body: 867 full time, 1 part time; 100% male, 0% female; 0% American Indian, 1% Asian, 6% black, 7% Hispanic, 3% multiracial, 0% Pacific Islander, 74% white, 7% international; 77% from in state; 91% live on campus; 54% of students in fraternities, N/A in sororities
Most popular majors: 16% History, General; 12% Political Science and Government, General; 11% Economics, General; 10% Biology/Biological Sciences, General; 9% Mathematics, General
Expenses: 2016-2017: $41,050; room/board: $9,600
Financial aid: (765) 361-6370; 75% of undergrads determined to have financial need; average aid package $33,277

IOWA

Briar Cliff University
Sioux City IA
(712) 279-5200
U.S. News ranking: Reg. Coll. (Mid. W), No. 30
Website: www.briarcliff.edu
Admissions email: admissions@briarcliff.edu
Private; founded 1930
Affiliation: Roman Catholic
Freshman admissions: selective; 2015-2016: 1,741 applied, 919 accepted. Either SAT or ACT required. ACT 25/75 percentile: 19-23. High school rank: 13% in top tenth, 38% in top quarter, 66% in top half
Early decision deadline: N/A, notification date: N/A
Early action deadline: N/A, notification date: N/A
Application deadline (fall): rolling
Undergraduate student body: 792 full time, 230 part time; 44% male, 56% female; 1% American Indian, 1% Asian, 7% black, 11% Hispanic, 2% multiracial, 1% Pacific Islander, 73% white, 4% international; 62% from in state; 47% live on campus; 0% of students in fraternities, 0% in sororities
Most popular majors: 30% Health Professions and Related Programs; 18% Business, Management, Marketing, and Related Support Services; 9% Education; 8% Parks, Recreation, Leisure, and Fitness Studies; 5% Biological and Biomedical Sciences
Expenses: 2016-2017: $28,608; room/board: $8,348
Financial aid: (712) 279-5239; 84% of undergrads determined to have financial need; average aid package $39,884

Buena Vista University
Storm Lake IA
(800) 383-9600
U.S. News ranking: Reg. Coll. (Mid. W), No. 24
Website: www.bvu.edu
Admissions email: admissions@bvu.edu
Private; founded 1891
Affiliation: Presbyterian

Freshman admissions: selective; 2015-2016: 1,372 applied, 934 accepted. Either SAT or ACT required. ACT 25/75 percentile: 19-24. High school rank: 15% in top tenth, 41% in top quarter, 73% in top half
Early decision deadline: N/A, notification date: N/A
Early action deadline: N/A, notification date: N/A
Application deadline (fall): rolling
Undergraduate student body: 872 full time, 9 part time; 48% male, 52% female; 0% American Indian, 2% Asian, 2% black, 7% Hispanic, 3% multiracial, 0% Pacific Islander, 74% white, 8% international; 75% from in state; 90% live on campus; 0% of students in fraternities, 0% in sororities
Most popular majors: 25% Business, Management, Marketing, and Related Support Services; 11% Biological and Biomedical Sciences; 11% Education; 10% Parks, Recreation, Leisure, and Fitness Studies; 7% Visual and Performing Arts
Expenses: 2016-2017: $32,210; room/board: $9,304
Financial aid: (712) 749-2164; 79% of undergrads determined to have financial need; average aid package $27,197

Central College
Pella IA
(641) 628-5286
U.S. News ranking: Nat. Lib. Arts, No. 132
Website: www.central.edu
Admissions email: admission@central.edu
Private; founded 1853
Affiliation: Reformed Church in America
Freshman admissions: more selective; 2015-2016: 3,071 applied, 1,974 accepted. Either SAT or ACT required. ACT 25/75 percentile: 20-26. High school rank: 23% in top tenth, 54% in top quarter, 85% in top half
Early decision deadline: N/A, notification date: N/A
Early action deadline: N/A, notification date: N/A
Application deadline (fall): 8/15
Undergraduate student body: 1,230 full time, 44 part time; 47% male, 53% female; 0% American Indian, 1% Asian, 2% black, 4% Hispanic, 1% multiracial, 0% Pacific Islander, 87% white, 0% international; 79% from in state; 91% live on campus; 3% of students in fraternities, 2% in sororities
Most popular majors: 24% Biological and Biomedical Sciences; 17% Business, Management, Marketing, and Related Support Services; 12% Social Sciences; 10% Education; 6% Psychology
Expenses: 2016-2017: $34,612; room/board: $9,980
Financial aid: (641) 628-5187; 82% of undergrads determined to have financial need; average aid package $28,501

Clarke University
Dubuque IA
(563) 588-6316
U.S. News ranking: Reg. Coll. (Mid. W), No. 17
Website: www.clarke.edu
Admissions email: admissions@clarke.edu
Private; founded 1843
Affiliation: Roman Catholic
Freshman admissions: selective; 2015-2016: 1,257 applied, 904 accepted. Either SAT or ACT required. ACT 25/75 percentile: 20-25. High school rank: 13% in top tenth, 42% in top quarter, 77% in top half
Early decision deadline: N/A, notification date: N/A
Early action deadline: N/A, notification date: N/A
Application deadline (fall): rolling
Undergraduate student body: 792 full time, 76 part time; 34% male, 66% female; N/A American Indian, 1% Asian, 4% black, 7% Hispanic, 2% multiracial, N/A Pacific Islander, 85% white, 1% international; 54% from in state; 48% live on campus; N/A of students in fraternities, N/A in sororities
Most popular majors: 28% Registered Nursing/Registered Nurse; 15% Business Administration and Management, General; 13% Psychology, General; 10% Elementary Education and Teaching; 5% Biology/Biological Sciences, General
Expenses: 2016-2017: $30,900; room/board: $9,200
Financial aid: (563) 588-6327; 87% of undergrads determined to have financial need; average aid package $25,080

Coe College
Cedar Rapids IA
(319) 399-8500
U.S. News ranking: Nat. Lib. Arts, No. 119
Website: www.coe.edu
Admissions email: admission@coe.edu
Private; founded 1851
Affiliation: Presbyterian
Freshman admissions: more selective; 2015-2016: 3,756 applied, 2,275 accepted. Either SAT or ACT required. ACT 25/75 percentile: 22-27. High school rank: 27% in top tenth, 55% in top quarter, 88% in top half
Early decision deadline: N/A, notification date: N/A
Early action deadline: 12/10, notification date: 1/20
Application deadline (fall): 3/1
Undergraduate student body: 1,357 full time, 59 part time; 42% male, 58% female; 0% American Indian, 3% Asian, 6% black, 9% Hispanic, 3% multiracial, 0% Pacific Islander, 74% white, 1% international; 45% from in state; 86% live on campus; 18% of students in fraternities, 28% in sororities
Most popular majors: 18% Business, Management, Marketing, and Related Support Services; 11% Biological and Biomedical Sciences; 10% Psychology; 7% Visual and Performing Arts

Expenses: 2016-2017: $41,000; room/board: $8,820
Financial aid: (319) 399-8540; 83% of undergrads determined to have financial need; average aid package $31,746

Cornell College
Mount Vernon IA
(800) 747-1112
U.S. News ranking: Nat. Lib. Arts, No. 90
Website: www.cornellcollege.edu
Admissions email: admissions@cornellcollege.edu
Private; founded 1853
Affiliation: United Methodist
Freshman admissions: more selective; 2015-2016: 1,934 applied, 1,366 accepted. Either SAT or ACT required. ACT 25/75 percentile: 23-29. High school rank: 22% in top tenth, 45% in top quarter, 88% in top half
Early decision deadline: 11/1, notification date: 12/15
Early action deadline: 12/1, notification date: 2/1
Application deadline (fall): 2/1
Undergraduate student body: 1,029 full time, 4 part time; 49% male, 51% female; 1% American Indian, 3% Asian, 5% black, 13% Hispanic, 3% multiracial, 0% Pacific Islander, 66% white, 3% international; 18% from in state; 93% live on campus; 16% of students in fraternities, 22% in sororities
Most popular majors: 15% Psychology; 11% Parks, Recreation, Leisure, and Fitness Studies; 9% Biological and Biomedical Sciences; 9% Social Sciences; 7% Biological and Biomedical Sciences
Expenses: 2016-2017: $39,900; room/board: $8,900
Financial aid: (319) 895-4216; 75% of undergrads determined to have financial need; average aid package $31,219

Dordt College
Sioux Center IA
(800) 343-6738
U.S. News ranking: Reg. Coll. (Mid. W), No. 8
Website: www.dordt.edu
Admissions email: admissions@dordt.edu
Private; founded 1955
Affiliation: Christian Reformed
Freshman admissions: selective; 2015-2016: 1,234 applied, 878 accepted. Either SAT or ACT required. ACT 25/75 percentile: 23-29. High school rank: 24% in top tenth, 47% in top quarter, 72% in top half
Early decision deadline: N/A, notification date: N/A
Early action deadline: N/A, notification date: N/A
Application deadline (fall): 8/1
Undergraduate student body: 1,351 full time, 34 part time; 52% male, 48% female; 0% American Indian, 1% Asian, 0% black, 2% Hispanic, 0% multiracial, 0% Pacific Islander, 81% white, 10% international; 40% from in state; 89% live on campus; 0% of students in fraternities, 0% in sororities

Most popular majors: 19% Business/Commerce, General; 18% Elementary Education and Teaching; 10% Engineering, General; 6% Parks, Recreation and Leisure Studies
Expenses: 2016-2017: $29,130; room/board: $8,730
Financial aid: (712) 722-6087; 68% of undergrads determined to have financial need; average aid package $24,197

Drake University
Des Moines IA
(800) 443-7253
U.S. News ranking: Reg. U. (Mid. W), No. 3
Website: www.drake.edu
Admissions email: admission@drake.edu
Private; founded 1881
Freshman admissions: more selective; 2015-2016: 6,514 applied, 4,356 accepted. Neither SAT nor ACT required. ACT 25/75 percentile: 24-30. High school rank: 37% in top tenth, 69% in top quarter, 93% in top half
Early decision deadline: N/A, notification date: N/A
Early action deadline: N/A, notification date: N/A
Application deadline (fall): rolling
Undergraduate student body: 3,167 full time, 171 part time; 44% male, 56% female; 0% American Indian, 3% Asian, 4% black, 4% Hispanic, 2% multiracial, 0% Pacific Islander, 79% white, 7% international; 31% from in state; 70% live on campus; 36% of students in fraternities, 29% in sororities
Most popular majors: 34% Business, Management, Marketing, and Related Services; 8% Biological and Biomedical Sciences; 8% Social Sciences; 7% Education
Expenses: 2016-2017: $35,206; room/board: $9,850
Financial aid: (515) 271-2905; 59% of undergrads determined to have financial need; average aid package $26,388

Graceland University
Lamoni IA
(866) 472-2352
U.S. News ranking: Reg. U. (Mid. W), No. 113
Website: www.graceland.edu
Admissions email: admissions@graceland.edu
Private; founded 1895
Affiliation: Community of Christ
Freshman admissions: selective; 2015-2016: 2,153 applied, 1,031 accepted. Either SAT or ACT required. ACT 25/75 percentile: 18-24. High school rank: 12% in top tenth, 18% in top quarter, 65% in top half
Early decision deadline: N/A, notification date: N/A
Early action deadline: N/A, notification date: N/A
Application deadline (fall): rolling
Undergraduate student body: 1,243 full time, 313 part time; 44% male, 56% female; 0% American Indian, 1% Asian, 10% black, 11% Hispanic, 4% multiracial, 1% Pacific Islander, 61% white, 3% international; 32% from in state; 70% live on campus; N/A

of students in fraternities, N/A in sororities
Most popular majors: 23% Health Professions and Related Programs; 21% Education; 16% Business, Management, Marketing, and Related Support Services; 7% Parks, Recreation, Leisure, and Fitness Studies; 4% Psychology
Expenses: 2016-2017: $27,010; room/board: $8,280
Financial aid: (641) 784-5136; 81% of undergrads determined to have financial need; average aid package $22,072

Grand View University
Des Moines IA
(515) 263-2810
U.S. News ranking: Reg. Coll. (Mid. W), No. 41
Website: admissions.grandview.edu/
Admissions email: admissions@grandview.edu
Private; founded 1896
Affiliation: Evangelical Lutheran Church in America
Freshman admissions: selective; 2015-2016: 784 applied, 770 accepted. Either SAT or ACT required. ACT 25/75 percentile: 18-23. High school rank: 14% in top tenth, 33% in top quarter, 68% in top half
Early decision deadline: N/A, notification date: N/A
Early action deadline: N/A, notification date: N/A
Application deadline (fall): 8/15
Undergraduate student body: 1,634 full time, 287 part time; 45% male, 55% female; 0% American Indian, 3% Asian, 8% black, 4% Hispanic, 3% multiracial, N/A Pacific Islander, 72% white, 2% international; 85% from in state; 43% live on campus; N/A of students in fraternities, N/A in sororities
Most popular majors: 21% Business, Management, Marketing, and Related Support Services; 13% Health Professions and Related Programs; 10% Education; 7% Parks, Recreation, Leisure, and Fitness Studies; 7% Visual and Performing Arts
Expenses: 2016-2017: $25,474; room/board: $8,172
Financial aid: (515) 263-2820; 83% of undergrads determined to have financial need; average aid package $16,688

Grinnell College
Grinnell IA
(800) 247-0113
U.S. News ranking: Nat. Lib. Arts, No. 19
Website: www.grinnell.edu
Admissions email: askgrin@grinnell.edu
Private; founded 1846
Freshman admissions: most selective; 2015-2016: 6,414 applied, 1,598 accepted. Either SAT or ACT required. ACT 25/75 percentile: 30-33. High school rank: 81% in top tenth, 96% in top quarter, 100% in top half
Early decision deadline: 11/15, notification date: 12/15
Early action deadline: N/A, notification date: N/A
Application deadline (fall): 1/15

Undergraduate student body: 1,665 full time, 40 part time; 45% male, 55% female; 0% American Indian, 7% Asian, 6% black, 7% Hispanic, 5% multiracial, 0% Pacific Islander, 56% white, 16% international; 12% from in state; 88% live on campus; 0% of students in fraternities, 0% in sororities
Most popular majors: 25% Social Sciences; 15% Biological and Biomedical Sciences; 11% Foreign Languages, Literatures, and Linguistics; 8% Psychology; 7% English Language and Literature/Letters
Expenses: 2016-2017: $48,758; room/board: $11,980
Financial aid: (641) 269-3250; 68% of undergrads determined to have financial need; average aid package $45,009

Iowa State University
Ames IA
(800) 262-3810
U.S. News ranking: Nat. U., No. 111
Website: www.iastate.edu
Admissions email: admissions@iastate.edu
Public; founded 1858
Freshman admissions: more selective; 2015-2016: 19,164 applied, 16,702 accepted. Either SAT or ACT required. ACT 25/75 percentile: 22-28. High school rank: 22% in top tenth, 54% in top quarter, 91% in top half
Early decision deadline: N/A, notification date: N/A
Early action deadline: N/A, notification date: N/A
Application deadline (fall): rolling
Undergraduate student body: 28,202 full time, 1,832 part time; 57% male, 43% female; 0% American Indian, 3% Asian, 3% black, 5% Hispanic, 2% multiracial, 0% Pacific Islander, 76% white, 7% international; 69% from in state; 41% live on campus; 12% of students in fraternities, 20% in sororities
Most popular majors: 19% Business, Management, Marketing, and Related Support Services; 19% Engineering; 6% Biological and Biomedical Sciences; 4% Education
Expenses: 2016-2017: $7,969 in state, $21,483 out of state; room/board: $8,356
Financial aid: (515) 294-2223; 52% of undergrads determined to have financial need; average aid package $11,920

Iowa Wesleyan University
Mount Pleasant IA
(319) 385-6231
U.S. News ranking: Reg. Coll. (Mid. W), No. 60
Website: www.iw.edu
Admissions email: admit@iw.edu
Private; founded 1842
Affiliation: United Methodist
Freshman admissions: selective; 2015-2016: 4,981 applied, 2,472 accepted. Either SAT or ACT required. ACT 25/75 percentile: 19-23. High school rank: 9% in top tenth, 35% in top quarter, 63% in top half

Early decision deadline: N/A, notification date: N/A
Early action deadline: N/A, notification date: N/A
Application deadline (fall): N/A
Undergraduate student body: 387 full time, 69 part time; 41% male, 59% female; N/A American Indian, N/A Asian, N/A black, N/A Hispanic, N/A multiracial, N/A Pacific Islander, N/A white, N/A international; N/A from in state; 80% live on campus; N/A of students in fraternities, N/A in sororities
Most popular majors: 34% Teacher Education, Multiple Levels; 19% Business Administration and Management, General; 18% Registered Nursing/Registered Nurse
Expenses: 2016-2017: $29,146; room/board: $10,054
Financial aid: (319) 385-6242; 90% of undergrads determined to have financial need; average aid package $21,746

Kaplan University[1]
Davenport IA
(800) 987-7734
U.S. News ranking: Reg. U. (Mid. W), unranked
Website: www.kaplan.edu
Admissions email: N/A
For-profit
Application deadline (fall): N/A
Undergraduate student body: N/A full time, N/A part time
Expenses: 2015-2016: $14,241; room/board: N/A
Financial aid: (866) 428-2008

Loras College
Dubuque IA
(800) 245-6727
U.S. News ranking: Reg. Coll. (Mid. W), No. 11
Website: www.loras.edu
Admissions email: admissions@loras.edu
Private; founded 1839
Affiliation: Roman Catholic
Freshman admissions: selective; 2015-2016: 1,250 applied, 1,187 accepted. Either SAT or ACT required. ACT 25/75 percentile: 21-26. High school rank: 22% in top tenth, 46% in top quarter, 77% in top half
Early decision deadline: N/A, notification date: N/A
Early action deadline: N/A, notification date: N/A
Application deadline (fall): rolling
Undergraduate student body: 1,418 full time, 44 part time; 52% male, 48% female; 0% American Indian, 1% Asian, 2% black, 6% Hispanic, 2% multiracial, 0% Pacific Islander, 84% white, 1% international; 38% from in state; 68% live on campus; 4% of students in fraternities, 5% in sororities
Most popular majors: 6% Marketing/Marketing Management, General; 6% Psychology, General; 5% Biology/Biological Sciences, General; 5% Finance, General; 5% Elementary Education and Teaching
Expenses: 2016-2017: $31,525; room/board: $7,700
Financial aid: (563) 588-7136; 74% of undergrads determined to have financial need; average aid package $24,670

Luther College

Decorah IA
(563) 387-1287
U.S. News ranking: Nat. Lib. Arts, No. 90
Website: www.luther.edu
Admissions email: admissions@luther.edu
Private; founded 1861
Affiliation: Lutheran
Freshman admissions: more selective; 2015-2016: 3,896 applied, 2,606 accepted. Either SAT or ACT required. ACT 25/75 percentile: 23-29. High school rank: 31% in top tenth, 62% in top quarter, 90% in top half
Early decision deadline: N/A, notification date: N/A
Early action deadline: N/A, notification date: N/A
Application deadline (fall): rolling
Undergraduate student body: 2,303 full time, 34 part time; 45% male, 55% female; 0% American Indian, 2% Asian, 2% black, 4% Hispanic, 2% multiracial, 0% Pacific Islander, 84% white, 6% international; 32% from in state; 90% live on campus; 1% of students in fraternities, 2% in sororities
Most popular majors: 15% Biology/Biological Sciences, General; 11% Psychology, General; 9% Music, General; 9% Business Administration and Management, General; 6% Elementary Education and Teaching
Expenses: 2016-2017: $40,040; room/board: $8,500
Financial aid: (563) 387-1018; 69% of undergrads determined to have financial need; average aid package $31,400

Maharishi University of Management[1]

Fairfield IA
(641) 472-1110
U.S. News ranking: Reg. U. (Mid. W), unranked
Website: www.mum.edu
Admissions email: admissions@mum.edu
Private
Application deadline (fall): N/A
Undergraduate student body: N/A full time, N/A part time
Expenses: 2015-2016: $26,530; room/board: $7,400
Financial aid: (641) 472-1156

Morningside College

Sioux City IA
(712) 274-5111
U.S. News ranking: Reg. U. (Mid. W), No. 56
Website: www.morningside.edu
Admissions email: mscadm@morningside.edu
Private; founded 1894
Affiliation: United Methodist
Freshman admissions: selective; 2015-2016: 4,556 applied, 2,551 accepted. Either SAT or ACT required. ACT 25/75 percentile: 20-26. High school rank: 16% in top tenth, 43% in top quarter, 76% in top half
Early decision deadline: N/A, notification date: N/A
Early action deadline: N/A, notification date: N/A
Application deadline (fall): rolling
Undergraduate student body: 1,277 full time, 30 part time; 47%

male, 53% female; 1% American Indian, 1% Asian, 1% black, 7% Hispanic, 2% multiracial, 0% Pacific Islander, 79% white, 5% international; 65% from in state; 60% live on campus; 4% of students in fraternities, 3% in sororities
Most popular majors: 24% Business, Management, Marketing, and Related Support Services; 21% Education; 17% Biological and Biomedical Sciences; 11% Health Professions and Related Programs; 8% Psychology
Expenses: 2016-2017: $29,094; room/board: $9,210
Financial aid: (712) 274-5159; 83% of undergrads determined to have financial need; average aid package $23,373

Mount Mercy University

Cedar Rapids IA
(319) 368-6460
U.S. News ranking: Reg. U. (Mid. W), No. 49
Website: www.mtmercy.edu
Admissions email: admission@mtmercy.edu
Private; founded 1928
Affiliation: Roman Catholic
Freshman admissions: selective; 2015-2016: 1,108 applied, 672 accepted. Either SAT or ACT required. ACT 25/75 percentile: 19-23. High school rank: 12% in top tenth, 37% in top quarter, 82% in top half
Early decision deadline: N/A, notification date: N/A
Early action deadline: N/A, notification date: N/A
Application deadline (fall): rolling
Undergraduate student body: 957 full time, 586 part time; 29% male, 71% female; 1% American Indian, 1% Asian, 7% black, 2% Hispanic, 2% multiracial, 0% Pacific Islander, 79% white, 5% international; 88% from in state; 41% live on campus; 0% of students in fraternities, 0% in sororities
Most popular majors: 16% Registered Nursing/Registered Nurse; 13% Nursing Education; 10% Business/Commerce, General; 6% Accounting; 6% Criminal Justice/Law Enforcement Administration
Expenses: 2016-2017: $29,496; room/board: $8,900
Financial aid: (319) 368-6467; 72% of undergrads determined to have financial need; average aid package $22,178

Northwestern College

Orange City IA
(712) 707-7130
U.S. News ranking: Reg. Coll. (Mid. W), No. 6
Website: www.nwciowa.edu
Admissions email: admissions@nwciowa.edu
Private; founded 1882
Affiliation: Reformed Church in America
Freshman admissions: more selective; 2015-2016: 1,234 applied, 890 accepted. Either SAT or ACT required. ACT 25/75 percentile: 22-28. High school

rank: 25% in top tenth, 57% in top quarter, 88% in top half
Early decision deadline: N/A, notification date: N/A
Early action deadline: N/A, notification date: N/A
Application deadline (fall): rolling
Undergraduate student body: 1,062 full time, 59 part time; 42% male, 58% female; 0% American Indian, 1% Asian, 2% black, 5% Hispanic, 2% multiracial, 0% Pacific Islander, 83% white, 3% international; 55% from in state; 87% live on campus; 0% of students in fraternities, 0% in sororities
Most popular majors: 15% Business Administration and Management, General; 15% Elementary Education and Teaching; 12% Registered Nursing/Registered Nurse; 7% Biology/Biological Sciences, General; 7% Kinesiology and Exercise Science
Expenses: 2016-2017: $29,500; room/board: $8,900
Financial aid: (712) 707-7131; 73% of undergrads determined to have financial need; average aid package $24,640

Simpson College

Indianola IA
(515) 961-1624
U.S. News ranking: Nat. Lib. Arts, No. 149
Website: www.simpson.edu
Admissions email: admiss@simpson.edu
Private; founded 1860
Affiliation: United Methodist
Freshman admissions: selective; 2015-2016: 1,271 applied, 1,137 accepted. Either SAT or ACT required. ACT 25/75 percentile: 21-27. High school rank: 24% in top tenth, 52% in top quarter, 83% in top half
Early decision deadline: N/A, notification date: N/A
Early action deadline: N/A, notification date: N/A
Application deadline (fall): rolling
Undergraduate student body: 1,426 full time, 197 part time; 46% male, 54% female; 0% American Indian, 2% Asian, 2% black, 3% Hispanic, 1% multiracial, 0% Pacific Islander, 88% white, 1% international; N/A from in state; N/A live on campus; 23% of students in fraternities, 22% in sororities
Most popular majors: 22% Business/Commerce, General; 8% Criminal Justice/Safety Studies; 8% Elementary Education and Teaching; 6% Computer and Information Sciences, General
Expenses: 2016-2017: $35,876; room/board: $7,963
Financial aid: (515) 961-1630; 82% of undergrads determined to have financial need; average aid package $26,643

St. Ambrose University

Davenport IA
(563) 333-6300
U.S. News ranking: Reg. U. (Mid. W), No. 35
Website: www.sau.edu
Admissions email: admit@sau.edu

Private; founded 1882
Affiliation: Roman Catholic
Freshman admissions: selective; 2015-2016: 2,546 applied, 1,858 accepted. Either SAT or ACT required. ACT 25/75 percentile: 20-25. High school rank: 15% in top tenth, 40% in top quarter, 74% in top half
Early decision deadline: N/A, notification date: N/A
Early action deadline: N/A, notification date: N/A
Application deadline (fall): rolling
Undergraduate student body: 2,259 full time, 269 part time; 43% male, 57% female; 0% American Indian, 1% Asian, 3% black, 6% Hispanic, 2% multiracial, 0% Pacific Islander, 80% white, 3% international; 41% from in state; 64% live on campus; 0% of students in fraternities, 0% in sororities
Most popular majors: 25% Business, Management, Marketing, and Related Support Services; 20% Health Professions and Related Programs; 13% Psychology; 12% Education; 5% Biological and Biomedical Sciences
Expenses: 2016-2017: $29,150; room/board: $9,869
Financial aid: (563) 333-6314; 76% of undergrads determined to have financial need; average aid package $20,864

University of Dubuque

Dubuque IA
(800) 722-5583
U.S. News ranking: Reg. U. (Mid. W), No. 108
Website: www.dbq.edu
Admissions email: admssns@univ.dbq.edu
Private; founded 1852
Affiliation: Presbyterian
Freshman admissions: less selective; 2015-2016: 1,457 applied, 1,128 accepted. Either SAT or ACT required. SAT 25/75 percentile: 780-980. High school rank: 5% in top tenth, 25% in top quarter, 49% in top half
Early decision deadline: N/A, notification date: N/A
Early action deadline: N/A, notification date: N/A
Application deadline (fall): rolling
Undergraduate student body: 1,626 full time, 220 part time; 59% male, 41% female; 0% American Indian, 3% Asian, 15% black, 9% Hispanic, 3% multiracial, 0% Pacific Islander, 61% white, 4% international
Most popular majors: Information not available
Expenses: 2015-2016: $29,161; room/board: $8,790
Financial aid: (563) 589-3396

University of Iowa

Iowa City IA
(319) 335-3847
U.S. News ranking: Nat. U., No. 82
Website: www.uiowa.edu
Admissions email: admissions@uiowa.edu
Public; founded 1847
Freshman admissions: more selective; 2015-2016: 26,222 applied, 21,171 accepted. Either SAT or ACT required. ACT 25/75 percentile: 23-28. High school

rank: 28% in top tenth, 60% in top quarter, 90% in top half
Early decision deadline: N/A, notification date: N/A
Early action deadline: N/A, notification date: N/A
Application deadline (fall): 5/1
Undergraduate student body: 19,911 full time, 3,446 part time; 48% male, 52% female; 0% American Indian, 4% Asian, 3% black, 7% Hispanic, 3% multiracial, 0% Pacific Islander, 67% white, 12% international; 66% from in state; 26% live on campus; 13% of students in fraternities, 18% in sororities
Most popular majors: 19% Business, Management, Marketing, and Related Support Services; 12% Parks, Recreation, Leisure, and Fitness Studies; 10% Social Sciences; 8% Engineering
Expenses: 2016-2017: $8,325 in state, $28,413 out of state; room/board: $9,728
Financial aid: (319) 335-1450; 48% of undergrads determined to have financial need; average aid package $14,382

University of Northern Iowa

Cedar Falls IA
(800) 772-2037
U.S. News ranking: Reg. U. (Mid. W), No. 20
Website: www.uni.edu/
Admissions email: admissions@uni.edu
Public; founded 1876
Freshman admissions: selective; 2015-2016: 5,364 applied, 4,271 accepted. Either SAT or ACT required. ACT 25/75 percentile: 20-25. High school rank: 18% in top tenth, 48% in top quarter, 84% in top half
Early decision deadline: N/A, notification date: N/A
Early action deadline: N/A, notification date: N/A
Application deadline (fall): 8/15
Undergraduate student body: 9,127 full time, 1,042 part time; 43% male, 57% female; 0% American Indian, 1% Asian, 3% black, 3% Hispanic, 2% multiracial, 0% Pacific Islander, 83% white, 4% international; 94% from in state; 74% live on campus; 4% of students in fraternities, 6% in sororities
Most popular majors: 18% Business, Management, Marketing, and Related Support Services; 16% Education; 7% Social Sciences; 6% Biological and Biomedical Sciences
Expenses: 2016-2017: $8,059 in state, $18,551 out of state; room/board: $8,630
Financial aid: (319) 273-2700; 60% of undergrads determined to have financial need; average aid package $8,329

Upper Iowa University

Fayette IA
(563) 425-5281
U.S. News ranking: Reg. U. (Mid. W), second tier
Website: www.uiu.edu
Admissions email: admission@uiu.edu

More at usnews.com/college

Private; founded 1857
Freshman admissions: selective; 2015-2016: 1,797 applied, 1,184 accepted. Either SAT or ACT required. ACT 25/75 percentile: 17-22. High school rank: 7% in top tenth, 19% in top quarter, 39% in top half
Early decision deadline: N/A, notification date: N/A
Early action deadline: N/A, notification date: N/A
Application deadline (fall): rolling
Undergraduate student body: 2,455 full time, 1,656 part time; 38% male, 62% female; N/A American Indian, N/A Asian, N/A black, N/A Hispanic, N/A multiracial, N/A Pacific Islander, N/A white, N/A international
Most popular majors: Information not available
Expenses: 2015-2016: $28,073; room/board: $8,057
Financial aid: (563) 425-5274

Waldorf College[1]
Forest City IA
(641) 585-8112
U.S. News ranking: Reg. Coll. (Mid. W), second tier
Website: www.waldorf.edu
Admissions email: admissions@waldorf.edu
For-profit
Application deadline (fall): N/A
Undergraduate student body: N/A full time, N/A part time
Expenses: 2015-2016: $20,884; room/board: $6,994
Financial aid: (641) 585-8120

Wartburg College
Waverly IA
(319) 352-8264
U.S. News ranking: Nat. Lib. Arts, No. 132
Website: www.wartburg.edu
Admissions email: admissions@wartburg.edu
Private; founded 1852
Affiliation: Lutheran
Freshman admissions: more selective; 2015-2016: 2,147 applied, 1,585 accepted. Either SAT or ACT required. ACT 25/75 percentile: 21-27. High school rank: 26% in top tenth, 58% in top quarter, 83% in top half
Early decision deadline: N/A, notification date: N/A
Early action deadline: 12/1, notification date: N/A
Application deadline (fall): rolling
Undergraduate student body: 1,474 full time, 63 part time; 48% male, 52% female; 0% American Indian, 1% Asian, 5% black, 3% Hispanic, 2% multiracial, 0% Pacific Islander, 77% white, 8% international; 72% from in state; 82% live on campus; 0% of students in fraternities, 0% in sororities
Most popular majors: 21% Business/Commerce, General; 16% Biology/Biological Sciences, General; 9% Elementary Education and Teaching; 8% Social Sciences, General
Expenses: 2016-2017: $38,380; room/board: $9,460
Financial aid: (319) 352-8262; 72% of undergrads determined to have financial need; average aid package $28,353

William Penn University[1]
Oskaloosa IA
(641) 673-1012
U.S. News ranking: Reg. U. (Mid. W), second tier
Website: www.wmpenn.edu
Admissions email: admissions@wmpenn.edu
Private
Application deadline (fall): N/A
Undergraduate student body: N/A full time, N/A part time
Expenses: 2015-2016: $23,930; room/board: $6,544
Financial aid: (641) 673-1040

KANSAS

Baker University
Baldwin City KS
(800) 873-4282
U.S. News ranking: Reg. U. (Mid. W), No. 47
Website: www.bakeru.edu
Admissions email: admission@bakeru.edu
Private; founded 1858
Affiliation: United Methodist
Freshman admissions: selective; 2015-2016: 889 applied, 729 accepted. Either SAT or ACT required. ACT 25/75 percentile: 20-25. High school rank: 17% in top tenth, 43% in top quarter, 75% in top half
Early decision deadline: N/A, notification date: N/A
Early action deadline: N/A, notification date: N/A
Application deadline (fall): rolling
Undergraduate student body: 790 full time, 199 part time; 52% male, 48% female; 3% American Indian, 1% Asian, 10% black, 7% Hispanic, 2% multiracial, 1% Pacific Islander, 70% white, 3% international; 68% from in state; 82% live on campus; 31% of students in fraternities, 44% in sororities
Most popular majors: 19% Business Administration and Management, General; 14% Kinesiology and Exercise Science; 8% Elementary Education and Teaching; 7% Sociology; 6% Psychology, General
Expenses: 2016-2017: $27,980; room/board: $8,270
Financial aid: (785) 594-4595; 72% of undergrads determined to have financial need; average aid package $28,945

Benedictine College
Atchison KS
(800) 467-5340
U.S. News ranking: Reg. Coll. (Mid. W), No. 14
Website: www.benedictine.edu
Admissions email: bcadmiss@benedictine.edu
Private; founded 1859
Affiliation: Roman Catholic
Freshman admissions: selective; 2015-2016: 2,345 applied, 2,325 accepted. Either SAT or ACT required. ACT 25/75 percentile: 21-28. High school rank: 24% in top tenth, 49% in top quarter, 78% in top half
Early decision deadline: N/A, notification date: N/A
Early action deadline: N/A, notification date: N/A

Application deadline (fall): rolling
Undergraduate student body: 1,857 full time, 276 part time; 45% male, 55% female; 0% American Indian, 1% Asian, 3% black, 5% Hispanic, 5% multiracial, 0% Pacific Islander, 80% white, 3% international; 25% from in state; 82% live on campus; 0% of students in fraternities, 0% in sororities
Most popular majors: 21% Business, Management, Marketing, and Related Support Services; 20% Education; 16% Social Sciences; 8% Health Professions and Related Programs; 8% Theology and Religious Vocations
Expenses: 2016-2017: $27,480; room/board: $9,510
Financial aid: (913) 360-7484; 66% of undergrads determined to have financial need; average aid package $21,288

Bethany College
Lindsborg KS
(800) 826-2281
U.S. News ranking: Reg. Coll. (Mid. W), second tier
Website: www.bethanylb.edu
Admissions email: admissions@bethanylb.edu
Private; founded 1881
Affiliation: Evangelical Luteran Chuch in America (ELCA)
Freshman admissions: selective; 2015-2016: 1,650 applied, 1,638 accepted. Either SAT or ACT required. ACT 25/75 percentile: 18-23. High school rank: 9% in top tenth, 22% in top quarter, 50% in top half
Early decision deadline: N/A, notification date: N/A
Early action deadline: N/A, notification date: N/A
Application deadline (fall): rolling
Undergraduate student body: 620 full time, 78 part time; 59% male, 41% female; 0% American Indian, 1% Asian, 14% black, 16% Hispanic, 2% multiracial, N/A Pacific Islander, 59% white, 7% international
Most popular majors: 14% Biology/Biological Sciences, General; 11% Business, Management, Marketing, and Related Support Services, Other; 11% Criminology; 11% Finance, General; 8% Psychology, General
Expenses: 2015-2016: $25,900; room/board: $8,100
Financial aid: (785) 227-3311

Bethel College
North Newton KS
(800) 522-1887
U.S. News ranking: Nat. Lib. Arts, second tier
Website: www.bethelks.edu
Admissions email: admissions@bethelks.edu
Private; founded 1887
Affiliation: Mennonite Church USA
Freshman admissions: more selective; 2015-2016: 862 applied, 459 accepted. Either SAT or ACT required. ACT 25/75 percentile: 18-24. High school rank: 22% in top tenth, 41% in top quarter, 67% in top half
Early decision deadline: N/A, notification date: N/A
Early action deadline: N/A, notification date: N/A

Application deadline (fall): rolling
Undergraduate student body: 509 full time, 16 part time; 48% male, 52% female; 1% American Indian, 1% Asian, 14% black, 6% Hispanic, 4% multiracial, 0% Pacific Islander, 70% white, 2% international; 67% from in state; 63% live on campus; 0% of students in fraternities, 0% in sororities
Most popular majors: 36% Health Professions and Related Programs; 18% Biological and Biomedical Sciences; 12% Education; 12% Public Administration and Social Service Professions; 3% Business, Management, Marketing, and Related Support Services
Expenses: 2016-2017: $26,920; room/board: $8,990
Financial aid: (316) 284-5232; 85% of undergrads determined to have financial need; average aid package $25,688

Central Christian College
McPherson KS
(800) 835-0078
U.S. News ranking: Reg. Coll. (Mid. W), second tier
Website: www.centralchristian.edu/
Admissions email: rick.wyatt@centralchristian.edu
Private; founded 1884
Affiliation: Free Metodist Church of North America
Freshman admissions: selective; 2015-2016: 703 applied, 293 accepted. Neither SAT nor ACT required. ACT 25/75 percentile: 17-24. High school rank: 6% in top tenth, 23% in top quarter, 45% in top half
Early decision deadline: N/A, notification date: N/A
Early action deadline: 11/30, notification date: 12/1
Application deadline (fall): rolling
Undergraduate student body: 1,120 full time, 34 part time; 49% male, 51% female; 2% American Indian, 1% Asian, 28% black, 11% Hispanic, 2% multiracial, 0% Pacific Islander, 49% white, 0% international; 22% from in state; 22% live on campus; N/A of students in fraternities, N/A in sororities
Most popular majors: 13% Organizational Leadership; 11% Psychology, General; 7% Kinesiology and Exercise Science; 7% Liberal Arts and Sciences/Liberal Studies; 7% Youth Ministry
Expenses: 2015-2016: $14,501; room/board: $7,600
Financial aid: (620) 241-0723

Donnelly College
Kansas City KS
(913) 621-8700
U.S. News ranking: Reg. Coll. (Mid. W), unranked
Website: donnelly.edu
Admissions email: N/A
Private; founded 1949
Affiliation: Catholic
Freshman admissions: N/A; 2015-2016: 251 applied, 251 accepted. Neither SAT nor ACT required. ACT 25/75 percentile: N/A. High school rank: N/A

Early decision deadline: N/A, notification date: N/A
Early action deadline: N/A, notification date: N/A
Application deadline (fall): rolling
Undergraduate student body: 196 full time, 66 part time; 32% male, 68% female; N/A American Indian, 5% Asian, 32% black, 41% Hispanic, 6% multiracial, N/A Pacific Islander, 10% white, 6% international; 68% from in state; N/A live on campus; N/A of students in fraternities, N/A in sororities
Most popular majors: 8% Non-Profit/Public/Organizational Management
Expenses: 2015-2016: $6,822; room/board: $7,438
Financial aid: (913) 621-8700

Emporia State University
Emporia KS
(620) 341-5465
U.S. News ranking: Reg. U. (Mid. W), No. 108
Website: www.emporia.edu
Admissions email: go2esu@emporia.edu
Public; founded 1863
Freshman admissions: selective; 2015-2016: 1,736 applied, 1,510 accepted. Neither SAT nor ACT required. ACT 25/75 percentile: 19-25. High school rank: 13% in top tenth, 36% in top quarter, 69% in top half
Early decision deadline: N/A, notification date: N/A
Early action deadline: N/A, notification date: N/A
Application deadline (fall): rolling
Undergraduate student body: 3,579 full time, 285 part time; 40% male, 60% female; 1% American Indian, 1% Asian, 5% black, 7% Hispanic, 7% multiracial, 0% Pacific Islander, 70% white, 8% international; 91% from in state; 25% live on campus; 11% of students in fraternities, 10% in sororities
Most popular majors: 23% Education; 13% Business, Management, Marketing, and Related Support Services; 11% Health Professions and Related Programs; 10% Social Sciences; 6% Liberal Arts and Sciences, General Studies and Humanities
Expenses: 2015-2016: $6,136 in state, $18,524 out of state; room/board: $7,968
Financial aid: (620) 341-5457; 62% of undergrads determined to have financial need; average aid package $8,900

Fort Hays State University
Hays KS
(800) 628-3478
U.S. News ranking: Reg. U. (Mid. W), second tier
Website: www.fhsu.edu
Admissions email: tigers@fhsu.edu
Public; founded 1902
Freshman admissions: selective; 2015-2016: 2,337 applied, 2,007 accepted. Neither SAT nor ACT required. ACT 25/75 percentile: N/A. High school rank: N/A
Early decision deadline: N/A, notification date: N/A

Early action deadline: N/A, notification date: N/A
Application deadline (fall): rolling
Undergraduate student body: 5,705 full time, 6,126 part time; 39% male, 61% female; 0% American Indian, 1% Asian, 4% black, 7% Hispanic, 2% multiracial, 0% Pacific Islander, 57% white, 29% international; 69% from in state; 11% live on campus; 2% of students in fraternities, 2% in sororities
Most popular majors: Information not available
Expenses: 2015-2016: $4,654 in state, $13,657 out of state; room/board: $7,512
Financial aid: (785) 628-4408

Friends University
Wichita KS
(316) 295-5100
U.S. News ranking: Reg. U. (Mid. W), second tier
Website: www.friends.edu
Admissions email: learn@friends.edu
Private; founded 1898
Affiliation: Quaker
Freshman admissions: selective; 2015-2016: 713 applied, 416 accepted. Either SAT or ACT required. ACT 25/75 percentile: 19-24. High school rank: 12% in top tenth, 37% in top quarter, 60% in top half
Early decision deadline: N/A, notification date: N/A
Early action deadline: N/A, notification date: N/A
Application deadline (fall): rolling
Undergraduate student body: 1,025 full time, 434 part time; 45% male, 55% female; 1% American Indian, 2% Asian, 11% black, 5% Hispanic, 7% multiracial, 0% Pacific Islander, 70% white, 0% international
Most popular majors: 35% Business, Management, Marketing, and Related Support Services; 5% Biological and Biomedical Sciences; 4% Education; 4% Visual and Performing Arts; 4% Psychology
Expenses: 2016-2017: $26,730; room/board: $7,590
Financial aid: (316) 295-5200; 81% of undergrads determined to have financial need; average aid package $15,845

Kansas State University
Manhattan KS
(785) 532-6250
U.S. News ranking: Nat. U., No. 135
Website: www.k-state.edu
Admissions email: k-state@k-state.edu
Public; founded 1863
Freshman admissions: selective; 2015-2016: 9,178 applied, 8,712 accepted. Neither SAT nor ACT required. ACT 25/75 percentile: 22-28. High school rank: 22% in top tenth, 47% in top quarter, 75% in top half
Early decision deadline: N/A, notification date: N/A
Early action deadline: N/A, notification date: N/A
Application deadline (fall): rolling
Undergraduate student body: 17,935 full time, 1,924 part

time; 52% male, 48% female; 0% American Indian, 1% Asian, 4% black, 7% Hispanic, 3% multiracial, 0% Pacific Islander, 78% white, 6% international; 82% from in state; 23% live on campus; N/A of students in fraternities, N/A in sororities
Most popular majors: 19% Business, Management, Marketing, and Related Support Services; 10% Engineering; 9% Social Sciences; 8% Family and Consumer Sciences/Human Sciences
Expenses: 2015-2016: $9,350 in state, $23,429 out of state; room/board: $8,430
Financial aid: (785) 532-6420; 50% of undergrads determined to have financial need; average aid package $11,504

Kansas Wesleyan University
Salina KS
(785) 827-5541
U.S. News ranking: Reg. Coll. (Mid. W), No. 45
Website: www.kwu.edu
Admissions email: admissions@kwu.edu
Private; founded 1886
Affiliation: United Methodist
Freshman admissions: selective; 2015-2016: 818 applied, 504 accepted. Either SAT or ACT required. ACT 25/75 percentile: 20-24. High school rank: 14% in top tenth, 29% in top quarter, 78% in top half
Early decision deadline: N/A, notification date: N/A
Early action deadline: N/A, notification date: N/A
Application deadline (fall): rolling
Undergraduate student body: 619 full time, 71 part time; 51% male, 49% female; 1% American Indian, 0% Asian, 9% black, 15% Hispanic, 2% multiracial, 0% Pacific Islander, 69% white, 2% international; 48% from in state; 66% live on campus; N/A of students in fraternities, N/A in sororities
Most popular majors: 22% Health Professions and Related Programs; 19% Business, Management, Marketing, and Related Support Services; 11% Parks, Recreation, Leisure, and Fitness Studies; 8% Education; 5% Homeland Security, Law Enforcement, Firefighting and Related Protective Services
Expenses: 2016-2017: $28,000; room/board: $8,600
Financial aid: (785) 827-5541; 87% of undergrads determined to have financial need; average aid package $21,506

McPherson College[1]
McPherson KS
(800) 365-7402
U.S. News ranking: Reg. Coll. (Mid. W), No. 38
Website: www.mcpherson.edu
Admissions email: admissions@mcpherson.edu
Private; founded 1887
Affiliation: Church of the Brethren
Application deadline (fall): 8/1
Undergraduate student body: N/A full time, N/A part time

Expenses: 2015-2016: $25,236; room/board: $8,441
Financial aid: (620) 241-0731

MidAmerica Nazarene University
Olathe KS
(913) 971-3380
U.S. News ranking: Reg. U. (Mid. W), No. 115
Website: www.mnu.edu
Admissions email: admissions@mnu.edu
Private; founded 1966
Affiliation: International Church of the Nazarene
Freshman admissions: selective; 2015-2016: 873 applied, 533 accepted. Either SAT or ACT required. Average composite ACT score: 22. High school rank: N/A
Early decision deadline: N/A, notification date: N/A
Early action deadline: N/A, notification date: N/A
Application deadline (fall): 8/1
Undergraduate student body: 1,068 full time, 310 part time; 42% male, 58% female; 1% American Indian, 1% Asian, 13% black, 4% Hispanic, 5% multiracial, 1% Pacific Islander, 60% white, 0% international
Most popular majors: 40% Health Professions and Related Programs; 30% Business, Management, Marketing, and Related Support Services; 5% Education; 5% Parks, Recreation, Leisure, and Fitness Studies
Expenses: 2016-2017: $27,650; room/board: $7,900
Financial aid: (913) 791-3298

Newman University
Wichita KS
(877) 639-6268
U.S. News ranking: Reg. U. (Mid. W), second tier
Website: www.newmanu.edu
Admissions email: admissions@newmanu.edu
Private; founded 1933
Affiliation: Roman Catholic
Freshman admissions: selective; 2015-2016: 1,284 applied, 715 accepted. Neither SAT nor ACT required. ACT 25/75 percentile: 20-27. High school rank: 26% in top tenth, 53% in top quarter, 85% in top half
Early decision deadline: N/A, notification date: N/A
Early action deadline: N/A, notification date: N/A
Application deadline (fall): rolling
Undergraduate student body: 1,030 full time, 1,724 part time; 38% male, 62% female; 1% American Indian, 5% Asian, 5% black, 13% Hispanic, 3% multiracial, 0% Pacific Islander, 67% white, 6% international; 84% from in state; 24% live on campus; N/A of students in fraternities, N/A in sororities
Most popular majors: 20% Health Professions and Related Programs; 16% Biological and Biomedical Sciences; 14% Education; 13% Business, Management, Marketing, and Related Support Services; 8% Psychology
Expenses: 2015-2016: $26,030; room/board: $7,340
Financial aid: (316) 942-4291

Ottawa University
Ottawa KS
(785) 242-5200
U.S. News ranking: Reg. Coll. (Mid. W), No. 47
Website: www.ottawa.edu
Admissions email: admiss@ottawa.edu
Private; founded 1865
Affiliation: American Baptist
Freshman admissions: selective; 2015-2016: 1,002 applied, 410 accepted. Neither SAT nor ACT required. ACT 25/75 percentile: 18-23. High school rank: 8% in top tenth, 28% in top quarter, 61% in top half
Early decision deadline: N/A, notification date: N/A
Early action deadline: N/A, notification date: N/A
Application deadline (fall): rolling
Undergraduate student body: 614 full time, 16 part time; 60% male, 40% female; 5% American Indian, 1% Asian, 13% black, 3% Hispanic, 3% multiracial, 0% Pacific Islander, 61% white, N/A international; 59% from in state; 69% live on campus; N/A of students in fraternities, N/A in sororities
Most popular majors: 15% Kinesiology and Exercise Science; 14% Business Administration and Management, General; 10% Biology/Biological Sciences, General; 10% Elementary Education and Teaching; 9% Public Administration and Social Service Professions
Expenses: 2016-2017: $27,121; room/board: $9,250
Financial aid: (785) 242-5200; 87% of undergrads determined to have financial need; average aid package $13,176

Pittsburg State University
Pittsburg KS
(800) 854-7488
U.S. News ranking: Reg. U. (Mid. W), No. 94
Website: www.pittstate.edu
Admissions email: psuadmit@pittstate.edu
Public; founded 1903
Freshman admissions: selective; 2015-2016: 2,631 applied, 2,169 accepted. Either SAT or ACT required. ACT 25/75 percentile: 19-24. High school rank: 31% in top tenth, 46% in top quarter, 74% in top half
Early decision deadline: N/A, notification date: N/A
Early action deadline: N/A, notification date: N/A
Application deadline (fall): rolling
Undergraduate student body: 5,455 full time, 638 part time; 53% male, 47% female; 1% American Indian, 1% Asian, 4% black, 5% Hispanic, 6% multiracial, 0% Pacific Islander, 79% white, 3% international; 72% from in state; N/A live on campus; N/A of students in fraternities, N/A in sororities
Most popular majors: 8% Registered Nursing, Nursing Administration, Nursing Research and Clinical Nursing; 7% Teacher Education and Professional Development, Specific Levels and Methods; 6% Business/Commerce, General; 6%

Psychology, General; 6% Teacher Education and Professional Development, Specific Subject Areas
Expenses: 2016-2017: $6,758 in state, $17,542 out of state; room/board: $7,572
Financial aid: (620) 235-4240; 65% of undergrads determined to have financial need; average aid package $6,452

Southwestern College
Winfield KS
(620) 229-6236
U.S. News ranking: Reg. U. (Mid. W), No. 115
Website: www.sckans.edu
Admissions email: scadmit@sckans.edu
Private; founded 1885
Affiliation: United Methodist
Freshman admissions: selective; 2015-2016: 362 applied, 330 accepted. Either SAT or ACT required. ACT 25/75 percentile: 19-24. High school rank: 8% in top tenth, 34% in top quarter, 75% in top half
Early decision deadline: N/A, notification date: N/A
Early action deadline: N/A, notification date: N/A
Application deadline (fall): 8/25
Undergraduate student body: 481 full time, 709 part time; 59% male, 41% female; 2% American Indian, 1% Asian, 12% black, 8% Hispanic, 3% multiracial, 0% Pacific Islander, 54% white, 5% international; 48% from in state; 25% live on campus; N/A of students in fraternities, N/A in sororities
Most popular majors: 42% Business, Management, Marketing, and Related Support Services; 12% Homeland Security, Law Enforcement, Firefighting and Related Protective Services; 11% Education; 9% Computer and Information Sciences and Support Services; 7% Health Professions and Related Programs
Expenses: 2016-2017: $27,250; room/board: $7,250
Financial aid: (620) 229-6215; 78% of undergrads determined to have financial need; average aid package $21,780

Sterling College
Sterling KS
(800) 346-1017
U.S. News ranking: Reg. Coll. (Mid. W), No. 56
Website: www.sterling.edu
Admissions email: admissions@sterling.edu
Private; founded 1887
Affiliation: Presbyterian
Freshman admissions: selective; 2015-2016: 1,118 applied, 463 accepted. Either SAT or ACT required. ACT 25/75 percentile: 19-24. High school rank: 9% in top tenth, 20% in top quarter, 52% in top half
Early decision deadline: N/A, notification date: N/A
Early action deadline: N/A, notification date: N/A
Application deadline (fall): rolling
Undergraduate student body: 614 full time, 90 part time; 52% male, 48% female; 3% American

Indian, 1% Asian, 12% black, 15% Hispanic, 0% multiracial, 0% Pacific Islander, 65% white, 0% international
Most popular majors: Information not available
Expenses: 2016-2017: $24,250; room/board: $7,216
Financial aid: (620) 278-4207; 87% of undergrads determined to have financial need; average aid package $22,395

Tabor College
Hillsboro KS
(620) 947-3121
U.S. News ranking: Reg. Coll. (Mid. W), No. 41
Website: www.tabor.edu
Admissions email: admissions@tabor.edu
Private; founded 1908
Affiliation: Mennonite Brethren
Freshman admissions: selective; 2015-2016: 592 applied, 328 accepted. Either SAT or ACT required. ACT 25/75 percentile: 19-25. High school rank: 13% in top tenth, 36% in top quarter, 66% in top half
Early decision deadline: N/A, notification date: N/A
Early action deadline: N/A, notification date: N/A
Application deadline (fall): rolling
Undergraduate student body: 551 full time, 136 part time; 52% male, 48% female; 1% American Indian, 1% Asian, 10% black, 13% Hispanic, 4% multiracial, 0% Pacific Islander, 64% white, 2% international; 46% from in state; 89% live on campus; N/A of students in fraternities, N/A in sororities
Most popular majors: 26% Registered Nursing, Nursing Administration, Nursing Research and Clinical Nursing, Other; 16% Marketing/Marketing Management, General; 9% Elementary Education and Teaching; 7% Christian Studies; 4% Psychology, General
Expenses: 2016-2017: $26,590; room/board: $9,280
Financial aid: (620) 947-3121; 79% of undergrads determined to have financial need; average aid package $22,141

University of Kansas
Lawrence KS
(785) 864-3911
U.S. News ranking: Nat. U., No. 118
Website: www.ku.edu/
Admissions email: adm@ku.edu
Public; founded 1865
Freshman admissions: more selective; 2015-2016: 15,155 applied, 14,165 accepted. Either SAT or ACT required. ACT 25/75 percentile: 22-28. High school rank: 26% in top tenth, 57% in top quarter, 88% in top half
Early decision deadline: N/A, notification date: N/A
Early action deadline: N/A, notification date: N/A
Application deadline (fall): rolling
Undergraduate student body: 17,191 full time, 2,054 part time; 50% male, 50% female; 0% American Indian, 4% Asian, 4% black, 7% Hispanic, 5% multiracial, 0% Pacific Islander, 72% white, 6% international;

73% from in state; 25% live on campus; 18% of students in fraternities, 25% in sororities
Most popular majors: 16% Business, Management, Marketing, and Related Support Services; 12% Health Professions and Related Programs; 9% Engineering; 8% Social Sciences
Expenses: 2016-2017: $10,549 in state, $25,932 out of state; room/board: $9,586
Financial aid: (785) 864-4700; 47% of undergrads determined to have financial need; average aid package $14,363

University of St. Mary
Leavenworth KS
(913) 758-6118
U.S. News ranking: Reg. U. (Mid. W), second tier
Website: www.stmary.edu
Admissions email: admiss@stmary.edu
Private; founded 1923
Affiliation: Roman Catholic
Freshman admissions: selective; 2015-2016: 933 applied, 458 accepted. Either SAT or ACT required. ACT 25/75 percentile: 19-23. High school rank: 10% in top tenth, 34% in top quarter, 65% in top half
Early decision deadline: N/A, notification date: N/A
Early action deadline: N/A, notification date: N/A
Application deadline (fall): rolling
Undergraduate student body: 625 full time, 250 part time; 40% male, 60% female; 0% American Indian, 1% Asian, 13% black, 16% Hispanic, 3% multiracial, 1% Pacific Islander, 57% white, 1% international
Most popular majors: Information not available
Expenses: 2015-2016: $26,340; room/board: $7,750
Financial aid: (800) 752-7043

Washburn University
Topeka KS
(785) 670-1030
U.S. News ranking: Reg. U. (Mid. W), No. 94
Website: www.washburn.edu
Admissions email: admissions@washburn.edu
Public; founded 1865
Freshman admissions: selective; 2015-2016: 1,458 applied, 1,440 accepted. ACT required. ACT 25/75 percentile: 19-25. High school rank: 13% in top tenth, 34% in top quarter, 67% in top half
Early decision deadline: N/A, notification date: N/A
Early action deadline: N/A, notification date: N/A
Application deadline (fall): 8/1
Undergraduate student body: 3,767 full time, 2,026 part time; 41% male, 59% female; N/A American Indian, N/A Asian, N/A black, N/A Hispanic, N/A multiracial, N/A Pacific Islander, N/A white, N/A international; 93% from in state; 15% live on campus; 7% of students in fraternities, 8% in sororities
Most popular majors: 28% Health Professions and Related Programs; 13% Business, Management, Marketing, and Related Support Services; 8%

Education; 7% Homeland Security, Law Enforcement, Firefighting and Related Protective Services
Expenses: 2015-2016: $7,910 in state, $17,750 out of state; room/board: $6,830
Financial aid: (785) 670-1151; 60% of undergrads determined to have financial need; average aid package $9,867

Wichita State University
Wichita KS
(316) 978-3085
U.S. News ranking: Nat. U., second tier
Website: www.wichita.edu
Admissions email: admissions@wichita.edu
Public; founded 1895
Freshman admissions: selective; 2015-2016: 5,431 applied, 5,145 accepted. Neither SAT nor ACT required. ACT 25/75 percentile: 21-26. High school rank: 20% in top tenth, 45% in top quarter, 78% in top half
Early decision deadline: N/A, notification date: N/A
Early action deadline: N/A, notification date: N/A
Application deadline (fall): rolling
Undergraduate student body: 8,684 full time, 3,007 part time; 47% male, 53% female; 1% American Indian, 7% Asian, 6% black, 11% Hispanic, 4% multiracial, 0% Pacific Islander, 63% white, 6% international; 93% from in state; 9% live on campus; 4% of students in fraternities, 4% in sororities
Most popular majors: 19% Business, Management, Marketing, and Related Support Services; 17% Health Professions and Related Programs; 13% Engineering; 9% Education; 5% Parks, Recreation, Leisure, and Fitness Studies
Expenses: 2015-2016: $7,528 in state, $15,851 out of state; room/board: $10,930
Financial aid: (316) 978-3430; 41% of undergrads determined to have financial need; average aid package $7,455

KENTUCKY

Alice Lloyd College
Pippa Passes KY
(888) 280-4252
U.S. News ranking: Nat. Lib. Arts, second tier
Website: www.alc.edu
Admissions email: admissions@alc.edu
Private; founded 1923
Freshman admissions: selective; 2015-2016: 4,811 applied, N/A accepted. Either SAT or ACT required. ACT 25/75 percentile: 19-24. High school rank: 17% in top tenth, 49% in top quarter, 86% in top half
Early decision deadline: N/A, notification date: N/A
Early action deadline: N/A, notification date: N/A
Application deadline (fall): 7/1
Undergraduate student body: 592 full time, 24 part time; 45% male, 55% female; 0% American Indian, 0% Asian, 1% black, 0%

Hispanic, 0% multiracial, 0% Pacific Islander, 96% white, 0% international
Most popular majors: 22% Biological and Biomedical Sciences; 19% Education; 14% Business, Management, Marketing, and Related Support Services; 13% Social Sciences; 10% History
Expenses: 2016-2017: $11,550; room/board: $6,240
Financial aid: (606) 368-6059; 90% of undergrads determined to have financial need; average aid package $13,179

Asbury University
Wilmore KY
(800) 888-1818
U.S. News ranking: Reg. U. (S), No. 14
Website: www.asbury.edu
Admissions email: admissions@asbury.edu
Private; founded 1890
Affiliation: Christian non-denominational
Freshman admissions: more selective; 2015-2016: 1,620 applied, 921 accepted. Either SAT or ACT required. ACT 25/75 percentile: 21-27. High school rank: 26% in top tenth, 51% in top quarter, 82% in top half
Early decision deadline: N/A, notification date: N/A
Early action deadline: N/A, notification date: N/A
Application deadline (fall): rolling
Undergraduate student body: 1,353 full time, 321 part time; 40% male, 60% female; 0% American Indian, 1% Asian, 4% black, 2% Hispanic, 6% multiracial, 0% Pacific Islander, 81% white, 2% international; 55% from in state; 85% live on campus; 0% of students in fraternities, 0% in sororities
Most popular majors: 11% Elementary Education and Teaching; 7% Psychology, General; 6% Social Work
Expenses: 2015-2016: $27,934; room/board: $6,336
Financial aid: (800) 888-1818

Bellarmine University
Louisville KY
(502) 272-8131
U.S. News ranking: Reg. U. (S), No. 12
Website: www.bellarmine.edu
Admissions email: admissions@bellarmine.edu
Private; founded 1950
Affiliation: Roman Catholic
Freshman admissions: selective; 2015-2016: 5,885 applied, 4,940 accepted. Either SAT or ACT required. ACT 25/75 percentile: 22-27. High school rank: 25% in top tenth, 59% in top quarter, 85% in top half
Early decision deadline: N/A, notification date: N/A
Early action deadline: 11/1, notification date: 11/15
Application deadline (fall): 8/15
Undergraduate student body: 2,459 full time, 192 part time; 35% male, 65% female; 0% American Indian, 2% Asian, 4% black, 3% Hispanic, 3% multiracial, 0% Pacific Islander, 85% white, 1% international; 67% from in state; 43% live on campus; 1%

of students in fraternities, 1% in sororities
Most popular majors: 36% Health Professions and Related Programs; 14% Business, Management, Marketing, and Related Support Services; 9% Psychology; 6% Biological and Biomedical Sciences; 6% Parks, Recreation, Leisure, and Fitness Studies
Expenses: 2016-2017: $39,350; room/board: $11,470
Financial aid: (502) 452-8124; 78% of undergrads determined to have financial need; average aid package $29,769

Berea College
Berea KY
(859) 985-3500
U.S. News ranking: Nat. Lib. Arts, No. 60
Website: www.berea.edu
Admissions email: admissions@berea.edu
Private; founded 1855
Freshman admissions: more selective; 2015-2016: 1,635 applied, 597 accepted. Either SAT or ACT required. ACT 25/75 percentile: 22-26. High school rank: 24% in top tenth, 67% in top quarter, 96% in top half
Early decision deadline: N/A, notification date: N/A
Early action deadline: N/A, notification date: N/A
Application deadline (fall): 4/30
Undergraduate student body: 1,592 full time, 51 part time; 43% male, 57% female; 0% American Indian, 2% Asian, 16% black, 8% Hispanic, 5% multiracial, 0% Pacific Islander, 60% white, 8% international; 47% from in state; 85% live on campus; N/A of students in fraternities, N/A in sororities
Most popular majors: 8% Biological and Biomedical Sciences; 8% Visual and Performing Arts; 7% Business, Management, Marketing, and Related Support Services; 7% Social Sciences
Expenses: 2016-2017: $570; room/board: $6,472
Financial aid: (859) 985-3310; 100% of undergrads determined to have financial need; average aid package $31,939

Brescia University
Owensboro KY
(270) 686-4241
U.S. News ranking: Reg. Coll. (S), No. 32
Website: www.brescia.edu
Admissions email: admissions@brescia.edu
Private; founded 1950
Affiliation: Roman Catholic
Freshman admissions: selective; 2015-2016: 4,153 applied, 1,991 accepted. Either SAT or ACT required. ACT 25/75 percentile: 19-24. High school rank:
Early decision deadline: N/A, notification date: N/A
Early action deadline: N/A, notification date: N/A
Application deadline (fall): rolling
Undergraduate student body: 770 full time, 273 part time; 23% male, 77% female; 1% American Indian, 0% Asian, 13% black,

6% Hispanic, 1% multiracial, 0% Pacific Islander, 66% white, 1% international; N/A from in state; 45% live on campus; 0% of students in fraternities, 0% in sororities
Most popular majors: 40% Social Work; 15% Psychology, General; 10% Audiology/Audiologist and Speech-Language Pathology/Pathologist; 10% Business/Commerce, General; 5% Liberal Arts and Sciences/Liberal Studies
Expenses: 2016-2017: $21,534; room/board: $9,050
Financial aid: (270) 686-4253; 78% of undergrads determined to have financial need; average aid package $10,381

Campbellsville University
Campbellsville KY
(270) 789-5220
U.S. News ranking: Reg. U. (S), No. 98
Website: www.campbellsville.edu
Admissions email: admissions@campbellsville.edu
Private; founded 1906
Affiliation: Baptist
Freshman admissions: selective; 2015-2016: 2,579 applied, 1,949 accepted. Either SAT or ACT required. ACT 25/75 percentile: 18-24. High school rank: 16% in top tenth, 40% in top quarter, 68% in top half
Early decision deadline: N/A, notification date: N/A
Early action deadline: N/A, notification date: N/A
Application deadline (fall): rolling
Undergraduate student body: 1,879 full time, 818 part time; 43% male, 57% female; 0% American Indian, 0% Asian, 12% black, 2% Hispanic, 1% multiracial, 0% Pacific Islander, 73% white, 10% international; 85% from in state; 47% live on campus; N/A of students in fraternities, N/A in sororities
Most popular majors: 24% Business/Commerce, General; 11% Adult and Continuing Education and Teaching; 11% Social Work; 9% Criminal Justice/Law Enforcement Administration; 8% Theology/Theological Studies
Expenses: 2016-2017: $24,596; room/board: $8,772
Financial aid: (270) 789-5013; 89% of undergrads determined to have financial need; average aid package $18,694

Centre College
Danville KY
(859) 238-5350
U.S. News ranking: Nat. Lib. Arts, No. 44
Website: www.centre.edu
Admissions email: admission@centre.edu
Private; founded 1819
Freshman admissions: more selective; 2015-2016: 2,716 applied, 1,933 accepted. Either SAT or ACT required. ACT 25/75 percentile: 26-31. High school rank: 54% in top tenth, 84% in top quarter, 97% in top half
Early decision deadline: 11/15, notification date: 12/15

Early action deadline: 12/1, notification date: 1/15
Application deadline (fall): 1/15
Undergraduate student body: 1,362 full time, 5 part time; 50% male, 50% female; 0% American Indian, 4% Asian, 5% black, 3% Hispanic, 3% multiracial, 0% Pacific Islander, 77% white, 7% international; 53% from in state; 98% live on campus; 40% of students in fraternities, 41% in sororities
Most popular majors: 22% Economics, General; 9% Biology/Biological Sciences, General; 9% History, General; 9% International/Global Studies; 9% Political Science and Government, General
Expenses: 2016-2017: $39,300; room/board: $9,950
Financial aid: (859) 238-5365; 56% of undergrads determined to have financial need; average aid package $30,006

Eastern Kentucky University
Richmond KY
(800) 465-9191
U.S. News ranking: Reg. U. (S), No. 79
Website: www.eku.edu
Admissions email: admissions@eku.edu
Public; founded 1906
Freshman admissions: selective; 2015-2016: 10,215 applied, 7,215 accepted. Either SAT or ACT required. ACT 25/75 percentile: 19-25. High school rank: 12% in top tenth, 35% in top quarter, 68% in top half
Early decision deadline: N/A, notification date: N/A
Early action deadline: N/A, notification date: N/A
Application deadline (fall): 8/1
Undergraduate student body: 11,332 full time, 2,995 part time; 43% male, 57% female; 0% American Indian, 1% Asian, 6% black, 2% Hispanic, 2% multiracial, 0% Pacific Islander, 84% white, 2% international; 87% from in state; 29% live on campus; 10% of students in fraternities, 7% in sororities
Most popular majors: 15% Homeland Security, Law Enforcement, Firefighting and Related Protective Services; 13% Health Professions and Related Programs; 9% Liberal Arts and Sciences, General Studies and Humanities; 8% Business, Management, Marketing, and Related Support Services; 8% Education
Expenses: 2016-2017: $8,868 in state, $18,180 out of state; room/board: $8,666
Financial aid: (859) 622-2361; 72% of undergrads determined to have financial need; average aid package $10,771

Georgetown College
Georgetown KY
(502) 863-8009
U.S. News ranking: Nat. Lib. Arts, No. 168
Website: www.georgetowncollege.edu
Admissions email: admissions@georgetowncollege.edu

Private; founded 1829
Affiliation: Baptist
Freshman admissions: selective; 2015-2016: 2,145 applied, 1,452 accepted. Either SAT or ACT required. ACT 25/75 percentile: 20-25. High school rank: 17% in top tenth, 44% in top quarter, 80% in top half
Early decision deadline: N/A, notification date: N/A
Early action deadline: N/A, notification date: N/A
Application deadline (fall): 8/15
Undergraduate student body: 907 full time, 77 part time; 47% male, 53% female; 0% American Indian, 1% Asian, 7% black, 4% Hispanic, 4% multiracial, 0% Pacific Islander, 79% white, 1% international; 76% from in state; 91% live on campus; 27% of students in fraternities, 35% in sororities
Most popular majors: 13% Business/Commerce, General; 12% Biology/Biological Sciences, General; 10% Kinesiology and Exercise Science; 10% Psychology, General
Expenses: 2016-2017: $35,850; room/board: $9,050
Financial aid: (502) 863-8027; 83% of undergrads determined to have financial need; average aid package $29,935

Kentucky Christian University[1]
Grayson KY
(800) 522-3181
U.S. News ranking: Reg. Coll. (S), No. 32
Website: www.kcu.edu
Admissions email: knights@kcu.edu
Private; founded 1919
Affiliation: Christian Church/Church of Christ
Application deadline (fall): 8/1
Undergraduate student body: N/A full time, N/A part time
Expenses: 2015-2016: $17,810; room/board: $7,800
Financial aid: (606) 474-3226

Kentucky State University
Frankfort KY
(800) 325-1716
U.S. News ranking: Reg. Coll. (S), No. 16
Website: www.kysu.edu
Admissions email: admissions@kysu.edu
Public; founded 1886
Freshman admissions: selective; 2015-2016: 4,666 applied, 1,787 accepted. Either SAT or ACT required. ACT 25/75 percentile: 17-22. High school rank: 4% in top tenth, 26% in top quarter, 58% in top half
Early decision deadline: N/A, notification date: N/A
Early action deadline: N/A, notification date: N/A
Application deadline (fall): 7/1
Undergraduate student body: 1,100 full time, 333 part time; 41% male, 59% female; 0% American Indian, 1% Asian, 57% black, 3% Hispanic, 2% multiracial, 0% Pacific Islander, 27% white, 0% international; 68% from in

state; 35% live on campus; 2% of students in fraternities, 4% in sororities
Most popular majors: 13% Liberal Arts and Sciences/Liberal Studies; 10% Criminal Justice/Safety Studies; 9% Business/Commerce, General; 9% Psychology, General; 7% Registered Nursing/Registered Nurse
Expenses: 2015-2016: $7,754 in state, $18,056 out of state; room/board: $6,690
Financial aid: (502) 597-5960; 91% of undergrads determined to have financial need; average aid package $15,866

Kentucky Wesleyan College
Owensboro KY
(800) 999-0592
U.S. News ranking: Reg. Coll. (S), No. 13
Website: www.kwc.edu/page.php?page=354
Admissions email: rsmith@kwc.edu
Private; founded 1858
Affiliation: United Methodist
Freshman admissions: selective; 2015-2016: N/A applied, N/A accepted. Either SAT or ACT required. ACT 25/75 percentile: 20-26. High school rank: N/A
Early decision deadline: N/A, notification date: N/A
Early action deadline: N/A, notification date: N/A
Application deadline (fall): rolling
Undergraduate student body: 665 full time, 28 part time; 53% male, 47% female; 0% American Indian, 0% Asian, 15% black, 1% Hispanic, 0% multiracial, 0% Pacific Islander, 73% white, 0% international
Most popular majors: Information not available
Expenses: 2016-2017: $24,050; room/board: $8,480
Financial aid: (270) 926-3111; 83% of undergrads determined to have financial need; average aid package $18,630

Lindsey Wilson College
Columbia KY
(270) 384-8100
U.S. News ranking: Reg. U. (S), second tier
Website: www.lindsey.edu
Admissions email: admissions@lindsey.edu
Private; founded 1903
Affiliation: United Methodist
Freshman admissions: selective; 2015-2016: 2,787 applied, 1,998 accepted. Neither SAT nor ACT required. ACT 25/75 percentile: 19-24. High school rank: 13% in top tenth, 36% in top quarter, 72% in top half
Early decision deadline: N/A, notification date: N/A
Early action deadline: N/A, notification date: N/A
Application deadline (fall): rolling
Undergraduate student body: 2,071 full time, 127 part time; 41% male, 59% female; 0% American Indian, 0% Asian, 9% black, 1% Hispanic, 2% multiracial, 0% Pacific Islander, 69% white, 0% international; 81% from in

state; 50% live on campus; N/A of students in fraternities, N/A in sororities
Most popular majors: 56% Public Administration and Social Service Professions; 8% Business Administration and Management, General; 5% Criminal Justice/Safety Studies; 5% Physiological Psychology/Psychobiology
Expenses: 2016-2017: $23,762; room/board: $9,120
Financial aid: (270) 384-8022; 94% of undergrads determined to have financial need; average aid package $19,168

Midway University
Midway KY
(800) 755-0031
U.S. News ranking: Reg. U. (S), No. 69
Website: www.midway.edu
Admissions email: admissions@midway.edu
Private; founded 1847
Affiliation: Christian Church (Disciples of Christ)
Freshman admissions: selective; 2015-2016: 333 applied, 193 accepted. Either SAT or ACT required. ACT 25/75 percentile: 20-25. High school rank: 15% in top tenth, 42% in top quarter, 96% in top half
Early decision deadline: N/A, notification date: N/A
Early action deadline: N/A, notification date: N/A
Application deadline (fall): rolling
Undergraduate student body: 596 full time, 348 part time; 14% male, 86% female; 0% American Indian, 0% Asian, 9% black, 4% Hispanic, 2% multiracial, N/A Pacific Islander, 75% white, 5% international
Most popular majors: Information not available
Expenses: 2016-2017: $23,350; room/board: $8,400
Financial aid: (859) 846-5745

Morehead State University
Morehead KY
(606) 783-2000
U.S. News ranking: Reg. U. (S), No. 72
Website: www.moreheadstate.edu
Admissions email: admissions@moreheadstate.edu
Public; founded 1887
Freshman admissions: selective; 2015-2016: 4,888 applied, 4,174 accepted. Either SAT or ACT required. ACT 25/75 percentile: 20-25. High school rank: 18% in top tenth, 44% in top quarter, 75% in top half
Early decision deadline: N/A, notification date: N/A
Early action deadline: N/A, notification date: N/A
Application deadline (fall): rolling
Undergraduate student body: 6,209 full time, 3,574 part time; 40% male, 60% female; 0% American Indian, 0% Asian, 4% black, 1% Hispanic, 2% multiracial, 0% Pacific Islander, 89% white, 2% international; 88% from in state; 40% live on campus; 5% of students in fraternities, 7% in sororities
Most popular majors: 13% General Studies; 8% Registered Nursing/

Registered Nurse; 8% Social Work; 5% Business/Commerce, General; 4% Sociology
Expenses: 2016-2017: $8,496 in state, $12,744 out of state; room/board: $8,892
Financial aid: (606) 783-2011; 77% of undergrads determined to have financial need; average aid package $11,462

Murray State University
Murray KY
(270) 809-3741
U.S. News ranking: Reg. U. (S), No. 35
Website: www.murraystate.edu
Admissions email: admissions@murraystate.edu
Public; founded 1922
Freshman admissions: selective; 2015-2016: 4,874 applied, 4,416 accepted. Either SAT or ACT required. ACT 25/75 percentile: 20-26. High school rank: 18% in top tenth, 45% in top quarter, 75% in top half
Early decision deadline: N/A, notification date: N/A
Early action deadline: N/A, notification date: N/A
Application deadline (fall): 8/15
Undergraduate student body: 7,162 full time, 2,106 part time; 41% male, 59% female; 0% American Indian, 1% Asian, 8% black, 2% Hispanic, 2% multiracial, 0% Pacific Islander, 81% white, 4% international; 74% from in state; 32% live on campus; 17% of students in fraternities, 19% in sororities
Most popular majors: 8% General Studies; 7% Registered Nursing/Registered Nurse; 6% Veterinary/Animal Health Technology/Technician and Veterinary Assistant; 5% Business/Commerce, General; 5% Elementary Education and Teaching
Expenses: 2016-2017: $7,944 in state, $21,648 out of state; room/board: $8,588
Financial aid: (270) 809-2546; 61% of undergrads determined to have financial need; average aid package $13,456

Northern Kentucky University
Highland Heights KY
(800) 637-9948
U.S. News ranking: Reg. U. (S), No. 82
Website: www.nku.edu
Admissions email: admitnku@nku.edu
Public; founded 1968
Freshman admissions: selective; 2015-2016: 7,397 applied, 6,797 accepted. Either SAT or ACT required. ACT 25/75 percentile: 20-26. High school rank: 11% in top tenth, 32% in top quarter, 64% in top half
Early decision deadline: N/A, notification date: N/A
Early action deadline: N/A, notification date: N/A
Application deadline (fall): 8/15
Undergraduate student body: 9,268 full time, 3,263 part time; 44% male, 56% female; 0% American Indian, 1% Asian, 7% black, 3% Hispanic, 2% multiracial, 0%

Pacific Islander, 82% white, 3% international; 69% from in state; 16% live on campus; 10% of students in fraternities, 14% in sororities
Most popular majors: 8% Organizational Behavior Studies; 6% Registered Nursing/Registered Nurse; 5% Psychology, General; 4% Social Work
Expenses: 2016-2017: $9,384 in state, $18,384 out of state; room/board: $9,526
Financial aid: (859) 572-5143; 65% of undergrads determined to have financial need; average aid package $10,840

Spalding University[1]
Louisville KY
(502) 585-7111
U.S. News ranking: Nat. U., second tier
Website: www.spalding.edu
Admissions email: admissions@spalding.edu
Private; founded 1814
Affiliation: Roman Catholic
Application deadline (fall): rolling
Undergraduate student body: N/A full time, N/A part time
Expenses: 2015-2016: $24,000; room/board: $8,400
Financial aid: (502) 585-9911

Sullivan University[1]
Louisville KY
(502) 456-6504
U.S. News ranking: Reg. U. (S), unranked
Website: www.sullivan.edu
Admissions email: admissions@sullivan.edu
Private
Application deadline (fall): N/A
Undergraduate student body: N/A full time, N/A part time
Expenses: 2015-2016: $19,740; room/board: $9,720
Financial aid: (800) 844-1354

Thomas More College
Crestview Hills KY
(800) 825-4557
U.S. News ranking: Reg. U. (S), No. 79
Website: www.thomasmore.edu
Admissions email: admissions@thomasmore.edu
Private; founded 1921
Affiliation: Roman Catholic
Freshman admissions: selective; 2015-2016: 1,531 applied, 1,352 accepted. Either SAT or ACT required. ACT 25/75 percentile: 20-24. High school rank: 11% in top tenth, 31% in top quarter, 61% in top half
Early decision deadline: N/A, notification date: N/A
Early action deadline: N/A, notification date: N/A
Application deadline (fall): rolling
Undergraduate student body: 1,272 full time, 459 part time; 45% male, 55% female; 0% American Indian, 0% Asian, 7% black, 2% Hispanic, 3% multiracial, 0% Pacific Islander, 76% white, 1% international; 51% from in state; 30% live on campus; 3% of students in fraternities, 3% in sororities

Most popular majors: 37% Business Administration and Management, General; 8% Biology/Biological Sciences, General; 6% Registered Nursing/Registered Nurse; 5% Psychology, General; 4% English Language and Literature, General
Expenses: 2016-2017: $29,450; room/board: $7,990
Financial aid: (859) 344-3319; 74% of undergrads determined to have financial need; average aid package $19,287

Transylvania University
Lexington KY
(859) 233-8242
U.S. News ranking: Nat. Lib. Arts, No. 83
Website: www.transy.edu
Admissions email: admissions@transy.edu
Private; founded 1780
Affiliation: Christian Church (Disciples of Christ)
Freshman admissions: more selective; 2015-2016: 1,538 applied, 1,425 accepted. Neither SAT nor ACT required. ACT 25/75 percentile: 24-30. High school rank: 39% in top tenth, 76% in top quarter, 91% in top half
Early decision deadline: N/A, notification date: N/A
Early action deadline: 12/1, notification date: 1/15
Application deadline (fall): rolling
Undergraduate student body: 1,049 full time, 7 part time; 42% male, 58% female; 0% American Indian, 2% Asian, 3% black, 6% Hispanic, 3% multiracial, 0% Pacific Islander, 79% white, 4% international; 78% from in state; 65% live on campus; 44% of students in fraternities, 55% in sororities
Most popular majors: 11% Psychology, General; 10% Business/Commerce, General; 9% Biology/Biological Sciences, General; 9% Spanish Language and Literature; 7% Accounting
Expenses: 2016-2017: $35,830; room/board: $9,860
Financial aid: (859) 233-8239; 67% of undergrads determined to have financial need; average aid package $27,620

Union College[1]
Barbourville KY
(800) 489-8646
U.S. News ranking: Reg. U. (S), second tier
Website: www.unionky.edu
Admissions email: enroll@unionky.edu
Private
Application deadline (fall): N/A
Undergraduate student body: N/A full time, N/A part time
Expenses: 2016-2017: $25,060; room/board: $7,325
Financial aid: (606) 546-1229; 86% of undergrads determined to have financial need; average aid package $22,110

University of Kentucky
Lexington KY
(859) 257-2000
U.S. News ranking: Nat. U., No. 133
Website: www.uky.edu
Admissions email: admissions@uky.edu
Public; founded 1865
Freshman admissions: more selective; 2015-2016: 18,432 applied, 16,685 accepted. Either SAT or ACT required. ACT 25/75 percentile: 22-28. High school rank: 30% in top tenth, 58% in top quarter, 86% in top half
Early decision deadline: N/A, notification date: N/A
Early action deadline: 12/1, notification date: N/A
Application deadline (fall): rolling
Undergraduate student body: 21,199 full time, 1,506 part time; 47% male, 53% female; 0% American Indian, 2% Asian, 8% black, 4% Hispanic, 3% multiracial, 0% Pacific Islander, 76% white, 3% international; 70% from in state; 28% live on campus; 20% of students in fraternities, 34% in sororities
Most popular majors: 5% Biology/Biological Sciences, General; 5% Marketing/Marketing Management, General; 5% Physical Education Teaching and Coaching; 5% Registered Nursing/Registered Nurse; 4% Psychology, General
Expenses: 2016-2017: $11,484 in state, $26,334 out of state; room/board: $12,184
Financial aid: (859) 257-3172; 52% of undergrads determined to have financial need; average aid package $11,128

University of Louisville
Louisville KY
(502) 852-6531
U.S. News ranking: Nat. U., No. 171
Website: www.louisville.edu
Admissions email: admitme@louisville.edu
Public; founded 1798
Freshman admissions: selective; 2015-2016: 9,430 applied, 6,758 accepted. Either SAT or ACT required. ACT 25/75 percentile: 22-29. High school rank: 11% in top tenth, 29% in top quarter, 53% in top half
Early decision deadline: N/A, notification date: N/A
Early action deadline: N/A, notification date: N/A
Application deadline (fall): 8/25
Undergraduate student body: 12,336 full time, 3,433 part time; 50% male, 50% female; 0% American Indian, 3% Asian, 11% black, 4% Hispanic, 4% multiracial, 0% Pacific Islander, 76% white, 1% international; 84% from in state; 27% live on campus; 20% of students in fraternities, 18% in sororities
Most popular majors: 13% Business, Management, Marketing, and Related Support Services; 10% Parks, Recreation, Leisure, and Fitness Studies; 10% Engineering; 9% Health Professions and Related Programs

Expenses: 2015-2016: $10,738 in state, $24,626 out of state; room/board: $8,120
Financial aid: (502) 852-5511; 60% of undergrads determined to have financial need; average aid package $11,632

University of Pikeville
Pikeville KY
(606) 218-5251
U.S. News ranking: Nat. Lib. Arts, second tier
Website: www.pc.edu/
Admissions email: wewantyou@pc.edu
Private; founded 1889
Affiliation: Presbyterian Church (USA)
Freshman admissions: selective; 2015-2016: 2,408 applied, 2,408 accepted. Either SAT or ACT required. ACT 25/75 percentile: 18-23. High school rank: 14% in top tenth, 27% in top quarter, 61% in top half
Early decision deadline: N/A, notification date: N/A
Early action deadline: N/A, notification date: N/A
Application deadline (fall): rolling
Undergraduate student body: 1,220 full time, 686 part time; 46% male, 54% female; 0% American Indian, 1% Asian, 12% black, 2% Hispanic, 0% multiracial, 0% Pacific Islander, 81% white, 4% international; 80% from in state; 58% live on campus; 3% of students in fraternities, N/A in sororities
Most popular majors: 20% Business, Management, Marketing, and Related Support Services; 17% Biological and Biomedical Sciences; 10% Psychology; 9% Homeland Security, Law Enforcement, Firefighting and Related Protective Services
Expenses: 2016-2017: $19,600; room/board: $9,100
Financial aid: (606) 218-5253; 98% of undergrads determined to have financial need; average aid package $20,777

University of the Cumberlands
Williamsburg KY
(800) 343-1609
U.S. News ranking: Nat. U., second tier
Website: www.ucumberlands.edu
Admissions email: admiss@ucumberlands.edu
Private; founded 1888
Affiliation: Baptist
Freshman admissions: selective; 2015-2016: 2,440 applied, 1,667 accepted. Either SAT or ACT required. ACT 25/75 percentile: 19-25. High school rank: 17% in top tenth, 40% in top quarter, 74% in top half
Early decision deadline: N/A, notification date: N/A
Early action deadline: N/A, notification date: N/A
Application deadline (fall): 8/15
Undergraduate student body: 1,670 full time, 1,230 part time; 44% male, 56% female; 0% American Indian, 0% Asian, 6% black, 2% Hispanic, 1% multiracial, 0% Pacific Islander, 76% white, 5% international; 68% from in

state; 62% live on campus; 0% of students in fraternities, 0% in sororities
Most popular majors: 34% Business, Management, Marketing, and Related Support Services; 16% Psychology; 9% Parks, Recreation, Leisure, and Fitness Studies; 8% Biological and Biomedical Sciences; 7% Public Administration and Social Service Professions
Expenses: 2016-2017: $23,000; room/board: $9,000
Financial aid: (800) 532-0828; 85% of undergrads determined to have financial need; average aid package $19,977

Western Kentucky University
Bowling Green KY
(270) 745-2551
U.S. News ranking: Reg. U. (S), No. 31
Website: www.wku.edu
Admissions email: admission@wku.edu
Public; founded 1906
Freshman admissions: selective; 2015-2016: 8,957 applied, 8,303 accepted. Either SAT or ACT required. ACT 25/75 percentile: 19-26. High school rank: 22% in top tenth, 44% in top quarter, 74% in top half
Early decision deadline: N/A, notification date: N/A
Early action deadline: N/A, notification date: N/A
Application deadline (fall): 8/1
Undergraduate student body: 13,152 full time, 4,158 part time; 43% male, 57% female; 0% American Indian, 1% Asian, 10% black, 3% Hispanic, 3% multiracial, 0% Pacific Islander, 76% white, 6% international; 81% from in state; 32% live on campus; 13% of students in fraternities, 17% in sororities
Most popular majors: 9% Registered Nursing/Registered Nurse; 5% Elementary Education and Teaching; 4% Biology/Biological Sciences, General; 4% Business Administration and Management, General; 4% Psychology, General
Expenses: 2016-2017: $9,912 in state, $24,792 out of state; room/board: $7,713
Financial aid: (270) 745-2755; 62% of undergrads determined to have financial need; average aid package $13,896

LOUISIANA

Centenary College of Louisiana
Shreveport LA
(800) 234-4448
U.S. News ranking: Nat. Lib. Arts, No. 146
Website: www.centenary.edu
Admissions email: admission@centenary.edu
Private; founded 1825
Affiliation: United Methodist
Freshman admissions: more selective; 2015-2016: 747 applied, 501 accepted. Either SAT or ACT required. ACT 25/75 percentile: 21-28. High school rank: 27% in top tenth, 54% in top quarter, 78% in top half

Early decision deadline: N/A, notification date: N/A
Early action deadline: 12/1, notification date: 1/15
Application deadline (fall): 8/1
Undergraduate student body: 513 full time, 10 part time; 44% male, 56% female; 1% American Indian, 3% Asian, 35% black, 6% Hispanic, 5% multiracial, 0% Pacific Islander, 48% white, 2% international
Most popular majors: 23% Biology/Biological Sciences, General; 14% Business Administration and Management, General; 7% Psychology, General; 6% Geology/Earth Science, General
Expenses: 2016-2017: $35,430; room/board: $12,980
Financial aid: (318) 869-5137; 78% of undergrads determined to have financial need; average aid package $24,955

Dillard University
New Orleans LA
(800) 216-6637
U.S. News ranking: Nat. Lib. Arts, second tier
Website: www.dillard.edu
Admissions email: admissions@dillard.edu
Private; founded 1869
Freshman admissions: selective; 2015-2016: 4,615 applied, 2,197 accepted. Either SAT or ACT required. ACT 25/75 percentile: 17-20. High school rank: 10% in top tenth, 35% in top quarter, 68% in top half
Early decision deadline: N/A, notification date: N/A
Early action deadline: N/A, notification date: N/A
Application deadline (fall): 8/1
Undergraduate student body: 1,133 full time, 52 part time; 27% male, 73% female; N/A American Indian, N/A Asian, 91% black, 0% Hispanic, 1% multiracial, N/A Pacific Islander, 0% white, 2% international; 37% from in state; 50% live on campus; 5% of students in fraternities, 5% in sororities
Most popular majors: 19% Registered Nursing/Registered Nurse; 13% Psychology, General; 13% Public Health, General; 10% Sociology; 8% Biology/Biological Sciences, General
Expenses: 2016-2017: $17,531; room/board: $9,873
Financial aid: (504) 816-4677; 93% of undergrads determined to have financial need; average aid package $15,450

Grambling State University
Grambling LA
(318) 274-6183
Website: www.gram.edu/
Admissions email: admissions@gram.edu
Public
Freshman admissions: less selective; 2015-2016: 3,584 applied, 1,370 accepted. ACT required. ACT 25/75 percentile: 16-20. High school rank: 6% in top tenth, 19% in top quarter, 51% in top half

Early decision deadline: N/A, notification date: N/A
Early action deadline: N/A, notification date: N/A
Application deadline (fall): 8/15
Undergraduate student body: 3,320 full time, 263 part time; 43% male, 57% female; 0% American Indian, 0% Asian, 91% black, 1% Hispanic, 2% multiracial, 0% Pacific Islander, 1% white, 4% international; 70% from in state; 41% live on campus; 2% of students in fraternities, 2% in sororities
Most popular majors: 24% Criminal Justice/Safety Studies; 11% Social Work; 7% Psychology, General; 5% Business Administration and Management, General
Expenses: 2016-2017: $7,063 in state, $16,086 out of state; room/board: $8,638
Financial aid: (318) 274-6056; 82% of undergrads determined to have financial need; average aid package $6,734

Louisiana College
Pineville LA
(318) 487-7259
U.S. News ranking: Reg. U. (S), second tier
Website: www.lacollege.edu
Admissions email: admissions@lacollege.edu
Private; founded 1906
Affiliation: Southern Baptist
Freshman admissions: selective; 2015-2016: 756 applied, 525 accepted. Either SAT or ACT required. ACT 25/75 percentile: 18-23. High school rank: N/A
Early decision deadline: N/A, notification date: N/A
Early action deadline: 12/1, notification date: N/A
Application deadline (fall): rolling
Undergraduate student body: 859 full time, 48 part time; 53% male, 47% female; 1% American Indian, 1% Asian, 28% black, 3% Hispanic, 1% multiracial, 0% Pacific Islander, 63% white, 3% international; 90% from in state; N/A live on campus; N/A of students in fraternities, N/A in sororities
Most popular majors: 24% Health Professions and Related Programs; 17% Education; 10% Business, Management, Marketing, and Related Support Services; 9% Theology and Religious Vocations; 7% Biological and Biomedical Sciences
Expenses: 2016-2017: $15,678; room/board: $5,479
Financial aid: (318) 487-7386

Louisiana State University–Alexandria
Alexandria LA
(318) 473-6417
U.S. News ranking: Nat. Lib. Arts, second tier
Website: www.lsua.edu
Admissions email: admissions@lsua.edu
Public; founded 1960
Freshman admissions: selective; 2015-2016: 2,279 applied, 1,545 accepted. Either SAT or ACT required. ACT 25/75 percentile: 18-22. High school

rank: 9% in top tenth, 29% in top quarter, 67% in top half
Early decision deadline: N/A, notification date: N/A
Early action deadline: N/A, notification date: N/A
Application deadline (fall): 8/1
Undergraduate student body: 1,741 full time, 1,363 part time; 35% male, 65% female; 4% American Indian, 1% Asian, 18% black, 3% Hispanic, 3% multiracial, 0% Pacific Islander, 67% white, 3% international; 97% from in state; 9% live on campus; 0% of students in fraternities, 0% in sororities
Most popular majors: Information not available
Expenses: 2015-2016: $6,158 in state, $13,150 out of state; room/board: $7,770
Financial aid: (318) 473-6423; 61% of undergrads determined to have financial need; average aid package $13,440

Louisiana State University–Baton Rouge
Baton Rouge LA
(225) 578-1175
U.S. News ranking: Nat. U., No. 135
Website: www.lsu.edu
Admissions email: admissions@lsu.edu
Public; founded 1860
Freshman admissions: more selective; 2015-2016: 17,429 applied, 13,480 accepted. Either SAT or ACT required. ACT 25/75 percentile: 23-28. High school rank: 26% in top tenth, 52% in top quarter, 82% in top half
Early decision deadline: N/A, notification date: N/A
Early action deadline: N/A, notification date: N/A
Application deadline (fall): 4/15
Undergraduate student body: 23,602 full time, 2,554 part time; 48% male, 52% female; 0% American Indian, 4% Asian, 12% black, 6% Hispanic, 2% multiracial, 0% Pacific Islander, 73% white, 2% international; 83% from in state; 24% live on campus; 17% of students in fraternities, 28% in sororities
Most popular majors: 21% Business, Management, Marketing, and Related Support Services; 13% Engineering; 10% Education; 8% Biological and Biomedical Sciences
Expenses: 2015-2016: $9,842 in state, $27,005 out of state; room/board: $11,200
Financial aid: (225) 578-3103; 46% of undergrads determined to have financial need; average aid package $16,038

Louisiana State University–Shreveport
Shreveport LA
(318) 797-5061
U.S. News ranking: Reg. U. (S), second tier
Website: www.lsus.edu
Admissions email: admissions@pilot.lsus.edu
Public; founded 1967

Freshman admissions: less selective; 2015-2016: 602 applied, 489 accepted. Either SAT or ACT required. ACT 25/75 percentile: 20-25. High school rank: N/A
Early decision deadline: N/A, notification date: N/A
Early action deadline: N/A, notification date: N/A
Application deadline (fall): rolling
Undergraduate student body: 1,826 full time, 950 part time; 40% male, 60% female; 1% American Indian, 2% Asian, 23% black, 5% Hispanic, 4% multiracial, 0% Pacific Islander, 57% white, 2% international; 93% from in state; 0% live on campus; 1% of students in fraternities, 1% in sororities
Most popular majors: 22% Business, Management, Marketing, and Related Support Services; 14% Liberal Arts and Sciences, General Studies and Humanities; 11% Biological and Biomedical Sciences; 10% Health Professions and Related Programs; 9% Education
Expenses: 2015-2016: $6,903 in state, $20,057 out of state; room/board: $9,073
Financial aid: (318) 797-5363

Louisiana Tech University
Ruston LA
(318) 257-3036
U.S. News ranking: Nat. U., No. 202
Website: www.latech.edu
Admissions email: bulldog@latech.edu
Public; founded 1894
Freshman admissions: more selective; 2015-2016: 6,378 applied, 4,072 accepted. Either SAT or ACT required. ACT 25/75 percentile: 21-27. High school rank: 24% in top tenth, 49% in top quarter, 81% in top half
Early decision deadline: N/A, notification date: N/A
Early action deadline: N/A, notification date: N/A
Application deadline (fall): rolling
Undergraduate student body: 7,386 full time, 3,296 part time; 52% male, 48% female; 0% American Indian, 1% Asian, 14% black, 4% Hispanic, 3% multiracial, 0% Pacific Islander, 68% white, 3% international; 98% from in state; 15% live on campus; N/A of students in fraternities, 5% in sororities
Most popular majors: 17% Business, Management, Marketing, and Related Support Services; 13% Engineering; 7% Biological and Biomedical Sciences; 6% Health Professions and Related Programs; 5% Education
Expenses: 2015-2016: $8,853 in state, $25,851 out of state; room/board: $6,702
Financial aid: (318) 257-2643; 56% of undergrads determined to have financial need; average aid package $11,565

Loyola University New Orleans

New Orleans LA
(800) 456-9652
U.S. News ranking: Reg. U. (S), No. 10
Website: www.loyno.edu
Admissions email: admit@loyno.edu
Private; founded 1912
Affiliation: Roman Catholic (Jesuit)
Freshman admissions: selective; 2015-2016: 3,591 applied, 3,243 accepted. Either SAT or ACT required. ACT 25/75 percentile: 22-28. High school rank: 8% in top tenth, 20% in top quarter, 39% in top half
Early decision deadline: N/A, notification date: N/A
Early action deadline: 11/15, notification date: 12/19
Application deadline (fall): rolling
Undergraduate student body: 2,510 full time, 181 part time; 40% male, 60% female; 1% American Indian, 4% Asian, 17% black, 16% Hispanic, 4% multiracial, 0% Pacific Islander, 51% white, 3% international; 41% from in state; 49% live on campus; 9% of students in fraternities, 21% in sororities
Most popular majors: 12% Psychology, General; 8% Music Management; 6% Criminology; 4% Creative Writing
Expenses: 2016-2017: $38,504; room/board: $13,204
Financial aid: (504) 865-3231; 71% of undergrads determined to have financial need; average aid package $30,614

McNeese State University

Lake Charles LA
(337) 475-5356
U.S. News ranking: Reg. U. (S), No. 98
Website: www.mcneese.edu
Admissions email: admissions@mcneese.edu
Public; founded 1939
Freshman admissions: selective; 2015-2016: 3,002 applied, 2,463 accepted. Either SAT or ACT required. ACT 25/75 percentile: 20-24. High school rank: 18% in top tenth, 41% in top quarter, 73% in top half
Early decision deadline: N/A, notification date: N/A
Early action deadline: N/A, notification date: N/A
Application deadline (fall): 8/15
Undergraduate student body: 5,721 full time, 1,744 part time; 41% male, 59% female; 1% American Indian, 2% Asian, 18% black, 3% Hispanic, 2% multiracial, 0% Pacific Islander, 68% white, 7% international; 92% from in state; 10% live on campus; N/A of students in fraternities, N/A in sororities
Most popular majors: 13% General Studies; 13% Registered Nursing/Registered Nurse; 6% Engineering, General; 6% Business Administration and Management, General; 6% Kinesiology and Exercise Science
Expenses: 2016-2017: $7,290 in state, $18,366 out of state; room/board: $8,014
Financial aid: (337) 475-5065

Nicholls State University

Thibodaux LA
(985) 448-4507
U.S. News ranking: Reg. U. (S), No. 102
Website: www.nicholls.edu
Admissions email: nicholls@nicholls.edu
Public; founded 1948
Freshman admissions: selective; 2015-2016: 2,399 applied, 2,164 accepted. Either SAT or ACT required. ACT 25/75 percentile: 20-24. High school rank: 17% in top tenth, 42% in top quarter, 75% in top half
Early decision deadline: N/A, notification date: N/A
Early action deadline: N/A, notification date: N/A
Application deadline (fall): rolling
Undergraduate student body: 4,591 full time, 903 part time; 37% male, 63% female; 2% American Indian, 1% Asian, 20% black, 3% Hispanic, 3% multiracial, 0% Pacific Islander, 68% white, 2% international; 94% from in state; 25% live on campus; 12% of students in fraternities, 14% in sororities
Most popular majors: 23% Business, Management, Marketing, and Related Support Services; 18% Health Professions and Related Programs; 14% Multi/Interdisciplinary Studies; 7% Education; 5% Personal and Culinary Services
Expenses: 2016-2017: $7,276 in state, $20,562 out of state; room/board: $7,200
Financial aid: (985) 448-4048; 64% of undergrads determined to have financial need; average aid package $9,548

Northwestern State University of Louisiana[1]

Natchitoches LA
(800) 426-3754
U.S. News ranking: Reg. U. (S), second tier
Website: www.nsula.edu
Admissions email: admissions@nsula.edu
Public; founded 1884
Application deadline (fall): 7/6
Undergraduate student body: N/A full time, N/A part time
Expenses: 2015-2016: $7,006 in state, $17,794 out of state; room/board: $8,584
Financial aid: (318) 357-5961

Our Lady of Holy Cross College[1]

New Orleans LA
(504) 398-2175
U.S. News ranking: Reg. Coll. (S), No. 56
Website: www.olhcc.edu
Admissions email: admissions@olhcc.edu
Private
Application deadline (fall): N/A
Undergraduate student body: N/A full time, N/A part time
Expenses: 2016-2017: $11,632; room/board: N/A
Financial aid: (504) 398-2165; 89% of undergrads determined to have financial need; average aid package $7,801

Southeastern Louisiana University

Hammond LA
(985) 549-5637
U.S. News ranking: Reg. U. (S), second tier
Website: www.selu.edu
Admissions email: admissions@selu.edu
Public; founded 1925
Freshman admissions: selective; 2015-2016: 3,738 applied, 3,242 accepted. Either SAT or ACT required. ACT 25/75 percentile: 20-24. High school rank: 10% in top tenth, 31% in top quarter, 61% in top half
Early decision deadline: N/A, notification date: N/A
Early action deadline: N/A, notification date: N/A
Application deadline (fall): 8/1
Undergraduate student body: 9,580 full time, 3,987 part time; 39% male, 61% female; 0% American Indian, 1% Asian, 18% black, 8% Hispanic, 7% multiracial, 0% Pacific Islander, 64% white, 2% international; 96% from in state; 21% live on campus; 7% of students in fraternities, 7% in sororities
Most popular majors: 23% Business, Management, Marketing, and Related Support Services; 13% Health Professions and Related Programs; 12% Liberal Arts and Sciences, General Studies and Humanities; 12% Education; 5% Psychology
Expenses: 2015-2016: $7,280 in state, $19,758 out of state; room/board: $8,252
Financial aid: (985) 549-2244; 63% of undergrads determined to have financial need; average aid package $9,597

Southern University and A&M College

Baton Rouge LA
(225) 771-2430
U.S. News ranking: Reg. U. (S), second tier
Website: www.subr.edu/
Admissions email: admit@subr.edu
Public; founded 1880
Freshman admissions: less selective; 2015-2016: N/A applied, N/A accepted. Either SAT or ACT required. ACT 25/75 percentile: 17-21. High school rank: 1% in top tenth, 7% in top quarter, 29% in top half
Early decision deadline: N/A, notification date: N/A
Early action deadline: N/A, notification date: N/A
Application deadline (fall): 7/1
Undergraduate student body: 4,580 full time, 858 part time; 35% male, 65% female; 0% American Indian, 0% Asian, 92% black, 1% Hispanic, 2% multiracial, 0% Pacific Islander, 3% white, 1% international
Most popular majors: 15% Health Professions and Related Programs; 8% Business, Management, Marketing, and Related Support Services; 7% Homeland Security, Law Enforcement, Firefighting and Related Protective Services; 6% Engineering; 4% Psychology

Expenses: 2015-2016: $7,346 in state, $17,696 out of state; room/board: $8,003
Financial aid: (225) 771-2790

Southern University–New Orleans[1]

New Orleans LA
(504) 286-5314
U.S. News ranking: Reg. U. (S), second tier
Website: www.suno.edu
Admissions email: N/A
Public
Application deadline (fall): N/A
Undergraduate student body: N/A full time, N/A part time
Expenses: 2015-2016: $5,827 in state, $5,827 out of state; room/board: $7,530
Financial aid: (504) 286-5263

Tulane University

New Orleans LA
(504) 865-5731
U.S. News ranking: Nat. U., No. 39
Website: www.tulane.edu
Admissions email: undergrad.admission@tulane.edu
Private; founded 1834
Freshman admissions: most selective; 2015-2016: 26,257 applied, 8,008 accepted. Either SAT or ACT required. ACT 25/75 percentile: 29-32. High school rank: 55% in top tenth, 85% in top quarter, 96% in top half
Early decision deadline: N/A, notification date: N/A
Early action deadline: 11/15, notification date: 12/15
Application deadline (fall): 1/15
Undergraduate student body: 6,624 full time, 38 part time; 41% male, 59% female; 0% American Indian, 4% Asian, 4% black, 6% Hispanic, 4% multiracial, 0% Pacific Islander, 77% white, 3% international; 24% from in state; 45% live on campus; 31% of students in fraternities, 51% in sororities
Most popular majors: 23% Business, Management, and Related Support Services; 15% Social Sciences; 9% Biological and Biomedical Sciences; 8% Health Professions and Related Programs; 6% Psychology
Expenses: 2016-2017: $51,010; room/board: $13,844
Financial aid: (504) 865-5723; 34% of undergrads determined to have financial need; average aid package $43,183

University of Louisiana–Lafayette

Lafayette LA
(337) 482-6553
U.S. News ranking: Nat. U., second tier
Website: www.louisiana.edu
Admissions email: enroll@louisiana.edu
Public; founded 1898
Freshman admissions: selective; 2015-2016: 10,899 applied, 6,023 accepted. Either SAT or ACT required. ACT 25/75 percentile: 21-25. High school rank: 21% in top tenth, 46% in top quarter, 77% in top half

Early decision deadline: N/A, notification date: N/A
Early action deadline: N/A, notification date: N/A
Application deadline (fall): rolling
Undergraduate student body: 12,867 full time, 3,003 part time; 44% male, 56% female; 0% American Indian, 2% Asian, 22% black, 4% Hispanic, 2% multiracial, 0% Pacific Islander, 67% white, 2% international; 92% from in state; 20% live on campus; 9% of students in fraternities, 12% in sororities
Most popular majors: 19% Health Professions and Related Programs; 16% Business, Management, Marketing, and Related Support Services; 12% Education; 10% Liberal Arts and Sciences, General Studies and Humanities; 9% Engineering
Expenses: 2015-2016: $8,256 in state, $21,984 out of state; room/board: N/A
Financial aid: (337) 482-6506; 58% of undergrads determined to have financial need; average aid package $9,772

University of Louisiana–Monroe

Monroe LA
(318) 342-5430
U.S. News ranking: Nat. U., second tier
Website: www.ulm.edu
Admissions email: admissions@ulm.edu
Public; founded 1931
Freshman admissions: selective; 2015-2016: 3,187 applied, 2,997 accepted. Either SAT or ACT required. ACT 25/75 percentile: 20-25. High school rank: 22% in top tenth, 52% in top quarter, 80% in top half
Early decision deadline: N/A, notification date: N/A
Early action deadline: N/A, notification date: N/A
Application deadline (fall): rolling
Undergraduate student body: 5,034 full time, 2,472 part time; 36% male, 64% female; 0% American Indian, 2% Asian, 25% black, 2% Hispanic, 3% multiracial, 0% Pacific Islander, 62% white, 3% international; 91% from in state; 29% live on campus; N/A of students in fraternities, N/A in sororities
Most popular majors: 9% General Studies; 9% Pharmacy, Pharmaceutical Sciences, and Administration, Other; 8% Psychology, General; 7% Registered Nursing/Registered Nurse; 6% Business Administration and Management, General
Expenses: 2015-2016: $7,658 in state, $19,758 out of state; room/board: $7,334
Financial aid: (318) 342-5320

University of New Orleans

New Orleans LA
(504) 280-6595
U.S. News ranking: Nat. U., second tier
Website: www.uno.edu
Admissions email: unopec@uno.edu
Public; founded 1956

BEST COLLEGES

Freshman admissions: selective; 2015-2016: 3,932 applied, 2,267 accepted. Either SAT or ACT required. ACT 25/75 percentile: 20-24. High school rank: 14% in top tenth, 32% in top quarter, 60% in top half
Early decision deadline: N/A, notification date: N/A
Early action deadline: N/A, notification date: N/A
Application deadline (fall): 7/25
Undergraduate student body: 4,847 full time, 1,754 part time; 50% male, 50% female; 0% American Indian, 8% Asian, 16% black, 11% Hispanic, 4% multiracial, 0% Pacific Islander, 54% white, 5% international; 94% from in state; 10% live on campus; N/A of students in fraternities, N/A in sororities
Most popular majors: 31% Business, Management, Marketing, and Related Support Services; 10% Biological and Biomedical Sciences; 10% Multi/Interdisciplinary Studies; 9% Engineering; 7% Psychology
Expenses: 2015-2016: $8,094 in state, $21,911 out of state; room/board: $9,515
Financial aid: (504) 280-6603; 74% of undergrads determined to have financial need; average aid package $10,148

Xavier University of Louisiana

New Orleans LA
(504) 520-7388
U.S. News ranking: Reg. U. (S), No. 27
Website: www.xula.edu
Admissions email: apply@xula.edu
Private; founded 1915
Affiliation: Roman Catholic
Freshman admissions: selective; 2015-2016: 4,847 applied, 3,187 accepted. Either SAT or ACT required. ACT 25/75 percentile: 20-26. High school rank: 31% in top tenth, 57% in top quarter, 81% in top half
Early decision deadline: N/A, notification date: N/A
Early action deadline: N/A, notification date: N/A
Application deadline (fall): 7/1
Undergraduate student body: 2,242 full time, 124 part time; 27% male, 73% female; 0% American Indian, 10% Asian, 76% black, 4% Hispanic, 3% multiracial, 0% Pacific Islander, 4% white, 2% international; 59% from in state; 46% live on campus; 1% of students in fraternities, 1% in sororities
Most popular majors: 37% Biological and Biomedical Sciences; 14% Physical Sciences; 13% Psychology; 9% Business, Management, Marketing, and Related Support Services; 6% Health Professions and Related Programs
Expenses: 2016-2017: $23,046; room/board: $8,523
Financial aid: (504) 520-7517; 84% of undergrads determined to have financial need; average aid package $22,203

MAINE

Bates College

Lewiston ME
(855) 228-3755
U.S. News ranking: Nat. Lib. Arts, No. 27
Website: www.bates.edu
Admissions email: admission@bates.edu
Private; founded 1855
Freshman admissions: most selective; 2015-2016: 5,651 applied, 1,231 accepted. Neither SAT nor ACT required. SAT 25/75 percentile: 1190-1416. High school rank: 72% in top tenth, 97% in top quarter, 97% in top half
Early decision deadline: 11/15, notification date: 12/20
Early action deadline: N/A, notification date: N/A
Application deadline (fall): 1/1
Undergraduate student body: 1,792 full time, N/A part time; 49% male, 51% female; 0% American Indian, 4% Asian, 5% black, 8% Hispanic, 4% multiracial, N/A Pacific Islander, 71% white, 7% international
Most popular majors: 28% Social Sciences; 11% Biological and Biomedical Sciences; 8% English Language and Literature/Letters; 8% Psychology; 7% Foreign Languages, Literatures, and Linguistics
Expenses: 2016-2017: $50,310; room/board: $14,190
Financial aid: (207) 786-6096; 43% of undergrads determined to have financial need; average aid package $43,568

Bowdoin College

Brunswick ME
(207) 725-3100
U.S. News ranking: Nat. Lib. Arts, No. 6
Website: www.bowdoin.edu
Admissions email: admissions@bowdoin.edu
Private; founded 1794
Freshman admissions: most selective; 2015-2016: 6,790 applied, 1,010 accepted. Neither SAT nor ACT required. SAT 25/75 percentile: 1375-1535. High school rank: 84% in top tenth, 98% in top quarter, 100% in top half
Early decision deadline: 11/15, notification date: 12/15
Early action deadline: N/A, notification date: N/A
Application deadline (fall): 1/1
Undergraduate student body: 1,794 full time, 5 part time; 50% male, 50% female; 0% American Indian, 7% Asian, 5% black, 12% Hispanic, 6% multiracial, 0% Pacific Islander, 63% white, 5% international; 10% from in state; 91% live on campus; N/A of students in fraternities, N/A in sororities
Most popular majors: 16% Political Science and Government, General; 13% Economics, General; 10% Mathematics, General; 7% Biology/Biological Sciences, General
Expenses: 2016-2017: $49,900; room/board: $13,600

Colby College

Waterville ME
(800) 723-3032
U.S. News ranking: Nat. Lib. Arts, No. 12
Website: www.colby.edu
Admissions email: admissions@colby.edu
Private; founded 1813
Affiliation: None
Freshman admissions: most selective; 2015-2016: 7,593 applied, 1,710 accepted. Neither SAT nor ACT required. SAT 25/75 percentile: 1270-1460. High school rank: 63% in top tenth, 93% in top quarter, 97% in top half
Early decision deadline: 11/15, notification date: 12/15
Early action deadline: N/A, notification date: N/A
Application deadline (fall): 1/1
Undergraduate student body: 1,857 full time, N/A part time; 48% male, 52% female; 0% American Indian, 6% Asian, 3% black, 6% Hispanic, 5% multiracial, 0% Pacific Islander, 62% white, 11% international; 13% from in state; 94% live on campus; N/A of students in fraternities, N/A in sororities
Most popular majors: 25% Social Sciences; 11% Multi/Interdisciplinary Studies; 10% Biological and Biomedical Sciences; 7% English Language and Literature/Letters; 7% Physical Sciences
Expenses: 2016-2017: $50,960; room/board: $13,100
Financial aid: (800) 723-3032; 37% of undergrads determined to have financial need; average aid package $43,845

College of the Atlantic

Bar Harbor ME
(800) 528-0025
U.S. News ranking: Nat. Lib. Arts, No. 83
Website: www.coa.edu/
Admissions email: inquiry@coa.edu
Private; founded 1969
Freshman admissions: more selective; 2015-2016: 400 applied, 302 accepted. Neither SAT nor ACT required. SAT 25/75 percentile: 1130-1350. High school rank: 26% in top tenth, 47% in top quarter, 95% in top half
Early decision deadline: 12/1, notification date: 12/15
Early action deadline: N/A, notification date: N/A
Application deadline (fall): 2/1
Undergraduate student body: 328 full time, 10 part time; 30% male, 70% female; 0% American Indian, 3% Asian, 1% black, 5% Hispanic, 2% multiracial, 0% Pacific Islander, 72% white, 17% international; 22% from in state; 50% live on campus; 0% of students in fraternities, 0% in sororities
Most popular majors: Information not available
Expenses: 2016-2017: $43,542; room/board: $9,747

Financial aid: (207) 725-3273; 45% of undergrads determined to have financial need; average aid package $43,352

Colby College

Waterville ME
(800) 723-3032
U.S. News ranking: Nat. Lib. Arts, No. 12

Husson University

Bangor ME
(207) 941-7100
U.S. News ranking: Reg. U. (N), second tier
Website: www.husson.edu
Admissions email: admit@husson.edu
Private; founded 1898
Freshman admissions: less selective; 2015-2016: 2,066 applied, 1,610 accepted. Either SAT or ACT required. SAT 25/75 percentile: 860-1070. High school rank: 11% in top tenth, 39% in top quarter, 73% in top half
Early decision deadline: N/A, notification date: N/A
Early action deadline: N/A, notification date: N/A
Application deadline (fall): 8/15
Undergraduate student body: 2,217 full time, 474 part time; 46% male, 54% female; 1% American Indian, 1% Asian, 4% black, 2% Hispanic, 1% multiracial, 0% Pacific Islander, 88% white, 3% international; 79% from in state; 39% live on campus; 3% of students in fraternities, 6% in sororities
Most popular majors: 29% Business Administration, Management and Operations; 20% Health Professions and Related Programs; 12% Psychology, General; 11% Communications Technologies/Technicians and Support Services; 11% Criminal Justice and Corrections
Expenses: 2016-2017: $16,500; room/board: $9,220
Financial aid: (207) 941-7156; 87% of undergrads determined to have financial need; average aid package $12,149

Maine College of Art

Portland ME
(800) 699-1509
U.S. News ranking: Arts, unranked
Website: www.meca.edu
Admissions email: admissions@meca.edu
Private; founded 1882
Freshman admissions: N/A; 2015-2016: 411 applied, 403 accepted. Neither SAT nor ACT required. SAT 25/75 percentile: N/A. High school rank: N/A
Early decision deadline: N/A, notification date: N/A
Early action deadline: 12/1, notification date: 12/24
Application deadline (fall): rolling
Undergraduate student body: 411 full time, 19 part time; 30% male, 70% female; 0% American Indian, 2% Asian, 1% black, 5% Hispanic, 4% multiracial, N/A Pacific Islander, 85% white, 1% international; 30% from in state; 47% live on campus; N/A of students in fraternities, N/A in sororities
Most popular majors: Information not available
Expenses: 2016-2017: $32,872; room/board: $11,186

Financial aid: (800) 528-0025; 85% of undergrads determined to have financial need; average aid package $38,120

Maine Maritime Academy

Castine ME
(207) 326-2206
U.S. News ranking: Reg. Coll. (N), No. 5
Website: www.mainemaritime.edu
Admissions email: admissions@mma.edu
Public; founded 1941
Freshman admissions: selective; 2015-2016: 777 applied, 606 accepted. Either SAT or ACT required. SAT 25/75 percentile: 950-1150. High school rank: 17% in top tenth, 44% in top quarter, 81% in top half
Early decision deadline: N/A, notification date: N/A
Early action deadline: 11/30, notification date: 2/1
Application deadline (fall): 3/31
Undergraduate student body: 969 full time, 28 part time; 86% male, 14% female; 1% American Indian, 1% Asian, 1% black, 1% Hispanic, 0% multiracial, 0% Pacific Islander, 91% white, 0% international; 73% from in state; 65% live on campus; 0% of students in fraternities, 0% in sororities
Most popular majors: 34% Engineering Technologies and Engineering-Related Fields, Other; 24% Naval Architecture and Marine Engineering; 23% Marine Science/Merchant Marine Officer; 14% International Business/Trade/Commerce; 5% Biological and Biomedical Sciences, Other
Expenses: 2016-2017: $18,108 in state, $26,158 out of state; room/board: $10,030
Financial aid: (207) 326-2339; 74% of undergrads determined to have financial need; average aid package $10,285

St. Joseph's College[1]

Standish ME
(207) 893-7746
U.S. News ranking: Reg. U. (N), No. 137
Website: www.sjcme.edu
Admissions email: admission@sjcme.edu
Private
Application deadline (fall): N/A
Undergraduate student body: N/A full time, N/A part time
Expenses: 2015-2016: $32,620; room/board: $12,510
Financial aid: (800) 752-1266

Thomas College

Waterville ME
(800) 339-7001
U.S. News ranking: Reg. U. (N), second tier
Website: www.thomas.edu
Admissions email: admiss@thomas.edu
Private; founded 1894
Freshman admissions: selective; 2015-2016: N/A applied, N/A accepted. Neither SAT nor ACT required. ACT 25/75 percentile: 22-22. High school rank: N/A

Financial aid: (207) 775-3052; 80% of undergrads determined to have financial need; average aid package $20,330

Early decision deadline: N/A, notification date: N/A
Early action deadline: N/A, notification date: N/A
Application deadline (fall): rolling
Undergraduate student body: 808 full time, 404 part time; 48% male, 52% female; 0% American Indian, 1% Asian, 4% black, 2% Hispanic, 9% multiracial, 0% Pacific Islander, 75% white, 2% international; 81% from in state; 67% live on campus; 1% of students in fraternities, 0% in sororities
Most popular majors: 19% Business Administration and Management, General; 18% Criminal Justice/Safety Studies; 14% Psychology, General; 12% Accounting; 8% Sport and Fitness Administration/Management
Expenses: 2016-2017: $25,150; room/board: $10,800
Financial aid: (207) 859-1112; 87% of undergrads determined to have financial need; average aid package $26,868

Unity College
Unity ME
(207) 948-3131
U.S. News ranking: Reg. Coll. (N), No. 15
Website: www.unity.edu
Admissions email: admissions@unity.edu
Private; founded 1965
Freshman admissions: selective; 2015-2016: 831 applied, 756 accepted. Neither SAT nor ACT required. SAT 25/75 percentile: 880-1150. High school rank: 18% in top tenth, 32% in top quarter, 63% in top half
Early decision deadline: N/A, notification date: N/A
Early action deadline: 12/15, notification date: 12/31
Application deadline (fall): 6/15
Undergraduate student body: 638 full time, 27 part time; 49% male, 51% female; 1% American Indian, 2% Asian, 1% black, 2% Hispanic, 4% multiracial, 0% Pacific Islander, 88% white, 0% international; 27% from in state; 72% live on campus; 0% of students in fraternities, 0% in sororities
Most popular majors: 31% Wildlife Biology; 4% Outdoor Education
Expenses: 2016-2017: $27,070; room/board: $10,100
Financial aid: (207) 948-3131; 85% of undergrads determined to have financial need; average aid package $19,960

University of Maine
Orono ME
(877) 486-2364
U.S. News ranking: Nat. U., No. 183
Website: www.umaine.edu
Admissions email: um-admit@maine.edu
Public; founded 1865
Freshman admissions: selective; 2015-2016: 11,044 applied, 10,073 accepted. Either SAT or ACT required. SAT 25/75 percentile: 960-1210. High school rank: 19% in top tenth, 46% in top quarter, 80% in top half

Early decision deadline: N/A, notification date: N/A
Early action deadline: 12/15, notification date: 1/31
Application deadline (fall): rolling
Undergraduate student body: 8,120 full time, 1,177 part time; 52% male, 48% female; 1% American Indian, 2% Asian, 2% black, 3% Hispanic, 3% multiracial, 0% Pacific Islander, 82% white, 2% international; 73% from in state; 39% live on campus; N/A of students in fraternities, N/A in sororities
Most popular majors: 13% Business, Management, Marketing, and Related Support Services; 12% Engineering; 9% Education; 9% Social Sciences; 7% Health Professions and Related Programs
Expenses: 2016-2017: $10,628 in state, $29,498 out of state; room/board: $10,164
Financial aid: (207) 581-1324; 71% of undergrads determined to have financial need; average aid package $16,316

University of Maine–Augusta
Augusta ME
(207) 621-3465
U.S. News ranking: Reg. Coll. (N), second tier
Website: www.uma.edu
Admissions email: umaadm@maine.edu
Public; founded 1965
Freshman admissions: least selective; 2015-2016: 747 applied, 728 accepted. Neither SAT nor ACT required. SAT 25/75 percentile: 780-1000. High school rank: N/A
Early decision deadline: N/A, notification date: N/A
Early action deadline: N/A, notification date: N/A
Application deadline (fall): 9/1
Undergraduate student body: 1,663 full time, 3,020 part time; 28% male, 72% female; 2% American Indian, 1% Asian, 1% black, 2% Hispanic, 2% multiracial, 0% Pacific Islander, 78% white, 0% international
Most popular majors: 44% Health Professions and Related Programs; 18% Liberal Arts and Sciences, General Studies and Humanities; 12% Business, Management, Marketing, and Related Support Services; 8% Homeland Security, Law Enforcement, Firefighting and Related Protective Services; 5% Computer and Information Sciences and Support Services
Expenses: 2016-2017: $7,448 in state, $16,688 out of state; room/board: N/A
Financial aid: (207) 621-3163; 87% of undergrads determined to have financial need; average aid package $9,281

University of Maine–Farmington
Farmington ME
(207) 778-7050
U.S. News ranking: Reg. Coll. (N), No. 7
Website: www.farmington.edu
Admissions email: umfadmit@maine.edu

Public; founded 1864
Freshman admissions: selective; 2015-2016: 1,614 applied, 1,346 accepted. Neither SAT nor ACT required. SAT 25/75 percentile: 870-1115. High school rank: 13% in top tenth, 40% in top quarter, 74% in top half
Early decision deadline: N/A, notification date: N/A
Early action deadline: 11/15, notification date: 12/15
Application deadline (fall): rolling
Undergraduate student body: 1,688 full time, 107 part time; 35% male, 65% female; 1% American Indian, 1% Asian, 2% black, 2% Hispanic, 2% multiracial, 0% Pacific Islander, 87% white, 0% international; 84% from in state; 53% live on campus; N/A of students in fraternities, N/A in sororities
Most popular majors: 34% Education; 16% Health Professions and Related Programs; 13% Psychology; 8% English Language and Literature/Letters; 6% Business, Management, Marketing, and Related Support Services
Expenses: 2016-2017: $9,217 in state, $18,305 out of state; room/board: $8,970
Financial aid: (207) 778-7100; 80% of undergrads determined to have financial need; average aid package $13,678

University of Maine–Fort Kent
Fort Kent ME
(207) 834-7600
U.S. News ranking: Reg. Coll. (N), No. 23
Website: www.umfk.maine.edu
Admissions email: umfkadm@maine.edu
Public; founded 1878
Freshman admissions: least selective; 2015-2016: 215 applied, 192 accepted. Neither SAT nor ACT required. SAT 25/75 percentile: 800-980. High school rank: 1% in top tenth, 7% in top quarter, 39% in top half
Early decision deadline: N/A, notification date: N/A
Early action deadline: N/A, notification date: N/A
Application deadline (fall): rolling
Undergraduate student body: 583 full time, 976 part time; 31% male, 69% female; 1% American Indian, 1% Asian, 4% black, 2% Hispanic, 2% multiracial, 0% Pacific Islander, 75% white, 11% international; 87% from in state; 29% live on campus; 1% of students in fraternities, 2% in sororities
Most popular majors: 52% Health Professions and Related Programs; 14% Business, Management, Marketing, and Related Support Services; 8% Education; 7% Liberal Arts and Sciences, General Studies and Humanities; 7% Social Sciences
Expenses: 2016-2017: $7,575 in state, $11,205 out of state; room/board: $7,910
Financial aid: (888) 879-8635; 74% of undergrads determined to have financial need; average aid package $11,480

University of Maine–Machias
Machias ME
(888) 468-6866
U.S. News ranking: Nat. Lib. Arts, second tier
Website: www.umm.maine.edu
Admissions email: ummadmissions@maine.edu
Public; founded 1909
Freshman admissions: less selective; 2015-2016: 449 applied, 389 accepted. Either SAT or ACT required. SAT 25/75 percentile: 770-1010. High school rank: N/A
Early decision deadline: N/A, notification date: N/A
Early action deadline: 12/15, notification date: N/A
Application deadline (fall): 8/15
Undergraduate student body: 409 full time, 377 part time; 33% male, 67% female; 4% American Indian, 0% Asian, 4% black, 5% Hispanic, 2% multiracial, N/A Pacific Islander, 77% white, 2% international; 82% from in state; 41% live on campus; 4% of students in fraternities, 5% in sororities
Most popular majors: 20% Community Psychology; 18% Biology/Biological Sciences, General; 14% Entrepreneurship/Entrepreneurial Studies; 14% Teacher Education and Professional Development, Specific Levels and Methods; 12% Parks, Recreation and Leisure Studies
Expenses: 2015-2016: $7,480 in state, $19,370 out of state; room/board: $8,466
Financial aid: (207) 255-1203

University of Maine–Presque Isle
Presque Isle ME
(207) 768-9532
U.S. News ranking: Reg. Coll. (N), No. 27
Website: www.umpi.edu
Admissions email: admissions@umpi.edu
Public; founded 1903
Freshman admissions: less selective; 2015-2016: 1,442 applied, 1,112 accepted. Neither SAT nor ACT required. SAT 25/75 percentile: 791-1060. High school rank: 3% in top tenth, 15% in top quarter, 45% in top half
Early decision deadline: N/A, notification date: N/A
Early action deadline: N/A, notification date: N/A
Application deadline (fall): rolling
Undergraduate student body: 675 full time, 614 part time; 36% male, 64% female; 3% American Indian, 0% Asian, 3% black, 2% Hispanic, 3% multiracial, 0% Pacific Islander, 79% white, 8% international; 96% from in state; 29% live on campus; N/A of students in fraternities, N/A in sororities
Most popular majors: 17% Education; 17% Business, Management, Marketing, and Related Support Services; 15% Liberal Arts and Sciences, General Studies and Humanities; 9% Public Administration and Social Service Professions; 9% Psychology

Expenses: 2016-2017: $7,436 in state, $11,066 out of state; room/board: $8,044
Financial aid: (207) 768-9511; 77% of undergrads determined to have financial need; average aid package $11,848

University of New England
Biddeford ME
(207) 283-0171
U.S. News ranking: Reg. U. (N), No. 80
Website: www.une.edu
Admissions email: admissions@une.edu
Private; founded 1831
Freshman admissions: selective; 2015-2016: 4,416 applied, 3,760 accepted. Either SAT or ACT required. SAT 25/75 percentile: 960-1170. High school rank: N/A
Early decision deadline: N/A, notification date: N/A
Early action deadline: 12/1, notification date: 12/31
Application deadline (fall): 2/15
Undergraduate student body: 2,268 full time, 1,533 part time; 31% male, 69% female; 0% American Indian, 3% Asian, 1% black, 0% Hispanic, 1% multiracial, 0% Pacific Islander, 80% white, 0% international; 32% from in state; 62% live on campus; N/A of students in fraternities, N/A in sororities
Most popular majors: 45% Health Professions and Related Programs; 29% Biological and Biomedical Sciences; 8% Parks, Recreation, Leisure, and Fitness Studies; 4% Psychology; 4% Social Sciences
Expenses: 2016-2017: $35,630; room/board: $13,250
Financial aid: (207) 602-2342

University of Southern Maine
Portland ME
(207) 780-5670
U.S. News ranking: Reg. U. (N), second tier
Website: www.usm.maine.edu
Admissions email: usmadm@usm.maine.edu
Public; founded 1878
Freshman admissions: less selective; 2015-2016: 3,402 applied, 2,986 accepted. Either SAT or ACT required. SAT 25/75 percentile: 860-1100. High school rank: 5% in top tenth, 26% in top quarter, 60% in top half
Early decision deadline: N/A, notification date: N/A
Early action deadline: N/A, notification date: N/A
Application deadline (fall): rolling
Undergraduate student body: 3,730 full time, 2,396 part time; 44% male, 56% female; 1% American Indian, 2% Asian, 4% black, 2% Hispanic, 3% multiracial, 0% Pacific Islander, 82% white, 1% international; 89% from in state; 20% live on campus; N/A of students in fraternities, N/A in sororities
Most popular majors: 19% Health Professions and Related Programs; 19% Business, Management, Marketing, and

Related Support Services; 13% Social Sciences; 4% Biological and Biomedical Sciences
Expenses: 2016-2017: $8,920 in state, $21,280 out of state; room/board: $9,400
Financial aid: (207) 780-5250; 75% of undergrads determined to have financial need; average aid package $13,356

MARYLAND

Bowie State University
Bowie MD
(301) 860-3415
U.S. News ranking: Reg. U. (N), second tier
Website: www.bowiestate.edu
Admissions email: ugradadmissions@bowiestate.edu
Public; founded 1865
Affiliation: None
Freshman admissions: less selective; 2015-2016: 3,180 applied, 1,680 accepted. Either SAT or ACT required. SAT 25/75 percentile: 810-960. High school rank: N/A
Early decision deadline: N/A, notification date: N/A
Early action deadline: N/A, notification date: N/A
Application deadline (fall): rolling
Undergraduate student body: 3,533 full time, 782 part time; 38% male, 62% female; 0% American Indian, 1% Asian, 86% black, 3% Hispanic, 4% multiracial, 0% Pacific Islander, 3% white, 1% international; 91% from in state; 40% live on campus; 20% of students in fraternities, 30% in sororities
Most popular majors: Information not available
Expenses: 2016-2017: $7,880 in state, $18,416 out of state; room/board: $10,970
Financial aid: (301) 860-3540; 84% of undergrads determined to have financial need; average aid package $8,940

Capitol Technology University[1]
Laurel MD
(800) 950-1992
U.S. News ranking: Engineering, unranked
Website: captechu.edu/
Admissions email: N/A
Private
Application deadline (fall): N/A
Undergraduate student body: N/A full time, N/A part time
Expenses: 2015-2016: $23,508; room/board: $6,964
Financial aid: (301) 369-2800

Coppin State University
Baltimore MD
(410) 951-3600
U.S. News ranking: Reg. U. (N), second tier
Website: www.coppin.edu
Admissions email: admissions@coppin.edu
Public; founded 1900
Freshman admissions: less selective; 2015-2016: 4,453 applied, 1,656 accepted. Either SAT or ACT required. SAT 25/75

percentile: 810-970. High school rank: N/A
Early decision deadline: N/A, notification date: N/A
Early action deadline: N/A, notification date: N/A
Application deadline (fall): rolling
Undergraduate student body: 2,007 full time, 661 part time; 26% male, 74% female; 0% American Indian, 0% Asian, 85% black, 2% Hispanic, 1% multiracial, 0% Pacific Islander, 2% white, 7% international
Most popular majors: Information not available
Expenses: 2015-2016: $7,346 in state, $12,870 out of state; room/board: $9,616
Financial aid: (410) 951-3636

Frostburg State University
Frostburg MD
(301) 687-4201
U.S. News ranking: Reg. U. (N), No. 122
Website: www.frostburg.edu
Admissions email: fsuadmissions@frostburg.edu
Public; founded 1898
Freshman admissions: less selective; 2015-2016: 3,911 applied, 2,481 accepted. Either SAT or ACT required. SAT 25/75 percentile: 860-1060. High school rank: 9% in top tenth, 27% in top quarter, 61% in top half
Early decision deadline: 12/15, notification date: N/A
Early action deadline: N/A, notification date: N/A
Application deadline (fall): rolling
Undergraduate student body: 4,176 full time, 785 part time; 49% male, 51% female; 0% American Indian, 2% Asian, 31% black, 5% Hispanic, 4% multiracial, 0% Pacific Islander, 55% white, 1% international; 94% from in state; 31% live on campus; N/A of students in fraternities, N/A in sororities
Most popular majors: 11% Business Administration and Management, General; 9% Psychology, General; 9% Registered Nursing/Registered Nurse; 7% Liberal Arts and Sciences/Liberal Studies
Expenses: 2016-2017: $8,702 in state, $21,226 out of state; room/board: $10,052
Financial aid: (301) 687-4301; 60% of undergrads determined to have financial need; average aid package $8,946

Goucher College
Baltimore MD
(410) 337-6100
U.S. News ranking: Nat. Lib. Arts, No. 113
Website: www.goucher.edu
Admissions email: admissions@goucher.edu
Private; founded 1885
Freshman admissions: selective; 2015-2016: 3,577 applied, 2,777 accepted. Neither SAT nor ACT required. SAT 25/75 percentile: 980-1220. High school rank: 22% in top tenth, 47% in top quarter, 84% in top half

Early decision deadline: 11/15, notification date: 12/15
Early action deadline: 12/1, notification date: 2/1
Application deadline (fall): 2/1
Undergraduate student body: 1,452 full time, 26 part time; 32% male, 68% female; 0% American Indian, 4% Asian, 12% black, 9% Hispanic, 4% multiracial, 0% Pacific Islander, 65% white, 3% international; 27% from in state; 82% live on campus; N/A of students in fraternities, N/A in sororities
Most popular majors: 15% Social Sciences; 12% Psychology; 11% Visual and Performing Arts; 8% Foreign Languages, Literatures, and Linguistics; 6% Business, Management, Marketing, and Related Support Services
Expenses: 2016-2017: $43,416; room/board: $12,300
Financial aid: (410) 337-6141; 64% of undergrads determined to have financial need; average aid package $32,780

Hood College
Frederick MD
(800) 922-1599
U.S. News ranking: Reg. U. (N), No. 38
Website: www.hood.edu
Admissions email: admission@hood.edu
Private; founded 1893
Affiliation: United Church of Christ
Freshman admissions: selective; 2015-2016: 1,636 applied, 1,288 accepted. Neither SAT nor ACT required. SAT 25/75 percentile: 910-1170. High school rank: 21% in top tenth, 42% in top quarter, 75% in top half
Early decision deadline: N/A, notification date: N/A
Early action deadline: N/A, notification date: N/A
Application deadline (fall): rolling
Undergraduate student body: 1,179 full time, 98 part time; 37% male, 63% female; 0% American Indian, 3% Asian, 12% black, 9% Hispanic, 5% multiracial, 0% Pacific Islander, 63% white, 2% international; 77% from in state; 55% live on campus; 0% of students in fraternities, 0% in sororities
Most popular majors: 11% Education; 9% Psychology; 8% Biological and Biomedical Sciences; 8% English Language and Literature/Letters; 7% Business, Management, Marketing, and Related Support Services
Expenses: 2016-2017: $36,540; room/board: $12,200
Financial aid: (301) 696-3411; 78% of undergrads determined to have financial need; average aid package $26,419

Johns Hopkins University
Baltimore MD
(410) 516-8171
U.S. News ranking: Nat. U., No. 10
Website: www.jhu.edu
Admissions email: gotojhu@jhu.edu

Private; founded 1876
Freshman admissions: most selective; 2015-2016: 24,718 applied, 3,252 accepted. Either SAT or ACT required. SAT 25/75 percentile: 1400-1550. High school rank: 92% in top tenth, 99% in top quarter, 100% in top half
Early decision deadline: 11/1, notification date: 12/15
Early action deadline: N/A, notification date: N/A
Application deadline (fall): 1/1
Undergraduate student body: 5,972 full time, 552 part time; 46% male, 54% female; 0% American Indian, 22% Asian, 6% black, 13% Hispanic, 5% multiracial, 0% Pacific Islander, 42% white, 10% international; 12% from in state; 52% live on campus; 20% of students in fraternities, 33% in sororities
Most popular majors: 11% Public Health, General; 10% Bioengineering and Biomedical Engineering; 7% International Relations and Affairs; 7% Neuroscience; 6% Economics, General
Expenses: 2016-2017: $50,410; room/board: $14,976
Financial aid: (410) 516-8028; 48% of undergrads determined to have financial need; average aid package $39,344

Loyola University Maryland
Baltimore MD
(410) 617-5012
U.S. News ranking: Reg. U. (N), No. 3
Website: www.loyola.edu
Admissions email: admissions@loyola.edu
Private; founded 1852
Affiliation: Roman Catholic
Freshman admissions: more selective; 2015-2016: 13,867 applied, 8,449 accepted. Neither SAT nor ACT required. SAT 25/75 percentile: 1110-1280. High school rank: 26% in top tenth, 62% in top quarter, 91% in top half
Early decision deadline: N/A, notification date: N/A
Early action deadline: 11/1, notification date: 1/15
Application deadline (fall): 1/15
Undergraduate student body: 4,021 full time, 47 part time; 42% male, 58% female; 0% American Indian, 4% Asian, 6% black, 9% Hispanic, 2% multiracial, 0% Pacific Islander, 78% white, 0% international; 18% from in state; 81% live on campus; 0% of students in fraternities, 0% in sororities
Most popular majors: 35% Business/Commerce, General; 9% Psychology, General; 9% Social Sciences, General; 7% Biological and Physical Sciences
Expenses: 2016-2017: $46,595; room/board: $15,090
Financial aid: (410) 617-2576; 57% of undergrads determined to have financial need; average aid package $30,520

Maryland Institute College of Art
Baltimore MD
(410) 225-2222
U.S. News ranking: Arts, unranked
Website: www.mica.edu
Admissions email: admissions@mica.edu
Private; founded 1826
Freshman admissions: N/A; 2015-2016: 3,818 applied, 1,808 accepted. Either SAT or ACT required. SAT 25/75 percentile: N/A. High school rank: N/A
Early decision deadline: 11/15, notification date: 12/15
Early action deadline: N/A, notification date: N/A
Application deadline (fall): 2/1
Undergraduate student body: 1,743 full time, 24 part time; 26% male, 74% female; 0% American Indian, 13% Asian, 6% black, 3% Hispanic, 10% multiracial, 0% Pacific Islander, 49% white, 16% international; 20% from in state; 88% live on campus; N/A of students in fraternities, N/A in sororities
Most popular majors: Information not available
Expenses: 2016-2017: $45,400; room/board: $12,450
Financial aid: (410) 225-2285

McDaniel College
Westminster MD
(800) 638-5005
U.S. News ranking: Nat. Lib. Arts, No. 128
Website: www.mcdaniel.edu
Admissions email: admissions@mcdaniel.edu
Private; founded 1867
Freshman admissions: selective; 2015-2016: 2,864 applied, 2,286 accepted. Either SAT or ACT required. SAT 25/75 percentile: 960-1180. High school rank: 26% in top tenth, 51% in top quarter, 82% in top half
Early decision deadline: 1/15, notification date: 2/1
Early action deadline: 12/1, notification date: 12/15
Application deadline (fall): rolling
Undergraduate student body: 1,613 full time, 50 part time; 46% male, 54% female; 0% American Indian, 4% Asian, 14% black, 6% Hispanic, 0% multiracial, 0% Pacific Islander, 69% white, 1% international; 66% from in state; 80% live on campus; 12% of students in fraternities, 18% in sororities
Most popular majors: 12% Social Sciences; 10% Parks, Recreation, Leisure, and Fitness Studies; 9% Business, Management, Marketing, and Related Support Services; 9% Visual and Performing Arts; 8% Psychology
Expenses: 2016-2017: $40,580; room/board: $10,800
Financial aid: (410) 857-2233; 76% of undergrads determined to have financial need; average aid package $32,792

Morgan State University

Baltimore MD
(800) 332-6674
U.S. News ranking: Nat. U., second tier
Website: www.morgan.edu
Admissions email: admissions@morgan.edu
Public; founded 1867
Freshman admissions: less selective; 2015-2016: 5,090 applied, 3,396 accepted. Neither SAT nor ACT required. SAT 25/75 percentile: 840-970. High school rank: N/A
Early decision deadline: N/A, notification date: N/A
Early action deadline: 11/15, notification date: 2/15
Application deadline (fall): rolling
Undergraduate student body: 5,597 full time, 722 part time; 46% male, 54% female; 0% American Indian, 1% Asian, 83% black, 4% Hispanic, 3% multiracial, 0% Pacific Islander, 2% white, 7% international; 81% from in state; 32% live on campus; N/A of students in fraternities, N/A in sororities
Most popular majors: 25% Business, Management, Marketing, and Related Support Services; 13% Engineering; 8% Education; 8% Social Sciences
Expenses: 2016-2017: $7,636 in state, $17,504 out of state; room/board: $10,490
Financial aid: (443) 885-3170; 81% of undergrads determined to have financial need; average aid package $22,738

Mount St. Mary's University

Emmitsburg MD
(800) 448-4347
U.S. News ranking: Reg. U. (N), No. 27
Website: www.msmary.edu
Admissions email: admissions@msmary.edu
Private; founded 1808
Affiliation: Roman Catholic
Freshman admissions: selective; 2015-2016: 6,113 applied, 4,105 accepted. Either SAT or ACT required. SAT 25/75 percentile: 910-1130. High school rank: 14% in top tenth, 31% in top quarter, 62% in top half
Early decision deadline: N/A, notification date: N/A
Early action deadline: 12/1, notification date: 12/25
Application deadline (fall): 3/1
Undergraduate student body: 1,689 full time, 106 part time; 46% male, 54% female; 0% American Indian, 3% Asian, 12% black, 9% Hispanic, 5% multiracial, 0% Pacific Islander, 69% white, 1% international; 55% from in state; 81% live on campus; N/A of students in fraternities, N/A in sororities
Most popular majors: 20% Business/Commerce, General; 12% Criminology; 7% Accounting; 7% Biology/Biological Sciences, General; 7% Elementary Education and Teaching
Expenses: 2016-2017: $39,000; room/board: $12,610

Financial aid: (301) 447-5207; 69% of undergrads determined to have financial need; average aid package $25,643

Notre Dame of Maryland University

Baltimore MD
(410) 532-5330
U.S. News ranking: Reg. U. (N), No. 51
Website: www.ndm.edu
Admissions email: admiss@ndm.edu
Private; founded 1895
Affiliation: Roman Catholic
Freshman admissions: selective; 2015-2016: 834 applied, 433 accepted. Either SAT or ACT required. SAT 25/75 percentile: 960-1180. High school rank: 28% in top tenth, 55% in top quarter, 84% in top half
Early decision deadline: N/A, notification date: N/A
Early action deadline: 12/1, notification date: 12/15
Application deadline (fall): rolling
Undergraduate student body: 516 full time, 497 part time; 5% male, 95% female; 1% American Indian, 7% Asian, 27% black, 6% Hispanic, 0% multiracial, 0% Pacific Islander, 56% white, 2% international; 100% from in state; 0% live on campus; 0% of students in fraternities, 0% in sororities
Most popular majors: 54% Registered Nursing/Registered Nurse; 10% Liberal Arts and Sciences, General Studies and Humanities, Other; 8% Multi-/Interdisciplinary Studies, Other; 4% Biology/Biological Sciences, General; 4% Business Administration and Management, General
Expenses: 2015-2016: $33,670; room/board: $10,930
Financial aid: (410) 532-5369

Salisbury University

Salisbury MD
(410) 543-6161
U.S. News ranking: Reg. U. (N), No. 67
Website: www.salisbury.edu/
Admissions email: admissions@salisbury.edu
Public; founded 1925
Freshman admissions: selective; 2015-2016: 8,360 applied, 5,069 accepted. Neither SAT nor ACT required. SAT 25/75 percentile: 1080-1240. High school rank: 20% in top tenth, 54% in top quarter, 89% in top half
Early decision deadline: 11/15, notification date: 12/15
Early action deadline: 12/1, notification date: 1/15
Application deadline (fall): 1/15
Undergraduate student body: 7,148 full time, 701 part time; 43% male, 57% female; 1% American Indian, 3% Asian, 13% black, 4% Hispanic, 4% multiracial, 0% Pacific Islander, 71% white, 1% international; 86% from in state; 42% live on campus; 10% of students in fraternities, 10% in sororities
Most popular majors: 7% Kinesiology and Exercise Science; 7% Psychology,

General; 6% Biology/Biological Sciences, General; 6% Business Administration and Management, General
Expenses: 2016-2017: $9,364 in state, $17,776 out of state; room/board: $11,350
Financial aid: (410) 543-6165; 53% of undergrads determined to have financial need; average aid package $8,076

Sojourner-Douglass College[1]

Baltimore MD
(800) 732-2630
U.S. News ranking: Reg. Coll. (N), unranked
Website: www.sdc.edu/
Admissions email: N/A
Private
Application deadline (fall): N/A
Undergraduate student body: N/A full time, N/A part time
Expenses: 2015-2016: $9,830; room/board: N/A
Financial aid: (410) 276-0306

Stevenson University

Stevenson MD
(410) 486-7001
U.S. News ranking: Reg. U. (N), No. 75
Website: www.stevenson.edu/
Admissions email: admissions@stevenson.edu
Private; founded 1947
Freshman admissions: selective; 2015-2016: 5,747 applied, 3,433 accepted. Either SAT or ACT required. SAT 25/75 percentile: 900-1110. High school rank: 18% in top tenth, 48% in top quarter, 81% in top half
Early decision deadline: N/A, notification date: N/A
Early action deadline: N/A, notification date: N/A
Application deadline (fall): rolling
Undergraduate student body: 3,122 full time, 578 part time; 33% male, 67% female; 0% American Indian, 3% Asian, 27% black, 5% Hispanic, 4% multiracial, 0% Pacific Islander, 57% white, 0% international; 83% from in state; 42% live on campus; 0% of students in fraternities, 2% in sororities
Most popular majors: 23% Business, Management, Marketing, and Related Support Services; 21% Health Professions and Related Programs; 9% Homeland Security, Law Enforcement, Firefighting and Related Protective Services; 8% Computer and Information Sciences and Support Services; 7% Education
Expenses: 2016-2017: $33,168; room/board: $12,702
Financial aid: (443) 334-2559; 78% of undergrads determined to have financial need; average aid package $20,067

St. John's College

Annapolis MD
(410) 626-2522
U.S. News ranking: Nat. Lib. Arts, No. 53
Website: sjc.edu
Admissions email: annapolis.admissions@sjc.edu

Private; founded 1696
Freshman admissions: more selective; 2015-2016: 332 applied, 260 accepted. Neither SAT nor ACT required. SAT 25/75 percentile: 1220-1450. High school rank: 29% in top tenth, 60% in top quarter, 87% in top half
Early decision deadline: N/A, notification date: N/A
Early action deadline: 1/15, notification date: 2/15
Application deadline (fall): rolling
Undergraduate student body: 406 full time, 0 part time; 55% male, 45% female; 0% American Indian, 4% Asian, 2% black, 6% Hispanic, 2% multiracial, 0% Pacific Islander, 69% white, 14% international; 45% from in state; 74% live on campus; 0% of students in fraternities, 0% in sororities
Most popular majors: 100% Liberal Arts and Sciences, General Studies and Humanities
Expenses: 2016-2017: $50,353; room/board: $11,888
Financial aid: (410) 626-2502; 70% of undergrads determined to have financial need; average aid package $37,419

St. Mary's College of Maryland

St. Mary's City MD
(800) 492-7181
U.S. News ranking: Nat. Lib. Arts, No. 99
Website: www.smcm.edu
Admissions email: admissions@smcm.edu
Public; founded 1840
Freshman admissions: selective; 2015-2016: 1,675 applied, 1,320 accepted. Either SAT or ACT required. SAT 25/75 percentile: 1030-1260. High school rank: N/A
Early decision deadline: N/A, notification date: N/A
Early action deadline: 11/15, notification date: 12/20
Application deadline (fall): 2/15
Undergraduate student body: 1,683 full time, 63 part time; 43% male, 57% female; 0% American Indian, 3% Asian, 8% black, 8% Hispanic, 5% multiracial, N/A Pacific Islander, 72% white, 1% international; 92% from in state; 84% live on campus; N/A of students in fraternities, N/A in sororities
Most popular majors: 14% Psychology, General; 12% Biology/Biological Sciences, General; 11% Economics, General; 9% English Language and Literature, General; 8% Political Science and Government, General
Expenses: 2016-2017: $14,192 in state, $29,340 out of state; room/board: $12,658
Financial aid: (240) 895-3000; 48% of undergrads determined to have financial need; average aid package $13,099

Towson University

Towson MD
(410) 704-2113
U.S. News ranking: Reg. U. (N), No. 51
Website: www.towson.edu
Admissions email: admissions@towson.edu
Public; founded 1866
Freshman admissions: selective; 2015-2016: 10,947 applied, 8,033 accepted. Either SAT or ACT required. SAT 25/75 percentile: 1000-1170. High school rank: 18% in top tenth, 45% in top quarter, 84% in top half
Early decision deadline: N/A, notification date: N/A
Early action deadline: N/A, notification date: N/A
Application deadline (fall): 1/15
Undergraduate student body: 16,768 full time, 2,281 part time; 40% male, 60% female; 0% American Indian, 5% Asian, 18% black, 6% Hispanic, 4% multiracial, 0% Pacific Islander, 61% white, 2% international; 86% from in state; 26% live on campus; 12% of students in fraternities, 11% in sororities
Most popular majors: 14% Business, Management, Marketing, and Related Support Services; 12% Health Professions and Related Programs; 10% Education; 10% Social Sciences
Expenses: 2016-2017: $9,408 in state, $21,076 out of state; room/board: $11,754
Financial aid: (410) 704-4236; 55% of undergrads determined to have financial need; average aid package $9,937

United States Naval Academy

Annapolis MD
(410) 293-4361
U.S. News ranking: Nat. Lib. Arts, No. 12
Website: www.usna.edu
Admissions email: webmail@usna.edu
Public; founded 1845
Freshman admissions: more selective; 2015-2016: 16,101 applied, 1,373 accepted. Either SAT or ACT required. SAT 25/75 percentile: 1180-1380. High school rank: 58% in top tenth, 80% in top quarter, 94% in top half
Early decision deadline: N/A, notification date: N/A
Early action deadline: N/A, notification date: N/A
Application deadline (fall): 1/31
Undergraduate student body: 4,525 full time, 0 part time; 75% male, 25% female; 0% American Indian, 7% Asian, 7% black, 11% Hispanic, 8% multiracial, 1% Pacific Islander, 64% white, 1% international; 6% from in state; 100% live on campus; 0% of students in fraternities, 0% in sororities
Most popular majors: 10% Economics, General; 10% Systems Engineering; 9% Political Science and Government, General; 8% Mechanical Engineering; 8% Oceanography, Chemical and Physical
Expenses: N/A

Financial aid: N/A; 0% of undergrads determined to have financial need

University of Baltimore
Baltimore MD
(410) 837-4777
U.S. News ranking: Reg. U. (N), second tier
Website: www.ubalt.edu
Admissions email: admissions@ubalt.edu
Public; founded 1925
Freshman admissions: less selective; 2015-2016: 504 applied, 303 accepted. Either SAT or ACT required. SAT 25/75 percentile: 865-1080. High school rank: N/A
Early decision deadline: N/A, notification date: N/A
Early action deadline: N/A, notification date: N/A
Application deadline (fall): rolling
Undergraduate student body: 2,056 full time, 1,288 part time; 42% male, 58% female; 0% American Indian, 5% Asian, 47% black, 5% Hispanic, 4% multiracial, 0% Pacific Islander, 34% white, 2% international; 96% from in state; N/A live on campus; N/A of students in fraternities, N/A in sororities
Most popular majors: 33% Business/Commerce, General; 10% Criminal Justice/Police Science; 10% Health Services Administration; 6% Animation, Interactive Technology, Video Graphics and Special Effects; 5% Public Administration and Social Service Professions
Expenses: 2016-2017: $8,596 in state, $20,242 out of state; room/board: N/A
Financial aid: (410) 837-4763; 71% of undergrads determined to have financial need; average aid package $11,043

University of Maryland–Baltimore County
Baltimore MD
(410) 455-2291
U.S. News ranking: Nat. U., No. 159
Website: www.umbc.edu
Admissions email: admissions@umbc.edu
Public; founded 1963
Freshman admissions: more selective; 2015-2016: 10,629 applied, 6,316 accepted. SAT required. SAT 25/75 percentile: 1110-1310. High school rank: 27% in top tenth, 56% in top quarter, 83% in top half
Early decision deadline: N/A, notification date: N/A
Early action deadline: 11/1, notification date: 12/15
Application deadline (fall): 2/1
Undergraduate student body: 9,592 full time, 1,651 part time; 55% male, 45% female; 0% American Indian, 20% Asian, 17% black, 6% Hispanic, 4% multiracial, 0% Pacific Islander, 44% white, 4% international; 94% from in state; 35% live on campus; 4% of students in fraternities, 6% in sororities
Most popular majors: 16% Biological and Biomedical

Sciences; 15% Computer and Information Sciences and Support Services; 13% Psychology; 13% Social Sciences; 7% Engineering
Expenses: 2016-2017: $11,264 in state, $24,492 out of state; room/board: $11,568
Financial aid: (410) 455-2387; 53% of undergrads determined to have financial need; average aid package $10,482

University of Maryland–College Park
College Park MD
(301) 314-8385
U.S. News ranking: Nat. U., No. 60
Website: www.maryland.edu
Admissions email: um-admit@umd.edu
Public; founded 1856
Freshman admissions: more selective; 2015-2016: 28,301 applied, 12,637 accepted. Either SAT or ACT required. SAT 25/75 percentile: 1210-1420. High school rank: 70% in top tenth, 88% in top quarter, 98% in top half
Early decision deadline: N/A, notification date: N/A
Early action deadline: 11/1, notification date: 1/31
Application deadline (fall): 1/20
Undergraduate student body: 25,547 full time, 1,896 part time; 53% male, 47% female; 0% American Indian, 16% Asian, 13% black, 9% Hispanic, 4% multiracial, 0% Pacific Islander, 52% white, 4% international; 79% from in state; 42% live on campus; 15% of students in fraternities, 19% in sororities
Most popular majors: 8% Biology/Biological Sciences, General; 6% Criminology; 5% Economics, General; 5% Psychology, General; 4% Accounting
Expenses: 2016-2017: $10,181 in state, $32,045 out of state; room/board: $11,758
Financial aid: (301) 314-9000; 42% of undergrads determined to have financial need; average aid package $13,562

University of Maryland–Eastern Shore
Princess Anne MD
(410) 651-6410
U.S. News ranking: Nat. U., second tier
Website: www.umes.edu
Admissions email: umesadmissions@umes.edu
Public; founded 1886
Freshman admissions: less selective; 2015-2016: 7,249 applied, 3,556 accepted. Either SAT or ACT required. SAT 25/75 percentile: 750-930. High school rank: N/A
Early decision deadline: N/A, notification date: N/A
Early action deadline: N/A, notification date: N/A
Application deadline (fall): 6/30
Undergraduate student body: 3,291 full time, 452 part time; 46% male, 54% female; 0% American Indian, 1% Asian, 75% black,

3% Hispanic, 8% multiracial, 0% Pacific Islander, 10% white, 3% international
Most popular majors: 19% Criminal Justice/Police Science; 8% Biology/Biological Sciences, General; 8% Business Administration and Management, General; 8% Sociology; 7% Kinesiology and Exercise Science
Expenses: 2016-2017: $7,804 in state, $17,188 out of state; room/board: $9,388
Financial aid: (410) 651-6172; 82% of undergrads determined to have financial need; average aid package $11,687

University of Maryland University College
Adelphi MD
(800) 888-8682
U.S. News ranking: Reg. U. (N), unranked
Website: www.umuc.edu/
Admissions email: enroll@umuc.edu
Public; founded 1947
Freshman admissions: N/A; 2015-2016: 1,453 applied, 1,453 accepted. Neither SAT nor ACT required. ACT 25/75 percentile: N/A. High school rank: N/A
Early decision deadline: N/A, notification date: N/A
Early action deadline: N/A, notification date: N/A
Application deadline (fall): rolling
Undergraduate student body: 8,578 full time, 28,776 part time; 54% male, 46% female; 1% American Indian, 4% Asian, 27% black, 12% Hispanic, 4% multiracial, 1% Pacific Islander, 42% white, 1% international; 44% from in state; N/A live on campus; N/A of students in fraternities, N/A in sororities
Most popular majors: 43% Computer and Information Sciences and Support Services; 23% Business, Management, Marketing, and Related Support Services; 8% Psychology; 7% Homeland Security, Law Enforcement, Firefighting and Related Protective Services
Expenses: 2016-2017: $7,056 in state, $12,336 out of state; room/board: N/A
Financial aid: (301) 985-7510; 61% of undergrads determined to have financial need; average aid package $7,420

Washington Adventist University
Takoma Park MD
(301) 891-4080
U.S. News ranking: Reg. U. (N), second tier
Website: www.wau.edu
Admissions email: enroll@wau.edu
Private; founded 1904
Affiliation: Seventh-day Adventist
Freshman admissions: less selective; 2015-2016: 1,237 applied, 455 accepted. Either SAT or ACT required. SAT 25/75 percentile: 700-930. High school rank: N/A
Early decision deadline: N/A, notification date: N/A
Early action deadline: N/A, notification date: N/A
Application deadline (fall): 8/1

Undergraduate student body: 659 full time, 218 part time; 48% male, 52% female; 1% American Indian, 5% Asian, 45% black, 10% Hispanic, 1% multiracial, 0% Pacific Islander, 7% white, 22% international
Most popular majors: Information not available
Expenses: 2016-2017: $23,400; room/board: $8,930
Financial aid: (301) 891-4005; 95% of undergrads determined to have financial need; average aid package $10,500

Washington College
Chestertown MD
(410) 778-7700
U.S. News ranking: Nat. Lib. Arts, No. 99
Website: www.washcoll.edu
Admissions email: adm.off@washcoll.edu
Private; founded 1782
Freshman admissions: more selective; 2015-2016: 6,847 applied, 3,702 accepted. Either SAT or ACT required. SAT 25/75 percentile: 1070-1290. High school rank: 36% in top tenth, 60% in top quarter, 87% in top half
Early decision deadline: 11/15, notification date: 12/15
Early action deadline: 12/1, notification date: 1/15
Application deadline (fall): 2/15
Undergraduate student body: 1,400 full time, 23 part time; 44% male, 56% female; 1% American Indian, 2% Asian, 5% black, 3% Hispanic, 2% multiracial, 0% Pacific Islander, 73% white, 10% international; 47% from in state; 85% live on campus; 8% of students in fraternities, 11% in sororities
Most popular majors: 20% Social Sciences; 18% Business, Management, Marketing, and Related Support Services; 10% Biological and Biomedical Sciences; 9% Psychology; 7% English Language and Literature/Letters
Expenses: 2016-2017: $43,850; room/board: $10,612
Financial aid: (410) 778-7214; 60% of undergrads determined to have financial need; average aid package $31,250

MASSACHUSETTS

American International College
Springfield MA
(413) 205-3201
U.S. News ranking: Nat. U., second tier
Website: www.aic.edu
Admissions email: inquiry@aic.edu
Private; founded 1885
Freshman admissions: less selective; 2015-2016: 2,053 applied, 1,315 accepted. Either SAT or ACT required. SAT 25/75 percentile: 790-980. High school rank: N/A
Early decision deadline: N/A, notification date: N/A
Early action deadline: N/A, notification date: N/A
Application deadline (fall): rolling
Undergraduate student body: 1,392 full time, 94 part time; 40%

male, 60% female; 0% American Indian, 1% Asian, 25% black, 14% Hispanic, 3% multiracial, 0% Pacific Islander, 39% white, 3% international; 61% from in state; 50% live on campus; N/A of students in fraternities, N/A in sororities
Most popular majors: 39% Health Professions and Related Programs; 16% Business, Management, Marketing, and Related Support Services; 11% Homeland Security, Law Enforcement, Firefighting and Related Protective Services; 9% Social Sciences; 7% Psychology
Expenses: 2016-2017: $33,140; room/board: $13,490
Financial aid: (413) 205-3259; 91% of undergrads determined to have financial need; average aid package $26,741

Amherst College
Amherst MA
(413) 542-2328
U.S. News ranking: Nat. Lib. Arts, No. 2
Website: www.amherst.edu
Admissions email: admission@amherst.edu
Private; founded 1821
Freshman admissions: most selective; 2015-2016: 8,568 applied, 1,210 accepted. Either SAT or ACT required. SAT 25/75 percentile: 1360-1560. High school rank: 86% in top tenth, 96% in top quarter, 100% in top half
Early decision deadline: 11/15, notification date: 12/15
Early action deadline: N/A, notification date: N/A
Application deadline (fall): 1/1
Undergraduate student body: 1,795 full time, 0 part time; 50% male, 50% female; 0% American Indian, 14% Asian, 12% black, 13% Hispanic, 5% multiracial, 0% Pacific Islander, 42% white, 10% international; 14% from in state; 98% live on campus; 0% of students in fraternities, 0% in sororities
Most popular majors: 15% Economics, General; 12% Mathematics, General; 11% English Language and Literature, General; 10% History, General; 9% Psychology, General
Expenses: 2016-2017: $52,476; room/board: $13,710
Financial aid: (413) 542-2296; 58% of undergrads determined to have financial need; average aid package $50,255

Anna Maria College
Paxton MA
(508) 849-3360
U.S. News ranking: Reg. U. (N), second tier
Website: www.annamaria.edu
Admissions email: admissions@annamaria.edu
Private; founded 1946
Affiliation: Roman Catholic
Freshman admissions: less selective; 2015-2016: 1,785 applied, 1,429 accepted. Neither SAT nor ACT required. ACT 25/75 percentile: N/A. High school rank: N/A
Early decision deadline: N/A, notification date: N/A

Early action deadline: N/A, notification date: N/A
Application deadline (fall): rolling
Undergraduate student body: 811 full time, 317 part time; 39% male, 61% female; 0% American Indian, 2% Asian, 11% black, 8% Hispanic, 2% multiracial, 0% Pacific Islander, 69% white, 0% international
Most popular majors: Information not available
Expenses: 2016-2017: $36,110; room/board: $13,510
Financial aid: (508) 849-3366; 88% of undergrads determined to have financial need; average aid package $25,076

Assumption College
Worcester MA
(866) 477-7776
U.S. News ranking: Reg. U. (N), No. 23
Website: www.assumption.edu
Admissions email: admiss@assumption.edu
Private; founded 1904
Affiliation: Roman Catholic
Freshman admissions: selective; 2015-2016: 4,769 applied, 3,614 accepted. Neither SAT nor ACT required. SAT 25/75 percentile: 1020-1210. High school rank: 12% in top tenth, 43% in top quarter, 81% in top half
Early decision deadline: N/A, notification date: N/A
Early action deadline: 11/1, notification date: 12/15
Application deadline (fall): 2/15
Undergraduate student body: 1,975 full time, 12 part time; 41% male, 59% female; 0% American Indian, 2% Asian, 6% black, 7% Hispanic, 2% multiracial, 0% Pacific Islander, 75% white, 2% international; 65% from in state; 87% live on campus; 0% of students in fraternities, 0% in sororities
Most popular majors: 10% Biology/Biological Sciences, General; 10% Rehabilitation and Therapeutic Professions, Other; 9% Psychology, General; 8% English Language and Literature, General; 7% Business Administration and Management, General
Expenses: 2016-2017: $36,260; room/board: $11,660
Financial aid: (508) 767-7158; 75% of undergrads determined to have financial need; average aid package $26,588

Babson College
Babson Park MA
(781) 239-5522
U.S. News ranking: Business, unranked
Website: www.babson.edu
Admissions email: ugradadmission@babson.edu
Private; founded 1919
Freshman admissions: N/A; 2015-2016: 7,516 applied, 1,977 accepted. Either SAT or ACT required. SAT 25/75 percentile: N/A. High school rank: N/A
Early decision deadline: 11/1, notification date: 12/15
Early action deadline: 11/1, notification date: 1/1
Application deadline (fall): 1/3

Undergraduate student body: 2,141 full time, 0 part time; 52% male, 48% female; 0% American Indian, 12% Asian, 5% black, 10% Hispanic, 2% multiracial, 0% Pacific Islander, 38% white, 26% international; 27% from in state; 79% live on campus; 17% of students in fraternities, 25% in sororities
Most popular majors: 23% Finance, General; 13% Economics, General; 12% Marketing/Marketing Management, General; 8% Entrepreneurship/Entrepreneurial Studies; 8% Management Sciences and Quantitative Methods
Expenses: 2016-2017: $48,288; room/board: $15,376
Financial aid: (781) 239-4219; 44% of undergrads determined to have financial need; average aid package $39,883

Bard College at Simon's Rock
Great Barrington MA
(800) 234-7186
U.S. News ranking: Nat. Lib. Arts, No. 144
Website: www.simons-rock.edu
Admissions email: admit@simons-rock.edu
Private; founded 1966
Freshman admissions: more selective; 2015-2016: 199 applied, 178 accepted. Neither SAT nor ACT required. SAT 25/75 percentile: 1250-1400. High school rank: 60% in top tenth, 81% in top quarter, 96% in top half
Early decision deadline: N/A, notification date: N/A
Early action deadline: N/A, notification date: N/A
Application deadline (fall): 5/1
Undergraduate student body: 323 full time, 6 part time; 40% male, 60% female; 0% American Indian, 10% Asian, 4% black, 3% Hispanic, 6% multiracial, N/A Pacific Islander, 54% white, 14% international; 29% from in state; 92% live on campus; N/A of students in fraternities, N/A in sororities
Most popular majors: 21% Visual and Performing Arts; 14% Multi/Interdisciplinary Studies; 13% English Language and Literature/Letters; 10% Social Sciences; 6% Computer and Information Sciences and Support Services
Expenses: 2016-2017: $51,797; room/board: $14,060
Financial aid: (413) 528-7297; 75% of undergrads determined to have financial need; average aid package $36,635

Bay Path University
Longmeadow MA
(413) 565-1331
U.S. News ranking: Reg. U. (N), No. 122
Website: www.baypath.edu
Admissions email: admiss@baypath.edu
Private; founded 1897
Freshman admissions: less selective; 2015-2016: 1,148 applied, 887 accepted. Neither SAT nor ACT required. SAT 25/75 percentile: 850-1050.

High school rank: 18% in top tenth, 42% in top quarter, 76% in top half
Early decision deadline: N/A, notification date: N/A
Early action deadline: 12/15, notification date: 1/2
Application deadline (fall): 8/1
Undergraduate student body: 1,471 full time, 385 part time; 0% male, 100% female; 0% American Indian, 14% black, 19% Hispanic, 2% multiracial, 0% Pacific Islander, 55% white, 0% international; 57% from in state; 45% live on campus; N/A of students in fraternities, N/A in sororities
Most popular majors: 28% Business, Management, Marketing, and Related Support Services; 19% Psychology; 14% Liberal Arts and Sciences, General Studies and Humanities; 10% Education; 9% Health Professions and Related Programs
Expenses: 2016-2017: $32,793; room/board: $12,610
Financial aid: (413) 565-1261; 92% of undergrads determined to have financial need; average aid package $26,070

Bay State College
Boston MA
(617) 217-9000
U.S. News ranking: Reg. Coll. (N), second tier
Website: www.baystate.edu
Admissions email: N/A
For-profit; founded 1946
Freshman admissions: least selective; 2015-2016: N/A applied, N/A accepted. Neither SAT nor ACT required. ACT 25/75 percentile: N/A. High school rank: N/A
Early decision deadline: N/A, notification date: N/A
Early action deadline: N/A, notification date: N/A
Application deadline (fall): rolling
Undergraduate student body: 649 full time, 430 part time; 33% male, 67% female; N/A American Indian, N/A Asian, N/A black, N/A Hispanic, N/A multiracial, N/A Pacific Islander, N/A white, N/A international
Most popular majors: 44% Business Administration and Management, General; 20% Criminal Justice/Safety Studies; 20% Fashion Merchandising; 10% Arts, Entertainment, and Media Management, General; 6% Registered Nursing/Registered Nurse
Expenses: 2016-2017: $27,750; room/board: $13,000
Financial aid: (617) 217-9186; 77% of undergrads determined to have financial need

Becker College[1]
Worcester MA
(877) 523-2537
U.S. News ranking: Reg. Coll. (N), second tier
Website: www.beckercollege.edu
Admissions email: admissions@beckercollege.edu
Private; founded 1784
Application deadline (fall): rolling
Undergraduate student body: N/A full time, N/A part time

Expenses: 2016-2017: $37,272; room/board: $12,850
Financial aid: (508) 791-9241; 84% of undergrads determined to have financial need; average aid package $21,722

Bentley University
Waltham MA
(781) 891-2244
U.S. News ranking: Reg. U. (N), No. 3
Website: www.bentley.edu
Admissions email: ugadmission@bentley.edu
Private; founded 1917
Freshman admissions: more selective; 2015-2016: 8,346 applied, 3,532 accepted. Either SAT or ACT required. SAT 25/75 percentile: 1140-1330. High school rank: 38% in top tenth, 72% in top quarter, 93% in top half
Early decision deadline: 11/15, notification date: 12/31
Early action deadline: N/A, notification date: N/A
Application deadline (fall): 1/7
Undergraduate student body: 4,137 full time, 66 part time; 59% male, 41% female; 0% American Indian, 8% Asian, 3% black, 7% Hispanic, 2% multiracial, 0% Pacific Islander, 62% white, 14% international; 45% from in state; 79% live on campus; 11% of students in fraternities, 11% in sororities
Most popular majors: 19% Finance, General; 16% Business, Management, Marketing, and Related Support Services, Other; 14% Marketing/Marketing Management, General; 13% Accounting; 10% Accounting and Finance
Expenses: 2016-2017: $45,760; room/board: $15,130
Financial aid: (781) 891-3441; 43% of undergrads determined to have financial need; average aid package $35,525

Berklee College of Music
Boston MA
(800) 237-5533
U.S. News ranking: Arts, unranked
Website: www.berklee.edu
Admissions email: admissions@berklee.edu
Private; founded 1945
Freshman admissions: N/A; 2015-2016: 7,682 applied, 2,012 accepted. Neither SAT nor ACT required. SAT 25/75 percentile: N/A. High school rank: N/A
Early decision deadline: N/A, notification date: N/A
Early action deadline: 11/1, notification date: 1/31
Application deadline (fall): 1/15
Undergraduate student body: 4,291 full time, 821 part time; 67% male, 33% female; 0% American Indian, 4% Asian, 5% black, 8% Hispanic, 5% multiracial, 0% Pacific Islander, 36% white, 33% international; 15% from in state; 27% live on campus; 0% of students in fraternities, 0% in sororities
Most popular majors: 96% Visual and Performing Arts; 3% Health Professions and Related Programs; 2% Education

Expenses: 2016-2017: $41,398; room/board: $18,000
Financial aid: (617) 747-2274; 36% of undergrads determined to have financial need; average aid package $17,173

Boston Architectural College
Boston MA
(617) 585-0123
U.S. News ranking: Arts, unranked
Website: www.the-bac.edu
Admissions email: admissions@the-bac.edu
Private; founded 1889
Freshman admissions: N/A; 2015-2016: 43 applied, 43 accepted. Neither SAT nor ACT required. SAT 25/75 percentile: N/A. High school rank: N/A
Early decision deadline: N/A, notification date: N/A
Early action deadline: N/A, notification date: N/A
Application deadline (fall): rolling
Undergraduate student body: 328 full time, 60 part time; 59% male, 41% female; 0% American Indian, 8% Asian, 8% black, 14% Hispanic, 4% multiracial, 0% Pacific Islander, 45% white, 12% international
Most popular majors: Information not available
Expenses: 2016-2017: $20,666; room/board: $13,280
Financial aid: (617) 585-0125; 57% of undergrads determined to have financial need; average aid package $11,128

Boston College
Chestnut Hill MA
(617) 552-3100
U.S. News ranking: Nat. U., No. 31
Website: www.bc.edu
Admissions email: N/A
Private; founded 1863
Affiliation: Roman Catholic (Jesuit)
Freshman admissions: most selective; 2015-2016: 29,486 applied, 8,405 accepted. Either SAT or ACT required. SAT 25/75 percentile: 1260-1470. High school rank: 79% in top tenth, 95% in top quarter, 99% in top half
Early decision deadline: N/A, notification date: N/A
Early action deadline: 11/1, notification date: 12/25
Application deadline (fall): 1/1
Undergraduate student body: 9,192 full time, 0 part time; 47% male, 53% female; 0% American Indian, 10% Asian, 4% black, 10% Hispanic, 3% multiracial, 0% Pacific Islander, 63% white, 6% international; 25% from in state; 84% live on campus; 0% of students in fraternities, 0% in sororities
Most popular majors: 12% Economics, General; 10% Finance, General; 7% Biology/Biological Sciences, General; 7% Psychology, General
Expenses: 2016-2017: $51,296; room/board: $13,818
Financial aid: (617) 552-3320; 40% of undergrads determined to have financial need; average aid package $39,958

Boston Conservatory[1]
Boston MA
(617) 912-9153
U.S. News ranking: Arts, unranked
Website:
www.bostonconservatory.edu
Admissions email: admissions@
bostonconservatory.edu
Private
Application deadline (fall): N/A
Undergraduate student body: N/A
full time, N/A part time
Expenses: 2015-2016: $43,800;
room/board: $17,242
Financial aid: (617) 912-9147

Boston University
Boston MA
(617) 353-2300
U.S. News ranking: Nat. U.,
No. 39
Website: www.bu.edu
Admissions email:
admissions@bu.edu
Private; founded 1839
Freshman admissions: more
selective; 2015-2016: 54,781
applied, 17,871 accepted.
Either SAT or ACT required. SAT
25/75 percentile: 1200-1410.
High school rank: 58% in top
tenth, 89% in top quarter, 99%
in top half
Early decision deadline: 11/1,
notification date: 12/15
Early action deadline: N/A,
notification date: N/A
Application deadline (fall): 1/3
Undergraduate student body:
16,585 full time, 1,347 part
time; 40% male, 60% female;
0% American Indian, 14% Asian,
4% black, 11% Hispanic, 4%
multiracial, 0% Pacific Islander,
43% white, 20% international;
20% from in state; 75% live
on campus; 5% of students in
fraternities, 15% in sororities
Most popular majors: 20%
Business, Management,
Marketing, and Related Support
Services; 15% Social Sciences;
9% Health Professions and
Related Programs; 8% Biological
and Biomedical Sciences
Expenses: 2016-2017: $50,240;
room/board: $14,870
Financial aid: (617) 353-2965;
36% of undergrads determined
to have financial need; average
aid package $38,952

Brandeis University
Waltham MA
(781) 736-3500
U.S. News ranking: Nat. U.,
No. 34
Website: www.brandeis.edu
Admissions email: admissions@
brandeis.edu
Private; founded 1948
Freshman admissions: most
selective; 2015-2016: 10,528
applied, 3,582 accepted. Either
SAT or ACT required. SAT 25/75
percentile: 1250-1470. High
school rank: 71% in top tenth,
91% in top quarter, 98% in
top half
Early decision deadline: 11/1,
notification date: 12/15
Early action deadline: N/A,
notification date: N/A
Application deadline (fall): 1/1
Undergraduate student body: 3,602
full time, 19 part time; 43%
male, 57% female; 0% American

Indian, 13% Asian, 5% black,
7% Hispanic, 3% multiracial,
0% Pacific Islander, 47% white,
20% international; 26% from in
state; 79% live on campus; 0%
of students in fraternities, 0% in
sororities
Most popular majors: 10% Biology/
Biological Sciences, General;
9% Economics, General; 9%
Psychology, General; 8%
Business/Commerce, General;
7% Health Policy Analysis
Expenses: 2016-2017: $51,570;
room/board: $14,380
Financial aid: (781) 736-3700;
50% of undergrads determined
to have financial need; average
aid package $41,869

Bridgewater State University
Bridgewater MA
(508) 531-1237
U.S. News ranking: Reg. U. (N),
No. 118
Website: www.bridgew.edu/
admissions
Admissions email: admission@
bridgew.edu
Public; founded 1840
Freshman admissions: less
selective; 2015-2016: 5,867
applied, 4,371 accepted. Either
SAT or ACT required. SAT 25/75
percentile: 890-1100. High
school rank: N/A
Early decision deadline: N/A,
notification date: N/A
Early action deadline: 11/15,
notification date: 12/15
Application deadline (fall): rolling
Undergraduate student body: 7,933
full time, 1,675 part time; 41%
male, 59% female; 0% American
Indian, 2% Asian, 9% black,
6% Hispanic, 3% multiracial,
0% Pacific Islander, 78% white,
0% international; 96% from in
state; 41% live on campus; N/A
of students in fraternities, N/A in
sororities
Most popular majors: 20%
Education; 16% Business,
Management, Marketing, and
Related Support Services; 12%
Psychology; 11% Homeland
Security, Law Enforcement,
Firefighting and Related
Protective Services
Expenses: 2016-2017: $9,610
in state, $15,750 out of state;
room/board: $12,200
Financial aid: (508) 531-1341;
69% of undergrads determined
to have financial need; average
aid package $8,092

Cambridge College[1]
Cambridge MA
(800) 877-4723
U.S. News ranking: Reg. U. (N),
unranked
Website:
www.cambridgecollege.edu
Admissions email: N/A
Private; founded 1971
Application deadline (fall): rolling
Undergraduate student body: N/A
full time, N/A part time
Expenses: 2015-2016: $14,004;
room/board: N/A
Financial aid: (800) 877-4723

Clark University
Worcester MA
(508) 793-7431
U.S. News ranking: Nat. U.,
No. 74
Website: www.clarku.edu
Admissions email:
admissions@clarku.edu
Private; founded 1887
Freshman admissions: more
selective; 2015-2016: 8,045
applied, 4,430 accepted. Neither
SAT nor ACT required. SAT
25/75 percentile: 1120-1340.
High school rank: 44% in top
tenth, 77% in top quarter, 99%
in top half
Early decision deadline: 11/1,
notification date: 12/15
Early action deadline: 11/1,
notification date: 12/15
Application deadline (fall): 1/15
Undergraduate student body: 2,320
full time, 77 part time; 40%
male, 60% female; 0% American
Indian, 7% Asian, 4% black,
7% Hispanic, 2% multiracial,
0% Pacific Islander, 57% white,
15% international; 37% from in
state; 70% live on campus; N/A
of students in fraternities, N/A in
sororities
Most popular majors: 17%
Psychology; 7% Biology, General;
7% Economics; 6% History
Expenses: 2016-2017: $43,150;
room/board: $8,450
Financial aid: (508) 793-7478;
59% of undergrads determined
to have financial need; average
aid package $34,304

College of Our Lady of the Elms
Chicopee MA
(800) 255-3567
U.S. News ranking: Reg. U. (N),
No. 101
Website: www.elms.edu
Admissions email:
admissions@elms.edu
Private
Affiliation: Roman Catholic,
founded by Sisters of Saint
Joseph of Springfield
Freshman admissions: less
selective; 2015-2016: 832
applied, 623 accepted. Either
SAT or ACT required. SAT 25/75
percentile: 870-1070. High
school rank: N/A
Early decision deadline: N/A,
notification date: N/A
Early action deadline: N/A,
notification date: N/A
Application deadline (fall): rolling
Undergraduate student body: 969
full time, 342 part time; 24%
male, 76% female; 0% American
Indian, 2% Asian, 7% black,
10% Hispanic, 0% multiracial,
0% Pacific Islander, 56% white,
0% international; 77% from in
state; 30% live on campus; 0%
of students in fraternities, 0% in
sororities
Most popular majors: 44%
Health Professions and Related
Programs; 11% Business,
Management, Marketing, and
Public Administration and
Social Service Professions; 10%
Education; 7% Psychology
Expenses: 2016-2017: $33,470;
room/board: $12,236

Financial aid: (413) 594-2761;
90% of undergrads determined
to have financial need; average
aid package $22,272

College of the Holy Cross
Worcester MA
(508) 793-2443
U.S. News ranking: Nat. Lib. Arts,
No. 32
Website: www.holycross.edu
Admissions email: admissions@
holycross.edu
Private; founded 1843
Affiliation: Roman Catholic
(Jesuit)
Freshman admissions: more
selective; 2015-2016: 6,595
applied, 2,442 accepted. Neither
SAT nor ACT required. SAT
25/75 percentile: 1220-1380.
High school rank: 61% in top
tenth, 89% in top quarter, 100%
in top half
Early decision deadline: 12/15,
notification date: 1/15
Early action deadline: N/A,
notification date: N/A
Application deadline (fall): 1/15
Undergraduate student body: 2,885
full time, 31 part time; 50%
male, 50% female; 0% American
Indian, 5% Asian, 3% black,
10% Hispanic, 3% multiracial,
0% Pacific Islander, 70% white,
2% international; 38% from in
state; 91% live on campus; 0%
of students in fraternities, 0% in
sororities
Most popular majors: 34% Social
Sciences; 13% Psychology; 9%
English Language and Literature/
Letters; 8% Foreign Languages,
Literatures, and Linguistics;
7% Biological and Biomedical
Sciences
Expenses: 2016-2017: $48,940;
room/board: $13,225
Financial aid: (508) 793-2266;
52% of undergrads determined
to have financial need; average
aid package $37,255

Curry College
Milton MA
(800) 669-0686
U.S. News ranking: Reg. U. (N),
second tier
Website: www.curry.edu
Admissions email:
curryadm@curry.edu
Private; founded 1879
Freshman admissions: less
selective; 2015-2016: 5,554
applied, 4,871 accepted. Neither
SAT nor ACT required. SAT
25/75 percentile: 840-1030.
High school rank: 4% in top
tenth, 21% in top quarter, 52%
in top half
Early decision deadline: N/A,
notification date: N/A
Early action deadline: 12/1,
notification date: 12/15
Application deadline (fall): rolling
Undergraduate student body: 2,012
full time, 716 part time; 38%
male, 62% female; 0% American
Indian, 2% Asian, 9% black,
6% Hispanic, 2% multiracial,
0% Pacific Islander, 69% white,
2% international; 76% from in
state; 54% live on campus; 0%
of students in fraternities, 0% in
sororities

Most popular majors: 45%
Health Professions and Related
Programs; 12% Business,
Management, Marketing, and
Related Support Services;
12% Homeland Security, Law
Enforcement, Firefighting and
Related Protective Services; 8%
Psychology
Expenses: 2016-2017: $37,505;
room/board: $14,310
Financial aid: (617) 333-2146;
75% of undergrads determined
to have financial need; average
aid package $25,720

Dean College
Franklin MA
(508) 541-1508
U.S. News ranking: Reg. Coll. (N),
No. 19
Website: www.dean.edu
Admissions email:
admission@dean.edu
Private; founded 1865
Freshman admissions: least
selective; 2015-2016: 2,384
applied, 1,607 accepted. Neither
SAT nor ACT required. SAT
25/75 percentile: 720-940. High
school rank: N/A
Early decision deadline: N/A,
notification date: N/A
Early action deadline: 12/1,
notification date: 1/15
Application deadline (fall): rolling
Undergraduate student body: 1,113
full time, 269 part time; 55%
male, 45% female; 0% American
Indian, 1% Asian, 8% black, 8%
Hispanic, 0% multiracial, 0%
Pacific Islander, 31% white, N/A
international
Most popular majors: 31%
Business Administration and
Management, General; 28%
Dance, General; 22% Liberal Arts
and Sciences/Liberal Studies;
18% Drama and Dramatics/
Theatre Arts, General; 1%
Crafts/Craft Design, Folk Art and
Artisanry
Expenses: 2016-2017: $36,660;
room/board: $15,732
Financial aid: (508) 541-1519;
73% of undergrads determined
to have financial need; average
aid package $25,493

Eastern Nazarene College
Quincy MA
(617) 745-3711
U.S. News ranking: Reg. U. (N),
second tier
Website: www.enc.edu
Admissions email: info@enc.edu
Private; founded 1918
Affiliation: Nazarene
Freshman admissions: less
selective; 2015-2016: 1,129
applied, 692 accepted. Either
SAT or ACT required. SAT 25/75
percentile: 840-1110. High
school rank: N/A
Early decision deadline: N/A,
notification date: N/A
Early action deadline: N/A,
notification date: N/A
Application deadline (fall): rolling
Undergraduate student body: 904
full time, 9 part time; 37% male,
63% female; 0% American
Indian, 2% Asian, 24% black,
12% Hispanic, 4% multiracial,
0% Pacific Islander, 53% white,
3% international

Most popular majors: Information not available
Expenses: 2016-2017: $30,815; room/board: $9,140
Financial aid: (617) 745-3869

Emerson College
Boston MA
(617) 824-8600
U.S. News ranking: Reg. U. (N), No. 8
Website: www.emerson.edu
Admissions email: admission@ emerson.edu
Private; founded 1880
Freshman admissions: more selective; 2015-2016: 8,618 applied, 4,225 accepted. Either SAT or ACT required. SAT 25/75 percentile: 1100-1310. High school rank: 27% in top tenth, 67% in top quarter, 95% in top half
Early decision deadline: N/A, notification date: N/A
Early action deadline: 11/1, notification date: 12/15
Application deadline (fall): 1/15
Undergraduate student body: 3,734 full time, 55 part time; 40% male, 60% female; 0% American Indian, 4% Asian, 3% black, 11% Hispanic, 4% multiracial, 0% Pacific Islander, 67% white, 7% international; 26% from in state; 57% live on campus; 2% of students in fraternities, 3% in sororities
Most popular majors: 30% Cinematography and Film/Video Production; 15% Marketing/ Marketing Management, General; 13% Creative Writing; 2% Communication Disorders Sciences and Services
Expenses: 2016-2017: $40,796; room/board: $16,320
Financial aid: (617) 824-8655; 64% of undergrads determined to have financial need; average aid package $21,254

Emmanuel College
Boston MA
(617) 735-9715
U.S. News ranking: Nat. Lib. Arts, second tier
Website: www.emmanuel.edu
Admissions email: enroll@ emmanuel.edu
Private; founded 1919
Affiliation: Roman Catholic
Freshman admissions: selective; 2015-2016: 5,692 applied, 4,463 accepted. Neither SAT nor ACT required. SAT 25/75 percentile: 1030-1210. High school rank: N/A
Early decision deadline: N/A, notification date: N/A
Early action deadline: 11/1, notification date: 12/15
Application deadline (fall): 2/15
Undergraduate student body: 1,775 full time, 211 part time; 26% male, 74% female; 0% American Indian, 4% Asian, 5% black, 9% Hispanic, 2% multiracial, 0% Pacific Islander, 71% white, 2% international; 55% from in state; 73% live on campus; N/A of students in fraternities, N/A in sororities
Most popular majors: 16% Business, Management, Marketing, and Related Support Services; 14% Biological and

Biomedical Sciences; 10% Psychology; 9% Education
Expenses: 2016-2017: $37,540; room/board: $14,270
Financial aid: (617) 735-9938; 81% of undergrads determined to have financial need; average aid package $26,071

Endicott College
Beverly MA
(978) 921-1000
U.S. News ranking: Reg. U. (N), No. 51
Website: www.endicott.edu
Admissions email: admission@ endicott.edu
Private; founded 1939
Freshman admissions: selective; 2015-2016: 3,997 applied, 2,912 accepted. Neither SAT nor ACT required. SAT 25/75 percentile: 980-1170. High school rank: 15% in top tenth, 44% in top quarter, 77% in top half
Early decision deadline: N/A, notification date: N/A
Early action deadline: N/A, notification date: N/A
Application deadline (fall): 2/15
Undergraduate student body: 2,806 full time, 452 part time; 40% male, 60% female; 0% American Indian, 1% Asian, 3% black, 5% Hispanic, 1% multiracial, 0% Pacific Islander, 83% white, 2% international; 47% from in state; 92% live on campus; N/A of students in fraternities, N/A in sororities
Most popular majors: 15% Business Administration and Management, General; 9% Psychology, General; 8% Hospitality Administration/ Management, General; 8% Sport and Fitness Administration/ Management
Expenses: 2016-2017: $31,312; room/board: $14,500
Financial aid: (978) 232-2070; 64% of undergrads determined to have financial need; average aid package $20,795

Fisher College
Boston MA
(617) 236-8818
U.S. News ranking: Reg. Coll. (N), No. 31
Website: www.fisher.edu
Admissions email: admissions@fisher.edu
Private; founded 1903
Freshman admissions: least selective; 2015-2016: 2,674 applied, 1,875 accepted. Neither SAT nor ACT required. SAT 25/75 percentile: 700-920. High school rank: N/A
Early decision deadline: N/A, notification date: N/A
Early action deadline: N/A, notification date: N/A
Application deadline (fall): rolling
Undergraduate student body: 1,232 full time, 706 part time; 29% male, 71% female; 0% American Indian, 1% Asian, 11% black, 10% Hispanic, 2% multiracial, 0% Pacific Islander, 30% white, 9% international; 78% from in state; 20% live on campus; N/A of students in fraternities, N/A in sororities

Most popular majors: 40% Business, Management, Marketing, and Related Support Services; 15% Health Professions and Related Programs; 13% Education; 10% Liberal Arts and Sciences, General Studies and Humanities
Expenses: 2016-2017: $29,640; room/board: $15,459
Financial aid: (617) 236-8821; 65% of undergrads determined to have financial need; average aid package $18,078

Fitchburg State University
Fitchburg MA
(978) 665-3144
U.S. News ranking: Reg. U. (N), second tier
Website: www.fitchburgstate.edu
Admissions email: admissions@ fitchburgstate.edu
Public; founded 1894
Freshman admissions: less selective; 2015-2016: 3,998 applied, 2,989 accepted. Either SAT or ACT required. SAT 25/75 percentile: 890-1090. High school rank: N/A
Early decision deadline: N/A, notification date: N/A
Early action deadline: N/A, notification date: N/A
Application deadline (fall): rolling
Undergraduate student body: 3,466 full time, 804 part time; 46% male, 54% female; 0% American Indian, 2% Asian, 9% black, 10% Hispanic, 3% multiracial, 0% Pacific Islander, 73% white, 1% international; 92% from in state; 41% live on campus; 1% of students in fraternities, 3% in sororities
Most popular majors: 16% Visual and Performing Arts; 12% Business, Management, Marketing, and Related Support Services; 12% Multi/ Interdisciplinary Studies; 8% Parks, Recreation, Leisure, and Fitness Studies; 7% Homeland Security, Law Enforcement, Firefighting and Related Protective Services
Expenses: 2016-2017: $10,620 in state, $16,215 out of state; room/board: $10,200
Financial aid: (978) 665-3156; 66% of undergrads determined to have financial need; average aid package $10,582

Framingham State University
Framingham MA
(508) 626-4500
U.S. News ranking: Reg. U. (N), second tier
Website: www.framingham.edu
Admissions email: admissions@ framingham.edu
Public; founded 1839
Freshman admissions: less selective; 2015-2016: 4,803 applied, 3,401 accepted. Either SAT or ACT required. SAT 25/75 percentile: 870-1080. High school rank: 6% in top tenth, 19% in top quarter, 60% in top half
Early decision deadline: N/A, notification date: N/A
Early action deadline: 11/15, notification date: 12/15

Application deadline (fall): rolling
Undergraduate student body: 3,826 full time, 652 part time; 37% male, 63% female; 0% American Indian, 3% Asian, 8% black, 11% Hispanic, 4% multiracial, 0% Pacific Islander, 72% white, 0% international; 96% from in state; 50% live on campus; N/A of students in fraternities, N/A in sororities
Most popular majors: 19% Social Sciences; 16% Business, Management, Marketing, and Related Support Services; 12% Family and Consumer Sciences/Human Sciences; 10% Psychology; 8% Communications Technologies/Technicians and Support Services
Expenses: 2015-2016: $8,700 in state, $14,780 out of state; room/board: $10,834
Financial aid: (508) 626-4534

Franklin W. Olin College of Engineering
Needham MA
(781) 292-2222
U.S. News ranking: Engineering, unranked
Website: www.olin.edu/
Admissions email: info@olin.edu
Private; founded 1997
Freshman admissions: N/A; 2015-2016: 1,075 applied, 118 accepted. Either SAT or ACT required. SAT 25/75 percentile: N/A. High school rank: N/A
Early decision deadline: N/A, notification date: N/A
Early action deadline: N/A, notification date: N/A
Application deadline (fall): 1/1
Undergraduate student body: 342 full time, 28 part time; 50% male, 50% female; 0% American Indian, 16% Asian, 0% black, 5% Hispanic, 7% multiracial, 0% Pacific Islander, 53% white, 8% international; 14% from in state; 100% live on campus; 0% of students in fraternities, 0% in sororities
Most popular majors: 47% Engineering, General; 32% Mechanical Engineering; 21% Electrical and Electronics Engineering
Expenses: 2016-2017: $47,330; room/board: $15,800
Financial aid: N/A; 45% of undergrads determined to have financial need; average aid package $42,254

Gordon College
Wenham MA
(866) 464-6736
U.S. News ranking: Nat. Lib. Arts, No. 171
Website: www.gordon.edu
Admissions email: admissions@ gordon.edu
Private; founded 1889
Affiliation: multi-denominational
Freshman admissions: selective; 2015-2016: 1,832 applied, 1,708 accepted. Either SAT or ACT required. SAT 25/75 percentile: 950-1230. High school rank: 26% in top tenth, 61% in top quarter, 83% in top half
Early decision deadline: 10/15, notification date: 12/1

Early action deadline: 11/15, notification date: 12/1
Application deadline (fall): 8/1
Undergraduate student body: 1,644 full time, 50 part time; 38% male, 62% female; 0% American Indian, 4% Asian, 4% black, 7% Hispanic, 4% multiracial, 0% Pacific Islander, 72% white, 8% international; 32% from in state; 87% live on campus; N/A of students in fraternities, N/A in sororities
Most popular majors: 7% Business/Commerce, General; 7% Biology/Biological Sciences, General; 6% Psychology, General; 6% English Language and Literature, General
Expenses: 2016-2017: $36,060; room/board: $10,412
Financial aid: (978) 867-4246; 67% of undergrads determined to have financial need; average aid package $23,819

Hampshire College[1]
Amherst MA
(413) 559-5471
U.S. News ranking: Nat. Lib. Arts, unranked
Website: www.hampshire.edu
Admissions email: admissions@ hampshire.edu
Private; founded 1965
Application deadline (fall): 1/15
Undergraduate student body: N/A full time, N/A part time
Expenses: 2015-2016: $49,048; room/board: $12,950
Financial aid: (413) 559-5484

Harvard University
Cambridge MA
(617) 495-1551
U.S. News ranking: Nat. U., No. 2
Website: www.college.harvard.edu
Admissions email: college@ fas.harvard.edu
Private; founded 1636
Freshman admissions: most selective; 2015-2016: 37,307 applied, 2,080 accepted. Either SAT or ACT required. SAT 25/75 percentile: 1400-1600. High school rank: 95% in top tenth, 99% in top quarter, 100% in top half
Early decision deadline: N/A, notification date: N/A
Early action deadline: 11/1, notification date: 12/16
Application deadline (fall): 1/1
Undergraduate student body: 6,698 full time, 1 part time; 53% male, 47% female; 0% American Indian, 20% Asian, 7% black, 10% Hispanic, 6% multiracial, 0% Pacific Islander, 42% white, 12% international; 17% from in state; 99% live on campus; N/A of students in fraternities, N/A in sororities
Most popular majors: 29% Social Sciences, General; 14% Biology/Biological Sciences, General; 9% History, General; 9% Mathematics, General; 7% Physical Sciences
Expenses: 2016-2017: $47,074; room/board: $15,951
Financial aid: (617) 495-1581; 55% of undergrads determined to have financial need; average aid package $51,393

Lasell College

Newton MA
(617) 243-2225
U.S. News ranking: Reg. U. (N),
No. 131
Website: www.lasell.edu
Admissions email: info@lasell.edu
Private; founded 1851
Freshman admissions: less
selective; 2015-2016: 3,171
applied, 2,478 accepted. Either
SAT or ACT required. SAT 25/75
percentile: 870-1060. High
school rank: N/A
Early decision deadline: N/A,
notification date: N/A
Early action deadline: 11/15,
notification date: 12/1
Application deadline (fall): rolling
Undergraduate student body: 1,788
full time, 27 part time; 34%
male, 66% female; 0% American
Indian, 2% Asian, 5% black,
8% Hispanic, 3% multiracial,
0% Pacific Islander, 72% white,
6% international; 56% from in
state; 74% live on campus; 0%
of students in fraternities, 0% in
sororities
Most popular majors: 9% Sport
and Fitness Administration/
Management; 8% Fashion
Merchandising; 8% Business
Administration and Management,
General
Expenses: 2016-2017: $33,600;
room/board: $13,900
Financial aid: (617) 243-2227;
79% of undergrads determined
to have financial need; average
aid package $25,377

Lesley University

Cambridge MA
(617) 349-8800
U.S. News ranking: Nat. U.,
No. 197
Website: www.lesley.edu
Admissions email: lcadmissions@
lesley.edu
Private; founded 1909
Freshman admissions: selective;
2015-2016: 3,115 applied,
2,135 accepted. Either SAT
or ACT required. SAT 25/75
percentile: 960-1170. High
school rank: 15% in top tenth,
44% in top quarter, 80% in
top half
Early decision deadline: N/A,
notification date: N/A
Early action deadline: 12/1,
notification date: 12/23
Application deadline (fall): rolling
Undergraduate student body: 1,364
full time, 156 part time; 25%
male, 75% female; 0% American
Indian, 4% Asian, 4% black,
10% Hispanic, 4% multiracial,
0% Pacific Islander, 71% white,
2% international; 43% from in
state; 60% live on campus; N/A
of students in fraternities, N/A in
sororities
Most popular majors: Information
not available
Expenses: 2016-2017: $25,750;
room/board: $15,300
Financial aid: (617) 349-8581

Massachusetts College of Art and Design

Boston MA
(617) 879-7222
U.S. News ranking: Arts, unranked
Website: www.massart.edu
Admissions email: admissions@
massart.edu
Public; founded 1873
Freshman admissions: N/A;
2015-2016: 1,273 applied, 908
accepted. Either SAT or ACT
required. SAT 25/75 percentile:
N/A. High school rank: N/A
Early decision deadline: N/A,
notification date: N/A
Early action deadline: 12/1,
notification date: 1/5
Application deadline (fall): 2/1
Undergraduate student body: 1,547
full time, 320 part time; 29%
male, 71% female; 0% American
Indian, 8% Asian, 3% black,
10% Hispanic, 1% multiracial,
0% Pacific Islander, 63% white,
4% international; 67% from in
state; 38% live on campus; N/A
of students in fraternities, N/A in
sororities
Most popular majors: Information
not available
Expenses: 2016-2017: $12,200
in state, $32,800 out of state;
room/board: $13,100
Financial aid: (617) 879-7850;
52% of undergrads determined
to have financial need; average
aid package $10,741

Massachusetts College of Liberal Arts

North Adams MA
(413) 662-5410
U.S. News ranking: Nat. Lib. Arts,
second tier
Website: www.mcla.edu
Admissions email:
admissions@mcla.edu
Public; founded 1894
Freshman admissions: selective;
2015-2016: 2,091 applied,
1,535 accepted. Either SAT
or ACT required. SAT 25/75
percentile: 890-1130. High
school rank: 16% in top tenth,
43% in top quarter, 76% in
top half
Early decision deadline: N/A,
notification date: N/A
Early action deadline: 12/1,
notification date: 12/15
Application deadline (fall): rolling
Undergraduate student body: 1,280
full time, 177 part time; 37%
male, 63% female; 1% American
Indian, 2% Asian, 9% black,
8% Hispanic, 3% multiracial,
N/A Pacific Islander, 74% white,
0% international; 75% from in
state; 59% live on campus; N/A
of students in fraternities, N/A in
sororities
Most popular majors: 15% English
Language and Literature/Letters;
14% Business, Management,
Marketing, and Related
Support Services; 13% Multi/
Interdisciplinary Studies; 10%
Psychology; 8% Visual and
Performing Arts
Expenses: 2015-2016: $9,475
in state, $18,420 out of state;
room/board: $9,828

Financial aid: (413) 662-5219;
77% of undergrads determined
to have financial need; average
aid package $15,142

Massachusetts Institute of Technology

Cambridge MA
(617) 253-3400
U.S. News ranking: Nat. U., No. 7
Website: web.mit.edu/
Admissions email:
admissions@mit.edu
Private; founded 1861
Freshman admissions: most
selective; 2015-2016: 18,306
applied, 1,519 accepted. Either
SAT or ACT required. SAT 25/75
percentile: 1430-1580. High
school rank: 98% in top tenth,
100% in top quarter, 100% in
top half
Early decision deadline: N/A,
notification date: N/A
Early action deadline: 11/1,
notification date: 12/20
Application deadline (fall): 1/1
Undergraduate student body: 4,492
full time, 35 part time; 54%
male, 46% female; 0% American
Indian, 25% Asian, 6% black,
15% Hispanic, 6% multiracial,
0% Pacific Islander, 37% white,
10% international; 10% from in
state; 94% live on campus; 48%
of students in fraternities, 36%
in sororities
Most popular majors: 39%
Engineering; 23% Computer
and Information Sciences
and Support Services; 9%
Mathematics and Statistics;
8% Biological and Biomedical
Sciences; 8% Physical Sciences
Expenses: 2016-2017: $48,452;
room/board: $14,210
Financial aid: (617) 253-4971;
59% of undergrads determined
to have financial need; average
aid package $43,807

Massachusetts Maritime Academy

Buzzards Bay MA
(800) 544-3411
U.S. News ranking: Reg. U. (N),
No. 18
Website: www.maritime.edu
Admissions email: admissions@
maritime.edu
Public; founded 1891
Freshman admissions: selective;
2015-2016: 825 applied, 610
accepted. Either SAT or ACT
required. SAT 25/75 percentile:
980-1160. High school rank: N/A
Early decision deadline: N/A,
notification date: N/A
Early action deadline: 11/1,
notification date: 12/31
Application deadline (fall): rolling
Undergraduate student body: 1,506
full time, 65 part time; 87%
male, 13% female; 0% American
Indian, 1% Asian, 1% black,
4% Hispanic, 3% multiracial,
N/A Pacific Islander, 87% white,
1% international; 79% from in
state; 96% live on campus; N/A
of students in fraternities, N/A in
sororities
Most popular majors: 24%
Naval Architecture and Marine
Engineering; 20% Engineering,
Other; 19% Marine Science/
Merchant Marine Officer

Expenses: 2016-2017: $8,004
in state, $24,600 out of state;
room/board: $11,978
Financial aid: (508) 830-5087;
38% of undergrads determined
to have financial need; average
aid package $12,026

Merrimack College

North Andover MA
(978) 837-5100
U.S. News ranking: Reg. U. (N),
No. 57
Website: www.merrimack.edu
Admissions email: Admission@
Merrimack.edu
Private; founded 1947
Affiliation: Roman Catholic
Freshman admissions: selective;
2015-2016: 7,751 applied,
6,121 accepted. Neither SAT
nor ACT required. SAT 25/75
percentile: 890-1100. High
school rank: 7% in top tenth,
26% in top quarter, 59% in
top half
Early decision deadline: 11/15,
notification date: 12/15
Early action deadline: 11/15,
notification date: 12/15
Application deadline (fall): 2/15
Undergraduate student body: 3,058
full time, 133 part time; 48%
male, 52% female; 0% American
Indian, 1% Asian, 3% black,
5% Hispanic, 1% multiracial,
0% Pacific Islander, 73% white,
5% international; 69% from in
state; 74% live on campus; 1%
of students in fraternities, 5% in
sororities
Most popular majors: 10%
Business Administration
and Management, General;
10% Human Development,
Family Studies, and Related
Services, Other; 7% Marketing/
Marketing Management, General;
6% Criminal Justice/Law
Enforcement Administration
Expenses: 2016-2017: $38,425;
room/board: $14,345
Financial aid: (978) 837-5196;
71% of undergrads determined
to have financial need; average
aid package $22,288

Montserrat College of Art[1]

Beverly MA
(978) 921-4242
U.S. News ranking: Arts, unranked
Website: www.montserrat.edu
Admissions email: admissions@
montserrrat.edu
Private; founded 1970
Application deadline (fall): N/A
Undergraduate student body: N/A
full time, N/A part time
Expenses: 2016-2017: $30,800;
room/board: $9,250
Financial aid: (978) 921-4242

Mount Holyoke College

South Hadley MA
(413) 538-2023
U.S. News ranking: Nat. Lib. Arts,
No. 36
Website: www.mtholyoke.edu
Admissions email: admission@
mtholyoke.edu
Private; founded 1837
Freshman admissions: more
selective; 2015-2016: 3,858
applied, 1,932 accepted. Neither

SAT nor ACT required. SAT
25/75 percentile: 1230-1465.
High school rank: 58% in top
tenth, 90% in top quarter, 97%
in top half
Early decision deadline: 11/15,
notification date: 1/1
Early action deadline: N/A,
notification date: N/A
Application deadline (fall): 1/15
Undergraduate student body: 2,095
full time, 31 part time; 0% male
100% female; 0% American
Indian, 10% Asian, 6% black,
8% Hispanic, 4% multiracial,
0% Pacific Islander, 45% white,
26% international; 25% from in
state; 95% live on campus; N/A
of students in fraternities, N/A in
sororities
Most popular majors: 10%
Psychology, General; 9%
Economics, General; 8% English
Language and Literature, General
8% International Relations and
Affairs; 7% Political Science and
Government, General
Expenses: 2016-2017: $45,866;
room/board: $13,440
Financial aid: (413) 538-2291;
65% of undergrads determined
to have financial need; average
aid package $36,895

Mount Ida College

Newton MA
(617) 928-4535
U.S. News ranking: Reg. Coll. (N),
No. 27
Website: www.mountida.edu
Admissions email: admissions@
mountida.edu
Private; founded 1899
Freshman admissions: less
selective; 2015-2016: 2,319
applied, 1,467 accepted. Either
SAT or ACT required. SAT 25/75
percentile: 800-1010. High
school rank: N/A
Early decision deadline: N/A,
notification date: N/A
Early action deadline: N/A,
notification date: N/A
Application deadline (fall): rolling
Undergraduate student body: 1,241
full time, 79 part time; 33%
male, 67% female; 0% American
Indian, 2% Asian, 9% black,
10% Hispanic, 2% multiracial,
0% Pacific Islander, 63% white,
8% international; 66% from in
state; 61% live on campus; 0%
of students in fraternities, 0% in
sororities
Most popular majors: 20%
Veterinary/Animal Health
Technology/Technician and
Veterinary Assistant; 13%
Dental Hygiene/Hygienist; 9%
Criminal Justice/Safety Studies;
8% Business Administration
and Management, General; 7%
Fashion Merchandising
Expenses: 2016-2017: $33,820;
room/board: $13,000
Financial aid: (617) 928-4785;
81% of undergrads determined
to have financial need; average
aid package $24,618

National Graduate School of Quality Management
Falmouth MA
(800) 838-2580
U.S. News ranking: Business, unranked
Website: www.ngs.edu
Admissions email: N/A
Private; founded 1993
Freshman admissions: N/A; 2015-2016: N/A applied, N/A accepted. Neither SAT nor ACT required. SAT 25/75 percentile: N/A. High school rank: N/A
Early decision deadline: N/A, notification date: N/A
Early action deadline: N/A, notification date: N/A
Application deadline (fall): N/A
Undergraduate student body: 111 full time, N/A part time; 77% male, 23% female; N/A American Indian, 3% Asian, 28% black, 11% Hispanic, N/A multiracial, N/A Pacific Islander, 58% white, N/A international
Most popular majors: Information not available
Expenses: 2015-2016: $10,320; room/board: N/A
Financial aid: (800) 838-2580

Newbury College
Brookline MA
(617) 730-7007
U.S. News ranking: Reg. Coll. (N), unranked
Website: www.newbury.edu/
Admissions email: info@newbury.edu
Private; founded 1962
Freshman admissions: N/A; 2015-2016: 2,580 applied, 2,040 accepted. Neither SAT nor ACT required. SAT 25/75 percentile: 740-940. High school rank: N/A
Early decision deadline: N/A, notification date: N/A
Early action deadline: N/A, notification date: N/A
Application deadline (fall): rolling
Undergraduate student body: 778 full time, 87 part time; 44% male, 56% female; 0% American Indian, 5% Asian, 36% black, 15% Hispanic, 6% multiracial, 0% Pacific Islander, 36% white, 3% international, 78% from in state; 38% live on campus; 0% of students in fraternities, 0% in sororities
Most popular majors: 16% Psychology, General; 13% Business Administration and Management, General; 10% Hospitality Administration/Management, General; 10% Restaurant, Culinary, and Catering Management/Manager; 7% Sport and Fitness Administration/Management
Expenses: 2016-2017: $33,518; room/board: $14,150
Financial aid: (617) 730-7100; 91% of undergrads determined to have financial need; average aid package $23,964

New England College of Business and Finance[1]
Boston MA
(800) 997-1673
U.S. News ranking: Business, unranked
Website: www.necb.edu/
Admissions email: N/A
For-profit
Application deadline (fall): N/A
Undergraduate student body: N/A full time, N/A part time
Expenses: 2015-2016: $10,525; room/board: N/A
Financial aid: N/A

New England Conservatory of Music
Boston MA
(617) 585-1101
U.S. News ranking: Arts, unranked
Website: www.newenglandconservatory.edu
Admissions email: admission@newenglandconservatory.edu
Private; founded 1867
Freshman admissions: N/A; 2015-2016: 1,170 applied, 379 accepted. Neither SAT nor ACT required. SAT 25/75 percentile: N/A. High school rank: N/A
Early decision deadline: N/A, notification date: N/A
Early action deadline: N/A, notification date: N/A
Application deadline (fall): 12/1
Undergraduate student body: 369 full time, 38 part time; 56% male, 44% female; 0% American Indian, 10% Asian, 3% black, 3% Hispanic, 6% multiracial, 0% Pacific Islander, 39% white, 35% international; 12% from in state; 30% live on campus; 0% of students in fraternities, 0% in sororities
Most popular majors: Information not available
Expenses: 2016-2017: $44,755; room/board: $13,900
Financial aid: (617) 585-1110; 44% of undergrads determined to have financial need; average aid package $27,364

New England Institute of Art[1]
Brookline MA
(800) 903-4425
U.S. News ranking: Arts, unranked
Website: www.artinstitutes.edu/boston/
Admissions email: N/A
For-profit
Application deadline (fall): N/A
Undergraduate student body: N/A full time, N/A part time
Expenses: 2015-2016: $18,636; room/board: N/A
Financial aid: N/A

Nichols College
Dudley MA
(800) 470-3379
U.S. News ranking: Business, unranked
Website: www.nichols.edu/
Admissions email: admissions@nichols.edu
Private; founded 1815
Freshman admissions: N/A; 2015-2016: 2,260 applied, 1,881 accepted. Neither SAT nor ACT required. SAT 25/75 percentile: N/A. High school rank: 3% in top tenth, 16% in top quarter, 44% in top half
Early decision deadline: N/A, notification date: N/A
Early action deadline: 12/1, notification date: N/A
Application deadline (fall): rolling
Undergraduate student body: 1,150 full time, 117 part time; 62% male, 38% female; 0% American Indian, 1% Asian, 7% black, 6% Hispanic, 4% multiracial, 0% Pacific Islander, 81% white, 1% international; 60% from in state; 70% live on campus; 0% of students in fraternities, 0% in sororities
Most popular majors: 33% Business/Commerce, General; 16% Sport and Fitness Administration/Management; 8% Marketing/Marketing Management, General; 7% Criminal Justice/Law Enforcement Administration; 5% Business Administration and Management, General
Expenses: 2016-2017: $33,400; room/board: $13,500
Financial aid: (508) 213-2278; 79% of undergrads determined to have financial need; average aid package $31,843

Northeastern University
Boston MA
(617) 373-2200
U.S. News ranking: Nat. U., No. 39
Website: www.northeastern.edu/
Admissions email: admissions@neu.edu
Private; founded 1898
Freshman admissions: most selective; 2015-2016: 50,523 applied, 14,388 accepted. Either SAT or ACT required. ACT 25/75 percentile: 31-34. High school rank: 70% in top tenth, 94% in top quarter, 99% in top half
Early decision deadline: 11/1, notification date: 12/15
Early action deadline: 11/1, notification date: 12/31
Application deadline (fall): 1/1
Undergraduate student body: 13,664 full time, 33 part time; 50% male, 50% female; 0% American Indian, 12% Asian, 4% black, 7% Hispanic, 4% multiracial, 0% Pacific Islander, 48% white, 20% international; 30% from in state; 48% live on campus; 8% of students in fraternities, 12% in sororities
Most popular majors: 23% Business, Management, Marketing, and Related Support Services; 15% Health Professions and Related Programs; 14% Engineering; 10% Social Sciences; 8% Biological and Biomedical Sciences
Expenses: 2016-2017: $47,655; room/board: $15,600
Financial aid: (617) 373-3190; 37% of undergrads determined to have financial need; average aid package $29,567

Pine Manor College
Chestnut Hill MA
(617) 731-7104
U.S. News ranking: Nat. Lib. Arts, second tier
Website: www.pmc.edu
Admissions email: admission@pmc.edu
Private; founded 1911
Freshman admissions: least selective; 2015-2016: 764 applied, 542 accepted. Either SAT or ACT required. SAT 25/75 percentile: 680-860. High school rank: N/A
Early decision deadline: N/A, notification date: N/A
Early action deadline: N/A, notification date: N/A
Application deadline (fall): rolling
Undergraduate student body: 438 full time, 10 part time; 43% male, 57% female; 1% American Indian, 2% Asian, 25% black, 14% Hispanic, 7% multiracial, N/A Pacific Islander, 4% white, 35% international
Most popular majors: 28% Biology/Biological Sciences, General; 23% Business Administration and Management, General; 18% Psychology, General; 13% Sociology
Expenses: 2015-2016: $27,250; room/board: $12,980
Financial aid: (617) 731-7129

Salem State University
Salem MA
(978) 542-6200
U.S. News ranking: Reg. U. (N), second tier
Website: www.salemstate.edu
Admissions email: admissions@salemstate.edu
Public; founded 1854
Freshman admissions: less selective; 2015-2016: 5,164 applied, 3,868 accepted. Either SAT or ACT required. SAT 25/75 percentile: 880-1070. High school rank: N/A
Early decision deadline: N/A, notification date: N/A
Early action deadline: 11/15, notification date: 1/1
Application deadline (fall): rolling
Undergraduate student body: 5,919 full time, 1,580 part time; 39% male, 61% female; 0% American Indian, 3% Asian, 9% black, 12% Hispanic, 3% multiracial, 0% Pacific Islander, 68% white, 3% international; 96% from in state; 32% live on campus; N/A of students in fraternities, N/A in sororities
Most popular majors: 20% Business, Management, Marketing, and Related Support Services; 15% Health Professions and Related Programs; 9% Education; 8% Homeland Security, Law Enforcement, Firefighting and Related Protective Services; 8% Psychology
Expenses: 2015-2016: $9,246 in state, $15,508 out of state; room/board: $12,101
Financial aid: (978) 542-6139

Simmons College
Boston MA
(800) 345-8468
U.S. News ranking: Reg. U. (N), No. 11
Website: www.simmons.edu
Admissions email: ugadm@simmons.edu
Private; founded 1899
Freshman admissions: more selective; 2015-2016: 4,576 applied, 2,635 accepted. Either SAT or ACT required. SAT 25/75 percentile: 1060-1240. High school rank: 35% in top tenth, 72% in top quarter, 97% in top half
Early decision deadline: N/A, notification date: N/A
Early action deadline: 11/1, notification date: 12/15
Application deadline (fall): 2/1
Undergraduate student body: 1,599 full time, 142 part time; 0% male, 100% female; 0% American Indian, 9% Asian, 7% black, 9% Hispanic, 4% multiracial, 0% Pacific Islander, 67% white, 3% international; 60% from in state; 60% live on campus; 0% of students in fraternities, 0% in sororities
Most popular majors: 41% Health Professions and Related Programs; 9% Social Sciences; 8% Business, Management, Marketing, and Related Support Services; 6% Parks, Recreation, Leisure, and Fitness Studies; 5% Psychology
Expenses: 2015-2016: $37,380; room/board: $14,040
Financial aid: (617) 521-2001; 78% of undergrads determined to have financial need; average aid package $28,976

Smith College
Northampton MA
(413) 585-2500
U.S. News ranking: Nat. Lib. Arts, No. 12
Website: www.smith.edu
Admissions email: admission@smith.edu
Private; founded 1871
Freshman admissions: more selective; 2015-2016: 5,006 applied, 1,897 accepted. Neither SAT nor ACT required. SAT 25/75 percentile: 1240-1460. High school rank: 62% in top tenth, 90% in top quarter, 100% in top half
Early decision deadline: 11/15, notification date: 12/15
Early action deadline: N/A, notification date: N/A
Application deadline (fall): 1/15
Undergraduate student body: 2,460 full time, 18 part time; 0% male, 100% female; 0% American Indian, 12% Asian, 5% black, 10% Hispanic, 5% multiracial, 0% Pacific Islander, 45% white, 14% international; 18% from in state; 95% live on campus; N/A of students in fraternities, N/A in sororities
Most popular majors: 10% Economics, General; 9% Psychology, General; 8% Political Science and Government, General; 6% Biology/Biological Sciences, General; 5% Sociology
Expenses: 2016-2017: $47,904; room/board: $16,010

Financial aid: (413) 585-2530; 60% of undergrads determined to have financial need; average aid package $45,628

Springfield College
Springfield MA
(413) 748-3136
U.S. News ranking: Reg. U. (N), No. 27
Website: www.springfieldcollege.edu
Admissions email: admissions@springfiledcollege.edu
Private; founded 1885
Freshman admissions: selective; 2015-2016: 4,112 applied, 2,638 accepted. Either SAT or ACT required. SAT 25/75 percentile: 930-1140. High school rank: 16% in top tenth, 33% in top quarter, 74% in top half
Early decision deadline: 12/1, notification date: 2/1
Early action deadline: N/A, notification date: N/A
Application deadline (fall): 4/1
Undergraduate student body: 2,129 full time, 31 part time; 49% male, 51% female; 0% American Indian, 1% Asian, 5% black, 6% Hispanic, 2% multiracial, 0% Pacific Islander, 81% white, 3% international; 43% from in state; 83% live on campus; N/A of students in fraternities, N/A in sororities
Most popular majors: 10% Kinesiology and Exercise Science; 7% Physical Therapy/Therapist; 7% Psychology, General; 7% Sport and Fitness Administration/Management; 6% Physical Education Teaching and Coaching
Expenses: 2016-2017: $35,475; room/board: $11,890
Financial aid: (413) 748-3108; 80% of undergrads determined to have financial need; average aid package $26,129

Stonehill College
Easton MA
(508) 565-1373
U.S. News ranking: Nat. Lib. Arts, No. 108
Website: www.stonehill.edu
Admissions email: admission@stonehill.edu
Private; founded 1948
Affiliation: Roman Catholic
Freshman admissions: selective; 2015-2016: 5,892 applied, 4,429 accepted. Neither SAT nor ACT required. SAT 25/75 percentile: 1020-1220. High school rank: 27% in top tenth, 59% in top quarter, 89% in top half
Early decision deadline: 12/1, notification date: 12/31
Early action deadline: 11/1, notification date: 12/31
Application deadline (fall): 1/15
Undergraduate student body: 2,470 full time, 24 part time; 40% male, 60% female; 0% American Indian, 2% Asian, 5% black, 4% Hispanic, 2% multiracial, 0% Pacific Islander, 83% white, 1% international; 58% from in state; 91% live on campus; 0% of students in fraternities, 0% in sororities

Most popular majors: 20% Business, Management, Marketing, and Related Support Services; 14% Social Sciences; 11% Biological and Biomedical Sciences; 11% Psychology
Expenses: 2016-2017: $39,900; room/board: $15,130
Financial aid: (508) 565-1088; 69% of undergrads determined to have financial need; average aid package $30,209

Suffolk University
Boston MA
(617) 573-8460
U.S. News ranking: Nat. U., No. 188
Website: www.suffolk.edu
Admissions email: admission@suffolk.edu
Private; founded 1906
Freshman admissions: selective; 2015-2016: 8,650 applied, 7,127 accepted. Neither SAT nor ACT required. SAT 25/75 percentile: 910-1120. High school rank: 11% in top tenth, 40% in top quarter, 73% in top half
Early decision deadline: N/A, notification date: N/A
Early action deadline: 11/15, notification date: 12/15
Application deadline (fall): 2/15
Undergraduate student body: 5,232 full time, 333 part time; 46% male, 54% female; 0% American Indian, 8% Asian, 6% black, 12% Hispanic, 2% multiracial, 0% Pacific Islander, 40% white, 23% international; 68% from in state; 24% live on campus; N/A of students in fraternities, N/A in sororities
Most popular majors: 38% Business, Management, Marketing, and Related Support Services; 16% Social Sciences; 7% Psychology; 5% Visual and Performing Arts
Expenses: 2016-2017: $35,578; room/board: $14,730
Financial aid: (617) 573-8470; 58% of undergrads determined to have financial need; average aid package $25,827

Tufts University
Medford MA
(617) 627-3170
U.S. News ranking: Nat. U., No. 27
Website: www.tufts.edu
Admissions email: admissions.inquiry@ase.tufts.edu
Private; founded 1852
Freshman admissions: most selective; 2015-2016: 19,063 applied, 3,069 accepted. Either SAT or ACT required. SAT 25/75 percentile: 1370-1520. High school rank: N/A
Early decision deadline: 11/1, notification date: 12/15
Early action deadline: N/A, notification date: N/A
Application deadline (fall): 1/1
Undergraduate student body: 5,215 full time, 75 part time; 50% male, 50% female; 0% American Indian, 11% Asian, 4% black, 6% Hispanic, 4% multiracial, 0% Pacific Islander, 58% white, 9% international; 24% from in state; 65% live on campus; 18% of students in fraternities, 18% in sororities

Most popular majors: 29% Social Sciences; 9% Biological and Biomedical Sciences; 9% Engineering; 7% Multi/Interdisciplinary Studies; 7% Visual and Performing Arts
Expenses: 2016-2017: $52,430; room/board: $13,566
Financial aid: (617) 627-2000; 37% of undergrads determined to have financial need; average aid package $42,319

University of Massachusetts–Amherst
Amherst MA
(413) 545-0222
U.S. News ranking: Nat. U., No. 74
Website: www.umass.edu
Admissions email: mail@admissions.umass.edu
Public; founded 1863
Freshman admissions: more selective; 2015-2016: 40,010 applied, 23,308 accepted. Either SAT or ACT required. SAT 25/75 percentile: 1130-1310. High school rank: 32% in top tenth, 73% in top quarter, 97% in top half
Early decision deadline: N/A, notification date: N/A
Early action deadline: 11/1, notification date: 12/31
Application deadline (fall): 1/15
Undergraduate student body: 21,098 full time, 1,650 part time; 51% male, 49% female; 0% American Indian, 9% Asian, 4% black, 5% Hispanic, 3% multiracial, 0% Pacific Islander, 67% white, 4% international; 80% from in state; 58% live on campus; 8% of students in fraternities, 6% in sororities
Most popular majors: 15% Business, Management, Marketing, and Related Support Services; 10% Biological and Biomedical Sciences; 10% Social Sciences; 8% Health Professions and Related Programs; 8% Psychology
Expenses: 2015-2016: $13,790 in state, $30,123 out of state; room/board: $12,028
Financial aid: (413) 545-0801; 57% of undergrads determined to have financial need; average aid package $16,338

University of Massachusetts–Boston
Boston MA
(617) 287-6000
U.S. News ranking: Nat. U., No. 220
Website: www.umb.edu
Admissions email: enrollment.info@umb.edu
Public; founded 1964
Freshman admissions: selective; 2015-2016: 9,365 applied, 6,467 accepted. SAT required. SAT 25/75 percentile: 950-1160. High school rank: N/A
Early decision deadline: N/A, notification date: N/A
Early action deadline: 11/1, notification date: 1/31
Application deadline (fall): 3/1
Undergraduate student body: 9,384 full time, 3,565 part time; 45% male, 55% female; 0% American

Indian, 12% Asian, 16% black, 13% Hispanic, 3% multiracial, 0% Pacific Islander, 36% white, 11% international; 95% from in state; N/A live on campus; N/A of students in fraternities, N/A in sororities
Most popular majors: 18% Business, Management, Marketing, and Related Support Services; 17% Health Professions and Related Programs; 13% Psychology; 11% Social Sciences; 7% Biological and Biomedical Sciences
Expenses: 2016-2017: $13,435 in state, $32,023 out of state; room/board: N/A
Financial aid: (617) 287-6300; 66% of undergrads determined to have financial need; average aid package $15,370

University of Massachusetts–Dartmouth
North Dartmouth MA
(508) 999-8605
U.S. News ranking: Nat. U., No. 220
Website: www.umassd.edu
Admissions email: admissions@umassd.edu
Public; founded 1895
Freshman admissions: selective; 2015-2016: 7,591 applied, 5,789 accepted. Either SAT or ACT required. SAT 25/75 percentile: 920-1130. High school rank: 13% in top tenth, 38% in top quarter, 74% in top half
Early decision deadline: N/A, notification date: N/A
Early action deadline: 11/15, notification date: 12/15
Application deadline (fall): rolling
Undergraduate student body: 6,254 full time, 1,041 part time; 52% male, 48% female; 0% American Indian, 4% Asian, 14% black, 8% Hispanic, 3% multiracial, 0% Pacific Islander, 64% white, 1% international; 95% from in state; 56% live on campus; N/A of students in fraternities, N/A in sororities
Most popular majors: 27% Business, Management, and Related Support Services; 13% Engineering; 13% Health Professions and Related Programs; 9% Social Sciences; 9% Visual and Performing Arts
Expenses: 2015-2016: $12,588 in state, $19,270 out of state; room/board: $11,622
Financial aid: (508) 999-8632; 72% of undergrads determined to have financial need; average aid package $16,535

University of Massachusetts–Lowell
Lowell MA
(978) 934-3931
U.S. News ranking: Nat. U., No. 152
Website: www.uml.edu
Admissions email: admissions@uml.edu
Public; founded 1894
Freshman admissions: selective; 2015-2016: 10,638 applied, 6,020 accepted. Either SAT

or ACT required. SAT 25/75 percentile: 1070-1270. High school rank: 20% in top tenth, 49% in top quarter, 85% in top half
Early decision deadline: N/A, notification date: N/A
Early action deadline: 11/1, notification date: 12/15
Application deadline (fall): 2/1
Undergraduate student body: 9,743 full time, 3,523 part time; 62% male, 38% female; 0% American Indian, 9% Asian, 6% black, 10% Hispanic, 3% multiracial, 0% Pacific Islander, 64% white, 3% international; 91% from in state; 38% live on campus; N/A of students in fraternities, N/A in sororities
Most popular majors: 18% Business, Management, Marketing, and Related Support Services; 15% Engineering; 11% Computer and Information Sciences and Support Services; 11% Health Professions and Related Programs; 11% Homeland Security, Law Enforcement, Firefighting and Related Protective Services
Expenses: 2015-2016: $13,427 in state, $29,125 out of state; room/board: $11,670
Financial aid: (978) 934-4226; 60% of undergrads determined to have financial need; average aid package $15,497

Wellesley College
Wellesley MA
(781) 283-2270
U.S. News ranking: Nat. Lib. Arts, No. 3
Website: www.wellesley.edu
Admissions email: admission@wellesley.edu
Private; founded 1870
Freshman admissions: most selective; 2015-2016: 4,555 applied, 1,380 accepted. Either SAT or ACT required. SAT 25/75 percentile: 1290-1490. High school rank: 80% in top tenth, 95% in top quarter, 100% in top half
Early decision deadline: 11/1, notification date: 12/15
Early action deadline: N/A, notification date: N/A
Application deadline (fall): 1/15
Undergraduate student body: 2,188 full time, 168 part time; 3% male, 97% female; 0% American Indian, 23% Asian, 5% black, 11% Hispanic, 6% multiracial, N/A Pacific Islander, 39% white, 12% international; 16% from in state; 98% live on campus; N/A of students in fraternities, N/A in sororities
Most popular majors: 15% Economics, General; 11% Political Science and Government, General; 10% Research and Experimental Psychology, Other; 6% Computer and Information Sciences, General; 6% Neuroscience
Expenses: 2016-2017: $48,802; room/board: $15,114
Financial aid: (781) 283-2360; 63% of undergrads determined to have financial need; average aid package $44,218

Wentworth Institute of Technology
Boston MA
(617) 989-4000
U.S. News ranking: Reg. U. (N), No. 57
Website: www.wit.edu
Admissions email: admissions@wit.edu
Private; founded 1904
Freshman admissions: selective; 2015-2016: 6,975 applied, 4,648 accepted. Either SAT or ACT required. SAT 25/75 percentile: 1010-1210. High school rank: N/A
Early decision deadline: N/A, notification date: N/A
Early action deadline: N/A, notification date: N/A
Application deadline (fall): rolling
Undergraduate student body: 3,902 full time, 422 part time; 80% male, 20% female; 0% American Indian, 7% Asian, 4% black, 3% Hispanic, 6% multiracial, N/A Pacific Islander, 60% white, 7% international; 65% from in state; 51% live on campus; N/A of students in fraternities, N/A in sororities
Most popular majors: 25% Business, Management, Marketing, and Related Support Services; 22% Engineering Technologies and Engineering-Related Fields; 15% Engineering; 13% Computer and Information Sciences and Support Services
Expenses: 2016-2017: $31,840; room/board: $13,500
Financial aid: (617) 989-4020; 72% of undergrads determined to have financial need; average aid package $20,095

Western New England University
Springfield MA
(413) 782-1321
U.S. News ranking: Reg. U. (N), No. 67
Website: www.wne.edu
Admissions email: learn@wne.edu
Private; founded 1919
Freshman admissions: selective; 2015-2016: 6,207 applied, 5,024 accepted. Either SAT or ACT required. SAT 25/75 percentile: 960-1180. High school rank: 22% in top tenth, 47% in top quarter, 78% in top half
Early decision deadline: N/A, notification date: N/A
Early action deadline: N/A, notification date: N/A
Application deadline (fall): rolling
Undergraduate student body: 2,578 full time, 155 part time; 61% male, 39% female; 0% American Indian, 3% Asian, 6% black, 8% Hispanic, 1% multiracial, 0% Pacific Islander, 73% white, 3% international; 50% from in state; 65% live on campus; N/A of students in fraternities, N/A in sororities
Most popular majors: 27% Business, Management, Marketing, and Related Support Services; 20% Engineering; 9% Psychology; 9% Homeland Security, Law Enforcement, Firefighting and Related

Protective Services; 5% Parks, Recreation, Leisure, and Fitness Studies
Expenses: 2016-2017: $34,874; room/board: $13,214
Financial aid: (413) 796-2080; 78% of undergrads determined to have financial need; average aid package $25,170

Westfield State University
Westfield MA
(413) 572-5218
U.S. News ranking: Reg. U. (N), No. 118
Website: www.westfield.ma.edu
Admissions email: admissions@westfield.ma.edu
Public; founded 1839
Freshman admissions: less selective; 2015-2016: 5,140 applied, 4,092 accepted. Either SAT or ACT required. SAT 25/75 percentile: 910-1090. High school rank: 8% in top tenth, 25% in top quarter, 64% in top half
Early decision deadline: N/A, notification date: N/A
Early action deadline: N/A, notification date: N/A
Application deadline (fall): 3/30
Undergraduate student body: 4,963 full time, 653 part time; 46% male, 54% female; 0% American Indian, 2% Asian, 4% black, 9% Hispanic, 4% multiracial, 0% Pacific Islander, 77% white, 0% international; 93% from in state; 60% live on campus; 0% of students in fraternities, 0% in sororities
Most popular majors: 15% Liberal Arts and Sciences, General Studies and Humanities; 14% Business, Management, and Related Support Services; 13% Homeland Security, Law Enforcement, Firefighting and Related Protective Services; 10% Education; 9% Psychology
Expenses: 2016-2017: $9,275 in state, $15,355 out of state; room/board: $10,396
Financial aid: (413) 572-5218; 65% of undergrads determined to have financial need; average aid package $8,335

Wheaton College
Norton MA
(508) 286-8251
U.S. News ranking: Nat. Lib. Arts, No. 77
Website: www.wheatoncollege.edu
Admissions email: admission@wheatoncollege.edu
Private; founded 1834
Freshman admissions: more selective; 2015-2016: 4,322 applied, 2,790 accepted. Neither SAT nor ACT required. SAT 25/75 percentile: 1100-1330. High school rank: 26% in top tenth, 60% in top quarter, 89% in top half
Early decision deadline: 11/15, notification date: 12/15
Early action deadline: 11/15, notification date: 1/15
Application deadline (fall): 1/15
Undergraduate student body: 1,567 full time, 31 part time; 36% male, 64% female; 0% American Indian, 5% Asian, 6% black,

7% Hispanic, 3% multiracial, 0% Pacific Islander, 67% white, 10% international; 37% from in state; 95% live on campus; 0% of students in fraternities, 0% in sororities
Most popular majors: 22% Social Sciences; 13% Biological and Biomedical Sciences; 12% Psychology; 12% Visual and Performing Arts
Expenses: 2016-2017: $49,012; room/board: $12,500
Financial aid: (508) 286-8232; 64% of undergrads determined to have financial need; average aid package $38,407

Wheelock College
Boston MA
(617) 879-2206
U.S. News ranking: Reg. U. (N), No. 85
Website: www.wheelock.edu
Admissions email: undergrad@wheelock.edu
Private; founded 1888
Freshman admissions: less selective; 2015-2016: 1,331 applied, 1,270 accepted. Either SAT or ACT required. SAT 25/75 percentile: 810-1062. High school rank: 11% in top tenth, 33% in top quarter, 57% in top half
Early decision deadline: N/A, notification date: N/A
Early action deadline: 12/1, notification date: 12/20
Application deadline (fall): 5/1
Undergraduate student body: 797 full time, 14 part time; 16% male, 84% female; N/A American Indian, 4% Asian, 13% black, 11% Hispanic, 3% multiracial, 0% Pacific Islander, 60% white, 2% international; 61% from in state; 64% live on campus; 0% of students in fraternities, 0% in sororities
Most popular majors: 17% Counseling Psychology; 16% Developmental and Child Psychology; 11% Social Work; 9% Human Development and Family Studies, General
Expenses: 2015-2016: $33,835; room/board: $14,000
Financial aid: (617) 879-2206

Williams College
Williamstown MA
(413) 597-2211
U.S. News ranking: Nat. Lib. Arts, No. 1
Website: www.williams.edu
Admissions email: admission@williams.edu
Private; founded 1793
Freshman admissions: most selective; 2015-2016: 6,883 applied, 1,212 accepted. Either SAT or ACT required. SAT 25/75 percentile: 1330-1550. High school rank: 93% in top tenth, 98% in top quarter, 100% in top half
Early decision deadline: 11/15, notification date: 12/15
Early action deadline: N/A, notification date: N/A
Application deadline (fall): 1/1
Undergraduate student body: 2,065 full time, 34 part time; 49% male, 51% female; 0% American Indian, 12% Asian, 8% black, 13% Hispanic, 6% multiracial, 0% Pacific Islander, 54% white,

8% international; 13% from in state; 93% live on campus; 0% of students in fraternities, 0% in sororities
Most popular majors: 17% Economics, General; 13% English Language and Literature, General; 12% History, General; 12% Psychology, General; 11% Biology/Biological Sciences, General
Expenses: 2016-2017: $51,790; room/board: $13,690
Financial aid: (413) 597-4181; 49% of undergrads determined to have financial need; average aid package $50,057

Worcester Polytechnic Institute
Worcester MA
(508) 831-5286
U.S. News ranking: Nat. U., No. 60
Website: admissions.wpi.edu
Admissions email: admissions@wpi.edu
Private; founded 1865
Freshman admissions: more selective; 2015-2016: 10,172 applied, 4,938 accepted. Neither SAT nor ACT required. SAT 25/75 percentile: 1210-1420. High school rank: 65% in top tenth, 91% in top quarter, 98% in top half
Early decision deadline: N/A, notification date: N/A
Early action deadline: 1/1, notification date: 2/10
Application deadline (fall): 2/1
Undergraduate student body: 4,158 full time, 141 part time; 67% male, 33% female; 0% American Indian, 5% Asian, 2% black, 8% Hispanic, 3% multiracial, 0% Pacific Islander, 63% white, 12% international; 43% from in state; 49% live on campus; 31% of students in fraternities, 49% in sororities
Most popular majors: 19% Mechanical Engineering; 11% Bioengineering and Biomedical Engineering; 11% Chemical Engineering; 11% Computer Science; 9% Electrical and Electronics Engineering
Expenses: 2016-2017: $46,994; room/board: $13,736
Financial aid: (508) 831-5469; 64% of undergrads determined to have financial need; average aid package $35,920

Worcester State University
Worcester MA
(508) 929-8040
U.S. News ranking: Reg. U. (N), No. 118
Website: www.worcester.edu
Admissions email: admissions@worcester.edu
Public; founded 1874
Freshman admissions: selective; 2015-2016: 3,703 applied, 2,539 accepted. Either SAT or ACT required. SAT 25/75 percentile: 925-1110. High school rank: N/A
Early decision deadline: N/A, notification date: N/A
Early action deadline: 11/15, notification date: 12/15

Application deadline (fall): 3/1
Undergraduate student body: 4,117 full time, 1,397 part time; 41% male, 59% female; 0% American Indian, 4% Asian, 8% black, 9% Hispanic, 3% multiracial, 0% Pacific Islander, 71% white, 1% international; 96% from in state; 30% live on campus; N/A of students in fraternities, N/A in sororities
Most popular majors: 21% Health Professions and Related Programs; 17% Business, Management, Marketing, and Related Support Services; 12% Psychology; 8% Biological and Biomedical Sciences; 8% Homeland Security, Law Enforcement, Firefighting and Related Protective Services
Expenses: 2015-2016: $8,857 in state, $14,937 out of state; room/board: $11,560
Financial aid: (508) 929-8056; 63% of undergrads determined to have financial need; average aid package $12,444

MICHIGAN

Adrian College
Adrian MI
(800) 877-2246
U.S. News ranking: Reg. Coll. (Mid. W), No. 15
Website: www.adrian.edu
Admissions email: admissions@adrian.edu
Private; founded 1859
Affiliation: The United Methodist Church
Freshman admissions: selective; 2015-2016: 5,294 applied, 3,231 accepted. Either SAT or ACT required. ACT 25/75 percentile: 19-24. High school rank: 28% in top tenth, 60% in top quarter, 84% in top half
Early decision deadline: N/A, notification date: N/A
Early action deadline: N/A, notification date: N/A
Application deadline (fall): rolling
Undergraduate student body: 1,609 full time, 78 part time; 53% male, 47% female; 0% American Indian, 0% Asian, 9% black, 5% Hispanic, 4% multiracial, 0% Pacific Islander, 72% white, 0% international; 78% from in state; 88% live on campus; 19% of students in fraternities, 19% in sororities
Most popular majors: 21% Business, Management, Marketing, and Related Support Services; 13% Parks, Recreation, Leisure, and Fitness Studies; 11% Biological and Biomedical Sciences; 11% Visual and Performing Arts; 8% Homeland Security, Law Enforcement, Firefighting and Related Protective Services
Expenses: 2016-2017: $34,890; room/board: $10,740
Financial aid: (517) 264-3107; 86% of undergrads determined to have financial need; average aid package $27,456

Albion College

Albion MI
(800) 858-6770
U.S. News ranking: Nat. Lib. Arts,
No. 122
Website: www.albion.edu/
Admissions email:
admission@albion.edu
Private; founded 1835
Affiliation: United Methodist
Freshman admissions: selective;
2015-2016: 2,803 applied,
2,227 accepted. Either SAT
or ACT required. ACT 25/75
percentile: 22-27. High school
rank: N/A
Early decision deadline: N/A,
notification date: N/A
Early action deadline: 12/1,
notification date: 1/15
Application deadline (fall): rolling
Undergraduate student body: 1,359
full time, 17 part time; 50%
male, 50% female; 0% American
Indian, 2% Asian, 6% black, 5%
Hispanic, 3% multiracial, 0%
Pacific Islander, 77% white, 3%
international; 88% from in state;
90% live on campus; 37% of
students in fraternities, 30% in
sororities
Most popular majors: 14% Biology/
Biological Sciences, General;
10% Psychology, General;
8% Economics, General; 6%
Business Administration and
Management, General; 5%
Kinesiology and Exercise Science
Expenses: 2016-2017: $41,040;
room/board: $11,610
Financial aid: (517) 629-0440;
74% of undergrads determined
to have financial need; average
aid package $32,521

Alma College

Alma MI
(800) 321-2562
U.S. News ranking: Nat. Lib. Arts,
No. 146
Website: www.alma.edu
Admissions email:
admissions@alma.edu
Private; founded 1886
Affiliation: Presbyterian
Freshman admissions: selective;
2015-2016: 2,479 applied,
1,675 accepted. Either SAT
or ACT required. ACT 25/75
percentile: 21-27. High school
rank: 22% in top tenth, 50% in
top quarter, 81% in top half
Early decision deadline: N/A,
notification date: N/A
Early action deadline: N/A,
notification date: N/A
Application deadline (fall): rolling
Undergraduate student body: 1,335
full time, 50 part time; 43%
male, 57% female; 0% American
Indian, 1% Asian, 4% black, 4%
Hispanic, 2% multiracial, 0%
Pacific Islander, 83% white, 1%
international; 92% from in state;
88% live on campus; 24% of
students in fraternities, 25% in
sororities
Most popular majors: 16%
Health Professions and Related
Programs; 15% Business,
Management, Marketing, and
Related Support Services; 10%
Biological and Biomedical
Sciences; 9% Psychology; 8%
Visual and Performing Arts
Expenses: 2016-2017: $37,310;
room/board: $10,238

Financial aid: (989) 463-7347;
83% of undergrads determined
to have financial need; average
aid package $24,758

Andrews University

Berrien Springs MI
(800) 253-2874
U.S. News ranking: Nat. U.,
No. 183
Website: www.andrews.edu
Admissions email:
enroll@andrews.edu
Private; founded 1874
Affiliation: Seventh-day Adventist
Freshman admissions: more
selective; 2015-2016: 2,201
applied, 863 accepted. Either
SAT or ACT required. ACT 25/75
percentile: 20-27. High school
rank: 17% in top tenth, 40% in
top quarter, 76% in top half
Early decision deadline: N/A,
notification date: N/A
Early action deadline: N/A,
notification date: N/A
Application deadline (fall): rolling
Undergraduate student body: 1,415
full time, 318 part time; 44%
male, 56% female; 0% American
Indian, 15% Asian, 19% black,
14% Hispanic, 2% multiracial,
0% Pacific Islander, 29% white,
18% international; 36% from in
state; 60% live on campus; N/A
of students in fraternities, N/A in
sororities
Most popular majors: 21%
Health Professions and Related
Programs; 10% Biological
and Biomedical Sciences;
10% Business, Management,
Marketing, and Related Support
Services; 6% Visual and
Performing Arts; 5% Foreign
Languages, Literatures, and
Linguistics
Expenses: 2016-2017: $27,684;
room/board: $8,742
Financial aid: (269) 471-3334;
61% of undergrads determined
to have financial need; average
aid package $28,271

Aquinas College

Grand Rapids MI
(616) 732-4460
U.S. News ranking: Reg. U.
(Mid. W), No. 56
Website: www.aquinas.edu
Admissions email: admissions@
aquinas.edu
Private; founded 1886
Affiliation: Roman Catholic
Freshman admissions: selective;
2015-2016: 2,635 applied,
1,908 accepted. Either SAT
or ACT required. ACT 25/75
percentile: 21-26. High school
rank: N/A
Early decision deadline: N/A,
notification date: N/A
Early action deadline: N/A,
notification date: N/A
Application deadline (fall): rolling
Undergraduate student body: 1,537
full time, 250 part time; 40%
male, 60% female; 0% American
Indian, 1% Asian, 3% black,
6% Hispanic, 3% multiracial,
0% Pacific Islander, 82% white,
1% international; 94% from in
state; 51% live on campus; N/A
of students in fraternities, N/A in
sororities

Most popular majors: 17%
Business, Management,
Marketing, and Related Support
Services; 9% Education; 8%
Psychology; 8% Social Sciences;
7% Biological and Biomedical
Sciences
Expenses: 2016-2017: $30,062;
room/board: $8,814
Financial aid: (616) 632-2893;
80% of undergrads determined
to have financial need; average
aid package $22,169

Baker College of Flint[1]

Flint MI
(810) 766-4000
U.S. News ranking: Reg. Coll.
(Mid. W), unranked
Website: www.baker.edu
Admissions email:
troy.crowe@baker.edu
Private
Application deadline (fall): N/A
Undergraduate student body: N/A
full time, N/A part time
Expenses: 2015-2016: $8,640;
room/board: $5,400
Financial aid: (810) 766-4202

Calvin College

Grand Rapids MI
(616) 526-6106
U.S. News ranking: Reg. Coll.
(Mid. W), No. 1
Website: www.calvin.edu
Admissions email:
admissions@calvin.edu
Private; founded 1876
Affiliation: Christian Reformed
Freshman admissions: more
selective; 2015-2016: 3,824
applied, 2,840 accepted. Either
SAT or ACT required. ACT 25/75
percentile: 23-30. High school
rank: 28% in top tenth, 56% in
top quarter, 82% in top half
Early decision deadline: N/A,
notification date: N/A
Early action deadline: N/A,
notification date: N/A
Application deadline (fall): 8/15
Undergraduate student body: 3,713
full time, 156 part time; 45%
male, 55% female; 0% American
Indian, 4% Asian, 3% black,
4% Hispanic, 4% multiracial,
0% Pacific Islander, 74% white,
10% international; 56% from in
state; 59% live on campus; 0%
of students in fraternities, 0% in
sororities
Most popular majors: 8% Business
Administration and Management,
General; 8% Engineering,
General; 6% Registered
Nursing/Registered Nurse; 5%
Psychology, General; 4% Biology/
Biological Sciences, General
Expenses: 2016-2017: $31,730;
room/board: $9,840
Financial aid: (616) 526-6137;
63% of undergrads determined
to have financial need; average
aid package $23,099

Central Michigan University

Mount Pleasant MI
(989) 774-3076
U.S. News ranking: Nat. U.,
No. 202
Website: www.cmich.edu
Admissions email:
cmuadmit@cmich.edu
Public; founded 1892

Freshman admissions: selective;
2015-2016: 18,269 applied,
12,674 accepted. Either SAT
or ACT required. ACT 25/75
percentile: 20-24. High school
rank: 17% in top tenth, 40% in
top quarter, 75% in top half
Early decision deadline: N/A,
notification date: N/A
Early action deadline: N/A,
notification date: N/A
Application deadline (fall): 7/1
Undergraduate student body:
17,709 full time, 2,789 part
time; 44% male, 56% female;
1% American Indian, 1% Asian,
8% black, 4% Hispanic, 3%
multiracial, 0% Pacific Islander,
79% white, 2% international;
95% from in state; 36% live
on campus; 7% of students in
fraternities, 8% in sororities
Most popular majors: 24%
Business, Management,
Marketing, and Related Support
Services; 11% Education;
8% Psychology; 8% Parks,
Recreation, Leisure, and Fitness
Studies
Expenses: 2016-2017: $12,150
in state, $23,670 out of state;
room/board: $9,406
Financial aid: (989) 774-3674;
58% of undergrads determined
to have financial need; average
aid package $13,496

Cleary University

Ann Arbor MI
(734) 332-4477
U.S. News ranking: Business,
unranked
Website: www.cleary.edu
Admissions email:
admissions@cleary.edu
Private; founded 1883
Freshman admissions: N/A;
2015-2016: 123 applied, 85
accepted. Either SAT or ACT
required. SAT 25/75 percentile:
N/A. High school rank: N/A
Early decision deadline: N/A,
notification date: N/A
Early action deadline: N/A,
notification date: N/A
Application deadline (fall): N/A
Undergraduate student body: 206
full time, 249 part time; 49%
male, 51% female; 0% American
Indian, 1% Asian, 6% black, 3%
Hispanic, N/A multiracial, N/A
Pacific Islander, 79% white, 2%
international
Most popular majors: Information
not available
Expenses: 2016-2017: $17,500;
room/board: $9,600
Financial aid: (800) 686-1883

College for Creative Studies[1]

Detroit MI
(313) 664-7425
U.S. News ranking: Arts, unranked
Website: www.
collegeforcreativestudies.edu
Admissions email: admissions@
collegeforcreativestudies.edu
Private; founded 1906
Application deadline (fall): 7/1
Undergraduate student body: N/A
full time, N/A part time
Expenses: 2015-2016: $38,950;
room/board: N/A
Financial aid: (313) 664-7495

Cornerstone University

Grand Rapids MI
(616) 222-1426
U.S. News ranking: Reg. U.
(Mid. W), No. 79
Website: www.cornerstone.edu
Admissions email: admissions@
cornerstone.edu
Private; founded 1941
Affiliation: Protestant
Freshman admissions: selective;
2015-2016: 2,618 applied,
1,910 accepted. Either SAT
or ACT required. ACT 25/75
percentile: 20-25. High school
rank: 13% in top tenth, 37% in
top quarter, 73% in top half
Early decision deadline: N/A,
notification date: N/A
Early action deadline: N/A,
notification date: N/A
Application deadline (fall): rolling
Undergraduate student body: 1,486
full time, 539 part time; 39%
male, 61% female; 1% American
Indian, 1% Asian, 14% black,
4% Hispanic, 1% multiracial,
0% Pacific Islander, 77% white,
2% international; 76% from in
state; 60% live on campus; 0%
of students in fraternities, 0% in
sororities
Most popular majors: 44%
Business, Management,
Marketing, and Related Support
Services; 13% Psychology; 9%
Education; 8% Theology and
Religious Vocations
Expenses: 2016-2017: $26,860;
room/board: $8,810
Financial aid: (616) 222-1424;
82% of undergrads determined
to have financial need; average
aid package $20,646

Davenport University

Grand Rapids MI
(866) 925-3884
U.S. News ranking: Reg. U.
(Mid. W), second tier
Website: www.davenport.edu
Admissions email: Davenport.
Admissions@davenport.edu
Private; founded 1866
Freshman admissions: less
selective; 2015-2016: 2,216
applied, 1,978 accepted. Neither
SAT nor ACT required. ACT
25/75 percentile: 19-24. High
school rank: N/A
Early decision deadline: N/A,
notification date: N/A
Early action deadline: N/A,
notification date: N/A
Application deadline (fall): rolling
Undergraduate student body: 2,339
full time, 4,002 part time; 41%
male, 59% female; 0% American
Indian, 2% Asian, 13% black,
1% Hispanic, 3% multiracial,
0% Pacific Islander, 66% white,
2% international
Most popular majors: 19%
Business Administration and
Management, General; 11%
Business/Commerce, General;
10% Health Information/Medical
Records Technology/Technician;
8% Registered Nursing/
Registered Nurse; 7% Accounting
Expenses: 2016-2017: $19,775;
room/board: $9,132
Financial aid: (616) 451-3511

Eastern Michigan University
Ypsilanti MI
(734) 487-3060
U.S. News ranking: Nat. U., second tier
Website: www.emich.edu/
Admissions email: undergraduate.admissions@emich.edu
Public; founded 1849
Freshman admissions: selective; 2015-2016: 14,228 applied, 10,639 accepted. Either SAT or ACT required. ACT 25/75 percentile: 19-25. High school rank: 13% in top tenth, 39% in top quarter, 76% in top half
Early decision deadline: N/A, notification date: N/A
Early action deadline: N/A, notification date: N/A
Application deadline (fall): rolling
Undergraduate student body: 13,071 full time, 4,709 part time; 41% male, 59% female; 0% American Indian, 2% Asian, 20% black, 5% Hispanic, 4% multiracial, 0% Pacific Islander, 65% white, 2% international; 90% from in state; 22% live on campus; N/A of students in fraternities, N/A in sororities
Most popular majors: 20% Business, Management, Marketing, and Related Support Services; 15% Health Professions and Related Programs; 12% Education; 7% Multi/ Interdisciplinary Studies; 7% Social Sciences
Expenses: 2016-2017: $10,704 in state, $28,524 out of state; room/board: $9,592
Financial aid: (734) 487-0455; 70% of undergrads determined to have financial need; average aid package $9,435

Ferris State University
Big Rapids MI
(231) 591-2100
U.S. News ranking: Reg. U. (Mid. W), No. 74
Website: www.ferris.edu
Admissions email: admissions@ferris.edu
Public; founded 1884
Freshman admissions: selective; 2015-2016: 10,299 applied, 8,052 accepted. Either SAT or ACT required. ACT 25/75 percentile: 19-24. High school rank: N/A
Early decision deadline: N/A, notification date: N/A
Early action deadline: N/A, notification date: N/A
Application deadline (fall): 8/1
Undergraduate student body: 9,103 full time, 4,220 part time; 48% male, 52% female; 1% American Indian, 2% Asian, 8% black, 4% Hispanic, 3% multiracial, 0% Pacific Islander, 79% white, 1% international; 94% from in state; 26% live on campus; 4% of students in fraternities, 4% in sororities
Most popular majors: 19% Criminal Justice/Police Science; 9% Registered Nursing/ Registered Nurse; 8% Business Administration and Management, General; 5% Pharmacy; 4% Health/Health Care Administration/Management

Expenses: 2016-2017: $11,290 in state, $18,048 out of state; room/board: $9,652
Financial aid: (231) 591-2110; 71% of undergrads determined to have financial need; average aid package $11,330

Finlandia University[1]
Hancock MI
(906) 487-7274
U.S. News ranking: Reg. Coll. (Mid. W), second tier
Website: www.finlandia.edu
Admissions email: N/A
Private
Application deadline (fall): N/A
Undergraduate student body: N/A full time, N/A part time
Expenses: 2015-2016: $22,110; room/board: $7,648
Financial aid: (906) 487-7240

Grace Bible College
Grand Rapids MI
(616) 538-2330
U.S. News ranking: Reg. Coll. (Mid. W), second tier
Website: www.gbcol.edu
Admissions email: enrollment@gbcol.edu
Private; founded 1939
Affiliation: Grace Gospel Fellowship
Freshman admissions: selective; 2015-2016: 881 applied, 398 accepted. Either SAT or ACT required. ACT 25/75 percentile: 19-23. High school rank: 4% in top tenth, 30% in top quarter, 47% in top half
Early decision deadline: N/A, notification date: N/A
Early action deadline: N/A, notification date: N/A
Application deadline (fall): rolling
Undergraduate student body: 774 full time, 51 part time; 48% male, 52% female; 1% American Indian, 0% Asian, 21% black, 5% Hispanic, 5% multiracial, 3% Pacific Islander, 61% white, 0% international; 31% from in state; 16% live on campus; N/A of students in fraternities, N/A in sororities
Most popular majors: 34% Bible/Biblical Studies; 23% Music, Other; 21% Public Administration and Social Service Professions; 16% Religious Education; 6% Multi-/ Interdisciplinary Studies, Other
Expenses: 2015-2016: $12,268; room/board: $7,400
Financial aid: (800) 968-1887

Grand Valley State University
Allendale MI
(800) 748-0246
U.S. News ranking: Reg. U. (Mid. W), No. 27
Website: www.gvsu.edu
Admissions email: admissions@gvsu.edu
Public; founded 1960
Freshman admissions: selective; 2015-2016: 16,987 applied, 13,784 accepted. Either SAT or ACT required. ACT 25/75 percentile: 21-26. High school rank: 17% in top tenth, 46% in top quarter, 85% in top half
Early decision deadline: N/A, notification date: N/A

Early action deadline: N/A, notification date: N/A
Application deadline (fall): 5/1
Undergraduate student body: 19,377 full time, 2,595 part time; 41% male, 59% female; 0% American Indian, 2% Asian, 5% black, 5% Hispanic, 3% multiracial, 0% Pacific Islander, 83% white, 1% international; 94% from in state; 28% live on campus; N/A of students in fraternities, N/A in sororities
Most popular majors: 19% Business, Management, Marketing, and Related Support Services; 18% Health Professions and Related Programs; 8% Education; 7% Psychology; 5% Social Sciences
Expenses: 2015-2016: $11,363 in state, $16,044 out of state; room/board: $8,360
Financial aid: (616) 331-3234; 59% of undergrads determined to have financial need; average aid package $9,534

Hillsdale College
Hillsdale MI
(517) 607-2327
U.S. News ranking: Nat. Lib. Arts, No. 83
Website: www.hillsdale.edu
Admissions email: admissions@hillsdale.edu
Private; founded 1844
Affiliation: Christian
Freshman admissions: more selective; 2015-2016: 1,859 applied, 930 accepted. Either SAT or ACT required. ACT 25/75 percentile: 27-31. High school rank: N/A
Early decision deadline: 11/1, notification date: 12/1
Early action deadline: N/A, notification date: N/A
Application deadline (fall): 4/1
Undergraduate student body: 1,451 full time, 39 part time; 49% male, 51% female; N/A American Indian, N/A Asian, N/A black, N/A Hispanic, N/A multiracial, N/A Pacific Islander, N/A white, 1% international; 35% from in state; 71% live on campus; 26% of students in fraternities, 36% in sororities
Most popular majors: 14% History, General; 13% English Language and Literature, General; 10% Economics, General; 9% Political Science and Government, General; 8% Finance, General
Expenses: 2016-2017: $25,522; room/board: $10,200
Financial aid: (517) 607-2350; 55% of undergrads determined to have financial need; average aid package $16,833

Hope College
Holland MI
(616) 395-7850
U.S. News ranking: Nat. Lib. Arts, No. 108
Website: www.hope.edu
Admissions email: admissions@hope.edu
Private; founded 1866
Affiliation: Reformed Church in America
Freshman admissions: more selective; 2015-2016: 4,420 applied, 3,184 accepted. Either SAT or ACT required. ACT 25/75 percentile: 24-29. High school

rank: 34% in top tenth, 65% in top quarter, 92% in top half
Early decision deadline: N/A, notification date: N/A
Early action deadline: N/A, notification date: N/A
Application deadline (fall): rolling
Undergraduate student body: 3,216 full time, 160 part time; 40% male, 60% female; 0% American Indian, 2% Asian, 3% black, 8% Hispanic, 2% multiracial, 0% Pacific Islander, 84% white, 1% international; 68% from in state; 77% live on campus; 10% of students in fraternities, 10% in sororities
Most popular majors: 12% Education, General; 12% Business Administration and Management, General; 9% Psychology, General; 8% Biology/ Biological Sciences, General; 7% Behavioral Sciences
Expenses: 2016-2017: $31,560; room/board: $9,690
Financial aid: (616) 395-7765; 57% of undergrads determined to have financial need; average aid package $24,744

Jackson College[1]
Jackson MI
(517) 796-8571
U.S. News ranking: Reg. Coll. (Mid. W), unranked
Website: www.jccmi.edu/
Admissions email: N/A
Public
Application deadline (fall): N/A
Undergraduate student body: N/A full time, N/A part time
Expenses: 2015-2016: $5,040 in state, $6,912 out of state; room/ board: $8,000
Financial aid: N/A

Kalamazoo College
Kalamazoo MI
(800) 253-3602
U.S. News ranking: Nat. Lib. Arts, No. 68
Website: www.kzoo.edu
Admissions email: admission@kzoo.edu
Private; founded 1833
Freshman admissions: more selective; 2015-2016: 2,455 applied, 1,759 accepted. Neither SAT nor ACT required. ACT 25/75 percentile: 26-30. High school rank: 40% in top tenth, 79% in top quarter, 97% in top half
Early decision deadline: 11/1, notification date: 12/1
Early action deadline: 11/1, notification date: 12/20
Application deadline (fall): 1/15
Undergraduate student body: 1,434 full time, 9 part time; 44% male, 56% female; 0% American Indian, 7% Asian, 6% black, 10% Hispanic, 5% multiracial, 0% Pacific Islander, 60% white, 7% international; 66% from in state; 66% live on campus; 0% of students in fraternities, 0% in sororities
Most popular majors: 19% Social Sciences; 13% Biological and Biomedical Sciences; 12% Psychology; 11% Business, Management, Marketing, and Related Support Services; 8% Physical Sciences
Expenses: 2016-2017: $44,757; room/board: $9,174

Financial aid: (269) 337-7192; 68% of undergrads determined to have financial need; average aid package $35,822

Kettering University
Flint MI
(800) 955-4464
U.S. News ranking: Reg. U. (Mid. W), No. 31
Website: www.kettering.edu
Admissions email: admissions@kettering.edu
Private; founded 1919
Freshman admissions: more selective; 2015-2016: 2,478 applied, 1,737 accepted. Either SAT or ACT required. ACT 25/75 percentile: 24-29. High school rank: 32% in top tenth, 65% in top quarter, 93% in top half
Early decision deadline: N/A, notification date: N/A
Early action deadline: 11/15, notification date: 12/15
Application deadline (fall): rolling
Undergraduate student body: 1,760 full time, 81 part time; 81% male, 19% female; 0% American Indian, 4% Asian, 4% black, 4% Hispanic, 3% multiracial, 0% Pacific Islander, 76% white, 5% international; 83% from in state; 35% live on campus; 34% of students in fraternities, 31% in sororities
Most popular majors: 84% Engineering; 8% Computer and Information Sciences and Support Services; 4% Business, Management, Marketing, and Related Support Services; 2% Biological and Biomedical Sciences; 2% Physical Sciences
Expenses: 2016-2017: $39,790; room/board: $7,780
Financial aid: (810) 762-7859; 75% of undergrads determined to have financial need; average aid package $21,047

Kuyper College[1]
Grand Rapids MI
(800) 511-3749
U.S. News ranking: Reg. Coll. (Mid. W), No. 60
Website: www.kuyper.edu
Admissions email: admissions@kuyper.edu
Private
Application deadline (fall): N/A
Undergraduate student body: N/A full time, N/A part time
Expenses: 2015-2016: $19,544; room/board: $7,260
Financial aid: (616) 222-3000

Lake Superior State University
Sault Ste. Marie MI
(906) 635-2231
U.S. News ranking: Reg. Coll. (Mid. W), No. 53
Website: www.lssu.edu
Admissions email: admissions@lssu.edu
Public; founded 1946
Freshman admissions: selective; 2015-2016: 1,587 applied, 1,459 accepted. Neither SAT nor ACT required. ACT 25/75 percentile: 19-24. High school rank: 12% in top tenth, 35% in top quarter, 68% in top half
Early decision deadline: N/A, notification date: N/A

Early action deadline: N/A, notification date: N/A
Application deadline (fall): rolling
Undergraduate student body: 1,807 full time, 442 part time; 49% male, 51% female; 8% American Indian, 1% Asian, 1% black, 2% Hispanic, 1% multiracial, 0% Pacific Islander, 80% white, 7% international; 94% from in state; 40% live on campus; N/A of students in fraternities, N/A in sororities
Most popular majors: 23% Homeland Security, Law Enforcement, Firefighting and Related Protective Services; 17% Business, Management, Marketing, and Related Support Services; 11% Health Professions and Related Programs; 7% Parks, Recreation, Leisure, and Fitness Studies; 5% Biological and Biomedical Sciences
Expenses: 2015-2016: $10,580 in state, $15,788 out of state; room/board: $9,290
Financial aid: (906) 635-2678

Lawrence Technological University
Southfield MI
(248) 204-3160
U.S. News ranking: Reg. U. (Mid. W), No. 40
Website: www.ltu.edu
Admissions email: admissions@ltu.edu
Private; founded 1932
Freshman admissions: more selective; 2015-2016: 2,147 applied, 1,187 accepted. Either SAT or ACT required. ACT 25/75 percentile: 22-29. High school rank: 24% in top tenth, 50% in top quarter, 82% in top half
Early decision deadline: N/A, notification date: N/A
Early action deadline: N/A, notification date: N/A
Application deadline (fall): rolling
Undergraduate student body: 1,657 full time, 1,122 part time; 78% male, 22% female; 0% American Indian, 2% Asian, 7% black, 4% Hispanic, 2% multiracial, 0% Pacific Islander, 64% white, 17% international; 95% from in state; 26% live on campus; 8% of students in fraternities, 17% in sororities
Most popular majors: 30% Engineering, General; 9% Business Administration and Management, General; 9% Computer Science; 7% Engineering Technologies and Engineering-Related Fields
Expenses: 2016-2017: $31,140; room/board: $10,107
Financial aid: (248) 204-2280; 61% of undergrads determined to have financial need; average aid package $24,348

Madonna University
Livonia MI
(734) 432-5339
U.S. News ranking: Reg. U. (Mid. W), No. 86
Website: www.madonna.edu
Admissions email: admissions@madonna.edu
Private; founded 1947
Affiliation: Roman Catholic

Freshman admissions: selective; 2015-2016: 972 applied, 582 accepted. Either SAT or ACT required. ACT 25/75 percentile: 20-24. High school rank: 19% in top tenth, 43% in top quarter, 77% in top half
Early decision deadline: N/A, notification date: N/A
Early action deadline: 11/1, notification date: N/A
Application deadline (fall): N/A
Undergraduate student body: 1,456 full time, 1,431 part time; 32% male, 68% female; 0% American Indian, 1% Asian, 12% black, 4% Hispanic, 2% multiracial, 0% Pacific Islander, 63% white, 17% international; 99% from in state; 8% live on campus; N/A of students in fraternities, N/A in sororities
Most popular majors: 24% Health Professions and Related Programs; 20% Homeland Security, Law Enforcement, Firefighting and Related Protective Services; 19% Business, Management, Marketing, and Related Support Services; 5% Education; 4% Public Administration and Social Service Professions
Expenses: 2016-2017: $19,500; room/board: $9,550
Financial aid: (734) 432-5662; 70% of undergrads determined to have financial need; average aid package $11,514

Marygrove College[1]
Detroit MI
(313) 927-1240
U.S. News ranking: Reg. U. (Mid. W), second tier
Website: www.marygrove.edu
Admissions email: info@marygrove.edu
Private
Affiliation: Roman Catholic
Application deadline (fall): rolling
Undergraduate student body: N/A full time, N/A part time
Expenses: 2015-2016: $20,930; room/board: $7,100
Financial aid: (313) 927-1692

Michigan State University
East Lansing MI
(517) 355-8332
U.S. News ranking: Nat. U., No. 82
Website: www.msu.edu/
Admissions email: admis@msu.edu
Public; founded 1855
Freshman admissions: more selective; 2015-2016: 35,300 applied, 23,397 accepted. Either SAT or ACT required. ACT 25/75 percentile: 23-28. High school rank: 31% in top tenth, 67% in top quarter, 95% in top half
Early decision deadline: N/A, notification date: N/A
Early action deadline: 10/17, notification date: 11/20
Application deadline (fall): rolling
Undergraduate student body: 35,645 full time, 3,498 part time; 50% male, 50% female; 0% American Indian, 5% Asian, 7% black, 4% Hispanic, 3% multiracial, 0% Pacific Islander, 67% white, 13% international; 88% from in state; 39% live

on campus; 8% of students in fraternities, 7% in sororities
Most popular majors: 18% Business, Management, Marketing, and Related Support Services; 11% Social Sciences; 10% Biological and Biomedical Sciences; 6% Engineering
Expenses: 2016-2017: $14,070 in state, $39,090 out of state; room/board: $9,734
Financial aid: (517) 353-5940; 48% of undergrads determined to have financial need; average aid package $12,914

Michigan Technological University
Houghton MI
(906) 487-2335
U.S. News ranking: Nat. U., No. 118
Website: www.mtu.edu
Admissions email: mtu4u@mtu.edu
Public; founded 1885
Freshman admissions: more selective; 2015-2016: 5,386 applied, 4,063 accepted. Either SAT or ACT required. ACT 25/75 percentile: 24-29. High school rank: 28% in top tenth, 62% in top quarter, 92% in top half
Early decision deadline: N/A, notification date: N/A
Early action deadline: N/A, notification date: N/A
Application deadline (fall): rolling
Undergraduate student body: 5,352 full time, 369 part time; 73% male, 27% female; 0% American Indian, 1% Asian, 1% black, 2% Hispanic, 3% multiracial, 0% Pacific Islander, 86% white, 4% international; 77% from in state; 47% live on campus; 8% of students in fraternities, 14% in sororities
Most popular majors: 57% Engineering; 7% Business, Management, Marketing, and Related Support Services; 7% Computer and Information Sciences and Support Services; 4% Engineering Technologies and Engineering-Related Fields
Expenses: 2016-2017: $14,634 in state, $30,968 out of state; room/board: $10,105
Financial aid: (906) 487-2622; 64% of undergrads determined to have financial need; average aid package $14,294

Northern Michigan University
Marquette MI
(906) 227-2650
U.S. News ranking: Reg. U. (Mid. W), No. 79
Website: www.nmu.edu
Admissions email: admiss@nmu.edu
Public; founded 1899
Freshman admissions: selective; 2015-2016: 5,827 applied, 4,067 accepted. Either SAT or ACT required. ACT 25/75 percentile: 19-24. High school rank: N/A
Early decision deadline: N/A, notification date: N/A
Early action deadline: N/A, notification date: N/A
Application deadline (fall): rolling

Undergraduate student body: 6,664 full time, 764 part time; 45% male, 55% female; 2% American Indian, 1% Asian, 2% black, 3% Hispanic, 3% multiracial, 0% Pacific Islander, 85% white, 1% international
Most popular majors: 14% Health Professions and Related Programs; 13% Business, Management, Marketing, and Related Support Services; 11% Biological and Biomedical Sciences; 9% Visual and Performing Arts; 7% Education
Expenses: 2016-2017: $9,620 in state, $15,020 out of state; room/board: $9,286
Financial aid: (906) 227-2327; 69% of undergrads determined to have financial need; average aid package $9,689

Northwestern Michigan College[1]
Traverse City MI
(855) 346-3662
U.S. News ranking: Reg. Coll. (Mid. W), unranked
Website: www.nmc.edu/
Admissions email: N/A
Public
Application deadline (fall): N/A
Undergraduate student body: N/A full time, N/A part time
Expenses: 2015-2016: $6,163 in state, $7,902 out of state; room/board: $9,325
Financial aid: N/A

Northwood University
Midland MI
(989) 837-4273
U.S. News ranking: Business, unranked
Website: www.northwood.edu
Admissions email: miadmit@northwood.edu
Private; founded 1959
Freshman admissions: N/A; 2015-2016: 2,192 applied, 1,506 accepted. Either SAT or ACT required. SAT 25/75 percentile: N/A. High school rank: 13% in top tenth, 34% in top quarter, 70% in top half
Early decision deadline: N/A, notification date: N/A
Early action deadline: N/A, notification date: N/A
Application deadline (fall): rolling
Undergraduate student body: 1,416 full time, 53 part time; 64% male, 36% female; 0% American Indian, 0% Asian, 7% black, 3% Hispanic, 2% multiracial, 1% Pacific Islander, 78% white, 6% international; 87% from in state; 44% live on campus; 8% of students in fraternities, 13% in sororities
Most popular majors: 20% Business Administration and Management, General; 16% Marketing/Marketing Management, General; 13% Accounting; 12% Finance, General; 11% Sport and Fitness Administration/Management
Expenses: 2015-2016: $24,170; room/board: $9,590
Financial aid: (989) 837-4230

Oakland University
Rochester MI
(248) 370-3360
U.S. News ranking: Nat. U., second tier
Website: www.oakland.edu
Admissions email: visit@oakland.edu
Public; founded 1957
Freshman admissions: selective; 2015-2016: 10,162 applied, 8,169 accepted. Either SAT or ACT required. ACT 25/75 percentile: 20-26. High school rank: 15% in top tenth, 46% in top quarter, 79% in top half
Early decision deadline: N/A, notification date: N/A
Early action deadline: N/A, notification date: N/A
Application deadline (fall): 8/1
Undergraduate student body: 12,887 full time, 3,906 part time; 43% male, 57% female; 0% American Indian, 4% Asian, 8% black, 3% Hispanic, 3% multiracial, 0% Pacific Islander, 75% white, 2% international; 99% from in state; 16% live on campus; 3% of students in fraternities, 5% in sororities
Most popular majors: 27% Health Professions and Related Programs; 15% Business, Management, Marketing, and Related Support Services; 6% Biological and Biomedical Sciences; 6% Psychology
Expenses: 2015-2016: $12,431 in state, $24,735 out of state; room/board: $9,250
Financial aid: (248) 370-2550; 62% of undergrads determined to have financial need; average aid package $13,444

Olivet College
Olivet MI
(269) 749-7635
U.S. News ranking: Reg. Coll. (Mid. W), No. 48
Website: www.olivetcollege.edu
Admissions email: admissions@olivetcollege.edu
Private; founded 1844
Affiliation: United Church of Christ
Freshman admissions: less selective; 2015-2016: 3,378 applied, 1,921 accepted. Either SAT or ACT required. ACT 25/75 percentile: 17-22. High school rank: N/A
Early decision deadline: N/A, notification date: N/A
Early action deadline: N/A, notification date: N/A
Application deadline (fall): rolling
Undergraduate student body: 877 full time, 112 part time; 59% male, 41% female; 0% American Indian, 1% Asian, 13% black, 6% Hispanic, 3% multiracial, N/A Pacific Islander, 75% white, 1% international
Most popular majors: 37% Criminal Justice/Safety Studies; 11% Biology/Biological Sciences, General; 10% Health and Physical Education/Fitness, General; 10% Business Administration and Management, General; 9% Insurance
Expenses: 2016-2017: $25,560; room/board: $8,950

Financial aid: (269) 749-7102; 93% of undergrads determined to have financial need; average aid package $18,750

Robert B. Miller College[1]

Battle Creek MI
(269) 660-8021
U.S. News ranking: Reg. Coll. (Mid. W), unranked
Website: www.millercollege.edu
Admissions email: N/A
Private
Application deadline (fall): N/A
Undergraduate student body: N/A full time, N/A part time
Expenses: 2015-2016: $11,970; room/board: N/A
Financial aid: (269) 660-8021

Rochester College[1]

Rochester Hills MI
(248) 218-2031
U.S. News ranking: Reg. Coll. (Mid. W), No. 58
Website: www.rc.edu
Admissions email: admissions@rc.edu
Private; founded 1959
Affiliation: Church of Christ
Application deadline (fall): rolling
Undergraduate student body: N/A full time, N/A part time
Expenses: 2015-2016: $22,129; room/board: $6,750
Financial aid: (248) 218-2028

Saginaw Valley State University

University Center MI
(989) 964-4200
U.S. News ranking: Reg. U. (Mid. W), second tier
Website: www.svsu.edu
Admissions email: admissions@svsu.edu
Public; founded 1963
Freshman admissions: selective; 2015-2016: 7,023 applied, 5,349 accepted. Either SAT or ACT required. ACT 25/75 percentile: 19-25. High school rank: 18% in top tenth, 43% in top quarter, 75% in top half
Early decision deadline: N/A, notification date: N/A
Early action deadline: N/A, notification date: N/A
Application deadline (fall): rolling
Undergraduate student body: 7,377 full time, 1,386 part time; 43% male, 57% female; 0% American Indian, 1% Asian, 9% black, 4% Hispanic, 2% multiracial, 0% Pacific Islander, 71% white, 8% international; 99% from in state; 31% live on campus; 3% of students in fraternities, 3% in sororities
Most popular majors: 13% Registered Nursing/Registered Nurse; 9% Social Work; 6% Criminal Justice/Safety Studies; 6% Elementary Education and Teaching; 5% Health/Medical Preparatory Programs, Other
Expenses: 2015-2016: $8,968 in state, $21,061 out of state; room/board: $8,917
Financial aid: (989) 964-4103; 56% of undergrads determined to have financial need; average aid package $8,212

Siena Heights University

Adrian MI
(517) 264-7180
U.S. News ranking: Reg. U. (Mid. W), second tier
Website: www.sienaheights.edu
Admissions email: admissions@sienaheights.edu
Private; founded 1919
Affiliation: Roman Catholic
Freshman admissions: selective; 2015-2016: 1,777 applied, 1,377 accepted. Neither SAT nor ACT required. ACT 25/75 percentile: 18-26. High school rank: 12% in top tenth, 32% in top quarter, 67% in top half
Early decision deadline: N/A, notification date: N/A
Early action deadline: N/A, notification date: N/A
Application deadline (fall): 8/1
Undergraduate student body: 1,310 full time, 1,182 part time; 42% male, 58% female; 0% American Indian, 1% Asian, 12% black, 6% Hispanic, 2% multiracial, N/A Pacific Islander, 58% white, 3% international
Most popular majors: 20% Health Professions and Related Programs; 18% Business, Management, Marketing, and Related Support Services; 13% Homeland Security, Law Enforcement, Firefighting and Related Protective Services; 10% Public Administration and Social Service Professions; 7% Liberal Arts and Sciences, General Studies and Humanities
Expenses: 2016-2017: $24,856; room/board: $10,400
Financial aid: (517) 264-7130

Spring Arbor University

Spring Arbor MI
(800) 968-0011
U.S. News ranking: Reg. U. (Mid. W), No. 63
Website: www.arbor.edu/
Admissions email: admissions@arbor.edu
Private; founded 1873
Affiliation: Free Methodist
Freshman admissions: selective; 2015-2016: 1,546 applied, 1,065 accepted. Either SAT or ACT required. ACT 25/75 percentile: 20-26. High school rank: 23% in top tenth, 48% in top quarter, 75% in top half
Early decision deadline: N/A, notification date: N/A
Early action deadline: N/A, notification date: N/A
Application deadline (fall): 8/1
Undergraduate student body: 1,703 full time, 732 part time; 32% male, 68% female; 0% American Indian, 1% Asian, 10% black, 3% Hispanic, 3% multiracial, 0% Pacific Islander, 74% white, 1% international
Most popular majors: 13% Teacher Education and Professional Development, Specific Subject Areas; 10% Social Work; 8% Psychology, General; 4% Biology/Biological Sciences, General; 4% Health and Physical Education/Fitness, General
Expenses: 2016-2017: $26,730; room/board: $9,270

University of Detroit Mercy

Detroit MI
(313) 993-1245
U.S. News ranking: Reg. U. (Mid. W), No. 24
Website: www.udmercy.edu
Admissions email: admissions@udmercy.edu
Private; founded 1877
Affiliation: Catholic
Freshman admissions: selective; 2015-2016: 4,450 applied, 3,269 accepted. Either SAT or ACT required. ACT 25/75 percentile: 22-27. High school rank: 20% in top tenth, 45% in top quarter, 81% in top half
Early decision deadline: N/A, notification date: N/A
Early action deadline: N/A, notification date: N/A
Application deadline (fall): 3/1
Undergraduate student body: 2,081 full time, 591 part time; 36% male, 64% female; 0% American Indian, 5% Asian, 15% black, 4% Hispanic, 3% multiracial, 0% Pacific Islander, 65% white, 5% international; 95% from in state; 30% live on campus; 9% of students in fraternities, 7% in sororities
Most popular majors: 52% Registered Nursing/Registered Nurse; 10% Biology/Biological Sciences, General; 5% Business Administration and Management, General; 4% Dental Hygiene/Hygienist
Expenses: 2016-2017: $39,882; room/board: $9,224
Financial aid: (313) 993-3350; 72% of undergrads determined to have financial need; average aid package $31,113

University of Michigan–Ann Arbor

Ann Arbor MI
(734) 764-7433
U.S. News ranking: Nat. U., No. 27
Website: www.umich.edu
Admissions email: N/A
Public; founded 1817
Freshman admissions: most selective; 2015-2016: 51,761 applied, 13,584 accepted. Either SAT or ACT required. ACT 25/75 percentile: 29-33. High school rank: 73% in top tenth, 94% in top quarter, 99% in top half
Early decision deadline: N/A, notification date: N/A
Early action deadline: 11/1, notification date: 12/24
Application deadline (fall): 2/1
Undergraduate student body: 27,258 full time, 1,054 part time; 51% male, 49% female; 0% American Indian, 13% Asian, 4% black, 5% Hispanic, 3% multiracial, 0% Pacific Islander, 62% white, 7% international; 62% from in state; 34% live on campus; 17% of students in fraternities, 24% in sororities
Most popular majors: 7% Business Administration and Management, General; 7% Economics, General; 7% Experimental Psychology;

5% Physiological Psychology/Psychobiology; 5% Political Science and Government, General
Expenses: 2015-2016: $13,856 in state, $43,476 out of state; room/board: $10,554
Financial aid: (734) 763-4119; 38% of undergrads determined to have financial need; average aid package $22,694

University of Michigan–Dearborn

Dearborn MI
(313) 593-5100
U.S. News ranking: Reg. U. (Mid. W), No. 40
Website: www.umd.umich.edu
Admissions email: admissions@umd.umich.edu
Public; founded 1959
Freshman admissions: more selective; 2015-2016: 5,312 applied, 3,318 accepted. Either SAT or ACT required. ACT 25/75 percentile: 21-27. High school rank: 28% in top tenth, 59% in top quarter, 90% in top half
Early decision deadline: N/A, notification date: N/A
Early action deadline: N/A, notification date: N/A
Application deadline (fall): rolling
Undergraduate student body: 5,035 full time, 2,167 part time; 52% male, 48% female; 0% American Indian, 7% Asian, 10% black, 6% Hispanic, 3% multiracial, 0% Pacific Islander, 69% white, 2% international; 96% from in state; N/A live on campus; 2% of students in fraternities, 3% in sororities
Most popular majors: 18% Business, Management, Marketing, and Related Support Services; 12% Engineering; 11% Psychology; 9% Biological and Biomedical Sciences; 9% Social Sciences
Expenses: 2015-2016: $11,524 in state, $23,866 out of state; room/board: N/A
Financial aid: (313) 593-5300; 63% of undergrads determined to have financial need; average aid package $10,084

University of Michigan–Flint

Flint MI
(810) 762-3300
U.S. News ranking: Reg. U. (Mid. W), No. 108
Website: www.umflint.edu
Admissions email: admissions@umflint.edu
Public; founded 1956
Freshman admissions: selective; 2015-2016: 3,918 applied, 2,883 accepted. Either SAT or ACT required. ACT 25/75 percentile: 18-24. High school rank: 16% in top tenth, 40% in top quarter, 76% in top half
Early decision deadline: N/A, notification date: N/A
Early action deadline: N/A, notification date: N/A
Application deadline (fall): 8/18
Undergraduate student body: 4,006 full time, 2,862 part time; 40% male, 60% female; 1% American Indian, 2% Asian, 14% black, 4% Hispanic, 3% multiracial, 0% Pacific Islander, 67% white,

6% international; 98% from in state; 4% live on campus; 6% of students in fraternities, 6% in sororities
Most popular majors: 35% Health Professions and Related Programs; 15% Business, Management, Marketing, and Related Support Services; 7% Psychology; 7% Education; 6% Biological and Biomedical Sciences
Expenses: 2015-2016: $10,458 in state, $19,980 out of state; room/board: $8,178
Financial aid: (810) 762-3444

Walsh College of Accountancy and Business Administration[1]

Troy MI
(248) 823-1610
U.S. News ranking: Business, unranked
Website: www.walshcollege.edu
Admissions email: admissions@walshcollege.edu
Private; founded 1922
Application deadline (fall): N/A
Undergraduate student body: N/A full time, N/A part time
Expenses: 2015-2016: $12,570; room/board: N/A
Financial aid: (248) 823-1665

Wayne State University

Detroit MI
(313) 577-3577
U.S. News ranking: Nat. U., second tier
Website: www.wayne.edu/
Admissions email: admissions@wayne.edu
Public; founded 1868
Freshman admissions: selective; 2015-2016: 10,009 applied, 7,994 accepted. Either SAT or ACT required. ACT 25/75 percentile: 20-26. High school rank: 22% in top tenth, 51% in top quarter, 78% in top half
Early decision deadline: N/A, notification date: N/A
Early action deadline: N/A, notification date: N/A
Application deadline (fall): 8/1
Undergraduate student body: 11,907 full time, 5,762 part time; 45% male, 55% female; 0% American Indian, 8% Asian, 19% black, 5% Hispanic, 3% multiracial, 0% Pacific Islander, 57% white, 2% international; 99% from in state; 12% live on campus; N/A of students in fraternities, N/A in sororities
Most popular majors: 12% Psychology, General; 8% Health Professions and Related Clinical Sciences, Other; 6% Biology/Biological Sciences, General; 4% Criminal Justice/Safety Studies; 3% Accounting
Expenses: 2015-2016: $12,745 in state, $27,443 out of state; room/board: $10,061
Financial aid: (313) 577-3378; 74% of undergrads determined to have financial need; average aid package $11,212

Western Michigan University
Kalamazoo MI
(269) 387-2000
U.S. News ranking: Nat. U., No. 194
Website: www.wmich.edu
Admissions email: ask-wmu@wmich.edu
Public; founded 1903
Freshman admissions: selective; 2015-2016: 15,175 applied, 12,501 accepted. Either SAT or ACT required. ACT 25/75 percentile: 19-25. High school rank: 13% in top tenth, 36% in top quarter, 70% in top half
Early decision deadline: N/A, notification date: N/A
Early action deadline: N/A, notification date: N/A
Application deadline (fall): rolling
Undergraduate student body: 15,416 full time, 3,151 part time; 51% male, 49% female; 0% American Indian, 2% Asian, 12% black, 5% Hispanic, 3% multiracial, 0% Pacific Islander, 72% white, 4% international; 92% from in state; 27% live on campus; 5% of students in fraternities, 7% in sororities
Most popular majors: 19% Business, Management, Marketing, and Related Support Services; 10% Health Professions and Related Programs; 8% Education; 7% Multi/Interdisciplinary Studies; 7% Psychology
Expenses: 2015-2016: $11,029 in state, $25,713 out of state; room/board: $9,238
Financial aid: (269) 387-6000; 61% of undergrads determined to have financial need; average aid package $13,600

MINNESOTA

Augsburg College
Minneapolis MN
(612) 330-1001
U.S. News ranking: Reg. U. (Mid. W), No. 30
Website: www.augsburg.edu
Admissions email: admissions@augsburg.edu
Private; founded 1869
Affiliation: Lutheran
Freshman admissions: selective; 2015-2016: 2,925 applied, 1,731 accepted. Either SAT or ACT required. ACT 25/75 percentile: 19-24. High school rank: N/A
Early decision deadline: N/A, notification date: N/A
Early action deadline: N/A, notification date: N/A
Application deadline (fall): 8/1
Undergraduate student body: 1,970 full time, 504 part time; 47% male, 53% female; 1% American Indian, 7% Asian, 11% black, 6% Hispanic, 2% multiracial, 0% Pacific Islander, 53% white, 3% international; 82% from in state; 38% live on campus; N/A of students in fraternities, N/A in sororities
Most popular majors: 28% Business, Management, Marketing, and Related Support Services; 12% Health Professions and Related Programs; 8% Social Sciences; 7% Education; 7% Psychology

Expenses: 2015-2016: $35,465; room/board: $9,380
Financial aid: (612) 330-1046

Bemidji State University
Bemidji MN
(218) 755-2040
U.S. News ranking: Reg. U. (Mid. W), No. 115
Website: www.bemidjistate.edu
Admissions email: admissions@bemidjistate.edu
Public; founded 1919
Freshman admissions: selective; 2015-2016: 2,566 applied, 2,407 accepted. Either SAT or ACT required. ACT 25/75 percentile: 19-24. High school rank: 7% in top tenth, 23% in top quarter, 56% in top half
Early decision deadline: N/A, notification date: N/A
Early action deadline: N/A, notification date: N/A
Application deadline (fall): rolling
Undergraduate student body: 3,410 full time, 1,329 part time; 43% male, 57% female; 3% American Indian, 1% Asian, 2% black, 2% Hispanic, 3% multiracial, N/A Pacific Islander, 85% white, 2% international; 90% from in state; 28% live on campus; N/A of students in fraternities, N/A in sororities
Most popular majors: 20% Business, Management, Marketing, and Related Support Services; 18% Health Professions and Related Programs; 12% Education; 7% Biological and Biomedical Sciences; 7% Homeland Security, Law Enforcement, Firefighting and Related Protective Services
Expenses: 2016-2017: $8,386 in state, $8,386 out of state; room/board: $7,920
Financial aid: (218) 755-4143; 60% of undergrads determined to have financial need; average aid package $9,556

Bethany Lutheran College
Mankato MN
(507) 344-7331
U.S. News ranking: Nat. Lib. Arts, second tier
Website: www.blc.edu
Admissions email: admiss@blc.edu
Private; founded 1927
Affiliation: Evangelical Lutheran Synod
Freshman admissions: selective; 2015-2016: 347 applied, 296 accepted. Either SAT or ACT required. ACT 25/75 percentile: 20-26. High school rank: 14% in top tenth, 35% in top quarter, 66% in top half
Early decision deadline: N/A, notification date: N/A
Early action deadline: N/A, notification date: N/A
Application deadline (fall): 7/1
Undergraduate student body: 490 full time, 34 part time; 45% male, 55% female; 0% American Indian, 0% Asian, 3% black, 3% Hispanic, 1% multiracial, 0% Pacific Islander, 88% white, 3% international; 77% from in state; 67% live on campus; N/A of students in fraternities, N/A in sororities

Most popular majors: 21% Business, Management, Marketing, and Related Support Services; 19% Visual and Performing Arts; 17% Biological and Biomedical Sciences; 8% Education
Expenses: 2016-2017: $25,890; room/board: $7,960
Financial aid: (507) 344-7307; 82% of undergrads determined to have financial need; average aid package $21,100

Bethel University
St. Paul MN
(800) 255-8706
U.S. News ranking: Reg. U. (Mid. W), No. 22
Website: www.bethel.edu
Admissions email: undergrad-admissions@bethel.edu
Private; founded 1871
Affiliation: Converge Worldwide (former Baptist General Conference)
Freshman admissions: more selective; 2015-2016: 1,531 applied, 1,453 accepted. Either SAT or ACT required. ACT 25/75 percentile: 22-27. High school rank: 26% in top tenth, 57% in top quarter, 86% in top half
Early decision deadline: N/A, notification date: N/A
Early action deadline: N/A, notification date: N/A
Application deadline (fall): rolling
Undergraduate student body: 2,444 full time, 540 part time; 38% male, 62% female; 0% American Indian, 4% Asian, 5% black, 4% Hispanic, 2% multiracial, 0% Pacific Islander, 78% white, 0% international; 79% from in state; 72% live on campus; 0% of students in fraternities, 0% in sororities
Most popular majors: 15% Business, Management, Marketing, and Related Support Services; 15% Education; 13% Health Professions and Related Programs; 6% Psychology
Expenses: 2016-2017: $35,160; room/board: $10,110
Financial aid: (800) 255-8706; 73% of undergrads determined to have financial need; average aid package $25,995

Capella University[1]
Minneapolis MN
(888) 227-3552
U.S. News ranking: Nat. U., unranked
Website: www.capella.edu
Admissions email: admissionsoffice@capella.edu
For-profit
Application deadline (fall): N/A
Undergraduate student body: N/A full time, N/A part time
Expenses: 2015-2016: $13,176; room/board: N/A
Financial aid: (612) 977-5233

Carleton College
Northfield MN
(507) 222-4190
U.S. News ranking: Nat. Lib. Arts, No. 7
Website: www.carleton.edu
Admissions email: admissions@carleton.edu
Private; founded 1866

Freshman admissions: most selective; 2015-2016: 6,722 applied, 1,388 accepted. Either SAT or ACT required. ACT 25/75 percentile: 29-33. High school rank: 71% in top tenth, 96% in top quarter, 100% in top half
Early decision deadline: 11/15, notification date: 12/15
Early action deadline: N/A, notification date: N/A
Application deadline (fall): 1/15
Undergraduate student body: 1,997 full time, 17 part time; 48% male, 52% female; 0% American Indian, 8% Asian, 4% black, 7% Hispanic, 5% multiracial, 0% Pacific Islander, 63% white, 10% international; 18% from in state; 96% live on campus; 0% of students in fraternities, 0% in sororities
Most popular majors: 17% Social Sciences; 16% Physical Sciences; 10% Biological and Biomedical Sciences; 10% Computer and Information Sciences and Support Services; 10% Visual and Performing Arts
Expenses: 2016-2017: $50,874; room/board: $13,197
Financial aid: (507) 646-4138; 56% of undergrads determined to have financial need; average aid package $41,059

College of St. Benedict
St. Joseph MN
(320) 363-5060
U.S. News ranking: Nat. Lib. Arts, No. 87
Website: www.csbsju.edu
Admissions email: admissions@csbsju.edu
Private; founded 1913
Affiliation: Roman Catholic (Benedictine)
Freshman admissions: more selective; 2015-2016: 1,858 applied, 1,389 accepted. Either SAT or ACT required. ACT 25/75 percentile: 22-27. High school rank: 31% in top tenth, 61% in top quarter, 93% in top half
Early decision deadline: N/A, notification date: N/A
Early action deadline: 11/15, notification date: 12/15
Application deadline (fall): N/A
Undergraduate student body: 1,927 full time, 16 part time; 0% male, 100% female; 1% American Indian, 6% Asian, 3% black, 6% Hispanic, 1% multiracial, 0% Pacific Islander, 79% white, 4% international; 84% from in state; 90% live on campus; N/A of students in fraternities, N/A in sororities
Most popular majors: 13% Psychology, General; 10% Rhetoric and Composition; 9% Nutrition Sciences; 9% Registered Nursing/Registered Nurse; 8% Business Administration and Management, General
Expenses: 2016-2017: $42,271; room/board: $10,535
Financial aid: (320) 363-5388; 70% of undergrads determined to have financial need; average aid package $34,374

College of St. Scholastica
Duluth MN
(218) 723-6046
U.S. News ranking: Reg. U. (Mid. W), No. 35
Website: www.css.edu
Admissions email: admissions@css.edu
Private; founded 1912
Affiliation: Roman Catholic
Freshman admissions: selective; 2015-2016: 3,589 applied, 2,206 accepted. Either SAT or ACT required. ACT 25/75 percentile: 20-26. High school rank: 23% in top tenth, 48% in top quarter, 87% in top half
Early decision deadline: N/A, notification date: N/A
Early action deadline: N/A, notification date: N/A
Application deadline (fall): rolling
Undergraduate student body: 2,277 full time, 567 part time; 29% male, 71% female; 2% American Indian, 2% Asian, 3% black, 3% Hispanic, 3% multiracial, 0% Pacific Islander, 83% white, 3% international; 85% from in state; 49% live on campus; 0% of students in fraternities, 0% in sororities
Most popular majors: 44% Health Professions and Related Programs; 18% Business, Management, Marketing, and Related Support Services; 10% Biological and Biomedical Sciences; 9% Public Administration and Social Service Professions; 6% Psychology
Expenses: 2016-2017: $35,326; room/board: $9,314
Financial aid: (218) 723-6047; 79% of undergrads determined to have financial need; average aid package $23,917

Concordia College–Moorhead
Moorhead MN
(800) 699-9897
U.S. News ranking: Nat. Lib. Arts, No. 115
Website: www.concordiacollege.edu
Admissions email: admissions@cord.edu
Private; founded 1891
Affiliation: Evangelical Lutheran Church in America
Freshman admissions: more selective; 2015-2016: 2,278 applied, 1,781 accepted. Either SAT or ACT required. ACT 25/75 percentile: 22-28. High school rank: 31% in top tenth, 59% in top quarter, 87% in top half
Early decision deadline: N/A, notification date: N/A
Early action deadline: N/A, notification date: N/A
Application deadline (fall): rolling
Undergraduate student body: 2,125 full time, 37 part time; 40% male, 60% female; 1% American Indian, 2% Asian, 2% black, 2% Hispanic, 2% multiracial, 0% Pacific Islander, 85% white, 3% international; 71% from in state; 61% live on campus; 0% of students in fraternities, 0% in sororities
Most popular majors: 12% Business Administration, Management and Operations; 12% Education, General; 9%

Biology, General; 8% Visual and Performing Arts, General
Expenses: 2016-2017: $36,878; room/board: $7,810
Financial aid: (218) 299-3010; 72% of undergrads determined to have financial need; average aid package $28,327

Concordia University–St. Paul
St. Paul MN
(651) 641-8230
U.S. News ranking: Reg. U. (Mid. W), No. 103
Website: www.csp.edu
Admissions email: admissions@csp.edu
Private; founded 1893
Affiliation: Lutheran Church–Missouri Synod
Freshman admissions: selective; 2015-2016: 1,483 applied, 822 accepted. ACT required. ACT 25/75 percentile: 18-24. High school rank: 11% in top tenth, 30% in top quarter, 58% in top half
Early decision deadline: N/A, notification date: N/A
Early action deadline: N/A, notification date: N/A
Application deadline (fall): 8/1
Undergraduate student body: 1,382 full time, 1,185 part time; 42% male, 58% female; 1% American Indian, 7% Asian, 13% black, 4% Hispanic, 4% multiracial, 0% Pacific Islander, 64% white, 5% international; 73% from in state; 21% live on campus; N/A of students in fraternities, N/A in sororities
Most popular majors: 40% Business, Management, Marketing, and Related Support Services; 11% Parks, Recreation, Leisure, and Fitness Studies; 8% Education; 7% Homeland Security, Law Enforcement, Firefighting and Related Protective Services; 6% Psychology
Expenses: 2016-2017: $21,250; room/board: $8,500
Financial aid: (651) 603-6300; 74% of undergrads determined to have financial need; average aid package $14,167

Crown College
St. Bonifacius MN
(952) 446-4142
U.S. News ranking: Reg. Coll. (Mid. W), No. 48
Website: www.crown.edu
Admissions email: admissions@crown.edu
Private; founded 1916
Affiliation: Christian and Missionary Alliance
Freshman admissions: selective; 2015-2016: 1,047 applied, 532 accepted. Either SAT or ACT required. ACT 25/75 percentile: 19-25. High school rank: N/A
Early decision deadline: N/A, notification date: N/A
Early action deadline: N/A, notification date: N/A
Application deadline (fall): 8/20
Undergraduate student body: 735 full time, 245 part time; 47% male, 53% female; 1% American Indian, 6% Asian, 6% black, 6% Hispanic, 2% multiracial, 0% Pacific Islander, 74% white,

4% international; 63% from in state; 72% live on campus; 0% of students in fraternities, 0% in sororities
Most popular majors: 15% Religious Education; 10% Business Administration and Management, General; 10% Counseling Psychology; 10% Registered Nursing/Registered Nurse
Expenses: 2016-2017: $24,700; room/board: $8,240
Financial aid: (952) 446-4177; 85% of undergrads determined to have financial need; average aid package $17,776

Dunwoody College of Technology
Minneapolis MN
(800) 292-4625
U.S. News ranking: Reg. Coll. (Mid. W), No. 53
Website: www.dunwoody.edu
Admissions email: admissions@dunwoody.edu
Private; founded 1914
Freshman admissions: selective; 2015-2016: N/A applied, N/A accepted. Neither SAT nor ACT required. ACT 25/75 percentile: N/A. High school rank: 14% in top tenth, 41% in top quarter, 76% in top half
Early decision deadline: N/A, notification date: N/A
Early action deadline: N/A, notification date: N/A
Application deadline (fall): rolling
Undergraduate student body: 898 full time, 196 part time; 86% male, 14% female; 1% American Indian, 6% Asian, 6% black, 2% Hispanic, 2% multiracial, N/A Pacific Islander, 78% white, 0% international; 98% from in state; N/A live on campus; N/A of students in fraternities, N/A in sororities
Most popular majors: 53% Business Administration and Management, General; 26% Interior Design; 12% Manufacturing Engineering; 9% Computer Science
Expenses: 2016-2017: $21,325; room/board: N/A
Financial aid: N/A; 87% of undergrads determined to have financial need; average aid package $8,651

Gustavus Adolphus College
St. Peter MN
(507) 933-7676
U.S. News ranking: Nat. Lib. Arts, No. 77
Website: www.gac.edu
Admissions email: admission@gac.edu
Private; founded 1862
Affiliation: Lutheran–ELCA
Freshman admissions: more selective; 2015-2016: 4,657 applied, 3,123 accepted. Neither SAT nor ACT required. ACT 25/75 percentile: 24-30. High school rank: 30% in top tenth, 65% in top quarter, 94% in top half
Early decision deadline: N/A, notification date: N/A
Early action deadline: 11/1, notification date: 11/20

Application deadline (fall): rolling
Undergraduate student body: 2,342 full time, 44 part time; 47% male, 53% female; 0% American Indian, 4% Asian, 2% black, 4% Hispanic, 3% multiracial, 0% Pacific Islander, 82% white, 4% international; 82% from in state; 88% live on campus; 16% of students in fraternities, 18% in sororities
Most popular majors: 12% Business/Commerce, General; 11% Biology/Biological Sciences, General; 11% Psychology, General
Expenses: 2016-2017: $42,840; room/board: $9,400
Financial aid: (507) 933-7527; 70% of undergrads determined to have financial need; average aid package $37,120

Hamline University
St. Paul MN
(651) 523-2207
U.S. News ranking: Reg. U. (Mid. W), No. 20
Website: www.hamline.edu
Admissions email: admission@hamline.edu
Private; founded 1854
Affiliation: United Methodist
Freshman admissions: selective; 2015-2016: 3,995 applied, 2,892 accepted. Either SAT or ACT required. ACT 25/75 percentile: 21-28. High school rank: 17% in top tenth, 47% in top quarter, 81% in top half
Early decision deadline: 11/1, notification date: 11/15
Early action deadline: 12/1, notification date: N/A
Application deadline (fall): rolling
Undergraduate student body: 2,121 full time, 108 part time; 42% male, 58% female; 0% American Indian, 6% Asian, 6% black, 7% Hispanic, 6% multiracial, 0% Pacific Islander, 72% white, 1% international; 79% from in state; 41% live on campus; N/A of students in fraternities, N/A in sororities
Most popular majors: 13% Business, Management, Marketing, and Related Support Services; 12% Social Sciences; 11% Psychology; 8% English Language and Literature/Letters; 8% Multi/Interdisciplinary Studies
Expenses: 2016-2017: $39,149; room/board: $9,894
Financial aid: (651) 523-3000; 83% of undergrads determined to have financial need; average aid package $29,204

Macalester College
St. Paul MN
(651) 696-6357
U.S. News ranking: Nat. Lib. Arts, No. 24
Website: www.macalester.edu
Admissions email: admissions@macalester.edu
Private; founded 1874
Freshman admissions: most selective; 2015-2016: 6,030 applied, 2,353 accepted. Either SAT or ACT required. ACT 25/75 percentile: 29-32. High school rank: 65% in top tenth, 95% in top quarter, 100% in top half

Early decision deadline: 11/15, notification date: 12/15
Early action deadline: N/A, notification date: N/A
Application deadline (fall): 1/15
Undergraduate student body: 2,138 full time, 34 part time; 40% male, 60% female; 0% American Indian, 7% Asian, 2% black, 6% Hispanic, 5% multiracial, 0% Pacific Islander, 66% white, 14% international; 18% from in state; 61% live on campus; 0% of students in fraternities, 0% in sororities
Most popular majors: 24% Social Sciences; 11% Biological and Biomedical Sciences; 10% Multi/Interdisciplinary Studies; 8% Foreign Languages, Literatures, and Linguistics; 7% Psychology
Expenses: 2016-2017: $50,639; room/board: $11,266
Financial aid: (651) 696-6214; 69% of undergrads determined to have financial need; average aid package $42,348

Metropolitan State University[1]
St. Paul MN
(651) 772-7600
U.S. News ranking: Reg. U. (Mid. W), second tier
Website: www.metrostate.edu
Admissions email: admissions@metrostate.edu
Public
Application deadline (fall): N/A
Undergraduate student body: N/A full time, N/A part time
Expenses: 2015-2016: $7,566 in state, $14,394 out of state; room/board: $9,402
Financial aid: (651) 772-7670

Minneapolis College of Art and Design
Minneapolis MN
(612) 874-3760
U.S. News ranking: Arts, unranked
Website: www.mcad.edu
Admissions email: admissions@mcad.edu
Private; founded 1886
Freshman admissions: N/A; 2015-2016: 556 applied, 367 accepted. Either SAT or ACT required. SAT 25/75 percentile: N/A. High school rank: N/A
Early decision deadline: N/A, notification date: N/A
Early action deadline: 12/1, notification date: 12/14
Application deadline (fall): 4/1
Undergraduate student body: 659 full time, 22 part time; 34% male, 66% female; 1% American Indian, 8% Asian, 4% black, 6% Hispanic, 3% multiracial, 0% Pacific Islander, 59% white, 0% international; 58% from in state; 56% live on campus; 0% of students in fraternities, 0% in sororities
Most popular majors: 20% Graphic Design; 8% Animation, Interactive Technology, Video Graphics and Special Effects; 7% Photography
Expenses: 2015-2016: $35,326; room/board: N/A
Financial aid: (612) 874-3782

Minnesota State University–Mankato
Mankato MN
(507) 389-1822
U.S. News ranking: Reg. U. (Mid. W), No. 103
Website: www.mnsu.edu
Admissions email: admissions@mnsu.edu
Public; founded 1867
Freshman admissions: selective; 2015-2016: 10,134 applied, 6,752 accepted. ACT required. ACT 25/75 percentile: 20-24. High school rank: 7% in top tenth, 23% in top quarter, 65% in top half
Early decision deadline: N/A, notification date: N/A
Early action deadline: N/A, notification date: N/A
Application deadline (fall): rolling
Undergraduate student body: 11,038 full time, 2,110 part time; 48% male, 52% female; 0% American Indian, 4% Asian, 5% black, 4% Hispanic, 3% multiracial, 0% Pacific Islander, 76% white, 6% international
Most popular majors: 17% Business, Management, Marketing, and Related Support Services; 14% Health Professions and Related Programs; 7% Parks, Recreation, Leisure, and Fitness Studies; 7% Psychology; 6% Education
Expenses: 2016-2017: $7,836 in state, $15,580 out of state; room/board: $8,430
Financial aid: (507) 389-1866; 57% of undergrads determined to have financial need; average aid package $9,218

Minnesota State University–Moorhead
Moorhead MN
(800) 593-7246
U.S. News ranking: Reg. U. (Mid. W), No. 115
Website: www.mnstate.edu
Admissions email: admissions@mnstate.edu
Public; founded 1887
Freshman admissions: selective; 2015-2016: 2,544 applied, 2,084 accepted. Either SAT or ACT required. ACT 25/75 percentile: 20-25. High school rank: 10% in top tenth, 35% in top quarter, 74% in top half
Early decision deadline: N/A, notification date: N/A
Early action deadline: N/A, notification date: N/A
Application deadline (fall): 8/1
Undergraduate student body: 4,324 full time, 921 part time; 40% male, 60% female; 1% American Indian, 1% Asian, 3% black, 3% Hispanic, 3% multiracial, 0% Pacific Islander, 78% white, 7% international
Most popular majors: 17% Health Professions and Related Programs; 15% Business, Management, Marketing, and Related Support Services; 11% Visual and Performing Arts; 9% Education
Expenses: 2016-2017: $8,120 in state, $15,256 out of state; room/board: $8,076
Financial aid: (218) 477-2251; 60% of undergrads determined to have financial need; average aid package $3,303

North Central University

Minneapolis MN
(800) 289-6222
U.S. News ranking: Reg. Coll. (Mid. W), No. 44
Website: www.northcentral.edu
Admissions email: admissions@northcentral.edu
Private; founded 1930
Affiliation: Assemblies of God
Freshman admissions: selective; 2015-2016: 1,313 applied, 700 accepted. Either SAT or ACT required. ACT 25/75 percentile: 18-27. High school rank: 15% in top tenth, 41% in top quarter, 68% in top half
Early decision deadline: N/A, notification date: N/A
Early action deadline: N/A, notification date: N/A
Application deadline (fall): rolling
Undergraduate student body: 1,001 full time, 181 part time; 43% male, 57% female; N/A American Indian, 3% Asian, 3% black, 5% Hispanic, 3% multiracial, 0% Pacific Islander, 78% white, 2% international; 60% from in state; 85% live on campus; N/A of students in fraternities, N/A in sororities
Most popular majors: 8% Elementary Education and Teaching; 8% Intercultural/Multicultural and Diversity Studies; 7% Human Development and Family Studies, General; 7% Pastoral Studies/Counseling; 6% Psychology, General
Expenses: 2016-2017: $22,240; room/board: $6,790
Financial aid: (612) 343-4485; 83% of undergrads determined to have financial need; average aid package $16,769

Southwest Minnesota State University

Marshall MN
(507) 537-6286
U.S. News ranking: Reg. U. (Mid. W), second tier
Website: www.smsu.edu
Admissions email: N/A
Public; founded 1963
Freshman admissions: selective; 2015-2016: 2,013 applied, 1,289 accepted. ACT required. ACT 25/75 percentile: 19-24. High school rank: 5% in top tenth, 21% in top quarter, 58% in top half
Early decision deadline: N/A, notification date: N/A
Early action deadline: N/A, notification date: N/A
Application deadline (fall): 9/1
Undergraduate student body: 2,089 full time, 4,654 part time; 41% male, 59% female; 1% American Indian, 3% Asian, 6% black, 2% Hispanic, N/A multiracial, 0% Pacific Islander, 82% white, 5% international; 83% from in state; 34% live on campus; N/A of students in fraternities, N/A in sororities
Most popular majors: 28% Business, Management, Marketing, and Related Support Services; 16% Education; 9% Parks, Recreation, Leisure, and Fitness Studies; 5% Public Administration and Social Service Professions; 5% Social Sciences

Expenses: 2016-2017: $8,336 in state, $8,336 out of state; room/board: $7,686
Financial aid: (507) 537-6281; 66% of undergrads determined to have financial need; average aid package $8,786

St. Catherine University

St. Paul MN
(800) 945-4599
U.S. News ranking: Reg. U. (Mid. W), No. 15
Website: www.stkate.edu
Admissions email: admissions@stkate.edu
Private; founded 1905
Affiliation: Roman Catholic
Freshman admissions: selective; 2015-2016: 2,999 applied, 2,021 accepted. Either SAT or ACT required. ACT 25/75 percentile: 21-26. High school rank: 25% in top tenth, 68% in top quarter, 93% in top half
Early decision deadline: N/A, notification date: N/A
Early action deadline: N/A, notification date: N/A
Application deadline (fall): rolling
Undergraduate student body: 2,128 full time, 1,192 part time; 3% male, 97% female; 1% American Indian, 12% Asian, 9% black, 7% Hispanic, 3% multiracial, 0% Pacific Islander, 64% white, 1% international; 88% from in state; 41% live on campus; N/A of students in fraternities, N/A in sororities
Most popular majors: 32% Registered Nursing/Registered Nurse; 6% Public Health Education and Promotion; 5% Business Administration and Management, General; 5% English Language and Literature, General; 5% Psychology, General
Expenses: 2016-2017: $36,884; room/board: $9,010
Financial aid: (651) 690-6540; 84% of undergrads determined to have financial need; average aid package $34,000

St. Cloud State University

St. Cloud MN
(320) 308-2244
U.S. News ranking: Reg. U. (Mid. W), No. 115
Website: www.stcloudstate.edu
Admissions email: scsu4u@stcloudstate.edu
Public; founded 1869
Freshman admissions: selective; 2015-2016: 6,110 applied, 5,267 accepted. Either SAT or ACT required. ACT 25/75 percentile: 19-25. High school rank: 5% in top tenth, 20% in top quarter, 64% in top half
Early decision deadline: N/A, notification date: N/A
Early action deadline: N/A, notification date: N/A
Application deadline (fall): 8/1
Undergraduate student body: 9,132 full time, 4,498 part time; 47% male, 53% female; 0% American Indian, 6% Asian, 7% black, 3% Hispanic, 3% multiracial, 0% Pacific Islander, 73% white, 7% international; 93% from in

state; 15% live on campus; 1% of students in fraternities, 1% in sororities
Most popular majors: 25% Business Administration and Management, General; 10% Curriculum and Instruction; 8% Communication Sciences and Disorders, General; 8% Psychology, General
Expenses: 2015-2016: $7,814 in state, $15,732 out of state; room/board: $7,930
Financial aid: (320) 308-2047; 60% of undergrads determined to have financial need; average aid package $9,708

St. John's University

Collegeville MN
(320) 363-5060
U.S. News ranking: Nat. Lib. Arts, No. 77
Website: www.csbsju.edu
Admissions email: admissions@csbsju.edu
Private; founded 1857
Affiliation: Roman Catholic (Benedictine)
Freshman admissions: more selective; 2015-2016: 1,607 applied, 1,191 accepted. ACT 25/75 percentile: 23-28. High school rank: 21% in top tenth, 48% in top quarter, 86% in top half
Early decision deadline: N/A, notification date: N/A
Early action deadline: 11/15, notification date: 12/15
Application deadline (fall): 1/15
Undergraduate student body: 1,712 full time, 30 part time; 100% male, 0% female; 1% American Indian, 3% Asian, 3% black, 6% Hispanic, 1% multiracial, 0% Pacific Islander, 80% white, 5% international; 80% from in state; 90% live on campus; N/A of students in fraternities, N/A in sororities
Most popular majors: 17% Business Administration and Management, General; 14% Accounting; 10% Biology/Biological Sciences, General; 7% Economics, General; 5% Rhetoric and Composition
Expenses: 2016-2017: $41,732; room/board: $9,892
Financial aid: (320) 363-3664; 68% of undergrads determined to have financial need; average aid package $31,681

St. Mary's University of Minnesota

Winona MN
(507) 457-1700
U.S. News ranking: Reg. U. (Mid. W), No. 49
Website: www.smumn.edu
Admissions email: admissions@smumn.edu
Private; founded 1912
Affiliation: Roman Catholic
Freshman admissions: selective; 2015-2016: 1,447 applied, 1,123 accepted. Either SAT or ACT required. ACT 25/75 percentile: 19-26. High school rank: 17% in top tenth, 39% in top quarter, 71% in top half
Early decision deadline: N/A, notification date: N/A

Early action deadline: N/A, notification date: N/A
Application deadline (fall): 5/1
Undergraduate student body: 1,228 full time, 530 part time; 46% male, 54% female; 0% American Indian, 2% Asian, 7% black, 5% Hispanic, 1% multiracial, 0% Pacific Islander, 59% white, 3% international; 56% from in state; 93% live on campus; 4% of students in fraternities, 3% in sororities
Most popular majors: 10% Business/Commerce, General; 6% Business Administration and Management, General; 6% Marketing/Marketing Management, General; 5% Criminal Justice/Police Science; 5% Human Resources Management/Personnel Administration, General
Expenses: 2016-2017: $32,575; room/board: $8,635
Financial aid: (507) 457-1438; 76% of undergrads determined to have financial need; average aid package $24,134

St. Olaf College

Northfield MN
(507) 786-3025
U.S. News ranking: Nat. Lib. Arts, No. 53
Website: wp.stolaf.edu/
Admissions email: admissions@stolaf.edu
Private; founded 1874
Affiliation: Lutheran
Freshman admissions: more selective; 2015-2016: 7,571 applied, 2,723 accepted. Either SAT or ACT required. ACT 25/75 percentile: 26-31. High school rank: 43% in top tenth, 77% in top quarter, 96% in top half
Early decision deadline: 11/15, notification date: 12/15
Early action deadline: N/A, notification date: N/A
Application deadline (fall): 1/15
Undergraduate student body: 3,005 full time, 41 part time; 43% male, 57% female; 0% American Indian, 6% Asian, 2% black, 5% Hispanic, 4% multiracial, 0% Pacific Islander, 75% white, 7% international; 42% from in state; 93% live on campus; N/A of students in fraternities, N/A in sororities
Most popular majors: 17% Social Sciences; 12% Biological and Biomedical Sciences; 10% Visual and Performing Arts; 8% Physical Sciences; 8% Psychology
Expenses: 2016-2017: $44,180; room/board: $10,080
Financial aid: (507) 646-3019; 68% of undergrads determined to have financial need; average aid package $35,916

University of Minnesota–Crookston

Crookston MN
(800) 232-6466
U.S. News ranking: Reg. Coll. (Mid. W), No. 40
Website: www.crk.umn.edu
Admissions email: UMCinfo@umn.edu
Public; founded 1966
Freshman admissions: selective; 2015-2016: 1,073 applied, 839 accepted. Either SAT or ACT

required. ACT 25/75 percentile: 19-25. High school rank: 11% in top tenth, 37% in top quarter, 68% in top half
Early decision deadline: N/A, notification date: N/A
Early action deadline: N/A, notification date: N/A
Application deadline (fall): rolling
Undergraduate student body: 1,281 full time, 1,542 part time; 47% male, 53% female; 0% American Indian, 2% Asian, 7% black, 4% Hispanic, 2% multiracial, 0% Pacific Islander, 78% white, 5% international; 72% from in state; 30% live on campus; 3% of students in fraternities, N/A in sororities
Most popular majors: 37% Business, Management, Marketing, and Related Support Services; 11% Health Professions and Related Programs; 6% Multi/Interdisciplinary Studies
Expenses: 2015-2016: $11,646 in state, $11,646 out of state; room/board: $8,093
Financial aid: (218) 281-8576; 68% of undergrads determined to have financial need; average aid package $11,388

University of Minnesota–Duluth

Duluth MN
(218) 726-7171
U.S. News ranking: Reg. U. (Mid. W), No. 47
Website: www.d.umn.edu
Admissions email: umdadmis@d.umn.edu
Public; founded 1947
Freshman admissions: selective; 2015-2016: 7,491 applied, 5,696 accepted. Either SAT or ACT required. ACT 25/75 percentile: 22-26. High school rank: 19% in top tenth, 44% in top quarter, 86% in top half
Early decision deadline: N/A, notification date: N/A
Early action deadline: N/A, notification date: N/A
Application deadline (fall): 8/1
Undergraduate student body: 8,621 full time, 1,216 part time; 53% male, 47% female; 0% American Indian, 3% Asian, 2% black, 3% Hispanic, 3% multiracial, 0% Pacific Islander, 86% white, 2% international; 89% from in state; 32% live on campus; N/A of students in fraternities, N/A in sororities
Most popular majors: 18% Business, Management, Marketing, and Related Support Services; 12% Engineering; 10% Biological and Biomedical Sciences; 9% Social Sciences; 8% Psychology
Expenses: 2015-2016: $13,082 in state, $17,032 out of state; room/board: $7,210
Financial aid: (218) 726-8000; 58% of undergrads determined to have financial need; average aid package $11,993

University of Minnesota–Morris

Morris MN
(888) 866-3382
U.S. News ranking: Nat. Lib. Arts, No. 140
Website: www.morris.umn.edu
Admissions email: admissions@morris.umn.edu
Public; founded 1959
Freshman admissions: more selective; 2015-2016: 3,619 applied, 2,164 accepted. Either SAT or ACT required. ACT 25/75 percentile: 22-28. High school rank: 24% in top tenth, 55% in top quarter, 90% in top half
Early decision deadline: N/A, notification date: N/A
Early action deadline: N/A, notification date: N/A
Application deadline (fall): 3/15
Undergraduate student body: 1,704 full time, 152 part time; 46% male, 54% female; 6% American Indian, 3% Asian, 2% black, 4% Hispanic, 11% multiracial, 0% Pacific Islander, 62% white, 11% international; 87% from in state; 56% live on campus; 0% of students in fraternities, 0% in sororities
Most popular majors: 13% Social Sciences; 12% English Language and Literature/Letters; 11% Biological and Biomedical Sciences; 10% Physical Sciences; 10% Psychology
Expenses: 2015-2016: $12,846 in state, $12,846 out of state; room/board: $7,804
Financial aid: (320) 589-6035; 61% of undergrads determined to have financial need; average aid package $12,973

University of Minnesota–Twin Cities

Minneapolis MN
(800) 752-1000
U.S. News ranking: Nat. U., No. 71
Website: www.umn.edu
Admissions email: N/A
Public; founded 1851
Freshman admissions: more selective; 2015-2016: 46,165 applied, 20,579 accepted. Either SAT or ACT required. ACT 25/75 percentile: 26-31. High school rank: 49% in top tenth, 85% in top quarter, 99% in top half
Early decision deadline: N/A, notification date: N/A
Early action deadline: N/A, notification date: N/A
Application deadline (fall): rolling
Undergraduate student body: 29,168 full time, 4,903 part time; 48% male, 52% female; 0% American Indian, 9% Asian, 4% black, 4% Hispanic, 4% multiracial, 0% Pacific Islander, 70% white, 9% international; 73% from in state; 23% live on campus; N/A of students in fraternities, N/A in sororities
Most popular majors: 12% Biological and Biomedical Sciences; 11% Engineering; 11% Social Sciences; 9% Business, Management, Marketing, and Related Support Services; 7% Psychology

University of Northwestern–St. Paul

St. Paul MN
(800) 827-6827
U.S. News ranking: Reg. U. (Mid. W), No. 40
Website: www.unwsp.edu
Admissions email: admissions@unwsp.edu
Private; founded 1902
Affiliation: Christian nondenominational
Freshman admissions: selective; 2015-2016: 1,327 applied, 1,153 accepted. Either SAT or ACT required. ACT 25/75 percentile: 21-27. High school rank: 22% in top tenth, 49% in top quarter, 84% in top half
Early decision deadline: N/A, notification date: N/A
Early action deadline: N/A, notification date: N/A
Application deadline (fall): 8/1
Undergraduate student body: 1,958 full time, 1,312 part time; 39% male, 61% female; 0% American Indian, 4% Asian, 3% black, 4% Hispanic, 3% multiracial, 0% Pacific Islander, 84% white, 1% international
Most popular majors: Information not available
Expenses: 2016-2017: $29,370; room/board: $9,060
Financial aid: (651) 631-5212

University of St. Thomas

St. Paul MN
(651) 962-6150
U.S. News ranking: Nat. U., No. 118
Website: www.stthomas.edu
Admissions email: admissions@stthomas.edu
Private; founded 1885
Affiliation: Roman Catholic
Freshman admissions: selective; 2015-2016: 5,436 applied, 4,564 accepted. Either SAT or ACT required. ACT 25/75 percentile: 24-29. High school rank: 24% in top tenth, 56% in top quarter, 89% in top half
Early decision deadline: N/A, notification date: N/A
Early action deadline: N/A, notification date: N/A
Application deadline (fall): rolling
Undergraduate student body: 5,952 full time, 288 part time; 54% male, 46% female; 0% American Indian, 3% Asian, 3% black, 5% Hispanic, 3% multiracial, 0% Pacific Islander, 83% white, 1% international; 79% from in state; 41% live on campus; N/A of students in fraternities, N/A in sororities
Most popular majors: 41% Business, Management, Marketing, and Related Support Services; 7% Biological and Biomedical Sciences; 7% Social Sciences; 6% Engineering

Expenses: 2016-2017: $39,594; room/board: $9,760
Financial aid: (651) 962-6550; 57% of undergrads determined to have financial need; average aid package $25,744

Walden University[1]

Minneapolis MN
(866) 492-5336
U.S. News ranking: Nat. U., unranked
Website: www.waldenu.edu/
Admissions email: N/A
For-profit; founded 1970
Application deadline (fall): rolling
Undergraduate student body: N/A full time, N/A part time
Expenses: 2015-2016: $12,075; room/board: N/A
Financial aid: N/A

Winona State University

Winona MN
(507) 457-5100
U.S. News ranking: Reg. U. (Mid. W), No. 71
Website: www.winona.edu
Admissions email: admissions@winona.edu
Public; founded 1858
Freshman admissions: selective; 2015-2016: 6,780 applied, 4,235 accepted. Either SAT or ACT required. ACT 25/75 percentile: 20-25. High school rank: 9% in top tenth, 30% in top quarter, 69% in top half
Early decision deadline: N/A, notification date: N/A
Early action deadline: N/A, notification date: N/A
Application deadline (fall): 7/16
Undergraduate student body: 7,061 full time, 941 part time; 39% male, 61% female; 0% American Indian, 2% Asian, 2% black, 3% Hispanic, 2% multiracial, 0% Pacific Islander, 87% white, 3% international; 70% from in state; 30% live on campus; N/A of students in fraternities, N/A in sororities
Most popular majors: 19% Business, Management, Marketing, and Related Support Services; 19% Health Professions and Related Programs; 13% Education; 8% Parks, Recreation, Leisure, and Fitness Studies
Expenses: 2016-2017: $9,075 in state, $14,772 out of state; room/board: $8,460
Financial aid: (507) 457-5090; 59% of undergrads determined to have financial need; average aid package $7,757

MISSISSIPPI

Alcorn State University

Alcorn State MS
(601) 877-6147
U.S. News ranking: Reg. U. (S), No. 89
Website: www.alcorn.edu
Admissions email: ebarnes@alcorn.edu
Public; founded 1871
Freshman admissions: less selective; 2015-2016: 3,010 applied, 2,425 accepted. Either SAT or ACT required. ACT 25/75

percentile: 16-20. High school rank: 0% in top tenth, 0% in top quarter, 70% in top half
Early decision deadline: N/A, notification date: N/A
Early action deadline: N/A, notification date: N/A
Application deadline (fall): rolling
Undergraduate student body: 2,556 full time, 355 part time; 36% male, 64% female; 0% American Indian, 0% Asian, 93% black, 0% Hispanic, 2% multiracial, 0% Pacific Islander, 3% white, 1% international; 81% from in state; 57% live on campus; N/A of students in fraternities, N/A in sororities
Most popular majors: 25% Biological and Biomedical Sciences; 8% Liberal Arts and Sciences, General Studies and Humanities; 7% Business, Management, Marketing, and Related Support Services; 5% Homeland Security, Law Enforcement, Firefighting and Related Protective Services; 5% Public Administration and Social Service Professions
Expenses: 2016-2017: $6,552 in state, $6,552 out of state; room/board: $9,356
Financial aid: (601) 877-6190; 47% of undergrads determined to have financial need; average aid package $14,742

Belhaven University

Jackson MS
(601) 968-5940
U.S. News ranking: Reg. U. (S), No. 52
Website: www.belhaven.edu
Admissions email: admission@belhaven.edu
Private; founded 1883
Affiliation: Presbyterian
Freshman admissions: selective; 2015-2016: 3,053 applied, 1,551 accepted. Either SAT or ACT required. ACT 25/75 percentile: 20-24. High school rank: 15% in top tenth, 43% in top quarter, 69% in top half
Early decision deadline: N/A, notification date: N/A
Early action deadline: N/A, notification date: N/A
Application deadline (fall): rolling
Undergraduate student body: 1,403 full time, 1,348 part time; 35% male, 65% female; 0% American Indian, 2% Asian, 36% black, 6% Hispanic, 2% multiracial, 0% Pacific Islander, 41% white, 8% international; N/A from in state; 78% live on campus; N/A of students in fraternities, N/A in sororities
Most popular majors: 31% Business, Management, Marketing, and Related Support Services; 12% Social Sciences; 9% Visual and Performing Arts; 8% Parks, Recreation, Leisure, and Fitness Studies; 7% Health Professions and Related Programs
Expenses: 2016-2017: $23,016; room/board: $8,000
Financial aid: (601) 968-5934; 79% of undergrads determined to have financial need; average aid package $22,762

Blue Mountain College

Blue Mountain MS
(662) 685-4161
U.S. News ranking: Reg. Coll. (S), No. 7
Website: www.bmc.edu
Admissions email: admissions@bmc.edu
Private; founded 1873
Affiliation: Southern Baptist
Freshman admissions: selective; 2015-2016: 326 applied, 125 accepted. Either SAT or ACT required. ACT 25/75 percentile: 18-24. High school rank: 17% in top tenth, 37% in top quarter, 65% in top half
Early decision deadline: N/A, notification date: N/A
Early action deadline: N/A, notification date: N/A
Application deadline (fall): rolling
Undergraduate student body: 397 full time, 60 part time; 43% male, 57% female; 0% American Indian, 0% Asian, 10% black, 1% Hispanic, 1% multiracial, 0% Pacific Islander, 85% white, 2% international; 80% from in state; 54% live on campus; 0% of students in fraternities, 0% in sororities
Most popular majors: 23% Psychology, General; 19% Bible/Biblical Studies; 18% Elementary Education and Teaching; 12% Business Administration and Management, General; 7% Biology/Biological Sciences, General
Expenses: 2016-2017: $11,212; room/board: $5,839
Financial aid: (662) 685-4771; 78% of undergrads determined to have financial need; average aid package $9,864

Delta State University[1]

Cleveland MS
(662) 846-4018
U.S. News ranking: Reg. U. (S), second tier
Website: www.deltastate.edu
Admissions email: admissions@deltastate.edu
Public; founded 1924
Application deadline (fall): 8/1
Undergraduate student body: N/A full time, N/A part time
Expenses: 2015-2016: $6,112 in state, $6,112 out of state; room/board: $7,064
Financial aid: (662) 846-4670

Jackson State University

Jackson MS
(601) 979-2100
U.S. News ranking: Nat. U., second tier
Website: www.jsums.edu
Admissions email: admappl@jsums.edu
Public; founded 1877
Freshman admissions: selective; 2015-2016: 8,035 applied, 5,425 accepted. Either SAT or ACT required. ACT 25/75 percentile: 17-21. High school rank:
Early decision deadline: N/A, notification date: N/A
Early action deadline: N/A, notification date: N/A
Application deadline (fall): 9/2

Undergraduate student body: 6,678 full time, 797 part time; 37% male, 63% female; 0% American Indian, 0% Asian, 91% black, 0% Hispanic, 1% multiracial, 0% Pacific Islander, 4% white, 2% international; 77% from in state; 34% live on campus; 1% of students in fraternities, 1% in sororities Most popular majors: 18% Education; 14% Business, Management, Marketing, and Related Support Services; 12% Multi/Interdisciplinary Studies; 8% Homeland Security, Law Enforcement, Firefighting and Related Protective Services; 8% Public Administration and Social Service Professions Expenses: 2016-2017: $7,261 in state, $17,614 out of state; room/board: $10,078 Financial aid: (601) 979-2227; 92% of undergrads need; average aid package $11,255

Millsaps College

Jackson MS
(601) 974-1050
U.S. News ranking: Nat. Lib. Arts, No. 90
Website: www.millsaps.edu
Admissions email: admissions@ millsaps.edu
Private; founded 1890
Affiliation: United Methodist
Freshman admissions: more selective; 2015-2016: 3,657 applied, 1,925 accepted. Either SAT or ACT required. ACT 25/75 percentile: 23-28. High school rank: 34% in top tenth, 64% in top quarter, 90% in top half
Early decision deadline: N/A, notification date: N/A
Early action deadline: 11/15, notification date: 1/15
Application deadline (fall): 7/1
Undergraduate student body: 750 full time, 11 part time; 50% male, 50% female; 1% American Indian, 3% Asian, 13% black, 4% Hispanic, 0% multiracial, 0% Pacific Islander, 72% white, 4% international; 45% from in state; 90% live on campus; 62% of students in fraternities, 58% in sororities
Most popular majors: 29% Business, Management, Marketing, and Related Support Services; 22% Biological and Biomedical Sciences; 9% Psychology; 9% Social Sciences
Expenses: 2016-2017: $37,110; room/board $14,303
Financial aid: (601) 974-1220; 59% of undergrads determined to have financial need; average aid package $31,657

Mississippi College

Clinton MS
(601) 925-3800
U.S. News ranking: Reg. U. (S), No. 31
Website: www.mc.edu
Admissions email: enrollment-services@mc.edu
Private; founded 1826
Affiliation: Mississippi Baptist Convention
Freshman admissions: selective; 2015-2016: 2,581 applied, 1,635 accepted. Either SAT or ACT required. ACT 25/75

percentile: 21-27. High school rank: 33% in top tenth, 60% in top quarter, 85% in top half
Early decision deadline: N/A, notification date: N/A
Early action deadline: N/A, notification date: N/A
Application deadline (fall): rolling
Undergraduate student body: 2,677 full time, 327 part time; 40% male, 60% female; 1% American Indian, 2% Asian, 19% black, 3% Hispanic, 1% multiracial, 0% Pacific Islander, 67% white, 5% international; 71% from in state; 64% live on campus; 10% of students in fraternities, 24% in sororities
Most popular majors: 12% Registered Nursing/Registered Nurse; 11% Kinesiology and Exercise Science; 7% Biomedical Sciences, General; 7% Business Administration and Management, General; 6% Elementary Education and Teaching
Expenses: 2016-2017: $16,740; room/board: $9,190
Financial aid: (601) 925-3319; 52% of undergrads determined to have financial need; average aid package $15,035

Mississippi State University

Mississippi State MS
(662) 325-2224
U.S. News ranking: Nat. U., No. 176
Website: www.msstate.edu
Admissions email: admit@ admissions.msstate.edu
Public; founded 1878
Freshman admissions: more selective; 2015-2016: 12,701 applied, 9,113 accepted. Either SAT or ACT required. ACT 25/75 percentile: 20-27. High school rank: 26% in top tenth, 52% in top quarter, 82% in top half
Early decision deadline: N/A, notification date: N/A
Early action deadline: N/A, notification date: N/A
Application deadline (fall): rolling
Undergraduate student body: 16,023 full time, 1,398 part time; 51% male, 49% female; 1% American Indian, 1% Asian, 20% black, 2% Hispanic, 2% multiracial, 0% Pacific Islander, 72% white, 1% international; 72% from in state; 27% live on campus; 20% of students in fraternities, 23% in sororities
Most popular majors: 19% Business, Management, Marketing, and Related Support Services; 14% Engineering; 9% Parks, Recreation, Leisure, and Fitness Studies; 8% Education; 5% Psychology
Expenses: 2015-2016: $7,502 in state, $20,142 out of state; room/board: $9,068
Financial aid: (662) 325-2450

Mississippi University for Women

Columbus MS
(662) 329-7106
U.S. News ranking: Reg. U. (S), No. 43
Website: www.muw.edu
Admissions email: admissions@muw.edu

Public; founded 1884
Freshman admissions: selective; 2015-2016: 671 applied, 645 accepted. Either SAT or ACT required. ACT 25/75 percentile: 18-24. High school rank: 24% in top tenth, 54% in top quarter, 84% in top half
Early decision deadline: N/A, notification date: N/A
Early action deadline: N/A, notification date: N/A
Application deadline (fall): rolling
Undergraduate student body: 1,976 full time, 494 part time; 20% male, 80% female; 0% American Indian, 0% Asian, 37% black, 0% Hispanic, 0% multiracial, 0% Pacific Islander, 57% white, 4% international; 85% from in state; 25% live on campus; 10% of students in fraternities, 13% in sororities
Most popular majors: 52% Registered Nursing/Registered Nurse; 6% Business Administration and Management, General; 5% Public Health Education and Promotion; 4% Health and Physical Education/Fitness, General; 4% Speech-Language Pathology/Pathologist
Expenses: 2016-2017: $6,065 in state, $16,634 out of state; room/board: $6,808
Financial aid: (662) 329-7114; 76% of undergrads determined to have financial need; average aid package $9,263

Mississippi Valley State University

Itta Bena MS
(662) 254-3344
U.S. News ranking: Reg. U. (S), second tier
Website: www.mvsu.edu
Admissions email: admsn@mvsu.edu
Public; founded 1950
Freshman admissions: less selective; 2015-2016: 2,310 applied, 1,748 accepted. Either SAT or ACT required. ACT 25/75 percentile: 16-19. High school rank: N/A
Early decision deadline: N/A, notification date: N/A
Early action deadline: N/A, notification date: N/A
Application deadline (fall): 8/17
Undergraduate student body: 1,704 full time, 244 part time; 41% male, 59% female; N/A American Indian, 0% Asian, 91% black, 1% Hispanic, 0% multiracial, N/A Pacific Islander, 3% white, N/A international
Most popular majors: 31% Education; 22% Business, Management, Marketing, and Related Support Services; 15% Public Administration and Social Service Professions; 9% Homeland Security, Law Enforcement, Firefighting and Related Protective Services
Expenses: 2015-2016: $5,936 in state, $5,936 out of state; room/board: $7,177
Financial aid: (662) 254-3335

Rust College

Holly Springs MS
(662) 252-8000
U.S. News ranking: Reg. Coll. (S), No. 52
Website: www.rustcollege.edu
Admissions email: admissions@ rustcollege.edu
Private; founded 1866
Affiliation: United Methodist
Freshman admissions: less selective; 2015-2016: 5,307 applied, 856 accepted. ACT required. ACT 25/75 percentile: 14-18. High school rank: N/A
Early decision deadline: N/A, notification date: N/A
Early action deadline: N/A, notification date: N/A
Application deadline (fall): rolling
Undergraduate student body: 795 full time, 61 part time; 40% male, 60% female; N/A American Indian, N/A Asian, 96% black, N/A Hispanic, N/A multiracial, N/A Pacific Islander, 0% white, 3% international; 51% from in state; N/A live on campus; N/A of students in fraternities, N/A in sororities
Most popular majors: 26% Biology/Biological Sciences, General; 14% Kindergarten/Preschool Education and Teaching; 9% Business Administration and Management, General; 8% Social Work
Expenses: 2016-2017: $9,500; room/board: $4,100
Financial aid: (662) 252-8000; 100% of undergrads determined to have financial need; average aid package $12,426

Tougaloo College

Tougaloo MS
(601) 977-7765
U.S. News ranking: Nat. Lib. Arts, second tier
Website: www.tougaloo.edu
Admissions email: information@ mail.tougaloo.edu
Private; founded 1869
Affiliation: United Church Disciples of Christ
Freshman admissions: less selective; 2015-2016: 2,321 applied, 908 accepted. Either SAT or ACT required. ACT 25/75 percentile: 15-20. High school rank: 19% in top tenth, 25% in top quarter, 80% in top half
Early decision deadline: N/A, notification date: N/A
Early action deadline: 11/1, notification date: 12/1
Application deadline (fall): 7/1
Undergraduate student body: 816 full time, 47 part time; 35% male, 65% female; 0% American Indian, N/A Asian, 99% black, 0% Hispanic, N/A multiracial, N/A Pacific Islander, 0% white, N/A international; 80% from in state; 75% live on campus; 5% of students in fraternities, 1% in sororities
Most popular majors: 17% Sociology; 13% Biology/Biological Sciences, General; 9% Economics, General; 8% Chemistry, General
Expenses: 2016-2017: $10,600; room/board: $6,330
Financial aid: (601) 977-7769; 94% of undergrads determined to have financial need; average aid package $12,500

University of Mississippi

University MS
(662) 915-7226
U.S. News ranking: Nat. U., No. 135
Website: www.olemiss.edu
Admissions email: admissions@ olemiss.edu
Public; founded 1844
Freshman admissions: more selective; 2015-2016: 18,059 applied, 14,217 accepted. Neither SAT nor ACT required. ACT 25/75 percentile: 21-28. High school rank: 24% in top tenth, 49% in top quarter, 78% in top half
Early decision deadline: N/A, notification date: N/A
Early action deadline: N/A, notification date: N/A
Application deadline (fall): rolling
Undergraduate student body: 17,395 full time, 1,390 part time; 44% male, 56% female; 0% American Indian, 2% Asian, 14% black, 3% Hispanic, 2% multiracial, 0% Pacific Islander, 78% white, 1% international; 58% from in state; 27% live on campus; 35% of students in fraternities, 48% in sororities
Most popular majors: 6% Elementary Education and Teaching; 6% General Studies; 5% Accounting; 5% Marketing/Marketing Management, General; 5% Psychology, General
Expenses: 2016-2017: $7,744 in state, $22,012 out of state; room/board: $10,002
Financial aid: (662) 915-7175; 50% of undergrads determined to have financial need; average aid package $9,219

University of Southern Mississippi

Hattiesburg MS
(601) 266-5000
U.S. News ranking: Nat. U., No. 220
Website: www.usm.edu/admissions
Admissions email: admissions@usm.edu
Public; founded 1910
Freshman admissions: selective; 2015-2016: 6,046 applied, 3,509 accepted. Either SAT or ACT required. ACT 25/75 percentile: 19-26. High school rank: N/A
Early decision deadline: N/A, notification date: N/A
Early action deadline: N/A, notification date: N/A
Application deadline (fall): rolling
Undergraduate student body: 10,300 full time, 1,540 part time; 36% male, 64% female; 0% American Indian, 1% Asian, 30% black, 3% Hispanic, 2% multiracial, 0% Pacific Islander, 61% white, 1% international; 84% from in state; 27% live on campus; 10% of students in fraternities, 14% in sororities
Most popular majors: 7% Elementary Education and Teaching; 7% Registered Nursing/Registered Nurse; 7% Psychology, General; 4% Business Administration and Management, General; 4% Biology/Biological Sciences, General

Expenses: 2016-2017: $7,224 in state, $16,094 out of state; room/board: $9,060
Financial aid: (601) 266-4774; 77% of undergrads determined to have financial need; average aid package $10,743

William Carey University
Hattiesburg MS
(601) 318-6103
U.S. News ranking: Reg. U. (S), No. 41
Website: www.wmcarey.edu
Admissions email: admissions@wmcarey.edu
Private; founded 1892
Affiliation: Baptist
Freshman admissions: selective; 2015-2016: 842 applied, 479 accepted. Either SAT or ACT required. ACT 25/75 percentile: 20-27. High school rank: 33% in top tenth, 54% in top quarter, 84% in top half
Early decision deadline: N/A, notification date: N/A
Early action deadline: N/A, notification date: N/A
Application deadline (fall): rolling
Undergraduate student body: 1,850 full time, 637 part time; 37% male, 63% female; 1% American Indian, 1% Asian, 31% black, 2% Hispanic, 0% multiracial, 0% Pacific Islander, 60% white, 4% international; 88% from in state; 32% live on campus; 5% of students in fraternities, 8% in sororities
Most popular majors: 25% Registered Nursing/Registered Nurse; 19% Psychology, General; 18% Elementary Education and Teaching; 11% Biology/Biological Sciences, General; 10% Business Administration and Management, General
Expenses: 2016-2017: $11,700; room/board: $4,260
Financial aid: (601) 318-6153; 92% of undergrads determined to have financial need; average aid package $16,500

MISSOURI

Avila University[1]
Kansas City MO
(816) 501-2400
U.S. News ranking: Reg. U. (Mid. W), second tier
Website: www.Avila.edu
Admissions email: admissions@mail.avila.edu
Private
Application deadline (fall): N/A
Undergraduate student body: N/A full time, N/A part time
Expenses: 2015-2016: $26,450; room/board: $7,410
Financial aid: (816) 501-3600

Central Methodist University
Fayette MO
(660) 248-6251
U.S. News ranking: Reg. Coll. (Mid. W), No. 26
Website: www.centralmethodist.edu
Admissions email: admissions@centralmethodist.edu
Private; founded 1854

Affiliation: United Methodist
Freshman admissions: selective; 2015-2016: 1,430 applied, 827 accepted. Either SAT or ACT required. ACT 25/75 percentile: 20-25. High school rank: 13% in top tenth, 42% in top quarter, 79% in top half
Early decision deadline: N/A, notification date: N/A
Early action deadline: N/A, notification date: N/A
Application deadline (fall): rolling
Undergraduate student body: 1,072 full time, 22 part time; 48% male, 52% female; 0% American Indian, 0% Asian, 8% black, 3% Hispanic, 3% multiracial, 0% Pacific Islander, 78% white, 4% international; 87% from in state; 61% live on campus; 16% of students in fraternities, 22% in sororities
Most popular majors: 18% Health Professions and Related Programs; 17% Education; 15% Business, Management, Marketing, and Related Support Services; 11% Biological and Biomedical Sciences; 6% Homeland Security, Law Enforcement, Firefighting and Related Protective Services
Expenses: 2016-2017: $23,010; room/board: $7,550
Financial aid: (660) 248-6244; 79% of undergrads determined to have financial need; average aid package $19,348

College of the Ozarks
Point Lookout MO
(800) 222-0525
U.S. News ranking: Reg. Coll. (Mid. W), No. 4
Website: www.cofo.edu
Admissions email: admiss4@cofo.edu
Private; founded 1906
Affiliation: Evangelical Christian Interdenominational
Freshman admissions: selective; 2015-2016: 3,122 applied, 386 accepted. Either SAT or ACT required. ACT 25/75 percentile: 21-25. High school rank: 23% in top tenth, 61% in top quarter, 91% in top half
Early decision deadline: N/A, notification date: N/A
Early action deadline: N/A, notification date: N/A
Application deadline (fall): rolling
Undergraduate student body: 1,432 full time, 10 part time; 47% male, 53% female; 0% American Indian, 1% Asian, 1% black, 2% Hispanic, 2% multiracial, 0% Pacific Islander, 93% white, 2% international; 81% from in state; 82% live on campus; 0% of students in fraternities, 0% in sororities
Most popular majors: 14% Business, Management, Marketing, and Related Support Services; 11% Education, General; 7% Health Professions and Related Programs; 7% Homeland Security, Law Enforcement, Firefighting and Related Protective Services
Expenses: 2016-2017: $18,930; room/board: $6,800
Financial aid: (417) 334-6411; 93% of undergrads determined to have financial need; average aid package $20,102

Columbia College
Columbia MO
(573) 875-7352
U.S. News ranking: Reg. U. (Mid. W), unranked
Website: www.ccis.edu
Admissions email: admissions@ccis.edu
Private; founded 1851
Affiliation: Christian Church (Disciples of Christ)
Freshman admissions: N/A; 2015-2016: N/A applied, N/A accepted. Neither SAT nor ACT required. ACT 25/75 percentile: N/A. High school rank: N/A
Early decision deadline: N/A, notification date: N/A
Early action deadline: N/A, notification date: N/A
Application deadline (fall): rolling
Undergraduate student body: 8,180 full time, 5,708 part time; 41% male, 59% female; N/A American Indian, N/A Asian, N/A black, N/A Hispanic, N/A multiracial, N/A Pacific Islander, N/A white, N/A international
Most popular majors: Information not available
Expenses: 2015-2016: $8,240; room/board: $6,302
Financial aid: (573) 875-7390

Cottey College
Nevada MO
(888) 526-8839
U.S. News ranking: Reg. Coll. (Mid. W), No. 22
Website: www.cottey.edu/
Admissions email: N/A
Private; founded 1884
Freshman admissions: selective; 2015-2016: 412 applied, 303 accepted. Either SAT or ACT required. ACT 25/75 percentile: 20-26. High school rank: 15% in top tenth, 41% in top quarter, 75% in top half
Early decision deadline: N/A, notification date: N/A
Early action deadline: N/A, notification date: N/A
Application deadline (fall): rolling
Undergraduate student body: 289 full time, 31 part time; 0% male, 100% female; 2% American Indian, 2% Asian, 8% black, 10% Hispanic, 5% multiracial, 0% Pacific Islander, 59% white, 14% international
Most popular majors: Information not available
Expenses: 2016-2017: $19,300; room/board: $7,000
Financial aid: N/A; 76% of undergrads determined to have financial need; average aid package $20,584

Culver-Stockton College
Canton MO
(800) 537-1883
U.S. News ranking: Reg. Coll. (Mid. W), No. 30
Website: www.culver.edu
Admissions email: admissions@culver.edu
Private; founded 1853
Affiliation: Christian Church (Disciples of Christ)
Freshman admissions: selective; 2015-2016: 2,913 applied, 1,628 accepted. Either SAT or ACT required. ACT 25/75 percentile: 18-23. High school

rank: 11% in top tenth, 27% in top quarter, 61% in top half
Early decision deadline: N/A, notification date: N/A
Early action deadline: N/A, notification date: N/A
Application deadline (fall): rolling
Undergraduate student body: 926 full time, 123 part time; 49% male, 51% female; N/A American Indian, 0% Asian, 13% black, 5% Hispanic, 2% multiracial, 0% Pacific Islander, 71% white, 8% international; 54% from in state; 76% live on campus; 36% of students in fraternities, 39% in sororities
Most popular majors: 18% Business Administration and Management, General; 12% Psychology, General; 10% Sport and Fitness Administration/Management; 9% Criminal Justice/Law Enforcement Administration; 8% Registered Nursing/Registered Nurse
Expenses: 2016-2017: $25,415; room/board: $8,110
Financial aid: (573) 288-6307; 80% of undergrads determined to have financial need; average aid package $20,594

Drury University
Springfield MO
(417) 873-7205
U.S. News ranking: Reg. U. (Mid. W), No. 11
Website: www.drury.edu
Admissions email: druryad@drury.edu
Private; founded 1873
Affiliation: Christian Church (Disciples of Christ)
Freshman admissions: more selective; 2015-2016: 1,423 applied, 927 accepted. Either SAT or ACT required. ACT 25/75 percentile: 20-31. High school rank: 28% in top tenth, 59% in top quarter, 88% in top half
Early decision deadline: N/A, notification date: N/A
Early action deadline: N/A, notification date: N/A
Application deadline (fall): 5/1
Undergraduate student body: 1,291 full time, 24 part time; 45% male, 55% female; 0% American Indian, 2% Asian, 3% black, 4% Hispanic, 2% multiracial, 0% Pacific Islander, 76% white, 13% international; 86% from in state; 61% live on campus; 22% of students in fraternities, 27% in sororities
Most popular majors: 14% Psychology; 13% Business, Management, Marketing, and Related Support Services; 9% Biological and Biomedical Sciences; 7% Education
Expenses: 2016-2017: $25,905; room/board: $7,480
Financial aid: (417) 873-7312; 68% of undergrads determined to have financial need; average aid package $19,058

Evangel University
Springfield MO
(800) 382-6435
U.S. News ranking: Reg. U. (Mid. W), second tier
Website: www.evangel.edu
Admissions email: admissions@evangel.edu
Private; founded 1955

Affiliation: Assemblies of God
Freshman admissions: selective; 2015-2016: 1,483 applied, 912 accepted. Either SAT or ACT required. ACT 25/75 percentile: 20-26. High school rank: N/A
Early decision deadline: N/A, notification date: N/A
Early action deadline: N/A, notification date: N/A
Application deadline (fall): rolling
Undergraduate student body: 1,559 full time, 165 part time; 45% male, 55% female; 1% American Indian, 2% Asian, 4% black, 4% Hispanic, 3% multiracial, 0% Pacific Islander, 78% white, 1% international
Most popular majors: 13% Bible/Biblical Studies; 13% Business Administration and Management, General; 7% Psychology, General; 6% Elementary Education and Teaching; 5% Biology/Biological Sciences, General
Expenses: 2016-2017: $21,956; room/board: $7,882
Financial aid: (417) 865-2815; 84% of undergrads determined to have financial need; average aid package $16,542

Fontbonne University
St. Louis MO
(314) 889-1400
U.S. News ranking: Reg. U. (Mid. W), No. 91
Website: www.fontbonne.edu
Admissions email: admissions@fontbonne.edu
Private; founded 1923
Affiliation: Roman Catholic
Freshman admissions: selective; 2015-2016: 494 applied, 478 accepted. Either SAT or ACT required. ACT 25/75 percentile: 20-25. High school rank: N/A
Early decision deadline: N/A, notification date: N/A
Early action deadline: N/A, notification date: N/A
Application deadline (fall): rolling
Undergraduate student body: 902 full time, 203 part time; 31% male, 69% female; 0% American Indian, 1% Asian, 15% black, 2% Hispanic, 2% multiracial, 0% Pacific Islander, 71% white, 7% international; 76% from in state; 34% live on campus; N/A of students in fraternities, N/A in sororities
Most popular majors: 12% Office Management and Supervision; 5% Social Work; 4% Special Education and Teaching, General; 4% Speech-Language Pathology/Pathologist; 3% Apparel and Textiles, General
Expenses: 2016-2017: $24,610; room/board: $9,107
Financial aid: (314) 889-1414

Hannibal-LaGrange University
Hannibal MO
(800) 454-1119
U.S. News ranking: Reg. Coll. (Mid. W), No. 58
Website: www.hlg.edu
Admissions email: admissions@hlg.edu
Private; founded 1858
Affiliation: Southern Baptist Convention
Freshman admissions: less selective; 2015-2016: N/A

applied, 283 accepted. Either SAT or ACT required. ACT 25/75 percentile: N/A. High school rank: N/A
Early decision deadline: N/A, notification date: N/A
Early action deadline: N/A, notification date: N/A
Application deadline (fall): 8/27
Undergraduate student body: 799 full time, 303 part time; 40% male, 60% female; 1% American Indian, 0% Asian, 5% black, 2% Hispanic, 2% multiracial, N/A Pacific Islander, 82% white, 7% international
Most popular majors: Business Administration and Management, General; Criminal Justice/Safety Studies; Elementary Education and Teaching; Organizational Leadership; Registered Nursing/Registered Nurse
Expenses: 2015-2016: $21,110; room/board: $7,608
Financial aid: (573) 221-3675

Harris-Stowe State University
St. Louis MO
(314) 340-3300
U.S. News ranking: Reg. Coll. (Mid. W), second tier
Website: www.hssu.edu
Admissions email: admissions@hssu.edu
Public; founded 1857
Freshman admissions: least selective; 2015-2016: 2,573 applied, 1,321 accepted. Either SAT or ACT required. ACT 25/75 percentile: 14-18. High school rank: 4% in top tenth, 20% in top quarter, 56% in top half
Early decision deadline: N/A, notification date: N/A
Early action deadline: N/A, notification date: N/A
Application deadline (fall): rolling
Undergraduate student body: 1,036 full time, 354 part time; 33% male, 67% female; 0% American Indian, 0% Asian, 82% black, 2% Hispanic, 3% multiracial, N/A Pacific Islander, 7% white, 0% international; 92% from in state; 30% live on campus; N/A of students in fraternities, N/A in sororities
Most popular majors: 22% Business Administration and Management, General; 19% Criminal Justice/Safety Studies; 13% Education, General; 10% Elementary Education and Teaching; 9% Accounting
Expenses: 2016-2017: $5,220 in state, $9,853 out of state; room/board: $9,250
Financial aid: (314) 340-3500; 81% of undergrads determined to have financial need; average aid package $9,248

Kansas City Art Institute[1]
Kansas City MO
(800) 522-5224
U.S. News ranking: Arts, unranked
Website: www.kcai.edu
Admissions email: admiss@kcai.edu
Private; founded 1885
Application deadline (fall): rolling
Undergraduate student body: N/A full time, N/A part time

Expenses: 2015-2016: $35,270; room/board: $10,240
Financial aid: (816) 802-3448

Lincoln University
Jefferson City MO
(573) 681-5599
U.S. News ranking: Reg. U. (Mid. W), second tier
Website: www.lincolnu.edu
Admissions email: enroll@lincolnu.edu
Public; founded 1866
Freshman admissions: less selective; 2015-2016: N/A applied, N/A accepted. Either SAT or ACT required. ACT 25/75 percentile: 15-19. High school rank: 6% in top tenth, 23% in top quarter, 61% in top half
Early decision deadline: N/A, notification date: N/A
Early action deadline: N/A, notification date: N/A
Application deadline (fall): rolling
Undergraduate student body: 1,974 full time, 847 part time; 45% male, 55% female; 0% American Indian, 0% Asian, 52% black, 2% Hispanic, 4% multiracial, 0% Pacific Islander, 36% white, 2% international; 85% from in state; 33% live on campus; N/A of students in fraternities, N/A in sororities
Most popular majors: 14% Liberal Arts and Sciences/Liberal Studies; 10% Business Administration and Management, General; 7% Criminal Justice/Law Enforcement Administration; 7% Elementary Education and Teaching; 7% Psychology, General
Expenses: 2015-2016: $7,042 in state, $13,432 out of state; room/board: $10,400
Financial aid: (573) 681-6156; 84% of undergrads determined to have financial need; average aid package $10,522

Lindenwood University
St. Charles MO
(636) 949-4949
U.S. News ranking: Nat. U., second tier
Website: www.lindenwood.edu
Admissions email: admissions@lindenwood.edu
Private; founded 1827
Freshman admissions: selective; 2015-2016: 4,156 applied, 2,302 accepted. Neither SAT nor ACT required. ACT 25/75 percentile: 20-25. High school rank: 10% in top tenth, 33% in top quarter, 70% in top half
Early decision deadline: N/A, notification date: N/A
Early action deadline: N/A, notification date: N/A
Application deadline (fall): rolling
Undergraduate student body: 7,297 full time, 988 part time; 45% male, 55% female; 0% American Indian, 1% Asian, 13% black, 4% Hispanic, 3% multiracial, 0% Pacific Islander, 56% white, 12% international; 64% from in state; 56% live on campus; 3% of students in fraternities, 4% in sororities
Most popular majors: 17% Business/Commerce, General; 7% General Studies; 5%

Criminal Justice/Safety Studies; 5% Kinesiology and Exercise Science; 4% Psychology, General
Expenses: 2016-2017: $16,332; room/board: $8,800
Financial aid: (636) 949-4923; 57% of undergrads determined to have financial need; average aid package $10,149

Maryville University of St. Louis
St Louis MO
(800) 627-9855
U.S. News ranking: Nat. U., No. 164
Website: www.maryville.edu
Admissions email: admissions@maryville.edu
Private; founded 1872
Freshman admissions: more selective; 2015-2016: 1,457 applied, 1,053 accepted. Neither SAT nor ACT required. ACT 25/75 percentile: 23-27. High school rank: 25% in top tenth, 59% in top quarter, 90% in top half
Early decision deadline: N/A, notification date: N/A
Early action deadline: N/A, notification date: N/A
Application deadline (fall): 8/15
Undergraduate student body: 1,915 full time, 880 part time; 31% male, 69% female; 0% American Indian, 2% Asian, 8% black, 3% Hispanic, 2% multiracial, 0% Pacific Islander, 75% white, 4% international; 79% from in state; 24% live on campus; 0% of students in fraternities, 0% in sororities
Most popular majors: 38% Health Professions and Related Programs; 22% Business, Management, Marketing, and Related Support Services; 10% Psychology; 6% Visual and Performing Arts; 4% Biological and Biomedical Sciences
Expenses: 2016-2017: $27,958; room/board: $10,400
Financial aid: (314) 529-9360; 70% of undergrads determined to have financial need; average aid package $22,644

Missouri Baptist University[1]
St. Louis MO
(314) 434-2290
U.S. News ranking: Reg. U. (Mid. W), second tier
Website: www.mobap.edu
Admissions email: admissions@mobap.edu
Private; founded 1964
Affiliation: Baptist
Application deadline (fall): rolling
Undergraduate student body: N/A full time, N/A part time
Expenses: 2015-2016: $23,886; room/board: $9,510
Financial aid: (314) 392-2366

Missouri Southern State University
Joplin MO
(417) 781-6778
U.S. News ranking: Reg. Coll. (Mid. W), second tier
Website: www.mssu.edu
Admissions email: admissions@mssu.edu
Public; founded 1937

Freshman admissions: selective; 2015-2016: 2,333 applied, 2,196 accepted. Either SAT or ACT required. ACT 25/75 percentile: 19-25. High school rank: 14% in top tenth, 39% in top quarter, 70% in top half
Early decision deadline: N/A, notification date: N/A
Early action deadline: N/A, notification date: N/A
Application deadline (fall): rolling
Undergraduate student body: 4,210 full time, 1,522 part time; 44% male, 56% female; 3% American Indian, 2% Asian, 6% black, 5% Hispanic, 1% multiracial, 0% Pacific Islander, 77% white, 3% international; 83% from in state; 14% live on campus; 1% of students in fraternities, 2% in sororities
Most popular majors: 26% Business, Management, Marketing, and Related Support Services; 13% Education; 11% Health Professions and Related Programs; 11% Homeland Security, Law Enforcement, Firefighting and Related Protective Services; 6% Biological and Biomedical Sciences
Expenses: 2016-2017: $5,877 in state, $11,283 out of state; room/board: $6,627
Financial aid: (417) 625-9325; 55% of undergrads determined to have financial need; average aid package $8,665

Missouri State University[1]
Springfield MO
(800) 492-7900
U.S. News ranking: Reg. U. (Mid. W), No. 71
Website: www.missouristate.edu
Admissions email: info@missouristate.edu
Public; founded 1906
Application deadline (fall): 7/20
Undergraduate student body: N/A full time, N/A part time
Expenses: 2015-2016: $7,060 in state, $13,930 out of state; room/board: $7,868
Financial aid: (417) 836-5262

Missouri University of Science & Technology
Rolla MO
(573) 341-4165
U.S. News ranking: Nat. U., No. 164
Website: www.mst.edu
Admissions email: admissions@mst.edu
Public; founded 1870
Freshman admissions: more selective; 2015-2016: 3,592 applied, 3,164 accepted. Either SAT or ACT required. ACT 25/75 percentile: 25-31. High school rank: 44% in top tenth, 74% in top quarter, 94% in top half
Early decision deadline: N/A, notification date: N/A
Early action deadline: N/A, notification date: N/A
Application deadline (fall): 7/1
Undergraduate student body: 6,168 full time, 673 part time; 77% male, 23% female; 0% American Indian, 3% Asian, 4% black, 3% Hispanic, 3% multiracial,

0% Pacific Islander, 78% white, 6% international; 78% from in state; 30% live on campus; N/A of students in fraternities, N/A in sororities
Most popular majors: 66% Engineering; 9% Computer and Information Sciences and Support Services; 5% Biological and Biomedical Sciences; 5% Engineering Technologies and Engineering-Related Fields; 4% Physical Sciences
Expenses: 2016-2017: $9,628 in state, $26,152 out of state; room/board: $9,935
Financial aid: (573) 341-4282; 56% of undergrads determined to have financial need; average aid package $15,692

Missouri Valley College
Marshall MO
(660) 831-4114
U.S. News ranking: Reg. Coll. (Mid. W), second tier
Website: www.moval.edu
Admissions email: admissions@moval.edu
Private; founded 1889
Affiliation: Presbyterian Church
Freshman admissions: selective; 2015-2016: 2,879 applied, 1,312 accepted. Either SAT or ACT required. ACT 25/75 percentile: N/A. High school rank: 28% in top tenth, 37% in top quarter, 59% in top half
Early decision deadline: N/A, notification date: N/A
Early action deadline: N/A, notification date: N/A
Application deadline (fall): rolling
Undergraduate student body: 1,349 full time, 363 part time; 57% male, 43% female; 1% American Indian, 1% Asian, 18% black, 4% Hispanic, 4% multiracial, 1% Pacific Islander, 52% white, 11% international
Most popular majors: Information not available
Expenses: 2015-2016: $19,000; room/board: $8,400
Financial aid: (660) 831-4171

Missouri Western State University[1]
St. Joseph MO
(816) 271-4266
U.S. News ranking: Reg. Coll. (Mid. W), second tier
Website: www.missouriwestern.edu
Admissions email: admission@missouriwestern.edu
Public; founded 1969
Application deadline (fall): rolling
Undergraduate student body: N/A full time, N/A part time
Expenses: 2015-2016: $6,651 in state, $12,809 out of state; room/board: $7,590
Financial aid: (816) 271-4361

Northwest Missouri State University
Maryville MO
(800) 633-1175
U.S. News ranking: Reg. U. (Mid. W), No. 94
Website: www.nwmissouri.edu
Admissions email: admissions@nwmissouri.edu
Public; founded 1905

More at usnews.com/college

Freshman admissions: selective; 2015-2016: 5,009 applied, 3,754 accepted. Either SAT or ACT required. ACT 25/75 percentile: 20-25. High school rank: 16% in top tenth, 40% in top quarter, 77% in top half
Early decision deadline: N/A, notification date: N/A
Early action deadline: N/A, notification date: N/A
Application deadline (fall): rolling
Undergraduate student body: 4,974 full time, 644 part time; 44% male, 56% female; 0% American Indian, 1% Asian, 7% black, 4% Hispanic, 3% multiracial, 0% Pacific Islander, 79% white, 6% international; 71% from in state; 41% live on campus; 18% of students in fraternities, 18% in sororities
Most popular majors: 22% Business, Management, Marketing, and Related Support Services; 19% Education; 11% Psychology; 5% Parks, Recreation, Leisure, and Fitness Studies
Expenses: 2016-2017: $9,179 in state, $15,500 out of state; room/board: $8,558
Financial aid: (660) 562-1363; 68% of undergrads determined to have financial need; average aid package $9,623

Park University
Parkville MO
(800) 745-7275
U.S. News ranking: Reg. U. (Mid. W), second tier
Website: www.park.edu
Admissions email: admissions@ mail.park.edu
Private; founded 1875
Freshman admissions: selective; 2015-2016: 954 applied, 396 accepted. ACT required. Average composite ACT score: 22. High school rank: 10% in top tenth, 35% in top quarter, 65% in top half
Early decision deadline: N/A, notification date: N/A
Early action deadline: N/A, notification date: N/A
Application deadline (fall): 8/1
Undergraduate student body: 4,777 full time, 6,752 part time; 53% male, 47% female; N/A American Indian, N/A Asian, N/A black, N/A Hispanic, N/A multiracial, N/A Pacific Islander, N/A white, N/A international
Most popular majors: 53% Business, Management, Marketing, and Related Support Services; 16% Psychology; 10% Homeland Security, Law Enforcement, Firefighting and Related Protective Services; 4% Health Professions and Related Programs; 3% Computer and Information Sciences and Support Services
Expenses: 2016-2017: $12,130; room/board: $7,710
Financial aid: (816) 584-6190; 84% of undergrads determined to have financial need; average aid package $10,589

Ranken Technical College[1]
Saint Louis MO
(866) 472-6536
U.S. News ranking: Reg. Coll. (Mid. W), unranked
Website: www.ranken.edu
Admissions email: N/A
Private
Application deadline (fall): N/A
Undergraduate student body: N/A full time, N/A part time
Expenses: 2015-2016: $14,457; room/board: $5,200
Financial aid: (314) 286-4862

Rockhurst University
Kansas City MO
(816) 501-4100
U.S. News ranking: Reg. U. (Mid. W), No. 15
Website: www.rockhurst.edu
Admissions email: admissions@ rockhurst.edu
Private; founded 1910
Affiliation: Roman Catholic (Jesuit)
Freshman admissions: more selective; 2015-2016: 2,774 applied, 2,041 accepted. Either SAT or ACT required. ACT 25/75 percentile: 23-28. High school rank: 28% in top tenth, 56% in top quarter, 83% in top half
Early decision deadline: N/A, notification date: N/A
Early action deadline: N/A, notification date: N/A
Application deadline (fall): rolling
Undergraduate student body: 1,442 full time, 635 part time; 40% male, 60% female; 0% American Indian, 3% Asian, 4% black, 8% Hispanic, 3% multiracial, 0% Pacific Islander, 72% white, 2% international; 66% from in state; 53% live on campus; 31% of students in fraternities, 49% in sororities
Most popular majors: 29% Health Professions and Related Programs; 17% Business, Management, Marketing, and Related Support Services; 10% Biological and Biomedical Sciences; 9% Psychology; 8% Social Sciences
Expenses: 2016-2017: $35,670; room/board: $9,380
Financial aid: (816) 501-4100; 71% of undergrads determined to have financial need; average aid package $27,825

Saint Louis University
St. Louis MO
(314) 977-2500
U.S. News ranking: Nat. U., No. 96
Website: www.slu.edu
Admissions email: admission@slu.edu
Private; founded 1818
Affiliation: Roman Catholic–Jesuit
Freshman admissions: more selective; 2015-2016: 13,216 applied, 8,273 accepted. Either SAT or ACT required. ACT 25/75 percentile: 25-31. High school rank: 42% in top tenth, 70% in top quarter, 91% in top half
Early decision deadline: N/A, notification date: N/A
Early action deadline: N/A, notification date: N/A

Application deadline (fall): 8/20
Undergraduate student body: 7,488 full time, 760 part time; 41% male, 59% female; 0% American Indian, 9% Asian, 6% black, 6% Hispanic, 4% multiracial, 0% Pacific Islander, 67% white, 5% international; 37% from in state; 51% live on campus; 18% of students in fraternities, 27% in sororities
Most popular majors: 11% Registered Nursing/Registered Nurse; 6% Biology/Biological Sciences, General; 6% Kinesiology and Exercise Science; 5% Accounting; 4% Psychology, General
Expenses: 2016-2017: $40,726; room/board: $10,640
Financial aid: (314) 977-2350; 55% of undergrads determined to have financial need; average aid package $26,811

Southeast Missouri State University
Cape Girardeau MO
(573) 651-2590
U.S. News ranking: Reg. U. (Mid. W), No. 103
Website: www.semo.edu
Admissions email: admissions@semo.edu
Public; founded 1873
Freshman admissions: selective; 2015-2016: 4,622 applied, 3,896 accepted. Either SAT or ACT required. ACT 25/75 percentile: 20-25. High school rank: 17% in top tenth, 44% in top quarter, 76% in top half
Early decision deadline: N/A, notification date: N/A
Early action deadline: N/A, notification date: N/A
Application deadline (fall): 7/1
Undergraduate student body: 7,924 full time, 2,663 part time; 44% male, 56% female; 0% American Indian, 1% Asian, 10% black, 2% Hispanic, 0% multiracial, 0% Pacific Islander, 77% white, 7% international; 83% from in state; 31% live on campus; 15% of students in fraternities, 15% in sororities
Most popular majors: 9% Liberal Arts and Sciences, General Studies and Humanities; 7% Registered Nursing, Nursing Administration, Nursing Research and Clinical Nursing; 7% Teacher Education and Professional Development, Specific Levels and Methods; 7% Teacher Education and Professional Development, Specific Subject Areas
Expenses: 2016-2017: $6,990 in state, $12,375 out of state; room/board: $8,508
Financial aid: (573) 651-2253; 62% of undergrads determined to have financial need; average aid package $8,882

Southwest Baptist University[1]
Bolivar MO
(800) 526-5859
U.S. News ranking: Reg. U. (Mid. W), second tier
Website: www.sbuniv.edu
Admissions email: dcrowder@sbuniv.edu
Private
Application deadline (fall): N/A

Undergraduate student body: N/A full time, N/A part time
Expenses: 2015-2016: $21,908; room/board: $7,160
Financial aid: (417) 328-1822

Stephens College
Columbia MO
(800) 876-7207
U.S. News ranking: Reg. U. (Mid. W), No. 79
Website: www.stephens.edu
Admissions email: apply@stephens.edu
Private; founded 1833
Freshman admissions: selective; 2015-2016: 1,219 applied, 826 accepted. Either SAT or ACT required. ACT 25/75 percentile: 20-24. High school rank: 19% in top tenth, 45% in top quarter, 80% in top half
Early decision deadline: 11/15, notification date: 12/1
Early action deadline: 1/1, notification date: 1/15
Application deadline (fall): rolling
Undergraduate student body: 595 full time, 121 part time; 1% male, 99% female; 1% American Indian, 1% Asian, 15% black, 5% Hispanic, 6% multiracial, 1% Pacific Islander, 69% white, 0% international
Most popular majors: 16% Counselor Education/School Counseling and Guidance Services; 13% Health Information/Medical Records Administration/Administrator; 10% Organizational Leadership; 8% Fashion Merchandising; 7% Fashion/Apparel Design
Expenses: 2016-2017: $29,754; room/board: $10,220
Financial aid: (573) 876-7106

Truman State University
Kirksville MO
(660) 785-4114
U.S. News ranking: Reg. U. (Mid. W), No. 8
Website: www.truman.edu
Admissions email: admissions@ truman.edu
Public; founded 1867
Freshman admissions: more selective; 2015-2016: 3,900 applied, 3,080 accepted. Either SAT or ACT required. ACT 25/75 percentile: 25-30. High school rank: 47% in top tenth, 79% in top quarter, 97% in top half
Early decision deadline: N/A, notification date: N/A
Early action deadline: N/A, notification date: N/A
Application deadline (fall): rolling
Undergraduate student body: 5,207 full time, 646 part time; 41% male, 59% female; 0% American Indian, 2% Asian, 4% black, 3% Hispanic, 3% multiracial, 0% Pacific Islander, 80% white, 7% international; 83% from in state; 48% live on campus; 8% of students in fraternities, 10% in sororities
Most popular majors: 10% Kinesiology and Exercise Science; 9% Biology/Biological Sciences, General; 9% Business Administration and Management, General; 9% Psychology, General; 7% English Language and Literature, General

Expenses: 2015-2016: $7,430 in state, $13,654 out of state; room/board: $8,480
Financial aid: (660) 785-4130; 52% of undergrads determined to have financial need; average aid package $12,375

University of Central Missouri
Warrensburg MO
(660) 543-4290
U.S. News ranking: Reg. U. (Mid. W), No. 86
Website: www.ucmo.edu
Admissions email: admit@ucmo.edu
Public; founded 1871
Freshman admissions: selective; 2015-2016: 4,818 applied, 3,828 accepted. Neither SAT nor ACT required. ACT 25/75 percentile: 19-24. High school rank: 11% in top tenth, 33% in top quarter, 68% in top half
Early decision deadline: N/A, notification date: N/A
Early action deadline: N/A, notification date: N/A
Application deadline (fall): 8/19
Undergraduate student body: 8,120 full time, 1,881 part time; 45% male, 55% female; 0% American Indian, 1% Asian, 11% black, 4% Hispanic, 4% multiracial, 0% Pacific Islander, 77% white, 2% international; 90% from in state; 35% live on campus; 12% of students in fraternities, 14% in sororities
Most popular majors: 15% Health Professions and Related Programs; 14% Education; 13% Business, Management, Marketing, and Related Support Services; 10% Homeland Security, Law Enforcement, Firefighting and Related Protective Services; 9% Engineering Technologies and Engineering-Related Fields
Expenses: 2016-2017: $7,322 in state, $13,767 out of state; room/board: $8,318
Financial aid: (660) 543-4040; 61% of undergrads determined to have financial need; average aid package $8,814

University of Missouri
Columbia MO
(573) 882-7786
U.S. News ranking: Nat. U., No. 111
Website: www.missouri.edu
Admissions email: mu4u@missouri.edu
Public; founded 1839
Freshman admissions: more selective; 2015-2016: 21,988 applied, 17,180 accepted. Either SAT or ACT required. ACT 25/75 percentile: 24-29. High school rank: 28% in top tenth, 58% in top quarter, 87% in top half
Early decision deadline: N/A, notification date: N/A
Early action deadline: N/A, notification date: N/A
Application deadline (fall): rolling
Undergraduate student body: 26,027 full time, 1,785 part time; 48% male, 52% female; 0% American Indian, 2% Asian, 8% black, 4% Hispanic, 3% multiracial, 0% Pacific Islander, 79% white, 4% international;

75% from in state; 25% live on campus; N/A of students in fraternities, N/A in sororities
Most popular majors: 15% Business, Management, Marketing, and Related Support Services; 14% Health Professions and Related Programs; 8% Engineering; 6% Biological and Biomedical Sciences
Expenses: 2016-2017: $9,518 in state, $25,892 out of state; room/board: $10,298
Financial aid: (573) 882-7506; 48% of undergrads determined to have financial need; average aid package $15,239

University of Missouri–Kansas City

Kansas City MO
(816) 235-1111
U.S. News ranking: Nat. U., No. 210
Website: www.umkc.edu
Admissions email: admit@umkc.edu
Public; founded 1929
Freshman admissions: selective; 2015-2016: 4,428 applied, 2,777 accepted. Either SAT or ACT required. ACT 25/75 percentile: 21-28. High school rank: 32% in top tenth, 57% in top quarter, 82% in top half
Early decision deadline: N/A, notification date: N/A
Early action deadline: N/A, notification date: N/A
Application deadline (fall): rolling
Undergraduate student body: 6,636 full time, 4,617 part time; 43% male, 57% female; 0% American Indian, 7% Asian, 15% black, 8% Hispanic, 5% multiracial, 0% Pacific Islander, 58% white, 4% international; 80% from in state; 23% live on campus; N/A of students in fraternities, N/A in sororities
Most popular majors: 14% Business/Commerce, General; 11% Registered Nursing/Registered Nurse; 10% Liberal Arts and Sciences/Liberal Studies; 6% Psychology, General
Expenses: 2016-2017: $9,551 in state, $22,714 out of state; room/board: $10,010
Financial aid: (816) 235-1154; 66% of undergrads determined to have financial need; average aid package $10,216

University of Missouri–St. Louis

St. Louis MO
(314) 516-5451
U.S. News ranking: Nat. U., No. 220
Website: www.umsl.edu
Admissions email: admissions@umsl.edu
Public; founded 1963
Freshman admissions: more selective; 2015-2016: 1,770 applied, 1,343 accepted. Either SAT or ACT required. ACT 25/75 percentile: 21-27. High school rank: 29% in top tenth, 61% in top quarter, 91% in top half
Early decision deadline: N/A, notification date: N/A
Early action deadline: N/A, notification date: N/A
Application deadline (fall): 9/16

Undergraduate student body: 5,711 full time, 7,858 part time; 42% male, 58% female; 0% American Indian, 5% Asian, 19% black, 3% Hispanic, 3% multiracial, 0% Pacific Islander, 63% white, 3% international; 89% from in state; 9% live on campus; 1% of students in fraternities, 1% in sororities
Most popular majors: 23% Business, Management, Marketing, and Related Support Services; 13% Health Professions and Related Programs; 11% Social Sciences; 9% Education
Expenses: 2016-2017: $10,065 in state, $26,277 out of state; room/board: $9,220
Financial aid: (314) 516-5526; 71% of undergrads determined to have financial need; average aid package $11,655

Washington University in St. Louis

St. Louis MO
(800) 638-0700
U.S. News ranking: Nat. U., No. 19
Website: www.wustl.edu
Admissions email: admissions@wustl.edu
Private; founded 1853
Freshman admissions: most selective; 2015-2016: 29,259 applied, 4,898 accepted. Either SAT or ACT required. ACT 25/75 percentile: 32-34. High school rank: 89% in top tenth, 100% in top quarter, 100% in top half
Early decision deadline: 11/15, notification date: 12/15
Early action deadline: N/A, notification date: N/A
Application deadline (fall): 1/15
Undergraduate student body: 6,819 full time, 685 part time; 47% male, 53% female; 0% American Indian, 19% Asian, 6% black, 7% Hispanic, 4% multiracial, 0% Pacific Islander, 55% white, 8% international; 7% from in state; 78% live on campus; 30% of students in fraternities, 30% in sororities
Most popular majors: 19% Engineering; 15% Pre-Medicine/Pre-Medical Studies; 14% Social Sciences; 13% Business, Management, Marketing, and Related Support Services; 11% Biological and Biomedical Sciences
Expenses: 2016-2017: $49,770; room/board: $15,596
Financial aid: (888) 547-6670; 43% of undergrads determined to have financial need; average aid package $40,466

Webster University

St. Louis MO
(314) 246-7800
U.S. News ranking: Reg. U. (Mid. W), No. 24
Website: www.webster.edu
Admissions email: admit@webster.edu
Private; founded 1915
Freshman admissions: more selective; 2015-2016: 1,994 applied, 1,119 accepted. Either SAT or ACT required. ACT 25/75

percentile: 21-27. High school rank: 20% in top tenth, 47% in top quarter, 76% in top half
Early decision deadline: N/A, notification date: N/A
Early action deadline: N/A, notification date: N/A
Application deadline (fall): 8/1
Undergraduate student body: 2,318 full time, 448 part time; 45% male, 55% female; 0% American Indian, 2% Asian, 13% black, 5% Hispanic, 3% multiracial, 0% Pacific Islander, 64% white, 5% international; 73% from in state; 31% live on campus; 0% of students in fraternities, 3% in sororities
Most popular majors: 16% Business Administration and Management, General; 5% Cinematography and Film/Video Production; 5% Education, General; 5% Psychology, General; 5% Registered Nursing/Registered Nurse
Expenses: 2016-2017: $26,300; room/board: $11,190
Financial aid: (314) 968-6992; 80% of undergrads determined to have financial need; average aid package $22,312

Westminster College

Fulton MO
(800) 475-3361
U.S. News ranking: Nat. Lib. Arts, No. 149
Website: www.westminster-mo.edu
Admissions email: admissions@westminster-mo.edu
Private; founded 1851
Affiliation: Presbyterian
Freshman admissions: selective; 2015-2016: 1,789 applied, 1,139 accepted. Either SAT or ACT required. ACT 25/75 percentile: 21-26. High school rank: 21% in top tenth, 40% in top quarter, 75% in top half
Early decision deadline: N/A, notification date: N/A
Early action deadline: N/A, notification date: N/A
Application deadline (fall): rolling
Undergraduate student body: 919 full time, 21 part time; 57% male, 43% female; 2% American Indian, 0% Asian, 9% black, 3% Hispanic, 1% multiracial, 1% Pacific Islander, 65% white, 15% international; 81% from in state; 84% live on campus; 48% of students in fraternities, 35% in sororities
Most popular majors: 26% Business, Management, Marketing, and Related Support Services; 11% Biological and Biomedical Sciences; 10% Education; 9% Social Sciences; 7% Foreign Languages, Literatures, and Linguistics
Expenses: 2016-2017: $24,540; room/board: $9,480
Financial aid: (573) 592-5364; 64% of undergrads determined to have financial need; average aid package $21,714

William Jewell College

Liberty MO
(888) 253-9355
U.S. News ranking: Nat. Lib. Arts, No. 154
Website: www.jewell.edu
Admissions email: admission@william.jewell.edu
Private; founded 1849
Freshman admissions: more selective; 2015-2016: 1,456 applied, 719 accepted. Neither SAT nor ACT required. ACT 25/75 percentile: 23-28. High school rank: 30% in top tenth, 59% in top quarter, 90% in top half
Early decision deadline: N/A, notification date: N/A
Early action deadline: N/A, notification date: N/A
Application deadline (fall): 8/15
Undergraduate student body: 1,026 full time, 27 part time; 42% male, 58% female; 0% American Indian, 1% Asian, 4% black, 4% Hispanic, 6% multiracial, 0% Pacific Islander, 78% white, 5% international; 60% from in state; 84% live on campus; 34% of students in fraternities, 40% in sororities
Most popular majors: 33% Health Professions and Related Programs; 19% Business, Management, Marketing, and Related Support Services; 10% Psychology; 7% Education; 7% Social Sciences
Expenses: 2016-2017: $32,930; room/board: $9,280
Financial aid: (888) 253-9355; 72% of undergrads determined to have financial need; average aid package $28,156

William Woods University

Fulton MO
(573) 592-4221
U.S. News ranking: Reg. U. (Mid. W), No. 91
Website: www.williamwoods.edu
Admissions email: admissions@williamwoods.edu
Private; founded 1870
Affiliation: Disciples of Christ
Freshman admissions: selective; 2015-2016: 682 applied, 636 accepted. Either SAT or ACT required. ACT 25/75 percentile: 19-26. High school rank: 38% in top tenth, 57% in top quarter, 76% in top half
Early decision deadline: N/A, notification date: N/A
Early action deadline: N/A, notification date: N/A
Application deadline (fall): rolling
Undergraduate student body: 843 full time, 157 part time; 26% male, 75% female; 0% American Indian, 0% Asian, 4% black, 2% Hispanic, 2% multiracial, 0% Pacific Islander, 71% white, 1% international; 63% from in state; 63% live on campus; 35% of students in fraternities, 35% in sororities
Most popular majors: 20% Business Administration and Management, General; 12% Sign Language Interpretation and Translation; 5% Education, General; 5% Sport and Fitness Administration/Management

Expenses: 2016-2017: $23,040; room/board: $9,300
Financial aid: (573) 592-4232; 72% of undergrads determined to have financial need; average aid package $17,009

MONTANA

Carroll College

Helena MT
(406) 447-4384
U.S. News ranking: Reg. Coll. (W), No. 1
Website: www.carroll.edu
Admissions email: admission@carroll.edu
Private; founded 1909
Affiliation: Roman Catholic
Freshman admissions: more selective; 2015-2016: 3,513 applied, 2,252 accepted. Either SAT or ACT required. ACT 25/75 percentile: 22-27. High school rank: 23% in top tenth, 60% in top quarter, 88% in top half
Early decision deadline: N/A, notification date: N/A
Early action deadline: 12/1, notification date: 1/1
Application deadline (fall): 5/1
Undergraduate student body: 1,406 full time, 63 part time; 42% male, 58% female; 1% American Indian, 2% Asian, 1% black, 5% Hispanic, 2% multiracial, 0% Pacific Islander, 81% white, 1% international; 45% from in state; 60% live on campus; 0% of students in fraternities, 0% in sororities
Most popular majors: 31% Health Professions and Related Programs; 14% Biological and Biomedical Sciences; 11% Business, Management, Marketing, and Related Support Services; 8% Education; 7% Psychology
Expenses: 2016-2017: $33,192; room/board: $9,372
Financial aid: (406) 447-5423; 66% of undergrads determined to have financial need; average aid package $22,653

Montana State University

Bozeman MT
(406) 994-2452
U.S. News ranking: Nat. U., No. 210
Website: www.montana.edu
Admissions email: admissions@montana.edu
Public; founded 1893
Freshman admissions: selective; 2015-2016: 14,816 applied, 12,277 accepted. Either SAT or ACT required. ACT 25/75 percentile: 21-28. High school rank: 18% in top tenth, 42% in top quarter, 73% in top half
Early decision deadline: N/A, notification date: N/A
Early action deadline: N/A, notification date: N/A
Application deadline (fall): rolling
Undergraduate student body: 11,671 full time, 2,036 part time; 55% male, 45% female; 2% American Indian, 1% Asian, 1% black, 4% Hispanic, 3% multiracial, 0% Pacific Islander, 86% white, 3% international;

61% from in state; 25% live on campus; 2% of students in fraternities, 2% in sororities
Most popular majors: 10% Business/Commerce, General; 10% Registered Nursing/Registered Nurse; 5% Mechanical Engineering; 4% Psychology, General; 3% Elementary Education and Teaching
Expenses: 2016-2017: $7,031 in state, $23,042 out of state; room/board: $8,900
Financial aid: (406) 994-2845; 49% of undergrads determined to have financial need; average aid package $11,350

Montana State University–Billings
Billings MT
(406) 657-2158
U.S. News ranking: Reg. U. (W), second tier
Website: www.msubillings.edu
Admissions email: admissions@msubillings.edu
Public; founded 1927
Freshman admissions: selective; 2015-2016: 1,470 applied, 1,463 accepted. Neither SAT nor ACT required. ACT 25/75 percentile: 18-24. High school rank: 8% in top tenth, 31% in top quarter, 63% in top half
Early decision deadline: N/A, notification date: N/A
Early action deadline: N/A, notification date: N/A
Application deadline (fall): rolling
Undergraduate student body: 2,701 full time, 1,333 part time; 38% male, 62% female; 4% American Indian, 1% Asian, 1% black, 5% Hispanic, 3% multiracial, 0% Pacific Islander, 82% white, 3% international; 90% from in state; 11% live on campus; N/A of students in fraternities, N/A in sororities
Most popular majors: 28% Business/Commerce, General; 23% Education; 8% Liberal Arts and Sciences/Liberal Studies; 6% Psychology, General; 5% Homeland Security, Law Enforcement, Firefighting and Related Protective Services
Expenses: 2016-2017: $8,808 in state, $17,718 out of state; room/board: $7,510
Financial aid: (406) 657-2188; 61% of undergrads determined to have financial need; average aid package $9,671

Montana State University–Northern[1]
Havre MT
(406) 265-3704
U.S. News ranking: Reg. Coll. (W), second tier
Website: www.msun.edu
Admissions email: admissions@msun.edu
Public
Application deadline (fall): N/A
Undergraduate student body: N/A full time, N/A part time
Expenses: 2015-2016: $5,329 in state, $17,408 out of state; room/board: $6,300
Financial aid: (406) 265-3787

Montana Tech of the University of Montana
Butte MT
(406) 496-4256
U.S. News ranking: Reg. Coll. (W), No. 4
Website: www.mtech.edu
Admissions email: enrollment@mtech.edu
Public; founded 1893
Freshman admissions: more selective; 2015-2016: 969 applied, 857 accepted. Either SAT or ACT required. ACT 25/75 percentile: 23-27. High school rank: 23% in top tenth, 56% in top quarter, 88% in top half
Early decision deadline: N/A, notification date: N/A
Early action deadline: N/A, notification date: N/A
Application deadline (fall): rolling
Undergraduate student body: 2,235 full time, 535 part time; 62% male, 38% female; 2% American Indian, 1% Asian, 1% black, 2% Hispanic, 0% multiracial, 0% Pacific Islander, 78% white, 11% international; 84% from in state; 11% live on campus; 0% of students in fraternities, 0% in sororities
Most popular majors: 22% Petroleum Engineering; 15% Engineering, General; 13% Business/Commerce, General; 7% Mining and Mineral Engineering; 7% Occupational Health and Industrial Hygiene
Expenses: 2016-2017: $6,881 in state, $21,007 out of state; room/board: $8,932
Financial aid: (406) 496-4212; 57% of undergrads determined to have financial need; average aid package $11,164

Rocky Mountain College
Billings MT
(406) 657-1026
U.S. News ranking: Reg. Coll. (W), No. 9
Website: www.rocky.edu
Admissions email: admissions@rocky.edu
Private; founded 1878
Affiliation: United Church of Christ, Methodist, and Presbyterian
Freshman admissions: selective; 2015-2016: 1,424 applied, 994 accepted. Either SAT or ACT required. ACT 25/75 percentile: 20-25. High school rank: 13% in top tenth, 38% in top quarter, 75% in top half
Early decision deadline: N/A, notification date: N/A
Early action deadline: N/A, notification date: N/A
Application deadline (fall): rolling
Undergraduate student body: 893 full time, 45 part time; 53% male, 47% female; 2% American Indian, 1% Asian, 3% black, 6% Hispanic, 4% multiracial, 1% Pacific Islander, 78% white, 4% international; 57% from in state; 51% live on campus; N/A of students in fraternities, N/A in sororities
Most popular majors: 26% Business Administration and Management, General; 13% Biology/Biological Sciences, General; 11% Kinesiology and Exercise Science; 7% Airline/Commercial/Professional Pilot and Flight Crew
Expenses: 2016-2017: $26,665; room/board: $8,133
Financial aid: (406) 657-1031; 75% of undergrads determined to have financial need; average aid package $22,332

University of Great Falls
Great Falls MT
(406) 791-5200
U.S. News ranking: Reg. Coll. (W), No. 19
Website: www.ugf.edu
Admissions email: enroll@ugf.edu
Private; founded 1932
Affiliation: Roman Catholic
Freshman admissions: less selective; 2015-2016: 828 applied, 693 accepted. Either SAT or ACT required. ACT 25/75 percentile: 17-22. High school rank: N/A
Early decision deadline: N/A, notification date: N/A
Early action deadline: N/A, notification date: N/A
Application deadline (fall): 9/1
Undergraduate student body: 610 full time, 442 part time; 33% male, 67% female; 2% American Indian, 3% Asian, 3% black, 7% Hispanic, 0% multiracial, 1% Pacific Islander, 76% white, 0% international; 38% from in state; 38% live on campus; 0% of students in fraternities, 0% in sororities
Most popular majors: 29% Health Professions and Related Programs; 12% Education; 9% Biological and Biomedical Sciences; 8% Business, Management, Marketing, and Related Support Services; 8% Social Sciences
Expenses: 2016-2017: $24,184; room/board: $8,300
Financial aid: (406) 791-5235; 78% of undergrads determined to have financial need; average aid package $19,092

University of Montana
Missoula MT
(800) 462-8636
U.S. News ranking: Nat. U., No. 214
Website: www.umt.edu
Admissions email: admiss@umontana.edu
Public; founded 1893
Freshman admissions: selective; 2015-2016: 4,863 applied, 4,476 accepted. Either SAT or ACT required. ACT 25/75 percentile: 20-27. High school rank: 18% in top tenth, 39% in top quarter, 72% in top half
Early decision deadline: N/A, notification date: N/A
Early action deadline: N/A, notification date: N/A
Application deadline (fall): rolling
Undergraduate student body: 7,605 full time, 1,127 part time; 46% male, 54% female; 3% American Indian, 1% Asian, 1% black, 4% Hispanic, 4% multiracial, 0% Pacific Islander, 79% white, 3% international; 74% from in state; N/A live on campus; 6% of students in fraternities, 6% in sororities

Most popular majors: 17% Business, Management, Marketing, and Related Support Services; 13% Social Sciences; 8% Education
Expenses: 2016-2017: $6,446 in state, $24,562 out of state; room/board: $8,826
Financial aid: (406) 243-5373; 60% of undergrads determined to have financial need; average aid package $13,619

University of Montana–Western
Dillon MT
(877) 683-7331
U.S. News ranking: Reg. Coll. (W), No. 8
Website: www.umwestern.edu
Admissions email: admissions@umwestern.edu
Public; founded 1893
Freshman admissions: less selective; 2015-2016: 721 applied, 532 accepted. Either SAT or ACT required. ACT 25/75 percentile: 17-22. High school rank: 4% in top tenth, 21% in top quarter, 49% in top half
Early decision deadline: N/A, notification date: N/A
Early action deadline: N/A, notification date: N/A
Application deadline (fall): rolling
Undergraduate student body: 1,170 full time, 299 part time; 39% male, 61% female; 2% American Indian, 1% Asian, 1% black, 3% Hispanic, 1% multiracial, 0% Pacific Islander, 85% white, 0% international; 76% from in state; 26% live on campus; N/A of students in fraternities, N/A in sororities
Most popular majors: 36% Education; 22% Business/Commerce, General; 9% Biology/Biological Sciences, General
Expenses: 2016-2017: $5,502 in state, $15,770 out of state; room/board: $7,122
Financial aid: (406) 683-7511; 65% of undergrads determined to have financial need; average aid package $3,569

NEBRASKA

Bellevue University[1]
Bellevue NE
(800) 756-7920
U.S. News ranking: Reg. U. (Mid. W), unranked
Website: www.bellevue.edu
Admissions email: info@bellevue.edu
Private
Application deadline (fall): N/A
Undergraduate student body: N/A full time, N/A part time
Expenses: 2015-2016: $7,050; room/board: $6,285
Financial aid: (402) 293-3763

Chadron State College[1]
Chadron NE
(308) 432-6263
U.S. News ranking: Reg. U. (Mid. W), unranked
Website: www.csc.edu
Admissions email: inquire@csc.edu
Public; founded 1911

Application deadline (fall): N/A
Undergraduate student body: N/A full time, N/A part time
Expenses: 2015-2016: $6,220 in state, $6,250 out of state; room/board: $6,840
Financial aid: (308) 432-6230

College of St. Mary[1]
Omaha NE
(402) 399-2407
U.S. News ranking: Reg. U. (Mid. W), No. 94
Website: www.csm.edu
Admissions email: enroll@csm.edu
Private; founded 1923
Affiliation: Catholic
Application deadline (fall): rolling
Undergraduate student body: N/A full time, N/A part time
Expenses: 2015-2016: $28,964; room/board: $7,400
Financial aid: (402) 399-2362

Concordia University
Seward NE
(800) 535-5494
U.S. News ranking: Reg. U. (Mid. W), No. 40
Website: www.cune.edu
Admissions email: admiss@cune.edu
Private; founded 1894
Affiliation: Lutheran Church-Missouri Synod
Freshman admissions: selective; 2015-2016: 1,380 applied, 1,072 accepted. Either SAT or ACT required. ACT 25/75 percentile: 20-27. High school rank: 17% in top tenth, 43% in top quarter, 72% in top half
Early decision deadline: N/A, notification date: N/A
Early action deadline: N/A, notification date: N/A
Application deadline (fall): 8/1
Undergraduate student body: 1,215 full time, 263 part time; 49% male, 51% female; 0% American Indian, 1% Asian, 4% black, 6% Hispanic, 0% multiracial, 0% Pacific Islander, 75% white, 2% international; 47% from in state; 60% live on campus; 0% of students in fraternities, 0% in sororities
Most popular majors: 30% Education; 16% Business, Management, Marketing, and Related Support Services; 10% Biological and Biomedical Sciences; 8% Psychology; 7% Multi/Interdisciplinary Studies
Expenses: 2016-2017: $28,480; room/board: $7,800
Financial aid: (402) 643-7270; 74% of undergrads determined to have financial need; average aid package $21,969

Creighton University
Omaha NE
(800) 282-5835
U.S. News ranking: Reg. U. (Mid. W), No. 1
Website: www.creighton.edu
Admissions email: admissions@creighton.edu
Private; founded 1878
Affiliation: Roman Catholic (Jesuit)
Freshman admissions: more selective; 2015-2016: 9,747 applied, 6,870 accepted. Either SAT or ACT required. ACT 25/75

percentile: 24-29. High school rank: 37% in top tenth, 68% in top quarter, 92% in top half
Early decision deadline: N/A, notification date: N/A
Early action deadline: N/A, notification date: N/A
Application deadline (fall): 2/15
Undergraduate student body: 3,909 full time, 254 part time; 43% male, 57% female; 0% American Indian, 10% Asian, 2% black, 8% Hispanic, 4% multiracial, 0% Pacific Islander, 71% white, 3% international; 25% from in state; 60% live on campus; 30% of students in fraternities, 46% in sororities
Most popular majors: 23% Health Professions and Related Programs; 18% Business, Management, Marketing, and Related Support Services; 10% Biological and Biomedical Sciences; 8% Social Sciences; 6% Psychology
Expenses: 2016-2017: $37,606; room/board: $10,600
Financial aid: (402) 280-2731; 55% of undergrads determined to have financial need; average aid package $27,934

Doane University
Crete NE
(402) 826-8222
U.S. News ranking: Nat. Lib. Arts, No. 149
Website: www.doane.edu
Admissions email: admissions@doane.edu
Private; founded 1872
Freshman admissions: selective; 2015-2016: 1,892 applied, 1,449 accepted. ACT required. ACT 25/75 percentile: 20-26. High school rank: 12% in top tenth, 38% in top quarter, 76% in top half
Early decision deadline: N/A, notification date: N/A
Early action deadline: N/A, notification date: N/A
Application deadline (fall): rolling
Undergraduate student body: 1,048 full time, 9 part time; 53% male, 47% female; 0% American Indian, 1% Asian, 3% black, 7% Hispanic, 3% multiracial, 0% Pacific Islander, 82% white, 2% international; 79% from in state; 78% live on campus; 17% of students in fraternities, 21% in sororities
Most popular majors: 21% Education; 15% Business, Management, Marketing, and Related Support Services; 12% Biological and Biomedical Sciences; 11% Visual and Performing Arts; 7% Social Sciences
Expenses: 2016-2017: $30,434; room/board: $8,750
Financial aid: (402) 826-8260; 77% of undergrads determined to have financial need; average aid package $22,419

Grace University[1]
Omaha NE
(402) 449-2831
U.S. News ranking: Reg. Coll. (Mid. W), second tier
Website: www.graceuniversity.edu
Admissions email: admissions@graceuniversity.edu
Private

Application deadline (fall): N/A
Undergraduate student body: N/A full time, N/A part time
Expenses: 2015-2016: $20,548; room/board: $7,076
Financial aid: (402) 449-2810

Hastings College
Hastings NE
(800) 532-7642
U.S. News ranking: Reg. Coll. (Mid. W), No. 16
Website: www.hastings.edu
Admissions email: hcadmissions@hastings.edu
Private; founded 1882
Affiliation: Presbyterian Church (USA)
Freshman admissions: selective; 2015-2016: 1,688 applied, 1,201 accepted. Either SAT or ACT required. ACT 25/75 percentile: 20-26. High school rank: 20% in top tenth, 45% in top quarter, 80% in top half
Early decision deadline: N/A, notification date: N/A
Early action deadline: N/A, notification date: N/A
Application deadline (fall): rolling
Undergraduate student body: 1,101 full time, 77 part time; 51% male, 49% female; 1% American Indian, 1% Asian, 4% black, 7% Hispanic, 4% multiracial, 0% Pacific Islander, 80% white, 2% international; 68% from in state; 70% live on campus; 27% of students in fraternities, 27% in sororities
Most popular majors: 22% Business, Management, Marketing, and Related Support Services; 22% Education; 12% Social Sciences; 11% Psychology; 9% Biological and Biomedical Sciences
Expenses: 2016-2017: $28,250; room/board: $8,880
Financial aid: (402) 461-7391; 73% of undergrads determined to have financial need; average aid package $22,932

Midland University
Fremont NE
(402) 941-6501
U.S. News ranking: Reg. Coll. (Mid. W), No. 48
Website: www.midlandu.edu/
Admissions email: admissions@midlandu.edu
Private; founded 1883
Affiliation: Lutheran
Freshman admissions: selective; 2015-2016: 1,745 applied, 1,058 accepted. Either SAT or ACT required. ACT 25/75 percentile: 18-23. High school rank: N/A
Early decision deadline: N/A, notification date: N/A
Early action deadline: N/A, notification date: N/A
Application deadline (fall): rolling
Undergraduate student body: 1,186 full time, 312 part time; 50% male, 50% female; 0% American Indian, 0% Asian, 3% black, 5% Hispanic, 21% multiracial, 0% Pacific Islander, 44% white, 2% international; 64% from in state; 36% live on campus; N/A of students in fraternities, N/A in sororities
Most popular majors: 21% Education, General; 20% Nursing Science; 19% Business/

Commerce, General; 14% Health and Physical Education/Fitness, General; 7% Biology/Biological Sciences, General
Expenses: 2015-2016: $29,400; room/board: $7,632
Financial aid: (402) 941-6520

Nebraska Wesleyan University
Lincoln NE
(402) 465-2218
U.S. News ranking: Reg. U. (Mid. W), No. 15
Website: www.nebrwesleyan.edu/undergraduate-admissions
Admissions email: admissions@nebrwesleyan.edu
Private; founded 1887
Affiliation: United Methodist
Freshman admissions: more selective; 2015-2016: 1,689 applied, 1,331 accepted. Either SAT or ACT required. ACT 25/75 percentile: 22-27. High school rank: 18% in top tenth, 50% in top quarter, 84% in top half
Early decision deadline: 12/1, notification date: N/A
Early action deadline: N/A, notification date: N/A
Application deadline (fall): 8/15
Undergraduate student body: 1,505 full time, 306 part time; 39% male, 61% female; 0% American Indian, 2% Asian, 2% black, 5% Hispanic, 2% multiracial, 0% Pacific Islander, 85% white, 1% international; 87% from in state; 70% live on campus; 17% of students in fraternities, 24% in sororities
Most popular majors: 20% Health Professions and Related Programs; 13% Business, Management, Marketing, and Related Support Services; 10% Education; 9% Multi/Interdisciplinary Studies; 7% Biological and Biomedical Sciences
Expenses: 2016-2017: $31,394; room/board: $8,758
Financial aid: (402) 465-2212; 72% of undergrads determined to have financial need; average aid package $20,873

Peru State College[1]
Peru NE
(402) 872-2221
U.S. News ranking: Reg. U. (Mid. W), unranked
Website: www.peru.edu
Admissions email: admissions@peru.edu
Public
Application deadline (fall): N/A
Undergraduate student body: N/A full time, N/A part time
Expenses: 2015-2016: $6,818 in state, $6,818 out of state; room/board: $7,106
Financial aid: (402) 872-2228

Union College
Lincoln NE
(800) 228-4600
U.S. News ranking: Reg. Coll. (Mid. W), No. 32
Website: www.ucollege.edu
Admissions email: ucenroll@ucollege.edu
Private; founded 1891
Affiliation: Seventh-day Adventist

Freshman admissions: selective; 2015-2016: 1,352 applied, 756 accepted. Either SAT or ACT required. ACT 25/75 percentile: 19-26. High school rank: 8% in top tenth, 25% in top quarter, 67% in top half
Early decision deadline: N/A, notification date: N/A
Early action deadline: N/A, notification date: N/A
Application deadline (fall): rolling
Undergraduate student body: 724 full time, 90 part time; 39% male, 61% female; 1% American Indian, 4% Asian, 8% black, 18% Hispanic, 5% multiracial, 1% Pacific Islander, 55% white, 8% international; 27% from in state; 74% live on campus; 0% of students in fraternities, 0% in sororities
Most popular majors: 37% Health Professions and Related Programs; 16% Business, Management, Marketing, and Related Support Services; 11% Education; 6% Biological and Biomedical Sciences; 6% Psychology
Expenses: 2016-2017: $22,538; room/board: $6,766
Financial aid: (402) 486-2505; 72% of undergrads determined to have financial need; average aid package $15,984

University of Nebraska–Kearney
Kearney NE
(308) 865-8526
U.S. News ranking: Reg. U. (Mid. W), No. 56
Website: www.unk.edu
Admissions email: admissionsug@unk.edu
Public; founded 1903
Freshman admissions: selective; 2015-2016: 2,511 applied, 2,144 accepted. Either SAT or ACT required. ACT 25/75 percentile: 20-25. High school rank: 17% in top tenth, 41% in top quarter, 76% in top half
Early decision deadline: N/A, notification date: N/A
Early action deadline: N/A, notification date: N/A
Application deadline (fall): 9/1
Undergraduate student body: 4,432 full time, 676 part time; 42% male, 58% female; 0% American Indian, 1% Asian, 2% black, 11% Hispanic, 2% multiracial, 0% Pacific Islander, 79% white, 5% international; 92% from in state; 35% live on campus; 13% of students in fraternities, 16% in sororities
Most popular majors: 15% Business Administration and Management, General; 13% Elementary Education and Teaching; 7% Operations Management and Supervision; 7% Parks, Recreation and Leisure Studies; 5% Psychology, General
Expenses: 2015-2016: $6,724 in state, $12,994 out of state; room/board: $9,230
Financial aid: (308) 865-8520; 64% of undergrads determined to have financial need; average aid package $10,919

University of Nebraska–Lincoln
Lincoln NE
(800) 742-8800
U.S. News ranking: Nat. U., No. 111
Website: www.unl.edu
Admissions email: Admissions@unl.edu
Public; founded 1869
Freshman admissions: more selective; 2015-2016: 9,724 applied, 7,425 accepted. Either SAT or ACT required. ACT 25/75 percentile: 22-28. High school rank: 26% in top tenth, 52% in top quarter, 83% in top half
Early decision deadline: N/A, notification date: N/A
Early action deadline: N/A, notification date: N/A
Application deadline (fall): 5/1
Undergraduate student body: 18,817 full time, 1,365 part time; 53% male, 47% female; 0% American Indian, 2% Asian, 3% black, 5% Hispanic, 3% multiracial, 0% Pacific Islander, 77% white, 8% international; 78% from in state; 41% live on campus; 19% of students in fraternities, 22% in sororities
Most popular majors: 23% Business, Management, Marketing, and Related Support Services; 10% Engineering; 8% Family and Consumer Sciences/Human Sciences; 7% Education
Expenses: 2016-2017: $8,628 in state, $23,148 out of state; room/board: $10,826
Financial aid: (402) 472-2030; 44% of undergrads determined to have financial need; average aid package $13,071

University of Nebraska–Omaha
Omaha NE
(402) 554-2393
U.S. News ranking: Nat. U., second tier
Website: www.unomaha.edu
Admissions email: unoadm@unomaha.edu
Public; founded 1908
Freshman admissions: selective; 2015-2016: 5,581 applied, 4,238 accepted. Either SAT or ACT required. ACT 25/75 percentile: 19-26. High school rank: 14% in top tenth, 38% in top quarter, 72% in top half
Early decision deadline: N/A, notification date: N/A
Early action deadline: N/A, notification date: N/A
Application deadline (fall): 8/1
Undergraduate student body: 9,607 full time, 2,881 part time; 48% male, 52% female; 0% American Indian, 3% Asian, 6% black, 11% Hispanic, 4% multiracial, 0% Pacific Islander, 69% white, 4% international; 92% from in state; 13% live on campus; 2% of students in fraternities, 2% in sororities
Most popular majors: 11% Criminal Justice/Safety Studies; 7% Business Administration and Management, General; 5% Finance, General; 5% Elementary Education and Teaching; 5% Psychology, General
Expenses: 2016-2017: $7,204 in state, $19,124 out of state; room/board: $8,916

Financial aid: (402) 554-2327; 46% of undergrads determined to have financial need; average aid package $9,379

Wayne State College
Wayne NE
(800) 228-9972
U.S. News ranking: Reg. U. (Mid. W), No. 94
Website: www.wsc.edu
Admissions email: admit1@wsc.edu
Public; founded 1909
Freshman admissions: selective; 2015-2016: 2,034 applied, 2,034 accepted. Neither SAT nor ACT required. ACT 25/75 percentile: 18-25. High school rank: 9% in top tenth, 29% in top quarter, 59% in top half
Early decision deadline: N/A, notification date: N/A
Early action deadline: N/A, notification date: N/A
Application deadline (fall): 8/21
Undergraduate student body: 2,611 full time, 302 part time; 43% male, 57% female; 1% American Indian, 1% Asian, 3% black, 7% Hispanic, 2% multiracial, 0% Pacific Islander, 82% white, 1% international; 87% from in state; 46% live on campus; N/A of students in fraternities, N/A in sororities
Most popular majors: 30% Education; 14% Business, Management, Marketing, and Related Support Services; 8% Parks, Recreation, Leisure, and Fitness Studies; 8% Psychology; 7% Homeland Security, Law Enforcement, Firefighting and Related Protective Services
Expenses: 2015-2016: $6,042 in state, $10,632 out of state; room/board: $6,760
Financial aid: (402) 375-7230; 69% of undergrads determined to have financial need; average aid package $9,082

York College
York NE
(800) 950-9675
U.S. News ranking: Reg. Coll. (Mid. W), second tier
Website: www.york.edu
Admissions email: enroll@york.edu
Private; founded 1890
Affiliation: Church of Christ
Freshman admissions: selective; 2015-2016: 650 applied, 300 accepted. Either SAT or ACT required. ACT 25/75 percentile: 16-20. High school rank: 8% in top tenth, 22% in top quarter, 59% in top half
Early decision deadline: N/A, notification date: N/A
Early action deadline: N/A, notification date: N/A
Application deadline (fall): 8/31
Undergraduate student body: 387 full time, 27 part time; 58% male, 42% female; 2% American Indian, 2% Asian, 15% black, 20% Hispanic, 0% multiracial, 0% Pacific Islander, 50% white, 0% international
Most popular majors: 20% Psychology, General; 13% Business Administration and Management, General; 10% Criminal Justice/Law Enforcement Administration; 9% Liberal Arts and Sciences/Liberal

Studies; 8% Biology/Biological Sciences, General
Expenses: 2015-2016: $17,600; room/board: $6,400
Financial aid: (402) 363-5624

NEVADA

College of Southern Nevada[1]
Las Vegas NV
(702) 651-5610
U.S. News ranking: Reg. Coll. (W), unranked
Website: www.csn.edu
Admissions email: N/A
Public; founded 1971
Application deadline (fall): rolling
Undergraduate student body: N/A full time, N/A part time
Expenses: 2015-2016: $2,805 in state, $9,450 out of state; room/board: N/A
Financial aid: (702) 651-5660

Great Basin College[1]
Elko NV
(775) 753-2102
U.S. News ranking: Reg. Coll. (W), unranked
Website: www.gbcnv.edu
Admissions email: N/A
Public
Application deadline (fall): N/A
Undergraduate student body: N/A full time, N/A part time
Expenses: 2015-2016: $2,805 in state, $9,450 out of state; room/board: $6,800
Financial aid: (775) 753-2399

Nevada State College[1]
Henderson NV
(702) 992-2130
U.S. News ranking: Reg. Coll. (W), unranked
Website: nsc.nevada.edu
Admissions email: N/A
Public; founded 2002
Application deadline (fall): rolling
Undergraduate student body: N/A full time, N/A part time
Expenses: 2015-2016: $4,738 in state, $15,423 out of state; room/board: N/A
Financial aid: (702) 992-2150

Sierra Nevada College
Incline Village NV
(866) 412-4636
U.S. News ranking: Reg. U. (W), second tier
Website: www.sierranevada.edu
Admissions email: admissions@sierranevada.edu
Private; founded 1969
Freshman admissions: less selective; 2015-2016: 554 applied, 364 accepted. Either SAT or ACT required. SAT 25/75 percentile: 870-1100. High school rank: 7% in top tenth, 9% in top quarter, 42% in top half
Early decision deadline: N/A, notification date: N/A
Early action deadline: N/A, notification date: N/A
Application deadline (fall): 8/22
Undergraduate student body: 486 full time, 21 part time; 61% male, 39% female; 3% American Indian, 4% Asian, 3% black, 5% Hispanic, 0% multiracial,

1% Pacific Islander, 72% white, 3% international; 20% from in state; 41% live on campus; N/A of students in fraternities, N/A in sororities
Most popular majors: 45% Business, Management, Marketing, and Related Support Services; 15% Multi/Interdisciplinary Studies; 8% Visual and Performing Arts; 8% Biological and Biomedical Sciences; 7% Psychology
Expenses: 2016-2017: $31,150; room/board: $12,332
Financial aid: (775) 831-1314; 66% of undergrads determined to have financial need; average aid package $25,480

University of Nevada–Las Vegas
Las Vegas NV
(702) 774-8658
U.S. News ranking: Nat. U., second tier
Website: www.unlv.edu
Admissions email: undergraduate.recruitment@unlv.edu
Public; founded 1957
Freshman admissions: selective; 2015-2016: 7,666 applied, 6,781 accepted. Either SAT or ACT required. SAT 25/75 percentile: 890-1120. High school rank: 23% in top tenth, 52% in top quarter, 82% in top half
Early decision deadline: N/A, notification date: N/A
Early action deadline: N/A, notification date: N/A
Application deadline (fall): 7/1
Undergraduate student body: 17,575 full time, 6,226 part time; 44% male, 56% female; 0% American Indian, 15% Asian, 8% black, 26% Hispanic, 9% multiracial, 1% Pacific Islander, 35% white, 4% international; 89% from in state; 7% live on campus; 8% of students in fraternities, 8% in sororities
Most popular majors: 33% Business, Management, Marketing, and Related Support Services; 8% Psychology; 6% Social Sciences; 6% Biological and Biomedical Sciences; 6% Homeland Security, Law Enforcement, Firefighting and Related Protective Services
Expenses: 2016-2017: $7,865 in state, $21,775 out of state; room/board: $10,710
Financial aid: (702) 895-3424; 64% of undergrads determined to have financial need; average aid package $11,291

University of Nevada–Reno
Reno NV
(775) 784-4700
U.S. News ranking: Nat. U., No. 197
Website: www.unr.edu
Admissions email: asknevada@unr.edu
Public; founded 1864
Freshman admissions: selective; 2015-2016: 9,538 applied, 8,208 accepted. Either SAT or ACT required. SAT 25/75 percentile: 970-1190. High

school rank: 24% in top tenth, 56% in top quarter, 89% in top half
Early decision deadline: N/A, notification date: N/A
Early action deadline: N/A, notification date: N/A
Application deadline (fall): 4/7
Undergraduate student body: 14,950 full time, 2,820 part time; 48% male, 52% female; 1% American Indian, 7% Asian, 4% black, 19% Hispanic, 6% multiracial, 1% Pacific Islander, 60% white, 1% international; 72% from in state; 22% live on campus; N/A of students in fraternities, N/A in sororities
Most popular majors: 17% Business, Management, Marketing, and Related Support Services; 12% Health Professions and Related Programs; 11% Biological and Biomedical Sciences; 11% Social Sciences; 10% Engineering
Expenses: 2016-2017: $7,142 in state, $21,052 out of state; room/board: $10,558
Financial aid: (775) 784-4666; 53% of undergrads determined to have financial need; average aid package $9,096

Western Nevada College[1]
Carson City NV
(775) 445-3000
U.S. News ranking: Reg. Coll. (W), unranked
Website: www.wnc.edu
Admissions email: N/A
Public; founded 1971
Application deadline (fall): rolling
Undergraduate student body: N/A full time, N/A part time
Expenses: 2015-2016: $2,805 in state, $9,450 out of state; room/board: N/A
Financial aid: (775) 445-3264

NEW HAMPSHIRE

Colby-Sawyer College[1]
New London NH
(800) 272-1015
U.S. News ranking: Reg. Coll. (N), unranked
Website: www.colby-sawyer.edu
Admissions email: admissions@colby-sawyer.edu
Private
Application deadline (fall): N/A
Undergraduate student body: N/A full time, N/A part time
Expenses: 2015-2016: $38,860; room/board: $13,000
Financial aid: (603) 526-3717

Daniel Webster College[1]
Nashua NH
(800) 325-6876
U.S. News ranking: Reg. U. (N), second tier
Website: www.dwc.edu
Admissions email: admissions@dwc.edu
Private; founded 1965
Application deadline (fall): rolling
Undergraduate student body: N/A full time, N/A part time

Expenses: 2015-2016: $15,630; room/board: $11,354
Financial aid: (603) 577-6590

Dartmouth College
Hanover NH
(603) 646-2875
U.S. News ranking: Nat. U., No. 11
Website: www.dartmouth.edu
Admissions email: admissions.office@dartmouth.edu
Private; founded 1769
Freshman admissions: most selective; 2015-2016: 20,507 applied, 2,250 accepted. Either SAT or ACT required. SAT 25/75 percentile: 1330-1560. High school rank: 91% in top tenth, 97% in top quarter, 100% in top half
Early decision deadline: 11/1, notification date: 12/15
Early action deadline: N/A, notification date: N/A
Application deadline (fall): 1/1
Undergraduate student body: 4,267 full time, 40 part time; 51% male, 49% female; 2% American Indian, 15% Asian, 7% black, 8% Hispanic, 5% multiracial, 0% Pacific Islander, 49% white, 8% international; 3% from in state; 87% live on campus; 46% of students in fraternities, 46% in sororities
Most popular majors: 17% Economics, General; 12% Political Science and Government, General; 7% History, General; 6% Biology/Biological Sciences, General; 6% Psychology, General
Expenses: 2016-2017: $51,438; room/board: $14,736
Financial aid: (603) 646-2451; 51% of undergrads determined to have financial need; average aid package $47,204

Franklin Pierce University
Rindge NH
(800) 437-0048
U.S. News ranking: Reg. U. (N), second tier
Website: www.franklinpierce.edu/
Admissions email: admissions@franklinpierce.edu
Private; founded 1962
Freshman admissions: less selective; 2015-2016: 3,740 applied, 2,981 accepted. Either SAT or ACT required. SAT 25/75 percentile: 830-1040. High school rank: 6% in top tenth, 30% in top quarter, 59% in top half
Early decision deadline: N/A, notification date: N/A
Early action deadline: N/A, notification date: N/A
Application deadline (fall): rolling
Undergraduate student body: 1,465 full time, 203 part time; 45% male, 55% female; 0% American Indian, 1% Asian, 5% black, 7% Hispanic, 2% multiracial, 0% Pacific Islander, 74% white, 4% international; 19% from in state; 87% live on campus; 0% of students in fraternities, 0% in sororities
Most popular majors: 19% Business, Management, Marketing, and Related Support Services; 14% Health Professions

and Related Programs; 7% Biological and Biomedical Sciences; 7% Education; 5% Visual and Performing Arts **Expenses:** 2016-2017: $34,050; room/board: $12,700 **Financial aid:** (603) 899-4186; 81% of undergrads determined to have financial need; average aid package $23,948

Granite State College
Concord NH
(603) 513-1391
U.S. News ranking: Reg. Coll. (N), unranked
Website: www.granite.edu
Admissions email: gsc.admissions@granite.edu
Public; founded 1972
Freshman admissions: N/A; 2015-2016: 233 applied, 233 accepted. Neither SAT nor ACT required. ACT 25/75 percentile: N/A. High school rank: N/A
Early decision deadline: N/A, notification date: N/A
Early action deadline: N/A, notification date: N/A
Application deadline (fall): rolling
Undergraduate student body: 1,021 full time, 849 part time; 25% male, 75% female; 0% American Indian, 1% Asian, 2% black, 3% Hispanic, 2% multiracial, 0% Pacific Islander, 85% white, 0% international; 84% from in state; N/A live on campus; N/A of students in fraternities, N/A in sororities
Most popular majors: 24% Business, Management, Marketing, and Related Support Services; 21% Psychology; 19% Multi/Interdisciplinary Studies; 11% Health Professions and Related Programs; 8% Education
Expenses: 2016-2017: $7,257 in state, $8,025 out of state; room/board: N/A
Financial aid: (603) 228-3000; 85% of undergrads determined to have financial need

Keene State College
Keene NH
(603) 358-2276
U.S. News ranking: Reg. U. (N), No. 72
Website: www.keene.edu
Admissions email: admissions@keene.edu
Public; founded 1909
Freshman admissions: less selective; 2015-2016: 5,674 applied, 4,464 accepted. Either SAT or ACT required. SAT 25/75 percentile: 880-1100. High school rank: 7% in top tenth, 23% in top quarter, 62% in top half
Early decision deadline: N/A, notification date: N/A
Early action deadline: N/A, notification date: N/A
Application deadline (fall): 4/1
Undergraduate student body: 4,097 full time, 162 part time; 44% male, 56% female; 0% American Indian, 1% Asian, 1% black, 4% Hispanic, 2% multiracial, 0% Pacific Islander, 87% white, 0% international; 44% from in state; 53% live on campus; 7% of students in fraternities, 7% in sororities
Most popular majors: 17% Education; 11% Health

Professions and Related Programs; 10% Psychology; 9% Engineering Technologies and Engineering-Related Fields; 9% Social Sciences
Expenses: 2016-2017: $13,613 in state, $21,997 out of state; room/board: $10,390
Financial aid: (603) 358-2280; 66% of undergrads determined to have financial need; average aid package $11,387

Mount Washington College[1]
Manchester NH
(888) 971-2190
U.S. News ranking: Reg. Coll. (N), unranked
Website: www.mountwashington.edu
Admissions email: N/A
For-profit;
Application deadline (fall): N/A
Undergraduate student body: N/A full time, N/A part time
Expenses: 2015-2016: $9,000; room/board: N/A
Financial aid: N/A

New England College
Henniker NH
(800) 521-7642
U.S. News ranking: Reg. U. (N), second tier
Website: www.nec.edu
Admissions email: admission@nec.edu
Private; founded 1946
Freshman admissions: less selective; 2015-2016: 4,987 applied, 4,875 accepted. Neither SAT nor ACT required. SAT 25/75 percentile: 790-1020. High school rank: 4% in top tenth, 16% in top quarter, 48% in top half
Early decision deadline: N/A, notification date: N/A
Early action deadline: N/A, notification date: N/A
Application deadline (fall): rolling
Undergraduate student body: 1,766 full time, 39 part time; 41% male, 59% female; 1% American Indian, 1% Asian, 24% black, 7% Hispanic, 1% multiracial, 0% Pacific Islander, 53% white, 3% international; 17% from in state; 34% live on campus; 10% of students in fraternities, 11% in sororities
Most popular majors: 25% Business, Management, Marketing, and Related Support Services; 11% Homeland Security, Law Enforcement, Firefighting and Related Protective Services; 11% Parks, Recreation, Leisure, and Fitness Studies; 9% Education
Expenses: 2016-2017: $35,492; room/board: $13,536
Financial aid: (603) 428-2414; 76% of undergrads determined to have financial need; average aid package $21,026

New Hampshire Institute of Art[1]
Manchester NH
(603) 836-2589
U.S. News ranking: Arts, unranked
Website: www.nhia.edu/
Admissions email: N/A
Private

Application deadline (fall): N/A
Undergraduate student body: N/A full time, N/A part time
Expenses: 2015-2016: $24,690; room/board: $10,810
Financial aid: N/A

Plymouth State University
Plymouth NH
(603) 535-2237
U.S. News ranking: Reg. U. (N), No. 104
Website: www.plymouth.edu
Admissions email: plymouthadmit@plymouth.edu
Public; founded 1871
Freshman admissions: less selective; 2015-2016: 6,626 applied, 4,875 accepted. Neither SAT nor ACT required. SAT 25/75 percentile: 880-1080. High school rank: 5% in top tenth, 21% in top quarter, 54% in top half
Early decision deadline: N/A, notification date: N/A
Early action deadline: N/A, notification date: N/A
Application deadline (fall): 4/1
Undergraduate student body: 3,855 full time, 250 part time; 51% male, 49% female; 0% American Indian, 2% Asian, 2% black, 2% Hispanic, 2% multiracial, 0% Pacific Islander, 81% white, 2% international; 56% from in state; 56% live on campus; 0% of students in fraternities, 3% in sororities
Most popular majors: 24% Business, Management, Marketing, and Related Support Services; 12% Education; 8% Parks, Recreation, Leisure, and Fitness Studies; 7% Homeland Security, Law Enforcement, Firefighting and Related Protective Services
Expenses: 2016-2017: $13,472 in state, $21,732 out of state; room/board: $11,008
Financial aid: (603) 535-2338; 69% of undergrads determined to have financial need; average aid package $11,750

Rivier University[1]
Nashua NH
(603) 888-1311
U.S. News ranking: Reg. U. (N), second tier
Website: rivier.edu
Admissions email: admissions@rivier.edu
Private
Application deadline (fall): rolling
Undergraduate student body: N/A full time, N/A part time
Expenses: 2015-2016: $29,700; room/board: $11,310
Financial aid: (603) 897-8533

Southern New Hampshire University
Manchester NH
(603) 645-9611
U.S. News ranking: Reg. U. (N), No. 101
Website: www.snhu.edu
Admissions email: admission@snhu.edu
Private; founded 1932

Freshman admissions: less selective; 2015-2016: 3,848 applied, 3,529 accepted. Neither SAT nor ACT required. SAT 25/75 percentile: 880-1090. High school rank: 6% in top tenth, 24% in top quarter, 56% in top half
Early decision deadline: N/A, notification date: N/A
Early action deadline: 11/15, notification date: 12/15
Application deadline (fall): rolling
Undergraduate student body: 2,977 full time, 52 part time; 48% male, 52% female; 0% American Indian, 1% Asian, 2% black, 3% Hispanic, 2% multiracial, 0% Pacific Islander, 68% white, 9% international; 49% from in state; 69% live on campus; 2% of students in fraternities, 3% in sororities
Most popular majors: 24% Business Administration and Management, General; 11% Psychology, General; 7% Corrections and Criminal Justice, Other; 6% Elementary Education and Teaching; 5% Computer and Information Sciences, General
Expenses: 2016-2017: $31,136; room/board: $12,062
Financial aid: (603) 645-9645; 72% of undergrads determined to have financial need; average aid package $21,947

St. Anselm College
Manchester NH
(603) 641-7500
U.S. News ranking: Nat. Lib. Arts, No. 115
Website: www.anselm.edu
Admissions email: admission@anselm.edu
Private; founded 1889
Affiliation: Roman Catholic (Benedictine)
Freshman admissions: more selective; 2015-2016: 3,955 applied, 2,883 accepted. Neither SAT nor ACT required. SAT 25/75 percentile: 1070-1250. High school rank: 31% in top tenth, 62% in top quarter, 89% in top half
Early decision deadline: N/A, notification date: N/A
Early action deadline: 11/15, notification date: 1/15
Application deadline (fall): 2/1
Undergraduate student body: 1,878 full time, 49 part time; 40% male, 60% female; 0% American Indian, 1% Asian, 2% black, 3% Hispanic, 2% multiracial, 0% Pacific Islander, 83% white, 1% international; 23% from in state; 92% live on campus; 0% of students in fraternities, 0% in sororities
Most popular majors: 18% Registered Nursing/Registered Nurse; 10% Criminology; 9% Business/Commerce, General; 7% Psychology, General
Expenses: 2016-2017: $38,826; room/board: $13,734
Financial aid: (603) 641-7110; 70% of undergrads determined to have financial need; average aid package $26,117

Thomas More College of Liberal Arts[1]
Merrimack NH
(800) 880-8308
U.S. News ranking: Nat. Lib. Arts, unranked
Website: www.thomasmorecollege.edu
Admissions email: admissions@thomasmorecollege.edu
Private
Affiliation: Roman Catholic
Application deadline (fall): rolling
Undergraduate student body: N/A full time, N/A part time
Expenses: 2016-2017: $20,400; room/board: $9,700
Financial aid: (800) 880-8308; 95% of undergrads determined to have financial need; average aid package $17,688

University of New Hampshire
Durham NH
(603) 862-1360
U.S. News ranking: Nat. U., No. 107
Website: www.unh.edu
Admissions email: admissions@unh.edu
Public; founded 1866
Freshman admissions: selective; 2015-2016: 19,255 applied, 15,137 accepted. Either SAT or ACT required. SAT 25/75 percentile: 1010-1210. High school rank: 18% in top tenth, 45% in top quarter, 86% in top half
Early decision deadline: N/A, notification date: N/A
Early action deadline: 11/15, notification date: 1/1
Application deadline (fall): 2/1
Undergraduate student body: 12,683 full time, 351 part time; 46% male, 54% female; 0% American Indian, 2% Asian, 1% black, 3% Hispanic, 2% multiracial, 0% Pacific Islander, 81% white, 2% international; 48% from in state; 56% live on campus; 11% of students in fraternities, 12% in sororities
Most popular majors: 17% Business Administration and Management, General; 7% Psychology, General; 5% Biomedical Sciences, General; 4% Mechanical Engineering
Expenses: 2016-2017: $17,624 in state, $31,424 out of state; room/board: $10,938
Financial aid: (603) 862-3600; 67% of undergrads determined to have financial need; average aid package $22,671

NEW JERSEY

Berkeley College
Woodland Park NJ
(800) 446-5400
U.S. News ranking: Business, unranked
Website: www.berkeleycollege.edu
Admissions email: admissions@berkeleycollege.edu
For-profit; founded 1931
Freshman admissions: N/A; 2015-2016: N/A applied, N/A accepted. Neither SAT nor ACT required. SAT 25/75 percentile: N/A. High school rank: N/A

Early decision deadline: N/A, notification date: N/A
Early action deadline: N/A, notification date: N/A
Application deadline (fall): rolling
Undergraduate student body: 3,189 full time, 624 part time; 27% male, 73% female; 0% American Indian, 2% Asian, 21% black, 34% Hispanic, N/A multiracial, 0% Pacific Islander, 15% white, 0% international
Most popular majors: 31% Business Administration and Management, General; 23% Criminal Justice/Law Enforcement Administration; 13% Fashion Merchandising; 11% Accounting; 6% Health/Health Care Administration/Management
Expenses: 2016-2017: $24,750; room/board: N/A
Financial aid: (973) 278-5400

Bloomfield College
Bloomfield NJ
(800) 848-4555
U.S. News ranking: Nat. Lib. Arts, second tier
Website: www.bloomfield.edu
Admissions email: admission@bloomfield.edu
Private; founded 1868
Affiliation: Presbyterian
Freshman admissions: least selective; 2015-2016: 3,027 applied, 1,807 accepted. Either SAT or ACT required. SAT 25/75 percentile: 770-950. High school rank: 3% in top tenth, 14% in top quarter, 42% in top half
Early decision deadline: N/A, notification date: N/A
Early action deadline: 12/1, notification date: 12/23
Application deadline (fall): 8/1
Undergraduate student body: 1,752 full time, 226 part time; 36% male, 64% female; 0% American Indian, 3% Asian, 50% black, 26% Hispanic, 1% multiracial, 0% Pacific Islander, 10% white, 4% international; 95% from in state; 30% live on campus; 4% of students in fraternities, 2% in sororities
Most popular majors: 17% Visual and Performing Arts; 15% Social Sciences; 14% Business, Management, Marketing, and Related Support Services; 14% Psychology; 13% Health Professions and Related Programs
Expenses: 2016-2017: $28,600; room/board: $11,500
Financial aid: (973) 748-9000; 93% of undergrads determined to have financial need; average aid package $25,767

Caldwell University
Caldwell NJ
(973) 618-3500
U.S. News ranking: Reg. U. (N), No. 104
Website: www.caldwell.edu
Admissions email: admissions@caldwell.edu
Private; founded 1939
Affiliation: Roman Catholic
Freshman admissions: selective; 2015-2016: 3,577 applied, 2,273 accepted. Either SAT or ACT required. SAT 25/75 percentile: 830-1070. High school rank: 14% in top tenth,

35% in top quarter, 69% in top half
Early decision deadline: N/A, notification date: N/A
Early action deadline: 12/1, notification date: 1/1
Application deadline (fall): rolling
Undergraduate student body: 1,417 full time, 195 part time; 29% male, 71% female; 1% American Indian, 4% Asian, 14% black, 19% Hispanic, 0% multiracial, 0% Pacific Islander, 39% white, 9% international; 91% from in state; 38% live on campus; 2% of students in fraternities, 7% in sororities
Most popular majors: 20% Psychology, General; 16% Business Administration and Management, General; 7% Registered Nursing/Registered Nurse; 6% Biology/Biological Sciences, General; 5% Accounting
Expenses: 2016-2017: $32,800; room/board: $12,600
Financial aid: (973) 618-3221; 77% of undergrads determined to have financial need; average aid package $24,199

Centenary College
Hackettstown NJ
(800) 236-8679
U.S. News ranking: Reg. U. (N), No. 131
Website: www.centenarycollege.edu
Admissions email: admissions@centenarycollege.edu
Private; founded 1867
Affiliation: United Methodist
Freshman admissions: less selective; 2015-2016: 1,186 applied, 1,029 accepted. Either SAT or ACT required. SAT 25/75 percentile: 830-1020. High school rank: N/A
Early decision deadline: N/A, notification date: N/A
Early action deadline: N/A, notification date: N/A
Application deadline (fall): 8/15
Undergraduate student body: 1,468 full time, 80 part time; 39% male, 61% female; 0% American Indian, 1% Asian, 11% black, 11% Hispanic, 0% multiracial, 0% Pacific Islander, 55% white, 4% international
Most popular majors: Information not available
Expenses: 2016-2017: $32,098; room/board: $10,946
Financial aid: (908) 852-1400

College of New Jersey
Ewing NJ
(609) 771-2131
U.S. News ranking: Reg. U. (N), No. 3
Website: www.tcnj.edu
Admissions email: admiss@tcnj.edu
Public; founded 1855
Freshman admissions: more selective; 2015-2016: 11,290 applied, 5,495 accepted. Either SAT or ACT required. SAT 25/75 percentile: 1120-1310. High school rank: 39% in top tenth, 79% in top quarter, 97% in top half
Early decision deadline: 11/1, notification date: 12/1

Early action deadline: N/A, notification date: N/A
Application deadline (fall): 2/1
Undergraduate student body: 6,486 full time, 272 part time; 41% male, 59% female; 0% American Indian, 10% Asian, 6% black, 12% Hispanic, 0% multiracial, 0% Pacific Islander, 66% white, 0% international; 94% from in state; 60% live on campus; 14% of students in fraternities, 11% in sororities
Most popular majors: 22% Teacher Education and Professional Development, Specific Levels and Methods; 20% Business Administration, Management and Operations; 7% Engineering, General; 7% Psychology, General; 5% Biology/Biological Sciences, General
Expenses: 2015-2016: $15,466 in state, $26,397 out of state; room/board: $12,498
Financial aid: (609) 771-2211; 52% of undergrads determined to have financial need; average aid package $10,664

College of St. Elizabeth
Morristown NJ
(973) 290-4700
U.S. News ranking: Reg. U. (N), No. 122
Website: www.cse.edu
Admissions email: apply@cse.edu
Private; founded 1899
Affiliation: Catholic
Freshman admissions: least selective; 2015-2016: 804 applied, 508 accepted. Either SAT or ACT required. SAT 25/75 percentile: 709-903. High school rank: N/A
Early decision deadline: N/A, notification date: N/A
Early action deadline: N/A, notification date: N/A
Application deadline (fall): rolling
Undergraduate student body: 534 full time, 271 part time; 6% male, 94% female; 1% American Indian, 2% Asian, 41% black, 22% Hispanic, 3% multiracial, N/A Pacific Islander, 22% white, 4% international; 95% from in state; 39% live on campus; N/A of students in fraternities, N/A in sororities
Most popular majors: 39% Registered Nursing/Registered Nurse; 11% Legal Professions and Studies, Other; 11% Psychology, General; 8% Business Administration and Management, General; 5% Dietetics/Dietitian
Expenses: 2016-2017: $32,282; room/board: $12,744
Financial aid: (973) 290-4445

Drew University
Madison NJ
(973) 408-3739
U.S. News ranking: Nat. Lib. Arts, No. 108
Website: www.drew.edu
Admissions email: cadm@drew.edu
Private; founded 1867
Affiliation: Methodist
Freshman admissions: selective; 2015-2016: 3,025 applied, 2,127 accepted. Neither SAT nor ACT required. SAT 25/75

percentile: 990-1240. High school rank: 27% in top tenth, 65% in top quarter, 88% in top half
Early decision deadline: 11/16, notification date: 12/15
Early action deadline: N/A, notification date: N/A
Application deadline (fall): 2/15
Undergraduate student body: 1,412 full time, 38 part time; 39% male, 61% female; 0% American Indian, 6% Asian, 10% black, 10% Hispanic, 4% multiracial, 0% Pacific Islander, 56% white, 5% international; 68% from in state; 76% live on campus; N/A of students in fraternities, N/A in sororities
Most popular majors: 10% Economics, General; 9% Psychology, General; 8% Business Administration and Management, General; 7% Biology/Biological Sciences, General; 7% Drama and Dramatics/Theatre Arts, General
Expenses: 2016-2017: $47,752; room/board: $13,296
Financial aid: (973) 408-3112; 73% of undergrads determined to have financial need; average aid package $40,257

Fairleigh Dickinson University
Teaneck NJ
(800) 338-8803
U.S. News ranking: Reg. U. (N), No. 67
Website: www.fdu.edu
Admissions email: admissions@fdu.edu
Private; founded 1942
Freshman admissions: selective; 2015-2016: 11,339 applied, 7,362 accepted. Either SAT or ACT required. SAT 25/75 percentile: 910-1130. High school rank: 15% in top tenth, 41% in top quarter, 75% in top half
Early decision deadline: N/A, notification date: N/A
Early action deadline: N/A, notification date: N/A
Application deadline (fall): rolling
Undergraduate student body: 4,984 full time, 3,237 part time; 45% male, 55% female; 0% American Indian, 5% Asian, 12% black, 28% Hispanic, 2% multiracial, 0% Pacific Islander, 38% white, 5% international; 86% from in state; 37% live on campus; N/A of students in fraternities, N/A in sororities
Most popular majors: 34% Liberal Arts and Sciences, General Studies and Humanities; 15% Business, Management, Marketing, and Related Support Services; 9% Psychology; 6% Health Professions and Related Programs
Expenses: 2015-2016: $36,910; room/board: $12,756
Financial aid: (201) 692-2823

Felician College
Lodi NJ
(201) 559-6131
U.S. News ranking: Reg. U. (N), second tier
Website: www.felician.edu
Admissions email: admissions@felician.edu

Private; founded 1942
Affiliation: Roman Catholic
Freshman admissions: less selective; 2015-2016: 1,763 applied, 1,389 accepted. Either SAT or ACT required. SAT 25/75 percentile: 790-970. High school rank: 12% in top tenth, 30% in top quarter, 66% in top half
Early decision deadline: N/A, notification date: N/A
Early action deadline: 11/15, notification date: 12/23
Application deadline (fall): rolling
Undergraduate student body: 1,388 full time, 221 part time; 28% male, 72% female; 0% American Indian, 5% Asian, 22% black, 28% Hispanic, 1% multiracial, 0% Pacific Islander, 30% white, 2% international; 92% from in state; 28% live on campus; N/A of students in fraternities, N/A in sororities
Most popular majors: 45% Health Professions and Related Programs; 15% Business, Management, Marketing, and Related Support Services; 9% Biological and Biomedical Sciences; 7% Homeland Security, Law Enforcement, Firefighting and Related Protective Services; 6% Education
Expenses: 2016-2017: $33,090; room/board: $12,380
Financial aid: (201) 559-6010; 91% of undergrads determined to have financial need; average aid package $23,340

Georgian Court University
Lakewood NJ
(800) 458-8422
U.S. News ranking: Reg. U. (N), No. 122
Website: www.georgian.edu
Admissions email: admissions@georgian.edu
Private; founded 1908
Affiliation: Roman Catholic
Freshman admissions: less selective; 2015-2016: 1,322 applied, 963 accepted. Either SAT or ACT required. SAT 25/75 percentile: 840-1050. High school rank: 7% in top tenth, 28% in top quarter, 64% in top half
Early decision deadline: N/A, notification date: N/A
Early action deadline: 11/15, notification date: 12/30
Application deadline (fall): 8/1
Undergraduate student body: 1,249 full time, 279 part time; 26% male, 74% female; 0% American Indian, 2% Asian, 14% black, 10% Hispanic, 2% multiracial, 0% Pacific Islander, 59% white, 1% international; 95% from in state; 29% live on campus; N/A of students in fraternities, N/A in sororities
Most popular majors: 30% Psychology, General; 9% Registered Nursing/Registered Nurse; 8% Business Administration and Management, General; 8% English Language and Literature, General; 5% History, General
Expenses: 2016-2017: $31,618; room/board: $10,808

BEST COLLEGES

Financial aid: (732) 364-2200; 83% of undergrads determined to have financial need; average aid package $26,505

Kean University
Union NJ
(908) 737-7100
U.S. News ranking: Reg. U. (N), second tier
Website: www.kean.edu
Admissions email: admitme@kean.edu
Public; founded 1855
Freshman admissions: less selective; 2015-2016: 7,944 applied, 5,900 accepted. Either SAT or ACT required. SAT 25/75 percentile: 840-1020. High school rank: 11% in top tenth, 28% in top quarter, 66% in top half
Early decision deadline: N/A, notification date: N/A
Early action deadline: 12/1, notification date: N/A
Application deadline (fall): 8/15
Undergraduate student body: 9,192 full time, 2,622 part time; 40% male, 60% female; 0% American Indian, 5% Asian, 20% black, 27% Hispanic, 2% multiracial, 0% Pacific Islander, 36% white, 2% international; 98% from in state; 15% live on campus; N/A of students in fraternities, N/A in sororities
Most popular majors: 16% Psychology, General; 7% Biology/Biological Sciences, General; 7% Business Administration and Management, General; 6% Criminal Justice/Law Enforcement Administration
Expenses: 2015-2016: $11,581 in state, $18,183 out of state; room/board: $12,565
Financial aid: (908) 737-3190; 73% of undergrads determined to have financial need; average aid package $10,442

Monmouth University
West Long Branch NJ
(800) 543-9671
U.S. News ranking: Reg. U. (N), No. 38
Website: www.monmouth.edu
Admissions email: admission@monmouth.edu
Private; founded 1933
Freshman admissions: selective; 2015-2016: 8,486 applied, 6,651 accepted. Either SAT or ACT required. SAT 25/75 percentile: 950-1120. High school rank: 14% in top tenth, 39% in top quarter, 77% in top half
Early decision deadline: N/A, notification date: N/A
Early action deadline: 12/1, notification date: 1/15
Application deadline (fall): 3/1
Undergraduate student body: 4,450 full time, 243 part time; 42% male, 58% female; 0% American Indian, 3% Asian, 5% black, 11% Hispanic, 2% multiracial, 0% Pacific Islander, 74% white, 1% international; 86% from in state; 46% live on campus; 16% of students in fraternities, 15% in sororities
Most popular majors: 23% Business, Management, Marketing, and Related Support Services; 11% Education;

7% Homeland Security, Law Enforcement, Firefighting and Related Protective Services; 7% Psychology
Expenses: 2016-2017: $35,364; room/board: $13,038
Financial aid: (732) 571-3463; 72% of undergrads determined to have financial need; average aid package $22,813

Montclair State University
Montclair NJ
(973) 655-4444
U.S. News ranking: Nat. U., No. 176
Website: www.montclair.edu
Admissions email: undergraduate.admissions@montclair.edu
Public; founded 1908
Freshman admissions: selective; 2015-2016: 11,990 applied, 8,401 accepted. Neither SAT nor ACT required. SAT 25/75 percentile: 870-1090. High school rank: 10% in top tenth, 37% in top quarter, 79% in top half
Early decision deadline: N/A, notification date: N/A
Early action deadline: N/A, notification date: N/A
Application deadline (fall): 3/1
Undergraduate student body: 14,433 full time, 1,903 part time; 38% male, 62% female; 0% American Indian, 5% Asian, 11% black, 25% Hispanic, 3% multiracial, 0% Pacific Islander, 44% white, 2% international; 97% from in state; 31% live on campus; 0% of students in fraternities, 0% in sororities
Most popular majors: 14% Business Administration and Management, General; 11% Psychology, General; 6% Family and Consumer Sciences/Human Sciences, General; 5% Biology/Biological Sciences, General; 5% Multi-/Interdisciplinary Studies, Other
Expenses: 2015-2016: $11,771 in state, $20,318 out of state; room/board: $13,884
Financial aid: (973) 655-4461; 67% of undergrads determined to have financial need; average aid package $9,619

New Jersey City University
Jersey City NJ
(888) 441-6528
U.S. News ranking: Reg. U. (N), second tier
Website: www.njcu.edu/
Admissions email: admissions@njcu.edu
Public; founded 1927
Freshman admissions: least selective; 2015-2016: 2,789 applied, 2,419 accepted. Either SAT or ACT required. SAT 25/75 percentile: 760-970. High school rank: 9% in top tenth, 29% in top quarter, 61% in top half
Early decision deadline: N/A, notification date: N/A
Early action deadline: N/A, notification date: N/A
Undergraduate student body: 4,826 full time, 1,491 part time; 40% male, 60% female; 0% American Indian, 7% Asian, 21% black, 35% Hispanic, 2% multiracial,

1% Pacific Islander, 23% white, 3% international; 99% from in state; 4% live on campus; 2% of students in fraternities, 1% in sororities
Most popular majors: 15% Registered Nursing, Nursing Administration, Nursing Research and Clinical Nursing, Other; 14% Psychology, General; 13% Business Administration and Management, General; 9% Corrections and Criminal Justice, Other; 7% Accounting
Expenses: 2015-2016: $11,180 in state, $20,009 out of state; room/board: $11,858
Financial aid: (201) 200-3173; 86% of undergrads determined to have financial need; average aid package $10,141

New Jersey Institute of Technology
Newark NJ
(973) 596-3300
U.S. News ranking: Nat. U., No. 135
Website: www.njit.edu
Admissions email: admissions@njit.edu
Public; founded 1881
Freshman admissions: more selective; 2015-2016: 6,045 applied, 3,673 accepted. Either SAT or ACT required. SAT 25/75 percentile: 1110-1310. High school rank: 31% in top tenth, 59% in top quarter, 87% in top half
Early decision deadline: N/A, notification date: N/A
Early action deadline: N/A, notification date: N/A
Application deadline (fall): 3/1
Undergraduate student body: 6,178 full time, 1,830 part time; 76% male, 24% female; 0% American Indian, 22% Asian, 9% black, 22% Hispanic, 3% multiracial, 0% Pacific Islander, 33% white, 4% international; 92% from in state; 23% live on campus; 8% of students in fraternities, 5% in sororities
Most popular majors: 39% Engineering; 18% Computer and Information Sciences and Support Services; 14% Engineering Technologies and Engineering-Related Fields; 7% Business, Management, Marketing, and Related Support Services
Expenses: 2016-2017: $16,108 in state, $30,326 out of state; room/board: $13,300
Financial aid: (973) 596-3479; 70% of undergrads determined to have financial need; average aid package $13,693

Princeton University
Princeton NJ
(609) 258-3060
U.S. News ranking: Nat. U., No. 1
Website: www.princeton.edu
Admissions email: uaoffice@princeton.edu
Private; founded 1746
Freshman admissions: most selective; 2015-2016: 27,290 applied, 1,948 accepted. Either SAT or ACT required. SAT 25/75 percentile: 1390-1590. High

school rank: 94% in top tenth, 98% in top quarter, 100% in top half
Early decision deadline: N/A, notification date: N/A
Early action deadline: 11/1, notification date: 12/15
Application deadline (fall): 1/1
Undergraduate student body: 5,277 full time, 125 part time; 52% male, 48% female; 0% American Indian, 22% Asian, 8% black, 9% Hispanic, 4% multiracial, 0% Pacific Islander, 45% white, 11% international; 18% from in state; 96% live on campus; 0% of students in fraternities, 0% in sororities
Most popular majors: 12% Public Policy Analysis, General; 9% Computer Engineering, General; 9% Economics, General; 6% History, General; 6% Psychology, General
Expenses: 2016-2017: $45,320; room/board: $14,770
Financial aid: (609) 258-3330; 59% of undergrads determined to have financial need; average aid package $46,220

Ramapo College of New Jersey
Mahwah NJ
(201) 684-7300
U.S. News ranking: Reg. U. (N), No. 27
Website: www.ramapo.edu
Admissions email: admissions@ramapo.edu
Public; founded 1969
Freshman admissions: selective; 2015-2016: 7,106 applied, 3,783 accepted. Either SAT or ACT required. SAT 25/75 percentile: 990-1195. High school rank: 10% in top tenth, 25% in top quarter, 52% in top half
Early decision deadline: 11/1, notification date: 12/5
Early action deadline: N/A, notification date: N/A
Application deadline (fall): 3/1
Undergraduate student body: 4,992 full time, 669 part time; 45% male, 55% female; 0% American Indian, 7% Asian, 5% black, 13% Hispanic, 1% multiracial, 0% Pacific Islander, 64% white, 1% international; 95% from in state; 49% live on campus; 7% of students in fraternities, 3% in sororities
Most popular majors: 17% Business Administration and Management, General; 15% Psychology, General; 7% Nursing Science; 6% Accounting
Expenses: 2016-2017: $13,920 in state, $23,006 out of state; room/board: $11,640
Financial aid: (201) 684-7549; 56% of undergrads determined to have financial need; average aid package $16,242

Rider University
Lawrenceville NJ
(609) 896-5042
U.S. News ranking: Reg. U. (N), No. 23
Website: www.rider.edu
Admissions email: admissions@rider.edu
Private; founded 1865

Freshman admissions: selective; 2015-2016: 9,851 applied, 6,798 accepted. Either SAT or ACT required. SAT 25/75 percentile: 910-1110. High school rank: 14% in top tenth, 37% in top quarter, 75% in top half
Early decision deadline: N/A, notification date: N/A
Early action deadline: 11/15, notification date: 12/15
Application deadline (fall): rolling
Undergraduate student body: 3,685 full time, 443 part time; 43% male, 57% female; 0% American Indian, 5% Asian, 12% black, 12% Hispanic, 3% multiracial, 0% Pacific Islander, 62% white, 3% international; 77% from in state; 55% live on campus; 5% of students in fraternities, 10% in sororities
Most popular majors: 10% Elementary Education and Teaching; 10% Psychology, General; 8% Accounting; 6% Business Administration and Management, General; 6% Finance, General
Expenses: 2016-2017: $39,820; room/board: $14,230
Financial aid: (609) 896-5360; 74% of undergrads determined to have financial need; average aid package $27,656

Rowan University
Glassboro NJ
(856) 256-4200
U.S. News ranking: Reg. U. (N), No. 20
Website: www.rowan.edu
Admissions email: admissions@rowan.edu
Public; founded 1923
Freshman admissions: selective; 2015-2016: 12,158 applied, 6,860 accepted. Either SAT or ACT required. SAT 25/75 percentile: 1000-1230. High school rank: N/A
Early decision deadline: N/A, notification date: N/A
Early action deadline: N/A, notification date: N/A
Application deadline (fall): 3/1
Undergraduate student body: 11,710 full time, 1,459 part time; 54% male, 46% female; 0% American Indian, 5% Asian, 10% black, 13% Hispanic, 3% multiracial, 0% Pacific Islander, 65% white, 1% international; 95% from in state; 37% live on campus; 5% of students in fraternities, 4% in sororities
Most popular majors: 14% Business, Management, Marketing, and Related Support Services; 12% Education; 9% Psychology; 8% Biological and Biomedical Sciences
Expenses: 2016-2017: $12,864 in state, $20,978 out of state; room/board: $11,627
Financial aid: (856) 256-4250; 64% of undergrads determined to have financial need; average aid package $9,060

More at usnews.com/college

Rutgers University–Camden
Camden NJ
(856) 225-6104
U.S. News ranking: Reg. U. (N), No. 32
Website: www.rutgers.edu/
Admissions email: camden@ugadm.rutgers.edu
Public; founded 1927
Freshman admissions: selective; 2015-2016: 7,518 applied, 4,389 accepted. Either SAT or ACT required. SAT 25/75 percentile: 920-1120. High school rank: 15% in top tenth, 44% in top quarter, 81% in top half
Early decision deadline: N/A, notification date: N/A
Early action deadline: N/A, notification date: N/A
Application deadline (fall): rolling
Undergraduate student body: 3,931 full time, 968 part time; 42% male, 58% female; 0% American Indian, 9% Asian, 16% black, 13% Hispanic, 4% multiracial, 0% Pacific Islander, 55% white, 1% international
Most popular majors: 17% Registered Nursing/Registered Nurse; 11% Business Administration and Management, General; 11% Psychology, General; 8% Criminal Justice/Safety Studies; 7% Accounting
Expenses: 2016-2017: $14,298 in state, $29,441 out of state; room/board: $11,908
Financial aid: (856) 225-6039; 79% of undergrads determined to have financial need; average aid package $11,986

Rutgers University–Newark
Newark NJ
(973) 353-5205
U.S. News ranking: Nat. U., No. 135
Website: rutgers-newark.rutgers.edu
Admissions email: admissions@ugadm.rutgers.edu
Public; founded 1908
Freshman admissions: selective; 2015-2016: 11,646 applied, 7,529 accepted. Either SAT or ACT required. SAT 25/75 percentile: 930-1130. High school rank: 19% in top tenth, 50% in top quarter, 85% in top half
Early decision deadline: N/A, notification date: N/A
Early action deadline: N/A, notification date: N/A
Application deadline (fall): rolling
Undergraduate student body: 6,212 full time, 1,501 part time; 48% male, 52% female; 0% American Indian, 21% Asian, 19% black, 27% Hispanic, 2% multiracial, 0% Pacific Islander, 25% white, 4% international
Most popular majors: 15% Accounting; 13% Psychology, General; 12% Criminal Justice/Safety Studies; 10% Finance, General; 7% Air Force JROTC/ROTC
Expenses: 2016-2017: $13,829 in state, $29,480 out of state; room/board: $13,459

Rutgers University– New Brunswick
Piscataway NJ
(732) 932-4636
U.S. News ranking: Nat. U., No. 70
Website: www.rutgers.edu
Admissions email: admissions@ugadm.rutgers.edu
Public; founded 1766
Freshman admissions: more selective; 2015-2016: 35,340 applied, 20,657 accepted. Either SAT or ACT required. SAT 25/75 percentile: 1110-1340. High school rank: 38% in top tenth, 76% in top quarter, 97% in top half
Early decision deadline: N/A, notification date: N/A
Early action deadline: N/A, notification date: N/A
Application deadline (fall): rolling
Undergraduate student body: 33,392 full time, 2,092 part time; 50% male, 50% female; 0% American Indian, 26% Asian, 7% black, 13% Hispanic, 3% multiracial, 0% Pacific Islander, 42% white, 7% international
Most popular majors: 7% Psychology, General; 5% Biology/Biological Sciences, General; 4% Kinesiology and Exercise Science; 4% Human Resources Management/Personnel Administration, General
Expenses: 2016-2017: $14,372 in state, $30,023 out of state; room/board: $12,260
Financial aid: (732) 932-7057; 54% of undergrads determined to have financial need; average aid package $13,477

Seton Hall University
South Orange NJ
(973) 761-9332
U.S. News ranking: Nat. U., No. 118
Website: www.shu.edu
Admissions email: thehall@shu.edu
Private; founded 1856
Affiliation: Roman Catholic
Freshman admissions: selective; 2015-2016: 14,108 applied, 10,757 accepted. Either SAT or ACT required. SAT 25/75 percentile: 1060-1230. High school rank: 30% in top tenth, 60% in top quarter, 90% in top half
Early decision deadline: N/A, notification date: N/A
Early action deadline: 11/15, notification date: 12/30
Application deadline (fall): rolling
Undergraduate student body: 5,588 full time, 502 part time; 44% male, 56% female; 0% American Indian, 9% Asian, 10% black, 19% Hispanic, 3% multiracial, 0% Pacific Islander, 51% white, 3% international; 74% from in state; 41% live on campus; 9% of students in fraternities, 11% in sororities
Most popular majors: 19% Registered Nursing/Registered Nurse; 9% Biology/Biological Sciences, General; 8%

Humanities/Humanistic Studies; 7% Finance, General; 4% Psychology, General
Expenses: 2016-2017: $39,258; room/board: $14,732
Financial aid: (973) 761-9350

Stevens Institute of Technology
Hoboken NJ
(201) 216-5194
U.S. News ranking: Nat. U., No. 71
Website: www.stevens.edu
Admissions email: admissions@stevens.edu
Private; founded 1870
Freshman admissions: more selective; 2015-2016: 6,540 applied, 2,849 accepted. Neither SAT nor ACT required. SAT 25/75 percentile: 1240-1425. High school rank: 66% in top tenth, 93% in top quarter, 100% in top half
Early decision deadline: 11/15, notification date: 12/15
Early action deadline: N/A, notification date: N/A
Application deadline (fall): 2/1
Undergraduate student body: 2,648 full time, 225 part time; 70% male, 30% female; 0% American Indian, 11% Asian, 2% black, 9% Hispanic, N/A multiracial, N/A Pacific Islander, 66% white, 4% international; 63% from in state; 71% live on campus; 25% of students in fraternities, 25% in sororities
Most popular majors: 26% Mechanical Engineering; 9% Business Administration and Management, General; 9% Civil Engineering, General; 8% Chemical Engineering; 7% Computer Science
Expenses: 2016-2017: $48,838; room/board: $13,500
Financial aid: (201) 216-5555; 64% of undergrads determined to have financial need; average aid package $29,910

Stockton University
Galloway NJ
(609) 652-4261
U.S. News ranking: Reg. U. (N), No. 51
Website: www.stockton.edu
Admissions email: admissions@stockton.edu
Public; founded 1969
Freshman admissions: selective; 2015-2016: 5,483 applied, 3,532 accepted. Either SAT or ACT required. SAT 25/75 percentile: 980-1180. High school rank: 21% in top tenth, 54% in top quarter, 95% in top half
Early decision deadline: N/A, notification date: N/A
Early action deadline: N/A, notification date: N/A
Application deadline (fall): 5/1
Undergraduate student body: 7,378 full time, 430 part time; 41% male, 59% female; 0% American Indian, 5% Asian, 7% black, 11% Hispanic, 3% multiracial, 0% Pacific Islander, 72% white, 0% international; 99% from in state; 38% live on campus; 7% of students in fraternities, 7% in sororities

Most popular majors: 14% Business Administration and Management, General; 11% Psychology, General; 9% Biology/Biological Sciences, General; 9% Criminology; 6% Health Professions and Related Programs
Expenses: 2015-2016: $12,820 in state, $19,472 out of state; room/board: $11,707
Financial aid: (609) 652-4201; 71% of undergrads determined to have financial need; average aid package $16,165

St. Peter's University
Jersey City NJ
(201) 761-7100
U.S. News ranking: Reg. U. (N), No. 99
Website: www.spc.edu
Admissions email: admissions@spc.edu
Private; founded 1872
Affiliation: Roman Catholic (Jesuit)
Freshman admissions: less selective; 2015-2016: 4,528 applied, 3,048 accepted. Neither SAT nor ACT required. SAT 25/75 percentile: 810-1010. High school rank: 13% in top tenth, 36% in top quarter, 69% in top half
Early decision deadline: N/A, notification date: N/A
Early action deadline: 12/15, notification date: 1/31
Application deadline (fall): 8/31
Undergraduate student body: 2,208 full time, 317 part time; 38% male, 62% female; 1% American Indian, 7% Asian, 25% black, 37% Hispanic, 2% multiracial, 1% Pacific Islander, 18% white, 2% international; 89% from in state; 31% live on campus; N/A of students in fraternities, N/A in sororities
Most popular majors: 22% Business, Management, Marketing, and Related Support Services; 13% Health Professions and Related Programs; 12% Biological and Biomedical Sciences; 9% Homeland Security, Law Enforcement, Firefighting and Related Protective Services; 7% Social Sciences
Expenses: 2016-2017: $35,192; room/board: $14,956
Financial aid: (201) 915-4929; 90% of undergrads determined to have financial need; average aid package $29,763

Thomas Edison State University
Trenton NJ
(888) 442-8372
U.S. News ranking: Reg. U. (N), unranked
Website: www.tesu.edu
Admissions email: admissions@tesu.edu
Public; founded 1972
Freshman admissions: N/A; 2015-2016: N/A applied, N/A accepted. Neither SAT nor ACT required. ACT 25/75 percentile: N/A. High school rank: N/A
Early decision deadline: N/A, notification date: N/A
Early action deadline: N/A, notification date: N/A

Application deadline (fall): rolling
Undergraduate student body: 149 full time, 17,441 part time; 54% male, 46% female; 1% American Indian, 4% Asian, 15% black, 9% Hispanic, 2% multiracial, 1% Pacific Islander, 53% white, 1% international
Most popular majors: Information not available
Expenses: 2015-2016: $6,266 in state, $9,167 out of state; room/board: N/A
Financial aid: (609) 633-9658

William Paterson University of New Jersey
Wayne NJ
(973) 720-2125
U.S. News ranking: Reg. U. (N), No. 104
Website: www.wpunj.edu/
Admissions email: admissions@wpunj.edu
Public; founded 1855
Freshman admissions: selective; 2015-2016: 9,851 applied, 7,318 accepted. Either SAT or ACT required. SAT 25/75 percentile: 900-1080. High school rank: N/A
Early decision deadline: N/A, notification date: N/A
Early action deadline: 12/1, notification date: 1/15
Application deadline (fall): 6/1
Undergraduate student body: 7,721 full time, 1,677 part time; 45% male, 55% female; 0% American Indian, 7% Asian, 16% black, 28% Hispanic, 3% multiracial, N/A Pacific Islander, 43% white, 0% international; 98% from in state; N/A live on campus; 2% of students in fraternities, 3% in sororities
Most popular majors: 19% Business, Management, Marketing, and Related Support Services; 12% Psychology; 10% Education; 9% Health Professions and Related Programs
Expenses: 2016-2017: $12,574 in state, $20,466 out of state; room/board: $11,103
Financial aid: (973) 720-2202; 74% of undergrads determined to have financial need; average aid package $10,488

NEW MEXICO

Eastern New Mexico University[1]
Portales NM
(505) 562-2178
U.S. News ranking: Reg. U. (W), second tier
Website: www.enmu.edu
Admissions email: admissions.office@enmu.edu
Public
Application deadline (fall): N/A
Undergraduate student body: N/A full time, N/A part time
Expenses: 2015-2016: $4,858 in state, $10,633 out of state; room/board: $6,452
Financial aid: (800) 367-3668

New Mexico Highlands University

Las Vegas NM
(505) 454-3439
U.S. News ranking: Reg. U. (W), second tier
Website: www.nmhu.edu
Admissions email: admissions@nmhu.edu
Public; founded 1893
Freshman admissions: less selective; 2015-2016: 993 applied, 993 accepted. Neither SAT nor ACT required. ACT 25/75 percentile: 15-20. High school rank: 2% in top tenth, 15% in top quarter, 45% in top half
Early decision deadline: N/A, notification date: N/A
Early action deadline: N/A, notification date: N/A
Application deadline (fall): rolling
Undergraduate student body: 1,474 full time, 759 part time; 38% male, 62% female; 8% American Indian, 1% Asian, 6% black, 56% Hispanic, 1% multiracial, 1% Pacific Islander, 21% white, 6% international; 81% from in state; 21% live on campus; N/A of students in fraternities, N/A in sororities
Most popular majors: 34% Health Professions and Related Programs; 24% Education; 16% Business, Management, Marketing, and Related Support Services; 6% Homeland Security, Law Enforcement, Firefighting and Related Protective Services; 4% Biological and Biomedical Sciences
Expenses: 2016-2017: $5,550 in state, $8,650 out of state; room/board: $7,154
Financial aid: (505) 454-3430; 76% of undergrads determined to have financial need; average aid package $1,832

New Mexico Institute of Mining and Technology

Socorro NM
(505) 835-5424
U.S. News ranking: Reg. U. (W), No. 27
Website: www.nmt.edu
Admissions email: admission@admin.nmt.edu
Public; founded 1889
Freshman admissions: more selective; 2015-2016: 1,628 applied, 398 accepted. Either SAT or ACT required. ACT 25/75 percentile: 23-29. High school rank: 36% in top tenth, 68% in top quarter, 91% in top half
Early decision deadline: N/A, notification date: N/A
Early action deadline: N/A, notification date: N/A
Application deadline (fall): 8/1
Undergraduate student body: 1,423 full time, 194 part time; 70% male, 30% female; 3% American Indian, 3% Asian, 2% black, 29% Hispanic, 5% multiracial, 0% Pacific Islander, 53% white, 3% international; 86% from in state; 45% live on campus; 0% of students in fraternities, 0% in sororities
Most popular majors: 23% Mechanical Engineering; 16% Petroleum Engineering; 7%

Biology/Biological Sciences, General; 7% Computer and Information Sciences, General; 7% Physics, General
Expenses: 2016-2017: $6,891 in state, $20,041 out of state; room/board: $7,942
Financial aid: (505) 835-5333; 51% of undergrads determined to have financial need; average aid package $12,676

New Mexico State University

Las Cruces NM
(505) 646-3121
U.S. News ranking: Nat. U., No. 220
Website: www.nmsu.edu
Admissions email: admissions@nmsu.edu
Public; founded 1888
Freshman admissions: selective; 2015-2016: 7,427 applied, 4,848 accepted. Either SAT or ACT required. ACT 25/75 percentile: 18-24. High school rank: 19% in top tenth, 46% in top quarter, 78% in top half
Early decision deadline: N/A, notification date: N/A
Early action deadline: N/A, notification date: N/A
Application deadline (fall): rolling
Undergraduate student body: 10,419 full time, 2,107 part time; 47% male, 53% female; 2% American Indian, 1% Asian, 3% black, 55% Hispanic, 2% multiracial, 0% Pacific Islander, 29% white, 5% international; 75% from in state; 18% live on campus; 5% of students in fraternities, 5% in sororities
Most popular majors: 7% Criminal Justice/Safety Studies; 6% Liberal Arts and Sciences/Liberal Studies; 5% Registered Nursing/Registered Nurse; 4% Psychology, General; 3% Biology/Biological Sciences, General
Expenses: 2016-2017: $6,729 in state, $21,234 out of state; room/board: $7,988
Financial aid: (505) 646-4105; 66% of undergrads determined to have financial need; average aid package $13,164

Northern New Mexico University[1]

Espanola NM
(505) 747-2111
U.S. News ranking: Reg. Coll. (W), unranked
Website: nnmc.edu
Admissions email: N/A
Public
Application deadline (fall): N/A
Undergraduate student body: N/A full time, N/A part time
Expenses: 2016-2017: $2,280 in state, $6,516 out of state; room/board: N/A
Financial aid: (505) 747-2128

Santa Fe University of Art and Design

Santa Fe NM
(505) 473-6937
U.S. News ranking: Arts, unranked
Website: www.santafeuniversity.edu

Admissions email: admissions@santafeuniversity.edu
For-profit; founded 1859
Freshman admissions: N/A; 2015-2016: 642 applied, 641 accepted. Neither SAT nor ACT required. SAT 25/75 percentile: N/A. High school rank: N/A
Early decision deadline: N/A, notification date: N/A
Early action deadline: N/A, notification date: N/A
Application deadline (fall): rolling
Undergraduate student body: 909 full time, 10 part time; 49% male, 51% female; 3% American Indian, 3% Asian, 8% black, 26% Hispanic, 8% multiracial, 2% Pacific Islander, 45% white, 5% international
Most popular majors: 23% Cinematography and Film/Video Production; 18% Drama and Dramatics/Theatre Arts, General; 15% Music, General; 12% Fine/Studio Arts, General; 8% Creative Writing
Expenses: 2015-2016: $31,346; room/board: $8,946
Financial aid: (505) 473-6454

St. John's College

Santa Fe NM
(505) 984-6060
U.S. News ranking: Nat. Lib. Arts, No. 83
Website: www.sjc.edu/admissions-and-aid
Admissions email: santafe.admissions@sjc.edu
Private; founded 1964
Freshman admissions: more selective; 2015-2016: 177 applied, 144 accepted. Neither SAT nor ACT required. SAT 25/75 percentile: 1160-1420. High school rank: 26% in top tenth, 57% in top quarter, 88% in top half
Early decision deadline: N/A, notification date: N/A
Early action deadline: 1/15, notification date: 2/15
Application deadline (fall): rolling
Undergraduate student body: 318 full time, 6 part time; 57% male, 43% female; 0% American Indian, 3% Asian, 0% black, 12% Hispanic, 4% multiracial, 0% Pacific Islander, 60% white, 20% international; 8% from in state; 85% live on campus; N/A of students in fraternities, N/A in sororities
Most popular majors: 100% Liberal Arts and Sciences/Liberal Studies
Expenses: 2016-2017: $51,148; room/board: $11,162
Financial aid: (505) 984-6073; 90% of undergrads determined to have financial need; average aid package $34,650

University of New Mexico

Albuquerque NM
(505) 277-8900
U.S. News ranking: Nat. U., No. 176
Website: www.unm.edu
Admissions email: apply@unm.edu
Public; founded 1889
Freshman admissions: selective; 2015-2016: 13,517 applied, 6,780 accepted. Either SAT or ACT required. ACT 25/75

percentile: 19-25. High school rank: N/A
Early decision deadline: N/A, notification date: N/A
Early action deadline: N/A, notification date: N/A
Application deadline (fall): rolling
Undergraduate student body: 16,085 full time, 4,437 part time; 45% male, 55% female; 6% American Indian, 3% Asian, 2% black, 47% Hispanic, 3% multiracial, 0% Pacific Islander, 35% white, 1% international; 93% from in state; 8% live on campus; 5% of students in fraternities, 6% in sororities
Most popular majors: 15% Business, Management, Marketing, and Related Support Services; 10% Education; 10% Psychology; 8% Biological and Biomedical Sciences; 7% Social Sciences
Expenses: 2015-2016: $7,071 in state, $21,302 out of state; room/board: $8,690
Financial aid: (505) 277-3012

University of the Southwest[1]

Hobbs NM
(575) 392-6563
U.S. News ranking: Reg. U. (W), second tier
Website: www.usw.edu
Admissions email: admissions@usw.edu
Private; founded 1962
Application deadline (fall): rolling
Undergraduate student body: N/A full time, N/A part time
Expenses: 2015-2016: $14,616; room/board: $7,078
Financial aid: (505) 392-6561

Western New Mexico University[1]

Silver City NM
(505) 538-6127
U.S. News ranking: Reg. U. (W), unranked
Website: www.wnmu.edu
Admissions email: admissions@wnmu.edu
Public; founded 1893
Application deadline (fall): 8/1
Undergraduate student body: N/A full time, N/A part time
Expenses: 2015-2016: $5,704 in state, $13,364 out of state; room/board: $9,410
Financial aid: (575) 538-6173

NEW YORK

Adelphi University

Garden City NY
(800) 233-5744
U.S. News ranking: Nat. U., No. 146
Website: www.adelphi.edu
Admissions email: admissions@adelphi.edu
Private; founded 1896
Freshman admissions: selective; 2015-2016: 9,367 applied, 6,762 accepted. Neither SAT nor ACT required. SAT 25/75 percentile: 1010-1220. High school rank: 23% in top tenth, 54% in top quarter, 87% in top half

Early decision deadline: N/A, notification date: N/A
Early action deadline: 12/1, notification date: 12/31
Application deadline (fall): rolling
Undergraduate student body: 4,414 full time, 438 part time; 32% male, 68% female; 0% American Indian, 9% Asian, 9% black, 15% Hispanic, 2% multiracial, 0% Pacific Islander, 54% white, 4% international; 93% from in state; 24% live on campus; 10% of students in fraternities, 8% in sororities
Most popular majors: 31% Registered Nursing/Registered Nurse; 8% Psychology, General; 6% Business Administration and Management, General; 4% Social Work; 4% Sport and Fitness Administration/Management
Expenses: 2015-2016: $34,034; room/board: $14,210
Financial aid: (516) 877-3365; 72% of undergrads determined to have financial need; average aid package $20,100

Alfred University

Alfred NY
(800) 541-9229
U.S. News ranking: Nat. Lib. Arts, No. 159
Website: www.alfred.edu
Admissions email: admissions@alfred.edu
Private; founded 1836
Freshman admissions: selective; 2015-2016: 3,640 applied, 2,490 accepted. Either SAT or ACT required. SAT 25/75 percentile: 920-1150. High school rank: 15% in top tenth, 43% in top quarter, 77% in top half
Early decision deadline: 12/1, notification date: 12/15
Early action deadline: N/A, notification date: N/A
Application deadline (fall): rolling
Undergraduate student body: 1,760 full time, 46 part time; 50% male, 50% female; 0% American Indian, 2% Asian, 9% black, 7% Hispanic, 3% multiracial, 0% Pacific Islander, 66% white, 2% international; 80% from in state; 76% live on campus; 0% of students in fraternities, 0% in sororities
Most popular majors: 31% Visual and Performing Arts; 15% Engineering; 14% Business, Management, Marketing, and Related Support Services; 9% Psychology; 4% Health Professions and Related Programs
Expenses: 2016-2017: $31,070; room/board: $12,196
Financial aid: (607) 871-2159; 87% of undergrads determined to have financial need; average aid package $29,107

Bard College

Annandale on Hudson NY
(845) 758-7472
U.S. News ranking: Nat. Lib. Arts, No. 49
Website: www.bard.edu
Admissions email: admission@bard.edu
Private; founded 1860
Freshman admissions: more selective; 2015-2016: 7,044 applied, 2,266 accepted. Neither

SAT nor ACT required. SAT 25/75 percentile: 1160-1370. High school rank: 49% in top tenth, 76% in top quarter, 96% in top half
Early decision deadline: 11/1, notification date: N/A
Early action deadline: 11/1, notification date: 1/1
Application deadline (fall): 1/1
Undergraduate student body: 1,946 full time, 77 part time; 45% male, 55% female; 1% American Indian, 6% Asian, 8% black, 1% Hispanic, N/A multiracial, N/A Pacific Islander, 63% white, 10% international; 34% from in state; 73% live on campus; N/A of students in fraternities, N/A in sororities
Most popular majors: 28% Visual and Performing Arts; 13% Social Sciences; 12% English Language and Literature/Letters; 10% Foreign Languages, Literatures, and Linguistics; 5% Physical Sciences
Expenses: 2016-2017: $51,384; room/board: $14,540
Financial aid: (845) 758-7525; 67% of undergrads determined to have financial need; average aid package $40,737

Barnard College
New York NY
(212) 854-2014
U.S. News ranking: Nat. Lib. Arts, No. 27
Website: www.barnard.edu
Admissions email: admissions@barnard.edu
Private; founded 1889
Freshman admissions: most selective; 2015-2016: 6,655 applied, 1,306 accepted. Either SAT or ACT required. SAT 25/75 percentile: 1260-1450. High school rank: 81% in top tenth, 94% in top quarter, 99% in top half
Early decision deadline: 11/1, notification date: 12/15
Early action deadline: N/A, notification date: N/A
Application deadline (fall): 1/1
Undergraduate student body: 2,511 full time, 37 part time; 0% male, 100% female; 0% American Indian, 14% Asian, 7% black, 12% Hispanic, 6% multiracial, 0% Pacific Islander, 53% white, 8% international; 26% from in state; 91% live on campus; 0% of students in fraternities, 20% in sororities
Most popular majors: 30% Social Sciences; 13% Psychology; 10% English Language and Literature/Letters; 10% Visual and Performing Arts; 9% Biological and Biomedical Sciences
Expenses: 2016-2017: $50,394; room/board: $15,598
Financial aid: (212) 854-2154; 41% of undergrads determined to have financial need; average aid package $45,817

Berkeley College
New York NY
(212) 986-4343
U.S. News ranking: Business, unranked
Website: www.berkeleycollege.edu
Admissions email: admissions@berkeleycollege.edu

For-profit; founded 1931
Freshman admissions: N/A; 2015-2016: N/A applied, N/A accepted. Neither SAT nor ACT required. SAT 25/75 percentile: N/A. High school rank: N/A
Early decision deadline: N/A, notification date: N/A
Early action deadline: N/A, notification date: N/A
Application deadline (fall): rolling
Undergraduate student body: 3,876 full time, 527 part time; 36% male, 64% female; 0% American Indian, 3% Asian, 25% black, 21% Hispanic, 0% multiracial, 0% Pacific Islander, 8% white, 15% international; 88% from in state; 7% live on campus; N/A of students in fraternities, N/A in sororities
Most popular majors: 24% Business Administration and Management, General; 19% Criminal Justice/Law Enforcement Administration; 18% Fashion Merchandising; 9% Health/Health Care Administration/Management; 8% Accounting
Expenses: 2016-2017: $24,750; room/board: $12,600
Financial aid: (212) 986-4343

Binghamton University–SUNY
Binghamton NY
(607) 777-2171
U.S. News ranking: Nat. U., No. 86
Website: www.binghamton.edu
Admissions email: admit@binghamton.edu
Public; founded 1946
Freshman admissions: more selective; 2015-2016: 30,616 applied, 13,010 accepted. Either SAT or ACT required. SAT 25/75 percentile: 1230-1383. High school rank: N/A
Early decision deadline: N/A, notification date: N/A
Early action deadline: 11/1, notification date: 1/15
Application deadline (fall): rolling
Undergraduate student body: 13,054 full time, 437 part time; 52% male, 48% female; 0% American Indian, 14% Asian, 5% black, 10% Hispanic, 2% multiracial, 0% Pacific Islander, 56% white, 10% international; 92% from in state; 51% live on campus; 14% of students in fraternities, 10% in sororities
Most popular majors: 15% Business Administration and Management, General; 12% Psychology, General; 11% Biology/Biological Sciences, General; 10% Engineering, General; 6% English Language and Literature, General
Expenses: 2015-2016: $9,044 in state, $22,164 out of state; room/board: $13,198
Financial aid: (607) 777-2428; 48% of undergrads determined to have financial need; average aid package $12,867

Boricua College
New York NY
(212) 694-1000
U.S. News ranking: Reg. Coll. (N), unranked
Website: www.boricuacollege.edu/
Admissions email: acruz@boricuacollege.edu
Private; founded 1973
Freshman admissions: N/A; 2015-2016: 271 applied, 190 accepted. Neither SAT nor ACT required. ACT 25/75 percentile: N/A. High school rank: N/A
Early decision deadline: N/A, notification date: N/A
Early action deadline: N/A, notification date: N/A
Application deadline (fall): rolling
Undergraduate student body: 925 full time, N/A part time; 25% male, 75% female; N/A American Indian, N/A Asian, 14% black, 82% Hispanic, N/A multiracial, 0% Pacific Islander, 0% white, N/A international
Most popular majors: 42% Community Organization and Advocacy; 35% Multicultural Education; 16% Business Administration and Management, General
Expenses: 2015-2016: $10,625; room/board: N/A
Financial aid: (212) 694-1000

Briarcliffe College[1]
Bethpage NY
(888) 348-4999
U.S. News ranking: Reg. Coll. (N), unranked
Website: www.briarcliffe.edu
Admissions email: N/A
For-profit
Application deadline (fall): N/A
Undergraduate student body: N/A full time, N/A part time
Expenses: 2015-2016: $14,349; room/board: N/A
Financial aid: N/A

Canisius College
Buffalo NY
(800) 843-1517
U.S. News ranking: Reg. U. (N), No. 23
Website: www.canisius.edu
Admissions email: admissions@canisius.edu
Private; founded 1870
Affiliation: Roman Catholic
Freshman admissions: selective; 2015-2016: 4,209 applied, 3,661 accepted. Either SAT or ACT required. SAT 25/75 percentile: 950-1180. High school rank: 18% in top tenth, 50% in top quarter, 88% in top half
Early decision deadline: N/A, notification date: N/A
Early action deadline: N/A, notification date: N/A
Application deadline (fall): rolling
Undergraduate student body: 2,538 full time, 133 part time; 46% male, 54% female; N/A American Indian, N/A Asian, N/A black, N/A Hispanic, N/A multiracial, N/A Pacific Islander, N/A white, N/A international; 91% from in state; 46% live on campus; 1% of students in fraternities, 1% in sororities
Most popular majors: 23% Business, Management, Marketing, and Related Support

Services; 14% Biological and Biomedical Sciences; 11% Psychology; 10% Social Sciences; 9% Education
Expenses: 2016-2017: $35,424; room/board $13,022
Financial aid: (716) 888-2300; 77% of undergrads determined to have financial need; average aid package $29,531

Cazenovia College
Cazenovia NY
(800) 654-3210
U.S. News ranking: Reg. Coll. (N), No. 8
Website: www.cazenovia.edu
Admissions email: admission@cazenovia.edu
Private; founded 1824
Freshman admissions: less selective; 2015-2016: 2,307 applied, 1,880 accepted. Neither SAT nor ACT required. SAT 25/75 percentile: 840-1060. High school rank: 12% in top tenth, 35% in top quarter, 71% in top half
Early decision deadline: N/A, notification date: N/A
Early action deadline: N/A, notification date: N/A
Application deadline (fall): rolling
Undergraduate student body: 943 full time, 129 part time; 26% male, 74% female; 0% American Indian, 1% Asian, 8% black, 6% Hispanic, 2% multiracial, 0% Pacific Islander, 69% white, 0% international; 85% from in state; 97% live on campus; N/A of students in fraternities, N/A in sororities
Most popular majors: 29% Business, Management, Marketing, and Related Support Services; 27% Visual and Performing Arts; 13% Public Administration and Social Service Professions; 11% Homeland Security, Law Enforcement, Firefighting and Related Protective Services; 4% Education
Expenses: 2016-2017: $32,674; room/board: $13,198
Financial aid: (315) 655-7887; 91% of undergrads determined to have financial need; average aid package $30,850

Clarkson University
Potsdam NY
(800) 527-6577
U.S. News ranking: Nat. U., No. 129
Website: www.clarkson.edu
Admissions email: admission@clarkson.edu
Private; founded 1896
Freshman admissions: more selective; 2015-2016: 6,906 applied, 4,700 accepted. Either SAT or ACT required. SAT 25/75 percentile: 1080-1290. High school rank: 36% in top tenth, 72% in top quarter, 95% in top half
Early decision deadline: 12/1, notification date: 1/1
Early action deadline: N/A, notification date: N/A
Application deadline (fall): 1/15
Undergraduate student body: 3,185 full time, 72 part time; 70% male, 30% female; 0% American Indian, 3% Asian, 2% black, 4% Hispanic, 2% multiracial, 0%

Pacific Islander, 84% white, 3% international; 74% from in state; 84% live on campus; 10% of students in fraternities, 12% in sororities
Most popular majors: 53% Engineering, General; 20% Business Administration and Management, General; 8% Biology/Biological Sciences, General; 4% Psychology, General
Expenses: 2016-2017: $46,132; room/board: $14,558
Financial aid: (315) 268-6479; 82% of undergrads determined to have financial need; average aid package $40,757

Colgate University
Hamilton NY
(315) 228-7401
U.S. News ranking: Nat. Lib. Arts, No. 12
Website: www.colgate.edu
Admissions email: admission@mail.colgate.edu
Private; founded 1819
Freshman admissions: most selective; 2015-2016: 8,724 applied, 2,387 accepted. Either SAT or ACT required. SAT 25/75 percentile: 1250-1450. High school rank: 75% in top tenth, 94% in top quarter, 99% in top half
Early decision deadline: 11/15, notification date: 12/15
Early action deadline: N/A, notification date: N/A
Application deadline (fall): 1/15
Undergraduate student body: 2,834 full time, 19 part time; 45% male, 55% female; 0% American Indian, 4% Asian, 4% black, 9% Hispanic, 3% multiracial, 0% Pacific Islander, 67% white, 9% international; 27% from in state; 90% live on campus; 11% of students in fraternities, 21% in sororities
Most popular majors: 12% Economics, General; 8% History, General; 8% Political Science and Government, General; 7% English Language and Literature, General; 6% Neuroscience
Expenses: 2016-2017: $51,955; room/board: $13,075
Financial aid: (315) 228-7431; 38% of undergrads determined to have financial need; average aid package $47,563

College at Brockport–SUNY
Brockport NY
(585) 395-2751
U.S. News ranking: Reg. U. (N), No. 61
Website: www.brockport.edu
Admissions email: admit@brockport.edu
Public; founded 1835
Freshman admissions: selective; 2015-2016: 9,528 applied, 5,018 accepted. Either SAT or ACT required. SAT 25/75 percentile: 930-1120. High school rank: 11% in top tenth, 36% in top quarter, 79% in top half
Early decision deadline: N/A, notification date: N/A
Early action deadline: N/A, notification date: N/A
Application deadline (fall): 8/1

Undergraduate student body: 6,353 full time, 716 part time; 45% male, 55% female; 0% American Indian, 2% Asian, 10% black, 6% Hispanic, 2% multiracial, 0% Pacific Islander, 72% white, 1% international; 98% from in state; 28% live on campus; 1% of students in fraternities, 1% in sororities
Most popular majors: 17% Health Professions and Related Programs; 15% Business, Management, Marketing, and Related Support Services; 10% Parks, Recreation, Leisure, and Fitness Studies; 8% Psychology; 7% Homeland Security, Law Enforcement, Firefighting and Related Protective Services
Expenses: 2016-2017: $7,928 in state, $17,778 out of state; room/board: $12,418
Financial aid: (585) 395-2501; 72% of undergrads determined to have financial need; average aid package $10,767

College of Mount St. Vincent
Riverdale NY
(718) 405-3267
U.S. News ranking: Reg. U. (N), No. 128
Website: www.mountsaintvincent.edu
Admissions email: admissions.office@mountsaintvincent.edu
Private; founded 1847
Affiliation: Roman Catholic
Freshman admissions: less selective; 2015-2016: 2,734 applied, 2,353 accepted. Either SAT or ACT required. SAT 25/75 percentile: 810-990. High school rank: 5% in top tenth, 19% in top quarter, 64% in top half
Early decision deadline: N/A, notification date: N/A
Early action deadline: 11/1, notification date: 12/1
Undergraduate student body: 1,508 full time, 86 part time; 31% male, 69% female; 0% American Indian, 10% Asian, 15% black, 38% Hispanic, 5% multiracial, 0% Pacific Islander, 27% white, 2% international; 86% from in state; 54% live on campus; 0% of students in fraternities, 0% in sororities
Most popular majors: 43% Health Professions and Related Programs; 14% Business, Management, Marketing, and Related Support Services; 10% Psychology; 8% Social Sciences
Expenses: 2016-2017: $24,680; room/board: $8,720
Financial aid: (718) 405-3290; 78% of undergrads determined to have financial need; average aid package $15,864

College of New Rochelle
New Rochelle NY
(800) 933-5923
U.S. News ranking: Reg. U. (N), No. 75
Website: www.cnr.edu
Admissions email: admission@cnr.edu
Private; founded 1904
Affiliation: Roman Catholic
Freshman admissions: selective; 2015-2016: 1,727 applied, 546

accepted. Either SAT or ACT required. SAT 25/75 percentile: 870-1030. High school rank: 17% in top tenth, 47% in top quarter, 79% in top half
Early decision deadline: N/A, notification date: N/A
Early action deadline: N/A, notification date: N/A
Application deadline (fall): rolling
Undergraduate student body: 505 full time, 68 part time; 6% male, 94% female; 0% American Indian, 7% Asian, 38% black, 29% Hispanic, 1% multiracial, 1% Pacific Islander, 15% white, 1% international; 92% from in state; 33% live on campus; 0% of students in fraternities, 0% in sororities
Most popular majors: 53% Registered Nursing/Registered Nurse; 12% Psychology, General; 6% Social Work; 5% Biology/Biological Sciences, General
Expenses: 2016-2017: $34,960; room/board: $13,208
Financial aid: (914) 654-5224; 93% of undergrads determined to have financial need; average aid package $27,025

College of Saint Rose
Albany NY
(518) 454-5150
U.S. News ranking: Reg. U. (N), No. 67
Website: www.strose.edu
Admissions email: admit@strose.edu
Private; founded 1920
Freshman admissions: selective; 2015-2016: 5,599 applied, 4,578 accepted. Neither SAT nor ACT required. SAT 25/75 percentile: 950-1130. High school rank: 14% in top tenth, 40% in top quarter, 73% in top half
Early decision deadline: N/A, notification date: N/A
Early action deadline: 12/1, notification date: 12/15
Application deadline (fall): 5/1
Undergraduate student body: 2,540 full time, 153 part time; 35% male, 65% female; 0% American Indian, 2% Asian, 10% black, 6% Hispanic, 7% multiracial, 0% Pacific Islander, 67% white, 2% international; 88% from in state; 48% live on campus; N/A of students in fraternities, N/A in sororities
Most popular majors: 25% Education; 15% Business, Management, Marketing, and Related Support Services; 10% Visual and Performing Arts; 8% Psychology
Expenses: 2016-2017: $30,692; room/board: $12,356
Financial aid: (518) 458-5424; 84% of undergrads determined to have financial need; average aid package $18,862

The College of Westchester
White Plains NY
(855) 403-7722
U.S. News ranking: Reg. Coll. (N), unranked
Website: www.cw.edu/
Admissions email: N/A
For-profit

Freshman admissions: N/A; 2015-2016: N/A applied, N/A accepted. Neither SAT nor ACT required. ACT 25/75 percentile: N/A. High school rank: N/A
Early decision deadline: N/A, notification date: N/A
Early action deadline: N/A, notification date: N/A
Application deadline (fall): N/A
Undergraduate student body: 847 full time, 220 part time; 35% male, 65% female; 0% American Indian, 2% Asian, 39% black, 41% Hispanic, 2% multiracial, N/A Pacific Islander, 12% white, N/A international
Most popular majors: Information not available
Expenses: 2015-2016: $21,015; room/board: N/A
Financial aid: N/A

Columbia University
New York NY
(212) 854-2522
U.S. News ranking: Nat. U., No. 5
Website: www.columbia.edu
Admissions email: ugrad-ask@columbia.edu
Private; founded 1754
Freshman admissions: most selective; 2015-2016: 36,250 applied, 2,220 accepted. Either SAT or ACT required. SAT 25/75 percentile: 1400-1590. High school rank: 96% in top tenth, 99% in top quarter, 100% in top half
Early decision deadline: 11/1, notification date: 12/15
Early action deadline: N/A, notification date: N/A
Application deadline (fall): 1/1
Undergraduate student body: 6,102 full time, 0 part time; 52% male, 48% female; 2% American Indian, 22% Asian, 12% black, 12% Hispanic, N/A multiracial, N/A Pacific Islander, 34% white, 14% international; 33% from in state; 94% live on campus; 8% of students in fraternities, 10% in sororities
Most popular majors: 22% Engineering; 22% Social Sciences; 9% Biological and Biomedical Sciences; 5% English Language and Literature/Letters; 5% Foreign Languages, Literatures, and Linguistics
Expenses: 2015-2016: $53,000; room/board: $12,860
Financial aid: (212) 854-3711; 49% of undergrads determined to have financial need; average aid package $49,348

Concordia College
Bronxville NY
(800) 937-2655
U.S. News ranking: Reg. Coll. (N), No. 22
Website: www.concordia-ny.edu
Admissions email: admission@concordia-ny.edu
Private; founded 1881
Affiliation: Lutheran
Freshman admissions: least selective; 2015-2016: 1,024 applied, 731 accepted. Neither SAT nor ACT required. SAT 25/75 percentile: 790-1000. High school rank: N/A
Early decision deadline: N/A, notification date: N/A
Early action deadline: 11/15, notification date: 12/15

Application deadline (fall): 8/15
Undergraduate student body: 809 full time, 149 part time; 35% male, 65% female; 0% American Indian, 4% Asian, 17% black, 24% Hispanic, 2% multiracial, 0% Pacific Islander, 34% white, 13% international
Most popular majors: Business Administration, Management and Operations
Expenses: 2016-2017: $30,550; room/board: $11,575
Financial aid: (914) 337-9300; 73% of undergrads determined to have financial need; average aid package $24,885

Cooper Union
New York NY
(212) 353-4120
U.S. News ranking: Reg. Coll. (N), No. 1
Website: www.cooper.edu
Admissions email: admissions@cooper.edu
Private; founded 1859
Freshman admissions: most selective; 2015-2016: 3,258 applied, 426 accepted. Either SAT or ACT required. SAT 25/75 percentile: 1240-1510. High school rank: 85% in top tenth, 90% in top quarter, 95% in top half
Early decision deadline: 12/1, notification date: 12/22
Early action deadline: N/A, notification date: N/A
Application deadline (fall): 1/9
Undergraduate student body: 893 full time, 8 part time; 67% male, 33% female; N/A American Indian, 17% Asian, 3% black, 9% Hispanic, 9% multiracial, N/A Pacific Islander, 31% white, 18% international; 53% from in state; 0% live on campus; 1% of students in fraternities, 0% in sororities
Most popular majors: 54% Engineering; 32% Visual and Performing Arts
Expenses: 2016-2017: $43,850; room/board: $15,910
Financial aid: (212) 353-4113; 41% of undergrads determined to have financial need; average aid package $38,228

Cornell University
Ithaca NY
(607) 255-5241
U.S. News ranking: Nat. U., No. 15
Website: www.cornell.edu
Admissions email: admissions@cornell.edu
Private; founded 1865
Freshman admissions: most selective; 2015-2016: 41,900 applied, 6,315 accepted. Either SAT or ACT required. SAT 25/75 percentile: 1330-1530. High school rank: 89% in top tenth, 97% in top quarter, 100% in top half
Early decision deadline: 11/1, notification date: 12/15
Early action deadline: N/A, notification date: N/A
Application deadline (fall): 1/1
Undergraduate student body: 14,315 full time, 0 part time; 48% male, 52% female; 0% American Indian, 18% Asian, 6% black, 12% Hispanic, 4% multiracial, 0% Pacific Islander,

41% white, 10% international; 35% from in state; 55% live on campus; 33% of students in fraternities, 34% in sororities
Most popular majors: 17% Engineering; 15% Biological and Biomedical Sciences; 13% Business, Management, Marketing, and Related Support Services; 10% Social Sciences
Expenses: 2016-2017: $50,953; room/board: $13,950
Financial aid: (607) 255-5145; 46% of undergrads determined to have financial need; average aid package $44,859

CUNY–Baruch College
New York NY
(646) 312-1400
U.S. News ranking: Reg. U. (N), No. 20
Website: www.baruch.cuny.edu
Admissions email: admissions@baruch.cuny.edu
Public; founded 1919
Freshman admissions: more selective; 2015-2016: 19,864 applied, 6,443 accepted. SAT required. SAT 25/75 percentile: 1100-1320. High school rank: 48% in top tenth, 78% in top quarter, 93% in top half
Early decision deadline: 12/13, notification date: 1/7
Early action deadline: N/A, notification date: N/A
Application deadline (fall): 2/1
Undergraduate student body: 11,233 full time, 4,021 part time; 51% male, 49% female; 0% American Indian, 32% Asian, 9% black, 22% Hispanic, 2% multiracial, 0% Pacific Islander, 23% white, 11% international; 97% from in state; 2% live on campus; N/A of students in fraternities, N/A in sororities
Most popular majors: 23% Finance, General; 18% Accounting; 11% Sales, Distribution, and Marketing Operations, General; 9% Business/Corporate Communications; 7% Business Administration and Management, General
Expenses: 2016-2017: $7,301 in state, $17,771 out of state; room/board: $13,768
Financial aid: (646) 312-1360; 64% of undergrads determined to have financial need; average aid package $5,761

CUNY– Brooklyn College
Brooklyn NY
(718) 951-5001
U.S. News ranking: Reg. U. (N), No. 75
Website: www.brooklyn.cuny.edu
Admissions email: adminqry@brooklyn.cuny.edu
Public; founded 1930
Freshman admissions: selective; 2015-2016: 20,324 applied, 7,583 accepted. Either SAT or ACT required. SAT 25/75 percentile: 970-1180. High school rank: 18% in top tenth, 50% in top quarter, 78% in top half
Early decision deadline: N/A, notification date: N/A
Early action deadline: N/A, notification date: N/A

Application deadline (fall): 2/1
Undergraduate student body: 10,175 full time, 4,032 part time; 41% male, 59% female; 0% American Indian, 18% Asian, 22% black, 22% Hispanic, 2% multiracial, 0% Pacific Islander, 33% white, 4% international; 99% from in state; N/A live on campus; 3% of students in fraternities, 3% in sororities
Most popular majors: 21% Business Administration and Management, General; 16% Psychology, General; 11% Accounting; 5% Biology/Biological Sciences, General; 3% Audiology/Audiologist and Speech-Language Pathology/Pathologist
Expenses: 2016-2017: $6,838 in state, $17,308 out of state; room/board: N/A
Financial aid: (718) 951-5045; 91% of undergrads determined to have financial need; average aid package $7,500

CUNY–City College
New York NY
(212) 650-6977
U.S. News ranking: Reg. U. (N), No. 85
Website: www.ccny.cuny.edu
Admissions email: admissions@ccny.cuny.edu
Public; founded 1847
Freshman admissions: selective; 2015-2016: 24,735 applied, 9,794 accepted. SAT required. SAT 25/75 percentile: 970-1230. High school rank: N/A
Early decision deadline: N/A, notification date: N/A
Early action deadline: N/A, notification date: N/A
Application deadline (fall): 1/15
Undergraduate student body: 9,735 full time, 3,605 part time; 50% male, 50% female; 0% American Indian, 25% Asian, 16% black, 35% Hispanic, 2% multiracial, 0% Pacific Islander, 15% white, 6% international; 99% from in state; N/A live on campus; N/A of students in fraternities, N/A in sororities
Most popular majors: 17% Psychology; 14% Engineering; 13% Social Sciences; 10% Visual and Performing Arts; 7% Biological and Biomedical Sciences
Expenses: 2016-2017: $6,689 in state, $13,799 out of state; room/board: N/A
Financial aid: (212) 650-5819; 89% of undergrads determined to have financial need; average aid package $9,140

CUNY–College of Staten Island
Staten Island NY
(718) 982-2010
U.S. News ranking: Reg. U. (N), second tier
Website: www.csi.cuny.edu
Admissions email: admissions@csi.cuny.edu
Public; founded 1976
Freshman admissions: less selective; 2015-2016: 13,051 applied, 13,051 accepted. Either SAT or ACT required. SAT 25/75 percentile: 910-1100. High school rank: N/A

Early decision deadline: N/A, notification date: N/A
Early action deadline: N/A, notification date: N/A
Application deadline (fall): rolling
Undergraduate student body: 9,693 full time, 3,113 part time; 44% male, 56% female; 0% American Indian, 12% Asian, 15% black, 17% Hispanic, N/A multiracial, N/A Pacific Islander, 52% white, 3% international; 99% from in state; 3% live on campus; 0% of students in fraternities, 0% in sororities
Most popular majors: 18% Business, Management, Marketing, and Related Support Services; 18% Psychology; 11% Health Professions and Related Programs; 10% Social Sciences; 7% Education
Expenses: 2015-2016: $6,809 in state, $17,279 out of state; room/board: $16,832
Financial aid: (718) 982-2030; 68% of undergrads determined to have financial need; average aid package $8,502

CUNY–Hunter College
New York NY
(212) 772-4490
U.S. News ranking: Reg. U. (N), No. 42
Website: www.hunter.cuny.edu
Admissions email: admissions@hunter.cuny.edu
Public; founded 1870
Freshman admissions: more selective; 2015-2016: 28,041 applied, 10,878 accepted. Either SAT or ACT required. SAT 25/75 percentile: 1070-1260. High school rank: 24% in top tenth, 57% in top quarter, 87% in top half
Early decision deadline: N/A, notification date: N/A
Early action deadline: N/A, notification date: N/A
Application deadline (fall): 3/15
Undergraduate student body: 12,033 full time, 4,517 part time; 35% male, 65% female; 0% American Indian, 28% Asian, 11% black, 21% Hispanic, N/A multiracial, N/A Pacific Islander, 33% white, 6% international
Most popular majors: Information not available
Expenses: 2016-2017: $6,780 in state, $14,340 out of state; room/board: $10,573
Financial aid: (212) 772-4820; 83% of undergrads determined to have financial need; average aid package $8,700

CUNY–John Jay College of Criminal Justice
New York NY
(212) 237-8866
U.S. News ranking: Reg. U. (N), No. 108
Website: www.jjay.cuny.edu/
Admissions email: admissions@jjay.cuny.edu
Public; founded 1965
Freshman admissions: less selective; 2015-2016: 13,398 applied, 6,971 accepted. Either SAT or ACT required. SAT 25/75 percentile: 860-1050. High school rank: N/A

Early decision deadline: N/A, notification date: N/A
Early action deadline: N/A, notification date: N/A
Application deadline (fall): 5/31
Undergraduate student body: 10,130 full time, 2,839 part time; 43% male, 57% female; 0% American Indian, 12% Asian, 20% black, 42% Hispanic, 0% multiracial, 0% Pacific Islander, 23% white, 3% international; 96% from in state; N/A live on campus; N/A of students in fraternities, N/A in sororities
Most popular majors: 52% Criminal Justice/Law Enforcement Administration; 17% Forensic Psychology; 17% Social Sciences; 3% Legal Professions and Studies; 3% Public Administration
Expenses: 2016-2017: $6,510 in state, $16,530 out of state; room/board: N/A
Financial aid: (212) 237-8151; 77% of undergrads determined to have financial need; average aid package $9,034

CUNY–Lehman College
Bronx NY
(718) 960-8131
U.S. News ranking: Reg. U. (N), second tier
Website: www.lehman.cuny.edu
Admissions email: undergraduate.admissions@lehman.cuny.edu
Public; founded 1968
Freshman admissions: less selective; 2015-2016: 14,076 applied, 4,216 accepted. Either SAT or ACT required. SAT 25/75 percentile: 860-1000. High school rank: N/A
Early decision deadline: N/A, notification date: N/A
Early action deadline: N/A, notification date: N/A
Application deadline (fall): 10/1
Undergraduate student body: 6,259 full time, 4,541 part time; 32% male, 68% female; 0% American Indian, 7% Asian, 32% black, 50% Hispanic, N/A multiracial, N/A Pacific Islander, 8% white, 3% international; 93% from in state; N/A live on campus; N/A of students in fraternities, N/A in sororities
Most popular majors: 21% Business, Management, Marketing, and Related Support Services; 14% Health Professions and Related Programs; 9% Social Sciences; 8% Public Administration and Social Service Professions; 7% Psychology
Expenses: 2016-2017: $6,230 in state, $13,040 out of state; room/board: N/A
Financial aid: (718) 960-8545; 88% of undergrads determined to have financial need; average aid package $4,859

CUNY–Medgar Evers College
Brooklyn NY
(718) 270-6024
U.S. News ranking: Reg. Coll. (N), second tier
Website: www.mec.cuny.edu
Admissions email: enroll@mec.cuny.edu
Public; founded 1969

Freshman admissions: least selective; 2015-2016: N/A applied, N/A accepted. Neither SAT nor ACT required. SAT 25/75 percentile: 690-860. High school rank: N/A
Early decision deadline: N/A, notification date: N/A
Early action deadline: N/A, notification date: N/A
Application deadline (fall): rolling
Undergraduate student body: 4,513 full time, 2,252 part time; 28% male, 72% female; 1% American Indian, 2% Asian, 67% black, 13% Hispanic, 0% multiracial, 0% Pacific Islander, 1% white, 1% international
Most popular majors: Biology/Biological Sciences, General; Business/Commerce, General; Health Professions and Related Programs; Psychology, General; Public Administration and Social Service Professions
Expenses: 2015-2016: $6,225 in state, $16,245 out of state; room/board: N/A
Financial aid: (718) 270-6038

CUNY–New York City College of Technology
Brooklyn NY
(718) 260-5500
U.S. News ranking: Reg. Coll. (N), second tier
Website: www.citytech.cuny.edu
Admissions email: admissions@citytech.cuny.edu
Public; founded 1946
Freshman admissions: least selective; 2015-2016: 16,881 applied, 12,443 accepted. Neither SAT nor ACT required. SAT 25/75 percentile: 740-950. High school rank: N/A
Early decision deadline: N/A, notification date: N/A
Early action deadline: N/A, notification date: N/A
Application deadline (fall): 2/1
Undergraduate student body: 10,821 full time, 6,603 part time; 56% male, 44% female; 0% American Indian, 20% Asian, 29% black, 32% Hispanic, 1% multiracial, 0% Pacific Islander, 12% white, 5% international; 97% from in state; N/A live on campus; N/A of students in fraternities, N/A in sororities
Most popular majors: 14% Hospitality Administration/Management, General; 13% Information Science/Studies; 11% Registered Nursing/Registered Nurse; 11% Design and Visual Communications, General; 10% Public Administration and Social Service Professions
Expenses: 2015-2016: $6,669 in state, $13,779 out of state; room/board: N/A
Financial aid: (718) 260-5700

CUNY–Queens College
Flushing NY
(718) 997-5600
U.S. News ranking: Reg. U. (N), No. 38
Website: www.qc.edu/
Admissions email: applyto@uapc.cuny.edu
Public; founded 1937

Freshman admissions: more selective; 2015-2016: 18,416 applied, 7,447 accepted. Either SAT or ACT required. SAT 25/75 percentile: 1020-1200. High school rank: 36% in top tenth, 66% in top quarter, 99% in top half
Early decision deadline: N/A, notification date: N/A
Early action deadline: N/A, notification date: N/A
Application deadline (fall): 2/1
Undergraduate student body: 11,555 full time, 4,545 part time; 44% male, 56% female; 0% American Indian, 27% Asian, 9% black, 29% Hispanic, 1% multiracial, 0% Pacific Islander, 29% white, 5% international; 98% from in state; 2% live on campus; 1% of students in fraternities, 1% in sororities
Most popular majors: 18% Psychology, General; 12% Accounting; 8% Sociology; 7% Economics, General; 5% English Language and Literature, General
Expenses: 2016-2017: $6,938 in state, $17,408 out of state; room/board: N/A
Financial aid: (718) 997-5101; 66% of undergrads determined to have financial need; average aid package $7,425

CUNY–York College
Jamaica NY
(718) 262-2165
U.S. News ranking: Reg. Coll. (N), second tier
Website: www.york.cuny.edu
Admissions email: admissions@york.cuny.edu
Public; founded 1966
Freshman admissions: least selective; 2015-2016: 13,889 applied, 8,695 accepted. SAT required. SAT 25/75 percentile: 770-950. High school rank: N/A
Early decision deadline: N/A, notification date: N/A
Early action deadline: N/A, notification date: N/A
Application deadline (fall): 6/1
Undergraduate student body: 5,226 full time, 3,220 part time; 35% male, 65% female; 1% American Indian, 24% Asian, 42% black, 20% Hispanic, 0% multiracial, 0% Pacific Islander, 7% white, 5% international; 99% from in state; 0% live on campus; 0% of students in fraternities, 0% in sororities
Most popular majors: Information not available
Expenses: 2016-2017: $6,748 in state, $17,218 out of state; room/board: N/A
Financial aid: (718) 262-2230; 77% of undergrads determined to have financial need; average aid package $6,914

Daemen College
Amherst NY
(800) 462-7652
U.S. News ranking: Reg. U. (N), second tier
Website: www.daemen.edu
Admissions email: admissions@daemen.edu
Private; founded 1947
Freshman admissions: selective; 2015-2016: 3,047 applied, 1,514 accepted. Either SAT or ACT required. SAT 25/75

percentile: 920-1140. High school rank: 19% in top tenth, 51% in top quarter, 86% in top half
Early decision deadline: N/A, notification date: N/A
Early action deadline: N/A, notification date: N/A
Application deadline (fall): rolling
Undergraduate student body: 1,678 full time, 352 part time; 28% male, 72% female; 0% American Indian, 2% Asian, 12% black, 7% Hispanic, 1% multiracial, 0% Pacific Islander, 73% white, 1% international; 96% from in state; 34% live on campus; 6% of students in fraternities, 5% in sororities
Most popular majors: 34% Registered Nursing/Registered Nurse; 15% Natural Sciences; 7% Physician Assistant; 7% Health and Wellness, General; 6% Business Administration and Management, General
Expenses: 2016-2017: $26,940; room/board: $12,425
Financial aid: (716) 839-8254; 69% of undergrads determined to have financial need; average aid package $23,791

Dominican College
Orangeburg NY
(845) 359-3533
U.S. News ranking: Reg. U. (N), second tier
Website: www.dc.edu
Admissions email: admissions@dc.edu
Private; founded 1952
Freshman admissions: least selective; 2015-2016: 1,959 applied, 1,400 accepted. Either SAT or ACT required. SAT 25/75 percentile: 780-960. High school rank: N/A
Early decision deadline: N/A, notification date: N/A
Early action deadline: N/A, notification date: N/A
Application deadline (fall): rolling
Undergraduate student body: 1,356 full time, 196 part time; 34% male, 66% female; N/A American Indian, 7% Asian, 17% black, 29% Hispanic, 14% multiracial, N/A Pacific Islander, 32% white, 1% international; 76% from in state; 50% live on campus; N/A of students in fraternities, N/A in sororities
Most popular majors: 33% Health Professions and Related Programs; 16% Business, Management, Marketing, and Related Support Services; 11% Social Sciences; 7% Education; 7% Homeland Security, Law Enforcement, Firefighting and Related Protective Services
Expenses: 2016-2017: $27,438; room/board: $12,420
Financial aid: (845) 359-7800; average aid package $22,346

Dowling College[1]
Oakdale Long Island NY
(631) 244-3030
U.S. News ranking: Reg. U. (N), second tier
Website: www.dowling.edu
Admissions email: admissions@dowling.edu
Private; founded 1955
Application deadline (fall): rolling

Undergraduate student body: N/A full time, N/A part time
Expenses: 2015-2016: $29,100; room/board: N/A
Financial aid: (631) 244-3303

D'Youville College
Buffalo NY
(716) 829-7600
U.S. News ranking: Reg. U. (N), second tier
Website: www.dyc.edu
Admissions email: admissions@dyc.edu
Private; founded 1908
Freshman admissions: selective; 2015-2016: 1,216 applied, 854 accepted. Either SAT or ACT required. SAT 25/75 percentile: 900-1130. High school rank: N/A
Early decision deadline: N/A, notification date: N/A
Early action deadline: N/A, notification date: N/A
Application deadline (fall): rolling
Undergraduate student body: 1,419 full time, 396 part time; 26% male, 74% female; 1% American Indian, 3% Asian, 7% black, 4% Hispanic, 2% multiracial, 0% Pacific Islander, 74% white, 5% international; 93% from in state; 17% live on campus; 0% of students in fraternities, 0% in sororities
Most popular majors: 69% Health Professions and Related Programs; 10% Business, Management, Marketing, and Related Support Services; 10% Multi/Interdisciplinary Studies; 6% Biological and Biomedical Sciences; 1% Social Sciences
Expenses: 2016-2017: $25,210; room/board: $11,570
Financial aid: (716) 829-7500; 84% of undergrads determined to have financial need; average aid package $19,088

Elmira College
Elmira NY
(800) 935-6472
U.S. News ranking: Nat. Lib. Arts, No. 174
Website: www.elmira.edu
Admissions email: admissions@elmira.edu
Private; founded 1855
Freshman admissions: selective; 2015-2016: 2,387 applied, 1,818 accepted. Neither SAT nor ACT required. SAT 25/75 percentile: 910-1130. High school rank: 26% in top tenth, 61% in top quarter, 86% in top half
Early decision deadline: N/A, notification date: N/A
Early action deadline: N/A, notification date: N/A
Application deadline (fall): rolling
Undergraduate student body: 1,123 full time, 165 part time; 30% male, 70% female; 0% American Indian, 2% Asian, 4% black, 3% Hispanic, 2% multiracial, N/A Pacific Islander, 80% white, 5% international; 63% from in state; 88% live on campus; N/A of students in fraternities, N/A in sororities
Most popular majors: 23% Health Professions and Related Programs; 17% Business, Management, Marketing, and Related Support Services; 16%

Education; 8% English Language and Literature/Letters
Expenses: 2016-2017: $41,900; room/board: $12,000
Financial aid: (607) 735-1728; 81% of undergrads determined to have financial need; average aid package $31,328

Excelsior College[1]
Albany NY
(518) 464-8500
U.S. News ranking: Reg. U. (N), unranked
Website: www.excelsior.edu
Admissions email: admissions@excelsior.edu
Private; founded 1971
Application deadline (fall): rolling
Undergraduate student body: N/A full time, N/A part time
Expenses: N/A
Financial aid: (518) 464-8500

Farmingdale State College–SUNY
Farmingdale NY
(631) 420-2200
U.S. News ranking: Reg. Coll. (N), No. 17
Website: www.farmingdale.edu
Admissions email: admissions@farmingdale.edu
Public; founded 1912
Freshman admissions: selective; 2015-2016: 5,256 applied, 2,313 accepted. Either SAT or ACT required. SAT 25/75 percentile: 910-1080. High school rank: 5% in top tenth, 25% in top quarter, 70% in top half
Early decision deadline: N/A, notification date: N/A
Early action deadline: N/A, notification date: N/A
Application deadline (fall): 6/1
Undergraduate student body: 6,388 full time, 2,260 part time; 57% male, 43% female; 0% American Indian, 7% Asian, 10% black, 17% Hispanic, 2% multiracial, 0% Pacific Islander, 60% white, 3% international; 100% from in state; 7% live on campus; 3% of students in fraternities, 4% in sororities
Most popular majors: 25% Business, Management, and Related Support Services; 14% Engineering Technologies and Engineering-Related Fields; 11% Health Professions and Related Programs; 11% Homeland Security, Law Enforcement, Firefighting and Related Protective Services; 10% Multi/Interdisciplinary Studies
Expenses: 2015-2016: $7,808 in state, $17,658 out of state; room/board: $12,500
Financial aid: (631) 420-2328; 55% of undergrads determined to have financial need; average aid package $7,949

Fashion Institute of Technology
New York NY
(212) 217-3760
U.S. News ranking: Reg. Coll. (N), unranked
Website: www.fitnyc.edu
Admissions email: FITinfo@fitnyc.edu

Public; founded 1944
Freshman admissions: N/A; 2015-2016: 4,753 applied, 1,948 accepted. Neither SAT nor ACT required. ACT 25/75 percentile: N/A. High school rank: N/A
Early decision deadline: N/A, notification date: N/A
Early action deadline: N/A, notification date: N/A
Application deadline (fall): 1/1
Undergraduate student body: 7,409 full time, 1,983 part time; 15% male, 85% female; 0% American Indian, 10% Asian, 9% black, 17% Hispanic, 4% multiracial, 0% Pacific Islander, 47% white, 14% international; 69% from in state; 21% live on campus; 0% of students in fraternities, 0% in sororities
Most popular majors: 25% Fashion Merchandising; 19% Fashion/Apparel Design; 9% International Marketing; 5% Commercial and Advertising Art
Expenses: 2015-2016: $7,200 in state, $20,322 out of state; room/board: $13,291
Financial aid: (212) 217-7439; 52% of undergrads determined to have financial need; average aid package $11,458

Five Towns College
Dix Hills NY
(631) 424-7000
U.S. News ranking: Reg. Coll. (N), second tier
Website: www.ftc.edu
Admissions email: admissions@ftc.edu
For-profit; founded 1972
Freshman admissions: less selective; 2015-2016: 382 applied, 238 accepted. Either SAT or ACT required. SAT 25/75 percentile: 770-980. High school rank: 7% in top tenth, 16% in top quarter, 36% in top half
Early decision deadline: 10/15, notification date: 11/1
Early action deadline: N/A, notification date: N/A
Application deadline (fall): rolling
Undergraduate student body: 611 full time, 43 part time; 68% male, 32% female; 1% American Indian, 4% Asian, 20% black, 15% Hispanic, 4% multiracial, 0% Pacific Islander, 50% white, N/A international; 92% from in state; 23% live on campus; N/A of students in fraternities, N/A in sororities
Most popular majors: 44% Business Administration and Management, General; 19% Music, General; 17% Film/Cinema/Video Studies; 7% Music Teacher Education; 5% Drama and Dramatics/Theatre Arts, General
Expenses: 2016-2017: $19,700; room/board: $12,270
Financial aid: (631) 424-7000; 84% of undergrads determined to have financial need; average aid package $14,821

Fordham University
New York NY
(800) 367-3426
U.S. News ranking: Nat. U., No. 60
Website: www.fordham.edu
Admissions email: enroll@fordham.edu

Private; founded 1841
Affiliation: Roman Catholic
Freshman admissions: more selective; 2015-2016: 42,811 applied, 20,366 accepted. Either SAT or ACT required. SAT 25/75 percentile: 1170-1350. High school rank: 46% in top tenth, 79% in top quarter, 97% in top half
Early decision deadline: 11/1, notification date: 12/20
Early action deadline: 11/1, notification date: 12/20
Application deadline (fall): 1/1
Undergraduate student body: 8,329 full time, 526 part time; 44% male, 56% female; 0% American Indian, 10% Asian, 4% black, 14% Hispanic, 3% multiracial, 0% Pacific Islander, 59% white, 7% international; 45% from in state; 55% live on campus; N/A of students in fraternities, N/A in sororities
Most popular majors: 12% Business Administration and Management, General; 7% Economics, General; 7% Finance, General; 7% Psychology, General
Expenses: 2015-2016: $47,317; room/board: $16,350
Financial aid: (718) 817-3800

Hamilton College
Clinton NY
(800) 843-2655
U.S. News ranking: Nat. Lib. Arts, No. 12
Website: www.hamilton.edu
Admissions email: admission@hamilton.edu
Private; founded 1812
Freshman admissions: most selective; 2015-2016: 5,434 applied, 1,348 accepted. Either SAT or ACT required. SAT 25/75 percentile: 1300-1470. High school rank: 77% in top tenth, 96% in top quarter, 100% in top half
Early decision deadline: 11/15, notification date: 12/15
Early action deadline: N/A, notification date: N/A
Application deadline (fall): 1/1
Undergraduate student body: 1,862 full time, 10 part time; 49% male, 51% female; 0% American Indian, 7% Asian, 5% black, 7% Hispanic, 3% multiracial, 0% Pacific Islander, 63% white, 6% international; 30% from in state; 100% live on campus; 28% of students in fraternities, 21% in sororities
Most popular majors: 11% Economics, General; 8% Mathematics, General; 8% Political Science and Government, General; 6% Psychology, General; 4% International Relations and Affairs
Expenses: 2016-2017: $51,240; room/board: $13,010
Financial aid: (315) 859-4434; 48% of undergrads determined to have financial need; average aid package $45,553

Hartwick College
Oneonta NY
(607) 431-4150
U.S. News ranking: Nat. Lib. Arts, No. 159
Website: www.hartwick.edu
Admissions email: admissions@hartwick.edu
Private; founded 1797
Freshman admissions: selective; 2015-2016: 2,692 applied, 2,174 accepted. Neither SAT nor ACT required. SAT 25/75 percentile: 910-1110. High school rank: 6% in top tenth, 25% in top quarter, 83% in top half
Early decision deadline: 11/15, notification date: 11/25
Early action deadline: N/A, notification date: N/A
Application deadline (fall): rolling
Undergraduate student body: 1,353 full time, 39 part time; 40% male, 60% female; 0% American Indian, 2% Asian, 9% black, 7% Hispanic, 0% multiracial, 0% Pacific Islander, 67% white, 3% international; 75% from in state; 77% live on campus; 5% of students in fraternities, 8% in sororities
Most popular majors: 16% Business Administration, Management and Operations; 14% Registered Nursing, Nursing Administration, Nursing Research and Clinical Nursing; 12% Biology, General; 9% Psychology, General; 7% Sociology
Expenses: 2016-2017: $42,860; room/board: $11,510
Financial aid: (607) 431-4130; 83% of undergrads determined to have financial need; average aid package $33,342

Hilbert College[1]
Hamburg NY
(716) 649-7900
U.S. News ranking: Reg. Coll. (N), unranked
Website: www.hilbert.edu/
Admissions email: admissions@hilbert.edu
Private
Application deadline (fall): N/A
Undergraduate student body: N/A full time, N/A part time
Expenses: 2015-2016: $20,700; room/board: $9,380
Financial aid: (716) 649-7900

Hobart and William Smith Colleges
Geneva NY
(315) 781-3622
U.S. News ranking: Nat. Lib. Arts, No. 65
Website: www.hws.edu
Admissions email: admissions@hws.edu
Private; founded 1822
Freshman admissions: more selective; 2015-2016: 4,488 applied, 2,549 accepted. Neither SAT nor ACT required. SAT 25/75 percentile: 1170-1340. High school rank: 30% in top tenth, 65% in top quarter, 92% in top half
Early decision deadline: 11/15, notification date: 12/15
Early action deadline: N/A, notification date: N/A
Application deadline (fall): 2/1

Undergraduate student body: 2,270 full time, 74 part time; 51% male, 49% female; 0% American Indian, 3% Asian, 5% black, 6% Hispanic, 0% multiracial, 0% Pacific Islander, 72% white, 6% international; 41% from in state; 90% live on campus; 20% of students in fraternities; N/A in sororities
Most popular majors: 12% Economics, General; 7% Biology/Biological Sciences, General; 7% Demography and Population Studies; 6% Psychology, General
Expenses: 2016-2017: $51,523; room/board: $13,050
Financial aid: (315) 781-3315; 64% of undergrads determined to have financial need; average aid package $35,131

Hofstra University
Hempstead NY
(516) 463-6700
U.S. News ranking: Nat. U., No. 133
Website: www.hofstra.edu
Admissions email: admission@hofstra.edu
Private; founded 1935
Freshman admissions: more selective; 2015-2016: 27,991 applied, 17,090 accepted. Neither SAT nor ACT required. SAT 25/75 percentile: 1090-1260. High school rank: 27% in top tenth, 63% in top quarter, 91% in top half
Early decision deadline: N/A, notification date: N/A
Early action deadline: 11/15, notification date: 12/15
Application deadline (fall): rolling
Undergraduate student body: 6,417 full time, 407 part time; 46% male, 54% female; 0% American Indian, 9% Asian, 8% black, 14% Hispanic, 2% multiracial, 1% Pacific Islander, 57% white, 4% international; 64% from in state; 47% live on campus; 8% of students in fraternities, 9% in sororities
Most popular majors: 7% Psychology, General; 6% Accounting; 6% Marketing/Marketing Management, General
Expenses: 2016-2017: $42,160; room/board: $13,800
Financial aid: (516) 463-6680; 66% of undergrads determined to have financial need; average aid package $27,000

Houghton College
Houghton NY
(800) 777-2556
U.S. News ranking: Nat. Lib. Arts, No. 144
Website: www.houghton.edu
Admissions email: admission@houghton.edu
Private; founded 1883
Affiliation: The Wesleyan Church
Freshman admissions: selective; 2015-2016: 737 applied, 696 accepted. Either SAT or ACT required. SAT 25/75 percentile: 990-1250. High school rank: 27% in top tenth, 61% in top quarter, 87% in top half
Early decision deadline: N/A, notification date: N/A
Early action deadline: N/A, notification date: N/A
Application deadline (fall): rolling

Undergraduate student body: 990 full time, 24 part time; 36% male, 64% female; 0% American Indian, 2% Asian, 3% black, 2% Hispanic, 4% multiracial, 0% Pacific Islander, 78% white, 11% international; 68% from in state; 81% live on campus; N/A of students in fraternities, N/A in sororities
Most popular majors: 22% Business, Management, Marketing, and Related Support Services; 18% Education; 12% Biological and Biomedical Sciences; 9% Visual and Performing Arts
Expenses: 2016-2017: $30,336; room/board: $8,754
Financial aid: (585) 567-9328; 81% of undergrads determined to have financial need; average aid package $23,990

Iona College
New Rochelle NY
(914) 633-2502
U.S. News ranking: Reg. U. (N), No. 75
Website: www.iona.edu/info
Admissions email: admissions@iona.edu
Private; founded 1940
Affiliation: Roman Catholic
Freshman admissions: less selective; 2015-2016: 9,587 applied, 8,744 accepted. Either SAT or ACT required. SAT 25/75 percentile: 890-1100. High school rank: 8% in top tenth, 25% in top quarter, 56% in top half
Early decision deadline: N/A, notification date: N/A
Early action deadline: 12/1, notification date: 12/22
Application deadline (fall): 2/15
Undergraduate student body: 2,959 full time, 312 part time; 49% male, 51% female; 0% American Indian, 2% Asian, 8% black, 22% Hispanic, 2% multiracial, 0% Pacific Islander, 58% white, 3% international; 75% from in state; 41% live on campus; 6% of students in fraternities, 12% in sororities
Most popular majors: 36% Business, Management, Marketing, and Related Support Services; 9% Homeland Security, Law Enforcement, Firefighting and Related Protective Services; 8% Psychology; 6% Health Professions and Related Programs
Expenses: 2016-2017: $36,584; room/board: $14,400
Financial aid: (914) 633-2497; 81% of undergrads determined to have financial need; average aid package $24,168

Ithaca College
Ithaca NY
(800) 429-4274
U.S. News ranking: Reg. U. (N), No. 6
Website: www.ithaca.edu
Admissions email: admission@ithaca.edu
Private; founded 1892
Freshman admissions: more selective; 2015-2016: 16,519 applied, 11,072 accepted. Neither SAT nor ACT required. SAT 25/75 percentile: 1100-1270. High school rank: 23% in

top tenth, 63% in top quarter, 91% in top half
Early decision deadline: 11/1, notification date: 12/15
Early action deadline: 12/1, notification date: 2/1
Application deadline (fall): 2/1
Undergraduate student body: 6,206 full time, 117 part time; 42% male, 58% female; 0% American Indian, 4% Asian, 6% black, 8% Hispanic, 3% multiracial, 0% Pacific Islander, 71% white, 2% international; 45% from in state; 69% live on campus; 1% of students in fraternities, 0% in sororities
Most popular majors: 17% Visual and Performing Arts; 16% Health Professions and Related Programs; 12% Business, Management, Marketing, and Related Support Services; 5% Biological and Biomedical Sciences
Expenses: 2016-2017: $41,776; room/board: $14,990
Financial aid: (607) 274-3131; 68% of undergrads determined to have financial need; average aid package $34,400

Jamestown Business College[1]
Jamestown NY
(716) 664-5100
U.S. News ranking: Business, unranked
Website: www.jamestownbusinesscollege.edu/
Admissions email: N/A
For-profit
Application deadline (fall): N/A
Undergraduate student body: N/A full time, N/A part time
Expenses: 2015-2016: $12,300; room/board: N/A
Financial aid: N/A

Juilliard School
New York NY
(212) 799-5000
U.S. News ranking: Arts, unranked
Website: www.juilliard.edu
Admissions email: admissions@juilliard.edu
Private; founded 1905
Freshman admissions: N/A; 2015-2016: 2,551 applied, 164 accepted. Neither SAT nor ACT required. SAT 25/75 percentile: N/A. High school rank: N/A
Early decision deadline: N/A, notification date: N/A
Early action deadline: N/A, notification date: N/A
Application deadline (fall): 12/1
Undergraduate student body: 488 full time, 76 part time; 52% male, 48% female; 0% American Indian, 15% Asian, 4% black, 7% Hispanic, 6% multiracial, 0% Pacific Islander, 39% white, 28% international; 11% from in state; N/A live on campus; N/A of students in fraternities, N/A in sororities
Most popular majors: Information not available
Expenses: 2016-2017: $41,760; room/board: $15,380
Financial aid: (212) 799-5000; 75% of undergrads determined to have financial need; average aid package $32,822

Keuka College
Keuka Park NY
(315) 279-5254
U.S. News ranking: Reg. U. (N), No. 131
Website: www.keuka.edu
Admissions email: admissions@mail.keuka.edu
Private; founded 1890
Affiliation: American Baptist
Freshman admissions: less selective; 2015-2016: 2,290 applied, 1,756 accepted. Neither SAT nor ACT required. ACT 25/75 percentile: N/A. High school rank: N/A
Early decision deadline: N/A, notification date: N/A
Early action deadline: N/A, notification date: N/A
Application deadline (fall): rolling
Undergraduate student body: 1,336 full time, 388 part time; 26% male, 74% female; 1% American Indian, 1% Asian, 9% black, 4% Hispanic, 2% multiracial, 0% Pacific Islander, 74% white, 3% international; N/A from in state; 80% live on campus; N/A of students in fraternities, N/A in sororities
Most popular majors: 34% Health Professions and Related Programs; 22% Public Administration and Social Service Professions; 20% Business, Management, Marketing, and Related Support Services; 8% Homeland Security, Law Enforcement, Firefighting and Related Protective Services; 7% Education
Expenses: 2016-2017: $29,421; room/board: $11,070
Financial aid: (315) 279-5232; 84% of undergrads determined to have financial need; average aid package $20,979

The King's College[1]
New York NY
(212) 659-3610
U.S. News ranking: Nat. Lib. Arts, second tier
Website: www.tkc.edu/
Admissions email: admissions@tkc.edu
Private; founded 1938
Affiliation: Christian nondenominational
Application deadline (fall): rolling
Undergraduate student body: N/A full time, N/A part time
Expenses: 2016-2017: $34,320; room/board: N/A
Financial aid: (212) 659-7200; 73% of undergrads determined to have financial need; average aid package $26,187

Le Moyne College
Syracuse NY
(315) 445-4300
U.S. News ranking: Reg. U. (N), No. 16
Website: www.lemoyne.edu
Admissions email: admission@lemoyne.edu
Private; founded 1946
Affiliation: Roman Catholic (Jesuit)
Freshman admissions: selective; 2015-2016: 6,877 applied, 4,247 accepted. Neither SAT nor ACT required. SAT 25/75 percentile: 980-1170. High school rank: 22% in top tenth,

55% in top quarter, 88% in top half
Early decision deadline: N/A, notification date: N/A
Early action deadline: 11/15, notification date: 12/15
Application deadline (fall): rolling
Undergraduate student body: 2,495 full time, 382 part time; 40% male, 60% female; 0% American Indian, 2% Asian, 5% black, 5% Hispanic, 2% multiracial, 0% Pacific Islander, 80% white, 1% international; 95% from in state; 59% live on campus; 0% of students in fraternities, 0% in sororities
Most popular majors: 16% Biology/Biological Sciences, General; 14% Psychology, General; 8% Registered Nursing/Registered Nurse; 6% Business Administration, Management and Operations, Other
Expenses: 2016-2017: $33,030; room/board: $12,970
Financial aid: (315) 445-4400; 82% of undergrads determined to have financial need; average aid package $25,276

LIM College
New York NY
(800) 677-1323
U.S. News ranking: Business, unranked
Website: www.limcollege.edu/html/home.htm
Admissions email: admissions@limcollege.edu
For-profit; founded 1939
Freshman admissions: N/A; 2015-2016: 1,242 applied, 983 accepted. Either SAT or ACT required. SAT 25/75 percentile: N/A. High school rank: N/A
Early decision deadline: N/A, notification date: N/A
Early action deadline: 11/15, notification date: 12/15
Application deadline (fall): rolling
Undergraduate student body: 1,428 full time, 87 part time; 7% male, 93% female; 1% American Indian, 6% Asian, 15% black, 12% Hispanic, 1% multiracial, 1% Pacific Islander, 55% white, 4% international; 39% from in state; 27% live on campus; 0% of students in fraternities, 0% in sororities
Most popular majors: 59% Fashion Merchandising; 28% Marketing/Marketing Management, General; 8% Business Administration and Management, General; 5% Design and Visual Communications, General; 0% International Business/Trade/Commerce
Expenses: 2015-2016: $24,825; room/board: $19,850
Financial aid: (800) 677-1323

LIU Post
Brookville NY
(516) 299-2900
U.S. News ranking: Reg. U. (N), No. 114
Website: www.liu.edu
Admissions email: post-enroll@liu.edu
Private; founded 1954
Freshman admissions: less selective; 2015-2016: 6,371 applied, 5,134 accepted. Either SAT or ACT required. SAT 25/75

percentile: 910-1110. High school rank: N/A
Early decision deadline: N/A, notification date: N/A
Early action deadline: 12/1, notification date: 12/31
Application deadline (fall): rolling
Undergraduate student body: 3,090 full time, 3,134 part time; 42% male, 58% female; 0% American Indian, 4% Asian, 12% black, 14% Hispanic, 2% multiracial, 0% Pacific Islander, 46% white, 9% international; 92% from in state; 31% live on campus; 5% of students in fraternities, 9% in sororities
Most popular majors: 14% Business Administration and Management, General; 7% Criminal Justice/Law Enforcement Administration; 7% Psychology, General; 5% Clinical Nutrition/Nutritionist; 4% Accounting
Expenses: 2016-2017: $36,256; room/board: $13,426
Financial aid: (516) 299-2338; 75% of undergrads determined to have financial need; average aid package $21,577

Manhattan College
Riverdale NY
(718) 862-7200
U.S. News ranking: Reg. U. (N), No. 15
Website: www.manhattan.edu
Admissions email: admit@manhattan.edu
Private; founded 1853
Affiliation: Roman Catholic
Freshman admissions: selective; 2015-2016: 8,313 applied, 5,557 accepted. SAT required. SAT 25/75 percentile: 990-1190. High school rank: 23% in top tenth, 51% in top quarter, 84% in top half
Early decision deadline: 11/15, notification date: 12/15
Early action deadline: N/A, notification date: N/A
Application deadline (fall): rolling
Undergraduate student body: 3,384 full time, 192 part time; 55% male, 45% female; 0% American Indian, 5% Asian, 4% black, 21% Hispanic, 2% multiracial, 0% Pacific Islander, 57% white, 3% international; 69% from in state; 57% live on campus; 3% of students in fraternities, 5% in sororities
Most popular majors: 31% Engineering; 22% Business, Management, Marketing, and Related Support Services; 11% Education
Expenses: 2016-2017: $40,345; room/board: $15,010
Financial aid: (718) 862-7100; 77% of undergrads determined to have financial need

Manhattan School of Music[1]
New York NY
(212) 749-2802
U.S. News ranking: Arts, unranked
Website: www.msmnyc.edu
Admissions email: admission@msmnyc.edu
Private; founded 1917
Application deadline (fall): rolling
Undergraduate student body: N/A full time, N/A part time

Expenses: 2015-2016: $42,500; room/board: $12,260
Financial aid: (212) 749-2802

Manhattanville College
Purchase NY
(914) 323-5464
U.S. News ranking: Nat. Lib. Arts, second tier
Website: www.mville.edu
Admissions email: admissions@mville.edu
Private; founded 1841
Freshman admissions: selective; 2015-2016: 4,033 applied, 2,989 accepted. Neither SAT nor ACT required. SAT 25/75 percentile: 960-1150. High school rank: 7% in top tenth, 22% in top quarter, 67% in top half
Early decision deadline: N/A, notification date: N/A
Early action deadline: 12/1, notification date: 12/31
Application deadline (fall): rolling
Undergraduate student body: 1,714 full time, 88 part time; 34% male, 66% female; 0% American Indian, 1% Asian, 8% black, 17% Hispanic, 2% multiracial, 0% Pacific Islander, 36% white, 9% international; 64% from in state; 66% live on campus; 0% of students in fraternities, 0% in sororities
Most popular majors: 15% Business Administration and Management, General; 12% Psychology, General; 12% Social Sciences, General; 6% Sociology
Expenses: 2016-2017: $36,920; room/board: $14,520
Financial aid: (914) 323-5357; 68% of undergrads determined to have financial need; average aid package $29,892

Marist College
Poughkeepsie NY
(845) 575-3226
U.S. News ranking: Reg. U. (N), No. 9
Website: www.marist.edu
Admissions email: admissions@marist.edu
Private; founded 1929
Freshman admissions: more selective; 2015-2016: 9,213 applied, 4,142 accepted. Neither SAT nor ACT required. SAT 25/75 percentile: 1050-1250. High school rank: 26% in top tenth, 61% in top quarter, 87% in top half
Early decision deadline: 11/15, notification date: 12/15
Early action deadline: 11/15, notification date: 1/15
Application deadline (fall): 2/1
Undergraduate student body: 4,874 full time, 702 part time; 41% male, 59% female; 0% American Indian, 3% Asian, 4% black, 9% Hispanic, 2% multiracial, 0% Pacific Islander, 78% white, 2% international; 53% from in state; 69% live on campus; 3% of students in fraternities, 3% in sororities
Most popular majors: 26% Business, Management, Marketing, and Related Support Services; 13% Psychology; 8% Visual and Performing Arts; 6% Homeland Security, Law

Enforcement, Firefighting and Related Protective Services
Expenses: 2016-2017: $35,050; room/board: $15,105
Financial aid: (845) 575-3230; 56% of undergrads determined to have financial need; average aid package $19,674

Marymount Manhattan College
New York NY
(212) 517-0430
U.S. News ranking: Nat. Lib. Arts, second tier
Website: www.mmm.edu
Admissions email: admissions@mmm.edu
Private; founded 1936
Freshman admissions: selective; 2015-2016: 4,459 applied, 3,737 accepted. Either SAT or ACT required. SAT 25/75 percentile: 930-1150. High school rank: N/A
Early decision deadline: N/A, notification date: N/A
Early action deadline: N/A, notification date: N/A
Application deadline (fall): rolling
Undergraduate student body: 1,711 full time, 217 part time; 23% male, 77% female; 1% American Indian, 4% Asian, 10% black, 18% Hispanic, 1% multiracial, 0% Pacific Islander, 57% white, 5% international; 41% from in state; 38% live on campus; N/A of students in fraternities, N/A in sororities
Most popular majors: 40% Visual and Performing Arts; 12% Business, Management, Marketing, and Related Support Services; 6% Psychology; 5% Multi/Interdisciplinary Studies
Expenses: 2016-2017: $30,290; room/board: $15,990
Financial aid: (212) 517-0480

Medaille College
Buffalo NY
(716) 880-2200
U.S. News ranking: Reg. U. (N), second tier
Website: www.medaille.edu
Admissions email: admissionsug@medaille.edu
Private; founded 1937
Freshman admissions: less selective; 2015-2016: 1,320 applied, 381 accepted. Either SAT or ACT required. ACT 25/75 percentile: N/A. High school rank: N/A
Early decision deadline: N/A, notification date: N/A
Early action deadline: N/A, notification date: N/A
Application deadline (fall): rolling
Undergraduate student body: 1,442 full time, 79 part time; 32% male, 68% female; 1% American Indian, 2% Asian, 24% black, 7% Hispanic, 3% multiracial, 0% Pacific Islander, 55% white, 0% international
Most popular majors: Information not available
Expenses: 2015-2016: $26,252; room/board: $12,460
Financial aid: (716) 880-2256

Mercy College
Dobbs Ferry NY
(877) 637-2946
U.S. News ranking: Reg. U. (N), unranked
Website: www.mercy.edu
Admissions email: admissions@mercy.edu
Private; founded 1950
Freshman admissions: N/A; 2015-2016: 5,573 applied, 3,661 accepted. Neither SAT nor ACT required. ACT 25/75 percentile: N/A. High school rank: N/A
Early decision deadline: N/A, notification date: N/A
Early action deadline: 12/1, notification date: 1/2
Application deadline (fall): rolling
Undergraduate student body: 5,392 full time, 2,624 part time; 31% male, 69% female; 0% American Indian, 4% Asian, 23% black, 35% Hispanic, 1% multiracial, 0% Pacific Islander, 27% white, 1% international; 93% from in state; 13% live on campus; N/A of students in fraternities, N/A in sororities
Most popular majors: 22% Social Sciences; 14% Psychology; 13% Health Professions and Related Programs; 9% Business, Management, Marketing, and Related Support Services; 7% Homeland Security, Law Enforcement, Firefighting and Related Protective Services
Expenses: 2016-2017: $18,392; room/board: $13,700
Financial aid: (914) 378-3421; 87% of undergrads determined to have financial need; average aid package $13,100

Metropolitan College of New York
New York NY
(800) 338-4465
U.S. News ranking: Reg. U. (N), second tier
Website: www.metropolitan.edu/
Admissions email: N/A
Private; founded 1964
Freshman admissions: less selective; 2015-2016: 333 applied, 176 accepted. Neither SAT nor ACT required. ACT 25/75 percentile: N/A. High school rank: N/A
Early decision deadline: N/A, notification date: N/A
Early action deadline: N/A, notification date: N/A
Application deadline (fall): rolling
Undergraduate student body: 685 full time, 94 part time; 26% male, 74% female; 1% American Indian, 2% Asian, 57% black, 22% Hispanic, 1% multiracial, N/A Pacific Islander, 3% white, 3% international; 96% from in state; N/A live on campus; N/A of students in fraternities, N/A in sororities
Most popular majors: 47% Public Administration and Social Service Professions; 28% Business, Management, Marketing, and Related Support Services; 21% Health Professions and Related Programs; 5% Social Sciences
Expenses: 2016-2017: $18,730; room/board: N/A
Financial aid: (212) 343-1234; 95% of undergrads determined to have financial need; average aid package $16,524

Molloy College
Rockville Centre NY
(516) 323-4000
U.S. News ranking: Reg. U. (N), No. 44
Website: www.molloy.edu
Admissions email: admissions@molloy.edu
Private; founded 1955
Affiliation: Roman Catholic
Freshman admissions: selective; 2015-2016: 3,550 applied, 2,681 accepted. Either SAT or ACT required. SAT 25/75 percentile: 970-1150. High school rank: 17% in top tenth, 56% in top quarter, 83% in top half
Early decision deadline: N/A, notification date: N/A
Early action deadline: 12/1, notification date: 12/15
Application deadline (fall): rolling
Undergraduate student body: 2,753 full time, 672 part time; 25% male, 75% female; 0% American Indian, 7% Asian, 12% black, 15% Hispanic, 1% multiracial, 0% Pacific Islander, 60% white, 0% international; 97% from in state; 8% live on campus; N/A of students in fraternities, N/A in sororities
Most popular majors: 54% Health Professions and Related Programs; 11% Education; 10% Business, Management, Marketing, and Related Support Services; 5% Homeland Security, Law Enforcement, Firefighting and Related Protective Services; 5% Psychology
Expenses: 2016-2017: $29,100; room/board: $14,250
Financial aid: (516) 256-2217; 83% of undergrads determined to have financial need; average aid package $15,825

Monroe College
Bronx NY
(800) 556-6676
U.S. News ranking: Reg. Coll. (N), No. 26
Website: www.monroecollege.edu
Admissions email: N/A
For-profit; founded 1933
Freshman admissions: least selective; 2015-2016: 4,146 applied, 1,878 accepted. Neither SAT nor ACT required. SAT 25/75 percentile: 715-870. High school rank: N/A
Early decision deadline: N/A, notification date: N/A
Early action deadline: 12/15, notification date: 1/31
Application deadline (fall): rolling
Undergraduate student body: 4,524 full time, 1,613 part time; 37% male, 63% female; 0% American Indian, 1% Asian, 44% black, 40% Hispanic, 0% multiracial, 0% Pacific Islander, 2% white, 10% international; 92% from in state; 14% live on campus; 0% of students in fraternities, 0% in sororities
Most popular majors: 24% Criminal Justice/Law Enforcement Administration; 18% Business Administration and Management, General; 15% Health Services Administration; 13% Hospitality Administration/Management, General; 10% Accounting

Morrisville State College
Morrisville NY
(315) 684-6046
U.S. News ranking: Reg. Coll. (N), No. 21
Website: www.morrisville.edu
Admissions email: admissions@morrisville.edu
Public; founded 1908
Freshman admissions: less selective; 2015-2016: 3,935 applied, 2,293 accepted. Neither SAT nor ACT required. SAT 25/75 percentile: 830-1010. High school rank: 7% in top tenth, 19% in top quarter, 54% in top half
Early decision deadline: N/A, notification date: N/A
Early action deadline: N/A, notification date: N/A
Application deadline (fall): rolling
Undergraduate student body: 2,531 full time, 409 part time; 52% male, 48% female; 1% American Indian, 1% Asian, 18% black, 8% Hispanic, 2% multiracial, 0% Pacific Islander, 68% white, 1% international; 96% from in state; 42% live on campus; N/A of students in fraternities, N/A in sororities
Most popular majors: 21% Business, Management, Marketing, and Related Support Services; 17% Homeland Security, Law Enforcement, Firefighting and Related Protective Services; 12% Computer and Information Sciences and Support Services; 10% Mechanic and Repair Technologies/Technicians
Expenses: 2016-2017: $8,270 in state, $13,340 out of state; room/board: $14,000
Financial aid: (315) 684-6289; 85% of undergrads determined to have financial need; average aid package $9,880

Mount St. Mary College
Newburgh NY
(845) 569-3488
U.S. News ranking: Reg. U. (N), No. 110
Website: www.msmc.edu
Admissions email: admissions@msmc.edu
Private; founded 1959
Affiliation: Roman Catholic
Freshman admissions: less selective; 2015-2016: 3,625 applied, 3,247 accepted. Either SAT or ACT required. SAT 25/75 percentile: 880-1055. High school rank: 7% in top tenth, 32% in top quarter, 73% in top half
Early decision deadline: N/A, notification date: N/A
Early action deadline: N/A, notification date: N/A
Application deadline (fall): 8/15
Undergraduate student body: 1,780 full time, 377 part time; 29% male, 71% female; 1% American Indian, 2% Asian, 7% black, 15% Hispanic, 1% multiracial, 0% Pacific Islander, 61% white, 0% international; 89% from in state; 48% live on campus; N/A of students in fraternities, N/A in sororities
Most popular majors: 25% Health Professions and Related Programs; 18% Business, Management, Marketing, and Related Support Services; 9% Psychology; 8% History; 7% English Language and Literature/Letters
Expenses: 2016-2017: $29,048; room/board: $14,104
Financial aid: (845) 569-3298; 80% of undergrads determined to have financial need; average aid package $18,243

Nazareth College
Rochester NY
(585) 389-2860
U.S. News ranking: Reg. U. (N), No. 38
Website: www.naz.edu
Admissions email: admissions@naz.edu
Private; founded 1924
Freshman admissions: selective; 2015-2016: 3,677 applied, 2,778 accepted. Neither SAT nor ACT required. SAT 25/75 percentile: 970-1170. High school rank: 27% in top tenth, 58% in top quarter, 86% in top half
Early decision deadline: 11/15, notification date: 12/15
Early action deadline: N/A, notification date: N/A
Application deadline (fall): 2/1
Undergraduate student body: 1,974 full time, 134 part time; 29% male, 71% female; 0% American Indian, 3% Asian, 7% black, 5% Hispanic, 2% multiracial, 0% Pacific Islander, 76% white, 2% international; 92% from in state; 56% live on campus; 0% of students in fraternities, 0% in sororities
Most popular majors: 24% Health Professions and Related Programs; 12% Education; 11% Visual and Performing Arts; 10% Business, Management, Marketing, and Related Support Services; 7% Public Administration and Social Service Professions
Expenses: 2016-2017: $32,424; room/board: $13,150
Financial aid: (585) 389-2310; 82% of undergrads determined to have financial need; average aid package $26,453

New School
New York NY
(800) 292-3040
U.S. News ranking: Nat. U., No. 129
Website: www.newschool.edu
Admissions email: admission@newschool.edu
Private; founded 1919
Freshman admissions: selective; 2015-2016: 7,339 applied, 4,889 accepted. Neither SAT nor ACT required. SAT 25/75 percentile: 1000-1250. High school rank: 15% in top tenth, 41% in top quarter, 75% in top half

Early decision deadline: 11/1, notification date: 12/20
Early action deadline: N/A, notification date: N/A
Application deadline (fall): 1/15
Undergraduate student body: 5,971 full time, 821 part time; 27% male, 73% female; 0% American Indian, 9% Asian, 6% black, 12% Hispanic, 4% multiracial, 0% Pacific Islander, 33% white, 32% international; 19% from in state; 24% live on campus; N/A of students in fraternities, N/A in sororities
Most popular majors: 68% Visual and Performing Arts; 12% Liberal Arts and Sciences, General Studies and Humanities; 5% English Language and Literature/Letters
Expenses: 2016-2017: $45,535; room/board: $18,420
Financial aid: (212) 229-8930; 46% of undergrads determined to have financial need; average aid package $25,189

New York Institute of Technology
Old Westbury NY
(516) 686-7520
U.S. News ranking: Reg. U. (N), No. 32
Website: www.nyit.edu
Admissions email: admissions@nyit.edu
Private; founded 1955
Freshman admissions: selective; 2015-2016: 8,566 applied, 5,805 accepted. Either SAT or ACT required. SAT 25/75 percentile: 1060-1248. High school rank: 22% in top tenth, 52% in top quarter, 88% in top half
Early decision deadline: N/A, notification date: N/A
Early action deadline: N/A, notification date: N/A
Application deadline (fall): rolling
Undergraduate student body: 3,553 full time, 496 part time; 64% male, 36% female; 0% American Indian, 15% Asian, 8% black, 13% Hispanic, 1% multiracial, 0% Pacific Islander, 20% white, 18% international; 90% from in state; 19% live on campus; 3% of students in fraternities, 4% in sororities
Most popular majors: 17% Engineering; 12% Business, Management, Marketing, and Related Support Services; 11% Biological and Biomedical Sciences
Expenses: 2016-2017: $35,160; room/board: $13,570
Financial aid: (516) 686-7680; 69% of undergrads determined to have financial need; average aid package $21,382

New York University
New York NY
(212) 998-4500
U.S. News ranking: Nat. U., No. 36
Website: www.nyu.edu
Admissions email: admissions@nyu.edu
Private; founded 1831
Freshman admissions: more selective; 2015-2016: 56,092 applied, 18,738 accepted. Either SAT or ACT required. SAT

25/75 percentile: 1250-1470. High school rank: 56% in top tenth, 88% in top quarter, 98% in top half
Early decision deadline: 11/1, notification date: 12/15
Early action deadline: N/A, notification date: N/A
Application deadline (fall): 1/1
Undergraduate student body: 24,480 full time, 1,242 part time; 43% male, 57% female; 0% American Indian, 20% Asian, 5% black, 12% Hispanic, 4% multiracial, 0% Pacific Islander, 34% white, 17% international; 36% from in state; 44% live on campus; 7% of students in fraternities, 6% in sororities
Most popular majors: 20% Visual and Performing Arts; 16% Social Sciences; 14% Business, Management, Marketing, and Related Support Services; 9% Liberal Arts and Sciences, General Studies and Humanities; 8% Health Professions and Related Programs
Expenses: 2016-2017: $49,062; room/board: $17,578
Financial aid: (212) 998-4444; 53% of undergrads determined to have financial need; average aid package $36,042

Niagara University
Niagara University NY
(716) 286-8700
U.S. News ranking: Reg. U. (N), No. 44
Website: www.niagara.edu
Admissions email: admissions@niagara.edu
Private; founded 1856
Affiliation: Roman Catholic (Vincentian)
Freshman admissions: selective; 2015-2016: 3,987 applied, 1,910 accepted. Either SAT or ACT required. SAT 25/75 percentile: 930-1133. High school rank: 14% in top tenth, 44% in top quarter, 78% in top half
Early decision deadline: N/A, notification date: N/A
Early action deadline: 12/10, notification date: 1/7
Application deadline (fall): 8/30
Undergraduate student body: 2,862 full time, 352 part time; 38% male, 62% female; 1% American Indian, 1% Asian, 5% black, 4% Hispanic, 2% multiracial, N/A Pacific Islander, 68% white, 13% international; 92% from in state; 43% live on campus; N/A of students in fraternities, N/A in sororities
Most popular majors: 30% Business, Management, Marketing, and Related Support Services; 27% Education; 8% Homeland Security, Law Enforcement, Firefighting and Related Protective Services; 5% Biological and Biomedical Sciences; 5% Health Professions and Related Programs
Expenses: 2016-2017: $30,950; room/board: $12,700
Financial aid: (716) 286-8686; 77% of undergrads determined to have financial need; average aid package $24,532

Nyack College
Nyack NY
(800) 336-9225
U.S. News ranking: Reg. U. (N), second tier
Website: www.nyack.edu
Admissions email: admissions@nyack.edu
Private; founded 1882
Affiliation: Christian & Missionary Alliance
Freshman admissions: least selective; 2015-2016: 489 applied, 482 accepted. Neither SAT nor ACT required. SAT 25/75 percentile: 770-1030. High school rank: 6% in top tenth, 20% in top quarter, 57% in top half
Early decision deadline: N/A, notification date: N/A
Early action deadline: N/A, notification date: N/A
Application deadline (fall): rolling
Undergraduate student body: 1,300 full time, 245 part time; 39% male, 61% female; 1% American Indian, 8% Asian, 30% black, 31% Hispanic, 2% multiracial, 0% Pacific Islander, 20% white, 6% international; 70% from in state; 72% live on campus; N/A of students in fraternities, N/A in sororities
Most popular majors: 31% Organizational Behavior Studies; 8% Business Administration and Management, General; 8% Multi/Interdisciplinary Studies; 7% Psychology, General; 6% Registered Nursing/Registered Nurse
Expenses: 2016-2017: $24,850; room/board: $9,200
Financial aid: (845) 358-1710; 83% of undergrads determined to have financial need; average aid package $20,421

Pace University
New York NY
(212) 346-1323
U.S. News ranking: Nat. U., No. 188
Website: www.pace.edu
Admissions email: infoctr@pace.edu
Private; founded 1906
Freshman admissions: selective; 2015-2016: 17,038 applied, 14,283 accepted. Neither SAT nor ACT required. SAT 25/75 percentile: 940-1160. High school rank: 17% in top tenth, 43% in top quarter, 75% in top half
Early decision deadline: N/A, notification date: N/A
Early action deadline: 12/1, notification date: 1/1
Application deadline (fall): 2/15
Undergraduate student body: 7,579 full time, 1,168 part time; 41% male, 59% female; 0% American Indian, 8% Asian, 11% black, 14% Hispanic, 4% multiracial, 0% Pacific Islander, 50% white, 9% international; 58% from in state; 42% live on campus; 4% of students in fraternities, 5% in sororities
Most popular majors: 34% Business, Management, Marketing, and Related Support Services; 11% Health Professions and Related Programs; 9% Psychology; 7% Visual and Performing Arts

Expenses: 2016-2017: $42,772; room/board: $18,280
Financial aid: (212) 346-1300; 71% of undergrads determined to have financial need; average aid package $30,427

Paul Smith's College[1]
Paul Smiths NY
(800) 421-2605
U.S. News ranking: Reg. Coll. (N), No. 31
Website: www.paulsmiths.edu
Admissions email: admiss@paulsmiths.edu
Private
Application deadline (fall): N/A
Undergraduate student body: N/A full time, N/A part time
Expenses: 2016-2017: $25,723; room/board: $11,290
Financial aid: (518) 327-6220; 90% of undergrads determined to have financial need; average aid package $21,950

Plaza College[1]
Forest Hills NY
(718) 779-1430
U.S. News ranking: Reg. Coll. (N), unranked
Website: www.plazacollege.edu
Admissions email: N/A
For-profit; founded 1916
Application deadline (fall): rolling
Undergraduate student body: N/A full time, N/A part time
Expenses: 2015-2016: $11,350; room/board: N/A
Financial aid: (718) 779-1430

Pratt Institute
Brooklyn NY
(718) 636-3514
U.S. News ranking: Arts, unranked
Website: www.pratt.edu
Admissions email: admissions@pratt.edu
Private; founded 1887
Freshman admissions: N/A; 2015-2016: 4,819 applied, 3,186 accepted. Either SAT or ACT required. SAT 25/75 percentile: N/A. High school rank: N/A
Early decision deadline: N/A, notification date: N/A
Early action deadline: 11/1, notification date: 12/15
Application deadline (fall): 1/5
Undergraduate student body: 3,103 full time, 123 part time; 31% male, 69% female; 0% American Indian, 15% Asian, 4% black, 10% Hispanic, 2% multiracial, 0% Pacific Islander, 40% white, 27% international; 42% from in state; 54% live on campus; 5% of students in fraternities, 4% in sororities
Most popular majors: 12% Graphic Design; 9% Industrial and Product Design; 8% Interior Design
Expenses: 2016-2017: $48,154; room/board: $12,026
Financial aid: (718) 636-3599; 80% of undergrads determined to have financial need; average aid package $22,733

Purchase College–SUNY
Purchase NY
(914) 251-6300
U.S. News ranking: Nat. Lib. Arts, second tier
Website: www.purchase.edu
Admissions email: admissions@purchase.edu
Public; founded 1967
Freshman admissions: selective; 2015-2016: 7,928 applied, 3,235 accepted. Either SAT or ACT required. SAT 25/75 percentile: 960-1180. High school rank: N/A
Early decision deadline: N/A, notification date: N/A
Early action deadline: 11/15, notification date: 12/15
Application deadline (fall): 7/15
Undergraduate student body: 3,747 full time, 368 part time; 44% male, 56% female; 0% American Indian, 4% Asian, 10% black, 18% Hispanic, 5% multiracial, 0% Pacific Islander, 55% white, 2% international; 85% from in state; 67% live on campus; 0% of students in fraternities, 0% in sororities
Most popular majors: 45% Visual and Performing Arts; 15% Liberal Arts and Sciences, General Studies and Humanities; 11% Social Sciences; 5% Psychology
Expenses: 2016-2017: $8,267 in state, $18,117 out of state; room/board: $12,576
Financial aid: (914) 251-6350; 62% of undergrads determined to have financial need; average aid package $9,669

Rensselaer Polytechnic Institute
Troy NY
(518) 276-6216
U.S. News ranking: Nat. U., No. 39
Website: www.rpi.edu
Admissions email: admissions@rpi.edu
Private; founded 1824
Freshman admissions: most selective; 2015-2016: 17,752 applied, 7,432 accepted. Either SAT or ACT required. SAT 25/75 percentile: 1280-1490. High school rank: 72% in top tenth, 94% in top quarter, 99% in top half
Early decision deadline: 11/1, notification date: 12/12
Early action deadline: N/A, notification date: N/A
Application deadline (fall): 2/1
Undergraduate student body: 5,845 full time, 19 part time; 69% male, 31% female; 0% American Indian, 10% Asian, 3% black, 8% Hispanic, 7% multiracial, 0% Pacific Islander, 59% white, 11% international; 33% from in state; 57% live on campus; 30% of students in fraternities, 16% in sororities
Most popular majors: 56% Engineering; 10% Computer and Information Sciences and Support Services; 7% Business, Management, Marketing, and Related Support Services; 6% Biological and Biomedical Sciences; 5% Physical Sciences
Expenses: 2016-2017: $50,797; room/board: $14,630

Financial aid: (518) 276-6813; 61% of undergrads determined to have financial need; average aid package $36,894

Roberts Wesleyan College
Rochester NY
(585) 594-6400
U.S. News ranking: Reg. U. (N), No. 101
Website: www.roberts.edu
Admissions email: admissions@roberts.edu
Private; founded 1866
Affiliation: Free Methodist
Freshman admissions: selective; 2015-2016: 1,330 applied, 882 accepted. Either SAT or ACT required. SAT 25/75 percentile: 950-1180. High school rank: 24% in top tenth, 47% in top quarter, 84% in top half
Early decision deadline: N/A, notification date: N/A
Early action deadline: N/A, notification date: N/A
Application deadline (fall): 8/20
Undergraduate student body: 1,215 full time, 109 part time; 31% male, 69% female; 0% American Indian, 2% Asian, 11% black, 5% Hispanic, 3% multiracial, 0% Pacific Islander, 74% white, 3% international; 92% from in state; 66% live on campus; 0% of students in fraternities, 0% in sororities
Most popular majors: 35% Health Professions and Related Programs; 27% Business, Management, Marketing, and Related Support Services; 9% Education; 5% Liberal Arts and Sciences, General Studies and Humanities; 4% Psychology
Expenses: 2016-2017: $29,540; room/board: $10,212
Financial aid: (585) 594-6150; 85% of undergrads determined to have financial need; average aid package $21,951

Rochester Institute of Technology
Rochester NY
(585) 475-6631
U.S. News ranking: Nat. U., No. 107
Website: www.rit.edu
Admissions email: admissions@rit.edu
Private; founded 1829
Freshman admissions: more selective; 2015-2016: 18,598 applied, 10,652 accepted. Either SAT or ACT required. SAT 25/75 percentile: 1130-1350. High school rank: 36% in top tenth, 70% in top quarter, 96% in top half
Early decision deadline: 11/15, notification date: 12/15
Early action deadline: N/A, notification date: N/A
Application deadline (fall): 1/15
Undergraduate student body: 11,536 full time, 1,071 part time; 67% male, 33% female; 0% American Indian, 8% Asian, 5% black, 7% Hispanic, 3% multiracial, 0% Pacific Islander, 66% white, 6% international; 54% from in state; 55% live on campus; 5% of students in fraternities, 6% in sororities

Most popular majors: 19% Engineering; 15% Computer and Information Sciences and Support Services; 15% Visual and Performing Arts; 13% Engineering Technologies and Engineering-Related Fields; 9% Business, Management, Marketing, and Related Support Services
Expenses: 2016-2017: $38,568; room/board: $12,500
Financial aid: (585) 475-2186; 74% of undergrads determined to have financial need; average aid package $25,500

The Sage Colleges
Troy NY
(888) 837-9724
U.S. News ranking: Reg. U. (N), No. 85
Website: www.sage.edu
Admissions email: tscadm@sage.edu
Private; founded 1916
Freshman admissions: selective; 2015-2016: 2,487 applied, 1,345 accepted. Neither SAT nor ACT required. SAT 25/75 percentile: 850-1070. High school rank: 18% in top tenth, 48% in top quarter, 84% in top half
Early decision deadline: N/A, notification date: N/A
Early action deadline: N/A, notification date: N/A
Application deadline (fall): rolling
Undergraduate student body: 1,419 full time, 228 part time; 20% male, 80% female; 0% American Indian, 3% Asian, 13% black, 9% Hispanic, 3% multiracial, 0% Pacific Islander, 63% white, 0% international; 92% from in state; 56% live on campus; N/A of students in fraternities, N/A in sororities
Most popular majors: 27% Health Professions and Related Programs; 13% Social Sciences; 11% Business, Management, Marketing, and Related Support Services; 10% Biological and Biomedical Sciences; 9% Visual and Performing Arts
Expenses: 2016-2017: $28,805; room/board: $12,420
Financial aid: (518) 244-2215; 92% of undergrads determined to have financial need

Sarah Lawrence College
Bronxville NY
(914) 395-2510
U.S. News ranking: Nat. Lib. Arts, No. 59
Website: www.slc.edu
Admissions email: slcadmit@sarahlawrence.edu
Private; founded 1926
Freshman admissions: more selective; 2015-2016: 2,814 applied, 1,502 accepted. Neither SAT nor ACT required. SAT 25/75 percentile: 1170-1390. High school rank: 37% in top tenth, 71% in top quarter, 90% in top half
Early decision deadline: 11/1, notification date: 12/15
Early action deadline: N/A, notification date: N/A
Application deadline (fall): 1/15

Undergraduate student body: 1,327 full time, 21 part time; 28% male, 72% female; 0% American Indian, 5% Asian, 4% black, 10% Hispanic, 7% multiracial, 0% Pacific Islander, 53% white, 13% international; 21% from in state; 83% live on campus; 0% of students in fraternities, 0% in sororities
Most popular majors: 100% Liberal Arts and Sciences, General Studies and Humanities
Expenses: 2016-2017: $52,550; room/board: $14,440
Financial aid: (914) 395-2570; 59% of undergrads determined to have financial need; average aid package $37,481

School of Visual Arts
New York NY
(212) 592-2100
U.S. News ranking: Arts, unranked
Website: www.schoolofvisualarts.edu/
Admissions email: admissions@sva.edu
For-profit; founded 1947
Freshman admissions: N/A; 2015-2016: 3,648 applied, 2,697 accepted. Either SAT or ACT required. SAT 25/75 percentile: N/A. High school rank: N/A
Early decision deadline: N/A, notification date: N/A
Early action deadline: N/A, notification date: N/A
Application deadline (fall): N/A
Undergraduate student body: 3,466 full time, 241 part time; 35% male, 65% female; 0% American Indian, 14% Asian, 6% black, 5% Hispanic, 0% multiracial, 0% Pacific Islander, 34% white, 37% international
Most popular majors: Information not available
Expenses: 2016-2017: $36,500; room/board: $18,300
Financial aid: (212) 592-2030; 45% of undergrads determined to have financial need; average aid package $16,736

Siena College
Loudonville NY
(888) 287-4362
U.S. News ranking: Nat. Lib. Arts, No. 122
Website: www.siena.edu
Admissions email: admissions@siena.edu
Private; founded 1937
Affiliation: Roman Catholic
Freshman admissions: selective; 2015-2016: 8,919 applied, 4,978 accepted. Neither SAT nor ACT required. SAT 25/75 percentile: 980-1200. High school rank: 21% in top tenth, 50% in top quarter, 84% in top half
Early decision deadline: 12/1, notification date: 1/1
Early action deadline: 12/1, notification date: 1/7
Application deadline (fall): 2/15
Undergraduate student body: 3,007 full time, 115 part time; 49% male, 51% female; 0% American Indian, 4% Asian, 4% black, 7% Hispanic, 2% multiracial, 0% Pacific Islander, 80% white, 1% international; 81% from in state; 80% live on campus; N/A of students in fraternities, N/A in sororities

Most popular majors: 13% Accounting; 13% Psychology, General; 11% Marketing/Marketing Management, General; 9% Biology/Biological Sciences, General; 7% Management Science
Expenses: 2016-2017: $34,611; room/board: $14,105
Financial aid: (518) 783-2427; 77% of undergrads determined to have financial need; average aid package $28,100

Skidmore College
Saratoga Springs NY
(518) 580-5570
U.S. News ranking: Nat. Lib. Arts, No. 38
Website: www.skidmore.edu
Admissions email: admissions@skidmore.edu
Private; founded 1903
Freshman admissions: more selective; 2015-2016: 8,508 applied, 3,105 accepted. Neither SAT nor ACT required. SAT 25/75 percentile: 1110-1343. High school rank: 41% in top tenth, 72% in top quarter, 96% in top half
Early decision deadline: 11/15, notification date: 12/15
Early action deadline: N/A, notification date: N/A
Application deadline (fall): 1/15
Undergraduate student body: 2,603 full time, 31 part time; 39% male, 61% female; 0% American Indian, 6% Asian, 4% black, 8% Hispanic, 4% multiracial, 0% Pacific Islander, 64% white, 10% international; 32% from in state; 92% live on campus; 0% of students in fraternities, 0% in sororities
Most popular majors: 20% Social Sciences; 14% Visual and Performing Arts; 13% Business, Management, Marketing, and Related Support Services; 9% Psychology; 8% English Language and Literature/Letters
Expenses: 2015-2016: $48,970; room/board: $13,072
Financial aid: (518) 580-5750; 42% of undergrads determined to have financial need; average aid package $43,500

St. Bonaventure University
St. Bonaventure NY
(800) 462-5050
U.S. News ranking: Reg. U. (N), No. 27
Website: www.sbu.edu
Admissions email: admissions@sbu.edu
Private; founded 1858
Affiliation: Roman Catholic
Freshman admissions: selective; 2015-2016: 2,985 applied, 1,969 accepted. Either SAT or ACT required. SAT 25/75 percentile: 930-1170. High school rank: 19% in top tenth, 47% in top quarter, 74% in top half
Early decision deadline: N/A, notification date: N/A
Early action deadline: N/A, notification date: N/A
Application deadline (fall): 7/1
Undergraduate student body: 1,633 full time, 54 part time; 51% male, 49% female; 0% American

Indian, 4% Asian, 6% black, 7% Hispanic, 3% multiracial, 0% Pacific Islander, 69% white, 2% international; 73% from in state; 75% live on campus; 0% of students in fraternities, 0% in sororities
Most popular majors: 13% Special Education and Teaching, General; 11% Accounting; 8% Biology/Biological Sciences, General; 7% Marketing/Marketing Management, General
Expenses: 2016-2017: $32,331; room/board: $11,456
Financial aid: (716) 375-2528; 72% of undergrads determined to have financial need; average aid package $24,764

St. Francis College
Brooklyn Heights NY
(718) 489-5200
U.S. News ranking: Reg. Coll. (N), No. 9
Website: www.sfc.edu
Admissions email: admissions@stfranciscollege.edu
Private; founded 1884
Freshman admissions: less selective; 2015-2016: 2,747 applied, 2,164 accepted. Either SAT or ACT required. SAT 25/75 percentile: 810-1000. High school rank: N/A
Early decision deadline: N/A, notification date: N/A
Early action deadline: N/A, notification date: N/A
Application deadline (fall): rolling
Undergraduate student body: 2,393 full time, 205 part time; 42% male, 58% female; 1% American Indian, 4% Asian, 19% black, 20% Hispanic, 2% multiracial, 1% Pacific Islander, 40% white, 4% international; 96% from in state; 6% live on campus; 7% of students in fraternities, 3% in sororities
Most popular majors: 13% Business Administration, Management and Operations; 10% Psychology, General; 8% Biology, General; 6% Teacher Education and Professional Development, Specific Levels and Methods
Expenses: 2016-2017: $25,300; room/board: $14,250
Financial aid: (718) 489-5255; 72% of undergrads determined to have financial need; average aid package $15,460

St. John Fisher College
Rochester NY
(585) 385-8064
U.S. News ranking: Nat. U., No. 146
Website: www.sjfc.edu
Admissions email: admissions@sjfc.edu
Private; founded 1948
Affiliation: Roman Catholic
Freshman admissions: selective; 2015-2016: 4,586 applied, 2,860 accepted. Either SAT or ACT required. SAT 25/75 percentile: 1000-1170. High school rank: 22% in top tenth, 57% in top quarter, 91% in top half
Early decision deadline: 12/1, notification date: 1/16

Early action deadline: N/A, notification date: N/A
Application deadline (fall): rolling
Undergraduate student body: 2,619 full time, 186 part time; 40% male, 60% female; 0% American Indian, 4% Asian, 4% black, 4% Hispanic, 2% multiracial, 0% Pacific Islander, 84% white, 0% international; 97% from in state; 50% live on campus; 0% of students in fraternities, 0% in sororities
Most popular majors: 24% Business, Management, Marketing, and Related Support Services; 22% Health Professions and Related Programs; 10% Education; 10% Social Sciences; 8% Biological and Biomedical Sciences
Expenses: 2016-2017: $31,880; room/board: $11,740
Financial aid: (585) 385-8042; 81% of undergrads determined to have financial need; average aid package $21,604

St. John's University
Queens NY
(718) 990-2000
U.S. News ranking: Nat. U., No. 164
Website: www.stjohns.edu/
Admissions email: admission@stjohns.edu
Private; founded 1870
Affiliation: Roman Catholic
Freshman admissions: selective; 2015-2016: 36,105 applied, 23,428 accepted. Either SAT or ACT required. SAT 25/75 percentile: 960-1180. High school rank: 21% in top tenth, 48% in top quarter, 81% in top half
Early decision deadline: N/A, notification date: N/A
Early action deadline: N/A, notification date: N/A
Application deadline (fall): rolling
Undergraduate student body: 11,051 full time, 5,159 part time; 43% male, 57% female; 0% American Indian, 17% Asian, 19% black, 12% Hispanic, 5% multiracial, 0% Pacific Islander, 34% white, 5% international; 71% from in state; 29% live on campus; 8% of students in fraternities, 5% in sororities
Most popular majors: 19% Business, Management, Marketing, and Related Support Services; 10% Health Professions and Related Programs; 9% Homeland Security, Law Enforcement, Firefighting and Related Protective Services; 8% Biological and Biomedical Sciences
Expenses: 2016-2017: $39,460; room/board: $16,600
Financial aid: (718) 990-2000; 81% of undergrads determined to have financial need; average aid package $27,611

St. Joseph's College New York
Brooklyn NY
(718) 940-5800
U.S. News ranking: Reg. U. (N), No. 80
Website: www.sjcny.edu
Admissions email: longislandas@sjcny.edu

Private; founded 1916
Freshman admissions: selective; 2015-2016: 3,220 applied, 2,187 accepted. Either SAT or ACT required. SAT 25/75 percentile: 910-1110. High school rank: N/A
Early decision deadline: N/A, notification date: N/A
Early action deadline: N/A, notification date: N/A
Application deadline (fall): 8/31
Undergraduate student body: 3,157 full time, 721 part time; 34% male, 66% female; 1% American Indian, 3% Asian, 10% black, 13% Hispanic, 1% multiracial, 0% Pacific Islander, 61% white, N/A international; 98% from in state; N/A live on campus; N/A of students in fraternities, N/A in sororities
Most popular majors: 19% Special Education and Teaching, General; 11% Business Administration and Management, General; 8% Psychology, General; 7% Criminal Justice/Law Enforcement Administration; 7% Rhetoric and Composition
Expenses: 2016-2017: $25,130; room/board: N/A
Financial aid: (718) 636-6808; 77% of undergrads determined to have financial need; average aid package $12,371

St. Lawrence University
Canton NY
(315) 229-5261
U.S. News ranking: Nat. Lib. Arts, No. 53
Website: www.stlawu.edu
Admissions email: admissions@stlawu.edu
Private; founded 1856
Freshman admissions: more selective; 2015-2016: 5,876 applied, 2,713 accepted. Neither SAT nor ACT required. SAT 25/75 percentile: 1100-1310. High school rank: 45% in top tenth, 77% in top quarter, 95% in top half
Early decision deadline: 11/1, notification date: N/A
Early action deadline: N/A, notification date: N/A
Application deadline (fall): 2/1
Undergraduate student body: 2,404 full time, 31 part time; 45% male, 55% female; 0% American Indian, 2% Asian, 3% black, 4% Hispanic, 2% multiracial, 0% Pacific Islander, 79% white, 9% international; 41% from in state; 99% live on campus; 10% of students in fraternities, 15% in sororities
Most popular majors: 32% Social Sciences; 12% Biological and Biomedical Sciences; 10% Psychology; 7% English Language and Literature/Letters; 5% History
Expenses: 2016-2017: $51,200; room/board: $13,190
Financial aid: (315) 229-5265; 57% of undergrads determined to have financial need; average aid package $40,981

Stony Brook University–SUNY
Stony Brook NY
(631) 632-6868
U.S. News ranking: Nat. U., No. 96
Website: www.stonybrook.edu
Admissions email: enroll@stonybrook.edu
Public; founded 1957
Freshman admissions: more selective; 2015-2016: 34,146 applied, 13,995 accepted. Either SAT or ACT required. SAT 25/75 percentile: 1150-1380. High school rank: 46% in top tenth, 79% in top quarter, 96% in top half
Early decision deadline: N/A, notification date: N/A
Early action deadline: N/A, notification date: N/A
Application deadline (fall): rolling
Undergraduate student body: 15,714 full time, 1,117 part time; 54% male, 46% female; 0% American Indian, 24% Asian, 7% black, 11% Hispanic, 2% multiracial, 0% Pacific Islander, 36% white, 13% international; 92% from in state; 51% live on campus; 3% of students in fraternities, 3% in sororities
Most popular majors: 13% Health Professions and Related Programs; 12% Psychology, General; 9% Biology/Biological Sciences, General; 8% Business Administration and Management, General; 7% Registered Nursing/Registered Nurse
Expenses: 2016-2017: $9,026 in state, $26,266 out of state; room/board: $12,790
Financial aid: (631) 632-6840; 55% of undergrads determined to have financial need; average aid package $12,500

St. Thomas Aquinas College
Sparkill NY
(845) 398-4100
U.S. News ranking: Reg. U. (N), No. 99
Website: www.stac.edu
Admissions email: admissions@stac.edu
Private; founded 1952
Freshman admissions: less selective; 2015-2016: 1,918 applied, 1,513 accepted. Either SAT or ACT required. SAT 25/75 percentile: 830-1050. High school rank: 12% in top tenth, 34% in top quarter, 59% in top half
Early decision deadline: N/A, notification date: N/A
Early action deadline: N/A, notification date: N/A
Application deadline (fall): rolling
Undergraduate student body: 1,117 full time, 579 part time; 44% male, 56% female; 0% American Indian, 3% Asian, 10% black, 22% Hispanic, 1% multiracial, 0% Pacific Islander, 52% white, 3% international; 87% from in state; 34% live on campus; N/A of students in fraternities, N/A in sororities
Most popular majors: 12% Business Administration and Management, General; 9% Psychology, General; 7% Marketing, Other; 7% Social Sciences, General

Expenses: 2016-2017: $29,600; room/board: $12,390
Financial aid: (845) 398-4097; 78% of undergrads determined to have financial need; average aid package $16,100

SUNY Buffalo State
Buffalo NY
(716) 878-4017
U.S. News ranking: Reg. U. (N), No. 110
Website: www.buffalostate.edu
Admissions email: admissions@buffalostate.edu
Public; founded 1871
Freshman admissions: less selective; 2015-2016: 13,679 applied, 8,524 accepted. Either SAT or ACT required. SAT 25/75 percentile: 800-990. High school rank: 8% in top tenth, 28% in top quarter, 65% in top half
Early decision deadline: N/A, notification date: N/A
Early action deadline: N/A, notification date: N/A
Application deadline (fall): rolling
Undergraduate student body: 8,137 full time, 1,050 part time; 43% male, 57% female; 0% American Indian, 3% Asian, 28% black, 12% Hispanic, 3% multiracial, 0% Pacific Islander, 51% white, 2% international; 97% from in state; 34% live on campus; 1% of students in fraternities, 1% in sororities
Most popular majors: 13% Business, Management, Marketing, and Related Support Services; 13% Education; 9% Social Sciences; 8% Homeland Security, Law Enforcement, Firefighting and Related Protective Services
Expenses: 2015-2016: $7,669 in state, $17,519 out of state; room/board: $12,404
Financial aid: (716) 878-4901; 65% of undergrads determined to have financial need; average aid package $13,977

SUNY College– Cortland
Cortland NY
(607) 753-4711
U.S. News ranking: Reg. U. (N), No. 61
Website: www.cortland.edu/admissions
Admissions email: admissions@cortland.edu
Public; founded 1868
Freshman admissions: selective; 2015-2016: 11,060 applied, 5,623 accepted. Neither SAT nor ACT required. SAT 25/75 percentile: 960-1110. High school rank: 11% in top tenth, 39% in top quarter, 80% in top half
Early decision deadline: N/A, notification date: N/A
Early action deadline: 11/15, notification date: 1/1
Application deadline (fall): rolling
Undergraduate student body: 6,179 full time, 104 part time; 44% male, 56% female; 0% American Indian, 1% Asian, 6% black, 11% Hispanic, 2% multiracial, 0% Pacific Islander, 74% white, 1% international; 96% from in

state; N/A live on campus; N/A of students in fraternities, N/A in sororities
Most popular majors: 27% Education; 17% Parks, Recreation, Leisure, and Fitness Studies; 10% Social Sciences; 8% Health Professions and Related Programs
Expenses: 2015-2016: $8,050 in state, $17,900 out of state; room/board: $12,200
Financial aid: (607) 753-4717

SUNY College of Agriculture and Technology– Cobleskill
Cobleskill NY
(518) 255-5525
U.S. News ranking: Reg. Coll. (N), No. 17
Website: www.cobleskill.edu
Admissions email: admissionsoffice@cobleskill.edu
Public; founded 1911
Freshman admissions: least selective; 2015-2016: 3,107 applied, 2,760 accepted. Neither SAT nor ACT required. SAT 25/75 percentile: 760-1000. High school rank: 5% in top tenth, 17% in top quarter, 51% in top half
Early decision deadline: N/A, notification date: N/A
Early action deadline: N/A, notification date: N/A
Application deadline (fall): rolling
Undergraduate student body: 2,337 full time, 109 part time; 47% male, 53% female; 1% American Indian, 1% Asian, 13% black, 8% Hispanic, N/A multiracial, N/A Pacific Islander, 70% white, 1% international; 93% from in state; 59% live on campus; N/A of students in fraternities, N/A in sororities
Most popular majors: 16% Business, Management, Marketing, and Related Support Services; 5% Biological and Biomedical Sciences
Expenses: 2015-2016: $8,231 in state, $18,071 out of state; room/board: $12,948
Financial aid: (518) 255-5623; 77% of undergrads determined to have financial need; average aid package $7,364

SUNY College of Environmental Science and Forestry
Syracuse NY
(315) 470-6600
U.S. News ranking: Nat. U., No. 99
Website: www.esf.edu
Admissions email: esfinfo@esf.edu
Public; founded 1911
Freshman admissions: more selective; 2015-2016: 1,619 applied, 841 accepted. Either SAT or ACT required. SAT 25/75 percentile: 1120-1300. High school rank: 34% in top tenth, 72% in top quarter, 97% in top half
Early decision deadline: 12/1, notification date: 1/15
Early action deadline: N/A, notification date: N/A
Application deadline (fall): rolling

Undergraduate student body: 1,731 full time, 108 part time; 54% male, 46% female; 0% American Indian, 3% Asian, 1% black, 5% Hispanic, 3% multiracial, 0% Pacific Islander, 81% white, 2% international; 82% from in state; 35% live on campus; 5% of students in fraternities, 5% in sororities
Most popular majors: 38% Environmental Biology; 15% Engineering, General; 3% Chemistry, General
Expenses: 2016-2017: $7,770 in state, $17,620 out of state; room/board: $14,860
Financial aid: (315) 470-6706; 61% of undergrads determined to have financial need; average aid package $15,400

SUNY College of Technology–Alfred
Alfred NY
(800) 425-3733
U.S. News ranking: Reg. Coll. (N), No. 12
Website: www.alfredstate.edu/alfred/Default.asp
Admissions email: admissions@alfredstate.edu
Public; founded 1908
Freshman admissions: less selective; 2015-2016: 4,912 applied, 2,790 accepted. Neither SAT nor ACT required. SAT 25/75 percentile: 840-1080. High school rank: N/A
Early decision deadline: N/A, notification date: N/A
Early action deadline: N/A, notification date: N/A
Application deadline (fall): rolling
Undergraduate student body: 3,378 full time, 321 part time; 62% male, 38% female; 0% American Indian, 1% Asian, 10% black, 7% Hispanic, 2% multiracial, 0% Pacific Islander, 76% white, 2% international; 96% from in state; 64% live on campus; 4% of students in fraternities, 3% in sororities
Most popular majors: 48% Business, Management, Marketing, and Related Support Services; 30% Engineering Technologies and Engineering-Related Fields; 9% Communications Technologies/Technicians and Support Services; 9% Computer and Information Sciences and Support Services; 3% Homeland Security, Law Enforcement, Firefighting and Related Protective Services
Expenses: 2016-2017: $8,075 in state, $17,925 out of state; room/board: $11,820
Financial aid: (607) 587-4251; 83% of undergrads determined to have financial need; average aid package $11,523

SUNY College of Technology–Canton
Canton NY
(800) 388-7123
U.S. News ranking: Reg. Coll. (N), No. 23
Website: www.canton.edu/
Admissions email: admissions@canton.edu
Public; founded 1906

Freshman admissions: less selective; 2015-2016: 2,836 applied, 2,403 accepted. Neither SAT nor ACT required. SAT 25/75 percentile: 800-1000. High school rank: 4% in top tenth, 16% in top quarter, 48% in top half
Early decision deadline: N/A, notification date: N/A
Early action deadline: N/A, notification date: N/A
Application deadline (fall): rolling
Undergraduate student body: 2,641 full time, 543 part time; 44% male, 56% female; 1% American Indian, 1% Asian, 14% black, 10% Hispanic, 2% multiracial, 0% Pacific Islander, 67% white, 2% international; 97% from in state; 38% live on campus; 1% of students in fraternities, 1% in sororities
Most popular majors: 12% Legal Assistant/Paralegal; 11% Finance, General; 9% Business Administration and Management, General; 9% Corrections and Criminal Justice, Other; 9% Registered Nursing/Registered Nurse
Expenses: 2016-2017: $7,968 in state, $17,818 out of state; room/board: $12,150
Financial aid: (315) 386-7616; 85% of undergrads determined to have financial need; average aid package $10,886

SUNY College of Technology–Delhi
Delhi NY
(607) 746-4550
U.S. News ranking: Reg. Coll. (N), No. 19
Website: www.delhi.edu/
Admissions email: enroll@delhi.edu
Public; founded 1913
Freshman admissions: least selective; 2015-2016: 5,476 applied, 2,984 accepted. Neither SAT nor ACT required. ACT 25/75 percentile: N/A. High school rank: 3% in top tenth, 18% in top quarter, 50% in top half
Early decision deadline: N/A, notification date: N/A
Early action deadline: N/A, notification date: N/A
Application deadline (fall): rolling
Undergraduate student body: 2,548 full time, 873 part time; 46% male, 54% female; 0% American Indian, 4% Asian, 16% black, 14% Hispanic, N/A multiracial, N/A Pacific Islander, 61% white, N/A international; 97% from in state; 49% live on campus; N/A of students in fraternities, N/A in sororities
Most popular majors: 42% Health Professions and Related Programs; 9% Personal and Culinary Services; 6% Homeland Security, Law Enforcement, Firefighting and Related Protective Services; 4% Business, Management, Marketing, and Related Support Services
Expenses: 2015-2016: $8,075 in state, $12,465 out of state; room/board: $11,330

Financial aid: (607) 746-4570; 78% of undergrads determined to have financial need; average aid package $10,890

SUNY College–Old Westbury

Old Westbury NY
(516) 876-3073
U.S. News ranking: Reg. U. (N), second tier
Website: www.oldwestbury.edu
Admissions email: enroll@oldwestbury.edu
Public; founded 1965
Freshman admissions: less selective; 2015-2016: 4,474 applied, 2,241 accepted. Either SAT or ACT required. SAT 25/75 percentile: 910-1080. High school rank: N/A
Early decision deadline: N/A, notification date: N/A
Early action deadline: N/A, notification date: N/A
Application deadline (fall): rolling
Undergraduate student body: 3,522 full time, 603 part time; 42% male, 58% female; 0% American Indian, 10% Asian, 30% black, 22% Hispanic, 3% multiracial, 0% Pacific Islander, 30% white, 1% international; 99% from in state; 19% live on campus; 2% of students in fraternities, 2% in sororities
Most popular majors: 16% Psychology, General; 11% Accounting; 9% Business Administration and Management, General; 8% Criminology
Expenses: 2015-2016: $7,643 in state, $17,493 out of state; room/board: $10,390
Financial aid: (516) 876-3222

SUNY College–Oneonta

Oneonta NY
(607) 436-2524
U.S. News ranking: Reg. U. (N), No. 44
Website: www.oneonta.edu
Admissions email: admissions@oneonta.edu
Public; founded 1889
Freshman admissions: selective; 2015-2016: 11,427 applied, 5,567 accepted. Either SAT or ACT required. SAT 25/75 percentile: 1000-1170. High school rank: N/A
Early decision deadline: N/A, notification date: N/A
Early action deadline: 11/15, notification date: 12/1
Application deadline (fall): rolling
Undergraduate student body: 5,754 full time, 96 part time; 40% male, 60% female; 0% American Indian, 2% Asian, 3% black, 11% Hispanic, 2% multiracial, 0% Pacific Islander, 78% white, 1% international; 99% from in state; 58% live on campus; 10% of students in fraternities, 10% in sororities
Most popular majors: 12% Education; 11% Family and Consumer Sciences/Human Sciences; 10% Visual and Performing Arts; 9% Psychology
Expenses: 2015-2016: $7,520 in state, $17,170 out of state; room/board: $11,530
Financial aid: (607) 436-2532

SUNY College–Potsdam

Potsdam NY
(315) 267-2180
U.S. News ranking: Reg. U. (N), No. 95
Website: www.potsdam.edu
Admissions email: admissions@potsdam.edu
Public; founded 1816
Freshman admissions: selective; 2015-2016: 4,976 applied, 3,678 accepted. Neither SAT nor ACT required. SAT 25/75 percentile: 877-1150. High school rank: 15% in top tenth, 25% in top quarter, 43% in top half
Early decision deadline: N/A, notification date: N/A
Early action deadline: N/A, notification date: N/A
Application deadline (fall): rolling
Undergraduate student body: 3,504 full time, 110 part time; 43% male, 57% female; 2% American Indian, 2% Asian, 10% black, 13% Hispanic, 2% multiracial, 0% Pacific Islander, 65% white, 1% international; 97% from in state; 60% live on campus; 1% of students in fraternities, 2% in sororities
Most popular majors: 18% Education; 14% Visual and Performing Arts; 9% Psychology; 8% Business, Management, Marketing, and Related Support Services; 8% Social Sciences
Expenses: 2015-2016: $7,923 in state, $17,773 out of state; room/board: $11,870
Financial aid: (315) 267-2162; 74% of undergrads determined to have financial need; average aid package $14,563

SUNY Empire State College

Saratoga Springs NY
(518) 587-2100
U.S. News ranking: Reg. U. (N), unranked
Website: www.esc.edu
Admissions email: admissions@esc.edu
Public; founded 1971
Freshman admissions: N/A; 2015-2016: 1,177 applied, 991 accepted. Neither SAT nor ACT required. ACT 25/75 percentile: N/A. High school rank: N/A
Early decision deadline: N/A, notification date: N/A
Early action deadline: N/A, notification date: N/A
Application deadline (fall): rolling
Undergraduate student body: 4,278 full time, 6,529 part time; 38% male, 62% female; 0% American Indian, 2% Asian, 16% black, 12% Hispanic, 2% multiracial, 0% Pacific Islander, 60% white, 5% international; 94% from in state; N/A live on campus; N/A of students in fraternities, N/A in sororities
Most popular majors: 37% Business, Management, Marketing, and Related Support Services; 25% Public Administration and Social Service Professions; 7% Psychology; 6% Physical Sciences; 6% Health Professions and Related Programs

Expenses: 2015-2016: $6,985 in state, $16,835 out of state; room/board: N/A
Financial aid: (518) 587-2100

SUNY–Fredonia

Fredonia NY
(800) 252-1212
U.S. News ranking: Reg. U. (N), No. 61
Website: www.fredonia.edu
Admissions email: admissions.office@fredonia.edu
Public; founded 1826
Freshman admissions: selective; 2015-2016: 5,824 applied, 3,451 accepted. Either SAT or ACT required. SAT 25/75 percentile: 920-1160. High school rank: 15% in top tenth, 38% in top quarter, 77% in top half
Early decision deadline: 11/1, notification date: 12/1
Early action deadline: N/A, notification date: N/A
Application deadline (fall): rolling
Undergraduate student body: 4,458 full time, 124 part time; 44% male, 56% female; 0% American Indian, 2% Asian, 6% black, 7% Hispanic, 2% multiracial, 0% Pacific Islander, 78% white, 2% international; 97% from in state; 50% live on campus; N/A of students in fraternities, N/A in sororities
Most popular majors: 14% Education; 13% Business, Management, Marketing, and Related Support Services; 13% Visual and Performing Arts; 6% Psychology
Expenses: 2016-2017: $8,074 in state, $17,924 out of state; room/board: $12,590
Financial aid: (716) 673-3253; 70% of undergrads determined to have financial need; average aid package $10,785

SUNY–Geneseo

Geneseo NY
(585) 245-5571
U.S. News ranking: Reg. U. (N), No. 14
Website: www.geneseo.edu
Admissions email: admissions@geneseo.edu
Public; founded 1871
Freshman admissions: more selective; 2015-2016: 9,118 applied, 6,632 accepted. Either SAT or ACT required. SAT 25/75 percentile: 1100-1290. High school rank: 36% in top tenth, 74% in top quarter, 95% in top half
Early decision deadline: 11/15, notification date: 12/15
Early action deadline: N/A, notification date: N/A
Application deadline (fall): 1/1
Undergraduate student body: 5,470 full time, 113 part time; 40% male, 60% female; 0% American Indian, 6% Asian, 3% black, 7% Hispanic, 3% multiracial, 0% Pacific Islander, 74% white, 2% international; 98% from in state; 56% live on campus; 22% of students in fraternities, 26% in sororities
Most popular majors: 17% Social Sciences; 14% Psychology; 13% Biological and Biomedical Sciences; 13% Business, Management, Marketing, and

Related Support Services; 10% Education
Expenses: 2016-2017: $8,176 in state, $18,026 out of state; room/board: $12,264
Financial aid: (585) 245-5731; 50% of undergrads determined to have financial need; average aid package $11,162

SUNY Maritime College

Throggs Neck NY
(718) 409-7221
U.S. News ranking: Reg. U. (N), No. 80
Website: www.sunymaritime.edu
Admissions email: admissions@sunymaritime.edu
Public; founded 1874
Freshman admissions: selective; 2015-2016: 1,342 applied, 917 accepted. Either SAT or ACT required. SAT 25/75 percentile: 1030-1200. High school rank: 13% in top tenth, 34% in top quarter, 79% in top half
Early decision deadline: 11/1, notification date: 12/15
Early action deadline: N/A, notification date: N/A
Application deadline (fall): 1/31
Undergraduate student body: 1,630 full time, 46 part time; 90% male, 10% female; 0% American Indian, 5% Asian, 4% black, 11% Hispanic, 2% multiracial, 0% Pacific Islander, 71% white, 3% international; 76% from in state; 85% live on campus; N/A of students in fraternities, N/A in sororities
Most popular majors: 37% Marine Science/Merchant Marine Officer; 20% Business, Management, Marketing, and Related Support Services, Other; 18% Mechanical Engineering; 8% Industrial Engineering; 8% Naval Architecture and Marine Engineering
Expenses: 2016-2017: $7,834 in state, $17,684 out of state; room/board: $11,948
Financial aid: (718) 409-7254; 57% of undergrads determined to have financial need; average aid package $8,382

SUNY–New Paltz

New Paltz NY
(845) 257-3200
U.S. News ranking: Reg. U. (N), No. 20
Website: www.newpaltz.edu
Admissions email: admissions@newpaltz.edu
Public; founded 1828
Freshman admissions: selective; 2015-2016: 14,655 applied, 6,084 accepted. Either SAT or ACT required. SAT 25/75 percentile: 1025-1210. High school rank: 30% in top tenth, 74% in top quarter, 100% in top half
Early decision deadline: N/A, notification date: N/A
Early action deadline: 11/15, notification date: 12/15
Application deadline (fall): 4/1
Undergraduate student body: 6,165 full time, 534 part time; 38% male, 62% female; 0% American Indian, 6% Asian, 6% black, 17% Hispanic, 2% multiracial, 0% Pacific Islander, 63% white,

2% international; 97% from in state; 47% live on campus; 5% of students in fraternities, 5% in sororities
Most popular majors: 14% Business, Management, Marketing, and Related Support Services; 14% Social Sciences; 11% Education; 11% Visual and Performing Arts
Expenses: 2016-2017: $7,800 in state, $17,650 out of state; room/board: $12,000
Financial aid: (845) 257-3250; 58% of undergrads determined to have financial need; average aid package $10,744

SUNY–Oswego

Oswego NY
(315) 312-2250
U.S. News ranking: Reg. U. (N), No. 44
Website: www.oswego.edu
Admissions email: admiss@oswego.edu
Public; founded 1861
Freshman admissions: selective; 2015-2016: 10,885 applied, 5,552 accepted. Either SAT or ACT required. SAT 25/75 percentile: 1010-1190. High school rank: 14% in top tenth, 52% in top quarter, 85% in top half
Early decision deadline: N/A, notification date: N/A
Early action deadline: N/A, notification date: N/A
Application deadline (fall): rolling
Undergraduate student body: 6,778 full time, 326 part time; 50% male, 50% female; 0% American Indian, 3% Asian, 7% black, 10% Hispanic, 2% multiracial, 0% Pacific Islander, 75% white, 1% international; 97% from in state; 60% live on campus; 7% of students in fraternities, 6% in sororities
Most popular majors: 10% Business Administration and Management, General; 8% Psychology, General; 6% Criminal Justice/Law Enforcement Administration; 4% Health Teacher Education
Expenses: 2015-2016: $7,881 in state, $17,731 out of state; room/board: $12,690
Financial aid: (315) 312-2248; 68% of undergrads determined to have financial need; average aid package $11,108

SUNY–Plattsburgh

Plattsburgh NY
(888) 673-0012
U.S. News ranking: Reg. U. (N), No. 72
Website: www.plattsburgh.edu
Admissions email: admissions@plattsburgh.edu
Public; founded 1889
Freshman admissions: selective; 2015-2016: 8,261 applied, 4,105 accepted. Either SAT or ACT required. SAT 25/75 percentile: 980-1200. High school rank: 11% in top tenth, 39% in top quarter, 77% in top half
Early decision deadline: N/A, notification date: N/A
Early action deadline: N/A, notification date: N/A
Application deadline (fall): rolling

Undergraduate student body: 4,960 full time, 417 part time; 44% male, 56% female; 0% American Indian, 3% Asian, 7% black, 10% Hispanic, 2% multiracial, 0% Pacific Islander, 68% white, 6% international; 94% from in state; 50% live on campus; 9% of students in fraternities, 10% in sororities
Most popular majors: 21% Business, Management, Marketing, and Related Support Services; 9% Health Professions and Related Programs; 8% Homeland Security, Law Enforcement, Firefighting and Related Protective Services; 8% Psychology
Expenses: 2016-2017: $7,895 in state, $17,745 out of state; room/board: $12,080
Financial aid: (518) 564-4061; 64% of undergrads determined to have financial need; average aid package $13,136

SUNY Polytechnic Institute
Utica NY
(315) 792-7500
U.S. News ranking: Reg. U. (N), No. 18
Website: www.sunypoly.edu
Admissions email: admissions@sunyit.edu
Public; founded 1966
Freshman admissions: selective; 2015-2016: 2,319 applied, 1,402 accepted. Either SAT or ACT required. SAT 25/75 percentile: 960-1310. High school rank: 28% in top tenth, 59% in top quarter, 91% in top half
Early decision deadline: N/A, notification date: N/A
Early action deadline: 11/15, notification date: 12/15
Application deadline (fall): 7/15
Undergraduate student body: 1,742 full time, 340 part time; 64% male, 36% female; 0% American Indian, 4% Asian, 7% black, 7% Hispanic, 2% multiracial, 0% Pacific Islander, 79% white, 1% international; 99% from in state; 38% live on campus; N/A of students in fraternities, N/A in sororities
Most popular majors: 15% Business Administration and Management, General; 12% Registered Nursing/Registered Nurse; 11% Mechanical Engineering/Mechanical Technology/Technician; 7% Psychology, General; 6% Computer and Information Sciences, General
Expenses: 2016-2017: $7,890 in state, $17,740 out of state; room/board: $13,170
Financial aid: (315) 792-7210; 68% of undergrads determined to have financial need; average aid package $10,058

Syracuse University
Syracuse NY
(315) 443-3611
U.S. News ranking: Nat. U., No. 60
Website: syr.edu
Admissions email: orange@syr.edu
Private; founded 1870

Freshman admissions: more selective; 2015-2016: 33,254 applied, 16,071 accepted. Either SAT or ACT required. SAT 25/75 percentile: 1090-1290. High school rank: 35% in top tenth, 70% in top quarter, 95% in top half
Early decision deadline: 11/15, notification date: N/A
Early action deadline: N/A, notification date: N/A
Application deadline (fall): 1/1
Undergraduate student body: 14,566 full time, 630 part time; 45% male, 55% female; 1% American Indian, 8% Asian, 8% black, 11% Hispanic, 3% multiracial, 0% Pacific Islander, 55% white, 12% international; 37% from in state; 75% live on campus; 28% of students in fraternities, 32% in sororities
Most popular majors: 14% Business, Management, Marketing, and Related Support Services; 12% Social Sciences; 11% Visual and Performing Arts; 9% Engineering
Expenses: 2016-2017: $45,022; room/board: $15,217
Financial aid: (315) 443-1513; 55% of undergrads determined to have financial need; average aid package $36,050

Touro College
New York NY
(212) 463-0400
U.S. News ranking: Reg. U. (N), second tier
Website: www.touro.edu/
Admissions email: lasadmit@touro.edu
Private; founded 1971
Affiliation: Jewish
Freshman admissions: selective; 2015-2016: 2,201 applied, 751 accepted. Neither SAT nor ACT required. SAT 25/75 percentile: 950-1240. High school rank: N/A
Early decision deadline: N/A, notification date: N/A
Early action deadline: N/A, notification date: N/A
Application deadline (fall): rolling
Undergraduate student body: 4,977 full time, 1,857 part time; 30% male, 70% female; 0% American Indian, 4% Asian, 16% black, 9% Hispanic, 0% multiracial, 0% Pacific Islander, 63% white, 4% international; 89% from in state; 0% live on campus; 0% of students in fraternities, 0% in sororities
Most popular majors: 23% Psychology; 17% Health Professions and Related Programs; 17% Multi/Interdisciplinary Studies; 14% Business, Management, Marketing, and Related Support Services; 9% Biological and Biomedical Sciences
Expenses: 2016-2017: $16,980; room/board: $11,970
Financial aid: (718) 252-7800; 85% of undergrads determined to have financial need; average aid package $10,319

Union College
Schenectady NY
(888) 843-6688
U.S. News ranking: Nat. Lib. Arts, No. 38
Website: www.union.edu
Admissions email: admissions@union.edu
Private; founded 1795
Freshman admissions: more selective; 2015-2016: 5,996 applied, 2,297 accepted. Neither SAT nor ACT required. SAT 25/75 percentile: 1240-1400. High school rank: 71% in top tenth, 87% in top quarter, 97% in top half
Early decision deadline: 11/15, notification date: 12/15
Early action deadline: N/A, notification date: N/A
Application deadline (fall): 1/15
Undergraduate student body: 2,226 full time, 43 part time; 54% male, 46% female; 0% American Indian, 6% Asian, 4% black, 7% Hispanic, 2% multiracial, N/A Pacific Islander, 73% white, 7% international; 34% from in state; 89% live on campus; 37% of students in fraternities, 42% in sororities
Most popular majors: 14% Economics, General; 10% Political Science and Government, General; 8% Psychology, General; 7% Mechanical Engineering; 6% Biology/Biological Sciences, General
Expenses: 2016-2017: $51,696; room/board: $12,678
Financial aid: (518) 388-6123; 50% of undergrads determined to have financial need; average aid package $41,663

United States Merchant Marine Academy
Kings Point NY
(516) 773-5391
U.S. News ranking: Reg. Coll. (N), No. 3
Website: www.usmma.edu
Admissions email: admissions@usmma.edu
Public; founded 1943
Freshman admissions: more selective; 2015-2016: 1,662 applied, 255 accepted. Either SAT or ACT required. SAT 25/75 percentile: 1183-1351. High school rank: 35% in top tenth, 68% in top quarter, 93% in top half
Early decision deadline: N/A, notification date: N/A
Early action deadline: N/A, notification date: N/A
Application deadline (fall): 3/1
Undergraduate student body: 904 full time, 0 part time; 83% male, 17% female; 2% American Indian, 7% Asian, 3% black, 10% Hispanic, 0% multiracial, 0% Pacific Islander, 75% white, 1% international; N/A from in state; 100% live on campus; 0% of students in fraternities, 0% in sororities
Most popular majors: 35% Transportation and Materials Moving, Other; 23% Systems Engineering; 19% Engineering, General; 16% Marine Transportation, Other; 7% Engineering, Other

Expenses: 2015-2016: $1,107 in state, $1,107 out of state; room/board: $4,000
Financial aid: (516) 773-5295; 12% of undergrads determined to have financial need; average aid package $6,500

United States Military Academy
West Point NY
(845) 938-4041
U.S. News ranking: Nat. Lib. Arts, No. 19
Website: www.usma.edu
Admissions email: admissions@usma.edu
Public; founded 1802
Freshman admissions: more selective; 2015-2016: 14,635 applied, 1,486 accepted. Either SAT or ACT required. ACT 25/75 percentile: 26-31. High school rank: 52% in top tenth, 77% in top quarter, 94% in top half
Early decision deadline: N/A, notification date: N/A
Early action deadline: N/A, notification date: N/A
Application deadline (fall): 2/28
Undergraduate student body: 4,348 full time, 0 part time; 81% male, 19% female; 1% American Indian, 6% Asian, 10% black, 12% Hispanic, 3% multiracial, 1% Pacific Islander, 65% white, 1% international; 7% from in state; 100% live on campus; 0% of students in fraternities, 0% in sororities
Most popular majors: 27% Engineering; 19% Social Sciences; 7% Business, Management, Marketing, and Related Support Services; 7% Foreign Languages, Literatures, and Linguistics; 6% Multi/Interdisciplinary Studies
Expenses: N/A
Financial aid: (845) 938-4262; 0% of undergrads determined to have financial need; average aid package $0

University at Albany–SUNY
Albany NY
(518) 442-5435
U.S. News ranking: Nat. U., No. 146
Website: www.albany.edu
Admissions email: ugadmissions@albany.edu
Public; founded 1844
Freshman admissions: selective; 2015-2016: 22,337 applied, 12,608 accepted. Either SAT or ACT required. SAT 25/75 percentile: 1000-1170. High school rank: 16% in top tenth, 46% in top quarter, 86% in top half
Early decision deadline: N/A, notification date: N/A
Early action deadline: 11/15, notification date: 11/15
Application deadline (fall): 3/1
Undergraduate student body: 12,223 full time, 685 part time; 51% male, 49% female; 0% American Indian, 8% Asian, 16% black, 15% Hispanic, 3% multiracial, 0% Pacific Islander, 49% white, 6% international; 95% from in state; 59% live on campus; 1% of students in fraternities, 2% in sororities

Most popular majors: 27% Social Sciences; 14% English Language and Literature/Letters; 12% Business, Management, Marketing, and Related Support Services; 11% Biological and Biomedical Sciences; 11% Psychology
Expenses: 2016-2017: $9,124 in state, $22,244 out of state; room/board: $12,941
Financial aid: (518) 442-5757; 64% of undergrads determined to have financial need; average aid package $10,933

University at Buffalo–SUNY
Buffalo NY
(716) 645-6900
U.S. News ranking: Nat. U., No. 99
Website: www.buffalo.edu
Admissions email: ub-admissions@buffalo.edu
Public; founded 1846
Freshman admissions: more selective; 2015-2016: 23,629 applied, 14,175 accepted. Either SAT or ACT required. SAT 25/75 percentile: 1060-1260. High school rank: 30% in top tenth, 64% in top quarter, 91% in top half
Early decision deadline: N/A, notification date: N/A
Early action deadline: 11/15, notification date: N/A
Application deadline (fall): rolling
Undergraduate student body: 18,452 full time, 1,499 part time; 56% male, 44% female; 0% American Indian, 14% Asian, 7% black, 6% Hispanic, 2% multiracial, 0% Pacific Islander, 48% white, 16% international; 97% from in state; 35% live on campus; 1% of students in fraternities, 2% in sororities
Most popular majors: 17% Social Sciences; 17% Business, Management, Marketing, and Related Support Services; 14% Engineering; 12% Psychology; 9% Biological and Biomedical Sciences
Expenses: 2016-2017: $9,770 in state, $26,270 out of state; room/board: $12,292
Financial aid: (866) 838-7257; 58% of undergrads determined to have financial need; average aid package $9,246

University of Rochester
Rochester NY
(585) 275-3221
U.S. News ranking: Nat. U., No. 32
Website: www.rochester.edu
Admissions email: admit@admissions.rochester.edu
Private; founded 1850
Freshman admissions: most selective; 2015-2016: 17,912 applied, 6,058 accepted. Neither SAT nor ACT required. SAT 25/75 percentile: 1240-1470. High school rank: 68% in top tenth, 91% in top quarter, 98% in top half
Early decision deadline: 11/1, notification date: 12/15
Early action deadline: N/A, notification date: N/A
Application deadline (fall): 1/5

Undergraduate student body: 6,046 full time, 258 part time; 50% male, 50% female; 0% American Indian, 11% Asian, 5% black, 7% Hispanic, 3% multiracial, 0% Pacific Islander, 48% white, 18% international; 41% from in state; 76% live on campus; 22% of students in fraternities, 24% in sororities
Most popular majors: 16% Health Professions and Related Programs; 16% Social Sciences; 13% Biological and Biomedical Sciences; 13% Engineering; 9% Psychology
Expenses: 2016-2017: $50,142; room/board: $14,890
Financial aid: (585) 275-3226; 52% of undergrads determined to have financial need; average aid package $42,392

Utica College
Utica NY
(315) 792-3006
U.S. News ranking: Reg. U. (N), No. 122
Website: www.utica.edu
Admissions email: admiss@utica.edu
Private; founded 1946
Freshman admissions: less selective; 2015-2016: 5,151 applied, 4,270 accepted. Neither SAT nor ACT required. SAT 25/75 percentile: 880-1100. High school rank: 9% in top tenth, 33% in top quarter, 63% in top half
Early decision deadline: 11/1, notification date: 12/15
Early action deadline: 11/15, notification date: 12/15
Application deadline (fall): rolling
Undergraduate student body: 2,410 full time, 674 part time; 39% male, 61% female; 1% American Indian, 3% Asian, 11% black, 8% Hispanic, 3% multiracial, 0% Pacific Islander, 67% white, 2% international; 82% from in state; 35% live on campus; 2% of students in fraternities, 2% in sororities
Most popular majors: 47% Health Professions and Related Programs; 20% Homeland Security, Law Enforcement, Firefighting and Related Protective Services; 9% Business, Management, Marketing, and Related Support Services; 6% Science Technologies/Technicians; 4% Biological and Biomedical Sciences
Expenses: 2016-2017: $19,996; room/board: $10,434
Financial aid: (315) 792-3179; 87% of undergrads determined to have financial need; average aid package $26,564

Vassar College
Poughkeepsie NY
(845) 437-7300
U.S. News ranking: Nat. Lib. Arts, No. 12
Website: www.vassar.edu
Admissions email: admission@vassar.edu
Private; founded 1861
Freshman admissions: most selective; 2015-2016: 7,556 applied, 1,947 accepted. Either SAT or ACT required. SAT 25/75 percentile: 1330-1490. High

school rank: 72% in top tenth, 96% in top quarter, 99% in top half
Early decision deadline: 11/15, notification date: 12/15
Early action deadline: N/A, notification date: N/A
Application deadline (fall): 1/1
Undergraduate student body: 2,421 full time, 14 part time; 44% male, 56% female; 0% American Indian, 11% Asian, 5% black, 11% Hispanic, 6% multiracial, N/A Pacific Islander, 59% white, 7% international; 26% from in state; 96% live on campus; N/A of students in fraternities, N/A in sororities
Most popular majors: 26% Social Sciences; 12% Biological and Biomedical Sciences; 12% Visual and Performing Arts; 8% Foreign Languages, Literatures, and Linguistics; 7% English Language and Literature/Letters
Expenses: 2016-2017: $53,090; room/board: $12,400
Financial aid: (845) 437-5320; 60% of undergrads determined to have financial need; average aid package $50,304

Vaughn College of Aeronautics and Technology
Flushing NY
(718) 429-6600
U.S. News ranking: Reg. Coll. (N), No. 9
Website: www.vaughn.edu
Admissions email: admitme@vaughn.edu
Private; founded 1932
Freshman admissions: selective; 2015-2016: 748 applied, 553 accepted. SAT required. SAT 25/75 percentile: 890-1121. High school rank: N/A
Early decision deadline: N/A, notification date: N/A
Early action deadline: N/A, notification date: N/A
Application deadline (fall): rolling
Undergraduate student body: 1,224 full time, 302 part time; 87% male, 13% female; 0% American Indian, 10% Asian, 19% black, 34% Hispanic, 3% multiracial, 2% Pacific Islander, 14% white, 4% international; 89% from in state; 12% live on campus; 0% of students in fraternities, 0% in sororities
Most popular majors: 54% Aviation/Airway Management and Operations; 28% Mechanical Engineering/Mechanical Technology/Technician; 7% Business Administration and Management, General; 6% Mechanical Engineering; 5% Avionics Maintenance Technology/Technician
Expenses: 2016-2017: $23,640; room/board: $12,860
Financial aid: (718) 429-6600; 83% of undergrads determined to have financial need; average aid package $12,917

Villa Maria College[1]
Buffalo NY
(716) 202-2989
U.S. News ranking: Reg. Coll. (N), unranked
Website: www.villa.edu/
Admissions email: N/A

Private
Application deadline (fall): N/A
Undergraduate student body: N/A full time, N/A part time
Expenses: 2015-2016: $20,260; room/board: N/A
Financial aid: N/A

Wagner College
Staten Island NY
(718) 390-3411
U.S. News ranking: Reg. U. (N), No. 35
Website: www.wagner.edu
Admissions email: adm@wagner.edu
Private; founded 1883
Freshman admissions: selective; 2015-2016: 2,803 applied, 1,920 accepted. Neither SAT nor ACT required. SAT 25/75 percentile: 1030-1230. High school rank: 31% in top tenth, 62% in top quarter, 88% in top half
Early decision deadline: N/A, notification date: N/A
Early action deadline: 12/1, notification date: 1/5
Application deadline (fall): 2/15
Undergraduate student body: 1,709 full time, 41 part time; 37% male, 63% female; 0% American Indian, 3% Asian, 7% black, 11% Hispanic, 2% multiracial, 0% Pacific Islander, 66% white, 3% international; 46% from in state; 67% live on campus; 5% of students in fraternities, 10% in sororities
Most popular majors: 22% Business, Management, Marketing, and Related Support Services; 17% Visual and Performing Arts; 11% Biological and Biomedical Sciences; 11% Psychology; 9% Biological and Biomedical Sciences
Expenses: 2016-2017: $43,980; room/board: $13,260
Financial aid: (718) 390-3183; 64% of undergrads determined to have financial need; average aid package $29,073

Webb Institute
Glen Cove NY
(516) 671-8355
U.S. News ranking: Engineering, unranked
Website: www.webb.edu
Admissions email: admissions@webb.edu
Private; founded 1889
Freshman admissions: N/A; 2015-2016: 105 applied, 38 accepted. Either SAT or ACT required. SAT 25/75 percentile: N/A. High school rank: 78% in top tenth, 88% in top quarter, 100% in top half
Early decision deadline: 10/15, notification date: 12/15
Early action deadline: N/A, notification date: N/A
Application deadline (fall): 2/15
Undergraduate student body: 91 full time, 0 part time; 81% male, 19% female; N/A American Indian, 11% Asian, N/A black, N/A Hispanic, 8% multiracial, N/A Pacific Islander, 77% white, 1% international; 20% from in state; 100% live on campus; 0% of students in fraternities, 0% in sororities

Most popular majors: 100% Naval Architecture and Marine Engineering
Expenses: 2016-2017: $47,400; room/board: $14,400
Financial aid: (516) 671-2213

Wells College
Aurora NY
(800) 952-9355
U.S. News ranking: Nat. Lib. Arts, No. 174
Website: www.wells.edu
Admissions email: admissions@wells.edu
Private; founded 1868
Freshman admissions: less selective; 2015-2016: N/A applied, N/A accepted. Neither SAT nor ACT required. SAT 25/75 percentile: 900-1090. High school rank: N/A
Early decision deadline: 12/15, notification date: 1/15
Early action deadline: 12/15, notification date: 1/15
Application deadline (fall): 3/1
Undergraduate student body: 558 full time, 14 part time; 33% male, 67% female; 1% American Indian, 2% Asian, 15% black, 11% Hispanic, 0% multiracial, 0% Pacific Islander, 62% white, 1% international; 62% from in state; 95% live on campus; N/A of students in fraternities, N/A in sororities
Most popular majors: 14% Psychology, General; 11% Liberal Arts and Sciences, General Studies and Humanities, Other; 10% Biology/Biological Sciences, General; 9% Sociology; 7% Biochemistry
Expenses: 2016-2017: $38,530; room/board: $13,360
Financial aid: (315) 364-3289; 95% of undergrads determined to have financial need; average aid package $35,598

Yeshiva University
New York NY
(212) 960-5277
U.S. News ranking: Nat. U., No. 66
Website: www.yu.edu
Admissions email: yuadmit@ymail.yu.edu
Private; founded 1886
Freshman admissions: more selective; 2015-2016: 1,558 applied, 1,254 accepted. Either SAT or ACT required. SAT 25/75 percentile: 1130-1370. High school rank: N/A
Early decision deadline: 11/1, notification date: 12/15
Early action deadline: N/A, notification date: N/A
Application deadline (fall): 2/1
Undergraduate student body: 2,691 full time, 53 part time; 55% male, 45% female; 0% American Indian, N/A Asian, N/A black, 0% Hispanic, 0% multiracial, N/A Pacific Islander, 94% white, 5% international; 34% from in state; N/A live on campus; N/A of students in fraternities, N/A in sororities
Most popular majors: 16% Biology/Biological Sciences, General; 14% Psychology, General; 12% Accounting; 6% Economics, General; 5% Business Administration and Management, General

Expenses: 2016-2017: $40,670; room/board: $12,135
Financial aid: (212) 960-5399; 56% of undergrads determined to have financial need; average aid package $31,978

NORTH CAROLINA

Appalachian State University
Boone NC
(828) 262-2120
U.S. News ranking: Reg. U. (S), No. 9
Website: www.appstate.edu
Admissions email: admissions@appstate.edu
Public; founded 1899
Freshman admissions: selective; 2015-2016: 13,083 applied, 8,684 accepted. Either SAT or ACT required. SAT 25/75 percentile: 1060-1240. High school rank: 21% in top tenth, 61% in top quarter, 92% in top half
Early decision deadline: N/A, notification date: N/A
Early action deadline: N/A, notification date: N/A
Application deadline (fall): 3/15
Undergraduate student body: 15,351 full time, 939 part time; 46% male, 54% female; 0% American Indian, 2% Asian, 3% black, 4% Hispanic, 3% multiracial, 0% Pacific Islander, 85% white, 1% international; 92% from in state; 34% live on campus; 9% of students in fraternities, 14% in sororities
Most popular majors: 18% Business, Management, Marketing, and Related Support Services; 12% Education; 9% Health Professions and Related Programs; 7% Parks, Recreation, Leisure, and Fitness Studies; 7% Psychology
Expenses: 2016-2017: $6,541 in state, $21,057 out of state; room/board: $8,100
Financial aid: (828) 262-2190; 52% of undergrads determined to have financial need; average aid package $9,759

Barton College
Wilson NC
(800) 345-4973
U.S. News ranking: Reg. Coll. (S), No. 13
Website: www.barton.edu
Admissions email: enroll@barton.edu
Private; founded 1902
Affiliation: Christian Church (Disciples of Christ)
Freshman admissions: selective; 2015-2016: 2,920 applied, 1,220 accepted. Either SAT or ACT required. SAT 25/75 percentile: 850-1050. High school rank: 11% in top tenth, 38% in top quarter, 74% in top half
Early decision deadline: N/A, notification date: N/A
Early action deadline: N/A, notification date: N/A
Application deadline (fall): rolling
Undergraduate student body: 911 full time, 74 part time; 30% male, 70% female; 1% American Indian, 1% Asian, 21% black, 6% Hispanic, 3% multiracial,

0% Pacific Islander, 56% white, 4% international
Most popular majors: Information not available
Expenses: 2016-2017: $29,052; room/board: $9,634
Financial aid: (252) 399-6323; 91% of undergrads determined to have financial need; average aid package $21,135

Belmont Abbey College
Belmont NC
(704) 461-6665
U.S. News ranking: Reg. Coll. (S), No. 10
Website: www.belmontabbeycollege.edu
Admissions email: admissions@bac.edu
Private; founded 1876
Affiliation: Roman Catholic
Freshman admissions: less selective; 2015-2016: 1,967 applied, 1,335 accepted. Neither SAT nor ACT required. SAT 25/75 percentile: 900-1130. High school rank: N/A
Early decision deadline: N/A, notification date: N/A
Early action deadline: N/A, notification date: N/A
Application deadline (fall): 8/1
Undergraduate student body: 1,385 full time, 110 part time; 46% male, 54% female; 0% American Indian, 1% Asian, 22% black, 1% Hispanic, 0% multiracial, 0% Pacific Islander, 45% white, 2% international; 70% from in state; 49% live on campus; 5% of students in fraternities, 5% in sororities
Most popular majors: 22% Business Administration and Management, General; 13% Education, General; 11% Liberal Arts and Sciences/Liberal Studies; 9% Accounting; 6% Sport and Fitness Administration/Management
Expenses: 2016-2017: $18,500; room/board: $10,386
Financial aid: (704) 825-6718; 72% of undergrads determined to have financial need; average aid package $11,893

Bennett College
Greensboro NC
(336) 370-8624
U.S. News ranking: Reg. Coll. (S), No. 9
Website: www.bennett.edu
Admissions email: admiss@bennett.edu
Private; founded 1873
Affiliation: United Methodist
Freshman admissions: least selective; 2015-2016: 1,478 applied, 1,402 accepted. Either SAT or ACT required. SAT 25/75 percentile: 633-778. High school rank: 5% in top tenth, 16% in top quarter, 41% in top half
Early decision deadline: N/A, notification date: N/A
Early action deadline: N/A, notification date: N/A
Application deadline (fall): rolling
Undergraduate student body: 502 full time, 81 part time; 1% male, 99% female; 0% American Indian, N/A Asian, 83% black, 3% Hispanic, 3% multiracial, 0% Pacific Islander, 0% white,

N/A international; 45% from in state; 63% live on campus; N/A of students in fraternities, 5% in sororities
Most popular majors: 17% Business Administration and Management, General; 17% Social Work; 10% Biology/Biological Sciences, General; 10% Multi-/Interdisciplinary Studies, Other
Expenses: 2015-2016: $18,150; room/board: N/A
Financial aid: (336) 517-2205

Brevard College
Brevard NC
(828) 884-8300
U.S. News ranking: Reg. Coll. (S), No. 22
Website: www.brevard.edu
Admissions email: admissions@brevard.edu
Private; founded 1853
Affiliation: Methodist
Freshman admissions: less selective; 2015-2016: 3,215 applied, 1,320 accepted. Neither SAT nor ACT required. SAT 25/75 percentile: 840-1060. High school rank: 5% in top tenth, 18% in top quarter, 51% in top half
Early decision deadline: N/A, notification date: N/A
Early action deadline: N/A, notification date: N/A
Application deadline (fall): rolling
Undergraduate student body: 715 full time, 14 part time; 55% male, 45% female; 1% American Indian, 1% Asian, 13% black, 3% Hispanic, 2% multiracial, 0% Pacific Islander, 70% white, 4% international; 60% from in state; 77% live on campus; 0% of students in fraternities, 0% in sororities
Most popular majors: 18% Visual and Performing Arts; 17% Parks, Recreation, Leisure, and Fitness Studies; 12% Business, Management, Marketing, and Related Support Services; 11% Multi/Interdisciplinary Studies; 11% Psychology
Expenses: 2016-2017: $27,790; room/board: $9,868
Financial aid: (828) 884-8287; 76% of undergrads determined to have financial need; average aid package $22,027

Campbell University
Buies Creek NC
(910) 893-1320
U.S. News ranking: Reg. U. (S), No. 30
Website: www.campbell.edu
Admissions email: adm@mailcenter.campbell.edu
Private; founded 1887
Affiliation: Baptist
Freshman admissions: selective; 2015-2016: 6,626 applied, 4,870 accepted. Either SAT or ACT required. SAT 25/75 percentile: 900-1110. High school rank: 25% in top tenth, 54% in top quarter, 85% in top half
Early decision deadline: N/A, notification date: N/A
Early action deadline: N/A, notification date: N/A
Application deadline (fall): rolling

Undergraduate student body: 3,623 full time, 832 part time; 48% male, 52% female; 1% American Indian, 2% Asian, 17% black, 7% Hispanic, 3% multiracial, 0% Pacific Islander, 62% white, 2% international; 82% from in state; N/A live on campus; 2% of students in fraternities, 2% in sororities
Most popular majors: 13% Business Administration and Management, General; 7% Science Technologies/Technicians, Other; 6% Information Technology; 6% Psychology, General; 6% Social Sciences, General
Expenses: 2016-2017: $30,050; room/board: $10,760
Financial aid: (910) 893-1310; 80% of undergrads determined to have financial need; average aid package $20,600

Catawba College
Salisbury NC
(800) 228-2922
U.S. News ranking: Reg. Coll. (S), No. 4
Website: www.catawba.edu
Admissions email: admission@catawba.edu
Private; founded 1851
Affiliation: United Church of Christ
Freshman admissions: selective; 2015-2016: 3,117 applied, 991 accepted. Neither SAT nor ACT required. SAT 25/75 percentile: 870-1110. High school rank: 13% in top tenth, 39% in top quarter, 73% in top half
Early decision deadline: N/A, notification date: N/A
Early action deadline: N/A, notification date: N/A
Application deadline (fall): rolling
Undergraduate student body: 1,203 full time, 67 part time; 48% male, 52% female; 0% American Indian, 1% Asian, 18% black, 5% Hispanic, 3% multiracial, 0% Pacific Islander, 69% white, 3% international; 77% from in state; 69% live on campus; N/A of students in fraternities, N/A in sororities
Most popular majors: 31% Business, Management, Marketing, and Related Support Services; 17% Education; 13% Visual and Performing Arts; 8% Biological and Biomedical Sciences; 8% Parks, Recreation, Leisure, and Fitness Studies
Expenses: 2016-2017: $29,333; room/board: $10,487
Financial aid: (704) 637-4416; 83% of undergrads determined to have financial need; average aid package $23,858

Chowan University
Murfreesboro NC
(252) 398-1236
U.S. News ranking: Reg. Coll. (S), second tier
Website: www.chowan.edu
Admissions email: admission@chowan.edu
Private; founded 1848
Affiliation: Baptist
Freshman admissions: least selective; 2015-2016: 4,829 applied, 2,982 accepted. Either SAT or ACT required. SAT 25/75 percentile: 700-860. High school

rank: 3% in top tenth, 11% in top quarter, 34% in top half
Early decision deadline: N/A, notification date: N/A
Early action deadline: N/A, notification date: N/A
Application deadline (fall): rolling
Undergraduate student body: 1,453 full time, 69 part time; 46% male, 54% female; 0% American Indian, 0% Asian, 71% black, 4% Hispanic, 5% multiracial, 0% Pacific Islander, 17% white, 2% international; 55% from in state; 86% live on campus; 13% of students in fraternities, 12% in sororities
Most popular majors: 15% Health and Physical Education/Fitness, General; 14% Biomedical Sciences, General; 14% Business Administration and Management, General; 12% Psychology, General; 10% Social Sciences, General
Expenses: 2016-2017: $23,930; room/board: $8,950
Financial aid: (252) 398-1229; 94% of undergrads determined to have financial need; average aid package $20,776

Davidson College
Davidson NC
(800) 768-0380
U.S. News ranking: Nat. Lib. Arts, No. 9
Website: www.davidson.edu
Admissions email: admission@davidson.edu
Private; founded 1837
Affiliation: Presbyterian Church (USA)
Freshman admissions: most selective; 2015-2016: 5,382 applied, 1,191 accepted. Either SAT or ACT required. SAT 25/75 percentile: 1260-1440. High school rank: 74% in top tenth, 97% in top quarter, 99% in top half
Early decision deadline: 11/15, notification date: 12/15
Early action deadline: N/A, notification date: N/A
Application deadline (fall): 1/2
Undergraduate student body: 1,784 full time, 0 part time; 50% male, 50% female; 1% American Indian, 5% Asian, 7% black, 8% Hispanic, 4% multiracial, 0% Pacific Islander, 68% white, 6% international; 25% from in state; 94% live on campus; 39% of students in fraternities, 70% in sororities
Most popular majors: 13% Political Science and Government, General; 12% Biology/Biological Sciences, General; 11% Economics, General; 10% Psychology, General; 7% English Language and Literature, General
Expenses: 2016-2017: $48,376; room/board: $13,547
Financial aid: (704) 894-2232; 52% of undergrads determined to have financial need; average aid package $42,181

Duke University
Durham NC
(919) 684-3214
U.S. News ranking: Nat. U., No. 8
Website: www.duke.edu/
Admissions email: N/A
Private; founded 1838
Affiliation: Methodist

Freshman admissions: most selective; 2015-2016: 30,112 applied, 3,566 accepted. Either SAT or ACT required. SAT 25/75 percentile: 1360-1550. High school rank: 91% in top tenth, 98% in top quarter, 100% in top half
Early decision deadline: 11/1, notification date: 12/15
Early action deadline: N/A, notification date: N/A
Application deadline (fall): 1/2
Undergraduate student body: 6,611 full time, 28 part time; 51% male, 49% female; 1% American Indian, 22% Asian, 10% black, 7% Hispanic, 2% multiracial, 0% Pacific Islander, 46% white, 10% international; 13% from in state; 82% live on campus; 30% of students in fraternities, 39% in sororities
Most popular majors: 10% Public Policy Analysis, General; 9% Biology/Biological Sciences, General; 9% Economics, General; 7% Bioengineering and Biomedical Engineering; 6% Psychology, General
Expenses: 2016-2017: $51,265; room/board: $15,116
Financial aid: (919) 684-6225; 43% of undergrads determined to have financial need; average aid package $47,640

East Carolina University
Greenville NC
(252) 328-6640
U.S. News ranking: Nat. U., No. 210
Website: www.ecu.edu
Admissions email: admis@ecu.edu
Public; founded 1907
Freshman admissions: selective; 2015-2016: 16,871 applied, 11,647 accepted. Either SAT or ACT required. SAT 25/75 percentile: 980-1130. High school rank: 16% in top tenth, 44% in top quarter, 80% in top half
Early decision deadline: N/A, notification date: N/A
Early action deadline: N/A, notification date: N/A
Application deadline (fall): 3/1
Undergraduate student body: 19,336 full time, 3,703 part time; 42% male, 58% female; 1% American Indian, 3% Asian, 16% black, 6% Hispanic, 3% multiracial, 0% Pacific Islander, 69% white, 0% international; 88% from in state; 26% live on campus; 13% of students in fraternities, 15% in sororities
Most popular majors: 18% Health Professions and Related Programs; 17% Business, Management, Marketing, and Related Support Services; 9% Education; 7% Biological and Biomedical Sciences
Expenses: 2016-2017: $6,946 in state, $22,904 out of state; room/board: $9,426
Financial aid: (252) 328-6610; 61% of undergrads determined to have financial need; average aid package $10,523

Elizabeth City State University

Elizabeth City NC
(252) 335-3305
U.S. News ranking: Reg. U. (S), No. 89
Website: www.ecsu.edu
Admissions email: admissions@mail.ecsu.edu
Public; founded 1891
Freshman admissions: least selective; 2015-2016: 1,531 applied, 1,071 accepted. Either SAT or ACT required. SAT 25/75 percentile: 760-940. High school rank: 1% in top tenth, 8% in top quarter, 40% in top half
Early decision deadline: N/A, notification date: N/A
Early action deadline: N/A, notification date: N/A
Application deadline (fall): 8/1
Undergraduate student body: 1,405 full time, 130 part time; 43% male, 57% female; 0% American Indian, 0% Asian, 74% black, 2% Hispanic, 1% multiracial, 0% Pacific Islander, 14% white, 0% international; 91% from in state; 58% live on campus; N/A of students in fraternities, N/A in sororities
Most popular majors: 14% Business, Management, Marketing, and Related Support Services; 14% Education; 11% Homeland Security, Law Enforcement, Firefighting and Related Protective Services; 9% Social Sciences; 7% Biological and Biomedical Sciences
Expenses: 2016-2017: $4,858 in state, $17,829 out of state; room/board: $7,601
Financial aid: (252) 335-3282; 43% of undergrads determined to have financial need; average aid package $10,839

Elon University

Elon NC
(800) 334-8448
U.S. News ranking: Reg. U. (S), No. 1
Website: www.elon.edu
Admissions email: admissions@elon.edu
Private; founded 1889
Freshman admissions: more selective; 2015-2016: 10,256 applied, 5,866 accepted. Either SAT or ACT required. SAT 25/75 percentile: 1110-1290. High school rank: 24% in top tenth, 68% in top quarter, 90% in top half
Early decision deadline: 11/1, notification date: 12/1
Early action deadline: 11/10, notification date: 12/20
Application deadline (fall): 1/10
Undergraduate student body: 5,735 full time, 168 part time; 41% male, 59% female; 0% American Indian, 2% Asian, 6% black, 5% Hispanic, 2% multiracial, 0% Pacific Islander, 82% white, 2% international; 28% from in state; 62% live on campus; 18% of students in fraternities, 39% in sororities
Most popular majors: 30% Business/Commerce, General; 6% Psychology, General; 5% Health and Physical Education/Fitness; 4% Biology, General
Expenses: 2016-2017: $33,104; room/board: $11,495

Fayetteville State University

Fayetteville NC
(910) 672-1371
U.S. News ranking: Reg. U. (S), No. 102
Website: www.uncfsu.edu
Admissions email: admissions@uncfsu.edu
Public; founded 1867
Freshman admissions: less selective; 2015-2016: 3,945 applied, 2,383 accepted. Either SAT or ACT required. SAT 25/75 percentile: 790-930. High school rank: 5% in top tenth, 20% in top quarter, 60% in top half
Early decision deadline: N/A, notification date: N/A
Early action deadline: N/A, notification date: N/A
Application deadline (fall): 6/30
Undergraduate student body: 4,055 full time, 1,451 part time; 32% male, 68% female; 3% American Indian, 1% Asian, 64% black, 6% Hispanic, 0% multiracial, 0% Pacific Islander, 19% white, 0% international
Most popular majors: 15% Registered Nursing/Registered Nurse; 14% Criminal Justice/Safety Studies; 13% Psychology, General; 11% Business Administration and Management, General; 6% Sociology
Expenses: 2016-2017: $5,455 in state, $17,063 out of state; room/board: N/A
Financial aid: (910) 672-1325; 86% of undergrads determined to have financial need; average aid package $10,117

Gardner-Webb University

Boiling Springs NC
(800) 253-6472
U.S. News ranking: Nat. U., No. 220
Website: www.gardner-webb.edu
Admissions email: admissions@gardner-webb.edu
Private; founded 1905
Affiliation: Baptist
Freshman admissions: selective; 2015-2016: 2,537 applied, 2,014 accepted. Either SAT or ACT required. SAT 25/75 percentile: 850-1080. High school rank: 20% in top tenth, 51% in top quarter, 85% in top half
Early decision deadline: N/A, notification date: N/A
Early action deadline: N/A, notification date: N/A
Application deadline (fall): rolling
Undergraduate student body: 2,096 full time, 519 part time; 34% male, 66% female; 1% American Indian, 1% Asian, 17% black, 3% Hispanic, 0% multiracial, 0% Pacific Islander, 67% white, 1% international; 78% from in state; 51% live on campus; N/A of students in fraternities, N/A in sororities
Most popular majors: 23% Psychology; 20% Business, Management, Marketing, and Related Support Services;

20% Health Professions and Related Programs; 7% Homeland Security, Law Enforcement, Firefighting and Related Protective Services; 5% Biological and Biomedical Sciences
Expenses: 2016-2017: $29,850; room/board: $9,780
Financial aid: (704) 406-4243; 80% of undergrads determined to have financial need; average aid package $23,594

Greensboro College[1]

Greensboro NC
(336) 272-7102
U.S. News ranking: Reg. Coll. (S), No. 51
Website: www.gborocollege.edu
Admissions email: admissions@gborocollege.edu
Private
Application deadline (fall): N/A
Undergraduate student body: N/A full time, N/A part time
Expenses: 2015-2016: $26,900; room/board: $10,100
Financial aid: (336) 272-7102

Guilford College

Greensboro NC
(800) 992-7759
U.S. News ranking: Nat. Lib. Arts, No. 146
Website: www.guilford.edu
Admissions email: admission@guilford.edu
Private; founded 1837
Affiliation: Quaker
Freshman admissions: selective; 2015-2016: 2,775 applied, 1,743 accepted. Neither SAT nor ACT required. SAT 25/75 percentile: 910-1170. High school rank: 14% in top tenth, 39% in top quarter, 76% in top half
Early decision deadline: N/A, notification date: N/A
Early action deadline: 12/15, notification date: 1/1
Application deadline (fall): 8/10
Undergraduate student body: 1,554 full time, 363 part time; 47% male, 53% female; 0% American Indian, 3% Asian, 22% black, 7% Hispanic, 3% multiracial, 0% Pacific Islander, 63% white, 2% international; 71% from in state; 74% live on campus; 0% of students in fraternities, 0% in sororities
Most popular majors: 16% Business, Management, Marketing, and Related Support Services; 9% Psychology; 7% Homeland Security, Law Enforcement, Firefighting and Related Protective Services; 5% Social Sciences
Expenses: 2015-2016: $34,090; room/board: $9,556
Financial aid: (336) 316-2165

High Point University

High Point NC
(800) 345-6993
U.S. News ranking: Reg. Coll. (S), No. 1
Website: www.highpoint.edu
Admissions email: admiss@highpoint.edu
Private; founded 1924
Affiliation: United Methodist

Freshman admissions: selective; 2015-2016: 10,910 applied, 7,909 accepted. Either SAT or ACT required. SAT 25/75 percentile: 1012-1196. High school rank: 25% in top tenth, 54% in top quarter, 80% in top half
Early decision deadline: 11/1, notification date: 11/28
Early action deadline: 11/14, notification date: 12/16
Application deadline (fall): 7/1
Undergraduate student body: 4,323 full time, 48 part time; 40% male, 60% female; 0% American Indian, 2% Asian, 5% black, 4% Hispanic, 5% multiracial, 0% Pacific Islander, 79% white, 3% international; 24% from in state; 94% live on campus; 17% of students in fraternities, 32% in sororities
Most popular majors: 34% Business, Management, Marketing, and Related Support Services; 9% Visual and Performing Arts; 7% Education; 6% Biological and Biomedical Sciences
Expenses: 2016-2017: $33,405; room/board: $12,572
Financial aid: (336) 841-9128; 42% of undergrads determined to have financial need; average aid package $14,960

Johnson C. Smith University

Charlotte NC
(704) 378-1010
U.S. News ranking: Nat. Lib. Arts, second tier
Website: www.jcsu.edu
Admissions email: admissions@jcsu.edu
Private; founded 1867
Freshman admissions: least selective; 2015-2016: 4,346 applied, 1,983 accepted. Either SAT or ACT required. SAT 25/75 percentile: 700-880. High school rank: 5% in top tenth, 15% in top quarter, 47% in top half
Early decision deadline: N/A, notification date: N/A
Early action deadline: N/A, notification date: N/A
Application deadline (fall): rolling
Undergraduate student body: 1,322 full time, 53 part time; 39% male, 61% female; 0% American Indian, 0% Asian, 79% black, 5% Hispanic, 2% multiracial, 0% Pacific Islander, 0% white, 4% international; 60% from in state; 65% live on campus; 3% of students in fraternities, 4% in sororities
Most popular majors: 21% Business Administration and Management, General; 15% Criminology; 9% Biology/Biological Sciences, General; 8% Information Technology
Expenses: 2016-2017: $18,236; room/board: $7,100
Financial aid: (704) 378-1035; 80% of undergrads determined to have financial need; average aid package $16,672

Lees-McRae College

Banner Elk NC
(828) 898-8723
U.S. News ranking: Reg. Coll. (S), No. 23
Website: www.lmc.edu
Admissions email: admissions@lmc.edu
Private; founded 1900
Affiliation: Presbyterian Church (U.S.A.)
Freshman admissions: selective; 2015-2016: 1,400 applied, 931 accepted. Neither SAT nor ACT required. ACT 25/75 percentile: 18-24. High school rank: 5% in top tenth, 27% in top quarter, 51% in top half
Early decision deadline: N/A, notification date: N/A
Early action deadline: N/A, notification date: N/A
Application deadline (fall): rolling
Undergraduate student body: 1,028 full time, 5 part time; 34% male, 66% female; 0% American Indian, 1% Asian, 7% black, 4% Hispanic, 1% multiracial, 0% Pacific Islander, 67% white, 2% international; 74% from in state; 59% live on campus; N/A of students in fraternities, N/A in sororities
Most popular majors: 35% Registered Nursing/Registered Nurse; 10% Criminal Justice/Law Enforcement Administration; 10% Elementary Education and Teaching; 9% Wildlife Biology; 6% Biology/Biological Sciences, General
Expenses: 2016-2017: $26,198; room/board: $10,392
Financial aid: (828) 898-8793; 85% of undergrads determined to have financial need; average aid package $23,930

Lenoir-Rhyne University

Hickory NC
(828) 328-7300
U.S. News ranking: Reg. U. (S), No. 56
Website: www.lr.edu
Admissions email: admission@lr.edu
Private; founded 1891
Affiliation: Evangelical Lutheran Church in America
Freshman admissions: selective; 2015-2016: 3,994 applied, 3,369 accepted. Either SAT or ACT required. SAT 25/75 percentile: 880-1100. High school rank: N/A
Early decision deadline: N/A, notification date: N/A
Early action deadline: 11/7, notification date: 11/21
Application deadline (fall): rolling
Undergraduate student body: 1,378 full time, 209 part time; 42% male, 58% female; 1% American Indian, 1% Asian, 15% black, 5% Hispanic, 3% multiracial, 0% Pacific Islander, 69% white, 2% international; 82% from in state; 51% live on campus; 13% of students in fraternities, 8% in sororities
Most popular majors: 22% Health Professions and Related Programs; 17% Parks, Recreation, Leisure, and Fitness Studies; 16% Business, Management, Marketing, and Related Support Services; 7%

BEST COLLEGES

Education; 7% Social Sciences
Expenses: 2016-2017: $33,730;
room/board: $11,600
Financial aid: (828) 328-7304;
86% of undergrads determined
to have financial need; average
aid package $26,974

Livingstone College
Salisbury NC
(704) 216-6001
U.S. News ranking: Reg. Coll. (S),
second tier
Website: www.livingstone.edu/
Admissions email: admissions@
livingstone.edu
Private; founded 1879
Affiliation: African Methodist
Episcopal Zion
Freshman admissions: least
selective; 2015-2016: 4,574
applied, 3,260 accepted. Either
SAT or ACT required. SAT 25/75
percentile: 640-810. High school
rank: 2% in top tenth, 7% in top
quarter, 25% in top half
Early decision deadline: N/A,
notification date: N/A
Early action deadline: N/A,
notification date: N/A
Application deadline (fall): rolling
Undergraduate student body: 1,250
full time, 12 part time; 51%
male, 49% female; 0% American
Indian, 0% Asian, 81% black,
1% Hispanic, 0% multiracial,
0% Pacific Islander, 0% white,
0% international; 35% from in
state; 83% live on campus; 5%
of students in fraternities, 5% in
sororities
Most popular majors: 18%
Business Administration and
Management, General; 18%
Criminal Justice/Safety Studies;
17% Social Work; 11% Biology/
Biological Sciences, General; 9%
Sport and Fitness Administration/
Management
Expenses: 2016-2017: $17,763;
room/board: $6,596
Financial aid: (704) 216-6069;
97% of undergrads determined
to have financial need; average
aid package $13,016

Mars Hill University
Mars Hill NC
(866) 642-4968
U.S. News ranking: Reg. Coll. (S),
No. 20
Website: www.mhc.edu
Admissions email:
admissions@mhc.edu
Private; founded 1856
Freshman admissions: less
selective; 2015-2016: 3,010
applied, 1,835 accepted. Either
SAT or ACT required. SAT 25/75
percentile: 810-990. High school
rank: 5% in top tenth, 19% in
top quarter, 56% in top half
Early decision deadline: N/A,
notification date: N/A
Early action deadline: N/A,
notification date: N/A
Application deadline (fall): rolling
Undergraduate student body: 1,284
full time, 111 part time; 49%
male, 51% female; 1% American
Indian, 1% Asian, 22% black,
3% Hispanic, 1% multiracial,
0% Pacific Islander, 68% white,
0% international; 74% from in
state; 69% live on campus; 7%
of students in fraternities, 11%
in sororities

Most popular majors: 22%
Business, Management,
Marketing, and Related
Support Services; 20%
Education; 9% Biological and
Biomedical Sciences; 8% Public
Administration and Social Service
Professions; 8% Visual and
Performing Arts
Expenses: 2016-2017: $30,534;
room/board: $9,282
Financial aid: (828) 689-1103;
64% of undergrads determined
to have financial need; average
aid package $21,882

Meredith College
Raleigh NC
(919) 760-8581
U.S. News ranking: Nat. Lib. Arts,
No. 154
Website: www.meredith.edu
Admissions email: admissions@
meredith.edu
Private; founded 1891
Freshman admissions: selective;
2015-2016: 1,721 applied,
1,033 accepted. Either SAT
or ACT required. SAT 25/75
percentile: 920-1130. High
school rank: 20% in top tenth,
48% in top quarter, 84% in
top half
Early decision deadline: 10/30,
notification date: 11/1
Early action deadline: N/A,
notification date: N/A
Application deadline (fall): rolling
Undergraduate student body: 1,616
full time, 63 part time; 0% male,
100% female; 1% American
Indian, 3% Asian, 10% black,
3% Hispanic, 4% multiracial,
0% Pacific Islander, 71% white,
5% international; 91% from in
state; 58% live on campus; N/A
of students in fraternities, N/A in
sororities
Most popular majors: 14% Biology/
Biological Sciences, General;
10% Psychology, General; 6%
Business Administration and
Management, General; 6%
Child Development; 6% Fashion
Merchandising
Expenses: 2016-2017: $34,906;
room/board: $10,390
Financial aid: (919) 760-8565;
75% of undergrads determined
to have financial need; average
aid package $24,977

Methodist University
Fayetteville NC
(910) 630-7027
U.S. News ranking: Reg. U. (S),
No. 87
Website: www.methodist.edu
Admissions email: admissions@
methodist.edu
Private; founded 1956
Affiliation: United Methodist
Freshman admissions: selective;
2015-2016: 4,783 applied,
2,590 accepted. Either SAT
or ACT required. ACT 25/75
percentile: 18-23. High school
rank: 11% in top tenth, 33% in
top quarter, 70% in top half
Early decision deadline: N/A,
notification date: N/A
Early action deadline: N/A,
notification date: N/A
Application deadline (fall): rolling
Undergraduate student body: 1,986
full time, 239 part time; 55%
male, 45% female; 1% American
Indian, 1% Asian, 19% black,

7% Hispanic, 4% multiracial,
0% Pacific Islander, 48% white,
8% international; 66% from in
state; 58% live on campus; 8%
of students in fraternities, 12%
in sororities
Most popular majors: Information
not available
Expenses: 2016-2017: $31,980;
room/board: N/A
Financial aid: (910) 630-7193;
80% of undergrads determined
to have financial need; average
aid package $16,570

Montreat College
Montreat NC
(800) 622-6968
U.S. News ranking: Reg. U. (S),
second tier
Website: www.montreat.edu
Admissions email: admissions@
montreat.edu
Private; founded 1916
Affiliation: Non-denominational
Christian
Freshman admissions: less
selective; 2015-2016: 819
applied, 442 accepted. Either
SAT or ACT required. SAT 25/75
percentile: 850-1060. High
school rank: 9% in top tenth,
26% in top quarter, 60% in
top half
Early decision deadline: N/A,
notification date: N/A
Early action deadline: N/A,
notification date: N/A
Application deadline (fall): rolling
Undergraduate student body: 506
full time, 302 part time; 46%
male, 54% female; 1% American
Indian, 2% Asian, 16% black,
3% Hispanic, 3% multiracial,
0% Pacific Islander, 64% white,
5% international; 42% from in
state; 80% live on campus; N/A
of students in fraternities, N/A in
sororities
Most popular majors: 46%
Business, Management,
Marketing, and Related Support
Services; 24% Psychology;
9% Biological and Biomedical
Sciences; 6% Theology and
Religious Vocations; 5% Parks,
Recreation, Leisure, and Fitness
Studies
Expenses: 2015-2016: $25,720;
room/board: $8,266
Financial aid: (800) 545-4656

North Carolina A&T State University
Greensboro NC
(336) 334-7946
U.S. News ranking: Nat. U.,
second tier
Website: www.ncat.edu
Admissions email:
uadmit@ncat.edu
Public; founded 1891
Freshman admissions: less
selective; 2015-2016: 8,162
applied, 4,855 accepted. Either
SAT or ACT required. SAT 25/75
percentile: 830-990. High school
rank: 9% in top tenth, 33% in
top quarter, 75% in top half
Early decision deadline: N/A,
notification date: N/A
Early action deadline: N/A,
notification date: N/A
Application deadline (fall): 6/15
Undergraduate student body: 8,494
full time, 859 part time; 46%
male, 54% female; 0% American

Indian, 1% Asian, 83% black,
3% Hispanic, 3% multiracial,
0% Pacific Islander, 5% white,
2% international; 82% from in
state; 42% live on campus; 45%
of students in fraternities, 45%
in sororities
Most popular majors: 14%
Engineering; 12% Business,
Management, Marketing, and
Related Support Services; 8%
Liberal Arts and Sciences,
General Studies and Humanities;
8% Psychology
Expenses: 2016-2017: $6,372
in state, $19,132 out of state;
room/board: $7,153
Financial aid: (336) 334-7973;
85% of undergrads determined
to have financial need; average
aid package $14,265

North Carolina Central University
Durham NC
(919) 530-6298
U.S. News ranking: Reg. U. (S),
No. 72
Website: www.nccu.edu
Admissions email:
admissions@nccu.edu
Public; founded 1910
Freshman admissions: less
selective; 2015-2016: 7,651
applied, 5,040 accepted. Either
SAT or ACT required. SAT 25/75
percentile: 800-940. High school
rank: 6% in top tenth, 22% in
top quarter, 66% in top half
Early decision deadline: N/A,
notification date: N/A
Early action deadline: N/A,
notification date: N/A
Application deadline (fall): rolling
Undergraduate student body: 5,247
full time, 921 part time; 34%
male, 66% female; 0% American
Indian, 1% Asian, 81% black,
4% Hispanic, 5% multiracial,
0% Pacific Islander, 6% white,
0% international; 91% from in
state; 48% live on campus; 1%
of students in fraternities, 1% in
sororities
Most popular majors: 13%
Business Administration and
Management, General; 13%
Psychology, General; 12%
Criminal Justice/Safety Studies;
12% Family and Consumer
Sciences/Human Sciences,
General; 11% Public Health
Education and Promotion
Expenses: 2016-2017: $5,882
in state, $18,340 out of state;
room/board: $8,270
Financial aid: (919) 530-6180;
91% of undergrads determined
to have financial need; average
aid package $11,745

North Carolina State University–Raleigh
Raleigh NC
(919) 515-2434
U.S. News ranking: Nat. U.,
No. 92
Website: admissions.ncsu.edu
Admissions email: undergrad-
admissions@ncsu.edu
Public; founded 1887
Freshman admissions: more
selective; 2015-2016: 21,099
applied, 10,579 accepted.
Either SAT or ACT required. SAT
25/75 percentile: 1160-1330.
High school rank: 51% in top

tenth, 87% in top quarter, 99%
in top half
Early decision deadline: N/A,
notification date: N/A
Early action deadline: 10/15,
notification date: 1/30
Application deadline (fall): 1/15
Undergraduate student body:
21,023 full time, 3,088 part
time; 55% male, 45% female;
0% American Indian, 5% Asian,
6% black, 5% Hispanic, 4%
multiracial, 0% Pacific Islander,
74% white, 4% international;
90% from in state; 32% live
on campus; 11% of students in
fraternities, 17% in sororities
Most popular majors: 24%
Engineering; 14% Business,
Management, Marketing, and
Related Support Services; 10%
Biological and Biomedical
Sciences; 5% Social Sciences
Expenses: 2016-2017: $8,880
in state, $26,399 out of state;
room/board: $10,635
Financial aid: (919) 515-2421;
49% of undergrads determined
to have financial need; average
aid package $12,834

North Carolina Wesleyan College
Rocky Mount NC
(800) 488-6292
U.S. News ranking: Reg. Coll. (S),
No. 47
Website: www.ncwc.edu
Admissions email: adm@ncwc.edu
Private; founded 1956
Affiliation: Methodist
Freshman admissions: less
selective; 2015-2016: 3,102
applied, 1,720 accepted. Neither
SAT nor ACT required. SAT
25/75 percentile: 760-970.
High school rank: 10% in top
tenth, 30% in top quarter, 59%
in top half
Early decision deadline: N/A,
notification date: N/A
Early action deadline: N/A,
notification date: N/A
Application deadline (fall): rolling
Undergraduate student body: 1,726
full time, 393 part time; 41%
male, 59% female; 1% American
Indian, 1% Asian, 46% black,
2% Hispanic, 2% multiracial,
0% Pacific Islander, 32% white,
5% international; 88% from in
state; 31% live on campus; N/A
of students in fraternities, N/A in
sororities
Most popular majors: 33%
Business Administration
and Management, General;
23% Criminal Justice/Law
Enforcement Administration;
19% Psychology, General; 11%
Accounting; 8% Computer and
Information Sciences, General
Expenses: 2016-2017: $29,400;
room/board: $9,850
Financial aid: (252) 985-5200;
90% of undergrads determined
to have financial need; average
aid package $17,843

Pfeiffer University
Misenheimer NC
(800) 338-2060
U.S. News ranking: Reg. U. (S),
No. 84
Website: www.pfeiffer.edu
Admissions email:
admissions@pfeiffer.edu

More at usnews.com/college

Private; founded 1885
Affiliation: Methodist
Freshman admissions: less selective; 2015-2016: 1,627 applied, 757 accepted. Either SAT or ACT required. SAT 25/75 percentile: 805-1060. High school rank: 8% in top tenth, 28% in top quarter, 62% in top half
Early decision deadline: N/A, notification date: N/A
Early action deadline: N/A, notification date: N/A
Application deadline (fall): rolling
Undergraduate student body: 817 full time, 100 part time; 42% male, 58% female; 0% American Indian, 1% Asian, 21% black, 3% Hispanic, 2% multiracial, 0% Pacific Islander, 52% white, 6% international; 81% from in state; 51% live on campus; N/A of students in fraternities, N/A in sororities
Most popular majors: 34% Health/ Health Care Administration/ Management; 21% Business Administration and Management, General; 8% Marriage and Family Therapy/Counseling; 6% Organizational Leadership; 4% Criminal Justice/Safety Studies
Expenses: 2016-2017: $28,995; room/board: $10,700
Financial aid: (800) 338-2060; 89% of undergrads determined to have financial need; average aid package $23,825

Queens University of Charlotte

Charlotte NC
(800) 849-0202
U.S. News ranking: Reg. U. (S), No. 22
Website: www.queens.edu
Admissions email: admissions@queens.edu
Private; founded 1857
Affiliation: Presbyterian
Freshman admissions: selective; 2015-2016: 2,111 applied, 1,417 accepted. Either SAT or ACT required. SAT 25/75 percentile: 940-1150. High school rank: 15% in top tenth, 44% in top quarter, 79% in top half
Early decision deadline: N/A, notification date: N/A
Early action deadline: 12/1, notification date: 12/15
Application deadline (fall): 9/8
Undergraduate student body: 1,343 full time, 298 part time; 31% male, 69% female; 1% American Indian, 3% Asian, 17% black, 8% Hispanic, 1% multiracial, 0% Pacific Islander, 55% white, 7% international; 59% from in state; 69% live on campus; 9% of students in fraternities, 25% in sororities
Most popular majors: 29% Health Professions and Related Programs; 15% Business, Management, Marketing, and Related Support Services; 9% Visual and Performing Arts; 6% Social Sciences
Expenses: 2016-2017: $32,430; room/board: $10,944
Financial aid: (704) 337-2225; 64% of undergrads determined to have financial need; average aid package $21,954

Salem College

Winston-Salem NC
(336) 721-2621
U.S. News ranking: Nat. Lib. Arts, No. 122
Website: www.salem.edu
Admissions email: admissions@salem.edu
Private; founded 1772
Affiliation: Moravian Church in America
Freshman admissions: more selective; 2015-2016: 903 applied, 563 accepted. Either SAT or ACT required. ACT 25/75 percentile: 21-29. High school rank: 37% in top tenth, 73% in top quarter, 99% in top half
Early decision deadline: N/A, notification date: N/A
Early action deadline: N/A, notification date: N/A
Application deadline (fall): rolling
Undergraduate student body: 768 full time, 170 part time; 4% male, 96% female; 0% American Indian, 5% Asian, 36% black, 19% Hispanic, 5% multiracial, 0% Pacific Islander, 26% white, 1% international; 73% from in state; 60% live on campus; 0% of students in fraternities, 0% in sororities
Most popular majors: 11% Education, General; 10% Biology/ Biological Sciences, General; 9% Business Administration and Management, General; 8% Psychology, General
Expenses: 2016-2017: $27,406; room/board: $11,500
Financial aid: (336) 721-2808; 88% of undergrads determined to have financial need; average aid package $29,201

Shaw University[1]

Raleigh NC
(800) 214-6683
U.S. News ranking: Reg. Coll. (S), second tier
Website: www.shawu.edu
Admissions email: admission@shawu.edu
Private; founded 1865
Affiliation: Baptist
Application deadline (fall): 7/30
Undergraduate student body: N/A full time, N/A part time
Expenses: 2015-2016: $16,580; room/board: $8,158
Financial aid: (919) 546-8240

Southeastern Baptist Theological Seminary

Wake Forest NC
(800) 284-6317
U.S. News ranking: Reg. U. (S), unranked
Website: www.sebts.edu/
Admissions email: N/A
Private; founded 1950
Affiliation: Southern Baptist
Freshman admissions: N/A; 2015-2016: 126 applied, 124 accepted. Neither SAT nor ACT required. ACT 25/75 percentile: N/A. High school rank: N/A
Early decision deadline: N/A, notification date: N/A
Early action deadline: N/A, notification date: N/A
Application deadline (fall): 7/20
Undergraduate student body: 239 full time, 179 part time; 68% male, 32% female; N/A American Indian, 3% Asian, 5% black, 3%

Hispanic, N/A multiracial, N/A Pacific Islander, 87% white, 0% international
Most popular majors: Information not available
Expenses: 2015-2016: $8,124; room/board: $4,068
Financial aid: N/A

St. Augustine's University

Raleigh NC
(919) 516-4012
U.S. News ranking: Reg. Coll. (S), No. 49
Website: www.st-aug.edu
Admissions email: admissions@st-aug.edu
Private; founded 1867
Affiliation: Episcopal
Freshman admissions: least selective; 2015-2016: 2,581 applied, 1,488 accepted. Either SAT or ACT required. ACT 25/75 percentile: 14-18. High school rank: N/A
Early decision deadline: N/A, notification date: N/A
Early action deadline: N/A, notification date: N/A
Application deadline (fall): rolling
Undergraduate student body: 798 full time, 12 part time; 53% male, 47% female; 1% American Indian, 0% Asian, 94% black, 1% Hispanic, N/A multiracial, N/A Pacific Islander, 1% white, 2% international
Most popular majors: 12% Criminal Justice and Corrections; 8% Psychology, General; 7% Health Professions and Related Programs; 7% Sociology; 6% Business Administration, Management and Operations
Expenses: 2016-2017: $17,890; room/board: $7,692
Financial aid: (919) 516-4131; 82% of undergrads determined to have financial need; average aid package $5,134

University of Mount Olive

Mount Olive NC
(919) 658-2502
U.S. News ranking: Reg. Coll. (S), No. 32
Website: www.umo.edu/
Admissions email: admissions@umo.edu
Private; founded 1951
Affiliation: Original Free Will Baptist
Freshman admissions: less selective; 2015-2016: 2,262 applied, 1,143 accepted. Neither SAT nor ACT required. SAT 25/75 percentile: 795-1020. High school rank: N/A
Early decision deadline: N/A, notification date: N/A
Early action deadline: N/A, notification date: N/A
Application deadline (fall): rolling
Undergraduate student body: 1,393 full time, 1,858 part time; 33% male, 67% female; 1% American Indian, 1% Asian, 29% black, 3% Hispanic, 6% multiracial, 0% Pacific Islander, 50% white, 3% international
Most popular majors: 34% Business, Management, Marketing, and Related Support Services; 20% Health Professions and Related Programs; 18%

Homeland Security, Law Enforcement, Firefighting and Related Protective Services; 15% Education
Expenses: 2015-2016: $18,400; room/board: $7,400
Financial aid: (919) 658-2502

University of North Carolina– Asheville

Asheville NC
(828) 251-6481
U.S. News ranking: Nat. Lib. Arts, No. 159
Website: www.unca.edu
Admissions email: admissions@unca.edu
Public; founded 1927
Freshman admissions: selective; 2015-2016: 3,324 applied, 2,617 accepted. Either SAT or ACT required. SAT 25/75 percentile: 1050-1250. High school rank: 21% in top tenth, 52% in top quarter, 91% in top half
Early decision deadline: N/A, notification date: N/A
Early action deadline: 11/15, notification date: 12/15
Application deadline (fall): 2/15
Undergraduate student body: 3,296 full time, 562 part time; 44% male, 56% female; 1% American Indian, 2% Asian, 4% black, 5% Hispanic, 4% multiracial, 0% Pacific Islander, 80% white, 1% international; 89% from in state; 39% live on campus; 3% of students in fraternities, 3% in sororities
Most popular majors: 12% Psychology, General; 6% Biology/ Biological Sciences, General; 6% Business Administration and Management, General; 6% Public Health Education and Promotion
Expenses: 2016-2017: $6,977 in state, $23,372 out of state; room/board: $8,746
Financial aid: (828) 251-6535; 57% of undergrads determined to have financial need; average aid package $11,858

University of North Carolina– Chapel Hill

Chapel Hill NC
(919) 966-3621
U.S. News ranking: Nat. U., No. 30
Website: www.unc.edu
Admissions email: unchelp@ admissions.unc.edu
Public; founded 1789
Freshman admissions: most selective; 2015-2016: 31,953 applied, 9,510 accepted. Either SAT or ACT required. SAT 25/75 percentile: 1200-1390. High school rank: 77% in top tenth, 96% in top quarter, 99% in top half
Early decision deadline: N/A, notification date: N/A
Early action deadline: 10/15, notification date: 1/31
Application deadline (fall): 1/15
Undergraduate student body: 17,645 full time, 770 part time; 42% male, 58% female; 1% American Indian, 10% Asian, 8% black, 8% Hispanic, 4% multiracial, 0% Pacific Islander,

64% white, 2% international; 83% from in state; 52% live on campus; 18% of students in fraternities, 18% in sororities
Most popular majors: 9% Biology, General; 8% Psychology, General; 8% Economics
Expenses: 2016-2017: $8,834 in state, $33,916 out of state; room/board: $11,218
Financial aid: (919) 962-8396; 43% of undergrads determined to have financial need; average aid package $19,538

University of North Carolina– Charlotte

Charlotte NC
(704) 687-5507
U.S. News ranking: Nat. U., No. 202
Website: www.uncc.edu/
Admissions email: admissions@uncc.edu
Public; founded 1946
Freshman admissions: selective; 2015-2016: 16,383 applied, 10,372 accepted. Either SAT or ACT required. SAT 25/75 percentile: 1010-1180. High school rank: 22% in top tenth, 57% in top quarter, 87% in top half
Early decision deadline: N/A, notification date: N/A
Early action deadline: 11/1, notification date: 1/30
Application deadline (fall): 6/1
Undergraduate student body: 19,765 full time, 2,967 part time; 52% male, 48% female; 0% American Indian, 6% Asian, 17% black, 9% Hispanic, 4% multiracial, 0% Pacific Islander, 60% white, 2% international; 95% from in state; 23% live on campus; 8% of students in fraternities, 11% in sororities
Most popular majors: 18% Business, Management, Marketing, and Related Support Services; 9% Social Sciences; 8% Health Professions and Related Programs; 7% Engineering; 7% Psychology
Expenses: 2016-2017: $6,617 in state, $20,193 out of state; room/board: $11,940
Financial aid: (704) 687-2461; 64% of undergrads determined to have financial need; average aid package $10,587

University of North Carolina– Greensboro

Greensboro NC
(336) 334-5243
U.S. News ranking: Nat. U., No. 220
Website: www.uncg.edu/
Admissions email: admissions@uncg.edu
Public; founded 1891
Freshman admissions: selective; 2015-2016: 10,566 applied, 6,192 accepted. Either SAT or ACT required. SAT 25/75 percentile: 940-1110. High school rank: 13% in top tenth, 41% in top quarter, 79% in top half
Early decision deadline: N/A, notification date: N/A

Early action deadline: N/A, notification date: N/A
Application deadline (fall): 3/1
Undergraduate student body: 13,450 full time, 2,501 part time; 34% male, 66% female; 0% American Indian, 5% Asian, 28% black, 8% Hispanic, 4% multiracial, 0% Pacific Islander, 52% white, 2% international; 95% from in state; 34% live on campus; N/A of students in fraternities, N/A in sororities
Most popular majors: 18% Business, Management, Marketing, and Related Support Services; 9% Education; 8% Social Sciences; 8% Health Professions and Related Programs; 7% Visual and Performing Arts
Expenses: 2015-2016: $6,733 in state, $21,595 out of state; room/board: $8,252
Financial aid: (336) 334-5702

University of North Carolina–Pembroke
Pembroke NC
(910) 521-6262
U.S. News ranking: Reg. U. (S), No. 91
Website: www.uncp.edu
Admissions email: admissions@uncp.edu
Public; founded 1887
Freshman admissions: less selective; 2015-2016: 4,596 applied, 3,418 accepted. Either SAT or ACT required. SAT 25/75 percentile: 830-990. High school rank: 11% in top tenth, 34% in top quarter, 73% in top half
Early decision deadline: N/A, notification date: N/A
Early action deadline: N/A, notification date: N/A
Application deadline (fall): 7/31
Undergraduate student body: 4,572 full time, 1,108 part time; 39% male, 61% female; 15% American Indian, 2% Asian, 36% black, 6% Hispanic, 2% multiracial, 0% Pacific Islander, 37% white, 1% international; 98% from in state; 39% live on campus; 6% of students in fraternities, 3% in sororities
Most popular majors: 11% Business Administration and Management, General; 11% Sociology; 11% Criminal Justice/Safety Studies; 10% Health and Physical Education/Fitness, General; 10% Education, General
Expenses: 2016-2017: $5,816 in state, $16,760 out of state; room/board: $8,576
Financial aid: (910) 521-6255; 81% of undergrads determined to have financial need; average aid package $10,030

University of North Carolina School of the Arts
Winston-Salem NC
(336) 770-3291
U.S. News ranking: Arts, unranked
Website: www.uncsa.edu
Admissions email: admissions@uncsa.edu
Public; founded 1963
Freshman admissions: N/A; 2015-2016: 887 applied, 305

accepted. Either SAT or ACT required. SAT 25/75 percentile: N/A. High school rank: 16% in top tenth, 43% in top quarter, 76% in top half
Early decision deadline: N/A, notification date: N/A
Early action deadline: N/A, notification date: N/A
Application deadline (fall): 3/15
Undergraduate student body: 838 full time, 18 part time; 49% male, 51% female; 0% American Indian, 2% Asian, 9% black, 8% Hispanic, 5% multiracial, 0% Pacific Islander, 72% white, 2% international; 51% from in state; 63% live on campus; N/A of students in fraternities, N/A in sororities
Most popular majors: 42% Cinematography and Film/Video Production; 22% Technical Theatre/Theatre Design and Technology; 15% Music Performance, General; 14% Drama and Dramatics/Theatre Arts, General; 7% Dance, General
Expenses: 2016-2017: $9,139 in state, $24,609 out of state; room/board: $8,779
Financial aid: (336) 770-3297; 63% of undergrads determined to have financial need; average aid package $13,104

University of North Carolina–Wilmington
Wilmington NC
(910) 962-3243
U.S. News ranking: Reg. U. (S), No. 16
Website: www.uncw.edu
Admissions email: admissions@uncw.edu
Public; founded 1947
Freshman admissions: more selective; 2015-2016: 11,444 applied, 6,976 accepted. Either SAT or ACT required. ACT 25/75 percentile: 23-27. High school rank: 24% in top tenth, 63% in top quarter, 95% in top half
Early decision deadline: N/A, notification date: N/A
Early action deadline: 11/1, notification date: 1/20
Application deadline (fall): 2/1
Undergraduate student body: 11,635 full time, 1,583 part time; 39% male, 61% female; 1% American Indian, 2% Asian, 5% black, 5% Hispanic, 3% multiracial, 0% Pacific Islander, 78% white, 1% international; 87% from in state; 31% live on campus; 4% of students in fraternities, 9% in sororities
Most popular majors: 19% Business, Management, Marketing, and Related Support Services; 10% Health Professions and Related Programs; 9% Biological and Biomedical Sciences; 9% Social Sciences; 8% Education
Expenses: 2016-2017: $6,952 in state, $20,920 out of state; room/board: $10,060
Financial aid: (910) 962-3177; 56% of undergrads determined to have financial need; average aid package $9,823

Wake Forest University
Winston-Salem NC
(336) 758-5201
U.S. News ranking: Nat. U., No. 27
Website: www.wfu.edu
Admissions email: admissions@wfu.edu
Private; founded 1834
Freshman admissions: most selective; 2015-2016: 13,281 applied, 3,903 accepted. Neither SAT nor ACT required. SAT 25/75 percentile: 1200-1410. High school rank: 77% in top tenth, 93% in top quarter, 98% in top half
Early decision deadline: 11/15, notification date: N/A
Early action deadline: N/A, notification date: N/A
Application deadline (fall): 1/1
Undergraduate student body: 4,807 full time, 64 part time; 47% male, 53% female; 0% American Indian, 5% Asian, 6% black, 7% Hispanic, 3% multiracial, 0% Pacific Islander, 72% white, 7% international; 22% from in state; 77% live on campus; 35% of students in fraternities, 57% in sororities
Most popular majors: Information not available
Expenses: 2016-2017: $49,308; room/board: $14,748
Financial aid: (336) 758-5154; 33% of undergrads determined to have financial need; average aid package $44,843

Warren Wilson College
Asheville NC
(800) 934-3536
U.S. News ranking: Nat. Lib. Arts, No. 159
Website: www.warren-wilson.edu
Admissions email: admit@warren-wilson.edu
Private; founded 1894
Freshman admissions: more selective; 2015-2016: 809 applied, 678 accepted. Neither SAT nor ACT required. ACT 25/75 percentile: 21-28. High school rank: 17% in top tenth, 53% in top quarter, 77% in top half
Early decision deadline: 11/15, notification date: 12/1
Early action deadline: 11/1, notification date: 12/1
Application deadline (fall): rolling
Undergraduate student body: 741 full time, 12 part time; 40% male, 60% female; 1% American Indian, 1% Asian, 4% black, 9% Hispanic, 3% multiracial, 0% Pacific Islander, 76% white, 2% international; 26% from in state; 88% live on campus; 0% of students in fraternities, 0% in sororities
Most popular majors: 9% Visual and Performing Arts, General; 9% Psychology, General; 7% Social Work; 7% Creative Writing
Expenses: 2016-2017: $33,970; room/board: $10,250
Financial aid: (828) 771-2082; 76% of undergrads determined to have financial need; average aid package $29,978

Western Carolina University
Cullowhee NC
(828) 227-7317
U.S. News ranking: Reg. U. (S), No. 37
Website: www.wcu.edu
Admissions email: admiss@email.wcu.edu
Public; founded 1889
Freshman admissions: selective; 2015-2016: 17,702 applied, 7,127 accepted. Either SAT or ACT required. ACT 25/75 percentile: 20-24. High school rank: 11% in top tenth, 38% in top quarter, 80% in top half
Early decision deadline: N/A, notification date: N/A
Early action deadline: 11/15, notification date: 12/15
Application deadline (fall): 3/1
Undergraduate student body: 7,440 full time, 1,381 part time; 45% male, 55% female; 1% American Indian, 1% Asian, 6% black, 6% Hispanic, 4% multiracial, 0% Pacific Islander, 79% white, 2% international; 93% from in state; N/A live on campus; N/A of students in fraternities, N/A in sororities
Most popular majors: 18% Health Professions and Related Programs; 16% Business, Management, Marketing, and Related Support Services; 13% Education; 8% Homeland Security, Law Enforcement, Firefighting and Related Protective Services; 6% Psychology
Expenses: 2015-2016: $6,903 in state, $17,296 out of state; room/board: N/A
Financial aid: (828) 227-7290; 68% of undergrads determined to have financial need; average aid package $11,557

William Peace University[1]
Raleigh NC
(919) 508-2214
U.S. News ranking: Nat. Lib. Arts, second tier
Website: www.peace.edu
Admissions email: admissions@peace.edu
Private; founded 1857
Affiliation: Presbyterian Church (USA)
Application deadline (fall): rolling
Undergraduate student body: N/A full time, N/A part time
Expenses: 2015-2016: $25,850; room/board: $9,900
Financial aid: (919) 508-2249

Wingate University
Wingate NC
(800) 755-5550
U.S. News ranking: Reg. U. (S), No. 37
Website: www.wingate.edu/admissions
Admissions email: admit@wingate.edu
Private; founded 1896
Freshman admissions: selective; 2015-2016: 8,018 applied, 5,597 accepted. Either SAT or ACT required. SAT 25/75 percentile: 930-1130. High school rank: 19% in top tenth, 49% in top quarter, 86% in top half

Early decision deadline: N/A, notification date: N/A
Early action deadline: N/A, notification date: N/A
Application deadline (fall): rolling
Undergraduate student body: 1,969 full time, 54 part time; 40% male, 60% female; 0% American Indian, 2% Asian, 16% black, 3% Hispanic, 4% multiracial, 0% Pacific Islander, 63% white, 5% international; 78% from in state; 77% live on campus; 4% of students in fraternities, 10% in sororities
Most popular majors: 15% Business, Management, Marketing, and Related Support Services; 14% Biological and Biomedical Sciences; 11% Parks, Recreation, Leisure, and Fitness Studies; 11% Psychology
Expenses: 2016-2017: $29,170; room/board: $10,780
Financial aid: (704) 233-8209; 81% of undergrads determined to have financial need; average aid package $22,679

Winston-Salem State University[1]
Winston-Salem NC
(336) 750-2070
U.S. News ranking: Reg. U. (S), No. 91
Website: www.wssu.edu
Admissions email: admissions@wssu.edu
Public; founded 1892
Application deadline (fall): 3/15
Undergraduate student body: N/A full time, N/A part time
Expenses: 2015-2016: $5,707 in state, $15,523 out of state; room/board: $9,503
Financial aid: (336) 750-3280

NORTH DAKOTA

Bismarck State College
Bismarck ND
(701) 224-2459
U.S. News ranking: Reg. Coll. (Mid. W), No. 56
Website: www.bismarckstate.edu
Admissions email: bsc.admissions@bismarckstate.edu
Public; founded 1939
Freshman admissions: less selective; 2015-2016: 1,067 applied, 1,067 accepted. Neither SAT nor ACT required. ACT 25/75 percentile: 17-23. High school rank: 3% in top tenth, 11% in top quarter, 36% in top half
Early decision deadline: N/A, notification date: N/A
Early action deadline: N/A, notification date: N/A
Application deadline (fall): rolling
Undergraduate student body: 2,281 full time, 1,797 part time; 57% male, 43% female; 2% American Indian, 1% Asian, 4% black, 3% Hispanic, 3% multiracial, 0% Pacific Islander, 86% white, 0% international; 75% from in state; 11% live on campus; 0% of students in fraternities, 0% in sororities
Most popular majors: 100% Operations Management and Supervision

Expenses: 2015-2016: $3,604 in state, $8,383 out of state; room/board: $7,151
Financial aid: (701) 224-5494

Dickinson State University
Dickinson ND
(701) 483-2175
U.S. News ranking: Reg. Coll. (Mid. W), No. 43
Website: www.dickinsonstate.com
Admissions email: dsu.hawks@dsu.nodak.edu
Public; founded 1918
Freshman admissions: selective; 2015-2016: 521 applied, 321 accepted. Neither SAT nor ACT required. ACT 25/75 percentile: 18-22. High school rank: N/A
Early decision deadline: N/A, notification date: N/A
Early action deadline: 4/15, notification date: N/A
Application deadline (fall): 8/15
Undergraduate student body: 896 full time, 414 part time; 40% male, 60% female; 1% American Indian, 1% Asian, 4% black, 5% Hispanic, 3% multiracial, 0% Pacific Islander, 77% white, 6% international; 62% from in state; 21% live on campus; 0% of students in fraternities, 0% in sororities
Most popular majors: 35% Business, Management, Marketing, and Related Support Services; 21% Education; 9% Parks, Recreation, Leisure, and Fitness Studies; 6% Multi/Interdisciplinary Studies; 5% Health Professions and Related Programs
Expenses: 2016-2017: $6,348 in state, $8,918 out of state; room/board: $6,750
Financial aid: (701) 483-2371; 54% of undergrads determined to have financial need; average aid package $10,341

Mayville State University
Mayville ND
(701) 788-4667
U.S. News ranking: Reg. Coll. (Mid. W), No. 53
Website: www.mayvillestate.edu
Admissions email: masuadmissions@mayvillestate.edu
Public; founded 1889
Freshman admissions: selective; 2015-2016: 336 applied, 180 accepted. ACT required. ACT 25/75 percentile: 17-22. High school rank: N/A
Early decision deadline: N/A, notification date: N/A
Early action deadline: N/A, notification date: N/A
Application deadline (fall): rolling
Undergraduate student body: 638 full time, 453 part time; 43% male, 57% female; 1% American Indian, 0% Asian, 8% black, 5% Hispanic, 3% multiracial, 1% Pacific Islander, 78% white, 3% international; 57% from in state; 32% live on campus; 0% of students in fraternities, 0% in sororities
Most popular majors: Adult and Continuing Education and Teaching; Business Administration and Management,

General; General Studies; Physical Education Teaching and Coaching
Expenses: 2015-2016: $7,830 in state, $10,295 out of state; room/board: $6,976
Financial aid: (701) 788-4767

Minot State University
Minot ND
(701) 858-3350
U.S. News ranking: Reg. U. (Mid. W), second tier
Website: www.minotstateu.edu
Admissions email: askmsu@minotstateu.edu
Public; founded 1913
Freshman admissions: selective; 2015-2016: 840 applied, 477 accepted. Either SAT or ACT required. ACT 25/75 percentile: 19-24. High school rank: 6% in top tenth, 20% in top quarter, 60% in top half
Early decision deadline: N/A, notification date: N/A
Early action deadline: N/A, notification date: N/A
Application deadline (fall): rolling
Undergraduate student body: 2,021 full time, 1,043 part time; 39% male, 61% female; 1% American Indian, 2% Asian, 6% black, 6% Hispanic, 4% multiracial, 0% Pacific Islander, 66% white, 13% international; 83% from in state; 21% live on campus; N/A of students in fraternities, N/A in sororities
Most popular majors: 22% Business Administration and Management, General; 20% Elementary Education and Teaching; 17% Registered Nursing/Registered Nurse; 12% Social Work; 6% Criminal Justice/Safety Studies
Expenses: 2016-2017: $6,568 in state, $6,568 out of state; room/board: $6,164
Financial aid: (701) 858-3375; 45% of undergrads determined to have financial need; average aid package $10,190

North Dakota State University
Fargo ND
(701) 231-8643
U.S. News ranking: Nat. U., No. 188
Website: www.ndsu.edu
Admissions email: NDSU.Admission@ndsu.edu
Public; founded 1890
Freshman admissions: selective; 2015-2016: 5,311 applied, 4,974 accepted. Either SAT or ACT required. ACT 25/75 percentile: 21-26. High school rank: 15% in top tenth, 41% in top quarter, 76% in top half
Early decision deadline: N/A, notification date: N/A
Early action deadline: N/A, notification date: N/A
Application deadline (fall): rolling
Undergraduate student body: 10,676 full time, 1,361 part time; 55% male, 45% female; 1% American Indian, 1% Asian, 3% black, 2% Hispanic, 2% multiracial, 0% Pacific Islander, 87% white, 2% international; 43% from in state; 36% live on campus; 5% of students in fraternities, 2% in sororities

Most popular majors: 15% Health Professions and Related Programs; 15% Business, Management, Marketing, and Related Support Services; 14% Engineering; 7% Biological and Biomedical Sciences
Expenses: 2016-2017: $9,046 in state, $19,790 out of state; room/board: $8,136
Financial aid: (800) 726-3188; 51% of undergrads determined to have financial need; average aid package $11,266

University of Jamestown
Jamestown ND
(701) 252-3467
U.S. News ranking: Reg. Coll. (Mid. W), No. 24
Website: www.jc.edu
Admissions email: admissions@jc.edu
Private; founded 1884
Affiliation: Presbyterian
Freshman admissions: selective; 2015-2016: 1,131 applied, 735 accepted. Either SAT or ACT required. ACT 25/75 percentile: 18-28. High school rank: 20% in top tenth, 41% in top quarter, 79% in top half
Early decision deadline: N/A, notification date: N/A
Early action deadline: N/A, notification date: N/A
Application deadline (fall): rolling
Undergraduate student body: 846 full time, 42 part time; 48% male, 52% female; 1% American Indian, 2% Asian, 5% black, 7% Hispanic, 0% multiracial, 1% Pacific Islander, 78% white, 6% international; 47% from in state; 76% live on campus; N/A of students in fraternities, N/A in sororities
Most popular majors: 19% Registered Nursing/Registered Nurse; 8% Business Administration and Management, General; 8% Kinesiology and Exercise Science; 7% Elementary Education and Teaching; 5% Criminal Justice/Safety Studies
Expenses: 2016-2017: $20,480; room/board: $7,066
Financial aid: (701) 252-3467; 65% of undergrads determined to have financial need; average aid package $15,952

University of Mary
Bismarck ND
(701) 355-8030
U.S. News ranking: Reg. U. (Mid. W), No. 94
Website: www.umary.edu
Admissions email: marauder@umary.edu
Private; founded 1959
Affiliation: Christian, Catholic, and Benedictine.
Freshman admissions: selective; 2015-2016: 982 applied, 803 accepted. Either SAT or ACT required. ACT 25/75 percentile: 20-26. High school rank: 15% in top tenth, 45% in top quarter, 77% in top half
Early decision deadline: N/A, notification date: N/A
Early action deadline: N/A, notification date: N/A
Application deadline (fall): rolling
Undergraduate student body: 784 full time, 494 part time; 40% male, 60% female; 1% American Indian, 0% Asian, 4% black, 6% Hispanic, 3% multiracial, 0% Pacific Islander, 81% white,

Undergraduate student body: 1,706 full time, 343 part time; 36% male, 64% female; 2% American Indian, 1% Asian, 2% black, 4% Hispanic, 2% multiracial, 0% Pacific Islander, 84% white, 1% international
Most popular majors: Information not available
Expenses: 2016-2017: $17,644; room/board: $6,482
Financial aid: (701) 355-8079; 63% of undergrads determined to have financial need; average aid package $12,152

University of North Dakota
Grand Forks ND
(800) 225-5863
U.S. News ranking: Nat. U., No. 202
Website: und.edu
Admissions email: admissions@und.edu
Public; founded 1883
Freshman admissions: selective; 2015-2016: 4,920 applied, 4,029 accepted. Either SAT or ACT required. ACT 25/75 percentile: 21-26. High school rank: 17% in top tenth, 41% in top quarter, 77% in top half
Early decision deadline: N/A, notification date: N/A
Early action deadline: N/A, notification date: N/A
Application deadline (fall): rolling
Undergraduate student body: 9,120 full time, 2,457 part time; 57% male, 43% female; 1% American Indian, 2% Asian, 2% black, 3% Hispanic, 3% multiracial, 0% Pacific Islander, 83% white, 4% international; 40% from in state; 29% live on campus; 10% of students in fraternities, 11% in sororities
Most popular majors: 7% Registered Nursing/Registered Nurse; 6% Psychology, General; 5% Airline/Commercial/Professional Pilot and Flight Crew; 5% Mechanical Engineering; 4% Biology/Biological Sciences, General
Expenses: 2015-2016: $4,965 in state, $18,899 out of state; room/board: $7,492
Financial aid: (701) 777-3121

Valley City State University
Valley City ND
(701) 845-7101
U.S. News ranking: Reg. Coll. (Mid. W), No. 33
Website: www.vcsu.edu
Admissions email: enrollment.services@vcsu.edu
Public; founded 1890
Freshman admissions: selective; 2015-2016: 403 applied, 348 accepted. Either SAT or ACT required. ACT 25/75 percentile: 18-23. High school rank: N/A
Early decision deadline: N/A, notification date: N/A
Early action deadline: N/A, notification date: N/A
Application deadline (fall): rolling
Undergraduate student body: 784 full time, 494 part time; 40% male, 60% female; 1% American Indian, 0% Asian, 4% black, 6% Hispanic, 3% multiracial, 0% Pacific Islander, 81% white,

3% international; 64% from in state; 35% live on campus; 1% of students in fraternities, 1% in sororities
Most popular majors: 40% Elementary Education and Teaching; 12% Business Administration and Management, General; 4% Biology/Biological Sciences, General; 4% Health and Physical Education/Fitness, General
Expenses: 2016-2017: $7,196 in state, $16,016 out of state; room/board: $6,352
Financial aid: (701) 845-7412; 58% of undergrads determined to have financial need; average aid package $11,899

OHIO

Antioch University[1]
Yellow Springs OH
(937) 769-1818
U.S. News ranking: Reg. U. (Mid. W), unranked
Website: midwest.antioch.edu
Admissions email: admission. aum@antioch.edu
Private; founded 1852
Application deadline (fall): rolling
Undergraduate student body: N/A full time, N/A part time
Expenses: 2016-2017: $16,010; room/board: N/A
Financial aid: N/A

Art Academy of Cincinnati[1]
Cincinnati OH
(513) 562-8740
U.S. News ranking: Arts, unranked
Website: www.artacademy.edu
Admissions email: admissions@artacademy.edu
Private; founded 1869
Application deadline (fall): rolling
Undergraduate student body: N/A full time, N/A part time
Expenses: 2015-2016: $27,788; room/board: $9,100
Financial aid: (513) 562-8751

Ashland University
Ashland OH
(419) 289-5052
U.S. News ranking: Nat. U., No. 214
Website: www.ashland.edu/admissions
Admissions email: enrollme@ashland.edu
Private; founded 1878
Affiliation: Brethren Church
Freshman admissions: selective; 2015-2016: 3,470 applied, 2,556 accepted. Either SAT or ACT required. ACT 25/75 percentile: 20-25. High school rank: 18% in top tenth, 48% in top quarter, 78% in top half
Early decision deadline: N/A, notification date: N/A
Early action deadline: N/A, notification date: N/A
Application deadline (fall): rolling
Undergraduate student body: 2,609 full time, 1,107 part time; 47% male, 53% female; 0% American Indian, 1% Asian, 5% black, 3% Hispanic, 2% multiracial, 0% Pacific Islander, 67% white, 2% international

Most popular majors: 19% Nursing Practice; 4% Business Administration and Management, General; 4% Education/Teaching of Individuals with Multiple Disabilities; 4% Exercise Physiology
Expenses: 2016-2017: $20,392; room/board: $9,602
Financial aid: (419) 289-5002; 75% of undergrads determined to have financial need; average aid package $17,081

Baldwin Wallace University
Berea OH
(440) 826-2222
U.S. News ranking: Reg. U. (Mid. W), No. 15
Website: www.bw.edu
Admissions email: admission@bw.edu
Private; founded 1845
Affiliation: United Methodist
Freshman admissions: selective; 2015-2016: 4,363 applied, 2,626 accepted. Neither SAT nor ACT required. ACT 25/75 percentile: 20-27. High school rank: 19% in top tenth, 45% in top quarter, 81% in top half
Early decision deadline: N/A, notification date: N/A
Early action deadline: N/A, notification date: N/A
Application deadline (fall): rolling
Undergraduate student body: 3,056 full time, 326 part time; 45% male, 55% female; 0% American Indian, 1% Asian, 9% black, 5% Hispanic, 5% multiracial, 0% Pacific Islander, 78% white, 1% international; 79% from in state; 63% live on campus; 13% of students in fraternities, 24% in sororities
Most popular majors: 22% Business, Management, Marketing, and Related Support Services; 11% Health Professions and Related Programs; 11% Visual and Performing Arts; 9% Education; 9% Biological and Biomedical Sciences
Expenses: 2016-2017: $30,776; room/board: $8,748
Financial aid: (440) 826-2108; 75% of undergrads determined to have financial need; average aid package $23,601

Bluffton University
Bluffton OH
(800) 488-3257
U.S. News ranking: Reg. Coll. (Mid. W), No. 29
Website: www.bluffton.edu
Admissions email: admissions@bluffton.edu
Private; founded 1899
Affiliation: Mennonite Church USA
Freshman admissions: selective; 2015-2016: 1,652 applied, 885 accepted. Either SAT or ACT required. ACT 25/75 percentile: 18-23. High school rank: 12% in top tenth, 25% in top quarter, 67% in top half
Early decision deadline: N/A, notification date: N/A
Early action deadline: N/A, notification date: N/A
Application deadline (fall): rolling
Undergraduate student body: 746 full time, 164 part time; 48% male, 52% female; 0% American

Indian, 0% Asian, 6% black, 4% Hispanic, 3% multiracial, 0% Pacific Islander, 85% white, 0% international; 88% from in state; 88% live on campus; 0% of students in fraternities, 0% in sororities
Most popular majors: 17% Organizational Behavior Studies; 16% Social Work; 10% Business Administration and Management, General; 7% Sport and Fitness Administration/Management
Expenses: 2016-2017: $30,762; room/board: $10,188
Financial aid: (419) 358-3266; 87% of undergrads determined to have financial need; average aid package $25,468

Bowling Green State University
Bowling Green OH
(419) 372-2478
U.S. News ranking: Nat. U., No. 194
Website: www.bgsu.edu
Admissions email: choosebgsu@bgsu.edu
Public; founded 1910
Freshman admissions: selective; 2015-2016: 14,887 applied, 11,240 accepted. Either SAT or ACT required. ACT 25/75 percentile: 20-25. High school rank: 12% in top tenth, 36% in top quarter, 71% in top half
Early decision deadline: N/A, notification date: N/A
Early action deadline: N/A, notification date: N/A
Application deadline (fall): 7/15
Undergraduate student body: 13,214 full time, 1,120 part time; 43% male, 57% female; 0% American Indian, 1% Asian, 10% black, 4% Hispanic, 3% multiracial, 0% Pacific Islander, 78% white, 2% international; 88% from in state; 42% live on campus; 12% of students in fraternities, 11% in sororities
Most popular majors: 5% Liberal Arts and Sciences/Liberal Studies; 4% Education, Other; 4% Psychology, General; 4% Biology/Biological Sciences, General; 4% Kindergarten/Preschool Education and Teaching
Expenses: 2015-2016: $10,796 in state, $18,332 out of state; room/board: N/A
Financial aid: (419) 372-2651; 69% of undergrads determined to have financial need; average aid package $14,008

Capital University
Columbus OH
(866) 544-6175
U.S. News ranking: Reg. U. (Mid. W), No. 38
Website: www.capital.edu
Admissions email: admission@capital.edu
Private; founded 1830
Affiliation: Lutheran
Freshman admissions: selective; 2015-2016: 3,718 applied, 2,685 accepted. Either SAT or ACT required. ACT 25/75 percentile: 22-28. High school rank: 16% in top tenth, 47% in top quarter, 81% in top half
Early decision deadline: N/A, notification date: N/A

Early action deadline: N/A, notification date: N/A
Application deadline (fall): 5/1
Undergraduate student body: 2,514 full time, 251 part time; 42% male, 58% female; 0% American Indian, 1% Asian, 10% black, 4% Hispanic, 5% multiracial, 0% Pacific Islander, 75% white, 2% international; 90% from in state; 59% live on campus; 3% of students in fraternities, 6% in sororities
Most popular majors: 19% Health Professions and Related Programs; 12% Business, Management, Marketing, and Related Support Services; 12% Education; 11% Visual and Performing Arts; 9% Social Sciences
Expenses: 2016-2017: $33,492; room/board: $9,790
Financial aid: (614) 236-6511; 82% of undergrads determined to have financial need; average aid package $27,112

Case Western Reserve University
Cleveland OH
(216) 368-4450
U.S. News ranking: Nat. U., No. 37
Website: www.case.edu
Admissions email: admission@case.edu
Private; founded 1826
Freshman admissions: most selective; 2015-2016: 22,807 applied, 8,271 accepted. Either SAT or ACT required. ACT 25/75 percentile: 30-33. High school rank: 71% in top tenth, 91% in top quarter, 99% in top half
Early decision deadline: 11/1, notification date: 12/15
Early action deadline: 11/1, notification date: 12/15
Application deadline (fall): 1/15
Undergraduate student body: 5,019 full time, 102 part time; 55% male, 45% female; 0% American Indian, 20% Asian, 5% black, 6% Hispanic, 4% multiracial, 0% Pacific Islander, 52% white, 11% international; 40% from in state; 80% live on campus; 34% of students in fraternities, 39% in sororities
Most popular majors: 10% Registered Nursing/Registered Nurse; 9% Biology/Biological Sciences, General; 9% Mechanical Engineering; 8% Bioengineering and Biomedical Engineering; 8% Psychology, General
Expenses: 2016-2017: $46,006; room/board: $14,298
Financial aid: (216) 368-3866; 51% of undergrads determined to have financial need; average aid package $39,782

Cedarville University
Cedarville OH
(800) 233-2784
U.S. News ranking: Reg. Coll. (Mid. W), No. 12
Website: www.cedarville.edu
Admissions email: admissions@cedarville.edu
Private; founded 1887
Affiliation: Baptist

Freshman admissions: more selective; 2015-2016: 3,159 applied, 2,344 accepted. Either SAT or ACT required. ACT 25/75 percentile: 23-28. High school rank: 30% in top tenth, 61% in top quarter, 86% in top half
Early decision deadline: N/A, notification date: N/A
Early action deadline: N/A, notification date: N/A
Application deadline (fall): 8/1
Undergraduate student body: 3,014 full time, 339 part time; 48% male, 52% female; 0% American Indian, 2% Asian, 2% black, 3% Hispanic, 3% multiracial, 0% Pacific Islander, 87% white, 2% international; 39% from in state; 84% live on campus; 0% of students in fraternities, 0% in sororities
Most popular majors: 19% Health Professions and Related Programs; 11% Engineering; 10% Education; 8% Business, Management, Marketing, and Related Support Services
Expenses: 2016-2017: $28,110; room/board: $6,880
Financial aid: (937) 766-7866; 67% of undergrads determined to have financial need; average aid package $18,493

Central State University
Wilberforce OH
(937) 376-6348
U.S. News ranking: Reg. Coll. (Mid. W), second tier
Website: www.centralstate.edu
Admissions email: admissions@centralstate.edu
Public; founded 1887
Freshman admissions: less selective; 2015-2016: 6,502 applied, 2,568 accepted. Either SAT or ACT required. ACT 25/75 percentile: 14-18. High school rank: 7% in top tenth, 20% in top quarter, 48% in top half
Early decision deadline: N/A, notification date: N/A
Early action deadline: N/A, notification date: N/A
Application deadline (fall): rolling
Undergraduate student body: 1,649 full time, 143 part time; 45% male, 55% female; 0% American Indian, 0% Asian, 95% black, 1% Hispanic, 1% multiracial, 0% Pacific Islander, 1% white, 1% international; 57% from in state; 62% live on campus; 1% of students in fraternities, 1% in sororities
Most popular majors: 27% Business, Management, Marketing, and Related Support Services; 14% Psychology; 13% Education; 11% Homeland Security, Law Enforcement, Firefighting and Related Protective Services
Expenses: 2016-2017: $6,246 in state, $8,096 out of state; room/board: $9,934
Financial aid: (937) 376-6579; 75% of undergrads determined to have financial need

Cleveland Institute of Art
Cleveland OH
(216) 421-7418
U.S. News ranking: Arts, unranked
Website: www.cia.edu
Admissions email: admissions@cia.edu
Private; founded 1882
Freshman admissions: N/A; 2015-2016: 738 applied, 479 accepted. Either SAT or ACT required. SAT 25/75 percentile: N/A. High school rank: 17% in top tenth, 36% in top quarter, 74% in top half
Early decision deadline: N/A, notification date: N/A
Early action deadline: 12/1, notification date: 12/15
Application deadline (fall): rolling
Undergraduate student body: 600 full time, 6 part time; 43% male, 57% female; 0% American Indian, 4% Asian, 9% black, 5% Hispanic, 4% multiracial, N/A Pacific Islander, 69% white, 10% international; 65% from in state; 35% live on campus; N/A of students in fraternities, N/A in sororities
Most popular majors: 23% Industrial and Product Design; 10% Painting; 6% Drawing; 6% Medical Illustration/Medical Illustrator
Expenses: 2016-2017: $39,585; room/board: $11,854
Financial aid: (216) 421-7425; 79% of undergrads determined to have financial need; average aid package $28,164

Cleveland Institute of Music
Cleveland OH
(216) 795-3107
U.S. News ranking: Arts, unranked
Website: www.cim.edu/
Admissions email: admission@cim.edu
Private; founded 1920
Freshman admissions: N/A; 2015-2016: 442 applied, 223 accepted. Neither SAT nor ACT required. SAT 25/75 percentile: N/A. High school rank: N/A
Early decision deadline: N/A, notification date: N/A
Early action deadline: N/A, notification date: N/A
Application deadline (fall): 12/1
Undergraduate student body: 236 full time, 2 part time; 50% male, 50% female; 0% American Indian, 0% Asian, 0% black, 0% Hispanic, N/A multiracial, N/A Pacific Islander, 4% white, 20% international
Most popular majors: Information not available
Expenses: 2016-2017: $48,656; room/board: $14,382
Financial aid: (216) 791-5000; 61% of undergrads determined to have financial need; average aid package $33,332

Cleveland State University
Cleveland OH
(216) 687-2100
U.S. News ranking: Nat. U., second tier
Website: www.csuohio.edu
Admissions email: admissions@csuohio.edu
Public; founded 1964
Freshman admissions: selective; 2015-2016: 7,544 applied, 4,876 accepted. Either SAT or ACT required. Either SAT percentile: 19-25. High school rank: 15% in top tenth, 39% in top quarter, 71% in top half
Early decision deadline: N/A, notification date: N/A
Early action deadline: 5/1, notification date: N/A
Application deadline (fall): 8/16
Undergraduate student body: 9,135 full time, 3,308 part time; 48% male, 52% female; 0% American Indian, 3% Asian, 17% black, 4% Hispanic, 3% multiracial, 0% Pacific Islander, 64% white, 3% international; 96% from in state; 8% live on campus; 1% of students in fraternities, 1% in sororities
Most popular majors: Information not available
Expenses: 2016-2017: $9,786 in state, $13,028 out of state; room/board: $10,648
Financial aid: (216) 687-2054; 65% of undergrads determined to have financial need; average aid package $8,839

College of Wooster
Wooster OH
(800) 877-9905
U.S. News ranking: Nat. Lib. Arts, No. 62
Website: www.wooster.edu/
Admissions email: admissions@wooster.edu
Private; founded 1866
Freshman admissions: more selective; 2015-2016: 5,748 applied, 3,178 accepted. Either SAT or ACT required. ACT 25/75 percentile: 25-30. High school rank: 46% in top tenth, 70% in top quarter, 92% in top half
Early decision deadline: 11/1, notification date: 11/15
Early action deadline: 11/15, notification date: 12/31
Application deadline (fall): 2/15
Undergraduate student body: 2,027 full time, 23 part time; 45% male, 55% female; 1% American Indian, 5% Asian, 8% black, 5% Hispanic, 0% multiracial, 0% Pacific Islander, 69% white, 9% international; 39% from in state; 99% live on campus; 18% of students in fraternities, 25% in sororities
Most popular majors: 24% Social Sciences; 13% Biological and Biomedical Sciences; 9% Philosophy and Religious Studies; 8% History; 7% Physical Sciences
Expenses: 2016-2017: $46,860; room/board: $11,040
Financial aid: (330) 263-2317; 63% of undergrads determined to have financial need; average aid package $39,377

Columbus College of Art and Design
Columbus OH
(614) 222-3261
U.S. News ranking: Arts, unranked
Website: www.ccad.edu
Admissions email: admissions@ccad.edu
Private; founded 1879
Freshman admissions: N/A; 2015-2016: 696 applied, 544 accepted. Neither SAT nor ACT required. SAT 25/75 percentile: N/A. High school rank: N/A
Early decision deadline: N/A, notification date: N/A
Early action deadline: 12/1, notification date: 12/20
Application deadline (fall): 8/22
Undergraduate student body: 1,038 full time, 48 part time; 36% male, 64% female; 0% American Indian, 3% Asian, 10% black, 5% Hispanic, 5% multiracial, 0% Pacific Islander, 67% white, 8% international; 83% from in state; 37% live on campus; N/A of students in fraternities, N/A in sororities
Most popular majors: Information not available
Expenses: 2016-2017: $33,480; room/board: $9,150
Financial aid: (614) 222-3295; 79% of undergrads determined to have financial need; average aid package $21,630

Defiance College
Defiance OH
(800) 520-4632
U.S. News ranking: Reg. Coll. (Mid. W), No. 38
Website: www.defiance.edu
Admissions email: admissions@defiance.edu
Private; founded 1850
Affiliation: United Church of Christ
Freshman admissions: selective; 2015-2016: 1,197 applied, 787 accepted. Either SAT or ACT required. ACT 25/75 percentile: 19-24. High school rank: 11% in top tenth, 19% in top quarter, 69% in top half
Early decision deadline: N/A, notification date: N/A
Early action deadline: N/A, notification date: N/A
Application deadline (fall): rolling
Undergraduate student body: 571 full time, 95 part time; 53% male, 47% female; 0% American Indian, 1% Asian, 8% black, 6% Hispanic, 3% multiracial, N/A Pacific Islander, 80% white, 2% international; 72% from in state; 50% live on campus; 6% of students in fraternities, 6% in sororities
Most popular majors: 23% Business Administration and Management, General; 17% Education, General; 14% Sport and Fitness Administration/Management; 12% Criminal Justice/Police Science; 6% Social Work
Expenses: 2016-2017: $31,680; room/board: $9,950
Financial aid: (419) 783-2376; 88% of undergrads determined to have financial need; average aid package $23,106

Denison University
Granville OH
(740) 587-6276
U.S. News ranking: Nat. Lib. Arts, No. 51
Website: www.denison.edu
Admissions email: admissions@denison.edu
Private; founded 1831
Freshman admissions: more selective; 2015-2016: 6,110 applied, 2,932 accepted. Neither SAT nor ACT required. ACT 25/75 percentile: 26-31. High school rank: 55% in top tenth, 78% in top quarter, 96% in top half
Early decision deadline: 11/15, notification date: N/A
Early action deadline: N/A, notification date: N/A
Application deadline (fall): 1/15
Undergraduate student body: 2,253 full time, 29 part time; 43% male, 57% female; 0% American Indian, 4% Asian, 7% black, 10% Hispanic, 4% multiracial, 0% Pacific Islander, 66% white, 8% international; 28% from in state; 99% live on campus; 21% of students in fraternities, 34% in sororities
Most popular majors: 29% Social Sciences; 11% Biological and Biomedical Sciences; 8% Psychology; 7% Visual and Performing Arts
Expenses: 2016-2017: $48,960; room/board: $11,970
Financial aid: (740) 587-6279; 53% of undergrads determined to have financial need; average aid package $40,899

Franciscan University of Steubenville
Steubenville OH
(740) 283-6226
U.S. News ranking: Reg. U. (Mid. W), No. 22
Website: www.franciscan.edu
Admissions email: admissions@franciscan.edu
Private; founded 1946
Affiliation: Roman Catholic
Freshman admissions: more selective; 2015-2016: 1,741 applied, 1,368 accepted. Either SAT or ACT required. ACT 25/75 percentile: 23-28. High school rank: 25% in top tenth, 55% in top quarter, 80% in top half
Early decision deadline: N/A, notification date: N/A
Early action deadline: N/A, notification date: N/A
Application deadline (fall): rolling
Undergraduate student body: 2,007 full time, 96 part time; 39% male, 61% female; 0% American Indian, 2% Asian, 1% black, 10% Hispanic, 2% multiracial, 0% Pacific Islander, 83% white, 1% international; 21% from in state; 79% live on campus; 0% of students in fraternities, 0% in sororities
Most popular majors: 27% Theology/Theological Studies; 10% Accounting; 10% Registered Nursing/Registered Nurse; 7% Psychology, General
Expenses: 2016-2017: $25,680; room/board: $8,300
Financial aid: (740) 283-6226; 63% of undergrads determined to have financial need; average aid package $14,871

Franklin University[1]
Columbus OH
(614) 341-6256
U.S. News ranking: Business, unranked
Website: www.franklin.edu
Admissions email: info@franklin.edu
Private; founded 1902
Application deadline (fall): rolling
Undergraduate student body: N/A full time, N/A part time
Expenses: 2015-2016: $11,641; room/board: $13,978
Financial aid: (614) 797-4700

Heidelberg University
Tiffin OH
(419) 448-2330
U.S. News ranking: Nat. Lib. Arts, second tier
Website: www.heidelberg.edu
Admissions email: adminfo@heidelberg.edu
Private; founded 1850
Affiliation: United Church of Christ
Freshman admissions: selective; 2015-2016: 1,147 applied, 905 accepted. Either SAT or ACT required. ACT 25/75 percentile: 19-25. High school rank: N/A
Early decision deadline: N/A, notification date: N/A
Early action deadline: N/A, notification date: N/A
Application deadline (fall): 8/1
Undergraduate student body: 1,014 full time, 20 part time; 52% male, 48% female; 0% American Indian, 1% Asian, 7% black, 2% Hispanic, 4% multiracial, 0% Pacific Islander, 76% white, 0% international; 85% from in state; 78% live on campus; 17% of students in fraternities, 35% in sororities
Most popular majors: 15% Business, Management, Marketing, and Related Support Services; 15% Health Professions and Related Programs; 9% Social Sciences; 8% Education; 7% Biological and Biomedical Sciences
Expenses: 2016-2017: $29,200; room/board: $10,000
Financial aid: (419) 448-2293; 88% of undergrads determined to have financial need; average aid package $23,317

Hiram College
Hiram OH
(800) 362-5280
U.S. News ranking: Nat. Lib. Arts, No. 149
Website: www.hiram.edu
Admissions email: admission@hiram.edu
Private; founded 1850
Freshman admissions: selective; 2015-2016: 1,864 applied, 1,074 accepted. Either SAT or ACT required. ACT 25/75 percentile: 20-27. High school rank: 17% in top tenth, 45% in top quarter, 77% in top half
Early decision deadline: N/A, notification date: N/A
Early action deadline: N/A, notification date: N/A
Application deadline (fall): rolling
Undergraduate student body: 912 full time, 188 part time; 48% male, 52% female; 0% American Indian, 1% Asian, 17% black,

4% Hispanic, 3% multiracial, 0% Pacific Islander, 68% white, 2% international; 81% from in state; 79% live on campus; 4% of students in fraternities, 9% in sororities
Most popular majors: 17% Accounting and Finance; 13% Business Administration and Management, General; 8% Registered Nursing/Registered Nurse; 5% Biology/Biological Sciences, General
Expenses: 2015-2016: $32,830; room/board: $10,190
Financial aid: (330) 569-5107

John Carroll University
University Heights OH
(216) 397-4294
U.S. News ranking: Reg. U. (Mid. W), No. 7
Website: www.jcu.edu
Admissions email: admission@jcu.edu
Private; founded 1886
Affiliation: Roman Catholic (Jesuit)
Freshman admissions: selective; 2015-2016: 4,087 applied, 3,352 accepted. Either SAT or ACT required. ACT 25/75 percentile: 22-28. High school rank: 19% in top tenth, 41% in top quarter, 79% in top half
Early decision deadline: N/A, notification date: N/A
Early action deadline: N/A, notification date: N/A
Application deadline (fall): 2/1
Undergraduate student body: 2,990 full time, 163 part time; 51% male, 49% female; 0% American Indian, 2% Asian, 5% black, 3% Hispanic, 2% multiracial, N/A Pacific Islander, 86% white, 2% international; 68% from in state; 58% live on campus; 10% of students in fraternities, 21% in sororities
Most popular majors: 27% Business, Management, Marketing, and Related Support Services; 13% Social Sciences; 9% Psychology; 8% Biological and Biomedical Sciences
Expenses: 2016-2017: $38,490; room/board: $11,250
Financial aid: (216) 397-4248; 72% of undergrads determined to have financial need; average aid package $29,415

Kent State University
Kent OH
(330) 672-2444
U.S. News ranking: Nat. U., No. 188
Website: www.kent.edu
Admissions email: kentadm@kent.edu
Public; founded 1910
Freshman admissions: selective; 2015-2016: 15,772 applied, 13,369 accepted. Either SAT or ACT required. ACT 25/75 percentile: 21-25. High school rank: 14% in top tenth, 39% in top quarter, 77% in top half
Early decision deadline: N/A, notification date: N/A
Early action deadline: N/A, notification date: N/A
Application deadline (fall): 5/1
Undergraduate student body: 20,660 full time, 2,947 part

time; 40% male, 60% female; 0% American Indian, 1% Asian, 9% black, 3% Hispanic, 3% multiracial, 0% Pacific Islander, 75% white, 6% international; 87% from in state; 28% live on campus; N/A of students in fraternities, N/A in sororities
Most popular majors: 20% Business, Management, Marketing, and Related Support Services; 18% Health Professions and Related Programs; 9% Education; 7% Psychology; 6% Visual and Performing Arts
Expenses: 2016-2017: $10,012 in state, $18,376 out of state; room/board: $10,720
Financial aid: (330) 672-2972; 63% of undergrads determined to have financial need; average aid package $10,028

Kenyon College
Gambier OH
(740) 427-5776
U.S. News ranking: Nat. Lib. Arts, No. 27
Website: www.kenyon.edu
Admissions email: admissions@kenyon.edu
Private; founded 1824
Freshman admissions: more selective; 2015-2016: 7,076 applied, 1,703 accepted. Either SAT or ACT required. SAT 25/75 percentile: 1240-1420. High school rank: 61% in top tenth, 84% in top quarter, 97% in top half
Early decision deadline: 11/15, notification date: 12/18
Early action deadline: N/A, notification date: N/A
Application deadline (fall): 1/15
Undergraduate student body: 1,699 full time, 12 part time; 45% male, 55% female; 0% American Indian, 4% Asian, 4% black, 7% Hispanic, 4% multiracial, 0% Pacific Islander, 73% white, 5% international; 17% from in state; 100% live on campus; 18% of students in fraternities, 20% in sororities
Most popular majors: 15% English Language and Literature, General; 10% Economics, General; 8% International/Global Studies; 6% Molecular Biology; 6% Political Science and Government, General
Expenses: 2016-2017: $51,200; room/board: $12,130
Financial aid: (740) 427-5430; 43% of undergrads determined to have financial need; average aid package $42,699

Lake Erie College
Painesville OH
(800) 916-0904
U.S. News ranking: Reg. U. (Mid. W), No. 115
Website: www.lec.edu
Admissions email: admissions@lec.edu
Private; founded 1856
Freshman admissions: selective; 2015-2016: 1,712 applied, 964 accepted. Neither SAT nor ACT required. ACT 25/75 percentile: 19-23. High school rank: N/A
Early decision deadline: N/A, notification date: N/A
Early action deadline: N/A, notification date: N/A

Application deadline (fall): 8/1
Undergraduate student body: 804 full time, 194 part time; 49% male, 51% female; 0% American Indian, 0% Asian, 10% black, 2% Hispanic, 3% multiracial, N/A Pacific Islander, 77% white, 4% international; 75% from in state; 62% live on campus; N/A of students in fraternities, N/A in sororities
Most popular majors: 27% Business, Management, Marketing, and Related Support Services; 12% Education; 10% Biological and Biomedical Sciences; 8% Homeland Security, Law Enforcement, Firefighting and Related Protective Services
Expenses: 2016-2017: $29,960; room/board: $9,178
Financial aid: (440) 375-7100; 82% of undergrads determined to have financial need; average aid package $22,722

Lourdes University
Sylvania OH
(419) 885-5291
U.S. News ranking: Reg. U. (Mid. W), second tier
Website: www.lourdes.edu
Admissions email: admissionslcadmits@lourdes.edu
Private; founded 1958
Affiliation: Roman Catholic
Freshman admissions: selective; 2015-2016: 692 applied, 479 accepted. Either SAT or ACT required. ACT 25/75 percentile: 18-24. High school rank: 6% in top tenth, 24% in top quarter, 57% in top half
Early decision deadline: N/A, notification date: N/A
Early action deadline: N/A, notification date: N/A
Application deadline (fall): rolling
Undergraduate student body: 878 full time, 359 part time; 30% male, 70% female; 0% American Indian, 0% Asian, 13% black, 7% Hispanic, 3% multiracial, 0% Pacific Islander, 74% white, 1% international
Most popular majors: 35% Registered Nursing/Registered Nurse; 9% Multi-/Interdisciplinary Studies, Other; 8% Social Work; 7% Accounting and Finance; 5% Business Administration and Management, General
Expenses: 2015-2016: $19,370; room/board: $9,100
Financial aid: (419) 824-3732

Malone University
Canton OH
(330) 471-8145
U.S. News ranking: Reg. U. (Mid. W), No. 69
Website: www.malone.edu
Admissions email: admissions@malone.edu
Private; founded 1892
Affiliation: Evangelical Friends
Freshman admissions: selective; 2015-2016: 1,168 applied, 804 accepted. Either SAT or ACT required. ACT 25/75 percentile: 19-25. High school rank: 13% in top tenth, 42% in top quarter, 72% in top half
Early decision deadline: N/A, notification date: N/A

Early action deadline: N/A, notification date: N/A
Application deadline (fall): rolling
Undergraduate student body: 1,171 full time, 196 part time; 40% male, 60% female; 0% American Indian, 1% Asian, 8% black, 3% Hispanic, 2% multiracial, 0% Pacific Islander, 85% white, 1% international; 87% from in state; 60% live on campus; 0% of students in fraternities, 0% in sororities
Most popular majors: 16% Registered Nursing/Registered Nurse; 13% Business Administration, Management and Operations, Other; 4% Kinesiology and Exercise Science
Expenses: 2016-2017: $29,422; room/board: $9,028
Financial aid: (330) 471-8159; 87% of undergrads determined to have financial need; average aid package $22,543

Marietta College
Marietta OH
(800) 331-7896
U.S. News ranking: Reg. Coll. (Mid. W), No. 8
Website: www.marietta.edu
Admissions email: admit@marietta.edu
Private; founded 1797
Freshman admissions: selective; 2015-2016: 2,863 applied, 2,062 accepted. Either SAT or ACT required. ACT 25/75 percentile: 21-27. High school rank: 30% in top tenth, 56% in top quarter, 84% in top half
Early decision deadline: N/A, notification date: N/A
Early action deadline: N/A, notification date: N/A
Application deadline (fall): 4/15
Undergraduate student body: 1,177 full time, 69 part time; 62% male, 38% female; 0% American Indian, 1% Asian, 6% black, 2% Hispanic, 3% multiracial, N/A Pacific Islander, 70% white, 14% international; 64% from in state; 76% live on campus; 10% of students in fraternities, 22% in sororities
Most popular majors: 25% Petroleum Engineering; 6% Marketing/Marketing Management, General; 6% Psychology, General; 4% Geology/Earth Science, General; 4% Sport and Fitness Administration/Management
Expenses: 2016-2017: $35,330; room/board: $11,100
Financial aid: (740) 376-4712; 72% of undergrads determined to have financial need; average aid package $28,439

Miami University–Oxford
Oxford OH
(513) 529-2531
U.S. News ranking: Nat. U., No. 79
Website: www.MiamiOH.edu
Admissions email: admission@MiamiOH.edu
Public; founded 1809
Freshman admissions: more selective; 2015-2016: 27,454 applied, 17,980 accepted. Either SAT or ACT required. ACT 25/75 percentile: 26-30. High school

rank: 36% in top tenth, 68% in top quarter, 94% in top half
Early decision deadline: 11/15, notification date: 12/15
Early action deadline: 12/1, notification date: 2/1
Application deadline (fall): 2/1
Undergraduate student body: 16,023 full time, 364 part time; 49% male, 51% female; 0% American Indian, 2% Asian, 3% black, 4% Hispanic, 3% multiracial, 0% Pacific Islander, 77% white, 10% international; 65% from in state; 46% live on campus; 23% of students in fraternities, 31% in sororities
Most popular majors: 26% Business, Management, Marketing, and Related Support Services; 8% Education; 8% Social Sciences; 7% Parks, Recreation, Leisure, and Fitness Studies
Expenses: 2016-2017: $14,288 in state, $31,592 out of state; room/board: $12,014
Financial aid: (513) 529-8734; 35% of undergrads determined to have financial need; average aid package $13,240

Mount St. Joseph University
Cincinnati OH
(513) 244-4531
U.S. News ranking: Reg. U. (Mid. W), No. 79
Website: www.msj.edu
Admissions email: admission@mail.msj.edu
Private; founded 1920
Affiliation: Catholic
Freshman admissions: selective; 2015-2016: 2,187 applied, 1,138 accepted. Either SAT or ACT required. ACT 25/75 percentile: 19-24. High school rank: 9% in top tenth, 34% in top quarter, 59% in top half
Early decision deadline: N/A, notification date: N/A
Early action deadline: N/A, notification date: N/A
Application deadline (fall): 8/15
Undergraduate student body: 1,098 full time, 307 part time; 43% male, 57% female; 0% American Indian, 1% Asian, 11% black, 1% Hispanic, 4% multiracial, 0% Pacific Islander, 78% white, 0% international; 84% from in state; 23% live on campus; N/A of students in fraternities, N/A in sororities
Most popular majors: Information not available
Expenses: 2016-2017: $28,300; room/board: $9,048
Financial aid: (513) 244-4418; 62% of undergrads determined to have financial need; average aid package $20,324

Mount Vernon Nazarene University
Mount Vernon OH
(866) 462-6868
U.S. News ranking: Reg. U. (Mid. W), No. 86
Website: www.gotomvnu.com
Admissions email: admissions@mvnu.edu
Private; founded 1968
Affiliation: Nazarene

Freshman admissions: selective; 2015-2016: 1,059 applied, 822 accepted. Either SAT or ACT required. ACT 25/75 percentile: 20-25. High school rank: 15% in top tenth, 30% in top quarter, 52% in top half
Early decision deadline: N/A, notification date: N/A
Early action deadline: N/A, notification date: N/A
Application deadline (fall): 7/15
Undergraduate student body: 1,466 full time, 322 part time; 38% male, 62% female; 0% American Indian, 0% Asian, 5% black, 2% Hispanic, 2% multiracial, 0% Pacific Islander, 85% white, 1% international; 92% from in state; 58% live on campus; 0% of students in fraternities, 0% in sororities
Most popular majors: 34% Business, Management, Marketing, and Related Support Services; 17% Public Administration and Social Service Professions; 8% Health Professions and Related Programs; 8% Theology and Religious Vocations; 6% Education
Expenses: 2016-2017: $26,950; room/board: $7,550
Financial aid: (740) 392-6868; 71% of undergrads determined to have financial need; average aid package $22,264

Muskingum University
New Concord OH
(740) 826-8137
U.S. News ranking: Reg. U. (Mid. W), No. 63
Website: www.muskingum.edu
Admissions email: adminfo@muskingum.edu
Private; founded 1837
Affiliation: Presbyterian Church (USA)
Freshman admissions: selective; 2015-2016: 1,977 applied, 1,461 accepted. Either SAT or ACT required. ACT 25/75 percentile: 18-24. High school rank: 12% in top tenth, 33% in top quarter, 63% in top half
Early decision deadline: N/A, notification date: N/A
Early action deadline: N/A, notification date: N/A
Application deadline (fall): 8/1
Undergraduate student body: 1,415 full time, 268 part time; 44% male, 56% female; 0% American Indian, 1% Asian, 5% black, 2% Hispanic, 3% multiracial, 0% Pacific Islander, 78% white, 3% international; 92% from in state; 71% live on campus; 18% of students in fraternities, 38% in sororities
Most popular majors: 19% Business, Management, Marketing, and Related Support Services; 18% Health Professions and Related Programs; 14% Education; 9% Psychology
Expenses: 2016-2017: $27,090; room/board: $10,650
Financial aid: (740) 826-8139; 85% of undergrads determined to have financial need; average aid package $22,299

Notre Dame College of Ohio[1]

Cleveland OH
(216) 373-5355
U.S. News ranking: Reg. U. (Mid. W), second tier
Website: www.notredamecollege.edu
Admissions email: admissions@ndc.edu
Private; founded 1922
Affiliation: Roman Catholic
Application deadline (fall): rolling
Undergraduate student body: N/A full time, N/A part time
Expenses: 2015-2016: $27,520; room/board: $9,904
Financial aid: (216) 373-5263

Oberlin College

Oberlin OH
(440) 775-8411
U.S. News ranking: Nat. Lib. Arts, No. 24
Website: www.oberlin.edu
Admissions email: college.admissions@oberlin.edu
Private; founded 1833
Freshman admissions: more selective; 2015-2016: 7,815 applied, 2,249 accepted. Either SAT or ACT required. SAT 25/75 percentile: 1260-1450. High school rank: 61% in top tenth, 95% in top quarter, 99% in top half
Early decision deadline: 11/15, notification date: 12/10
Early action deadline: N/A, notification date: N/A
Application deadline (fall): 1/15
Undergraduate student body: 2,897 full time, 15 part time; 44% male, 56% female; N/A American Indian, 4% Asian, 5% black, 8% Hispanic, 6% multiracial, 0% Pacific Islander, 68% white, 8% international
Most popular majors: 16% Visual and Performing Arts; 8% Education; 7% Economics; 6% English Language and Literature/Letters
Expenses: 2016-2017: $52,002; room/board: $14,010
Financial aid: (440) 775-8142; 57% of undergrads determined to have financial need; average aid package $39,414

Ohio Christian University

Circleville OH
(877) 762-8669
U.S. News ranking: Reg. Coll. (Mid. W), second tier
Website: www.ohiochristian.edu/
Admissions email: enroll@ohiochristian.edu
Private; founded 1948
Affiliation: Protestant
Freshman admissions: less selective; 2015-2016: N/A applied, N/A accepted. Either SAT or ACT required. ACT 25/75 percentile: 17-22. High school rank: N/A
Early decision deadline: N/A, notification date: N/A
Early action deadline: N/A, notification date: N/A
Application deadline (fall): N/A
Undergraduate student body: 2,485 full time, 1,448 part time; 38% male, 62% female; 0% American Indian, 1% Asian, 27% black, 4% Hispanic, 2% multiracial,

0% Pacific Islander, 51% white, 1% international
Most popular majors: Information not available
Expenses: 2015-2016: $18,840; room/board: $7,500
Financial aid: (740) 477-7758

Ohio Dominican University[1]

Columbus OH
(614) 251-4500
U.S. News ranking: Reg. U. (Mid. W), No. 108
Website: www.ohiodominican.edu
Admissions email: admissions@ohiodominican.edu
Private; founded 1911
Affiliation: Roman Catholic
Application deadline (fall): rolling
Undergraduate student body: N/A full time, N/A part time
Expenses: 2015-2016: $30,270; room/board: $10,530
Financial aid: (614) 251-4778

Ohio Northern University

Ada OH
(888) 408-4668
U.S. News ranking: Reg. Coll. (Mid. W), No. 6
Website: www.onu.edu
Admissions email: admissions-ug@onu.edu
Private; founded 1871
Affiliation: Methodist
Freshman admissions: selective; 2015-2016: 3,108 applied, 2,146 accepted. Either SAT or ACT required. ACT 25/75 percentile: 23-28. High school rank: 32% in top tenth, 60% in top quarter, 85% in top half
Early decision deadline: N/A, notification date: N/A
Early action deadline: N/A, notification date: N/A
Application deadline (fall): 8/15
Undergraduate student body: 2,143 full time, 258 part time; 55% male, 45% female; 0% American Indian, 1% Asian, 3% black, 1% Hispanic, 3% multiracial, 0% Pacific Islander, 84% white, 4% international; 83% from in state; 68% live on campus; 24% of students in fraternities, 27% in sororities
Most popular majors: 17% Business, Management, Marketing, and Related Support Services; 15% Engineering; 14% Health Professions and Related Programs; 10% Biological and Biomedical Sciences; 6% Visual and Performing Arts
Expenses: 2016-2017: $29,820; room/board: $11,050
Financial aid: (419) 772-2272

Ohio State University–Columbus

Columbus OH
(614) 292-3980
U.S. News ranking: Nat. U., No. 54
Website: www.osu.edu
Admissions email: askabuckeye@osu.edu
Public; founded 1870
Freshman admissions: more selective; 2015-2016: 40,240 applied, 19,872 accepted. Either SAT or ACT required. ACT 25/75 percentile: 27-31. High school

rank: 62% in top tenth, 95% in top quarter, 99% in top half
Early decision deadline: N/A, notification date: N/A
Early action deadline: 11/15, notification date: 1/15
Application deadline (fall): 2/1
Undergraduate student body: 41,117 full time, 4,172 part time; 52% male, 48% female; 0% American Indian, 6% Asian, 6% black, 4% Hispanic, 3% multiracial, 0% Pacific Islander, 71% white, 7% international; 83% from in state; 26% live on campus; 9% of students in fraternities, 10% in sororities
Most popular majors: 6% Psychology, General; 4% Finance, General; 3% Biology/Biological Sciences, General; 3% Marketing/Marketing Management, General
Expenses: 2016-2017: $10,037 in state, $29,229 out of state; room/board: $11,666
Financial aid: (614) 292-0300; 49% of undergrads determined to have financial need; average aid package $13,083

Ohio University

Athens OH
(740) 593-4100
U.S. News ranking: Nat. U., No. 146
Website: www.ohio.edu
Admissions email: admissions@ohio.edu
Public; founded 1804
Freshman admissions: selective; 2015-2016: 21,000 applied, 15,628 accepted. Either SAT or ACT required. ACT 25/75 percentile: 22-26. High school rank: 16% in top tenth, 43% in top quarter, 81% in top half
Early decision deadline: N/A, notification date: N/A
Early action deadline: N/A, notification date: N/A
Undergraduate student body: 17,392 full time, 6,121 part time; 41% male, 59% female; 0% American Indian, 1% Asian, 5% black, 3% Hispanic, 3% multiracial, 0% Pacific Islander, 83% white, 3% international; 85% from in state; 46% live on campus; 8% of students in fraternities, 11% in sororities
Most popular majors: 38% Registered Nursing/Registered Nurse; 4% Liberal Arts and Sciences, General Studies and Humanities, Other; 3% Business Administration and Management, General
Expenses: 2016-2017: $11,744 in state, $21,208 out of state; room/board: $12,268
Financial aid: (740) 593-4141; 57% of undergrads determined to have financial need; average aid package $9,035

Ohio Wesleyan University

Delaware OH
(740) 368-3020
U.S. News ranking: Nat. Lib. Arts, No. 95
Website: web.owu.edu
Admissions email: owuadmit@owu.edu
Private; founded 1842
Affiliation: Methodist

Freshman admissions: more selective; 2015-2016: 3,949 applied, 2,955 accepted. Neither SAT nor ACT required. ACT 25/75 percentile: 22-28. High school rank: 23% in top tenth, 52% in top quarter, 84% in top half
Early decision deadline: 11/15, notification date: 11/30
Early action deadline: 1/15, notification date: N/A
Application deadline (fall): 3/1
Undergraduate student body: 1,659 full time, 16 part time; 47% male, 53% female; 0% American Indian, 3% Asian, 8% black, 5% Hispanic, 5% multiracial, N/A Pacific Islander, 70% white, 6% international; 47% from in state; 91% live on campus; 46% of students in fraternities, 34% in sororities
Most popular majors: 14% Biological and Biomedical Sciences; 14% Library Science; 12% Business, Management, Marketing, and Related Support Services; 9% Psychology; 9% Visual and Performing Arts
Expenses: 2016-2017: $44,090; room/board: $11,770
Financial aid: (740) 368-3050; 68% of undergrads determined to have financial need; average aid package $34,536

Otterbein University

Westerville OH
(614) 823-1500
U.S. News ranking: Reg. U. (Mid. W), No. 11
Website: www.otterbein.edu
Admissions email: UOtterB@Otterbein.edu
Private; founded 1847
Affiliation: United Methodist
Freshman admissions: more selective; 2015-2016: 2,917 applied, 2,197 accepted. Either SAT or ACT required. ACT 25/75 percentile: 21-26. High school rank: 27% in top tenth, 60% in top quarter, 86% in top half
Early decision deadline: N/A, notification date: N/A
Early action deadline: N/A, notification date: N/A
Application deadline (fall): rolling
Undergraduate student body: 2,122 full time, 221 part time; 39% male, 61% female; 0% American Indian, 2% Asian, 6% black, 2% Hispanic, 4% multiracial, 0% Pacific Islander, 76% white, 1% international; 88% from in state; 53% live on campus; 28% of students in fraternities, 28% in sororities
Most popular majors: 18% Health Professions and Related Programs; 12% Business, Management, Marketing, and Related Support Services; 12% Visual and Performing Arts; 11% Education
Expenses: 2016-2017: $31,874; room/board: $10,108
Financial aid: (614) 823-1502; 76% of undergrads determined to have financial need; average aid package $23,663

Shawnee State University

Portsmouth OH
(800) 959-2778
U.S. News ranking: Reg. Coll. (Mid. W), second tier
Website: www.shawnee.edu
Admissions email: To_SSU@shawnee.edu
Public; founded 1986
Freshman admissions: selective; 2015-2016: 3,694 applied, 2,765 accepted. Neither SAT nor ACT required. ACT 25/75 percentile: N/A. High school rank: 15% in top tenth, 35% in top quarter, 64% in top half
Early decision deadline: N/A, notification date: N/A
Early action deadline: N/A, notification date: N/A
Application deadline (fall): rolling
Undergraduate student body: 3,098 full time, 648 part time; 44% male, 56% female; 1% American Indian, 0% Asian, 6% black, 1% Hispanic, 2% multiracial, 0% Pacific Islander, 86% white, 1% international; 89% from in state; 24% live on campus; 1% of students in fraternities, 1% in sororities
Most popular majors: 13% Registered Nursing, Nursing Administration, Nursing Research and Clinical Nursing; 12% Business Administration and Management, General; 6% Psychology, General; 5% Biology/Biological Sciences, General; 4% Sport and Fitness Administration/Management
Expenses: 2016-2017: $7,364 in state, $12,761 out of state; room/board: $9,766
Financial aid: (740) 351-4243

Tiffin University

Tiffin OH
(419) 448-3423
U.S. News ranking: Reg. U. (Mid. W), second tier
Website: www.tiffin.edu
Admissions email: admiss@tiffin.edu
Private; founded 1888
Freshman admissions: less selective; 2015-2016: 2,668 applied, 2,485 accepted. Neither SAT nor ACT required. ACT 25/75 percentile: 18-23. High school rank: N/A
Early decision deadline: N/A, notification date: N/A
Early action deadline: N/A, notification date: N/A
Application deadline (fall): rolling
Undergraduate student body: 1,821 full time, 638 part time; 48% male, 52% female; 0% American Indian, 0% Asian, 14% black, 3% Hispanic, 3% multiracial, 0% Pacific Islander, 44% white, 10% international; 74% from in state; 58% live on campus; 2% of students in fraternities, 2% in sororities
Most popular majors: 36% Business, Management, Marketing, and Related Support Services; 36% Homeland Security, Law Enforcement, Firefighting and Related Protective Services; 13% Psychology; 4% Parks, Recreation, Leisure, and Fitness Studies; 3% Health Professions and Related Programs

Expenses: 2015-2016: $22,165; room/board: $10,196
Financial aid: (419) 448-3357

Union Institute and University
Cincinnati OH
(513) 487-1239
U.S. News ranking: Nat. U., unranked
Website: www.myunion.edu
Admissions email: admissions@myunion.edu
Private; founded 1694
Freshman admissions: N/A; 2015-2016: N/A applied, N/A accepted. Neither SAT nor ACT required. ACT 25/75 percentile: N/A. High school rank: N/A
Early decision deadline: N/A, notification date: N/A
Early action deadline: N/A, notification date: N/A
Application deadline (fall): rolling
Undergraduate student body: 554 full time, 534 part time; 47% male, 53% female; 0% American Indian, 1% Asian, 18% black, 32% Hispanic, 2% multiracial, 1% Pacific Islander, 36% white, N/A international
Most popular majors: 59% Criminal Justice/Law Enforcement Administration; 20% Child Development; 5% Liberal Arts and Sciences/Liberal Studies; 4% Crisis/Emergency/Disaster Management; 4% Maternal and Child Health
Expenses: 2015-2016: $12,144; room/board: N/A
Financial aid: (513) 487-1127

University of Akron
Akron OH
(330) 972-7077
U.S. News ranking: Nat. U., second tier
Website: www.uakron.edu
Admissions email: admissions@uakron.edu
Public; founded 1870
Freshman admissions: selective; 2015-2016: 15,166 applied, 14,650 accepted. Either SAT or ACT required. ACT 25/75 percentile: 19-26. High school rank: 16% in top tenth, 38% in top quarter, 68% in top half
Early decision deadline: N/A, notification date: N/A
Early action deadline: 11/1, notification date: 12/15
Application deadline (fall): 8/1
Undergraduate student body: 15,175 full time, 3,862 part time; 53% male, 47% female; 0% American Indian, 2% Asian, 12% black, 2% Hispanic, 4% multiracial, 0% Pacific Islander, 74% white, 2% international; 95% from in state; 17% live on campus; N/A of students in fraternities, N/A in sororities
Most popular majors: 20% Business, Management, Marketing, and Related Support Services; 15% Health Professions and Related Programs; 11% Education; 11% Engineering
Expenses: 2015-2016: $10,509 in state, $19,040 out of state; room/board: $11,322
Financial aid: (330) 972-7032; 70% of undergrads determined to have financial need; average aid package $7,871

University of Cincinnati
Cincinnati OH
(513) 556-1100
U.S. News ranking: Nat. U., No. 135
Website: www.uc.edu
Admissions email: admissions@uc.edu
Public; founded 1819
Freshman admissions: more selective; 2015-2016: 17,275 applied, 13,101 accepted. Either SAT or ACT required. ACT 25/75 percentile: 23-28. High school rank: 21% in top tenth, 47% in top quarter, 83% in top half
Early decision deadline: N/A, notification date: N/A
Early action deadline: N/A, notification date: N/A
Application deadline (fall): 3/1
Undergraduate student body: 21,060 full time, 3,994 part time; 50% male, 50% female; 0% American Indian, 3% Asian, 7% black, 3% Hispanic, 3% multiracial, 0% Pacific Islander, 75% white, 4% international; 84% from in state; 20% live on campus; N/A of students in fraternities, N/A in sororities
Most popular majors: 18% Business, Management, Marketing, and Related Support Services; 17% Health Professions and Related Programs; 9% Engineering; 7% Visual and Performing Arts
Expenses: 2016-2017: $11,000 in state, $26,334 out of state; room/board: $10,964
Financial aid: (513) 556-6982; 54% of undergrads determined to have financial need; average aid package $8,826

University of Cincinnati– UC Blue Ash College[1]
Cincinnati OH
(513) 745-5700
U.S. News ranking: Reg. Coll. (Mid. W), unranked
Website: www.rwc.uc.edu/
Admissions email: N/A
Public
Application deadline (fall): N/A
Undergraduate student body: N/A full time, N/A part time
Expenses: 2015-2016: $6,746 in state, $15,544 out of state; room/board: N/A
Financial aid: (513) 745-5700

University of Dayton
Dayton OH
(937) 229-4411
U.S. News ranking: Nat. U., No. 111
Website: www.udayton.edu
Admissions email: admission@udayton.edu
Private; founded 1850
Affiliation: Roman Catholic (Marianist)
Freshman admissions: more selective; 2015-2016: 16,968 applied, 9,760 accepted. Either SAT or ACT required. ACT 25/75 percentile: 24-29. High school rank: 25% in top tenth, 58% in top quarter, 88% in top half
Early decision deadline: N/A, notification date: N/A

Early action deadline: 12/15, notification date: 2/1
Application deadline (fall): rolling
Undergraduate student body: 8,205 full time, 460 part time; 53% male, 47% female; 0% American Indian, 1% Asian, 3% black, 3% Hispanic, 2% multiracial, 0% Pacific Islander, 78% white, 11% international; 56% from in state; 72% live on campus; 16% of students in fraternities, 22% in sororities
Most popular majors: 29% Business, Management, Marketing, and Related Support Services; 14% Engineering; 8% Education; 7% Health Professions and Related Programs
Expenses: 2016-2017: $40,940; room/board: $12,680
Financial aid: (937) 229-4311; 54% of undergrads determined to have financial need; average aid package $27,319

University of Findlay
Findlay OH
(800) 548-0932
U.S. News ranking: Reg. U. (Mid. W), No. 56
Website: www.findlay.edu
Admissions email: admissions@findlay.edu
Private; founded 1882
Affiliation: Churches of God General Conference
Freshman admissions: more selective; 2015-2016: 3,106 applied, 2,357 accepted. Either SAT or ACT required. ACT 25/75 percentile: 20-25. High school rank: 43% in top tenth, 45% in top quarter, 90% in top half
Early decision deadline: N/A, notification date: N/A
Early action deadline: N/A, notification date: N/A
Application deadline (fall): rolling
Undergraduate student body: 2,704 full time, 1,008 part time; 38% male, 62% female; 0% American Indian, 1% Asian, 4% black, 2% Hispanic, 2% multiracial, 0% Pacific Islander, 81% white, 10% international; 81% from in state; 40% live on campus; 2% of students in fraternities, 2% in sororities
Most popular majors: 30% Health Professions and Related Programs; 16% Business, Management, Marketing, and Related Support Services; 8% Education; 6% Parks, Recreation, Leisure, and Fitness Studies
Expenses: 2016-2017: $32,402; room/board: $9,538
Financial aid: (419) 434-4792; 64% of undergrads determined to have financial need; average aid package $23,792

University of Mount Union
Alliance OH
(330) 823-2590
U.S. News ranking: Reg. Coll. (Mid. W), No. 10
Website: www.mountunion.edu/
Admissions email: admission@mountunion.edu
Private; founded 1846
Affiliation: United Methodist
Freshman admissions: selective; 2015-2016: 2,289 applied,

1,717 accepted. Either SAT or ACT required. ACT 25/75 percentile: 21-26. High school rank: 22% in top tenth, 50% in top quarter, 80% in top half
Early decision deadline: N/A, notification date: N/A
Early action deadline: N/A, notification date: N/A
Application deadline (fall): rolling
Undergraduate student body: 2,058 full time, 36 part time; 50% male, 50% female; 1% American Indian, 1% Asian, 6% black, 2% Hispanic, 3% multiracial, 0% Pacific Islander, 82% white, 2% international; 85% from in state; 75% live on campus; 15% of students in fraternities, 32% in sororities
Most popular majors: 22% Business, Management, Marketing, and Related Support Services; 12% Parks, Recreation, Leisure, and Fitness Studies; 11% Education; 7% Biological and Biomedical Sciences; 6% Psychology
Expenses: 2016-2017: $29,120; room/board: $9,850
Financial aid: (877) 543-9185; 79% of undergrads determined to have financial need; average aid package $22,699

University of Northwestern Ohio[1]
Lima OH
(419) 998-3120
U.S. News ranking: Reg. Coll. (Mid. W), unranked
Website: www.unoh.edu/
Admissions email: info@unoh.edu
Private
Application deadline (fall): N/A
Undergraduate student body: N/A full time, N/A part time
Expenses: 2015-2016: $9,930; room/board: $6,750
Financial aid: (419) 998-3140

University of Rio Grande
Rio Grande OH
(740) 245-7208
U.S. News ranking: Reg. Coll. (Mid. W), unranked
Website: www.rio.edu
Admissions email: admissions@rio.edu
Private; founded 1876
Freshman admissions: N/A; 2015-2016: 1,909 applied, 1,325 accepted. Neither SAT nor ACT required. Average composite ACT score: 19. High school rank: 5% in top tenth, 20% in top quarter, 49% in top half
Early decision deadline: N/A, notification date: N/A
Early action deadline: N/A, notification date: N/A
Application deadline (fall): rolling
Undergraduate student body: 1,550 full time, 451 part time; 35% male, 65% female; 0% American Indian, 0% Asian, 4% black, 1% Hispanic, 0% multiracial, 0% Pacific Islander, 79% white, 1% international; 95% from in state; 17% live on campus; 2% of students in fraternities, 1% in sororities
Most popular majors: Information not available
Expenses: 2015-2016: $23,860; room/board: $9,920

Financial aid: (740) 245-7218; 92% of undergrads determined to have financial need; average aid package $7,444

University of Toledo
Toledo OH
(419) 530-8888
U.S. News ranking: Nat. U., second tier
Website: www.utoledo.edu
Admissions email: enroll@utnet.utoledo.edu
Public; founded 1872
Freshman admissions: selective; 2015-2016: 10,678 applied, 9,952 accepted. Either SAT or ACT required. ACT 25/75 percentile: 20-26. High school rank: 16% in top tenth, 42% in top quarter, 70% in top half
Early decision deadline: N/A, notification date: N/A
Early action deadline: N/A, notification date: N/A
Application deadline (fall): rolling
Undergraduate student body: 12,714 full time, 3,350 part time; 52% male, 48% female; 0% American Indian, 2% Asian, 12% black, 5% Hispanic, 3% multiracial, 0% Pacific Islander, 69% white, 6% international; 80% from in state; 19% live on campus; N/A of students in fraternities, N/A in sororities
Most popular majors: 21% Business, Management, Marketing, and Related Support Services; 18% Health Professions and Related Programs; 11% Engineering; 7% Multi/Interdisciplinary Studies; 5% Education
Expenses: 2015-2016: $9,568 in state, $18,906 out of state; room/board: $10,492
Financial aid: (419) 530-8700

Urbana University[1]
Urbana OH
(937) 484-1356
U.S. News ranking: Reg. Coll. (Mid. W), unranked
Website: www.urbana.edu
Admissions email: admiss@urbana.edu
Private
Application deadline (fall): N/A
Undergraduate student body: N/A full time, N/A part time
Expenses: 2015-2016: $22,012; room/board: $9,024
Financial aid: (937) 484-1355

Ursuline College
Pepper Pike OH
(440) 449-4203
U.S. News ranking: Reg. U. (Mid. W), No. 63
Website: www.ursuline.edu
Admissions email: admission@ursuline.edu
Private; founded 1871
Affiliation: Roman Catholic
Freshman admissions: selective; 2015-2016: 723 applied, 636 accepted. Either SAT or ACT required. ACT 25/75 percentile: 19-24. High school rank: 16% in top tenth, 45% in top quarter, 74% in top half
Early decision deadline: N/A, notification date: N/A
Early action deadline: N/A, notification date: N/A

Application deadline (fall): 2/1
Undergraduate student body: 441 full time, 214 part time; 7% male, 93% female; N/A American Indian, 1% Asian, 26% black, 3% Hispanic, 3% multiracial, N/A Pacific Islander, 62% white, 2% international; 92% from in state; 25% live on campus; N/A of students in fraternities, N/A in sororities
Most popular majors: 53% Health Professions and Related Programs; 16% Business, Management, Marketing, and Related Support Services; 6% Psychology; 5% Biological and Biomedical Sciences
Expenses: 2016-2017: $29,940; room/board: $9,964
Financial aid: (440) 646-8309; 87% of undergrads determined to have financial need; average aid package $23,184

Walsh University
North Canton OH
(800) 362-9846
U.S. News ranking: Reg. U. (Mid. W), No. 49
Website: www.walsh.edu
Admissions email: admissions@walsh.edu
Private; founded 1958
Affiliation: Roman Catholic
Freshman admissions: selective; 2015-2016: 1,447 applied, 1,162 accepted. Either SAT or ACT required. ACT 25/75 percentile: 18-27. High school rank: 17% in top tenth, 43% in top quarter, 76% in top half
Early decision deadline: N/A, notification date: N/A
Early action deadline: N/A, notification date: N/A
Application deadline (fall): 8/15
Undergraduate student body: 1,878 full time, 396 part time; 40% male, 60% female; 0% American Indian, 1% Asian, 6% black, 3% Hispanic, 2% multiracial, 0% Pacific Islander, 75% white, 1% international; 93% from in state; 48% live on campus; 0% of students in fraternities, 0% in sororities
Most popular majors: 37% Business, Management, Marketing, and Related Support Services; 18% Health Professions and Related Programs; 14% Education; 12% Biological and Biomedical Sciences; 5% Psychology
Expenses: 2016-2017: $28,720; room/board: $10,240
Financial aid: (330) 490-7150; 84% of undergrads determined to have financial need; average aid package $21,031

Wilberforce University[1]
Wilberforce OH
(800) 367-8568
U.S. News ranking: Reg. Coll. (Mid. W), second tier
Website: www.wilberforce.edu
Admissions email: admissions@wilberforce.edu
Private
Application deadline (fall): N/A
Undergraduate student body: N/A full time, N/A part time

Expenses: 2015-2016: $13,475; room/board: $6,456
Financial aid: (800) 367-8565

Wilmington College[1]
Wilmington OH
(937) 382-6661
U.S. News ranking: Reg. Coll. (Mid. W), No. 45
Website: www2.wilmington.edu
Admissions email: admission@wilmington.edu
Private; founded 1870
Affiliation: Religious Society of Friends
Undergraduate student body: N/A full time, N/A part time
Expenses: 2015-2016: $24,500; room/board: $9,500
Financial aid: (937) 382-6661

Wittenberg University
Springfield OH
(937) 327-6314
U.S. News ranking: Nat. Lib. Arts, No. 154
Website: www5.wittenberg.edu
Admissions email: admission@wittenberg.edu
Private; founded 1845
Affiliation: Lutheran
Freshman admissions: more selective; 2015-2016: 6,487 applied, 4,986 accepted. Neither SAT nor ACT required. ACT 25/75 percentile: 22-28. High school rank: 19% in top tenth, 46% in top quarter, 78% in top half
Early decision deadline: 11/15, notification date: 12/1
Early action deadline: 12/1, notification date: 1/1
Application deadline (fall): rolling
Undergraduate student body: 1,760 full time, 105 part time; 43% male, 57% female; 0% American Indian, 1% Asian, 7% black, 3% Hispanic, 6% multiracial, N/A Pacific Islander, 81% white, 1% international; 74% from in state; 86% live on campus; 28% of students in fraternities, 36% in sororities
Most popular majors: 18% Social Sciences; 14% Business, Management, Marketing, and Related Support Services; 10% Biological and Biomedical Sciences; 8% Psychology; 7% Education
Expenses: 2016-2017: $38,090; room/board: $10,126
Financial aid: (937) 327-7321; 79% of undergrads determined to have financial need; average aid package $31,718

Wright State University
Dayton OH
(937) 775-5700
U.S. News ranking: Nat. U., second tier
Website: www.wright.edu
Admissions email: admissions@wright.edu
Public; founded 1964
Freshman admissions: selective; 2015-2016: 5,560 applied, 5,336 accepted. Either SAT or ACT required. ACT 25/75 percentile: 19-25. High school rank: 17% in top tenth, 37% in top quarter, 68% in top half

Early decision deadline: N/A, notification date: N/A
Early action deadline: N/A, notification date: N/A
Application deadline (fall): 8/22
Undergraduate student body: 9,940 full time, 2,782 part time; 48% male, 52% female; 0% American Indian, 2% Asian, 12% black, 3% Hispanic, 4% multiracial, 0% Pacific Islander, 72% white, 5% international; 98% from in state; 20% live on campus; 3% of students in fraternities, 6% in sororities
Most popular majors: 12% Business Administration and Management, General; 9% Registered Nursing/Registered Nurse; 8% Psychology, General; 5% Biology/Biological Sciences, General; 5% Mechanical Engineering
Expenses: 2016-2017: $8,730 in state, $17,098 out of state; room/board: $11,376
Financial aid: (937) 873-5721; 64% of undergrads determined to have financial need; average aid package $10,444

Xavier University
Cincinnati OH
(877) 982-3648
U.S. News ranking: Reg. U. (Mid. W), No. 4
Website: www.xavier.edu
Admissions email: xuadmit@xavier.edu
Private; founded 1831
Affiliation: Roman Catholic (Jesuit)
Freshman admissions: selective; 2015-2016: 10,661 applied, 7,631 accepted. Either SAT or ACT required. ACT 25/75 percentile: 22-27. High school rank: 23% in top tenth, 53% in top quarter, 84% in top half
Early decision deadline: N/A, notification date: N/A
Early action deadline: N/A, notification date: N/A
Application deadline (fall): rolling
Undergraduate student body: 4,231 full time, 341 part time; 46% male, 54% female; 0% American Indian, 3% Asian, 10% black, 5% Hispanic, 4% multiracial, 0% Pacific Islander, 72% white, 2% international; 48% from in state; 52% live on campus; N/A of students in fraternities, N/A in sororities
Most popular majors: 26% Business, Management, Marketing, and Related Support Services; 12% Liberal Arts and Sciences, General Studies and Humanities; 10% Health Professions and Related Programs; 7% Biological and Biomedical Sciences; 6% Social Sciences
Expenses: 2016-2017: $36,150; room/board: $11,730
Financial aid: (513) 745-3142; 58% of undergrads determined to have financial need; average aid package $21,546

Youngstown State University
Youngstown OH
(877) 468-6978
U.S. News ranking: Reg. U. (Mid. W), second tier
Website: www.ysu.edu
Admissions email: enroll@ysu.edu
Public; founded 1908
Freshman admissions: selective; 2015-2016: 7,281 applied, 5,152 accepted. Either SAT or ACT required. ACT 25/75 percentile: 18-24. High school rank: 12% in top tenth, 30% in top quarter, 61% in top half
Early decision deadline: N/A, notification date: N/A
Early action deadline: N/A, notification date: N/A
Application deadline (fall): 8/1
Undergraduate student body: 8,628 full time, 2,545 part time; 48% male, 52% female; 0% American Indian, 1% Asian, 11% black, 4% Hispanic, 3% multiracial, 0% Pacific Islander, 76% white, 1% international; 88% from in state; 11% live on campus; 2% of students in fraternities, 2% in sororities
Most popular majors: 7% Criminal Justice/Safety Studies; 6% Social Work; 5% General Studies; 5% Registered Nursing/Registered Nurse; 5% Accounting
Expenses: 2015-2016: $8,317 in state, $14,317 out of state; room/board: $8,645
Financial aid: (330) 941-3399; 75% of undergrads determined to have financial need; average aid package $9,010

OKLAHOMA

Bacone College[1]
Muskogee OK
(888) 682-5514
U.S. News ranking: Reg. Coll. (W), second tier
Website: www.bacone.edu/
Admissions email: admissions@bacone.edu
Private
Application deadline (fall): rolling
Undergraduate student body: N/A full time, N/A part time
Expenses: 2015-2016: $24,500; room/board: $9,500
Financial aid: (888) 682-5514

Cameron University
Lawton OK
(580) 581-2289
U.S. News ranking: Reg. U. (W), second tier
Website: www.cameron.edu
Admissions email: admissions@cameron.edu
Public; founded 1908
Freshman admissions: less selective; 2015-2016: 1,048 applied, 1,045 accepted. Neither SAT nor ACT required. ACT 25/75 percentile: 17-22. High school rank: 3% in top tenth, 11% in top quarter, 37% in top half
Early decision deadline: N/A, notification date: N/A
Early action deadline: N/A, notification date: N/A
Application deadline (fall): rolling
Undergraduate student body: 3,176 full time, 1,564 part time; 39%

male, 61% female; 6% American Indian, 2% Asian, 15% black, 12% Hispanic, 8% multiracial, 1% Pacific Islander, 49% white, 5% international; 85% from in state; 9% live on campus; 2% of students in fraternities, 2% in sororities
Most popular majors: 11% Business Administration and Management, General; 9% Corrections and Criminal Justice, Other; 9% Psychology, General; 7% Elementary Education and Teaching; 6% Health and Physical Education/Fitness, General
Expenses: 2015-2016: $5,580 in state, $14,190 out of state; room/board: $4,888
Financial aid: (580) 581-2293; 69% of undergrads determined to have financial need; average aid package $10,316

East Central University[1]
Ada OK
(580) 559-5239
U.S. News ranking: Reg. U. (W), second tier
Website: www.ecok.edu
Admissions email: parmstro@ecok.edu
Public
Application deadline (fall): N/A
Undergraduate student body: N/A full time, N/A part time
Expenses: 2015-2016: $5,874 in state, $14,182 out of state; room/board: $5,350
Financial aid: (580) 559-5242

Langston University
Langston OK
(405) 466-3231
U.S. News ranking: Reg. U. (W), unranked
Website: www.lunet.edu
Admissions email: admission@speedy.lunet.edu
Public; founded 1897
Freshman admissions: N/A; 2015-2016: 9,324 applied, 5,643 accepted. Neither SAT nor ACT required. Average composite ACT score: 16. High school rank: N/A
Early decision deadline: N/A, notification date: N/A
Early action deadline: N/A, notification date: N/A
Application deadline (fall): rolling
Undergraduate student body: 1,965 full time, 193 part time; 36% male, 64% female; 1% American Indian, 0% Asian, 90% black, 1% Hispanic, 0% multiracial, 0% Pacific Islander, 6% white, 1% international; 62% from in state; 36% live on campus; N/A of students in fraternities, N/A in sororities
Most popular majors: 25% Health Professions and Related Programs; 16% Business, Management, Marketing, and Related Support Services; 14% Education; 9% Psychology; 7% Liberal Arts and Sciences, General Studies and Humanities
Expenses: 2015-2016: $5,042 in state, $12,370 out of state; room/board: $9,272
Financial aid: (405) 466-3282; 91% of undergrads determined to have financial need; average aid package $10,930

Mid-America Christian University[1]
Oklahoma City OK
(888) 436-3035
U.S. News ranking: Reg. U. (W), unranked
Website: www.macu.edu
Admissions email: info@macu.edu
Private
Application deadline (fall): N/A
Undergraduate student body: N/A full time, N/A part time
Expenses: 2015-2016: $16,798; room/board: $7,790
Financial aid: (405) 691-3800

Northeastern State University
Tahlequah OK
(918) 444-2200
U.S. News ranking: Reg. U. (W), second tier
Website: www.nsuok.edu
Admissions email: nsuinfo@nsuok.edu
Public; founded 1846
Freshman admissions: selective; 2015-2016: 1,512 applied, 1,388 accepted. ACT required. ACT 25/75 percentile: 19-23. High school rank: 20% in top tenth, 47% in top quarter, 83% in top half
Early decision deadline: N/A, notification date: N/A
Early action deadline: N/A, notification date: N/A
Application deadline (fall): rolling
Undergraduate student body: 5,001 full time, 2,043 part time; 39% male, 61% female; 20% American Indian, 2% Asian, 4% black, 5% Hispanic, 17% multiracial, 0% Pacific Islander, 49% white, 2% international; 94% from in state; 16% live on campus; 2% of students in fraternities, 2% in sororities
Most popular majors: 10% Elementary Education and Teaching; 8% Psychology, General; 6% Accounting; 6% Criminal Justice/Law Enforcement Administration; 5% Kinesiology and Exercise Science
Expenses: 2016-2017: $5,714 in state, $13,377 out of state; room/board: $7,466
Financial aid: (918) 456-5511; 69% of undergrads determined to have financial need; average aid package $12,699

Northwestern Oklahoma State University
Alva OK
(580) 327-8545
U.S. News ranking: Reg. U. (W), second tier
Website: www.nwosu.edu
Admissions email: recruit@nwosu.edu
Public; founded 1897
Freshman admissions: selective; 2015-2016: 857 applied, 415 accepted. Either SAT or ACT required. ACT 25/75 percentile: 18-22. High school rank: 10% in top tenth, 27% in top quarter, 64% in top half
Early decision deadline: N/A, notification date: N/A
Early action deadline: N/A, notification date: N/A
Application deadline (fall): rolling

Undergraduate student body: 1,532 full time, 442 part time; 44% male, 56% female; 7% American Indian, 1% Asian, 7% black, 8% Hispanic, 0% multiracial, 1% Pacific Islander, 62% white, 7% international; 79% from in state; 51% live on campus; N/A of students in fraternities, N/A in sororities
Most popular majors: 10% Business Administration and Management, General; 10% Parks, Recreation, Leisure, and Fitness Studies, Other; 10% Registered Nursing/Registered Nurse; 9% Psychology, General; 6% Elementary Education and Teaching
Expenses: 2015-2016: $6,112 in state, $12,562 out of state; room/board: $4,400
Financial aid: (580) 327-8542

Oklahoma Baptist University
Shawnee OK
(405) 585-5000
U.S. News ranking: Reg. Coll. (W), No. 5
Website: www.okbu.edu
Admissions email: admissions@okbu.edu
Private; founded 1910
Affiliation: Southern Baptist Convention
Freshman admissions: selective; 2015-2016: 4,785 applied, 3,590 accepted. Either SAT or ACT required. ACT 25/75 percentile: 20-25. High school rank: 23% in top tenth, 49% in top quarter, 90% in top half
Early decision deadline: N/A, notification date: N/A
Early action deadline: N/A, notification date: N/A
Application deadline (fall): 8/1
Undergraduate student body: 1,774 full time, 87 part time; 40% male, 60% female; 6% American Indian, 1% Asian, 7% black, 3% Hispanic, 8% multiracial, 0% Pacific Islander, 70% white, 3% international; 51% from in state; 67% live on campus; 3% of students in fraternities, 11% in sororities
Most popular majors: 22% Health Professions and Related Programs; 16% Education; 12% Theology and Religious Vocations; 9% Business, Management, Marketing, and Related Support Services; 6% Psychology
Expenses: 2016-2017: $25,310; room/board: $7,010
Financial aid: (405) 878-2016; 73% of undergrads determined to have financial need; average aid package $21,800

Oklahoma Christian University
Oklahoma City OK
(405) 425-5050
U.S. News ranking: Reg. U. (W), No. 41
Website: www.oc.edu/
Admissions email: info@oc.edu
Private; founded 1950
Affiliation: Church of Christ
Freshman admissions: selective; 2015-2016: 2,597 applied, 1,535 accepted. Either SAT or ACT required. ACT 25/75

percentile: 21-28. High school rank: 24% in top tenth, 49% in top quarter, 79% in top half
Early decision deadline: N/A, notification date: N/A
Early action deadline: N/A, notification date: N/A
Application deadline (fall): rolling
Undergraduate student body: 1,910 full time, 89 part time; 50% male, 50% female; 2% American Indian, 1% Asian, 5% black, 6% Hispanic, 6% multiracial, 0% Pacific Islander, 72% white, 8% international; 42% from in state; 82% live on campus; 25% of students in fraternities, 34% in sororities
Most popular majors: 19% Business, Management, Marketing, and Related Support Services; 15% Engineering; 10% Education; 8% Visual and Performing Arts; 7% Liberal Arts and Sciences, General Studies and Humanities
Expenses: 2016-2017: $20,840; room/board: $7,290
Financial aid: (405) 425-5190; 63% of undergrads determined to have financial need; average aid package $22,894

Oklahoma City University
Oklahoma City OK
(405) 208-5050
U.S. News ranking: Reg. U. (W), No. 23
Website: www.okcu.edu
Admissions email: uadmissions@okcu.edu
Private; founded 1904
Affiliation: United Methodist
Freshman admissions: more selective; 2015-2016: 1,562 applied, 1,096 accepted. Either SAT or ACT required. ACT 25/75 percentile: 23-29. High school rank: 34% in top tenth, 61% in top quarter, 88% in top half
Early decision deadline: N/A, notification date: N/A
Early action deadline: N/A, notification date: N/A
Application deadline (fall): rolling
Undergraduate student body: 1,609 full time, 195 part time; 35% male, 65% female; 3% American Indian, 2% Asian, 6% black, 9% Hispanic, 8% multiracial, 0% Pacific Islander, 61% white, 11% international; 52% from in state; 50% live on campus; 10% of students in fraternities, 25% in sororities
Most popular majors: 26% Adult Health Nurse/Nursing; 23% General Studies; 7% Dance, General; 6% Acting; 4% Music Performance, General
Expenses: 2016-2017: $30,726; room/board: $9,814
Financial aid: (405) 208-5211; 63% of undergrads determined to have financial need; average aid package $19,902

Oklahoma Panhandle State University[1]
Goodwell OK
(800) 664-6778
U.S. News ranking: Reg. Coll. (W), second tier
Website: www.opsu.edu
Admissions email: opsu@opsu.edu
Public; founded 1909

Application deadline (fall): rolling
Undergraduate student body: N/A full time, N/A part time
Expenses: 2015-2016: $7,461 in state, $7,461 out of state; room/board: $5,344
Financial aid: (580) 349-1580

Oklahoma State University
Stillwater OK
(405) 744-5358
U.S. News ranking: Nat. U., No. 152
Website: osu.okstate.edu
Admissions email: admissions@okstate.edu
Public; founded 1890
Freshman admissions: more selective; 2015-2016: 12,501 applied, 9,392 accepted. Either SAT or ACT required. ACT 25/75 percentile: 22-27. High school rank: 27% in top tenth, 56% in top quarter, 85% in top half
Early decision deadline: N/A, notification date: N/A
Early action deadline: N/A, notification date: N/A
Application deadline (fall): rolling
Undergraduate student body: 18,336 full time, 2,710 part time; 51% male, 49% female; 5% American Indian, 2% Asian, 5% black, 6% Hispanic, 9% multiracial, 0% Pacific Islander, 70% white, 3% international; 73% from in state; 47% live on campus; 18% of students in fraternities, 27% in sororities
Most popular majors: 27% Business, Management, Marketing, and Related Support Services; 10% Engineering; 7% Family and Consumer Sciences/Human Sciences; 6% Education
Expenses: 2016-2017: $7,778 in state, $20,978 out of state; room/board: $8,190
Financial aid: (405) 744-6604; 50% of undergrads determined to have financial need; average aid package $13,914

Oklahoma State University Institute of Technology–Okmulgee
Okmulgee OK
(918) 293-4680
U.S. News ranking: Reg. Coll. (W), No. 20
Website: www.osuit.edu/admissions
Admissions email: osuit.admissions@okstate.edu
Public; founded 1946
Freshman admissions: less selective; 2015-2016: 2,050 applied, 852 accepted. Either SAT or ACT required. ACT 25/75 percentile: 16-20. High school rank: 2% in top tenth, 16% in top quarter, 50% in top half
Early decision deadline: N/A, notification date: N/A
Early action deadline: N/A, notification date: N/A
Application deadline (fall): rolling
Undergraduate student body: 1,770 full time, 706 part time; 63% male, 37% female; 14% American Indian, 1% Asian, 5% black, 5% Hispanic, 9% multiracial, 0% Pacific Islander, 61% white, 1% international; 90% from in state; 29% live

on campus; 0% of students in fraternities, 0% in sororities
Most popular majors: 74% Computer and Information Systems Security/Information Assurance; 20% Instrumentation Technology/Technician; 6% Civil Engineering Technology/Technician
Expenses: 2016-2017: $5,100 in state, $10,710 out of state; room/board: $6,554
Financial aid: (800) 722-4471; 65% of undergrads determined to have financial need; average aid package $7,600

Oklahoma State University–Oklahoma City
Oklahoma City OK
(405) 945-3224
U.S. News ranking: Reg. Coll. (W), unranked
Website: www.osuokc.edu/
Admissions email: admissions@osuokc.edu
Public; founded 1961
Freshman admissions: N/A; 2015-2016: 2,412 applied, 795 accepted. Neither SAT nor ACT required. ACT 25/75 percentile: N/A. High school rank: N/A
Early decision deadline: N/A, notification date: N/A
Early action deadline: N/A, notification date: N/A
Application deadline (fall): rolling
Undergraduate student body: 1,874 full time, 4,085 part time; 40% male, 60% female; 4% American Indian, 3% Asian, 14% black, 11% Hispanic, 12% multiracial, N/A Pacific Islander, 53% white, N/A international; 96% from in state; N/A live on campus; N/A of students in fraternities, N/A in sororities
Most popular majors: Information not available
Expenses: 2015-2016: $2,859 in state, $7,719 out of state; room/board: N/A
Financial aid: (405) 945-3319

Oklahoma Wesleyan University
Bartlesville OK
(866) 222-8226
U.S. News ranking: Reg. U. (W), No. 74
Website: www.okwu.edu
Admissions email: admissions@okwu.edu
Private; founded 1972
Affiliation: The Wesleyan Church
Freshman admissions: selective; 2015-2016: 2,092 applied, 1,982 accepted. Either SAT or ACT required. ACT 25/75 percentile: 18-25. High school rank: 9% in top tenth, 25% in top quarter, 50% in top half
Early decision deadline: N/A, notification date: N/A
Early action deadline: N/A, notification date: N/A
Application deadline (fall): rolling
Undergraduate student body: 615 full time, 553 part time; 38% male, 62% female; 37% American Indian, 1% Asian, 8% black, 8% Hispanic, 0% multiracial, 0% Pacific Islander, 59% white, 5% international

Most popular majors: 38% Nursing Science; 11% Business, Management, Marketing, and Related Support Services, Other; 9% Nursing Science; 6% Theological and Ministerial Studies, Other; 5% Theological and Ministerial Studies, Other **Expenses:** 2016-2017: $25,070; room/board: $8,136 **Financial aid:** (918) 335-6282; 77% of undergrads determined to have financial need; average aid package $16,249

Oral Roberts University

Tulsa OK
(800) 678-8876
U.S. News ranking: Reg. U. (W), No. 44
Website: www.oru.edu
Admissions email: admissions@oru.edu
Private; founded 1963
Affiliation: Christian interdenominational
Freshman admissions: selective; 2015-2016: 2,376 applied, 513 accepted. Either SAT or ACT required. ACT 25/75 percentile: 19-24. High school rank: 19% in top tenth, 38% in top quarter, 67% in top half
Early decision deadline: N/A, notification date: N/A
Early action deadline: N/A, notification date: N/A
Application deadline (fall): rolling
Undergraduate student body: 2,513 full time, 544 part time; 42% male, 58% female; 3% American Indian, 2% Asian, 15% black, 9% Hispanic, 6% multiracial, 0% Pacific Islander, 50% white, 8% international; 49% from in state; 66% live on campus; 0% of students in fraternities, 0% in sororities
Most popular majors: 22% Business, Management, Marketing, and Related Support Services; 13% Theology and Religious Vocations; 8% Education; 8% Health Professions and Related Programs
Expenses: 2016-2017: $25,678; room/board: $10,348
Financial aid: (918) 495-7088; 70% of undergrads determined to have financial need; average aid package $23,541

Rogers State University

Claremore OK
(918) 343-7545
U.S. News ranking: Reg. Coll. (W), second tier
Website: www.rsu.edu/
Admissions email: info@rsu.edu
Public; founded 1909
Freshman admissions: less selective; 2015-2016: 1,057 applied, 865 accepted. Either SAT or ACT required. ACT 25/75 percentile: 16-18. High school rank: 11% in top tenth, 33% in top quarter, 66% in top half
Early decision deadline: N/A, notification date: N/A
Early action deadline: N/A, notification date: N/A
Application deadline (fall): rolling
Undergraduate student body: 2,452 full time, 1,622 part time;

38% male, 62% female; 31% American Indian, 2% Asian, 4% black, 0% Hispanic, 0% multiracial, 0% Pacific Islander, 62% white, 0% international; 96% from in state; 15% live on campus; 0% of students in fraternities, 1% in sororities
Most popular majors: 28% Business, Management, Marketing, and Related Support Services; 12% Psychology; 11% Health Professions and Related Programs; 10% Biological and Biomedical Sciences; 10% Multi-Interdisciplinary Studies
Expenses: 2016-2017: $6,430 in state, $14,080 out of state; room/board: $8,357
Financial aid: (918) 343-7553; 68% of undergrads determined to have financial need; average aid package $9,530

Southeastern Oklahoma State University

Durant OK
(580) 745-2060
U.S. News ranking: Reg. U. (W), second tier
Website: www.se.edu
Admissions email: admissions@se.edu
Public; founded 1909
Freshman admissions: selective; 2015-2016: 1,051 applied, 759 accepted. Either SAT or ACT required. ACT 25/75 percentile: 18-23. High school rank: 13% in top tenth, 41% in top quarter, 78% in top half
Early decision deadline: N/A, notification date: N/A
Early action deadline: N/A, notification date: N/A
Application deadline (fall): rolling
Undergraduate student body: 2,451 full time, 761 part time; 46% male, 54% female; 30% American Indian, 1% Asian, 7% black, 6% Hispanic, 0% multiracial, 0% Pacific Islander, 56% white, 0% international
Most popular majors: 20% Engineering Technologies and Engineering-Related Fields; 13% Liberal Arts and Sciences, General Studies and Humanities; 12% Education; 10% Business, Management, Marketing, and Related Support Services; 10% Psychology
Expenses: 2015-2016: $5,975 in state, $14,613 out of state; room/board: $6,487
Financial aid: (580) 745-2186; 82% of undergrads determined to have financial need; average aid package $8,479

Southern Nazarene University[1]

Bethany OK
(405) 491-6324
U.S. News ranking: Reg. U. (W), second tier
Website: www.snu.edu
Admissions email: admissions@snu.edu
Private; founded 1899
Affiliation: Nazarene
Application deadline (fall): 8/6
Undergraduate student body: N/A full time, N/A part time

Expenses: 2015-2016: $23,320; room/board: $8,120
Financial aid: (405) 491-6310

Southwestern Christian University[1]

Bethany OK
(405) 789-7661
U.S. News ranking: Reg. Coll. (W), No. 22
Website: www.swcu.edu/
Admissions email: admissions@swcu.edu
Private; founded 1946
Affiliation: Pentecostal
Application deadline (fall): rolling
Undergraduate student body: N/A full time, N/A part time
Expenses: 2015-2016: $12,830; room/board: $6,733
Financial aid: N/A

Southwestern Oklahoma State University

Weatherford OK
(580) 774-3782
U.S. News ranking: Reg. U. (W), second tier
Website: www.swosu.edu
Admissions email: admissions@swosu.edu
Public; founded 1901
Freshman admissions: selective; 2015-2016: 2,876 applied, 2,341 accepted. Neither SAT nor ACT required. ACT 25/75 percentile: 19-24. High school rank: 22% in top tenth, 47% in top quarter, 78% in top half
Early decision deadline: N/A, notification date: N/A
Early action deadline: N/A, notification date: N/A
Application deadline (fall): rolling
Undergraduate student body: 3,485 full time, 873 part time; 42% male, 58% female; 4% American Indian, 2% Asian, 5% black, 8% Hispanic, 7% multiracial, 0% Pacific Islander, 67% white, 5% international; 90% from in state; 27% live on campus; 3% of students in fraternities, 6% in sororities
Most popular majors: 20% Registered Nursing/Registered Nurse; 15% Business Administration and Management, General; 7% Parks, Recreation and Leisure Facilities Management, General; 7% Elementary Education and Teaching; 6% Health Professions and Related Clinical Sciences, Other
Expenses: 2016-2017: $6,090 in state, $12,540 out of state; room/board: $5,220
Financial aid: (580) 774-3786; 60% of undergrads determined to have financial need; average aid package $5,667

St. Gregory's University

Shawnee OK
(405) 878-5444
U.S. News ranking: Reg. Coll. (W), No. 17
Website: www.stgregorys.edu
Admissions email: admissions@stgregorys.edu
Private; founded 1915

Affiliation: Roman Catholic–Benedictine
Freshman admissions: selective; 2015-2016: 382 applied, 234 accepted. Either SAT or ACT required. ACT 25/75 percentile: 18-23. High school rank: N/A
Early decision deadline: N/A, notification date: N/A
Early action deadline: N/A, notification date: N/A
Application deadline (fall): N/A
Undergraduate student body: 473 full time, 132 part time; 44% male, 56% female; 10% American Indian, 1% Asian, 8% black, 12% Hispanic, 8% multiracial, 0% Pacific Islander, 55% white, 3% international
Most popular majors: Information not available
Expenses: 2015-2016: $20,280; room/board: $4,085
Financial aid: (405) 878-5412

University of Central Oklahoma

Edmond OK
(405) 974-2727
U.S. News ranking: Reg. U. (W), No. 88
Website: www.uco.edu/em/become-a-broncho/index.asp
Admissions email: onestop@uco.edu
Public; founded 1890
Freshman admissions: selective; 2015-2016: 5,122 applied, 3,581 accepted. Either SAT or ACT required. ACT 25/75 percentile: 19-24. High school rank: 11% in top tenth, 35% in top quarter, 68% in top half
Early decision deadline: N/A, notification date: N/A
Early action deadline: N/A, notification date: N/A
Application deadline (fall): rolling
Undergraduate student body: 10,686 full time, 4,381 part time; 42% male, 58% female; 4% American Indian, 3% Asian, 9% black, 9% Hispanic, 4% multiracial, 0% Pacific Islander, 58% white, 7% international; 97% from in state; 9% live on campus; 2% of students in fraternities, 3% in sororities
Most popular majors: 14% General Studies; 6% Business Administration and Management, General; 5% Psychology, General; 4% Registered Nursing/Registered Nurse; 4% Finance, General
Expenses: 2016-2017: $6,096 in state, $14,972 out of state; room/board: $7,130
Financial aid: (405) 974-3334; 58% of undergrads determined to have financial need; average aid package $10,494

University of Oklahoma

Norman OK
(405) 325-2252
U.S. News ranking: Nat. U., No. 111
Website: www.ou.edu
Admissions email: admrec@ou.edu
Public; founded 1890
Freshman admissions: more selective; 2015-2016: 12,002 applied, 9,318 accepted. Either SAT or ACT required. ACT 25/75 percentile: 24-29. High school

rank: 37% in top tenth, 68% in top quarter, 93% in top half
Early decision deadline: N/A, notification date: N/A
Early action deadline: N/A, notification date: N/A
Application deadline (fall): 2/1
Undergraduate student body: 18,910 full time, 3,222 part time; 49% male, 51% female; 4% American Indian, 6% Asian, 5% black, 9% Hispanic, 7% multiracial, 0% Pacific Islander, 62% white, 4% international; 68% from in state; 30% live on campus; 22% of students in fraternities, 29% in sororities
Most popular majors: 7% Health Professions and Related Programs; 4% Business, Management, Marketing, and Related Support Services; 4% Liberal Arts and Sciences, General Studies and Humanities; 4% Psychology
Expenses: 2015-2016: $8,065 in state, $21,451 out of state; room/board: $9,742
Financial aid: (405) 325-4521; 45% of undergrads determined to have financial need; average aid package $13,218

University of Science and Arts of Oklahoma

Chickasha OK
(405) 574-1357
U.S. News ranking: Nat. Lib. Arts, second tier
Website: www.usao.edu
Admissions email: usao-admissions@usao.edu
Public; founded 1908
Freshman admissions: selective; 2015-2016: 706 applied, 466 accepted. Either SAT or ACT required. ACT 25/75 percentile: 19-24. High school rank: 25% in top tenth, 47% in top quarter, 78% in top half
Early decision deadline: N/A, notification date: N/A
Early action deadline: N/A, notification date: N/A
Application deadline (fall): 8/30
Undergraduate student body: 787 full time, 101 part time; 34% male, 66% female; 14% American Indian, 1% Asian, 5% black, 7% Hispanic, 0% multiracial, 0% Pacific Islander, 63% white, 8% international; 86% from in state; 55% live on campus; 2% of students in fraternities, 13% in sororities
Most popular majors: 28% Business, Management, Marketing, and Related Support Services; 18% Education; 17% Parks, Recreation, Leisure, and Fitness Studies; 14% Psychology; 12% Social Sciences
Expenses: 2016-2017: $7,200 in state, $17,550 out of state; room/board: $5,720
Financial aid: (405) 574-1240; 65% of undergrads determined to have financial need; average aid package $10,627

University of Tulsa

Tulsa OK
(918) 631-2307
U.S. News ranking: Nat. U.,
No. 86
Website: utulsa.edu
Admissions email:
admission@utulsa.edu
Private; founded 1894
Affiliation: Presbyterian
Freshman admissions: most
selective; 2015-2016: 6,762
applied, 2,847 accepted. Either
SAT or ACT required. ACT 25/75
percentile: 26-32. High school
rank: 74% in top tenth, 91% in
top quarter, 99% in top half
Early decision deadline: N/A,
notification date: N/A
Early action deadline: 11/1,
notification date: 12/15
Application deadline (fall): rolling
Undergraduate student body: 3,359
full time, 119 part time; 58%
male, 42% female; 3% American
Indian, 4% Asian, 5% black,
5% Hispanic, 1% multiracial,
0% Pacific Islander, 56% white,
26% international; 57% from in
state; 71% live on campus; 20%
of students in fraternities, 22%
in sororities
Most popular majors: 23%
Business, Management,
Marketing, and Related Support
Services; 23% Engineering; 7%
Health Professions and Related
Programs; 6% Biological and
Biomedical Sciences; 6% Social
Sciences
Expenses: 2016-2017: $38,796;
room/board: $11,116
Financial aid: (918) 631-2526;
40% of undergrads determined
to have financial need; average
aid package $26,970

OREGON

Art Institute of Portland[1]

Portland OR
(888) 228-6528
U.S. News ranking: Arts, unranked
Website: www.artinstitutes.edu/
portland/
Admissions email: N/A
For-profit
Application deadline (fall): N/A
Undergraduate student body: N/A
full time, N/A part time
Expenses: 2015-2016: $17,412;
room/board: $8,874
Financial aid: N/A

Corban University

Salem OR
(800) 845-3005
U.S. News ranking: Reg. U. (W),
No. 68
Website: www.corban.edu
Admissions email:
admissions@corban.edu
Private; founded 1935
Affiliation: Evangelical
Freshman admissions: selective;
2015-2016: 3,108 applied, 949
accepted. Either SAT or ACT
required. SAT 25/75 percentile:
940-1160. High school rank:
33% in top tenth, 60% in top
quarter, 89% in top half
Early decision deadline: N/A,
notification date: N/A
Early action deadline: N/A,
notification date: N/A

Application deadline (fall): 8/1
Undergraduate student body: 949
full time, 113 part time; 38%
male, 62% female; 1% American
Indian, 4% Asian, 1% black,
3% Hispanic, 8% multiracial,
0% Pacific Islander, 76% white,
1% international; N/A from in
state; 59% live on campus; N/A
of students in fraternities, N/A in
sororities
Most popular majors: 25%
Business, Management,
Marketing, and Related Support
Services; 22% Psychology;
11% Education; 6% Health
Professions and Related
Programs; 4% Theology and
Religious Vocations
Expenses: 2016-2017: $30,640;
room/board: $9,666
Financial aid: (503) 375-7006;
76% of undergrads determined
to have financial need; average
aid package $22,261

Eastern Oregon University

La Grande OR
(541) 962-3393
U.S. News ranking: Reg. U. (W),
second tier
Website: www.eou.edu
Admissions email:
admissions@eou.edu
Public; founded 1929
Freshman admissions: less
selective; 2015-2016: 994
applied, 967 accepted. Either
SAT or ACT required. SAT 25/75
percentile: 840-1050. High
school rank: 11% in top tenth,
37% in top quarter, 72% in
top half
Early decision deadline: N/A,
notification date: N/A
Early action deadline: 2/1,
notification date: N/A
Application deadline (fall): 9/1
Undergraduate student body: 1,759
full time, 1,369 part time; 38%
male, 62% female; 2% American
Indian, 2% Asian, 3% black,
5% Hispanic, 3% multiracial,
1% Pacific Islander, 76% white,
1% international; 73% from in
state; 11% live on campus; N/A
of students in fraternities, N/A in
sororities
Most popular majors: 31%
Business, Management,
Marketing, and Related Support
Services; 24% Liberal Arts and
Sciences, General Studies and
Humanities; 7% Social Sciences;
7% Education; 6% Parks,
Recreation, Leisure, and Fitness
Studies
Expenses: 2016-2017: $8,073
in state, $18,804 out of state;
room/board: $9,642
Financial aid: (541) 962-3551;
77% of undergrads determined
to have financial need; average
aid package $9,436

George Fox University

Newberg OR
(800) 765-4369
U.S. News ranking: Reg. U. (W),
No. 23
Website: www.georgefox.edu
Admissions email:
admissions@georgefox.edu
Private; founded 1891
Affiliation: Evangelical Friends

Freshman admissions: selective;
2015-2016: 3,001 applied,
2,346 accepted. Either SAT
or ACT required. SAT 25/75
percentile: 960-1200. High
school rank: 26% in top tenth,
56% in top quarter, 82% in
top half
Early decision deadline: N/A,
notification date: N/A
Early action deadline: 11/15,
notification date: 12/23
Application deadline (fall): rolling
Undergraduate student body: 2,361
full time, 230 part time; 44%
male, 56% female; 1% American
Indian, 4% Asian, 2% black,
11% Hispanic, 6% multiracial,
0% Pacific Islander, 68% white,
4% international; 58% from in
state; 55% live on campus; N/A
of students in fraternities, N/A in
sororities
Most popular majors: 26%
Business, Management,
Marketing, and Related
Support Services; 13% Multi/
Interdisciplinary Studies; 9%
Health Professions and Related
Programs; 9% Visual and
Performing Arts; 6% Biological
and Biomedical Sciences
Expenses: 2016-2017: $33,730;
room/board: $10,528
Financial aid: (503) 554-2290;
75% of undergrads determined
to have financial need; average
aid package $23,776

Lewis & Clark College

Portland OR
(800) 444-4111
U.S. News ranking: Nat. Lib. Arts,
No. 87
Website: www.lclark.edu
Admissions email:
admissions@lclark.edu
Private; founded 1867
Freshman admissions: more
selective; 2015-2016: 7,368
applied, 4,629 accepted. Neither
SAT nor ACT required. SAT
25/75 percentile: 1190-1390.
High school rank: 48% in top
tenth, 82% in top quarter, 97%
in top half
Early decision deadline: 11/1,
notification date: 12/15
Early action deadline: 11/1,
notification date: 12/31
Application deadline (fall): 3/1
Undergraduate student body: 2,178
full time, 31 part time; 39%
male, 61% female; 1% American
Indian, 6% Asian, 2% black,
10% Hispanic, 4% multiracial,
0% Pacific Islander, 66% white,
5% international; 11% from in
state; 70% live on campus; 0%
of students in fraternities, 0% in
sororities
Most popular majors: 18% Social
Sciences; 15% Psychology;
11% Biological and Biomedical
Sciences; 9% Visual and
Performing Arts
Expenses: 2016-2017: $46,894;
room/board: $11,638
Financial aid: (503) 768-7090;
60% of undergrads determined
to have financial need; average
aid package $42,467

Linfield College

McMinnville OR
(800) 640-2287
U.S. News ranking: Nat. Lib. Arts,
No. 128
Website: www.linfield.edu
Admissions email:
admission@linfield.edu
Private; founded 1858
Affiliation: American Baptist
Freshman admissions: selective;
2015-2016: 2,330 applied,
1,955 accepted. Either SAT
or ACT required. SAT 25/75
percentile: 950-1160. High
school rank: 26% in top tenth,
59% in top quarter, 91% in
top half
Early decision deadline: N/A,
notification date: N/A
Early action deadline: 11/1,
notification date: 1/15
Application deadline (fall): rolling
Undergraduate student body: 1,663
full time, 37 part time; 40%
male, 60% female; 1% American
Indian, 5% Asian, 2% black,
13% Hispanic, 13% multiracial,
1% Pacific Islander, 60% white,
3% international; 47% from in
state; 77% live on campus; 25%
of students in fraternities, 31%
in sororities
Most popular majors: 19%
Business, Management,
Marketing, and Related Support
Services; 13% Social Sciences;
11% Education; 7% Biological
and Biomedical Sciences; 7%
Visual and Performing Arts
Expenses: 2016-2017: $40,105;
room/board: $11,905
Financial aid: (503) 883-2225;
77% of undergrads determined
to have financial need; average
aid package $32,727

Marylhurst University[1]

Marylhurst OR
(503) 699-6268
U.S. News ranking: Reg. U. (W),
unranked
Website: www.marylhurst.edu
Admissions email:
admissions@marylhurst.edu
Private
Application deadline (fall): N/A
Undergraduate student body: N/A
full time, N/A part time
Expenses: 2015-2016: $20,835;
room/board: N/A
Financial aid: (503) 699-6253

Northwest Christian University

Eugene OR
(541) 684-7201
U.S. News ranking: Reg. U. (W),
second tier
Website: www.nwcu.edu
Admissions email:
admissions@nwcu.edu
Private; founded 1895
Affiliation: Christian Church
(Disciples of Christ)
Freshman admissions: selective;
2015-2016: 369 applied, 251
accepted. Either SAT or ACT
required. SAT 25/75 percentile:
910-1075. High school rank: N/A
Early decision deadline: N/A,
notification date: N/A
Early action deadline: N/A,
notification date: N/A
Application deadline (fall): rolling

Undergraduate student body: 421
full time, 112 part time; 40%
male, 60% female; 3% American
Indian, 2% Asian, 3% black,
9% Hispanic, 3% multiracial,
1% Pacific Islander, 77% white,
N/A international; 76% from in
state; 48% live on campus; N/A
of students in fraternities, N/A in
sororities
Most popular majors: 36%
Business, Management,
Marketing, and Related Support
Services; 25% Education;
17% Psychology; 7% Multi/
Interdisciplinary Studies; 6%
Biological and Biomedical
Sciences
Expenses: 2016-2017: $27,930;
room/board: $8,650
Financial aid: (541) 684-7203;
81% of undergrads determined
to have financial need; average
aid package $20,482

Oregon College of Art and Craft

Portland OR
(800) 390-0632
U.S. News ranking: Arts, unranked
Website: www.ocac.edu/
Admissions email:
admissions@ocac.edu
Private; founded 1907
Freshman admissions: N/A;
2015-2016: 147 applied, 66
accepted. Neither SAT nor ACT
required. SAT 25/75 percentile:
N/A. High school rank: 9% in top
tenth, 32% in top quarter, 60%
in top half
Early decision deadline: N/A,
notification date: N/A
Early action deadline: N/A,
notification date: N/A
Application deadline (fall): rolling
Undergraduate student body: 94
full time, 17 part time; 18%
male, 82% female; 1% American
Indian, 3% Asian, 1% black,
12% Hispanic, 10% multiracial,
0% Pacific Islander, 68% white,
0% international
Most popular majors: 100%
Crafts/Craft Design, Folk Art and
Artisanry
Expenses: 2015-2016: $29,580;
room/board: $8,000
Financial aid: N/A

Oregon Institute of Technology

Klamath Falls OR
(541) 885-1155
U.S. News ranking: Reg. Coll.
(W), No. 3
Website: www.oit.edu
Admissions email: oit@oit.edu
Public; founded 1947
Freshman admissions: selective;
2015-2016: 1,487 applied, 84%
accepted. Either SAT or ACT
required. SAT 25/75 percentile:
920-1170. High school rank:
18% in top tenth, 49% in top
quarter, 88% in top half
Early decision deadline: N/A,
notification date: N/A
Early action deadline: N/A,
notification date: N/A
Application deadline (fall): 9/7
Undergraduate student body: 2,37_
full time, 2,352 part time; 53%
male, 47% female; 1% America_
Indian, 6% Asian, 2% black,
8% Hispanic, 6% multiracial,
1% Pacific Islander, 69% white

1% international; 73% from in state; 13% live on campus; N/A of students in fraternities, N/A in sororities
Most popular majors: 48% Health Professions and Related Programs; 14% Engineering; 14% Engineering Technologies and Engineering-Related Fields; 8% Business, Management, Marketing, and Related Support Services; 6% Psychology
Expenses: 2016-2017: $9,625 in state, $27,326 out of state; room/board: $9,206
Financial aid: (541) 885-1280; 70% of undergrads determined to have financial need; average aid package $7,634

Oregon State University
Corvallis OR
(541) 737-4411
U.S. News ranking: Nat. U., No. 143
Website: oregonstate.edu
Admissions email: osuadmit@oregonstate.edu
Public; founded 1868
Freshman admissions: selective; 2015-2016: 14,058 applied, 11,016 accepted. Either SAT or ACT required. SAT 25/75 percentile: 970-1240. High school rank: 24% in top tenth, 54% in top quarter, 89% in top half
Early decision deadline: N/A, notification date: N/A
Early action deadline: 11/1, notification date: 12/20
Application deadline (fall): 9/1
Undergraduate student body: 18,493 full time, 6,119 part time; 54% male, 46% female; 1% American Indian, 7% Asian, 1% black, 9% Hispanic, 7% multiracial, 0% Pacific Islander, 67% white, 6% international; 71% from in state; 17% live on campus; 6% of students in fraternities, 13% in sororities
Most popular majors: 15% Engineering; 13% Business, Management, Marketing, and Related Support Services; 10% Family and Consumer Sciences/Human Sciences; 6% Social Sciences
Expenses: 2016-2017: $10,366 in state, $28,846 out of state; room/board: $12,153
Financial aid: (541) 737-2241; 54% of undergrads determined to have financial need; average aid package $13,244

Pacific Northwest College of Art[1]
Portland OR
(800) 818-7622
U.S. News ranking: Arts, unranked
Website: www.pnca.edu
Admissions email: admissions@pnca.edu
Private
Application deadline (fall): N/A
Undergraduate student body: N/A full time, N/A part time
Expenses: 2015-2016: $33,070; room/board: $11,198
Financial aid: (503) 821-8976

Pacific University
Forest Grove OR
(800) 677-6712
U.S. News ranking: Reg. U. (W), No. 22
Website: www.pacificu.edu
Admissions email: admissions@pacificu.edu
Private; founded 1849
Freshman admissions: selective; 2015-2016: 3,004 applied, 2,374 accepted. Either SAT or ACT required. SAT 25/75 percentile: 990-1190. High school rank: N/A
Early decision deadline: N/A, notification date: N/A
Early action deadline: N/A, notification date: N/A
Application deadline (fall): 8/15
Undergraduate student body: 1,881 full time, 43 part time; 40% male, 60% female; 1% American Indian, 12% Asian, 2% black, 13% Hispanic, 12% multiracial, 3% Pacific Islander, 52% white, 2% international
Most popular majors: Information not available
Expenses: 2016-2017: $41,054; room/board: $11,822
Financial aid: (503) 352-2222; 79% of undergrads determined to have financial need; average aid package $30,168

Portland State University
Portland OR
(503) 725-3511
U.S. News ranking: Nat. U., second tier
Website: www.pdx.edu
Admissions email: admissions@pdx.edu
Public; founded 1946
Freshman admissions: selective; 2015-2016: 6,299 applied, 5,397 accepted. Neither SAT nor ACT required. SAT 25/75 percentile: 930-1160. High school rank: 11% in top tenth, 36% in top quarter, 79% in top half
Early decision deadline: N/A, notification date: N/A
Early action deadline: N/A, notification date: N/A
Application deadline (fall): rolling
Undergraduate student body: 14,606 full time, 7,374 part time; 47% male, 53% female; 1% American Indian, 8% Asian, 4% black, 12% Hispanic, 6% multiracial, 1% Pacific Islander, 57% white, 7% international; 84% from in state; 10% live on campus; 1% of students in fraternities, 1% in sororities
Most popular majors: 17% Business, Management, Marketing, and Related Support Services; 15% Social Sciences; 8% Health Professions and Related Programs; 8% Psychology; 6% Liberal Arts and Sciences, General Studies and Humanities
Expenses: 2016-2017: $8,337 in state, $24,852 out of state; room/board: $10,260
Financial aid: (503) 725-3461; 68% of undergrads determined to have financial need; average aid package $9,590

Reed College[1]
Portland OR
(503) 777-7511
U.S. News ranking: Nat. Lib. Arts, No. 87
Website: www.reed.edu/
Admissions email: admission@reed.edu
Private
Application deadline (fall): N/A
Undergraduate student body: N/A full time, N/A part time
Expenses: 2015-2016: $49,940; room/board: $12,590
Financial aid: (503) 777-7223

Southern Oregon University
Ashland OR
(541) 552-6411
U.S. News ranking: Reg. U. (W), No. 76
Website: www.sou.edu
Admissions email: admissions@sou.edu
Public; founded 1926
Freshman admissions: selective; 2015-2016: 2,411 applied, 2,296 accepted. Either SAT or ACT required. SAT 25/75 percentile: 910-1150. High school rank: N/A
Early decision deadline: N/A, notification date: N/A
Early action deadline: N/A, notification date: N/A
Application deadline (fall): rolling
Undergraduate student body: 3,686 full time, 1,715 part time; 40% male, 60% female; 1% American Indian, 2% Asian, 3% black, 11% Hispanic, 9% multiracial, 1% Pacific Islander, 60% white, 3% international
Most popular majors: 17% Business, Management, Marketing, and Related Support Services; 10% Psychology; 7% Homeland Security, Law Enforcement, Firefighting and Related Protective Services; 5% Education
Expenses: 2015-2016: $8,145 in state, $22,365 out of state; room/board: $12,105
Financial aid: (541) 552-6754

University of Oregon
Eugene OR
(800) 232-3825
U.S. News ranking: Nat. U., No. 103
Website: www.uoregon.edu
Admissions email: uoadmit@uoregon.edu
Public; founded 1876
Freshman admissions: selective; 2015-2016: 22,000 applied, 16,328 accepted. Either SAT or ACT required. SAT 25/75 percentile: 1000-1230. High school rank: 29% in top tenth, 64% in top quarter, 93% in top half
Early decision deadline: N/A, notification date: N/A
Early action deadline: 11/1, notification date: 12/15
Application deadline (fall): 1/15
Undergraduate student body: 18,630 full time, 1,908 part time; 47% male, 53% female; 0% American Indian, 6% Asian, 2% black, 10% Hispanic, 7% multiracial, 0% Pacific Islander, 60% white, 14% international; 59% from in state; 20% live

on campus; 15% of students in fraternities, 20% in sororities
Most popular majors: 11% Business/Commerce, General; 7% Psychology, General; 7% Social Sciences, General; 6% Economics, General; 5% Physiology, General
Expenses: 2016-2017: $10,762 in state, $33,442 out of state; room/board: $12,210
Financial aid: (541) 346-3221; 45% of undergrads determined to have financial need; average aid package $10,400

University of Portland
Portland OR
(888) 627-5601
U.S. News ranking: Reg. U. (W), No. 7
Website: www.up.edu
Admissions email: admission@up.edu
Private; founded 1901
Affiliation: Roman Catholic
Freshman admissions: more selective; 2015-2016: 11,202 applied, 6,939 accepted. Either SAT or ACT required. SAT 25/75 percentile: 1090-1300. High school rank: 45% in top tenth, 77% in top quarter, 96% in top half
Early decision deadline: N/A, notification date: N/A
Early action deadline: N/A, notification date: N/A
Application deadline (fall): 2/1
Undergraduate student body: 3,698 full time, 72 part time; 41% male, 59% female; 0% American Indian, 12% Asian, 1% black, 11% Hispanic, 8% multiracial, 2% Pacific Islander, 61% white, 3% international; 30% from in state; 57% live on campus; 0% of students in fraternities, 0% in sororities
Most popular majors: 20% Health Professions and Related Programs; 15% Business, Management, Marketing, and Related Support Services; 14% Engineering; 10% Biological and Biomedical Sciences; 8% Foreign Languages, Literatures, and Linguistics
Expenses: 2016-2017: $42,014; room/board: $14,220
Financial aid: (503) 943-7311; 62% of undergrads determined to have financial need; average aid package $29,500

Warner Pacific College
Portland OR
(503) 517-1020
U.S. News ranking: Reg. Coll. (W), No. 6
Website: www.warnerpacific.edu
Admissions email: admissions@warnerpacific.edu
Private; founded 1937
Affiliation: Church of God
Freshman admissions: less selective; 2015-2016: 781 applied, 738 accepted. Either SAT or ACT required. SAT 25/75 percentile: 800-1070. High school rank: 3% in top tenth, 7% in top quarter, 44% in top half
Early decision deadline: N/A, notification date: N/A
Early action deadline: N/A, notification date: N/A

Application deadline (fall): rolling
Undergraduate student body: 487 full time, 36 part time; 44% male, 56% female; 2% American Indian, 7% Asian, 12% black, 23% Hispanic, 4% multiracial, 1% Pacific Islander, 43% white, 2% international; 66% from in state; 45% live on campus; N/A of students in fraternities, N/A in sororities
Most popular majors: 18% Business, Management, Marketing, and Related Support Services; 13% Family and Consumer Sciences/Human Sciences; 11% Theology and Religious Vocations; 9% Education; 8% Biological and Biomedical Sciences
Expenses: 2016-2017: $22,710; room/board: $8,900
Financial aid: (503) 517-1017; 83% of undergrads determined to have financial need; average aid package $17,768

Western Oregon University
Monmouth OR
(503) 838-8211
U.S. News ranking: Reg. U. (W), No. 67
Website: www.wou.edu
Admissions email: wolfgram@wou.edu
Public; founded 1856
Freshman admissions: less selective; 2015-2016: 3,327 applied, 2,920 accepted. Neither SAT nor ACT required. SAT 25/75 percentile: 840-1070. High school rank: 11% in top tenth, 35% in top quarter, 71% in top half
Early decision deadline: N/A, notification date: N/A
Early action deadline: N/A, notification date: N/A
Application deadline (fall): rolling
Undergraduate student body: 4,059 full time, 749 part time; 40% male, 60% female; 2% American Indian, 4% Asian, 4% black, 11% Hispanic, 0% multiracial, 2% Pacific Islander, 66% white, 5% international; 82% from in state; 26% live on campus; 1% of students in fraternities, 1% in sororities
Most popular majors: 17% Business/Commerce, General; 14% Criminal Justice/Law Enforcement Administration; 13% Multi-/Interdisciplinary Studies, Other; 9% Education, General; 9% Psychology, General
Expenses: 2016-2017: $8,796 in state, $22,056 out of state; room/board: $9,638
Financial aid: (503) 838-8475; 83% of undergrads determined to have financial need; average aid package $9,705

Willamette University
Salem OR
(877) 542-2787
U.S. News ranking: Nat. Lib. Arts, No. 72
Website: www.willamette.edu
Admissions email: LIBARTS@willamette.edu
Private; founded 1842
Affiliation: United Methodist
Freshman admissions: more selective; 2015-2016: 6,332

applied, 4,935 accepted. Either SAT or ACT required. SAT 25/75 percentile: 1100-1330. High school rank: 40% in top tenth, 73% in top quarter, 97% in top half
Early decision deadline: N/A, notification date: N/A
Early action deadline: 12/1, notification date: 1/15
Application deadline (fall): 2/1
Undergraduate student body: 1,977 full time, 162 part time; 43% male, 57% female; 1% American Indian, 9% Asian, 2% black, 12% Hispanic, 10% multiracial, 0% Pacific Islander, 62% white, 1% international; 22% from in state; 68% live on campus; 28% of students in fraternities, 25% in sororities
Most popular majors: 29% Social Sciences; 12% Biological and Biomedical Sciences; 10% English Language and Literature/Letters; 8% Visual and Performing Arts; 7% Foreign Languages, Literatures, and Linguistics
Expenses: 2016-2017: $47,217; room/board: $11,600
Financial aid: (503) 370-6273; 62% of undergrads determined to have financial need; average aid package $34,259

PENNSYLVANIA

Albright College
Reading PA
(800) 252-1856
U.S. News ranking: Nat. Lib. Arts, second tier
Website: www.albright.edu
Admissions email: admission@alb.edu
Private; founded 1856
Affiliation: United Methodist
Freshman admissions: selective; 2015-2016: 7,645 applied, 3,759 accepted. Neither SAT nor ACT required. SAT 25/75 percentile: 960-1150. High school rank: 16% in top tenth, 38% in top quarter, 73% in top half
Early decision deadline: N/A, notification date: N/A
Early action deadline: N/A, notification date: N/A
Application deadline (fall): rolling
Undergraduate student body: 2,219 full time, 25 part time; 39% male, 61% female; 1% American Indian, 3% Asian, 21% black, 11% Hispanic, 1% multiracial, 0% Pacific Islander, 58% white, 3% international; 62% from in state; 65% live on campus; 15% of students in fraternities, 20% in sororities
Most popular majors: 33% Business, Management, Marketing, and Related Support Services; 16% Psychology; 13% Social Sciences; 8% Visual and Performing Arts; 5% Computer and Information Sciences and Support Services
Expenses: 2016-2017: $41,544; room/board: $11,188
Financial aid: (610) 921-7515; 89% of undergrads determined to have financial need; average aid package $34,550

Allegheny College
Meadville PA
(800) 521-5293
U.S. News ranking: Nat. Lib. Arts, No. 77
Website: www.allegheny.edu
Admissions email: admissions@allegheny.edu
Private; founded 1815
Affiliation: United Methodist
Freshman admissions: more selective; 2015-2016: 4,324 applied, 2,955 accepted. Neither SAT nor ACT required. SAT 25/75 percentile: 1013-1250. High school rank: 35% in top tenth, 65% in top quarter, 91% in top half
Early decision deadline: 11/15, notification date: 12/15
Early action deadline: N/A, notification date: N/A
Application deadline (fall): 2/15
Undergraduate student body: 1,890 full time, 41 part time; 46% male, 54% female; 0% American Indian, 2% Asian, 6% black, 7% Hispanic, 5% multiracial, 0% Pacific Islander, 76% white, 3% international; 52% from in state; 93% live on campus; 28% of students in fraternities, 29% in sororities
Most popular majors: 15% Psychology, General; 12% Biology/Biological Sciences, General; 10% Economics, General; 8% English Language and Literature, General; 7% Political Science and Government, General
Expenses: 2016-2017: $44,250; room/board: $11,170
Financial aid: (800) 835-7780; 72% of undergrads determined to have financial need; average aid package $36,790

Alvernia University
Reading PA
(610) 796-8220
U.S. News ranking: Reg. U. (N), No. 114
Website: www.alvernia.edu
Admissions email: admissions@alvernia.edu
Private; founded 1958
Affiliation: Roman Catholic
Freshman admissions: selective; 2015-2016: 1,670 applied, 1,240 accepted. Either SAT or ACT required. SAT 25/75 percentile: 900-1090. High school rank: 10% in top tenth, 35% in top quarter, 65% in top half
Early decision deadline: N/A, notification date: N/A
Early action deadline: N/A, notification date: N/A
Application deadline (fall): rolling
Undergraduate student body: 1,765 full time, 593 part time; 28% male, 72% female; 0% American Indian, 2% Asian, 13% black, 7% Hispanic, 1% multiracial, 0% Pacific Islander, 69% white, 0% international; 83% from in state; 43% live on campus; N/A of students in fraternities, N/A in sororities
Most popular majors: 36% Health Professions and Related Programs; 16% Business, Management, Marketing, and Related Support Services; 13% Homeland Security, Law Enforcement, Firefighting and Related Protective Services;

6% Education; 6% Public Administration and Social Service Professions
Expenses: 2016-2017: $32,270; room/board: $11,240
Financial aid: (610) 796-8356; 78% of undergrads determined to have financial need; average aid package $19,663

Arcadia University
Glenside PA
(215) 572-2910
U.S. News ranking: Reg. U. (N), No. 42
Website: www.arcadia.edu
Admissions email: admiss@arcadia.edu
Private; founded 1853
Freshman admissions: selective; 2015-2016: 9,641 applied, 5,713 accepted. Either SAT or ACT required. SAT 25/75 percentile: 996-1200. High school rank: 28% in top tenth, 60% in top quarter, 88% in top half
Early decision deadline: N/A, notification date: N/A
Early action deadline: N/A, notification date: N/A
Application deadline (fall): rolling
Undergraduate student body: 2,380 full time, 260 part time; 31% male, 69% female; 0% American Indian, 5% Asian, 9% black, 8% Hispanic, 4% multiracial, 0% Pacific Islander, 68% white, 3% international; 61% from in state; 54% live on campus; 0% of students in fraternities, 0% in sororities
Most popular majors: 15% Biology/Biological Sciences, General; 11% Psychology, General; 8% International Business/Trade/Commerce; 5% Teacher Education and Professional Development, Specific Subject Areas, Other; 4% International/Global Studies
Expenses: 2016-2017: $40,920; room/board: $13,500
Financial aid: (215) 572-2980; 75% of undergrads determined to have financial need; average aid package $30,044

The Art Institute of Philadelphia[1]
Philadelphia PA
(855) 270-5167
U.S. News ranking: Arts, unranked
Website: www.artinstitutes.edu/philadelphia
Admissions email: N/A
For-profit
Application deadline (fall): N/A
Undergraduate student body: N/A full time, N/A part time
Expenses: 2015-2016: $17,916; room/board: $11,373
Financial aid: N/A

Art Institute of Pittsburgh[1]
Pittsburgh PA
(800) 275-2470
U.S. News ranking: Arts, unranked
Website: www.artinstitutes.edu/pittsburgh/Admissions
Admissions email: aip@aii.edu
For-profit
Application deadline (fall): N/A
Undergraduate student body: N/A full time, N/A part time

Expenses: 2015-2016: $17,628; room/board: $10,656
Financial aid: N/A

Bloomsburg University of Pennsylvania
Bloomsburg PA
(570) 389-4316
U.S. News ranking: Reg. U. (N), No. 104
Website: www.bloomu.edu
Admissions email: buadmiss@bloomu.edu
Public; founded 1839
Freshman admissions: less selective; 2015-2016: 9,795 applied, 8,592 accepted. Either SAT or ACT required. SAT 25/75 percentile: 880-1080. High school rank: 8% in top tenth, 26% in top quarter, 61% in top half
Early decision deadline: N/A, notification date: N/A
Early action deadline: N/A, notification date: 5/1
Application deadline (fall): rolling
Undergraduate student body: 8,439 full time, 719 part time; 43% male, 57% female; 0% American Indian, 1% Asian, 9% black, 6% Hispanic, 3% multiracial, 0% Pacific Islander, 80% white, 1% international; 90% from in state; 44% live on campus; N/A of students in fraternities, N/A in sororities
Most popular majors: 18% Business Administration and Management, General; 6% Psychology, General; 4% Criminal Justice/Safety Studies
Expenses: 2016-2017: $10,154 in state, $21,012 out of state; room/board:
Financial aid: (570) 389-4297; 65% of undergrads determined to have financial need; average aid package $9,011

Bryn Athyn College of the New Church
Bryn Athyn PA
(267) 502-6000
U.S. News ranking: Nat. Lib. Arts, second tier
Website: www.brynathyn.edu
Admissions email: admissions@brynathyn.edu
Private; founded 1877
Affiliation: General Church of the New Jerusalem
Freshman admissions: less selective; 2015-2016: 439 applied, 185 accepted. Either SAT or ACT required. SAT 25/75 percentile: 785-1105. High school rank: N/A
Early decision deadline: N/A, notification date: N/A
Early action deadline: N/A, notification date: N/A
Application deadline (fall): rolling
Undergraduate student body: 264 full time, 9 part time; 53% male, 47% female; 0% American Indian, 3% Asian, 20% black, 10% Hispanic, 0% multiracial, 0% Pacific Islander, 62% white, 4% international; 74% from in state; 61% live on campus; N/A of students in fraternities, N/A in sororities

Most popular majors: Business, Management, Marketing, and Related Support Services; Education; History; Multi/Interdisciplinary Studies; Psychology
Expenses: 2015-2016: $19,353; room/board: $11,202
Financial aid: (267) 502-2630

Bryn Mawr College
Bryn Mawr PA
(610) 526-5152
U.S. News ranking: Nat. Lib. Arts, No. 31
Website: www.brynmawr.edu
Admissions email: admissions@brynmawr.edu
Private; founded 1885
Freshman admissions: more selective; 2015-2016: 2,890 applied, 1,113 accepted. Neither SAT nor ACT required. SAT 25/75 percentile: 1240-1460. High school rank: 63% in top tenth, 88% in top quarter, 98% in top half
Early decision deadline: 11/15, notification date: 12/15
Early action deadline: N/A, notification date: N/A
Application deadline (fall): 1/15
Undergraduate student body: 1,332 full time, 14 part time; 0% male, 100% female; 0% American Indian, 12% Asian, 6% black, 9% Hispanic, 5% multiracial, 0% Pacific Islander, 36% white, 23% international; 17% from in state; 93% live on campus; N/A of students in fraternities, N/A in sororities
Most popular majors: 24% Social Sciences, General; 15% Psychology, General; 10% Biology/Biological Sciences, General; 9% Foreign Languages and Literatures, General; 9% Mathematics, General
Expenses: 2016-2017: $48,790; room/board: $15,370
Financial aid: (610) 526-5245; 51% of undergrads determined to have financial need; average aid package $44,283

Bucknell University
Lewisburg PA
(570) 577-3000
U.S. News ranking: Nat. Lib. Arts, No. 32
Website: www.bucknell.edu
Admissions email: admissions@bucknell.edu
Private; founded 1846
Freshman admissions: more selective; 2015-2016: 10,967 applied, 2,718 accepted. Either SAT or ACT required. SAT 25/75 percentile: 1210-1390. High school rank: 65% in top tenth, 91% in top quarter, 99% in top half
Early decision deadline: 11/15, notification date: 12/15
Early action deadline: N/A, notification date: N/A
Application deadline (fall): 1/15
Undergraduate student body: 3,533 full time, 36 part time; 48% male, 52% female; 0% American Indian, 4% Asian, 3% black, 6% Hispanic, 4% multiracial, N/A Pacific Islander, 77% white, 5% international; 23% from in state; 91% live on campus; 41% of students in fraternities, 47% in sororities

Most popular majors: 10% Economics, General; 7% Political Science and Government, General; 6% Accounting and Finance; 6% Biology/Biological Sciences, General; 6% Psychology, General
Expenses: 2016-2017: $51,960; room/board: $12,656
Financial aid: (570) 577-1331; 42% of undergrads determined to have financial need; average aid package $31,500

Cabrini University
Radnor PA
(610) 902-8552
U.S. News ranking: Reg. U. (N), No. 131
Website: www.cabrini.edu
Admissions email: admit@cabrini.edu
Private; founded 1957
Affiliation: Roman Catholic
Freshman admissions: less selective; 2015-2016: 2,544 applied, 1,843 accepted. Neither SAT nor ACT required. ACT 25/75 percentile: N/A. High school rank: N/A
Early decision deadline: N/A, notification date: N/A
Early action deadline: N/A, notification date: N/A
Application deadline (fall): rolling
Undergraduate student body: 1,310 full time, 267 part time; 37% male, 63% female; 0% American Indian, 1% Asian, 20% black, 7% Hispanic, 4% multiracial, 0% Pacific Islander, 63% white, 0% international; 70% from in state; 64% live on campus; N/A of students in fraternities, N/A in sororities
Most popular majors: 25% Business, Management, and Related Support Services, Other; 12% Education, General; 11% Psychology, General; 11% Social Sciences, General
Expenses: 2015-2016: $30,752; room/board: $12,738
Financial aid: (610) 902-8420

Cairn University
Langhorne PA
(215) 702-4235
U.S. News ranking: Reg. U. (N), No. 137
Website: cairn.edu/
Admissions email: admissions@cairn.edu
Private; founded 1913
Affiliation: Evangelical
Freshman admissions: less selective; 2015-2016: 390 applied, 385 accepted. Either SAT or ACT required. SAT 25/75 percentile: 850-1095. High school rank: 7% in top tenth, 27% in top quarter, 60% in top half
Early decision deadline: N/A, notification date: N/A
Early action deadline: N/A, notification date: N/A
Application deadline (fall): rolling
Undergraduate student body: 724 full time, 59 part time; 46% male, 54% female; 0% American Indian, 4% Asian, 14% black, 7% Hispanic, 2% multiracial, 0% Pacific Islander, 72% white, 2% international
Most popular majors: Information not available

Expenses: 2016-2017: $25,246; room/board: $9,583
Financial aid: (215) 702-4246; 81% of undergrads determined to have financial need; average aid package $19,882

California University of Pennsylvania
California PA
(724) 938-4404
U.S. News ranking: Reg. U. (N), second tier
Website: www.calu.edu/
Admissions email: inquiry@calu.edu
Public; founded 1852
Freshman admissions: less selective; 2015-2016: 3,691 applied, 3,049 accepted. SAT required. SAT 25/75 percentile: 820-1020. High school rank: 8% in top tenth, 23% in top quarter, 55% in top half
Early decision deadline: N/A, notification date: N/A
Early action deadline: N/A, notification date: N/A
Application deadline (fall): 8/22
Undergraduate student body: 4,995 full time, 790 part time; 47% male, 53% female; 0% American Indian, 1% Asian, 12% black, 3% Hispanic, 3% multiracial, 0% Pacific Islander, 77% white, 1% international; 90% from in state; 30% live on campus; 3% of students in fraternities, 4% in sororities
Most popular majors: 14% Business, Management, Marketing, and Related Support Services; 13% Health Professions and Related Programs; 12% Parks, Recreation, Leisure, and Fitness Studies; 7% Homeland Security, Law Enforcement, Firefighting and Related Protective Services; 7% Education
Expenses: 2015-2016: $9,936 in state, $13,466 out of state; room/board: $10,086
Financial aid: (724) 938-4415

Carlow University
Pittsburgh PA
(412) 578-6059
U.S. News ranking: Reg. U. (N), No. 118
Website: www.carlow.edu
Admissions email: admissions@carlow.edu
Private; founded 1929
Affiliation: Roman Catholic
Freshman admissions: less selective; 2015-2016: 945 applied, 763 accepted. Either SAT or ACT required. SAT 25/75 percentile: 868-1063. High school rank: 12% in top tenth, 38% in top quarter, 75% in top half
Early decision deadline: N/A, notification date: N/A
Early action deadline: N/A, notification date: N/A
Application deadline (fall): rolling
Undergraduate student body: 1,040 full time, 359 part time; 12% male, 88% female; 0% American Indian, 1% Asian, 22% black, 2% Hispanic, 5% multiracial, 0% Pacific Islander, 61% white, 0% international; 95% from in

state; 31% live on campus; 6% of students in fraternities, 3% in sororities
Most popular majors: 27% Registered Nursing/Registered Nurse; 10% Biology/Biological Sciences, General; 9% Psychology, General; 6% Social Work
Expenses: 2016-2017: $27,764; room/board: $10,784
Financial aid: (412) 578-6058; 91% of undergrads determined to have financial need; average aid package $18,912

Carnegie Mellon University
Pittsburgh PA
(412) 268-2082
U.S. News ranking: Nat. U., No. 24
Website: www.cmu.edu
Admissions email: undergraduate-admissions@andrew.cmu.edu
Private; founded 1900
Freshman admissions: most selective; 2015-2016: 20,547 applied, 4,873 accepted. Either SAT or ACT required. SAT 25/75 percentile: 1360-1540. High school rank: 78% in top tenth, 95% in top quarter, 99% in top half
Early decision deadline: 11/1, notification date: 12/15
Early action deadline: N/A, notification date: N/A
Application deadline (fall): 1/1
Undergraduate student body: 6,234 full time, 220 part time; 54% male, 46% female; 0% American Indian, 27% Asian, 4% black, 8% Hispanic, 4% multiracial, 0% Pacific Islander, 30% white, 22% international; 16% from in state; 61% live on campus; 17% of students in fraternities, 14% in sororities
Most popular majors: 13% Information Technology; 9% Electrical and Electronics Engineering; 7% Business Administration and Management, General; 6% Computer Science; 6% Mechanical Engineering
Expenses: 2016-2017: $52,040; room/board: $13,270
Financial aid: (412) 268-8186; 43% of undergrads determined to have financial need; average aid package $37,013

Cedar Crest College
Allentown PA
(800) 360-1222
U.S. News ranking: Reg. Coll. (N), No. 6
Website: www.cedarcrest.edu
Admissions email: cccadmis@cedarcrest.edu
Private; founded 1867
Freshman admissions: selective; 2015-2016: 1,086 applied, 733 accepted. Either SAT or ACT required. SAT 25/75 percentile: 830-1080. High school rank: 16% in top tenth, 45% in top quarter, 79% in top half
Early decision deadline: N/A, notification date: N/A
Early action deadline: N/A, notification date: N/A
Application deadline (fall): rolling

Undergraduate student body: 775 full time, 613 part time; 10% male, 90% female; 0% American Indian, 3% Asian, 10% black, 15% Hispanic, 1% multiracial, 0% Pacific Islander, 62% white, 5% international; 87% from in state; 26% live on campus; N/A of students in fraternities, N/A in sororities
Most popular majors: 44% Health Professions and Related Programs; 12% Public Administration and Social Service Professions; 7% Psychology; 6% Business, Management, Marketing, and Related Support Services; 5% Family and Consumer Sciences/Human Sciences
Expenses: 2016-2017: $36,825; room/board: $10,933
Financial aid: (610) 740-3785; 92% of undergrads determined to have financial need; average aid package $28,069

Central Penn College[1]
Summerdale PA
(800) 759-2727
U.S. News ranking: Reg. Coll. (N), unranked
Website: www.centralpenn.edu
Admissions email: admissions@centralpenn.edu
For-profit
Application deadline (fall): N/A
Undergraduate student body: N/A full time, N/A part time
Expenses: 2015-2016: $17,151; room/board: $6,798
Financial aid: (800) 759-2727

Chatham University
Pittsburgh PA
(800) 837-1290
U.S. News ranking: Reg. U. (N), No. 72
Website: www.chatham.edu
Admissions email: admissions@chatham.edu
Private; founded 1869
Freshman admissions: selective; 2015-2016: 1,490 applied, 817 accepted. Neither SAT nor ACT required. SAT 25/75 percentile: 955-1145. High school rank: 23% in top tenth, 53% in top quarter, 87% in top half
Early decision deadline: N/A, notification date: N/A
Early action deadline: N/A, notification date: N/A
Application deadline (fall): 8/1
Undergraduate student body: 667 full time, 367 part time; 17% male, 83% female; 1% American Indian, 2% Asian, 10% black, 5% Hispanic, 2% multiracial, 0% Pacific Islander, 72% white, 3% international; 81% from in state; 52% live on campus; N/A of students in fraternities, N/A in sororities
Most popular majors: 26% Health Professions and Related Programs; 12% Biological and Biomedical Sciences; 11% Business, Management, Marketing, and Related Support Services; 10% Visual and Performing Arts; 9% Psychology
Expenses: 2016-2017: $35,475; room/board: $11,042
Financial aid: (412) 365-1777; 81% of undergrads determined to have financial need; average aid package $26,184

Chestnut Hill College
Philadelphia PA
(215) 248-7001
U.S. News ranking: Reg. U. (N), No. 137
Website: www.chc.edu
Admissions email: chcapply@chc.edu
Private; founded 1924
Affiliation: Roman Catholic
Freshman admissions: less selective; 2015-2016: 1,215 applied, 1,125 accepted. Either SAT or ACT required. SAT 25/75 percentile: 850-1080. High school rank: 9% in top tenth, 28% in top quarter, 47% in top half
Early decision deadline: N/A, notification date: N/A
Early action deadline: N/A, notification date: N/A
Application deadline (fall): rolling
Undergraduate student body: 1,148 full time, 295 part time; 33% male, 67% female; 0% American Indian, 2% Asian, 37% black, 9% Hispanic, 3% multiracial, 0% Pacific Islander, 39% white, 3% international; 64% from in state; 52% live on campus; 0% of students in fraternities, 0% in sororities
Most popular majors: 22% Public Administration and Social Service Professions; 16% Business, Management, Marketing, and Related Support Services; 16% Homeland Security, Law Enforcement, Firefighting and Related Protective Services; 15% Education; 7% Psychology
Expenses: 2016-2017: $34,130; room/board: $10,300
Financial aid: (215) 248-7182; 84% of undergrads determined to have financial need; average aid package $22,043

Cheyney University of Pennsylvania
Cheyney PA
(610) 399-2275
U.S. News ranking: Nat. Lib. Arts, second tier
Website: www.cheyney.edu
Admissions email: abrown@cheyney.edu
Public; founded 1837
Freshman admissions: selective; 2015-2016: 1,700 applied, 685 accepted. Neither SAT nor ACT required. ACT 25/75 percentile: N/A. High school rank: N/A
Early decision deadline: N/A, notification date: N/A
Early action deadline: N/A, notification date: N/A
Application deadline (fall): N/A
Undergraduate student body: 619 full time, 67 part time; 50% male, 50% female; 0% American Indian, 0% Asian, 82% black, 5% Hispanic, 4% multiracial, 0% Pacific Islander, 2% white, 0% international
Most popular majors: Information not available
Expenses: 2015-2016: $9,344 in state, $14,162 out of state; room/board: $11,252
Financial aid: (610) 399-2302

Clarion University of Pennsylvania

Clarion PA
(814) 393-2306
U.S. News ranking: Reg. U. (N), second tier
Website: www.clarion.edu
Admissions email: admissions@clarion.edu
Public; founded 1867
Freshman admissions: less selective; 2015-2016: 2,215 applied, 2,128 accepted. Either SAT or ACT required. SAT 25/75 percentile: 840-1030. High school rank: 11% in top tenth, 27% in top quarter, 59% in top half
Early decision deadline: N/A, notification date: N/A
Early action deadline: N/A, notification date: N/A
Application deadline (fall): rolling
Undergraduate student body: 3,703 full time, 852 part time; 37% male, 63% female; 0% American Indian, 1% Asian, 8% black, 1% Hispanic, 2% multiracial, 0% Pacific Islander, 85% white, 1% international; 93% from in state; 37% live on campus; 8% of students in fraternities, 11% in sororities
Most popular majors: 24% Health Professions and Related Programs; 19% Business, Management, Marketing, and Related Support Services; 11% Liberal Arts and Sciences, General Studies and Humanities; 10% Education
Expenses: 2015-2016: $10,190 in state, $13,720 out of state; room/board: $9,792
Financial aid: (814) 393-2315; 80% of undergrads determined to have financial need; average aid package $9,572

Curtis Institute of Music[1]

Philadelphia PA
(215) 717-3117
U.S. News ranking: Arts, unranked
Website: www.curtis.edu
Admissions email: admissions@curtis.edu
Private; founded 1924
Application deadline (fall): 12/12
Undergraduate student body: N/A full time, N/A part time
Expenses: 2015-2016: $2,525; room/board: $14,709
Financial aid: (215) 717-3165

Delaware Valley University

Doylestown PA
(215) 489-2211
U.S. News ranking: Reg. U. (N), No. 114
Website: www.delval.edu
Admissions email: admitme@delval.edu
Private; founded 1896
Freshman admissions: less selective; 2015-2016: 2,594 applied, 1,782 accepted. Either SAT or ACT required. SAT 25/75 percentile: 870-1110. High school rank: 11% in top tenth, 35% in top quarter, 67% in top half
Early decision deadline: N/A, notification date: N/A

DeSales University

Center Valley PA
(610) 282-4443
U.S. News ranking: Reg. U. (N), No. 61
Website: www.desales.edu
Admissions email: admiss@desales.edu
Private; founded 1964
Affiliation: Roman Catholic
Freshman admissions: selective; 2015-2016: 2,706 applied, 2,100 accepted. Either SAT or ACT required. SAT 25/75 percentile: 890-1180. High school rank: 21% in top tenth, 47% in top quarter, 75% in top half
Early decision deadline: N/A, notification date: N/A
Early action deadline: N/A, notification date: N/A
Application deadline (fall): 8/1
Undergraduate student body: 1,738 full time, 553 part time; 40% male, 60% female; 1% American Indian, 2% Asian, 4% black, 12% Hispanic, 0% multiracial, 0% Pacific Islander, 75% white, 0% international; 72% from in state; 60% live on campus; 0% of students in fraternities, 0% in sororities
Most popular majors: 23% Business, Management, Marketing, and Related Support Services; 22% Health Professions and Related Programs; 10% Psychology; 10% Visual and Performing Arts; 7% Homeland Security, Law Enforcement, Firefighting and Related Protective Services
Expenses: 2016-2017: $34,850; room/board: $12,412
Financial aid: (610) 282-1100; 78% of undergrads determined to have financial need; average aid package $24,108

Dickinson College

Carlisle PA
(800) 644-1773
U.S. News ranking: Nat. Lib. Arts, No. 41
Website: www.dickinson.edu
Admissions email: admissions@dickinson.edu
Private; founded 1783

Freshman admissions: more selective; 2015-2016: 6,031 applied, 2,841 accepted. Neither SAT nor ACT required. SAT 25/75 percentile: 1190-1380. High school rank: N/A
Early decision deadline: 11/15, notification date: 12/15
Early action deadline: 12/1, notification date: 2/15
Application deadline (fall): 2/1
Undergraduate student body: 2,391 full time, 29 part time; 42% male, 58% female; 0% American Indian, 3% Asian, 4% black, 6% Hispanic, 4% multiracial, 0% Pacific Islander, 72% white, 10% international; 22% from in state; 94% live on campus; 14% of students in fraternities, 26% in sororities
Most popular majors: 9% International Business/Trade/Commerce; 8% Political Science and Government, General; 7% Economics, General; 7% Psychology, General; 6% English Language and Literature, General
Expenses: 2016-2017: $51,180; room/board: $12,794
Financial aid: (717) 245-1308; 54% of undergrads determined to have financial need; average aid package $40,650

Drexel University

Philadelphia PA
(800) 237-3935
U.S. News ranking: Nat. U., No. 96
Website: www.drexel.edu
Admissions email: enroll@drexel.edu
Private; founded 1891
Freshman admissions: more selective; 2015-2016: 28,758 applied, 21,494 accepted. Either SAT or ACT required. SAT 25/75 percentile: 1095-1310. High school rank: 42% in top tenth, 69% in top quarter, 91% in top half
Early decision deadline: N/A, notification date: N/A
Early action deadline: 11/1, notification date: 12/15
Application deadline (fall): 1/15
Undergraduate student body: 11,776 full time, 2,362 part time; 51% male, 49% female; 0% American Indian, 13% Asian, 7% black, 6% Hispanic, 3% multiracial, 1% Pacific Islander, 54% white, 13% international
Most popular majors: Information not available
Expenses: 2016-2017: $51,030; room/board: $14,367
Financial aid: (215) 895-2537; 60% of undergrads determined to have financial need; average aid package $34,747

Duquesne University

Pittsburgh PA
(412) 396-6222
U.S. News ranking: Nat. U., No. 124
Website: www.duq.edu
Admissions email: admissions@duq.edu
Private; founded 1878
Affiliation: Roman Catholic
Freshman admissions: selective; 2015-2016: 7,354 applied, 5,562 accepted. Neither SAT nor ACT required. SAT 25/75 percentile: 1040-1210. High

school rank: 23% in top tenth, 54% in top quarter, 86% in top half
Early decision deadline: 11/1, notification date: 11/15
Early action deadline: 12/1, notification date: 1/15
Application deadline (fall): 7/1
Undergraduate student body: 5,720 full time, 241 part time; 38% male, 62% female; 0% American Indian, 2% Asian, 5% black, 3% Hispanic, 3% multiracial, 0% Pacific Islander, 81% white, 4% international; 74% from in state; 56% live on campus; 17% of students in fraternities, 23% in sororities
Most popular majors: 28% Business, Management, Marketing, and Related Support Services; 25% Health Professions and Related Programs; 9% Biological and Biomedical Sciences; 6% Education
Expenses: 2016-2017: $35,062; room/board: $11,760
Financial aid: (412) 396-6607; 67% of undergrads determined to have financial need; average aid package $24,318

Eastern University

St. Davids PA
(610) 341-5967
U.S. News ranking: Reg. U. (N), No. 91
Website: www.eastern.edu
Admissions email: ugadm@eastern.edu
Private; founded 1952
Affiliation: American Baptist
Freshman admissions: selective; 2015-2016: 2,941 applied, 1,536 accepted. Either SAT or ACT required. SAT 25/75 percentile: 920-1170. High school rank: 20% in top tenth, 44% in top quarter, 78% in top half
Early decision deadline: N/A, notification date: N/A
Early action deadline: N/A, notification date: N/A
Application deadline (fall): rolling
Undergraduate student body: 1,851 full time, 333 part time; 30% male, 70% female; 0% American Indian, 2% Asian, 23% black, 17% Hispanic, 1% multiracial, 0% Pacific Islander, 50% white, 2% international; 41% from in state; 76% live on campus; N/A of students in fraternities, N/A in sororities
Most popular majors: 13% Business Administration and Management, General; 7% Nursing Practice; 7% Social Work; 6% Psychology, General
Expenses: 2016-2017: $31,140; room/board: $10,674
Financial aid: (610) 341-5842; 83% of undergrads determined to have financial need; average aid package $21,501

East Stroudsburg University of Pennsylvania

East Stroudsburg PA
(570) 422-3542
U.S. News ranking: Reg. U. (N), No. 131
Website: www.esu.edu
Admissions email: undergrads@po-box.esu.edu

Public; founded 1893
Freshman admissions: less selective; 2015-2016: 6,517 applied, 5,027 accepted. Neither SAT nor ACT required. SAT 25/75 percentile: 840-1030. High school rank: 7% in top tenth, 23% in top quarter, 57% in top half
Early decision deadline: N/A, notification date: N/A
Early action deadline: N/A, notification date: N/A
Application deadline (fall): 5/1
Undergraduate student body: 5,644 full time, 522 part time; 44% male, 56% female; 0% American Indian, 2% Asian, 14% black, 12% Hispanic, 4% multiracial, 0% Pacific Islander, 66% white, 1% international; 70% from in state; 46% live on campus; 5% of students in fraternities, 4% in sororities
Most popular majors: 15% Business Administration and Management, General; 15% Public Health, General; 11% Parks, Recreation and Leisure Facilities Management, General; 9% Biology/Biological Sciences, General; 9% Psychology, General
Expenses: 2015-2016: $9,684 in state, $20,502 out of state; room/board: $8,126
Financial aid: (570) 422-2800; 53% of undergrads determined to have financial need; average aid package $7,583

Edinboro University of Pennsylvania[1]

Edinboro PA
(888) 846-2676
U.S. News ranking: Reg. U. (N), second tier
Website: www.edinboro.edu
Admissions email: eup_admissions@edinboro.edu
Public; founded 1857
Application deadline (fall): rolling
Undergraduate student body: N/A full time, N/A part time
Expenses: 2016-2017: $9,535 in state, $13,065 out of state; room/board: $11,154
Financial aid: (814) 732-5555

Elizabethtown College

Elizabethtown PA
(717) 361-1400
U.S. News ranking: Nat. Lib. Arts, No. 115
Website: www.etown.edu
Admissions email: admissions@etown.edu
Private; founded 1899
Affiliation: Brethren
Freshman admissions: selective; 2015-2016: 3,453 applied, 2,442 accepted. Either SAT or ACT required. SAT 25/75 percentile: 1000-1230. High school rank: 31% in top tenth, 63% in top quarter, 88% in top half
Early decision deadline: N/A, notification date: N/A
Early action deadline: N/A, notification date: N/A
Application deadline (fall): rolling
Undergraduate student body: 1,755 full time, 19 part time; 38% male, 62% female; 0% American Indian, 2% Asian, 3% black, 4% Hispanic, 2% multiracial, 0% Pacific Islander, 86% white,

3% international; 67% from in state; 87% live on campus; N/A of students in fraternities, N/A in sororities
Most popular majors: 19% Business, Management, Marketing, and Related Support Services; 13% Health Professions and Related Programs; 12% Biological and Biomedical Sciences; 9% Education; 8% Social Sciences
Expenses: 2015-2016: $41,710; room/board: $10,140
Financial aid: (717) 361-1404

Franklin and Marshall College
Lancaster PA
(717) 291-3953
U.S. News ranking: Nat. Lib. Arts, No. 47
Website: www.fandm.edu
Admissions email: admission@fandm.edu
Private; founded 1787
Freshman admissions: more selective; 2015-2016: 7,146 applied, 2,305 accepted. Neither SAT nor ACT required. SAT 25/75 percentile: 1210-1400. High school rank: 48% in top tenth, 80% in top quarter, 97% in top half
Early decision deadline: 11/15, notification date: 12/15
Early action deadline: N/A, notification date: N/A
Application deadline (fall): 1/15
Undergraduate student body: 2,217 full time, 32 part time; 48% male, 52% female; 0% American Indian, 5% Asian, 6% black, 8% Hispanic, 2% multiracial, 0% Pacific Islander, 59% white, 14% international; 27% from in state; 99% live on campus; 20% of students in fraternities, 30% in sororities
Most popular majors: 13% Business Administration and Management, General; 12% Political Science and Government, General; 8% Economics, General; 6% Psychology, General; 5% Creative Writing
Expenses: 2016-2017: $52,290; room/board: $13,120
Financial aid: (717) 291-3991; 52% of undergrads determined to have financial need; average aid package $46,531

Gannon University
Erie PA
(814) 871-7240
U.S. News ranking: Reg. U. (N), No. 51
Website: www.gannon.edu
Admissions email: admissions@gannon.edu
Private; founded 1925
Affiliation: Roman Catholic
Freshman admissions: selective; 2015-2016: 4,213 applied, 3,192 accepted. Either SAT or ACT required. SAT 25/75 percentile: 923-1130. High school rank: 24% in top tenth, 50% in top quarter, 81% in top half
Early decision deadline: N/A, notification date: N/A
Early action deadline: N/A, notification date: N/A

Application deadline (fall): rolling
Undergraduate student body: 2,531 full time, 584 part time; 44% male, 56% female; 0% American Indian, 2% Asian, 5% black, 3% Hispanic, 2% multiracial, 0% Pacific Islander, 76% white, 9% international; 73% from in state; 44% live on campus; 14% of students in fraternities, 15% in sororities
Most popular majors: 34% Health Professions and Related Programs; 15% Business, Management, Marketing, and Related Support Services; 10% Parks, Recreation, Leisure, and Fitness Studies; 9% Biological and Biomedical Sciences; 5% Homeland Security, Law Enforcement, Firefighting and Related Protective Services
Expenses: 2016-2017: $30,042; room/board: $11,990
Financial aid: (814) 871-7337; 78% of undergrads determined to have financial need; average aid package $24,840

Geneva College
Beaver Falls PA
(724) 847-6500
U.S. News ranking: Reg. U. (N), No. 80
Website: www.geneva.edu
Admissions email: admissions@geneva.edu
Private; founded 1848
Affiliation: Reformed Presbyterian Church of North America
Freshman admissions: selective; 2015-2016: 1,678 applied, 1,230 accepted. Either SAT or ACT required. SAT 25/75 percentile: 900-1180. High school rank: 19% in top tenth, 51% in top quarter, 78% in top half
Early decision deadline: N/A, notification date: N/A
Early action deadline: N/A, notification date: N/A
Application deadline (fall): rolling
Undergraduate student body: 1,378 full time, 88 part time; 49% male, 51% female; 0% American Indian, 0% Asian, 9% black, 1% Hispanic, 3% multiracial, 0% Pacific Islander, 84% white, 1% international; 74% from in state; 62% live on campus; 0% of students in fraternities, 0% in sororities
Most popular majors: 9% Higher Education/Higher Education Administration; 9% Organizational Leadership; 9% Public Administration and Social Service Professions; 8% Business Administration and Management, General; 7% Counseling Psychology
Expenses: 2016-2017: $25,680; room/board: $9,770
Financial aid: (724) 847-6530; 82% of undergrads determined to have financial need; average aid package $20,649

Gettysburg College
Gettysburg PA
(800) 431-0803
U.S. News ranking: Nat. Lib. Arts, No. 51
Website: www.gettysburg.edu
Admissions email: admiss@gettysburg.edu
Private; founded 1832

Affiliation: Lutheran
Freshman admissions: more selective; 2015-2016: 6,386 applied, 2,540 accepted. Either SAT or ACT required. SAT 25/75 percentile: 1210-1350. High school rank: 56% in top tenth, 82% in top quarter, 98% in top half
Early decision deadline: 11/15, notification date: 12/15
Early action deadline: N/A, notification date: N/A
Application deadline (fall): 1/15
Undergraduate student body: 2,430 full time, 24 part time; 47% male, 53% female; 0% American Indian, 2% Asian, 3% black, 5% Hispanic, 2% multiracial, N/A Pacific Islander, 79% white, 5% international; 26% from in state; 94% live on campus; 31% of students in fraternities, 33% in sororities
Most popular majors: 24% Social Sciences, General; 13% Biology/Biological Sciences, General; 8% English Language and Literature, General; 8% Psychology, General; 7% Business/Commerce, General
Expenses: 2016-2017: $50,860; room/board: $12,140
Financial aid: (717) 337-6611; 62% of undergrads determined to have financial need; average aid package $38,861

Grove City College
Grove City PA
(724) 458-2100
U.S. News ranking: Nat. Lib. Arts, No. 122
Website: www.gcc.edu
Admissions email: admissions@gcc.edu
Private; founded 1876
Affiliation: Undenominational
Freshman admissions: more selective; 2015-2016: 1,541 applied, 1,248 accepted. Either SAT or ACT required. SAT 25/75 percentile: 1076-1309. High school rank: 40% in top tenth, 68% in top quarter, 91% in top half
Early decision deadline: 11/15, notification date: 12/15
Early action deadline: N/A, notification date: N/A
Application deadline (fall): 2/1
Undergraduate student body: 2,396 full time, 48 part time; 50% male, 50% female; 0% American Indian, 2% Asian, 1% black, 1% Hispanic, 3% multiracial, 0% Pacific Islander, 92% white, 1% international; 53% from in state; 95% live on campus; 18% of students in fraternities, 19% in sororities
Most popular majors: 8% General Literature; 7% Mechanical Engineering; 6% Biology/Biological Sciences, General; 6% Business Administration and Management, General
Expenses: 2016-2017: $16,630; room/board: $9,062
Financial aid: (724) 458-3300; 42% of undergrads determined to have financial need; average aid package $7,103

Gwynedd Mercy University
Gwynedd Valley PA
(215) 681-5510
U.S. News ranking: Reg. U. (N), No. 137
Website: www.gmercyu.edu/
Admissions email: admissions@gmercyu.edu
Private; founded 1948
Affiliation: Roman Catholic
Freshman admissions: less selective; 2015-2016: 850 applied, 785 accepted. Either SAT or ACT required. SAT 25/75 percentile: 830-1010. High school rank: 8% in top tenth, 25% in top quarter, 59% in top half
Early decision deadline: N/A, notification date: N/A
Early action deadline: N/A, notification date: N/A
Application deadline (fall): 8/20
Undergraduate student body: 1,826 full time, 174 part time; 24% male, 76% female; 0% American Indian, 5% Asian, 23% black, 5% Hispanic, N/A multiracial, N/A Pacific Islander, 57% white, 0% international; 89% from in state; 20% live on campus; N/A of students in fraternities, N/A in sororities
Most popular majors: 46% Health Professions and Related Programs; 30% Business, Management, Marketing, and Related Support Services; 5% Education; 5% Homeland Security, Law Enforcement, Firefighting and Related Protective Services; 3% Psychology
Expenses: 2016-2017: $32,480; room/board: $11,300
Financial aid: (215) 641-5570; 80% of undergrads determined to have financial need; average aid package $20,474

Harrisburg University of Science and Technology
Harrisburg PA
(717) 901-5150
U.S. News ranking: Reg. U. (N), second tier
Website: www.harrisburgu.edu
Admissions email: admissions@harrisburgu.edu
Private; founded 2001
Freshman admissions: less selective; 2015-2016: N/A applied, N/A accepted. Neither SAT nor ACT required. ACT 25/75 percentile: N/A. High school rank: N/A
Early decision deadline: N/A, notification date: N/A
Early action deadline: N/A, notification date: N/A
Application deadline (fall): rolling
Undergraduate student body: 330 full time, 104 part time; 56% male, 44% female; 1% American Indian, 6% Asian, 36% black, 10% Hispanic, 5% multiracial, 1% Pacific Islander, 40% white, 0% international
Most popular majors: 52% Computer and Information Sciences, General; 32% Natural Sciences
Expenses: 2016-2017: $23,900; room/board: $9,700

Financial aid: N/A; 95% of undergrads determined to have financial need; average aid package $19,386

Haverford College
Haverford PA
(610) 896-1350
U.S. News ranking: Nat. Lib. Arts, No. 12
Website: www.haverford.edu
Admissions email: admission@haverford.edu
Private; founded 1833
Freshman admissions: most selective; 2015-2016: 3,467 applied, 852 accepted. Either SAT or ACT required. SAT 25/75 percentile: 1320-1530. High school rank: 96% in top tenth, 100% in top quarter, 100% in top half
Early decision deadline: 11/15, notification date: 12/15
Early action deadline: N/A, notification date: N/A
Application deadline (fall): 1/15
Undergraduate student body: 1,233 full time, N/A part time; 49% male, 51% female; 0% American Indian, 10% Asian, 7% black, 10% Hispanic, 4% multiracial, N/A Pacific Islander, 61% white, 7% international; 13% from in state; 99% live on campus; N/A of students in fraternities, N/A in sororities
Most popular majors: 24% Social Sciences, General; 15% Physical Sciences; 10% English Language and Literature, General; 9% Biology/Biological Sciences, General; 9% Psychology, General
Expenses: 2016-2017: $51,024; room/board: $15,466
Financial aid: (610) 896-1350; 51% of undergrads determined to have financial need; average aid package $46,600

Holy Family University
Philadelphia PA
(215) 637-3050
U.S. News ranking: Reg. U. (N), second tier
Website: www.holyfamily.edu
Admissions email: admissions@holyfamily.edu
Private; founded 1954
Affiliation: Roman Catholic
Freshman admissions: less selective; 2015-2016: 1,328 applied, 982 accepted. Either SAT or ACT required. SAT 25/75 percentile: 820-1010. High school rank: 10% in top tenth, 25% in top quarter, 62% in top half
Early decision deadline: N/A, notification date: N/A
Early action deadline: N/A, notification date: N/A
Application deadline (fall): rolling
Undergraduate student body: 1,432 full time, 613 part time; 27% male, 73% female; 0% American Indian, 4% Asian, 9% black, 7% Hispanic, N/A multiracial, N/A Pacific Islander, 62% white, 0% international; 84% from in state; 17% live on campus; N/A of students in fraternities, N/A in sororities
Most popular majors: 46% Health Professions and Related Programs; 18% Business, Management, Marketing, and Related Support Services; and

Education; 8% Homeland Security, Law Enforcement, Firefighting and Related Protective Services; 8% Psychology
Expenses: 2016-2017: $29,750; room/board: $13,576
Financial aid: (215) 637-5538; 86% of undergrads determined to have financial need; average aid package $20,660

Immaculata University
Immaculata PA
(877) 428-6329
U.S. News ranking: Nat. U., No. 152
Website: www.immaculata.edu
Admissions email: admiss@immaculata.edu
Private; founded 1920
Affiliation: Roman Catholic
Freshman admissions: less selective; 2015-2016: 1,586 applied, 1,250 accepted. Either SAT or ACT required. SAT 25/75 percentile: 860-1080. High school rank: N/A
Early decision deadline: N/A, notification date: N/A
Early action deadline: N/A, notification date: N/A
Application deadline (fall): rolling
Undergraduate student body: 1,021 full time, 769 part time; 28% male, 72% female; 0% American Indian, 2% Asian, 14% black, 5% Hispanic, 2% multiracial, 0% Pacific Islander, 74% white, 1% international; 71% from in state; 42% live on campus; 2% of students in fraternities, 13% in sororities
Most popular majors: 65% Health Professions and Related Programs; 14% Business, Management, Marketing, and Related Support Services; 5% Education; 3% Homeland Security, Law Enforcement, Firefighting and Related Protective Services; 3% Parks, Recreation, Leisure, and Fitness Studies
Expenses: 2016-2017: $35,210; room/board: $12,500
Financial aid: (610) 647-4400; 75% of undergrads determined to have financial need; average aid package $21,029

Indiana University of Pennsylvania
Indiana PA
(800) 442-6830
U.S. News ranking: Nat. U., second tier
Website: www.iup.edu
Admissions email: admissions-inquiry@iup.edu
Public; founded 1875
Freshman admissions: less selective; 2015-2016: 9,566 applied, 8,451 accepted. Either SAT or ACT required. SAT 25/75 percentile: 860-1060. High school rank: 8% in top tenth, 26% in top quarter, 62% in top half
Early decision deadline: N/A, notification date: N/A
Early action deadline: N/A, notification date: N/A
Application deadline (fall): rolling
Undergraduate student body: 10,740 full time, 797 part time; 45% male, 55% female; 0%

American Indian, 1% Asian, 12% black, 4% Hispanic, 4% multiracial, 0% Pacific Islander, 75% white, 4% international; 94% from in state; 33% live on campus; 8% of students in fraternities, 8% in sororities
Most popular majors: 24% Business, Management, Marketing, and Related Support Services; 17% Social Sciences; 9% Health Professions and Related Programs; 6% Visual and Performing Arts; 6% Parks, Recreation, Leisure, and Fitness Studies
Expenses: 2016-2017: $11,368 in state, $21,034 out of state; room/board: $12,402
Financial aid: (724) 357-2218; 71% of undergrads determined to have financial need; average aid package $9,845

Juniata College
Huntingdon PA
(877) 586-4282
U.S. News ranking: Nat. Lib. Arts, No. 108
Website: www.juniata.edu
Admissions email: admissions@juniata.edu
Private; founded 1876
Freshman admissions: selective; 2015-2016: 2,604 applied, 2,003 accepted. Neither SAT nor ACT required. SAT 25/75 percentile: 1020-1250. High school rank: 30% in top tenth, 58% in top quarter, 91% in top half
Early decision deadline: 11/15, notification date: 12/23
Early action deadline: N/A, notification date: N/A
Application deadline (fall): 2/15
Undergraduate student body: 1,512 full time, 58 part time; 44% male, 56% female; 0% American Indian, 4% Asian, 3% black, 4% Hispanic, 2% multiracial, 0% Pacific Islander, 73% white, 8% international; 66% from in state; 82% live on campus; 0% of students in fraternities, 0% in sororities
Most popular majors: 20% Biological and Biomedical Sciences; 11% Physical Sciences; 11% Business, Management, Marketing, and Related Support Services; 7% Social Sciences
Expenses: 2016-2017: $42,170; room/board: $11,590
Financial aid: (814) 641-3142; 72% of undergrads determined to have financial need; average aid package $31,957

Keystone College
La Plume PA
(570) 945-8000
U.S. News ranking: Reg. Coll. (N), No. 29
Website: www.keystone.edu
Admissions email: admissions@keystone.edu
Private; founded 1868
Freshman admissions: least selective; 2015-2016: 999 applied, 977 accepted. Either SAT or ACT required. SAT 25/75 percentile: 800-1010. High school rank: N/A
Early decision deadline: N/A, notification date: N/A

Early action deadline: N/A, notification date: N/A
Application deadline (fall): 7/1
Undergraduate student body: 1,149 full time, 260 part time; 39% male, 61% female; 0% American Indian, 1% Asian, 7% black, 6% Hispanic, 2% multiracial, 0% Pacific Islander, 77% white, 0% international
Most popular majors: Information not available
Expenses: 2015-2016: $25,300; room/board: $10,500
Financial aid: (877) 426-5534

King's College
Wilkes-Barre PA
(888) 546-4772
U.S. News ranking: Reg. U. (N), No. 57
Website: www.kings.edu
Admissions email: admissions@kings.edu
Private; founded 1946
Affiliation: Catholic
Freshman admissions: selective; 2015-2016: 3,244 applied, 2,322 accepted. Neither SAT nor ACT required. SAT 25/75 percentile: 930-1130. High school rank: 15% in top tenth, 42% in top quarter, 70% in top half
Early decision deadline: N/A, notification date: N/A
Early action deadline: N/A, notification date: N/A
Application deadline (fall): rolling
Undergraduate student body: 1,801 full time, 188 part time; 51% male, 49% female; 0% American Indian, 2% Asian, 3% black, 7% Hispanic, 2% multiracial, 0% Pacific Islander, 78% white, 2% international; 74% from in state; 50% live on campus; 0% of students in fraternities, 0% in sororities
Most popular majors: 13% Accounting; 11% Business Administration and Management, General; 9% Criminal Justice/ Safety Studies; 8% Elementary Education and Teaching; 8% Health Professions and Related Clinical Sciences, Other
Expenses: 2015-2016: $33,090; room/board: $11,958
Financial aid: (570) 208-5868; 80% of undergrads determined to have financial need; average aid package $23,731

Kutztown University of Pennsylvania
Kutztown PA
(610) 683-4060
U.S. News ranking: Reg. U. (N), No. 128
Website: www.kutztown.edu
Admissions email: admissions@kutztown.edu
Public; founded 1866
Freshman admissions: less selective; 2015-2016: 8,136 applied, 6,599 accepted. Either SAT or ACT required. SAT 25/75 percentile: 860-1050. High school rank: 5% in top tenth, 19% in top quarter, 54% in top half
Early decision deadline: N/A, notification date: N/A
Early action deadline: N/A, notification date: N/A
Application deadline (fall): rolling

Undergraduate student body: 7,808 full time, 485 part time; 46% male, 54% female; 0% American Indian, 1% Asian, 8% black, 7% Hispanic, 3% multiracial, 0% Pacific Islander, 77% white, 1% international; 89% from in state; 45% live on campus; 3% of students in fraternities, 11% in sororities
Most popular majors: 19% Business Administration and Management, General; 11% Psychology, General; 9% English Language and Literature, General; 6% Criminal Justice/ Safety Studies; 5% Parks, Recreation and Leisure Studies
Expenses: 2015-2016: $9,411 in state, $20,229 out of state; room/board: $9,598
Financial aid: (610) 683-4077; 71% of undergrads determined to have financial need; average aid package $8,583

Lafayette College
Easton PA
(610) 330-5100
U.S. News ranking: Nat. Lib. Arts, No. 36
Website: www.lafayette.edu
Admissions email: admissions@lafayette.edu
Private; founded 1826
Freshman admissions: more selective; 2015-2016: 7,465 applied, 2,258 accepted. Either SAT or ACT required. SAT 25/75 percentile: 1200-1380. High school rank: 70% in top tenth, 93% in top quarter, 98% in top half
Early decision deadline: 11/15, notification date: 12/15
Early action deadline: N/A, notification date: N/A
Application deadline (fall): 1/15
Undergraduate student body: 2,491 full time, 42 part time; 51% male, 49% female; 0% American Indian, 4% Asian, 5% black, 6% Hispanic, 2% multiracial, 0% Pacific Islander, 67% white, 9% international; 19% from in state; 94% live on campus; 17% of students in fraternities, 34% in sororities
Most popular majors: 32% Social Sciences; 19% Engineering; 12% Biological and Biomedical Sciences; 8% Psychology; 7% Visual and Performing Arts
Expenses: 2016-2017: $48,885; room/board: $14,470
Financial aid: (610) 330-5055; 32% of undergrads determined to have financial need; average aid package $43,569

La Roche College
Pittsburgh PA
(800) 838-4572
U.S. News ranking: Reg. Coll. (N), No. 23
Website: www.laroche.edu
Admissions email: admissions@laroche.edu
Private; founded 1963
Affiliation: Roman Catholic
Freshman admissions: less selective; 2015-2016: 1,167 applied, 1,114 accepted. Either SAT or ACT required. SAT 25/75 percentile: 830-1040. High school rank: 7% in top tenth, 29% in top quarter, 69% in top half

Early decision deadline: N/A, notification date: N/A
Early action deadline: N/A, notification date: N/A
Application deadline (fall): rolling
Undergraduate student body: 1,162 full time, 236 part time; 44% male, 56% female; 0% American Indian, 1% Asian, 8% black, 2% Hispanic, 2% multiracial, 0% Pacific Islander, 62% white, 16% international; 92% from in state; 46% live on campus; N/A of students in fraternities, N/A in sororities
Most popular majors: 10% Psychology, General; 8% Management Science; 7% Criminal Justice/Safety Studies; 7% Medical Radiologic Technology/Science - Radiation Therapist; 7% Registered Nursing/Registered Nurse
Expenses: 2016-2017: $27,000; room/board: $10,924
Financial aid: (412) 536-1120; 69% of undergrads determined to have financial need; average aid package $27,782

La Salle University
Philadelphia PA
(215) 951-1500
U.S. News ranking: Reg. U. (N), No. 35
Website: www.lasalle.edu
Admissions email: admiss@lasalle.edu
Private; founded 1863
Affiliation: Roman Catholic
Freshman admissions: selective; 2015-2016: 5,797 applied, 4,542 accepted. Either SAT or ACT required. SAT 25/75 percentile: 890-1100. High school rank: 15% in top tenth, 36% in top quarter, 69% in top half
Early decision deadline: N/A, notification date: N/A
Early action deadline: 11/15, notification date: 12/15
Application deadline (fall): rolling
Undergraduate student body: 3,354 full time, 593 part time; 37% male, 63% female; 0% American Indian, 5% Asian, 18% black, 12% Hispanic, 2% multiracial, 0% Pacific Islander, 55% white, 2% international; 68% from in state; 55% live on campus; 10% of students in fraternities, 13% in sororities
Most popular majors: 23% Registered Nursing/Registered Nurse; 8% Marketing/Marketing Management, General; 7% Health and Wellness, General; 7% Psychology, General
Expenses: 2016-2017: $41,100; room/board: $14,690
Financial aid: (215) 951-1070; 82% of undergrads determined to have financial need; average aid package $31,501

Lebanon Valley College
Annville PA
(717) 867-6181
U.S. News ranking: Reg. U. (N), No. 23
Website: www.lvc.edu
Admissions email: admission@lvc.edu
Private; founded 1866
Affiliation: Methodist

More at usnews.com/college

Freshman admissions: selective; 2015-2016: 3,329 applied, 2,413 accepted. Neither SAT nor ACT required. SAT 25/75 percentile: 1000-1210. High school rank: 35% in top tenth, 69% in top quarter, 92% in top half
Early decision deadline: 11/1, notification date: 12/1
Early action deadline: N/A, notification date: N/A
Application deadline (fall): rolling
Undergraduate student body: 1,608 full time, 113 part time; 47% male, 53% female; 0% American Indian, 2% Asian, 3% black, 5% Hispanic, 2% multiracial, 0% Pacific Islander, 84% white, 0% international; 79% from in state; 80% live on campus; 7% of students in fraternities, 12% in sororities
Most popular majors: 27% Education; 13% Business, Management, Marketing, and Related Support Services; 10% Health Professions and Related Programs; 9% Social Sciences; 8% Visual and Performing Arts
Expenses: 2016-2017: $40,550; room/board: $10,980
Financial aid: (717) 867-6126; 86% of undergrads determined to have financial need; average aid package $30,078

Lehigh University
Bethlehem PA
(610) 758-3100
U.S. News ranking: Nat. U., No. 44
Website: www.lehigh.edu
Admissions email: admissions@lehigh.edu
Private; founded 1865
Freshman admissions: more selective; 2015-2016: 12,843 applied, 3,905 accepted. Either SAT or ACT required. SAT 25/75 percentile: 1230-1420. High school rank: 60% in top tenth, 89% in top quarter, 98% in top half
Early decision deadline: 11/15, notification date: 12/15
Early action deadline: N/A, notification date: N/A
Application deadline (fall): 1/1
Undergraduate student body: 5,001 full time, 74 part time; 56% male, 44% female; 0% American Indian, 9% Asian, 4% black, 9% Hispanic, 3% multiracial, 0% Pacific Islander, 66% white, 8% international; 27% from in state; 67% live on campus; 40% of students in fraternities, 45% in sororities
Most popular majors: 12% Finance, General; 8% Mechanical Engineering; 7% Accounting; 5% Chemical Engineering; 5% Logistics, Materials, and Supply Chain Management
Expenses: 2016-2017: $48,320; room/board: $12,690
Financial aid: (610) 758-3181; 39% of undergrads determined to have financial need; average aid package $41,131

Lincoln University
Lincoln University PA
(800) 790-0191
U.S. News ranking: Reg. U. (N), second tier
Website: www.lincoln.edu
Admissions email: admiss@lu.lincoln.edu
Public; founded 1854
Freshman admissions: least selective; 2015-2016: 3,318 applied, 3,032 accepted. Either SAT or ACT required. SAT 25/75 percentile: 740-930. High school rank: 4% in top tenth, 19% in top quarter, 40% in top half
Early decision deadline: N/A, notification date: N/A
Early action deadline: N/A, notification date: N/A
Application deadline (fall): rolling
Undergraduate student body: 1,546 full time, 150 part time; 38% male, 62% female; 0% American Indian, 0% Asian, 86% black, 1% Hispanic, 2% multiracial, 0% Pacific Islander, 1% white, 4% international; 44% from in state; N/A live on campus; N/A of students in fraternities, N/A in sororities
Most popular majors: 13% Homeland Security, Law Enforcement, Firefighting and Related Protective Services; 13% Social Sciences; 12% Public Administration and Social Service Professions; 9% Computer and Information Sciences and Support Services
Expenses: 2016-2017: $11,099 in state, $15,990 out of state; room/board: $9,268
Financial aid: (800) 561-2606; 90% of undergrads determined to have financial need; average aid package $12,064

Lock Haven University of Pennsylvania
Lock Haven PA
(570) 893-2027
U.S. News ranking: Reg. U. (N), No. 137
Website: www.lhup.edu
Admissions email: admissions@lhup.edu
Public; founded 1870
Freshman admissions: less selective; 2015-2016: 3,415 applied, 3,133 accepted. Either SAT or ACT required. SAT 25/75 percentile: 850-1050. High school rank: 9% in top tenth, 29% in top quarter, 64% in top half
Early decision deadline: N/A, notification date: N/A
Early action deadline: N/A, notification date: N/A
Application deadline (fall): rolling
Undergraduate student body: 3,894 full time, 326 part time; 43% male, 57% female; 0% American Indian, 1% Asian, 9% black, 2% Hispanic, 1% multiracial, 0% Pacific Islander, 84% white, 1% international; 95% from in state; 34% live on campus; 3% of students in fraternities, 4% in sororities
Most popular majors: 11% Health Professions and Related Clinical Sciences, Other; 10% Criminal Justice/Law Enforcement Administration; 8% Business Administration and Management, General; 7% Sport and Fitness

Administration/Management; 6% Parks, Recreation and Leisure Facilities Management, General
Expenses: 2015-2016: $9,380 in state, $18,050 out of state; room/board: $9,050
Financial aid: (570) 893-2344; 57% of undergrads determined to have financial need; average aid package $8,602

Lycoming College
Williamsport PA
(800) 345-3920
U.S. News ranking: Nat. Lib. Arts, No. 154
Website: www.lycoming.edu
Admissions email: admissions@lycoming.edu
Private; founded 1812
Affiliation: Methodist
Freshman admissions: selective; 2015-2016: 1,845 applied, 1,314 accepted. Neither SAT nor ACT required. SAT 25/75 percentile: 920-1140. High school rank: 17% in top tenth, 37% in top quarter, 75% in top half
Early decision deadline: 11/1, notification date: 11/15
Early action deadline: 11/15, notification date: 12/1
Application deadline (fall): 3/1
Undergraduate student body: 1,272 full time, 17 part time; 47% male, 53% female; 0% American Indian, 1% Asian, 9% black, 6% Hispanic, 3% multiracial, N/A Pacific Islander, 70% white, 5% international; 64% from in state; 88% live on campus; 13% of students in fraternities, 20% in sororities
Most popular majors: 21% Business, Management, Marketing, and Related Support Services; 19% Social Sciences; 11% Biological and Biomedical Sciences; 11% Psychology; 8% Visual and Performing Arts
Expenses: 2016-2017: $37,162; room/board: $11,418
Financial aid: (570) 321-4040; 82% of undergrads determined to have financial need; average aid package $32,731

Mansfield University of Pennsylvania
Mansfield PA
(800) 577-6826
U.S. News ranking: Reg. U. (N), No. 131
Website: www.mansfield.edu
Admissions email: admissns@mansfield.edu
Public; founded 1857
Freshman admissions: less selective; 2015-2016: 2,017 applied, 1,742 accepted. Neither SAT nor ACT required. SAT 25/75 percentile: 850-1070. High school rank: 10% in top tenth, 30% in top quarter, 64% in top half
Early decision deadline: N/A, notification date: N/A
Early action deadline: N/A, notification date: N/A
Application deadline (fall): rolling
Undergraduate student body: 2,048 full time, 207 part time; 40% male, 60% female; 0% American Indian, 1% Asian, 9% black, 3% Hispanic, 2% multiracial, 0% Pacific Islander, 82% white,

0% international; 83% from in state; 51% live on campus; N/A of students in fraternities, N/A in sororities
Most popular majors: 14% Visual and Performing Arts; 13% Health Professions and Related Programs; 12% Social Sciences; 10% Homeland Security, Law Enforcement, Firefighting and Related Protective Services; 8% Business, Management, Marketing, and Related Support Services
Expenses: 2016-2017: $12,360 in state, $21,570 out of state; room/board: $11,880
Financial aid: (570) 662-4878; 83% of undergrads determined to have financial need; average aid package $9,671

Marywood University
Scranton PA
(570) 348-6234
U.S. News ranking: Reg. U. (N), No. 51
Website: www.marywood.edu
Admissions email: YourFuture@marywood.edu
Private; founded 1915
Affiliation: Roman Catholic
Freshman admissions: selective; 2015-2016: 2,273 applied, 1,603 accepted. Either SAT or ACT required. SAT 25/75 percentile: 930-1120. High school rank: 13% in top tenth, 48% in top quarter, 80% in top half
Early decision deadline: N/A, notification date: N/A
Early action deadline: N/A, notification date: N/A
Application deadline (fall): rolling
Undergraduate student body: 1,768 full time, 165 part time; 32% male, 68% female; 0% American Indian, 2% Asian, 2% black, 6% Hispanic, 2% multiracial, 0% Pacific Islander, 79% white, 1% international; 70% from in state; 39% live on campus; 0% of students in fraternities, 7% in sororities
Most popular majors: 24% Health Professions and Related Programs; 14% Business, Management, Marketing, and Related Support Services; 11% Visual and Performing Arts; 9% Psychology; 7% Education
Expenses: 2015-2016: $32,692; room/board: $13,900
Financial aid: (570) 348-6225; 82% of undergrads determined to have financial need; average aid package $24,292

Mercyhurst University
Erie PA
(814) 824-2202
U.S. News ranking: Reg. U. (N), No. 61
Website: www.mercyhurst.edu
Admissions email: admug@mercyhurst.edu
Private; founded 1926
Affiliation: Roman Catholic
Freshman admissions: selective; 2015-2016: 2,749 applied, 2,242 accepted. Neither SAT nor ACT required. SAT 25/75 percentile: 910-1160. High school rank: 11% in top tenth, 25% in top quarter, 70% in top half

Early decision deadline: N/A, notification date: N/A
Early action deadline: N/A, notification date: N/A
Application deadline (fall): rolling
Undergraduate student body: 2,403 full time, 88 part time; 44% male, 56% female; 0% American Indian, 1% Asian, 4% black, 3% Hispanic, 0% multiracial, 0% Pacific Islander, 44% white, 11% international; 56% from in state; 71% live on campus; 0% of students in fraternities, 0% in sororities
Most popular majors: 23% Business, Management, Marketing, and Related Support Services; 13% Military Technologies and Applied Sciences; 12% Homeland Security, Law Enforcement, Firefighting and Related Protective Services; 10% Health Professions and Related Programs; 9% Biological and Biomedical Sciences
Expenses: 2016-2017: $34,480; room/board: $11,624
Financial aid: (814) 824-2288; 71% of undergrads determined to have financial need; average aid package $26,019

Messiah College
Mechanicsburg PA
(717) 691-6000
U.S. News ranking: Reg. Coll. (N), No. 4
Website: www.messiah.edu
Admissions email: admiss@messiah.edu
Private; founded 1909
Affiliation: Christian interdenominational
Freshman admissions: selective; 2015-2016: 2,469 applied, 1,950 accepted. Either SAT or ACT required. SAT 25/75 percentile: 1010-1250. High school rank: 32% in top tenth, 63% in top quarter, 91% in top half
Early decision deadline: N/A, notification date: N/A
Early action deadline: N/A, notification date: N/A
Application deadline (fall): rolling
Undergraduate student body: 2,681 full time, 138 part time; 39% male, 61% female; 0% American Indian, 2% Asian, 3% black, 4% Hispanic, 3% multiracial, 0% Pacific Islander, 83% white, 4% international; 63% from in state; 86% live on campus; N/A of students in fraternities, N/A in sororities
Most popular majors: 8% Registered Nursing/Registered Nurse; 6% Engineering, General; 6% Business Administration and Management, General; 5% Psychology, General; 4% Elementary Education and Teaching
Expenses: 2016-2017: $33,180; room/board: $9,920
Financial aid: (717) 691-6007; 72% of undergrads determined to have financial need; average aid package $23,080

Millersville University of Pennsylvania

Millersville PA
(717) 871-4625
U.S. News ranking: Reg. U. (N), No. 95
Website: www.millersville.edu
Admissions email: Admissions@millersville.edu
Public; founded 1855
Freshman admissions: selective; 2015-2016: 6,053 applied, 4,422 accepted. Either SAT or ACT required. SAT 25/75 percentile: 900-1100. High school rank: 9% in top tenth, 29% in top quarter, 66% in top half
Early decision deadline: N/A, notification date: N/A
Early action deadline: N/A, notification date: N/A
Application deadline (fall): rolling
Undergraduate student body: 6,152 full time, 932 part time; 44% male, 56% female; 0% American Indian, 3% Asian, 9% black, 8% Hispanic, 3% multiracial, 0% Pacific Islander, 76% white, 0% international; 95% from in state; 33% live on campus; 3% of students in fraternities, 4% in sororities
Most popular majors: 11% Education; 10% Business, Management, Marketing, and Related Support Services; 9% Social Sciences; 8% Psychology
Expenses: 2015-2016: $10,918 in state, $20,108 out of state; room/board: $11,795
Financial aid: (717) 872-3026; 69% of undergrads determined to have financial need; average aid package $8,454

Misericordia University

Dallas PA
(570) 674-6264
U.S. News ranking: Reg. U. (N), No. 44
Website: www.misericordia.edu/
Admissions email: admiss@misericordia.edu
Private; founded 1924
Affiliation: Roman Catholic
Freshman admissions: selective; 2015-2016: 1,956 applied, 1,398 accepted. Either SAT or ACT required. SAT 25/75 percentile: 970-1140. High school rank: 24% in top tenth, 56% in top quarter, 84% in top half
Early decision deadline: N/A, notification date: N/A
Early action deadline: N/A, notification date: N/A
Application deadline (fall): rolling
Undergraduate student body: 1,792 full time, 608 part time; 32% male, 68% female; 0% American Indian, 1% Asian, 2% black, 3% Hispanic, 1% multiracial, 0% Pacific Islander, 92% white, 0% international; 75% from in state; 42% live on campus; 0% of students in fraternities, 0% in sororities
Most popular majors: 17% Business Administration and Management, General; 13% Health Professions and Related Programs; 12% Registered Nursing/Registered Nurse;

7% Health/Health Care Administration/Management; 7% Psychology, General
Expenses: 2016-2017: $30,740; room/board: $13,150
Financial aid: (570) 674-6280; 80% of undergrads determined to have financial need; average aid package $21,666

Moore College of Art & Design

Philadelphia PA
(215) 965-4015
U.S. News ranking: Arts, unranked
Website: www.moore.edu
Admissions email: admiss@moore.edu
Private; founded 1848
Freshman admissions: N/A; 2015-2016: 557 applied, 310 accepted. Neither SAT nor ACT required. SAT 25/75 percentile: N/A. High school rank: N/A
Early decision deadline: N/A, notification date: N/A
Early action deadline: N/A, notification date: N/A
Application deadline (fall): rolling
Undergraduate student body: 391 full time, 14 part time; 0% male, 100% female; 0% American Indian, 3% Asian, 21% black, 7% Hispanic, 6% multiracial, 0% Pacific Islander, 59% white, 1% international; 60% from in state; 39% live on campus; 0% of students in fraternities, 0% in sororities
Most popular majors: 21% Fashion/Apparel Design; 15% Fine/Studio Arts, General; 14% Interior Design; 12% Photography
Expenses: 2015-2016: $36,828; room/board: $13,836
Financial aid: (215) 965-4042

Moravian College

Bethlehem PA
(610) 861-1320
U.S. News ranking: Nat. Lib. Arts, No. 159
Website: www.moravian.edu
Admissions email: admissions@moravian.edu
Private; founded 1742
Affiliation: Moravian Church
Freshman admissions: selective; 2015-2016: 2,737 applied, 2,041 accepted. Either SAT or ACT required. SAT 25/75 percentile: 930-1090. High school rank: 10% in top tenth, 38% in top quarter, 72% in top half
Early decision deadline: N/A, notification date: N/A
Early action deadline: N/A, notification date: N/A
Application deadline (fall): 3/1
Undergraduate student body: 1,691 full time, 140 part time; 45% male, 55% female; 0% American Indian, 1% Asian, 4% black, 9% Hispanic, 2% multiracial, 0% Pacific Islander, 72% white, 6% international; 66% from in state; 70% live on campus; 16% of students in fraternities, 27% in sororities
Most popular majors: 20% Business, Management, Marketing, and Related Support Services; 18% Social Sciences; 15% Health Professions and Related Programs; 9% Biological

and Biomedical Sciences; 9% Visual and Performing Arts
Expenses: 2016-2017: $40,287; room/board: $12,090
Financial aid: (610) 861-1330; 81% of undergrads determined to have financial need; average aid package $28,686

Mount Aloysius College

Cresson PA
(814) 886-6383
U.S. News ranking: Reg. Coll. (N), No. 29
Website: www.mtaloy.edu
Admissions email: admissions@mtaloy.edu
Private; founded 1853
Affiliation: Roman Catholic (Sisters of Mercy)
Freshman admissions: less selective; 2015-2016: 1,485 applied, 1,082 accepted. Either SAT or ACT required. SAT 25/75 percentile: 860-1020. High school rank: N/A
Early decision deadline: N/A, notification date: N/A
Early action deadline: N/A, notification date: N/A
Application deadline (fall): rolling
Undergraduate student body: 1,176 full time, 627 part time; 29% male, 71% female; 0% American Indian, 0% Asian, 3% black, 1% Hispanic, 0% multiracial, 0% Pacific Islander, 78% white, 2% international; 94% from in state; 34% live on campus; N/A of students in fraternities, N/A in sororities
Most popular majors: 38% Health Professions and Related Programs; 17% Business, Management, Marketing, and Related Support Services; 11% Liberal Arts and Sciences, General Studies and Humanities; 10% Biological and Biomedical Sciences; 8% Homeland Security, Law Enforcement, Firefighting and Related Protective Services
Expenses: 2016-2017: $21,850; room/board: $9,940
Financial aid: (814) 886-6357; 88% of undergrads determined to have financial need; average aid package $14,500

Muhlenberg College

Allentown PA
(484) 664-3200
U.S. News ranking: Nat. Lib. Arts, No. 65
Website: www.muhlenberg.edu
Admissions email: admissions@muhlenberg.edu
Private; founded 1848
Affiliation: Lutheran
Freshman admissions: more selective; 2015-2016: 5,015 applied, 2,426 accepted. Neither SAT nor ACT required. SAT 25/75 percentile: 1110-1320. High school rank: 41% in top tenth, 71% in top quarter, 94% in top half
Early decision deadline: 2/15, notification date: 12/1
Early action deadline: N/A, notification date: N/A
Application deadline (fall): 2/15
Undergraduate student body: 2,307 full time, 90 part time; 40% male, 60% female; 0% American

Indian, 3% Asian, 3% black, 7% Hispanic, 2% multiracial, 0% Pacific Islander, 75% white, 3% international; 27% from in state; 91% live on campus; 19% of students in fraternities, 27% in sororities
Most popular majors: 14% Business Administration and Management, General; 11% Psychology, General; 8% Drama and Dramatics/Theatre Arts, General; 5% Biology/Biological Sciences, General
Expenses: 2016-2017: $48,310; room/board: $11,090
Financial aid: (484) 664-3174; 48% of undergrads determined to have financial need; average aid package $34,606

Neumann University

Aston PA
(610) 558-5616
U.S. News ranking: Reg. U. (N), second tier
Website: www.neumann.edu
Admissions email: neumann@neumann.edu
Private; founded 1965
Affiliation: Roman Catholic
Freshman admissions: less selective; 2015-2016: 2,253 applied, 2,046 accepted. Either SAT or ACT required. SAT 25/75 percentile: 820-990. High school rank: N/A
Early decision deadline: N/A, notification date: N/A
Early action deadline: N/A, notification date: N/A
Application deadline (fall): rolling
Undergraduate student body: 1,806 full time, 597 part time; 36% male, 64% female; 0% American Indian, 1% Asian, 22% black, 2% Hispanic, 2% multiracial, 0% Pacific Islander, 54% white, 1% international; 69% from in state; 32% live on campus; N/A of students in fraternities, N/A in sororities
Most popular majors: 18% Liberal Arts and Sciences/Liberal Studies; 16% Registered Nursing, Nursing Administration, Nursing Research and Clinical Nursing, Other; 11% Psychology, General; 8% Criminal Justice/Safety Studies; 8% Education/Teaching of Individuals in Elementary Special Education Programs
Expenses: 2016-2017: $28,580; room/board: $12,158
Financial aid: (610) 558-5521; 74% of undergrads determined to have financial need; average aid package $13,570

Peirce College

Philadelphia PA
(888) 467-3472
U.S. News ranking: Reg. Coll. (N), unranked
Website: www.peirce.edu
Admissions email: info@peirce.edu
Private; founded 1865
Freshman admissions: N/A; 2015-2016: N/A applied, N/A accepted. Neither SAT nor ACT required. ACT 25/75 percentile: N/A. High school rank: N/A
Early decision deadline: N/A, notification date: N/A
Early action deadline: N/A, notification date: N/A
Application deadline (fall): rolling

Undergraduate student body: 304 full time, 1,339 part time; 28% male, 72% female; 0% American Indian, 2% Asian, 69% black, 8% Hispanic, 0% multiracial, 0% Pacific Islander, 20% white, 0% international; 92% from in state; N/A live on campus; N/A of students in fraternities, N/A in sororities
Most popular majors: 58% Business, Management, Marketing, and Related Support Services; 18% Legal Professions and Studies; 15% Computer and Information Sciences and Support Services; 8% Health Professions and Related Programs
Expenses: 2015-2016: $14,184; room/board: N/A
Financial aid: (215) 670-9370

Pennsylvania Academy of the Fine Arts[1]

Philadelphia PA
(215) 972-7625
U.S. News ranking: Arts, unranked
Website: www.pafa.org/
Admissions email: admissions@pafa.edu
Private
Application deadline (fall): N/A
Undergraduate student body: N/A full time, N/A part time
Expenses: 2015-2016: $34,410; room/board: $14,368
Financial aid: N/A

Pennsylvania College of Art and Design[1]

Lancaster PA
(717) 396-7833
U.S. News ranking: Arts, unranked
Website: www.pcad.edu
Admissions email: N/A
Private; founded 1982
Application deadline (fall): rolling
Undergraduate student body: N/A full time, N/A part time
Expenses: 2015-2016: $22,800; room/board: $9,623
Financial aid: (800) 689-0379

Pennsylvania College of Technology

Williamsport PA
(570) 327-4761
U.S. News ranking: Reg. Coll. (N), No. 13
Website: www.pct.edu
Admissions email: admissions@pct.edu
Public; founded 1941
Freshman admissions: less selective; 2015-2016: 3,144 applied, 2,672 accepted. Neither SAT nor ACT required. SAT 25/75 percentile: 840-1050. High school rank: 7% in top tenth, 22% in top quarter, 56% in top half
Early decision deadline: N/A, notification date: N/A
Early action deadline: N/A, notification date: N/A
Application deadline (fall): 7/1
Undergraduate student body: 4,619 full time, 895 part time; 64% male, 36% female; 0% American Indian, 1% Asian, 3% black, 3% Hispanic, 2% multiracial, 0% Pacific Islander, 88% white, 1% international; 89% from in

state; 28% live on campus; N/A of students in fraternities, N/A in sororities
Most popular majors: 30% Engineering Technologies and Engineering-Related Fields; 22% Health Professions and Related Programs; 16% Business, Management, Marketing, and Related Support Services; 10% Computer and Information Sciences and Support Services; 9% Construction Trades
Expenses: 2016-2017: $16,350 in state, $23,220 out of state; room/board: $10,546
Financial aid: (570) 327-4766; 79% of undergrads determined to have financial need; average aid package $4,089

Pennsylvania State University–University Park
University Park PA
(814) 865-5471
U.S. News ranking: Nat. U., No. 50
Website: www.psu.edu
Admissions email: admissions@psu.edu
Public; founded 1855
Freshman admissions: more selective; 2015-2016: 53,472 applied, 27,440 accepted. Either SAT or ACT required. SAT 25/75 percentile: 1090-1300. High school rank: 41% in top tenth, 82% in top quarter, 98% in top half
Early decision deadline: N/A, notification date: N/A
Early action deadline: N/A, notification date: N/A
Application deadline (fall): rolling
Undergraduate student body: 39,520 full time, 1,222 part time; 54% male, 46% female; 0% American Indian, 6% Asian, 4% black, 6% Hispanic, 3% multiracial, 0% Pacific Islander, 69% white, 11% international; 69% from in state; 34% live on campus; 18% of students in fraternities, 19% in sororities
Most popular majors: 15% Business, Management, Marketing, and Related Support Services; 15% Engineering; 8% Social Sciences; 6% Biological and Biomedical Sciences
Expenses: 2016-2017: $17,900 in state, $32,382 out of state; room/board: $11,860
Financial aid: (814) 865-6301; 47% of undergrads determined to have financial need; average aid package $11,584

Philadelphia University
Philadelphia PA
(215) 951-2800
U.S. News ranking: Reg. U. (N), No. 60
Website: www.philau.edu
Admissions email: admissions@philau.edu
Private; founded 1884
Freshman admissions: selective; 2015-2016: 4,129 applied, 2,651 accepted. Either SAT or ACT required. SAT 25/75 percentile: 980-1180. High school rank: 17% in top tenth, 41% in top quarter, 79% in top half

---

Early decision deadline: N/A, notification date: N/A
Early action deadline: N/A, notification date: N/A
Application deadline (fall): rolling
Undergraduate student body: 2,449 full time, 349 part time; 33% male, 67% female; 0% American Indian, 5% Asian, 15% black, 8% Hispanic, 2% multiracial, 0% Pacific Islander, 55% white, 4% international; 59% from in state; 50% live on campus; 1% of students in fraternities, 1% in sororities
Most popular majors: 28% Business, Management, Marketing, and Related Support Services; 17% Health Professions and Related Programs; 16% Visual and Performing Arts; 6% Psychology
Expenses: 2016-2017: $37,800; room/board: $12,570
Financial aid: (215) 951-2940; 78% of undergrads determined to have financial need; average aid package $26,759

Point Park University
Pittsburgh PA
(800) 321-0129
U.S. News ranking: Reg. U. (N), No. 110
Website: www.pointpark.edu
Admissions email: enroll@pointpark.edu
Private; founded 1960
Freshman admissions: selective; 2015-2016: 4,021 applied, 2,836 accepted. Either SAT or ACT required. SAT 25/75 percentile: 880-1090. High school rank: 12% in top tenth, 34% in top quarter, 70% in top half
Early decision deadline: N/A, notification date: N/A
Early action deadline: N/A, notification date: N/A
Application deadline (fall): rolling
Undergraduate student body: 2,643 full time, 545 part time; 43% male, 57% female; 0% American Indian, 1% Asian, 15% black, 3% Hispanic, 4% multiracial, 0% Pacific Islander, 71% white, 4% international; 76% from in state; 32% live on campus; N/A of students in fraternities, N/A in sororities
Most popular majors: 11% Business, Management, Marketing, and Related Support Services, Other; 9% Drama and Dramatics/Theatre Arts, General; 8% Business Administration and Management, General; 7% Dance, General; 6% Criminal Justice/Safety Studies
Expenses: 2016-2017: $29,030; room/board: $10,840
Financial aid: (412) 392-3930; 92% of undergrads determined to have financial need; average aid package $22,313

Robert Morris University
Moon Township PA
(412) 397-5200
U.S. News ranking: Nat. U., No. 188
Website: www.rmu.edu
Admissions email: admissions@rmu.edu

Private; founded 1921
Freshman admissions: selective; 2015-2016: 6,579 applied, 5,109 accepted. Either SAT or ACT required. SAT 25/75 percentile: 940-1150. High school rank: 18% in top tenth, 45% in top quarter, 76% in top half
Early decision deadline: N/A, notification date: N/A
Early action deadline: N/A, notification date: N/A
Application deadline (fall): rolling
Undergraduate student body: 3,965 full time, 532 part time; 56% male, 44% female; 0% American Indian, 1% Asian, 6% black, 2% Hispanic, 3% multiracial, 0% Pacific Islander, 75% white, 11% international; 87% from in state; 51% live on campus; 9% of students in fraternities, 15% in sororities
Most popular majors: 12% Registered Nursing/Registered Nurse; 10% Accounting; 9% Business Administration and Management, General; 8% Engineering, General
Expenses: 2016-2017: $28,250; room/board: $12,590
Financial aid: (412) 262-8545; 71% of undergrads determined to have financial need; average aid package $20,964

Rosemont College
Rosemont PA
(800) 331-0708
U.S. News ranking: Reg. U. (N), No. 137
Website: www.rosemont.edu
Admissions email: admissions@rosemont.edu
Private; founded 1921
Affiliation: Roman Catholic
Freshman admissions: less selective; 2015-2016: 875 applied, 618 accepted. Either SAT or ACT required. SAT 25/75 percentile: 780-1025. High school rank: 28% in top tenth, 46% in top quarter, 74% in top half
Early decision deadline: N/A, notification date: N/A
Early action deadline: N/A, notification date: N/A
Application deadline (fall): rolling
Undergraduate student body: 456 full time, 73 part time; 35% male, 65% female; N/A American Indian, 5% Asian, 40% black, 6% Hispanic, 4% multiracial, N/A Pacific Islander, 38% white, 2% international; 73% from in state; 79% live on campus; N/A of students in fraternities, N/A in sororities
Most popular majors: 25% Business/Commerce, General; 14% Education, General; 6% Biology/Biological Sciences, General; 6% English Language and Literature, General; 6% Visual and Performing Arts, General
Expenses: 2015-2016: $32,500; room/board: $13,400
Financial aid: (610) 527-0200

Saint Vincent College
Latrobe PA
(800) 782-5549
U.S. News ranking: Nat. Lib. Arts, No. 149
Website: www.stvincent.edu
Admissions email: admission@stvincent.edu
Private; founded 1846
Affiliation: Roman Catholic
Freshman admissions: selective; 2015-2016: 1,908 applied, 1,332 accepted. Either SAT or ACT required. SAT 25/75 percentile: 950-1160. High school rank: 17% in top tenth, 44% in top quarter, 75% in top half
Early decision deadline: N/A, notification date: N/A
Early action deadline: N/A, notification date: N/A
Application deadline (fall): 5/1
Undergraduate student body: 1,590 full time, 62 part time; 53% male, 47% female; 1% American Indian, 2% Asian, 5% black, 3% Hispanic, 1% multiracial, 0% Pacific Islander, 85% white, 1% international; 81% from in state; 75% live on campus; 0% of students in fraternities, 0% in sororities
Most popular majors: 27% Business, Management, Marketing, and Related Support Services; 15% Biological and Biomedical Sciences; 9% Psychology; 8% Social Sciences
Expenses: 2016-2017: $33,426; room/board: $10,488
Financial aid: (724) 537-4540; 78% of undergrads determined to have financial need; average aid package $28,300

Seton Hill University
Greensburg PA
(724) 838-4255
U.S. News ranking: Reg. U. (N), No. 44
Website: www.setonhill.edu
Admissions email: admit@setonhill.edu
Private; founded 1883
Affiliation: Roman Catholic
Freshman admissions: selective; 2015-2016: 2,093 applied, 1,600 accepted. Neither SAT nor ACT required. SAT 25/75 percentile: 930-1170. High school rank: 18% in top tenth, 52% in top quarter, 78% in top half
Early decision deadline: N/A, notification date: N/A
Early action deadline: N/A, notification date: N/A
Application deadline (fall): 8/15
Undergraduate student body: 1,493 full time, 127 part time; 35% male, 65% female; 0% American Indian, 1% Asian, 8% black, 4% Hispanic, 2% multiracial, 0% Pacific Islander, 83% white, 1% international; 74% from in state; 56% live on campus; 0% of students in fraternities, 0% in sororities
Most popular majors: 20% Business, Management, Marketing, and Related Support Services; 11% Visual and Performing Arts; 10% Education; 10% Health Professions and Related Programs; 8% Biological and Biomedical Sciences

---

Expenses: 2015-2016: $32,420; room/board: $10,868
Financial aid: (724) 838-4293; 87% of undergrads determined to have financial need; average aid package $24,211

Shippensburg University of Pennsylvania
Shippensburg PA
(717) 477-1231
U.S. News ranking: Reg. U. (N), No. 95
Website: www.ship.edu
Admissions email: admiss@ship.edu
Public; founded 1871
Freshman admissions: less selective; 2015-2016: 6,126 applied, 5,461 accepted. Either SAT or ACT required. SAT 25/75 percentile: 880-1080. High school rank: 9% in top tenth, 28% in top quarter, 64% in top half
Early decision deadline: N/A, notification date: N/A
Early action deadline: N/A, notification date: N/A
Application deadline (fall): rolling
Undergraduate student body: 5,665 full time, 362 part time; 50% male, 50% female; 0% American Indian, 1% Asian, 10% black, 5% Hispanic, 3% multiracial, 0% Pacific Islander, 78% white, 0% international; 93% from in state; 34% live on campus; 8% of students in fraternities, 9% in sororities
Most popular majors: 10% Psychology, General; 8% Business Administration and Management, General; 6% Criminal Justice/Safety Studies; 6% Marketing/Marketing Management, General
Expenses: 2016-2017: $3,022 in state, $19,308 out of state; room/board: $11,756
Financial aid: (717) 477-1131; 69% of undergrads determined to have financial need; average aid package $8,373

Slippery Rock University of Pennsylvania
Slippery Rock PA
(800) 929-4778
U.S. News ranking: Reg. U. (N), No. 75
Website: www.sru.edu
Admissions email: asktherock@sru.edu
Public; founded 1889
Freshman admissions: selective; 2015-2016: 5,781 applied, 3,952 accepted. Either SAT or ACT required. SAT 25/75 percentile: 910-1080. High school rank: 10% in top tenth, 36% in top quarter, 76% in top half
Early decision deadline: N/A, notification date: N/A
Early action deadline: N/A, notification date: N/A
Application deadline (fall): rolling
Undergraduate student body: 7,057 full time, 526 part time; 43% male, 57% female; 0% American Indian, 1% Asian, 5% black, 2% Hispanic, 3% multiracial, 0% Pacific Islander, 86% white,

1% international; 89% from in state; 37% live on campus; 1% of students in fraternities, 2% in sororities

Most popular majors: 22% Health Professions and Related Programs; 11% Business, Management, Marketing, and Related Support Services; 10% Education; 9% Parks, Recreation, Leisure, and Fitness Studies; 7% Social Sciences

Expenses: 2015-2016: $9,645 in state, $13,175 out of state; room/board: $10,022

Financial aid: (724) 738-2044; 69% of undergrads determined to have financial need; average aid package $8,933

St. Francis University

Loretto PA
(814) 472-3100
U.S. News ranking: Reg. U. (N), No. 27
Website: www.francis.edu/undergraduate_admissions
Admissions email: admissions@francis.edu
Private; founded 1847
Affiliation: Roman Catholic
Freshman admissions: selective; 2015-2016: 1,932 applied, 1,432 accepted. Either SAT or ACT required. SAT 25/75 percentile: 930-1160. High school rank: 30% in top tenth, 58% in top quarter, 83% in top half
Early decision deadline: N/A, notification date: N/A
Early action deadline: N/A, notification date: N/A
Application deadline (fall): 7/30
Undergraduate student body: 1,600 full time, 133 part time; 38% male, 62% female; 0% American Indian, 2% Asian, 7% black, 1% Hispanic, 1% multiracial, 0% Pacific Islander, 83% white, 3% international
Most popular majors: 11% Physician Assistant; 9% Occupational Therapy/Therapist; 8% Physical Therapy/Therapist; 4% Adult Health Nurse/Nursing; 4% Marketing/Marketing Management, General
Expenses: 2015-2016: $32,178; room/board: $10,500
Financial aid: (814) 472-3010

St. Joseph's University

Philadelphia PA
(610) 660-1300
U.S. News ranking: Reg. U. (N), No. 11
Website: www.sju.edu
Admissions email: admit@sju.edu
Private; founded 1851
Affiliation: Roman Catholic (Jesuit)
Freshman admissions: selective; 2015-2016: 8,352 applied, 6,830 accepted. Neither SAT nor ACT required. SAT 25/75 percentile: 1050-1230. High school rank: 19% in top tenth, 48% in top quarter, 83% in top half
Early decision deadline: N/A, notification date: N/A
Early action deadline: 11/15, notification date: 12/25
Application deadline (fall): rolling
Undergraduate student body: 4,624 full time, 771 part time; 45% male, 55% female; 0% American

Indian, 2% Asian, 7% black, 6% Hispanic, 2% multiracial, 0% Pacific Islander, 80% white, 2% international; 48% from in state; N/A live on campus; N/A of students in fraternities, N/A in sororities
Most popular majors: 50% Business, Management, Marketing, and Related Support Services; 8% Social Sciences; 7% Education; 6% Biological and Biomedical Sciences; 6% Psychology
Expenses: 2016-2017: $43,020; room/board: $14,524
Financial aid: (610) 660-1556; 53% of undergrads determined to have financial need; average aid package $25,959

Susquehanna University

Selinsgrove PA
(800) 326-9672
U.S. News ranking: Nat. Lib. Arts, No. 132
Website: www.susqu.edu
Admissions email: suadmiss@susqu.edu
Private; founded 1858
Affiliation: Lutheran
Freshman admissions: selective; 2015-2016: 5,304 applied, 4,033 accepted. Neither SAT nor ACT required. SAT 25/75 percentile: 1010-1220. High school rank: 26% in top tenth, 57% in top quarter, 87% in top half
Early decision deadline: 11/15, notification date: 12/1
Early action deadline: 11/1, notification date: 12/1
Application deadline (fall): rolling
Undergraduate student body: 2,114 full time, 82 part time; 45% male, 55% female; 0% American Indian, 2% Asian, 6% black, 6% Hispanic, 3% multiracial, 0% Pacific Islander, 81% white, 2% international; 50% from in state; 92% live on campus; 18% of students in fraternities, 14% in sororities
Most popular majors: 16% Business/Commerce, General; 9% Psychology, General; 7% Creative Writing; 7% Biology/Biological Sciences, General
Expenses: 2016-2017: $43,720; room/board: $11,620
Financial aid: (570) 372-4450; 77% of undergrads determined to have financial need; average aid package $32,605

Swarthmore College

Swarthmore PA
(610) 328-8300
U.S. News ranking: Nat. Lib. Arts, No. 4
Website: www.swarthmore.edu
Admissions email: admissions@swarthmore.edu
Private; founded 1864
Freshman admissions: most selective; 2015-2016: 7,818 applied, 976 accepted. Either SAT or ACT required. SAT 25/75 percentile: 1340-1530. High school rank: 88% in top tenth, 99% in top quarter, 100% in top half
Early decision deadline: 11/15, notification date: 12/15

Early action deadline: N/A, notification date: N/A
Application deadline (fall): 1/1
Undergraduate student body: 1,571 full time, 10 part time; 50% male, 50% female; 0% American Indian, 17% Asian, 6% black, 13% Hispanic, 8% multiracial, 0% Pacific Islander, 42% white, 11% international; 13% from in state; 95% live on campus; 11% of students in fraternities, 6% in sororities
Most popular majors: 24% Social Sciences; 13% Biological and Biomedical Sciences; 9% Computer and Information Sciences and Support Services; 8% Visual and Performing Arts; 7% Foreign Languages, Literatures, and Linguistics
Expenses: 2016-2017: $49,104; room/board: $14,446
Financial aid: (610) 328-8358; 52% of undergrads determined to have financial need; average aid package $45,907

Temple University

Philadelphia PA
(215) 204-7200
U.S. News ranking: Nat. U., No. 118
Website: www.temple.edu
Admissions email: askanowl@temple.edu
Public; founded 1884
Freshman admissions: selective; 2015-2016: 28,886 applied, 16,084 accepted. Neither SAT nor ACT required. SAT 25/75 percentile: 1050-1250. High school rank: 22% in top tenth, 54% in top quarter, 90% in top half
Early decision deadline: N/A, notification date: N/A
Early action deadline: 11/1, notification date: 1/10
Application deadline (fall): 3/1
Undergraduate student body: 25,318 full time, 3,291 part time; 49% male, 51% female; 0% American Indian, 11% Asian, 13% black, 6% Hispanic, 3% multiracial, 0% Pacific Islander, 56% white, 6% international; 82% from in state; 21% live on campus; 3% of students in fraternities, 5% in sororities
Most popular majors: 21% Business, Management, Marketing, and Related Support Services; 8% Visual and Performing Arts; 6% Parks, Recreation, Leisure, and Fitness Studies; 6% Education
Expenses: 2016-2017: $15,688 in state, $25,994 out of state; room/board: $11,146
Financial aid: (215) 204-8760; 69% of undergrads determined to have financial need; average aid package $17,767

Thiel College

Greenville PA
(800) 248-4435
U.S. News ranking: Nat. Lib. Arts, second tier
Website: www.thiel.edu
Admissions email: admission@thiel.edu
Private; founded 1866
Affiliation: Lutheran
Freshman admissions: less selective; 2015-2016: 2,275 applied, 1,399 accepted. Either

SAT or ACT required. SAT 25/75 percentile: 790-1010. High school rank: 9% in top tenth, 13% in top quarter, 90% in top half
Early decision deadline: N/A, notification date: N/A
Early action deadline: N/A, notification date: N/A
Application deadline (fall): rolling
Undergraduate student body: 903 full time, 23 part time; 54% male, 46% female; 0% American Indian, 0% Asian, 9% black, 2% Hispanic, 3% multiracial, 0% Pacific Islander, 77% white, 4% international; 61% from in state; 92% live on campus; 24% of students in fraternities, 28% in sororities
Most popular majors: 38% Business, Management, and Related Support Services; 12% Psychology; 8% Biological and Biomedical Sciences; 6% Homeland Security, Law Enforcement, Firefighting and Related Protective Services; 6% Social Sciences
Expenses: 2016-2017: $29,740; room/board: $11,700
Financial aid: (724) 589-2178; 91% of undergrads determined to have financial need; average aid package $24,045

University of Pennsylvania

Philadelphia PA
(215) 898-7507
U.S. News ranking: Nat. U., No. 8
Website: www.upenn.edu
Admissions email: info@admissions.ugao.upenn.edu
Private; founded 1740
Freshman admissions: most selective; 2015-2016: 37,268 applied, 3,787 accepted. Either SAT or ACT required. SAT 25/75 percentile: 1380-1550. High school rank: 95% in top tenth, 99% in top quarter, 100% in top half
Early decision deadline: 11/1, notification date: 12/15
Early action deadline: N/A, notification date: N/A
Application deadline (fall): 1/5
Undergraduate student body: 9,444 full time, 282 part time; 50% male, 50% female; 0% American Indian, 20% Asian, 7% black, 10% Hispanic, 4% multiracial, 0% Pacific Islander, 44% white, 12% international; 19% from in state; 54% live on campus; N/A of students in fraternities, N/A in sororities
Most popular majors: 13% Finance, General; 6% Registered Nursing/Registered Nurse; 5% Economics, General; 4% Biology/Biological Sciences, General
Expenses: 2016-2017: $51,464; room/board: $14,536
Financial aid: (215) 898-1988; 47% of undergrads determined to have financial need; average aid package $43,542

University of Pittsburgh

Pittsburgh PA
(412) 624-7488
U.S. News ranking: Nat. U., No. 68
Website: www.oafa.pitt.edu/
Admissions email: oafa@pitt.edu
Public; founded 1787
Freshman admissions: more selective; 2015-2016: 30,626 applied, 16,503 accepted. Either SAT or ACT required. SAT 25/75 percentile: 1180-1350. High school rank: 50% in top tenth, 83% in top quarter, 99% in top half
Early decision deadline: N/A, notification date: N/A
Early action deadline: N/A, notification date: N/A
Application deadline (fall): rolling
Undergraduate student body: 17,887 full time, 1,021 part time; 49% male, 51% female; 0% American Indian, 9% Asian, 5% black, 3% Hispanic, 3% multiracial, 0% Pacific Islander, 74% white, 4% international; 73% from in state; 44% live on campus; 10% of students in fraternities, 10% in sororities
Most popular majors: 17% Business, Management, Marketing, and Related Support Services; 13% Health Professions and Related Programs; 11% Social Sciences; 11% Engineering; 8% Psychology
Expenses: 2016-2017: $18,618 in state, $29,758 out of state; room/board: $10,950
Financial aid: (412) 624-7488; 53% of undergrads determined to have financial need; average aid package $16,229

University of Scranton

Scranton PA
(570) 941-7540
U.S. News ranking: Reg. U. (N), No. 6
Website: www.scranton.edu
Admissions email: admissions@scranton.edu
Private; founded 1888
Affiliation: Roman Catholic (Jesuit)
Freshman admissions: selective; 2015-2016: 10,049 applied, 7,256 accepted. Either SAT or ACT required. SAT 25/75 percentile: 1030-1230. High school rank: 34% in top tenth, 62% in top quarter, 88% in top half
Early decision deadline: N/A, notification date: N/A
Early action deadline: 11/15, notification date: 12/15
Application deadline (fall): 3/1
Undergraduate student body: 3,713 full time, 197 part time; 42% male, 58% female; 0% American Indian, 2% Asian, 2% black, 9% Hispanic, 3% multiracial, 0% Pacific Islander, 82% white, 1% international; 41% from in state; 64% live on campus; N/A of students in fraternities, N/A in sororities
Most popular majors: 11% Biology/Biological Sciences, General; 9% Registered Nursing/Registered Nurse; 7% Kinesiology and Exercise Science; 6% Health Professions and Related Clinical Sciences, Other; 5% Business

Administration and Management, General
Expenses: 2016-2017: $42,162; room/board: $14,264
Financial aid: (570) 941-7700; 70% of undergrads determined to have financial need; average aid package $26,642

University of the Arts
Philadelphia PA
(215) 717-6049
U.S. News ranking: Arts, unranked
Website: www.uarts.edu
Admissions email: admissions@uarts.edu
Private; founded 1876
Freshman admissions: N/A; 2015-2016: 1,608 applied, 1,185 accepted. Either SAT or ACT required. SAT 25/75 percentile: N/A. High school rank: N/A.
Early decision deadline: N/A, notification date: N/A
Early action deadline: N/A, notification date: N/A
Application deadline (fall): rolling
Undergraduate student body: 1,671 full time, 41 part time; 40% male, 60% female; 0% American Indian, 3% Asian, 14% black, 10% Hispanic, 5% multiracial, 1% Pacific Islander, 62% white, 5% international; 41% from in state; 32% live on campus; 0% of students in fraternities, 0% in sororities
Most popular majors: 15% Dance, General; 8% Graphic Design; 7% Film/Video and Photographic Arts, Other; 7% Photography
Expenses: 2016-2017: $41,464; room/board: $15,120
Financial aid: (215) 717-6170; 77% of undergrads determined to have financial need; average aid package $27,008

University of Valley Forge[1]
Phoenixville PA
(800) 432-8322
U.S. News ranking: Reg. Coll. (N), No. 33
Website: www.valleyforge.edu/
Admissions email: admissions@valleyforge.edu
Private
Application deadline (fall): N/A
Undergraduate student body: N/A full time, N/A part time
Expenses: 2015-2016: $20,394; room/board: $8,116
Financial aid: (610) 917-1498

Ursinus College
Collegeville PA
(610) 409-3200
U.S. News ranking: Nat. Lib. Arts, No. 95
Website: www.ursinus.edu
Admissions email: Admissions@Ursinus.edu
Private; founded 1869
Freshman admissions: selective; 2015-2016: 2,634 applied, 2,176 accepted. Neither SAT nor ACT required. SAT 25/75 percentile: 1040-1250. High school rank: 25% in top tenth, 53% in top quarter, 89% in top half
Early decision deadline: 2/1, notification date: 2/15

Early action deadline: 1/1, notification date: 1/31
Application deadline (fall): rolling
Undergraduate student body: 1,632 full time, 11 part time; 47% male, 53% female; 0% American Indian, 5% Asian, 6% black, 6% Hispanic, 3% multiracial, 0% Pacific Islander, 74% white, 2% international; 55% from in state; 96% live on campus; 19% of students in fraternities, 25% in sororities
Most popular majors: 16% Economics, General; 13% Biology/Biological Sciences, General; 11% Psychology, General; 8% Exercise Physiology
Expenses: 2016-2017: $49,370; room/board: $12,320
Financial aid: (610) 409-3600; 75% of undergrads determined to have financial need; average aid package $34,460

Villanova University
Villanova PA
(610) 519-4000
U.S. News ranking: Nat. U., No. 50
Website: www.villanova.edu
Admissions email: gotovu@villanova.edu
Private; founded 1842
Affiliation: Roman Catholic
Freshman admissions: more selective; 2015-2016: 16,206 applied, 7,761 accepted. Either SAT or ACT required. SAT 25/75 percentile: 1200-1400. High school rank: 55% in top tenth, 87% in top quarter, 98% in top half
Early decision deadline: N/A, notification date: N/A
Early action deadline: 11/1, notification date: 12/20
Application deadline (fall): 1/15
Undergraduate student body: 6,400 full time, 594 part time; 49% male, 51% female; 0% American Indian, 7% Asian, 5% black, 8% Hispanic, 2% multiracial, 0% Pacific Islander, 74% white, 2% international; 22% from in state; 69% live on campus; 17% of students in fraternities, 42% in sororities
Most popular majors: 33% Business, Management, Marketing, and Related Support Services; 11% Engineering; 11% Social Sciences; 10% Health Professions and Related Programs
Expenses: 2016-2017: $49,280; room/board: $13,066
Financial aid: (610) 519-4010; 49% of undergrads determined to have financial need; average aid package $35,466

Washington and Jefferson College
Washington PA
(724) 223-6025
U.S. News ranking: Nat. Lib. Arts, No. 99
Website: www.washjeff.edu
Admissions email: admission@washjeff.edu
Private; founded 1781
Freshman admissions: more selective; 2015-2016: 6,835 applied, 2,971 accepted. Neither

SAT nor ACT required. SAT 25/75 percentile: 1060-1250. High school rank: 34% in top tenth, 64% in top quarter, 93% in top half
Early decision deadline: 12/1, notification date: 12/15
Early action deadline: 1/15, notification date: 2/15
Application deadline (fall): 3/1
Undergraduate student body: 1,342 full time, 8 part time; 52% male, 48% female; 0% American Indian, 2% Asian, 5% black, 4% Hispanic, 3% multiracial, 0% Pacific Islander, 81% white, 3% international; 78% from in state; 95% live on campus; 34% of students in fraternities, 39% in sororities
Most popular majors: 12% Psychology, General; 10% Business/Commerce, General; 7% Accounting; 7% English Language and Literature, General; 6% Economics, General
Expenses: 2016-2017: $44,900; room/board: $11,854
Financial aid: (724) 223-6019; 79% of undergrads determined to have financial need; average aid package $33,603

Waynesburg University
Waynesburg PA
(800) 225-7393
U.S. News ranking: Reg. U. (N), No. 85
Website: www.waynesburg.edu/
Admissions email: admissions@waynesburg.edu
Private; founded 1849
Affiliation: Presbyterian
Freshman admissions: selective; 2015-2016: 1,418 applied, 1,214 accepted. Either SAT or ACT required. SAT 25/75 percentile: 905-1100. High school rank: 17% in top tenth, 48% in top quarter, 82% in top half
Early decision deadline: N/A, notification date: N/A
Early action deadline: N/A, notification date: N/A
Application deadline (fall): rolling
Undergraduate student body: 1,329 full time, 101 part time; 40% male, 60% female; 0% American Indian, 1% Asian, 3% black, 1% Hispanic, 2% multiracial, 0% Pacific Islander, 91% white, 0% international; 80% from in state; 70% live on campus; N/A of students in fraternities, N/A in sororities
Most popular majors: 25% Nursing Practice; 7% Criminal Justice/Law Enforcement Administration; 6% Psychology, General; 5% Business Administration and Management, General
Expenses: 2016-2017: $22,800; room/board: $9,490
Financial aid: (724) 852-3208; 83% of undergrads determined to have financial need; average aid package $17,749

West Chester University of Pennsylvania
West Chester PA
(610) 436-3414
U.S. News ranking: Reg. U. (N), No. 61
Website: www.wcupa.edu/
Admissions email: ugadmiss@wcupa.edu
Public; founded 1871
Freshman admissions: selective; 2015-2016: 12,624 applied, 7,408 accepted. Either SAT or ACT required. SAT 25/75 percentile: 980-1160. High school rank: 12% in top tenth, 40% in top quarter, 79% in top half
Early decision deadline: N/A, notification date: N/A
Early action deadline: N/A, notification date: N/A
Application deadline (fall): rolling
Undergraduate student body: 12,781 full time, 1,440 part time; 41% male, 59% female; 0% American Indian, 2% Asian, 11% black, 5% Hispanic, 3% multiracial, 0% Pacific Islander, 78% white, 0% international; 88% from in state; 36% live on campus; 12% of students in fraternities, 16% in sororities
Most popular majors: 18% Business, Management, Marketing, and Related Support Services; 16% Health Professions and Related Programs; 13% Education; 8% English Language and Literature/Letters; 8% Psychology
Expenses: 2015-2016: $9,462 in state, $20,280 out of state; room/board: $12,780
Financial aid: (610) 436-2627; 59% of undergrads determined to have financial need; average aid package $7,785

Westminster College
New Wilmington PA
(800) 942-8033
U.S. News ranking: Nat. Lib. Arts, No. 119
Website: www.westminster.edu
Admissions email: admis@westminster.edu
Private; founded 1852
Affiliation: Presbyterian Church (USA)
Freshman admissions: selective; 2015-2016: 1,762 applied, 1,657 accepted. Either SAT or ACT required. SAT 25/75 percentile: 940-1070. High school rank: 24% in top tenth, 43% in top quarter, 64% in top half
Early decision deadline: N/A, notification date: N/A
Early action deadline: 11/15, notification date: 12/1
Application deadline (fall): 5/1
Undergraduate student body: 1,093 full time, 29 part time; 45% male, 55% female; 0% American Indian, 1% Asian, 3% black, 1% Hispanic, 2% multiracial, 0% Pacific Islander, 77% white, 0% international; 78% from in state; 71% live on campus; 22% of students in fraternities, 38% in sororities

Most popular majors: 17% Business, Management, Marketing, and Related Support Services; 16% Education; 14% Biological and Biomedical Sciences; 12% Social Sciences
Expenses: 2016-2017: $35,210; room/board: $10,690
Financial aid: (724) 946-7102; 83% of undergrads determined to have financial need; average aid package $27,070

Widener University
Chester PA
(610) 499-4126
U.S. News ranking: Nat. U., No. 183
Website: www.widener.edu
Admissions email: admissions.office@widener.edu
Private; founded 1821
Freshman admissions: selective; 2015-2016: 5,421 applied, 3,686 accepted. Either SAT or ACT required. SAT 25/75 percentile: 930-1120. High school rank: 12% in top tenth, 41% in top quarter, 81% in top half
Early decision deadline: N/A, notification date: N/A
Early action deadline: N/A, notification date: N/A
Application deadline (fall): rolling
Undergraduate student body: 2,954 full time, 600 part time; 44% male, 56% female; 0% American Indian, 4% Asian, 13% black, 5% Hispanic, 2% multiracial, 0% Pacific Islander, 69% white, 4% international; 60% from in state; 47% live on campus; 10% of students in fraternities, 9% in sororities
Most popular majors: 26% Health Professions and Related Programs; 19% Business, Management, Marketing, and Related Support Services; 15% Education; 9% Psychology; 5% Biological and Biomedical Sciences
Expenses: 2016-2017: $42,870; room/board: $13,616
Financial aid: (610) 499-4174; 79% of undergrads determined to have financial need; average aid package $31,740

Wilkes University
Wilkes-Barre PA
(570) 408-4400
U.S. News ranking: Reg. U. (N), No. 85
Website: www.wilkes.edu
Admissions email: admissions@wilkes.edu
Private; founded 1933
Freshman admissions: selective; 2015-2016: 3,164 applied, 2,586 accepted. Either SAT or ACT required. SAT 25/75 percentile: 930-1176. High school rank: 25% in top tenth, 50% in top quarter, 80% in top half
Early decision deadline: N/A, notification date: N/A
Early action deadline: N/A, notification date: N/A
Application deadline (fall): rolling
Undergraduate student body: 2,254 full time, 167 part time; 52% male, 48% female; 0% American Indian, 3% Asian, 4% black,

6% Hispanic, 4% multiracial, 0% Pacific Islander, 73% white, 9% international; 82% from in state; 41% live on campus; 0% of students in fraternities, 0% in sororities
Most popular majors: 16% Business, Management, Marketing, and Related Support Services; 14% Engineering; 14% Health Professions and Related Programs; 8% Psychology
Expenses: 2016-2017: $33,568; room/board: $13,746
Financial aid: (570) 408-4346; 80% of undergrads determined to have financial need; average aid package $24,966

Wilson College
Chambersburg PA
(800) 421-8402
U.S. News ranking: Reg. Coll. (N), No. 13
Website: www.wilson.edu
Admissions email: admissions@wilson.edu
Private; founded 1869
Affiliation: Presbyterian Church (USA)
Freshman admissions: selective; 2015-2016: 879 applied, 401 accepted. Neither SAT nor ACT required. SAT 25/75 percentile: 820-1050. High school rank: 19% in top tenth, 43% in top quarter, 74% in top half
Early decision deadline: N/A, notification date: N/A
Early action deadline: N/A, notification date: N/A
Application deadline (fall): rolling
Undergraduate student body: 438 full time, 250 part time; 17% male, 83% female; 0% American Indian, 1% Asian, 7% black, 4% Hispanic, 3% multiracial, 0% Pacific Islander, 65% white, 8% international; 74% from in state; 62% live on campus; 0% of students in fraternities, 0% in sororities
Most popular majors: 43% Health Services Administration; 9% Business Administration and Management, General; 6% Animal-Assisted Therapy; 5% Biology/Biological Sciences, General
Expenses: 2016-2017: $24,430; room/board: $11,190
Financial aid: (717) 262-2016; 96% of undergrads determined to have financial need; average aid package $21,589

York College of Pennsylvania
York PA
(717) 849-1600
U.S. News ranking: Reg. U. (N), No. 91
Website: www.ycp.edu
Admissions email: admissions@ycp.edu
Private; founded 1787
Freshman admissions: selective; 2015-2016: 13,235 applied, 5,694 accepted. Either SAT or ACT required. SAT 25/75 percentile: 960-1150. High school rank: 4% in top tenth, 30% in top quarter, 71% in top half
Early decision deadline: N/A, notification date: N/A

Early action deadline: N/A, notification date: N/A
Application deadline (fall): rolling
Undergraduate student body: 4,077 full time, 460 part time; 45% male, 55% female; 0% American Indian, 2% Asian, 5% black, 6% Hispanic, 4% multiracial, 0% Pacific Islander, 83% white, 0% international; 58% from in state; 57% live on campus; 4% of students in fraternities, 6% in sororities
Most popular majors: 17% Business, Management, Marketing, and Related Support Services; 15% Health Professions and Related Programs; 9% Education; 9% Homeland Security, Law Enforcement, Firefighting and Related Protective Services
Expenses: 2016-2017: $18,780; room/board: $10,460
Financial aid: (717) 849-1682; 67% of undergrads determined to have financial need; average aid package $14,371

RHODE ISLAND

Brown University
Providence RI
(401) 863-2378
U.S. News ranking: Nat. U., No. 14
Website: www.brown.edu
Admissions email: admission@brown.edu
Private; founded 1764
Freshman admissions: most selective; 2015-2016: 30,396 applied, 2,875 accepted. Either SAT or ACT required. SAT 25/75 percentile: 1370-1560. High school rank: 91% in top tenth, 100% in top quarter, 100% in top half
Early decision deadline: 11/1, notification date: 12/15
Early action deadline: N/A, notification date: N/A
Application deadline (fall): 1/1
Undergraduate student body: 6,318 full time, 334 part time; 47% male, 53% female; 0% American Indian, 13% Asian, 7% black, 11% Hispanic, 6% multiracial, 0% Pacific Islander, 43% white, 12% international; 6% from in state; 76% live on campus; 12% of students in fraternities, 9% in sororities
Most popular majors: 11% Biology/Biological Sciences, General; 9% Economics, General; 5% Computer Science; 4% History, General; 4% Neuroscience
Expenses: 2016-2017: $51,367; room/board: $13,200
Financial aid: (401) 863-2721; 45% of undergrads determined to have financial need; average aid package $46,775

Bryant University
Smithfield RI
(800) 622-7001
U.S. News ranking: Reg. U. (N), No. 9
Website: www.bryant.edu
Admissions email: admission@bryant.edu
Private; founded 1863
Freshman admissions: selective; 2015-2016: 6,705 applied, 4,849 accepted. Neither SAT

nor ACT required. SAT 25/75 percentile: 1090-1250. High school rank: 24% in top tenth, 58% in top quarter, 90% in top half
Early decision deadline: 11/17, notification date: 12/15
Early action deadline: 12/1, notification date: 1/15
Application deadline (fall): 2/2
Undergraduate student body: 3,379 full time, 80 part time; 59% male, 41% female; 0% American Indian, 5% Asian, 4% black, 7% Hispanic, 1% multiracial, 0% Pacific Islander, 73% white, 8% international; 12% from in state; 82% live on campus; 5% of students in fraternities, 11% in sororities
Most popular majors: 20% Accounting; 18% Finance, General; 14% Marketing/Marketing Management, General; 10% Business Administration and Management, General; 8% International Business/Trade/Commerce
Expenses: 2016-2017: $40,962; room/board: $14,684
Financial aid: (401) 232-6020; 62% of undergrads determined to have financial need; average aid package $24,591

Johnson & Wales University
Providence RI
(800) 342-5598
U.S. News ranking: Reg. U. (N), No. 67
Website: www.jwu.edu
Admissions email: admissions.pvd@jwu.edu
Private; founded 1914
Freshman admissions: less selective; 2015-2016: 11,971 applied, 9,807 accepted. Neither SAT nor ACT required. SAT 25/75 percentile: 852-1070. High school rank: N/A
Early decision deadline: N/A, notification date: N/A
Early action deadline: N/A, notification date: N/A
Application deadline (fall): rolling
Undergraduate student body: 8,185 full time, 583 part time; 40% male, 60% female; 0% American Indian, 1% Asian, 11% black, 11% Hispanic, 8% multiracial, 0% Pacific Islander, 56% white, 9% international; 19% from in state; 44% live on campus; N/A of students in fraternities, N/A in sororities
Most popular majors: 29% Foodservice Systems Administration/Management; 12% Parks, Recreation and Leisure Facilities Management, General; 10% Hotel/Motel Administration/Management; 8% Business Administration and Management, General; 7% Culinary Arts/Chef Training
Expenses: 2016-2017: $30,746; room/board: N/A
Financial aid: (401) 598-1468; 71% of undergrads determined to have financial need; average aid package $20,363

New England Institute of Technology
East Greenwich RI
(401) 467-7744
U.S. News ranking: Reg. Coll. (N), unranked
Website: www.neit.edu/
Admissions email: NEITAdmissions@neit.edu
Private; founded 1940
Freshman admissions: N/A; 2015-2016: N/A applied, N/A accepted. Neither SAT nor ACT required. ACT 25/75 percentile: N/A. High school rank: N/A
Early decision deadline: N/A, notification date: N/A
Early action deadline: N/A, notification date: N/A
Application deadline (fall): rolling
Undergraduate student body: 2,369 full time, 444 part time; 67% male, 33% female; 1% American Indian, 2% Asian, 5% black, 11% Hispanic, 2% multiracial, 0% Pacific Islander, 65% white, 4% international
Most popular majors: Information not available
Expenses: 2016-2017: $24,651; room/board: N/A
Financial aid: (800) 736-7744

Providence College
Providence RI
(401) 865-2535
U.S. News ranking: Reg. U. (N), No. 1
Website: www.providence.edu
Admissions email: pcadmiss@providence.edu
Private; founded 1917
Affiliation: Roman Catholic
Freshman admissions: selective; 2015-2016: 10,215 applied, 5,800 accepted. Neither SAT nor ACT required. SAT 25/75 percentile: 1050-1250. High school rank: 9% in top tenth, 69% in top quarter, 94% in top half
Early decision deadline: 12/1, notification date: 1/1
Early action deadline: 11/15, notification date: 1/1
Application deadline (fall): 1/15
Undergraduate student body: 3,911 full time, 290 part time; 44% male, 56% female; 0% American Indian, 1% Asian, 4% black, 8% Hispanic, 2% multiracial, 0% Pacific Islander, 77% white, 2% international; 15% from in state; 76% live on campus; N/A of students in fraternities, N/A in sororities
Most popular majors: 33% Business, Management, Marketing, and Related Support Services; 12% Social Sciences; 9% Biological and Biomedical Sciences; 7% Health Professions and Related Programs; 7% Psychology
Expenses: 2016-2017: $46,970; room/board: $13,790
Financial aid: (401) 865-2286; 56% of undergrads determined to have financial need; average aid package $27,900

Rhode Island College
Providence RI
(800) 669-5760
U.S. News ranking: Reg. U. (N), No. 137
Website: www.ric.edu
Admissions email: admissions@ric.edu
Public; founded 1854
Freshman admissions: less selective; 2015-2016: 4,732 applied, 3,389 accepted. Either SAT or ACT required. SAT 25/75 percentile: 800-1030. High school rank: 11% in top tenth, 35% in top quarter, 75% in top half
Early decision deadline: N/A, notification date: N/A
Early action deadline: N/A, notification date: N/A
Application deadline (fall): 3/15
Undergraduate student body: 5,581 full time, 1,865 part time; 32% male, 68% female; 0% American Indian, 3% Asian, 8% black, 16% Hispanic, 2% multiracial, 0% Pacific Islander, 62% white, 0% international; 86% from in state; 15% live on campus; N/A of students in fraternities, N/A in sororities
Most popular majors: 16% Health Professions and Related Programs; 16% Education; 16% Business, Management, Marketing, and Related Support Services; 12% Psychology; 10% Public Administration and Social Service Professions
Expenses: 2016-2017: $8,206 in state, $19,867 out of state; room/board: $10,794
Financial aid: (401) 456-8033; 69% of undergrads determined to have financial need; average aid package $9,009

Rhode Island School of Design
Providence RI
(401) 454-6300
U.S. News ranking: Arts, unranked
Website: www.risd.edu
Admissions email: admissions@risd.edu
Private; founded 1877
Freshman admissions: N/A; 2015-2016: 2,516 applied, 904 accepted. Either SAT or ACT required. SAT 25/75 percentile: N/A. High school rank: N/A
Early decision deadline: 11/1, notification date: 12/7
Early action deadline: N/A, notification date: N/A
Application deadline (fall): 2/1
Undergraduate student body: 2,014 full time, 0 part time; 32% male, 68% female; 0% American Indian, 19% Asian, 2% black, 8% Hispanic, 4% multiracial, 0% Pacific Islander, 31% white, 26% international; 5% from in state; 60% live on campus; 0% of students in fraternities, 0% in sororities
Most popular majors: 14% Industrial and Product Design; 11% Graphic Design; 9% Film/Video and Photographic Arts, Other
Expenses: 2016-2017: $47,110; room/board: $12,850
Financial aid: (401) 454-6636; 39% of undergrads determined to have financial need; average aid package $28,805

Roger Williams University

Bristol RI
(401) 254-3500
U.S. News ranking: Reg. U. (N), No. 35
Website: www.rwu.edu
Admissions email: admit@rwu.edu
Private; founded 1956
Freshman admissions: selective; 2015-2016: 9,597 applied, 7,532 accepted. Neither SAT nor ACT required. SAT 25/75 percentile: 1030-1200. High school rank: N/A
Early decision deadline: N/A, notification date: N/A
Early action deadline: 11/1, notification date: 12/1
Application deadline (fall): 2/1
Undergraduate student body: 3,956 full time, 599 part time; 48% male, 52% female; 0% American Indian, 1% Asian, 2% black, 6% Hispanic, 2% multiracial, 0% Pacific Islander, 75% white, 5% international; 18% from in state; 75% live on campus; 0% of students in fraternities, 0% in sororities
Most popular majors: 25% Business, Management, Marketing, and Related Support Services; 11% Homeland Security, Law Enforcement, Firefighting and Related Protective Services; 7% Biological and Biomedical Sciences; 7% Psychology
Expenses: 2016-2017: $32,100; room/board: $15,086
Financial aid: (401) 254-3100; 60% of undergrads determined to have financial need; average aid package $21,411

Salve Regina University

Newport RI
(888) 467-2583
U.S. News ranking: Reg. U. (N), No. 32
Website: www.salve.edu
Admissions email: sruadmis@salve.edu
Private; founded 1934
Affiliation: Roman Catholic
Freshman admissions: selective; 2015-2016: 4,582 applied, 3,322 accepted. Neither SAT nor ACT required. SAT 25/75 percentile: 1020-1170. High school rank: 15% in top tenth, 49% in top quarter, 84% in top half
Early decision deadline: N/A, notification date: N/A
Early action deadline: 11/1, notification date: 12/25
Application deadline (fall): rolling
Undergraduate student body: 1,995 full time, 163 part time; 28% male, 72% female; 0% American Indian, 1% Asian, 2% black, 6% Hispanic, 2% multiracial, 0% Pacific Islander, 81% white, 1% international; 23% from in state; 60% live on campus; 0% of students in fraternities, 0% in sororities
Most popular majors: 17% Registered Nursing/Registered Nurse; 10% Business Administration and Management, General; 10% Marketing/Marketing Management, General;

9% Criminal Justice/Law Enforcement Administration; 7% Psychology, General
Expenses: 2016-2017: $37,820; room/board: $13,650
Financial aid: (401) 341-2901; 77% of undergrads determined to have financial need; average aid package $26,100

University of Rhode Island

Kingston RI
(401) 874-7100
U.S. News ranking: Nat. U., No. 159
Website: www.uri.edu
Admissions email: admission@uri.edu
Public; founded 1892
Freshman admissions: selective; 2015-2016: 21,261 applied, 15,200 accepted. Either SAT or ACT required. SAT 25/75 percentile: 1010-1190. High school rank: 19% in top tenth, 50% in top quarter, 86% in top half
Early decision deadline: N/A, notification date: N/A
Early action deadline: 12/1, notification date: 1/31
Application deadline (fall): 2/1
Undergraduate student body: 12,293 full time, 1,348 part time; 46% male, 54% female; 0% American Indian, 3% Asian, 5% black, 9% Hispanic, 3% multiracial, 0% Pacific Islander, 71% white, 1% international; 55% from in state; 44% live on campus; 17% of students in fraternities, 22% in sororities
Most popular majors: 8% Registered Nursing/Registered Nurse; 6% Psychology, General; 5% Kinesiology and Exercise Science; 5% Human Development and Family Studies, General
Expenses: 2015-2016: $12,862 in state, $28,852 out of state; room/board: $11,956
Financial aid: (401) 874-9500; 87% of undergrads determined to have financial need; average aid package $16,530

SOUTH CAROLINA

Allen University[1]

Columbia SC
(803) 376-5735
U.S. News ranking: Nat. Lib. Arts, second tier
Website: www.allenuniversity.edu
Admissions email: admissions@allenuniversity.edu
Private; founded 1870
Affiliation: African Methodist Episcopal
Application deadline (fall): rolling
Undergraduate student body: N/A full time, N/A part time
Expenses: 2015-2016: $13,540; room/board: $6,560
Financial aid: (803) 376-5736

Anderson University

Anderson SC
(864) 231-5607
U.S. News ranking: Reg. U. (S), No. 67
Website: www.andersonuniversity.edu
Admissions email: admission@andersonuniversity.edu
Private; founded 1911
Affiliation: South Carolina Baptist Convention
Freshman admissions: selective; 2015-2016: 3,322 applied, 1,825 accepted. Either SAT or ACT required. SAT 25/75 percentile: 950-1183. High school rank: 37% in top tenth, 62% in top quarter, 87% in top half
Early decision deadline: N/A, notification date: N/A
Early action deadline: N/A, notification date: N/A
Application deadline (fall): rolling
Undergraduate student body: 2,397 full time, 427 part time; 32% male, 68% female; 1% American Indian, 1% Asian, 7% black, 2% Hispanic, 0% multiracial, 1% Pacific Islander, 62% white, 26% international; 81% from in state; 53% live on campus; 0% of students in fraternities, 0% in sororities
Most popular majors: 24% Education; 18% Business, Management, Marketing, and Related Support Services; 9% Visual and Performing Arts; 8% Parks, Recreation, Leisure, and Fitness Studies; 7% Homeland Security, Law Enforcement, Firefighting and Related Protective Services
Expenses: 2016-2017: $26,510; room/board: $9,174
Financial aid: (864) 231-2070; 80% of undergrads determined to have financial need; average aid package $18,340

Benedict College[1]

Columbia SC
(803) 253-5143
U.S. News ranking: Reg. Coll. (S), second tier
Website: www.benedict.edu
Admissions email: admissions@benedict.edu
Private; founded 1870
Affiliation: Baptist
Application deadline (fall): rolling
Undergraduate student body: N/A full time, N/A part time
Expenses: 2015-2016: $18,288; room/board: $8,104
Financial aid: (803) 253-5105

Charleston Southern University

Charleston SC
(843) 863-7050
U.S. News ranking: Reg. U. (S), No. 98
Website: www.csuniv.edu
Admissions email: enroll@csuniv.edu
Private; founded 1964
Affiliation: Baptist
Freshman admissions: selective; 2015-2016: 4,390 applied, 2,643 accepted. Either SAT or ACT required. SAT 25/75 percentile: 910-1110. High

school rank: 20% in top tenth, 47% in top quarter, 82% in top half
Early decision deadline: N/A, notification date: N/A
Early action deadline: N/A, notification date: N/A
Application deadline (fall): rolling
Undergraduate student body: 2,796 full time, 385 part time; 37% male, 63% female; 1% American Indian, 2% Asian, 26% black, 3% Hispanic, 2% multiracial, 0% Pacific Islander, 61% white, 1% international
Most popular majors: 13% Registered Nursing/Registered Nurse; 11% Health and Physical Education/Fitness, General; 7% Biology/Biological Sciences, General; 6% Criminal Justice/Law Enforcement Administration; 5% Psychology, General
Expenses: 2016-2017: $24,140; room/board: $9,600
Financial aid: (843) 863-7050

The Citadel

Charleston SC
(843) 953-5230
U.S. News ranking: Reg. U. (S), No. 3
Website: www.citadel.edu/root/
Admissions email: admissions@citadel.edu
Public; founded 1842
Freshman admissions: selective; 2015-2016: 2,436 applied, 1,864 accepted. Either SAT or ACT required. SAT 25/75 percentile: 980-1180. High school rank: 11% in top tenth, 34% in top quarter, 70% in top half
Early decision deadline: N/A, notification date: N/A
Early action deadline: N/A, notification date: N/A
Application deadline (fall): rolling
Undergraduate student body: 2,461 full time, 210 part time; 90% male, 10% female; 1% American Indian, 2% Asian, 9% black, 6% Hispanic, 4% multiracial, 0% Pacific Islander, 77% white, 1% international; 61% from in state; 100% live on campus; 0% of students in fraternities, 0% in sororities
Most popular majors: 28% Business Administration and Management, General; 16% Criminal Justice/Law Enforcement Administration; 13% Engineering, General; 10% Social Sciences, General; 7% Secondary Education and Teaching
Expenses: 2015-2016: $11,364 in state, $31,780 out of state; room/board: $6,381
Financial aid: (843) 953-5187; 56% of undergrads determined to have financial need; average aid package $16,019

Claflin University

Orangeburg SC
(803) 535-5340
U.S. News ranking: Nat. Lib. Arts, second tier
Website: www.claflin.edu
Admissions email: mike.zeigler@claflin.edu
Private; founded 1869
Affiliation: United Methodist

Freshman admissions: least selective; 2015-2016: 5,418 applied, 2,239 accepted. Either SAT or ACT required. SAT 25/75 percentile: 720-910. High school rank: 8% in top tenth, 26% in top quarter, 59% in top half
Early decision deadline: N/A, notification date: N/A
Early action deadline: N/A, notification date: N/A
Application deadline (fall): rolling
Undergraduate student body: 1,807 full time, 44 part time; 36% male, 64% female; 1% American Indian, 1% Asian, 92% black, 2% Hispanic, 0% multiracial, 0% Pacific Islander, 1% white, 2% international
Most popular majors: Information not available
Expenses: 2016-2017: $16,098; room/board: $11,116
Financial aid: (803) 535-5334; 95% of undergrads determined to have financial need; average aid package $14,957

Clemson University

Clemson SC
(864) 656-2287
U.S. News ranking: Nat. U., No. 66
Website: www.clemson.edu
Admissions email: cuadmissions@clemson.edu
Public; founded 1889
Freshman admissions: more selective; 2015-2016: 22,396 applied, 11,483 accepted. Either SAT or ACT required. ACT 25/75 percentile: 27-31. High school rank: 56% in top tenth, 88% in top quarter, 98% in top half
Early decision deadline: N/A, notification date: N/A
Early action deadline: N/A, notification date: N/A
Application deadline (fall): 5/1
Undergraduate student body: 17,238 full time, 778 part time; 53% male, 47% female; 0% American Indian, 2% Asian, 7% black, 3% Hispanic, 3% multiracial, 0% Pacific Islander, 83% white, 1% international; 67% from in state; 41% live on campus; 18% of students in fraternities, 32% in sororities
Most popular majors: 19% Business, Management, Marketing, and Related Support Services; 17% Engineering; 9% Biological and Biomedical Sciences; 7% Health Professions and Related Programs
Expenses: 2015-2016: $14,240 in state, $32,796 out of state; room/board: $8,718
Financial aid: (864) 656-2280; 46% of undergrads determined to have financial need; average aid package $11,367

Coastal Carolina University

Conway SC
(843) 349-2170
U.S. News ranking: Reg. U. (S), No. 62
Website: www.coastal.edu
Admissions email: admissions@coastal.edu
Public; founded 1954
Freshman admissions: selective; 2015-2016: 17,252 applied, 10,291 accepted. Either SAT

or ACT required. SAT 25/75 percentile: 910-1080. High school rank: 9% in top tenth, 31% in top quarter, 69% in top half
Early decision deadline: N/A, notification date: N/A
Early action deadline: N/A, notification date: N/A
Application deadline (fall): 8/1
Undergraduate student body: 8,771 full time, 844 part time; 47% male, 53% female; 0% American Indian, 1% Asian, 20% black, 4% Hispanic, 5% multiracial, 0% Pacific Islander, 68% white, 1% international; 49% from in state; 42% live on campus; 4% of students in fraternities, 6% in sororities
Most popular majors: 8% Business Administration and Management, General; 6% Kinesiology and Exercise Science; 6% Marine Biology and Biological Oceanography; 6% Psychology, General
Expenses: 2015-2016: $10,530 in state, $24,320 out of state; room/board: $8,690
Financial aid: (843) 349-2313; 70% of undergrads determined to have financial need; average aid package $10,106

Coker College
Hartsville SC
(843) 383-8050
U.S. News ranking: Reg. Coll. (S), No. 6
Website: www.coker.edu
Admissions email: admissions@coker.edu
Private; founded 1908
Freshman admissions: selective; 2015-2016: 1,483 applied, 737 accepted. Either SAT or ACT required. ACT 25/75 percentile: 18-22. High school rank: N/A
Early decision deadline: N/A, notification date: N/A
Early action deadline: N/A, notification date: N/A
Application deadline (fall): 8/1
Undergraduate student body: 957 full time, 246 part time; 39% male, 61% female; 1% American Indian, 1% Asian, 33% black, 4% Hispanic, 2% multiracial, 0% Pacific Islander, 55% white, 1% international; 76% from in state; 44% live on campus; 0% of students in fraternities, 0% in sororities
Most popular majors: 23% Business/Commerce, General; 14% Sport and Fitness Administration/Management; 10% Psychology, General; 9% Criminology
Expenses: 2016-2017: $27,624; room/board: $8,568
Financial aid: (843) 383-8055; 87% of undergrads determined to have financial need; average aid package $19,876

College of Charleston
Charleston SC
(843) 953-5670
U.S. News ranking: Reg. U. (S), No. 10
Website: www.cofc.edu
Admissions email: admissions@cofc.edu
Public; founded 1770

Freshman admissions: selective; 2015-2016: 11,722 applied, 9,043 accepted. Either SAT or ACT required. SAT 25/75 percentile: 1030-1210. High school rank: 21% in top tenth, 54% in top quarter, 90% in top half
Early decision deadline: N/A, notification date: N/A
Early action deadline: 11/1, notification date: 1/1
Application deadline (fall): 4/1
Undergraduate student body: 9,590 full time, 878 part time; 37% male, 63% female; 0% American Indian, 2% Asian, 7% black, 5% Hispanic, 4% multiracial, 0% Pacific Islander, 80% white, 1% international; 65% from in state; 31% live on campus; 19% of students in fraternities, 24% in sororities
Most popular majors: 24% Business, Management, Marketing, and Related Support Services; 12% Biological and Biomedical Sciences; 10% Visual and Performing Arts; 9% Social Sciences
Expenses: 2015-2016: $11,360 in state, $28,904 out of state; room/board: $10,900
Financial aid: (843) 953-5540; 49% of undergrads determined to have financial need; average aid package $13,547

Columbia College
Columbia SC
(800) 277-1301
U.S. News ranking: Reg. U. (S), No. 47
Website: www.columbiasc.edu
Admissions email: admissions@columbiasc.edu
Private; founded 1854
Affiliation: United Methodist
Freshman admissions: less selective; 2015-2016: 515 applied, 459 accepted. Either SAT or ACT required. SAT 25/75 percentile: 840-1070. High school rank: 15% in top tenth, 47% in top quarter, 78% in top half
Early decision deadline: N/A, notification date: N/A
Early action deadline: N/A, notification date: N/A
Application deadline (fall): rolling
Undergraduate student body: 1,033 full time, 354 part time; 23% male, 77% female; 1% American Indian, 1% Asian, 34% black, 4% Hispanic, 3% multiracial, 0% Pacific Islander, 55% white, 2% international; 93% from in state; 34% live on campus; 0% of students in fraternities, 0% in sororities
Most popular majors: 15% Social Work; 14% Psychology, General; 9% Behavioral Sciences; 9% Business Administration and Management, General; 8% Speech-Language Pathology/Pathologist
Expenses: 2015-2016: $28,100; room/board: $7,400
Financial aid: (803) 786-3612

Columbia International University
Columbia SC
(800) 777-2227
U.S. News ranking: Reg. U. (S), No. 43
Website: www.ciu.edu
Admissions email: N/A
Private; founded 1923
Affiliation: Evangelical multi-denominational
Freshman admissions: selective; 2015-2016: 553 applied, 188 accepted. Either SAT or ACT required. SAT 25/75 percentile: 930-1130. High school rank: 23% in top tenth, 42% in top quarter, 74% in top half
Early decision deadline: N/A, notification date: N/A
Early action deadline: N/A, notification date: N/A
Application deadline (fall): 8/1
Undergraduate student body: 495 full time, 54 part time; 51% male, 49% female; 0% American Indian, 2% Asian, 10% black, 4% Hispanic, 2% multiracial, N/A Pacific Islander, 71% white, 4% international; 57% from in state; 65% live on campus; N/A of students in fraternities, N/A in sororities
Most popular majors: Information not available
Expenses: 2015-2016: $20,430; room/board: $7,530
Financial aid: (803) 754-4100

Converse College
Spartanburg SC
(864) 596-9040
U.S. News ranking: Reg. U. (S), No. 31
Website: www.converse.edu
Admissions email: info@converse.edu
Private; founded 1889
Freshman admissions: selective; 2015-2016: 1,316 applied, 760 accepted. Either SAT or ACT required. ACT 25/75 percentile: 20-25. High school rank: 20% in top tenth, 48% in top quarter, 85% in top half
Early decision deadline: N/A, notification date: N/A
Early action deadline: N/A, notification date: N/A
Application deadline (fall): rolling
Undergraduate student body: 745 full time, 49 part time; 0% male, 100% female; N/A American Indian, N/A Asian, N/A black, N/A Hispanic, N/A multiracial, N/A Pacific Islander, N/A white, N/A international
Most popular majors: 20% Visual and Performing Arts; 19% Education; 18% Psychology; 9% Biological and Biomedical Sciences; 8% Business, Management, Marketing, and Related Support Services
Expenses: 2016-2017: $17,350; room/board: $10,300
Financial aid: (864) 596-9019; 84% of undergrads determined to have financial need; average aid package $15,291

Erskine College
Due West SC
(864) 379-8838
U.S. News ranking: Nat. Lib. Arts, second tier
Website: www.erskine.edu
Admissions email: admissions@erskine.edu
Private; founded 1839
Affiliation: Associate Reformed Presbyterian
Freshman admissions: selective; 2015-2016: 991 applied, 637 accepted. Either SAT or ACT required. SAT 25/75 percentile: 880-1110. High school rank: 17% in top tenth, 31% in top quarter, 72% in top half
Early decision deadline: N/A, notification date: N/A
Early action deadline: N/A, notification date: N/A
Application deadline (fall): rolling
Undergraduate student body: 615 full time, 7 part time; 54% male, 46% female; 1% American Indian, 1% Asian, 13% black, 4% Hispanic, 0% multiracial, 0% Pacific Islander, 67% white, 0% international
Most popular majors: 18% Biological and Biomedical Sciences; 18% Business, Management, Marketing, and Related Support Services; 9% English Language and Literature/Letters; 8% Parks, Recreation, Leisure, and Fitness Studies; 8% Physical Sciences
Expenses: 2016-2017: $34,560; room/board: $10,900
Financial aid: (864) 379-8832; 100% of undergrads determined to have financial need; average aid package $23,800

Francis Marion University
Florence SC
(843) 661-1231
U.S. News ranking: Reg. U. (S), No. 84
Website: www.fmarion.edu
Admissions email: admissions@fmarion.edu
Public; founded 1970
Freshman admissions: less selective; 2015-2016: 3,681 applied, 2,167 accepted. Either SAT or ACT required. SAT 25/75 percentile: 820-1030. High school rank: 13% in top tenth, 39% in top quarter, 78% in top half
Early decision deadline: N/A, notification date: N/A
Early action deadline: N/A, notification date: N/A
Application deadline (fall): 8/1
Undergraduate student body: 3,172 full time, 412 part time; 32% male, 68% female; 0% American Indian, 1% Asian, 47% black, 2% Hispanic, 2% multiracial, 0% Pacific Islander, 46% white, 1% international; 97% from in state; 45% live on campus; 1% of students in fraternities, 5% in sororities
Most popular majors: 17% Business, Management, Marketing, and Related Support Services; 16% Health Professions and Related Programs; 15% Biological and Biomedical Sciences; 10% Social Sciences; 9% Psychology

Expenses: 2015-2016: $10,632 in state, $19,668 out of state; room/board: $7,472
Financial aid: (843) 661-1190; 77% of undergrads determined to have financial need; average aid package $12,609

Furman University
Greenville SC
(864) 294-2034
U.S. News ranking: Nat. Lib. Arts, No. 53
Website: www.furman.edu/
Admissions email: admissions@furman.edu
Private; founded 1826
Freshman admissions: more selective; 2015-2016: 5,043 applied, 3,268 accepted. Neither SAT nor ACT required. SAT 25/75 percentile: 1100-1320. High school rank: 39% in top tenth, 71% in top quarter, 92% in top half
Early decision deadline: 11/1, notification date: 11/15
Early action deadline: 11/1, notification date: 12/20
Application deadline (fall): 1/15
Undergraduate student body: 2,623 full time, 108 part time; 43% male, 57% female; 0% American Indian, 2% Asian, 5% black, 4% Hispanic, 2% multiracial, 0% Pacific Islander, 78% white, 6% international; 28% from in state; 96% live on campus; 33% of students in fraternities, 58% in sororities
Most popular majors: 9% Health Professions and Related Clinical Sciences, Other; 8% Business Administration, Management and Operations; 6% Biology, General
Expenses: 2016-2017: $47,164; room/board: $11,864
Financial aid: (864) 294-2204; 43% of undergrads determined to have financial need; average aid package $37,314

Lander University
Greenwood SC
(864) 388-8307
U.S. News ranking: Reg. Coll. (S), No. 19
Website: www.lander.edu
Admissions email: admissions@lander.edu
Public; founded 1872
Freshman admissions: selective; 2015-2016: 2,614 applied, 1,620 accepted. Either SAT or ACT required. SAT 25/75 percentile: 860-1060. High school rank: 14% in top tenth, 40% in top quarter, 75% in top half
Early decision deadline: N/A, notification date: N/A
Early action deadline: N/A, notification date: N/A
Application deadline (fall): rolling
Undergraduate student body: 2,446 full time, 213 part time; 31% male, 69% female; 0% American Indian, 0% Asian, 29% black, 1% Hispanic, 2% multiracial, 0% Pacific Islander, 58% white, 4% international; 95% from in state; 49% live on campus; N/A of students in fraternities, N/A in sororities
Most popular majors: 21% Business Administration and Management, General; 13% Registered Nursing/Registered

Nurse; 10% Psychology, General; 7% Kinesiology and Exercise Science; 7% Sociology
Expenses: 2016-2017: $11,200 in state, $20,800 out of state; room/board: $8,583
Financial aid: (864) 388-8340; 77% of undergrads determined to have financial need; average aid package $11,268

Limestone College
Gaffney SC
(864) 488-4554
U.S. News ranking: Reg. Coll. (S), No. 41
Website: www.limestone.edu
Admissions email: admiss@limestone.edu
Private; founded 1845
Affiliation: Christian nondenominational
Freshman admissions: less selective; 2015-2016: 3,195 applied, 1,653 accepted. Either SAT or ACT required. SAT 25/75 percentile: 810-1010. High school rank: 5% in top tenth, 19% in top quarter, 50% in top half
Early decision deadline: N/A, notification date: N/A
Early action deadline: N/A, notification date: N/A
Application deadline (fall): 8/22
Undergraduate student body: 1,227 full time, 0 part time; 63% male, 37% female; 0% American Indian, 0% Asian, 34% black, 4% Hispanic, 3% multiracial, 0% Pacific Islander, 48% white, 9% international; 58% from in state; 69% live on campus; 1% of students in fraternities, 2% in sororities
Most popular majors: 22% Business, Management, Marketing, and Related Support Services; 11% Social Sciences; 9% Computer and Information Sciences and Support Services; 9% Liberal Arts and Sciences, General Studies and Humanities
Expenses: 2016-2017: $23,900; room/board: $8,350
Financial aid: (864) 488-8231; 92% of undergrads determined to have financial need; average aid package $19,588

Morris College[1]
Sumter SC
(803) 934-3225
U.S. News ranking: Reg. Coll. (S), unranked
Website: www.morris.edu
Admissions email: dcalhoun@morris.edu
Private
Application deadline (fall): N/A
Undergraduate student body: N/A full time, N/A part time
Expenses: 2015-2016: $12,649; room/board: $5,216
Financial aid: (803) 934-3238

Newberry College
Newberry SC
(800) 845-4955
U.S. News ranking: Reg. Coll. (S), No. 16
Website: www.newberry.edu/
Admissions email: admissions@newberry.edu
Private; founded 1856
Affiliation: Evangelical Lutheran Church of America

Freshman admissions: selective; 2015-2016: 1,171 applied, 656 accepted. Either SAT or ACT required. SAT 25/75 percentile: 850-1070. High school rank: 12% in top tenth, 32% in top quarter, 63% in top half
Early decision deadline: N/A, notification date: N/A
Early action deadline: N/A, notification date: N/A
Application deadline (fall): rolling
Undergraduate student body: 1,031 full time, 33 part time; 54% male, 46% female; 0% American Indian, 0% Asian, 26% black, 4% Hispanic, 4% multiracial, 0% Pacific Islander, 59% white, 4% international; 76% from in state; 82% live on campus; 21% of students in fraternities, 26% in sororities
Most popular majors: 25% Business Administration and Management, General; 14% Parks, Recreation and Leisure Studies; 10% Registered Nursing/Registered Nurse; 9% Biology/Biological Sciences, General; 9% Education, General
Expenses: 2016-2017: $25,600; room/board: $9,790
Financial aid: (803) 321-5120; 87% of undergrads determined to have financial need; average aid package $22,608

North Greenville University
Tigerville SC
(864) 977-7001
U.S. News ranking: Reg. U. (S), No. 84
Website: www.ngu.edu
Admissions email: admissions@ngu.edu
Private; founded 1892
Affiliation: Southern Baptist Convention
Freshman admissions: selective; 2015-2016: 1,593 applied, 919 accepted. Either SAT or ACT required. ACT 25/75 percentile: 22-30. High school rank: 24% in top tenth, 37% in top quarter, 75% in top half
Early decision deadline: N/A, notification date: N/A
Early action deadline: N/A, notification date: N/A
Application deadline (fall): rolling
Undergraduate student body: 2,209 full time, 272 part time; 50% male, 50% female; 0% American Indian, 0% Asian, 8% black, 3% Hispanic, 2% multiracial, 0% Pacific Islander, 80% white, 0% international; N/A from in state; 67% live on campus; N/A of students in fraternities, N/A in sororities
Most popular majors: 17% Liberal Arts and Sciences/Liberal Studies; 15% Sport and Fitness Administration/Management; 12% Business Administration and Management, General; 11% Elementary Education and Teaching; 10% Bible/Biblical Studies
Expenses: 2016-2017: $17,594; room/board: $9,892
Financial aid: (864) 977-7058; 57% of undergrads determined to have financial need; average aid package $5,783

Presbyterian College
Clinton SC
(864) 833-8230
U.S. News ranking: Nat. Lib. Arts, No. 119
Website: www.presby.edu
Admissions email: admissions@presby.edu
Private; founded 1880
Affiliation: Presbyterian Church (USA)
Freshman admissions: selective; 2015-2016: 2,072 applied, 1,291 accepted. Neither SAT nor ACT required. SAT 25/75 percentile: 970-1190. High school rank: 27% in top tenth, 56% in top quarter, 91% in top half
Early decision deadline: 11/1, notification date: 12/1
Early action deadline: 11/15, notification date: 12/15
Application deadline (fall): 6/30
Undergraduate student body: 990 full time, 74 part time; 47% male, 53% female; 0% American Indian, 1% Asian, 14% black, 3% Hispanic, 2% multiracial, 0% Pacific Islander, 77% white, 1% international; 35% from in state; 98% live on campus; 36% of students in fraternities, 51% in sororities
Most popular majors: 20% Business, Management, Marketing, and Related Support Services; 17% Biological and Biomedical Sciences; 13% Psychology; 8% Social Sciences; 7% History
Expenses: 2015-2016: $36,130; room/board: $9,750
Financial aid: (864) 833-8289; 77% of undergrads determined to have financial need; average aid package $34,081

South Carolina State University
Orangeburg SC
(803) 536-7185
U.S. News ranking: Reg. U. (S), second tier
Website: www.scsu.edu
Admissions email: admissions@scsu.edu
Public; founded 1896
Freshman admissions: least selective; 2015-2016: 2,445 applied, 2,320 accepted. Either SAT or ACT required. SAT 25/75 percentile: 680-840. High school rank: 3% in top tenth, 13% in top quarter, 34% in top half
Early decision deadline: N/A, notification date: N/A
Early action deadline: N/A, notification date: N/A
Application deadline (fall): 7/31
Undergraduate student body: 2,303 full time, 347 part time; 49% male, 51% female; 0% American Indian, 1% Asian, 96% black, 0% Hispanic, 0% multiracial, 0% Pacific Islander, 2% white, 0% international; 80% from in state; 44% live on campus; 20% of students in fraternities, 20% in sororities
Most popular majors: 12% Biology/Biological Sciences, General; 12% Family and Consumer Sciences/Human Sciences, General; 6% Social Work; 5% Criminal Justice/Law Enforce-

ment Administration; 5% Physical Education Teaching and Coaching
Expenses: 2015-2016: $10,088 in state, $19,856 out of state; room/board: $9,402
Financial aid: (803) 536-7067

Southern Wesleyan University[1]
Central SC
(864) 644-5550
U.S. News ranking: Reg. U. (S), No. 96
Website: www.swu.edu
Admissions email: admissions@swu.edu
Private
Application deadline (fall): N/A
Undergraduate student body: N/A full time, N/A part time
Expenses: 2015-2016: $23,620; room/board: $9,420
Financial aid: (864) 644-5500

University of South Carolina
Columbia SC
(803) 777-7700
U.S. News ranking: Nat. U., No. 107
Website: www.sc.edu
Admissions email: admissions-ugrad@sc.edu
Public; founded 1801
Freshman admissions: more selective; 2015-2016: 25,736 applied, 16,611 accepted. Either SAT or ACT required. SAT 25/75 percentile: 1110-1290. High school rank: 30% in top tenth, 65% in top quarter, 94% in top half
Early decision deadline: N/A, notification date: N/A
Early action deadline: 10/15, notification date: 12/20
Application deadline (fall): 12/1
Undergraduate student body: 23,613 full time, 1,624 part time; 46% male, 54% female; 0% American Indian, 3% Asian, 9% black, 4% Hispanic, 4% multiracial, 0% Pacific Islander, 76% white, 2% international; 61% from in state; 29% live on campus; 17% of students in fraternities, 35% in sororities
Most popular majors: 6% Physiology, Pathology and Related Sciences; 6% Biology, General; 5% Research and Experimental Psychology; 5% Finance and Financial Management Services
Expenses: 2016-2017: $11,854 in state, $31,282 out of state; room/board: $9,700
Financial aid: (803) 777-8134; 53% of undergrads determined to have financial need; average aid package $9,402

University of South Carolina–Aiken
Aiken SC
(803) 641-3366
U.S. News ranking: Reg. Coll. (S), No. 5
Website: web.usca.edu/
Admissions email: admit@sc.edu
Public; founded 1961
Freshman admissions: selective; 2015-2016: 2,341 applied,

1,338 accepted. Either SAT or ACT required. SAT 25/75 percentile: 880-1080. High school rank: 13% in top tenth, 43% in top quarter, 81% in top half
Early decision deadline: N/A, notification date: N/A
Early action deadline: N/A, notification date: N/A
Application deadline (fall): 8/1
Undergraduate student body: 2,594 full time, 762 part time; 36% male, 64% female; 0% American Indian, 1% Asian, 27% black, 4% Hispanic, 4% multiracial, 0% Pacific Islander, 58% white, 4% international; 88% from in state; 29% live on campus; 7% of students in fraternities, 8% in sororities
Most popular majors: 21% Health Professions and Related Programs; 17% Business, Management, and Related Support Services; 13% Parks, Recreation, Leisure, and Fitness Studies; 11% Education; 9% Social Sciences
Expenses: 2015-2016: $9,878 in state, $19,472 out of state; room/board: $7,290
Financial aid: (803) 641-3476; 70% of undergrads determined to have financial need; average aid package $10,739

University of South Carolina–Beaufort
Bluffton SC
(843) 208-8000
U.S. News ranking: Reg. Coll. (S), No. 37
Website: www.uscb.edu
Admissions email: admissions@uscb.edu
Public; founded 1959
Freshman admissions: less selective; 2015-2016: 1,970 applied, 1,236 accepted. Either SAT or ACT required. SAT 25/75 percentile: 830-1020. High school rank: 7% in top tenth, 27% in top quarter, 58% in top half
Early decision deadline: N/A, notification date: N/A
Early action deadline: N/A, notification date: N/A
Application deadline (fall): rolling
Undergraduate student body: 1,656 full time, 324 part time; 36% male, 64% female; 0% American Indian, 1% Asian, 22% black, 7% Hispanic, 4% multiracial, 0% Pacific Islander, 57% white, 1% international
Most popular majors: 23% Business Administration and Management, General; 16% Hospitality Administration/ Management, General; 11% Psychology, General; 9% Registered Nursing/Registered Nurse; 8% Social Sciences, General
Expenses: 2015-2016: $9,818 in state, $19,994 out of state; room/board: $8,297
Financial aid: (843) 521-3104

University of South Carolina–Upstate

Spartanburg SC
(864) 503-5246
U.S. News ranking: Reg. Coll. (S), No. 10
Website: www.uscupstate.edu/
Admissions email: admissions@uscupstate.edu
Public; founded 1967
Freshman admissions: less selective; 2015-2016: 3,956 applied, 2,262 accepted. Either SAT or ACT required. SAT 25/75 percentile: 860-1040. High school rank: 9% in top tenth, 35% in top quarter, 75% in top half
Early decision deadline: N/A, notification date: N/A
Early action deadline: N/A, notification date: N/A
Application deadline (fall): rolling
Undergraduate student body: 4,251 full time, 1,385 part time; 36% male, 64% female; 0% American Indian, 2% Asian, 29% black, 5% Hispanic, 4% multiracial, 0% Pacific Islander, 56% white, 2% international; 96% from in state; 12% live on campus; 2% of students in fraternities, 2% in sororities
Most popular majors: 28% Registered Nursing/Registered Nurse; 14% Non-Profit/Public/Organizational Management; 8% Liberal Arts and Sciences/Liberal Studies; 7% Psychology, General; 4% Education, General
Expenses: 2015-2016: $10,818 in state, $21,468 out of state; room/board: $7,848
Financial aid: (864) 503-5340; 78% of undergrads determined to have financial need; average aid package $9,429

Voorhees College[1]

Denmark SC
(803) 780-1030
U.S. News ranking: Reg. Coll. (S), second tier
Website: www.voorhees.edu
Admissions email: admissions@voorhees.edu
Private
Application deadline (fall): N/A
Undergraduate student body: N/A full time, N/A part time
Expenses: 2015-2016: $12,630; room/board: $7,346
Financial aid: (803) 780-1150

Winthrop University

Rock Hill SC
(803) 323-2191
U.S. News ranking: Reg. U. (S), No. 26
Website: www.winthrop.edu
Admissions email: admissions@winthrop.edu
Public; founded 1886
Freshman admissions: selective; 2015-2016: 4,876 applied, 3,272 accepted. Either SAT or ACT required. SAT 25/75 percentile: 910-1130. High school rank: 22% in top tenth, 51% in top quarter, 87% in top half
Early decision deadline: N/A, notification date: N/A
Early action deadline: N/A, notification date: N/A

Application deadline (fall): rolling
Undergraduate student body: 4,551 full time, 522 part time; 32% male, 68% female; 0% American Indian, 1% Asian, 30% black, 4% Hispanic, 4% multiracial, 0% Pacific Islander, 58% white, 2% international; 92% from in state; 51% live on campus; 3% of students in fraternities, 7% in sororities
Most popular majors: 23% Business, Management, Marketing, and Related Support Services; 14% Education; 9% Visual and Performing Arts; 8% Psychology
Expenses: 2016-2017: $14,510 in state, $28,090 out of state; room/board: $8,572
Financial aid: (803) 323-2189; 74% of undergrads determined to have financial need; average aid package $12,748

Wofford College

Spartanburg SC
(864) 597-4130
U.S. News ranking: Nat. Lib. Arts, No. 77
Website: www.wofford.edu
Admissions email: admissions@wofford.edu
Private; founded 1854
Affiliation: United Methodist
Freshman admissions: more selective; 2015-2016: 2,795 applied, 2,009 accepted. Either SAT or ACT required. ACT 25/75 percentile: 23-29. High school rank: 42% in top tenth, 72% in top quarter, 94% in top half
Early decision deadline: 11/1, notification date: 12/1
Early action deadline: 11/15, notification date: 2/1
Application deadline (fall): 2/1
Undergraduate student body: 1,573 full time, 40 part time; 50% male, 50% female; 0% American Indian, 3% Asian, 8% black, 3% Hispanic, 3% multiracial, 0% Pacific Islander, 81% white, 1% international; 55% from in state; 92% live on campus; 45% of students in fraternities, 54% in sororities
Most popular majors: 14% Biology/Biological Sciences, General; 10% Finance, General; 8% Business/Managerial Economics; 7% Accounting; 7% English Language and Literature, General
Expenses: 2016-2017: $40,245; room/board: $11,635
Financial aid: (864) 597-4160; 62% of undergrads determined to have financial need; average aid package $33,788

SOUTH DAKOTA

Augustana University

Sioux Falls SD
(605) 274-5516
U.S. News ranking: Reg. Coll. (Mid. W), No. 3
Website: www.augie.edu
Admissions email: admission@augie.edu
Private; founded 1860
Affiliation: ELCA Lutheran
Freshman admissions: more selective; 2015-2016: 1,463 applied, 952 accepted. Either SAT or ACT required. ACT 25/75 percentile: 23-28. High school

rank: 24% in top tenth, 59% in top quarter, 91% in top half
Early decision deadline: N/A, notification date: N/A
Early action deadline: N/A, notification date: N/A
Application deadline (fall): rolling
Undergraduate student body: 1,516 full time, 97 part time; 40% male, 60% female; 0% American Indian, 1% Asian, 2% black, 2% Hispanic, 2% multiracial, 0% Pacific Islander, 84% white, 8% international; 50% from in state; 72% live on campus; N/A of students in fraternities, N/A in sororities
Most popular majors: 17% Business, Management, Marketing, and Related Support Services; 14% Education, General; 11% Health Professions and Related Programs; 10% Parks, Recreation, Leisure, and Fitness Studies; 9% Foreign Languages, Literatures, and Linguistics
Expenses: 2016-2017: $30,944; room/board: $7,754
Financial aid: (605) 274-5216; 60% of undergrads determined to have financial need; average aid package $24,785

Black Hills State University

Spearfish SD
(800) 255-2478
U.S. News ranking: Reg. U. (Mid. W), second tier
Website: www.bhsu.edu
Admissions email: admissions@bhsu.edu
Public; founded 1883
Freshman admissions: less selective; 2015-2016: N/A applied, N/A accepted. Neither SAT nor ACT required. ACT 25/75 percentile: N/A. High school rank: N/A
Early decision deadline: N/A, notification date: N/A
Early action deadline: N/A, notification date: N/A
Application deadline (fall): N/A
Undergraduate student body: 2,238 full time, 1,658 part time; 36% male, 64% female; 3% American Indian, 0% Asian, 2% black, 5% Hispanic, 4% multiracial, 0% Pacific Islander, 83% white, 2% international
Most popular majors: Information not available
Expenses: 2015-2016: $8,004 in state, $10,586 out of state; room/board: $6,458
Financial aid: (605) 642-6145

Dakota State University

Madison SD
(888) 378-9988
U.S. News ranking: Reg. U. (Mid. W), No. 108
Website: www.dsu.edu
Admissions email: admissions@dsu.edu
Public; founded 1881
Freshman admissions: selective; 2015-2016: 911 applied, 740 accepted. Either SAT or ACT required. ACT 25/75 percentile: 20-25. High school rank: 6% in top tenth, 22% in top quarter, 51% in top half

Early decision deadline: N/A, notification date: N/A
Early action deadline: N/A, notification date: N/A
Application deadline (fall): rolling
Undergraduate student body: 1,251 full time, 1,569 part time; 55% male, 45% female; 1% American Indian, 1% Asian, 4% black, 4% Hispanic, 3% multiracial, 0% Pacific Islander, 84% white, 1% international; 66% from in state; 32% live on campus; 0% of students in fraternities, 0% in sororities
Most popular majors: 39% Computer and Information Sciences and Support Services; 18% Education; 12% Business, Management, Marketing, and Related Support Services; 7% Visual and Performing Arts; 6% Health Professions and Related Programs
Expenses: 2016-2017: $8,927 in state, $11,843 out of state; room/board: $6,411
Financial aid: (605) 256-5152; 68% of undergrads determined to have financial need; average aid package $8,116

Dakota Wesleyan University

Mitchell SD
(800) 333-8506
U.S. News ranking: Reg. Coll. (Mid. W), No. 33
Website: www.dwu.edu
Admissions email: admissions@dwu.edu
Private; founded 1885
Affiliation: United Methodist
Freshman admissions: selective; 2015-2016: 644 applied, 479 accepted. Either SAT or ACT required. ACT 25/75 percentile: 18-24. High school rank: 13% in top tenth, 34% in top quarter, 70% in top half
Early decision deadline: N/A, notification date: N/A
Early action deadline: N/A, notification date: N/A
Application deadline (fall): rolling
Undergraduate student body: 696 full time, 209 part time; 43% male, 57% female; 2% American Indian, 0% Asian, 2% black, 3% Hispanic, 3% multiracial, 0% Pacific Islander, 87% white, 2% international; 62% from in state; 64% live on campus; 0% of students in fraternities, 0% in sororities
Most popular majors: 11% Registered Nursing/Registered Nurse; 8% Business Administration and Management, General; 8% Criminal Justice/Safety Studies; 8% Educational Leadership and Administration, General; 8% Elementary Education and Teaching
Expenses: 2016-2017: $26,050; room/board: $6,900
Financial aid: (605) 995-2656; 68% of undergrads determined to have financial need; average aid package $25,212

Mount Marty College

Yankton SD
(800) 658-4552
U.S. News ranking: Reg. U. (Mid. W), No. 103
Website: www.mtmc.edu
Admissions email: mmcadmit@mtmc.edu
Private; founded 1936
Affiliation: Roman Catholic
Freshman admissions: selective; 2015-2016: 408 applied, 296 accepted. Either SAT or ACT required. ACT 25/75 percentile: 19-25. High school rank: 16% in top tenth, 45% in top quarter, 83% in top half
Early decision deadline: N/A, notification date: N/A
Early action deadline: N/A, notification date: N/A
Application deadline (fall): 8/30
Undergraduate student body: 494 full time, 553 part time; 42% male, 58% female; 4% American Indian, 1% Asian, 4% black, 8% Hispanic, 0% multiracial, 1% Pacific Islander, 80% white, N/A international; 59% from in state; 62% live on campus; N/A of students in fraternities, N/A in sororities
Most popular majors: 23% Registered Nursing/Registered Nurse; 15% Business Administration and Management, General; 15% Education, General; 9% Criminal Justice/Safety Studies
Expenses: 2016-2017: $25,330; room/board: $7,692
Financial aid: (605) 668-1589; 77% of undergrads determined to have financial need; average aid package $24,829

National American University[1]

Rapid City SD
(855) 448-2318
U.S. News ranking: Reg. Coll. (Mid. W), unranked
Website: www.national.edu/rc
Admissions email: N/A
For-profit
Application deadline (fall): N/A
Undergraduate student body: N/A full time, N/A part time
Expenses: 2015-2016: $13,647; room/board: N/A
Financial aid: (605) 394-4880

Northern State University

Aberdeen SD
(800) 678-5330
U.S. News ranking: Reg. U. (Mid. W), No. 103
Website: www.northern.edu
Admissions email: admissions@northern.edu
Public; founded 1901
Freshman admissions: selective; 2015-2016: 1,253 applied, 947 accepted. Either SAT or ACT required. ACT 25/75 percentile: 19-25. High school rank: 9% in top tenth, 24% in top quarter, 57% in top half
Early decision deadline: N/A, notification date: N/A
Early action deadline: N/A, notification date: N/A
Application deadline (fall): rolling

Undergraduate student body: 1,372 full time, 1,619 part time; 43% male, 57% female; 3% American Indian, 2% Asian, 2% black, 4% Hispanic, 2% multiracial, 0% Pacific Islander, 83% white, 4% international; 75% from in state; 40% live on campus; N/A of students in fraternities, N/A in sororities
Most popular majors: 32% Business, Management, Marketing, and Related Support Services; 22% Education; 9% Biological and Biomedical Sciences; 7% Liberal Arts and Sciences, General Studies and Humanities; 7% Social Sciences
Expenses: 2016-2017: $7,887 in state, $10,803 out of state; room/board: $7,520
Financial aid: (605) 626-2640; 64% of undergrads determined to have financial need; average aid package $10,441

South Dakota School of Mines and Technology
Rapid City SD
(605) 394-2414
U.S. News ranking: Engineering, unranked
Website: www.sdsmt.edu
Admissions email: admissions@sdsmt.edu
Public; founded 1885
Freshman admissions: N/A; 2015-2016: 1,479 applied, 1,246 accepted. Either SAT or ACT required. SAT 25/75 percentile: N/A. High school rank: 23% in top tenth, 28% in top quarter, 82% in top half
Early decision deadline: N/A, notification date: N/A
Early action deadline: N/A, notification date: N/A
Application deadline (fall): rolling
Undergraduate student body: 2,055 full time, 430 part time; 79% male, 21% female; 2% American Indian, 1% Asian, 2% black, 4% Hispanic, 4% multiracial, 0% Pacific Islander, 84% white, 2% international; 48% from in state; 37% live on campus; 38% of students in fraternities, 53% in sororities
Most popular majors: 26% Mechanical Engineering; 13% Chemical Engineering; 10% Civil Engineering, General; 9% Electrical and Electronics Engineering; 8% Industrial Engineering
Expenses: 2016-2017: $11,170 in state, $14,230 out of state; room/board: $7,300
Financial aid: (605) 394-2274; 57% of undergrads determined to have financial need; average aid package $13,964

South Dakota State University
Brookings SD
(605) 688-4121
U.S. News ranking: Nat. U., No. 202
Website: www.sdstate.edu
Admissions email: SDSU_Admissions@sdstate.edu
Public; founded 1881
Freshman admissions: selective; 2015-2016: 5,060 applied, 4,640 accepted. Either SAT

or ACT required. ACT 25/75 percentile: 20-26. High school rank: 14% in top tenth, 36% in top quarter, 68% in top half
Early decision deadline: N/A, notification date: N/A
Early action deadline: N/A, notification date: N/A
Application deadline (fall): rolling
Undergraduate student body: 8,559 full time, 2,448 part time; 47% male, 53% female; 1% American Indian, 1% Asian, 2% black, 2% Hispanic, 2% multiracial, 0% Pacific Islander, 88% white, 4% international
Most popular majors: 24% Health Professions and Related Programs; 15% Communications Technologies/Technicians and Support Services; 7% Social Sciences; 6% Engineering; 6% Family and Consumer Sciences/Human Sciences
Expenses: 2016-2017: $8,172 in state, $11,403 out of state; room/board: $7,744
Financial aid: (605) 688-4695

University of Sioux Falls
Sioux Falls SD
(605) 331-6600
U.S. News ranking: Reg. U. (Mid. W), No. 79
Website: www.usiouxfalls.edu
Admissions email: admissions@usiouxfalls.edu
Private; founded 1883
Affiliation: American Baptist
Freshman admissions: selective; 2015-2016: 1,733 applied, 1,596 accepted. Either SAT or ACT required. ACT 25/75 percentile: 20-25. High school rank: 12% in top tenth, 35% in top quarter, 68% in top half
Early decision deadline: N/A, notification date: N/A
Early action deadline: N/A, notification date: N/A
Application deadline (fall): rolling
Undergraduate student body: 1,007 full time, 217 part time; 41% male, 59% female; 1% American Indian, 1% Asian, 4% black, 1% Hispanic, 3% multiracial, 0% Pacific Islander, 89% white, 1% international; 60% from in state; 47% live on campus; N/A of students in fraternities, N/A in sororities
Most popular majors: 24% Health Professions and Related Programs; 23% Business, Management, Marketing, and Related Support Services; 12% Education; 6% Psychology; 5% Parks, Recreation, Leisure, and Fitness Studies
Expenses: 2016-2017: $27,160; room/board: $7,140
Financial aid: (605) 331-6623; 74% of undergrads determined to have financial need; average aid package $18,867

University of South Dakota
Vermillion SD
(605) 677-5434
U.S. News ranking: Nat. U., No. 202
Website: www.usd.edu
Admissions email: admiss@usd.edu

Public; founded 1862
Freshman admissions: selective; 2015-2016: 4,218 applied, 3,102 accepted. Neither SAT nor ACT required. ACT 25/75 percentile: 20-25. High school rank: 21% in top tenth, 42% in top quarter, 72% in top half
Early decision deadline: N/A, notification date: N/A
Early action deadline: N/A, notification date: N/A
Application deadline (fall): rolling
Undergraduate student body: 4,961 full time, 2,474 part time; 38% male, 62% female; 1% American Indian, 1% Asian, 3% black, 3% Hispanic, 3% multiracial, 0% Pacific Islander, 86% white, 2% international; 70% from in state; 28% live on campus; 23% of students in fraternities, 14% in sororities
Most popular majors: 28% Health Professions and Related Programs; 10% Business, Management, Marketing, and Related Support Services; 7% Education; 6% Psychology; 5% Social Sciences
Expenses: 2016-2017: $8,457 in state, $11,688 out of state; room/board: $7,535
Financial aid: (605) 677-5446

TENNESSEE

Austin Peay State University
Clarksville TN
(931) 221-7661
U.S. News ranking: Reg. U. (S), No. 79
Website: www.apsu.edu
Admissions email: admissions@apsu.edu
Public; founded 1927
Freshman admissions: selective; 2015-2016: 3,625 applied, 3,174 accepted. Neither SAT nor ACT required. ACT 25/75 percentile: 19-24. High school rank: 13% in top tenth, 34% in top quarter, 70% in top half
Early decision deadline: N/A, notification date: N/A
Early action deadline: N/A, notification date: N/A
Application deadline (fall): 8/3
Undergraduate student body: 6,751 full time, 2,433 part time; 42% male, 58% female; 0% American Indian, 2% Asian, 20% black, 6% Hispanic, 6% multiracial, 0% Pacific Islander, 63% white, 0% international; 89% from in state; 16% live on campus; 8% of students in fraternities, 9% in sororities
Most popular majors: 13% Business, Management, Marketing, and Related Support Services; 12% Health Professions and Related Programs; 11% Parks, Recreation, Leisure, and Fitness Studies; 6% Computer and Information Sciences and Support Services
Expenses: 2015-2016: $7,801 in state, $24,583 out of state; room/board: $8,350
Financial aid: (931) 221-7907; 82% of undergrads determined to have financial need; average aid package $10,419

Belmont University
Nashville TN
(615) 460-6785
U.S. News ranking: Reg. U. (S), No. 6
Website: www.belmont.edu
Admissions email: buadmission@mail.belmont.edu
Private; founded 1890
Affiliation: Nondenominational Christian
Freshman admissions: more selective; 2015-2016: 6,145 applied, 4,934 accepted. Either SAT or ACT required. ACT 25/75 percentile: 23-28. High school rank: 30% in top tenth, 58% in top quarter, 89% in top half
Early decision deadline: N/A, notification date: N/A
Early action deadline: N/A, notification date: N/A
Application deadline (fall): 8/1
Undergraduate student body: 5,639 full time, 344 part time; 38% male, 62% female; 0% American Indian, 2% Asian, 5% black, 5% Hispanic, 4% multiracial, 0% Pacific Islander, 80% white, 1% international; 32% from in state; 55% live on campus; N/A of students in fraternities, N/A in sororities
Most popular majors: 38% Visual and Performing Arts; 13% Business, Management, Marketing, and Related Support Services; 11% Health Professions and Related Programs; 6% Communications Technologies/Technicians and Support Services
Expenses: 2016-2017: $31,390; room/board: $11,330
Financial aid: (615) 460-6403; 51% of undergrads determined to have financial need; average aid package $16,243

Bethel University
McKenzie TN
(731) 352-4030
U.S. News ranking: Reg. U. (S), second tier
Website: www.bethelu.edu
Admissions email: admissions@bethel-college.edu
Private; founded 1842
Affiliation: Cumberland Presbyterian Church
Freshman admissions: selective; 2015-2016: 1,149 applied, 965 accepted. Neither SAT nor ACT required. ACT 25/75 percentile: 17-22. High school rank: N/A
Early decision deadline: N/A, notification date: N/A
Early action deadline: N/A, notification date: N/A
Application deadline (fall): rolling
Undergraduate student body: 3,630 full time, 1,117 part time; 44% male, 56% female; 1% American Indian, 0% Asian, 36% black, 2% Hispanic, 1% multiracial, 0% Pacific Islander, 53% white, 1% international
Most popular majors: 40% Business, Management, Marketing, and Related Support Services; 33% Homeland Security, Law Enforcement, Firefighting and Related Protective Services; 10% Education; 10% Health Professions and Related Programs; 7% Biological and Biomedical Sciences

Expenses: 2016-2017: $15,764; room/board: $9,198
Financial aid: (731) 352-4233; 56% of undergrads determined to have financial need; average aid package $7,007

Bryan College
Dayton TN
(800) 277-9522
U.S. News ranking: Reg. U. (S), No. 72
Website: www.bryan.edu
Admissions email: admissions@bryan.edu
Private; founded 1930
Affiliation: Christian nondenominational
Freshman admissions: selective; 2015-2016: 716 applied, 326 accepted. Either SAT or ACT required. ACT 25/75 percentile: 19-25. High school rank: 18% in top tenth, 51% in top quarter, 75% in top half
Early decision deadline: N/A, notification date: N/A
Early action deadline: N/A, notification date: N/A
Application deadline (fall): rolling
Undergraduate student body: 838 full time, 582 part time; 46% male, 54% female; 0% American Indian, 0% Asian, 5% black, 4% Hispanic, 4% multiracial, 0% Pacific Islander, 81% white, 5% international; 36% from in state; 74% live on campus; 0% of students in fraternities, 0% in sororities
Most popular majors: 56% Business, Management, Marketing, and Related Support Services; 9% Psychology; 8% Education; 5% Parks, Recreation, Leisure, and Fitness Studies; 3% Theology and Religious Vocations
Expenses: 2016-2017: $24,450; room/board: $6,990
Financial aid: (423) 775-7339; 74% of undergrads determined to have financial need; average aid package $25,450

Carson-Newman University
Jefferson City TN
(800) 678-9061
U.S. News ranking: Reg. U. (S), No. 59
Website: www.cn.edu
Admissions email: admitme@cn.edu
Private; founded 1851
Affiliation: Baptist
Freshman admissions: selective; 2015-2016: 5,871 applied, 3,454 accepted. Either SAT or ACT required. ACT 25/75 percentile: 19-26. High school rank: N/A
Early decision deadline: N/A, notification date: N/A
Early action deadline: N/A, notification date: N/A
Application deadline (fall): rolling
Undergraduate student body: 1,691 full time, 61 part time; 42% male, 58% female; 0% American Indian, 1% Asian, 8% black, 2% Hispanic, 3% multiracial, 0% Pacific Islander, 83% white, 3% international; 77% from in state; 56% live on campus; N/A of students in fraternities, N/A in sororities

Most popular majors: 24% Education; 21% Health Professions and Related Programs; 20% Business, Management, Marketing, and Related Support Services; 5% Visual and Performing Arts; 4% Psychology
Expenses: 2016-2017: $26,360; room/board: $8,430
Financial aid: (865) 471-3247; 82% of undergrads determined to have financial need; average aid package $23,341

Christian Brothers University
Memphis TN
(901) 321-3205
U.S. News ranking: Reg. U. (S), No. 28
Website: www.cbu.edu
Admissions email: admissions@cbu.edu
Private; founded 1871
Affiliation: Roman Catholic
Freshman admissions: more selective; 2015-2016: 2,321 applied, 1,063 accepted. Either SAT or ACT required. ACT 25/75 percentile: 21-27. High school rank: 27% in top tenth, 60% in top quarter, 83% in top half
Early decision deadline: N/A, notification date: N/A
Early action deadline: N/A, notification date: N/A
Application deadline (fall): rolling
Undergraduate student body: 1,300 full time, 110 part time; 47% male, 53% female; 0% American Indian, 5% Asian, 29% black, 7% Hispanic, 3% multiracial, 0% Pacific Islander, 43% white, 6% international; 20% from in state; 40% live on campus; N/A of students in fraternities, N/A in sororities
Most popular majors: 11% Nursing Practice; 8% Natural Sciences; 8% Psychology, General; 7% Mechanical Engineering; 6% Biology/Biological Sciences, General
Expenses: 2016-2017: $30,780; room/board: $7,000
Financial aid: (901) 321-3305; 72% of undergrads determined to have financial need; average aid package $23,869

Cumberland University
Lebanon TN
(615) 444-2562
U.S. News ranking: Reg. U. (S), second tier
Website: www.cumberland.edu
Admissions email: admissions@cumberland.edu
Private; founded 1842
Freshman admissions: selective; 2015-2016: 695 applied, 341 accepted. ACT required. ACT 25/75 percentile: 19-23. High school rank: 13% in top tenth, 32% in top quarter, 70% in top half
Early decision deadline: N/A, notification date: N/A
Early action deadline: N/A, notification date: N/A
Application deadline (fall): rolling
Undergraduate student body: 987 full time, 319 part time; 39% male, 61% female; 1% American Indian, 1% Asian, 12% black,

3% Hispanic, 0% multiracial, 0% Pacific Islander, 63% white, 4% international
Most popular majors: 43% Registered Nursing/Registered Nurse; 7% Physical Education Teaching and Coaching; 6% Education, General; 4% Business Administration and Management, General; 4% Criminal Justice/Law Enforcement Administration
Expenses: 2016-2017: $21,210; room/board: $8,400
Financial aid: (615) 444-2562; 83% of undergrads determined to have financial need; average aid package $20,942

East Tennessee State University
Johnson City TN
(423) 439-4213
U.S. News ranking: Nat. U., second tier
Website: www.etsu.edu
Admissions email: go2etsu@etsu.edu
Public; founded 1911
Freshman admissions: selective; 2015-2016: 8,253 applied, 6,538 accepted. Either SAT or ACT required. ACT 25/75 percentile: 20-26. High school rank: 20% in top tenth, 47% in top quarter, 75% in top half
Early decision deadline: N/A, notification date: N/A
Early action deadline: N/A, notification date: N/A
Application deadline (fall): 8/15
Undergraduate student body: 9,455 full time, 1,937 part time; 44% male, 56% female; 0% American Indian, 1% Asian, 7% black, 2% Hispanic, 3% multiracial, 0% Pacific Islander, 82% white, 3% international; 86% from in state; 20% live on campus; 5% of students in fraternities, 5% in sororities
Most popular majors: 25% Health Professions and Related Programs; 12% Business, Management, Marketing, and Related Support Services; 7% Parks, Recreation, Leisure, and Fitness Studies; 6% Liberal Arts and Sciences, General Studies and Humanities; 5% Public Administration and Social Service Professions
Expenses: 2016-2017: $8,818 in state, $27,018 out of state; room/board: $7,952
Financial aid: (423) 439-4300; 80% of undergrads determined to have financial need; average aid package $10,220

Fisk University
Nashville TN
(888) 702-0022
U.S. News ranking: Nat. Lib. Arts, No. 171
Website: www.fisk.edu
Admissions email: admissions@fisk.edu
Private; founded 1866
Freshman admissions: selective; 2015-2016: 3,004 applied, 2,431 accepted. Either SAT or ACT required. ACT 25/75 percentile: 17-23. High school rank: 15% in top tenth, 46% in top quarter, 74% in top half
Early decision deadline: N/A, notification date: N/A

Early action deadline: N/A, notification date: N/A
Application deadline (fall): rolling
Undergraduate student body: 738 full time, 67 part time; 35% male, 65% female; 0% American Indian, 1% Asian, 87% black, 3% Hispanic, 1% multiracial, 0% Pacific Islander, 1% white, 0% international; 26% from in state; 74% live on campus; N/A of students in fraternities, N/A in sororities
Most popular majors: 22% Psychology; 10% Physical Sciences; 8% Social Sciences; 8% Visual and Performing Arts; 6% Foreign Languages, Literatures, and Linguistics
Expenses: 2016-2017: $21,480; room/board: $10,790
Financial aid: (615) 329-8585; 79% of undergrads determined to have financial need; average aid package $36,525

Freed-Hardeman University
Henderson TN
(800) 630-3480
U.S. News ranking: Reg. U. (S), No. 43
Website: www.fhu.edu
Admissions email: admissions@fhu.edu
Private; founded 1869
Affiliation: Church of Christ
Freshman admissions: selective; 2015-2016: 981 applied, 901 accepted. Either SAT or ACT required. ACT 25/75 percentile: 21-27. High school rank: 21% in top tenth, 52% in top quarter, 77% in top half
Early decision deadline: N/A, notification date: N/A
Early action deadline: N/A, notification date: N/A
Application deadline (fall): rolling
Undergraduate student body: 1,217 full time, 145 part time; 43% male, 57% female; 0% American Indian, 1% Asian, 5% black, 2% Hispanic, 2% multiracial, 0% Pacific Islander, 85% white, 2% international; 56% from in state; 85% live on campus; 0% of students in fraternities, 0% in sororities
Most popular majors: 12% Education; 11% Business, Management, Marketing, and Related Support Services; 11% Theology and Religious Vocations; 8% Multi/ Interdisciplinary Studies; 8% Public Administration and Social Service Professions
Expenses: 2016-2017: $21,500; room/board: $7,950
Financial aid: (731) 989-6662; 78% of undergrads determined to have financial need; average aid package $18,395

King University
Bristol TN
(423) 652-4861
U.S. News ranking: Reg. U. (S), No. 91
Website: www.king.edu
Admissions email: admissions@king.edu
Private; founded 1867
Affiliation: Presbyterian

Freshman admissions: selective; 2015-2016: 843 applied, 371 accepted. Either SAT or ACT required. ACT 25/75 percentile: 19-25. High school rank: 15% in top tenth, 43% in top quarter, 83% in top half
Early decision deadline: N/A, notification date: N/A
Early action deadline: N/A, notification date: N/A
Application deadline (fall): rolling
Undergraduate student body: 2,244 full time, 223 part time; 35% male, 65% female; 0% American Indian, 0% Asian, 6% black, 3% Hispanic, 2% multiracial, 0% Pacific Islander, 81% white, 3% international; 66% from in state; 13% live on campus; N/A of students in fraternities, N/A in sororities
Most popular majors: 40% Business Administration and Management, General; 36% Adult Health Nurse/Nursing; 5% Information Technology; 4% Psychology, General; 2% Biology/ Biological Sciences, General
Expenses: 2016-2017: $27,276; room/board: $8,180
Financial aid: (423) 652-4725; 88% of undergrads determined to have financial need; average aid package $13,766

Lane College
Jackson TN
(731) 426-7533
U.S. News ranking: Reg. Coll. (S), No. 56
Website: www.lanecollege.edu
Admissions email: admissions@lanecollege.edu
Private; founded 1882
Affiliation: Christian Methodist Episcopal
Freshman admissions: least selective; 2015-2016: 4,729 applied, 2,579 accepted. Either SAT or ACT required. ACT 25/75 percentile: 14-17. High school rank: 9% in top tenth, 30% in top quarter, 66% in top half
Early decision deadline: N/A, notification date: N/A
Early action deadline: N/A, notification date: N/A
Application deadline (fall): 7/1
Undergraduate student body: 1,351 full time, 25 part time; 54% male, 46% female; 0% American Indian, 0% Asian, 97% black, 0% Hispanic, 2% multiracial, N/A Pacific Islander, 0% white, 0% international; 58% from in state; 63% live on campus; 1% of students in fraternities, 1% in sororities
Most popular majors: 19% Business, Management, Marketing, and Related Support Services; 19% Homeland Security, Law Enforcement, Firefighting and Related Protective Services; 16% Biological and Biomedical Sciences; 13% Social Sciences
Expenses: 2015-2016: $9,930; room/board: $6,620
Financial aid: (731) 426-7535; 100% of undergrads determined to have financial need; average aid package $11,462

Lee University
Cleveland TN
(423) 614-8500
U.S. News ranking: Reg. U. (S), No. 56
Website: www.leeuniversity.edu
Admissions email: admissions@leeuniversity.edu
Private; founded 1918
Affiliation: Pentecostal
Freshman admissions: selective; 2015-2016: 2,141 applied, 1,830 accepted. Either SAT or ACT required. ACT 25/75 percentile: 21-27. High school rank: 19% in top tenth, 47% in top quarter, 76% in top half
Early decision deadline: N/A, notification date: N/A
Early action deadline: N/A, notification date: N/A
Application deadline (fall): rolling
Undergraduate student body: 3,785 full time, 775 part time; 41% male, 59% female; 1% American Indian, 1% Asian, 6% black, 4% Hispanic, 0% multiracial, 0% Pacific Islander, 79% white, 4% international; 43% from in state; 46% live on campus; 9% of students in fraternities, 8% in sororities
Most popular majors: 19% Theology and Religious Vocations; 16% Education; 11% Business, Management, Marketing, and Related Support Services; 10% Psychology
Expenses: 2016-2017: $15,770; room/board: $7,000
Financial aid: (423) 614-8300; 71% of undergrads determined to have financial need; average aid package $11,702

LeMoyne-Owen College
Memphis TN
(901) 435-1500
U.S. News ranking: Reg. Coll. (S), second tier
Website: www.loc.edu/
Admissions email: admission@loc.edu
Private; founded 1862
Affiliation: United Church of Christ
Freshman admissions: least selective; 2015-2016: 527 applied, 527 accepted. Either SAT or ACT required. ACT 25/75 percentile: 13-17. High school rank: N/A
Early decision deadline: N/A, notification date: N/A
Early action deadline: N/A, notification date: N/A
Application deadline (fall): 7/1
Undergraduate student body: 836 full time, 109 part time; 36% male, 64% female; N/A American Indian, N/A Asian, 98% black, 0% Hispanic, N/A multiracial, N/A Pacific Islander, 0% white, 1% international
Most popular majors: 47% Business Administration and Management, General; 7% Criminal Justice/Safety Studies; 5% Education, General; 5% Social Work; 4% Biology/ Biological Sciences, General
Expenses: 2016-2017: $10,900; room/board: N/A
Financial aid: (901) 942-7313

Lincoln Memorial University
Harrogate TN
(423) 869-6280
U.S. News ranking: Reg. U. (S), No. 59
Website: www.lmunet.edu
Admissions email: admissions@lmunet.edu
Private; founded 1897
Freshman admissions: selective; 2015-2016: 2,306 applied, 1,715 accepted. Either SAT or ACT required. ACT 25/75 percentile: 20-28. High school rank: N/A
Early decision deadline: N/A, notification date: N/A
Early action deadline: N/A, notification date: N/A
Application deadline (fall): rolling
Undergraduate student body: 1,220 full time, 455 part time; 28% male, 72% female; 0% American Indian, 1% Asian, 5% black, 0% Hispanic, 2% multiracial, 0% Pacific Islander, 83% white, 3% international
Most popular majors: 36% Health Professions and Related Programs; 17% Business, Management, Marketing, and Related Support Services; 9% Education; 7% Biological and Biomedical Sciences; 5% History
Expenses: 2016-2017: $21,050; room/board: $7,550
Financial aid: (423) 869-6336

Lipscomb University
Nashville TN
(615) 966-1776
U.S. News ranking: Nat. U., No. 176
Website: www.lipscomb.edu
Admissions email: admissions@lipscomb.edu
Private; founded 1891
Affiliation: Church of Christ
Freshman admissions: more selective; 2015-2016: 3,311 applied, 2,012 accepted. Either SAT or ACT required. ACT 25/75 percentile: 23-29. High school rank: 29% in top tenth, 57% in top quarter, 84% in top half
Early decision deadline: N/A, notification date: N/A
Early action deadline: N/A, notification date: N/A
Application deadline (fall): rolling
Undergraduate student body: 2,726 full time, 304 part time; 39% male, 61% female; 0% American Indian, 3% Asian, 7% black, 7% Hispanic, 2% multiracial, 0% Pacific Islander, 77% white, 2% international; 65% from in state; 51% live on campus; 23% of students in fraternities, 24% in sororities
Most popular majors: 19% Business, Management, Marketing, and Related Support Services; 14% Health Professions and Related Programs; 9% Education; 8% Psychology; 7% Biological and Biomedical Sciences
Expenses: 2016-2017: $29,756; room/board: $11,540
Financial aid: (615) 269-1791; 63% of undergrads determined to have financial need; average aid package $22,967

Martin Methodist College[1]
Pulaski TN
(931) 363-9804
U.S. News ranking: Reg. Coll. (S), unranked
Website: www.martinmethodist.edu
Admissions email: admit@martinmethodist.edu
Private
Application deadline (fall): N/A
Undergraduate student body: N/A full time, N/A part time
Expenses: 2015-2016: $23,100; room/board: $8,400
Financial aid: (931) 363-9821

Maryville College
Maryville TN
(865) 981-8092
U.S. News ranking: Nat. Lib. Arts, second tier
Website: www.maryvillecollege.edu
Admissions email: admissions@maryvillecollege.edu
Private; founded 1819
Affiliation: Presbyterian
Freshman admissions: selective; 2015-2016: 1,701 applied, 1,136 accepted. Either SAT or ACT required. ACT 25/75 percentile: 20-26. High school rank: 20% in top tenth, 42% in top quarter, 71% in top half
Early decision deadline: N/A, notification date: N/A
Early action deadline: N/A, notification date: N/A
Application deadline (fall): 5/1
Undergraduate student body: 1,178 full time, 35 part time; 46% male, 54% female; 0% American Indian, 1% Asian, 11% black, 3% Hispanic, 4% multiracial, 0% Pacific Islander, 78% white, 2% international; 71% from in state; 73% live on campus; 0% of students in fraternities, 0% in sororities
Most popular majors: 8% Psychology, General; 5% Accounting and Finance; 5% Business Administration and Management, General; 5% Professional, Technical, Business, and Scientific Writing
Expenses: 2016-2017: $33,524; room/board: $10,868
Financial aid: (865) 981-8100; 85% of undergrads determined to have financial need; average aid package $32,288

Memphis College of Art
Memphis TN
(800) 727-1088
U.S. News ranking: Arts, unranked
Website: www.mca.edu
Admissions email: info@mca.edu
Private; founded 1936
Freshman admissions: N/A; 2015-2016: 959 applied, 305 accepted. Either SAT or ACT required. SAT 25/75 percentile: N/A. High school rank: N/A
Early decision deadline: N/A, notification date: N/A
Early action deadline: N/A, notification date: N/A
Application deadline (fall): rolling
Undergraduate student body: 305 full time, 53 part time; 35% male, 65% female; 0% American Indian, 1% Asian, 29% black,

6% Hispanic, 3% multiracial, 0% Pacific Islander, 57% white, 0% international; 55% from in state; 47% live on campus; 0% of students in fraternities, 0% in sororities
Most popular majors: 63% Design and Visual Communications, General; 35% Fine/Studio Arts, General
Expenses: 2016-2017: $30,980; room/board: $8,600
Financial aid: (901) 272-5136; 86% of undergrads determined to have financial need; average aid package $22,996

Middle Tennessee State University
Murfreesboro TN
(615) 898-2111
U.S. News ranking: Nat. U., second tier
Website: www.mtsu.edu
Admissions email: admissions@mtsu.edu
Public; founded 1911
Freshman admissions: selective; 2015-2016: 8,164 applied, 5,927 accepted. Either SAT or ACT required. ACT 25/75 percentile: 19-25. High school rank: N/A
Early decision deadline: N/A, notification date: N/A
Early action deadline: N/A, notification date: N/A
Application deadline (fall): rolling
Undergraduate student body: 16,167 full time, 3,973 part time; 46% male, 54% female; 0% American Indian, 3% Asian, 22% black, 4% Hispanic, 3% multiracial, 0% Pacific Islander, 64% white, 3% international; 94% from in state; 15% live on campus; 6% of students in fraternities, 8% in sororities
Most popular majors: 15% Business, Management, Marketing, and Related Support Services; 10% Liberal Arts and Sciences, General Studies and Humanities; 9% Visual and Performing Arts; 7% Multi/Interdisciplinary Studies
Expenses: 2015-2016: $8,080 in state, $24,808 out of state; room/board: $8,106
Financial aid: (615) 898-2830; 75% of undergrads determined to have financial need; average aid package $9,714

Milligan College
Milligan College TN
(423) 461-8730
U.S. News ranking: Reg. U. (S), No. 22
Website: www.milligan.edu
Admissions email: admissions@milligan.edu
Private; founded 1866
Affiliation: Christian Churches/Churches of Christ
Freshman admissions: more selective; 2015-2016: 603 applied, 393 accepted. Either SAT or ACT required. ACT 25/75 percentile: 22-28. High school rank: 37% in top tenth, 65% in top quarter, 89% in top half
Early decision deadline: N/A, notification date: N/A
Early action deadline: N/A, notification date: N/A

Application deadline (fall): 8/1
Undergraduate student body: 785 full time, 107 part time; 37% male, 63% female; 0% American Indian, 2% Asian, 4% black, 6% Hispanic, 2% multiracial, 0% Pacific Islander, 82% white, 3% international; 60% from in state; 79% live on campus; N/A of students in fraternities, N/A in sororities
Most popular majors: 22% Business Administration and Management, General; 20% Registered Nursing/Registered Nurse; 10% Family and Consumer Sciences/Human Sciences; 10% Health and Physical Education/Fitness, General; 7% Psychology, General
Expenses: 2016-2017: $31,450; room/board: $6,700
Financial aid: (423) 461-8949; 80% of undergrads determined to have financial need; average aid package $22,434

Rhodes College
Memphis TN
(800) 844-5969
U.S. News ranking: Nat. Lib. Arts, No. 44
Website: www.rhodes.edu
Admissions email: adminfo@rhodes.edu
Private; founded 1848
Affiliation: Presbyterian (USA)
Freshman admissions: more selective; 2015-2016: 4,666 applied, 2,187 accepted. Either SAT or ACT required. ACT 25/75 percentile: 27-32. High school rank: 54% in top tenth, 83% in top quarter, 98% in top half
Early decision deadline: 11/1, notification date: 12/1
Early action deadline: 11/15, notification date: 1/15
Application deadline (fall): 1/15
Undergraduate student body: 2,032 full time, 14 part time; 43% male, 57% female; 0% American Indian, 6% Asian, 6% black, 5% Hispanic, 4% multiracial, 0% Pacific Islander, 74% white, 3% international; 26% from in state; 71% live on campus; 40% of students in fraternities, 62% in sororities
Most popular majors: 23% Social Sciences; 19% Biological and Biomedical Sciences; 13% Business, Management, Marketing, and Related Support Services; 10% Psychology; 6% English Language and Literature/Letters
Expenses: 2016-2017: $44,942; room/board: $11,068
Financial aid: (901) 843-3810; 39% of undergrads determined to have financial need; average aid package $34,932

Sewanee–University of the South
Sewanee TN
(800) 522-2234
U.S. News ranking: Nat. Lib. Arts, No. 47
Website: www.sewanee.edu
Admissions email: admiss@sewanee.edu
Private; founded 1857
Affiliation: Episcopal

Freshman admissions: more selective; 2015-2016: 4,509 applied, 1,830 accepted. Neither SAT nor ACT required. ACT 25/75 percentile: 26-30. High school rank: 29% in top tenth, 64% in top quarter, 91% in top half
Early decision deadline: 11/15, notification date: 12/15
Early action deadline: 12/1, notification date: 2/15
Application deadline (fall): 2/1
Undergraduate student body: 1,685 full time, 25 part time; 48% male, 52% female; 0% American Indian, 2% Asian, 4% black, 5% Hispanic, 3% multiracial, 0% Pacific Islander, 82% white, 3% international; 24% from in state; 99% live on campus; 60% of students in fraternities, 60% in sororities
Most popular majors: 22% Social Sciences; 13% English Language and Literature, General; 10% Biological and Biomedical Sciences; 9% History; 9% Psychology
Expenses: 2016-2017: $42,400; room/board: $12,100
Financial aid: (931) 598-1312; 48% of undergrads determined to have financial need; average aid package $31,512

South College[1]
Knoxville TN
(865) 251-1800
U.S. News ranking: Reg. U. (S), unranked
Website: www.southcollegetn.edu/
Admissions email: N/A
For-profit
Application deadline (fall): N/A
Undergraduate student body: N/A full time, N/A part time
Expenses: 2015-2016: $19,425; room/board: N/A
Financial aid: (865) 251-1800

Southern Adventist University
Collegedale TN
(423) 236-2844
U.S. News ranking: Reg. U. (S), No. 69
Website: www.southern.edu
Admissions email: admissions@southern.edu
Private; founded 1892
Affiliation: Seventh-day Adventist
Freshman admissions: selective; 2015-2016: 1,464 applied, 1,211 accepted. Either SAT or ACT required. ACT 25/75 percentile: 20-26. High school rank: N/A
Early decision deadline: N/A, notification date: N/A
Early action deadline: N/A, notification date: N/A
Application deadline (fall): rolling
Undergraduate student body: 2,226 full time, 447 part time; 43% male, 57% female; N/A American Indian, N/A Asian, N/A black, N/A Hispanic, N/A multiracial, N/A Pacific Islander, N/A white, N/A international; 35% from in state; N/A live on campus; N/A of students in fraternities, N/A in sororities
Most popular majors: Information not available

Expenses: 2016-2017: $21,150; room/board: $6,450
Financial aid: (423) 236-2835; 71% of undergrads determined to have financial need; average aid package $15,747

Tennessee State University
Nashville TN
(615) 963-5101
U.S. News ranking: Nat. U., second tier
Website: www.tnstate.edu
Admissions email: jcade@tnstate.edu
Public; founded 1912
Freshman admissions: less selective; 2015-2016: N/A applied, N/A accepted. Either SAT or ACT required. ACT 25/75 percentile: 16-20. High school rank: N/A
Early decision deadline: N/A, notification date: N/A
Early action deadline: N/A, notification date: N/A
Application deadline (fall): 7/1
Undergraduate student body: 5,975 full time, 1,289 part time; 40% male, 60% female; 0% American Indian, 1% Asian, 71% black, 1% Hispanic, 3% multiracial, N/A Pacific Islander, 13% white, 11% international
Most popular majors: Information not available
Expenses: 2016-2017: $7,234 in state, $20,208 out of state; room/board: $7,118
Financial aid: (615) 963-5701; 83% of undergrads determined to have financial need; average aid package $10,889

Tennessee Technological University
Cookeville TN
(800) 255-8881
U.S. News ranking: Nat. U., No. 220
Website: www.tntech.edu
Admissions email: admissions@tntech.edu
Public; founded 1915
Freshman admissions: more selective; 2015-2016: 5,786 applied, 3,953 accepted. Either SAT or ACT required. ACT 25/75 percentile: 21-27. High school rank: 33% in top tenth, 60% in top quarter, 84% in top half
Early decision deadline: N/A, notification date: N/A
Early action deadline: N/A, notification date: N/A
Application deadline (fall): rolling
Undergraduate student body: 8,709 full time, 1,092 part time; 56% male, 44% female; 0% American Indian, 2% Asian, 4% black, 3% Hispanic, 3% multiracial, 0% Pacific Islander, 81% white, 7% international; 97% from in state; 24% live on campus; N/A of students in fraternities, N/A in sororities
Most popular majors: 13% Teacher Education, Multiple Levels; 7% Mechanical Engineering; 6% Business Administration and Management, General; 6% Liberal Arts and Sciences/Liberal Studies; 5% Sport and Fitness Administration/Management

Expenses: 2016-2017: $8,300 in state, $24,800 out of state; room/board: $8,750
Financial aid: (931) 372-3073; 71% of undergrads determined to have financial need; average aid package $9,866

Tennessee Wesleyan College
Athens TN
(423) 746-5286
U.S. News ranking: Reg. Coll. (S), No. 16
Website: www.twcnet.edu
Admissions email: admissions@twcnet.edu
Private; founded 1857
Affiliation: United Methodist
Freshman admissions: selective; 2015-2016: 1,085 applied, 703 accepted. Either SAT or ACT required. ACT 25/75 percentile: 19-25. High school rank: 64% in top tenth, 64% in top quarter, 100% in top half
Early decision deadline: N/A, notification date: N/A
Early action deadline: N/A, notification date: N/A
Application deadline (fall): rolling
Undergraduate student body: 955 full time, 71 part time; 36% male, 64% female; 0% American Indian, 1% Asian, 6% black, 2% Hispanic, 3% multiracial, 0% Pacific Islander, 70% white, 0% international; 90% from in state; 35% live on campus; 2% of students in fraternities, 7% in sororities
Most popular majors: 36% Business, Management, Marketing, and Related Support Services; 27% Health Professions and Related Programs; 7% Multi/Interdisciplinary Studies; 7% Parks, Recreation, Leisure, and Fitness Studies; 5% Education
Expenses: 2016-2017: $23,000; room/board: $7,540
Financial aid: (423) 746-5209; 69% of undergrads determined to have financial need; average aid package $17,663

Trevecca Nazarene University
Nashville TN
(615) 248-1320
U.S. News ranking: Nat. U., second tier
Website: www.trevecca.edu
Admissions email: admissions_und@trevecca.edu
Private; founded 1901
Affiliation: Nazarene
Freshman admissions: selective; 2015-2016: 1,212 applied, 879 accepted. Either SAT or ACT required. ACT 25/75 percentile: 19-25. High school rank: N/A
Early decision deadline: N/A, notification date: N/A
Early action deadline: N/A, notification date: N/A
Application deadline (fall): 8/1
Undergraduate student body: 1,244 full time, 587 part time; 43% male, 57% female; 0% American Indian, 1% Asian, 11% black, 9% Hispanic, 3% multiracial, 0% Pacific Islander, 69% white, 1% international; 64% from in state; 45% live on campus; N/A of students in fraternities, N/A in sororities

Most popular majors: 42% Business, Management, Marketing, and Related Support Services; 8% Theology and Religious Vocations; 7% Health Professions and Related Programs; 6% Visual and Performing Arts; 5% Education
Expenses: 2016-2017: $24,624; room/board: $8,592
Financial aid: (615) 248-1242

Tusculum College
Greeneville TN
(800) 729-0256
U.S. News ranking: Reg. U. (S), No. 105
Website: www.tusculum.edu
Admissions email: admissions@tusculum.edu
Private; founded 1794
Affiliation: Presbyterian
Freshman admissions: selective; 2015-2016: 2,092 applied, 1,442 accepted. Either SAT or ACT required. ACT 25/75 percentile: 18-23. High school rank: N/A
Early decision deadline: N/A, notification date: N/A
Early action deadline: N/A, notification date: N/A
Application deadline (fall): rolling
Undergraduate student body: 1,505 full time, 114 part time; 44% male, 56% female; 1% American Indian, 0% Asian, 14% black, 3% Hispanic, 1% multiracial, 0% Pacific Islander, 74% white, 3% international; 77% from in state; 46% live on campus; N/A of students in fraternities, N/A in sororities
Most popular majors: 42% Business Administration and Management, General; 14% Education, General; 13% Psychology, General; 4% Biology/Biological Sciences, General; 4% Registered Nursing/Registered Nurse
Expenses: 2016-2017: $23,125; room/board: $8,500
Financial aid: (423) 636-7377; 85% of undergrads determined to have financial need; average aid package $16,087

Union University
Jackson TN
(800) 338-6466
U.S. News ranking: Nat. U., No. 169
Website: www.uu.edu
Admissions email: admissions@uu.edu
Private; founded 1823
Affiliation: Southern Baptist
Freshman admissions: more selective; 2015-2016: 1,830 applied, 1,265 accepted. Either SAT or ACT required. ACT 25/75 percentile: 22-29. High school rank: 34% in top tenth, 59% in top quarter, 88% in top half
Early decision deadline: N/A, notification date: N/A
Early action deadline: N/A, notification date: N/A
Application deadline (fall): rolling
Undergraduate student body: 2,172 full time, 657 part time; 39% male, 61% female; 0% American Indian, 1% Asian, 15% black, 2% Hispanic, 2% multiracial, 0% Pacific Islander, 75% white,

2% international; 58% from in state; 57% live on campus; 29% of students in fraternities, 20% in sororities
Most popular majors: 26% Health Professions and Related Programs; 19% Business, Management, Marketing, and Related Support Services; 7% Public Administration and Social Service Professions; 6% Education; 4% Psychology
Expenses: 2016-2017: $30,420; room/board: $9,400
Financial aid: (731) 661-5015; 66% of undergrads determined to have financial need; average aid package $20,643

University of Memphis
Memphis TN
(901) 678-2111
U.S. News ranking: Nat. U., second tier
Website: www.memphis.edu
Admissions email: recruitment@memphis.edu
Public; founded 1912
Freshman admissions: selective; 2015-2016: 7,556 applied, 6,955 accepted. Either SAT or ACT required. ACT 25/75 percentile: 20-26. High school rank: 15% in top tenth, 41% in top quarter, 75% in top half
Early decision deadline: N/A, notification date: N/A
Early action deadline: N/A, notification date: N/A
Application deadline (fall): 7/1
Undergraduate student body: 12,053 full time, 4,586 part time; 41% male, 59% female; 0% American Indian, 3% Asian, 37% black, 4% Hispanic, 4% multiracial, 0% Pacific Islander, 50% white, 1% international; 81% from in state; 14% live on campus; 3% of students in fraternities, 5% in sororities
Most popular majors: 18% Business, Management, Marketing, and Related Support Services; 12% Multi/Interdisciplinary Studies; 8% Education; 8% Health Professions and Related Programs; 6% Liberal Arts and Sciences, General Studies and Humanities
Expenses: 2015-2016: $8,903 in state, $20,615 out of state; room/board: $9,061
Financial aid: (901) 678-4825; 75% of undergrads determined to have financial need; average aid package $9,026

University of Tennessee
Knoxville TN
(865) 974-2184
U.S. News ranking: Nat. U., No. 103
Website: admissions.utk.edu/undergraduate
Admissions email: admissions@utk.edu
Public; founded 1794
Freshman admissions: more selective; 2015-2016: 17,081 applied, 13,032 accepted. Either SAT or ACT required. ACT 25/75 percentile: 24-30. High school rank: 54% in top tenth, 90% in top quarter, 100% in top half

Early decision deadline: N/A, notification date: N/A
Early action deadline: N/A, notification date: N/A
Application deadline (fall): 12/1
Undergraduate student body: 20,569 full time, 1,294 part time; 51% male, 49% female; 0% American Indian, 3% Asian, 7% black, 3% Hispanic, 3% multiracial, N/A Pacific Islander, 79% white, 1% international; 89% from in state; 33% live on campus; 16% of students in fraternities, 24% in sororities
Most popular majors: 21% Business, Management, Marketing, and Related Support Services; 10% Engineering; 8% Psychology; 8% Social Sciences
Expenses: 2016-2017: $12,668 in state, $30,858 out of state; room/board: $10,238
Financial aid: (865) 974-3131; 59% of undergrads determined to have financial need; average aid package $12,646

University of Tennessee–Chattanooga
Chattanooga TN
(423) 425-4662
U.S. News ranking: Reg. U. (S), No. 62
Website: www.utc.edu
Admissions email: utcmocs@utc.edu
Public; founded 1886
Freshman admissions: selective; 2015-2016: 6,752 applied, 5,349 accepted. Either SAT or ACT required. ACT 25/75 percentile: 21-26. High school rank: N/A
Early decision deadline: N/A, notification date: N/A
Early action deadline: N/A, notification date: N/A
Application deadline (fall): 5/1
Undergraduate student body: 8,763 full time, 1,321 part time; 44% male, 56% female; 0% American Indian, 2% Asian, 11% black, 3% Hispanic, 7% multiracial, 0% Pacific Islander, 75% white, 1% international; 94% from in state; 30% live on campus; 11% of students in fraternities, 17% in sororities
Most popular majors: 18% Business Administration and Management, General; 10% Education, General; 9% Kinesiology and Exercise Science; 7% Biology/Biological Sciences, General; 7% Health and Wellness, General
Expenses: 2015-2016: $8,356 in state, $24,474 out of state; room/board: $9,100
Financial aid: (423) 425-4677; 63% of undergrads determined to have financial need; average aid package $9,125

University of Tennessee–Martin
Martin TN
(800) 829-8861
U.S. News ranking: Reg. U. (S), No. 47
Website: www.utm.edu
Admissions email: admitme@utm.edu
Public; founded 1900

reshman admissions: selective;
2015-2016: 3,400 applied,
,368 accepted. Either SAT
r ACT required. ACT 25/75
ercentile: 20-25. High school
ank: 17% in top tenth, 46% in
op quarter, 80% in top half
arly decision deadline: N/A,
otification date: N/A
arly action deadline: N/A,
otification date: N/A
pplication deadline (fall): rolling
ndergraduate student body: 5,401
ull time, 1,034 part time; 42%
ale, 58% female; 0% American
ndian, 1% Asian, 15% black,
% Hispanic, 2% multiracial,
/A Pacific Islander, 77% white,
% international; 95% from in
tate; 30% live on campus; 13%
f students in fraternities, 15%
sororities
Most popular majors: 16%
usiness, Management,
Marketing, and Related
Support Services; 13% Multi/
nterdisciplinary Studies; 11%
Parks, Recreation, Leisure, and
itness Studies; 10% Education
xpenses: 2016-2017: $9,074
state, $14,834 out of state;
om/board: $7,764
inancial aid: (731) 587-7040;
6% of undergrads determined
have financial need; average
id package $13,557

Vanderbilt University

Nashville TN
800) 288-0432
U.S. News ranking: Nat. U.,
No. 15
Website: www.vanderbilt.edu
dmissions email: admissions@
anderbilt.edu
rivate; founded 1873
reshman admissions: most
elective; 2015-2016: 31,464
pplied, 3,674 accepted. Either
AT or ACT required. ACT 25/75
ercentile: 32-35. High school
ank: 91% in top tenth, 97% in
op quarter, 99% in top half
arly decision deadline: 11/1,
otification date: 12/15
arly action deadline: N/A,
otification date: N/A
pplication deadline (fall): 1/1
ndergraduate student body: 6,822
ull time, 61 part time; 50%
ale, 50% female; 0% American
ndian, 12% Asian, 8% black,
% Hispanic, 5% multiracial,
0% Pacific Islander, 55% white,
% international; 10% from in
tate; 92% live on campus; 35%
f students in fraternities, 53%
sororities
Most popular majors: 12%
conomics, General; 9% Multi-/
nterdisciplinary Studies,
ther; 9% Social Sciences,
eneral; 5% Political Science
nd Government, General; 4%
Neuroscience
xpenses: 2016-2017: $45,610;
oom/board: $14,962
inancial aid: (615) 322-3591;
9% of undergrads determined
have financial need; average
id package $46,002

Watkins College of Art, Design & Film[1]

Nashville TN
(615) 383-4848
U.S. News ranking: Arts, unranked
Website: www.watkins.edu
Admissions email:
admission@watkins.edu
Private
Application deadline (fall): N/A
Undergraduate student body: N/A
full time, N/A part time
Expenses: 2015-2016: $20,790;
room/board: $9,380
Financial aid: (615) 383-4848

Welch College

Nashville TN
(888) 979-3524
U.S. News ranking: Reg. Coll. (S),
No. 31
Website: www.welch.edu
Admissions email:
Recruit@welch.edu
Private; founded 1942
Affiliation: Free Will Baptist
Freshman admissions: selective;
2015-2016: 115 applied, 79
accepted. Either SAT or ACT
required. ACT 25/75 percentile:
17-25. High school rank: 39%
in top tenth, 52% in top quarter,
70% in top half
Early decision deadline: N/A,
notification date: N/A
Early action deadline: N/A,
notification date: N/A
Application deadline (fall): rolling
Undergraduate student body: 220
full time, 107 part time; 53%
male, 47% female; 1% American
Indian, 1% Asian, 7% black, 3%
Hispanic, 1% multiracial, 0%
Pacific Islander, 88% white, 0%
international; 44% from in state;
68% live on campus; 65% of
students in fraternities, 66% in
sororities
Most popular majors: 44%
Theology and Religious
Vocations; 22% Education;
14% Business, Management,
Marketing, and Related Support
Services; 8% Parks, Recreation,
Leisure, and Fitness Studies; 4%
Psychology
Expenses: 2016-2017: $17,920;
room/board: $7,260
Financial aid: (615) 844-5250;
89% of undergrads determined
to have financial need; average
aid package $13,994

TEXAS

Abilene Christian University

Abilene TX
(800) 460-6228
U.S. News ranking: Reg. U. (W),
No. 18
Website: www.acu.edu
Admissions email: info@
admissions.acu.edu
Private; founded 1906
Affiliation: Church of Christ
Freshman admissions: selective;
2015-2016: 10,804 applied,
5,393 accepted. Either SAT
or ACT required. SAT 25/75
percentile: 950-1180. High
school rank: 22% in top tenth,
58% in top quarter, 87% in
top half

Amberton University[1]

Garland TX
(972) 279-6511
U.S. News ranking: Reg. U. (W),
unranked
Website: www.amberton.edu
Admissions email:
advisor@amberton.edu
Private; founded 1981
Affiliation: Nondenominational
Christian
Application deadline (fall): rolling
Undergraduate student body: N/A
full time, N/A part time
Expenses: 2015-2016: $7,500;
room/board: N/A
Financial aid: (972) 279-6511

Angelo State University

San Angelo TX
(325) 942-2041
U.S. News ranking: Reg. U. (W),
second tier
Website: www.angelo.edu
Admissions email:
admissions@angelo.edu
Public; founded 1928
Freshman admissions: selective;
2015-2016: 3,822 applied,
2,934 accepted. Either SAT
or ACT required. ACT 25/75
percentile: 18-23. High school
rank: 14% in top tenth, 31% in
top quarter, 73% in top half
Early decision deadline: N/A,
notification date: N/A
Early action deadline: N/A,
notification date: N/A
Application deadline (fall): 8/29
Undergraduate student body: 4,756
full time, 2,517 part time; 44%
male, 56% female; 0% American
Indian, 1% Asian, 8% black,
32% Hispanic, 3% multiracial,
0% Pacific Islander, 52% white,
4% international; 97% from in
state; 20% live on campus; 5%
of students in fraternities, 3% in
sororities
Most popular majors: 14%
Health Professions and Related
Programs; 12% Business,
Management, Marketing, and
Related Support Services; 10%
Multi/Interdisciplinary Studies;

Early decision deadline: N/A,

notification date: N/A
Early action deadline: 11/1,
notification date: 12/1
Application deadline (fall): 2/15
Undergraduate student body: 3,582
full time, 178 part time; 41%
male, 59% female; 0% American
Indian, 1% Asian, 9% black,
16% Hispanic, 5% multiracial,
0% Pacific Islander, 64% white,
4% international; 86% from in
state; 48% live on campus; 26%
of students in fraternities, 33%
in sororities
Most popular majors: 7%
Registered Nursing/Registered
Nurse; 6% Accounting; 6%
Business Administration and
Management, General; 6%
Elementary Education and
Teaching; 6% Psychology,
General
Expenses: 2016-2017: $32,070;
room/board: $9,730
Financial aid: (325) 674-2643;
66% of undergrads determined
to have financial need; average
aid package $21,813

Austin College

Sherman TX
(800) 442-5363
U.S. News ranking: Nat. Lib. Arts,
No. 105
Website: www.austincollege.edu
Admissions email: admission@
austincollege.edu
Private; founded 1849
Affiliation: Presbyterian
Freshman admissions: more
selective; 2015-2016: 3,357
applied, 1,816 accepted. Either
SAT or ACT required. ACT 25/75
percentile: 22-28. High school
rank: 36% in top tenth, 71% in
top quarter, 93% in top half
Early decision deadline: 11/1,
notification date: 12/4
Early action deadline: 12/1,
notification date: 1/15
Application deadline (fall): N/A
Undergraduate student body: 1,242
full time, 13 part time; 47%
male, 53% female; 1% American
Indian, 13% Asian, 7% black,
19% Hispanic, 1% multiracial,
0% Pacific Islander, 53% white,
3% international; 91% from in
state; 82% live on campus; 25%
of students in fraternities, 18%
in sororities
Most popular majors: 15% Social
Sciences; 14% Business,
Management, Marketing, and
Related Support Services; 12%
Biological and Biomedical
Sciences; 9% Psychology; 8%
Foreign Languages, Literatures,
and Linguistics
Expenses: 2016-2017: $37,315;
room/board: $12,082
Financial aid: (903) 813-2900;
65% of undergrads determined
to have financial need; average
aid package $34,188

Baylor University

Waco TX
(800) 229-5678
U.S. News ranking: Nat. U.,
No. 71
Website: www.baylor.edu
Admissions email:
Admissions@Baylor.edu
Private; founded 1845
Affiliation: Baptist

9% Parks, Recreation, Leisure,
and Fitness Studies; 8%
Psychology
Expenses: 2016-2017: $8,038
in state, $20,278 out of state;
room/board: $7,666
Financial aid: (325) 942-2246;
65% of undergrads determined
to have financial need; average
aid package $11,582

Art Institute of Houston[1]

Houston TX
(800) 275-4244
U.S. News ranking: Arts, unranked
Website:
www.artinstitute.edu/houston/
Admissions email: N/A
For-profit
Application deadline (fall): N/A
Undergraduate student body: N/A
full time, N/A part time
Expenses: 2015-2016: $17,664;
room/board: $11,367
Financial aid: (713) 353-4311

Brazosport College[1]

Lake Jackson TX
(979) 230-3020
U.S. News ranking: Reg. Coll. (W),
unranked
Website: www.brazosport.edu
Admissions email: N/A
Public
Application deadline (fall): N/A
Undergraduate student body: N/A
full time, N/A part time
Expenses: 2015-2016: $3,405 in
state, $5,025 out of state; room/
board: N/A
Financial aid: (979) 230-0337

Concordia University Texas[1]

Austin TX
(800) 865-4282
U.S. News ranking: Reg. U. (W),
second tier
Website: www.concordia.edu
Admissions email: admissions@
concordia.edu
Private; founded 1926
Affiliation: Lutheran Church-
Missouri Synod
Application deadline (fall): 8/1
Undergraduate student body: N/A
full time, N/A part time
Expenses: 2015-2016: $28,160;
room/board: $9,287
Financial aid: (512) 486-1283

Dallas Baptist University

Dallas TX
(214) 333-5360
U.S. News ranking: Nat. U.,
No. 214
Website: www.dbu.edu
Admissions email:
admiss@dbu.edu
Private; founded 1898
Affiliation: Baptist
Freshman admissions: selective;
2015-2016: 2,949 applied,
1,236 accepted. Either SAT or

Freshman admissions: more

selective; 2015-2016: 32,136
applied, 14,033 accepted. Either
SAT or ACT required. ACT 25/75
percentile: 25-30. High school
rank: 42% in top tenth, 75% in
top quarter, 97% in top half
Early decision deadline: N/A,
notification date: N/A
Early action deadline: 11/1,
notification date: 1/15
Application deadline (fall): 2/1
Undergraduate student body:
13,946 full time, 243 part time;
42% male, 58% female; 0%
American Indian, 6% Asian,
7% black, 14% Hispanic, 5%
multiracial, 0% Pacific Islander,
64% white, 3% international;
73% from in state; 36% live
on campus; 15% of students in
fraternities, 28% in sororities
Most popular majors: 8% Biology/
Biological Sciences, General; 7%
Registered Nursing/Registered
Nurse; 5% Psychology, General;
4% Accounting; 4% Marketing/
Marketing Management, General
Expenses: 2016-2017: $42,006;
room/board: $11,632
Financial aid: (254) 710-2611;
55% of undergrads determined
to have financial need; average
aid package $27,366

ACT required. ACT 25/75 percentile: 19-24. High school rank: 19% in top tenth, 46% in top quarter, 77% in top half **Early decision deadline:** N/A, notification date: N/A **Early action deadline:** N/A, notification date: N/A **Application deadline (fall):** rolling **Undergraduate student body:** 2,421 full time, 894 part time; 40% male, 60% female; 1% American Indian, 2% Asian, 15% black, 15% Hispanic, 0% multiracial, 0% Pacific Islander, 60% white, 7% international; 94% from in state; 59% live on campus; 18% of students in fraternities, 20% in sororities **Most popular majors:** 17% Business Administration and Management, General; 12% Multi-/Interdisciplinary Studies, Other; 12% Psychology, General; 7% Religious Education **Expenses:** 2016-2017: $26,180; room/board: $7,533 **Financial aid:** (214) 333-5460; 60% of undergrads determined to have financial need; average aid package $14,972

East Texas Baptist University
Marshall TX
(800) 804-3828
U.S. News ranking: Reg. Coll. (W), No. 10
Website: www.etbu.edu
Admissions email: admissions@etbu.edu
Private; founded 1912
Affiliation: Baptist
Freshman admissions: selective; 2015-2016: 1,456 applied, 805 accepted. Either SAT or ACT required. ACT 25/75 percentile: 18-23. High school rank: 14% in top tenth, 42% in top quarter, 75% in top half **Early decision deadline:** N/A, notification date: N/A **Early action deadline:** N/A, notification date: N/A **Application deadline (fall):** 9/1 **Undergraduate student body:** 1,096 full time, 137 part time; 46% male, 54% female; 1% American Indian, 0% Asian, 20% black, 10% Hispanic, 3% multiracial, 0% Pacific Islander, 65% white, 1% international; 91% from in state; 85% live on campus; 1% of students in fraternities, 1% in sororities **Most popular majors:** 19% Multi/ Interdisciplinary Studies; 18% Education; 15% Business, Management, Marketing, and Related Support Services; 11% Health Professions and Related Programs; 6% Biological and Biomedical Sciences **Expenses:** 2016-2017: $24,700; room/board: $8,709 **Financial aid:** (903) 923-2137; 86% of undergrads determined to have financial need; average aid package $18,129

Hardin-Simmons University
Abilene TX
(325) 670-1206
U.S. News ranking: Reg. U. (W), No. 33
Website: www.hsutx.edu/
Admissions email: enroll@hsutx.edu
Private; founded 1891
Affiliation: Baptist
Freshman admissions: selective; 2015-2016: 1,595 applied, 957 accepted. Either SAT or ACT required. ACT 25/75 percentile: 19-25. High school rank: 20% in top tenth, 49% in top quarter, 79% in top half **Early decision deadline:** N/A, notification date: N/A **Early action deadline:** N/A, notification date: N/A **Application deadline (fall):** rolling **Undergraduate student body:** 1,475 full time, 163 part time; 46% male, 54% female; 0% American Indian, 1% Asian, 7% black, 15% Hispanic, 4% multiracial, 0% Pacific Islander, 71% white, 1% international; 96% from in state; 45% live on campus; 4% of students in fraternities, 5% in sororities **Most popular majors:** 12% Parks, Recreation, Leisure, and Fitness Studies; 12% Business, Management, Marketing, and Related Support Services; 12% Health Professions and Related Programs; 9% Biological and Biomedical Sciences; 8% Psychology **Expenses:** 2016-2017: $25,830; room/board: $8,138 **Financial aid:** (325) 670-5891; 73% of undergrads determined to have financial need; average aid package $22,285

Houston Baptist University
Houston TX
(281) 649-3211
U.S. News ranking: Reg. U. (W), No. 76
Website: www.hbu.edu
Admissions email: admissions@hbu.edu
Private; founded 1960
Affiliation: Baptist
Freshman admissions: selective; 2015-2016: 14,519 applied, 4,825 accepted. Either SAT or ACT required. SAT 25/75 percentile: 960-1150. High school rank: 25% in top tenth, 56% in top quarter, 80% in top half **Early decision deadline:** N/A, notification date: N/A **Early action deadline:** N/A, notification date: N/A **Application deadline (fall):** rolling **Undergraduate student body:** 2,117 full time, 133 part time; 39% male, 61% female; 0% American Indian, 10% Asian, 19% black, 30% Hispanic, 5% multiracial, 0% Pacific Islander, 27% white, 4% international; 96% from in state; 42% live on campus; 10% of students in fraternities, 14% in sororities **Most popular majors:** 17% Registered Nursing/Registered Nurse; 11% Biology/Biological

Sciences, General; 8% Business Administration and Management, General; 8% Kinesiology and Exercise Science; 7% Psychology, General **Expenses:** 2016-2017: $30,800; room/board: $7,858 **Financial aid:** (281) 649-3389; 72% of undergrads determined to have financial need; average aid package $26,018

Howard Payne University
Brownwood TX
(325) 649-8020
U.S. News ranking: Reg. Coll. (W), No. 7
Website: www.hputx.edu
Admissions email: enroll@hputx.edu
Private; founded 1889
Affiliation: Baptist
Freshman admissions: less selective; 2015-2016: 935 applied, 802 accepted. Either SAT or ACT required. SAT 25/75 percentile: 850-1060. High school rank: 17% in top tenth, 33% in top quarter, 65% in top half **Early decision deadline:** N/A, notification date: N/A **Early action deadline:** N/A, notification date: N/A **Application deadline (fall):** rolling **Undergraduate student body:** 951 full time, 128 part time; 53% male, 47% female; 0% American Indian, 0% Asian, 9% black, 22% Hispanic, 3% multiracial, 0% Pacific Islander, 61% white, 0% international; 98% from in state; 57% live on campus; 14% of students in fraternities, 17% in sororities **Most popular majors:** 20% Business, Management, Marketing, and Related Support Services; 19% Education; 9% Theology and Religious Vocations; 8% Social Sciences; 7% Psychology **Expenses:** 2016-2017: $26,630; room/board: $7,800 **Financial aid:** (325) 649-8014; 83% of undergrads determined to have financial need; average aid package $19,322

Huston-Tillotson University
Austin TX
(512) 505-3029
U.S. News ranking: Reg. Coll. (W), No. 23
Website: htu.edu/
Admissions email: admission@htu.edu
Private
Freshman admissions: least selective; 2015-2016: 2,210 applied, 1,048 accepted. Either SAT or ACT required. SAT 25/75 percentile: 680-900. High school rank: N/A **Early decision deadline:** N/A, notification date: N/A **Early action deadline:** N/A, notification date: N/A **Application deadline (fall):** 5/1 **Undergraduate student body:** 923 full time, 45 part time; 44% male, 56% female; 0% American Indian, 0% Asian, 67% black,

23% Hispanic, 0% multiracial, 0% Pacific Islander, 5% white, 4% international; 94% from in state; 35% live on campus; N/A of students in fraternities, N/A in sororities **Most popular majors:** 26% Business, Management, Marketing, and Related Support Services; 21% Parks, Recreation, Leisure, and Fitness Studies; 12% Homeland Security, Law Enforcement, Firefighting and Related Protective Services; 12% Liberal Arts and Sciences, General Studies and Humanities; 9% Education **Expenses:** 2015-2016: $14,346; room/board: $7,568 **Financial aid:** (512) 505-3031

Jarvis Christian College
Hawkins TX
(903) 730-4890
U.S. News ranking: Reg. Coll. (W), second tier
Website: www.jarvis.edu
Admissions email: Recruitment@jarvis.edu
Private; founded 1912
Affiliation: Christian Church (Disciples of Christ)
Freshman admissions: less selective; 2015-2016: 2,547 applied, 346 accepted. Either SAT or ACT required. ACT 25/75 percentile: 16-22. High school rank: 7% in top tenth, 14% in top quarter, 30% in top half **Early decision deadline:** N/A, notification date: N/A **Early action deadline:** N/A, notification date: N/A **Application deadline (fall):** 8/1 **Undergraduate student body:** 849 full time, 14 part time; 48% male, 52% female; 0% American Indian, 0% Asian, 83% black, 10% Hispanic, 0% multiracial, 0% Pacific Islander, 4% white, 1% international; 85% from in state; 55% live on campus; 5% of students in fraternities, 5% in sororities **Most popular majors:** 26% Parks, Recreation, Leisure, and Fitness Studies; 21% Business, Management, Marketing, and Related Support Services; 17% Homeland Security, Law Enforcement, Firefighting and Related Protective Services; 12% Education; 2% Biological and Biomedical Sciences **Expenses:** 2016-2017: $11,720; room/board: $8,440 **Financial aid:** (903) 769-5740; 97% of undergrads determined to have financial need; average aid package $17,753

Lamar University
Beaumont TX
(409) 880-8888
U.S. News ranking: Nat. U., second tier
Website: www.lamar.edu
Admissions email: admissions@lamar.edu
Public; founded 1923
Freshman admissions: less selective; 2015-2016: 4,529 applied, 3,583 accepted. Either SAT or ACT required. SAT 25/75 percentile: 860-1070. High

school rank: 16% in top tenth, 25% in top quarter, 73% in top half **Early decision deadline:** N/A, notification date: N/A **Early action deadline:** N/A, notification date: N/A **Application deadline (fall):** 8/10 **Undergraduate student body:** 6,314 full time, 2,860 part time; 43% male, 57% female; 0% American Indian, 5% Asian, 27% black, 15% Hispanic, 2% multiracial, 0% Pacific Islander, 48% white, 2% international; 97% from in state; 16% live on campus; 4% of students in fraternities, 2% in sororities **Most popular majors:** 16% Health Professions and Related Programs; 16% Multi-/ Interdisciplinary Studies, Other; 15% Business, Management, Marketing, and Related Support Services; 9% Engineering; 6% Homeland Security, Law Enforcement, Firefighting and Related Protective Services **Expenses:** 2016-2017: $9,901 in state, $22,141 out of state; room/board: $8,450 **Financial aid:** (409) 880-8450; 64% of undergrads determined to have financial need; average aid package $6,557

LeTourneau University
Longview TX
(903) 233-4300
U.S. News ranking: Reg. U. (W), No. 27
Website: www.letu.edu
Admissions email: admissions@letu.edu
Private; founded 1946
Affiliation: Christian interdenominational
Freshman admissions: more selective; 2015-2016: 2,203 applied, 1,002 accepted. Neither SAT nor ACT required. ACT 25/75 percentile: 22-29. High school rank: 32% in top tenth, 53% in top quarter, 85% in top half **Early decision deadline:** N/A, notification date: N/A **Early action deadline:** N/A, notification date: N/A **Application deadline (fall):** rolling **Undergraduate student body:** 1,262 full time, 1,024 part time; 51% male, 49% female; 0% American Indian, 1% Asian, 10% black, 10% Hispanic, 4% multiracial, 0% Pacific Islander, 66% white, 3% international; 59% from in state; 73% live on campus; N/A of students in fraternities, N/A in sororities **Most popular majors:** 30% Business, Management, and Related Support Services; 19% Engineering; 10% Education; 7% Transportation and Materials Moving; 6% Psychology **Expenses:** 2016-2017: $28,480; room/board: $9,770 **Financial aid:** (903) 233-3430; 86% of undergrads determined to have financial need; average aid package $21,389

ubbock Christian University

ubbock TX
306) 720-7151
.S. News ranking: Reg. U. (W),
o. 76
Vebsite: www.lcu.edu
dmissions email:
dmissions@lcu.edu
rivate; founded 1957
ffiliation: Churches of Christ
reshman admissions: selective;
015-2016: 867 applied, 833
ccepted. Either SAT or ACT
quired. ACT 25/75 percentile:
9-25. High school rank: 19%
 top tenth, 43% in top quarter,
4% in top half
arly decision deadline: N/A,
otification date: N/A
arly action deadline: N/A,
otification date: N/A
pplication deadline (fall): 6/1
ndergraduate student body: 1,271
ll time, 225 part time; 41%
ale, 59% female; 1% American
dian, 1% Asian, 5% black,
5% Hispanic, N/A multiracial,
% Pacific Islander, 66% white,
% international; 91% from in
ate; 34% live on campus; 21%
 students in fraternities, 17%
 sororities
lost popular majors: 27%
ealth Professions and Related
rograms; 15% Business,
lanagement, Marketing, and
elated Support Services; 12%
ducation; 9% Parks, Recreation,
eisure, and Fitness Studies; 5%
ublic Administration and Social
ervice Professions
xpenses: 2016-2017: $21,166;
om/board: $6,250
nancial aid: (800) 933-7601;
2% of undergrads determined
 have financial need; average
d package $15,015

McMurry University

bilene TX
325) 793-4700
.S. News ranking: Reg. Coll. (W),
lo. 13
Vebsite: www.mcm.edu
dmissions email:
dmissions@mcm.edu
rivate; founded 1923
ffiliation: Methodist
reshman admissions: less
elective; 2015-2016: 1,378
pplied, 735 accepted. Either
AT or ACT required. SAT 25/75
ercentile: 790-980. High school
ank: 10% in top tenth, 28% in
op quarter, 67% in top half
arly decision deadline: N/A,
otification date: N/A
arly action deadline: N/A,
otification date: N/A
pplication deadline (fall): 8/15
ndergraduate student body: 907
ll time, 162 part time; 55%
ale, 45% female; 1% American
dian, 1% Asian, 18% black,
5% Hispanic, 1% multiracial,
% Pacific Islander, 52% white,
% international; 96% from in
tate; 51% live on campus; 15%
 students in fraternities, 18%
 sororities
lost popular majors: 26%
usiness, Management,
larketing, and Related Support
ervices; 16% Education; 8%
arks, Recreation, Leisure, and
itness Studies; 8% Psychology;
% Social Sciences

Expenses: 2016-2017: $26,100;
room/board: $8,244
Financial aid: (325) 793-4709;
85% of undergrads determined
to have financial need; average
aid package $20,696

Midland College[1]

Midland TX
(432) 685-5502
U.S. News ranking: Reg. Coll. (W),
unranked
Website: www.midland.edu/
Admissions email:
pebensberger@midland.edu
Public
Application deadline (fall): N/A
Undergraduate student body: N/A
full time, N/A part time
Expenses: 2015-2016: $3,168 in
state, $4,128 out of state; room/
board: $4,700
Financial aid: (432) 685-4757

Midwestern State University

Wichita Falls TX
(800) 842-1922
U.S. News ranking: Reg. U. (W),
No. 82
Website: www.mwsu.edu
Admissions email:
admissions@mwsu.edu
Public; founded 1922
Freshman admissions: selective;
2015-2016: 2,854 applied,
2,169 accepted. Either SAT
or ACT required. SAT 25/75
percentile: 900-1090. High
school rank: 14% in top tenth,
39% in top quarter, 73% in
top half
Early decision deadline: N/A,
notification date: N/A
Early action deadline: 8/7,
notification date: N/A
Application deadline (fall): 8/1
Undergraduate student body: 4,055
full time, 1,232 part time; 42%
male, 58% female; 1% American
Indian, 3% Asian, 14% black,
17% Hispanic, 4% multiracial,
0% Pacific Islander, 52% white,
9% international; 92% from in
state; 28% live on campus; 8%
of students in fraternities, 10%
in sororities
Most popular majors: Information
not available
Expenses: 2016-2017: $8,294
in state, $10,244 out of state;
room/board: $7,370
Financial aid: (940) 397-4214;
60% of undergrads determined
to have financial need; average
aid package $9,851

Our Lady of the Lake University

San Antonio TX
(800) 436-6558
U.S. News ranking: Reg. U. (W),
No. 76
Website: www.ollusa.edu
Admissions email: admission@
lake.ollusa.edu
Private; founded 1895
Affiliation: Roman Catholic
Freshman admissions: less
selective; 2015-2016: 3,113
applied, 2,120 accepted. Either
SAT or ACT required. SAT 25/75
percentile: 840-1020. High

school rank: 9% in top tenth,
26% in top quarter, 58% in
top half
Early decision deadline: N/A,
notification date: N/A
Early action deadline: 11/14,
notification date: 12/31
Application deadline (fall): 8/1
Undergraduate student body: 1,343
full time, 185 part time; 31%
male, 69% female; 1% American
Indian, 1% Asian, 9% black,
70% Hispanic, 2% multiracial,
0% Pacific Islander, 13% white,
1% international; 97% from in
state; 39% live on campus; 5%
of students in fraternities, 5% in
sororities
Most popular majors: 13%
Business Administration
and Management, General;
13% Social Work; 11%
Communication Sciences
and Disorders, General; 10%
Psychology, General; 7% Criminal
Justice/Safety Studies
Expenses: 2016-2017: $27,140;
room/board: $7,872
Financial aid: (210) 434-6711;
86% of undergrads determined
to have financial need; average
aid package $21,495

Prairie View A&M University

Prairie View TX
(877) PVA-MU30
U.S. News ranking: Nat. U.,
second tier
Website: www.pvamu.edu
Admissions email:
admission@pvamu.edu
Public; founded 1876
Freshman admissions: least
selective; 2015-2016: 5,067
applied, 4,355 accepted. Either
SAT or ACT required. SAT 25/75
percentile: 770-930. High school
rank: 5% in top tenth, 14% in
top quarter, 57% in top half
Early decision deadline: N/A,
notification date: N/A
Early action deadline: N/A,
notification date: N/A
Application deadline (fall): 6/1
Undergraduate student body: 6,305
full time, 618 part time; 40%
male, 60% female; 0% American
Indian, 3% Asian, 86% black,
6% Hispanic, 1% multiracial,
0% Pacific Islander, 3% white,
2% international; 94% from in
state; 52% live on campus; 1%
of students in fraternities, 2% in
sororities
Most popular majors: 12%
Registered Nursing/Registered
Nurse; 9% Criminal Justice/
Safety Studies; 6% Biology/
Biological Sciences, General;
6% Psychology, General; 5%
Chemical Engineering
Expenses: 2015-2016: $9,745
in state, $22,272 out of state;
room/board: $8,419
Financial aid: (936) 857-2424;
87% of undergrads determined
to have financial need; average
aid package $14,796

Rice University

Houston TX
(713) 348-7423
U.S. News ranking: Nat. U.,
No. 15
Website: www.rice.edu
Admissions email:
admission@rice.edu
Private; founded 1912
Freshman admissions: most
selective; 2015-2016: 17,951
applied, 2,865 accepted. Either
SAT or ACT required. SAT 25/75
percentile: 1390-1560. High
school rank: 89% in top tenth,
96% in top quarter, 100% in
top half
Early decision deadline: 11/1,
notification date: 12/15
Early action deadline: N/A,
notification date: N/A
Application deadline (fall): 1/1
Undergraduate student body: 3,863
full time, 47 part time; 53%
male, 47% female; 0% American
Indian, 24% Asian, 7% black,
14% Hispanic, 4% multiracial,
0% Pacific Islander, 37% white,
12% international; 50% from in
state; 72% live on campus; N/A
of students in fraternities, N/A in
sororities
Most popular majors: 7%
Biochemistry; 6% Psychology,
General; 6% Chemical
Engineering; 6% Kinesiology and
Exercise Science; 5% Mechanical
Engineering
Expenses: 2016-2017: $43,918;
room/board: $13,750
Financial aid: (713) 348-4958;
38% of undergrads determined
to have financial need; average
aid package $40,421

Sam Houston State University

Huntsville TX
(936) 294-1828
U.S. News ranking: Nat. U.,
second tier
Website: www.shsu.edu
Admissions email:
admissions@shsu.edu
Public; founded 1879
Freshman admissions: selective;
2015-2016: 11,309 applied,
8,288 accepted. Either SAT
or ACT required. SAT 25/75
percentile: 880-1090. High
school rank: 15% in top tenth,
41% in top quarter, 88% in
top half
Early decision deadline: N/A,
notification date: N/A
Early action deadline: N/A,
notification date: N/A
Application deadline (fall): 8/1
Undergraduate student body:
14,117 full time, 3,284 part
time; 39% male, 61% female;
1% American Indian, 1% Asian,
19% black, 20% Hispanic, 3%
multiracial, 0% Pacific Islander,
53% white, 1% international;
98% from in state; 20% live
on campus; 2% of students in
fraternities, 2% in sororities
Most popular majors: 24%
Business, Management,
Marketing, and Related Support
Services; 20% Homeland
Security, Law Enforcement,
Firefighting and Related
Protective Services; 11% Multi/
Interdisciplinary Studies; 5%

Parks, Recreation, Leisure, and
Fitness Studies
Expenses: 2016-2017: $9,395
in state, $21,635 out of state;
room/board: $8,986
Financial aid: (936) 294-1774;
64% of undergrads determined
to have financial need; average
aid package $10,522

Schreiner University

Kerrville TX
(800) 343-4919
U.S. News ranking: Nat. Lib. Arts,
second tier
Website: www.schreiner.edu
Admissions email: admissions@
schreiner.edu
Private; founded 1923
Affiliation: Presbyterian
Freshman admissions: less
selective; 2015-2016: 943
applied, 850 accepted. Either
SAT or ACT required. SAT 25/75
percentile: 890-1090. High
school rank: 11% in top tenth,
36% in top quarter, 70% in
top half
Early decision deadline: N/A,
notification date: N/A
Early action deadline: N/A,
notification date: N/A
Application deadline (fall): 8/1
Undergraduate student body: 1,081
full time, 101 part time; 42%
male, 58% female; 0% American
Indian, 1% Asian, 4% black,
35% Hispanic, 3% multiracial,
0% Pacific Islander, 56% white,
1% international; 97% from in
state; 63% live on campus; N/A
of students in fraternities, N/A in
sororities
Most popular majors: 0%
Business, Management,
Marketing, and Related Support
Services; 0% Biological and
Biomedical Sciences; 0%
Health Professions and Related
Programs; 0% Psychology; 0%
Education
Expenses: 2016-2017: $25,750;
room/board: $9,806
Financial aid: (830) 792-7217;
88% of undergrads determined
to have financial need; average
aid package $18,744

Southern Methodist University

Dallas TX
(800) 323-0672
U.S. News ranking: Nat. U.,
No. 56
Website: www.smu.edu
Admissions email:
ugadmission@smu.edu
Private; founded 1911
Affiliation: United Methodist
Freshman admissions: more
selective; 2015-2016: 12,992
applied, 6,360 accepted. Either
SAT or ACT required. ACT 25/75
percentile: 28-32. High school
rank: 44% in top tenth, 75% in
top quarter, 93% in top half
Early decision deadline: 11/1,
notification date: 12/31
Early action deadline: 11/1,
notification date: 12/31
Application deadline (fall): 1/15
Undergraduate student body: 6,160
full time, 251 part time; 50%
male, 50% female; 0% American
Indian, 7% Asian, 5% black,
11% Hispanic, 4% multiracial,

BEST COLLEGES

0% Pacific Islander, 65% white, 8% international; 46% from in state; 57% live on campus; 28% of students in fraternities, 37% in sororities
Most popular majors: 22% Business, Management, Marketing, and Related Support Services; 14% Social Sciences; 10% Engineering; 7% Visual and Performing Arts
Expenses: 2016-2017: $50,358; room/board: $16,126
Financial aid: (214) 768-3016; 33% of undergrads determined to have financial need; average aid package $39,585

South Texas College[1]
McAllen TX
(956) 872-8323
U.S. News ranking: Reg. Coll. (W), unranked
Website: www.southtexascollege.edu/
Admissions email: N/A
Public
Application deadline (fall): N/A
Undergraduate student body: N/A full time, N/A part time
Expenses: 2015-2016: $3,770 in state, $4,440 out of state; room/board: N/A
Financial aid: (956) 872-8375

Southwestern Adventist University[1]
Keene TX
(817) 645-3921
U.S. News ranking: Reg. Coll. (W), No. 21
Website: www.swau.edu
Admissions email: admissions@swau.edu
Private; founded 1893
Affiliation: Seventh-day Adventist
Application deadline (fall): rolling
Undergraduate student body: N/A full time, N/A part time
Expenses: 2015-2016: $19,916; room/board: $7,400
Financial aid: (817) 645-3921

Southwestern Assemblies of God University
Waxahachie TX
(888) 937-7248
U.S. News ranking: Reg. U. (W), second tier
Website: www.sagu.edu/
Admissions email: admissions@sagu.edu
Private; founded 1927
Affiliation: Assemblies of God
Freshman admissions: selective; 2015-2016: 1,459 applied, 408 accepted. Either SAT or ACT required. ACT 25/75 percentile: 18-23. High school rank: N/A
Early decision deadline: N/A, notification date: N/A
Early action deadline: N/A, notification date: N/A
Application deadline (fall): rolling
Undergraduate student body: 1,420 full time, 241 part time; 48% male, 52% female; 2% American Indian, 1% Asian, 11% black, 21% Hispanic, 2% multiracial, 0% Pacific Islander, 63% white, 0% international; N/A from in

state; 85% live on campus; N/A of students in fraternities, N/A in sororities
Most popular majors: 20% Religious Education; 7% Business Administration and Management, General; 7% Elementary Education and Teaching; 7% General Studies; 7% Public Administration and Social Service Professions
Expenses: 2016-2017: $19,560; room/board: $7,144
Financial aid: N/A; 88% of undergrads determined to have financial need; average aid package $7,698

Southwestern Christian College[1]
Terrell TX
(972) 524-3341
U.S. News ranking: Reg. Coll. (W), unranked
Website: www.swcc.edu
Admissions email: N/A
Private
Application deadline (fall): N/A
Undergraduate student body: N/A full time, N/A part time
Expenses: 2016-2017: $8,074; room/board: $5,600
Financial aid: (972) 524-3341

Southwestern University
Georgetown TX
(800) 252-3166
U.S. News ranking: Nat. Lib. Arts, No. 95
Website: www.southwestern.edu
Admissions email: admission@southwestern.edu
Private; founded 1840
Affiliation: United Methodist
Freshman admissions: more selective; 2015-2016: 3,736 applied, 1,652 accepted. Either SAT or ACT required. SAT 25/75 percentile: 1040-1270. High school rank: 32% in top tenth, 68% in top quarter, 94% in top half
Early decision deadline: 11/1, notification date: 12/1
Early action deadline: 11/15, notification date: 2/15
Application deadline (fall): 7/1
Undergraduate student body: 1,499 full time, 16 part time; 43% male, 57% female; 0% American Indian, 4% Asian, 5% black, 22% Hispanic, 4% multiracial, 0% Pacific Islander, 62% white, 2% international; 88% from in state; 72% live on campus; 27% of students in fraternities, 23% in sororities
Most popular majors: 14% Business, Management, Marketing, and Related Support Services; 13% Biological and Biomedical Sciences; 12% Social Sciences; 10% Visual and Performing Arts; 7% Psychology
Expenses: 2016-2017: $39,060; room/board: $12,288
Financial aid: (512) 863-1259; 63% of undergrads determined to have financial need; average aid package $33,166

St. Edward's University
Austin TX
(512) 448-8500
U.S. News ranking: Reg. U. (W), No. 14
Website: www.stedwards.edu
Admissions email: seu.admit@stedwards.edu
Private; founded 1885
Affiliation: Roman Catholic
Freshman admissions: selective; 2015-2016: 5,034 applied, 3,899 accepted. Either SAT or ACT required. SAT 25/75 percentile: 1040-1220. High school rank: 24% in top tenth, 58% in top quarter, 86% in top half
Early decision deadline: N/A, notification date: N/A
Early action deadline: N/A, notification date: N/A
Application deadline (fall): 5/1
Undergraduate student body: 3,528 full time, 495 part time; 39% male, 61% female; 0% American Indian, 3% Asian, 4% black, 40% Hispanic, 4% multiracial, 0% Pacific Islander, 37% white, 9% international; 87% from in state; 39% live on campus; N/A of students in fraternities, N/A in sororities
Most popular majors: 10% Business Administration and Management, General; 10% Psychology, General; 5% Biology/Biological Sciences, General; 4% Finance, General
Expenses: 2016-2017: $40,828; room/board: $12,172
Financial aid: (512) 448-8520; 66% of undergrads determined to have financial need; average aid package $30,930

Stephen F. Austin State University
Nacogdoches TX
(936) 468-2504
U.S. News ranking: Reg. U. (W), No. 76
Website: www.sfasu.edu
Admissions email: admissions@sfasu.edu
Public; founded 1923
Freshman admissions: selective; 2015-2016: 11,382 applied, 7,008 accepted. Either SAT or ACT required. SAT 25/75 percentile: 890-1100. High school rank: 12% in top tenth, 40% in top quarter, 77% in top half
Early decision deadline: N/A, notification date: N/A
Early action deadline: N/A, notification date: N/A
Application deadline (fall): rolling
Undergraduate student body: 9,439 full time, 1,460 part time; 37% male, 63% female; 0% American Indian, 1% Asian, 21% black, 15% Hispanic, 3% multiracial, 0% Pacific Islander, 58% white, 1% international; 98% from in state; 44% live on campus; 15% of students in fraternities, 10% in sororities
Most popular majors: 20% Business Administration and Management, General; 15% Registered Nursing/

Registered Nurse; 13% Multi-/Interdisciplinary Studies, Other; 7% Kinesiology and Exercise Science; 5% Human Development and Family Studies, General
Expenses: 2015-2016: $9,342 in state, $21,042 out of state; room/board: $8,868
Financial aid: (936) 468-2403

St. Mary's University of San Antonio
San Antonio TX
(210) 436-3126
U.S. News ranking: Reg. U. (W), No. 21
Website: www.stmarytx.edu
Admissions email: uadm@stmarytx.edu
Private; founded 1852
Affiliation: Roman Catholic
Freshman admissions: selective; 2015-2016: 5,832 applied, 3,219 accepted. Either SAT or ACT required. SAT 25/75 percentile: 930-1130. High school rank: 25% in top tenth, 53% in top quarter, 81% in top half
Early decision deadline: N/A, notification date: N/A
Early action deadline: N/A, notification date: N/A
Application deadline (fall): rolling
Undergraduate student body: 2,196 full time, 113 part time; 46% male, 54% female; 0% American Indian, 2% Asian, 3% black, 70% Hispanic, 0% multiracial, 0% Pacific Islander, 15% white, 8% international; 92% from in state; 56% live on campus; 1% of students in fraternities, 1% in sororities
Most popular majors: 24% Business, Management, Marketing, and Related Support Services; 15% Social Sciences; 12% Biological and Biomedical Sciences; 10% Parks, Recreation, Leisure, and Fitness Studies; 9% Homeland Security, Law Enforcement, Firefighting and Related Protective Services
Expenses: 2016-2017: $28,200; room/board: $9,300
Financial aid: (210) 436-3141; 72% of undergrads determined to have financial need; average aid package $24,632

Sul Ross State University
Alpine TX
(432) 837-8050
U.S. News ranking: Reg. U. (W), second tier
Website: www.sulross.edu
Admissions email: admissions@sulross.edu
Public; founded 1917
Freshman admissions: least selective; 2015-2016: 1,142 applied, 913 accepted. Either SAT or ACT required. SAT 25/75 percentile: 740-940. High school rank: 3% in top tenth, 20% in top quarter, 56% in top half
Early decision deadline: N/A, notification date: N/A
Early action deadline: N/A, notification date: N/A

Application deadline (fall): rolling
Undergraduate student body: 1,25? full time, 900 part time; 43% male, 57% female; 0% American Indian, 0% Asian, 5% black, 69% Hispanic, 1% multiracial, 0% Pacific Islander, 22% white, 0% international
Most popular majors: Information not available
Expenses: 2015-2016: $7,211 in state, $18,911 out of state; room/board: $7,810
Financial aid: (432) 837-8059

Tarleton State University
Stephenville TX
(800) 687-8236
U.S. News ranking: Reg. U. (W), second tier
Website: www.tarleton.edu
Admissions email: uadm@tarleton.edu
Public; founded 1899
Freshman admissions: less selective; 2015-2016: 6,288 applied, 4,482 accepted. Either SAT or ACT required. SAT 25/75 percentile: 850-1050. High school rank: 9% in top tenth, 37% in top quarter, 87% in top half
Early decision deadline: N/A, notification date: N/A
Early action deadline: 3/1, notification date: N/A
Application deadline (fall): 7/21
Undergraduate student body: 8,309 full time, 2,441 part time; 39% male, 61% female; 1% American Indian, 1% Asian, 8% black, 18% Hispanic, 3% multiracial, 0% Pacific Islander, 68% white, 0% international; 98% from in state; 35% live on campus; N/A of students in fraternities, N/A in sororities
Most popular majors: 20% Business, Management, Marketing, and Related Support Services; 14% Multi-/Interdisciplinary Studies; 8% Homeland Security, Law Enforcement, Firefighting and Related Protective Services; 7% Parks, Recreation, Leisure, and Fitness Studies
Expenses: 2016-2017: $8,723 in state, $20,706 out of state; room/board: $9,970
Financial aid: (254) 968-9070; 64% of undergrads determined to have financial need; average aid package $8,874

Texas A&M International University
Laredo TX
(956) 326-2200
U.S. News ranking: Reg. U. (W), No. 68
Website: www.tamiu.edu
Admissions email: enroll@tamiu.edu
Public; founded 1970
Freshman admissions: less selective; 2015-2016: 6,161 applied, 2,931 accepted. Either SAT or ACT required. SAT 25/75 percentile: 810-1010. High

hool rank: 18% in top tenth,)% in top quarter, 84% in o half
rly decision deadline: N/A, tification date: N/A
rly action deadline: N/A, tification date: N/A
plication deadline (fall): 7/1
dergraduate student body: 4,586 ll time, 1,790 part time; 40% ale, 60% female; 0% American dian, 0% Asian, 0% black, 6% Hispanic, 0% multiracial, % Pacific Islander, 2% white, % international
ost popular majors: 19% usiness, Management, arketing, and Related Support rvices; 16% Homeland curity, Law Enforcement, refighting and Related otective Services; 13% ealth Professions and Related ograms; 12% Psychology; 9% ulti/Interdisciplinary Studies
penses: 2016-2017: $8,446 state, $20,149 out of state; om/board: $7,882
nancial aid: (956) 326-2225;)% of undergrads determined have financial need; average d package $9,774

exas A&M niversity– ollege Station

ollege Station TX
79) 845-3741
. News ranking: Nat. U.,). 74
ebsite: www.tamu.edu
missions email: missions@tamu.edu
blic; founded 1876
eshman admissions: more lective; 2015-2016: 33,970 plied, 22,371 accepted. ther SAT or ACT required. SAT 5/75 percentile: 1070-1310. gh school rank: 66% in top nth, 91% in top quarter, 99% top half
rly decision deadline: N/A, tification date: N/A
rly action deadline: N/A, tification date: N/A
plication deadline (fall): 12/1
dergraduate student body: 3,532 full time, 5,428 part ne; 51% male, 49% female; American Indian, 6% Asian, % black, 22% Hispanic, 3% ultiracial, 0% Pacific Islander, % white, 1% international; 7% from in state; 17% live campus; N/A of students in aternities, N/A in sororities
ost popular majors: 17% usiness, Management, arketing, and Related Support rvices; 14% Engineering; 10% ulti/Interdisciplinary Studies; % Biological and Biomedical iences
penses: 2015-2016: $10,176 state, $28,768 out of state; om/board: $10,338
nancial aid: (979) 845-3236; 5% of undergrads determined have financial need; average d package $16,178

Texas A&M University–Commerce

Commerce TX
(903) 886-5000
U.S. News ranking: Nat. U., second tier
Website: www.tamuc.edu/
Admissions email: Admissions@tamuc.edu
Public; founded 1889
Freshman admissions: less selective; 2015-2016: 7,195 applied, 3,413 accepted. Either SAT or ACT required. SAT 25/75 percentile: 680-1080. High school rank: 11% in top tenth, 35% in top quarter, 69% in top half
Early decision deadline: N/A, notification date: N/A
Early action deadline: N/A, notification date: N/A
Application deadline (fall): 8/15
Undergraduate student body: 5,445 full time, 2,197 part time; 41% male, 59% female; 1% American Indian, 1% Asian, 21% black, 17% Hispanic, 5% multiracial, 0% Pacific Islander, 52% white, 3% international; 98% from in state; 30% live on campus; 2% of students in fraternities, 3% in sororities
Most popular majors: 32% Multi/Interdisciplinary Studies; 16% Business, Management, Marketing, and Related Support Services; 7% Liberal Arts and Sciences, General Studies and Humanities; 6% Parks, Recreation, Leisure, and Fitness Studies; 5% Psychology
Expenses: 2016-2017: $7,898 in state, $20,138 out of state; room/board: $8,326
Financial aid: (903) 886-5096; 73% of undergrads determined to have financial need; average aid package $9,655

Texas A&M University–Corpus Christi

Corpus Christi TX
(361) 825-2624
U.S. News ranking: Nat. U., second tier
Website: www.tamucc.edu
Admissions email: admiss@tamucc.edu
Public; founded 1947
Freshman admissions: less selective; 2015-2016: 8,909 applied, 7,463 accepted. Either SAT or ACT required. SAT 25/75 percentile: 870-1070. High school rank: 10% in top tenth, 38% in top quarter, 74% in top half
Early decision deadline: N/A, notification date: N/A
Early action deadline: N/A, notification date: N/A
Application deadline (fall): 7/1
Undergraduate student body: 7,389 full time, 2,415 part time; 41% male, 59% female; 0% American Indian, 2% Asian, 7% black, 48% Hispanic, 1% multiracial, 0% Pacific Islander, 38% white, 3% international; 98% from in state; 22% live on campus; 4% of students in fraternities, 4% in sororities
Most popular majors: 18% Business, Management, Marketing, and Related Support Services; 18% Health Professions and Related Programs; 12% Multi/Interdisciplinary Studies; 9% Biological and Biomedical Sciences; 6% Psychology
Expenses: 2016-2017: $9,106 in state, $21,193 out of state; room/board: $9,195
Financial aid: (361) 825-2338; 62% of undergrads determined to have financial need; average aid package $8,951

Texas A&M University–Kingsville

Kingsville TX
(361) 593-2315
U.S. News ranking: Nat. U., second tier
Website: www.tamuk.edu
Admissions email: admissions@tamuk.edu
Public; founded 1925
Freshman admissions: selective; 2015-2016: 7,344 applied, 6,049 accepted. Either SAT or ACT required. ACT 25/75 percentile: 17-22. High school rank: 16% in top tenth, 43% in top quarter, 80% in top half
Early decision deadline: N/A, notification date: N/A
Early action deadline: N/A, notification date: N/A
Application deadline (fall): 8/1
Undergraduate student body: 5,077 full time, 1,528 part time; 53% male, 47% female; 0% American Indian, 1% Asian, 7% black, 70% Hispanic, 1% multiracial, 0% Pacific Islander, 18% white, 3% international; 99% from in state; 32% live on campus; N/A of students in fraternities, N/A in sororities
Most popular majors: 14% Health Professions and Related Programs; 14% Engineering; 12% Multi/Interdisciplinary Studies; 8% Social Sciences; 7% Business, Management, Marketing, and Related Support Services
Expenses: 2016-2017: $8,050 in state, $19,173 out of state; room/board: $8,530
Financial aid: (361) 593-2173; 77% of undergrads determined to have financial need; average aid package $12,301

Texas A&M University–Texarkana[1]

Texarkana TX
(903) 223-3069
U.S. News ranking: Reg. U. (W), second tier
Website: www.tamut.edu
Admissions email: admissions@tamut.edu
Public; founded 1971
Application deadline (fall): rolling
Undergraduate student body: N/A full time, N/A part time
Expenses: 2016-2017: $8,246 in state, $14,094 out of state; room/board: $7,194
Financial aid: (903) 223-3060; 70% of undergrads determined to have financial need; average aid package $13,273

Texas Christian University

Fort Worth TX
(817) 257-7490
U.S. News ranking: Nat. U., No. 82
Website: www.tcu.edu
Admissions email: frogmail@tcu.edu
Private; founded 1873
Affiliation: Christian Church (Disciples of Christ)
Freshman admissions: more selective; 2015-2016: 18,423 applied, 7,974 accepted. Either SAT or ACT required. ACT 25/75 percentile: 25-30. High school rank: 44% in top tenth, 76% in top quarter, 96% in top half
Early decision deadline: 11/1, notification date: 12/5
Early action deadline: 11/1, notification date: 12/15
Application deadline (fall): 2/15
Undergraduate student body: 8,586 full time, 308 part time; 40% male, 60% female; 1% American Indian, 3% Asian, 5% black, 11% Hispanic, 0% multiracial, 0% Pacific Islander, 73% white, 5% international; 55% from in state; 49% live on campus; 41% of students in fraternities, 55% in sororities
Most popular majors: 26% Business, Management, Marketing, and Related Support Services; 15% Health Professions and Related Programs; 8% Social Sciences; 6% Education
Expenses: 2016-2017: $42,670; room/board: $12,000
Financial aid: (817) 257-7858; 39% of undergrads determined to have financial need; average aid package $27,603

Texas College[1]

Tyler TX
(903) 593-8311
U.S. News ranking: Reg. Coll. (W), unranked
Website: www.texascollege.edu
Admissions email: cmarshall-biggins@texascollege.edu
Private
Application deadline (fall): N/A
Undergraduate student body: N/A full time, N/A part time
Expenses: 2015-2016: $10,008; room/board: $7,200
Financial aid: (903) 593-8311

Texas Lutheran University

Seguin TX
(800) 771-8521
U.S. News ranking: Reg. Coll. (W), No. 2
Website: www.tlu.edu
Admissions email: admissions@tlu.edu
Private; founded 1891
Affiliation: Evangelical Lutheran Church in America
Freshman admissions: selective; 2015-2016: 1,863 applied, 945 accepted. Either SAT or ACT required. SAT 25/75 percentile: 915-1115. High school rank: 20% in top tenth, 49% in top quarter, 82% in top half
Early decision deadline: 11/1, notification date: 12/15
Early action deadline: 12/15, notification date: 2/15
Application deadline (fall): 2/1
Undergraduate student body: 1,284 full time, 83 part time; 49% male, 51% female; 0% American Indian, 1% Asian, 9% black, 32% Hispanic, 0% multiracial, 0% Pacific Islander, 55% white, 0% international; 98% from in state; 60% live on campus; 7% of students in fraternities, 11% in sororities
Most popular majors: 21% Business, Management, Marketing, and Related Support Services; 16% Parks, Recreation, Leisure, and Fitness Studies; 12% Education; 11% Psychology; 8% Biological and Biomedical Sciences
Expenses: 2016-2017: $28,910; room/board: $9,320
Financial aid: (830) 372-8075; 81% of undergrads determined to have financial need; average aid package $25,716

Texas Southern University

Houston TX
(713) 313-7071
U.S. News ranking: Nat. U., second tier
Website: www.tsu.edu
Admissions email: admissions@tsu.edu
Public; founded 1947
Freshman admissions: least selective; 2015-2016: 10,487 applied, 5,338 accepted. Either SAT or ACT required. SAT 25/75 percentile: 725-900. High school rank: 5% in top tenth, 19% in top quarter, 53% in top half
Early decision deadline: 12/1, notification date: N/A
Early action deadline: N/A, notification date: N/A
Application deadline (fall): 8/1
Undergraduate student body: 5,884 full time, 812 part time; 43% male, 57% female; 1% American Indian, 2% Asian, 80% black, 6% Hispanic, N/A multiracial, 0% Pacific Islander, 2% white, 8% international; N/A from in state; 23% live on campus; 2% of students in fraternities, 3% in sororities
Most popular majors: 8% General Studies; 7% Biology/Biological Sciences, General; 7% Business Administration and Management, General; 6% Accounting; 6% Criminal Justice/Law Enforcement Administration
Expenses: 2015-2016: $8,726 in state, $20,426 out of state; room/board: $15,170
Financial aid: (713) 313-7071; 87% of undergrads determined to have financial need; average aid package $7,535

Texas State University

San Marcos TX
(512) 245-2364
U.S. News ranking: Nat. U., second tier
Website: www.txstate.edu
Admissions email: admissions@txstate.edu
Public; founded 1899
Freshman admissions: selective; 2015-2016: 20,711 applied, 14,672 accepted. Either SAT or ACT required. SAT 25/75 percentile: 930-1120. High school rank: 12% in top tenth, 48% in top quarter, 93% in top half
Early decision deadline: N/A, notification date: N/A
Early action deadline: N/A, notification date: N/A
Application deadline (fall): 5/1
Undergraduate student body: 27,369 full time, 6,111 part time; 43% male, 57% female; 0% American Indian, 2% Asian, 9% black, 35% Hispanic, 3% multiracial, 0% Pacific Islander, 49% white, 0% international; 98% from in state; 20% live on campus; 5% of students in fraternities, 5% in sororities
Most popular majors: 8% Multi-/Interdisciplinary Studies, Other; 6% Business Administration and Management, General; 6% Psychology, General; 5% Kinesiology and Exercise Science; 4% Marketing/Marketing Management, General
Expenses: 2016-2017: $10,218 in state, $22,458 out of state; room/board: $9,132
Financial aid: (512) 245-2315; 59% of undergrads determined to have financial need; average aid package $10,753

Texas Tech University

Lubbock TX
(806) 742-1480
U.S. News ranking: Nat. U., No. 176
Website: www.ttu.edu
Admissions email: admissions@ttu.edu
Public; founded 1923
Freshman admissions: selective; 2015-2016: 23,010 applied, 14,510 accepted. Either SAT or ACT required. SAT 25/75 percentile: 1030-1220. High school rank: 20% in top tenth, 55% in top quarter, 86% in top half
Early decision deadline: N/A, notification date: N/A
Early action deadline: N/A, notification date: N/A
Application deadline (fall): 8/1
Undergraduate student body: 26,121 full time, 3,116 part time; 55% male, 45% female; 0% American Indian, 3% Asian, 6% black, 23% Hispanic, 3% multiracial, 0% Pacific Islander, 60% white, 5% international; 94% from in state; 25% live on campus; 4% of students in fraternities, 8% in sororities
Most popular majors: 20% Business, Management, Marketing, and Related Support Services; 11% Engineering; 8% Multi/Interdisciplinary Studies;

8% Family and Consumer Sciences/Human Sciences
Expenses: 2016-2017: $10,622 in state, $22,861 out of state; room/board: $9,384
Financial aid: (806) 742-3681; 48% of undergrads determined to have financial need; average aid package $10,114

Texas Wesleyan University

Fort Worth TX
(817) 531-4422
U.S. News ranking: Reg. U. (W), No. 50
Website: www.txwes.edu
Admissions email: admission@txwes.edu
Private; founded 1890
Affiliation: Methodist
Freshman admissions: selective; 2015-2016: 3,062 applied, 1,407 accepted. Either SAT or ACT required. SAT 25/75 percentile: 928-1090. High school rank: 16% in top tenth, 42% in top quarter, 75% in top half
Early decision deadline: N/A, notification date: N/A
Early action deadline: N/A, notification date: N/A
Application deadline (fall): rolling
Undergraduate student body: 1,549 full time, 430 part time; 47% male, 53% female; 1% American Indian, 1% Asian, 13% black, 25% Hispanic, 4% multiracial, 0% Pacific Islander, 30% white, 26% international; 95% from in state; 23% live on campus; 2% of students in fraternities, 2% in sororities
Most popular majors: 19% Business, Management, Marketing, and Related Support Services; 16% Multi/Interdisciplinary Studies; 9% Psychology; 8% Education; 6% Homeland Security, Law Enforcement, Firefighting and Related Protective Services
Expenses: 2016-2017: $26,050; room/board: $9,084
Financial aid: (817) 531-4420; 61% of undergrads determined to have financial need; average aid package $24,264

Texas Woman's University

Denton TX
(940) 898-3188
U.S. News ranking: Nat. U., second tier
Website: www.twu.edu
Admissions email: admissions@twu.edu
Public; founded 1901
Freshman admissions: less selective; 2015-2016: 4,772 applied, 3,558 accepted. Neither SAT nor ACT required. SAT 25/75 percentile: 830-1050. High school rank: 18% in top tenth, 45% in top quarter, 80% in top half
Early decision deadline: N/A, notification date: N/A
Early action deadline: N/A, notification date: N/A
Application deadline (fall): 7/15
Undergraduate student body: 6,941 full time, 3,139 part time; 12% male, 88% female; 0% American

Indian, 8% Asian, 21% black, 28% Hispanic, 4% multiracial, 0% Pacific Islander, 38% white, 1% international; 99% from in state; 22% live on campus; 2% of students in fraternities, 1% in sororities
Most popular majors: 28% Health Professions and Related Programs; 14% Liberal Arts and Sciences, General Studies and Humanities; 11% Multi/Interdisciplinary Studies; 9% Business, Management, Marketing, and Related Support Services; 6% Family and Consumer Sciences/Human Sciences
Expenses: 2016-2017: $8,770 in state, $21,010 out of state; room/board: $7,578
Financial aid: (940) 898-3050; 71% of undergrads determined to have financial need; average aid package $10,906

Trinity University

San Antonio TX
(800) 874-6489
U.S. News ranking: Reg. U. (W), No. 1
Website: www.trinity.edu
Admissions email: admissions@trinity.edu
Private; founded 1869
Affiliation: Presbyterian
Freshman admissions: more selective; 2015-2016: 5,563 applied, 2,672 accepted. Either SAT or ACT required. ACT 25/75 percentile: 27-32. High school rank: 47% in top tenth, 75% in top quarter, 96% in top half
Early decision deadline: 11/1, notification date: 12/15
Early action deadline: 11/1, notification date: 12/15
Application deadline (fall): 2/1
Undergraduate student body: 2,228 full time, 45 part time; 48% male, 52% female; 0% American Indian, 6% Asian, 4% black, 20% Hispanic, 5% multiracial, 0% Pacific Islander, 55% white, 7% international; 76% from in state; 77% live on campus; 17% of students in fraternities, 29% in sororities
Most popular majors: 24% Business, Management, Marketing, and Related Support Services; 14% Social Sciences; 12% Biological and Biomedical Sciences; 7% Foreign Languages, Literatures, and Linguistics
Expenses: 2016-2017: $39,560; room/board: $12,754
Financial aid: (210) 999-8315; 41% of undergrads determined to have financial need; average aid package $35,251

University of Dallas

Irving TX
(800) 628-6999
U.S. News ranking: Reg. U. (W), No. 12
Website: www.udallas.edu
Admissions email: ugadmis@udallas.edu
Private; founded 1956
Affiliation: Roman Catholic
Freshman admissions: selective; 2015-2016: 2,228 applied, 1,436 accepted. Either SAT or ACT required. SAT 25/75

percentile: 1080-1340. High school rank: 39% in top tenth, 67% in top quarter, 88% in top half
Early decision deadline: N/A, notification date: N/A
Early action deadline: 11/1, notification date: 12/1
Application deadline (fall): 7/1
Undergraduate student body: 1,315 full time, 27 part time; 44% male, 56% female; 0% American Indian, 5% Asian, 2% black, 21% Hispanic, 3% multiracial, 0% Pacific Islander, 65% white, 2% international; 46% from in state; 68% live on campus; N/A in fraternities, N/A in sororities
Most popular majors: 17% Social Sciences; 14% Business, Management, Marketing, and Related Support Services; 12% Biological and Biomedical Sciences; 10% History; 9% English Language and Literature/Letters
Expenses: 2016-2017: $37,230; room/board: $11,540
Financial aid: (972) 721-5266; 62% of undergrads determined to have financial need; average aid package $30,216

University of Houston

Houston TX
(713) 743-1010
U.S. News ranking: Nat. U., No. 194
Website: www.uh.edu
Admissions email: admissions@uh.edu
Public; founded 1927
Freshman admissions: more selective; 2015-2016: 17,971 applied, 10,732 accepted. Either SAT or ACT required. SAT 25/75 percentile: 1050-1250. High school rank: 30% in top tenth, 64% in top quarter, 89% in top half
Early decision deadline: N/A, notification date: N/A
Early action deadline: N/A, notification date: N/A
Application deadline (fall): 7/1
Undergraduate student body: 24,909 full time, 9,807 part time; 51% male, 49% female; 0% American Indian, 22% Asian, 10% black, 32% Hispanic, 3% multiracial, 0% Pacific Islander, 26% white, 5% international; 98% from in state; 19% live on campus; 4% of students in fraternities, 4% in sororities
Most popular majors: 30% Business, Management, Marketing, and Related Support Services; 7% Psychology; 7% Social Sciences; 6% Biological and Biomedical Sciences
Expenses: 2015-2016: $10,710 in state, $25,410 out of state; room/board: $9,849
Financial aid: (713) 743-1010; 62% of undergrads determined to have financial need; average aid package $12,466

University of Houston–Clear Lake

Houston TX
(281) 283-2500
U.S. News ranking: Reg. U. (W), No. 74
Website: www.uhcl.edu
Admissions email: admissions@uhcl.edu
Public; founded 1974
Freshman admissions: selective; 2015-2016: 1,010 applied, 66 accepted. Either SAT or ACT required. SAT 25/75 percentile: 940-1120. High school rank: 16% in top tenth, 44% in top quarter, 75% in top half
Early decision deadline: N/A, notification date: N/A
Early action deadline: N/A, notification date: N/A
Application deadline (fall): 6/1
Undergraduate student body: 2,62 full time, 2,799 part time; 35% male, 65% female; 0% American Indian, 6% Asian, 9% black, 36% Hispanic, 3% multiracial, 0% Pacific Islander, 43% white 2% international; 100% from in state; 2% live on campus; N/A of students in fraternities, N/A i sororities
Most popular majors: 28% Multi-Interdisciplinary Studies; 27% Business, Management, Marketing, and Related Support Services; 8% Science Technologies/Technicians; 5% Social Sciences; 4% Parks, Recreation, Leisure, and Fitness Studies
Expenses: 2016-2017: $7,931 in state, $22,901 out of state; room/board: $9,704
Financial aid: (281) 283-2480; 67% of undergrads determined to have financial need; average aid package $8,085

University of Houston–Downtown

Houston TX
(713) 221-8522
U.S. News ranking: Reg. U. (W), second tier
Website: www.uhd.edu
Admissions email: uhdadmit@uhd.edu
Public; founded 1974
Freshman admissions: less selective; 2015-2016: 3,460 applied, 2,686 accepted. Either SAT or ACT required. SAT 25/7! percentile: 810-990. High scho rank: 6% in top tenth, 29% in top quarter, 74% in top half
Early decision deadline: N/A, notification date: N/A
Early action deadline: N/A, notification date: N/A
Application deadline (fall): 7/1
Undergraduate student body: 6,64 full time, 6,602 part time; 40% male, 60% female; 0% America Indian, 9% Asian, 23% black, 43% Hispanic, 1% multiracial, 0% Pacific Islander, 17% white 5% international; 99% from in state; N/A live on campus; 1% of students in fraternities, 1% i sororities
Most popular majors: 34% Business, Management, Marketing, and Related Support Services; 25% Multi/Interdisciplinary Studies;

% Homeland Security, Law
nforcement, Firefighting and
elated Protective Services; 8%
sychology
penses: 2016-2017: $6,938
state, $18,638 out of state;
om/board: N/A
nancial aid: (713) 221-8041;
% of undergrads determined
have financial need; average
d package $10,289

niversity of
ouston–Victoria
ctoria TX
77) 970-4848
S. News ranking: Reg. U. (W),
cond tier
ebsite: www.uhv.edu/
missions email: N/A
blic; founded 1973
eshman admissions: less
lective; 2015-2016: 4,117
plied, 2,202 accepted. Neither
T nor ACT required. SAT
/75 percentile: 790-970. High
hool rank: N/A
rly decision deadline: N/A,
tification date: N/A
rly action deadline: N/A,
tification date: N/A
plication deadline (fall): rolling
dergraduate student body: 1,536
l time, 1,467 part time; 35%
ale, 65% female; 0% American
dian, 7% Asian, 17% black,
% Hispanic, 2% multiracial,
% Pacific Islander, 35% white,
% international
st popular majors: 31%
siness, Management,
arketing, and Related
pport Services; 20% Multi/
terdisciplinary Studies; 14%
alth Professions and Related
ograms; 11% Psychology;
% Computer and Information
iences and Support Services
penses: 2015-2016: $7,086
state, $18,804 out of state;
om/board: $7,664
ancial aid: (877) 970-4848

niversity of
ary Hardin-Baylor
lton TX
54) 295-4520
S. News ranking: Reg. U. (W),
. 52
ebsite: www.umhb.edu
missions email:
mission@umhb.edu
vate; founded 1845
iliation: Baptist
eshman admissions: selective;
15-2016: 7,504 applied,
033 accepted. Either SAT
ACT required. SAT 25/75
rcentile: 930-1130. High
hool rank: 20% in top tenth,
% in top quarter, 84% in
half
rly decision deadline: N/A,
tification date: N/A
rly action deadline: N/A,
tification date: N/A
plication deadline (fall): rolling
dergraduate student body: 2,933
l time, 288 part time; 37%
ale, 63% female; 1% American
dian, 2% Asian, 15% black,
% Hispanic, 3% multiracial,
% Pacific Islander, 57% white,
% international; 98% from in
ate; 55% live on campus; N/A

of students in fraternities, N/A in
sororities
Most popular majors: 27%
Health Professions and Related
Programs; 13% Education;
12% Business, Management,
Marketing, and Related Support
Services; 8% Psychology; 5%
Liberal Arts and Sciences,
General Studies and Humanities
Expenses: 2016-2017: $26,550;
room/board: $7,590
Financial aid: (254) 295-4517;
78% of undergrads determined
to have financial need; average
aid package $17,157

University of
North Texas
Denton TX
(940) 565-2681
U.S. News ranking: Nat. U.,
second tier
Website: www.unt.edu
Admissions email:
undergrad@unt.edu
Public; founded 1890
Freshman admissions: selective;
2015-2016: 16,253 applied,
11,391 accepted. Either SAT
or ACT required. SAT 25/75
percentile: 990-1200. High
school rank: 21% in top tenth,
55% in top quarter, 89% in
top half
Early decision deadline: N/A,
notification date: N/A
Early action deadline: N/A,
notification date: N/A
Application deadline (fall): 8/1
Undergraduate student body:
24,957 full time, 5,546 part
time; 48% male, 52% female;
0% American Indian, 6% Asian,
13% black, 23% Hispanic, 4%
multiracial, 0% Pacific Islander,
49% white, 3% international;
97% from in state; 20% live
on campus; 5% of students in
fraternities, 6% in sororities
Most popular majors: 20%
Business, Management,
Marketing, and Related
Support Services; 13% Multi/
Interdisciplinary Studies; 9%
Visual and Performing Arts;
6% Liberal Arts and Sciences,
General Studies and Humanities
Expenses: 2016-2017: $10,519
in state, $22,759 out of state;
room/board: $8,690
Financial aid: (940) 565-2302;
61% of undergrads determined
to have financial need; average
aid package $11,049

University of
North Texas–Dallas
Dallas TX
(972) 780-3600
U.S. News ranking: Reg. U. (W),
No. 82
Website: www.untdallas.edu/
Admissions email: N/A
Public; founded 2010
Freshman admissions: less
selective; 2015-2016: 2,001
applied, 1,169 accepted. Either
SAT or ACT required. SAT 25/75
percentile: 830-987. High school
rank: 22% in top tenth, 24% in
top quarter, 78% in top half
Early decision deadline: N/A,
notification date: N/A
Early action deadline: N/A,
notification date: N/A

Application deadline (fall): 8/10
Undergraduate student body: 1,127
full time, 825 part time; 30%
male, 70% female; 0% American
Indian, 2% Asian, 35% black,
47% Hispanic, 1% multiracial,
0% Pacific Islander, 12% white,
1% international; 99% from in
state; N/A live on campus; N/A
of students in fraternities, N/A in
sororities
Most popular majors: 44% Multi/
Interdisciplinary Studies; 28%
Health Professions and Related
Programs; 17% Homeland
Security, Law Enforcement,
Firefighting and Related
Protective Services; 6%
Social Sciences; 3% Public
Administration and Social Service
Professions
Expenses: 2015-2016: $7,650
in state, $19,549 out of state;
room/board: $7,388
Financial aid: N/A

University of
St. Thomas
Houston TX
(713) 525-3500
U.S. News ranking: Reg. U. (W),
No. 29
Website: www.stthom.edu
Admissions email:
admissions@stthom.edu
Private; founded 1947
Affiliation: Roman Catholic
Freshman admissions: selective;
2015-2016: 866 applied, 682
accepted. Either SAT or ACT
required. SAT 25/75 percentile:
980-1210. High school rank:
29% in top tenth, 53% in top
quarter, 84% in top half
Early decision deadline: N/A,
notification date: N/A
Early action deadline: 12/1,
notification date: 12/15
Application deadline (fall): 5/1
Undergraduate student body: 1,362
full time, 443 part time; 41%
male, 59% female; 0% American
Indian, 12% Asian, 7% black,
40% Hispanic, 2% multiracial,
0% Pacific Islander, 28% white,
10% international; 97% from in
state; 14% live on campus; N/A
of students in fraternities, N/A in
sororities
Most popular majors: 24%
Business, Management,
Marketing, and Related Support
Services; 14% Biological and
Biomedical Sciences; 12% Social
Sciences; 8% Health Professions
and Related Programs; 7%
Liberal Arts and Sciences,
General Studies and Humanities
Expenses: 2016-2017: $31,520;
room/board: $8,500
Financial aid: (713) 525-2170;
57% of undergrads determined
to have financial need; average
aid package $22,061

University of
Texas–Arlington
Arlington TX
(817) 272-6287
U.S. News ranking: Nat. U.,
second tier
Website: www.uta.edu
Admissions email:
admissions@uta.edu
Public; founded 1895

Freshman admissions: selective;
2015-2016: 11,196 applied,
7,142 accepted. Either SAT
or ACT required. SAT 25/75
percentile: 950-1200. High
school rank: 32% in top tenth,
57% in top quarter, 98% in
top half
Early decision deadline: N/A,
notification date: N/A
Early action deadline: N/A,
notification date: N/A
Application deadline (fall): rolling
Undergraduate student body:
16,416 full time, 14,217 part
time; 40% male, 60% female;
0% American Indian, 11% Asian,
15% black, 25% Hispanic, 3%
multiracial, 0% Pacific Islander,
40% white, 5% international;
87% from in state; 11% live
on campus; 3% of students in
fraternities, 2% in sororities
Most popular majors: 39%
Health Professions and Related
Programs; 12% Business,
Management, Marketing, and
Related Support Services; 6%
Liberal Arts and Sciences,
General Studies and Humanities;
6% Biological and Biomedical
Sciences; 5% Engineering
Expenses: 2016-2017: $9,616
in state, $23,460 out of state;
room/board: $8,397
Financial aid: (817) 272-3568;
77% of undergrads determined
to have financial need; average
aid package $10,692

University of
Texas–Austin
Austin TX
(512) 475-7440
U.S. News ranking: Nat. U.,
No. 56
Website: www.utexas.edu
Admissions email: N/A
Public; founded 1883
Freshman admissions: more
selective; 2015-2016: 43,592
applied, 17,006 accepted.
Either SAT or ACT required. SAT
25/75 percentile: 1170-1390.
High school rank: 72% in top
tenth, 92% in top quarter, 98%
in top half
Early decision deadline: N/A,
notification date: N/A
Early action deadline: N/A,
notification date: N/A
Application deadline (fall): 12/1
Undergraduate student body:
36,565 full time, 3,054 part
time; 48% male, 52% female;
0% American Indian, 20% Asian,
4% black, 22% Hispanic, 4%
multiracial, 0% Pacific Islander,
44% white, 5% international;
95% from in state; 19% live
on campus; 15% of students in
fraternities, 18% in sororities
Most popular majors: 12%
Engineering; 12% Social
Sciences; 11% Business,
Management, Marketing, and
Related Support Services; 10%
Biological and Biomedical
Sciences
Expenses: 2016-2017: $9,806
in state, $34,676 out of state;
room/board: $11,456
Financial aid: (512) 475-6203;
42% of undergrads determined
to have financial need; average
aid package $12,717

University of
Texas–Dallas
Richardson TX
(972) 883-2270
U.S. News ranking: Nat. U.,
No. 146
Website: www.utdallas.edu
Admissions email:
interest@utdallas.edu
Public; founded 1969
Freshman admissions: more
selective; 2015-2016: 11,237
applied, 6,909 accepted. Either
SAT or ACT required. SAT 25/75
percentile: 1160-1370. High
school rank: 33% in top tenth,
64% in top quarter, 88% in
top half
Early decision deadline: N/A,
notification date: N/A
Early action deadline: N/A,
notification date: N/A
Application deadline (fall): 7/1
Undergraduate student body:
12,754 full time, 2,821 part
time; 57% male, 43% female;
0% American Indian, 29% Asian,
6% black, 18% Hispanic, 4%
multiracial, 0% Pacific Islander,
37% white, 3% international;
97% from in state; 27% live
on campus; 2% of students in
fraternities, 3% in sororities
Most popular majors: 28%
Business, Management,
Marketing, and Related Support
Services; 15% Biological and
Biomedical Sciences; 10%
Engineering; 8% Computer
and Information Sciences and
Support Services; 7% Psychology
Expenses: 2016-2017: $12,162
in state, $33,654 out of state;
room/board: $10,668
Financial aid: (972) 883-2941;
54% of undergrads determined
to have financial need; average
aid package $12,895

University of
Texas–El Paso
El Paso TX
(915) 747-5890
U.S. News ranking: Nat. U.,
second tier
Website: www.utep.edu
Admissions email:
futureminer@utep.edu
Public; founded 1914
Freshman admissions: less
selective; 2015-2016: 7,134
applied, 7,133 accepted. Either
SAT or ACT required. SAT 25/75
percentile: 820-1050. High
school rank: 18% in top tenth,
41% in top quarter, 69% in
top half
Early decision deadline: N/A,
notification date: N/A
Early action deadline: N/A,
notification date: N/A
Application deadline (fall): rolling
Undergraduate student body:
13,079 full time, 7,141 part
time; 46% male, 54% female;
0% American Indian, 1% Asian,
3% black, 83% Hispanic, 1%
multiracial, 0% Pacific Islander,
7% white, 5% international;
96% from in state; N/A live
on campus; N/A of students in
fraternities, N/A in sororities
Most popular majors: 18%
Business, Management,
Marketing, and Related Support
Services; 14% Health Professions

and Related Programs; 9% Engineering; 9% Multi/Interdisciplinary Studies; 8% Biological and Biomedical Sciences
Expenses: 2015-2016: $7,058 in state, $18,759 out of state; room/board: $9,114
Financial aid: (915) 747-5204; 79% of undergrads determined to have financial need; average aid package $12,613

University of Texas of the Permian Basin
Odessa TX
(432) 552-2605
U.S. News ranking: Reg. U. (W), No. 93
Website: www.utpb.edu
Admissions email: admissions@utpb.edu
Public; founded 1973
Freshman admissions: selective; 2015-2016: 1,154 applied, 975 accepted. Either SAT or ACT required. SAT 25/75 percentile: 880-1070. High school rank: 24% in top tenth, 54% in top quarter, 89% in top half
Early decision deadline: N/A, notification date: N/A
Early action deadline: N/A, notification date: N/A
Application deadline (fall): 8/24
Undergraduate student body: 2,138 full time, 3,026 part time; 44% male, 56% female; 1% American Indian, 2% Asian, 7% black, 47% Hispanic, 1% multiracial, 0% Pacific Islander, 41% white, 1% international; 96% from in state; 22% live on campus; 0% of students in fraternities, 0% in sororities
Most popular majors: 24% Business Administration and Management, General; 11% Psychology, General; 10% Multi-/Interdisciplinary Studies, Other; 8% Sociology; 7% Kinesiology and Exercise Science
Expenses: 2016-2017: $6,852 in state, $7,866 out of state; room/board: $10,800
Financial aid: (432) 552-2620; 61% of undergrads determined to have financial need; average aid package $10,440

University of Texas–Rio Grande Valley[1]
Edinburg TX
(956) 882-8983
U.S. News ranking: Nat. U., unranked
Website: www.utrgv.edu/en-us/
Admissions email: N/A
Public
Application deadline (fall): N/A
Undergraduate student body: N/A full time, N/A part time
Expenses: 2015-2016: $7,292 in state, $16,652 out of state; room/board: $7,632
Financial aid: N/A

University of Texas–San Antonio
San Antonio TX
(210) 458-4599
U.S. News ranking: Nat. U., second tier
Website: www.utsa.edu
Admissions email: prospects@utsa.edu
Public; founded 1969
Freshman admissions: selective; 2015-2016: 15,706 applied, 12,243 accepted. Either SAT or ACT required. SAT 25/75 percentile: 930-1150. High school rank: 19% in top tenth, 62% in top quarter, 92% in top half
Early decision deadline: N/A, notification date: N/A
Early action deadline: N/A, notification date: N/A
Application deadline (fall): 6/1
Undergraduate student body: 20,234 full time, 4,228 part time; 51% male, 49% female; 0% American Indian, 6% Asian, 9% black, 53% Hispanic, 3% multiracial, 0% Pacific Islander, 25% white, 3% international; 98% from in state; 14% live on campus; 4% of students in fraternities, 5% in sororities
Most popular majors: 25% Business, Management, Marketing, and Related Support Services; 7% Education; 7% Biological and Biomedical Sciences; 7% Engineering; 6% Parks, Recreation, Leisure, and Fitness Studies
Expenses: 2016-2017: $9,044 in state, $22,290 out of state; room/board: $8,074
Financial aid: (210) 458-8000; 66% of undergrads determined to have financial need; average aid package $9,516

University of Texas–Tyler
Tyler TX
(903) 566-7203
U.S. News ranking: Reg. U. (W), No. 88
Website: www.uttyler.edu
Admissions email: admrequest@uttyler.edu
Public; founded 1971
Freshman admissions: selective; 2015-2016: 2,468 applied, 1,591 accepted. Either SAT or ACT required. SAT 25/75 percentile: 970-1160. High school rank: 10% in top tenth, 35% in top quarter, 64% in top half
Early decision deadline: N/A, notification date: N/A
Early action deadline: N/A, notification date: N/A
Application deadline (fall): N/A
Undergraduate student body: 4,569 full time, 1,749 part time; 43% male, 57% female; 0% American Indian, 3% Asian, 9% black, 16% Hispanic, 8% multiracial, 0% Pacific Islander, 58% white, 2% international
Most popular majors: 21% Business, Management, Marketing, and Related Support Services; 21% Health Professions and Related Programs; 10% Multi/Interdisciplinary Studies;

8% Parks, Recreation, Leisure, and Fitness Studies; 7% Engineering
Expenses: 2015-2016: $7,321 in state, $19,236 out of state; room/board: $7,775
Financial aid: (903) 566-7180

University of the Incarnate Word
San Antonio TX
(210) 829-6005
U.S. News ranking: Reg. U. (W), No. 44
Website: www.uiw.edu
Admissions email: admis@uiwtx.edu
Private; founded 1881
Affiliation: Roman Catholic
Freshman admissions: less selective; 2015-2016: 4,050 applied, 3,735 accepted. Either SAT or ACT required. SAT 25/75 percentile: 860-1060. High school rank: 16% in top tenth, 40% in top quarter, 70% in top half
Early decision deadline: N/A, notification date: N/A
Early action deadline: N/A, notification date: N/A
Application deadline (fall): rolling
Undergraduate student body: 4,286 full time, 2,159 part time; 39% male, 61% female; 0% American Indian, 2% Asian, 7% black, 59% Hispanic, 1% multiracial, 0% Pacific Islander, 19% white, 5% international; 94% from in state; 18% live on campus; N/A of students in fraternities, N/A in sororities
Most popular majors: 14% Biology/Biological Sciences, General; 9% Registered Nursing/Registered Nurse; 6% Psychology, General; 5% Accounting; 4% Elementary Education and Teaching
Expenses: 2016-2017: $28,898; room/board: $11,880
Financial aid: (210) 829-6008; 74% of undergrads determined to have financial need; average aid package $21,045

West Texas A&M University
Canyon TX
(806) 651-2020
U.S. News ranking: Reg. U. (W), No. 91
Website: www.wtamu.edu
Admissions email: admissions@mail.wtamu.edu
Public; founded 1910
Freshman admissions: selective; 2015-2016: 5,557 applied, 3,717 accepted. Either SAT or ACT required. ACT 25/75 percentile: 18-23. High school rank: 14% in top tenth, 39% in top quarter, 75% in top half
Early decision deadline: N/A, notification date: N/A
Early action deadline: N/A, notification date: N/A
Application deadline (fall): rolling
Undergraduate student body: 5,681 full time, 1,598 part time; 45% male, 55% female; 1% American Indian, 1% Asian, 6% black, 27% Hispanic, 2% multiracial, 0% Pacific Islander, 60% white, 2% international; N/A from in state; N/A live on campus; 4% of students in fraternities, 5% in sororities
Most popular majors: 15% Business, Management, Marketing, and Related Support Services; 12% Multi/Interdisciplinary Studies; 11% Health Professions and Related Programs; 10% Liberal Arts and Sciences, General Studies and Humanities
Expenses: 2016-2017: $7,936 in state, $8,959 out of state; room/board: $7,196
Financial aid: (806) 651-2055; 61% of undergrads determined to have financial need; average aid package $8,609

applied, 544 accepted. Either SAT or ACT required. ACT 25/75 percentile: 16-23. High school rank: 10% in top tenth, 26% in top quarter, 56% in top half
Early decision deadline: N/A, notification date: N/A
Early action deadline: N/A, notification date: N/A
Application deadline (fall): rolling
Undergraduate student body: 1,045 full time, 2,776 part time; 52% male, 48% female; 1% American Indian, 2% Asian, 17% black, 28% Hispanic, 4% multiracial, 1% Pacific Islander, 42% white, 1% international; 68% from in state; 18% live on campus; 1% of students in fraternities, 2% in sororities
Most popular majors: 38% Business Administration and Management, General; 27% Liberal Arts and Sciences, General Studies and Humanities, Other; 8% Criminal Justice/Law Enforcement Administration; 8% Registered Nursing/Registered Nurse
Expenses: 2016-2017: $19,110; room/board: $7,296
Financial aid: (806) 291-3520; 69% of undergrads determined to have financial need; average aid package $13,254

Wade College[1]
Dallas TX
(888) 582-7042
U.S. News ranking: Reg. Coll. (W), unranked
Website: www.wadecollege.edu/
Admissions email: N/A
For-profit
Application deadline (fall): N/A
Undergraduate student body: N/A full time, N/A part time
Expenses: 2015-2016: $13,310; room/board: N/A
Financial aid: N/A

Wayland Baptist University
Plainview TX
(806) 291-3500
U.S. News ranking: Reg. U. (W), second tier
Website: www.wbu.edu
Admissions email: admityou@wbu.edu
Private; founded 1908
Affiliation: Southern Baptist Convention
Freshman admissions: less selective; 2015-2016: 550

Wiley College[1]
Marshall TX
(800) 658-6889
U.S. News ranking: Reg. Coll. (W), second tier
Website: www.wileyc.edu
Admissions email: admissions@wileyc.edu
Private; founded 1873
Affiliation: United Methodist
Application deadline (fall): rolling
Undergraduate student body: N/A full time, N/A part time
Expenses: 2015-2016: $11,828; room/board: $6,676
Financial aid: (903) 927-3210

UTAH

Brigham Young University–Provo
Provo UT
(801) 422-2507
U.S. News ranking: Nat. U., No. 68
Website: www.byu.edu
Admissions email: admissions@byu.edu
Private; founded 1875
Affiliation: Church of Jesus Christ of Latter-day Saints
Freshman admissions: more selective; 2015-2016: 13,376 applied, 6,427 accepted. Either SAT or ACT required. ACT 25/75 percentile: 27-31. High school rank: 54% in top tenth, 85% in top quarter, 98% in top half
Early decision deadline: N/A, notification date: N/A
Early action deadline: N/A, notification date: N/A
Application deadline (fall): 2/1
Undergraduate student body: 27,339 full time, 2,882 part time; 52% male, 48% female; 0% American Indian, 2% Asian, 0% black, 6% Hispanic, 4% multiracial, 1% Pacific Islander, 83% white, 3% international; 35% from in state; 19% live on campus; N/A of students in fraternities, N/A in sororities
Most popular majors: 12% Biological and Biomedical Sciences; 12% Business, Management, Marketing, and Related Support Services; 8% Education; 8% Health Professions and Related Programs; 8% Social Sciences
Expenses: 2016-2017: $5,300; room/board: $7,448
Financial aid: (801) 422-4104; 49% of undergrads determined to have financial need; average aid package $7,392

Dixie State University
Saint George UT
(435) 652-7702
U.S. News ranking: Reg. Coll. (W), unranked
Website: www.dixie.edu
Admissions email: admissions@dixie.edu
Public; founded 1911
Freshman admissions: N/A; 2015-2016: 4,041 applied, 4,041 accepted. Neither SAT nor ACT required. ACT 25/75 percentile 18-23. High school rank: 10% in top tenth, 28% in top quarter, 61% in top half

arly decision deadline: N/A,
otification date: N/A
arly action deadline: N/A,
otification date: N/A
pplication deadline (fall): 8/15
ndergraduate student body: 5,324
ll time, 3,179 part time; 47%
ale, 53% female; 1% American
dian, 1% Asian, 3% black,
1% Hispanic, 3% multiracial,
% Pacific Islander, 76% white,
% international; 81% from in
ate; 4% live on campus; N/A
* students in fraternities, N/A in
rorities
ost popular majors: 20%
usiness, Management,
arketing, and Related Support
ervices; 9% Education; 8%
ulti/Interdisciplinary Studies;
% Biological and Biomedical
ciences
xpenses: 2016-2017: $4,840
state, $13,855 out of state;
om/board: $5,615
nancial aid: (435) 652-7575;
4% of undergrads determined
have financial need; average
d package $10,014

now College[1]
phraim UT
35) 283-7144
S. News ranking: Reg. Coll. (W),
ranked
ebsite: www.snow.edu
lmissions email: N/A
blic
plication deadline (fall): N/A
ndergraduate student body: N/A
ll time, N/A part time
xpenses: 2015-2016: $3,484
state, $11,676 out of state;
om/board: $5,200
nancial aid: N/A

outhern Utah
niversity
edar City UT
35) 586-7740
S. News ranking: Reg. U. (W),
. 68
ebsite: www.suu.edu
dmissions email:
dmissionsinfo@suu.edu
blic; founded 1897
eshman admissions: selective;
015-2016: 8,387 applied,
050 accepted. Either SAT
ACT required. ACT 25/75
rcentile: 20-27. High school
nk: 18% in top tenth, 47% in
p quarter, 77% in top half
rly decision deadline: N/A
tification date: N/A
rly action deadline: N/A,
tification date: N/A
pplication deadline (fall): 5/1
ndergraduate student body: 5,647
ll time, 2,388 part time; 43%
ale, 57% female; 1% American
dian, 1% Asian, 2% black,
% Hispanic, 1% multiracial,
% Pacific Islander, 77% white,
% international; 79% from in
ate; 10% live on campus; N/A
students in fraternities, N/A in
rorities
ost popular majors: 19%
ducation; 13% Business,
anagement, Marketing, and
elated Support Services; 7%
ealth Professions and Related
ograms; 7% Visual and
erforming Arts; 6% Psychology

Expenses: 2016-2017: $6,530
in state, $19,810 out of state;
room/board: $7,067
Financial aid: (435) 586-7735;
62% of undergrads determined
to have financial need; average
aid package $11,356

University of Utah
Salt Lake City UT
(801) 581-8761
U.S. News ranking: Nat. U.,
No. 111
Website: www.utah.edu
Admissions email:
admissions@utah.edu
Public; founded 1850
Freshman admissions: more
selective; 2015-2016: 12,174
applied, 9,913 accepted. Either
SAT or ACT required. ACT 25/75
percentile: 21-28. High school
rank: 25% in top tenth, 53% in
top quarter, 86% in top half
Early decision deadline: N/A,
notification date: N/A
Early action deadline: 12/1,
notification date: 1/15
Application deadline (fall): 4/1
Undergraduate student body:
16,927 full time, 6,867 part
time; 56% male, 44% female;
0% American Indian, 6% Asian,
1% black, 11% Hispanic, 4%
multiracial, 1% Pacific Islander,
70% white, 6% international;
80% from in state; 13% live
on campus; 5% of students in
fraternities, 8% in sororities
Most popular majors: 7%
Psychology, General; 5%
Economics, General; 4% Human
Development and Family Studies,
General; 4% Kinesiology and
Exercise Science
Expenses: 2016-2017: $8,518
in state, $27,039 out of state;
room/board: $9,425
Financial aid: (801) 581-8788;
49% of undergrads determined
to have financial need; average
aid package $18,217

Utah State University
Logan UT
(435) 797-1079
U.S. News ranking: Nat. U.,
No. 220
Website: www.usu.edu
Admissions email: admit@usu.edu
Public; founded 1888
Freshman admissions: selective;
2015-2016: 16,158 applied,
15,620 accepted. Either SAT
or ACT required. ACT 25/75
percentile: 20-27. High school
rank: 21% in top tenth, 44% in
top quarter, 75% in top half
Early decision deadline: N/A,
notification date: N/A
Early action deadline: N/A,
notification date: N/A
Application deadline (fall): rolling
Undergraduate student body:
17,091 full time, 8,168 part
time; 47% male, 53% female;
2% American Indian, 1% Asian,
1% black, 6% Hispanic, 2%
multiracial, 0% Pacific Islander,
81% white, 2% international;
73% from in state; N/A live
on campus; 2% of students in
fraternities, 2% in sororities
Most popular majors: 10%
Communication Sciences and

Disorders, General; 8%
Economics, General; 4%
Physical Education Teaching
and Coaching; 4% Multi-/
Interdisciplinary Studies, Other;
4% Business Administration and
Management, General
Expenses: 2016-2017: $6,866
in state, $19,772 out of state;
room/board: $5,870
Financial aid: (435) 797-0173;
55% of undergrads determined
to have financial need; average
aid package $6,633

Utah Valley University
Orem UT
(801) 863-8466
U.S. News ranking: Reg. U. (W),
unranked
Website: www.uvu.edu/
Admissions email:
InstantInfo@uvu.edu
Public; founded 1941
Freshman admissions: N/A; 2015-
2016: 9,183 applied, 9,178
accepted. Neither SAT nor ACT
required. ACT 25/75 percentile:
18-24. High school rank: 8% in
top tenth, 25% in top quarter,
56% in top half
Early decision deadline: N/A,
notification date: N/A
Early action deadline: N/A,
notification date: N/A
Application deadline (fall): 8/1
Undergraduate student body:
17,173 full time, 15,853 part
time; 55% male, 45% female;
1% American Indian, 1% Asian,
1% black, 10% Hispanic, 3%
multiracial, 1% Pacific Islander,
77% white, 2% international;
84% from in state; N/A live
on campus; N/A of students in
fraternities, N/A in sororities
Most popular majors: 19%
Business, Management,
Marketing, and Related Support
Services; 12% Education; 10%
Psychology; 8% Transportation
and Materials Moving; 7%
Computer and Information
Sciences and Support Services
Expenses: 2016-2017: $5,530
in state, $15,690 out of state;
room/board: N/A
Financial aid: (801) 863-8442;
61% of undergrads determined
to have financial need; average
aid package $7,767

Weber State University
Ogden UT
(801) 626-6744
U.S. News ranking: Reg. U. (W),
No. 76
Website: weber.edu
Admissions email:
admissions@weber.edu
Public; founded 1889
Freshman admissions: selective;
2015-2016: 5,738 applied,
5,738 accepted. Neither SAT
nor ACT required. ACT 25/75
percentile: 18-24. High school
rank: 11% in top tenth, 29% in
top quarter, 60% in top half
Early decision deadline: N/A,
notification date: N/A
Early action deadline: N/A,
notification date: N/A
Application deadline (fall): 8/31

Undergraduate student body:
10,958 full time, 15,360 part
time; 45% male, 55% female;
1% American Indian, 2% Asian,
2% black, 10% Hispanic, 2%
multiracial, 1% Pacific Islander,
67% white, 2% international;
90% from in state; 4% live
on campus; 1% of students in
fraternities, 1% in sororities
Most popular majors: 14%
Registered Nursing/Registered
Nurse; 5% Selling Skills and
Sales Operations; 4% Computer
Science; 3% Accounting; 3%
Criminal Justice/Safety Studies
Expenses: 2016-2017: $5,524
in state, $14,750 out of state;
room/board: $8,000
Financial aid: (801) 626-7569;
60% of undergrads determined
to have financial need; average
aid package $6,056

Western Governors University[1]
Salt Lake City UT
(866) 225-5948
U.S. News ranking: Reg. U. (W),
unranked
Website: www.wgu.edu/
Admissions email: info@wgu.edu
Private; founded 1996
Application deadline (fall): rolling
Undergraduate student body: N/A
full time, N/A part time
Expenses: 2015-2016: $6,070;
room/board: N/A
Financial aid: (801) 327-8104

Westminster College
Salt Lake City UT
(801) 832-2200
U.S. News ranking: Reg. U. (W),
No. 20
Website:
www.westminstercollege.edu
Admissions email: admission@
westminstercollege.edu
Private; founded 1875
Freshman admissions: selective;
2015-2016: 2,001 applied,
1,920 accepted. Either SAT
or ACT required. ACT 25/75
percentile: 22-27. High school
rank: 20% in top tenth, 53% in
top quarter, 84% in top half
Early decision deadline: N/A,
notification date: N/A
Early action deadline: N/A,
notification date: N/A
Application deadline (fall): 8/16
Undergraduate student body: 2,037
full time, 122 part time; 44%
male, 56% female; 0% American
Indian, 2% Asian, 2% black,
10% Hispanic, 4% multiracial,
0% Pacific Islander, 73% white,
5% international; 60% from in
state; 32% live on campus; N/A
of students in fraternities, N/A in
sororities
Most popular majors: 24%
Business, Management,
Marketing, and Related Support
Services; 21% Health Professions
and Related Programs; 8%
Social Sciences; 7% Psychology;
6% Biological and Biomedical
Sciences
Expenses: 2016-2017: $32,104;
room/board: $8,974
Financial aid: (801) 832-2500;
59% of undergrads determined
to have financial need; average
aid package $23,686

Bennington College
Bennington VT
(800) 833-6845
U.S. News ranking: Nat. Lib. Arts,
No. 90
Website: www.bennington.edu
Admissions email: admissions@
bennington.edu
Private; founded 1932
Freshman admissions: more
selective; 2015-2016: 1,099
applied, 692 accepted. Neither
SAT nor ACT required. SAT
25/75 percentile: 1140-1400.
High school rank: N/A
Early decision deadline: 11/15,
notification date: 12/20
Early action deadline: 12/1,
notification date: 2/1
Application deadline (fall): 1/3
Undergraduate student body: 680
full time, 24 part time; 35%
male, 65% female; 1% American
Indian, 2% Asian, 2% black,
6% Hispanic, 5% multiracial,
0% Pacific Islander, 65% white,
13% international; 2% from in
state; 97% live on campus; 0%
of students in fraternities, 0% in
sororities
Most popular majors: 32%
Visual and Performing Arts;
20% English Language and
Literature/Letters; 10% Social
Sciences; 9% Foreign Languages,
Literatures, and Linguistics; 6%
Psychology
Expenses: 2016-2017: $50,570;
room/board: $14,520
Financial aid: (802) 440-4325;
66% of undergrads determined
to have financial need; average
aid package $38,747

Burlington College[1]
Burlington VT
(802) 862-9616
U.S. News ranking: Nat. Lib. Arts,
second tier
Website: www.burlington.edu
Admissions email: admissions@
burlington.edu
Private; founded 1972
Application deadline (fall): rolling
Undergraduate student body: N/A
full time, N/A part time
Expenses: 2016-2017: $21,500;
room/board: N/A
Financial aid: (802) 862-9616

Castleton State College[1]
Castleton VT
(800) 639-8521
U.S. News ranking: Reg. Coll.
(N), No. 9
Website: www.castleton.edu
Admissions email:
info@castleton.edu
Public; founded 1787
Application deadline (fall): rolling
Undergraduate student body: N/A
full time, N/A part time
Expenses: 2015-2016: $11,282
in state, $26,690 out of state;
room/board: $9,696
Financial aid: (802) 468-1292

Champlain College
Burlington VT
(800) 570-5858
U.S. News ranking: Reg. U. (N),
No. 91
Website: www.champlain.edu
Admissions email: admission@
champlain.edu
Private; founded 1878
Freshman admissions: selective;
2015-2016: 5,587 applied,
3,697 accepted. Either SAT
or ACT required. SAT 25/75
percentile: 1030-1260. High
school rank: 10% in top tenth,
34% in top quarter, 77% in
top half
Early decision deadline: 11/1,
notification date: 12/1
Early action deadline: N/A,
notification date: N/A
Application deadline (fall): 1/15
Undergraduate student body: 2,373
full time, 1,027 part time; 59%
male, 41% female; 0% American
Indian, 2% Asian, 5% black,
5% Hispanic, 3% multiracial,
0% Pacific Islander, 70% white,
1% international; 22% from in
state; 64% live on campus; N/A
of students in fraternities, N/A in
sororities
Most popular majors: 12%
Business Administration and
Management, General; 7%
Cyber/Computer Forensics
and Counterterrorism; 6%
Accounting; 6% Graphic Design
Expenses: 2016-2017: $38,660;
room/board: $14,472
Financial aid: (800) 570-5858;
69% of undergrads determined
to have financial need; average
aid package $24,860

College of St. Joseph
Rutland VT
(802) 773-5286
U.S. News ranking: Reg. Coll. (N),
second tier
Website: www.csj.edu
Admissions email:
admissions@csj.edu
Private; founded 1956
Affiliation: Roman Catholic
Freshman admissions: least
selective; 2015-2016: 231
applied, 161 accepted. Neither
SAT nor ACT required. SAT
25/75 percentile: 783-923.
High school rank: 2% in top
tenth, 10% in top quarter, 47%
in top half
Early decision deadline: N/A,
notification date: N/A
Early action deadline: N/A,
notification date: N/A
Application deadline (fall): 8/15
Undergraduate student body: 201
full time, 54 part time; 53%
male, 47% female; N/A American
Indian, N/A Asian, 27% black,
13% Hispanic, N/A multiracial,
N/A Pacific Islander, 61% white,
N/A international
Most popular majors: 20%
Business Administration and
Management, General; 10%
Accounting; 10% Psychology,
General; 10% Public
Administration and Social
Service Professions; 10%
Radiologic Technology/Science -
Radiographer
Expenses: 2016-2017: $22,550;
room/board: $11,250

Financial aid: (802) 773-5900;
95% of undergrads determined
to have financial need; average
aid package $25,775

Goddard College
Plainfield VT
(800) 906-8312
U.S. News ranking: Reg. U. (N),
unranked
Website: www.goddard.edu
Admissions email:
admissions@goddard.edu
Private; founded 1863
Freshman admissions: N/A;
2015-2016: N/A applied, N/A
accepted. Neither SAT nor ACT
required. ACT 25/75 percentile:
N/A. High school rank: N/A
Early decision deadline: N/A,
notification date: N/A
Early action deadline: N/A,
notification date: N/A
Application deadline (fall): rolling
Undergraduate student body: 177
full time, 7 part time; 36% male,
64% female; N/A American
Indian, N/A Asian, N/A black,
N/A Hispanic, N/A multiracial,
N/A Pacific Islander, N/A white,
N/A international; 29% from in
state; N/A live on campus; N/A
of students in fraternities, N/A in
sororities
Most popular majors: Information
not available
Expenses: 2016-2017: $15,786;
room/board: $1,598
Financial aid: (800) 468-4888;
76% of undergrads determined
to have financial need; average
aid package $8,221

Green Mountain College
Poultney VT
(802) 287-8208
U.S. News ranking: Reg. U. (N),
second tier
Website: www.greenmtn.edu
Admissions email:
admiss@greenmtn.edu
Private; founded 1834
Affiliation: United Methodist
Freshman admissions: less
selective; 2015-2016: 825
applied, 544 accepted. Neither
SAT nor ACT required. ACT
25/75 percentile: N/A. High
school rank: N/A
Early decision deadline: N/A,
notification date: N/A
Early action deadline: 11/1,
notification date: 12/14
Application deadline (fall): rolling
Undergraduate student body: 571
full time, 26 part time; 49%
male, 51% female; 1% American
Indian, 1% Asian, 4% black,
3% Hispanic, 1% multiracial,
N/A Pacific Islander, 53% white,
3% international; 15% from in
state; 85% live on campus; 0%
of students in fraternities, 0% in
sororities
Most popular majors: 18% Resort
Management; 11% Parks,
Recreation and Leisure Studies;
10% Resort Management; 8%
Business/Managerial Economics
Expenses: 2015-2016: $35,340;
room/board: $11,492
Financial aid: (802) 287-8210

Johnson State College
Johnson VT
(800) 635-2356
U.S. News ranking: Reg. U. (N),
second tier
Website: www.jsc.edu
Admissions email:
JSCAdmissions@jsc.edu
Public; founded 1828
Freshman admissions: less
selective; 2015-2016: N/A
applied, N/A accepted. Neither
SAT nor ACT required. ACT
25/75 percentile: N/A. High
school rank: N/A
Early decision deadline: N/A,
notification date: N/A
Early action deadline: N/A,
notification date: N/A
Application deadline (fall): rolling
Undergraduate student body: 949
full time, 410 part time; 33%
male, 67% female; 1% American
Indian, 1% Asian, 3% black, 3%
Hispanic, 3% multiracial, 0%
Pacific Islander, 81% white, 1%
international
Most popular majors: Information
not available
Expenses: 2015-2016: $11,018
in state, $23,714 out of state;
room/board: $9,696
Financial aid: (802) 635-1380

Landmark College[1]
Putney VT
(802) 387-6718
U.S. News ranking: Reg. Coll. (N),
unranked
Website: www.landmark.edu/
Admissions email: N/A
Private
Application deadline (fall): N/A
Undergraduate student body: N/A
full time, N/A part time
Expenses: 2015-2016: $51,330;
room/board: $10,710
Financial aid: N/A

Lyndon State College[1]
Lyndonville VT
(802) 626-6413
U.S. News ranking: Reg. Coll. (N),
second tier
Website: www.lyndonstate.edu
Admissions email: admissions@
lyndonstate.edu
Public; founded 1911
Application deadline (fall): rolling
Undergraduate student body: N/A
full time, N/A part time
Expenses: 2015-2016: $11,018
in state, $22,418 out of state;
room/board: $9,696
Financial aid: (802) 626-6218

Marlboro College
Marlboro VT
(800) 343-0049
U.S. News ranking: Nat. Lib. Arts,
No. 128
Website: www.marlboro.edu
Admissions email:
admissions@marlboro.edu
Private; founded 1946
Freshman admissions: selective;
2015-2016: 144 applied, 136
accepted. Neither SAT nor ACT
required. SAT 25/75 percentile:
1090-1360. High school rank:
17% in top tenth, 33% in top
quarter, 67% in top half
Early decision deadline: 11/15,
notification date: 12/1

Johnson State College (duplicate col)

Early action deadline: 1/15,
notification date: 2/1
Application deadline (fall): rolling
Undergraduate student body: 179
full time, 13 part time; 51%
male, 49% female; 1% American
Indian, 1% Asian, 0% black,
1% Hispanic, 5% multiracial,
0% Pacific Islander, 77% white,
2% international; 12% from in
state; 78% live on campus; 0%
of students in fraternities, 0% in
sororities
Most popular majors: 25% Visual
and Performing Arts; 18%
English Language and Literature/
Letters; 12% Social Sciences;
9% Philosophy and Religious
Studies
Expenses: 2016-2017: $40,030;
room/board: $10,802
Financial aid: (802) 258-9237;
83% of undergrads determined
to have financial need; average
aid package $31,863

Middlebury College
Middlebury VT
(802) 443-3000
U.S. News ranking: Nat. Lib. Arts,
No. 4
Website: www.middlebury.edu
Admissions email: admissions@
middlebury.edu
Private; founded 1800
Freshman admissions: most
selective; 2015-2016: 8,891
applied, 1,551 accepted. Either
SAT or ACT required. SAT 25/75
percentile: 1270-1500. High
school rank: 79% in top tenth,
95% in top quarter, 99% in
top half
Early decision deadline: 11/1,
notification date: 12/15
Early action deadline: N/A,
notification date: N/A
Application deadline (fall): 1/1
Undergraduate student body: 2,516
full time, 26 part time; 47%
male, 53% female; 0% American
Indian, 6% Asian, 3% black,
9% Hispanic, 5% multiracial,
0% Pacific Islander, 65% white,
11% international; 7% from in
state; 95% live on campus; 0%
of students in fraternities, 0% in
sororities
Most popular majors: 15%
Economics, General; 6% English
Language and Literature/Letters,
Other; 5% International/Global
Studies; 5% Psychology, General
Expenses: 2016-2017: $50,063;
room/board: $14,269
Financial aid: (802) 443-5158;
45% of undergrads determined
to have financial need; average
aid package $44,436

Norwich University
Northfield VT
(800) 468-6679
U.S. News ranking: Reg. U. (N),
No. 80
Website: www.norwich.edu
Admissions email:
nuadm@norwich.edu
Private; founded 1819
Freshman admissions: selective;
2015-2016: 3,530 applied,
2,016 accepted. Neither SAT
nor ACT required. SAT 25/75
percentile: 940-1160. High
school rank: 12% in top tenth,
38% in top quarter, 72% in
top half

Southern Vermont College (upper col)

Early decision deadline: N/A,
notification date: N/A
Early action deadline: N/A,
notification date: N/A
Application deadline (fall): rolling
Undergraduate student body: 2,28
full time, 577 part time; 78%
male, 22% female; 0% American
Indian, 3% Asian, 3% black,
7% Hispanic, 5% multiracial,
0% Pacific Islander, 77% white
2% international; 15% from in
state; 68% live on campus; N/A
of students in fraternities, N/A in
sororities
Most popular majors: 17%
Criminal Justice/Law
Enforcement Administration;
14% Intelligence, General; 6%
History, General; 6% Registered
Nursing/Registered Nurse; 5%
Business Administration and
Management, General
Expenses: 2016-2017: $37,354
room/board: $12,920
Financial aid: (802) 485-2015;
74% of undergrads determined
to have financial need; average
aid package $31,084

Southern Vermont College[1]
Bennington VT
(802) 447-6304
U.S. News ranking: Reg. Coll. (N)
second tier
Website: www.svc.edu
Admissions email: admis@svc.ed
Private; founded 1974
Application deadline (fall): N/A
Undergraduate student body: N/A
full time, N/A part time
Expenses: 2016-2017: $23,82(
room/board: $10,800
Financial aid: (877) 563-6076

Sterling College[1]
Craftsbury Common VT
(802) 586-7711
U.S. News ranking: Nat. Lib. Arts
unranked
Website: www.sterlingcollege.edi
Admissions email: admissions@
sterlingcollege.edu
Private; founded 1958
Application deadline (fall): rolling
Undergraduate student body: N/A
full time, N/A part time
Expenses: 2015-2016: $34,89(
room/board: $9,104
Financial aid: (802) 586-7711

St. Michael's College
Colchester VT
(800) 762-8000
U.S. News ranking: Nat. Lib. Arts
No. 99
Website: www.smcvt.edu
Admissions email:
admission@smcvt.edu
Private; founded 1904
Affiliation: Roman Catholic
Freshman admissions: selective;
2015-2016: 4,767 applied,
3,621 accepted. Neither SAT
nor ACT required. SAT 25/75
percentile: 1070-1260. High
school rank: 26% in top tenth,
56% in top quarter, 82% in
top half
Early decision deadline: N/A,
notification date: N/A
Early action deadline: 11/1,
notification date: 12/21
Application deadline (fall): 2/1

Undergraduate student body: 1,971 full time, 26 part time; 46% male, 54% female; 0% American Indian, 2% Asian, 3% black, 4% Hispanic, 2% multiracial, 4% Pacific Islander, 85% white, 3% international; 18% from in state; 95% live on campus; 0% of students in fraternities, 0% in sororities
Most popular majors: 20% Business, Management, Marketing, and Related Support Services; 14% Social Sciences; 11% Biological and Biomedical Sciences; 9% Psychology
Expenses: 2016-2017: $41,975; room/board: $11,300
Financial aid: (802) 654-3243; 74% of undergrads determined to have financial need; average aid package $28,135

University of Vermont
Burlington VT
(802) 656-3370
U.S. News ranking: Nat. U., No. 92
Website: www.uvm.edu
Admissions email: admissions@uvm.edu
Public; founded 1791
Freshman admissions: more selective; 2015-2016: 25,274 applied, 17,907 accepted. Either SAT or ACT required. SAT 25/75 percentile: 1100-1290. High school rank: 32% in top tenth, 74% in top quarter, 96% in top half
Early decision deadline: N/A, notification date: N/A
Early action deadline: 11/1, notification date: 12/15
Application deadline (fall): 1/15
Undergraduate student body: 9,991 full time, 982 part time; 44% male, 56% female; 0% American Indian, 3% Asian, 1% black, 3% Hispanic, 3% multiracial, 0% Pacific Islander, 82% white, 5% international; 29% from in state; 49% live on campus; 7% of students in fraternities, 8% in sororities
Most popular majors: 9% Business Administration and Management, General; 5% Psychology, General; 5% Mechanical Engineering; 5% Political Science and Government, General
Expenses: 2016-2017: $17,300 in state, $40,364 out of state; room/board: $11,578
Financial aid: (802) 656-5700; 55% of undergrads determined to have financial need; average aid package $23,942

Vermont Technical College
Randolph Center VT
(802) 728-1244
U.S. News ranking: Reg. Coll. (N), No. 15
Website: www.vtc.edu
Admissions email: admissions@vtc.edu
Public; founded 1866
Freshman admissions: less selective; 2015-2016: 554 applied, 376 accepted. Neither SAT nor ACT required. SAT 25/75 percentile: 830-1060. High school rank: 2% in top tenth, 14% in top quarter, 52% top half

Early decision deadline: N/A, notification date: N/A
Early action deadline: N/A, notification date: N/A
Application deadline (fall): rolling
Undergraduate student body: 1,068 full time, 478 part time; 53% male, 47% female; 1% American Indian, 1% Asian, 1% black, 2% Hispanic, 3% multiracial, 0% Pacific Islander, 87% white, 2% international; 84% from in state; N/A live on campus; N/A of students in fraternities, N/A in sororities
Most popular majors: Information not available
Expenses: 2016-2017: $14,401 in state, $26,223 out of state; room/board: $9,988
Financial aid: (800) 965-8790; 77% of undergrads determined to have financial need; average aid package $10,820

VIRGINIA

Averett University
Danville VA
(800) 283-7388
U.S. News ranking: Reg. Coll. (S), No. 20
Website: www.averett.edu
Admissions email: admit@averett.edu
Private; founded 1859
Affiliation: Baptist General Association of Virginia
Freshman admissions: less selective; 2015-2016: 2,250 applied, 1,378 accepted. Either SAT or ACT required. SAT 25/75 percentile: 800-1003. High school rank: 9% in top tenth, 27% in top quarter, 58% in top half
Early decision deadline: N/A, notification date: N/A
Early action deadline: N/A, notification date: N/A
Application deadline (fall): rolling
Undergraduate student body: 853 full time, 38 part time; 50% male, 50% female; 1% American Indian, 1% Asian, 33% black, 4% Hispanic, 0% multiracial, 0% Pacific Islander, 58% white, 4% international; 73% from in state; 61% live on campus; 2% of students in fraternities, 2% in sororities
Most popular majors: 13% Criminal Justice/Law Enforcement Administration; 10% Pre-Medicine/Pre-Medical Studies; 7% Management Science; 6% Teacher Education, Multiple Levels; 4% Political Science and Government, General
Expenses: 2016-2017: $31,980; room/board: $8,990
Financial aid: (434) 791-5646; 86% of undergrads determined to have financial need; average aid package $23,732

Bluefield College
Bluefield VA
(276) 326-4231
U.S. News ranking: Reg. Coll. (S), No. 37
Website: www.bluefield.edu
Admissions email: admissions@bluefield.edu
Private; founded 1922

Affiliation: Baptist
Freshman admissions: less selective; 2015-2016: 669 applied, 624 accepted. Either SAT or ACT required. SAT 25/75 percentile: 802-1036. High school rank: 7% in top tenth, 25% in top quarter, 59% in top half
Early decision deadline: N/A, notification date: N/A
Early action deadline: N/A, notification date: N/A
Application deadline (fall): rolling
Undergraduate student body: 815 full time, 144 part time; 43% male, 57% female; 0% American Indian, 1% Asian, 22% black, 4% Hispanic, 2% multiracial, 0% Pacific Islander, 65% white, 4% international; 67% from in state; 57% live on campus; N/A of students in fraternities, N/A in sororities
Most popular majors: 22% Public Administration and Social Service Professions; 21% Organizational Leadership; 12% Criminal Justice/Safety Studies; 11% Public Health/Community Nurse/Nursing; 8% Kinesiology and Exercise Science
Expenses: 2016-2017: $24,380; room/board: $8,928
Financial aid: (276) 326-4215; 85% of undergrads determined to have financial need; average aid package $15,315

Bridgewater College
Bridgewater VA
(800) 759-8328
U.S. News ranking: Nat. Lib. Arts, second tier
Website: www.bridgewater.edu
Admissions email: admissions@bridgewater.edu
Private; founded 1880
Affiliation: Church of the Brethren
Freshman admissions: selective; 2015-2016: 7,187 applied, 3,541 accepted. Either SAT or ACT required. SAT 25/75 percentile: 920-1125. High school rank: 15% in top tenth, 45% in top quarter, 82% in top half
Early decision deadline: N/A, notification date: N/A
Early action deadline: N/A, notification date: N/A
Application deadline (fall): 5/1
Undergraduate student body: 1,823 full time, 11 part time; 47% male, 53% female; 0% American Indian, 1% Asian, 11% black, 5% Hispanic, 5% multiracial, 0% Pacific Islander, 73% white, 1% international; 75% from in state; 83% live on campus; 0% of students in fraternities, 0% in sororities
Most popular majors: 19% Business, Management, Marketing, and Related Support Services; 14% Biological and Biomedical Sciences; 13% Parks, Recreation, Leisure, and Fitness Studies; 6% Psychology; 6% Social Sciences
Expenses: 2016-2017: $32,590; room/board: $11,920
Financial aid: (540) 828-5376; 80% of undergrads determined to have financial need; average aid package $28,318

Christopher Newport University
Newport News VA
(757) 594-7015
U.S. News ranking: Reg. U. (S), No. 14
Website: www.cnu.edu
Admissions email: admit@cnu.edu
Public; founded 1960
Freshman admissions: selective; 2015-2016: 7,366 applied, 4,427 accepted. Neither SAT nor ACT required. SAT 25/75 percentile: 1070-1250. High school rank: 17% in top tenth, 53% in top quarter, 88% in top half
Early decision deadline: 11/15, notification date: 12/15
Early action deadline: 12/1, notification date: 1/16
Application deadline (fall): 2/1
Undergraduate student body: 4,961 full time, 90 part time; 43% male, 57% female; 0% American Indian, 3% Asian, 8% black, 5% Hispanic, 5% multiracial, 0% Pacific Islander, 74% white, 0% international; 92% from in state; 74% live on campus; 17% of students in fraternities, 29% in sororities
Most popular majors: 15% Biology/Biological Sciences, General; 15% Psychology, General; 12% Business Administration and Management, General; 6% Political Science and Government, General
Expenses: 2016-2017: $13,054 in state, $24,280 out of state; room/board: $10,914
Financial aid: (757) 594-7170; 45% of undergrads determined to have financial need; average aid package $9,143

College of William and Mary
Williamsburg VA
(757) 221-4223
U.S. News ranking: Nat. U., No. 32
Website: www.wm.edu
Admissions email: admission@wm.edu
Public; founded 1693
Freshman admissions: most selective; 2015-2016: 14,952 applied, 5,153 accepted. Either SAT or ACT required. SAT 25/75 percentile: 1260-1460. High school rank: 81% in top tenth, 96% in top quarter, 100% in top half
Early decision deadline: 11/1, notification date: 12/1
Early action deadline: N/A, notification date: N/A
Application deadline (fall): 1/1
Undergraduate student body: 6,217 full time, 84 part time; 44% male, 56% female; 0% American Indian, 8% Asian, 7% black, 9% Hispanic, 4% multiracial, 0% Pacific Islander, 59% white, 6% international; 67% from in state; 74% live on campus; 26% of students in fraternities, 34% in sororities
Most popular majors: 24% Social Sciences; 11% Business, Management, Marketing, and Related Support Services; 10% Biological and Biomedical Sciences; 7% Psychology; 7% Multi/Interdisciplinary Studies

Expenses: 2016-2017: $18,687 in state, $41,718 out of state; room/board: $11,382
Financial aid: (757) 221-2420; 34% of undergrads determined to have financial need; average aid package $21,243

Eastern Mennonite University
Harrisonburg VA
(800) 368-2665
U.S. News ranking: Reg. U. (S), No. 41
Website: www.emu.edu
Admissions email: admiss@emu.edu
Private; founded 1917
Affiliation: Mennonite Church USA
Freshman admissions: selective; 2015-2016: 1,656 applied, 1,022 accepted. Either SAT or ACT required. SAT 25/75 percentile: 870-1130. High school rank: N/A
Early decision deadline: N/A, notification date: N/A
Early action deadline: N/A, notification date: N/A
Application deadline (fall): rolling
Undergraduate student body: 1,087 full time, 134 part time; 35% male, 65% female; 0% American Indian, 3% Asian, 10% black, 8% Hispanic, 2% multiracial, 0% Pacific Islander, 71% white, 3% international; 60% from in state; 62% live on campus; 0% of students in fraternities, 0% in sororities
Most popular majors: 35% Health Professions and Related Programs; 15% Business, Management, Marketing, and Related Support Services; 8% Liberal Arts and Sciences, General Studies and Humanities
Expenses: 2015-2016: $32,300; room/board: $10,250
Financial aid: (540) 432-4139

ECPI University
Virginia Beach VA
(866) 499-0336
U.S. News ranking: Reg. Coll. (S), unranked
Website: www.ecpi.edu/
Admissions email: ssaunders@ecpi.edu
For-profit; founded 1966
Freshman admissions: N/A; 2015-2016: 4,091 applied, 3,247 accepted. Neither SAT nor ACT required. ACT 25/75 percentile: N/A. High school rank: N/A
Early decision deadline: N/A, notification date: N/A
Early action deadline: N/A, notification date: N/A
Application deadline (fall): rolling
Undergraduate student body: 10,983 full time, 0 part time; 42% male, 58% female; 1% American Indian, 3% Asian, 41% black, 8% Hispanic, 3% multiracial, 0% Pacific Islander, 41% white, 0% international
Most popular majors: 10% Computer and Information Systems Security/Information Assurance; 5% Criminal Justice/Safety Studies; 5% Computer Technology/Computer Systems Technology; 3% Business Administration and Management, General; 1% Automation Engineer Technology/Technician

Expenses: 2015-2016: $14,755; room/board: N/A
Financial aid: N/A

Emory and Henry College

Emory VA
(800) 848-5493
U.S. News ranking: Nat. Lib. Arts, No. 174
Website: www.ehc.edu
Admissions email: ehadmiss@ehc.edu
Private; founded 1836
Affiliation: United Methodist
Freshman admissions: less selective; 2015-2016: 1,456 applied, 1,112 accepted. Either SAT or ACT required. SAT 25/75 percentile: 860-1090. High school rank: 10% in top tenth, 26% in top quarter, 63% in top half
Early decision deadline: 11/15, notification date: 12/15
Early action deadline: N/A, notification date: N/A
Application deadline (fall): rolling
Undergraduate student body: 1,007 full time, 17 part time; 52% male, 48% female; 1% American Indian, 1% Asian, 11% black, 4% Hispanic, 2% multiracial, 0% Pacific Islander, 73% white, 0% international; 66% from in state; 78% live on campus; 23% of students in fraternities, 33% in sororities
Most popular majors: 14% Social Sciences; 13% Education; 10% Business, Management, Marketing, and Related Support Services; 10% Visual and Performing Arts; 9% Psychology
Expenses: 2016-2017: $33,700; room/board: N/A
Financial aid: (276) 944-6229; 81% of undergrads determined to have financial need; average aid package $27,356

Ferrum College

Ferrum VA
(800) 868-9797
U.S. News ranking: Reg. Coll. (S), No. 32
Website: www.ferrum.edu
Admissions email: admissions@ferrum.edu
Private; founded 1913
Affiliation: United Methodist
Freshman admissions: least selective; 2015-2016: 3,020 applied, 2,203 accepted. Neither SAT nor ACT required. SAT 25/75 percentile: 770-1000. High school rank: 5% in top tenth, 16% in top quarter, 46% in top half
Early decision deadline: N/A, notification date: N/A
Early action deadline: N/A, notification date: N/A
Application deadline (fall): rolling
Undergraduate student body: 1,311 full time, 23 part time; 55% male, 45% female; 0% American Indian, 1% Asian, 33% black, 5% Hispanic, 6% multiracial, 0% Pacific Islander, 52% white, 1% international; 80% from in state; 89% live on campus; 4% of students in fraternities, 5% in sororities

Most popular majors: 12% Homeland Security, Law Enforcement, Firefighting and Related Protective Services; 11% Health Professions and Related Programs; 10% Business, Management, Marketing, and Related Support Services; 8% Education; 8% Public Administration and Social Service Professions
Expenses: 2016-2017: $31,915; room/board: $11,090
Financial aid: (540) 365-4282

George Mason University

Fairfax VA
(703) 993-2400
U.S. News ranking: Nat. U., No. 143
Website: www.gmu.edu
Admissions email: admissions@gmu.edu
Public; founded 1972
Freshman admissions: selective; 2015-2016: 18,987 applied, 15,138 accepted. Neither SAT nor ACT required. SAT 25/75 percentile: 1040-1250. High school rank: 21% in top tenth, 56% in top quarter, 92% in top half
Early decision deadline: N/A, notification date: N/A
Early action deadline: 11/1, notification date: 12/15
Application deadline (fall): 1/15
Undergraduate student body: 18,427 full time, 4,635 part time; 49% male, 51% female; 0% American Indian, 18% Asian, 10% black, 12% Hispanic, 4% multiracial, 0% Pacific Islander, 45% white, 4% international; 90% from in state; 26% live on campus; 6% of students in fraternities, 9% in sororities
Most popular majors: 8% Psychology, General; 6% Criminal Justice/Police Science; 5% Accounting; 5% Biology/ Biological Sciences, General; 5% Information Technology
Expenses: 2016-2017: $11,300 in state, $32,582 out of state; room/board: $10,730
Financial aid: (703) 993-2353; 56% of undergrads determined to have financial need; average aid package $12,514

Hampden-Sydney College

Hampden-Sydney VA
(800) 755-0733
U.S. News ranking: Nat. Lib. Arts, No. 105
Website: www.hsc.edu
Admissions email: hsapp@hsc.edu
Private; founded 1775
Affiliation: Presbyterian
Freshman admissions: selective; 2015-2016: 3,683 applied, 2,018 accepted. Either SAT or ACT required. SAT 25/75 percentile: 1000-1230. High school rank: 12% in top tenth, 37% in top quarter, 77% in top half
Early decision deadline: 11/15, notification date: 12/15
Early action deadline: 1/15, notification date: 2/15
Application deadline (fall): 3/1

Undergraduate student body: 1,085 full time, 2 part time; 100% male, 0% female; 0% American Indian, 1% Asian, 6% black, 2% Hispanic, 6% multiracial, 0% Pacific Islander, 81% white, 0% international; 71% from in state; 95% live on campus; 34% of students in fraternities, 0% in sororities
Most popular majors: 32% Social Sciences; 15% Business, Management, Marketing, and Related Support Services; 12% History; 11% Biological and Biomedical Sciences; 7% Psychology
Expenses: 2016-2017: $43,398; room/board: $13,286
Financial aid: (434) 223-6119; 64% of undergrads determined to have financial need; average aid package $32,493

Hampton University

Hampton VA
(757) 727-5328
U.S. News ranking: Reg. U. (S), No. 18
Website: www.hamptonu.edu
Admissions email: admissions@hamptonu.edu
Private; founded 1868
Freshman admissions: selective; 2015-2016: 10,258 applied, 7,083 accepted. Neither SAT nor ACT required. SAT 25/75 percentile: 940-1090. High school rank: 21% in top tenth, 54% in top quarter, 92% in top half
Early decision deadline: N/A, notification date: N/A
Early action deadline: 11/1, notification date: 12/31
Application deadline (fall): 3/1
Undergraduate student body: 3,264 full time, 155 part time; 34% male, 66% female; 0% American Indian, 0% Asian, 95% black, 1% Hispanic, 0% multiracial, 0% Pacific Islander, 2% white, 1% international; 27% from in state; 62% live on campus; 5% of students in fraternities, 4% in sororities
Most popular majors: 12% Psychology, General; 8% Biology/ Biological Sciences, General; 8% Business Administration and Management, General; 7% Registered Nursing/Registered Nurse
Expenses: 2016-2017: $24,127; room/board: $10,684
Financial aid: (800) 624-3341; 62% of undergrads determined to have financial need; average aid package $5,756

Hollins University

Roanoke VA
(800) 456-9595
U.S. News ranking: Nat. Lib. Arts, No. 105
Website: www.hollins.edu
Admissions email: huadm@hollins.edu
Private; founded 1842
Freshman admissions: selective; 2015-2016: 2,233 applied, 1,362 accepted. Either SAT or ACT required. SAT 25/75 percentile: 990-1210. High school rank: 23% in top tenth, 36% in top quarter, 93% in top half

Early decision deadline: 10/15, notification date: 11/1
Early action deadline: 11/15, notification date: 12/1
Application deadline (fall): rolling
Undergraduate student body: 621 full time, 18 part time; 0% male, 100% female; 1% American Indian, 3% Asian, 12% black, 7% Hispanic, 4% multiracial, 0% Pacific Islander, 64% white, 5% international; 53% from in state; 82% live on campus; 0% of students in fraternities, 0% in sororities
Most popular majors: 17% English Language and Literature/Letters; 14% Visual and Performing Arts; 12% Biological and Biomedical Sciences; 9% Business, Management, Marketing, and Related Support Services; 9% Psychology
Expenses: 2016-2017: $36,835; room/board: $12,800
Financial aid: (540) 362-6332; 82% of undergrads determined to have financial need; average aid package $34,672

James Madison University

Harrisonburg VA
(540) 568-5681
U.S. News ranking: Reg. U. (S), No. 8
Website: www.jmu.edu
Admissions email: admissions@jmu.edu
Public; founded 1908
Freshman admissions: selective; 2015-2016: 21,439 applied, 15,559 accepted. Either SAT or ACT required. SAT 25/75 percentile: 1040-1220. High school rank: 23% in top tenth, 41% in top quarter, 97% in top half
Early decision deadline: N/A, notification date: N/A
Early action deadline: 11/1, notification date: 1/15
Application deadline (fall): 1/15
Undergraduate student body: 18,433 full time, 963 part time; 41% male, 59% female; 0% American Indian, 4% Asian, 4% black, 6% Hispanic, 4% multiracial, 0% Pacific Islander, 76% white, 2% international; 76% from in state; 13% live on campus; 1% of students in fraternities, 5% in sororities
Most popular majors: 16% Health Professions and Related Programs; 15% Business, Management, Marketing, and Related Support Services; 8% Education; 7% Social Sciences
Expenses: 2016-2017: $10,342 in state, $26,116 out of state; room/board: $9,334
Financial aid: (540) 568-7820; 41% of undergrads determined to have financial need; average aid package $8,342

Liberty University

Lynchburg VA
(800) 543-5317
U.S. News ranking: Nat. U., second tier
Website: www.liberty.edu
Admissions email: admissions@liberty.edu
Private; founded 1971
Affiliation: Southern Baptist

Freshman admissions: selective; 2015-2016: 31,089 applied, 6,452 accepted. Either SAT or ACT required. SAT 25/75 percentile: 950-1190. High school rank: 23% in top tenth, 47% in top quarter, 78% in top half
Early decision deadline: N/A, notification date: N/A
Early action deadline: N/A, notification date: N/A
Application deadline (fall): rolling
Undergraduate student body: 27,671 full time, 22,192 part time; 42% male, 58% female; 0% American Indian, 1% Asian, 12% black, 5% Hispanic, 2% multiracial, 0% Pacific Islander, 47% white, 2% international; 26% from in state; 16% live on campus; N/A of students in fraternities, N/A in sororities
Most popular majors: 14% Business, Management, Marketing, and Related Support Services; 11% Health Professions and Related Programs; 8% Psychology; 7% Parks, Recreation, Leisure, and Fitness Studies
Expenses: 2016-2017: $23,020 room/board: $9,306
Financial aid: (434) 582-2270; 84% of undergrads determined to have financial need; average aid package $13,727

Longwood University

Farmville VA
(434) 395-2060
U.S. News ranking: Reg. U. (S), No. 31
Website: www.whylongwood.com
Admissions email: admissions@ longwood.edu
Public; founded 1839
Freshman admissions: less selective; 2015-2016: 4,716 applied, 3,721 accepted. Either SAT or ACT required. SAT 25/75 percentile: 890-1090. High school rank: 10% in top tenth, 34% in top quarter, 77% in top half
Early decision deadline: N/A, notification date: N/A
Early action deadline: 12/1, notification date: 1/15
Application deadline (fall): rolling
Undergraduate student body: 4,149 full time, 472 part time; 32% male, 68% female; 0% American Indian, 1% Asian, 9% black, 5% Hispanic, 4% multiracial, 0% Pacific Islander, 75% white, 1% international; 96% from in state; 69% live on campus; 17% of students in fraternities, 16% in sororities
Most popular majors: 19% Liberal Arts and Sciences, General Studies and Humanities; 11% Business, Management, Marketing, and Related Support Services; 9% Health Professions and Related Programs; 8% Social Sciences; 7% Psychology
Expenses: 2016-2017: $12,240 in state, $26,670 out of state; room/board: $10,685
Financial aid: (434) 395-2077; 56% of undergrads determined to have financial need; average aid package $13,973

Lynchburg College

Lynchburg VA
(434) 544-8300
U.S. News ranking: Reg. U. (S),
No. 35
Website: www.lynchburg.edu
Admissions email: admissions@
lynchburg.edu
Private; founded 1903
Affiliation: Christian Church
(Disciples of Christ)
Freshman admissions: selective;
2015-2016: 4,916 applied,
3,412 accepted. Either SAT
or ACT required. SAT 25/75
percentile: 910-1120. High
school rank: N/A
Early decision deadline: 11/15,
notification date: 12/15
Early action deadline: N/A,
notification date: N/A
Application deadline (fall): rolling
Undergraduate student body: 1,980
full time, 161 part time; 40%
male, 60% female; 0% American
Indian, 1% Asian, 11% black,
5% Hispanic, 4% multiracial,
0% Pacific Islander, 73% white,
3% international; 68% from in
state; 74% live on campus; 12%
of students in fraternities, 14%
in sororities
Most popular majors: 17%
Health Professions and Related
Programs; 14% Social Sciences;
13% Business, Management,
Marketing, and Related Support
Services; 11% Biological and
Biomedical Sciences; 6%
Education
Expenses: 2016-2017: $36,620;
room/board: $10,120
Financial aid: (434) 544-8228;
75% of undergrads determined
to have financial need; average
aid package $26,101

Mary Baldwin College

Staunton VA
(800) 468-2262
U.S. News ranking: Reg. U. (S),
No. 52
Website: www.mbc.edu
Admissions email: admit@mbc.edu
Private; founded 1842
Affiliation: Presbyterian
Freshman admissions: selective;
2015-2016: 5,407 applied,
2,693 accepted. Either SAT
or ACT required. SAT 25/75
percentile: 860-1140. High
school rank: 11% in top tenth,
32% in top quarter, 76% in
top half
Early decision deadline: 11/15,
notification date: 12/1
Early action deadline: N/A,
notification date: N/A
Application deadline (fall): rolling
Undergraduate student body: 897
full time, 415 part time; 7%
male, 93% female; 1% American
Indian, 2% Asian, 23% black,
6% Hispanic, 4% multiracial,
0% Pacific Islander, 58% white,
1% international
Most popular majors: 15%
Business, Management,
Marketing, and Related Support
Services; 13% Psychology;
8% History; 8% Public
Administration and Social Service
Professions; 8% Social Sciences
Expenses: 2016-2017: $30,635;
room/board: $9,230

Financial aid: (540) 887-7022;
91% of undergrads determined
to have financial need; average
aid package $21,628

Marymount University

Arlington VA
(703) 284-1500
U.S. News ranking: Reg. U. (S),
No. 43
Website: www.marymount.edu
Admissions email: admissions@
marymount.edu
Private; founded 1950
Affiliation: Roman Catholic
Freshman admissions: selective;
2015-2016: 2,143 applied,
1,838 accepted. Neither SAT
nor ACT required. SAT 25/75
percentile: 880-1110. High
school rank: 12% in top tenth,
37% in top quarter, 76% in
top half
Early decision deadline: N/A,
notification date: N/A
Early action deadline: N/A,
notification date: N/A
Application deadline (fall): rolling
Undergraduate student body: 2,089
full time, 234 part time; 34%
male, 66% female; 0% American
Indian, 8% Asian, 15% black,
17% Hispanic, 3% multiracial,
1% Pacific Islander, 40% white,
12% international; 61% from in
state; 33% live on campus; N/A
of students in fraternities, N/A in
sororities
Most popular majors: 24%
Registered Nursing/Registered
Nurse; 17% Business
Administration and Management,
General; 7% Psychology, General;
7% Public Health Education and
Promotion
Expenses: 2016-2017: $29,350;
room/board: $12,220
Financial aid: (703) 284-1530;
65% of undergrads determined
to have financial need; average
aid package $18,111

Norfolk State University

Norfolk VA
(757) 823-8396
U.S. News ranking: Reg. U. (S),
second tier
Website: www.nsu.edu
Admissions email:
admissions@nsu.edu
Public; founded 1935
Freshman admissions: least
selective; 2015-2016: 2,445
applied, 1,930 accepted. Either
SAT or ACT required. SAT 25/75
percentile: 700-910. High school
rank: 6% in top tenth, 22% in
top quarter, 59% in top half
Early decision deadline: N/A,
notification date: N/A
Early action deadline: N/A,
notification date: N/A
Undergraduate student body: 3,739
full time, 783 part time; 37%
male, 63% female; 0% American
Indian, 1% Asian, 84% black,
3% Hispanic, 4% multiracial,
0% Pacific Islander, 5% white,
0% international; 86% from in
state; 39% live on campus; N/A
of students in fraternities, N/A in
sororities
Most popular majors: 10%
Business/Commerce, General;

10% Multi-/Interdisciplinary
Studies, Other; 10% Psychology,
General; 10% Sociology; 8%
Social Work
Expenses: 2016-2017: $8,738
in state, $20,340 out of state;
room/board: $9,490
Financial aid: (757) 823-8381

Old Dominion University

Norfolk VA
(757) 683-3685
U.S. News ranking: Nat. U.,
No. 210
Website: www.odu.edu
Admissions email:
admissions@odu.edu
Public; founded 1930
Freshman admissions: selective;
2015-2016: 9,510 applied,
7,904 accepted. Either SAT
or ACT required. SAT 25/75
percentile: 920-1140. High
school rank: 8% in top tenth,
32% in top quarter, 71% in
top half
Early decision deadline: N/A,
notification date: N/A
Early action deadline: 12/1,
notification date: 1/15
Application deadline (fall): 2/1
Undergraduate student body:
15,358 full time, 4,743 part
time; 46% male, 54% female;
0% American Indian, 4% Asian,
27% black, 7% Hispanic, 6%
multiracial, 0% Pacific Islander,
47% white, 1% international;
93% from in state; 23% live
on campus; 8% of students in
fraternities, 8% in sororities
Most popular majors: 17%
Health Professions and Related
Programs; 15% Business,
Management, Marketing, and
Related Support Services; 13%
Social Sciences; 7% English
Language and Literature/Letters;
7% Psychology
Expenses: 2016-2017: $10,048
in state, $27,028 out of state;
room/board: $11,058
Financial aid: (757) 683-3683;
66% of undergrads determined
to have financial need; average
aid package $10,247

Radford University

Radford VA
(540) 831-5371
U.S. News ranking: Reg. U. (S),
No. 47
Website: www.radford.edu
Admissions email:
admissions@radford.edu
Public; founded 1910
Freshman admissions: less
selective; 2015-2016: 7,617
applied, 6,328 accepted. Neither
SAT nor ACT required. SAT
25/75 percentile: 890-1050.
High school rank: 6% in top
tenth, 18% in top quarter, 55%
in top half
Early decision deadline: N/A,
notification date: N/A
Early action deadline: 12/1,
notification date: 1/15
Application deadline (fall): rolling
Undergraduate student body: 8,522
full time, 358 part time; 44%
male, 56% female; 0% American
Indian, 1% Asian, 13% black,
7% Hispanic, 5% multiracial,

0% Pacific Islander, 71% white,
1% international; 95% from in
state; 34% live on campus; 14%
of students in fraternities, 15%
in sororities
Most popular majors: 9% Criminal
Justice/Safety Studies; 8%
Physical Education Teaching
and Coaching; 8% Multi-/
Interdisciplinary Studies, Other;
7% Psychology, General; 7%
Business Administration and
Management, General
Expenses: 2016-2017: $10,081
in state, $21,716 out of state;
room/board: $8,946
Financial aid: (540) 831-5408;
59% of undergrads determined
to have financial need; average
aid package $9,495

Randolph College

Lynchburg VA
(800) 745-7692
U.S. News ranking: Nat. Lib. Arts,
No. 132
Website:
www.randolphcollege.edu/
Admissions email: admissions@
randolphcollege.edu
Private; founded 1891
Affiliation: United Methodist
Freshman admissions: selective;
2015-2016: 1,207 applied, 972
accepted. Either SAT or ACT
required. SAT 25/75 percentile:
910-1120. High school rank:
13% in top tenth, 35% in top
quarter, 80% in top half
Early decision deadline: N/A,
notification date: N/A
Early action deadline: 12/1,
notification date: 1/1
Application deadline (fall): rolling
Undergraduate student body: 664
full time, 8 part time; 34% male,
66% female; 1% American
Indian, 2% Asian, 12% black,
5% Hispanic, 5% multiracial,
0% Pacific Islander, 67% white,
8% international; 60% from in
state; 84% live on campus; N/A
of students in fraternities, N/A in
sororities
Most popular majors: 15%
Biological and Biomedical
Sciences; 13% Social Sciences;
12% Visual and Performing Arts;
10% Business, Management,
Marketing, and Related Support
Services; 9% English Language
and Literature/Letters
Expenses: 2016-2017: $36,770;
room/board: $12,580
Financial aid: (434) 947-8128;
73% of undergrads determined
to have financial need; average
aid package $29,280

Randolph-Macon College

Ashland VA
(800) 888-1762
U.S. News ranking: Nat. Lib. Arts,
No. 132
Website: www.rmc.edu
Admissions email:
admissions@rmc.edu
Private; founded 1830
Affiliation: United Methodist
Freshman admissions: selective;
2015-2016: 2,968 applied,
1,790 accepted. Either SAT
or ACT required. SAT 25/75
percentile: 1000-1180. High

school rank: 21% in top tenth,
56% in top quarter, 86% in
top half
Early decision deadline: N/A,
notification date: N/A
Early action deadline: 11/15,
notification date: 1/1
Application deadline (fall): 3/1
Undergraduate student body: 1,391
full time, 27 part time; 45%
male, 55% female; 0% American
Indian, 2% Asian, 8% black, 5%
Hispanic, 4% multiracial, 0%
Pacific Islander, 78% white, 2%
international; 75% from in state;
85% live on campus; 27% of
students in fraternities, 28% in
sororities
Most popular majors: 14%
Psychology, General; 11%
Economics, Other; 10% Biology/
Biological Sciences, General; 8%
Sociology
Expenses: 2016-2017: $38,730;
room/board: $11,180
Financial aid: (804) 752-7259;
75% of undergrads determined
to have financial need; average
aid package $27,486

Regent University

Virginia Beach VA
(888) 718-1222
U.S. News ranking: Nat. U.,
second tier
Website: www.regent.edu
Admissions email:
admissions@regent.edu
Private; founded 1978
Affiliation: non-denominational
Freshman admissions: selective;
2015-2016: 1,665 applied,
1,426 accepted. Either SAT
or ACT required. SAT 25/75
percentile: 900-1150. High
school rank: 14% in top tenth,
34% in top quarter, 75% in
top half
Early decision deadline: N/A,
notification date: N/A
Early action deadline: N/A,
notification date: N/A
Application deadline (fall): 8/1
Undergraduate student body: 1,777
full time, 1,218 part time; 38%
male, 62% female; 1% American
Indian, 2% Asian, 25% black,
7% Hispanic, 5% multiracial,
0% Pacific Islander, 57% white,
1% international; 50% from in
state; 20% live on campus; 0%
of students in fraternities, 0% in
sororities
Most popular majors: 18%
Business Administration
and Management, General;
16% Divinity/Ministry; 15%
Psychology, General; 10%
English Language and Literature,
General
Expenses: 2016-2017: $16,700;
room/board: $8,250
Financial aid: (757) 352-4125;
77% of undergrads determined
to have financial need; average
aid package $11,173

Roanoke College

Salem VA
(540) 375-2270
U.S. News ranking: Nat. Lib. Arts,
No. 140
Website: www.roanoke.edu
Admissions email:
admissions@roanoke.edu
Private; founded 1842

Affiliation: Lutheran
Freshman admissions: selective; 2015-2016: 4,325 applied, 3,134 accepted. Either SAT or ACT required. SAT 25/75 percentile: 970-1200. High school rank: 15% in top tenth, 45% in top quarter, 78% in top half
Early decision deadline: 11/10, notification date: 11/26
Early action deadline: N/A, notification date: N/A
Application deadline (fall): 3/15
Undergraduate student body: 1,942 full time, 63 part time; 41% male, 59% female; 0% American Indian, 1% Asian, 6% black, 4% Hispanic, 4% multiracial, 0% Pacific Islander, 82% white, 2% international; 53% from in state; 76% live on campus; 18% of students in fraternities, 16% in sororities
Most popular majors: 14% Business Administration and Management, General; 11% Psychology, General; 8% Biology/Biological Sciences, General; 7% History, General
Expenses: 2016-2017: $41,054; room/board: $12,810
Financial aid: (540) 375-2235; 74% of undergrads determined to have financial need; average aid package $31,176

Shenandoah University

Winchester VA
(540) 665-4581
U.S. News ranking: Nat. U., No. 220
Website: www.su.edu
Admissions email: admit@su.edu
Private; founded 1875
Affiliation: United Methodist
Freshman admissions: selective; 2015-2016: 2,044 applied, 1,677 accepted. Either SAT or ACT required. SAT 25/75 percentile: 870-1123. High school rank: 15% in top tenth, 40% in top quarter, 78% in top half
Early decision deadline: N/A, notification date: N/A
Early action deadline: N/A, notification date: N/A
Application deadline (fall): rolling
Undergraduate student body: 1,927 full time, 83 part time; 41% male, 59% female; 1% American Indian, 3% Asian, 11% black, 6% Hispanic, 4% multiracial, 0% Pacific Islander, 59% white, 4% international; 62% from in state; 46% live on campus; N/A of students in fraternities, N/A in sororities
Most popular majors: 21% Registered Nursing/Registered Nurse; 8% Business Administration and Management, General; 7% Psychology, General; 5% Biology/Biological Sciences, General; 5% Physical Education Teaching and Coaching
Expenses: 2016-2017: $31,322; room/board: $9,990
Financial aid: (540) 665-4538; 76% of undergrads determined to have financial need; average aid package $29,543

Southern Virginia University[1]

Buena Vista VA
(540) 261-8401
U.S. News ranking: Nat. Lib. Arts, second tier
Website: svu.edu/
Admissions email: N/A
Private
Application deadline (fall): N/A
Undergraduate student body: N/A full time, N/A part time
Expenses: 2015-2016: $14,900; room/board: $7,500
Financial aid: N/A

Sweet Briar College

Sweet Briar VA
(800) 381-6142
U.S. News ranking: Nat. Lib. Arts, No. 140
Website: www.sbc.edu
Admissions email: admissions@sbc.edu
Private; founded 1901
Freshman admissions: selective; 2015-2016: 99 applied, 94 accepted. Either SAT or ACT required. SAT 25/75 percentile: 935-1230. High school rank: 25% in top tenth, 50% in top quarter, 67% in top half
Early decision deadline: N/A, notification date: N/A
Early action deadline: 11/1, notification date: N/A
Application deadline (fall): 2/1
Undergraduate student body: 310 full time, 6 part time; 5% male, 95% female; 2% American Indian, 3% Asian, 9% black, 9% Hispanic, 5% multiracial, N/A Pacific Islander, 71% white, 0% international; 52% from in state; 94% live on campus; N/A of students in fraternities, N/A in sororities
Most popular majors: 16% Business, Management, Marketing, and Related Support Services; 15% Social Sciences; 10% Visual and Performing Arts; 8% Foreign Languages, Literatures, and Linguistics; 8% Liberal Arts and Sciences, General Studies and Humanities
Expenses: 2016-2017: $36,425; room/board: $12,635
Financial aid: (434) 381-6156; 78% of undergrads determined to have financial need; average aid package $33,548

University of Mary Washington

Fredericksburg VA
(540) 654-2000
U.S. News ranking: Reg. U. (S), No. 16
Website: www.umw.edu
Admissions email: admit@umw.edu
Public; founded 1908
Freshman admissions: selective; 2015-2016: 5,549 applied, 4,588 accepted. Neither SAT nor ACT required. SAT 25/75 percentile: 1000-1210. High school rank: 14% in top tenth, 41% in top quarter, 84% in top half
Early decision deadline: 11/1, notification date: 12/7
Early action deadline: 11/15, notification date: 1/31

Application deadline (fall): rolling
Undergraduate student body: 3,796 full time, 524 part time; 36% male, 64% female; 0% American Indian, 4% Asian, 6% black, 8% Hispanic, 5% multiracial, 0% Pacific Islander, 70% white, 1% international; 89% from in state; 57% live on campus; N/A of students in fraternities, N/A in sororities
Most popular majors: 17% Social Sciences; 15% Business, Management, Marketing, and Related Support Services; 12% English Language and Literature/Letters; 11% Psychology; 8% Biological and Biomedical Sciences
Expenses: 2016-2017: $11,630 in state, $26,220 out of state; room/board: $11,118
Financial aid: (540) 654-2468; 43% of undergrads determined to have financial need; average aid package $9,260

University of Richmond

Univ. of Richmond VA
(804) 289-8640
U.S. News ranking: Nat. Lib. Arts, No. 27
Website: www.richmond.edu
Admissions email: admissions@richmond.edu
Private; founded 1830
Freshman admissions: more selective; 2015-2016: 9,977 applied, 3,104 accepted. Either SAT or ACT required. SAT 25/75 percentile: 1220-1420. High school rank: 61% in top tenth, 89% in top quarter, 97% in top half
Early decision deadline: 11/15, notification date: 12/15
Early action deadline: N/A, notification date: N/A
Application deadline (fall): 1/15
Undergraduate student body: 2,958 full time, 32 part time; 47% male, 53% female; 0% American Indian, 7% Asian, 6% black, 8% Hispanic, 4% multiracial, 0% Pacific Islander, 59% white, 9% international; 19% from in state; 90% live on campus; 17% of students in fraternities, 29% in sororities
Most popular majors: 36% Business, Management, Marketing, and Related Support Services; 14% Social Sciences; 9% Biological and Biomedical Sciences; 5% Psychology
Expenses: 2016-2017: $49,420; room/board: $11,460
Financial aid: (804) 289-8438; 40% of undergrads determined to have financial need; average aid package $44,771

University of Virginia

Charlottesville VA
(434) 982-3200
U.S. News ranking: Nat. U., No. 24
Website: www.virginia.edu
Admissions email: undergradadmission@virginia.edu
Public; founded 1819
Freshman admissions: most selective; 2015-2016: 30,840 applied, 9,186 accepted. Either

SAT or ACT required. SAT 25/75 percentile: 1250-1460. High school rank: 89% in top tenth, 97% in top quarter, 100% in top half
Early decision deadline: N/A, notification date: N/A
Early action deadline: 11/1, notification date: 1/31
Application deadline (fall): 1/1
Undergraduate student body: 15,816 full time, 920 part time; 44% male, 56% female; 0% American Indian, 13% Asian, 6% black, 6% Hispanic, 5% multiracial, 0% Pacific Islander, 60% white, 5% international; 28% from in state; 40% live on campus; 33% of students in fraternities, 33% in sororities
Most popular majors: 10% Economics, General; 9% Business/Commerce, General; 8% Biology/Biological Sciences, General; 8% International Relations and Affairs; 8% Psychology, General
Expenses: 2016-2017: $15,722 in state, $45,066 out of state; room/board: $10,726
Financial aid: (434) 982-6000; 33% of undergrads determined to have financial need; average aid package $25,522

University of Virginia–Wise

Wise VA
(888) 282-9324
U.S. News ranking: Nat. Lib. Arts, second tier
Website: www.uvawise.edu
Admissions email: admissions@uvawise.edu
Public; founded 1954
Freshman admissions: less selective; 2015-2016: 1,042 applied, 801 accepted. Either SAT or ACT required. SAT 25/75 percentile: 850-1040. High school rank: 31% in top tenth, 42% in top quarter, 75% in top half
Early decision deadline: N/A, notification date: N/A
Early action deadline: 12/1, notification date: 12/15
Application deadline (fall): 8/15
Undergraduate student body: 1,335 full time, 693 part time; 41% male, 59% female; 0% American Indian, 1% Asian, 12% black, 2% Hispanic, 0% multiracial, 0% Pacific Islander, 78% white, 0% international; 95% from in state; 25% live on campus; 5% of students in fraternities, 3% in sororities
Most popular majors: 17% Business, Management, Marketing, and Related Support Services; 16% Education; 12% Social Sciences; 11% Psychology; 8% Biological and Biomedical Sciences
Expenses: 2016-2017: $9,539 in state, $25,617 out of state; room/board: $10,346
Financial aid: (276) 328-0103; 79% of undergrads determined to have financial need; average aid package $17,477

Virginia Commonwealth University

Richmond VA
(800) 841-3638
U.S. News ranking: Nat. U., No. 164
Website: www.vcu.edu
Admissions email: ugrad@vcu.edu
Public; founded 1838
Freshman admissions: selective; 2015-2016: 16,293 applied, 11,798 accepted. Neither SAT nor ACT required. SAT 25/75 percentile: 990-1200. High school rank: 19% in top tenth, 49% in top quarter, 85% in top half
Early decision deadline: N/A, notification date: N/A
Early action deadline: N/A, notification date: N/A
Application deadline (fall): 1/15
Undergraduate student body: 20,411 full time, 3,640 part time; 42% male, 58% female; 0% American Indian, 13% Asian, 18% black, 8% Hispanic, 5% multiracial, 0% Pacific Islander, 49% white, 3% international; 93% from in state; 74% live on campus; N/A of students in fraternities, N/A in sororities
Most popular majors: 13% Business, Management, Marketing, and Related Support Services; 13% Visual and Performing Arts; 10% Psychology; 8% Biological and Biomedical Sciences; 7% Health Professions and Related Programs
Expenses: 2016-2017: $13,076 in state, $31,608 out of state; room/board: $9,919
Financial aid: (804) 828-6669; 57% of undergrads determined to have financial need; average aid package $10,648

Virginia Military Institute

Lexington VA
(800) 767-4207
U.S. News ranking: Nat. Lib. Arts, No. 72
Website: www.vmi.edu
Admissions email: admissions@vmi.edu
Public; founded 1839
Freshman admissions: selective; 2015-2016: 1,779 applied, 940 accepted. Either SAT or ACT required. SAT 25/75 percentile: 1040-1230. High school rank: 17% in top tenth, 46% in top quarter, 88% in top half
Early decision deadline: 11/15, notification date: 12/15
Early action deadline: N/A, notification date: N/A
Application deadline (fall): 2/1
Undergraduate student body: 1,717 full time, 0 part time; 89% male, 11% female; 1% American Indian, 4% Asian, 6% black, 5% Hispanic, 2% multiracial, 1% Pacific Islander, 80% white, 2% international; 60% from in state; 100% live on campus; N/A of students in fraternities, N/A in sororities
Most popular majors: 15% Civil Engineering, General; 12% International Relations and Affairs; 12% Psychology,

General; 11% History, General; 11% Biology/Biological Sciences, General
Expenses: 2016-2017: $17,492 in state, $41,801 out of state; room/board: $8,968
Financial aid: (540) 464-7208; 47% of undergrads determined to have financial need; average aid package $30,978

Virginia State University[1]
Petersburg VA
(804) 524-5902
U.S. News ranking: Reg. U. (S), second tier
Website: www.vsu.edu
Admissions email: admiss@vsu.edu
Public
Application deadline (fall): 5/1
Undergraduate student body: N/A full time, N/A part time
Expenses: 2015-2016: $8,226 in state, $17,760 out of state; room/board: $10,252
Financial aid: (804) 524-5992

Virginia Tech
Blacksburg VA
(540) 231-6267
U.S. News ranking: Nat. U., No. 74
Website: www.vt.edu
Admissions email: vtadmiss@vt.edu
Public; founded 1872
Freshman admissions: more selective; 2015-2016: 22,280 applied, 16,355 accepted. Either SAT or ACT required. SAT 25/75 percentile: 1100-1320. High school rank: 39% in top tenth, 80% in top quarter, 98% in top half
Early decision deadline: 11/1, notification date: 12/15
Early action deadline: N/A, notification date: N/A
Application deadline (fall): 1/15
Undergraduate student body: 24,841 full time, 543 part time; 57% male, 43% female; 0% American Indian, 9% Asian, 4% black, 5% Hispanic, 4% multiracial, 0% Pacific Islander, 68% white, 6% international; 76% from in state; 37% live on campus; 14% of students in fraternities, 18% in sororities
Most popular majors: 25% Engineering; 19% Business, Management, Marketing, and Related Support Services; 9% Family and Consumer Sciences/Human Sciences; 8% Biological and Biomedical Sciences; 8% Social Sciences
Expenses: 2016-2017: $12,852 in state, $29,371 out of state; room/board: $8,424
Financial aid: (540) 231-5179; 44% of undergrads determined to have financial need; average aid package $18,334

Virginia Union University
Richmond VA
(804) 257-5600
U.S. News ranking: Nat. Lib. Arts, second tier
Website: www.vuu.edu/
Admissions email: admissions@vuu.edu

Private; founded 1865
Affiliation: Baptist
Freshman admissions: least selective; 2015-2016: 7,337 applied, 3,598 accepted. Either SAT or ACT required. SAT 25/75 percentile: 680-860. High school rank: 7% in top tenth, 15% in top quarter, 46% in top half
Early decision deadline: N/A, notification date: N/A
Early action deadline: N/A, notification date: N/A
Application deadline (fall): 6/30
Undergraduate student body: 1,419 full time, 90 part time; 42% male, 58% female; 1% American Indian, 0% Asian, 94% black, 1% Hispanic, N/A multiracial, 0% Pacific Islander, 1% white, 0% international; 54% from in state; 71% live on campus; N/A of students in fraternities, N/A in sororities
Most popular majors: 22% Criminology; 12% Biology/Biological Sciences, General; 12% Business Administration and Management, General; 11% Psychology, General; 8% Computer and Information Sciences, General
Expenses: 2016-2017: $16,533; room/board: $8,413
Financial aid: (804) 257-5882; 96% of undergrads determined to have financial need; average aid package $13,234

Virginia Wesleyan College
Norfolk VA
(800) 737-8684
U.S. News ranking: Nat. Lib. Arts, second tier
Website: www.vwc.edu
Admissions email: admissions@vwc.edu
Private; founded 1961
Affiliation: United Methodist
Freshman admissions: less selective; 2015-2016: 1,850 applied, 1,712 accepted. Neither SAT nor ACT required. SAT 25/75 percentile: 860-1090. High school rank: 13% in top tenth, 33% in top quarter, 67% in top half
Early decision deadline: N/A, notification date: N/A
Early action deadline: N/A, notification date: N/A
Application deadline (fall): rolling
Undergraduate student body: 1,360 full time, 81 part time; 36% male, 64% female; 1% American Indian, 1% Asian, 24% black, 8% Hispanic, 5% multiracial, 0% Pacific Islander, 54% white, 1% international; 75% from in state; 57% live on campus; N/A of students in fraternities, N/A in sororities
Most popular majors: 15% Business Administration and Management, General; 13% Criminal Justice/Safety Studies; 9% Biology/Biological Sciences, General; 9% Psychology, General; 7% Parks, Recreation and Leisure Studies
Expenses: 2016-2017: $35,610; room/board: $8,768
Financial aid: (757) 455-3345; 83% of undergrads determined to have financial need; average aid package $23,622

Washington and Lee University
Lexington VA
(540) 463-8710
U.S. News ranking: Nat. Lib. Arts, No. 11
Website: www.wlu.edu
Admissions email: admissions@wlu.edu
Private; founded 1749
Freshman admissions: most selective; 2015-2016: 5,377 applied, 1,284 accepted. Either SAT or ACT required. ACT 25/75 percentile: 30-33. High school rank: 85% in top tenth, 99% in top quarter, 100% in top half
Early decision deadline: 11/1, notification date: 12/22
Early action deadline: N/A, notification date: N/A
Application deadline (fall): 1/1
Undergraduate student body: 1,851 full time, 3 part time; 51% male, 49% female; 0% American Indian, 3% Asian, 2% black, 3% Hispanic, 3% multiracial, 4% Pacific Islander, 82% white, 4% international; 14% from in state; 51% live on campus; 78% of students in fraternities, 81% in sororities
Most popular majors: 15% Business Administration and Management, General; 12% Accounting and Business/Management; 9% Economics, General; 7% Political Science and Government, General; 6% English Language and Literature, General
Expenses: 2016-2017: $48,267; room/board: $11,380
Financial aid: (540) 458-8717; 41% of undergrads determined to have financial need; average aid package $47,315

WASHINGTON

Art Institute of Seattle[1]
Seattle WA
(800) 275-2471
U.S. News ranking: Arts, unranked
Website: www.ais.edu
Admissions email: N/A
For-profit
Application deadline (fall): N/A
Undergraduate student body: N/A full time, N/A part time
Expenses: 2015-2016: $17,556; room/board: $12,456
Financial aid: N/A

Bellevue College[1]
Bellevue WA
(425) 564-1000
U.S. News ranking: Reg. Coll. (W), unranked
Website: bellevuecollege.edu
Admissions email: N/A
Public
Application deadline (fall): N/A
Undergraduate student body: N/A full time, N/A part time
Expenses: 2015-2016: $3,619 in state, $8,957 out of state; room/board: N/A
Financial aid: (425) 564-2227

Centralia College[1]
Centralia WA
(360) 736-9391
U.S. News ranking: Reg. Coll. (W), unranked
Website: www.centralia.edu/
Admissions email: N/A
Public
Application deadline (fall): N/A
Undergraduate student body: N/A full time, N/A part time
Expenses: 2015-2016: $4,188 in state, $4,600 out of state; room/board: $5,400
Financial aid: N/A

Central Washington University
Ellensburg WA
(509) 963-1211
U.S. News ranking: Reg. U. (W), No. 44
Website: www.cwu.edu
Admissions email: cwuadmis@cwu.edu
Public; founded 1891
Freshman admissions: less selective; 2015-2016: 4,959 applied, 4,039 accepted. Either SAT or ACT required. SAT 25/75 percentile: 870-1080. High school rank: N/A
Early decision deadline: N/A, notification date: N/A
Early action deadline: N/A, notification date: N/A
Application deadline (fall): rolling
Undergraduate student body: 9,069 full time, 1,913 part time; 49% male, 51% female; 1% American Indian, 4% Asian, 4% black, 14% Hispanic, 7% multiracial, 1% Pacific Islander, 59% white, 3% international; 93% from in state; 30% live on campus; N/A of students in fraternities, N/A in sororities
Most popular majors: 23% Business, Management, Marketing, and Related Support Services; 12% Education; 11% Social Sciences; 7% Homeland Security, Law Enforcement, Firefighting and Related Protective Services; 6% Psychology
Expenses: 2016-2017: $8,688 in state, $21,501 out of state; room/board: $9,316
Financial aid: (509) 963-1611; 64% of undergrads determined to have financial need; average aid package $11,490

City University of Seattle[1]
Seattle WA
(206) 239-4500
U.S. News ranking: Reg. U. (W), unranked
Website: www.cityu.edu
Admissions email: info@cityu.edu
Private; founded 1973
Application deadline (fall): rolling
Undergraduate student body: N/A full time, N/A part time
Expenses: 2015-2016: $16,500; room/board: N/A
Financial aid: (800) 426-5596

Columbia Basin College[1]
Pasco WA
(509) 547-0511
U.S. News ranking: Reg. Coll. (W), unranked
Website: www.columbiabasin.edu/
Admissions email: N/A
Public
Application deadline (fall): N/A
Undergraduate student body: N/A full time, N/A part time
Expenses: 2015-2016: $4,194 in state, $6,189 out of state; room/board: N/A
Financial aid: N/A

Cornish College of the Arts[1]
Seattle WA
(800) 726-ARTS
U.S. News ranking: Arts, unranked
Website: www.cornish.edu
Admissions email: admission@cornish.edu
Private; founded 1914
Application deadline (fall): rolling
Undergraduate student body: N/A full time, N/A part time
Expenses: 2016-2017: $38,820; room/board: $10,950
Financial aid: (206) 726-5014; 80% of undergrads determined to have financial need; average aid package $24,559

Eastern Washington University[1]
Cheney WA
(509) 359-2397
U.S. News ranking: Reg. U. (W), No. 61
Website: www.ewu.edu
Admissions email: admissions@ewu.edu
Public; founded 1882
Application deadline (fall): 5/15
Undergraduate student body: N/A full time, N/A part time
Expenses: 2015-2016: $8,204 in state, $22,321 out of state; room/board: $10,265
Financial aid: (509) 359-2314

Evergreen State College
Olympia WA
(360) 867-6170
U.S. News ranking: Reg. U. (W), No. 32
Website: www.evergreen.edu
Admissions email: admissions@evergreen.edu
Public; founded 1967
Freshman admissions: selective; 2015-2016: 1,744 applied, 1,707 accepted. Either SAT or ACT required. SAT 25/75 percentile: 940-1190. High school rank: 9% in top tenth, 25% in top quarter, 64% in top half
Early decision deadline: N/A, notification date: N/A
Early action deadline: N/A, notification date: N/A
Application deadline (fall): rolling
Undergraduate student body: 3,585 full time, 287 part time; 45% male, 55% female; 2% American Indian, 3% Asian, 5% black, 10% Hispanic, 8% multiracial, 0% Pacific Islander, 65% white,

0% international; 75% from in state; 23% live on campus; N/A of students in fraternities, N/A in sororities
Most popular majors: 82% Liberal Arts and Sciences/Liberal Studies; 18% Biological and Physical Sciences
Expenses: 2016-2017: $7,398 in state, $23,871 out of state; room/board: $9,360
Financial aid: (360) 867-6205; 69% of undergrads determined to have financial need; average aid package $12,714

Gonzaga University
Spokane WA
(800) 322-2584
U.S. News ranking: Reg. U. (W), No. 4
Website: www.gonzaga.edu
Admissions email: admissions@gonzaga.edu
Private; founded 1887
Affiliation: Roman Catholic
Freshman admissions: more selective; 2015-2016: 6,729 applied, 4,945 accepted. Either SAT or ACT required. SAT 25/75 percentile: 1090-1290. High school rank: 39% in top tenth, 71% in top quarter, 95% in top half
Early decision deadline: N/A, notification date: N/A
Early action deadline: 11/15, notification date: 1/15
Application deadline (fall): 2/1
Undergraduate student body: 4,972 full time, 69 part time; 46% male, 54% female; 1% American Indian, 5% Asian, 1% black, 10% Hispanic, 6% multiracial, 0% Pacific Islander, 72% white, 2% international; 50% from in state; 60% live on campus; N/A of students in fraternities, N/A in sororities
Most popular majors: 24% Business, Management, Marketing, and Related Support Services; 14% Social Sciences; 12% Engineering; 10% Biological and Biomedical Sciences
Expenses: 2016-2017: $39,730; room/board: $11,158
Financial aid: (509) 323-4049; 55% of undergrads determined to have financial need; average aid package $29,293

Heritage University[1]
Toppenish WA
(509) 865-8508
U.S. News ranking: Reg. U. (W), unranked
Website: www.heritage.edu
Admissions email: admissions@heritage.edu
Private
Application deadline (fall): N/A
Undergraduate student body: N/A full time, N/A part time
Expenses: 2015-2016: $19,122; room/board: N/A
Financial aid: (509) 865-8502

Lake Washington Institute of Technology
Kirkland WA
(425) 739-8104
U.S. News ranking: Reg. Coll. (W), unranked
Website: www.lwtech.edu/
Admissions email: N/A
Public
Freshman admissions: N/A; 2015-2016: 1,270 applied, 1,270 accepted. Neither SAT nor ACT required. ACT 25/75 percentile: N/A. High school rank: N/A
Early decision deadline: N/A, notification date: N/A
Early action deadline: N/A, notification date: N/A
Undergraduate student body: 2,118 full time, 2,272 part time; 40% male, 60% female; N/A American Indian, N/A Asian, N/A black, N/A Hispanic, N/A multiracial, N/A Pacific Islander, N/A white, N/A international
Most popular majors: Information not available
Expenses: 2015-2016: $3,880 in state, $9,218 out of state; room/board: N/A
Financial aid: N/A

North Seattle College[1]
Seattle WA
(206) 934-3663
U.S. News ranking: Reg. Coll. (W), unranked
Website: northseattle.edu/
Admissions email: N/A
Public
Application deadline (fall): N/A
Undergraduate student body: N/A full time, N/A part time
Expenses: 2015-2016: $4,458 in state, $9,693 out of state; room/board: N/A
Financial aid: N/A

Northwest University
Kirkland WA
(425) 889-5231
U.S. News ranking: Reg. U. (W), No. 68
Website: www.northwestu.edu
Admissions email: admissions@northwestu.edu
Private; founded 1934
Affiliation: Assembly of God
Freshman admissions: selective; 2015-2016: 766 applied, 488 accepted. Either SAT or ACT required. SAT 25/75 percentile: 840-1075. High school rank: N/A
Early decision deadline: N/A, notification date: N/A
Early action deadline: 11/15, notification date: 12/15
Application deadline (fall): rolling
Undergraduate student body: 905 full time, 25 part time; 34% male, 66% female; 1% American Indian, 5% Asian, 4% black, 8% Hispanic, 4% multiracial, 1% Pacific Islander, 71% white, 4% international; 81% from in state; N/A live on campus; N/A of students in fraternities, N/A in sororities
Most popular majors: 23% Registered Nursing/Registered Nurse; 9% Psychology, General; 8% Business Administration

and Management, General; 7% Elementary Education and Teaching
Expenses: 2016-2017: $29,200; room/board: $8,100
Financial aid: (425) 889-5336; 80% of undergrads determined to have financial need; average aid package $17,630

Olympic College[1]
Bremerton WA
(360) 792-6050
U.S. News ranking: Reg. Coll. (W), unranked
Website: www.olympic.edu
Admissions email: N/A
Public
Application deadline (fall): N/A
Undergraduate student body: N/A full time, N/A part time
Expenses: 2015-2016: $3,837 in state, $N/A out of state; room/board: $8,300
Financial aid: (800) 259-6718

Pacific Lutheran University
Tacoma WA
(800) 274-6758
U.S. News ranking: Reg. U. (W), No. 15
Website: www.plu.edu
Admissions email: admission@plu.edu
Private; founded 1890
Affiliation: Lutheran
Freshman admissions: selective; 2015-2016: 3,623 applied, 2,737 accepted. Either SAT or ACT required. SAT 25/75 percentile: 980-1230. High school rank: 50% in top tenth, 85% in top quarter, 96% in top half
Early decision deadline: N/A, notification date: N/A
Early action deadline: N/A, notification date: N/A
Application deadline (fall): N/A
Undergraduate student body: 2,774 full time, 86 part time; 38% male, 62% female; 1% American Indian, 8% Asian, 3% black, 8% Hispanic, 7% multiracial, 1% Pacific Islander, 67% white, 4% international; 79% from in state; 45% live on campus; N/A of students in fraternities, N/A in sororities
Most popular majors: 13% Business, Management, Marketing, and Related Support Services; 12% Social Sciences; 9% Health Professions and Related Programs; 8% Education; 7% Biological and Biomedical Sciences
Expenses: 2016-2017: $39,430; room/board: $10,330
Financial aid: (253) 535-7134; 74% of undergrads determined to have financial need; average aid package $35,634

Peninsula College[1]
Port Angeles WA
(360) 417-6340
U.S. News ranking: Reg. Coll. (W), unranked
Website: www.pencol.edu
Admissions email: N/A
Public
Application deadline (fall): N/A
Undergraduate student body: N/A full time, N/A part time

Expenses: 2015-2016: $4,191 in state, $4,591 out of state; room/board: N/A
Financial aid: (360) 417-6390

Seattle Central College[1]
Seattle WA
(206) 934-5450
U.S. News ranking: Reg. Coll. (W), unranked
Website: seattlecentral.edu/
Admissions email: N/A
Public
Application deadline (fall): N/A
Undergraduate student body: N/A full time, N/A part time
Expenses: 2015-2016: $3,891 in state, $9,083 out of state; room/board: N/A
Financial aid: N/A

Seattle Pacific University
Seattle WA
(800) 366-3344
U.S. News ranking: Nat. U., No. 159
Website: www.spu.edu
Admissions email: admissions@spu.edu
Private; founded 1891
Affiliation: Free Methodist
Freshman admissions: selective; 2015-2016: 5,227 applied, 4,266 accepted. Either SAT or ACT required. SAT 25/75 percentile: 1000-1230. High school rank: 1% in top tenth, 3% in top quarter, 12% in top half
Early decision deadline: N/A, notification date: N/A
Early action deadline: 11/15, notification date: 1/5
Application deadline (fall): 2/1
Undergraduate student body: 3,084 full time, 118 part time; 32% male, 68% female; 0% American Indian, 11% Asian, 4% black, 10% Hispanic, 8% multiracial, 0% Pacific Islander, 61% white, 4% international; 64% from in state; 52% live on campus; N/A of students in fraternities, N/A in sororities
Most popular majors: Information not available
Expenses: 2016-2017: $38,940; room/board: $10,824
Financial aid: (206) 281-2061; 71% of undergrads determined to have financial need; average aid package $32,666

Seattle University
Seattle WA
(206) 296-2000
U.S. News ranking: Reg. U. (W), No. 8
Website: www.seattleu.edu
Admissions email: admissions@seattleu.edu
Private; founded 1891
Affiliation: Roman Catholic (Jesuit)
Freshman admissions: more selective; 2015-2016: 7,806 applied, 5,700 accepted. Either SAT or ACT required. SAT 25/75 percentile: 1060-1280. High school rank: 38% in top tenth, 68% in top quarter, 93% in top half
Early decision deadline: N/A, notification date: N/A

Early action deadline: 11/15, notification date: 12/23
Application deadline (fall): rolling
Undergraduate student body: 4,480 full time, 231 part time; 40% male, 60% female; 0% American Indian, 16% Asian, 3% black, 9% Hispanic, 7% multiracial, 1% Pacific Islander, 44% white, 11% international; 43% from in state; 46% live on campus; 0% of students in fraternities, 0% in sororities
Most popular majors: 24% Business, Management, Marketing, and Related Support Services; 14% Health Professions and Related Programs; 7% Engineering; 7% Social Sciences; 6% Visual and Performing Arts
Expenses: 2016-2017: $41,265; room/board: $11,499
Financial aid: (206) 296-2000; 57% of undergrads determined to have financial need; average aid package $32,047

South Seattle College[1]
Seattle WA
(206) 764-5300
U.S. News ranking: Reg. Coll. (W), unranked
Website: southseattle.edu
Admissions email: N/A
Public
Application deadline (fall): N/A
Undergraduate student body: N/A full time, N/A part time
Expenses: 2015-2016: $4,130 in state, $9,550 out of state; room/board: N/A
Financial aid: (206) 934-5317

St. Martin's University
Lacey WA
(800) 368-8803
U.S. News ranking: Reg. U. (W), No. 40
Website: www.stmartin.edu
Admissions email: admissions@stmartin.edu
Private; founded 1895
Affiliation: Roman Catholic (Benedictine)
Freshman admissions: selective; 2015-2016: 945 applied, 880 accepted. Either SAT or ACT required. SAT 25/75 percentile: 918-1150. High school rank: 18% in top tenth, 55% in top quarter, 85% in top half
Early decision deadline: N/A, notification date: N/A
Early action deadline: N/A, notification date: N/A
Application deadline (fall): 7/31
Undergraduate student body: 1,008 full time, 341 part time; 51% male, 49% female; 1% American Indian, 5% Asian, 7% black, 14% Hispanic, 6% multiracial, 2% Pacific Islander, 55% white, 5% international; 69% from in state; 33% live on campus; 0% of students in fraternities, 0% in sororities
Most popular majors: 26% Business, Management, Marketing, and Related Support Services; 13% Engineering; 11% Psychology; 10% Education; 8% Biological and Biomedical Sciences
Expenses: 2016-2017: $34,356; room/board: $10,700

Financial aid: (360) 438-4397; 85% of undergrads determined to have financial need; average aid package $26,119

Trinity Lutheran College[1]
Everett WA
(425) 249-4741
U.S. News ranking: Reg. Coll. (W), No. 16
Website: www.tlc.edu/
Admissions email: admissions@tlc.edu
Private
Application deadline (fall): N/A
Undergraduate student body: N/A full time, N/A part time
Expenses: 2015-2016: $29,650; room/board: $8,350
Financial aid: (425) 249-4777

University of Puget Sound
Tacoma WA
(253) 879-3211
U.S. News ranking: Nat. Lib. Arts, No. 70
Website: www.pugetsound.edu
Admissions email: admission@pugetsound.edu
Private; founded 1888
Freshman admissions: more selective; 2015-2016: 5,827 applied, 4,616 accepted. Neither SAT nor ACT required. SAT 25/75 percentile: 1100-1340. High school rank: 37% in top tenth, 68% in top quarter, 94% in top half
Early decision deadline: 11/15, notification date: 12/15
Early action deadline: N/A, notification date: N/A
Application deadline (fall): 1/15
Undergraduate student body: 2,459 full time, 17 part time; 41% male, 59% female; 0% American Indian, 6% Asian, 1% black, 7% Hispanic, 8% multiracial, 0% Pacific Islander, 74% white, 0% international; 21% from in state; 66% live on campus; 27% of students in fraternities, 31% in sororities
Most popular majors: 17% Social Sciences; 12% Business, Management, Marketing, and Related Support Services; 11% Biological and Biomedical Sciences; 10% Foreign Languages, Literatures, and Linguistics; 8% Psychology
Expenses: 2016-2017: $46,552; room/board: $11,800
Financial aid: (800) 396-7192; 52% of undergrads determined to have financial need; average aid package $30,798

University of Washington
Seattle WA
(206) 543-9686
U.S. News ranking: Nat. U., No. 54
Website: www.washington.edu
Admissions email: askuwadm@u.washington.edu
Public; founded 1861
Freshman admissions: more selective; 2015-2016: 36,840 applied, 19,646 accepted. Either SAT or ACT required. SAT 25/75

percentile: 1120-1370. High school rank: 92% in top tenth, 98% in top quarter, 100% in top half
Early decision deadline: N/A, notification date: N/A
Early action deadline: N/A, notification date: N/A
Application deadline (fall): 12/1
Undergraduate student body: 28,377 full time, 2,686 part time; 48% male, 52% female; 0% American Indian, 24% Asian, 3% black, 7% Hispanic, 7% multiracial, 0% Pacific Islander, 42% white, 15% international; 83% from in state; 25% live on campus; 16% of students in fraternities, 15% in sororities
Most popular majors: 15% Social Sciences; 13% Biological and Biomedical Sciences; 11% Business, Management, Marketing, and Related Support Services; 9% Engineering
Expenses: 2016-2017: $10,753 in state, $34,791 out of state; room/board: $11,691
Financial aid: (206) 543-6101; 41% of undergrads determined to have financial need; average aid package $18,500

Walla Walla University
College Place WA
(509) 527-2327
U.S. News ranking: Reg. U. (W), No. 52
Website: www.wallawalla.edu
Admissions email: info@wallawalla.edu
Private; founded 1892
Affiliation: Seventh-day Adventist
Freshman admissions: selective; 2015-2016: 1,816 applied, 1,025 accepted. Either SAT or ACT required. SAT 25/75 percentile: 920-1160. High school rank: 15% in top tenth, 40% in top quarter, 70% in top half
Early decision deadline: N/A, notification date: N/A
Early action deadline: N/A, notification date: N/A
Application deadline (fall): rolling
Undergraduate student body: 1,556 full time, 98 part time; 50% male, 50% female; 1% American Indian, 7% Asian, 3% black, 14% Hispanic, 0% multiracial, 1% Pacific Islander, 69% white, 0% international; 36% from in state; N/A live on campus; N/A of students in fraternities, N/A in sororities
Most popular majors: 24% Health Professions and Related Programs; 14% Engineering; 10% Business, Management, Marketing, and Related Support Services; 7% Biological and Biomedical Sciences; 6% Education
Expenses: 2016-2017: $26,982; room/board: $6,990
Financial aid: (800) 656-2815; 65% of undergrads determined to have financial need; average aid package $21,488

Washington State University
Pullman WA
(888) 468-6978
U.S. News ranking: Nat. U., No. 143
Website: www.wsu.edu
Admissions email: admissions@wsu.edu
Public; founded 1890
Freshman admissions: selective; 2015-2016: 19,766 applied, 15,742 accepted. Either SAT or ACT required. SAT 25/75 percentile: 910-1150. High school rank: 34% in top tenth, 55% in top quarter, 84% in top half
Early decision deadline: N/A, notification date: N/A
Early action deadline: N/A, notification date: N/A
Application deadline (fall): rolling
Undergraduate student body: 21,384 full time, 3,086 part time; 48% male, 52% female; 1% American Indian, 5% Asian, 3% black, 13% Hispanic, 8% multiracial, 0% Pacific Islander, 63% white, 5% international; 90% from in state; 25% live on campus; 15% of students in fraternities, 20% in sororities
Most popular majors: 20% Business, Management, Marketing, and Related Support Services; 12% Social Sciences; 11% Engineering; 7% Health Professions and Related Programs
Expenses: 2016-2017: $11,041 in state, $25,673 out of state; room/board: $11,356
Financial aid: (509) 335-9711; 61% of undergrads determined to have financial need; average aid package $14,142

Western Washington University
Bellingham WA
(360) 650-3440
U.S. News ranking: Reg. U. (W), No. 18
Website: www.wwu.edu
Admissions email: admit@cc.wwu.edu
Public; founded 1893
Freshman admissions: selective; 2015-2016: 9,933 applied, 8,183 accepted. Either SAT or ACT required. SAT 25/75 percentile: 1000-1220. High school rank: 23% in top tenth, 54% in top quarter, 88% in top half
Early decision deadline: N/A, notification date: N/A
Early action deadline: N/A, notification date: N/A
Application deadline (fall): 1/31
Undergraduate student body: 13,247 full time, 1,155 part time; 45% male, 55% female; 0% American Indian, 7% Asian, 2% black, 8% Hispanic, 9% multiracial, 0% Pacific Islander, 73% white, 1% international; 91% from in state; 27% live on campus; N/A of students in fraternities, N/A in sororities
Most popular majors: 14% Business, Management, Marketing, and Related Support Services; 12% Social Sciences

Expenses: 2015-2016: $8,611 in state, $20,963 out of state; room/board: $10,341
Financial aid: (360) 650-3470; 50% of undergrads determined to have financial need; average aid package $14,324

Whitman College
Walla Walla WA
(509) 527-5176
U.S. News ranking: Nat. Lib. Arts, No. 41
Website: www.whitman.edu
Admissions email: admission@whitman.edu
Private; founded 1883
Freshman admissions: more selective; 2015-2016: 3,790 applied, 1,619 accepted. Either SAT or ACT required. SAT 25/75 percentile: 1200-1420. High school rank: 54% in top tenth, 88% in top quarter, 98% in top half
Early decision deadline: 11/15, notification date: 12/20
Early action deadline: N/A, notification date: N/A
Application deadline (fall): 1/15
Undergraduate student body: 1,430 full time, 40 part time; 42% male, 58% female; 0% American Indian, 5% Asian, 1% black, 7% Hispanic, 7% multiracial, 0% Pacific Islander, 73% white, 5% international; 36% from in state; 64% live on campus; 44% of students in fraternities, 44% in sororities
Most popular majors: 13% Biology/Biological Sciences, General; 9% Psychology, General; 6% Economics, General; 5% Political Science and Government, General
Expenses: 2016-2017: $47,862; room/board: $11,910
Financial aid: (509) 527-5178; 46% of undergrads determined to have financial need; average aid package $36,130

Whitworth University
Spokane WA
(800) 533-4668
U.S. News ranking: Reg. U. (W), No. 11
Website: www.whitworth.edu
Admissions email: admissions@whitworth.edu
Private; founded 1890
Affiliation: Presbyterian Church
Freshman admissions: selective; 2015-2016: 4,545 applied, 2,837 accepted. Neither SAT nor ACT required. SAT 25/75 percentile: 1060-1270. High school rank: N/A
Early decision deadline: N/A, notification date: N/A
Early action deadline: 11/30, notification date: 12/20
Application deadline (fall): 9/1
Undergraduate student body: 2,301 full time, 45 part time; 38% male, 62% female; 1% American Indian, 5% Asian, 2% black, 8% Hispanic, 6% multiracial, 0% Pacific Islander, 75% white, 2% international; 70% from in state; 53% live on campus; N/A of students in fraternities, N/A in sororities
Most popular majors: 14% Business, Management, Marketing, and Related Support Services; 12% Social Sciences

Most popular majors: 15% Business, Management, Marketing, and Related Support Services; 11% Social Sciences; 8% Physical Sciences; 8% Psychology; 7% Biological and Biomedical Sciences
Expenses: 2016-2017: $40,562; room/board: $11,170
Financial aid: (800) 533-4668; 68% of undergrads determined to have financial need; average aid package $32,974

WEST VIRGINIA

Alderson Broaddus University
Philippi WV
(800) 263-1549
U.S. News ranking: Reg. Coll. (S), No. 37
Website: www.ab.edu
Admissions email: admissions@ab.edu
Private; founded 1871
Affiliation: American Baptist
Freshman admissions: selective; 2015-2016: 4,206 applied, 2,258 accepted. Either SAT or ACT required. ACT 25/75 percentile: 19-23. High school rank: 11% in top tenth, 31% in top quarter, 69% in top half
Early decision deadline: N/A, notification date: N/A
Early action deadline: N/A, notification date: N/A
Application deadline (fall): 8/25
Undergraduate student body: 1,046 full time, 39 part time; 54% male, 46% female; 0% American Indian, 1% Asian, 16% black, 4% Hispanic, 1% multiracial, 0% Pacific Islander, 73% white, 5% international; 37% from in state; 85% live on campus; 4% of students in fraternities, 5% in sororities
Most popular majors: 29% Registered Nursing/Registered Nurse; 9% Biology/Biological Sciences, General; 7% Business Administration and Management, General; 7% Music Teacher Education; 6% Sport and Fitness Administration/Management
Expenses: 2016-2017: $25,350; room/board: $8,050
Financial aid: (304) 457-6354; 84% of undergrads determined to have financial need; average aid package $21,773

American Public University System
Charles Town WV
(877) 777-9081
U.S. News ranking: Reg. U. (S), unranked
Website: www.apus.edu
Admissions email: N/A
For-profit; founded 1991
Freshman admissions: N/A; 2015-2016: N/A applied, N/A accepted. Neither SAT nor ACT required. ACT 25/75 percentile: N/A. High school rank: N/A
Early decision deadline: N/A, notification date: N/A
Early action deadline: N/A, notification date: N/A
Application deadline (fall): rolling

Undergraduate student body: 3,759 full time, 39,129 part time; 64% male, 36% female; 1% American Indian, 2% Asian, 19% black, 11% Hispanic, 4% multiracial, 1% Pacific Islander, 57% white, 1% international
Most popular majors: 16% Business Administration and Management, General; 9% Criminal Justice/Safety Studies; 9% International/Global Studies; 6% Homeland Security; 6% Kinesiology and Exercise Science
Expenses: 2015-2016: $6,880; room/board: N/A
Financial aid: (877) 372-3535

Bethany College
Bethany WV
(304) 829-7611
U.S. News ranking: Nat. Lib. Arts, second tier
Website: www.bethanywv.edu
Admissions email: enrollment@bethanywv.edu
Private; founded 1840
Affiliation: Christian Church (Disciples of Christ)
Freshman admissions: less selective; 2015-2016: 1,168 applied, 820 accepted. Either SAT or ACT required. SAT 25/75 percentile: 780-1010. High school rank: 5% in top tenth, 21% in top quarter, 54% in top half
Early decision deadline: N/A, notification date: N/A
Early action deadline: N/A, notification date: N/A
Application deadline (fall): rolling
Undergraduate student body: 719 full time, 7 part time; 58% male, 42% female; 1% American Indian, 0% Asian, 18% black, 5% Hispanic, 2% multiracial, 0% Pacific Islander, 51% white, 2% international; 14% from in state; 98% live on campus; 19% of students in fraternities, 43% in sororities
Most popular majors: 16% Psychology; 15% Education; 9% Biological and Biomedical Sciences; 7% Public Administration and Social Service Professions
Expenses: 2016-2017: $27,438; room/board: $10,124
Financial aid: (304) 829-7141; 88% of undergrads determined to have financial need; average aid package $27,949

Bluefield State College
Bluefield WV
(304) 327-4065
U.S. News ranking: Reg. Coll. (S), No. 52
Website: www.bluefieldstate.edu
Admissions email: bscadmit@bluefieldstate.edu
Public; founded 1895
Freshman admissions: selective; 2015-2016: 618 applied, 475 accepted. Either SAT or ACT required. ACT 25/75 percentile: 17-22. High school rank: 31% in top tenth, 56% in top quarter, 82% in top half
Early decision deadline: N/A, notification date: N/A
Early action deadline: N/A, notification date: N/A

Application deadline (fall): rolling
Undergraduate student body: 1,217 full time, 269 part time; 40% male, 60% female; 0% American Indian, 1% Asian, 9% black, 1% Hispanic, 2% multiracial, 0% Pacific Islander, 85% white, 3% international; 97% from in state; 0% live on campus; 4% of students in fraternities, 4% in sororities
Most popular majors: 22% Liberal Arts and Sciences, General Studies and Humanities; 19% Engineering Technologies and Engineering-Related Fields; 16% Health Professions and Related Programs; 11% Social Sciences; 9% Education
Expenses: 2015-2016: $6,120 in state, $11,280 out of state; room/board: N/A
Financial aid: (304) 327-4020; 80% of undergrads determined to have financial need; average aid package $3,495

Concord University
Athens WV
(304) 384-5249
U.S. News ranking: Reg. U. (S), second tier
Website: www.concord.edu
Admissions email: admissions@concord.edu
Public; founded 1872
Freshman admissions: selective; 2015-2016: 1,483 applied, 1,267 accepted. Either SAT or ACT required. ACT 25/75 percentile: 19-24. High school rank: 21% in top tenth, 46% in top quarter, 78% in top half
Early decision deadline: N/A, notification date: N/A
Early action deadline: N/A, notification date: N/A
Application deadline (fall): rolling
Undergraduate student body: 1,953 full time, 189 part time; 44% male, 56% female; 1% American Indian, 1% Asian, 7% black, 1% Hispanic, 0% multiracial, 0% Pacific Islander, 86% white, 4% international; 87% from in state; 37% live on campus; N/A of students in fraternities, N/A in sororities
Most popular majors: 21% Business, Management, Marketing, and Related Support Services; 21% Liberal Arts and Sciences, General Studies and Humanities; 15% Education; 8% Social Sciences; 7% Public Administration and Social Service Professions
Expenses: 2016-2017: $7,080 in state, $15,564 out of state; room/board: $8,350
Financial aid: (304) 384-6069; 75% of undergrads determined to have financial need; average aid package $8,482

Davis and Elkins College[1]
Elkins WV
(304) 637-1230
U.S. News ranking: Nat. Lib. Arts, second tier
Website: www.davisandelkins.edu
Admissions email: admiss@davisandelkins.edu
Private
Application deadline (fall): N/A

Undergraduate student body: N/A full time, N/A part time
Expenses: 2015-2016: $27,492; room/board: $9,250
Financial aid: (304) 637-1373

Fairmont State University
Fairmont WV
(304) 367-4892
U.S. News ranking: Reg. U. (S), second tier
Website: www.fairmontstate.edu
Admissions email: admit@fairmontstate.edu
Public; founded 1865
Freshman admissions: selective; 2015-2016: 2,943 applied, 1,930 accepted. Either SAT or ACT required. ACT 25/75 percentile: 18-23. High school rank: 10% in top tenth, 33% in top quarter, 71% in top half
Early decision deadline: N/A, notification date: N/A
Early action deadline: N/A, notification date: N/A
Application deadline (fall): 8/15
Undergraduate student body: 3,259 full time, 548 part time; 45% male, 55% female; 0% American Indian, 0% Asian, 5% black, 2% Hispanic, 3% multiracial, 0% Pacific Islander, 86% white, 2% international; 91% from in state; 24% live on campus; N/A of students in fraternities, N/A in sororities
Most popular majors: 12% Civil Engineering Technology/Technician; 11% Criminal Justice/Safety Studies; 10% Education, General; 10% Registered Nursing/Registered Nurse; 8% General Studies
Expenses: 2016-2017: $6,620 in state, $13,970 out of state; room/board: $8,766
Financial aid: (304) 367-4213; 73% of undergrads determined to have financial need; average aid package $8,934

Glenville State College
Glenville WV
(304) 462-4128
U.S. News ranking: Reg. Coll. (S), No. 50
Website: www.glenville.edu
Admissions email: admissions@glenville.edu
Public; founded 1872
Freshman admissions: less selective; 2015-2016: 1,430 applied, 1,036 accepted. Either SAT or ACT required. ACT 25/75 percentile: 17-22. High school rank: 8% in top tenth, 26% in top quarter, 57% in top half
Early decision deadline: N/A, notification date: N/A
Early action deadline: N/A, notification date: N/A
Application deadline (fall): rolling
Undergraduate student body: 1,044 full time, 688 part time; 55% male, 45% female; 0% American Indian, 1% Asian, 19% black, 2% Hispanic, 1% multiracial, 0% Pacific Islander, 68% white, 0% international
Most popular majors: Information not available

Expenses: 2015-2016: $7,032 in state, $15,888 out of state; room/board: $9,702
Financial aid: (304) 462-4103; 83% of undergrads determined to have financial need; average aid package $14,287

Marshall University
Huntington WV
(800) 642-3499
U.S. News ranking: Reg. U. (S), No. 47
Website: www.marshall.edu
Admissions email: admissions@marshall.edu
Public; founded 1837
Freshman admissions: selective; 2015-2016: 4,911 applied, 4,317 accepted. Either SAT or ACT required. ACT 25/75 percentile: 20-25. High school rank: N/A
Early decision deadline: N/A, notification date: N/A
Early action deadline: N/A, notification date: N/A
Application deadline (fall): rolling
Undergraduate student body: 8,005 full time, 1,513 part time; 43% male, 57% female; 0% American Indian, 1% Asian, 7% black, 2% Hispanic, 3% multiracial, 0% Pacific Islander, 84% white, 1% international; 78% from in state; N/A live on campus; N/A of students in fraternities, N/A in sororities
Most popular majors: 18% Business, Management, Marketing, and Related Support Services; 16% Health Professions and Related Programs; 12% Liberal Arts and Sciences, General Studies and Humanities; 11% Education; 6% Psychology
Expenses: 2015-2016: $6,814 in state, $15,602 out of state; room/board: $8,984
Financial aid: (304) 696-3162; 71% of undergrads determined to have financial need; average aid package $10,347

Ohio Valley University
Vienna WV
(877) 446-8668
U.S. News ranking: Reg. Coll. (S), No. 45
Website: www.ovu.edu
Admissions email: admissions@ovu.edu
Private; founded 1958
Affiliation: Church of Christ
Freshman admissions: selective; 2015-2016: 882 applied, 415 accepted. Either SAT or ACT required. ACT 25/75 percentile: 17-22. High school rank: 8% in top tenth, 10% in top quarter, 41% in top half
Early decision deadline: N/A, notification date: N/A
Early action deadline: N/A, notification date: N/A
Application deadline (fall): 8/15
Undergraduate student body: 398 full time, 20 part time; 53% male, 47% female; N/A American Indian, 0% Asian, 12% black, 5% Hispanic, 4% multiracial, N/A Pacific Islander, 61% white, 9% international; 39% from in state; 60% live on campus; 50% of students in fraternities, 50% in sororities

Most popular majors: 29% Education; 23% Business, Management, Marketing, and Related Support Services; 8% Psychology; 8% Biological and Biomedical Sciences; 7% Theology and Religious Vocations
Expenses: 2016-2017: $20,460; room/board: $7,450
Financial aid: (304) 865-6075; 79% of undergrads determined to have financial need; average aid package $14,737

Salem International University[1]
Salem WV
(888) 235-5024
U.S. News ranking: Reg. U. (S), unranked
Website: www.salemu.edu
Admissions email: admissions@salemu.edu
For-profit
Application deadline (fall): N/A
Undergraduate student body: N/A full time, N/A part time
Expenses: 2015-2016: $17,700; room/board: $7,000
Financial aid: (304) 782-5303

Shepherd University
Shepherdstown WV
(304) 876-5212
U.S. News ranking: Nat. Lib. Arts, second tier
Website: www.shepherd.edu
Admissions email: admissions@shepherd.edu
Public; founded 1871
Freshman admissions: less selective; 2015-2016: 1,648 applied, 1,481 accepted. Either SAT or ACT required. SAT 25/75 percentile: 870-1093. High school rank: N/A
Early decision deadline: N/A, notification date: N/A
Early action deadline: N/A, notification date: N/A
Application deadline (fall): rolling
Undergraduate student body: 2,935 full time, 709 part time; 42% male, 58% female; 0% American Indian, 2% Asian, 10% black, 3% Hispanic, 2% multiracial, 0% Pacific Islander, 82% white, 0% international; 63% from in state; 34% live on campus; 3% of students in fraternities, 4% in sororities
Most popular majors: 14% Liberal Arts and Sciences, General Studies and Humanities; 13% Education; 11% Business, Management, Marketing, and Related Support Services; 9% Health Professions and Related Programs; 9% Parks, Recreation, Leisure, and Fitness Studies
Expenses: 2016-2017: $7,170 in state, $17,482 out of state; room/board: $10,054
Financial aid: (304) 876-5470; 65% of undergrads determined to have financial need; average aid package $12,194

University of Charleston
Charleston WV
(800) 995-4682
U.S. News ranking: Reg. U. (S), No. 72
Website: www.ucwv.edu
Admissions email: admissions@ucwv.edu
Private; founded 1888
Freshman admissions: selective; 2015-2016: 1,949 applied, 1,022 accepted. Either SAT or ACT required. ACT 25/75 percentile: 19-24. High school rank: N/A
Early decision deadline: N/A, notification date: N/A
Early action deadline: N/A, notification date: N/A
Application deadline (fall): rolling
Undergraduate student body: 1,292 full time, 435 part time; 52% male, 48% female; 1% American Indian, 1% Asian, 9% black, 2% Hispanic, 0% multiracial, 0% Pacific Islander, 58% white, 7% international; 57% from in state; 39% live on campus; 3% of students in fraternities, 3% in sororities
Most popular majors: 26% Business, Management, Marketing, and Related Support Services; 19% Health Professions and Related Programs; 12% Biological and Biomedical Sciences; 7% Psychology
Expenses: 2016-2017: $29,100; room/board: $9,100
Financial aid: (304) 357-4759; 84% of undergrads determined to have financial need; average aid package $19,719

West Liberty University
West Liberty WV
(304) 336-8076
U.S. News ranking: Reg. Coll. (S), No. 28
Website: www.westliberty.edu
Admissions email: admissions@westliberty.edu
Public; founded 1837
Freshman admissions: selective; 2015-2016: 1,692 applied, 1,220 accepted. Either SAT or ACT required. ACT 25/75 percentile: 18-24. High school rank: 15% in top tenth, 43% in top quarter, 74% in top half
Early decision deadline: N/A, notification date: N/A
Early action deadline: N/A, notification date: N/A
Application deadline (fall): rolling
Undergraduate student body: 1,847 full time, 319 part time; 40% male, 60% female; 0% American Indian, 1% Asian, 4% black, 1% Hispanic, 1% multiracial, 0% Pacific Islander, 79% white, 2% international; 68% from in state; 44% live on campus; 3% of students in fraternities, 4% in sororities
Most popular majors: 14% Business Administration and Management, General; 13% General Studies; 9% Kinesiology and Exercise Science; 9% Secondary Education and Teaching; 8% Criminal Justice/ Safety Studies

Expenses: 2015-2016: $6,702 in state, $14,112 out of state; room/board: $8,810
Financial aid: (304) 336-8016

West Virginia State University
Institute WV
(304) 766-4345
U.S. News ranking: Nat. Lib. Arts, second tier
Website: www.wvstateu.edu
Admissions email: admissions@wvstateu.edu
Public; founded 1891
Freshman admissions: selective; 2015-2016: 1,439 applied, 1,354 accepted. Either SAT or ACT required. ACT 25/75 percentile: 17-22. High school rank: N/A
Early decision deadline: N/A, notification date: N/A
Early action deadline: N/A, notification date: N/A
Application deadline (fall): 8/15
Undergraduate student body: 1,860 full time, 1,247 part time; 45% male, 55% female; 0% American Indian, 0% Asian, 14% black, 1% Hispanic, 10% multiracial, 0% Pacific Islander, 65% white, 1% international; 89% from in state; 17% live on campus; 1% of students in fraternities, 1% in sororities
Most popular majors: 15% General Studies; 10% Elementary Education and Teaching; 9% Criminal Justice/Safety Studies; 9% Secondary Education and Teaching; 8% Business Administration and Management, General
Expenses: 2016-2017: $6,996 in state, $15,572 out of state; room/board: $11,008
Financial aid: (304) 766-3131

West Virginia University
Morgantown WV
(304) 442-3146
U.S. News ranking: Nat. U., No. 183
Website: www.wvu.edu
Admissions email: tech-admissions@mail.wvu.edu
Public; founded 1867
Freshman admissions: selective; 2015-2016: 15,353 applied, 13,174 accepted. Either SAT or ACT required. ACT 25/75 percentile: 21-27. High school rank: 20% in top tenth, 46% in top quarter, 77% in top half
Early decision deadline: N/A, notification date: N/A
Early action deadline: N/A, notification date: N/A
Application deadline (fall): 8/1
Undergraduate student body: 20,532 full time, 1,966 part time; 54% male, 46% female; 0% American Indian, 1% Asian, 5% black, 4% Hispanic, 3% multiracial, 0% Pacific Islander, 81% white, 6% international; 47% from in state; 15% live on campus; N/A of students in fraternities, N/A in sororities
Most popular majors: 13% Engineering; 12% Business, Management, Marketing, and Related Support Services; 9% Multi/Interdisciplinary Studies; 8% Social Sciences

Expenses: 2015-2016: $7,632 in state, $21,432 out of state; room/board: $9,872
Financial aid: (800) 344-9881; 56% of undergrads determined to have financial need; average aid package $6,839

West Virginia University– Parkersburg[1]
Parkersburg WV
(304) 424-8220
U.S. News ranking: Reg. Coll. (S), unranked
Website: www.wvup.edu
Admissions email: info@mail.wvup.edu
Public
Application deadline (fall): rolling
Undergraduate student body: N/A full time, N/A part time
Expenses: 2015-2016: $3,216 in state, $11,559 out of state; room/board: N/A
Financial aid: (304) 424-8210

West Virginia Wesleyan College
Buckhannon WV
(800) 722-9933
U.S. News ranking: Reg. U. (S), No. 47
Website: www.wvwc.edu
Admissions email: admissions@wvwc.edu
Private; founded 1890
Affiliation: United Methodist
Freshman admissions: selective; 2015-2016: 1,782 applied, 1,376 accepted. Either SAT or ACT required. ACT 25/75 percentile: 20-25. High school rank: 25% in top tenth, 53% in top quarter, 82% in top half
Early decision deadline: N/A, notification date: N/A
Early action deadline: N/A, notification date: N/A
Application deadline (fall): rolling
Undergraduate student body: 1,363 full time, 26 part time; 45% male, 55% female; 0% American Indian, 0% Asian, 9% black, 2% Hispanic, 3% multiracial, 0% Pacific Islander, 79% white, 5% international; 60% from in state; 80% live on campus; 25% of students in fraternities, 25% in sororities
Most popular majors: 11% Parks, Recreation, Leisure, and Fitness Studies; 10% Business, Management, Marketing, and Related Support Services; 10% Education; 10% Psychology; 9% Physical Sciences
Expenses: 2016-2017: $29,752; room/board: $8,248
Financial aid: (304) 473-8080; 78% of undergrads determined to have financial need; average aid package $26,891

Wheeling Jesuit University
Wheeling WV
(800) 624-6992
U.S. News ranking: Reg. U. (S), No. 37
Website: www.wju.edu
Admissions email: admiss@wju.edu
Private; founded 1954

Affiliation: Jesuit, Roman Catholic
Freshman admissions: selective; 2015-2016: 799 applied, 732 accepted. Either SAT or ACT required. ACT 25/75 percentile: 20-25. High school rank: 12% in top tenth, 39% in top quarter, 71% in top half
Early decision deadline: N/A, notification date: N/A
Early action deadline: N/A, notification date: N/A
Application deadline (fall): rolling
Undergraduate student body: 858 full time, 185 part time; 48% male, 52% female; 0% American Indian, 1% Asian, 6% black, 3% Hispanic, 2% multiracial, 0% Pacific Islander, 75% white, 6% international; 31% from in state; 64% live on campus; N/A of students in fraternities, N/A in sororities
Most popular majors: 35% Health Professions and Related Programs; 19% Business, Management, Marketing, and Related Support Services; 9% Psychology; 6% Homeland Security, Law Enforcement, Firefighting and Related Protective Services; 6% Physical Sciences
Expenses: 2016-2017: $28,110; room/board: $7,796
Financial aid: (304) 243-2304; 74% of undergrads determined to have financial need; average aid package $25,293

WISCONSIN

Alverno College
Milwaukee WI
(414) 382-6100
U.S. News ranking: Reg. U. (Mid. W), No. 63
Website: www.alverno.edu
Admissions email: admissions@alverno.edu
Private; founded 1887
Affiliation: Roman Catholic
Freshman admissions: less selective; 2015-2016: 613 applied, 473 accepted. Either SAT or ACT required. ACT 25/75 percentile: 16-22. High school rank: 16% in top tenth, 36% in top quarter, 71% in top half
Early decision deadline: N/A, notification date: N/A
Early action deadline: N/A, notification date: N/A
Application deadline (fall): rolling
Undergraduate student body: 1,194 full time, 364 part time; 0% male, 100% female; 1% American Indian, 5% Asian, 15% black, 23% Hispanic, 4% multiracial, 0% Pacific Islander, 52% white, 0% international; 95% from in state; 15% live on campus; N/A of students in fraternities, 1% in sororities
Most popular majors: 38% Health Professions and Related Programs; 15% Liberal Arts and Sciences, General Studies and Humanities; 11% Business, Management, Marketing, and Related Support Services; 6% Psychology; 6% Biological and Biomedical Sciences
Expenses: 2016-2017: $26,932; room/board: $7,884

Financial aid: (414) 382-6046; 86% of undergrads determined to have financial need; average aid package $21,917

Beloit College
Beloit WI
(608) 363-2500
U.S. News ranking: Nat. Lib. Arts, No. 62
Website: www.beloit.edu
Admissions email: adniss@beloit.edu
Private; founded 1846
Freshman admissions: more selective; 2015-2016: 3,552 applied, 2,443 accepted. Neither SAT nor ACT required. ACT 25/75 percentile: 24-30. High school rank: 29% in top tenth, 64% in top quarter, 91% in top half
Early decision deadline: 11/1, notification date: 11/30
Early action deadline: 12/1, notification date: 12/15
Application deadline (fall): rolling
Undergraduate student body: 1,296 full time, 62 part time; 45% male, 55% female; 0% American Indian, 3% Asian, 5% black, 9% Hispanic, 3% multiracial, 0% Pacific Islander, 66% white, 9% international; 17% from in state; 87% live on campus; 19% of students in fraternities, 20% in sororities
Most popular majors: 21% Social Sciences; 11% Foreign Languages, Literatures, and Linguistics; 10% Physical Sciences; 9% English Language and Literature/Letters; 8% Visual and Performing Arts
Expenses: 2016-2017: $47,060; room/board: $8,146
Financial aid: (608) 363-2663; 68% of undergrads determined to have financial need; average aid package $37,008

Cardinal Stritch University
Milwaukee WI
(414) 410-4040
U.S. News ranking: Nat. U., second tier
Website: www.stritch.edu
Admissions email: admityou@stritch.edu
Private; founded 1937
Affiliation: Roman Catholic
Freshman admissions: selective; 2015-2016: 783 applied, 602 accepted. Neither SAT nor ACT required. ACT 25/75 percentile: 20-24. High school rank: 20% in top tenth, 46% in top quarter, 78% in top half
Early decision deadline: N/A, notification date: N/A
Early action deadline: N/A, notification date: N/A
Application deadline (fall): rolling
Undergraduate student body: 1,756 full time, 219 part time; 34% male, 66% female; 1% American Indian, 2% Asian, 21% black, 11% Hispanic, 3% multiracial, 0% Pacific Islander, 54% white, 6% international; 86% from in state; 14% live on campus; 3% of students in fraternities, 0% in sororities

Most popular majors: 42% Organizational Leadership; 15% Business Administration and Management, General; 6% Registered Nursing, Nursing Administration, Nursing Research and Clinical Nursing, Other; 5% Business/Commerce, General; 5% Human Resources Management/Personnel Administration, General
Expenses: 2016-2017: $28,212; room/board: $7,940
Financial aid: (414) 410-4048; 70% of undergrads determined to have financial need; average aid package $17,326

Carroll University
Waukesha WI
(262) 524-7220
U.S. News ranking: Reg. U. (Mid. W), No. 56
Website: www.carrollu.edu/
Admissions email: ccinfo@carrollu.edu
Private; founded 1846
Affiliation: Presbyterian Church (USA)
Freshman admissions: selective; 2015-2016: 2,337 applied, 2,196 accepted. Either SAT or ACT required. ACT 25/75 percentile: 21-26. High school rank: 21% in top tenth, 50% in top quarter, 84% in top half
Early decision deadline: N/A, notification date: N/A
Early action deadline: N/A, notification date: N/A
Application deadline (fall): rolling
Undergraduate student body: 2,752 full time, 287 part time; 35% male, 65% female; 0% American Indian, 3% Asian, 1% black, 7% Hispanic, 2% multiracial, 0% Pacific Islander, 83% white, 2% international; 75% from in state; 64% live on campus; N/A of students in fraternities, N/A in sororities
Most popular majors: 17% Kinesiology and Exercise Science; 11% Psychology, General; 9% Registered Nursing/Registered Nurse; 7% Business Administration and Management, General; 6% Biology/Biological Sciences, General
Expenses: 2016-2017: $30,388; room/board: $9,004
Financial aid: (262) 524-7296; 79% of undergrads determined to have financial need; average aid package $21,587

Carthage College
Kenosha WI
(262) 551-6000
U.S. News ranking: Nat. Lib. Arts, No. 154
Website: www.carthage.edu
Admissions email: admissions@carthage.edu
Private; founded 1847
Affiliation: Evangelical Lutheran Church in America
Freshman admissions: more selective; 2015-2016: 7,165 applied, 5,028 accepted. Either SAT or ACT required. ACT 25/75 percentile: 22-28. High school rank: 33% in top tenth, 58% in top quarter, 85% in top half
Early decision deadline: N/A, notification date: N/A

Early action deadline: N/A, notification date: N/A
Application deadline (fall): rolling
Undergraduate student body: 2,636 full time, 247 part time; 46% male, 54% female; 0% American Indian, 1% Asian, 4% black, 4% Hispanic, 3% multiracial, 0% Pacific Islander, 75% white, 1% international; 40% from in state; N/A live on campus; N/A of students in fraternities, N/A in sororities
Most popular majors: Information not available
Expenses: 2016-2017: $40,265; room/board: $10,974
Financial aid: (262) 551-6001; 79% of undergrads determined to have financial need; average aid package $30,411

Concordia University Wisconsin
Mequon WI
(262) 243-4300
U.S. News ranking: Reg. U. (Mid. W), No. 56
Website: www.cuw.edu
Admissions email: admissions@cuw.edu
Private; founded 1881
Affiliation: Lutheran Church–Missouri Synod
Freshman admissions: selective; 2015-2016: 2,837 applied, 1,959 accepted. ACT required. ACT 25/75 percentile: 20-26. High school rank: 20% in top tenth, 45% in top quarter, 77% in top half
Early decision deadline: N/A, notification date: N/A
Early action deadline: N/A, notification date: N/A
Application deadline (fall): 8/15
Undergraduate student body: 3,005 full time, 1,333 part time; 36% male, 64% female; 1% American Indian, 2% Asian, 15% black, 2% Hispanic, 3% multiracial, 0% Pacific Islander, 73% white, 2% international
Most popular majors: 16% Registered Nursing/Registered Nurse; 15% Business Administration and Management, General; 6% Occupational Therapy/Therapist; 5% Criminal Justice/Safety Studies; 4% Health/Health Care Administration/Management
Expenses: 2016-2017: $28,040; room/board: $10,330
Financial aid: (262) 243-4569; 80% of undergrads determined to have financial need; average aid package $20,419

Edgewood College
Madison WI
(608) 663-2294
U.S. News ranking: Nat. U., No. 171
Website: www.edgewood.edu
Admissions email: admissions@edgewood.edu
Private; founded 1927
Affiliation: Roman Catholic
Freshman admissions: selective; 2015-2016: 1,160 applied, 891 accepted. Either SAT or ACT required. ACT 25/75 percentile: 20-25. High school rank: 13% in top tenth, 45% in top quarter, 84% in top half

Early decision deadline: N/A, notification date: N/A
Early action deadline: N/A, notification date: N/A
Application deadline (fall): 8/15
Undergraduate student body: 1,550 full time, 263 part time; 30% male, 70% female; 0% American Indian, 3% Asian, 3% black, 6% Hispanic, 3% multiracial, 0% Pacific Islander, 80% white, 3% international; 93% from in state; 30% live on campus; N/A of students in fraternities, N/A in sororities
Most popular majors: 21% Registered Nursing/Registered Nurse; 9% Business/Commerce, General; 8% Psychology, General; 6% Business Administration and Management, General; 4% Elementary Education and Teaching
Expenses: 2016-2017: $27,530; room/board: $9,870
Financial aid: (608) 663-2305; 77% of undergrads determined to have financial need; average aid package $20,667

Herzing University[1]
Madison WI
(800) 596-0724
U.S. News ranking: Reg. U. (Mid. W), second tier
Website: www.herzing.edu/madison
Admissions email: info@msn.herzing.edu
For-profit
Application deadline (fall): N/A
Undergraduate student body: N/A full time, N/A part time
Expenses: 2015-2016: $13,090; room/board: $9,675
Financial aid: N/A

Lakeland College[1]
Plymouth WI
(920) 565-1226
U.S. News ranking: Reg. U. (Mid. W), second tier
Website: www.lakeland.edu
Admissions email: admissions@lakeland.edu
Private; founded 1862
Affiliation: United Church of Christ
Application deadline (fall): rolling
Undergraduate student body: N/A full time, N/A part time
Expenses: 2015-2016: $25,050; room/board: $8,530
Financial aid: (920) 565-1298

Lawrence University
Appleton WI
(800) 227-0982
U.S. News ranking: Nat. Lib. Arts, No. 60
Website: www.lawrence.edu/
Admissions email: admissions@lawrence.edu
Private; founded 1847
Freshman admissions: more selective; 2015-2016: 3,014 applied, 2,057 accepted. Neither SAT nor ACT required. ACT 25/75 percentile: 26-32. High school rank: 42% in top tenth, 77% in top quarter, 97% in top half
Early decision deadline: N/A, notification date: N/A
Early action deadline: 12/1, notification date: 1/25

Application deadline (fall): 1/15
Undergraduate student body: 1,515 full time, 46 part time; 45% male, 55% female; 0% American Indian, 5% Asian, 3% black, 7% Hispanic, 4% multiracial, 0% Pacific Islander, 70% white, 10% international; 29% from in state; 96% live on campus; 20% of students in fraternities, 14% in sororities
Most popular majors: 22% Visual and Performing Arts; 15% Biological and Biomedical Sciences; 13% Social Sciences; 9% Psychology; 6% English Language and Literature/Letters
Expenses: 2016-2017: $44,844; room/board: $9,654
Financial aid: (920) 832-6583; 62% of undergrads determined to have financial need; average aid package $35,483

Maranatha Baptist University
Watertown WI
(920) 206-2327
U.S. News ranking: Reg. Coll. (Mid. W), No. 48
Website: www.mbu.edu
Admissions email: admissions@mbu.edu
Private; founded 1968
Affiliation: Baptist
Freshman admissions: selective; 2015-2016: 338 applied, 232 accepted. Either SAT or ACT required. ACT 25/75 percentile: 20-26. High school rank: 13% in top tenth, 26% in top quarter, 40% in top half
Early decision deadline: N/A, notification date: N/A
Early action deadline: N/A, notification date: N/A
Application deadline (fall): rolling
Undergraduate student body: 633 full time, 272 part time; 43% male, 57% female; 0% American Indian, 1% Asian, 1% black, 3% Hispanic, 4% multiracial, 0% Pacific Islander, 87% white, 1% international; 26% from in state; 69% live on campus; N/A of students in fraternities, N/A in sororities
Most popular majors: 22% Education; 15% Multi/Interdisciplinary Studies; 14% Theology and Religious Vocations; 13% Health Professions and Related Programs; 13% Liberal Arts and Sciences, General Studies and Humanities
Expenses: 2016-2017: $14,260; room/board: $6,720
Financial aid: (920) 206-2319; 86% of undergrads determined to have financial need; average aid package $10,065

Marian University
Fond du Lac WI
(920) 923-7650
U.S. News ranking: Reg. U. (Mid. W), No. 113
Website: www.marianuniversity.edu
Admissions email: admissions@marianuniversity.edu
Private; founded 1936
Affiliation: Roman Catholic
Freshman admissions: selective; 2015-2016: 1,162 applied, 974 accepted. Either SAT or ACT

required. ACT 25/75 percentile: 17-23. High school rank: 11% in top tenth, 28% in top quarter, 64% in top half
Early decision deadline: N/A, notification date: N/A
Early action deadline: N/A, notification date: N/A
Application deadline (fall): rolling
Undergraduate student body: 1,287 full time, 266 part time; 29% male, 71% female; 0% American Indian, 1% Asian, 6% black, 6% Hispanic, 1% multiracial, 0% Pacific Islander, 82% white, 2% international; 87% from in state; 21% live on campus; 0% of students in fraternities, 4% in sororities
Most popular majors: 34% Health Professions and Related Programs; 19% Business, Management, Marketing, and Related Support Services; 14% Homeland Security, Law Enforcement, Firefighting and Related Protective Services; 7% Education; 7% Psychology
Expenses: 2016-2017: $28,280; room/board: $6,750
Financial aid: (920) 923-7614; 92% of undergrads determined to have financial need; average aid package $17,303

Marquette University
Milwaukee WI
(800) 222-6544
U.S. News ranking: Nat. U., No. 86
Website: www.marquette.edu
Admissions email: admissions@marquette.edu
Private; founded 1881
Affiliation: Roman Catholic (Jesuit)
Freshman admissions: more selective; 2015-2016: 20,486 applied, 15,202 accepted. Either SAT or ACT required. ACT 25/75 percentile: 24-30. High school rank: 34% in top tenth, 68% in top quarter, 94% in top half
Early decision deadline: N/A, notification date: N/A
Early action deadline: N/A, notification date: N/A
Application deadline (fall): 12/1
Undergraduate student body: 8,002 full time, 332 part time; 47% male, 53% female; 0% American Indian, 6% Asian, 4% black, 10% Hispanic, 4% multiracial, 0% Pacific Islander, 73% white, 4% international; 33% from in state; 52% live on campus; 4% of students in fraternities, 9% in sororities
Most popular majors: 28% Business, Management, Marketing, and Related Support Services; 10% Biological and Biomedical Sciences; 10% Engineering; 9% Social Sciences
Expenses: 2016-2017: $38,470; room/board: $11,440
Financial aid: (414) 288-0200; 57% of undergrads determined to have financial need; average aid package $25,701

Milwaukee Institute of Art and Design
Milwaukee WI
(414) 291-8070
U.S. News ranking: Arts, unranked
Website: www.miad.edu
Admissions email: admissions@miad.edu
Private; founded 1974
Freshman admissions: N/A; 2015-2016: 678 applied, 419 accepted. Neither SAT nor ACT required. SAT 25/75 percentile: N/A. High school rank: 10% in top tenth, 30% in top quarter, 63% in top half
Early decision deadline: N/A, notification date: N/A
Early action deadline: 12/1, notification date: 12/15
Application deadline (fall): 8/1
Undergraduate student body: 609 full time, 19 part time; 35% male, 65% female; 0% American Indian, 4% Asian, 7% black, 13% Hispanic, 5% multiracial, N/A Pacific Islander, 67% white, 1% international; 62% from in state; 38% live on campus; N/A in fraternities, N/A in sororities
Most popular majors: 15% Graphic Design; 15% Industrial and Product Design; 11% Fine/Studio Arts, General; 8% Painting
Expenses: 2016-2017: $34,920; room/board: $9,100
Financial aid: (414) 291-3272; 81% of undergrads determined to have financial need; average aid package $23,983

Milwaukee School of Engineering
Milwaukee WI
(800) 332-6763
U.S. News ranking: Reg. U. (Mid. W), No. 11
Website: www.msoe.edu
Admissions email: explore@msoe.edu
Private; founded 1903
Freshman admissions: more selective; 2015-2016: 2,326 applied, 1,511 accepted. Either SAT or ACT required. ACT 25/75 percentile: 25-30. High school rank: N/A
Early decision deadline: N/A, notification date: N/A
Early action deadline: N/A, notification date: N/A
Application deadline (fall): rolling
Undergraduate student body: 2,546 full time, 166 part time; 75% male, 25% female; 0% American Indian, 3% Asian, 2% black, 5% Hispanic, 2% multiracial, 0% Pacific Islander, 66% white, 13% international; 68% from in state; 39% live on campus; 5% of students in fraternities, 10% in sororities
Most popular majors: 69% Engineering; 14% Business, Management, Marketing, and Related Support Services; 12% Health Professions and Related Programs; 4% Engineering Technologies and Engineering-Related Fields
Expenses: 2016-2017: $37,980; room/board: $8,835

Mount Mary University
Milwaukee WI
(800) 321-6265
U.S. News ranking: Reg. U. (Mid. W), No. 86
Website: www.mtmary.edu
Admissions email: mmu-admiss@mtmary.ede
Private; founded 1913
Affiliation: Roman Catholic
Freshman admissions: selective; 2015-2016: 764 applied, 402 accepted. Either SAT or ACT required. ACT 25/75 percentile: 17-21. High school rank: 26% in top tenth, 50% in top quarter, 81% in top half
Early decision deadline: N/A, notification date: N/A
Early action deadline: N/A, notification date: N/A
Application deadline (fall): rolling
Undergraduate student body: 714 full time, 102 part time; 0% male, 100% female; 0% American Indian, 8% Asian, 19% black, 14% Hispanic, 4% multiracial, 0% Pacific Islander, 51% white, 2% international; 95% from in state; 26% live on campus; N/A of students in fraternities, N/A in sororities
Most popular majors: 12% Fashion/Apparel Design; 10% Occupational Therapy/Therapist; 10% Psychology, General; 8% Business Administration and Management, General; 8% Fashion Merchandising
Expenses: 2016-2017: $27,830; room/board: $8,200
Financial aid: (414) 256-1258; 93% of undergrads determined to have financial need; average aid package $22,588

Northland College
Ashland WI
(715) 682-1224
U.S. News ranking: Nat. Lib. Arts, No. 174
Website: www.northland.edu
Admissions email: admit@northland.edu
Private; founded 1892
Affiliation: United Church of Christ
Freshman admissions: more selective; 2015-2016: 852 applied, 487 accepted. Either SAT or ACT required. ACT 25/75 percentile: 21-28. High school rank: 22% in top tenth, 46% in top quarter, 74% in top half
Early decision deadline: N/A, notification date: N/A
Early action deadline: N/A, notification date: N/A
Application deadline (fall): rolling
Undergraduate student body: 513 full time, 28 part time; 51% male, 49% female; 2% American Indian, 0% Asian, 1% black, 6% Hispanic, 2% multiracial, 0% Pacific Islander, 83% white, 2% international; 51% from in state; 74% live on campus; 0% of students in fraternities, 0% in sororities

Most popular majors: 17% Biological and Biomedical Sciences; 10% Physical Sciences; 7% Education; 7% Public Administration and Social Service Professions
Expenses: 2016-2017: $33,432; room/board: $8,485
Financial aid: (715) 682-1255; 85% of undergrads determined to have financial need; average aid package $35,981

Ripon College
Ripon WI
(920) 748-8337
U.S. News ranking: Nat. Lib. Arts, No. 113
Website: www.ripon.edu
Admissions email: adminfo@ripon.edu
Private; founded 1851
Freshman admissions: more selective; 2015-2016: 1,874 applied, 1,239 accepted. Either SAT or ACT required. ACT 25/75 percentile: 21-27. High school rank: 21% in top tenth, 51% in top quarter, 80% in top half
Early decision deadline: N/A, notification date: N/A
Early action deadline: N/A, notification date: N/A
Application deadline (fall): rolling
Undergraduate student body: 785 full time, 9 part time; 50% male, 50% female; 1% American Indian, 1% Asian, 3% black, 5% Hispanic, 2% multiracial, 0% Pacific Islander, 84% white, 4% international; 74% from in state; 90% live on campus; 24% of students in fraternities, 19% in sororities
Most popular majors: 14% Business/Commerce, General; 11% Biology/Biological Sciences, General; 11% English Language and Literature, General; 11% Health and Physical Education/Fitness, General; 11% Psychology, General
Expenses: 2016-2017: $39,142; room/board: $7,770
Financial aid: (920) 748-8101; 84% of undergrads determined to have financial need; average aid package $30,737

Silver Lake College[1]
Manitowoc WI
(920) 686-6175
U.S. News ranking: Reg. U. (Mid. W), second tier
Website: www.sl.edu
Admissions email: admslc@silver.sl.edu
Private; founded 1935
Affiliation: Catholic
Application deadline (fall): 9/1
Undergraduate student body: N/A full time, N/A part time
Expenses: 2015-2016: $25,060; room/board: $9,715
Financial aid: (920) 686-6122

St. Norbert College
De Pere WI
(800) 236-4878
U.S. News ranking: Nat. Lib. Arts, No. 132
Website: www.snc.edu
Admissions email: admit@snc.edu
Private; founded 1898
Affiliation: Roman Catholic

University of Wisconsin–Eau Claire
Eau Claire WI
(715) 836-5415
U.S. News ranking: Reg. U. (Mid. W), No. 37
Website: www.uwec.edu
Admissions email: admissions@uwec.edu
Public; founded 1916
Freshman admissions: selective; 2015-2016: 5,810 applied, 4,950 accepted. Either SAT or ACT required. ACT 25/75 percentile: 22-26. High school rank: 18% in top tenth, 49% in top quarter, 91% in top half
Early decision deadline: N/A, notification date: N/A
Early action deadline: N/A, notification date: N/A
Application deadline (fall): 8/25
Undergraduate student body: 9,165 full time, 729 part time; 40% male, 60% female; 0% American Indian, 4% Asian, 1% black, 2% Hispanic, 2% multiracial, 0% Pacific Islander, 89% white, 2% international; 73% from in state; 41% live on campus; N/A of students in fraternities, N/A in sororities
Most popular majors: 20% Business, Management, Marketing, and Related Support Services; 14% Health Professions and Related Programs; 7% Education; 6% Psychology
Expenses: 2015-2016: $8,822 in state, $16,395 out of state; room/board: $7,322
Financial aid: (715) 836-3373; 54% of undergrads determined to have financial need; average aid package $9,686

University of Wisconsin–Green Bay
Green Bay WI
(920) 465-2111
U.S. News ranking: Reg. U. (Mid. W), No. 86
Website: www.uwgb.edu
Admissions email: uwgb@uwgb.edu
Public; founded 1965
Freshman admissions: selective; 2015-2016: 2,138 applied, 1,811 accepted. Either SAT or ACT required. ACT 25/75 percentile: 21-25. High school rank: N/A
Early decision deadline: N/A, notification date: N/A
Early action deadline: N/A, notification date: N/A
Application deadline (fall): rolling
Undergraduate student body: 4,007 full time, 2,521 part time; 33% male, 67% female; 1% American Indian, 3% Asian, 2% black, 4% Hispanic, 2% multiracial, 0% Pacific Islander, 86% white, 1% international; 93% from in state; 33% live on campus; 2% of students in fraternities, 2% in sororities
Most popular majors: 14% Business Administration and Management, General; 11% Liberal Arts and Sciences/Liberal Studies; 9% Human Biology; 9% Psychology, General; 9% Registered Nursing/Registered Nurse
Expenses: 2016-2017: $7,878 in state, $15,450 out of state; room/board: $7,186
Financial aid: (920) 465-2075; 65% of undergrads determined to have financial need; average aid package $8,862

University of Wisconsin–La Crosse
La Crosse WI
(608) 785-8939
U.S. News ranking: Reg. U. (Mid. W), No. 31
Website: www.uwlax.edu
Admissions email: admissions@uwlax.edu
Public; founded 1909
Freshman admissions: more selective; 2015-2016: 5,975 applied, 4,765 accepted. Either SAT or ACT required. ACT 25/75 percentile: 23-26. High school rank: 23% in top tenth, 61% in top quarter, 97% in top half
Early decision deadline: N/A, notification date: N/A
Early action deadline: N/A, notification date: N/A
Application deadline (fall): rolling
Undergraduate student body: 9,163 full time, 466 part time; 44% male, 56% female; 0% American Indian, 2% Asian, 1% black, 3% Hispanic, 3% multiracial, 0% Pacific Islander, 90% white, 1% international; 82% from in state; 37% live on campus; 1% of students in fraternities, 1% in sororities
Most popular majors: 21% Business, Management, Marketing, and Related Support Services; 15% Biological and Biomedical Sciences; 10% Psychology; 9% Health Professions and Related Programs; 9% Social Sciences

Expenses: 2015-2016: $8,832 in state, $16,783 out of state; room/board: $6,150
Financial aid: (608) 785-8604; 49% of undergrads determined to have financial need; average aid package $7,394

University of Wisconsin–Madison

Madison WI
(608) 262-3961
U.S. News ranking: Nat. U., No. 44
Website: www.wisc.edu
Admissions email: onwisconsin@admissions.wisc.edu
Public; founded 1848
Freshman admissions: more selective; 2015-2016: 32,780 applied, 16,121 accepted. Either SAT or ACT required. ACT 25/75 percentile: 27-31. High school rank: 54% in top tenth, 91% in top quarter, 99% in top half
Early decision deadline: N/A, notification date: N/A
Early action deadline: 11/2, notification date: 1/31
Application deadline (fall): 2/1
Undergraduate student body: 28,569 full time, 3,093 part time; 49% male, 51% female; 0% American Indian, 6% Asian, 2% black, 5% Hispanic, 3% multiracial, 0% Pacific Islander, 76% white, 8% international; 67% from in state; 26% live on campus; 9% of students in fraternities, 8% in sororities
Most popular majors: 8% Economics, General; 7% Biology/Biological Sciences, General; 5% Political Science and Government, General; 5% Psychology, General
Expenses: 2016-2017: $10,488 in state, $32,738 out of state; room/board: N/A
Financial aid: (608) 262-3060; 37% of undergrads determined to have financial need; average aid package $14,156

University of Wisconsin–Milwaukee

Milwaukee WI
(414) 229-2222
U.S. News ranking: Nat. U., second tier
Website: www.uwm.edu
Admissions email: uwmlook@uwm.edu
Public; founded 1956
Freshman admissions: selective; 2015-2016: 10,321 applied, 7,499 accepted. Neither SAT nor ACT required. ACT 25/75 percentile: 20-25. High school rank: 10% in top tenth, 28% in top quarter, 66% in top half
Early decision deadline: N/A, notification date: N/A
Early action deadline: N/A, notification date: N/A
Application deadline (fall): rolling
Undergraduate student body: 18,284 full time, 4,000 part time; 48% male, 52% female; 0% American Indian, 7% Asian, 8% black, 9% Hispanic, 4% multiracial, 0% Pacific Islander, 68% white, 4% international; 91% from in state; 19% live

on campus; N/A of students in fraternities, N/A in sororities
Most popular majors: 23% Business, Management, Marketing, and Related Support Services; 9% Health Professions and Related Programs; 7% Visual and Performing Arts; 6% Education
Expenses: 2015-2016: $9,429 in state, $19,603 out of state; room/board: $10,030
Financial aid: (414) 229-6300

University of Wisconsin–Oshkosh

Oshkosh WI
(920) 424-0202
U.S. News ranking: Reg. U. (Mid. W), No. 79
Website: www.uwosh.edu
Admissions email: oshadmuw@uwosh.edu
Public; founded 1871
Freshman admissions: selective; 2015-2016: 5,660 applied, 3,870 accepted. ACT required. ACT 25/75 percentile: 20-24. High school rank: 7% in top tenth, 31% in top quarter, 75% in top half
Early decision deadline: N/A, notification date: N/A
Early action deadline: N/A, notification date: N/A
Application deadline (fall): rolling
Undergraduate student body: 8,681 full time, 3,950 part time; 41% male, 59% female; 1% American Indian, 4% Asian, 2% black, 4% Hispanic, 2% multiracial, 0% Pacific Islander, 87% white, 1% international; 94% from in state; 32% live on campus; 3% of students in fraternities, 3% in sororities
Most popular majors: 18% Business, Management, Marketing, and Related Support Services; 14% Education; 13% Health Professions and Related Programs; 7% Public Administration and Social Service Professions
Expenses: 2016-2017: $7,500 in state, $15,100 out of state; room/board: $7,050
Financial aid: (920) 424-3377; 55% of undergrads determined to have financial need; average aid package $8,674

University of Wisconsin–Parkside

Kenosha WI
(262) 595-2355
U.S. News ranking: Nat. Lib. Arts, second tier
Website: www.uwp.edu
Admissions email: admissions@uwp.edu
Public; founded 1968
Freshman admissions: selective; 2015-2016: 1,662 applied, 1,356 accepted. Neither SAT nor ACT required. ACT 25/75 percentile: 18-23. High school rank: 12% in top tenth, 37% in top quarter, 72% in top half
Early decision deadline: N/A, notification date: N/A
Early action deadline: N/A, notification date: N/A
Application deadline (fall): rolling

Undergraduate student body: 3,272 full time, 1,028 part time; 48% male, 52% female; 0% American Indian, 3% Asian, 9% black, 13% Hispanic, 4% multiracial, 0% Pacific Islander, 69% white, 2% international; 82% from in state; 19% live on campus; 1% of students in fraternities, 1% in sororities
Most popular majors: 15% Business Administration and Management, General; 11% Criminal Justice/Safety Studies; 7% Psychology, General; 6% Accounting; 6% Biology/Biological Sciences, General
Expenses: 2016-2017: $7,367 in state, $15,356 out of state; room/board: $7,824
Financial aid: (262) 595-2004; 67% of undergrads determined to have financial need; average aid package $9,119

University of Wisconsin–Platteville

Platteville WI
(715) 608-1125
U.S. News ranking: Reg. U. (Mid. W), No. 94
Website: www.uwplatt.edu
Admissions email: admit@uwplatt.edu
Public; founded 1866
Freshman admissions: selective; 2015-2016: 4,401 applied, 3,393 accepted. Either SAT or ACT required. ACT 25/75 percentile: 21-26. High school rank: 11% in top tenth, 35% in top quarter, 75% in top half
Early decision deadline: N/A, notification date: N/A
Early action deadline: N/A, notification date: N/A
Application deadline (fall): rolling
Undergraduate student body: 7,109 full time, 869 part time; 65% male, 35% female; 0% American Indian, 1% Asian, 1% black, 3% Hispanic, 2% multiracial, 0% Pacific Islander, 90% white, 1% international; 75% from in state; 47% live on campus; 5% of students in fraternities, 7% in sororities
Most popular majors: 23% Engineering; 11% Education; 10% Homeland Security, Law Enforcement, Firefighting and Related Protective Services; 7% Engineering Technologies and Engineering-Related Fields
Expenses: 2016-2017: $7,488 in state, $15,339 out of state; room/board: $7,160
Financial aid: (608) 342-1836; 65% of undergrads determined to have financial need; average aid package $6,817

University of Wisconsin–River Falls

River Falls WI
(715) 425-3500
U.S. News ranking: Reg. U. (Mid. W), No. 91
Website: www.uwrf.edu
Admissions email: admit@uwrf.edu
Public; founded 1874
Freshman admissions: selective; 2015-2016: 2,467 applied, 2,215 accepted. Either SAT or ACT required. ACT 25/75

percentile: 20-25. High school rank: 10% in top tenth, 33% in top quarter, 69% in top half
Early decision deadline: N/A, notification date: N/A
Early action deadline: N/A, notification date: N/A
Application deadline (fall): rolling
Undergraduate student body: 4,917 full time, 590 part time; 39% male, 61% female; 0% American Indian, 3% Asian, 2% black, 3% Hispanic, 2% multiracial, 0% Pacific Islander, 89% white, 1% international; 50% from in state; 42% live on campus; N/A of students in fraternities, N/A in sororities
Most popular majors: 16% Business, Management, Marketing, and Related Support Services; 10% Education; 8% Biological and Biomedical Sciences
Expenses: 2015-2016: $7,937 in state, $15,510 out of state; room/board: $7,674
Financial aid: (715) 425-3141; 65% of undergrads determined to have financial need; average aid package $6,752

University of Wisconsin–Stevens Point

Stevens Point WI
(715) 346-2441
U.S. News ranking: Reg. U. (Mid. W), No. 49
Website: www.uwsp.edu
Admissions email: admiss@uwsp.edu
Public; founded 1894
Freshman admissions: selective; 2015-2016: 4,901 applied, 3,649 accepted. Neither SAT nor ACT required. ACT 25/75 percentile: 20-25. High school rank: 11% in top tenth, 33% in top quarter, 73% in top half
Early decision deadline: N/A, notification date: N/A
Early action deadline: N/A, notification date: N/A
Application deadline (fall): rolling
Undergraduate student body: 8,172 full time, 667 part time; 48% male, 52% female; 1% American Indian, 3% Asian, 2% black, 4% Hispanic, 2% multiracial, 0% Pacific Islander, 87% white, 2% international; 89% from in state; 39% live on campus; 2% of students in fraternities, 3% in sororities
Most popular majors: 10% Biology/Biological Sciences, General; 10% Business Administration and Management, General; 5% Psychology, General
Expenses: 2016-2017: $7,686 in state, $15,953 out of state; room/board: $7,180
Financial aid: (715) 346-4771; 59% of undergrads determined to have financial need; average aid package $9,048

University of Wisconsin–Stout

Menomonie WI
(715) 232-1411
U.S. News ranking: Reg. U. (Mid. W), No. 69
Website: www.uwstout.edu
Admissions email: admissions@uwstout.edu

Public; founded 1891
Freshman admissions: selective; 2015-2016: 3,535 applied, 2,964 accepted. Either SAT or ACT required. ACT 25/75 percentile: 20-24. High school rank: 8% in top tenth, 28% in top quarter, 67% in top half
Early decision deadline: N/A, notification date: N/A
Early action deadline: N/A, notification date: N/A
Application deadline (fall): rolling
Undergraduate student body: 6,841 full time, 1,547 part time; 54% male, 46% female; 4% American Indian, 0% Asian, 2% black, 1% Hispanic, 4% multiracial, 87% Pacific Islander, 0% white, 3% international; 68% from in state; 40% live on campus; 2% of students in fraternities, 3% in sororities
Most popular majors: 34% Business, Management, Marketing, and Related Support Services; 9% Education; 8% Engineering Technologies and Engineering-Related Fields; 8% Family and Consumer Sciences/Human Sciences; 8% Visual and Performing Arts
Expenses: 2015-2016: $9,203 in state, $16,949 out of state; room/board: N/A
Financial aid: (715) 232-1363; 57% of undergrads determined to have financial need; average aid package $10,734

University of Wisconsin–Superior

Superior WI
(715) 394-8230
U.S. News ranking: Reg. Coll. (Mid. W), No. 36
Website: www.uwsuper.edu
Admissions email: admissions@uwsuper.edu
Public; founded 1893
Freshman admissions: selective; 2015-2016: 995 applied, 712 accepted. Either SAT or ACT required. ACT 25/75 percentile: 19-23. High school rank: 10% in top tenth, 21% in top quarter, 59% in top half
Early decision deadline: N/A, notification date: N/A
Early action deadline: N/A, notification date: N/A
Application deadline (fall): 8/1
Undergraduate student body: 1,869 full time, 493 part time; 39% male, 61% female; 2% American Indian, 1% Asian, 2% black, 2% Hispanic, 3% multiracial, 0% Pacific Islander, 81% white, 8% international; 60% from in state; 33% live on campus; N/A of students in fraternities, N/A in sororities
Most popular majors: 13% Multi/Interdisciplinary Studies; 12% Biological and Biomedical Sciences; 11% Business, Management, Marketing, and Related Support Services; 11% Education
Expenses: 2015-2016: $8,036 in state, $15,609 out of state; room/board: $6,410
Financial aid: (715) 394-8200; 66% of undergrads determined to have financial need; average aid package $11,326

University of Wisconsin–Whitewater
Whitewater WI
(262) 472-1440
U.S. News ranking: Reg. U. (Mid. W), No. 49
Website: www.uww.edu
Admissions email: uwwadmit@mail.uww.edu
Public; founded 1868
Freshman admissions: selective; 2015-2016: 6,082 applied, 4,896 accepted. Either SAT or ACT required. ACT 25/75 percentile: 20-26. High school rank: 11% in top tenth, 32% in top quarter, 73% in top half
Early decision deadline: N/A, notification date: N/A
Early action deadline: N/A, notification date: N/A
Application deadline (fall): 5/1
Undergraduate student body: 9,963 full time, 1,179 part time; 50% male, 50% female; 0% American Indian, 2% Asian, 4% black, 6% Hispanic, 5% multiracial, 0% Pacific Islander, 82% white, 1% international; 84% from in state; 40% live on campus; N/A of students in fraternities, N/A in sororities
Most popular majors: 6% Accounting; 6% Finance, General; 6% Social Work; 5% Elementary Education and Teaching; 5% Psychology, General
Expenses: 2015-2016: $7,637 in state, $15,710 out of state; room/board: $7,082
Financial aid: (262) 472-1130; 52% of undergrads determined to have financial need; average aid package $8,131

Viterbo University[1]
La Crosse WI
(608) 796-3010
U.S. News ranking: Reg. U. (Mid. W), No. 115
Website: www.viterbo.edu
Admissions email: admission@viterbo.edu
Private
Application deadline (fall): N/A
Undergraduate student body: N/A full time, N/A part time
Expenses: 2015-2016: $25,050; room/board: $8,260
Financial aid: (608) 796-3900

Wisconsin Lutheran College
Milwaukee WI
(414) 443-8811
U.S. News ranking: Reg. Coll. (Mid. W), No. 20
Website: www.wlc.edu
Admissions email: admissions@wlc.edu
Private; founded 1973
Affiliation: Wisconsin Evangelical Lutheran Synod
Freshman admissions: selective; 2015-2016: 710 applied, 652 accepted. Either SAT or ACT required. ACT 25/75 percentile: 21-27. High school rank: 15% in top tenth, 37% in top quarter, 73% in top half
Early decision deadline: N/A, notification date: N/A
Early action deadline: N/A, notification date: N/A
Application deadline (fall): rolling
Undergraduate student body: 968 full time, 103 part time; 45% male, 55% female; 0% American Indian, 1% Asian, 5% black, 5% Hispanic, 2% multiracial, 0% Pacific Islander, 83% white, 2% international; 77% from in state; 59% live on campus; 0% of students in fraternities, 0% in sororities
Most popular majors: 19% Business Administration and Management, General; 8% Business Administration, Management and Operations, Other; 8% Psychology, General; 7% Biology/Biological Sciences, General; 7% Registered Nursing/Registered Nurse
Expenses: 2016-2017: $27,984; room/board: $9,620
Financial aid: (414) 443-8856; 81% of undergrads determined to have financial need; average aid package $20,438

WYOMING

University of Wyoming
Laramie WY
(307) 766-5160
U.S. News ranking: Nat. U., No. 171
Website: www.uwyo.edu
Admissions email: Why-wyo@uwyo.edu
Public; founded 1886
Freshman admissions: selective; 2015-2016: 4,657 applied, 4,455 accepted. Either SAT or ACT required. ACT 25/75 percentile: 22-27. High school rank: 22% in top tenth, 50% in top quarter, 81% in top half
Early decision deadline: N/A, notification date: N/A
Early action deadline: N/A, notification date: N/A
Application deadline (fall): 8/10
Undergraduate student body: 8,394 full time, 1,651 part time; 48% male, 52% female; 1% American Indian, 1% Asian, 1% black, 7% Hispanic, 3% multiracial, 0% Pacific Islander, 76% white, 4% international; 68% from in state; 24% live on campus; 6% of students in fraternities, 6% in sororities
Most popular majors: 10% Registered Nursing/Registered Nurse; 6% Elementary Education and Teaching; 5% Psychology, General; 4% Business Administration and Management, General; 4% Criminal Justice/Safety Studies
Expenses: 2016-2017: $5,055 in state, $16,215 out of state; room/board: $10,320
Financial aid: (307) 766-2116; 46% of undergrads determined to have financial need; average aid package $9,534

Centenary College of Louisiana 84, 136, D-54
Central Baptist College, AR 107, D-7
Central Christian College, KS 110, D-49
Central College, IA 84, 136, D-46
Central Connecticut State University 91, D-21
Centralia College, WA D-151
Central Methodist University, MO 109, D-77
Central Michigan University 77, 120, 123, 135, D-68
Central Penn College D-119
Central State University, OH 110, 113, D-108
Central Washington University 103, 104, D-151
Centre College, KY 80, D-52
Chadron State College, NE D-81
Chaminade University of Honolulu 103, D-34
Champlain College, VT 90, D-146
Chapman University, CA 102, 116, 139, D-11
Charleston Southern University, SC 96, 119, 123, D-129
Charter Oak State College, CT D-21
Chatham University, PA 90, 123, D-119
Chestnut Hill College, PA 91, D-119
Cheyney University of Pennsylvania 86, 113, D-119
Chicago State University 100, D-36
Chipola College, FL 108, D-24
Chowan University, NC 108, 172, D-102
Christian Brothers University, TN 94, 138, 171, D-134
Christopher Newport University, VA 92, 104, 138, D-147
The Citadel, SC 92, 104, 116 117, 171, D-129
City University of Seattle 119, 123, D-151
Claflin University, SC 86, 112, D-129
Claremont McKenna College, CA 80, 170, D-12
Clarion University of Pennsylvania 91, 122, D-120
Clark Atlanta University 77, 112, 172, D-30
Clarke University, IA 108, 139, 171, 172, D-46
Clarkson University, NY 76, 135, 170, D-89
Clark University, MA 74, 116, 135, 170, D-62
Clayton State University, GA 96, D-30
Cleary University, MI D-68
Clemson University, SC 74, 79, 114, 118, D-129
Cleveland Institute of Art D-108
Cleveland Institute of Music D-108
Cleveland State University 77, D-109
Coastal Carolina University, SC 94, 171, 172, D-129
Coe College, IA 84, 136, D-46
Cogswell Polytechnical College, CA D-12
Coker College, SC 107, D-130
Colby College, ME 80, 170, D-56
Colby-Sawyer College, NH D-83
Colgate University, NY 80, 170, D-89
College at Brockport–SUNY 90, D-89
College for Creative Studies, MI D-68
College of Central Florida D-24
College of Charleston, SC 92, 104, 138, D-130
College of Coastal Georgia 107, D-30
College of Idaho 84, D-35
College of Mount St. Vincent, NY 91, D-90
College of New Jersey 88, 104, 136, D-85
College of New Rochelle, NY 90, D-90
College of Our Lady of the Elms, MA 91, D-62
College of Saint Rose, NY 90, D-90
College of Southern Nevada D-83
College of St. Benedict, MN 82, 136, 172, D-72
College of St. Elizabeth, NJ 91, D-85
College of St. Joseph, VT 107, 172, D-146
College of St. Mary, NE 100, D-81
College of St. Scholastica, MN 98, 139, 172, D-72
College of the Atlantic, ME 82, 136, 170, D-56
College of the Holy Cross, MA 80, D-62
College of the Ozarks, MO 108, 139, 171, 173, D-77
The College of Westchester, NY D-90
College of William and Mary, VA 17, 72, 79, 114, D-147
College of Wooster, OH 82, 136, D-109
Colorado Christian University 104, D-19
Colorado College 80, 170, D-19
Colorado Mesa University 111, D-19
Colorado Mountain College D-19
Colorado School of Mines 74, 118, D-19
Colorado State University 76, 114, 120, 135, D-19
Colorado State University–Pueblo 104, D-19
Colorado Technical University 120, D-19
Columbia Basin College, WA D-151
Columbia College, MO 122, D-77
Columbia College, SC 94, D-130
Columbia College Chicago 100, D-36
Columbia International University, SC 94, D-130
Columbia University, NY 72, 118, 170, D-90
Columbus College of Art and Design, OH D-109
Columbus State University, GA 96, D-31
Concordia College, AL D-3
Concordia College, NY 106, D-90
Concordia College–Moorhead, MN 84, 136, D-72
Concordia University, CA 103, D-12
Concordia University, NE 98, 139, 171, D-81
Concordia University–St. Paul, MN 100, 120, D-73
Concordia University Texas 104, D-137
Concordia University Wisconsin 98, D-156
Concord University, WV 96, D-154
Connecticut College 80, D-21
Converse College, SC 94, 171, D-130
Cooper Union, NY 106, 117, 171, 173, D-90
Coppin State University, MD 91, 113, D-58
Corban University, OR 103, D-116
Cornell College, IA 82, 136, D-47
Cornell University, NY 21, 72, 114, 118, 170, D-90
Cornerstone University, MI 99, 123, D-68
Cornish College of the Arts, WA D-151
Cottey College, MO 108, 139, D-77
Covenant College, GA 84, 136, D-31
Creighton University, NE 98, 114, 119, 123, 139, D-81
Crowley's Ridge College, AR 108, D-7
Crown College, MN 110, D-73
Culver-Stockton College, MO 109, D-77
Cumberland University, TN 96, D-134
CUNY–Baruch College 88, 104, 114, 136, 173, D-90
CUNY–Brooklyn College 90, 173, D-90
CUNY–City College 90, 173, D-91
CUNY–College of Staten Island 91, D-91
CUNY–Hunter College 90, 104, 136, D-91
CUNY–John Jay College of Criminal Justice 91, D-91
CUNY–Lehman College 91, 173, D-91
CUNY–Medgar Evers College 107, D-91
CUNY–New York City College of Technology 107, D-91
CUNY–Queens College 88, 104, 136, 173, D-91
CUNY–York College 107, D-91
Curry College, MA 91, D-62
Curtis Institute of Music, PA D-120

D

Daemen College, NY 91, D-91
Dakota State University, SD 100, D-132
Dakota Wesleyan University, SD 109, 122, D-132
Dallas Baptist University 77, 122, D-137
Dalton State College, GA D-31
Daniel Webster College, NH 91, D-83
Dartmouth College, NH 72, 118, 170, 173, D-83
Darton State College, GA D-31
Davenport University, MI 100, D-68
Davidson College, NC 80, 170, 173, D-102
Davis and Elkins College, WV 86, D-154
Daytona State College, FL 119, 123, D-24
Dean College, MA 106, 171, D-62
Defiance College, OH 109, D-109
Delaware State University 91, 112, D-23
Delaware Valley University, PA 91, D-120
Delta State University, MS 96, D-75
Denison University, OH 82, D-109
DePaul University, IL 76, 114, 135, D-36
DePauw University, IN 82, 136, D-42
DeSales University, PA 90, D-120
DeVry University, IL 100, 122, D-36
Dickinson College, PA 80, D-120
Dickinson State University, ND 110, 111, D-107
Dillard University, LA 86, 112, 172, D-54
Dixie State University, UT D-144
Doane University, NE 84, D-82
Dominican College, NY 91, D-92
Dominican University, IL 98, 171, D-36
Dominican University of California 102, D-12
Donnelly College, KS D-49
Dordt College, IA 108, 117, 139, 171, D-47
Dowling College, NY 92, D-92
Drake University, IA 98, 139, D-47
Drew University, NJ 82, 136, D-85
Drexel University, PA 21, 74, 114 118, 120, 135, D-120
Drury University, MO 98, D-77
Duke University, NC 72, 118, 170, 173, D-102
Dunwoody College of Technology, MN 110, D-73
Duquesne University, PA 76, 116, 123 135, 170, 172, D-120
D'Youville College, NY 92, D-92

E

Earlham College, IN 82, 170, D-42
East Carolina University, NC 77, 135, D-102
East Central University, OK 104, D-113
Eastern Connecticut State University 90, D-21
Eastern Florida State College D-24
Eastern Illinois University 98, 104, D-36
Eastern Kentucky University 94, 120, D-52
Eastern Mennonite University, VA 94, D-147
Eastern Michigan University 77, D-69
Eastern Nazarene College, MA 92, D-62
Eastern New Mexico University 104, D-87
Eastern Oregon University 104, 120, D-116
Eastern University, PA 90, D-120
Eastern Washington University 103, 104, D-151
East Georgia State College 108, D-31
East Stroudsburg University of Pennsylvania 91, D-120
East Tennessee State University 78, D-134
East Texas Baptist University 111, 171, 172, D-138
East-West University, IL 86, D-37
Eckerd College, FL 84, D-25
ECPI University, VA D-147
Edgewood College, WI 76, 135, D-156
Edinboro University of Pennsylvania 92, D-120
Edward Waters College, FL 108, 113, D-25
Elizabeth City State University, NC 96, 112, D-103
Elizabethtown College, PA 84, 136, D-120
Elmhurst College, IL 98, 139, 171, D-37
Elmira College, NY 84, D-92
Elon University, NC 17, 18, 21 92, 114, 138, D-103
Embry-Riddle Aeronautical University, FL 92, 119 123, 138, D-25
Embry-Riddle Aeronautical University–Prescott, AZ 117
Emerson College, MA 88, 136, D-63
Emmanuel College, GA 107, 171, D-31
Emmanuel College, MA 86, 172, D-63
Emory and Henry College, VA 84, D-148
Emory University, GA 72, 114, 170, D-31
Emporia State University, KS 100, D-49
Endicott College, MA 90, 136, D-63
Erskine College, SC 86, 173, D-130
Eureka College, IL 109, D-37
Evangel University, MO 100, D-77
Everglades University, FL 107, D-25
Evergreen State College, WA 18, 102, 104, D-151
Excelsior College, NY D-92

F

Fairfield University, CT 88, 116, 136, D-21
Fairleigh Dickinson University, NJ 90, D-85
Fairmont State University, WV 96, D-154
Farmingdale State College–SUNY 106, D-92
Fashion Institute of Design & Merchandising, CA D-12
Fashion Institute of Technology, NY D-92
Faulkner University, AL 96, D-3
Fayetteville State University, NC 96, 112, D-103
Felician College, NJ 92, D-85
Ferris State University, MI 99, 120, 123, D-69
Ferrum College, VA 107, D-148

ACADEMIC INSIGHTS
YOUR SCHOOL BY THE NUMBERS

Designed for schools, U.S. News Academic Insights provides instant access to a rich historical archive of undergraduate and graduate school rankings data.

Advanced Visualizations
Take complex data and turn it into six easily understandable and exportable views.

Download Center
Export large data sets from the new Download Center to create custom reports.

Dedicated Account Management
Have access to full analyst support for training, troubleshooting and advanced reporting.

Peer-Group Analysis
Flexibility to create your own peer groups to compare your institution on more than 5 M+ data points.

Historical Trending
Find out how institutions have performed over time based on more than 350 metrics.

To request a demo visit **AI.USNEWS.COM**   or call **202.955.2121**

ACCOMPLISH *MORE* THAN YOU CAN IMAGINE

"Graduating as the valedictorian of my high school class, I was accepted to other top-tier colleges, and I had my choice of schools to attend, but I chose the Academy because I wanted to accomplish more than just earning a Bachelor's Degree.

"At West Point, I've developed physically, mentally, and academically, and I'm part of something bigger than myself. Every day is a new challenge, but I'm never alone. Every one of my classmates – the entire Corps of Cadets – is there for me, and they have my back, any place, every time.

"I came here as a city girl from Atlanta, but now I'm a leader, and when I graduate I'm going to be a warrior-scholar as a member of the Long Gray Line. I think that's pretty cool."

– *CDT Isabella Minter*

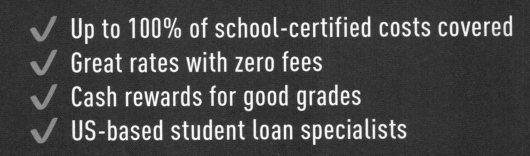

Up to 100% of school-certified costs covered

Great rates with zero fees

Cash rewards for good grades

US-based student loan specialists

DiscoverStudentLoans.com   1-800-STUDENT (788-3368)

DISCOVER® | STUDENT LOANS